DAVID WALLECHINSKY'S TWENTIETH CENTURY
History with the Boring Parts Left Out

ALSO BY DAVID WALLECHINSKY:

The People's Almanac (with Irving Wallace)
The People's Almanac #2 (with Irving Wallace)
The People's Almanac #3 (with Irving Wallace)
What Really Happened to the Class of '65? (with Michael Medved)
Midterm Report: The Class of '65
The Complete Book of the Olympics
The Book of Lists (with Amy Wallace)
Sports Illustrated Presents The Complete Book of the Summer Olympics

David Wallechinsky's Twentieth Century

History with the Boring Parts Left Out

by DAVID WALLECHINSKY

LITTLE, BROWN AND COMPANY
Boston   New York   Toronto   London

First Paperback Edition

Previously published as *The People's Almanac Presents the Twentieth Century*

The author is grateful for permission to include the following previously copyrighted materials:

"Subterranean Homesick Blues," "My Back Pages," and "The Times They Are A-Changing" by Bob Dylan. Copyright © by Special Rider Music. Reprinted by permission.

Excerpt from "Little Gidding" in *Four Quartets*, copyright 1943 by T. S. Eliot © renewed 1971 by Esme Valerie Eliot. Reprinted by permission of Harcourt Brace & Company.

"Brother Can You Spare a Dime" by Jay Gorney and E. Y. Harburg. Copyright © 1932 (renewed). Reprinted by permission of Warner Bros. Publications Inc.

"Boogie Woogie Amputee" by Barnes & Barnes. Reprinted by permission of Robert Haimer.

Excerpt from "This Be the Verse," by Philip Larkin. Reprinted by permission of the Marvell Press.

Excerpt from *No Surrender: My Thirty-Year War* by Hiroo Onoda. Reprinted by permission of Kodansha International Ltd.

"The Ballad of Lenin's Tomb" from *The Collected Poems of Robert Service* by Robert Service. Copyright 1940 by G. P. Putnam's Sons. Reprinted by permission.

Unabridged text of "The Little Boy and the Old Man" from *A Light in the Attic* by Shel Silverstein. Copyright © 1981 by Evil Eye Music, Inc. Reprinted by permission of HarperCollins Publishing Corporation.

"Do Not Go Gentle Into That Good Night" from *The Poems of Dylan Thomas*. Copyright © 1952 by Dylan Thomas. Reprinted by permission of New Directions Publishing Corporation.

"Over the Fire" from *The Uncelestial City* by Humbert Wolfe. Reprinted by permission of Lloyds Bank.

Library of Congress Cataloging-in-Publication Data
Wallechinsky, David.
    David Wallechinsky's twentieth century: history with the
boring parts left out / by David Wallechinsky. — 1st ed.
      p. cm.
    Includes index.
    ISBN 0-316-92095-9 (HC)   0-316-92056-8 (PB)
    1. Almanacs, American.   2. Handbooks, vade mecums, etc.
    3. Twentieth century—Miscellanea.   I. Title.
    AY64.W28   1995
    031.02—dc20   95-11568

MV-NY

10 9 8 7 6 5 4 3 2 1

Published simultaneously in Canada by Little, Brown & Company (Canada) Limited

Printed in the United States of America

To the memory of Irving Wallace and Irving Goodman. There are not enough Irvings left in this world.

They Wrote the Original Material

When "The Eds." is used, it means the material has been contributed by the editors of the *Almanac*. The authors, whose initials appear at the ends of the articles, are as follows:

A.B.C.	Andrew B. Cohen		J.B.M.	Joseph B. Morris
A.E.	Ann Elwood		J.E.	John Eastman
A.L.	Alan Linn		J.E.E.	Joan E. Eisenberg
A.R.	Alfred Rosa		J.F.K.	Janet F. Kunert
A.T.	Anita Taylor		J.L.	Jack Lukes
A.W.	Amy Wallace		J.L.K.	Jerold L. Kellman
B.B.	Barbara Bean		J.N.	James Natal
B.C.	Bill Carero		J.R.O.	James R. Orsag Jr.
B.F.	Bruce Felton		J.W.B.	James W. Blair
B.H.	Bill Henkin		J.Z.	John Zebrowski
B.S.	Betty Schaal		K.A.R.	Karla Rosenbusch
C.B.	Craig Buck		K.F.	Karen Feld
C.O.M.	Carol Orsag Madigan		K.H.J.	Kristine H. Johnson
C.P.	Carol Polsgrove		K.L.	Ken Lawless
C.S.	Carl Sifakis		L.A.C.	Lee A. Clayton
D.A.K.	Deborah A. Kent		L.B.W.	Laurence B. Winn
D.B.	Danny Biederman		L.C.	Linda Chase
D.C.	Don Cushman		L.Co.	Loren Coleman
D.R.	Dahlia Rudavsky		L.H.C.	Lewis H. Croce
D.W.	David Wallechinsky		L.S.	Linda Schallan
D.W.C.	Doug Cress		M.B.	Mike Baron
E.B.	Eugene Byrne		M.B.T.	Marguerite B. Thompson
E.Bi.	Esther Biederman		M.C.S.	Michael C. Sheeter
E.H.B.	Everett H. (Tevvy) Ball		M.D.C.	Micheal D. Clodfelter
E.S.L.	Elizabeth S. Lamb		M.E.R.	Marian E. Rudnyk
F.B.	Faubion Bowers		M.G.	Michael Grady
F.Br.	Fern Bryant		M.J.M.	Mary J. MacKenzie
F.D.	Frederick Drimmer		M.S.M.	Michael S. Medved
F.M.W.	Frank M. Woolley		M.S.S.	Michael S. Smith
F.W.S.	Francis W. Schruben		N.C.S.	Nancy C. Sorel
G.G.	George Gamester		N.H.	Nancy Herman
G.K.	Gary Kinder		N.J.M.R.	Norbert James Melvin Roy
G.P.W.	Gregory P. Wilkening		N.L.K.	Nancy Lois Kelton
H.L.R.	Helen L. Reitz		P.E.	Paul Eschholz
H.X.W.	Hunter X. Whitney		P.F.	Pamela Feinsilber
I.W.	Irving Wallace		P.G.	Paul Gerber
J.B.	Jeremy Beadle		P.H.	Paul Hoffman

CONTENTS

TO THE READER

When my father, Irving Wallace, and I began preparing the first *People's Almanac* in 1973, we adopted a working philosophy: learning should be fun, history should be fascinating. It is extremely difficult to make history boring, yet generations of teachers have beaten the odds and done it. By emphasizing the memorization of dates for future regurgitation on exams, many teachers have killed the learning spirit of their students and misled them into believing that history is not only uninteresting, but irrelevant. In *The Twentieth Century* you will find the important dates—in fact, I have tried to include the exact day on which events took place, rather than just the year—but these dates serve as a framework for the best part of history: good stories.

Another flaw in the teaching of history has been the deification of leaders, presenting them as two-dimensional decision makers who have nothing in common with normal human beings. In recent years, the popular media has swung to the opposite extreme, picking apart the personal lives of public figures to such an extent that they appear almost subhuman. In this book, as in previous volumes of *The People's Almanac* series, I have tried to portray important personages as they really are: human beings with strengths and weaknesses, whose public actions are influenced by their private lives.

In addition, I believe that history is made not just by the famous and the powerful, but by everyday people who live and die in relative obscurity. *The Twentieth Century* is sprinkled with "footnote people" like John Howard Griffin, who changed the color of his skin, and James Kilroy, whose scribbled name became a symbol of the common man. Their stories and others like them provide insights into the century that would otherwise be missed in the attempt to follow the big stories in the sweep of history.

The real world is a mixture of the serious and the absurd, of tragedies and amusements. *The Twentieth Century* reflects this diversity. You will find the major battles of the century and the great scientific discoveries, but you will also read about impostors, forgers, and bad predictions.

There are almost as many theories of history as there are history and philosophy professors seeking tenure. Some of them are even worthwhile. You won't find any of those theories in this book. You will, however, find plenty of raw material with which to compare those theories or to create your own.

In our introduction to the original *People's Almanac* my father and I wrote:

This is a reference book to be read for pleasure. This is an informative book that is meant to provide entertainment. This is a book in which to look up facts and also have fun. This is a book with a bias for the little known and the curious—occasionally lifting up a few historic rocks to see what crawls beneath.... This is a volume that attempts to go beyond often repeated, unchallenged data and offer behind-the-scenes, frequently omitted truths.

Twenty years later, I have tried to hold true to this description in *The Twentieth Century*. I hope that you enjoy it.

David Wallechinsky
The People's Almanac
P.O. Box 49699
Los Angeles, CA
90049

P.S. Technically speaking, the twentieth century began January 1, 1901, but in keeping with common usage, this book includes events that occurred in 1900.

THE TWENTIETH CENTURY: A BRIEF INTRODUCTION

It is commonplace when reviewing the twentieth century to marvel: "When the century began, who could have imagined that cars, movies, radios, and telephones would be taken for granted; that men would fly and walk on the moon, children would grow up with television as their baby-sitter and that the world economy would be dependent on computers?" It is true that these developments were unforeseen by all but the most clever of visionaries. Indeed, in the early years of the twentieth century, those people who believed in the possibility of air travel were considered not visionaries, but crackpots.

However, there have been many more developments in the twentieth century that were inconceivable as the nineteenth drew to a close. Few people imagined, for example, a World War—a conflict so contagious that it claimed victims from every inhabited continent. Fewer still guessed that this tragedy would be repeated, giving rise to the first manifestation of that twentieth-century phenomenon, the numbered sequel: World War II. How many people in the nineteenth century took seriously the future existence of a weapon so powerful that it could kill hundreds of thousands of people in a matter of seconds? And of those who did, how many imagined that such a weapon would actually be used?

Who could have imagined in the early 1900s that a radical philosophy, communism, would rule the lives of one-third of the world's population and then, more quickly than it arose, vanish outside of Asia? Who could have predicted that air and water pollution would become so bad, and that the degradation of the environment would become so serious, that international solutions would become necessary?

Many of the trends that have dominated the twentieth century were already in full swing before it began. In Europe and North America, it was the nineteenth century that saw the first shocks of industrialization, but it was the twentieth that experienced the major upheavals. In the United States, for example, 60 percent of Americans lived in rural areas in 1900. By 1920, as a result of the growth of industry, the majority of Americans lived in cities. Factories, having transformed the economy, began dying out, giving way to a postindustrial society. Labor unions, protecting the rights of workers against rich factory owners, were viewed sympathetically by most Americans on into the 1930s. By century's end, they were widely perceived as just another corrupt institution. In the countryside, meanwhile, family farms, the bedrock of nineteenth-century society, were overwhelmed by large corporations mass-producing food with machines, chemical fertilizers, and pesticides.

International trade has existed since before the days of Marco Polo, but only in the twentieth century has the economy of the various nations of the world become truly interdependent. In the 1980s, when nationalists in the United States launched a campaign to "Buy American," they discovered that no matter how hard they tried, it couldn't be done 100 percent. Even American-made automobiles were dependent on parts from Asia and Europe. In 1991, the United States went to war, sacrificing American lives to protect oil fields not in Texas, but in the Persian Gulf. Likewise, when human rights activists tried to promote a boycott of goods from China, they found themselves hardpressed to find toys for their children that hadn't been assembled in factories run by Chinese Communists.

One important change that has occurred in the twentieth century that has been largely ignored in the West by all but scholars is the end of colonialism. Almanacs for the year 1900 listed 54 independent nations. By 1995 that number had grown to 192. The demise of colonialism, though, did little to improve the lives of people in most of the former colonies. Africa is a particularly sad case in point. Most of Africa faces the twenty-first century not with vibrant, growing economies, but in poverty and chaos. Some of this is the fault of the richer European nations who, freed of the burdens of being colonial powers, are able to mine and

xix

farm African lands using the more efficient capitalist model. Nonetheless, most of the blame belongs to African leaders themselves. In 1964, the Organization of African Unity made the disastrous decision to retain colonial boundaries, despite the fact that these artificial frontiers cut right through natural tribal groupings and threw traditional antagonists into the same country. In addition, the majority of African rulers have used their positions to increase their personal wealth and power with little regard for the general good.

One thing that can be said of the twentieth century is that it has been the Century of Democracy. Most nations now hold some sort of elections, a fact that few people in the 1890s would have considered possible. Unfortunately, in most of the world, democracy has not lived up to its billing. Many authoritarian governments stage carefully controlled elections that the opposition has no chance of winning, merely to impress international trade partners and aid donors. Even truly democratic systems can be manipulated. After all, Adolf Hitler gained power by winning an election. Nor have elections guaranteed a sense of participation to the general citizenry. How else to explain that in the United States barely one-third of the voting-age population bothers to cast a ballot?

Like democracy, the concept of human rights already had a long history before the twentieth century. However, spurred by the Civil Rights Movement in the United States and the Anti-Apartheid Movement in South Africa, human rights has achieved a legitimacy not only among the world's peoples, but even among governments, which have, at the very least, been forced to pay lip service to the ideas of freedom of speech, freedom of the press, and freedom of religion. Clearly, though, the great achievements in the field of human rights lie ahead.

When the twentieth century began, proponents of equal rights for women were treated like believers in airplanes: amusing crackpots who were so strange they weren't even worth condemning. All that changed so rapidly that many young women of the 1990s don't understand what all the fuss was about. Women have been elected president or prime minister in nations as diverse as Iceland, Great Britain, Nicaragua, the Philippines, India, and Pakistan, although similar progress in the United States still seems a long way off.

One of the most bizarre trends of the twentieth century has been the growth of mass culture and its even more bizarre component, the democratization of celebrity. The star system already existed in the nineteenth century: composer Franz Liszt, for example, was besieged by swooning groupies. However, the advent of movies and then television has allowed millions of people to share experiences at the same time. Of course, these experiences are com-

pletely passive and they have damaged the growth of local and regional culture. Still, mass media has given people an opportunity to become aware of realities beyond their own.

It is very popular for intellectuals to decry the widespread obsession with celebrity gossip. Isn't it sick that people should be intensely involved in the personal lives of the famous, whom they will never meet? This is undoubtedly true; however, there is a positive side to celebrity gossip. Anyone who has lived in a small town or a closely knit neighborhood knows that most people have a natural curiosity about other people's lives, and this nosiness can be both disruptive and oppressive. When this curiosity is satisfied by following the private lives of celebrities, it relieves the pressure of neighborhood gossip, which can actually be more harmful than celebrity gossip.

Prior to the twentieth century, practically the only people who achieved national or international celebrity were political and military leaders, artists in various fields, and the occasional murderer. When Andy Warhol predicted that "in the future everyone will be famous for fifteen minutes," it appeared to be a statement made merely to attract attention, to gain publicity. In fact, it was surprisingly accurate. As pathetic as it may seem, it is now possible for a man to become well-known around the world simply because his wife cut off his penis.

As with mass culture, there is a bright side to the democratization of celebrity: everyday heroes, otherwise ignored, can now earn their day in the limelight, and their actions often serve as an inspiration to others. Rosa Parks is a good example. When she refused to move to the back of a bus in Montgomery, Alabama, in 1955, she might have gone to jail and been forgotten, as had happened to earlier civil rights protesters who had done the same thing in Kentucky in 1948. But the mass media made millions of people aware of Parks's act, and she became a symbol of resistance to an unfair system. When Italian bandits shot and killed the young son of American tourists, his parents donated their child's organs to Italians waiting for transplants. This act of compassion not only moved people on two continents, but it awoke an entire nation to the concept of organ donations.

For all the massive changes that have taken place in the twentieth century, certain things have stayed the same. As it became clear that technological developments were transforming society, many idealists predicted that war would become obsolete and violent crimes would disappear. Needless to say, nothing could be further from the truth. Torture, massacres, and mass slaughters are no less frequent in the 1990s than they were in the days of Attila the Hun. Indeed, a case could easily be made that things have gotten much worse. Even putting aside the horrors of warfare, in 1995 there was an average of almost seventy murders a day in the United States alone. The level of violence in the much-ballyhooed days of the Wild West pales in comparison.

The most obvious non-change in the twentieth century is that despite the billions of dollars pumped into medical research, everyone who is born eventually dies. It is as simple as that. Each person who dies leaves behind the subtle legacy of his or her actions and emotions. Whether we pay attention to them or not, we live our daily lives amidst this accumulation of legacies. Although it does not appear in books and on television, this too is history.

DAVID WALLECHINSKY'S TWENTIETH CENTURY
History with the Boring Parts Left Out

Chapter 1

QUOTEBOOK

ADDICTION

It is not heroin or cocaine that makes one an addict, it is the need to escape from a harsh reality. There are more television addicts, more baseball and football addicts, more movies addicts, and certainly more alcohol addicts in this country than there are narcotics addicts.

Shirley Chisholm,
testimony to House Select Committee on Crime,
September 17, 1969

ADVICE

Keep a clean nose
Watch the plain clothes
You don't need a weather man
To know which way the wind blows.

Bob Dylan,
"Subterranean Homesick Blues," 1965

Keep on truckin'.

Robert Crumb, catchphrase used
in cartoons from c. 1972

The world is divided into people who do things and people who get the credit. Try, if you can, to belong to the first class. There's far less competition.

Dwight Morrow, letter to his son,
in Harold Nicolson's *Dwight Morrow*, 1935

Never play cards with any man named "Doc." Never eat at any place called "Mom's." And never, ever, no matter what else you do in your whole life, never sleep with anyone whose troubles are worse than your own.

Dave Peltz

It ain't over till it's over.

Yogi Berra, 1973

But the whole thing, after all, may be put very simply. I believe that it is better to tell the truth than to lie. I believe that it is better to be free than to be a slave. And I believe that it is better to know than to be ignorant.

H. L. Mencken, *Living Philosophies*, 1931

Those who give advice are amazed that their wisdom does not always affect others; but the real amazement lies in the fact that most great advice does not even reach from the mouth of the advisor to his own ear.

Muhammad Hijazi,
Hazar Sokhan (A Thousand Sayings)

I got four things to live by: don't say nothin' that will hurt anybody; don't give advice—nobody will take it anyway; don't complain; don't explain.

Edward "Death Valley Scotty" Scott

AFRICAN AMERICANS

When we're unemployed, we're called lazy; when the whites are unemployed it's called a depression.

Jesse Jackson, interview with David Frost,
The Americans, 1970

I'm the world's original gradualist. I just think ninety-odd years is gradual enough.

Thurgood Marshall, reply to Eisenhower's call for
blacks' patience, *I. F. Stone's Weekly*, May 19, 1958

We [African Americans] turned the other cheek so often our heads seemed to revolve on the end of our necks like old stop-and-go signs. . . . We forgave as if forgiving was our talent.

Maya Angelou,
The Heart of a Woman, 1981

I am not tragically colored. There is no great sorrow dammed up in my soul, nor lurking behind my eyes. I do not mind at all. I do not belong to the sobbing school of Negrohood who hold that nature somehow has given them a low-down dirty deal and whose feelings are all hurt about it. Even in the helter-skelter skirmish that is my life, I have seen that the world is to the strong regardless of a little pigmentation more or

H. L. Mencken at work, 1948.

1

less. No, I do not weep at the world—I am too busy
sharpening my oyster knife.
> Zora Neale Hurston,
> "How It Feels to Be Colored Me," 1928

If a man calls me a nigger, he is calling me something I
am not. The nigger exists only in his own mind;
therefore his mind is the nigger. I must feel sorry for
such a man.
> Dick Gregory, The Shadow That Scares Me, 1968

No Viet Cong ever called me Nigger.
> Muhammad Ali

ANARCHISM
My political opinions lean more and more towards
anarchy. . . . The most improper job of any man, even
saints, is bossing other men.
> J. R. R. Tolkien,
> The Letters of J. R. R. Tolkien, 1981

AUSTRALIA
It's so empty and featureless, like a newspaper that
has been entirely censored. We used to drive for miles,
always expecting that round the next corner there
would be something to look at, and there never was.
That's the charm of Australia.
> Robert Morley, Robert Morley "Responsible
> Gentleman," 1966

BOSTON
And this is good old Boston,
The home of the bean and the cod,
Where the Lowells talk to the Cabots
And the Cabots talk only to God.
> John Collins Bossidy, verse spoken
> at Holy Cross College alumni dinner
> in Boston, Massachusetts, 1910

BUSINESS
He's a businessman. . . . I'll make him an offer he can't
refuse.
> Mario Puzo, The Godfather, 1969

My analysis . . . led me to formulate The Peter Principle: In a Hierarchy Every Employee Tends to Rise to
His Level of Incompetence . . . in time every post
tends to be occupied by an employee who is incompetent to carry out its duties. . . . Work is accomplished
by those employees who have not yet reached their
level of incompetence.
> Laurence Peter and Raymond Hall,
> The Peter Principle, 1969

CALAMITY
Calamity, n. A more than commonly plain and
unmistakable reminder that the affairs of this life are
not of our own ordering. Calamities are of two kinds:
misfortune to ourselves, and good fortune to others.
> Ambrose Bierce, The Devil's Dictionary, 1906

Ambrose Bierce, author of The Devil's Dictionary.

CANADA
Canada could have enjoyed:
English government,
French culture,
and American know-how.
Instead it ended up with:
English know-how,
French government,
and American culture.
> John Robert Colombo, "Oh Canada," 1965

In any world menu, Canada must be considered the
vichyssoise of nations—it's cold, half-French, and
difficult to stir.
> Stuart Keate, attributed

Canada is a country so square that even the female
impersonators are women.
> Richard Benner, screenplay, Outrageous!, 1977

CHOICES
Two roads diverged in a wood, and I—
I took the one less traveled by,
and that has made all the difference.
> Robert Frost,
> "The Road Not Taken," 1915

CITIES
Great cities are not like towns, only larger. They differ
from towns and suburbs in basic ways, and one of
these is that cities are, by definition, full of strangers.
> Jane Jacobs, The Death and Life of
> Great American Cities, 1961

CIVILIZATION

Armaments, universal debt and planned obsolescence—those are the three pillars of Western prosperity.
Aldous Huxley, *Island*, 1962

True civilization lies in the dominance of self and not in the dominance of other men.
Luther Standing Bear, *Land of the Spotted Eagle*, 1933

Civilization is more than the appreciation of the Fine Arts. We must not tie it down to museums and studios. I put forward as a general definition of civilization, that a civilized society is exhibiting the five qualities of Truth, Beauty, Adventure, Art, Peace.
Alfred North Whitehead, *Adventures of Ideas*, 1933

Journalist: Mr. Gandhi, what do you think of modern civilization?
Gandhi: *I think it would be a good idea.*
Mahatma Gandhi (Mohandas Karamchand Gandhi), on arrival in England, 1930

CLASS BARRIERS

[Question:] Do you think class barriers have broken down in Britain?
Of course they have, or I wouldn't be sitting here talking to someone like you.
Barbara Cartland, radio interview, 1978

COMMUNISM

From what I hear about Communism, I don't like it, because it isn't on the level.
Gary Cooper, testifying to the House Un-American Activities Committee, 1947

All animals are equal, but some animals are more equal than others.
George Orwell, *Animal Farm*, 1945

Whether you like it or not, history is on our side. We will bury you.
Nikita Khrushchev, address to ambassadors, Kremlin, September 27, 1956

Marxian Socialism must always remain a portent to the historians of Opinion—how a doctrine so illogical and so dull can have exercised so powerful and enduring an influence over the minds of men, and, through them, the events of history.
John Maynard Keynes, *The End of Laissez-Faire*, Third Impression, 1927

COMPROMISE

When you accept our views we shall be in full agreement with you.
Moshe Dayan to Cyrus Vance, August 10, 1977

CONSERVATISM

A conservative is someone who demands a square deal for the rich.
David Frost, *TVam*, 1983

DEMOCRACY

Democracy is the name we give the people whenever we need them.
Robert, Marquis de Flers and Arman de Caillavet, *L'habit vert*, May 31, 1913

Democracy means government by the uneducated, while aristocracy means government by the badly educated.
G. K. Chesterton, *New York Times*, 1931

Our great democracies still tend to think that a stupid man is more likely to be honest than a clever man, and our politicians take advantage of this prejudice by pretending to be even more stupid than nature has made them.
Bertrand Russell, *New Hopes for a Changing World*, 1951

Democracy is that system of government under which the people, having 35,717,342 native-born adult whites to choose from, including thousands who are handsome and many who are wise, pick out a Coolidge to be head of the States.
H. L. Mencken, *Prejudices, Fifth Series*, 1926

You can hold an important public office forever in our country with no qualifications for it but a clean nose, a photogenic face, and a closed mouth. If on top of that you look good on a horse, you are unbeatable.
Raymond Chandler, *The Long Goodbye*, 1953

Under democracy, one party always devotes its chief energies to trying to prove that the other party is unfit to rule—and both commonly succeed, and are right.
H. L. Mencken, *Minority Report*, 1956

Even though counting heads is not an ideal way to govern, at least it is better than breaking them.
Judge Learned Hand, speech to U.S. Federal Bar Association, March 8, 1932

Democracy is good. I say this because other systems are worse.
Jawaharlal Nehru

The death of democracy is not likely to be an assassination from ambush. It will be a slow extinction from apathy, indifference, and undernourishment.
Robert M. Hutchins, *Great Books*, 1954

DIETING

I went on a diet, swore off drinking and heavy eating, and in fourteen days I lost two weeks.
Joe E. Lewis

All the happiness depends on a leisurely breakfast.
John Gunther,
Newsweek, April 14, 1958

DIPLOMACY
A diplomat is a person who can tell you to go to hell in such a way that you actually look forward to the trip.
Caskie Stinnet, Out of the Red, 1960

DISSENT
The dissenter is every human being at those moments of his life when he resigns momentarily from the herd and thinks for himself.
Archibald MacLeish, The Nation, December 4, 1937

DOUBT
The trouble with the world is that the stupid are cocksure and the intelligent full of doubt.
Bertrand Russell, Autobiography, 1967

DREAMS
It is on the whole probable that we continually dream, but that consciousness makes such a noise that we do not hear it.
Carl Jung, quoted in Charles Rycroft,
The Innocence of Dreams

All the things one has forgotten scream for help in dreams.
Elias Canetti, Die Provinz der Menschen
(The Human Province), 1973

All men dream; but not equally. Those who dream by night in the dusty recesses of their minds wake in the day to find it was vanity; but dreamers of the day are dangerous men, for they may act their dream with open eyes, to make it possible.
T. E. Lawrence,
Seven Pillars of Wisdom, 1926

DULLARDS
There is no such thing on earth as an uninteresting subject; the only thing that can exist is an uninterested person.
G. K. Chesterton, Heretics, 1905

ENGLAND
The climate of England has been the world's most powerful colonizing impulse.
Russell Green

If I should die, think only this of me:
That there's some corner of a foreign field
That is forever England. There shall be
In that rich earth a richer dust concealed.
Rupert Brooke, "The Soldier," 1915

EQUALITY
The laws which force segregation do not presume the inferiority of a people; they assume an inherent equalness. It is the logic of the lawmakers that if a society does not erect artificial barriers between people at every point of contact, the people might fraternize and give their attention to the genuine, shared problems of the community.
Lorraine Hansberry, A Matter of Color, 1959

EVOLUTION
One of the odd things about evolution is why it has gone on so long, because you would have thought that any decent world would have stopped with the amoeba. It's an extraordinarily satisfying organism and we've been going into what you might call pathological complexity ever since, ending up, of course, with the Federal Reserve System.
Kenneth Boulding, "The World as an Economic Region," Regional Economic Policy, 1974

EXPERIENCE
Experience is a hard teacher because she gives the test first, the lesson afterwards.
Vernor Sanders Law, "How to Be a Winner,"
This Week, August 14, 1960

EXPERTS
Even when all the experts agree, they may well be mistaken.
Bertrand Russell, Autobiography, 1967

FALKLAND ISLANDS
The Falklands thing [the Falklands War of 1982] was a fight between two bald men over a comb.
Jorge Luis Borges, Time, February 14, 1983

FAME
The nice thing about being a celebrity is that when you bore people, they think it's their fault.
Henry Kissinger, Reader's Digest, April 1985

FORGIVENESS
The stupid neither forgive nor forget; the naïve forgive and forget; the wise forgive but do not forget.
Thomas Szasz, "Social Relations,"
The Second Sin, 1974

FRANCE
The French will only be united under the threat of danger. Nobody can simply bring together a country that has 265 kinds of cheese.
Charles de Gaulle, speech, 1952

FREEDOM
Freedom is an indivisible word. If we want to enjoy it, and fight for it, we must be prepared to extend it to everyone, whether they are rich or poor, whether they agree with us or not, no matter what their race or the colour of their skin.
Wendell Willkie, One World, 1943

Inequality is the inevitable consequence of liberty.
Salvador de Madariaga, Anarchy or Hierarchy, 1937

Freedom is not something that anybody can be given, freedom is something people take.
James Baldwin, Nobody Knows My Name, 1961

Freedom's just another word for nothing left to lose.
Kris Kristofferson and Fred Foster,
"Me and Bobby McGee," 1969

When people are free to do as they please, they usually imitate each other.
Eric Hoffer, *The Passionate State of Mind*, 1954

We have to believe in free-will. We've got no choice.
Isaac Bashevis Singer, *The Times*, June 21, 1982

FRIENDSHIP

Your friend is the man who knows all about you, and still likes you.
Elbert Hubbard, *The Notebook*, 1927

Friends are God's apology for relations.
Hugh Kingsmill, quoted in Michael Holroyd's
The Best of Kingsmill

To find a friend one must close one eye. To keep him—two.
Norman Douglas, *Almanac*, 1941

Friendship is unnecessary, like philosophy, like art. . . . It has no survival value; rather it is one of those things that give value to survival.
C. S. Lewis, *The Four Loves*, 1960

Acquaintance, n. A person whom we know well enough to borrow from, but not well enough to lend to. A degree of friendship called slight when its object is poor or obscure, and intimate when he is rich or famous.
Ambrose Bierce, *The Devil's Dictionary*, 1906

GERMANY

Germany is a machine for producing geniuses. Its crowning product was the German Jew which in suitably dramatic style it then tried to destroy.
Michel Tournier, *Observer*, January 29, 1983

THE GOOD LIFE

All the things I really like to do are either immoral, illegal, or fattening.
Alexander Woollcott, attributed

GOSSIP

When you are in trouble, people who call to sympathize are really looking for the particulars.
Edgar Watson Howe, *Country Town Sayings*, 1911

Some people will believe anything if you whisper it to them.
Louis B. Nizer, *Thinking on Your Feet*, 1940

GREATNESS

There is a great man who makes every man feel small. But the real great man is the man who makes every man feel great.
G. K. Chesterton, *Charles Dickens*, 1906

GUTS

Dorothy Parker: *Exactly what do you mean by "guts"?*
Hemingway: *I mean, "Grace under pressure."*
Ernest Hemingway, quoted in *The New Yorker*,
November 30, 1929

HAPPINESS

Happiness is an imaginary condition, formerly attributed by the living to the dead, now usually attributed by adults to children, and by children to adults.
Thomas Szasz, *The Second Sin*, 1974

HATRED

One of the reasons people cling to their hates so stubbornly is because they seem to sense, once hate is gone, that they will be forced to deal with pain.
James Baldwin, *Notes of a Native Son*, 1955

Hatred rarely does any harm to its object. It is the hater who suffers. His soul is warped and his life poisoned by dwelling on past injuries or projecting schemes of revenge. Rancor in the bosom is the foe of personal happiness.
Max Aitken, Baron Beaverbrook,
The Divine Propagandist, 1962

One of the most time-consuming things is to have an enemy.
E. B. White, "Letter from the East," *The New Yorker*,
February 22, 1958

One of the worst things about life is not how nasty the nasty people are. You know that already. It is how nasty the nice people can be.
Anthony Powell, *A Dance to the Music of Time:
The Kindly Ones*, 1962

THE HERD

There is no nonsense so arrant that it cannot be made the creed of the vast majority by adequate governmental action.
Bertrand Russell, *Unpopular Essays*, 1950

No one . . . has ever lost money by underestimating the intelligence of great masses of the plain people.
H. L. Mencken, *Chicago Tribune*, September 19, 1926

HEROES

Andrea: *Unhappy the land that has no heroes!* . . .
Galileo: *No. Unhappy the land that needs heroes.*
Bertolt Brecht, *Leben des Galilei* (Life of Galileo),
1939

HISTORY

That men do not learn much from the lessons of history is the most important of all the lessons that history has to teach.
Aldous Huxley, "Case of Voluntary Ignorance,"
Collected Essays, 1959

People are trapped in history and history is trapped in them.
James Baldwin, *Notes of a Native Son*, 1955

History is a vast early warning system.
     Norman Cousins, *Saturday Review*, April 15, 1978

History teaches us that men and nations behave wisely once they have exhausted all other alternatives.
                                        Abba Eban, 1970

Progress, far from consisting in change, depends on retentiveness. Those who cannot remember the past are condemned to repeat it.
     George Santayana, *The Life of Reason*, 1905

"Who controls the past," ran the Party slogan, "controls the future: who controls the present controls the past."
                              George Orwell, *1984*, 1949

The past is always being changed.
     Jorge Luis Borges, in an interview with Nicholas Shakespeare, *The Times*, October 6, 1983

History does not unfold: it piles up.
          Robert M. Adams, *Bad Mouth*, 1977

HOOVER, J. EDGAR
I'd much rather have that fellow inside my tent pissing out, than outside my tent pissing in.
     Lyndon B. Johnson, when asked why he retained J. Edgar Hoover at the FBI, *Guardian Weekly*, December 18, 1971

IDEALISM
I want to die a slave to principles, not to men.
                                        Emiliano Zapata

IDEAS
An idea isn't responsible for the people who believe in it.
          Don Marquis, *New York Sun*, c. 1918

You can kill a man, but you can't kill an idea.
     Myrlie Evers, on the death of her husband, Medgar, June 12, 1963

IMPERIALISM
The rest of mankind is the carving knife . . . while we are the fish and the meat.
                                        Sun Yat-sen

INCOMPETENCE
Human blunders usually do more to shape history than human wickedness.
A. J. P. Taylor, *The Origins of the Second World War*, 1961

INFERIORITY
No one can make you feel inferior without your consent.
     Eleanor Roosevelt, quoted in Don Peretz Elkins's *Glad to be Me*

INTELLIGENCE
The test of a first-rate intelligence is the ability to hold two opposed ideas in the mind at the same time, and still retain the ability to function. One should, for example, be able to see that things are hopeless and yet be determined to make them otherwise.
          F. Scott Fitzgerald, *The Crack-Up*, 1936

JAPAN
While we spend energy and imagination on inventing new ways of cleaning the floors of our houses, the Japanese solve the problem by not dirtying them in the first place.
     Bernard Rudofsky, *The Kimono Mind*, 1965

KNOWLEDGE
Knowledge fills a large brain; it merely inflates a small one.
     Sydney Harris, *Detroit Free Press*, January 7, 1982

LAWS
It may be true that the law cannot make a man love me, but it can keep him from lynching me, and I think that's pretty important.
                              Martin Luther King Jr.

LEADERSHIP
There are two ways of exerting one's strength: one is pushing down, the other is pulling up.
                              Booker T. Washington

It is no easy task to lead men. But it is easy enough to drive them.
                              Rabindranath Tagore

LEARNING
It is a great nuisance that knowledge can be acquired only by hard work.
          W. Somerset Maugham, *Cakes and Ale*, 1930

An educated man should know everything about something, and something about everything.
          Dame C. V. Wedgwood, address, Birkbeck College, 1963

Most of the most important experiences that truly educate cannot be arranged ahead of time with any precision.
Harold Taylor, "The Private World of the Man with a Book," *Saturday Review*, January 7, 1961

Teaching is not a lost art, but the regard for it is a lost tradition.
          Jacques Barzun, *Newsweek*, December 5, 1955

In teaching you cannot see the fruit of a day's work. It is invisible and remains so, maybe for twenty years.
          Jacques Barzun, *Teacher in America*, 1944

One of the things that is manifestly wrong with our school system is our thoughtless practice of hiring and assigning the youngest and the least experienced teachers for the lowest classes, when it should be quite the other way around.
Sydney Harris, Detroit Free Press, July 15, 1981

It is hard to convince a high-school student that he will encounter a lot of problems more difficult than those of algebra and geometry.
Edgar W. Howe, Country Town Sayings, 1911

Teachers are overworked and underpaid. True, it is an exacting and exhausting business, this damming up the flood of human potentialities.
George B. Leonard, Education and Ecstasy, 1968

I always loved learning and hated school.
I. F. Stone, "In Defense of the Campus Rebels," I. F. Stone's Weekly, May 19, 1969

I find that the three major administrative problems on a campus are sex for the students, athletics for the alumni and parking for the faculty.
Clark Kerr, Time, November 17, 1958

LIFE

Life is not a daily dying, not a pointless end, not an ashes-to-ashes and dust-to-dust, but a soaring and blinding gift snatched from eternity.
Irving Wallace, The Prize, 1962

He not busy being born is busy dying.
Bob Dylan, "It's Alright Ma, I'm Only Bleeding," 1965

Life is a tragedy when seen in close-up, but a comedy in long-shot.
Charlie Chaplin

Life is a sexually transmitted disease and there is a 100 percent mortality rate.
R. D. Laing, Observer, March 17, 1985

The real malady is fear of life, not death.
Naguib Mahfouz, Chatter on the Nile, 1966

If you want my final opinion on the mystery of life and all that, I can give it to you in a nutshell. The universe is like a safe to which there is a combination. But the combination is locked up in the safe.
Peter De Vries, Let Me Count the Ways, 1965

LOVE

And in the end, the love you take is equal to the love you make.
The Beatles, "The End," Abbey Road, 1969

The great tragedy of life is not that men perish, but that they cease to love.
W. Somerset Maugham, The Summing Up, 1938

Marcel Proust with female friends.

Impelled by a state of mind which is destined not to last, we make our irrevocable decisions.
Marcel Proust, In Search of Lost Time: The Prisoner, 1924

It is seldom indeed that one parts on good terms, because if one were on good terms one would not part.
Marcel Proust, In Search of Lost Time: The Prisoner, 1924

In the evening of life we shall be judged on love, and not one of us is going to come off very well, and were it not for my absolute faith in the loving forgiveness of my Lord I could not call on him to come.
Madeleine L'Engle, The Irrational Season, 1977

When a chap is in love, he will go out in all kinds of weather to keep an appointment with his beloved. Love can be demanding, in fact more demanding than law. It has its own imperatives—think of a mother sitting by the bedside of a sick child through the night, impelled only by love. Nothing is too much trouble for love.

Desmond Tutu

MANNERS

There is a truism about manners that can be stated didactically: Each generation believes that the manners of the generation that follows it have gone to hell in a hand basket.
Russell Lynes, "On Good Behavior," Architectural Digest, 1986

THE MEEK

It's going to be fun to watch and see how long the meek can keep the earth when they inherit it.

Kim Hubbard, *Abe Martin*, 1907

The meek shall inherit the earth, but not its mineral rights.

J. Paul Getty

MEN AND WOMEN

Men and women should live next door and visit each other once in a while.

Katharine Hepburn

MONEY

Money can't buy friends, but you can get a better class of enemy.

Spike Milligan, *Puckoon*, 1963

Money, it turned out, was exactly like sex, you thought of nothing else if you didn't have it and thought of other things if you did.

James Baldwin, "The Black Boy Looks at the White Boy," *Esquire*, May 1961

Let me tell you about the very rich. They are different from you and me. They possess and enjoy early, and it does something to them, makes them soft where we are hard, and cynical where we are trustful, in a way that, unless you were born rich, it is very difficult to understand. They think, deep in their hearts, that they are better than we are because we had to discover the compensations and refuges of life for ourselves. Even when they enter deep into our world or sink below us, they still think that they are better than we are. They are different.

F. Scott Fitzgerald, "The Rich Boy," *All the Sad Young Men*, 1926

God shows his contempt for wealth by the kind of person he selects to receive it.

Austin O'Malley, attributed, 1932

Leo, he who hesitates is poor.

Mel Brooks, screenplay, *The Producers*, 1968

Poor is a state of mind you never grow out of, but being broke is just a temporary condition.

Dick Gregory, *Nigger*, 1964

They say money talks, but the only thing it ever says to me is good-bye.

Paul Waner

In a consumer society there are inevitably two kinds of slaves: the prisoners of addiction and the prisoners of envy.

Ivan Illich, *Tools of Conviviality*, 1973

The customer is never wrong.

César Ritz, quoted in *Piccadilly to Pall Mall*, by R. Velilland and C. E. Jerningham

A bank is a place that will lend you money if you can prove that you don't need it.

Bob Hope, in Alan Harrington's *Life in the Crystal Palace*, 1959

If Patrick Henry thought that taxation without representation was bad, he should see how bad it is with representation.

Farmer's Almanac, 1966

In public services, we lag behind all the industrialized nations of the West, preferring that the public money go not to the people but to big business. The result is a unique society in which we have free enterprise for the poor and socialism for the rich.

Gore Vidal, "Edmund Wilson, Tax Dodger," *Reflections upon a Sinking Ship*, 1969

The instability of the economy is equaled only by the instability of economists.

John Henry Williams, *New York Times*, June 2, 1956

MOTIVATION

We were brought up with the value that as we sow, so shall we reap. We discarded the idea that anything we did was its own reward.

Janet Harris, *The Prime of Ms. America*, 1975

NATIONS

If people behaved in the way nations do they would all be put in straitjackets.

Tennessee Williams, BBC interview, 1970s

The great nations have always acted like gangsters, and the small nations like prostitutes.

Stanley Kubrick, *The Guardian*, June 5, 1963

Small nations are like indecently dressed women. They tempt the evil-minded.

Julius Nyerere, quoted in *The Reporter*, April 9, 1964

OPPRESSION

The most potent weapon in the hands of the oppressor is the mind of the oppressed.

Steve Biko, speech to the Cape Town Conference on Inter-racial Studies, 1971

I shall not rest quiet in Montparnasse.
I shall not lie easy at Winchelsea.
You may bury my body in Sussex grass,
You may bury my tongue at Champmédy.
I shall not be there, I shall rise and pass.
Bury my heart at Wounded Knee.

Stephen Vincent Benét, "American Names," *Yale Review*, Vol. 17, 1927

PATRIOTISM

Patriotism, as I see it, is often an arbitrary veneration of real estate above principles.

George Nathan, *Testament of a Critic*, 1931

I have never understood why one's affections must be confined, as once with women, to a single country.
John Kenneth Galbraith, *A Life in Our Times, 1981*

PESSIMISM
A pessimist is a man who looks both ways before crossing a one-way street.
Laurence J. Peter, *Peter's Quotations, 1977*

The optimist proclaims that we live in the best of all possible worlds; the pessimist fears that this is true.
James Branch Cabell, *The Silver Stallion, 1926*

PHILOSOPHERS
Philosophers are adults who persist in asking childish questions.
Isaiah Berlin, quoted in the *Listener, 1978*

POLITICS
In order to become the master, the politician poses as the servant.
Charles de Gaulle, 1970

The wrong sort of people are always in power because they would not be in power if they were not the wrong sort of people.
Jon Wynne Tyson, *Times Literary Supplement*

There are two major kinds of promises in politics: the promise made by candidates to the voters and the promises made by the candidates to persons and groups able to deliver the vote. Promises falling into the latter category are loosely called "patronage," and promises falling into the former category are most frequently called "lies."
Dick Gregory, *Dick Gregory's Political Primer, 1972*

Since a politician never believes what he says, he is always astonished when others do.
Charles de Gaulle, 1962

A candidate could easily commit political suicide if he were to come up with an unconventional thought during a presidential tour.
E. B. White, "Letter from the East," *The New Yorker,* November 3, 1956

The arithmetic of modern politics makes it tempting to overlook the very poor, because they are an inarticulate minority.
John Kenneth Galbraith

Politics, as a practice, whatever its professions, has always been the systematic organization of hatreds.
Henry Brooks Adams, *The Education of Henry Adams, 1907*

A politician was a person with whose politics you did not agree. When you did agree, he was a statesman.
David Lloyd George, speech, July 2, 1935

If a large city can, after intense intellectual efforts, choose for its mayor a man who merely will not steal from it, we consider it a triumph of the suffrage.
Frank Moore Colby, "On Seeing Ten Bad Plays," *The Colby Essays, 1926*

If we insist that public life be reserved for those whose personal history is pristine, we are not going to get paragons of virtue running our affairs. We will get the very rich, who contract out the messy things in life; the very dull, who have nothing to hide and nothing to show; and the very devious, expert at covering their tracks and ambitious enough to risk their discovery.
Charles Krauthammer, "Pietygate: School for Scandal," *Time,* September 10, 1984

I learned in business that you had to be very careful when you told somebody that's working for you to do something, because the chances were very high he'd do it. In government, you don't have to worry about that.
George P. Shultz, *New York Times,* October 14, 1984

I like to operate like a submarine on sonar. When I am picking up noise from both the left and right, I know my course is correct.
Gustavo Díaz Ordaz

Now I can go back to being ruthless again.
Robert F. Kennedy, on winning the race for the U.S. Senate, *Esquire,* April 1965

POSTERITY
You can keep the things of bronze and stone and give me one man to remember me just once a year.
Damon Runyon

POWER
Speak softly and carry a big stick.
Theodore Roosevelt, speech, September 2, 1901

Power is the great aphrodisiac.
Henry Kissinger, quoted in the *New York Times,* January 19, 1971

PREJUDICE
There is a tendency to judge a race, a nation, or a distinct group by its least worthy members.
Eric Hoffer, *The True Believer, 1951*

PROGRESS
What one generation sees as a luxury, the next sees as a necessity.
Anthony Crosland, *Observer, 1975*

PROMISE
Whom the gods wish to destroy they first call promising.
Cyril Connolly, *Enemies of Promise, 1938*

There is no heavier burden than a great potential.
Linus in *Peanuts,* by Charles Schulz, 1961

PROPAGANDA

The effectiveness of political and religious propaganda depends upon the methods employed, not on the doctrine taught. These doctrines may be true or false, wholesome or pernicious—it makes little or no difference. . . . Under favorable conditions, practically everybody can be converted to practically anything.

Aldous Huxley, Brave New World Revisited, 1958

The real struggle is not between East and West, or capitalism and communism, but between education and propaganda.

Martin Buber, in Encounter with Martin Buber, by Aubrey Hodes

PSYCHOANALYSIS

Psychoanalysis is confession without absolution.

G. K. Chesterton

PUBLIC OPINION

In a society in which there is no law, and in theory no compulsion, the only arbiter of behavior is public opinion. But public opinion, because of the tremendous urge to conformity in gregarious animals, is less tolerant than any system of law.

George Orwell, Collected Essays, 1968

PURITANISM

Puritanism—The haunting fear that someone, somewhere, may be happy.

H. L. Mencken, A Book of Burlesques, 1928

PURPOSE

There's something I would like to understand. And I don't think anyone can explain it. . . . There's your life. You begin it, feeling that it's something so precious and rare, so beautiful that it's like a sacred treasure. Now it's over, and it doesn't make any difference to anyone, and it isn't that they are indifferent, it's just that they don't know, they don't know what it means, that treasure of mine, and there's something about it that they should understand. I don't understand it myself, but there's something that should be understood by all of us. Only what is it? What?

Ayn Rand, We the Living, 1959

Life is either a daring adventure or nothing. To keep our faces toward change and behave like free spirits in the presence of fate is strength undefeatable.

Helen Keller, Let Us Have Faith, 1940

It is often easier to fight for principles than to live up to them.

Adlai Stevenson, speech, New York, August 27, 1952

The mark of the immature man is that he wants to die nobly for a cause, while the mark of the mature man is that he wants to live humbly for one.

Wilhelm Stekel, quoted in J. D. Salinger, Catcher in the Rye, 1951

Pray that your loneliness may spur you into finding something to live for, great enough to die for.

Dag Hammarskjöld, Diaries, 1951

QUOTATIONS

It would be nice if sometimes the kind things I say were considered worthy of quotation. It isn't difficult, you know, to be witty or amusing when one has something to say that is destructive, but damned hard to be clever and quotable when you are singing someone's praises.

Noël Coward, quoted in William Marchant's The Pleasure of His Company, 1981

RACISM

Racism is the snobbery of the poor.

Raymond Aron

REALISM

You may be sure that when a man begins to call himself a realist he is preparing to do something that he is secretly ashamed of doing.

Sydney J. Harris

REALITY

Human kind cannot bear too much reality.

T. S. Eliot, Murder in the Cathedral, 1935

RELATIVITY

When a man you like switches from what he said a year ago, or four years ago, he is a broad-minded person who has courage enough to change his mind with changing conditions. When a man you don't like does it, he is a liar who has broken his promises.

Franklin P. Adams, Nods and Becks, 1944

RESPONSIBILITY

The buck stops here.

Harry S. Truman, sign on his presidential desk

RETIREMENT

To retire is to begin to die.

Pablo Casals, contribution, Philadelphia Bulletin, reprinted October 28, 1973

REVOLUTION

Revolution is not a dinner party, not an essay, nor a painting, nor a piece of embroidery; it cannot be advanced softly, gradually, carefully, considerately, respectfully, politely, plainly, and modestly. A revolution is an insurrection, an act of violence by which one class overthrows another.

Mao Zedong, March 1927

A revolution is not a bed of roses. A revolution is a struggle to the death between the future and the past.

Fidel Castro

Revolution is always based on land. Revolution is never based on begging somebody for an integrated cup of coffee.

Malcolm X, Malcolm X Speaks, 1965

I am a revolutionist by birth, reading and principle. I am always on the side of the revolutionists because there never was a revolution unless there were some oppressive and intolerable conditions against which to revolt.

Mark Twain (Samuel Langhorne Clemens), interview, April 15, 1906, *New York Sun, Tribune, World,* in defense of Maksim Gorky

Revolution is the festival of the oppressed.

Germaine Greer

All successful revolutions are the kicking in of a rotten door.

John Kenneth Galbraith, *The Age of Uncertainty,* 1977

Every revolution evaporates and leaves behind only the slime of a new bureaucracy.

Franz Kafka, *The Great Wall of China: Aphorisms 1917–19,* 1931

A violent revolution has always brought forth a dictatorship of some kind or the other. . . . After a revolution, a new privileged class of rulers and exploiters grows up in the course of time to which the people at large is once again subject.

Jayaprakash Narayan

RUDENESS

It's not a slam at you when people are rude—it's a slam at the people they've met before.

F. Scott Fitzgerald, *The Last Tycoon,* 1941

Rudeness is the weak man's imitation of strength.

Eric Hoffer, *The Passionate State of Mind,* 1955

RULES

There was only one catch and that was Catch-22, which specified that a concern for one's own safety in the face of dangers that were real and immediate was the process of a rational mind. Orr was crazy and could be grounded. All he had to do was ask; and as soon as he did, he would no longer be crazy and would have to fly more missions. Orr would be crazy to fly more missions and sane if he didn't, but if he was sane he had to fly them. If he flew them he was crazy and didn't have to; but if he didn't want to he was sane and had to. Yossarian was moved very deeply by the absolute simplicity of this clause of Catch-22, and let out a respectful whistle.

Joseph Heller, *Catch-22,* 1961

RUSSIA

Communism was a good idea that was ruined because the first people to try it were Slavs.

Gore Vidal on television to Merv Griffin, 1976

SALVATION

Human salvation lies in the hands of the creatively maladjusted.

Martin Luther King Jr., *Strength to Love,* 1963

SAUDI ARABIA

We're Going To War To Defend People Who Won't Let Women Drive?

Protest button, 1991

SELF-IMAGE

The image of myself which I try to create in my own mind in order that I may love myself is very different from the image which I try to create in the minds of others in order that they may love me.

W. H. Auden, *The Dyer's Hand,* 1963

SEX

Whoever called it necking was a poor judge of anatomy.

Groucho Marx

[On masturbation:]
Don't knock it, it's sex with someone you love.

Woody Allen, *Annie Hall,* 1977

Murder is a crime. Describing murder is not. Sex is not a crime. Describing sex is.

Gershon Legman, quoted in *Maledicta* magazine, 1977

Of all sexual aberrations, chastity is the strangest.

Anatole France (Jacques Anatole Thibault)

He moved his lips about her ears and neck as though in thirsting search of an erogenous zone. A waste of time, he knew from experience. Erogenous zones were either everywhere or nowhere.

Joseph Heller, *Catch-22,* 1961

. . . and how he kissed me under the Moorish wall and I thought well as well him as another and then I asked him with my eyes to ask again yes and then he asked me would I yes to say yes my mountain flower and first I put my arms around him yes and drew him down to me so he could feel my breasts all perfume yes and his heart was going like mad and yes I said yes I will Yes.

James Joyce, *Ulysses,* 1922

Woman is: finally screwing and your groin and buttocks and thighs ache like hell and you're all wet and bloody and it wasn't like a Hollywood movie at all but Jesus, at least you're not a virgin anymore but is this what it's all about? And meanwhile he's asking "Did you come?"

Robin Morgan, *Sisterhood Is Powerful,* 1970

When modern women discovered the orgasm it was, combined with modern birth control, perhaps the biggest single nail in the coffin of male dominance.

Eva Figes, quoted in *The Descent of Woman,* by Elaine Morgan, 1972

Quite a few women told me, one way or another, that they thought it was sex, not youth, that's wasted on the young.

Janet Harris, *The Prime of Ms. America,* 1975

Whenever I hear people discussing birth control, I remember that I was the fifth.

Clarence Darrow

SINCERITY
When a person tells you, "I'll think it over and let you know"—you know.

Olin Miller

Sincerity is all that counts. It's a widespread modern heresy. Think again. Bolsheviks are sincere. Fascists are sincere. Lunatics are sincere. People who believe the earth is flat are sincere. They can't all be right. Better make certain first you've got something to be sincere about and with.

Tom Driberg, Daily Express, 1937

SINS
Christ died for our sins. Dare we make his martyrdom meaningless by not committing them?

Jules Feiffer

SOCIAL RESPONSIBILITY
I disapprove of what you say, but I will defend to the death your right to say it.

Evelyn Beatrice Hall, The Friends of Voltaire, 1906

Be part of the answer, not part of the problem.

Buell Gallagher, 1964

Pray for the dead and fight like hell for the living.

Mary "Mother Jones" Harris, Autobiography of Mother Jones, 1925

Goodbye, Bill. I die like a true-blue rebel.
Don't waste any time in mourning. Organize.
Joe Hill (Joseph Hillstrom), telegram to Bill Haywood before Hill's execution by firing squad, November 18, 1915

Years ago I began to recognize my kinship with all living beings. . . . I said then, and I say now, that while there is a lower class I am in it, while there is a criminal element, I am of it, while there is a soul in prison, I am not free.

Eugene V. Debs, speech at federal court, Cleveland, Ohio, September 11, 1918

In Germany, the Nazis came for the Communists and I didn't speak up because I was not a Communist. Then they came for the Jews and I didn't speak up because I was not a Jew. Then they came for the trade unionists and I didn't speak up because I was not a trade unionist. Then they came for the Catholics and I was a Protestant so I didn't speak up. Then they came for me. . . . By that time there was no one to speak up for anyone.

Martin Niemöller, 1945

Pierrot: I love humanity but I hate people.
Edna St. Vincent Millay, Aria da Capo, 1920

Edna St. Vincent Millay.

Blanche: I have always depended on the kindness of strangers.
Tennessee Williams, A Streetcar Named Desire, 1947

"Equality," I spoke the word
As if a wedding vow
Ah, but I was so much older then,
I'm younger than that now.

Bob Dylan, "My Back Pages," 1964

Ninotchka: Why should you carry other people's bags?
Porter: Well, that's my business, Madame.
Ninotchka: That's no business. That's social injustice.
Porter: That depends on the tip.
Charles Brackett, Billy Wilder, and D. M. Marshman Jr., screenplay, Ninotchka, 1939

STATESMANSHIP
The first requirement of a statesman is that he be dull. This is not always easy to achieve.

Dean Acheson, 1970

SUCCESS
It takes twenty years to make an overnight success.
Eddie Cantor, New York Times, October 20, 1963

The greatest accomplishment is not in never falling, but in rising again after you fall.

Vince Lombardi, in Jerry Kramer's Instant Replay, 1968

Later on I learned, especially in school, to value "success" and to hide "failure" so that I wouldn't be scolded or ridiculed. That wasn't the way I had started out, when both were interesting and failure was sometimes more interesting than success because it raised more questions.

Barry Stevens, Person to Person, 1967

As always, victory finds a hundred fathers, but defeat is an orphan.

Count Galeazzo Ciano, Diary, September 9, 1942

The penalty of success is to be bored by people who used to snub you.

Nancy Astor, Sunday Express, January 12, 1956

SWITZERLAND

The train passed fruit farms and clean villages and Swiss cycling in kerchiefs, calendar scenes that you admire for a moment before feeling an urge to move on to a new month.

Paul Theroux, The Great Railway Bazaar, 1975

In Italy, for 30 years under the Borgias, they had warfare, terror, murder and bloodshed, but they produced Michaelangelo, Leonardo da Vinci and the Renaissance. In Switzerland they had brotherly love; they had 500 years of democracy and peace—and what did they produce? The cuckoo clock.

Graham Greene, screenplay, The Third Man, 1949

TAKING CHANCES

An Immortal said: "In playing chess, there is no infallible way of winning, but there is an infallible way of not losing." He was asked what this infallible way could be, and replied: "It is not to play chess."

Feng Yula

If the creator had a purpose in equipping us with a neck, he surely meant us to stick it out.

Arthur Koestler, Encounter, 1970

TALKING

The opposite of talking isn't listening. The opposite of talking is waiting.

Fran Lebowitz, Social Studies, 1981

TECHNOLOGY

Our scientific power has outrun our spiritual power. We have guided missiles and misguided men.

Martin Luther King Jr., Strength to Love, 1963

THINKING

A great many people think they are thinking when they are rearranging their prejudices.

William James

We know what a person thinks not when he tells us what he thinks, but by his actions.

Isaac Bashevis Singer, New York Times Magazine, November 26, 1978

If you make people think they're thinking they'll love you: but if you really make them think, they'll hate you.

Don Marquis, Archy and Mehitabel, 1917

TIME

A good holiday is one spent among people whose notions of time are vaguer than yours.

J. B. Priestley

The necessity of not missing a train has taught us to account for minutes whereas among ancient Romans . . . the notions not of minutes but even of fixed hours barely existed.

Marcel Proust, In Search of Lost Time: Cities of the Plain, 1921–22

In theory one is aware that the earth revolves but in practice one does not perceive it, the ground upon which one treads seems not to move, and one can live undisturbed. So it is with Time in one's life.

Marcel Proust, In Search of Lost Time: Within a Budding Grove, 1919

In a real dark night of the soul it is always three in the morning, day after day.

F. Scott Fitzgerald, The Crack-Up, 1936

Three o'clock is always too late or too early for anything you want to do.

Jean-Paul Sartre, La Nausée (Nausea), 1938

TRUTH

I never give them hell. I just tell the truth, and they think it is hell.

Harry S. Truman, quoted in Look, April 3, 1953

It is hard to believe that a man is telling the truth when you know that you would lie if you were in his place.

H. L. Mencken, 1919

As scarce as truth is, the supply has always been in excess of the demand.

Henry Wheeler Shaw, Rocky Mountain News, June 5, 1980

UNITED STATES

The chief business of America is business.

Calvin Coolidge, speech, Washington, D.C., January 17, 1925

Violence is as American as cherry pie.

Hubert (H. Rap) Brown, Die, Nigger, Die, 1969

Racism is so universal in this country, so widespread and deep-seated, that it is invisible because it is so normal.

Shirley Chisholm, Unbought and Unbossed, 1970

To be black and conscious in America is to be in a constant state of rage.

James Baldwin

In America everybody is of the opinion that he has no social superiors, since all men are equal, but he does not admit that he has no social inferiors.

Bertrand Russell, Unpopular Essays, 1950

America is the only nation in history which miraculously has gone directly from barbarism to degeneration without the usual interval of civilization.

Georges Clemenceau, attributed

Americans think of themselves as a huge rescue squad on twenty-four-hour call to any spot on the globe where dispute and conflict may erupt.

Eldridge Cleaver, Soul on Ice, 1968

The best way to make Communists is to put the Americans into a place where there were no Communists before.

Norodom Sihanouk

Let's face it: Intellectual achievement and the intellectual elite are alien to the mainstream of American society. They are off to the side in a sub-section of esoteric isolation labeled "oddball," "high brow," "egghead," "double-dome."

Elmo Roper, "Roadblocks to Bookbuying," Publishers Weekly, June 16, 1958

Congress is so strange. A man gets up to speak and says nothing. Nobody listens—and then everybody disagrees.

Boris Marshalov, Reader's Digest, March 1941

Can any of you seriously say the Bill of Rights could get through Congress today? It wouldn't even get out of committee.

Ambrose Bierce, The Devil's Dictionary, 1906

In a land in which the tough guy is admired, politeness is widely considered to be effeminate.

Ashley Montagu, The American Way of Life, 1967

You can travel fifty thousand miles in America without once tasting a piece of good bread.

Henry Miller, "The Staff of Life," Remember to Remember, 1947

The Russians can give you arms, but only the United States can give you a selection.

Anwar el-Sadat, Newsweek, January 13, 1975

One comes to the United States—always, no matter how often—to see the future. It's what life in one's own country will be like, five, ten, twenty years from now.

Ehud Yonay, New York Times, November 26, 1972

I love America more than any other country in the world, and, exactly for this reason, I insist on the right to criticize her perpetually.

James Baldwin, Notes of a Native Son, 1955

WHITE PEOPLE

Whites tend to regard Africans as a separate breed. They do not look upon them as people with families of their own; they do not realize that they have emotions—that they fall in love like white people do; that they want to be with their wives and children like white people want to be with theirs; that they want to earn enough money to support their families properly, to feed and clothe them and send them to school. And what "house-boy" or "garden-boy" or laborer can ever hope to do this?

Nelson Mandela, statement during the Rivonia trial, April 20, 1964

The whites have always had the say in America. White people made Jesus white, angels white, the Last Supper white. If I threaten you, I'm blackmailing you. A black cat is bad luck. If you're put out of a club, you're blackballed. Angel's food cake is white; devil's food cake is black. Good guys in cowboy movies wear white hats. The bad guys always wore black hats.

Muhammad Ali

White men seem to have difficulty in realizing that people who live differently from themselves still might be traveling the upward and progressive road of life.

Luther Standing Bear, Land of the Spotted Eagle, 1933

You gotta say this for the white race—its self-confidence knows no bounds. Who else could go to a small island in the South Pacific where there's no poverty, no crime, no unemployment, no war and no worry—and call it a "primitive society"?

Dick Gregory, From the Back of the Bus, 1962

WILDERNESS

We did not think of the great open plains, the beautiful rolling hills, and the winding streams with tangled growth, as "wild." Only to the white man was nature a "wilderness" and only to him was the land infested with "wild" animals and "savage" people. To us it was tame. Earth was bountiful and we were surrounded with the blessings of the Great Mystery. Not until the hairy man from the east came and with brutal frenzy heaped injustices upon us and the families we loved was it "wild" for us. When the very animals of the forest began fleeing from his approach, then it was that for us the "Wild West" began.

Luther Standing Bear, Land of the Spotted Eagle, 1933

WOMEN

I'm furious about the Women's Liberationists. They keep getting up on soapboxes and proclaiming that women are brighter than men. That's true, but it should be kept very quiet or it ruins the whole racket.

Anita Loos, 1973

Women who seek to be equal to men lack ambition.

Bumper sticker

No woman, except for so-called deviants, seriously wishes to be male and have a penis. But most women *would like to have the privileges and opportunities that go with it.*

Eliana Gianini Belotti, *Little Girls*, 1973

People call me a feminist whenever I express sentiments that differentiate me from a doormat or a prostitute.

Rebecca West, 1913

Society considers the sex experiences of a man as attributes of his general development, while similar experiences in the life of a woman are looked upon as a terrible calamity, a loss of honor and of all that is good and noble in a human being.

Emma Goldman, "The Traffic in Women," *Anarchism and Other Essays*, 1911

It occurred to me when I was thirteen and wearing white gloves and Mary Janes and going to dancing school, that no one should have to dance backward all their lives.

Jill Ruckelshaus, speech, 1973

Twelve years ago, Barbara Jordan—another Texas woman—made the keynote address to this convention. Two women in 160 years is about par for the course. But if you give us a chance, we can perform. After all, Ginger Rogers did everything that Fred Astaire did, she just did it backwards and in high heels.

Ann W. Richards, Democratic National Convention, July 18, 1988

Woman's participation in political life . . . would involve the domestic calamity of a deserted home and the loss of the womanly qualities for which refined men adore women and marry them. . . . Doctors tell us, too, that thousands of children would be harmed or killed before birth by the injurious effect of untimely political excitement on their mothers.

Henry T. Finck, on woman's suffrage, *Independent*, January 31, 1901

Equal rights for the sexes will be achieved when mediocre women occupy high positions.

François Giroud

The more education a woman has, the wider the gap between men's and women's earnings for the same work.

Sandra Day O'Connor

Black women . . . are trained from childhood to become workers, and expect to be financially self-supporting for most of their lives. They know they will have to work, whether they are married or single; work to them, unlike to white women, is not a liberating goal, but rather an imposed lifelong necessity.

Gerda Lerner, *Black Women in White America*, 1972

Of my two "handicaps," being female put many more obstacles in my path than being black.

Shirley Chisholm, *Unbought and Unbossed*, 1970

From birth to age eighteen a girl needs good parents, from eighteen to thirty-five she needs good looks, from thirty-five to fifty-five she needs a good personality. From fifty-five on, she needs good cash.

Sophie Tucker, 1953

If women didn't exist all the money in the world would have no meaning.

Aristotle Onassis

Men want a woman whom they can turn on and off like a light switch.

Ian Fleming

I hate women because they always know where things are.

James Thurber

The great question that has never been answered, and which I have not been able to answer, despite my thirty years of research into the feminine soul, is "What does a woman want?"

Sigmund Freud to Marie Bonaparte

Why can't a woman be more like a man?
Men are so honest, so thoroughly square;
Eternally noble, historically fair;
Who, when you win, will always give your back a pat.
Why can't a woman be like that?

Alan Jay Lerner, "A Hymn to Him," 1956

Sigmund Freud.

Women have served all these centuries as looking-glasses possessing the magic and delicious power of reflecting the figure of man at twice its natural size.

Virginia Woolf, *A Room of One's Own*, 1929

Some of us are becoming the men we wanted to marry.

Gloria Steinem

Because women live creatively, they rarely experience the need to depict or write about that which to them is a primary experience and which men know only at a second remove. Women create naturally—men create artificially.

Ashley Montagu, *The Natural Superiority of Women*, 1952

The soldier's business is to take life. For that he is paid by the State, eulogized by political charlatans and upheld by public hysteria. But woman's function is to give life, yet neither the State nor politicians nor public opinion have ever made the slightest provision in return for the life woman has given.

Emma Goldman, "The Social Aspects of Birth Control," *Mother Earth*, April 1916

WORK

Work expands so as to fill the time available for its completion.

C. Northcote Parkinson, *Parkinson's Law*, 1958

YOUTH

The young always have the same problem—how to rebel and conform at the same time. They have now solved this by defying their parents and copying one another.

Quentin Crisp, *The Naked Civil Servant*, 1968
—D.W. and A.W.

Chapter 2

THE HIGH AND THE MIGHTY

WORLD LEADERS

NIKOLAI LENIN
(Vladimir Ilich Ulyanov)

VITAL STATISTICS

A firebrand speaker, a devoted foe of the Russian monarchy, and a man obsessed with Marxism and revolution, Lenin was the prime mover of the Russian Revolution and the creator of the Russian Communist Party, and a profound influence on the course of modern history.

Paul Axelrod summed up Lenin's total devotion: "There is not another man who for twenty-four hours of the day is taken up with the revolution, ... and who even in his sleep, dreams of nothing but revolution."

Lenin's Soviet Union was the first country controlled by Marxist revolutionaries, the beginning of a massive experiment in politics, economics, and social order that has proved to be almost a total failure.

Ironically, Lenin's father achieved the rank of a Russian nobleman. Born on May 4, 1870, Lenin had a quite ordinary childhood until two tragedies struck. In 1886 his father, only fifty-four years old, died of a cerebral hemorrhage, the same thing that eventually felled Lenin. A year later Lenin's older brother, Alexander, was executed for plotting to assassinate Czar Alexander III.

Lenin was short and stocky. Bald before he was twenty-five, he had a large head, small Mongoloid eyes, a high forehead, and a red beard. Bruce Lockhart, a British agent, said he had "a quizzing, half-contemptuous, half-smiling look."

Expelled from university for his political activities, he went on to study law on his own and become an attorney. As a young lawyer in Saint Petersburg, he became involved in the Marxist movement. For his revolutionary activities, he was imprisoned in 1895, then was exiled to Siberia in 1898. While in exile, he married a fellow revolutionary, Nadezhda Krupskaya. On their release in 1900, they moved to Switzerland.

His pamphlet *What Is to Be Done?*, penned in 1902, had an important influence on the growing revolutionary ferment in Russia. He broke from his fellow Marxists and founded the Bolshevik movement.

After the monarchy crumbled before the force of the revolution, and the provisional government, led by Alexandr Kerensky, collapsed in October 1917, Lenin and his Bolsheviks seized power. With the support of the secret police that he created, the Cheka, Lenin ruled with the iron grip of dictatorial powers.

V. I. Lenin, April 1917.

His control over the destiny of the new government was relatively short-lived. While his rival, Joseph Stalin, maneuvered for power, he suffered the first of a series of strokes in 1922. An invalid from then until his death, he succumbed to a cerebral hemorrhage on January 21, 1924.

PERSONAL LIFE

Like many revolutionaries, particularly those in turn-of-the-century czarist Russia, Vladimir Ulyanov came from a solid middle-class family. There was little indication during his happy childhood that he would grow up to devote his life to world revolution, to make his brand of communism a reality, and to rule (autocratically) a society of 150 million people under a regime dedicated to economic and social equality. Of course he was bright (alienated because of it) and rebellious (like many bright children). Full of contradictions, he was resentful of authority when applied to him, prone to use it ruthlessly against those who opposed him, gentle with it when dealing with those who accepted his power.

Vladimir's father, the son of a serf, had risen, through hard work and the assistance of a selfless brother, to become inspector of schools in Simbirsk. His mother was the daughter of a landowning physician.

As a child Vladimir was noisy and boisterous. Nicknamed "Little Barrel" because he was fat, he fell down more often than most children while learning to walk. People said it was because his head was too big for his body. Sometimes he was destructive; on one of his birthdays, he twisted the legs off the horses of a papier-mâché troika he had been given.

His quick mind and unusual ability to concentrate helped him excel in school. Already sharp edged, not quite involved, he was not popular with other students, though he often helped them with their homework. He was a reader; the nihilism of Goethe and Turgenev, whose books he devoured as an adolescent, affected him all his life.

In 1886 the first of the two major tragedies struck the family. Vladimir's father died of a cerebral hemorrhage. Vladimir was so upset by his father's death that twenty years later he said, "I was sixteen when I gave up religion."

Vladimir was particularly close to his older brother, Alexander, who was the one, according to townspeople, bound to succeed in life, the golden boy of the family. The summer after their father died, the two often played chess together. A neighbor girl who saw them doing so through a window said, "Why, they are like prisoners behind bars." Her words were prophetic; both brothers wound up in prison. (In fact, all five of the surviving Ulyanov children became revolutionaries, working against czarist law.) On May 20, 1887, Alexander was hung for participating in a conspiracy to assassinate Czar Alexander III. Vladimir's pragmatic response was: "We must find another way."

He tried to get on with his life, but it proved to be impossible. Because he was branded the brother of a revolutionary, doors were closed to him. Only with the help of his high-school principal was he accepted as a law student at Kazan University, and he had been there only three months when he was expelled for attending a peaceful protest meeting. Thenceforth no school would accept him.

So he tried gentleman farming ("The moment I started, I knew it wouldn't work out. My relations with the peasants became abnormal"); read *Das Kapital* (by 1889 he was a committed Marxist); and studied law on his own. Given permission to take the law examination, he passed first in a group of 124 in November 1891.

RISE TO POWER

It can be said that any emphasis on a personal life ended for Lenin when he moved to Saint Petersburg in 1893. True, he had relationships with women, but his wife was as much—maybe more—coworker as lover, and his two mistresses took second place to his revolutionary activities. He was only twenty-three years old when he made the move, but he was already bald and lined, and middle-aged in behavior as well as appearance, so his fellow revolutionaries nicknamed him "Starik" (Old Man). They lived under cover, shadowed by the secret police, sending messages in codes and invisible ink, wearing disguises, and operating under aliases. Their discussion groups were euphemistically known as pancake teas.

Lenin gathered Marxist workers into six-member cells, investigated industrial conditions and compiled statistical facts about them, and wrote inflammatory pamphlets full of phrases like "pillars of reaction" and "pack of little Judases" (the bureaucracy). At a Marxist study circle, he met his future wife, Nadezhda Krupskaya, then a feminine, white-skinned woman.

In 1895 he took the first of many trips abroad, where in Switzerland he first met tall, elegant Georgi Plekhanov, leader of the Social Democrats. Plekhanov believed in takeover of the government by the liberal bourgeoisie, while Lenin felt that only violent overthrow by an armed proletariat would do. Plekhanov said, after reading Lenin's pamphlets, "You show the bourgeoisie your behind. We, on the contrary, look them in the face." It was a graphic description of classic disagreement between them, which eventually split the party into two factions.

When Lenin returned to Russia later that year (1895), he carried a printing machine and illegal literature under the false bottom of his trunk; in his head were plans for a revolutionary newspaper. On the eve of its publication, he, with other leaders, including Julius Martov, was arrested. During Lenin's fifteen months in jail, in a comfortable cell with a table and a chair, he read innumerable books and communicated with the outside world through messages written in milk, which turned yellow when held over a candle flame. He kept milk in hollow bread pellets, which he swallowed when the peephole to his cell opened. Once he wrote, "Today I have eaten six inkpots."

After his jail term, we was exiled to southern Siberia (known as "Siberian Italy"). His sentence was a vacation compared with the exiles of more unfortunate political prisoners who landed in the icebound north. Krupskaya, also exiled, was able to get permission to join him as his fiancée. They were married in 1898.

In 1900, after they both had finished their exile, Lenin and Krupskaya left for Switzerland. With Plekhanov and others he started the newspaper *Iskra* (Spark) and the magazine *Zarya* (Dawn). The magazine, in which he first used the name N. Lenin, folded after three issues; the newspaper, which was smuggled into Russia, sometimes wrapped around bales of fish, was highly successful.

During those expatriate years, Lenin rose to a position of power among the Social Democrats, who split into the Bolsheviks (the majority, his faction) and the Mensheviks (the minority). His ideas were uncompromising and radical: outlawing of freedom of criticism in order to uphold party discipline, establishment of a terrorist intellectual elite to infiltrate institutions and destroy the aristocracy, merciless takeover of the government by an armed proletariat, abolition of the market system and of private ownership of the means of production, and membership in the party given only to those who were active revolutionaries (no fellow travelers). The Mensheviks, on the other hand, took a much milder view of things.

The 1905 massacre known as Bloody Sunday, in which Cossacks in Saint Petersburg fired on peaceful protesters led by Father Georgi Gapon, presaged uprisings in Russia. Lenin jettisoned theory for activism and began to make battle plans and draw up lists of weapons, including brass knuckles, barbed wire, and kerosene-soaked rags. He wrote, "Put Europe to the flames!" (he always saw the revolution as international) and sent a message to the Social Democratic Party in Saint Petersburg: "I am appalled, absolutely appalled, to know that for more than half a year you have been talking about bombs—and not a single bomb has been made." Under cover, he returned to Russia for two years, but the promised revolution did not occur, for the czar made enough concessions, among them the election of a relatively powerless Duma (parliament), to quiet unrest at least for a while.

Lenin went abroad again and eventually settled in Berne. When World War I broke out in 1914, many Socialists, to his disgust, betrayed one of the basic tenets of the party—to resist or overthrow governments that become involved in imperialist wars. He saw the cause of the war as colonialist expansion, encouraged by the desire of banks for superprofits and backed by workers who wanted a piece of the pie.

Then, on March 8, 1917, metalworkers in Saint Petersburg went on strike, a strike that grew until hundreds of thousands of people were milling in the streets. The czarist regime collapsed, and power went into the hands of the Duma, run by the bourgeoisie. Lenin, desperate to return to Russia, made a deal with the Germans. It was understood that if he seized power, Lenin would pull Russia out of the war and end fighting on Germany's eastern front. With this in mind, German leaders allowed Lenin and other Russian expatriate revolutionaries to cross Germany to the Swedish border on a sealed train.

His return to Russia was tumultuous. In Petrograd hordes of people carrying red-and-gold banners and torches cheered him. Standing on the turret of an armored car in the station square, he shouted, "Long live the worldwide Socialist revolution!"

His ideas, expounded in the "April Theses," written the next day, were not immediately accepted, possibly because they seemed too radical. The provisional government, headed by Alexandr Kerensky (son of Lenin's high-school principal), branded Lenin a traitor and accused him of being a German agent. Again a hunted man, he hid out, first in a barn loft, then in a hollowed-out haystack. Winter drove him into Finland, where he further developed the idea that the dictatorship of an armed proletariat would "wither away" into a classless, stateless, communist society, clearly the biggest error of his lifetime.

IN POWER

After the nearly bloodless October Revolution deposed the provisional government, Lenin, wearing a wig and disguised with a handkerchief as a man with a toothache, made his way to party headquarters, where, unrecognized, he was offered a roll and sausage by the Menshevik leader. In room 100, where the Military Revolutionary Committee sat, he took off his hat—and his wig came with it. It was a burlesque beginning to a seven-year reign of enormous power, one he had worked toward all his adult life. Then forty-seven, he was named president of the Society of People's Commissars (Communist Party), with dominion over a country of 150 million people, of whom 90 percent were illiterate. "It makes one's head spin," he said.

The problems of the new government were gigantic—to establish a new society, to make plans to administer it, and to end the war with Germany. The land was redistributed, some of it designated as collective farms. Factories, mines, banks, and utilities were taken over by the government; private capital and profits were no longer allowed. The Russian Orthodox Church was disestablished.

The new government was not recognized by the Allies, and Lenin worked out a disastrous peace treaty with the Germans and their allies at Brest Litovsk, in which, anxious to end the war, he gave away one-fourth of the land and nearly half the population of the country.

That same year, 1918, saw the beginning of civil war with the Whites, which was to drag on for two years. The Whites, a diverse group of anti-Communist forces, were supported by the Allies and held sway over vast portions of land. The Bolsheviks were supported only by the peasants and their own Workers' and Peasants' Red Army, led by Leon Trotsky, but it was enough for them to win.

That summer Lenin, leaving a factory, was shot by Fanya Kaplan, an intense Socialist Revolutionary, who opposed his dictatorial tendencies. Perhaps because of her poor sight (she was nearly blind), she succeeded only in wounding him. The Cheka, the terrorist secret police founded by Lenin earlier that year, executed more than 800 Socialist Revolutionaries in retaliation.

In 1919 famine and a typhus epidemic killed thousands. Bodies were stacked like cordwood in the cemeteries. Unhappy workers carried banners reading, "Down with Lenin and horse flesh. Give us the czar and pork." In 1920 and 1921 there was another famine, which affected nearly 27 million people. To turn the tide against disaster, Lenin put into effect his New Economic Plan, which provided for limited private business.

His health was beginning to fail. In May 1922 he had a minor stroke; less than a year later, he was further weakened by a second stroke. In the two years before his death, he tried to correct some of the abuses of his regime, asking for coexistence with capitalist countries, recognizing the inefficiency of his bureaucracy. In 1922 the Union of Soviet Socialist Republics was established.

In March 1923 Lenin was left speechless and paralyzed by a third stroke. Though he made a partial recovery, he never regained his former vitality and strength. On January 21, 1924, at the age of fifty-three, he died in convulsions, possibly poisoned on order of Joseph Stalin, his successor. His body was embalmed and put on display in a mausoleum in Red Square. Millions of people paid their last respects; some put wreaths made of wheat and steel near his coffin. The mausoleum in which Lenin's body was interred was a squat, square-topped pyramid of black and reddish stone inspired by the tomb of Tamerlane. Some historians suspect that the idea of embalming and displaying the remains of the venerated leader may have been influenced by the discovery, fifteen months before, of the tomb of Tutankhamen.

Although countless thousands of Russians filed past the exposed face of their great leader, Robert Service, in his poem "The Ballad of Lenin's Tomb," expressed skepticism of this veneration:

> They tell you he's a mummy—don't you make
>   that bright mistake.
> I tell you—he's a dummy; aye, a fiction and
>   a fake.

A footnote to the story of Lenin is the claim, by Eduard Radzinsky in a book published in 1991, that the murder of Czar Nicholas and his family was ordered personally by none other than Lenin.

LITTLE-KNOWN FACTS
Lenin had about twenty-five pseudonyms, including initials. Among them were Petrov, Tulin, Ilin, William Frey, Jacob Richter, Ivanov, I, L, and S.T.A.

He liked gadgets and tools. For example, he loved to sharpen pencils. His brother Dmitry said that he sharpened them with "a sort of special tenderness, so the letters came out like delicate threads." After he came into power, he had many telephones installed, five in his office alone. He enjoyed making long-distance calls and referred to telephones as "she." When he and Trotsky found themselves working at opposite ends of a long corridor, he jokingly suggested that they use roller skates.

Lenin had soft spots in his personality. Trotsky said he "had a way of falling in love with people." One of those people was a police spy, Roman Malinovski, who infiltrated revolutionary ranks. Though evidence seemed to prove Malinovski was a spy, Lenin did not want to believe it. He was unfailingly kind to people who worked for him and treated peasants with extreme courtesy. He always sent his mother a letter on his father's name day, even though he was not religiously inclined.

All his life he followed the same five-step plan for organizing material he wrote: a plan on a half-sheet of paper, a skeleton outline on the left-hand side of a folded full sheet of paper, revisions on the right-hand side, a draft in pencil, a final draft in ink.

Though he excelled at the study of languages in school, he had no facility for speaking them. Despite believing in the liberation of women (at least to work), he was not above a male-chauvinist remark. He once told Elizabeth de K., one of his mistresses, that he never knew a woman who could read *Das Kapital* straight through, figure out a railroad timetable, or play chess.

Lenin liked to ride bicycles.

He allowed nothing to move him from his political path. He said, "I can't listen to music too often. It affects your nerves, makes you want to say stupid nice things and stroke the heads of people who could create such beauty while living in this vile hell. And now you mustn't stroke anyone's head—you might get your hand bitten off."

He had two mistresses. The first was Elizabeth de K., a wealthy, cultured divorcée to whom he once said, "It is quite obvious that you will never make a Social Democrat." Her reply: "And you—you will never be anything but a Social Democrat." The second was Inessa Armand, a committed French Bolshevik, who died of typhus in 1919.

He disliked having photographs of himself in the newspapers.

During the last years of his life, before his strokes left him an invalid, he spent much time gathering mushrooms.

QUOTES BY LENIN

"Mankind may pass directly from capitalism into Socialism, i.e., into social ownership of the means of production.... Socialism is bound sooner or later to ripen into Communism, whose banner bears the motto: 'From each according to his ability, to each according to his needs.'"
—*The State and Revolution*, 1917; published 1918

"In a state worthy of the name there is no liberty. The people want to exercise power but what on earth would they do with it if it were given to them?"
—*The State and Revolution*

"We must hate—hatred is the basis of communism. Children must be taught to hate their parents if they are not communists."
—Speech to the Commissars of Education, Moscow, 1923

"Revolutions are the locomotives of history. Drive them full speed ahead and keep them on the rails."

"The ice is broken. The Soviets have conquered throughout the whole world. They have conquered first and foremost in the sense that they have won the sympathy of the proletarian masses.... Neither the bestiality of the imperialist bourgeoisie, nor the persecution and murder of Bolsheviks can take this conquest from the masses."
—After the triumph of the Third International

"Stalin is too coarse, and this fault, though tolerable in dealings among us communists, becomes unbearable in a General Secretary. Therefore I propose to the comrades to find some way of removing Stalin from his position and appointing somebody else who differs in all respects from Comrade Stalin in one characteristic—namely, someone more tolerant, more loyal, more polite and considerate to his comrades, less capricious, etc. This circumstance may seem to be a mere trifle, but I think that ... it is a trifle which may acquire a decisive importance."
—Postscript to a letter dictated to the Central Committee on December 23, 1922

QUOTES ABOUT LENIN

"Lenin's method leads to this: the party organization at first substitutes itself for the party as a whole. Then the central committee substitutes itself for the party organization, and finally a single dictator substitutes himself for the central committee."
—Leon Trotsky (Lev Davidovich Bronstein), 1906

"Vladimir Ilich Lenin stood before me even more firm and more inflexible than he had been at the London Congress. In those days he had been very agitated, and there were moments when it was obvious that the party split had given him a difficult time. Now he was in a quiet, rather cold and mocking mood, sternly rejecting all philosophical conversations and altogether on the alert. And at the same time there was in Capri another Lenin—a wonderful companion and lighthearted person with a lively and inexhaustible interest in the world around him, and very gentle in his relations with people."
—Maksim Gorky

"Lenin is an absolutely honest man, but a man with a one-track mind. For that reason his moral sense has been dulled. Lenin's socialism is a blunt socialism; he uses a big ax where a scalpel is needed."
—Viktor Chernov

"While Lenin was speaking, his face shrunk before my eyes. Furrows, great and small, innumerable, engraved themselves deeply on it. And every furrow was drawn by a grave trouble or a gnawing pain.... I was moved, shaken. In my mind I saw the picture of a crucified Christ of the medieval master Grünewald. I believe that the painting is known by the title The Man of Sorrows.... And as such a 'man of sorrows' Lenin appeared to me, burdened, pierced, oppressed with all the pain and all the suffering of the Russian working people."
—Clara Zetkin, in 1919

"Lenin is not in the least ambitious. I believe he never looks at himself, never glances in the mirror of history, never even thinks about what posterity will say about him—he simply does his work."
—Anatoli Vasilievich Lunacharski

"Their worst misfortune was his birth; their next worst—his death."
—Winston Churchill, referring to Lenin, *The World Crisis*, 1924
—A.E. and R.W.S.

WINSTON CHURCHILL

VITAL STATISTICS

Rarely in history has there been a more fortuitous coming together of the challenges of the day and the perfect man to meet them than there was on May 10, 1940, when, in the marauding shadow of Adolf Hitler, Winston Churchill replaced Neville Chamberlain as prime minister of England.

Born in 1874 near the end of the Victorian era, Churchill would live a long life and a wide one, encompassing the birth of aviation, two world wars and numerous minor conflicts, the rise and fall of Nazism, and the A-bomb. From the age of twenty-three on, Churchill seemed always to be at or near the center of military conflict and the government of his country.

Starting in Cuba in 1897, where as a journalist he heard his first shots fired in anger, through more newspaper assignments flung the world over, to off-and-on membership in Parliament, to various Cabinet positions close to the seat of power, and eventually to the role of prime minister at his country's and the world's darkest hour, Winston Churchill's sharp and imaginative mind, his moving oratory, and his abundant eccentricity made a mark on the history of the twentieth century that can never be forgotten.

In the darkest days of World War II, when Britain stood almost alone against Hitler, this man, looking like a cross between a bulldog and a fireplug, with his inspired and tireless leadership, his repeated "V for victory" sign, and his inspiring radio addresses to a beleaguered nation, provided courage and leadership.

Far from perfect, as a close examination of his life shows, he was nevertheless one of the giants of this and any century. He died on January 24, 1965.

PERSONAL LIFE

Winston Leonard Spencer Churchill was the first child born to Lord and Lady Randolph Churchill. He came into the world, early but healthy, on November 30, 1874, at Blenheim Palace, the Churchill family estate near Woodstock in Oxfordshire.

He would later earn a reputation not only as a great statesman but as a larger-than-life eccentric, and he inherited at least part of his idiosyncratic and whimsical behavior from his father. The story is told of Lord Randolph Churchill that he once escaped the interminable story of a club bore by hiring a waiter to listen to the end of it for him.

Proving that the apple falls not far from the tree, Winston was once subjected to a long and excruciatingly boring speech in the House of Commons in which the speaker was reciting statistics on brussels sprouts. An aged member at the back leaned forward with his ear trumpet poised to catch every word, whereupon Winston bellowed out, "Who is that idiot denying himself his natural advantages?"

But all this was in the future, as young Winston was brought up as was proper for an aristocratic child of the era. Although his parents grumbled about lack of money, they still entertained royally, kept a splendid establishment in London complete with a French cook, and were frequent guests at the great houses of London.

The boy, although loved by his parents, was raised mostly by governesses and nannies. His mother was remote and his father avoided a close, affectionate relationship with his son. He once suggested to Winston that he substitute "Father" for "Papa" in his letters home.

In April 1888 Winston was packed off to Harrow to continue his education. His performance as a scholar was nothing special except that it brought to the fore his phenomenal memory. The boy's main interests seemed to be military in nature—his skill in maneuvering his 1,500 lead soldiers seemed to outshine any intellectual abilities.

But, rather than encouragement from his father, he received reprimands. The boy, according to Lord Randolph's opinion, never did enough. He was chided on his "slovenly, happy-go-lucky harum scarum style of work."

Early on his skill as a speaker was duly noted—"bumptious and talkative" were terms used to describe the young man. Once, the victim of some schoolboy taunts and teasing, Churchill responded by marching up and down the dormitory bellowing that "one day [I] would be a great man when they [the boys] were nobodies."

Winston left Harrow and gained admission to the military academy, Sandhurst. It was at this point that the money troubles that were to plague him off and on throughout his life began. He mortgaged his allowance, visited pawnbrokers, and got to know moneylenders.

But, slim purse or not, Winston did well in the military environment of Sandhurst, studying tactics, fortification, musketry, riding, and military administration, and finishing twentieth in a class of 130. He believed military affairs were all a matter of common sense.

Lord Randolph's death in 1895 left Winston with complex feelings of loss and the exhilaration of finally being out of his father's tyrannical grip. At twenty-one the young man was ready to go his own way and make his mark on the world.

Winston's military career was only a brief interlude before he got down to the real business of his life, which was politics, and even while nominally serving the crown he was mostly working as a journalist covering skirmishes and hostilities in Cuba, India, and the Sudan. He sent back dispatches to prestigious London papers and earned substantial fees, laying the groundwork for his later reputation as a writer.

With soldiering and work as a war correspondent behind him, Winston Churchill stepped onto the stage he was born to trod when, in July 1897, he spoke at an outdoor fete of the Primrose League. He rose in favor of the Workmen's Compensation Bill. The audience loved him and he was extremely pleased with his performance. "With practice," he noted with acute prescience if not modesty, "I shall obtain great power on a public platform."

Speaking skills or not, he lost his first bid for a seat in Parliament when he sought the seat from Oldham in 1899. Disappointed but not dismayed, he set off to South Africa to cover the Boer War for the *Morning Post.* Captured while accompanying an armored train on a reconnaissance mission, he was said to have acted with exemplary bravery.

As a journalist he would probably have been released soon anyway, but Churchill decided to escape. He returned from his captivity famous, a hero to the man in the street. When he ran again for Parliament in 1900, he succeeded and entered that august body two months short of his twenty-sixth birthday.

In 1908 he married the woman who would be his wife until his death fifty-seven years later, Clementine Hozier. As impetuous as he could be in his political life, he was apparently a timid suitor. The story is told that he and Clementine, in their courting days, were out walking when a sudden rain began to fall. They found refuge in an ornamental temple to Diana overlooking a lake. They sat for an hour and nothing happened. Clementine noticed a beetle scuttling slowly across the floor and decided that if Winston didn't propose before the beetle reached a certain crack, he never would. Apparently Winston won the race.

RISE TO POWER

If Adolf Hitler had never been born and World War II had never been fought, then Winston Churchill would still have had what most men would consider an accomplished and rewarding career serving the crown. Even prior to the First World War, Churchill had served as an MP from Oldham and Dundee, and had been named, in succession, home secretary in 1910, first lord of the admiralty in 1911, chancellor of the duchy of Lancaster in 1915.

In 1917 he served as minister of munitions, and in 1919 he was named secretary for war (and air).

Although through all this he drew to himself as much controversy as such an eccentric and outspoken politician might be expected to, the only real blot on his career was his questionable handling of naval power in the Dardanelles in 1915. As first lord of the admiralty he ordered a naval expedition to free up the passage between the Aegean Sea and the Sea of Marmara in order

Winston Churchill with his fiancée, Clementine Hozier, one week before their marriage in 1908.

to break the stalemate on the western front and gain direct communication with Russia. The attack failed and many blamed Churchill.

Settling down to family life as much as a man of his restless energy could be expected to, he and Clementine bought Chartwell Manor in 1922.

As the shadow of Nazism and the specter of Hitler began to loom larger across the face of Europe, Churchill went on to win some and lose some—he was defeated for a seat in Parliament for the Abbey Division of Westminster in 1924, but was elected later that same year to represent Epping, and was appointed chancellor of the exchequer.

He was back in the headlines when he supported King Edward VIII during the controversial abdication crisis.

In 1939, with Hitler's troops rolling across the map of Europe, he was again appointed first lord of the admiralty. Britain was entering its darkest hour.

On the afternoon of May 9, 1940, Neville Chamberlain, Edward Wood (first earl of Halifax), and Churchill met at 10 Downing Street. The government chief whip, David Margesson, was also in attendance. Chamberlain had stepped down as prime minister. Chamberlain thought that perhaps Halifax should take the job, but he demurred, admitting that he did not have the qualities to lead a country at war. Winston Churchill accepted the job. Crowds greeted him with cries of "Good luck, Winnie. God bless you." He put on a brave face but dissolved into tears once out of their sight. "Poor people, poor people," he cried. "They trust me, and I can give them nothing but disaster for quite a long time."

IN POWER

Six weeks after he had taken office, Belgium had surrendered, France had fallen, and German troops stood poised to cross the English Channel. Two hundred twenty-four thousand British troops along with 110,000 of their French comrades had been evacuated from Dunkirk.

Asked by Paul Reynard, the French prime minister, what he intended to do if the Germans invaded, Churchill, jaw thrust forward, said he'd drown as many as he could of the invaders on their way over, and *frapper sur la tête* any that managed to crawl ashore. It was typical Winston Churchill and just an example of the fact that, in the coming months and years, what the man said and how he said it would be just as important as what he did.

Thus began the figure of Winston Churchill as not only leader of his people but also the very image for the world of pluck and determination against great odds. Clad in his quaint, old-fashioned overcoat, with the scruffy bow tie protruding, and his beaming face topped by an unfashionable hat, he marched about London with a cigar clenched in his teeth, with one

Winston Churchill, accompanied by his daughter Mary, flashes his famous "V for victory" sign, 1945.

hand clutching a cane and the other raised in a "V for victory."

The "V" sign was interpreted by all with its very British double meaning: an "up yours" to Adolf Hitler. His radio broadcasts galvanized a nation and gave courage to many throughout the world at war.

He made himself minister of defense as well as prime minister and there were niggling complaints that he intended to run the war by himself. Although some said of him that, like the Queen in *Alice in Wonderland*, he was capable of believing "as many as six impossible things before breakfast," he was a leader able to listen to advice and was commendably flexible in allowing his grand schemes to have the patina of reality added by his advisors.

The Middle East and the Mediterranean came to dominate his strategic thinking early in the war. British forces were already stationed there. His fixation with that part of the world, and later Italy, was to have far-reaching consequences. The tremendous drain of troops and resources would greatly complicate his relations with the United States.

In June 1941 Churchill proclaimed in a stirring radio broadcast that he intended to recognize Stalin's Russia as a full partner in the struggle to survive against Hitler. His speech, not authorized by the Cabinet, was one of his virtuoso performances but gave ammunition to those who thought he was taking too much into his own hands.

On August 9, 1941, one of the most important meetings in history took place as the British warship *Prince of Wales*, carrying Churchill, met with the USS *Augusta*, which brought Franklin Delano Roosevelt to Placentia Bay off Argentia, Newfoundland. It was to be the first of their nine wartime meetings and it cemented Anglo-American solidarity.

Churchill, according to FDR's aide, Harry Hopkins, was much impressed with the American president: "You'd have thought Winston was being carried up into the heavens to meet God!"

Churchill wanted Roosevelt to bring the

power of the United States into the war, and on December 7, 1941, when the Japanese attacked Pearl Harbor, a great step was taken in that direction. American sentiment was much more fully awake now to the fact that the conflict was indeed global.

In retrospect it might seem easy to assume that once the might of the United States came into the fray, success was assured, but it certainly didn't seem so at the time. The military might of Nazism proved daunting, and the strategy to overcome it had three main components, developed jointly by the Americans and the British: bombing, blockade, and the subversion of Germany. The ultimate goal was a large-scale invasion of western Europe.

At the Yalta Conference in February 1945 the big three Allied leaders came together—Churchill, Roosevelt, and Stalin—to make decisions that changed the map of Europe and created a power struggle that came to be called the Cold War. Roosevelt was gravely ill: Hopkins doubted that he heard "more than half of what went on."

Churchill, too, seemed distracted, "booming," according to Sir Alexander Cadogan, but "knowing nothing whatever of what he was talking about." Roosevelt and Churchill quarreled with each other; Stalin, quiet and restrained, crafty and powerful, was the most impressive of the three. Matters of vital importance were decided: the last-minute strategy for the final onslaught and the postwar zoning of Germany.

So much of Churchill's energy had been expended on standing up to Hitler and winning the war that some observers felt he had little left over to think through the political aftermath of the war.

"I never think of after the war," said his wife, Clementine, in the winter of 1944. "You see, I think Winston will die when it's over." When the war finally did end, Britain found itself virtually bankrupt, with a quarter of its national wealth destroyed, and deeply in debt. Churchill admitted that he felt "very lonely without a war."

He could have retired from politics in a blaze of glory, but that was not in the man. He still wanted to be in the fray, but with his return to a more peaceful life his marriage suffered from frequent quarrels, and he and Clementine spent much time apart. His relationship with his son, Randolph, suffered too, taking on some of the quality of Winston's relationship with his own father. "We have a deep animal love for one another," he said, "but every time we meet we have a bloody row."

As leader of the Opposition, Churchill could, with justification, claim to be the most famous man in the world. He traveled widely, sharing with the world his ideas about how the postwar world should be rebuilt. He spoke often on the theme of European unity.

By 1951 the question of his retirement was being asked with greater urgency. He was frequently exhausted, he had a heart condition, and he had survived three bouts of pneumonia. He was increasingly deaf, suffered from a violent irritation of his skin, and had a sensitive eye condition. His first minor stroke had come in 1949 and, although outwardly optimistic, he wrote in his diary: "This is the beginning of trouble. . . . but there can only be one end to it."

In February of 1952 he suffered another "spasm," as he referred to them, and for a few minutes the man who had never been at a loss for words, whose oratory had led a beleaguered people and given courage to the world, could not string together a simple sentence. In June 1953 he suffered the most serious of the strokes and was for a time paralyzed on his left side, unable to walk, and his speech was slurred. His memory began to fail.

In November 1954 he celebrated his eightieth birthday and the nation and world applauded him. Twenty-three thousand messages of congratulation poured in. At a special session of Parliament his portrait was unveiled. He detested it on sight, calling it, privately, "filthy and malignant," and had it secretly destroyed. Clementine rejected Salvador Dali's kind offer to paint another portrait.

Despite his ill health, he promised to stay in office to build a "sure and lasting peace." He bounced back for a time, but as resilient as he was, as determined to carry on, this human dynamo was simply running down. On the afternoon of April 5, 1955, he tendered his resignation to the queen and an era truly came to an end.

Depressed, bored, and lethargic, he suffered another "spasm" in the months immediately after his retirement. But, even if he was no longer at the center of power, he did carry on in his seat from Woodford in Parliament. He wrote, he painted, he developed a new passion: breeding and racing horses. One of his horses won more than £13,000 pounds in prize money and when it was time to put the horse to stud, he hesitated at "living off the immoral earnings of a horse." If his body had at least partially betrayed him, his wit had not.

Some would say the man lived too long. Noël Coward wrote of the old man "obsessed with a senile passion for Wendy [Reves, a young acquaintance]," chasing her "about the room with brimming eyes . . . staggering like a vast baby."

In 1958 preparations for his funeral were begun, code named "Hope Not," but not until a year after he had celebrated his ninetieth birthday did the great man finally die. His last coherent words were, "I'm so bored with it all."

As his funeral train passed, an unidentified observer noted a man standing at attention in his old RAF uniform, and a farmer, motionless, head bowed, cap in hand.

LITTLE-KNOWN FACTS
The man who became one of the great orators of our time had been, in his early days, plagued by

the inability to pronounce the letter s, slurring it more like sh. He consulted an expert on diseases of the throat and was relieved to find there was no organic problem—practice and perseverance corrected the difficulty.

Although he'd been a delicate child, he grew into a skilled, if lazy, athlete excelling in rifle shooting and fencing. His "quick and dashing attack" helped him win the 1892 public-school championship.

Most people are aware that Churchill was a skilled Sunday painter: the image of the man raptly concentrating on a watercolor, omnipresent cigar clenched between his teeth, is a common one. What few know is that he was also a skilled bricklayer and, in fact, for many years carried a union card. He could lay ninety bricks an hour, not a bad rate even for a pro.

Churchill loved to swim, and he did it with a style much like an exuberant whale. One afternoon at a party at the pool his bricklaying efforts helped build, he appeared wearing a Roman toga and a sombrero, both of which he flung at a bush as he then flung himself into the water, where he, as an observer put it, executed a "series of inexplicable front and back somersaults."

In April 1963 John F. Kennedy made him an honorary citizen of the United States of America.

QUOTES BY CHURCHILL

"Don't talk to me of naval tradition. It is all rum, sodomy and the lash."

—1911

"It is . . . nauseating to see Mr. Gandhi, a seditious Middle Temple lawyer, now posing as a fakir of a type well known in the East, striding half naked up the steps of the Viceregal Palace, while he is still organizing and conducting a defiant campaign of civil disobedience, to parley on equal terms with the representative of the King Emperor."

—Speech, Epping, February 23, 1931

"I cannot forecast to you the action of Russia. It is a riddle wrapped in a mystery inside an enigma; but perhaps there is a key. That key is Russian national interest."

—Speech, October 1, 1939

"I say to the House as I said to Ministers who have joined this government, I have nothing to offer but blood, toil, tears, and sweat. We have before us an ordeal of the most grievous kind. We have before us many, many months of struggle and suffering.

"You ask what is our policy? I say it is to wage war by land, sea, and air. War with all our might and with all the strength God has given us, and to wage war against a monstrous tyranny never surpassed in the dark and lamentable catalogue of human crime. That is our policy."

—Speech to the House of Commons, May 13, 1940

"Hitler knows he will have to break us in this island or lose the war. If we can stand up to him all Europe may

be freed and the life of the world may move forward into broad sunlit uplands; but if we fail, the whole world, including the United States and all that we have known and cared for, will sink into the abyss of a new dark age. . . . Let us therefore brace ourselves to our duty and so bear ourselves that if the British Commonwealth and Empire last for a thousand years, men will still say 'This was their finest hour.' "

—Speech to the House of Commons, June 18, 1940

"From Stettin in the Baltic to Trieste in the Adriatic, an iron curtain has descended across the continent."

—Speech, Fulton, Missouri, March 1946

"I have only one purpose, the destruction of Hitler, and my life is much simplified thereby. If Hitler invaded Hell I would make at least a favourable reference to the Devil in the House of Commons."

—The Grand Alliance, 1950

"[A desirable qualification for a young person who wishes to become a politician] is the ability to foretell what is going to happen tomorrow, next week, next month, and next year. And to have the ability afterwards to explain why it didn't happen."

QUOTES ABOUT CHURCHILL

"In private conversation he tries on speeches like a man trying on ties in his bedroom to see how he would look in them."

—Lionel Curtis, letter to Nancy Astor, 1912

"More than any man of his time he approaches an issue without mental reservations and obscure motives and restraints. He is not paralysed by the fear of consequences, not afraid to contemplate great changes. He knows that to deal in millions is as simple as to deal in pence, and that timidity is the unpardonable sin in politics."

—A. G. Gardiner

"He mobilized the English language and sent it to battle to steady his fellow countrymen and hearten those Europeans upon whom the long dark night of tyranny had descended."

—Edward R. Murrow

"The Russians in the late war were enormously impressed by Churchill at the table. His appetite for caviar and vodka convinced them that they were fighting on the right side."

—Robert Lewis Taylor, The Amazing Mr. Churchill
—R.W.S.

MAO ZEDONG

VITAL STATISTICS

Of all twentieth-century leaders, Mao Zedong has had a more profound and direct effect on more of the people of the planet than anyone else. Born of a peasant family a step or two up from dirt-poor on December 26, 1893, in the village of Shaoshan in Hunan Province, he rose from near the bottom of Chinese society to its very top, leading a revolution, dragging the planet's most populous nation into the twentieth century, and then ruling it with a commanding combination of acute intelligence, forceful will, and cunning guile.

As many as 40 million of his countrymen died thirty years before his birth in the bloody civil war called the Taiping Rebellion (1850–64), and the chaos of this great struggle colored his childhood. The last of the great dynasties, the Manchu-Qing was lurching to its close; China was both tempting to the commercial interests of foreign nations and ripe for revolution.

In 1911, when Mao was seventeen, the brittle and decrepit dynasty fell and a vigorous new leader, Sun Yat-sen (1866–1925) strode upon the scene, trailing in his wake a fresh sense of vigor and possibilities. Mao walked for days to join his forces and fight for a new China. Sun Yat-sen failed, and by 1916 China was in a condition very common in its long history: under the control of military men, some true patriots but others ruthless adventurers.

Working in the library of Peking University, the young Mao showed himself to be a dynamo of energy, drawn immediately to politics and protest.

In these days of ferment many of the ideas that would later change his nation were developing in his active, questing mind. He knew early on that China would have to undergo huge, painful reforms, and that there was an outside world, dominated by the West, that had to be dealt with from a position of strength.

The Russian Revolution provided an example and the Communist Party even sent advisers to help the Chinese stir up their own revolution and create their own Communist Party. But, again prescient beyond his years, Mao saw that domination by the Soviet Union was not desirable.

But before success in a Communist revolution was to be achieved, a victory must be won over the forces of the powerful rival party, the Kuomintang, founded by Sun Yat-sen but now led by Chiang Kai-shek, following Sun Yat-sen's death on March 25, 1925.

There followed years of armed struggle, with Mao leading his forces—he was, at the beginning of this process, only one leader of many— back and forth through the land, attacking when he could, retreating when that seemed wise. One of these horrendous peregrinations lasted a year and covered 6,000 miles and came to be mythologized in Chinese Communist lore as "the Long March."

During World War II the Communist Party and the Kuomintang clung to a tenuous truce while they fought to keep the Japanese out. All that changed in 1945 when the United States dropped

atom bombs on Hiroshima and Nagasaki. The warring factions in China were now free to go back to slaughtering each other.

In October 1949 Mao proclaimed the founding of the People's Republic of China as Chiang Kai-shek and his forces retreated offshore to Taiwan. In this year began the long, arduous struggle to bring China into the modern world economically, agriculturally, and socially.

In 1954 Mao led the "Great Leap Forward," a series of economic upheavals that mostly failed, and factions in the party began to try to reduce his powers. As a countermeasure he fomented the "Great Proletarian Cultural Revolution," an often bloody attack by China's youth on the establishment—but not on Mao himself, who by this time had acquired the status of a sort of god.

Aging, tired, and ill, he still managed to engineer one more astounding performance— his famous meeting with United States president Richard Nixon in 1972. On September 9, 1976, Mao died.

PERSONAL LIFE
Mao was born in the year of the snake in the traditional Chinese calendar and if his parents consulted a seer to learn what qualities to expect in their son, they would have learned that he would be flexible and cunning, with a powerful skill at survival and a dexterity for avoiding and foiling enemies. Not bad qualities for a revolutionary and leader of a vast, problem-filled nation such as China.

Hunan Province, the area from which Mao came, had long been known as isolated and backward, but in his time it was already becoming more important and connected to the rest of the country and beginning to provide some intellectual leadership.

The nation as well as his own personal life was in turmoil in Mao's growing-up years and later he would describe the dynamics of his family in the political terms with which he became so familiar. His father, he would say, was the ruling power, while Mao, his mother, and his brother were the opposition. Mao, hotheaded, was for direct confrontation, while his mother preferred more tactful and subtle methods. Both ways would blend into Mao's style as the years passed.

In spite of his peasant upbringing, and in common with so many other great leaders, Mao was an early and avid reader, seeking with books windows into a wider world. Although entrance into university was not open to him, he did manage to enroll in a teacher's training school and would, years later, describe his primary role in life as that of a teacher.

The young man looked around his nation and saw conditions deteriorating, even with the best efforts of Sun Yat-sen, whose "Land to the Tiller" program, while well-intentioned, did little to help the people. Absentee landlords who left behind cruel agents to collect rents by whatever means they could, growing debt, usury, and violence all plagued the people. Anyone, including Mao, who could look beyond his next meal saw the specter of foreign domination looming—most probably, and most dangerously, from Japan.

Mao moved to Peking (Beijing) in 1918 and obtained a modest post in the library of Peking University. It was a place of ferment for reform movements. Mao joined a Marxist study group and began, in that year of revolution in Russia, to gain the outlines of what could happen in China. What China lacked, he knew, was not the will or the power for revolution but the technique. He was determined to learn.

RISE TO POWER

Mao rose quickly in the ranks of revolutionary planning and, in 1921, when a group of thirteen men met in Shanghai to form a Communist Party, he was there. He returned to his native province, where he formed a local branch of the new Communist Party and a Marxist study group of his own. As Mao said, "Marxism is the arrow with which we will hit the target of the Chinese revolution."

However, when Russian help came in fomenting revolution, it was given not to the Communist Party but to the much larger, better-organized group, the Kuomintang, begun by Sun Yat-sen. With Soviet assistance Sun built an army and a modern party along Soviet lines. He prepared to march north from his base in Canton to do battle with the warlords and unify China.

The Communist Party had little choice but to obey Russia's edicts and cooperate with the Kuomintang. Mao, going against Marxist theory that stated that revolution must come from the proletariat, the urban working class, believed that, in China at least, the peasants would be the powerful force.

"The present upsurge of the peasant movement is a colossal event," he said. "Several million peasants will rise like a mighty storm, like a hurricane, a force so swift and violent that no power, however great, will be able to hold it back." This was Mao's unique observation, his key theoretical contribution to the revolution; the peasants would be the backbone of China's great revolution.

The struggle went on with an uneasy alliance between the Communists and the Kuomintang, now led by Chiang Kai-shek after Sun Yat-sen's death in 1925, and Mao was in the thick of it. With a massacre of thousands of Communists by the Kuomintang in 1927, open hostility began between the two groups.

For Mao it was a long, hard period of marching and countermarching, fighting, retreating, advancing, and covering great chunks of the huge country. In 1934, with Mao now the "chairman" of the party and the leader of his desperate army, the Kuomintang drove them from their sanctuary and there began the famous Long March, covering more than 6,000 miles as he led his people in search of another base from which to continue the fight.

Life at this point for Mao was nothing if not full of surprises. When the Japanese attacked Pearl Harbor in 1941 and the threat of Japanese domination of China again seemed imminent, he was forced again into an uneasy, unwelcome truce with the Kuomintang.

As soon as the fighting in the Pacific ended, however, with the United States dropping A-bombs on Japan, the struggle picked up again with the Kuomintang. America tried unsuccessfully to mediate the conflict but quickly gave up. The Kuomintang had a more modern fighting force, but the Communists had the fervor of millions of peasants—and they had Mao. Chiang Kai-shek fled to Taiwan.

In October 1949 Mao Zedong proclaimed the founding of the People's Republic of China, with him as its inspiration and, for the time being, its undisputed leader.

IN POWER

So much needed fixing, but Mao was full of energy and he had been thinking about how to solve the problems of his nation for years. The communism of China was, although based on the ideas of Marx, unique and quite different from that of Russia, with whom Mao and the Chinese had a sometimes uncomfortable relationship over the years.

Mao attacked, with mixed success, the problems of land reform, and the gigantic task of bringing China fully into the twentieth century in industrial production.

Ever an original thinker, he tried a grand experiment in 1956, a movement called the Hundred Flowers and the Hundred Schools. The Hundred Flowers were taken to be the arts, and the Hundred Schools the multiple, varying philosophies. There was to be room in China, Mao said, for all beliefs.

He apparently believed that this would be a way to bring many opinions into the fold, true communists all, and that this freedom would be used gently and discreetly. He was wrong. Suddenly the party and his own performance were being criticized widely and vigorously. There were demands for radical changes.

The only radical change that occurred was that the Hundred Flowers and the Hundred Schools was vigorously curtailed. At least Mao had a clearer picture now of who disagreed with him.

The next years were tumultuous in China and for Mao, marked with growing quarrels with Soviet Russia, increasing disputes about economic policy among Mao's underlings, and growing rivalries among the men closest to the great leader. China was, however, making real strides in agricultural production and industrial development. The nation was clearly in the midst of a vigorous industrial revolution, and the people were no longer starving.

The new nations of Asia were inclined to get along with the behemoth, China, and if the United States was overtly hostile, some of the nations of Europe—Holland and the Scandinavians, for example—were cautiously ready to treat China as an equal. The rift with the Soviets grew wider in 1956 when Nikita Khrushchev, with no warning to the Chinese, delivered his memorable speech denouncing Stalin's excesses.

Mao was a master of many things, survival probably being the most important. Apparently, and historians still argue over exactly what Mao had in mind, the Cultural Revolution of 1966 to 1969 was a ploy to gain control over rival factions. Whatever its intentions, the Cultural Revolution violently overthrew the established hierarchy of the party and threatened the collapse of the revolution into chaos.

It was Mao's way to reach past politicians and tap in to the love and loyalty of China's youth, engineered—some would use the word *brainwashed*—over the years by Mao's mammoth propaganda machine.

In August 1966 more than a million of the newly formed Red Guards massed in Peking with the slogan "To rebel is right." The average age of this mass of raw energy was fifteen to nineteen, with many even younger. They were urged by Mao and by their own leaders to ferret out traces of Western influence, any impure "traitors" to the cause. Important leaders were humiliated, paraded with dunce caps on their heads and derogatory slogans on placards around their necks.

Only Mao was above it all, even as the insane force of the Red Guards seemed to spin out of control. Exerting his undeniable power and force of personality, Mao began to put the brakes on the movement so that China more or less returned to normal by 1969.

Mao Zedong and Lin Biao in happier times. In 1971, Lin Biao died under mysterious circumstances after supposedly having plotted a coup against Mao.

Although Mao, according to his personal physician, had a very active sex life over the years, his sperm count was low. In spite of this, he fathered children by three of his wives—historians are not sure how many. The best guess is two and perhaps three sons by his first wife, Yang Kaihui; three or five daughters by He Zizhen; and probably two more daughters by Jiang Qinq. Jiang was his most interesting wife, the woman who became the leader of the infamous Gang of Four who carried out some of the most brutal excesses of the Cultural Revolution. In 1980–81, in a show trial, the unrepentant widow of Mao was declared responsible for the deaths of 34,000 people. She committed suicide on May 14, 1991, at age of seventy-eight.

Even the indomitable Mao could not last forever, and in 1972, sick with amyotrophic lateral sclerosis, known as Lou Gehrig's disease, his body ravaged by many years of mistreatment and hardship, he still had in him one more political surprise—he opened contact with the United States.

Mao was gravely ill while he made preparations for his historic meeting with Richard Nixon. He was suffering from pneumonia, congestive heart disease, and swelling of the internal organs, as well as from Lou Gehrig's disease. But he refused treatment until three weeks before the summit, when his doctor was allowed to begin a crash regime of medicine and therapy.

New uniforms were tailored for the bloated leader and he managed to meet the American president. The famous photographs of Mao shaking hands with Richard Nixon, after so many years of hostility between the two great nations, were mind-boggling, representing one of the watershed events of the century.

After Mao died in 1976, his embalmed body was placed on display and, say Chinese officials, will be forever.

LITTLE-KNOWN FACTS

Mao was a nightmare for his personal doctor, Li Zhisui, to try to take care of. He loved to gorge on fatty pork and lamb, as well as fish and vegetables swimming in cooking oil. He chain-smoked English cigarettes and, when admonished to cut down, declared, "Smoking is also a form of deep-breathing exercise, don't you think?"

As was common with many Chinese peasants, Mao didn't brush his teeth, preferring to rinse his mouth out with tea and then chew the leaves. His teeth turned green and would have provided a fortune in work for a periodontist. Why bother, was his attitude. "Does a tiger brush his teeth?" he demanded.

Bathing was considered a waste of time, too, with only an occasional rubdown with wet towels provided by servants while he worked. "These people," said his personal physician, Doctor Li, speaking of the peasant stock from whom Mao came, "have a three-bath philosophy. A bath at birth, one before marriage, and one at death."

Projecting a puritanical image to his fellow Chinese and to the world, Mao was a prodigious sexual athlete. In accord with the Taoist philosophy, he believed that the more women he slept with, the longer he would live, sometimes bedding three, four, or even five partners at the same time.

Some of the young women contracted a venereal disease from Mao, but he refused, according to his doctor, to take treatment. "Why are you getting so excited?" he asked. "If it doesn't bother me, it doesn't matter."

QUOTE BY MAO

"Every communist must grasp the truth: 'Political power grows out of the barrel of a gun.' Our principle is that the party commands the gun and the gun will never be allowed to command the party."
        —"Problems of War and Strategy"

QUOTES ABOUT MAO

"I adored him. When you first met him, he appeared easygoing, full of humor and nice talking. But when you stayed longer, you'd find he was merciless and would destroy anyone and anything blocking his ambition. He was not a healthy personality."
        —Mao's private doctor, Li Zhisui

"And the fascinating thing is how absolute power sort of deranges the professor of it, so that the boundary between fantasy and reality is obliterated because there's nothing to check his will. He was insulated in his own cocoon while everybody danced to his whims, and that has a lot to do with the tremendous disasters Mao wrought on the country as a whole because . . . his fantasies became reality."
        —Professor Andrew J. Nathan, an expert on Chinese politics at Columbia University

"But if you go carrying pictures of Chairman Mao, you ain't gonna make it with anyone anyhow."
        —John Lennon, "Revolution," 1968
        —R.W.S.

MIKHAIL GORBACHEV

VITAL STATISTICS

With a radical program of political and economic reforms, Mikhail Gorbachev, head of the Soviet Communist Party and leader of one of the most powerful nations on the planet, changed the face of his own land and dramatically affected its place in world affairs. He did this, surprising the so-called experts, in six turbulent years from 1985 to 1991, only to lose his position of power when the changes he began and the forces he unleashed defeated him.

Born on March 2, 1931, in the rural Russian village of Privolne in the Kuban region of Northern Caucasia, he was far from the center of Soviet power. The land was in the midst of enormous turmoil and change, with Stalin collectivizing agriculture and forcing on the people a series of five-year plans. With his tremendous energy and ambition, Mikhail was not a boy to be kept down on the farm.

He gained admission to the most distinguished educational institution in the Soviet Union, Moscow State University. As he studied law he also devoured books and ideas, and he married Raisa Titorenko, a social science student who was to become not just his wife but also a close partner who helped him mold his ideas.

He returned to Stavropol, near his home village, in 1955 and began his rise in the Communist Party organization. Because Stavropol was a vacation area for party brass, the young Gorbachev was able to meet the most powerful men in the government. He attracted the notice of Yuri Andropov, and when Andropov succeeded to power on the death of Leonid Brezhnev, Gorbachev became his chief assistant.

When Andropov died in early 1984, Gorbachev was passed over and lost out to another member of the party's older generation, Konstantin Chernenko. Chernenko didn't last long, dying the next year. Gorbachev was chosen Communist Party general secretary, making him the leader of his country.

He soon began to put into place his program of reforms, including glasnost (government accountability and freedom of information) and perestroika (the restructuring of the economic and political system). He released dissident Andrei Sakharov, ended the Afghan war, and began to negotiate substantial reductions in Soviet military strength. The world looked on in amazement. It was clear that the Soviet Union was now being led by a very different sort of man.

In 1986 he began a series of summit meetings with U.S. president Ronald Reagan. This new Soviet leader soon became a media star, a loved personality, mingling with crowds in New York City, pressing the flesh like an American politician running for election.

He won over Reagan, who had called the Soviet Union the "evil empire" in the Andropov years.

At home the most daring change came in 1989 when Gorbachev held elections in which members of his own party had to compete against opponents for the first time ever. In 1988 he took the post of Soviet president, so that now he had a power base outside the Communist Party.

Greeted with adulation in foreign countries, he was beset with serious problems at home. The various nationalities that made up the

Soviet Union clamored for independence; internal conflicts that had been suppressed by the power of the government now bubbled into open turmoil.

The economy threatened to collapse—it had worked in the old days, not well but enough, but now industrial and agricultural production declined dangerously and the people were close to a state of outright rebellion. It seemed that Gorbachev was more willing to make real changes in government and international affairs, but either unwilling or unable to do much to solve the problems of the nationalities and the economy.

In the political free-for-all that his nation had become, a rival emerged in the commanding presence of Boris Yeltsin. Yeltsin preempted Gorbachev's role as the leading advocate of economic change. While Gorbachev was on vacation in the Crimea in August 1991, he was captured in a bizarre coup, and then let go when Yeltsin engineered his release.

The Soviet Union had fallen apart, and Gorbachev didn't seem to know how to put it back together again. Yeltsin gained in power; Gorbachev resigned on Christmas Day, 1991.

PERSONAL LIFE
Gorbachev's life began in turmoil. His family were farmers and Stalin was in the midst of his drive to take farmland away from people who had owned it for generations and form the collective farms that communist theory maintained would be more efficient.

Anyone caught resisting was shipped off to exile in the far-flung prison camps of Siberia. Found guilty of hiding forty pounds of grain, Gorbachev's grandfather Andrei, his father's father, was sentenced to nine years. From this time on, what the young Gorbachev knew about how things really worked in the Soviet Union under Stalin formed a stark contrast to the party line.

But for an ambitious young man it was necessary to go along to get along, to rise in the Communist Party—and, early on, that was Gorbachev's goal. The memory of his grandfather's being shipped off to Siberia would remain with him, to profoundly affect the reforms he would instigate when he achieved true power.

His grandfather Andrei, released finally from the Siberian camp, brought Gorbachev up after his father, Sergei, went off to fight the Nazis. His grandmother taught him the old folktales and the words to Cossack songs; his love of language and the dramatic images of the old tales would help to make him a forceful storyteller and speaker years later.

He worked hard on the collective, and at the age of eighteen he was awarded the Order of the Red Banner of Labor. He was a local celebrity now, respected by the party members,

and in line for a spot in Moscow State University. To get into the university he had to pass a strict security check. With a family member who had been in Siberia, and having lived under Nazi occupation, he already had two strikes against him in competing for admission with the elite of the country and with returning war veterans. It is indicative of how favorably he had impressed local party officials that he got in at all.

But the fact is he did. He was on his way. On the long train ride through the ghosts of war-torn cities, through Stalingrad, through Voronezh, all in ruins, the young man saw for the first time the effects of war on his country.

At age nineteen he arrived in Moscow, a far cry from the rural area where he had been raised. He was a young man with many interests and a sharp intellect. "I have always shown interest in many things in different fields," he recalled later.

Contemporaries remember him as having an almost blind faith in himself, stubborn to a fault when he had made up his mind about something.

The ideology of Stalin was at its apogee; Gorbachev must have been vocal in his support of his policies and against "bourgeois liberalism," "cosmopolitanism," and all the stock enemies of the state. He would not otherwise have risen in the closely controlled Soviet Union of his time, and he did indeed rise: he became komsorg of his class, leader of the Komsomol, the party's youth group. He propagandized the party line and kept an eagle eye out for deviations among his classmates.

In 1952, when he was twenty-one, he became komsorg for his entire law school and was admitted as a full member of the Communist Party.

When did Gorbachev begin to believe in the reforms with which he later shocked his own nation and the world? For how many years was his support of the old line merely a way to rise in power? Only one man knows for certain the answers to these intriguing questions.

When Stalin died in 1953, and Nikita Khrushchev began a limited but still surprising process of thaw, Gorbachev and many others in the Soviet Union were forced into some ideological somersaults.

Stalin's death and Khrushchev's coming to power were important to Gorbachev's development, but a more significant event was to change his life and broaden his outlook at least as much. He met his future wife, Raisa Maximova Titorenko, a strong and intelligent young woman, a social science student and avid reader.

They married during their last year at the university and spent their wedding night in Gorbachev's dorm room, tactfully abandoned by all his roommates. The next night Raisa was back in her own dorm room and they did not live together for another several months.

RISE TO POWER

In June 1955 Gorbachev, his wife with him, returned to his native province to serve the party as a Komsomol organizer. He sought out a path to the top, and in 1964 enrolled at the Stavropol Agricultural Institute. In 1967 he completed his agricultural degree.

In Stavropol Gorbachev met and courted Yuri Andropov and, probably benefiting from the influence of Andropov, he was brought to Moscow in 1978 as the party official in charge of agricultural production.

The average member of the party ruling hierarchy was in his seventies; Gorbachev was only fifty-two and considered still too young and untested to hold high office. He had to wait until Brezhnev died and Andropov took over, and then live through the disappointment of being passed over for one of the party's older generation, Konstantin Chernenko, before his opportunity finally came.

Upon Chernenko's death in early 1985, Gorbachev was chosen Communist Party general secretary. The Soviet Union, and the world, would never be the same.

IN POWER

Raisa became, if possible, even more important to him now. He never left home without her. Always nearby, she was his sounding board. As a former teacher, she helped him with speeches and advised him on almost everything.

The man who would become inundated and eventually defeated by the myriad details of trying to reform his nation's economy and internal life had a clear strategy for international affairs: stanch the economic hemorrhaging of the arms race and convince the West to help save his country from economic disaster. He would take painful losses and offer many concessions, but he kept moving forward.

He became a consummate summiteer, forging relationships with President Reagan and Prime Minister Margaret Thatcher, for example, that no Soviet leader had ever even approached.

In negotiations Gorbachev, ever the pragmatist, could by turns bully or cajole. He seemed always in control. One senior intelligence analyst observed, "I have never seen Gorbachev *unintentionally* angry."

But if he was a master in one-on-one situations with foreign leaders, it was in public, with a crowd to play to, that his true genius came out.

In December 1987 Gorbachev, on a visit to the United States, horrified the U.S. Secret Service when his limo suddenly screeched to a halt on Washington's Sixteenth Street. "He's out," a police officer shouted into his handheld radio. "He's shaking hands!" Startled agents leaped up onto newspaper vending machines to keep their eyes on him as he worked the crowd like an American politician born to pressing the flesh. Gorbachev loved it and the people loved him.

The people in America, that is. At home he was facing a much harder sell. Russians were concerned mostly with the economy, with growing unrest in the republics. If the world loved glasnost, the home front was much less sure about perestroika.

Possibly the most triumphant moment of Gorbachev's life came far from home in November of 1989. He met in Italy with the president of the United States and the pope, back to back. Pomp and ceremony awaited him in the cobbled courtyard of Rome's Quirinal Palace as three large Zil bulletproof and bombproof limos, flown in from Moscow, wended their way through the narrow streets. It seemed all Rome crowded onto the sidewalks to welcome Gorbachev to the Eternal City.

Out of his limo, this short, pudgy figure walked the length of the courtyard. Instead of saluting the *granatieri* guards, he merely bowed his head. The two men met, one the leader of a religion that had long been unwelcome in the Soviet Union, the other the commander of a nuclear arsenal second to none on the planet. Within moments they were laughing and chatting.

At home, as always, it was a different story. The republics clamored for independence, and the economic future of this huge nation seemed hopeless. Russian economist Stanislav Shatlin had this explanation: "Until 1917 it was the bankers, the financiers, the entrepreneurs . . . there were lots of people with brains. They understood things. But we lost them."

Gorbachev wanted to change the economy in a land almost devoid of people who knew how to do it. Some critics complained vociferously that he went too slowly, was too timid, while the old guard cried he went too fast.

It wasn't only changes in international relations, in the organization of the republics, or the economy that were troubling; the people also had to accept a drastic new picture of their history. While Khrushchev had begun to criticize the Stalin years, Gorbachev continued in spades. "History must be seen as it is," he said. "Everything happened, there were mistakes—grave mistakes. . . . That was life, reality." Reality was a dose that went down hard.

If Gorbachev needed proof that he was becoming a Western-style politician, he had it in a powerful political rival, Boris Yeltsin. In an October 1989 poll conducted by the highly respected Moscow weekly *Argumenty i fakty*, Gorbachev found himself only the third-most popular political figure, behind Andrei Sakharov and his nemesis, Boris Yeltsin.

By early 1990 Gorbachev the leader had begun to unravel. In a last gasp Gorbachev controlled an emergency session of the Congress of People's Deputies and created a new office. He would be president, ruling by decree with the right to impose martial law on any republic or region.

Near the end of May, the government announced it was tripling bread prices as a move toward a "regulated market economy." Panic buying swept Moscow. Gorbachev, according to observers writing in the Western press, was "tense" and "halting."

Into the growing power vacuum created by his indecisiveness stepped the lumbering figure of Yeltsin. On June 8, 1990, Gorbachev lost his one-man rule as Yeltsin was elected president of Russia, the largest republic, and proclaimed the sovereignty of its laws. Yeltsin, leaping ahead of Gorbachev's economic thinking, accepted complete privitization.

In August 1991 a group of party conservatives staged a coup, capturing Gorbachev on vacation in the Crimea. Yeltsin saved him, leading a successful resistance to the coup. The handwriting on the wall was clear— Gorbachev's power was gone, the real power lay now with the republics, chief among them Russia and its president, Boris Yeltsin. On Christmas Day, 1991, Gorbachev retired from political office.

Still popular, he writes and travels, is sought as a speaker. He also serves as head of Green Cross, a worldwide environmental group.

Mikhail Gorbachev embraces capitalism.

LITTLE-KNOWN FACTS

The reddish blotch on Gorbachev's balding head became familiar to observers the world over. Many superstitious Russians, especially in isolated rural areas, saw dark meaning in the birthmark, as though perhaps he had been touched by the devil, or that it showed he was marked for infamy.

Gorbachev was a talented amateur thespian in high school. He even talked about trying to gain admission to a theatrical institute.

During his first year at Moscow State University, he and his roommates were awarded the "neatness award" for their personal neatness and the tidiness of their room.

After a confrontational meeting with Senator Edward M. Kennedy in 1986, an adviser handed Gorbachev a copy of Dale Carnegie's *How to Win Friends and Influence People.* He immediately ordered a Russian translation. At a meeting some weeks later of the U.S. Council on Foreign Relations, Arthur Hartman, then U.S. ambassador to Moscow, found Gorbachev a changed man. "He didn't begin with a long lecture, as he used to. Instead, in a very flattering way, he asked them questions, got them to pose their own questions . . . they were flattered and charmed."

QUOTES BY GORBACHEV

"The time has come when the threat of nuclear holocaust compels us to learn the great, difficult art of living together. . . . For, despite all our differences . . . we have something in common—our understanding that nuclear war is inadmissable, that it cannot be waged and that there will be no winner in a nuclear war."

—Speaking at a November 21, 1985,
news conference in Geneva

"A sincere man. I wish he could always be consistent without vacillating. I wish he wouldn't give in to pressure. And I would wish the same thing for myself. I wish he were more democratic. It wouldn't hurt him."

—Speaking on *Face the Nation,* December 22, 1991,
about his rival, Boris Yeltsin

QUOTES ABOUT GORBACHEV

"He isn't going to change the system. . . . He'll throw curves, knuckleballs, and spitters if he can get away with them. Of course Reagan has played a pitcher too, in that movie The Winning Team."

—Richard Nixon, 1985

"Gorbachev's intentions are serious, but the system resists and will resist. It may be an impossible mission."
    —Vladimir Voinovich, exiled Soviet author, 1987

"Where his predecessors were ponderous in diplomacy, Mr. Gorbachev is nimble. Where they were predictable, he has a facility for surprise. Where they were orthodox, he has used the pulpit of our open Western press to place before the world an image of a Soviet Union on the verge of far-reaching change at home and in world affairs."
    —Michael S. Dukakis, 1988
    —R.W.S.

U.S. PRESIDENTS

All the president is, is a glorified public relations man who spends his time flattering, kissing and kicking people to get them to do what they are supposed to do anyway.
    Harry S. Truman, letter to his sister,
    November 14, 1947

President Roosevelt proved that a president could serve for life. Truman proved that anyone could be elected. Eisenhower proved that your country can be run without a president.
    Nikita Khrushchev to Joe Curran, president,
    National Maritime Union, August 19, 1960

I wouldn't want a professional actor to be president of the United States, no matter how nice or bright he is because he's spent his entire life being moved about like a piece of furniture. He's used to being used. . . . I couldn't imagine an actor as president. I could imagine a director. After all, he's a hustler, a liar, a cheat—plainly presidential.
    Gore Vidal, American Film, April 1977

If presidents don't do it to their wives, they do it to the country.
    Mel Brooks, "The Two Thousand Year Old Man,"
    1960

WOODROW WILSON
Twenty-Eighth President

VITAL STATISTICS
Birth: Woodrow Wilson was born on December 28, 1856, in Staunton, Virginia, the last of eight American presidents born in Virginia. His given names were Thomas Woodrow and throughout his youth he was known as Tommy. At the age of twenty-four, however, Wilson officially dropped his first name. His birthplace, the former Presbyterian manse in Staunton, is located at 24 North Coalter Street and is open to the public.

Death: Wilson died in Washington, D.C., on February 3, 1924, at the age of sixty-seven. The cause of death was listed as apoplexy; Wilson had been in poor health and partially paralyzed since suffering a stroke while president in 1919.

He is buried in the Washington Cathedral—the only president buried in Washington, D.C. His last words, addressed to his wife, were "Edith, I'm a broken machine, but I'm ready."

BEFORE THE PRESIDENCY
Career: The son of a strong-willed Presbyterian minister, Wilson grew up in Georgia and the Carolinas, and always thought of himself as a loyal son of the South. At sixteen he entered North Carolina's Davidson College, but left after a few months because of poor health. A year later Wilson enrolled at the College of New Jersey (now Princeton), where he soon won distinction as an orator and debater. Even so, as one admiring biographer delicately put it, "His serious intellectual interests did not lead him to seek high marks in his classes." By the time he graduated in 1879 he had decided on a political career. As an initial step toward public office, he attended the University of Virginia School of Law, was admitted to the bar, and practiced for a year in Atlanta, Georgia. Wilson soon grew bored with the day-to-day details of legal work, and owing to his total disinterest in the commercial practice of law, was soon almost clientless. At the age of twenty-eight he sought refuge in an academic environment—this time as a graduate student in political science at Johns Hopkins University in Baltimore. He found much to criticize in the strict authoritarian instructional methods at Johns Hopkins, copied from those favored by German universities. In 1885 an expanded version of his Ph.D. thesis, *Congressional Government*, was published to widespread critical acclaim, giving young Wilson a preliminary taste of national attention. The book described the problems arising from the separation of the executive and legislative branches, and the resultant inordinate power of congressional committees. Its success helped launch Wilson's teaching career and gave him a glimpse of the literary life. "A man who wishes to make himself by utterance a force in the world, must—with as much love as possible— apply critical tests to himself," he wrote to a friend.

After brief teaching stints at Bryn Mawr College and Wesleyan University, he was appointed a full professor of jurisprudence and political economy at his beloved Princeton. Over the next ten years Wilson emerged as one of the "stars" of the Princeton faculty. During his academic career he produced thirty-five articles and nine books, including a biography of George Washington and a five-volume *History of the American People*. In 1902 the trustees of Princeton unanimously elected Wilson president of the university. He soon launched a program of educational innovation and reform that received much favorable publicity.

Personal Life: In April 1883 Wilson attended a church service in Rome, Georgia, where he met a girl with a "tip-tilted little nose, sweetly curved mouth, and hair like burnished copper." Ellen Axson, like Wilson, was the child of a Presbyterian minister. Along with her devotion to religion, Ellen maintained a strong interest in the fine arts. An accomplished painter, she spent several months just before her marriage to Wilson studying at the Art Students League in New York. The wedding took place on June 24, 1885, and two ministers presided over the ceremony: Wilson's father and Ellen's grandfather, the third clergyman in the family. On the surface the Wilsons maintained a proper and decorous relationship during their twenty-nine years of marriage, but in 1962, when, at long last, their remarkable love letters were published, the passionate, obsessive nature of their union was revealed. In a typical letter Wilson declared: "I would a thousand times rather repay you a tithe of the happiness you have brought me than make my name immortal without seeing you as the chief mission of my life. Ah, my little wife, do you know that my whole self has passed over into my allegiance for you?" Ellen bore Wilson three daughters, which was fortunate, because Wilson generally preferred the company of "clever" women to that of men. In 1914, while Wilson was president, Ellen died of Bright's disease at the age of fifty-four. Wilson sat beside her body for two days and was so stricken with grief that he came close to a nervous breakdown. His seemingly incurable depression was deepened by the fact that during the same week that his wife died, World War I had begun in Europe. Dr. Cary Grayson, the White House physician, took personal responsibility for providing Wilson with the emotional support and distraction that the president needed. Six months after Ellen's death, Grayson helped to engineer a meeting between Wilson and the beautiful Washington widow, Edith Bolling Galt. A romance quickly developed, and Wilson's top aides worried that an early remarriage might imperil the president's chances for reelection. Worse still, they feared that a new love interest might revive persistent (but totally unfounded) rumors that Wilson, while president of Princeton, had conducted an illicit affair with a divorcée in

Bermuda. Despite these warnings, Wilson married Edith Galt in a small, private ceremony at her Washington home on December 18, 1915, just sixteen months after Ellen's death. With no visible difficulty, Wilson transferred all the devotion he had felt for his first wife to the elegant and sophisticated Edith.

On the Way to the White House: As early as 1906 there was public speculation that Princeton's president might make a fine president of the United States. Wilson's original backers were conservatives who saw him as a safe-and-sound member of the eastern establishment, a forceful and eloquent speaker, and just the man to "save" the Democratic Party from left-wing reformers.

Wilson's much touted (and unsuccessful) struggle against Princeton's traditional "eating clubs" was often mentioned as an example of his struggle against entrenched privilege. In fact his campaign was actually nothing more than an attempt to introduce an Oxford- and Cambridge-style tutorial system to Princeton, deemphasizing what Wilson viewed as an unseemly preoccupation with sports and social life, by turning the eating clubs into separate colleges, each on its own quadrangle. When his academic reform proposals were rejected by influential alumni, who fondly remembered the university's sporting and social activities, Wilson was bitterly disappointed and said, "The side shows are swallowing up the circus." In a way he had the last laugh, because twenty years later Harvard, Yale, and Princeton all adopted versions of Wilson's reform scheme.

Surprisingly though, this schoolmasterly skirmish with the Princetonian old boys' network helped Wilson project a democratic image and gain popular appeal to reinforce his conservative support. Wilson accepted the New Jersey gubernatorial nomination when the Democratic bosses offered it to him in 1910 as a stepping-stone to the White House. With the misplaced support of one of the most corrupt political machines in America, Wilson was elected governor by a large margin; then he promptly turned against his former allies, pushing through legislation for direct primaries, workmen's compensation, and the regulation of public utilities. In 1912, after a scant two years in public office, Wilson took his progressive record to the people as a candidate for president. His stiff professorial manner seemed to alienate many voters, however, and in a key primary Wilson was crushed by a three-to-one margin. By the time of the Democratic convention, Wilson was still a candidate but decidedly an underdog in his quest for the nomination.

His Person: Wilson was a tall, lean man with sparse iron-gray hair and blue eyes hidden behind glittering, rimless glasses. His most prominent feature was his square, heavy lantern jaw, which, combined with a wide, thin-lipped mouth and arched eyebrows, gave him what he himself described as a Scottish Presbyterian face. Wilson had been a plain and ungainly youth, and throughout his life he thought of himself as particularly unattractive. He was fond of joking about his own forbidding appearance and liked to recite a self-derogatory limerick to his friends.

> For beauty I am not a star;
> There are others more handsome by far.
> But my face, I don't mind it,
> For I am behind it,
> It's the people in front that I jar.

Proud of his strong tenor voice (he had been a member of the Princeton Glee Club in his student days), Wilson often joined his daughters Margaret and Eleanor in a singing trio. In private social gatherings, he also did impersonations and was particularly fond of recounting dialect and black folk stories. Appearing cold and rigid in public, Wilson was always plagued by a painful sense of his own isolation. He once wrote: "The president of the United States is not made of steel or whipcord or leather. He is more utterly dependent on his friends, on their sympathy and belief in him, than any man he has ever known or read about. . . . He has many counselors, but few loving friends. The fire of life burns in him only as his heart is kept warm."

PRESIDENCY

Nomination: June 25, 1912

As the Democratic convention began in Baltimore, the leading candidate for the nomination was James Beauchamp "Champ" Clark, the popular Speaker of the House. Unlike Wilson, Clark was an old campaigner and had won an impressive string of primary victories. Clark had inherited William Jennings Bryan's old agrarian constituency, but although the Speaker won a majority of the votes on several early ballots, Wilson, combined with other minor candidates, managed to deprive him of the necessary two-thirds majority. When Bryan deserted Clark in Wilson's favor, swayed by Wilson's dramatic repudiation of the powerful Tammany Hall political machine's support, the former college president was finally nominated on the forty-sixth ballot.

Election: November 5, 1912

Wilson's election was assured from the very beginning by the bitter split in Republican ranks. After an unsuccessful drive to take the Republican nomination away from President William Howard Taft, former president Theodore Roosevelt led progressives out of the convention hall to organize their own party.

Under Roosevelt's leadership, the resulting Progressive, or "Bull Moose," Party was the most powerful third party in the history of presidential elections.

In the public debate on key issues, Wilson assumed a middle ground between the conservative Taft and the radical platform of the Roosevelt Progressives. Influenced by the crusading lawyer Louis D. Brandeis (later appointed by Wilson to the Supreme Court), Wilson developed a program known as the New Freedom, which aimed to end large business combinations and return the United States to the old days of wide-open opportunity and free-enterprise capitalism. Wilson loosened up considerably in taking his program to the public. He confided to a friend that the highlight of his campaign was the moment when a small-town well-wisher waved his arms at Wilson's train and shouted, "Hello, Woody!" On another occasion, as Wilson reached the climax of his speech, lashing out against the trusts, an unidentified citizen yelled, "Give it to 'em, Doc! You're all right."

Nevertheless, in the final tally Wilson actually pulled fewer votes than William Jennings Bryan had in any of his three unsuccessful tries as the Democratic candidate. But because of the Republican split, Wilson's 6,301,254 votes were enough for victory. Third-party candidate Roosevelt finished second with 4,127,788, while incumbent William Howard Taft polled only 3,485,531. In the electoral college, Wilson won easily, with 435 votes to 88 for Roosevelt and only 8 (the states of Utah and Vermont) for Taft. In short, Wilson had won the largest electoral majority in history up to that time, but his victory still represented a minority of the popular vote.

In this already complicated election, a strong fourth-party challenge was offered by the Socialists and their standard-bearer, Eugene V. Debs. Debs won nearly a million votes, or an impressive 6 percent of the national total.

First Term: March 4, 1913

On a cold and blustery day, Woodrow Wilson was sworn in by Chief Justice Edward Douglass White on the east portico of the Capitol. The Wilsons had insisted that there be no inaugural ball, and they retired to the White House for a quiet family evening before going to bed at "a reasonable hour."

Reelection: November 7, 1916

Despite an impressive record of domestic legislation in his first term, Wilson faced a tough fight for reelection. In 1916 the Republicans were united once again. The competent, colorless GOP candidate was Supreme Court Justice Charles Evans Hughes. Teddy Roosevelt grumbled about Hughes's lack of character and called him "the bearded lady" behind his back, but in the interests of party unity, he agreed to lead his Progressives back into the Republican fold.

There had been speculation that Wilson's remarriage would damage his chances of reelection, but the president's handsome new wife was in fact a valuable political asset. Republican gossip about the White House romance backfired, humanizing Wilson and infusing warmth into his austere presidential image.

The key issue for the Democrats was the fact that the United States remained at peace while the bloodiest war up to that point in history raged on in Europe. Wilson's campaign slogan was "He kept us out of war."

On election night it appeared that Hughes had won by a narrow margin. It was only after late returns arrived from rural California counties that it became clear Wilson had carried the state by the razor-thin margin of 4,000 votes, thereby winning the election. When a reporter called Hughes on the morning of November 5 with news from California, an aide loftily said, "The president can't be disturbed." "Well," drawled the reporter, "when he wakes up tell him he's no longer president." The closeness of the vote tantalized Republicans into hoping a recount would reverse the outcome, and Hughes waited two weeks before sending a telegram to Wilson conceding the election. Dryly commenting on the delay, Wilson said of the telegram: "It was a little moth-eaten when it got here, but quite legible."

Second Term: March 5, 1917
The inauguration was delayed one day when the scheduled Inauguration Day, March 4, fell on a Sunday. Wilson was once again sworn in by Chief Justice Edward D. White.

Just one month after the inauguration, the president who had "kept us out of war," and who had hoped to concentrate almost exclusively on domestic problems, sent his war message to Congress, leading the United States into World War I.

Vetoes: During his two terms Wilson vetoed forty-four bills. Only six of these vetoes were overridden by Congress.

His Eight Years as President:

PRO Wilson pushed through key reform legislation, including a reduction in the tariff; a stronger antitrust law; the establishment of the Federal Trade Commission to regulate unfair competition in business; and the institution of the Federal Reserve System, providing government, rather than private, control of the U.S. banking system.

CON Wilson's reforms, though significant, were as much a reflection of the progressive temper of the times as of presidential leadership. On several secondary issues Wilson showed his true colors. He attacked Roosevelt's proposal for a minimum-wage law as "paternalistic" and dismissed the question of woman's suffrage as "not a problem that is dealt with by the national government at all." Under Wilson's administration, a policy of racial segregation was instituted for the first time in federal offices. Wilson's attorney general, A. Mitchell Palmer, presided over the notorious "Big Red Scare," in which socialists and other radicals were ruthlessly persecuted in coast-to-coast raids and 249 "undesirables" were deported to Russia. Some of the undesirables shipped overseas were in fact American born, and the repressive operation against them was the first career triumph of an obscure young bureaucrat named J. Edgar Hoover. Wilson also introduced the first federal income tax, in 1914.

PRO Ignoring demands by hysterical interventionists for immediate American entry in the war, Wilson pursued a policy of neutrality that delayed U.S. participation for nearly three years and undoubtedly saved hundreds of thousands of American lives.

CON Wilson's talk of neutrality was a sham and a fraud. He and his top advisers showed a clear bias for the Allied cause. As American business interests became steadily more involved with Britain and France, Wilson adopted a policy that made war inevitable. While sincere pacifists such as William Jennings Bryan bitterly protested, the United States, like the European powers, followed a foreign policy designed to protect the interests of major capitalists, ignoring the risk of war. Wilson's highhanded intervention in Latin American affairs provided yet another illustration of this policy. In 1916, following over-the-border raids into New Mexico by Pancho Villa and the killing of U.S. citizens, Wilson ordered a punitive military action against Mexico, which led the United States to the brink of a second Mexican war, and caused lasting resentment south of the border.

PRO Once the United States decided to enter World War I, Wilson proved himself an able war leader. His idealistic definition of war aims, including the famous "Fourteen Points," helped to rally international support for the Allied cause. His aggressive action in organizing the home front to ensure victory demonstrated an efficient and imaginative use of the presidential war powers.

CON Though effective as propaganda, Wilson's lofty speeches about "making the world safe for democracy" were misleading and deceptive. World War I was a struggle between self-interested nation-states competing for economic and political advantage, not a crusade for justice or democracy. After all, the most backward and repressive ruler in the world, the czar of Russia, had been a key partner in the coalition described by Wilson as "the forces of decency." At the peace conference after the war, the hollow nature of Wilson's idealism was exposed for everyone to see. One by one, the much-heralded Fourteen Points were abandoned, and a selfish and vindictive peace was imposed—despite Wilson's earlier assurances to the German people. It was the obvious bankruptcy of Wilson's visionary war aims that led to the universal disillusionment that plagued the world after the war.

PRO   At the peace conference in Paris, Wilson struggled valiantly to defend his ideals. Without his influence, the final settlement would have been even harsher than it was. Most important for the future of the world was the fact that the treaty, at Wilson's insistence, included provisions for a League of Nations, intended to peacefully resolve future international conflicts. When Wilson returned home, however, he found that Senate Republicans—many motivated by partisan political considerations, were maneuvering to block Senate approval of the treaty. Wilson knew he was right, and refused to bargain with his political opponents. He boldly took his case directly to the people instead, hoping to influence the Senate decision. In the midst of his exhausting coast-to-coast speaking tour, the president suffered a stroke, leaving him partially paralyzed, a semi-invalid for the rest of his life. With his health broken, Wilson watched the Senate reject the treaty he had worked so hard to produce. Even more than Abraham Lincoln, Wilson was a tragic martyr to his ideals.

CON   Wilson's role in the peace conference was disfigured by an unparalleled and costly series of blunders. His first mistake was in attending the peace conference personally. If he had remained in the United States "above the battle," he might have been able to exert a greater influence on the proceedings. Second, even though the Republicans controlled Congress, Wilson stubbornly refused to invite a representative of the opposition to join him in the American delegation to the peace conference. Instead he gave the negotiations an inappropriately partisan flavor, surrounding himself with Democratic yes-men. Third—and most damaging—was Wilson's egotistical refusal to compromise with the Senate on even the smallest detail of his policy, virtually ensuring defeat of the treaty. Most historians agree that if Wilson had permitted some key "reservations" to be attached to the Versailles Treaty, the Senate would certainly have given its approval, and the United States would have entered the League of Nations. On the most controversial of these reservations—a

Woodrow Wilson with his wife, Edith, in Bismarck, North Dakota, nine days before his collapse. Edith Bolling Wilson became the first woman to take charge of the United States government.

restatement of the Constitution insisting that only the elected representatives in Congress, and not the League of Nations, could formally commit the United States to war—the senators were firmly in the right, and Wilson's rejection of compromise seems not only impractical but inexplicable. It was Wilson—not the Republican senators—who demanded final rejection of the league, after the key reservations had been attached. The illogical and uneasy peace that Wilson created in 1919 planted and nurtured the seeds of World War II. The enormously destructive influence of his neurotic personality must counterbalance the pity with which the president might otherwise be regarded.

AFTER THE PRESIDENCY
Incredibly, despite his broken health and the wreckage of his policies, Wilson hoped that the Democrats would nominate him for a third term. The convention turned elsewhere, choosing James M. Cox of Ohio, who unwisely agreed to champion the cause of the League of Nations, in effect turning the election into a referendum on Wilson's leadership. The result was the greatest landslide in American history up to that time—and an emphatic rejection of Wilsonian idealism. After a brief appearance at the inauguration of his Republican successor, the sixty-four-year-old former president bitterly retreated to a private home on S Street in Washington. There Wilson hoped to write a book that would advance his policies and justify his presidency. He never got farther than the first page—a formal dedication to his wife, Edith. On Armistice Day, 1923 (three months before his death), a throng of well-wishers gathered in front of his house. Overcome with emotion, Wilson appeared on the balcony and

made a brief speech. "I am not one of those that have the least anxiety about the triumph of the principle I have stood for," he told the crowd. "I have seen fools resist Providence before, and I have seen their destruction, as will come upon these again—utter destruction and contempt. That we shall prevail is as sure as that God reigns." The main headline in the *New York Times* the day Wilson's remarks appeared read—across three columns—HITLER FORCES RALLYING NEAR MUNICH.

PSYCHOHISTORY
As a boy, "Tommy" Wilson felt ugly, weak, and stupid, especially when he compared himself with his brilliant and much-admired father, the Reverend Joseph Ruggles Wilson. The boy developed serious difficulties in school—he failed to master reading until he was eleven—and became desperately afraid that he might disgrace his parents. Wilson convinced himself that the only way out of his dilemma was constant work—that pushing himself to the point of exhaustion was the road to success. This idea seemed to fuel the young man's psychic need for self-punishment—"deserved" punishment, since, when judged against the high standards set by his idealized parents, and his own grim Calvinist theology, he saw himself as imperfect and unworthy.

Another result of this chronically low self-esteem was Wilson's need to completely dominate his immediate environment. No one could disagree with him and remain his friend, and direct criticism was cause for banishment. As president he systematically dismissed all of his most trusted advisers, and felt comfortable only in the company of sycophants or admiring women. Anyone who dared challenge Wilson or his ideas was judged hopelessly misguided or utterly base. Compromise was alien to him. Sigmund Freud suggested that Wilson unconsciously identified himself as the second member of the Trinity, Jesus Christ, while his father, Joseph Ruggles Wilson, assumed the role of God the Father. In a speech during the treaty negotiations in 1919, Wilson asked his audience, "Why has Jesus Christ so far not succeeded in inducing the world to follow His teaching? It is because He taught the ideal without devising any practical means of attaining it. That is why I am proposing a practical scheme to carry out His aims." With such a messianic view of his own role, is it any wonder that Wilson seemed to seek ultimate martyrdom?

LITTLE-KNOWN FACTS
When Wilson was an undergraduate at the College of New Jersey, he wrote out on visiting cards: "Thomas Woodrow Wilson, Senator from Virginia." It was another twenty-five years, however, before he ran for public office and began to realize his political ambitions.

Wilson's first wife, Ellen, an accomplished artist, prepared crayon portraits of five of the men he most admired for her husband's study. Included were Daniel Webster, the American orator and lawyer; William Gladstone, the British statesman; Edmund Burke, British essayist and statesman; Walter Bagehot, British economist; and the Reverend Joseph Ruggles Wilson, Woodrow's father.

Washington etiquette was of little importance to Wilson. According to tradition, a president always walked ahead of his companions, even if those companions happened to be ladies, but Wilson refused to enter rooms before his wife, saying "a man who is a gentleman before becoming president should remain one afterwards."

In the White House, Wilson's daily breakfast was a glass of grapefruit juice and two raw eggs. His favorite lunch was chicken salad.

In 1915 a typographical error in the *Washington Post* made President Wilson the furious subject of lewd laughter. Describing an evening at the theater made notable by the attendance of the president and his new fiancée, a reporter wrote that instead of watching the performance, "the president spent most of his time entertaining Mrs. Galt." The word *entertaining* came out *entering* in the newspaper's earliest edition. After a White House aide detected the error and placed a desperate phone call to the managing editor, the offending edition was hastily retrieved from newsstands—but not before enough copies had been sold to convulse innumerable readers.

In the same vein was a riddle that made the rounds in Washington about the time of Wilson's second marriage:
"What did Mrs. Galt do when the president proposed to her?"
"She fell out of bed."

During the grim period following his stroke, Wilson enjoyed few amusements in the White House. Some of his happiest hours were those spent watching motion pictures, a plebian form of entertainment Wilson loved. One of his special favorites was D. W. Griffith's *Birth of a Nation*, which depicted the post–Civil War Reconstruction era with a pro-Southern, white supremicist bias that Wilson unselfconsciously shared.

QUOTES BY WILSON
"And let me again remind you that it is only by working with an energy which is almost superhuman and which looks to uninterested spectators like insanity that we can accomplish anything worth the achievement."
—Undergraduate essay, "The Ideal Statesman"

"Tolerance is an admirable intellectual gift; but it is worth little in politics. Politics is a way of causes; a joust of principles."
—Wilson at age twenty-one

"I have a sense of power in dealing with men collectively which I do not always feel in dealing with them singly. . . . One feels no sacrifice of pride necessary in courting the favor of an assembly of men such as he would have to make in seeking to please one man."

—Wilson at age twenty-seven

"The business of government is to organize the common interest against the special interests."

—1912

"Segregation is not humiliating but a benefit, and ought to be so regarded by you gentlemen. The only harm that will come will be if you cause the colored people of the country to think it is a humiliation."

—President Wilson to a delegation of black leaders, November 1913

"We are glad, now that we see the facts with no veil of false pretense about them, to fight thus for the ultimate peace of the world and for the liberation of its peoples, the German peoples included; for the rights of nations great and small and the privilege of men everywhere to choose their way of life and of obedience. The world must be made safe for democracy. . . . It is a fearful thing to lead this great peaceful people into war, into the most terrible and disastrous of all wars, civilization itself seeming to be in the balance. But the right is more precious than peace, and we shall fight for the things which we have always carried nearest our hearts."

—Declaration of war against Germany, April 2, 1917

"Better a thousand times to go down fighting than to dip your colors to dishonorable compromise."

—Wilson to his wife, 1919

"My constant embarrassment is to restrain the emotions that are inside of me. You may not believe it, but I sometimes feel like the fire from a far from extinct volcano, and if the lava does not seem to spill over it is because you are not high enough to see into the basin and see the caldron boil."

—Comment at presidential press conference

"If I said what I thought about those fellows in Congress, it would take a piece of asbestos two inches thick to hold it."

—On Senate opponents of the Versailles Treaty, August 12, 1919

"My fellow citizens, I believe in Divine Providence. If I did not I would go crazy."

—September 17, 1919, one week before his collapse

"Again and again mothers who lost their sons in France have come to me, and, taking my hand, have not only shed tears upon it, but they have added, 'God bless you, Mr. President!' Why should they pray God to bless me? I advised the Congress to create the situation that led to the death of their sons. I ordered their sons overseas. I consented to their sons' being put in the most difficult part of the battle line, where death was certain. . . . Why should they weep upon my hand and call down the blessings of God upon me? Because they believe that their boys died for something that vastly transcends any of the immediate and palpable objects of the war. They believe, and rightly believe, that their sons saved the liberty of the world."

—Speech in Pueblo, Colorado, September 26, 1919

"Sometimes people call me an idealist. Well, that is the way I know I am an American. . . . I do not say it in disparagement of any other great people—America is the only idealistic nation in the world."

—September 8, 1919

"Every man who takes office in Washington either grows or swells, and when I give a man office I watch him carefully to see whether he is growing or swelling."

—Speech, May 15, 1916

QUOTES ABOUT WILSON

"He had to hold the reins and do the driving alone; it was the only kind of leadership he knew."

—Arthur S. Link in Wilson: The Road to the White House

"He is an utterly selfish and cold-blooded politician always."

—Former president Theodore Roosevelt

"He thought that lying was justified in some instances, particularly where it involved the honor of a woman. . . . He thought it was also justified where it related to matters of public policy."

—Colonel E. M. House, Wilson's close friend and top aide

"That mulish enigma, that mountain of egotism and selfishness who lives in the White House."

—Former president William Howard Taft

"Father enjoyed the society of women, especially if they were what he called 'charming and conversable.' . . . Father once said, 'No man has ever been a success without having been surrounded by admiring females.'"

—Eleanor Wilson McAdoo

"Mr. Wilson bores me with his 14 Points; why, God Almighty has only 10."

—Georges Clemenceau, premier of France

"It would have been easy to lay the treaty and the covenant before the Senate as a bad lot, but the best he could do; but that would have been to confess weakness, to admire failure, something that Wilson could not do. He was schooled in the counsel of perfection and could give his approval to nothing less than perfection. So he brought home the perfect treaty and the impeccable covenant, and laid them both before his countrymen as the work of God."

—William Allen White

"Wilson, after all, stood for human decency. He stood weakly for human decency; but he stood where it is an honor to stand."

—Sigmund Freud and William Bullit in
Wilson: A Psychological Study
—**M.S.M.**

EDITH BOLLING WILSON
The Other Twenty-Eighth President

Thanks to American society's belated recognition of the equality of the sexes, the possibility of a woman's being elected president of the United States no longer raises eyebrows in alarm at the end of the twentieth century. But in an almost forgotten episode of early-twentieth-century American political history, a woman who staunchly opposed the campaign for female suffrage was hailed by newspapers in this nation and abroad as "Presidentress of the United States." Her name was Edith Bolling Galt Wilson. The second wife of Woodrow Wilson, Edith Wilson appointed herself a highly unofficial acting president during the long and crucial months following her husband's near-fatal incapacity.

The Bollings were direct descendants of the Indian princess Pocahontas. Reduced to poverty in the aftermath of the Civil War, William Bolling, a formerly prosperous planter, took his wife, Sallie White Bolling, to Wytheville, Virginia. Edith was born there on October 15, 1872, the seventh of nine children. Her father, a judge in the circuit court, had a modest income that permitted schooling for her brothers, but Edith stayed home, tutored in reading, writing, arithmetic, and French by her father and grandmother. Until she was nearly thirteen years old, Edith never left her rustic, impoverished hometown. Eventually she was sent to boarding school, where she received two years of formal education.

Edith's first husband was Norman Galt, a wealthy businessman who owned an exclusive jewelry store in Washington, D.C. When Galt died she successfully ran the store herself. Childless, she undertook the guardianship of a teenaged girl named Altrude Gordon, who later was engaged to White House physician Dr. Cary Grayson. Miss Gordon and her fiancé asked Edith to befriend Helen Bone, a young cousin of the president. Through Helen, Edith met Woodrow Wilson, a recent widower. To the great dismay of Colonel Edward House, the president's close adviser, Wilson soon married Edith Galt, who ended up replacing the colonel as Wilson's chief confidante.

On the evening of September 25, 1919, in the midst of a triumphant speaking tour rallying support for the League of Nations, President Wilson collapsed and was rushed back to the White House. On October 2 he suffered a paralytic stroke and was totally incapacitated until mid-November. During the next few months, he slowly regained a tenuous hold on the responsibilities of the presidential office. During this interval his wife embarked on "Mrs. Wilson's Stewardship," the words she herself used to describe her role. Some historians believe her stewardship lasted seventeen months, until the end of Wilson's second term.

A unique configuration of circumstances led Edith Wilson to become "acting president." She was strongly encouraged by Dr. F. X. Dercum, who implored her to take over, stressing that her husband's life depended upon her. He explained that the president had a blood clot in his brain. The clot would dissolve, and he would probably recover—but only if he was spared the chore of making decisions and shielded from all disturbing problems. Resignation was no answer, Dr. Dercum warned. The president's will to live would be gone, and the ratification of the peace treaty would be endangered, along with the League of Nations, the cause that meant the most to him. Dr. Grayson, Wilson's personal physician and friend, concurred in Dercum's oddly politicized prognosis. Both doctors agreed that the elevation of Vice President Thomas Riley Marshall to head of state would be calamitous. Marshall, the logical stand-in for Wilson by virtue of official rank, was a happy-go-lucky nonentity whose affability and entertaining speeches endeared him to everyone. It was he who coined the phrase "What this country needs is a good 5-cent cigar." However, at the prospect of assuming the presidency, Marshall simply dissolved. On one occasion, reminded that he might be duty-bound to take over Woodrow Wilson's job, he buried his head in his hands, struck speechless. Asked on another occasion what he would do if he became president, he blurted out, "I can't even think about it."

Secretary of State Robert Lansing was not much better suited to fill the role of chief of state. Nor, in all probability, did he know as much about foreign policy as Edith Wilson, who had been Wilson's confidante. In fact, all Lansing knew about Wilson's policies was what he had read in the newspapers. For that matter, Marshall knew little more. Marshall side-stepped Cabinet meetings, explaining that if he couldn't have the $75,000 a year that went along with the president's job, he wasn't going to do any of his work.

Lone wolf Woodrow Wilson had one alter ego upon whom he relied—his wife, Edith. He told her everything, and she helped him make all his decisions. When he agonized over accepting his political patron William Jennings Bryan's letter of resignation, Edith tipped the scales, urging him to replace Bryan. The secretary of state before Lansing, Bryan was an outspoken pacifist. Edith believed Bryan's disinclination to prepare for war was dangerous. Wilson deferred to Edith's opinion.

Edith had attended all of Wilson's private conferences. She was the only other person who knew the secret code by which Wilson communicated with Colonel House and his emissaries in Europe. Wilson taught her the code in February of 1915, and from then on he wrote his top-secret communications in longhand for Edith to encode in her own writing. Edith also decoded incoming messages during those four and a half years. Not another soul knew the mind of Wilson and the nuances of his foreign policy the way that Edith Wilson did. Thus she was eminently suited to the awesome cares thrust upon her by destiny, even if no one had voted for her.

Edith stood guard over her critically ill husband, warding off Cabinet members and other officials who "had to see the president." Joseph Tumulty, Wilson's loyal secretary, wore a hangdog expression, for he was routinely shunted aside. Now and then Edith would disappear into the sickroom, carefully closing the door behind her, to relay a message from some official to the president's ear. Emerging, she would report that "the President says . . ." Thus Edith screened all problems that would ordinarily reach the president, consulting with her husband, whose mind was lucid despite his physical condition, only as often as she deemed conducive to his recovery. It was Edith who decided which matters should be brought to his attention. She conferred with officials, freely dispensing advice; and when two department secretaries resigned, she personally handpicked men to replace them.

All papers, letters, and documents from the Cabinet and Congress went to Edith. She guided Wilson's faltering hand as he signed congressional bills. As a result, Senators who recognized Wilson's handwriting suspected Edith of forgery. Sometimes Edith conveyed the president's thoughts by scrawling replies directly on memorandums sent to him. Her large, round, distinctive handwriting would circle the margin of a question penned by some senator or Cabinet member, often to the perplexity of the recipient, as he turned the paper this way and that, trying to decipher the weaving, cryptic White House message.

Congress viewed Mrs. Wilson's activities with a good deal of consternation. Senator Albert Fall of New Mexico almost became violent, as he pounded on the table and thundered, "We have a petticoat Government! Mrs. Wilson is President!" An avalanche of newspaper criticism of her "regency" disheartened Edith, and some of the White House servants, alluding to her ancestry, churlishly complained about "being forced to work for an Indian."

As for the country's domestic affairs, it must be admitted that a number of "housekeeping chores" had to go by the board. A mining strike awaited the setting up of a commission to resolve it. Vacancies on a few commissions went temporarily unfilled. But then, Vice President Marshall had categorically refused to do "any of the President's work." At least Edith, although swamped by the demands of national leadership, was trying.

As to foreign affairs, in one crucial instance, Wilson failed to heed Edith's advice. When she asked him to consent to Senator Lodge's stipulations on U.S. entry into the League of Nations, Wilson stubbornly refused. Because Wilson's ego wouldn't allow him to compromise, the senator voted to keep the United States out of the league. Mrs. Wilson's political acumen might very well have positively changed the course of history if only her husband had listened to her.

Edith Wilson's initiative and determination won her praise as well as censure. The London Daily Mail reported that Mrs. Wilson was proving to be a perfectly capable "president." A member of the opposition party, a Republican journalist named Dolly Gann, exulted over the fact that a woman in the White House knew how to take over and act for the good of her country when necessary.

Wilson recovered and completed his term. Had it not been for Edith, he could long since have been removed from office for inability to perform his duties as president. And Thomas Marshall, who enjoyed being vice president because he had "no responsibilities," would have succeeded to the highest office in the land. Edith Wilson never wavered in her loyalty to her husband, the twenty-eighth president of the United States. After his death, she maintained her interest in the League of Nations and international cooperation, the cause in which he had so firmly believed.

There is no chance today of having another Edith Wilson acting as an American "presidentress." The Twenty-fifth Amendment, ratified February 10, 1967, clearly defines what happens in case the president is incapable of governing. The first official female president will have to be duly elected.

—R.Ho.

FRANKLIN ROOSEVELT
Thirty-Second President

VITAL STATISTICS
Birth: Franklin Delano Roosevelt was born on January 30, 1882, at Hyde Park, New York. His gracious Hudson River valley birthplace is usually described as an estate, but FDR himself

preferred to think of it as a farm. Visitors to the 187-acre site, now a historic landmark, can decide for themselves which title is more accurate. Hyde Park is located on U.S. Route 9, four miles north of Poughkeepsie.

Death: Roosevelt died on April 12, 1945, in the "Little White House" at Warm Springs, Georgia, where he had gone (under doctor's orders) to rest and prepare for the upcoming organizational meeting of the United Nations. On the morning of April 12, the president donned a crimson Harvard tie and his familiar black navy cape and went into the living room of his cottage to pose for a portrait. The artist worked quietly at her easel and Roosevelt glanced through a sheaf of papers, while the servants laid out lunch dishes on a nearby table. Suddenly the president raised a hand to his forehead and said softly, "I have a terrific headache." Then he slumped back in his chair, unconscious. Three hours later he was dead of a cerebral hemorrhage. Roosevelt, who was sixty-three, was buried in his garden at Hyde Park. A Roosevelt memorial, situated between the Potomac River and the Tidal Basin in Washington, D.C., was begun in 1994 and is scheduled to open in 1996.

BEFORE THE PRESIDENCY
Career: No American president came from a more patrician background than Franklin Roosevelt. His mother's family claimed that they could trace their genealogy all the way back to William the Conqueror. Between them, the Roosevelts and the Delanos boasted no fewer than twelve Mayflower ancestors. As a boy, Franklin was educated by private tutors and he toured Europe eight times before he was sixteen. At the proper time he attended Groton School (where 90 percent of the students were from Social Register families) and Harvard. Roosevelt was a mediocre student (maintaining a "gentlemanly" C average at Harvard) but a notable social success. His fifth cousin, Theodore Roosevelt, was then serving as president, and Franklin enjoyed a good deal of reflected glory. In his junior year he was elected editor of the *Harvard Crimson* and wrote ringing editorials urging the football team to victory and lamenting the decline in school spirit. After graduation he attended Columbia Law School but was thoroughly bored by his studies there. He flunked several courses and dropped out before winning his degree, but he absorbed enough information to pass a bar examination anyway and take his place in a fashionable New York law firm.

When Roosevelt was twenty-eight, the Democratic leaders in his home district became interested in the handsome young lawyer with the famous last name. Only one Democrat had carried the district since 1856, and now the party needed a state senate candidate. The main qualification was that the nominee be wealthy

enough to pay his own expenses in a hopeless cause. Roosevelt agreed to run, and then startled his neighbors with a flamboyant, person-to-person campaign in a red touring car. He won an upset victory, took his seat in Albany, and immediately identified himself with genteel reform elements. Though admirers have cited FDR's "courage" in defying the statewide Democratic machine, he was actually doing exactly what his overwhelmingly Republican constituents expected of him. In 1912 Roosevelt was an early supporter of Woodrow Wilson's presidential bid, and when Wilson was elected, the young state senator was rewarded with a post in the new administration. Roosevelt was appointed assistant secretary of the navy—a position that his cousin Teddy had made famous some fifteen years before. In the Navy Department, FDR proved a skillful and aggressive administrator with a knack for personal publicity. With the coming of World War I, the assistant secretary, long an advocate of increased naval power, gained stature as a prophet.

In 1920 the thirty-five-year-old Roosevelt was nominated by his party for the vice presidency, in the hope that his famous name would attract Progressive Republicans to the Democratic ticket. Though Roosevelt and his presidential running mate, James M. Cox, were crushed under the Harding landslide, FDR gained a reputation as a tireless and popular campaigner, and after the election his political prospects seemed brighter than ever. All of that came to an end in August 1921, while FDR was vacationing at his family's summer home at Campobello, in New Brunswick, Canada. While yachting with his sons, Roosevelt stopped to put out a forest fire on a small island, then refreshed himself with a swim in the icy waters of the bay. He suffered severe body shock, and that evening was overcome by a stab of pain and a chill. The next morning his legs failed him when he tried to stand up, and within fourteen hours he was paralyzed from the waist down. He had contracted polio, but it was more than a week before the doctors diagnosed his condition correctly. By that time Roosevelt, aged thirty-nine, had been permanently crippled. He would never regain the use of his legs.

Personal Life: Though he was considered a devastatingly handsome young man, Roosevelt showed no interest in women until his junior year at Harvard, when he fell in love with his fourth cousin, Eleanor Roosevelt. Eleanor was shy, plain, and insecure; an orphan; and the product of an unhappy childhood. What it was about her that attracted the dashing and fun-loving FDR remains a mystery, since Mrs. Roosevelt, in later life, destroyed his early letters to her. It may have been that Franklin was impressed by his cousin's brilliant mind, or by her social concern: Eleanor spent her free time as a volunteer in a Manhattan settlement house. It is also possible that he was swayed by her close connection to the family's most famous member: Eleanor was the daughter of Teddy Roosevelt's younger brother, and Uncle Ted appeared personally at the brilliant society wedding in 1905 to give away the bride.

Despite this auspicious beginning, the twenty-three-year-old FDR and his twenty-year-old wife ran into difficulties almost immediately. The first problem was Franklin's mother, an intelligent, strong-willed widow who wasn't about to give up her hold on her only child. She had moved to Boston to be close to Franklin during his years at Harvard, and now she insisted on setting up house with the young couple. She easily dominated the unassuming Eleanor and made all crucial decisions concerning the Roosevelt home.

There were also deeper tensions in the marriage: family papers, made public for the first time in 1971, show that Eleanor craved affection but always considered sex an ordeal, while Franklin had a healthier sexual appetite but was uncomfortable with genuine intimacy. In the early years of the marriage, FDR usually got his way, but in 1916, after the birth of her sixth child, Eleanor put her foot down. During the twenty-nine years of marriage that remained to them, the Roosevelts never slept together again. They maintained separate bedrooms and in the White House actually took over different wings of the mansion.

Not surprisingly, FDR looked for consolation outside his marriage. His first and most serious affair involved Lucy Mercer, his wife's beautiful and sophisticated social secretary. By the time Eleanor discovered a batch of love letters and found out about the affair, Franklin and Lucy were deeply in love. There was talk of a divorce and remarriage, but Roosevelt's mother squelched all such plans by threatening to cut off her son's generous financial allowance. Franklin was forced to give up Lucy Mercer, but his interest in her continued from a distance for the rest of his life.

In a sense, Roosevelt's paralysis probably strengthened his bond with Eleanor, but their relationship was one of mutual respect and dependence rather than personal intimacy. Medical reports prove that FDR's sexual prowess was unimpaired by polio, and rumors continued to link him with other women. Wartime gossip centered on a supposed romantic involvement between the president and the glamorous young Princess Martha of Norway. Then in 1973 FDR's son Elliott published a book in which he declared that Missy LeHand, his father's tall, slim, gray-eyed private secretary, was Roosevelt's mistress for ten years. Elliott also asserted that Eleanor not only knew about the relationship but approved of it— allowing Missy and Franklin to occupy adjoin-

ing bedrooms. In her 1981 book, Lillian Rogers Parks, a household maid, also claims that Missy was one of FDR's mistresses.

Though some Roosevelt intimates have doubted the accuracy of this account, there can be no question that as the years went by, Eleanor became more and more her own woman. In the White House she was without a doubt the most active and most controversial First Lady up to that time in American history, rivaled since, perhaps, only by Hillary Clinton. She wrote a daily newspaper column, held regular press conferences, chaired public works committees, and earned the nickname "Public Energy Number One." She also made countless far-flung inspection tours for her husband and filed the reports of her travels, in writing, in a small basket by FDR's bed. Roosevelt called her his "eyes and ears," and would often answer department heads by saying, "Yes, but, my missus tells me . . ." He was obviously proud of his brilliant wife, and she was no doubt devoted to him. The public knew nothing of the persistent problems in their marriage.

In 1944 Missy LeHand died of a stroke, and in his loneliness FDR turned once again to Lucy Mercer, now an aging but attractive widow. On several occasions he risked exposure to spend time with her; he once ordered an unscheduled stop on a presidential train so that he could spend half a day at Lucy's New Jersey home. Privileged observers noted a romantic, somewhat melancholy aspect in this "lonely hearts" relationship. Lucy was with Roosevelt in Warm Springs on the day that he died, but after his collapse she left hurriedly, before Eleanor and the press arrived on the scene.

On the Way to the White House: In the 1920s, FDR set out with unshakable confidence to prove to himself and his family that he need not live as an invalid. He worked tirelessly at a series of special exercises for his paralyzed legs, traveled to Georgia for water therapy, and accustomed himself to wheelchairs, or to crawling on his hands from room to room. Eventually his condition improved enough so that he was able to "walk," using a cane, eight-pound leg braces, and the supporting arm of one of his sons. This was an important triumph for FDR, because it allowed him to resume his political career: he could take the necessary steps from his chair to a speaker's platform, then lock his braces and hold the podium for support. At the 1924 Democratic convention, Roosevelt's appearance electrified the delegates, as he made a stirring speech nominating Al Smith for president. It seemed that FDR's handicap only served to increase his political appeal. Historian Paul Conkin has written that "polio made the aristocratic Roosevelt into an underdog. For him it replaced the log cabin." In 1928, when Al Smith finally won the Democratic presidential nomination, he asked

Roosevelt to run for governor of New York in order to lend strength to the ticket. Smith assured the hesitant FDR that the duties of the governorship need not interfere with continued therapy for his legs. "Don't hand me that baloney!" laughed Roosevelt, but he decided to make the race anyway. In the campaign that followed, Smith lost the state to Hoover by 100,000 votes, but the popular Roosevelt was elected governor by a narrow margin. With the coming of the depression, Roosevelt used his office to win relief for the hungry and unemployed in his state. In 1930 he ran for reelection and won by the biggest margin in the history of New York State up to that time. Despite lingering doubts concerning his physical incapacity, he automatically emerged as a leading contender for the Democratic presidential nomination in 1932. Early that year, at a meeting of Hoover's Cabinet, the subject of Roosevelt's possible candidacy was discussed; it was agreed that FDR could never be elected once the American people discovered that the polio victim was "only half a man."

His Person: FDR was six feet two inches tall and weighed about 190 pounds. Woodrow Wilson once described him as "the handsomest young giant I have ever seen." Roosevelt was always broad-shouldered, but after he lost the use of his legs he built up his arms and chest to prodigious strength. "Maybe my legs aren't so good," he once said, "but look at those shoulders! Jack Dempsey would be green with envy." While recovering from polio, he used to wrestle with his young sons on the floor, two at a time. Roosevelt had a high forehead and a roman nose and was almost always smiling. Political opponents cited his unfailing optimism, good humor, and charm as evidence of a shallow, flabby nature. Roosevelt could even make light of his own affliction. During one of her visits to the White House, Madame Chiang Kai-shek thoughtlessly told the president not to stand up as she rose to leave the room. "My dear child," laughed Roosevelt, tossing his head back in a characteristic gesture. "I couldn't stand up if I had to!" Visitors to Washington social functions, no matter how large, could always find the president by following the sound of his booming laughter. FDR's mellow, resonant voice, often described as "the best radio voice in the world," became a key political asset. Roosevelt was a steady, but never a problem, drinker, who generally enjoyed two or three cocktails a night. He was also a heavy smoker, and consumed thirty cigarettes a day despite doctor's orders to cut down. His long-stemmed cigarette holder, tilting upward from his toothy grin, became a Roosevelt trademark. Another trademark, the flowing black navy cape, had a practical justification: aides found it extremely awkward to help the crippled president in and

Franklin Delano Roosevelt at a press conference in Warm Springs, Georgia, April 4, 1939.

out of overcoats, and the cape greatly simplified matters. FDR developed a way of walking, supported by a son on one side and a cane on the other, that produced the illusion of mobility; it served as an apt metaphor for the determination that would lead him to the presidency.

PRESIDENCY
Nomination: June 27, 1932
As the Democratic convention assembled in Chicago, the delegates knew that the man they chose would be the next president. The "Hoover Depression" had made a Democratic victory a virtual certainty. FDR had won an impressive string of primary victories but had lost California to John Nance "Cactus Jack" Garner of Texas and had lost Massachusetts to his old friend Al Smith. On the first ballot, Roosevelt had more than half the delegate votes, but he fell short of the two-thirds necessary for nomination. As the convention completed its third ballot, it seemed that the opposition candidates might have enough strength to create a long-term deadlock. In desperation an agreement was reached: Garner, who was Speaker of the House, would get the vice presidential nod in exchange for releasing his delegates to Roosevelt. On the fourth ballot, FDR and Garner were duly nominated, and the confident Democrats moved on to the general election. As Senator W.G. McAdoo told Roosevelt: "Now all you have to do is stay alive until the election."

Election: November 8, 1932
The final election returns offered few surprises. Roosevelt polled 22,809,638 votes to 15,758,901 for Herbert Hoover, the Republican incumbent. Roosevelt carried forty-two of the forty-eight states and buried Hoover in the electoral college, 472 to 59. Much of Roosevelt's campaign rhetoric was naive and misleading; he promised, for instance, to cut federal spending at the same time he would increase relief. Nevertheless, the personality of the genial New Yorker seemed to catch on with the voters, as did his promise of a "new deal for the American people."

First Term: March 4, 1933
Roosevelt was sworn in by Chief Justice Charles Hughes at the east portico of the Capitol. The economic crisis had continued to worsen; now, with the nation near panic, the new president assured his countrymen: "This great nation will endure as it has endured, will revive and will prosper. So, first of all, let me assert my firm belief that the only thing we have to fear is fear itself—nameless, unreasoning, unjustified terror, which paralyzes needed efforts to convert retreat into advance."

Within a hundred days, Congress had approved all key aspects of Roosevelt's sweeping legislative program, setting up a host of new federal agencies and providing changes in nearly every aspect of American life.

Reelection: November 3, 1936
The Republicans had hysterically denounced nearly all of Roosevelt's reforms, and in the 1936 campaign they launched a crusade to "save America from Socialism." Their presidential candidate was a genial but colorless conservative named Alf Landon, who was dubbed by his supporters "the Kansas Coolidge." Another Landon nickname, "the Kansas Sunflower," led to a popular Democratic bumper sticker that read: "Sunflowers wilt in November." This proved an accurate prediction, as Roosevelt and Garner rolled up one of the greatest landslides in American history, carrying every state in the Union except Maine and Vermont. The final electoral tally was 523 to 8. The popular vote saw a record plurality of nearly 11 million.

Third Term: November 5, 1940
For months Roosevelt refused to say whether or not he would break tradition and run for a third term, but his hesitation prevented another Democrat from emerging as a strong contender. When the president finally announced that he would accept a "draft," many Democrats were unhappy, but they had little choice but to nominate him. The vice presidential nomination was another matter: Roosevelt wanted to replace retiring Vice President Garner with the secretary of agriculture, the radical Henry Wallace. The convention

seemed to favor a more conservative choice, and it was only the surprise appearance of Eleanor Roosevelt, making a forceful speech in behalf of her husband's choice, that secured the nomination for Wallace.

The Republicans entered the campaign with a new issue: the claim that Roosevelt's aid to Great Britain in the struggle with Hitler would lead the United States into an unnecessary war. Their candidate, however, agreed with Roosevelt on most key policy questions. Wendell Willkie was a political amateur who had used a strong grassroots organization to "steal" the Republican nomination from party professionals. Adding insult to injury was the fact that Willkie had been a Democrat all his life—and, in 1932, had actually contributed $150 to Roosevelt's campaign. Willkie, however, was a corporation lawyer; his business interests were threatened by the New Deal, and he soon began criticizing the administration. In the 1940 campaign he stumped the country with extraordinary vigor, pushing himself until his speaking voice grew hoarse and raspy. Wherever possible, the Republicans emphasized the third-term issue. "No man is good 3 times," proclaimed one of their slogans, while the Democrats answered: "Better a 3rd termer than a 3rd rater."

The election returns showed that Roosevelt's popularity had slipped significantly (Willkie won 45 percent of the vote), but "the Champ" still won by a comfortable margin. Roosevelt outpolled Willkie, 27,241,939 to 22,327,276. Willkie carried ten states (most of them in the Midwest) for 82 electoral votes to Roosevelt's 449.

Fourth Term: November 7, 1944
With the United States in the middle of the war, Roosevelt was not about to retire; though his health had deteriorated, he was determined to see the war through to its conclusion and play the leading role in forging international peace. His renomination by his party was a foregone conclusion, but once again the vice presidential slot was a subject of controversy. Conservatives were intent on dumping Wallace from the ticket, and in order to avoid a convention floor fight, FDR personally selected a compromise candidate—a little-known senator from Missouri named Harry S. Truman.

The Republicans, behind Governor Thomas E. Dewey of New York, waged a particularly bitter and personal campaign, whispering about the president's failing health and charging that "communist influences" had taken over the administration. Stung by these charges, Roosevelt was determined to show some of his old mettle. In October he greeted more than 3 million New Yorkers, campaigning in an open car in a blinding rain. In the end the Republicans were unable to shake Roosevelt's image as a war leader of international stature. Dewey was beaten by 3.5 million votes and lost the electoral college, 432 to 99.

On January 20, 1945, Roosevelt took the oath of office for the fourth time, in an austere, sparsely attended ceremony on the south portico of the White House. A light snow had fallen the night before and the thermometer registered only one degree above freezing; nevertheless, the president was bareheaded and without an overcoat while he delivered his six-minute address.

Two weeks later he traveled 14,000 miles to confer with Churchill and Stalin at Yalta. When he spoke to Congress after his return, he did so from a sitting position—the first time he had delivered a major speech without standing up. "I hope that you will pardon me for the unusual posture of sitting down," he said. "It makes it a lot easier for me not having to carry about ten pounds of steel around on the bottom of my legs." It was also the first time the president had ever referred to his braces in public. Five weeks later, Roosevelt was dead.

Vetoes: Roosevelt dominated Congress more completely than any other president in history, and he used his veto power with unparalleled zest. His 635 vetoes set an all-time record. Only nine of his vetoes were overridden by Congress. Old New Dealers tell the story that Roosevelt used to ask his aides to find something he could veto in order to remind Congress not to get "uppity."

His Twelve Years, Thirty-Nine Days as President:

PRO   Roosevelt restored the confidence of the people in their government at a time when that confidence was failing. He not only promised "action, and action now"; he kept that promise as well. It was only through his leadership that a disastrous social upheaval was avoided in the depression-torn United States. Responding to the worst domestic crisis in our history, FDR's magnificent buoyancy, self-assurance, and political skill gave the United States a new sense of purpose and direction.

CON   Roosevelt's enemies considered him a power-mad demagogue who expanded the powers of the presidency to dictatorial proportions. His infamous "court-packing" plan—which would have allowed him to appoint new justices and to remake the Supreme Court according to his will—showed his basic contempt for constitutional processes. In violating the unwritten law against a third term, he set the dangerous precedent of interminable one-man rule. In response to the excesses of the Roosevelt era, the nation wisely adopted the Twenty-second Amendment to the Constitution—limiting all future presidents to two terms only.

PRO   With its free-wheeling, experimental approach to America's problems, the New Deal provided jobs and relief for millions of hungry Americans. For the first time, government recognized its responsibility for the economic well-being of ordinary citizens. While the captains of industry howled, FDR began dismantling the mighty fortress of special privilege that had been built up over the course of a century: the Wagner Act guaranteed labor's right to organize, while other New Deal programs such as Social Security, the Tennessee Valley Authority, and the Works Progress Administration provided lasting benefits for the country and its citizens. The New Deal put an end to the bad old days of laissez-faire capitalism and moved the nation toward a more healthy and rational economic structure.

CON   After promising the voters that he would "balance the budget," FDR launched happily into an irresponsible spending spree, the likes of which had never been seen before. His massive give-away program encouraged the masses to develop "their wishbones more than their backbones." The effects of this paternalistic policy are still felt today, with a massive, all-powerful government bureaucracy overshadowing the life of the individual. The New Deal panaceas were not only costly but also ineffective in combating the depression. It was only the beginning of wartime production that returned prosperity to a nation dangerously weakened by six years of Roosevelt's ill-considered social experiments.

PRO   In an era of rampant isolationism, Roosevelt worked effectively to make his countrymen aware of their international responsibilities. His "Good Neighbor Policy" in Latin America was an unqualified success, restoring friendly relations after a generation of high-handed United States imperialism. He ordered diplomatic recognition of the Soviet Union, after sixteen years of blind hostility to the Communist regime. Against fierce domestic opposition, he provided crucial aid to Britain in its lonely fight against Hitler in 1940 and 1941. Without this support, England might well have succumbed to the Nazi onslaught.

CON   Roosevelt became aware of the Fascist menace too late to take effective action to stop it, and even then he failed to take the necessary steps to prepare the United States for war. He did nothing to prevent the appeasement of Hitler at Munich or elsewhere. During the Spanish Civil War, he supported the embargo of arms to Spanish Loyalists—thereby assuring the success of Franco's Fascists. The Japanese surprise attack on Pearl Harbor was the product of either gross incompetence on the part of the commander in chief or a deliberate willingness to sacrifice American lives to political expediency. It has often been suggested that the president knew a Japanese attack was coming—and welcomed it as a means of easing himself out of the controversial decision to lead the nation to war.

PRO Roosevelt's contributions to the Allied victory were enormous. He personally kept the alliance together through difficult times, and his eloquence and determination inspired millions of people throughout the world. As commander in chief, he chose an unusually gifted group of men for the top military positions, and then backed them up effectively. FDR showed great vision, though he angered Churchill with his insistence that a permanent postwar peace required the breakup of the old colonial empires. The United Nations—established by Roosevelt over the doubts of political opponents and other world leaders—is a permanent legacy of his wartime leadership, and of his firm belief that the United States could ill afford another period of isolationism in which it would turn its back on the world's problems. For Roosevelt the United Nations was, among other things, a way of ensuring for the United States a leading role in the postwar world.

CON During the war, FDR did absolutely nothing to rescue the doomed Jews of Europe—even

FDR was crippled by polio but hid his disability from the public by being photographed in semi-athletic poses.

after he learned that millions of them were being slaughtered by the Nazis. At home he approved the unconstitutional and inhuman internment of more than 100,000 Japanese Americans in the infamous "relocation camps." Throughout the war Roosevelt was naively confident that America's Soviet "allies" would keep their promises, and at the Yalta Conference he personally sanctioned Stalin's takeover of most of Eastern Europe. By the time of the Yalta meeting, Roosevelt's health was so bad that his performance was impaired: his mind wandered, and he found it hard to concentrate on the business at hand. With his doctor, Roosevelt had conspired to keep his failing health a secret from the American public, so as not to jeopardize his chances for a fourth term. Even Vice President Truman was left in the dark, and Roosevelt did nothing to prepare his successor for the enormous responsibilities of the wartime presidency.

PSYCHOHISTORY

At Hyde Park, Roosevelt enjoyed an unusually happy and secure childhood. He had his own pony at age four, his own twenty-one-foot sailboat at age sixteen. An only child, he called his mother "Sallie" and his father "Popsie" and absorbed all their attention. His father, a wealthy financier and country squire, was fifty-four when Franklin was born, and naturally he adored the boy. Father and son rode horses, hunted, swam, sailed, and every day they walked into town together to get the mail. By the time he went away to school, Franklin was used to being the center of attention, and even with his own wife and children, FDR was always something of the bright, favored child who could do no wrong. He was used to having his own way, and whether it was a mistress, a third term, or a reconstituted Supreme Court, he never questioned his right to get what he wanted. At every level, Roosevelt was filled with confidence that he could personally overcome any obstacle. In a strange way, his experience with polio only intensified this sense of personal invulnerability. "If you have spent two years in bed trying to wiggle your big toe," he said, "then anything else seems easy." In other words, since he had experienced physical paralysis and gone on to success, he could undertake anything and emerge, in the end, triumphant. As historian Richard Hofstadter has written, the essence of the New Deal was "Roosevelt's confidence that even when he was operating in unfamiliar territory he could do no wrong, commit no serious mistakes." How else can one explain a man who sincerely expected that his own personal charm would be enough to persuade Joseph Stalin to make key postwar concessions? There is a legend, fostered by Roosevelt admirers, that FDR used the years of his convalescence for wide reading on economic theory, and that out of this intellectual ferment came a new commitment to social change. While this was hardly the case (Roosevelt was never a very serious reader), it does seem probable that his sympathies, as well as his self-confidence, were deepened by his affliction. Once, while lecturing in Akron, Ohio, Eleanor Roosevelt received a cruel written question from a member of the audience: "Do you think your husband's illness has affected his mentality?" Eleanor paused for a moment and then replied: "I am glad that question was asked. The answer is Yes. Anyone who has gone through great suffering is bound to have a greater sympathy and understanding of the problems of mankind." The audience rose in a standing ovation.

LITTLE-KNOWN FACTS
At her wedding the orphaned Eleanor Roosevelt was given away by her uncle, President Theodore Roosevelt. After the ceremonies, reporters asked the president what he thought of his niece's marriage to her young fourth cousin, Franklin. Replied TR, "It is a good thing to keep the name in the family."

Building model ships and collecting stamps were FDR's favorite hobbies. At his death the sale of his personal stamp collection brought in more than $200,000.

Mark Twain was Roosevelt's favorite writer, and FDR is reputed to have taken the term *New Deal* from a chapter in *A Connecticut Yankee in King Arthur's Court*. Roosevelt once wrote: "If people like my choice of words and my oratorical style, it is largely due to my constant study of Twain's works."

While recovering from polio, FDR worked at various projects. He spent some time writing a movie script based on the history of the ship *Old Ironsides*, but he never succeeded in selling this product to Hollywood. He also invested money in several novel schemes, including a proposed intercity dirigible freight line.

Eleanor was often idiosyncratic in her supervision of the White House menus. Particularly fond of sweetbreads, she once ordered that they be served six times in a single week. This was too much for FDR, who sent his wife a note reading, "I am getting to the point where my stomach rebels, and this does not help my relations with foreign powers. I bit two of them today."

The Roosevelts hosted the first visit of a reigning British monarch to the United States. George VI and his wife, Elizabeth, spent a day and a night at the White House, and were introduced to that best of American foods—hot dogs—for the first time.

Roosevelt appointed not only the first woman Cabinet member (Secretary of Labor Frances Perkins) but also the first woman to represent the United States as ambassador to a foreign country. Shortly after taking the oath of office for the first time, he named Ruth Bryan Owens, daughter of the late Democratic warhorse William Jennings Bryan, as minister to Denmark.

During the war years, FDR's travel plans were kept secret for security reasons. It was during this period that the president's dog, Fala, won the nickname "the informer." That famous Scottish terrier insisted on being taken for a walk at every stop on a train trip, and the sight of him, accompanied by weary Secret Service agents, was a tip-off to reporters that the president was on board.

Informal Sunday night dinners became a White House tradition during the Roosevelt administrations. Invitations went out only to personal friends and special guests, and Eleanor would preside over the gatherings, standing at the end of the table and scrambling eggs personally in a silver chafing dish. On other occasions, Eleanor would use the dinner table as a forum for her political ideas, often arguing with her husband. "Mother, can't you see you are giving Father indigestion!" asked daughter Anna after one exhausting diatribe.

Speaking in Cleveland during his campaign for a third term, FDR assured his audience that "when the next four years are over, there will be another president." There were loud shouts of "No!" from the crowd, but FDR thrust his mouth close to the microphone and went right on talking so that the shouts, which suggested that he be elected permanently, would not be heard over the radio.

QUOTES BY ROOSEVELT
"A conservative is a man with two perfectly good legs, who, however, has never learned to walk."

"I have no expectation of making a hit every time I come to bat. What I seek is the highest possible batting average."

"The test of our progress is not whether we add more to the abundance of those who have much; it is whether we provide enough for those who have little."

"A man who has never gone to school may steal from a freight car, but if he has a university education he may steal the whole railroad."

"These unhappy times call for plans that build from the bottom up and not from the top down, that put their faith once more in the forgotten man at the bottom of the economic pyramid."
—1932

"One thing is sure. We have to do something. We have to do the best we know how at the moment. If it doesn't turn out right, we can modify it as we go along."
—1936

"These economic royalists complain that we seek to overthrow the institutions of America. What they really complain of is that we seek to take away their power. These economic royalists are unanimous in their hate for me—and I welcome their hatred."

—1936

"There is a mysterious cycle in human events. To some generations much is given. Of other generations much is expected. This generation of Americans has a rendezvous with destiny. . . . We are fighting to save a great and precious form of government for ourselves and for the world."

—Acceptance speech, June 27, 1936,
Democratic convention

"Yesterday, December 7, 1941—a date which will live in infamy—the United States of America was suddenly and deliberately attacked by naval and air forces of the Empire of Japan."

—Speech to Congress, December 8, 1941

"Never before have we had so little time in which to do so much."

—Quoted in The Hinge of Fate
by Winston S. Churchill, 1942

"More than an end to war, we want an end to the beginnings of all wars."

—Speech broadcast on the day after his death,
April 13, 1945

QUOTES ABOUT ROOSEVELT

"Dear Mr. President: This is just to tell you that everything is all right now. The man you sent found our house all right, and we went down to the bank with him and the mortgage can go on for a while longer. You remember I wrote you about losing the furniture too. Well, your man got it back for us. I never heard of a president like you."

—Letter to the White House, summer, 1933

"Meeting him is like opening a bottle of champagne."

—Winston Churchill

"He is a pleasant man, who, without any important qualifications for the office, would very much like to be president. . . . Here is a man who has made a good governor, who might make a good Cabinet officer, but who simply does not measure up to the tremendous demands of the office of president."

—Walter Lippmann, 1932

"One thing is sure—that the idea people get from his charming manner—that he is soft or flabby in disposition and character—is far from true. When he wants something a lot, he can be formidable; when crossed, he is hard, stubborn, resourceful, relentless."

—Presidential aide Raymond Moley

"The country is being run by a group of college professors. This Brain Trust is endeavoring to force socialism upon the American people."

—Senator Henry D. Hatfield of West Virginia

"He might have been happier with a wife who was completely uncritical. That I was never able to be. Nevertheless I think I sometimes acted as a spur. I was one of those who served his purposes."

—Eleanor Roosevelt, 1945

"Consider the world of 1994. It is manifestly not Adolf Hitler's world. . . . It is manifestly not Joseph Stalin's world. That world disintegrated before our eyes. . . . Nor is it Winston Churchill's world. Empire and its glories have long since vanished into the past. The world we live in today is Franklin Roosevelt's world. Of the figures who, for good or evil, bestrode the narrow world half a century ago, he would be the least surprised by the shape of things at the end of the century. For all his manifold foibles, flaws, follies, and there was a sufficiency of all of these, FDR deserves supreme credit as the twentieth-century statesman who saw most deeply into the grand movements of history."

—Arthur Schlesinger Jr., 1994
—M.S.M.

JOHN KENNEDY
Thirty-Fifth President

VITAL STATISTICS
Birth: John Fitzgerald Kennedy was born on May 29, 1917, in Brookline, Massachusetts. Brookline is an unpretentious suburb of Boston, and the gray frame house in which he spent his childhood was located in a middle-class neighborhood. The fabulous wealth for which his

John F. Kennedy in an official portrait.

family is celebrated came only in later years. Kennedy was the first president born in the twentieth century.

Death: Kennedy died on November 22, 1963, in Dallas, Texas, from bullet wounds in the neck and head. Kennedy was riding in a downtown motorcade when he was cut down by a sniper. The identity of the sniper—and other details of the assassination—are still a matter of controversy. (See "Assassinations," page 147.) Kennedy, who was forty-six, lived a shorter life than any other president. He was buried in Arlington National Cemetery, beneath a memorial "eternal flame." As E. B. White observed: "He died of exposure, but in a way that he would have settled for—in the line of duty, and with his friends and enemies all around, supporting him and shooting at him."

BEFORE THE PRESIDENCY

Career: Kennedy's maternal and paternal grandfathers were prominent Democratic ward bosses in an age when a handful of Irish "pols" ruled Boston. His father, however, purchased power in a different way. By age twenty-five Joe Kennedy had gained control of a bank in East Boston, and with subsequent investments in real estate, Hollywood, the stock market, and, during Prohibition, illicit liquor, he built a financial empire eventually worth $250 million. Naturally, he sent his children to the best schools, and young "Jack," the second-oldest, prepared for college at Choate School in Connecticut. Kennedy had a difficult time at prep school, and his housemaster wrote home, "He is casual and disorderly in almost all of his organization projects. Jack studies at the last minute, keeps appointments late, has little sense of material values, and can seldom locate his possessions." The young man came down with a mysterious illness; his letters of that time suggest a confused and sexually imaginative adolescent. After a month in the Mayo Clinic, during which he underwent a seemingly endless series of enemas, administered by nurses whom he charitably described as "the dirtiest minded bunch of females I've ever seen," he was finally sent home, where he immediately—and quite inexplicably—recovered. Though his popularity with his classmates won him election as "most likely to succeed," Kennedy graduated in the bottom half of his class.

In the choice of a college, Jack was naturally anxious to avoid direct competition with his brilliantly successful older brother, Joe Jr., so he steered clear of Harvard and enrolled instead at Princeton University. After two months, however, an attack of jaundice forced him to drop out of school and return home. By the time he was ready to start again the next year (1936), he had given in to the urgings of his family and agreed to join his brother at Harvard. As a student, Kennedy maintained a C average during his first two years, and devoted much of his time to athletics and chasing girls, until he seriously injured his back playing football. Then he fell in love with Frances Ann Cannon, daughter of a wealthy North Carolina family, whose parents, however, would not let her marry a Catholic. Jack took off the second semester of his junior year to travel through Europe. His father was then serving as U.S. ambassador to Great Britain (a reward for his generous support of FDR), and so young Kennedy was admitted to high-level political and diplomatic circles. Back at Harvard, he used this experience in his senior thesis—a study of England's complacency on the eve of World War II. Not only did this thesis win a magna cum laude from the political science department, but rewritten and retitled *Why England Slept*, it was also published and became a best-seller. Though Kennedy began to lean toward a writing career, after his graduation from Harvard he studied briefly at Stanford's Graduate School of Business, where in spite of recurrent problems with a venereal disease, he developed a plan of attack on the sorority houses. "Still can't get used to the co-eds," he wrote to a friend, "but . . . expect to cut one out of the herd and brand her shortly."

Then, in October 1941, as the United States moved close to war, Kennedy, whose draft number was "one" on the first drawing, accepted a commission in the navy. On the night of August 2, 1943, in the South Pacific, Lieutenant Kennedy was in command of PT-109 when it was rammed and sunk by a Japanese destroyer. He was thrown against the wall of the cockpit, severely aggravating the old football injury to his back, but he still managed to marshal the ten surviving members of his crew and swim with them to a nearby island. One of the men was too badly injured to swim, so Kennedy took the man's life preserver in his teeth and, for several hours, towed his wounded shipmate through the dark water. For his heroism, Kennedy won the Navy Medal and the Purple Heart, and he was sent back to a navy hospital in the United States for treatment of malaria and complications concerning his back. It was while he was still hospitalized that Jack learned that his older brother, Joe, had been killed while flying a dangerous mission over Europe. This in effect settled Jack's career plans: though he got a job as a reporter for the Hearst newspapers and continued to talk about a writing career, his family now demanded that he go into politics. As his father recalled years later: "I told him Joe was dead and it was his responsibility to run for Congress. He didn't want to. But I told him he had to." The Cambridge district, which the family selected as a target, was one in which John "Honey Fitz'

Fitzgerald—Jack's grandfather and a former mayor of Boston—still had a considerable following. An energetic, well-organized campaign, with the emphasis on the young candidate's distinguished military record, brought Kennedy an easy victory. In January 1947 he entered Congress, where he impressed one of his new colleagues as a "twenty-nine-year-old kid who looked nineteen and showed up for House debates in khaki pants with his shirttail out." This didn't seem to bother Jack's constituents, who twice reelected him by lopsided margins. In 1952 Congressman Kennedy felt ready to challenge the state's incumbent Republican senator, Henry Cabot Lodge. In the battle that followed, Kennedy dazzled the voters, while Papa Joe not only provided generous financing but also came through with a timely "business loan" of $500,000 to the failing *Boston Post*, following which the normally Republican paper soon came out strongly for Kennedy. In November, Eisenhower swept the state by 200,000 votes, but Kennedy managed to buck the Republican tide and beat Lodge by 70,000. At the age of thirty-five, Jack moved up to the U.S. Senate.

Personal Life: During Kennedy's years in the House of Representatives, he won national publicity as one of Washington's leading young bachelors; but when he began to entertain higher ambitions, it seemed time to find a wife as well. In 1952 he met Jacqueline Bouvier, the daughter of a socially prominent New York stockbroker and a former "deb queen of the year." The twenty-three-year-old Jackie, who had studied at Vassar and the Sorbonne, was working as an "inquiring camera girl" for a Washington newspaper. She was obviously fascinated by publicity and power, and some Washington friends tried several times to introduce her to Kennedy before they were finally brought together at a small dinner party. As Jack later recalled: "I reached across the asparagus and asked her for a date." The courtship that followed was frequently interrupted by Jack's trips to Massachusetts to campaign for the Senate. Nevertheless, he managed to keep in touch with Jackie. As she remembered it: "He was not the candy-and-flowers type, so every now and then he'd give me a book. He gave me *The Raven*, which is the life of Sam Houston, and also *Pilgrim's Way* by John Buchan." (Jackie's favorite reading, however, was Marcel Proust's *In Search of Lost Time*.) Kennedy and Jacqueline were married in a brilliant society wedding in Newport, Rhode Island, in 1953, when Jack was thirty-six and Jackie twenty-four. The 800-person guest list included the entire Senate.

During their ten years together, they seldom expressed their affection in public, but Kennedy was obviously proud of his brilliant and stylish wife. And, in spite of Jack's constant

philandering, a real and profound friendship grew between them. On one occasion he showed off her knowledge of antiquity by taking out a book on Greek civilization and quizzing her in front of their friends for half an hour. As president he was delighted with the attention that she received everywhere, and on a trip to Europe he once introduced himself as "the man who accompanied Jackie Kennedy to Paris." Over the course of the marriage, Jackie was pregnant five times, but she suffered two miscarriages and her last child, Patrick, died when he was two days old. Kennedy had never been particularly fond of children before his marriage, and once, when the four-year-old daughter of a friend recoiled rather than kiss him, the father quipped: "I don't think she quite caught that strong quality of love of children—so much of the candidate's makeup which has made him so dear to the hearts of all mothers." Nevertheless, when he had children of his own, Kennedy was a doting father. John Jr. and Caroline have gone on to distinguished lives of their own; Jackie, meanwhile, would survive her first husband by more than thirty years, dying of cancer on May 19, 1994.

As a bachelor, Kennedy had dated and bedded a dazzling succession of debutantes and Hollywood starlets. During his Senate campaign in 1952, his Republican opponents got hold of a snapshot showing the young congressman reclining on a Florida beach beside a nude and spectacularly buxom girl. His worried aides brought the photo to Kennedy's attention and the candidate studied it for a moment with obvious interest. Finally he smiled in recollection: "Yes, I remember her. She was great." When Kennedy was elected president, one of his top aides privately predicted, "This administration is going to do for sex what the last one did for golf." If, in retrospect, such a claim seems rather an overstatement, it's not because Kennedy didn't try. The list of presidential consorts is a long and varied one, chronicled in often lurid detail by such books as Thomas C. Reeves's *A Question of Character: A Life of John F. Kennedy* (1991). The most illustrious, perhaps, was Marilyn Monroe, whom Kennedy had first met back in the 1950s; her now-legendary (and stuporously sultry) rendition of "Happy Birthday Mr. President," sung in Madison Square Garden on the occasion of JFK's forty-fifth birthday, was telecast live nationwide. When she had finished and tottered off, Kennedy took the stage and said, "Thank you. I can now retire from politics after having had 'Happy Birthday' sung to me in such a sweet, wholesome way." Some three months later, Monroe was dead. In addition to the many nameless women quietly ushered into—and out of—the presidential quarters, there were such companions as Judith Exner, who also happened to be an intimate friend of the notorious mobster Sam Giancanna. Whatever JFK's other accomplishments, it is safe to say that, in terms of his personal life, he was the last major politician to be given a free ride by the Washington press corps.

On the Way to the White House: Kennedy never entirely gave up on his ambitions as a writer, and a successful book played a key role in his march to the presidency. In 1954 the condition of his back had deteriorated to such an extent that he couldn't walk without crutches, so he submitted to a painful and potentially dangerous spinal fusion operation. At first the surgery was unsuccessful, and for several days the thirty-seven-year-old senator lay close to death; only after a second operation did Kennedy begin to recover.

During the long months when he was unable to leave his bed at his father's Palm Beach home, Kennedy read extensively and began working on a book describing past United States senators who had bravely defied public opinion. Under the title *Profiles in Courage*, this book caused a mild sensation when it was published in 1956—it went on to become a best-seller and to win the Pulitzer Prize. Because of this book, Kennedy's name was inevitably associated with the idea of political courage—even though the bedridden senator had been conveniently absent during the stormy Senate debates on Joseph McCarthy's censure, and had even refused to declare himself on the issue. In the Democratic convention of 1956, Kennedy was widely respected as a young leader of national stature, and he made a strong bid for the vice presidential nomination. When Adlai Stevenson told the delegates to make their own choice for the second spot on the ticket, Kennedy was neck and neck with Senator Estes Kefauver, until Kefauver finally won on the third ballot. A graceful concession speech, however, meant that Jack's political prospects were brighter than ever. With their eyes on the 1960 presidential nomination, the Kennedys worked Jack's bid for reelection to the Senate in 1958; a landslide victory there could give Jack's national ambitions a powerful boost. Kennedy campaigned night and day to build up his vote, even though victory was assured from the very beginning. In November he won with a staggering majority of 875,000—an all-time record for the state of Massachusetts.

His Person: John Kennedy was six feet one inch tall, and he kept his weight at a photogenic 175 pounds. He had cool gray eyes and light brown hair—several shades lighter than it usually appeared in photographs. He was noted for his elegant and expensive wardrobe, and he always took great care with his clothing, changing at least twice each day, and often in a single day wearing as many as four different shirts. He

particularly disliked button-down collars, and ordered the members of his staff to stop wearing them. He also hated hats—convinced that they made him look silly. This created a problem with the hat industry when Kennedy was president—the public was so impressed with their hatless president that sales had dropped off sharply. Yet he continued to ignore pleas that he allow himself to be photographed in some fedora. This continued literally to his dying day, when he went through the Texas ritual of being presented a cowboy hat in Fort Worth, yet steadfastly refused to put it on despite the wishes of 2,000 Texans.

Kennedy widely promoted the image of himself as a physical-fitness enthusiast; despite his bad back, he enjoyed touch football, golf, and sailing; and he also exercised every day. He also, however, lived in constant physical pain, and by 1960 he was in many ways nearly a physical wreck. He suffered from severe spinal problems, Addison's disease, intense fevers, and recurrent bouts of venereal disease. Four times he received the Catholic Church's last rites. Kennedy himself was little interested in food—he was strictly a "meat and potatoes man" who, according to a close friend, "always ate as if somebody were about to grab his plate," and was a modest drinker. All his life he disliked people who put their hands on him, and despised the habits of old-time politicians who tried to throw friendly arms over his shoulders. Though he learned to shake hands with the public like any other politician, he was distinctly uncomfortable with handshakes that lasted more than a second.

Kennedy enjoyed going to the movies, and his favorites were westerns and Civil War pictures. If a film did not meet with his approval, however, he was reluctant to waste his time with it: he would tell his companions, "Let's haul it out of here," and expect them to leave the theater with him. His ability as a speed-reader was greatly celebrated—and, it now appears, somewhat exaggerated as well. The historian Richard Reeves, in his 1993 book *President Kennedy: Profile of Power*, recounts how Hugh Sidey of *Time* magazine, writing about Kennedy's speed-reading ability, was told by the speed-reading institute where the president had taken a course that Kennedy could read 800 words per minute. Kennedy found the number too low. "How about 1200?" Sidey asked. "That would do fine," Kennedy answered. Every morning he would read four newspapers in the course of fifteen minutes; he was impatient with people who digested material at a slower rate, and would sometimes tell them, "I asked you to read it—not to memorize it."

Everyone who met Jack Kennedy came away impressed by his sense of humor. He particularly enjoyed laughing at himself. Once, during the early stages of his campaign for the presidency, he told a private gathering in Washington: "I have just received the following telegram from my generous daddy. It says, 'Dear Jack: Don't buy a single vote more than necessary. I'll be damned if I'm going to pay for a landslide.' " His humor also had a sadistic edge and he delighted in embarrassing his friends and his staff. When his brother paid his daily visit to the presidential office, for instance, Kennedy would often call in his aide Kenny O'Donnell and say: "Now—tell Bobby why you think that idea of his is terrible."

At work or at play, Kennedy had to win, and his temper occasionally flared up at touch football partners who put out less than the maximum effort. Once, during the Bay of Pigs crisis, he tried to relax by playing checkers with his old friend Undersecretary of the Navy "Red" Fay. When it became clear that Fay was winning their first game, JFK deliberately upset the board. "One of those unfortunate incidents of life, Redhead," he smiled. "We'll never really know if the Undersecretary was going to outmaneuver the Commander-in-Chief strategically."

PRESIDENCY
Nomination: July 11, 1960
The main obstacle standing between Kennedy and the Democratic presidential nomination in 1960 was the belief that no Catholic could possibly be elected. Kennedy sought to overcome this religious prejudice by entering—and winning—a string of state primaries. With his generously financed, brilliantly organized campaigns and his fresh and youthful appeal, Kennedy easily outdistanced all his rivals. The decisive blow came in West Virginia—a state that was 95 percent Protestant—where Kennedy beat Senator Hubert Humphrey so badly that Humphrey was forced to withdraw from the race.

As the Democratic convention convened in Los Angeles, Kennedy had emerged as the clear choice of the northern liberal wing of his party and appeared close to a first-ballot victory. His chief convention rival was Senate Majority Leader Lyndon Johnson, who had the support of the South and the party's more conservative elements. At the last minute, an unexpected development jeopardized Kennedy's almost certain nomination: a strong drive to "draft" Adlai Stevenson for a third try as Democratic standard-bearer began to drain liberal strength from Kennedy. Senator Eugene McCarthy of Minnesota gave an impassioned nominating speech for Stevenson, and in the convention's longest and most emotional floor demonstration, delegates and the public showed their support for the Illinois leader. In the face of all this, Stevenson's repeated assurances that he was not a candidate began to lose credibility. Nevertheless, Kennedy's support remained surprisingly firm, and when the first roll call reached Wyoming, everyone at the convention knew that those fifteen

votes would put JFK over the top. As the convention paused in silence for a moment, the candidate's brother Teddy, in the middle of the Wyoming delegation, urged its members to use their votes to name a president. When the chairman of the delegation announced that all fifteen votes went to the Kennedy column, the convention went wild as JFK was nominated on the first ballot. The next day, in a bid for party unity and southern support, Kennedy asked that Lyndon Johnson be named as his running mate. Despite complaints from organized labor and Stevensonian liberals, this choice was finally accepted by the convention.

On Friday afternoon of convention week, in the shadows of the setting sun, Kennedy appeared before 90,000 people in the Los Angeles Coliseum to deliver his acceptance speech, in which he sounded the keynote for his campaign and his presidency:

> I stand tonight facing west on what was once the last frontier. From the lands that stretch 3,300 miles behind me, the pioneers of old gave up their safety, their comfort and sometimes their lives to build a new world here in the West....
>
> Today some would say that those struggles are all over, that all the horizons have been explored, that all the battles have been won, that there is no longer an American frontier. But the problems are not all solved and the battles are not all won, and we stand today on the edge of a new frontier—the frontier of the 1960s.... Beyond that frontier are uncharted problems of peace and war, unconquered pockets of ignorance and prejudice, unanswered questions of poverty and surplus.
>
> It would be easier to shrink back from that frontier, to look to the safe mediocrity of the past.... But I believe the times demand invention, innovation, imagination, decision. I am asking each of you to be new pioneers on that new frontier.

Election: November 8, 1960
To oppose Kennedy and Johnson, the Republicans chose Vice President Richard Nixon and Ambassador to the United Nations Henry Cabot Lodge—the same man Kennedy had beaten in a Massachusetts Senate race eight years before. In their campaign, Nixon and Lodge attempted to identify themselves with the popular Eisenhower, and to raise public doubts concerning Kennedy's maturity. Their national slogan "Experience counts" seemed to ignore the fact that Kennedy and Nixon had been first elected to Congress in the same year (1946), or that Nixon was only four years older than the forty-three-year-old JFK.

An unspoken issue throughout the campaign was the widespread fear that a Catholic president would allow his policies to be dictated by the Vatican. Kennedy decided to confront this issue head-on in a dramatic speech to a gathering of Protestant ministers in Houston. "Because I am a Catholic, and no Catholic has ever been elected president, it is apparently necessary for me to state once again—not what kind of church I believe in, for that should be important only to me, but what kind of America I believe in. I believe in an America where separation of Church and State is absolute, where no Catholic prelate would tell the president (should he be a Catholic) how to act and no Protestant minister would tell his parishioners for whom to vote." In the final analysis, Kennedy's religion may have won him as many votes among his fellow Catholics as it cost him in the rest of the population.

Easily the most celebrated moment of the campaign came on September 26, when Nixon and Kennedy met for the first of their four televised debates before a national audience estimated at 70 million. Most commentators expected that Nixon, with his reputation as a seasoned and effective TV performer, would demolish the inexperienced Kennedy. But the moment the two faces appeared on the screen, the entire election seemed to swing in Kennedy's direction. Nixon made the mistake of using dark-toned "lazy shave" face powder, and poor lighting threw deep shadows around his eyes. As historian Roger Butterfield expressed it, "He looked for all the world like a man with shaving and perspiration problems, glumly waiting for the commercial to tell him how not to offend." Kennedy, on the other hand, seemed cool and confident, in total command of the facts and the situation. After the first debate, the charge that JFK was too "young and inexperienced" for the presidency seemed to lose most of its potency.

Compared with these image differences, disagreements on the issues seemed unimportant. In fact, many liberals considered the candidates so similar that Kennedy partisan Arthur Schlesinger Jr. felt called upon to write a book called *Kennedy or Nixon: Does It Make Any Difference?*

In a bizarre sidelight to the campaign, strong differences did develop. For many months Vice President Nixon had been secretly urging an exile invasion of Cuba, and he was delighted when the CIA decided to go ahead with plans for the mission. Then, in the campaign, Kennedy came out publicly for the same proposal. Nixon was enraged; he felt that revealing his backing for the project would blow its cover. Facing what he considered "probably the most difficult decision of the campaign," Nixon decided: "There was only one thing I could do. The covert operation had to be protected at all costs. I must not even suggest by implication that the United States was rendering aid to rebel forces in and out of Cuba. In fact, I must go to the other extreme: I must attack the Kennedy proposal to provide such aid as wrong and irresponsible because it would violate our treaty commitments."

In other words, Nixon came out strongly against Nixon's plan.

On Election Day, Kennedy won with one of the shakiest mandates in American history. He polled 34,227,096 votes to Nixon's 34,108,546—a margin of only 49.9 percent to 49.6 percent. Most of the states had actually voted against Kennedy, as had majorities of whites, college graduates, high-income people, women, Protestants, farmers, senior citizens, and business and professional people. In the electoral college, with the help of Lyndon Johnson's strong appeal to the solid South and some disputed votes from Mayor Daley's Chicago, Kennedy won by the more comfortable margin of 303 to 219.

On Inauguration Day, January 20, 1961, Washington was blanketed by an unexpected snowstorm as temperatures plunged well below freezing. The city was plagued by traffic jams, and the spectators who gathered to watch the inaugural ceremonies stamped their feet, slapped their hands, and blew into cupped hands to keep warm.

At Kennedy's request, the aged poet Robert Frost made a special appearance on the inaugural platform. He read a poem that he had written in honor of the occasion:

Summoning artists to participate
In the august occasions of the state
Seems something artists ought to celebrate. . . .
A golden age of poetry and power
Of which this noonday's the beginning hour.

In the brilliant winter sunlight, the old man had difficulty reading his text; he eventually gave up his effort, and recited instead a poem he knew by heart.

As Kennedy stood up to take the oath of office from Chief Justice Earl Warren, he stunned the freezing crowd by stripping off his overcoat. His address, considered one of the most eloquent inaugurals in American history, contained more than a dozen ringing phrases that have since become shopworn political clichés. His most famous line had originally read: "Ask not what your country will do for you, but what you will do for your country." At the last moment he had scratched out the words *will* on his text and replaced them by *can*.

At the inaugural ball, Jack and Jackie dazzled the crowds. According to one of the president's few close friends, JFK "saw the whole thing and adored it . . . you knew this was one of his great moments, you could tell. Here was the reigning prince, and he was loving it."

The one thing I do not want to be called is First Lady. It sounds like a saddle horse.
Jacqueline Kennedy, in *The Kennedys*, by Peter Collier and David Horowitz, 1984

Since the 1965 publication of Arthur Schlesinger's narrative of the Kennedy presidency in *A Thousand Days*, countless books, ranging from the high and lucid to the low and lurid, have scoured much of the gleam and glitter off the Camelot image. One of the most compelling and credible of recent accounts, Reeves's *President Kennedy: Profile of Power*, portrays JFK not as the athletic idealist of lore, nor as the sleazy lecher of popular revisionist biography, nor yet as the driven compulsive of some scholarly psychohistories, but as a clear-headed cold warrior who suffered from a wide range of debilitating physical ailments, favored dispassionate analysis over moral argument, and, in such momentous events as the Cuban missile crisis, was able to combine tenacious courage with tough-minded tactical insight. Yet, rightly or wrongly, the complex realities of the Kennedy presidency remain inextricably intertwined with the symbolic role it has assumed in the American psyche, as a period that embodied the best America had to offer, and which, in its abrupt and tragic end, heralded the nation's moral passage from innocence to experience.

Vetoes: In his brief term, JFK vetoed only twenty-one bills—a smaller number than any president since Harding. None of his vetoes were overridden by Congress.

His 2 Years, 306 Days as President:

PRO Though the disastrous Bay of Pigs invasion had been planned and orchestrated by the previous administration, Kennedy took full responsibility for the fiasco—and learned never to trust military "experts" again. In the Cuban missile crisis of October 1962, Kennedy ignored his military advisers and took a cool and moderate course—which prevented the outbreak of nuclear war and brought about America's greatest Cold War victory. In his handling of the Laos situation, Kennedy also moved the world closer to peace by accepting a neutralist government and avoiding a U.S. commitment to an Asian land war. His success in negotiating a test ban treaty ended the threat of atmospheric fallout and was the first step toward international disarmament. Under Kennedy, the United States began to acknowledge its obligations to underdeveloped nations. The Peace Corps won worldwide praise, and JFK's generous "Alliance for Progress" made him a hero throughout Latin America, where, in annual visits, he urged leaders to implement land reforms or risk revolution. In that regard, the author William Manchester noted, "We can only describe [Kennedy] as prophetic."

CON In foreign policy, Kennedy lurched unsteadily from one crisis to another—it was his apparent ineptitude in the handling of the Bay of Pigs invasion that encouraged the Soviets to test his resolution by moving missiles to Cuba. In calling out American reserves to reinforce Berlin, Kennedy grossly overreacted to a perceived Soviet threat, and his inflated, warlike rhetoric consistently aggravated Cold War tensions. The big increases in military spending under Kennedy offer another example of dangerous saber rattling and provoked similar increases by the USSR. In committing the United States to the much-publicized "space race" with the Russians, Kennedy began a pointless competition that cost the American people some $50 billion.

PRO Kennedy championed a progressive and enlightened domestic program, including Medicare, aid to education, tax reform, and a strong new civil rights bill. In his successful effort to force the big steel companies to retract their announced price hike, Kennedy worked effectively to curb inflation and showed that a strong president can overcome corporate power. Under Kennedy, unemployment declined and America prospered.

CON Kennedy's handling of Congress was dismal and inept, and none of the major domestic proposals of his much-heralded New Frontier were enacted into law. His Senate minority leader Everett Dirksen aptly commented that a Kennedy legislative accommodation had "about as much impact as a snowflake on the bosom of the Potomac." In the first two years of his administration, Kennedy was often tardy and reluctant in his commitment to equal rights for black Americans, four times striking the name of Sammy Davis Jr. from invitation lists, for example, because he thought that the image of a black man with a white wife at the White House would have meant political disaster. As a candidate, he announced that a president could end discrimination in federal housing "with the stroke of a pen"; as president, it took him twenty-two months to pick up that pen.

PRO Kennedy brought new style, vigor, and intelligence to the presidency during his administration; the American people were fascinated by the First Family as never before. Kennedy's youthful leadership awakened the so-called "silent generation" from the long sleep of the Eisenhower years, and Americans developed a new commitment to the welfare of their country. In the White House, Kennedy entertained Nobel Prize winners, listened to classical music and Shakespeare, took an active interest in Washington architecture, and generally gave American cultural life an important boost.

CON Kennedy's "Camelot" was all glitter and no substance. It is true that JFK inspired a generation of Americans and raised them to a pitch of high excitement, but his promises were never followed by performance. The tense crisis atmosphere of the Kennedy years produced no significant progress for the American people. It was this gap between rhetoric and reality that caused much of the frustration and bitterness that came back to plague the nation in the late 1960s.

PRO   At the time of his death, Kennedy was just shifting his gears as president. All observers agree that his commitment to black America had deepened significantly in the last year of his life. On a host of other issues, Kennedy was preparing to move forward, preparing to take on the big oil companies and other corporations on such issues as tax reform and public welfare. His plan was to take his case to the people in a vigorous reelection campaign, and to sweep into office with him a more progressive and flexible Congress. He had also told his aides that as soon as possible after the election he intended to terminate the American commitment to the faltering government in South Vietnam. If Kennedy had lived, the United States might well have avoided the Vietnam War and entered a new era of social progress.

CON   Kennedy's fascination with "counterinsurgency" broadened U.S. commitments in Southeast Asia. Kennedy would probably have made the same mistakes that Johnson did. There is no reason to believe that his death had a major effect on the overall sweep of American history.

PSYCHOHISTORY

Jack Kennedy was a weak and sickly boy who was plagued by a host of childhood diseases. According to his brother Robert, "When we were growing up together, we used to laugh about the great risk a mosquito took in biting Jack—with some of his blood the mosquito was almost sure to die." As in the case of Theodore Roosevelt, this boyhood weakness was later reflected in a desperate emphasis on physical fitness and competition. This tendency was encouraged by Jack's father, who taught his sons that second-best was unacceptable. On one occasion, Joe Kennedy went so far as to send two of his children away from the dinner table because they had "goofed off" and lost a sailing race that day. "I can feel Pappy's eyes on the back of my neck," Kennedy told a friend when he was trying to decide about entering politics, and Papa Joe was always the driving force behind Jack's career. Even as president, Jack called his father at least once a day. The other dominant figure in Kennedy's life was his older brother, Joe Jr. "Joe was the star of our family," Jack once said. "He did everything better than the rest of us." In the family structure, with Joe two years older than Jack, and then five girls before Bobby and Teddy, it was only natural that

the two oldest boys should struggle for the leading position. They used to fight so fiercely at home that the younger children would run upstairs and hide, while the muscular Joe pounded away at his slender brother. The father insisted that no one interfere with these sometimes bloody struggles: Jack had to learn to fend for himself. Once, when the two boys were riding bicycles at each other, they both refused to turn aside: Joe was unhurt, but Jack required twenty-eight stitches. Though the brothers were friends at Harvard, and often ate together, the competition continued. Joe had the habit of moving in on Jack's dates, with the kind words "Get lost, baby brother." In later years, in the space race, in politics, and in a dozen other areas, Kennedy stridently declared that second-best was unacceptable. In taking this position, he was unconsciously recalling his own painful position as "second-best" in the Kennedy family. When his brother Joe was killed during the war, Jack was left to compete with a ghost. No matter how tough or successful he might seem, he could never fill his dead brother's shoes, and so he had to continue his struggle for the top. If Jack ever forgot about his own basic inadequacy, his mourning father was there to remind him. In 1957, when Jack was a U.S. senator and already widely discussed as a presidential possibility, a reporter went to Florida to talk with Joseph P. Kennedy Sr. As he was asked about his children, Kennedy happily ran down the list, obviously proud of their achievements. Then the reporter noted that Joe Jr., had been left out, and asked Kennedy to comment on his eldest. The father's reaction "was a terrible thing to see. He sat there at the table weeping, unable to speak or to control himself for almost five minutes. It seemed to the rest of us like an hour. Finally, he pulled himself together and wiped his eyes but still he couldn't talk. He gestured toward his wife and said, 'She can tell you about him. I can't.' " Jack's mother, Rose Kennedy, would outlive her husband and three of her sons, passing away on January 22, 1995, at the age of 104.

LITTLE-KNOWN FACTS

Kennedy was never particularly religious, but he made an effort to attend confession regularly. As president he was always worried that a priest might recognize the famous voice and then someday reveal the contents of the confession. In order to avoid recognition, Kennedy would drive to church with a group of Catholic Secret Service men and then find an inconspicuous place in the middle of their line as they lined up for confession. On one occasion this subterfuge proved such a miserable failure that the moment he stepped into the confessional, the priest said, "Good evening, Mr. President." Kennedy replied, "Good evening, Father," and then walked out immediately.

Kennedy was notoriously careless about
money. He never carried cash with him and was
always "borrowing" from friends—for restaurant checks, cab fares, or even the collection
plate at church. Occasionally, even his closest
friends became irritated with the fact that the
wealthy Kennedy made no effort to pay them
back.

Senator Barry Goldwater had a reputation as a
first-rate photographer, and he once took a
picture of President Kennedy and sent it to him
for an autograph. The picture came back with
this inscription:

For Barry Goldwater, whom I urge to follow the
career for which he has shown so much talent—
photography. From his friend, John Kennedy.

In his home state, Kennedy's name had acquired such magic by the late 1950s that another
John F. Kennedy—a stockroom worker at a razor
factory—got himself elected as treasurer of
Massachusetts simply by putting his name on
the ballot. His total campaign expenses were
$150—most of it for an election-night victory
party. Treasurer Kennedy drove around the state
in a chauffeur-driven limousine and appointed
many of his relatives to state positions.

Kennedy usually swam twice a day during
his presidency, in a White House pool that he
ordered heated to ninety degrees. On the wall
facing the pool, Kennedy had an artist paint a
floor-to-ceiling mural of a typical Massachusetts waterfront, complete with launches at
anchor, Cape Cod houses, and trees.

According to the polls, Kennedy's highest
rating as president came right after the Bay of
Pigs fiasco, as the American people rallied to
support their president in difficult times, and
82 percent expressed approval of his handling
of the job. No one was more amazed at this
development than Kennedy. "My God," he said,
"it's as bad as Eisenhower. The worse I do the
more popular I get."

In the fall of 1963, Kennedy appeared at a
Boston dinner honoring his brother Teddy—the
newly elected junior senator from Massachusetts. In the course of his speech, the president
joked about his own upcoming reelection bid in
1964. "My last campaign may be coming up very
shortly," he said, "but Teddy is around, and
therefore these dinners can go on indefinitely."

QUOTES BY KENNEDY
"Sure it's a big job, but I don't know anyone who can
do it better than I can."

"I had announced earlier this year that if successful I
would not consider campaign contributions as a
substitute for experience in appointing Ambassadors.
Ever since I made that statement I have not received
one single cent from my father."
—1960

"The political campaign won't tire me, for I have an
advantage. I can be myself."
—Spring, 1960

"The New Frontier of which I speak is not a set of
promises—it is a set of challenges. It sums up not what
I intend to offer the American people, but what I
intend to ask of them."
—Acceptance speech, July 1960

"Do you realize the responsibility I carry? I'm the only
person standing between Nixon and the White House."
—Said to Arthur Schlesinger, October 13, 1960

"Let us never negotiate out of fear, but let us never fear
to negotiate."
—Inaugural address, 1961

"If a free society cannot help the many who are poor, it
cannot save the few who are rich."
—Inaugural address, 1961

"All my life I've known better than to depend on the
experts. How could I have been so stupid, to let them
go ahead?"
—On the Bay of Pigs, April 1961

"When we got into office, the thing that surprised me
most was to find that things were just as bad as we'd
been saying they were."
—May 1961

"Those who make peaceful revolution impossible,
make violent revolution inevitable."
—To Latin-American diplomats, March 12, 1962

"There is a limitation upon the ability of the United
States to solve these problems . . . there are greater
limitations upon our ability to bring about a favorable
result than I had imagined. . . . It is much easier to
make the speeches than it is finally to make the
judgments. . . ."
—TV interview, 1962

QUOTES ABOUT KENNEDY
"What future historians may well note first about JFK
is what they note first about the Roman Emperor
Trajan—that he presided at the high-water mark of
empire."
—Richard Boeth, Newsweek, 1973

"Jack did like to have little things done for him without
hearing about the problems and the difficulties."
—Kenneth O'Donnell

"John Kennedy was a happy man, and those who knew
him well will always remember him that way."
—Paul "Red" Fay

"After long experience in sizing up people, I definitely
know you have the goods and you can go a long way.

President Kennedy greeting well-wishers in Fort Worth, Texas, on the morning of November 22, 1963.

Now aren't you foolish not to get all there is out of what God has given you."
—Joseph P. Kennedy, in a letter to his then fourteen-year-old son

"My son was rocked to political lullabies."
—Rose Kennedy

"It is true that we have a president with a face. And it is the face of a potential hero. But he embodies nothing, he personifies nothing, he is power, rather a quizzical power, without light or principle. . . . He learned too much and too early that victory goes to the discreet, that one does not speak one's opinion, that ideally one does not even develop one's opinion."
—Norman Mailer, 1963

"It is a good thing to have a brave man as our president in times as tough as these are."
—Ernest Hemingway

"I feel that I would hesitate to place the difficult decisions that the next president will have to make with someone who understands what courage is and admires it, but has not quite the independence to have it."
—Eleanor Roosevelt

"He seems to combine the best qualities of Elvis Presley and Franklin D. Roosevelt."
—An anonymous southern senator, 1960

"What a joy that literacy is no longer prima-facie evidence of treason, that syntax in no longer subversive at the White House."
—John Steinbeck

"You certainly can't say that the people of Dallas haven't given you a nice welcome."
—Mrs. John Connally, November 22, 1963

"We forgave, followed, and accepted because we liked the way he looked. And he had a pretty wife. Camelot was fun, even for the peasants, as long as it was televised to their huts."
—Joe McGinniss, The Selling of the President 1968, 1969

"Now I think that I should have known that he was magic all along. I did know it—but I should have guessed that it would be too much to ask to grow old with him and see our children grow up together. . . . So now he is a legend when he would have preferred to be a man."
—Jacqueline Kennedy, 1964
—M.S.M. and E.H.B.

RICHARD NIXON
Thirty-Seventh President

VITAL STATISTICS
Birth: Richard Milhous Nixon was born on
January 9, 1913, in the small frame house
adjoining his father's, Frank Nixon's, lemon
grove in Yorba Linda, California. Three of
Hannah Nixon's five sons were named for
English kings, and the future originator of the
"Imperial Presidency" was named after King
Richard the Lion-Hearted. When he was grow-
ing up, the nickname "Dick" was never used. As
his mother remembered, "I always called him
Richard, and he always called me Mother."

Death: Nixon died in New York City on April
22, 1994, following complications arising from
a massive stroke. He was eighty-one.

BEFORE THE PRESIDENCY
Career: When Richard was nine, his parents
gave up citrus farming and moved to nearby
Whittier, a small Quaker community fifteen
miles east of Los Angeles. Hannah Nixon's
family, the Milhouses, were well established in
Whittier, and they helped their hapless son-in-
law Frank set up a small gas station–grocery. As
a teenager, Richard spent much of his time
working in that store. He got up every day at
4:00 A.M. to drive the family's truck into Los
Angeles to pick up a load of vegetables. He
would rinse the produce and carefully set up a
display before putting in his full day at school.
Every afternoon he worked several more hours
at the store, then studied alone in his room until
midnight. Thanks to his iron self-discipline, he
did well in school and won a local reputation as
an intellectual. Nevertheless, he had to give up
his dreams of going to Harvard because his
struggling parents needed his help in the store.
After graduation from high school, Richard won
a scholarship to Whittier College—a scholarship established by his grandfather specifically
for members of the family. Richard continued
his grueling routine and high academic achievement, and polished his oratorical gifts, becoming a champion debater. Never popular with his
classmates, he managed to win his first election,
for student body president, by promising to
allow dancing on campus. Actually, Richard
himself seldom attended dances, but he
shrewdly convinced the administration that
chaperoned and tightly supervised dancing on
the campus was preferable to letting students
seek out less decorous amusements on their
own in the sinful atmosphere of nearby Los
Angeles, fifteen miles to the west. Graduating
second in his class of 109 students at Whittier,
Nixon won a full scholarship to the recently
established Duke University Law School in
Durham, North Carolina. There his marathon
sessions of uninterrupted study in the library

won him the nickname "Iron Butt." Other
classmates addressed him as "Gloomy Gus."
After finishing third in his law school class of
twenty-six, Nixon applied for jobs with New
York law firms, but he was turned down. He
also tried to become an FBI special agent (the
director of the FBI, J. Edgar Hoover, was one of
his personal heroes), but the bureau evidently
didn't consider him G-man material, and never
responded to Nixon's application. Keenly disappointed, Richard went back home to Whittier
and, remembering his grandfather had known
Thomas Bewley's grandfather years before,
asked for and got a job with the law firm of
Wingert and Bewley.
In 1937, ten days after he had been admitted
to the California bar, Nixon pleaded his first
case as a trial lawyer, representing Marie Schee,
a Los Angeles woman seeking to execute a
judgment to recover a bad debt. Accused by the
judge of unethical behavior during this case,
Nixon was threatened with disbarment; he was
also sued by his client for mishandling her case.
Thomas Bewley, the senior partner, settled with
Schee by giving her $4,800. It was such an
egregious blunder that Nixon actually made a
trip to Cuba to check out job possibilities there.
Fortunately for Nixon, Bewley decided not to
fire him.
With a salary of $250 a month, the young
lawyer was naturally anxious to improve his
financial position. He organized a company
called Citra-Frost, but despite eighteen months
of intensive effort by Nixon, the company's plan
to market frozen orange juice in plastic bags
failed to catch on. Thomas Bewley was city
attorney of Whittier, and he appointed his
young colleague to the post of assistant city
attorney. However, this new job also fell considerably short of appeasing the restless young
man's ambition. Shortly after Pearl Harbor,
Nixon went to Washington for a then relatively
high-paying job (sixty-one dollars a week) with
the tire-rationing department of the Office of
Price Administration. As a Quaker he was
automatically exempted from service in the
armed forces for conscientious objection during
the war, but after six months in Washington, he
probably realized service in uniform would be a
prerequisite for anyone running for office in the
postwar future. Nixon abandoned his Quaker
refusal to swear oaths and the pacifism that
went hand in hand with it, accepting a direct
commission in the navy. Assigned to the South
Pacific, Lieutenant Nixon divided his time
between serving as the operations officer for an
aerial transport squadron and playing poker.
Remote from combat on his Green Island duty
station, he built a little shack with a makeshift
bar, stocked with liquor he managed to "requisition." Officers and enlisted men alike, their
wallets bulging with unspent pay, flocked to
this gambling resort and found honest "Nick"
Nixon, the proprieter of the only game in town,

ready to play for high stakes. By the time his tour of duty was over, Nixon's poker acumen had netted him more than $10,000. It turned out to be his first campaign fund.

In 1946, newly returned to the United States and still working as a navy lawyer, Nixon read the following ad that 100 wealthy Republicans had placed in Whittier area newspapers:

WANTED: Congressman candidate with no previous political experience to defeat one man who has represented the district in the House for ten years. Any young man resident of district, preferably a veteran, fair education, may apply for the job.

The initial response to the ad was lukewarm, and someone (perhaps Nixon himself) suggested Nixon. The thirty-three-year-old Lieutenant Commander Nixon jumped at the chance to show local political bosses what he could do. After some hesitation, the Republican leaders agreed to sponsor him. As one of them put it: "He was the best of a bad lot." Nixon made his first campaign appearances improperly wearing his navy dress blue uniform, and attacked his opponent, incumbent congressman Jerry Voorhis, as a "friend of the communists." To "prove" his charges, Nixon repeatedly linked Voorhis with the left of center Congress of Industrial Organization's Political Action Committee (PAC). When a Voorhis aide complained to Nixon that he wasn't playing fair, Nixon told him: "You're missing the point. The point is to win." Actually, the Communist-influenced California PAC had bitterly opposed Voorhis—after all, the incumbent was a member of the House Un-American Activities Committee (HUAC) and a dedicated anti-Communist. But the national PAC had inexplicably endorsed Voorhis— thereby confusing everyone and inadvertently making Nixon's charges believable. The birth of Nixon's daughter Tricia was the unlikely turning point in the campaign. Voorhis routinely sent out a special pamphlet on infant care to all new parents in his district. On the cover of the pamphlet mailed to the Nixons, the congressman scrawled a friendly personal note: "Congratulations! I look forward to meeting you soon in public." Nixon pounced upon this innocuous pleasantry, reading it to his audiences at every speech, and claiming that it committed Voorhis to a series of public debates. Finally, Voorhis felt compelled to accept, and in five debates Nixon's aggressive attack rhetoric made mincemeat of his mild-mannered opponent. Nixon accused Congressman Voorhis of being "a lip service American, who is fronting for un-American elements, wittingly or otherwise." Three days before the election, he charged that Voorhis had "consistently voted the Moscow– PAC–Henry Wallace line in Congress."

On Election Day, drawing upon the momentum of a nationwide Republican trend, Nixon swamped his opponent, 65,586 to 49,994.

Across the country dozens of politicians— including Joseph McCarthy of Wisconsin— carefully studied Nixon's trailblazing use of "Communist influence" slander to destroy a political opponent. Although he was typically less virulent and more restrained than the notorious and unstable Senator McCarthy, Nixon is still often remembered as the originator of the 1950s Red-baiting craze.

In the Eightieth Congress, Nixon was naturally assigned to the House Un-American Activities Committee, and he was soon leading a crusade for tough new "antisubversive" legislation. His major proposal—introduced as the Mundt-Nixon bill—was so repressive that even Nixon's fellow Republican Thomas Dewey condemned it as an attempt "to beat down ideas with clubs." Though Congress refused to pass this legislation, its basic provisions were incorporated into the McCarran Internal Security Act of 1950, and the well-publicized debate it generated helped establish Nixon as the nation's most accomplished political witch-hunter. He solidified this reputation with his leadership in the celebrated Hiss case. When a former Communist editor of *Time* magazine named Whittaker Chambers appeared before the HUAC, accusing former State Department official Alger Hiss of Communist involvement, Nixon was at first the only one to believe the charges. In the months that followed, he pursued the case with such energy, persistence, and clever manipulation of the evidence and the press that Hiss was publicly discredited, while Nixon's name became a household word. (Eventually, enough evidence was marshaled to send Hiss to prison, not for espionage but for perjury. The facts of the Hiss case continue to be the subject of heated controversy.)

By 1948, facing reelection back in Whittier, Nixon had emerged as an astute professional politician, and by exploiting a loophole in California election law, he adroitly managed to get himself nominated by both the Republicans and the Democrats in the primaries. In 1950 the ruthless young congressman was hungry for bigger triumphs; he announced his candidacy for the U.S. Senate. His opponent was Congresswoman Helen Gahagan Douglas, a liberal and a former Hollywood actress, who was immediately dubbed "the Pink Lady" by Nixon. In what Nixon gleefully described as a "rocking, rolling campaign," the candidate once went so far as to publicly allude to the dignified Mrs. Douglas as "pink right down to her underwear." Another specimen of "hard-hitting" Nixon campaign literature, addressed directly to Mrs. Douglas, read: "You, *and you can't deny it*, have earned the praise of communist and procommunist newspapers for opposing the very things Nixon has stood for." The most widely circulated leaflet of the campaign was the infamous "Pink Sheet," printed on pink paper and distributed to more than 500,000 California voters. The leaflet trumpeted that on 354 separate occasions

Nixon's opponent had voted the same way as a "notorious communist-line congressman" from New York. This was a veiled reference to the mercurial Vito Marcantonio of New York, a Republican congressman who had, for reasons best known to himself, suddenly switched his affiliation to the American Labor Party. The pink sheet studiously omitted to report that on hundreds of other issues, Mrs. Douglas had *disagreed* with Marcantonio, or that even Nixon himself, on 112 different occasions, had voted *with* this same "notorious" left-winger. In a backhanded tribute to his shabby campaign tactics in this election, a small southern California paper, the *Independent Review*, first used the label "Tricky Dick" above Nixon's picture. The nickname seemed so fitting that it would follow Nixon for the rest of his life. Nevertheless, in his unprincipled bid for the Senate, Nixon won a handsome victory over his Democratic opponent—crushing Helen Douglas by a margin of nearly 700,000 votes.

As the Senate's youngest member (he was thirty-eight), Nixon spent most of his time supporting General Douglas MacArthur in his call for "victory" in Korea, and Generalissimo Chiang Kai-shek in his pleas for the (presumably U.S. fought and financed) "liberation" of the Chinese mainland. Nixon also found his way onto Joe McCarthy's Government Operations Committee and worked cheek by jowl with the Wisconsin senator in exposing purported and often fantastical instances of Communist subversion. And always, Nixon kept an eagerly attentive eye on the unfolding battle for the 1952 presidential nomination. The liberal-moderate wing of the Republican Party was working hard to assure the nomination of General Dwight Eisenhower and to block the selection of arch-conservative Robert Taft. The popular "Ike" was so politically untutored that his Republican handlers had to keep reminding him not to mention that he had never registered to vote before. Though Nixon was ideologically much closer to Taft, the moderate Republicans correctly surmised that the hungry young California senator could be counted upon to put personal advantage ahead of principle. New York governor Thomas E. Dewey, who was spearheading the Eisenhower drive, secretly told Nixon that if Ike were nominated, Nixon would be his most likely choice as a running mate. Inspired by that prospect, Nixon did everything he could to undercut Taft's candidacy, telling his conservative audiences that even though Taft would make a "fine president," he couldn't possibly be elected. At the Republican convention, Nixon performed further services to the Eisenhower cause by skillfully sandbagging the favorite-son candidacy of his fellow Californian, Governor Earl Warren. When Eisenhower finally won the nomination, he was persuaded to follow through on Dewey's earlier promise to Nixon. Many

In an early use of television campaigning, beleaguered vice-presidential candidate Richard Nixon addresses the public on September 23, 1952, in what became known as the Checkers Speech.

delegates still had their doubts about "Tricky Dick," but they lacked the energy to act on them. As one Republican recalled, "We took Dick Nixon not because he was right wing or left wing—but because he came from California and we were tired."

After the convention, the campaign got off to a promising start, with Ike and Dick hitting the Democrats hard with charges of corruption. But in mid-September, the *New York Post* began publishing stories that Nixon had himself been pocketing contributions of $900 a month from a secret fund raised in his behalf by a small group of California businessmen. These under-the-table funds were said to total $18,235.

Immediately, politicians of both parties demanded that Nixon resign from the ticket. Eisenhower refused to commit himself one way or another. Nixon began cracking under the pressure. In a famous phone conversation, he shouted at Eisenhower: "General—there comes a time in matters like this when you've either got to fish or cut bait." When Ike still declined to speak out, it became glaringly apparent, even to the increasingly desperate and agitated Nixon, that the general was merely waiting for the right moment to jettison his tarnished running mate from the ticket.

In a last-ditch effort to save himself, Nixon wheedled the Republican National Committee into buying $75,000 worth of television time so he could explain his $18,000 slush fund. Eisenhower finally agreed to allow Nixon to argue his case on television, but warned Nixon that he had better emerge from the burgeoning scandal "as clean as a hound's tooth." The resultant speech—broadcast live immediately after the top-rated Milton Berle show—was arguably the first pop-culture political classic. In his televised remarks, Nixon looked the camera right in the eye, and claimed:

Not one cent of the $18,000 or any other money of that type ever went to personal use. Every penny of it was used to pay for political expenses that I did not think should be charged to the taxpayers of the United States.

In fact, it would have been *illegal* for him to have charged such expenses to the taxpayer—which was precisely why the Nixon fund was a closely guarded secret. The candidate had apparently dipped into the illicit contributions to finance personal politicking, the kind that other senators were forced to pay for out of their salaries. The speech climaxed on a personal note:

One other thing I probably should tell you, because if I don't they'll probably be saying this about me too. We did get something, a gift, after the election. A man down in Texas heard Pat on the radio mention the fact that our two youngsters would like to have a dog. And, believe it or not, the day before we left on this campaign trip we got a message from Union Station in Baltimore saying they had a package for us. We went down to get it. You know what it was! It was a little cocker spaniel dog in a crate that he sent all the way from Texas. Black and white spotted. And our little girl Tricia, the six-year-old, named it Checkers. And you know, the kids love the dog, and I just want to say this right now, that regardless of what they say about it, we're gonna keep it.

Richard Nixon breaks into tears after Dwight Eisenhower agrees to keep him on the Republican ticket. Nixon once said, "I never cry—except in public."

As Nixon neared the conclusion of his speech, with only a few sentences left to go, the camera's red light flashed on, signifying he was off the air. "I'm terribly sorry I ran over," he said to his aide (and future secretary of state) William Rogers. "I loused it up, and I'm sorry." He thanked the technicians in the studio, then he gathered the notes from his desk, stacked them neatly, and threw them on the floor. "Dick, you did a terrific job," beamed his campaign manager, Murray Chotiner, patting him on the back. "No, it was a flop," Nixon dolefully insisted. "I couldn't get off in time." When he reached the dressing room, Nixon turned away from his friends and let loose the bitter tears he had been holding back.

Nevertheless, the public response to the speech was highly favorable, with calls and letters running 350 to 1 in Nixon's favor. Nixon's novel direct appeal to the voters on the new medium of television, effectively bypassing the critical print media, was a pioneering political gambit that has since become standard practice. The "Checkers" speech demonstrated that Nixon was one of the first major politicians to grasp the tantalizing political potential of the cathode ray tube.

Years later, in a revealing article for *TV Guide,* Nixon wrote, "Of all institutions arrayed against a president, none controls his fate more than television. . . . [TV reporters] are political actors, just like the president, ever mindful of their ratings, careful to preserve and build their power. They have to be outfoxed, outflanked, and outperformed."

Although Eisenhower appeared to have been privately disgusted by Nixon's maudlin performance, he was nevertheless forced to keep the resilient young Californian on the ticket. Greeting Nixon in Wheeling, West Virginia, Eisenhower grimly told him, "You're my boy," and the improbable team of Ike and Dick went on to a landslide victory in November. Presumably thinking of the decisive impact of the Checkers speech, defeated Democratic opponent Adlai Stevenson later said of Nixon, "He's the kind of politician who could chop down a redwood tree, and then mount the stump to make a speech for conservation."

PERSONAL LIFE

As he was growing up, Richard Nixon expressed little enthusiasm for the company of women. As one classmate recalled, "Oh, he used to dislike us girls so! He would make horrible faces at us. As a debater, his main theme in grammar school and the first years of high school was why he hated girls." This situation improved only slightly with time. As Nixon's mother recalled: "Richard was not much of a mixer in college, either. He never had any special buddy, and on the dates that he had during his college years he talked not of romance but about such things as what might have happened to the world if Persia had conquered the Greeks."

In 1938, after attending law school in North Carolina, Nixon was back in Whittier and beginning his legal career when a friend told him about a gorgeous redhead who had recently arrived in town. Pat Ryan had been hired to teach typing and shorthand at the local high school. Her real name was Thelma Catherine Ryan, but her father, an Irish miner in Ely, Nevada, had been so elated by his daughter's birth the day before Saint Patrick's day that he called her "Saint Patrick's Babe in the Morn." Eventually "Thelma" became more familiarly known as Pat. Pat spent most of her formative years nursing her mother, who died of cancer when Pat was thirteen, and her father, who died four years later. She nevertheless managed to finish high school, then went to New York and worked as a secretary and X-ray technician. Eventually she saved enough money to enroll at the University of Southern California. To support herself she worked in a department store and as a Hollywood extra in such films as *Becky Sharp* and *The Great Ziegfeld*. After graduating cum laude from USC, she accepted the teaching job at Whittier. She joined an amateur theater group to make new friends, and one night at rehearsal in walked Richard Nixon. He had come specifically to finesse an introduction to Pat, and seeking to get to know her better, he accepted a part in the play as a crusading district attorney—the second romantic lead. After rehearsal, Nixon drew Pat aside, and following a brief conversation, he asked her to marry him. She stared at him disbelievingly and blinked her eyes. "I thought he was nuts," she later reminisced. In the months that followed, Nixon pursued Pat with the same dogged intensity he later used on Alger Hiss. Pat was one of the most popular young women in Whittier, and she dated all of the town's most eligible bachelors. As she remembered it, Nixon "would drive me to meet other beaux, and wait around to take me home." After two full years of this curious courtship, Pat finally capitulated, albeit in the face of stiff maternal resistance from Hannah Nixon, who complained that her son's bride wasn't a Quaker. Pat converted to Nixon's faith and married him in an ornate hotel in Riverside, California, when Pat was twenty-eight and Richard was twenty-seven. Shortly thereafter, the couple moved into their first home—a small apartment over a garage.

One of the ties that bound the Nixon marriage together over the years was their shared capacity for hard work. As Pat once told a reporter: "I had to work. I haven't just sat back and thought of myself or what I wanted to do. I've kept working. I don't have time to worry about who I admire or who I identify with. I've never had it easy. I'm not like all you—all those people who

had it easy." Pat had mixed feelings about her husband's political career. Still, she loyally provided Nixon with the strength that allowed him to persevere. Just three minutes before going on the air with his Checkers speech, a panicky Nixon turned to Pat and said: "I can't go through with this." She reassured him, and sat next to him as he delivered the address. On the other hand, Pat continually urged Nixon to retire from politics. On two separate occasions she forced him to make written promises that he would quit. On both occasions Nixon, unable to help himself, soon broke his promises. In 1962, when he surprised her at a small dinner party with an impromptu announcement that he intended to run for governor of California, Pat "chewed him out" with such noisy vehemence that the evening was spoiled for everyone. Nevertheless, she followed her husband in all his political adventures and campaigned tirelessly in his behalf. Once, when she was asked if she weren't bored by the same tedious rally day after day, she answered: "I'm always interested in the rallies, they're so different. Some are outside; some are inside. Some have old people; some have young people."

> I have sacrificed everything in my life that I consider precious in order to advance the political career of my husband.
>
> Pat Nixon, in *Women at Work*,
> by Betty Medsger, 1975

When Pat was thirty-four, her daughter Tricia was born, and two years later daughter Julie came along. Perhaps not surprisingly, Nixon had little time to spend with his daughters. Just before Tricia's wedding, he wistfully told newsmen: "I was out making a political speech the day she was born. . . . I wasn't around much while she grew up. For the rest of the time, up to the present time, it seems I've always been saying good-bye—good-bye to her at airports."

During Nixon's White House years Pat spent much of her time alone. She and her husband often ate their meals in different parts of the mansion. The First Lady's personal staff was frequently outraged at what they perceived to be the callous way the president ignored Pat during public appearances, and the many weekends he spent in the Bahamas or at Camp David with his friend Bebe Rebozo—leaving Pat behind in Washington.

When asked about Nixon's career, Pat once commented: "The only thing I could do was help him, but it was not a life I would have chosen." Later, when a reporter suggested that she had had a good life, Pat raised her eyebrows and shot back, "I just don't tell all."

After being married to Richard for fifty-three

years, Pat Nixon died of cancer on June 22, 1993. In a rare public show of emotion, her husband said this about his first lady: "The best decision I ever made was choosing Pat to be my wife, my partner in life. I've had prestige, power, and even at times, some money. Those things come and go. But Pat stood by my side during good and bad times alike."

On the Way to the White House: Nixon proved to be an unusually active vice president. With Ike intent on remaining above politics, it fell to the vice president to serve as the Republicans' politician in chief. He ably demonstrated his presidential mettle twice, taking over the Oval Office for the first time during Ike's recuperation from a 1955 heart attack, and again serving as acting president when the general was laid up with ileitis in 1958. Nixon also sat in on most Cabinet meetings, usually listening in unobtrusive silence while others conducted the business of government. At one such meeting Nixon surprised his colleagues by pulling a mechanical drummer out of his pocket. He quickly wound up the toy, set it down on the long table, and let it march around for a few moments as the most powerful men in America looked on in bemused silence. Finally, Nixon explained the meaning of his demonstration: "We've got to drum up support for Republican candidates."

When Ike ran for reelection in 1956, he wanted to drop Nixon from the national ticket. He called the vice president in for a tense Oval Office meeting, and offered Nixon any post in the Cabinet (except secretary of state) if Nixon volunteered to step down. Nixon refused, falling back on his strong support from conservatives and Republican professionals. Ike realized he couldn't get rid of Nixon without a fight. The general reluctantly accepted Nixon as his running mate once again, but he pointedly snubbed the vice president socially and politically.

Nixon was deemed so trivial a personage in the Eisenhower administration's White House team that there were parts of the executive mansion that he had never seen until President Lyndon Johnson (who doubtless identified with Nixon's isolation from his own days as JFK's unwanted vice president) took him on a personal tour. Not even Eisenhower's heart attack and stroke—which brought Nixon to within the proverbial one heartbeat of the presidency— could persuade the general to take his vice president seriously. In 1960 Ike was asked at a press conference, "What major decisions of your administration has the vice president participated in?" Ike's uncharacteristically flippant response was: "If you give me a week, I might think of one."

By the beginning of 1959, it was clear that despite Eisenhower's distaste for him, Nixon would be virtually unopposed in his bid for the Republican presidential nomination in 1960. Expecting a hard fight against the Democrats, Nixon was eager to enhance his reputation as a major statesman, so he and his staff came up with the idea of a vice presidential trip to the Soviet Union. When this plan was discussed with officials in the State Department, their enthusiasm might charitably have been described as "muted." Nixon insisted, however, and he was finally granted permission to make the trip so long as it was clearly understood that the purpose of the visit was purely "ceremonial." Nixon's chief responsibility in Russia was to open a U.S. exhibition in a Moscow park. But while touring the grounds of the exhibit (including an American model kitchen), Nixon couldn't resist the opportunity to bait the Soviet bear in his den, taking on Soviet premier Nikita Khrushchev in a shouting match in front of the television cameras and the world press. Naturally, the subject was the relative strength of the United States versus the Soviet Union. "Now we were going at it toe-to-toe," Nixon later recalled in his book Six Crises. "To some, it may have looked as though we had both lost our tempers." (He was right—that was exactly how it looked.) "But," Nixon insisted, "exactly the opposite was true. I had full and complete control of my temper and was aware of it. I knew the value of keeping cool in a crisis." Despite Nixon's self-described composure, it was the ebullient Khrushchev who got off the best lines of the day. He told Nixon: "You don't know anything about communism except fear." Throwing an arm over a nearby smiling worker, Khrushchev asked, "Does this man look like a slave laborer?" Despite the inconsequential contents of the "kitchen debate," the American press felt obliged to report a Nixon victory—after all, the vice president was representing the United States. Soon after Nixon came home, his poll ratings soared, and he entered the 1960 presidential campaign as a heavy favorite against Senator John F. Kennedy.

Nixon's inept campaigning, however, soon managed to evaporate his initial strength. As one of his aides confessed after Nixon's defeat: "Dick didn't lose this election. Dick blew this election." One of candidate Nixon's problems was purely physical. While getting out of his car, Nixon had banged his knee so hard against the door that he had to be hospitalized in the middle of the campaign. When he managed to crack the same kneecap again, in exactly the same way, one of the reporters assigned to him could no longer hold back. "My God, he's trying to kill himself," he marveled. This second injury came on the very morning of Nixon's first "great debate" with Kennedy. Nixon's drawn and haggard appearance on the broadcast that evening was in large part due to his bad knee giving him almost constant pain. The debate itself—which he had agreed to in the foolhardy belief that he could humiliate Kennedy—was Nixon's biggest setback. Most listeners who heard the contest on the radio thought Nixon had clearly won, but on television the Republican's sweaty face and heavy five o'clock shadow proved notably less telegenic than the handsome and charismatic JFK.

Nixon had adamantly refused to wear heavy pancake makeup to cover his beard stubble under the heavy lights, and years later, before another television appearance, Franny, the same makeup artist whose services he had refused, was making him up for the cameras. Don Hewitt, who had produced and directed the first debate, remarked to Nixon that if he had let the artist do her job in 1960, he probably wouldn't have lost the election. Nixon thought it over for a moment and murmured, "You're probably right."

Nixon's campaign never fully recovered its momentum after the debates, and Nixon, in Murray Kempton's words, ended his election drive "wandering limply and wetly about the American heartland begging votes on the excuse that he had been too poor to have a pony when he was a boy." Nevertheless, the final result was so tantalizingly close that Nixon tortured himself for years with the thought that any one of his minor mistakes might have meant the crucial difference between victory and defeat. Even so, the 1960 presidential bid had been unusually restrained and gentlemanly by Nixon's previous standards. He refused to make an issue of JFK's Catholicism, for example, and refrained from making political hay out of father Joseph Kennedy's boozing, womanizing, rum-running past.

When the votes were finally tallied, Kennedy's razor-thin victory margin prompted many Republican leaders to urge Nixon to contest the results. To Nixon's credit, he refused to do so, replying that "the potential effects upon the country might be devastating."

Most observers agree that if Nixon had simply "retired" from politics after 1960, safely biding his time in private law practice, the Republicans would gladly have given him the party's support for a second try for the presidency in 1964. But Nixon was still smarting from the first defeat of his political career and, impelled by his private demons and on the emotional and political rebound after his defeat, he felt the need to prove himself a winner. He entered the race for the California governorship in 1962 against the incumbent, Pat Brown. Almost from the beginning, Nixon's campaign seemed to go badly, and he predicted to friends that he would lose. Preoccupied with national office, he was lamentably out of touch with California issues. One controversy that counted heavily against him was "the Hughes loan"—a secret transaction involving $200,000 that passed from billionaire Howard Hughes to Nixon's brother Donald.

More seriously damaging to his cause was the nearly universal belief that Nixon was interested in the California governorship only as a stepping-stone to the White House. Nixon bolstered that impression with a well-publicized slip in the last days of the campaign, describing himself as a candidate for "governor of the United States."

On Election Day, Brown easily defeated Nixon with a comfortable plurality of 350,000 votes. All night, Nixon bitterly watched the returns and stubbornly refused to concede defeat. The next morning, his suit rumpled and his eyes glassy, he was still watching the disheartening election returns on television. His press secretary, Herb Klein, told him that the reporters downstairs were demanding a statement. "Screw them," Nixon replied succinctly, and sent Klein to make a statement in his place. Klein was in front of television cameras from all major networks, trying his best to put a positive spin on the returns, when he was interrupted by a commotion behind him. Nixon unexpectedly walked into the room. Looking disheveled and distraught, the disappointed Nixon proceeded to regale the press with a tirade that has been aptly described as "a nervous breakdown in public." His jerky, convulsive gestures and nervous giggles reinforced the impression among viewers that here was a man who had been pushed to the outer fringes of sanity. Among Nixon's statements on that memorable day:

Now that all the members of the press are so delighted that I have lost.... I believe Governor Brown has a heart, even though he believes that I do not.... I did not win. I have no hard feelings against anybody, against any opponent, and least of all the people of California.... And as I leave the press, all I can say is this: For sixteen years, ever since the Hiss case, you've had a lot of fun—a lot of fun—that you've had an opportunity to attack me ... Just think about how much you're going to be missing: You won't have Nixon to kick around any more, because, gentlemen, this is my last press conference.

Two days later, ABC News ran a special entitled "The Political Obituary of Richard Nixon." The report of Nixon's political demise proved to be entirely premature. By 1964 Nixon was back on the campaign trail, stumping tirelessly for Republican candidates, even in the midst of what would turn out to be a Democratic landslide. Then, for his nonstop campaigning, he received the lion's share of the credit for Republican congressional gains of forty-seven seats in the house and three in the senate in the 1966 mid-term elections. Meanwhile, Nixon worked for a Wall Street law firm at a salary of $200,000 a year. Nixon told reporters that he enjoyed living in New York because it was "a fast track." He added, "Any person tends to vegetate unless he is moving on a fast track." By 1968 Nixon's own fast track, along with the gratitude of Republican political careerists throughout the country, brought him into contention once again as a leading candidate for the presidential nomination.

His Person: Nixon was five feet eleven and one-half inches tall and weighed 175 pounds, with brown eyes and dark hair. He had no illusions about his own attractiveness. "This is the face I've got," he once said. "I've got to accept it as it is." During the 1960 campaign, he refused to view tapes of his debates with Kennedy because he couldn't bear the way he looked on TV. Nixon's heavy growth of beard had always been widely caricatured, and during campaign tours he was forced to shave two or three times a day to keep himself presentable. When he was three years old, Nixon was seriously injured in a fall from a carriage, and his head was cut under its wheels. He had a long scar on the side of his head but hid it by carefully combing his hair over the injured site. This accident—which nearly killed him—left him permanently subject to motion sickness. Nixon also had problems with hay fever all his life.

As a boy, Nixon wore a tie and jacket to school, and his classmates often teased him for his solemn formality. During the White House years, when an old friend and business associate from Florida, Hoke T. Maroon, ventured to address Nixon as "Dick," the president snapped: "Don't you dare call me 'Dick.' I am the president of the United States. When you speak to me you call me 'Mr. President.' " Nixon always appeared to be more comfortable in his three-button business suits than in casual wear. While relaxing in the sun at Key Biscayne or San Clemente, he was often dressed primly in a sports jacket. During his solitary walks along the beach, he generally wore his black wing-tip dress shoes. After he became president, his wardrobe became more raffish, and he sported gold cufflinks emblazoned with the presidential eagle.

Nixon always had poor physical coordination. Childhood acquaintances agree that he had "two left feet." Because the Whittier College football team was short on players, Nixon was allowed to participate, but he warmed the bench for four years. Whenever he was put into the game, as one teammate recalled, everyone knew a five-yard penalty was coming up. "Richard had such determination to win that he would rush ahead before the play started. I knew he'd be offside just about every play." Nixon's predilection in later years for clumsily banging into car doors led to the serious knee injury that slowed down his campaign for the presidency in 1960. Having at last become president, his inveterate clumsiness continued to alarm observers. At one press conference, he raised his hands, beckoning the reporters in the room to stand up, while requesting of them, "Would you please be seated." Delivering a major speech, he was likely to point to the audience and say "I," then back at himself to say "you." Nixon was so habitually high-strung that when someone touched him lightly on the arm, he would jump as though struck by a blow.

PRESIDENCY
Nomination: August 5, 1968
As Murray Chotiner, Nixon's former campaign manager, so eloquently put it: "It was clear that Dick was going to be the party nominee in 1968. He had more brownie points than anyone." Some twenty years of active campaigning on behalf of Republican candidates in thousands of cities and towns across the country had made Richard Nixon the favorite of the old-guard professionals who ran the party. His actual policies were so amorphous that they offended almost no one. Nixon was a past master of the art of making a "strong statement" while committing himself to nothing. His statements about the Vietnam War were small masterpieces of political gobbledygook:

> Never has so much military, economic, and diplomatic power been used as ineffectively as in Vietnam. And if after all of this time and all of this sacrifice and all of this support there is still no end in sight, then I say the time has come for the American people to turn to new leadership not tied to the policies and mistakes of the past. I pledge to you: We will have an honorable end to the war in Vietnam.

Brilliantly calculated to attract both the advocates of escalation and the partisans of peace, such baffling pronouncements fell musically upon the ears of the victory-hungry Republican leaders. There were still lingering doubts about Nixon's personality, but the press began chronicling the regeneration of the "new Nixon." The ruthless political infighter was now forgotten. In his place stood a mellow, evenhanded elder statesman, one who impressed the nation with the calm wisdom of his foreign-policy articles in *Reader's Digest*.

If Nixon could prove himself in the primaries and dispell his loser's image, the nomination would be his for the asking. His chief opponent in the early stages of the campaign was Michigan governor George Romney, champion of the party's moderate-liberal wing. Romney soon managed to talk himself out of contention when he confided to an interviewer that he had formerly been "brainwashed" on the Vietnam War. Wags were soon telling each other that in Romney's case, a light rinse had been sufficient to change his mind. Facing certain defeat at Nixon's hands in the New Hampshire primary, Romney withdrew from the race. In the remaining primaries, no other

Republican was willing to challenge Nixon's lavishly financed campaign. As the Whittier Wonder sailed smoothly toward the convention in Miami, it appeared all but certain that he would dazzle the electorate with "the greatest comeback since the Resurrection of Jesus."

As the convention met, liberal Nelson Rockefeller and reactionary Ronald Reagan strenuously tried to chip enough delegates away from Nixon's "centrist" voting bloc to prevent his nomination on the first ballot. Reagan appeared to be making headway among southern delegates formally committed to Nixon until Nixon promised Senator J. Strom Thurmond of South Carolina and other influential southerners that he would choose a conservative as his running mate. By the time the balloting began, it was clear to everyone that Nixon had the nomination sewn up. The Republican delegates seemed disposed to agree with the sentiments of Maryland governor Spiro T. Agnew, who placed Nixon's name in nomination: "When a nation is in crisis and history speaks firmly to that nation, it needs a man to match the time. You don't create such a man—you don't discover such a man—you recognize such a man."

The only suspense left for the conventioneers centered on Nixon's choice of a running mate. In making his decision, the candidate told advisers he wanted to avoid a "super star" who might outshine him in the campaign ahead. Nixon succeeded beyond his wildest dreams, selecting Spiro Agnew. Press and public alike were aghast at the choice of the little-known and inexperienced Maryland governor. Agnew's only claim to fame was a headline-making tirade—directed at representatives of the Baltimore black community—in which the governor boisterously railed against "ready-mix, instantaneous, circuit-riding, Hanoi-visiting, caterwauling, riot-inciting, burn-America-down type of leaders." Even Agnew seemed incredulous that Nixon had selected him. "I stand here with a deep sense of the improbability of this moment," he said, formally accepting the nomination for the vice presidency.

Defiant in the face of widespread criticism, Nixon may have been remembering his own tenuous grasp on the vice presidency as he defended his choice of Agnew. "There is a mysticism about men," he said. "There is a quiet confidence. You look a man in the eye and you know he's got it. . . . Brains. This guy has got it. If he doesn't, Nixon has made a bum choice."

Election: November 5, 1968
Nixon entered the presidential race with a huge lead over his Democratic opponent, Vice President Hubert H. Humphrey. The Democrats were deeply divided over the Vietnam War, and Humphrey was still closely associated with the unpopular Johnson administration he had

served as vice president. Bobby Kennedy had been asassinated after winning the California primary, and Eugene McCarthy, the remaining "peace" candidate, suffered from his association in the popular mind with the wilder excesses of the antiwar activists. The bloody televised riots outside the Democratic convention in Chicago had made a mockery of the voluble Humphrey's "Politics of joy" slogan. Barring some disaster, Nixon was a sure winner, and the Republican strategists, mindful of Nixon's genius for snatching defeat from the jaws of victory, decided that the best way to avoid disaster was to keep Nixon away from people.

Former president Dwight Eisenhower's undiminished popularity was a "secret weapon" in the Republican arsenal. Throughout the campaign, the general lay close to death at Walter Reed Hospital. Drawing upon his Whittier College football days (or perhaps his viewing of Knute Rockne, All American, starring Ronald Reagan as "the Gipper"), Nixon exhorted Republican conventioneers: "Let's win this one for Ike!" Following Nixon's lead, Murray Chotiner invaded Ike's hospital room with TV cameras to film the general's endorsement of Nixon. The resulting footage horrified even Nixon's own staff. Ike, dressed in pajamas, was obviously a dying man, a microphone hanging limply from his neck. "No," said Nixon media wizard Harry Treleaven, "that's one thing I'm not going to do. I'm not going to make a commercial out of that." "If you can't get five minutes, how about at least one minute?" pleaded Chotiner. In the end, the Nixon staff finally contented themselves with Nixon's son-in-law-to-be, David Eisenhower, reading his grandfather's endorsement to the cameras.

Despite his repeated efforts to avoid the issue during the duration of the campaign, Nixon was forced to elaborate on his previous platitudes concerning the Vietnam War. He solemnly informed the nation that he had a "secret plan" to end the war but, ever the patriot, refused to divulge its contents for fear of compromising President Lyndon Johnson's negotiating position. The transparent hypocrisy of this position—combined with Agnew's unselfconscious use of sobriquets like "Fat Jap" and "Polack" in conversation—began to create serious doubts about the Nixon-Agnew ticket. Meanwhile, millions of "Peace Democrats," sobered by the likelihood that Nixon might actually become president of the United States, began streaming reluctantly back to the Humphrey column as the election went down to the wire.

Despite what was until then the most expensive campaign in U.S. history, Richard Nixon came within a hairsbreadth of blowing his "sure-thing" election. He actually polled 2.5 million fewer votes than he had garnered in his losing effort in 1960. His overall percentage of the popular vote was 43.4—lower than any winning candidate's since 1912. His victory was an inadvertant gift dumped in his lap by Alabama's George Wallace—the reactionary "American Independent" candidate, whose blustery law-and-order campaign drew nearly 10 million votes—or 13.5 percent of the total. Wallace won enough normally Democratic, blue-collar votes in key industrial states such as Illinois and Ohio to swing those states to Nixon—and with them the election. Nixon won 301 electoral votes to Humphrey's 191. But the difference in the popular vote was only 510,000—or a mere .7 percent. Wallace carried the states of the deepest South—Alabama, Arkansas, Georgia, Louisiana, and Mississippi—for a total of 46 electoral votes.

Inauguration: January 20, 1969
The fifty-six-year-old Nixon was sworn into office by Chief Justice Earl Warren at ceremonies on the east plaza of the Capitol. His inaugural address was distinguished chiefly by its haunting reminders of John Kennedy's inaugural address in 1961. Among the most striking parallels (Kennedy's words in italics):

Let this message be heard, by strong and weak alike . . .
Let the word go forth, to friend and foe alike . . .
Let all nations know . . .
Let every nation know . . .
Those who would be our adversaries, we invite to a peaceful competition . . .
To those nations who would make themselves our adversary, we offer not a pledge but a request: that both sides begin anew the quest for peace . . .
But to all those who would be tempted by weakness, let us leave no doubt that we will be as strong as we need to be, for as long we need to be . . .
We dare not tempt them with weakness, for only when our arms are strong beyond doubt can we be certain beyond doubt that they will never be employed . . .

At one of the inaugural balls that evening, Nixon forgot to introduce the First Lady, shattering a tradition as old as the ball itself. At the next ball, he first introduced his daughters, his son-in-law David Eisenhower, and then, as if an afterthought, finally his wife. "I just assumed that everybody knew the lady I was with," he said. Later, as he was about to step into his limousine to go to the next ball, Nixon had to be reminded by an aide that he had left Pat back at the ballroom, standing by herself. He gallantly sent a Secret Service man back to fetch her.

Moving into the White House the next day, Nixon banished each and every trace of his predecessor, Lyndon Johnson. Furniture, portraits, bookshelves, rocking chairs, even utilitarian items such as news tickers, television sets, and a console of telephones were carted away and consigned to oblivion. The rug was stripped from the floor and the paint from the walls. This scorched earth approach to redecorating was Nixon's way of announcing to official visitors around him that a bright new day had dawned in the White House. In fact, his administration was to be the darkest chapter in the history of the presidency.

Reelection: November 7, 1972
The full story behind Nixon's victory in 1972 may never be known (see page 471), but this much is already clear: the Nixon administration raised and spent more money than any other candidate in history, clamoring for millions of dollars of illegal corporate contributions. Every arm of government was politicized to an unprecedented degree in order to ensure Nixon's all-important reelection. A massive campaign of sabotage and espionage helped to divide and discredit the president's opponents. Though the Watergate transcripts later showed that Nixon was passionately concerned with every trivial detail of his own campaign, he persisted in the fiction—perhaps we should call it the Oval Office alibi—that he was too busy attending to "great issues" to bother himself with politics. On October 26 the president's envoy Henry Kissinger announced that "peace was at hand" in the Vietnam negotiations. It was, of course, "purest coincidence" that this announcement came less than two weeks before the elections. Kissinger's optimism subsequently proved "premature." A month after the votes were safely tallied in Nixon's favor, his administration leveled great swathes of Vietnam and slaughtered thousands of civilians in one of the most intensive bombing campaigns in history.

Meanwhile, the Democrats' internecine squabbling played directly into Nixon's hands. After an unusually bitter preconvention fight, the Democrats nominated Senator George McGovern of South Dakota—an outspoken antiwar liberal who had systematically alienated most of the party infrastructure: party regulars and labor leaders. McGovern infelicitously selected young Senator Thomas Eagleton of Missouri as his running mate, but shortly after the convention adjourned it was learned that the telegenic Eagleton had a history of psychiatric problems. After assuring the press and public that he stood behind Eagleton "1,000 percent," McGovern ejected Eagleton from the ticket with a hasty and none-too-subtle behind-the-scenes bum's rush. He thereby convinced many voters that he was every bit as slippery as Tricky Dick, although perhaps not quite so adept, and added the veneer of political duplicity to an image already badly tarnished by widespread suspicions of radicalism. As the campaign neared its climax, McGovern concentrated his fire on the mounting evidence of corruption in the Nixon administration. McGovern's damaged credibility, however, helped Nixon's men to portray their opponent's cries of White House corruption as business-as-usual political propaganda.

The American people voted overwhelmingly for "four more years" of the Nixon-Agnew leadership. Nixon's 60.7 percent of the popular vote was the highest percentage ever bestowed on a Republican candidate. Only three men in presidential history had won landslides of comparable proportions—Franklin Roosevelt, Lyndon Johnson, and Warren G. Harding. McGovern managed to carry Massachusetts and the District of Columbia for a total of seventeen electoral votes. Nixon won the rest of the Union, for an electoral tally of 531. He was the fifth presidential candidate to win the office after a prior defeat. (The others were Thomas Jefferson, Andrew Jackson, William Henry Harrison, and Grover Cleveland.) Nixon was also the first vice president since Martin Van Buren (in 1836) to be elected without first having succeeded to the office upon the death of his predecessor.

Second Inauguration: January 20, 1973
Nixon was sworn in for a second term by Chief Justice Warren Burger. In his inaugural address, he once more echoed his old nemesis John Kennedy: "Let each of us ask, not just what will government do for me—but what can I do for myself." Nixon included one particularly inspirational note in his speech: "Let us again learn to debate our differences with civility and decency, and let each of us reach out for that precious quality government cannot provide—a new level of respect for the rights of one another."

In the most expensive and elaborate inaugural festivities yet—a series of parades, concerts, balls, and receptions costing $94 million—the president's supporters deliriously ushered in what they confidently expected would be four more years of the Nixon-Agnew team.

Ultimately, they got only ten more months of Agnew and twenty more months of Nixon.

His 5 Years, 201 Days as President:

PRO The Nixon years marked a new emphasis in American foreign policy. Under the president's able leadership, the United States began to forego its costly and thankless role as "policeman of the world." The dangers and hysteria of the Cold War subsided as Nixon moved toward rapprochement with the Soviets. For the first time since 1950, America opened its eyes to China, establishing a promising dialogue with Beijing. Having inherited the war in Vietnam from his predecessors, Nixon finally managed to bring home the American troops and POWs and won, at long last, peace with honor. In the Middle East, Nixonian diplomacy brought about a cease-fire and negotiations between Arabs and Israelis, and the best chance for a peaceful settlement in Israel's twenty-five-year history. By the time Nixon left office, he had moved the world a giant step closer to his dream of a "new generation of peace." None of the scandals of his administration can obscure the glow of this monumental achievement.

CON Nixon's celebrated "detente" with Russia was more cosmetic than substantive—none of the key issues between the two superpowers were resolved, and Nixon failed in his drive for meaningful arms control agreements. The new policy toward China was inevitable, considering China's certain emergence from the militancy of the Mao Zedong era and the intensifying border disputes with the USSR. Nixon simply benefited from an inexorable trend in world affairs. In Vietnam he willfully continued a tragic war for four unnecessary years, at a cost of thousands of lives and billions of dollars. When direct U.S. involvement was finally terminated, Nixon accepted substantially the same settlement that Hanoi had proposed in 1968. His endless talk of peace with honor was only a sham. His invasion of Cambodia, his lies to the public and the Congress, his genocidal Christmas bombing of Vietnam in 1972, were the most cold-blooded media events in history, calculated more for political effect than for any military or strategic advantage. Despite the relentless Nixon-Kissinger public relations initiatives, the ruthless and cynical U.S. position in the India-Pakistan dispute, the threat of renewed fighting in the Middle East, the continuing bloodshed in Vietnam, and the CIA intervention in Chile support the conclusion that American policy under Nixon was just as immoral—and the world situation was just as precarious—as it had ever been.

PRO On the domestic scene, Nixon established a revenue-sharing program that restored a measure of balance and equality to the state-federal relationship. He set up the Council on Environmental Quality to address the problems arising from the accelerating consumption of limited natural resources and pollution. He ended the peacetime draft and helped to restore calm to the nation's campuses. He cut back on many of the wasteful programs of LBJ's "Great Society" that had been squandering the taxpayer's money.

CON Nixon's funding cutbacks gutted dozens of necessary programs providing health care, education, and job training services, as the government adopted a tacit policy of "benign neglect" toward the nation's poor. Meanwhile, Nixon urged increased federal spending on military-industrial boondoggles of questionable utility such as the antiballistic missile and the supersonic transport. On environmental issues,

Nixon invariably put the interests of big corporations (such as oil companies, automakers, and lumber barons) ahead of the needs of individuals. Most serious of all, his totally inept handling of the economy produced the most serious domestic crisis since the Great Depression—as inflation soared to unheard-of levels and the country skidded in and out of "Nixon recessions." Meanwhile, corporate profits reached all-time highs, and the administration offered the average citizen four interminable phases of economic waffling. By the time Nixon left office, all of America's most serious domestic problems had been notably exacerbated, and the standard of living had begun a slide, from which it has never fully recovered.

PRO Nixon made it clear that administration policy would not be affected by demonstrations in the streets. His firmness helped put an end to a dangerous cycle of ghetto and campus unrest. In 1973 Nixon upgraded the U.S. military alertness level to send an unmistakable warning to the Soviets to stay out of the Arab-Israeli war.

CON Nixon's "law and order" administration was nothing more than a grotesque euphemism for the most lawless regime in American history. The criminal activity started at the very top of the ticket and permeated almost every arm of the government. Even leaving Watergate aside, Nixon was clearly guilty of tax fraud in cheating the IRS out of the tidy sum of $500,000. He also contributed $17 million in public funds to an improvement of his own—a lavish series of resort homes. Meanwhile, Vice President Spiro Agnew specialized in less imaginative forms of graft, brazenly accepting thousands of dollars in bribes and payoffs. With these examples to inspire them, it is hardly surprising that Nixon appointees in every branch of government (including Cabinet members who pleaded guilty to or were indicted and convicted of Watergate-related crimes) disgraced themselves and abused the public trust. No one else in America has done as much as Nixon to cement Washington's reputation as "the crime capital of the world." Nixon ignored warnings of economic repercussions from King Faisal of Saudi Arabia if the United States continued its military aid to Israel. In 1973, after Israel's victory, the Arab states hit back at the United States by raising oil prices a whopping $30 per barrel and throwing the U.S. economy into a dangerous period of "stagflation": a stagnant growth rate coupled with rising inflation. Tens of thousands of Americans lost their jobs.

PRO In perpetrating the Watergate affair, Richard Nixon inadvertently performed his greatest service to his country. Thanks to Nixon, the people received an invaluable education concerning their constitutional rights, the criminal justice system, the importance of a free press, and the hypocrisy of many of their leaders. During the Nixon administration, Congress began to reassert its authority after a long period of dormancy, and the dangerous growth in presidential power was at last checked. At the very end of his presidency, Nixon fulfilled his promise to unite the country—as never before—with Americans of every political persuasion joining forces to demand his impeachment or resignation.

CON It is hard to decide which is more amazing in Nixon's handling of Watergate—the president's pervasive immorality or his thoroughgoing incompetence. Nixon will not only be remembered as the greatest liar in American history, he may also be memorialized as the most inept administrator. The antics of Nixon and his palace guard would be simply laughable had they not come so close to achieving their objective—subverting the rule of law and replacing it with the rule of the Nixon oligarchy. Nixon's efforts to steamroll the rights of citizens, spy on his political rivals, smear his real and imagined "enemies," intimidate the press, defy the courts, diminish Congress, and manipulate the FBI, CIA, and IRS for political leverage all proved—at least temporarily—successful. As historian Henry Steele Commager put it: "Other things being equal, we haven't had a *bad* president before now. Mr. Nixon is the first dangerous and wicked president."

RESIGNATION
July 24, 1974: The Supreme Court ruled unanimously that Nixon had no executive privilege or special power to withhold evidence in criminal proceedings and ordered him to turn over sixty-four previously unreleased White House tapes.

July 27, 1974: The House Judiciary Committee voted twenty-seven to eleven to recommend the impeachment of Richard Nixon. Even Nixon himself conceded that passage of an impeachment resolution by the full House was a "foregone conclusion." By August 5, 1973, half the respondents in a national Gallup poll said they didn't believe in Nixon's claims of innocence. By January 1974 another poll had 79 percent of those responding calling for Nixon's impeachment.

August 5, 1974: The president released to the public written transcripts of three tapes the Supreme Court had ordered him to surrender. The tapes revealed that Nixon personally ordered a cover-up of the facts of the Watergate affair within six days of the arrests following the final, unsuccessful break-in at Democratic national headquarters. The transcripts proved that

Nixon had been consistently lying to the public—and to members of his own family and staff—for more than two years. He began interrupting Kissinger's national security briefings with weird, inappropriate, sometimes salacious remarks. Even his signature had noticeably deteriorated, becoming little more than a straight horizontal line bisected with two crooked vertical marks.

August 8, 1974: Faced with the absolute certainty of impeachment and conviction, pressed by members of his own party, Nixon belatedly abandoned his intention of "stonewalling it" for a few more months. In a dramatic speech to the nation, he announced his resignation from the presidency—the first president in history to do so. In his speech, Nixon explained the situation with his trademark candor and sincerity: "I have concluded that because of the Watergate matter I might not have the support of the Congress that I would consider necessary. . . . I would say only that if some of my judgments were wrong, and some *were* wrong, they were made in what I believed at the time to be the best interest of the nation."

In anticipation of Nixon's resignation, the Dow-Jones averages shot up more than 27 points—Wall Street's third-largest rally of the year. By appropriate coincidence, August 8 has gone down in history not just as the day Nixon announced his resignation but also as the day that Napoléon Bonaparte sailed for Saint Helena in 1815 to spend the rest of his life in exile.

AFTER THE PRESIDENCY
Following a tear-soaked farewell to his staff in the East Room of the White House ("Only if you've been in the deepest valley can you ever know how magnificent it is to be on the highest mountain"), Nixon boarded an army helicopter and raised his arms one last time in his familiar V-for-victory gesture. Nixon was airborne somewhere over Missouri when Gerald Ford officially took the oath of office as Nixon's successor. The former president did not listen to the proceedings. He and Pat rode in silence—and in separate compartments—on their way "home" to San Clemente.

In the early weeks of his retirement, Nixon's health took a sudden turn for the worse, regrettably making it impossible for him to honor any of the court subpoenas that required his testimony. Meanwhile, Nixon set about writing his memoirs—for which he was to receive an advance estimated to be between $2 million and $3 million.

Just one month after Nixon's resignation, his hand-picked successor, Gerald Ford, granted the former president a "full, complete, and absolute pardon" for any crimes Nixon had committed in office, thereby shielding the former president from prosecution. In accepting the pardon (legally in itself an admission of wrongdoing), Nixon issued a statement that touched a new note of humility: "I was wrong in not acting more decisively and more forthrightly in dealing with Watergate. . . . I know that many fair-minded people believe that my motivation and actions in the Watergate affair were intentionally self-serving and illegal."

In the final years of his life, Nixon pulled off his last, and perhaps his greatest, reinvention of himself. He wrote his memoirs and eight books on global affairs, and became a valued counselor to presidents as ideologically diverse as Ronald Reagan and Bill Clinton. In short, the final updated edition of Richard Nixon personified the American "gray eminence/elder statesman" ideal. He went out of his way to make peace with former adversaries such as George McGovern, and gradually embarked on a systematic program of rehabilitating his name for the history books. His strategy consisted of these main points:

1. Don't hold any political office.
2. Don't appear too partisan.
3. Don't accept money for anything but writing or television interviews.
4. Don't speak in public too often.
5. When you do speak, limit your remarks solely to the field of foreign policy, your strong suit.

PSYCHOHISTORY
Frank Nixon, Richard's father, was a bitter, violent, and unpleasant man who was disliked by most of his Whittier neighbors. He often chased customers out of the family store with his noisy, bad-tempered harangues on political subjects. Having failed at nearly everything he tried—as a carpenter, lemon rancher, trolley operator, and service station manager—he often vented his frustrations on his five sons. He seems to have actually kicked the boys on occasion. It is reported that Richard, the second-oldest, submitted to these beatings "without a whimper." During his early years, the boy's only shelter in his unhappy and poverty-ridden home was his mother—an emotionally undemonstrative woman described by all who knew her as "a Quaker saint." She responded to her grim life and her difficult marriage with quiet resignation and iron self-control. "I have never heard her complain," one of her fellow Quakers remembered. "I have never heard her criticize anyone." Young Richard yearned to emulate Hannah's self-control, and his political rhetoric later in life constantly emphasized the virtues of discipline, self-mastery, and "keeping cool." "The best test of a man," he once said, "is not how well he does the things he likes, but how well he does the things he doesn't like." The fact that Richard could never fully conquer himself and live up

to his mother's teachings was a persistent and painful source of self-hate and a sense of worthlessness. His violent temper—in his mind the unwanted legacy of a despised father—was one aspect of his own personality that he could never accept. Accordingly, whenever Nixon began losing control, he had to assure himself—and everyone else—that he was actually keeping cool. Note, for instance, his fervent denials in Six Crises that he ever lost his temper at Khrushchev or Kennedy. Also note his insistence at his "last press conference" that "I do not say this in any bitterness" when everyone in the country could plainly see how bitter he was. Nixon, in short, was still trying desperately to be the kind of person who would please his mother— but knew, subconsciously at least, that he had utterly failed. His only resolution for this conflict was to talk like Hannah—mouthing platitudes about peace, gentleness, and restraint even as he brutally acted like Frank— forever violently lashing out at the enemies he saw everywhere.

When Richard was three years old, he nearly died after cracking his skull in a fall from a carriage. When he was four, he contracted pneumonia and once more lay close to death. Then, just before he reached adolescence, two of his brothers died—the oldest, Harold, after a long bout with tuberculosis, and the youngest, Arthur, as an unsuspected victim of tubercular meningitis. These experiences only deepened Richard's sense of guilt and unworthiness. His mother once took brother Harold for a protracted stay in smog-free Arizona, hoping to help his lungs. During her absence, nine-year-old Richard wrote her a pathetic little letter that began "My dear master" and concluded "From your good dog, Richard."

His older brother had been Nixon's main competitor for his mother's love and attention, and now, with that rival gone, Richard felt responsible for his death. Hannah Nixon herself sensed the pattern clearly. "I think that Richard may have felt a kind of guilt," she wrote, "that Harold and Arthur were dead and he was alive." The only way to overcome that guilt was to succeed—to prove to everyone that he deserved to survive, to remain alive while two idealized brothers had departed. In the words of political scientist James David Barber: "His political life—which is nearly his whole life— is a punishing one. At most he derives from it a grim satisfaction in endurance. . . . Nixon exerts extraordinary energies on a life which brings him back extraordinary hardships."

But those hardships were necessary if Nixon was to keep his balance. Unless his successes were tempered by failure and humiliation, he lived in unbearable tension—the tension of a man who feels that things are going "too well" and believes that his "triumphs" are in fact meaningless and undeserved. In 1952, after his nomination for the vice presidency at the age of thirty-nine, he left himself politically vulnerable by continuing to accept money from the "Nixon fund." In 1960, when he was running well ahead of Kennedy in the polls, he courted disaster by agreeing to televised debates. In 1972, while winning one of history's greatest landslides, he micromanaged his own undoing by his otherwise inexplicable mishandling of Watergate. Along with his fierce desire to win respect, to prove his strength at the expense of his enemies, came a desperate need to expose himself, to demonstrate his own unworthiness, to show the world that beneath the carefully composed mask of cool professionalism and self-control stood a vulnerable, painfully human man, an outsider fully as petty and bitter as Frank Nixon. How else can one explain Nixon's incredible "last press conference"—a masochistic orgy of self-exposure and public humiliation? How else can one explain his methodical tape-recording of precisely those "private" conversations that he must have known would discredit him?

Most comfortable when playing the pious martyr—a role echoing his "saintly," emotionally distant mother—Nixon found politics, from the beginning, the ideal venue for his self-dramatized inner struggle. Politics afforded him the "exquisite agony" of destroying himself in public, as well as the power he delighted in using to punish his invisible "enemies."

LITTLE-KNOWN FACTS

Nixon's mother once told the public about one of Richard's more obscure talents. "He was the best potato masher one could wish for," she recalled. "Even in these days, when I am visiting Richard and Pat in Washington, or when they visit me, he will take over the potato mashing. My feeling is that he actually enjoys it."

At Whittier College, the annual bonfire was a point of class pride. Each year the fire was fueled with scrap wood topped by an outhouse. The competition was to see which senior chairman could top the pile of debris with the largest outhouse, say, a two-holer, or even a three-holer. Young Nixon scored an immense and well-remembered triumph when his diligence turned up a four-holer. As writer Garry Wills suggests: "Picture the systematic intensity that went into this achievement."

After his Checkers speech Nixon received a congratulatory phone call from Hollywood producer Darryl Zanuck. "The most tremendous performance I've ever seen," Zanuck told him.

Occasionally, Nixon found it necessary to lash out physically at hecklers. During his trip to Peru as vice president, a man in the crowd spat on him. "As I saw his legs go by," Nixon remembered, "at least I had the satisfaction of planting a healthy kick on his shins. . . . Nothing I did all day made me feel better."

During one of his 1960 debates with Kennedy, Nixon demanded that his opponent "apologize" for the salty language being used by former president Harry Truman in Truman's vigorous anti-Nixon campaign. As Nixon pointed out to the television audience, "I can only say that I am very proud that President Eisenhower restored dignity and decency, and frankly, good language to the conduct of the presidency. And I can only hope—should I win this election—that I would approach President Eisenhower in maintaining the dignity of the office." Kennedy's reaction was off-camera laughter. A few minutes later, the debate over, Nixon retired to his dressing room and exploded in front of reporters. "That fucking bastard," he said. "He—he wasn't supposed to use notes!"

At the close of a business trip to Finland in 1965, Richard Nixon, then in private law practice, impulsively took a twenty-hour train ride to Moscow. At eleven o'clock at night, he knocked on Khrushchev's door. Khrushchev was occupied elsewhere. Nixon had to satisfy himself with a deputy director of Moscow State University and a perplexed Russian cop who happened by. Nixon unsuccessfully tried to interest both men in a nostalgic debate. In 1967, for no apparent reason, he went to Moscow once again, visiting Sokolniki Park, the site of his famous "kitchen debate" with Khrushchev eight years before. Once more Khrushchev himself was unavailable, and Nixon had to entertain himself by scoring rhetorical points against passersby.

Nixon was the first president in American history who managed to visit every state while in office.

While stumping for Republican candidates in 1970, Nixon was riding in a motorcade in Saint Petersburg, Florida, when a motorcycle policeman was thrown from his vehicle and severely injured. The president rushed to the suffering policeman's side and expressed his sympathies. The officer stoically apologized for the delay he had inadvertantly caused. There followed an interval of embarrassing silence, until Nixon blurted out: "Well, do you like the work?"

Nixon's favorite president was—of all people—Democrat Woodrow Wilson. Psychologists might point out that Wilson's martyrdom would naturally appeal to Nixon's own well-developed martyr complex. Moreover, Nixon obviously envied Wilson's intellectual credentials. "I think he was our greatest president of this century," Nixon once said. "You'll notice too that he was the best educated." When he moved into the White House, Nixon ordered that LBJ's desk be removed and had it replaced by the old, half-forgotten desk that had been used by President Wilson.

QUOTES BY NIXON

"The word politics causes some people lots of trouble. Let us be very clear—politics is not a dirty word."

"People go through that psychological bit nowadays. They think they should always be reevaluating themselves. I fight the battles as they come along. That sort of juvenile self-analysis is something I've never done."

"Those who have known great crisis . . . can never become adjusted to a more leisurely and orderly pace. They have drunk too deeply of the stuff which really makes life exciting and worth living to be satisfied with the froth."

"Frankly, most people are mentally and physically lazy. They believe you can get places by luck alone. They fail to do the hard grinding work required to get all the facts before reaching a decision."

"Your mind must always go, even while you're shaking hands and going through all the maneuvers. I developed the ability long ago to do one thing while thinking about another."

"Once you're in the stream of history you can't get out."

"It doesn't come natural to me to be a buddy-buddy boy. . . . I can't really let my hair down with anyone. No, not really with anyone, not even with my own family."

"I'm an introvert in an extrovert profession."

"I would have made a good pope."

"You know very well that whether you are on page one or page thirty depends on whether they fear you. It is just as simple as that."

"One vote is worth a hundred obscene slogans."

"You've got to have something where it doesn't appear that I am doing this in, you know, just in a—saying to hell with the Congress and to hell with the people, we are not going to tell you anything because of executive privilege. That they don't understand. But if you say, 'No, we are willing to cooperate,' and you've made a complete statement, but make it very incomplete. See, that is what I mean."

—1972

"I have never had much sympathy for the point of view 'It isn't whether you win or lose that counts, but how you play the game.' How you play the game does count. But one must put top consideration on the will, the desire, and the determination to win."

—1960

"Whenever any mother or father talks to his child, I hope he can look at the man in the White House, and whatever he may think of his politics, he will say, 'Well,

there is a man who maintains the kind of standards personally I would want my child to follow.' "
—Debate with Kennedy, 1960

"I believe that I spent too much time in the last campaign on substance and too little time on appearance; I paid too much attention to what I was going to say and too little to how I would look."
—1961

"What few disappointments have been my lot in the world of politics are as nothing compared to the mountain-top experiences which have been mine."
—1962

"From considerable experience in observing witnesses on the stand, I had learned that those who are lying or trying to cover up something generally make a common mistake—they tend to overreact, to overstate their case."
—Six Crises, 1962

"Let us begin by committing ourselves to the truth—to see it as it is, and tell it like it is—to find the truth, to speak the truth, and to live the truth."
—Presidential nomination acceptance speech, 1968

"All right. They still call me 'Tricky Dick.' It's a brutal thing to fight. The carefully cultivated impression is that Nixon is devious. I can overcome this impression in one way only: by absolute candor."
—1968

"There are some people, you know, they think the way to be a big man is to shout and stomp and raise hell—and then nothing ever really happens. I'm not like that . . . I never shoot blanks."
—Look, October 19, 1971

"Nobody is a friend of ours. Let's face it."
—September 15, 1972

"We are all in it together. This is war. We take a few shots and it will be over. We will give them a few shots and it will be over. Don't worry. I wouldn't want to be on the other side right now. Would you?"
—September 15, 1972

"We can't get the president involved in this. His people, that is one thing. We don't want to cover up, but there are ways."
—April 14, 1973

"I made my mistakes, but in all my years of public life I have never profited, never profited from public service. I have earned every cent. And in all of my years of public life I have never obstructed justice. And I think, too, that I could say that in my years of public life that I welcome this kind of examination

because people have got to know whether or not their president is a crook. Well, I am not a crook."
—November 17, 1973

"I have a quality which I guess I must have inherited from my Midwestern mother and father, which is that the tougher it gets, the cooler I get."
—1974

"Always give your best. Never get discouraged. Never be petty. Always remember: others may hate you. Those who hate you don't win unless you hate them. And then you destroy yourself."
—Farewell speech to White House staff, August 9, 1974

"When you're knocked down on the ropes, remember, life is 99 rounds, and, well, I still have a few rounds to go."

"I've always thought this country could run itself domestically without a president. You need a president for foreign policy, though."
—1968

"You know, I always wondered about that taping equipment, but I'm damn glad we have it, aren't you?"
—Nixon to Haldeman, April 25, 1973

QUOTES ABOUT NIXON

"Nixonland is a land of slander and scare, of lay innuendo, of a poison pen and the anonymous telephone call, and hustling, pushing, and shoving—the land of smash and grab and any thing to win."
—Adlai E. Stevenson, 1952

"Nixon went into politics the way other young men home from the war went into construction, or merchandising, or whatever—for lack of anything better to do. . . . The fact is that as a candidate for office, Nixon has consistently been a thoroughly second-rate politician, because he was made, not born."
—Stewart Alsop

"There is built into Nixon an automatic response mechanism triggered by opposition. Offer him the element of competition, tempt him with a fight, hint that someone might want to deprive him of some prize, and a tiger emerges from the camouflage he normally shows the world."
—Leonard Lurie

"Let's show them, Daddy—let's run!"
—Tricia Nixon, 1967

"Nixon is a shifty-eyed goddamn liar, and people know it. He's one of the few in the history of this country to run for high office talking out of both sides of his mouth at the same time and lying out of both sides."
—Harry S. Truman, 1961

"He's probably the most informed president there's ever been. I really can't understand how people can call him isolated. He's aware of everything that's going on."

—John Mitchell

"While he is likely to maintain a serious, almost brooding countenance in the company of three or four persons, he lights up like a Christmas tree when confronted with a crowd. He genuinely likes people."

—William Rogers

"I think basically he is shy, and like a lot of shy people he appears not to be warm."

—Rose Mary Woods

"One has the uneasy feeling that he is always on the verge of pronouncing himself the victim of some clandestine plot."

—Arthur Schlesinger Jr., 1968

"Let me say with absolute candor that I think he is the most civil man I ever worked for. He really does have some sense of your own feelings."

—Daniel P. Moynihan

"There were days when the entire White House seemed to be in the grip of a morbid obsession, not unlike the mood aboard the Pequod when Ahab was at the helm."

—Dan Rather

"The great division in retrospective appraisal of Nixon will be between those who regard his as the most inept of presidential performances, and those who will regard it as the most vicious."

—Richard E. Neustadt

"I don't think the son-of-a-bitch knows the difference between telling the truth and lying."

—Harry S. Truman

"The secret of Nixon's durability is his willingness to sacrifice former selves to the moment."

—Garry Wills, 1969

"He told us he was going to take crime out of the streets. He did. He took it into the damn White House."

—Reverend Ralph D. Abernathy

"President Nixon's motto was, if two wrongs don't make a right, try three."

—Norman Cousins, quoted by Christie Davies, Daily Telegraph, July 17, 1979

The Child Is Father to the Man:
"Dick always planned things out. He didn't do things accidentally. . . . Once, when he had just about as much of me as he could take, he cut loose and kept at it for a half to three-quarters of an hour. He went back a year or two, listing things I had done. He didn't leave out a thing. I was only eight, and he was ten, but I've had a lot of respect ever since for the way he can keep things in his mind."

—Donald Nixon

"I taught him how to cry, in a play by John Drinkwater called Bird in Hand. He tried conscientiously at rehearsals, and he'd get a pretty good lump in his throat and that was all. But on the evenings of the performance tears just ran right out of his eyes. It was beautifully done, those tears."
—Dr. Albert Upton, his Whittier College drama coach
—M.S.M. and N.H.

THE ANTI–HIGH AND MIGHTY

Everyone who leads large masses of people and is excessively idolized by them must be vigorously opposed, however enlightened or holy he may be, irrespective of his office or profession.

Kang Yu-wei

EMMA GOLDMAN

Emma Goldman was blamed for the assassination of President William McKinley, hounded from dozens of American cities and towns by mobs, was beaten, jailed, and ultimately deported by the agents of an ambitious young superpatriot named J. Edgar Hoover. A soldier, Raymond Buwalda, was court-martialed for

merely shaking Goldman's hand. He served ten months in prison for the offense, and was finally given a presidential pardon by Theodore Roosevelt, but Buwalda's freedom carried with it a severe reprimand for associating with "dangerous criminals."

Playwright S. N. Behrman recalled that his parents invoked "Red Emma's" name as a bogey to terrify naughty children into conformity. Yet today Goldman emerges from the history books as an idealistic, even motherly, figure whose courage and eloquence inspired many of the most important and influential American artists and activists of her era.

Her "shocking" ideas concerning the emancipation of women, birth control, and the folly of war (which during her lifetime inspired the press to dub her "the Most Dangerous Woman in America") now strike masses of people as evidence of her prescience and humanitarianism.

Emma Goldman was born on June 27, 1869, in Kovno, Lithuania. In 1881 her family moved to Saint Petersburg, where her father ran a small grocery. In 1885 the Goldmans emigrated to the United States, settling in Rochester, New York. As a teenager Emma found factory work at Garson and Mayer's, sewing ulsters ten and a half hours a day for $2.50 a week.

She married Jacob Kershner, but their honeymoon was blighted by his impotence. Goldman eventually divorced Kershner, but remarried him on the urging of family and friends, only to leave him for good when his problem proved incurable. She did not divorce Kershner the second time, and since her citizenship was based on her being Kershner's wife, her marital status would one day become a serious issue during her deportation trial.

Goldman became a famous advocate of free love, and she practiced what she preached, which accounts for a good deal of the vehemence directed against her by a repressive, puritanical society. While Goldman was hardly promiscuous by the freewheeling standards of the late twentieth century, her love life was a notorious scandal in her time.

Goldman moved to New York City in 1889 and came under the influence of radical editor Johann Most. Most's circle frequented Justus Schwab's Fifty-First Street saloon, an establishment so wicked and depraved that men and women entered by the same door.

Goldman had already been influenced by the harsh conditions she had seen and endured, and by the romantic idealism of her age. She steeped herself in the writings of Russian radicals such as Prince Peter Kropotkin, Nikolai Chernyshevski, and Mikhail Bakunin. When radicals accused of rioting in Chicago's Haymarket Square in 1886 were hung in the Cook County jail, she answered the call to the barricades. She fell in love with a young anarchist named Alexander Berkman, and the direction of her life was established.

On July 6, 1892, a battle broke out between strikers at the Homestead steel plant in Pittsburgh and 300 strike-busting Pinkerton operatives hired by industrialist Henry Clay Frick. Ten workers and three detectives were killed. Berkman decided to assassinate Frick in retaliation, but refused to take Goldman with him on his deadly mission. Determined to take part, however, Goldman revived her seamstress skills, making herself some provocative lingerie and pathetically trying to earn enough money to buy a gun by "going on the stroll" as a streetwalker on Fourteenth Street in New York City. Moved by what he took to be Goldman's naiveté, one of her would-be clients gave her the money she needed and sent her home untouched.

Berkman's attempt on Frick's life was equally unsuccessful, though he managed to shoot the industrialist three times before being subdued. Berkman was sentenced to twenty-two years in prison. Goldman's complicity in the act could not be proved, but she wrote articles praising her lover as the avenger of the Homestead men, thus making herself a target for the police.

On August 21, 1893, she addressed a rally of 4,000 in Union Square. A depression that would last for four years had already begun, creating a volatile social climate. Goldman was charged with inciting the unemployed to steal bread. As the soon-to-be-celebrated firebrand awaited trial, journalist Nellie Bly interviewed her in a New York City prison. Bly's article, appearing in the New York World on September 22, 1893, described Goldman as being about five feet tall and a trim 120 pounds, with expressive blue-gray eyes behind shell-rimmed glasses, a saucy turned-up nose, light brown hair falling loosely over her forehead, full lips, strong white teeth, and a mild pleasant voice. Nellie Bly also called her "a modern Joan of Arc." The judge sentenced Goldman to a year on Blackwell's Island.

Upon her release, Goldman went to Vienna to study nursing and midwifery. One of her lecturers was Sigmund Freud. In 1899, thanks to the generosity of Herman Miller, president of the Cleveland Brewing Company, and another philanthropist named Carl Stone, she was able to return to Europe to study medicine. Characteristically, she got involved in rallies against the Boer War and had a love affair with a Czech student named Hippolyte Havel. The benefactors underwriting her medical studies protested against these digressions, prompting Goldman to pen one of the best dismissals of a patron since Samuel Johnson scored off Philip Stanhope, fourth earl of Chesterfield, in 1755. She wrote, "E. G. the woman and her ideas are inseparable. She does not exist for the amusement of upstarts, nor will she permit anybody to dictate to her. Keep your money."

Goldman returned to the United States and continued to lecture. She was a spellbinder whose eloquence swept away many an audience. On September 6, 1901, as President McKinley was shaking hands with the crowd at the Temple of Music at the Pan-American Exposition in Buffalo, he was shot in the chest and stomach by a man named Leon Czolgosz, who had concealed a gun in a bandaged hand. McKinley died eight days later. Because Czolgosz had attended a Goldman lecture in Chicago, authorities tried to place her at the center of a conspiracy to assassinate the president. Prosecutors resorted to doctored testimony but still failed to make the charge stick. Even so, thanks to the yellow press, Goldman's guilt was widely assumed, especially since she had the effrontery to publicly defend assassin Czolgosz

Emma Goldman speaking in Union Square in New York City in 1916.

as a demented unfortunate who at least deserved a fair trial.

A law was passed in 1903 to deport alien anarchists. In this first "Red scare," many legislators also wanted to deport American-born and naturalized anarchists. When Goldman organized the Free Speech League to fight this repressive legislation, her name became so notorious that she had to call herself E. G. Smith, or not even dedicated liberals would associate with her.

Goldman's interests were not limited to politics. As the editor of *Mother Earth*, a radical magazine, she was instrumental in introducing American audiences to dramatists such as Henrik Ibsen and George Bernard Shaw. In 1911 the chief probation officer in Saint Louis was Roger Baldwin, a Harvard man who had once refused to hear Jack London speak because of his socialism. Invited to a Goldman lecture, Baldwin stoutly declined. He considered Goldman crazy. Upon being taunted with the narrowness of the Harvard outlook, he agreed to hear her.

Baldwin went to a crowded hall in the slums, where Goldman delivered a passionate, witty, and intellectual address that so moved him that

he became a social activist and founder of the American Civil Liberties Union. Novelist and poet Henry Miller was deeply affected when he heard her speak in San Diego in 1913. Historian Samuel Eliot Morison was in the audience when she spoke in England in the 1920s and called her "about the finest woman orator I have ever heard."

Still, many who had never heard Goldman speak hated what she represented. In 1912 her lover and manager, Dr. Ben L. Reitman, self-styled king of the hobos, was coated with tar and sagebrush by a San Diego mob, which also burned the initials IWW (for Industrial Workers of the World, the anarcho-syndicalist labor union) into his buttocks with a lighted cigar. When Goldman defied propriety by advocating birth control, she was jailed. When she challenged the war hysteria in 1917 by speaking against the draft, she was sentenced to two years in jail and then deported to Russia along with Alexander Berkman and other radicals.

The Emma Goldman who had been a thorn in the side of the Woodrow Wilson administration was even more critical of Lenin's Bolsheviks and their authoritarian Worker's Paradise.

She penned a scathing anti-Communist book entitled *My Disillusionment in Russia*, which was promptly seized and burned by U.S. customs agents as subversive literature. Leftists who refused to abide criticism of the Soviet experiment were now her most violent enemies, threatening to silence her by force.

While she was on a speaking tour in Canada, friends urged her to seek police protection. Goldman refused, saying, "I have never called for the police, but the police have often called for me." When the Spanish Civil War broke out, Goldman espoused the cause of the Catalonian anarchists, organizing the Anti-Fascist Solidarity with Rebecca West, George Orwell, and others. She died on May 14, 1940, after a stroke in Toronto. She is buried in Chicago's Forest Home Cemetery near her Haymarket comrades.

Goldman's impact was enormous. Her anar-chist journal, *Mother Earth*, wielded great influence between 1906 and 1917, when a police raid destroyed it. Theodore Dreiser urged her to write her autobiography, and Edna St. Vincent Millay headed the committee to raise money so she could. H. L. Mencken—no radical he—sang her praises and worked for her repatriation. Though she threw huge parties, called Red Balls, at which she danced the Anarchist's Slide dressed as a nun, she struck socialite Mabel Dodge as maternal. Educator John Dewey said, "Her reputation as a dangerous woman was built up entirely by a conjunction of yellow journalism and ill-advised police raids. She is a romantically idealistic person with a highly attractive personality." Emma Goldman may have been the bravest person of her era, facing down angry mobs to have her say against every form of tyranny that threatens the human spirit.

—K.L. and M.C.S.

Chapter 3

DISASTERS

THE SAN FRANCISCO EARTHQUAKE

San Francisco was no stranger to earthquakes. Lying on the San Andreas Fault, the city had experienced a sizable jolt in 1800, and another earthquake in 1857 had caused cracks in the earth as wide as thirty feet. By 1906 the city had become a major cosmopolitan area with a population of 400,000. Deep below the earth two of the world's great tectonic plates pushed past each other with a force that equaled the explosion of 6 million tons of TNT. The shock waves from the slippage on the fault line raced through the city at 7,000 miles per hour.

When: April 18, 1906, at 5:12 A.M.

Where: San Francisco, California.

The Loss: 2,500 dead; 300,000 homeless. Property damage exceeded $400 million.

The Disaster: A loud rumbling noise preceded the two major jolts of the quake. The first shock wave lasted for forty seconds. After an interval of ten seconds, the second jolt, lasting twenty-five seconds, hit. The city began to collapse like a giant house of cards. Cheaply constructed wood-frame and brick buildings crumbled instantly; anything built on a sandy landfill was a perfect target for the quake.

The new and "indestructible" city hall, which had taken twenty years and $6 million to build, was quickly destroyed; the dome was the only part of the building left intact. Floors of hotels collapsed one on top of the next. The spires of the city's great churches broke off and fell, like spears, on the people in the streets. As one observer later said: "Big buildings were crumbling as one might crush a biscuit in one's hand. Great gray clouds of dust shot up with flying timbers, and storms of masonry rained into the street. Wild, high jangles of smashing glass cut a sharp note into the frightful roaring. Ahead of me a great cornice crushed a man as if he were a maggot. . . . Everywhere men were on all fours in the street, like crawling bugs."

Those not buried under rubble poured into the streets, many of them half asleep and half dressed. One of the dazed survivors was the great operatic tenor Enrico Caruso, who was in the city to perform in *Carmen* at the Grand Opera House. Clutched in his hands was an autographed photograph of Theodore Roosevelt in a silver frame. Afraid that his voice might have been injured by the polluted air, Caruso supposedly tested his vocal abilities by singing loudly as he wandered through the streets. Upon leaving the city, Caruso vowed never to return, and he kept his word.

The greatest damage done to San Francisco was not caused by the earthquake but by the fires that soon broke out. Initially, there were fifty-three fires started by a variety of causes, including overturned stoves and heaters, and leaking gas from broken natural gas lines. One particularly devastating fire was started in a home on Hayes Street by a woman who was cooking a meal. Called the "Ham and Egg" fire, it was so intense and fast-moving that firefighters couldn't contain it.

Overall, firefighters fought a losing battle. Water mains all over the city were broken and the drop in water pressure rendered them useless. Thus, firefighters had to rely on water from a single water tower and from nearly forgotten underground cisterns, left over from the gold rush days. The fire department had thirty-eight horse-drawn fire engines, but some were trapped in collapsed fire stations. In addition, communication between fire officials was impossible because telephone and telegraph lines, as well as fire alarms, were inoperable.

Months earlier, Fire Chief Dennis Sullivan had warned government officials that the city was not prepared to deal with massive fires and had asked for money to study and implement new safety measures. However, no funds were appropriated. When the earthquake struck, Sullivan was critically injured in the Bush Street fire station when a wall of the adjoining California Hotel came crashing through the fire station. Sullivan, in a coma, was unable to provide leadership and expertise to his department; he died four days later.

In an attempt to halt the advancing flames, Mayor Eugene Schmitz ordered that firebreaks be created by dynamiting entire blocks of buildings. Assisting the fire department in the dynamiting effort were soldiers from the U.S. Army and the U.S. Navy as well as soldiers from the National Guard of California. However, many of the men were not experienced in the use of explosives, and the charges they set were too powerful. Instead of the buildings collapsing, they blew outward and started new fires. These explosion tactics ended up setting fire to Chinatown and unearthed thousands of escaping rats that carried bubonic plague. (A year after the fire, there were more than 150 reported cases of bubonic plague in the city.)

The dead and injured were everywhere. Some had been crushed by falling buildings; some had been engulfed by flames. Others were trampled to death by hordes of people and animals. Many people, stranded inside and on the roofs of burning buildings, jumped. Some, believing there was no way to escape a fiery death, asked police to shoot them—and the police complied. In one case, a policeman and several citizens tried in vain to free a man buried under burning wreckage. As one of the rescuers later said: "The helpless man watched in silence 'til the fire began burning his feet. Then he screamed and begged to be killed. The policeman took his name and address and shot him through the head."

The citizens of San Francisco valiantly fought the fires. They helped firefighters pull horseless fire engines through the streets and poured any available water on the flames. On Telegraph Hill, Italian residents raided their wine cellars and dumped more than a thousand gallons of wine on their burning homes.

As the fire neared the Montgomery Block, the employees of the Adolph Sutro Library scrambled to save a collection of 200,000 books, many of them valuable and irreplaceable. The books, loaded on wagons, were taken to a building across from city hall in an area untouched by fire. Hours later the entire collection went up in smoke. Ironically, the Montgomery Block was spared.

Panic swept through the city and thieves began looting. They broke into banks, bars, deserted homes and businesses. Brigadier General Frederick Funston, who had called in troops from the nearby Presidio garrison, ordered his men to restore order and shoot all looters. Mayor Schmitz subsequently made Funston's order official when he issued a proclamation "to kill any and all persons found engaged in looting or in the commission of any other crime." Vigilante squads joined up with the soldiers, and those who broke the law were swiftly executed.

Fire consumed the city for three days. The efforts of firemen, combined with a light rain, finally stopped the conflagration. An assessment of the damage was staggering. More than four square miles, or 514 city blocks, were annihilated. A total of 28,188 buildings were destroyed. Members of the San Francisco Real Estate Board passed a resolution stating that the disaster should be called not "the great earthquake" but "the great fire."

Aftermath: Thousands of insurance claims were filed with more than 200 insurance companies. Since most policies excluded coverage for earthquake damage, property owners claimed that fire had destroyed their buildings. While it was obvious that quite a bit of fraud was taking place, insurance companies had a difficult time separating the truth from the lies. In addition, it was rumored that many claimants had actually set fire to their damaged buildings, knowing that their insurance covered fire but not earthquake damage. Only five insurance companies were able to pay off all of their claims.

Following the disaster, the city made an amazing recovery. Within a few days some trains were running; within six weeks all the banks were back in business. In three years some 20,000 new buildings were completed—built to new fire and earthquake codes. The rebuilding program was so successful that San Francisco was chosen as the site for the Panama Pacific International Exposition of 1915. In nine years, San Francisco had made a complete comeback.

The Richter scale, which measures the intensity of earthquakes, wasn't around in 1906. Many seismologists today estimate that the earthquake was probably an 8.3 on the Richter scale; some, however, rank it lower, at 7.9.

—C.O.M.

THE TRIANGLE SHIRTWAIST FACTORY FIRE

It was five minutes before quitting time on Saturday afternoon at Manhattan's Triangle Shirtwaist Company factory. About 600 workers, most of them young women, Jewish and Italian immigrants in their teens and early twenties, were preparing to leave after a long and hard week of work. Scraps of material overflowed trash bins and cluttered the floors of the eighth- and ninth-story lofts jammed with row after row of sewing machines. The factory had been the center of a major strike the previous year. The factory had experienced several minor fires and had been reported by the fire department to the city's building department because of the inadequacy of its exits. The building itself was fireproof. Unfortunately, what was inside it—the fabric and the employees—was not. Suddenly, on the eighth floor, a smoldering fire in a bin of fabric waste erupted into a dangerous blaze. One of the young women noticed it and yelled "Fire!" and the panic began.

When: Saturday, March 25, 1911, at 4:40 P.M.

Where: The ten-story Asch Building on the corner of Washington Place and Greene Street in New York City.

The Loss: A total of 146 lives.

The Disaster: As soon as they heard the word *fire*, factory manager Samuel Bernstein and foreman Max Rother rang for the elevators, telephoned the fire department, and began dousing the fire with buckets of water. But the fire spread too quickly to be controlled by two water buckets. Within moments, the finished clothes hanging overhead were ignited, as were the cutting tables. Other men rushed to roll out a hose, but the valve was rusted shut and the hose was so rotted that it fell apart.

There were four elevators in the building, two for passengers and two for freight. One of these was out of service. Hundreds of screaming young women pushed their way through a narrow passageway to the main hallway and the elevators. One of the two elevator operators, Giuseppe Zito, made several trips up to the eighth floor, squeezing in fifteen women at a time. The other operator abandoned his post. Two passersby, a law student named Max Steinberg and an elevator operator from another building, Thomas Gregory, managed to make a few trips with the other elevators, but eventually all three machines were disabled when their cables burned. Thirty-six women leaped onto the roofs of the elevators and died in the elevator shafts.

Others attempted to flee by hurtling down the thirty-three-inch wide staircase, only to discover that the doors on the bottom floor opened inward; the press of women against the doors meant that they couldn't be opened. Another exit door was bolted shut, and the young workers struggled in vain until the fire followed them down the stairwell and burned them alive. Still others tried to run down the flimsy fire escape, but it collapsed immediately under the weight of so many people.

Many people, including the owners, Max Blanck and Isaac Harris, escaped by climbing onto the roof and crossing to adjoining buildings. One survivor, eighteen-year-old Pauline Grossman, saw three male employees on the eighth floor make a human chain of their bodies and swing across a narrow alleyway to a building on Greene Street. As more and more people crowded onto the human bridge, the weight on the center man became too great. His back was broken and he fell to the ground, as did the people trying to cross over him. Then the two other men lost their holds on the windowsills and fell as well.

Twenty-five-year-old Clotilda Terdanova had only one week more of work before she left the factory forever. In three weeks she was due to be married. In a panic she ran from window to window, finally breaking one open and leaping outside. Others, not realizing that she had been killed instantly, followed her lead. So many women jumped that the rescue efforts of the firemen, who had responded within eight minutes, were hampered by falling bodies. Corpses piled upon the sidewalk, making it difficult to unravel the hoses. Even when they were unobstructed, the hoses didn't reach beyond the sixth floor. Ladders were raised, but they stretched only as far as the seventh floor. The windows continued to fill with desperate women. Rescuers pulled out safety nets, but the women fell right through them. On the ground, horrified witnesses yelled up at the young women, "Don't jump! Don't jump!" But for many there was no choice: it was jump or be burned to death. One girl leaped from a window and her dress caught on a wire. The crowd watched helplessly as she hung in space until her dress burned and she fell to her death.

After eighteen minutes the fire was over, but the horror continued. Two girls, charred beyond recognition, were found in the ruins, their arms clasped around each other's necks. In the words of the *New York Times* account of the disaster, "Horrible cries had burst from the misery-stricken mob outside when these two were carried through the narrow street. . . . Everywhere burst anguished cries for sister, mother and wife, a dozen pet names in Italian and Yiddish rising in shrill agony above the deeper moan of the throng."

At the morgue the police used nightsticks to beat back the mob of family members looking for loved ones. Finally the morgue became too crowded and the bodies had to be moved to an adjoining pier. Twenty homeless men were pressed into service to lay out the bodies, and every opening in the morgue building and the covered pier was boarded up for fear grieving mourners, upon finding their dead relatives, would throw themselves into the water.

Aftermath: At the scene of the fire, Fire Chief Edward Croker complained bitterly that the Manufacturers' Association had, a week earlier, held a meeting on Wall Street to oppose his plan to build more and better fire escapes. He eventually resigned his post to lead a campaign for factory safety.

On April 5, 120,000 people marched in a funeral parade up Fifth Avenue. Six days later, owners Blanck and Harris were indicted for manslaughter. However, a grand jury eventually exonerated them. The tragedy, which could easily have been prevented, was treated by the county and state governments as if it were an act of God. On the other hand, significant safety and fire-prevention reforms were instituted all across the country. The International Ladies Garment Workers Union was also formed in direct response to the Triangle Shirtwaist tragedy. Although real changes did take place, the new awareness of workplace safety did not put an end to such disasters. As late as September 3, 1991, twenty-five workers at a chicken-processing plant operated by Imperial Food Products in Hamlet, North Carolina, were killed in a fire because there were no fire alarms or sprinkler systems. In addition, many exit doors were locked to prevent employees from stealing chicken parts. In the 1991 case, however, the owner, Emmett Roe, pleaded guilty to involuntary manslaughter and was sentenced to nineteen years and eleven months in prison, the harshest sentence ever for a workplace safety violation.

—D.W.

THE UNSINKABLE *TITANIC*

And as the smart ship grew
In stature, grace, and hue,
In shadowy silent distance grew the Iceberg too.

Alien they seemed to be:
Nor mortal eye could see
The intimate welding of their later history,

Or sign that they were bent
By paths coincident
On being anon twin halves of one august event,

Till the Spinner of the Years
Said "Now!" And each one hears,
And consummation comes, and jars two
hemispheres.

Thomas Hardy,
"The Convergence of the Twain," 1914

It was on a Friday afternoon that the *Titanic*, newest luxury-liner addition to Britain's White Star Fleet, departed from Queenstown, Ireland, on its maiden voyage from Southampton to New York. It carried 1,290 passengers, a crew of 903, and 3,814 sacks of mail. There was great excitement aboard as the big ship knifed its way through the Atlantic at twenty-three knots, a speed certain to set a new crossing record. A few hundred miles past the halfway point, lookouts in the crow's nest sighted an iceberg less than a quarter mile away. There was no time to stop or to swerve. The muffled grinding on impact gave little indication that the unsinkable *Titanic* had been fatally wounded.

When: Just before midnight on Sunday, April 14, 1912. Shortly after 2:00 A.M. the *Titanic* slid to its watery grave.
Where: 1,191 miles from New York.
The Loss: 1,493 passengers and crew members perished. The *Titanic* had cost more than $8 million.
The Disaster: It was just before midnight when the iceberg was spotted dead ahead, rising a hundred feet above the surface. Seconds later the *Titanic* rammed with a solid crunch on the

The iceberg that sank the Titanic. *The British luxury liner hit the killer berg at a speed of about 25 miles per hour.*

forward port side, then climbed the submerged iceberg, supposedly tearing out the forward end of the ship below the waterline. The sound was so muffled that no one was frightened. After a few minutes, the more curious passengers, in a happy mood, drifted on deck to look around and reach over the bow rail to touch the iceberg. They were unaware of a second danger: a fire that had broken out in the coal bunkers before leaving Southampton was still not extinguished. At 12:25 A.M., after having the damage assessed, Captain E. J. Smith ordered all persons assembled on the upper deck. With everyone in good spirits, this was accomplished in fifteen minutes. Passengers were informed of what had happened and of the captain's decision to abandon ship. There was no dissension or panic until at 12:50 A.M. Chief Officer William Murdock ordered: "Crews to the boats! Women and children first."

Cries of anguish were heard everywhere. Wives refused to leave their husbands. Crewmen began to grab women at random, shoving them forcibly into lifeboats. The seriousness of the situation struck home. Husbands cooperated, literally tossing women and children into the boats. By 2:00 A.M. all lifeboats were on the water.

Those in the lifeboats could see that the Titanic had sunk twenty-five feet to thirty feet, and its stern was out of the water. Lifeboat crews rowed furiously toward safety. A mile from the wounded liner survivors watched the Titanic break in two, the forward half slipping beneath the surface. For a moment the rear half righted itself, then there was an explosion and it too began to sink in the icy waters. Survivors later reported they could hear the ship's string orchestra playing as the huge aft section disappeared.

Many ships had picked up the Titanic's SOS signal: "Have struck iceberg. Badly damaged. Rush aid." The Carpathia arrived at the scene about 4:00 A.M. and took on board as many shocked and dazed survivors as it could find, then headed for New York.

Harold Bride, the Titanic's telegraph operator, reported that it was only by accident that the ship's radio was operational. It had gone out on Sunday, and he had managed to repair it just hours before the tragedy. Other survivors reported they had heard gunshots. Several told a story about crew members who were trying to get aboard lifeboats being shot. It was also said that Captain Smith shot himself before the Titanic went down. Later, when surviving crew members were questioned, they gave no credence to either story. The Carpathia, with 700 survivors aboard, arrived in New York at 9:00 A.M. on April 18.

Aftermath: Even hindsight isn't infallible in trying to pinpoint the cause of a disaster. After-the-fact experts agreed that the Titanic's captain, E. J. Smith, must have known of iceberg danger at least an hour before the disaster, yet there were no orders given to reduce speed. The weather was clear and cold, with excellent visibility. Apparently, to achieve a record crossing was very important. The captain, passengers, and crew firmly believed the Titanic's publicity, that it was unsinkable. All were afflicted with the "full speed ahead" euphoria. What could possibly happen to an unsinkable ship?

On July 30, 1912, the seventy-four-page report of the Court of Inquiry, held in London's Scottish Drill Hall, stated the following: "The Court, having carefully inquired into the circumstances of the above-mentioned shipping casualty, finds, for the reasons appearing in the annex hereto, that the loss of said ship was due to collision with an iceberg, brought about by the excessive speed at which the ship was being navigated." Nothing was said of the fact that the Titanic, capable of carrying 3,500 passengers and crew members, had lifeboats for a total of only 1,178.

In 1985 a joint American-French expedition, led by Dr. Robert Ballard of the Woods Hole Oceanographic Institution, discovered the Titanic lying in 13,000 feet of water in the North Atlantic. The two pieces of the ship were standing upright, 2,000 feet apart. In later expeditions, hundreds of artifacts were pulled from the water. And numerous photographs taken of the sunken liner have enabled researchers to study the disaster.

Photographs of the Titanic show no evidence of a huge gash in the ship's hull. The gash, supposedly caused by hitting the iceberg, has long been cited as the cause of the sinking. However, in 1993 a team of naval architects and marine engineers put forth a new theory. According to their analysis, the ship's hull was made of low-grade steel plates that fractured upon impact with the iceberg. The steel, which today would be considered substandard, was prone to brittle fractures when subjected to cold temperatures. The study concluded that better construction techniques and "a better quality of steel plate might have averted her loss or resulted in an even slower rate of flooding that may have saved more passengers and crew."

—F.M.W.

THE SINKING OF THE *LUSITANIA*

Prior to the involvement of the United States in World War I, the Lusitania, a great sleek grey-hound of the seas, was torpedoed and sunk by a German submarine. The tragedy happened so quickly that escape from the mortally wounded luxury liner was all but impossible.

When: Shortly after 2:00 P.M. on May 7, 1915.

Where: In the Celtic Sea, thirteen miles south of Old Head of Kinsale, Ireland.

The Loss: 1,195 passengers and crew members. Most of the victims were British; however, among the dead were 123 Americans. The 31,950-ton floating palace had cost an estimated $10 million.

The Disaster: The ill-fated *Lusitania* was cursed with problems from the time Cunard directors and the British Admiralty gave their specifications to designer Leonard Peskett. It was to be the fastest ship on the seas, carry 2,000 passengers plus a crew of 800, and cruise at twenty-four knots. Its huge engines—capable of developing 68,000 horsepower—and the four boiler rooms, containing twenty-five boilers and complicated controls, must all be fitted below a narrow waterline beam of 88 feet by 760 feet, leaving space for longitudinal watertight compartments along each side. This design left no place for fuel—the 6,600 tons of coal needed to power the *Lusitania* between Liverpool and New York.

Its watertight longitudinal compartments were transformed into coal bunkers, an expedient that would not be acceptable today. On top of this unstable power pack, Peskett added six decks, making the *Lusitania* taller than any other ship in use. On May 12, 1913, the giant liner went into dry dock to be armed with twelve guns. On August 4, England declared war on Germany; a month later, the *Lusitania* was registered as an armed auxiliary cruiser, yet it continued to carry passengers.

On the fateful voyage from New York to Liverpool, the *Lusitania*'s cargo was almost entirely contraband: 1,248 cases (fifty-one tons) of three-inch-diameter shrapnel shells, 1,639 copper ingots, 76 cases of brass rods, and 4,927 boxes of .303 caliber cartridges (1,000 rounds per box) that weighed over ten tons—in all, twenty-four pages of manifest, of which only one page was shown to obtain "clearance to sail."

On the morning of May 7, 1915, the *Lusitania*, heavily laden with passengers and cargo, was nearing the coast of Ireland. Captain William Turner expected momentary contact with his navy escort ship, the *Juno*. He had not been informed that the Admiralty had canceled the escort mission on May 5. Twelve years later British Commodore Joseph Kenworthy would write in his book *The Freedom of the Seas:* "The *Lusitania*, steaming at half speed straight through the submarine cruising ground of the Irish coast, was deliberately sent."

On May 6, after several British ships had been torpedoed, Vice-Admiral Charles Coke, at Queenstown, was forbidden to initiate retaliatory action or to send any messages via radio, but he chose to disregard orders. At 7:00 P.M. he sent a warning to Captain Turner: "Submarines active off south coast of Ireland." Though Turner's orders would not allow a deviation in his course, he did reduce his speed, and warned his passengers of danger. At 11:02 A.M. on the seventh, Vice-Admiral Coke sent a coded twelve-word message to the tug *Hellespont* to come to Queenstown immediately. Turner intercepted this message and decided to divert the *Lusitania* to Queenstown, twenty-five miles from his position thirteen miles off Old Head of Kinsale. The British Admiralty later denied that such a message was sent, but there is a certified copy of it in the naval station at Valentia.

At approximately 1:30 P.M. Walter Schwieger, commander of the German submarine *U-20*, satisfied with his toll of British shipping near Queenstown, was about to head for Germany with his last three torpedoes when he sighted the smoke of the *Lusitania* and changed course to intercept it. About 2:10 P.M. he fired a bow shot from 700 meters. Turner saw the torpedo approach before it struck the starboard side directly behind the bridge. There was a tremendous explosion. The great liner listed fifteen degrees. Then there was a second explosion, louder than the first. The bridge was demolished and the big ship stopped dead, its stern out of the water. Slowly it began to nose under to starboard.

The *Lusitania* had left New York with a shortage of engine-room crewmen and able seamen. Now there weren't enough seamen to man the forty-eight seventy-passenger lifeboats. Absolute panic reigned. There was no time and nothing worked right. Launching davits were frozen. Many of the twenty-six collapsible canvas lifeboats, stored beneath the twenty-two two-and-a-half-ton wooden boats, could not be lowered easily due to the fifteen-degree list. When the heavier boats were lowered, both collapsible boats and passengers were crushed against the hull. On the port side, lifeboats plunged into the sea. Within eighteen minutes, the luxury liner had settled under 300 feet of water. Afterward only scattered lifeboats could be seen floating on the ocean's surface. There were 764 survivors.

Aftermath: An inquiry in London produced one cargo manifest. In the United States a second cargo manifest was produced, and then the Cunard Lines produced a third manifest. All were different. Franklin D. Roosevelt found a fourth manifest in the papers of Woodrow Wilson. This fourth manifest, the carbon copy of the one that went down with the *Lusitania*, verified that the cargo was contraband. While the German submarine fired only one torpedo, there were two explosions onboard the *Lusitania*. It is generally believed that the second blast was caused when the ammunition ignited or when the giant boilers burst. Another plausible explanation is that the torpedo hit the coal bunkers, then almost empty, and that the large amount of leftover, and very volatile, coal dust exploded.

Years later it was reported that at least one crewman on the German submarine refused to take part in the attack on the *Lusitania*. His name was Charles Voegele, and his job was to fire the torpedo. He disobeyed orders, saying he would not fire on a ship carrying women and children. For his insubordination, Voegele was court-martialed and sentenced to three years in prison.

—F.M.W.

THE WORLDWIDE INFLUENZA EPIDEMIC

The worldwide influenza epidemic lasted just under a year, and before it had run its course, more than a billion people had been infected, including 25 million Americans. As it raced to every corner of the globe, it claimed the lives of millions of people, without regard to age, class, or ethnic origin. According to historian Alfred W. Crosby, author of *America's Forgotten Pandemic*: "Nothing else—no infection, no war, no famine—has ever killed so many in as short a period."

When: 1918 to 1919.

Where: Fort Riley, Kansas, then the world.

The Loss: More than 30 million people died.

The Disaster: The first outbreak of the flu occurred at Fort Riley, Kansas, in March 1918, when a soldier complained of fever, muscle aches, and a sore throat. Seven days later more than 500 soldiers at Fort Riley were sick, and the flu had spread to other nearby army camps. Doctors weren't worried, since the flu seemed rather mild and influenza wasn't high on the list of deadly diseases. World War I was in high gear and the military was far more concerned with getting American soldiers to the battlefields, particularly in France.

When American soldiers landed in France in the spring and summer of 1918, they brought the flu with them. Like wildfire, it spread through Europe, Asia, South America—even to remote islands in the South Pacific. The disease was called Flanders grippe in Great Britain, *Blitz Katarrh* in Germany, wrestler's fever in Japan, "the disease of the wind" in Persia. Because Spain was especially hard hit, many countries of the world mistakenly blamed the flu outbreak on Spain, calling the sickness "the Spanish influenza."

The flu seemed to strike in three waves, becoming more deadly with each assault. Victims complained of coughing, dizziness, muscular aches, and fever. Lung infections were common and many died from pneumonia. Since a single sneeze could project more than 85 million bacteria, the flu spread unchecked. Doctors could offer no cure, and many were finding it hard to believe that so many people were dying from the flu. Thus, doctors frequently misdiagnosed the flu as typhoid fever, cholera, scarlet fever—even appendicitis. Worldwide, hospitals were over-flowing and makeshift medical facilities had to be set up. Churches, schools, prisons, hotels, convents, post offices, and dance halls were quickly transformed to accommodate the massive flow of sick people.

In many countries the epidemic caused businesses and transportation systems to shut down owing to the lack of able-bodied staff. Food supplies were diminished as farms lay neglected. In Spain, many government offices were closed; in New Zealand, parliament had to be suspended; in England, more than a thousand German soldiers died in one prison camp. The entire population of one port city in Nigeria was hit with the flu, carried into the city by less than ten passengers on an arriving ship.

In the United States, the flu was taking its toll on civilians as well as soldiers. In the fall of 1918, 20 percent of all American soldiers stationed in the United States were sick. East Coast cities were the first to suffer, but the flu rapidly spread westward. In Philadelphia the death rate was 700 percent above normal. In Boston, hospitals were forced to house twenty patients to a room. In California one-third of the prisoners at San Quentin were afflicted. Because of the war, there was a shortage of doctors throughout the country; almost one-third of the nation's 140,000 doctors had enlisted.

In an attempt to cure the disease, Americans resorted to a great variety of home remedies. Some people covered themselves with bacon fat, while others gargled with salt water or lime juice. Some took very cold baths and others took very hot baths. Some wore small bags of camphor around their necks; some wore vinegar packs around their stomachs. They inhaled eucalyptus oil, ate red-pepper sandwiches, and sipped small amounts of strychnine. Those who were superstitious carried charms, and some put cucumber slices around their ankles to ward off the disease.

Americans lined up to be inoculated with an array of vaccines, but none of them worked. It was obvious that preventive measures were necessary, and people across the country began to wear antiflu masks. In some cities it was against the law to board a bus or trolley without a mask. Laws against coughing, sneezing, shaking hands, and spitting were enacted. In New

York City hundreds of people were arrested for spitting on "Spitless Sunday." Sales of alcohol and other disinfectants soared as people sanitized everything from telephones to buses and drinking fountains.

The surgeon general of the United States, Rupert Blue, asked Americans to refrain from participating in large public gatherings like parades and war rallies. At first Blue's request was ignored, but as the flu epidemic continued, people began to pay attention. Eventually, theaters and libraries, saloons and schools, were closed. Even churches were empty on Sundays. Many businesses went on half-day work schedules.

Despite the devastating effects of the epidemic, Americans pitched in to help one another and most tried to maintain some sense of humor. From coast to coast, children recited the jingle: "I had a little bird and its name was Enza. I opened the door and in-flew-Enza." People joked about their home remedies and poked fun at a Boston doctor who stated that "influenza is caused chiefly by excessive clothing." A newly-wed couple in San Francisco told friends that while making love they wore nothing but their antiflu masks.

Before the flu epidemic ended, it had affected people from all walks of life. King George V of Great Britain took to his bed, as did King Alfonso XIII of Spain and the U.S. assistant secretary of the navy, Franklin D. Roosevelt. American writer Katherine Anne Porter almost died from the flu and later wrote about the epidemic in *Pale Horse, Pale Rider*. In 1919, when world leaders met at the Paris Peace Conference to enact a treaty to end World War I, three of the main negotiators—British prime minister David Lloyd George, French premier Georges Clemenceau, and U.S. president Woodrow Wilson—were sick. While Lloyd George and Clemenceau seemed to be suffering from bad colds, Wilson had a severe case of the flu with a high fever and coughing spasms. It's speculated that Wilson's illness may have impaired his bargaining skills.

By the spring of 1919 the worldwide epidemic had subsided as mysteriously as it had erupted. Of all countries, India suffered the worst loss—12 million dead. In the United States, deaths were estimated at more than 550,000.

Aftermath: Historians and medical researchers who have studied the 1918 influenza epidemic say that it was unique because it spread so quickly and to so many parts of the world. In addition, they are puzzled by the fact that the majority of people who died were between the ages of twenty and forty, usually an age group that is best able to fight off the flu.

Not all historians believe that the epidemic started in the United States. Some believe it was brought into France by Chinese laborers or Russian soldiers, while others say it started in France when armies from different countries intermingled. Yet another group of researchers say that it is impossible to accurately determine the flu's point of origin. Most researchers, however, agree that the Spanish influenza did not start in Spain.

—C.O.M.

THE RUSSIAN FAMINE OF 1921

The rains had been meager in 1920 and nonexistent during the early months of the following year. By the spring of 1921, Russia's Bolshevik leaders knew that the prolonged drought was

Victims of the Russian famine of 1921 were reduced to cannibalism.

producing famine in the Volga region. At first the authorities tried to prevent word of the disaster from reaching the outside world. But by summer, newspapers in Western Europe were running accounts of peasants attempting to survive by eating grass, leaves, bark, and clay. Reports also told of Moscow residents fainting in the streets from hunger, as well as tales of cannibalism in the famine-affected area. Between 10 million and 30 million Russians were starving, and the Communist regime knew that it faced a difficult choice: issue a humiliating call for help or risk being overthrown. In August 1921 the call went out.

When: Spring 1921 through summer 1922.
Where: The Volga region of Russia, in the steppes to the south and east of Moscow.
The Loss: Between 2 million and 5 million lives.
The Disaster: Famine was no stranger to Russia. Starvation had stalked the land more than a

hundred times during the previous millennium. And while severe drought often precipitated the crises, culpability for mass death usually lay at the feet of the authorities—be they czars or, in this case, Communists.

V. I. Lenin and his Bolsheviks had been in power for less than four years when, in the summer of 1921, the continuing drought made a desert of a million square miles of farmland in the Volga River valley. Those years since the Russian Revolution had witnessed a terrible civil war between Lenin's Communist "Reds" and the counterrevolutionary "Whites." During the war, Lenin had issued several decrees in the name of "War Communism," decrees designed to place all the nation's resources under government control as it fought for survival. One decree in May 1918 authorized the Commissariat of Food to seize "surplus" peasant grain supplies; less than a year later, in January 1919, another decree gave the state power to "requisition" food supplies even if peasants were left with less than they needed to survive. Between 15 and 20 percent of the Russian agricultural output was requisitioned in 1919, about 30 percent in 1920. The peasants would face the onset of drought without a life-sustaining supply of grain from previous harvests.

Peasants resisted the requisition of their crops, leading to armed clashes with the Bolsheviks. As many as 2 million Russian men and women perished in what was called the Peasant War, culminating in the revolt of the Kronstadt naval base in March 1921. The Kronstadt rebels, siding with the peasants against the Bolsheviks, demanded an end to crop requisitions. Communist forces attacked the base, conquered it after two days of vicious fighting, and either executed or banished to concentration camps thousands of sailors taken prisoner. Lenin, realizing the extent of opposition to his regime, acknowledged in private: "We are barely holding on."

The crop requisition policy started producing spot famines even before drought brought on mass starvation. The Peasant War, a direct result of the requisition policy, turned millions of small farmers into refugees as they fled from homes and fields to escape the slaughter. Those who remained had little incentive to grow— only to have the government seize—bumper crops. As a result, once-productive fields went untended. The total acreage in cultivation declined from 214 million in 1916 to just 133 million in 1922. By 1921 the Russian economy was on the edge of full-scale collapse.

Lenin then made a strategic retreat. Early in 1921 he called off War Communism and replaced it with the New Economic Policy (NEP). Instead of forced crop requisitions, the government would impose only a moderate grain tax. But the NEP came too late for the peasants of the Volga region. The NEP could not replace their food reserves. When the drought struck, famine followed quickly in its wake.

The Central Committee of the Communist Party urged peasants not to flee, arguing that leaving the land would only compound the disaster. But in July 1921, the committee confessed that it was unable to alleviate the mass starvation. In early August the government finally made a public statement: "The starving regions have no grain stocks with which to relieve the famine, and shipments from other provinces can be only extremely limited. . . . The Soviet government welcomes the help of all providing it does not involve political considerations."

Yet it was not until Russian author Maksim Gorky appealed for foreign aid that an international rescue mission was launched. In late August the American Relief Administration (ARA)—headed by U.S. secretary of commerce (and future president) Herbert Hoover—started shipping food to Russia. At its peak, the ARA would feed more than 10 million Russians; nearly 2 million more would be saved from starvation by other relief organizations.

A member of one of those organizations, the International Committee for Russian Relief, reported that hunger-crazed peasants had taken to eating their own children, sisters, or brothers. Other observers confirmed that cannibalism was common in the Volga region. Relief workers gave up buying cheap sausages when some were discovered to contain human flesh.

Even worse, horses and cats were being slaughtered and consumed. The elimination of horses meant that fields could not be prepared for new crops; the destruction of cats would result in greater incidence of rat-borne diseases. As terrible as cannibalism was, it did not exacerbate the famine and threaten mass annihilation, as did the killing of horses and cats. An English Quaker described a peasant village in the fall of 1921:

> I saw in practically every home benches covered with birch or lime leaves. These are dried, pounded, mixed with acorns, some dirt and water, and then baked into a substance which they call bread, but which looks and smells like baked manure. The children cannot digest this food and they die. There are practically no babies and those that survive look ghastly. The mothers have no milk and pray that death may come quickly. Slow starvation is too painful. All the children have distended stomachs. . . . According to Government figures, ninety percent of the children between the ages of one and three have already died from the famine.

As desperate as the situation was, Kremlin leaders viewed relief efforts—especially those of Hoover's ARA—with deep suspicion. While it was clear that millions of Russians survived the famine only as a consequence of American intervention, Joseph Stalin expressed the fears of many top Bolsheviks when he warned that "the trading and all other sorts of missions and associations that are now pouring into Russia, trading with her and aiding her, are at the same time the most efficient spy agencies of the world bourgeoisie."

Ironically, it was the ARA's enormous success in defeating what the League of Nations labeled the worst famine in the history of modern Europe that secured the regime Stalin would shortly control. As the crisis came to an end in 1923, the Soviet government was able to stabi-

lize its authority. A huge harvest that year ended the food shortage, the economy recovered, and the reform measures of the NEP had a chance to take effect. Perhaps the most ardent anti-Communist in America, Herbert Hoover, had contributed greatly to bolstering the Bolshevik regime.

Yet, despite the heroic relief efforts, the Russian famine of 1921–22 claimed the lives of nearly 5 million people. More Russians died because of Leninist agricultural policies and the massive drought than had died during all of World War I.

—J.L.K.

THE CHINESE FLOOD OF 1938

The 4,000 years of recorded Chinese history include many references about the flooding of the Huang He, which is known in the West as the Yellow River. Running for approximately 3,400 miles, it's the sixth-longest river in the world. Nearly a mile wide at some locations, the Yellow River drains an area of more than 400,000 square miles and is considered the cause of more human casualties than any other of all the earth's great natural features.

Nature, however, hasn't been the only power to unleash the enormous fury of a Yellow River flood. During World War II, as Japan's conquering armies swarmed through China, the river's floodwaters were set free in a combined and unparalleled disaster. The great flood of 1938 was due to a deliberate act of man that manipulated a sometimes capricious, and often cruel, force of nature.

When: June 6 to June 8, 1938.

Where: The Yellow River at Huayuan (near Zhengzhou) in northern China.

The Loss: An estimated half million dead; 6 million rendered homeless.

The Disaster: The Japanese invasion of the Chinese mainland had penetrated deep into central China by the spring of 1938. With the soldiers of the Rising Sun on the verge of capturing Kaifeng, an ancient capital city, Chiang Kai-shek (the leader of the Nationalists) decided to enlist the power of the snowmelt-engorged Yellow River in the defense of China.

His plan was to destroy the river's dikes above Zhengzhou. Peasants living in the river's floodplain were offered money to evacuate. Adults received the equivalent of $1.77 and children 71¢ apiece to abandon their farms and homes. Unimpressed, most people stayed. Engineers of the Fifty-third Corps then exploded and dug through the ancient, thirty-two-foot-wide levees, which were already hard-pressed to contain the swollen river.

The Yellow River churned over its banks,

spread out over an estimated 9,000 square miles, and destroyed more than 4,000 villages. Approximately a half million Chinese perished in the flood, 6 million were rendered homeless, and untold numbers (often reported to be in the hundreds of thousands) died as a result of the famine that ensued when the crops were lost. The floodwaters managed to devastate the principal railroad line in the region, and a massive lake, with a 300-square-mile core that ran as deep as ten feet, was formed.

In addition to unleashing the flood, the Nationalist Army loaded a fleet of junks with trees, rocks, and cement and sank them to the river's bottom. The furious currents carried this massive heap as far as 135 miles downriver, where they jammed to cause a barrier to Japanese military movement. The breaks in the dike grew to be as wide as 500 feet, and the waters of the Yellow River continued to seek out low ground to such an extent that more than 100,000 Chinese found themselves marooned on pockets of high ground and faced with starvation.

The Japanese initially reacted by trying to restore the dikes, using both their soldiers and Chinese peasants as laborers. The challenge was hopeless as it was, and in addition the Nationalist Army took to shooting at repair crews. Within two weeks of the flood's inception, the Nationalists reported recapturing two cities as the heavily mechanized Japanese forces found themselves entrenched on mud-covered highways and in muddy fields. The flood contributed to the creation of a stalemate between the Chinese and the Japanese, and the shores that its runoff eventually established served as a kind of demarcation line between the two enemy forces for the remainder of the war.

Aftermath: No substantial effort was made to restore the dikes of the Yellow River until the surrender of the Japanese, seven years after the flood. During this time the river changed its course so that it no longer emptied into the sea north of the Shantung Peninsula—it now emptied into the sea 250 miles to the south, via the Huai River. A considerable volume of the floodwaters eventually drained into the Yangtze River. When peace finally came, more than 2 million acres of once-productive farmland remained water soaked.

The United Nations helped the Nationalists to restore the Yellow River to its preflood course in 1947. Three years later, with the Communists now in power, Chairman Mao Zedong embarked on a colossal campaign to bring flood control to the Yellow River valley. Up to 400,000 peasants labored to rebuild and improve 1,100 miles of dikes and put an end to the river's potential for creating cataclysm.

However, the storm of April 23, 1969, proved, once again, that nature can never fully be tamed. The storm caused the sea to surge twenty feet high as it struck a forty-five-mile length of coastline. Flood tides swept up the Yellow River for thirteen miles. Though the Chinese government did not release casualty counts, the Japanese press estimated that several hundred thousand lives were lost in this flood's onslaught.

—R.N.K.

THE DESTRUCTION OF THE *HINDENBURG*

Other than the storms that delayed its arrival by more than ten hours, the flight of the zeppelin *Hindenburg*, from Frankfurt, Germany, to Lakehurst, New Jersey, was uneventful and routine. Since 1928 at least 32,000 passengers had flown a total of more than 100,000 miles in German zeppelins without a single accident.

Then in the spring of 1937, on its arrival at Lakehurst, the big silver ship once again dropped its mooring lines to the ground. Navy and civilian workers grabbed them to guide the *Hindenburg* to its mooring mast.

As newsmen clicked their camera shutters and radio commentators recorded the arrival for

The Hindenburg *catches fire upon arrival at Lakehurst, New Jersey, May 6, 1937.*

a later broadcast, there was a puff of smoke at the zeppelin's stern, then a bigger one. The great *Hindenburg* was afire. Shortly thereafter, there was an explosion of hydrogen gas. In thirty-four seconds the graceful giant of the skies was a flaming funeral pyre.

When: At 7:25 P.M. on May 6, 1937.

Where: The Naval Air Station at Lakehurst, New Jersey.

The Loss: Fifteen passengers, twenty crewmen, and one line-handler were killed. The *Hindenburg*, last of the great zeppelins, had cost more than $5 million.

The Disaster: The *Hindenburg*, largest zeppelin in the world, more than 800 feet long, had sixteen gas bags containing a total of 7.2 million cubic feet of explosive hydrogen gas. Its four V-16 diesel engines with twenty-foot, four-bladed props developed 5,000 horsepower and drove the ship silently and vibrationlessly at a speed of up to eighty-four miles per hour. There were sleeping compartments with baths for fifty passengers and a crew of thirty, plus a first-class dining room, complete with china, fine linen, and real silverware. The ship even had a wine cellar and a lounge with a grand piano. The cost of a ticket aboard the luxury liner was $400.

Catwalks traversed the ship within its framework of sixteen ten-story-high rings and thirty-six longitudinal girders. Twenty-five fuel tanks carried 137,500 pounds of fuel to give the *Hindenburg* a 10,000-mile cruising range. Commissioned in March 1936, the LZ-129 had made ten round-trips between Germany and the United States. The airship, designed to use nonexplosive helium, was filled with hydrogen gas. The only source for helium was the United States, and the cost for more than 7 million cubic feet would have run about $600,000. The expense was unnecessary according to the Deutsche Zeppelin-Reederei Company, operators of the Graf Zeppelin passenger lines. Hydrogen was perfectly safe when handled by experts, and who were more expert than the Germans?

On the day it exploded, the *Hindenburg* was ten hours late on its arrival at Lakehurst, and rain, prevailing winds, and lightning prevented immediate landing. After the airship had cruised about for several hours, weather conditions changed and at 7:10 P.M. the luxury liner was 200 feet over the Naval Air Station. Passengers had collected their personal effects and were ready to disembark. Mooring lines were dropped. Twelve crewmen were at the nose ready to couple up. On the ground, 92 navy men and 139 civilians were grabbing lines to guide the LZ-129 to its mooring mast. At 7:25 the mooring was just minutes from being completed. Herbert Morrison of radio station WLS was recording the activity of mooring. Suddenly the commonplace became tragedy.

He shouted into his microphone: "It's burst into flames! Get out of the way, please, oh my, this is terrible, oh my, get out of the way, please! It's burning, bursting into flames and is falling on the mooring mast and all the folks, we—this is one of the worst catastrophes in the world! It's a terrific sight. Oh, the humanity and all the passengers!" Then the reporter burst into tears.

Seventy-seven hours out of Frankfurt, something had ignited the hydrogen gas. There was panic aboard the *Hindenburg*. Passengers broke out gondola windows to jump a hundred feet to their deaths. Then there was a loud, second explosion. In thirty-four seconds the zeppelin lay burning on the ground. Of those who managed to escape, badly burned, several died shortly thereafter. Of the ninety-seven people on board, thirty-five died horribly. There were sixty-two survivors.

Aftermath: The real cause of the disaster may never be known. The most widely accepted theory is that a spark was generated from the *Hindenburg's* wet outer shell and wet landing lines to the grounded structure, and the static electricity ignited hydrogen that had probably escaped from a ruptured gas bag. However, another theory suggested that the disaster was an act of sabotage intended to discredit Hitler and the Nazis. No evidence of sabotage was ever produced and both the German government and the U.S. Department of Commerce declared that the explosion was a result of natural causes.

Following the destruction of the *Hindenburg*, the German government made a concerted effort to get the United States to supply helium for use in German airships. Since the United States was already doing business with Nazi Germany and the need to replace the hydrogen in airships with helium was painfully obvious, the U.S. government agreed. A limited amount of helium was to be sold to the Germans, and the Munitions Control Board was set up to make sure that the helium would never be used for military purposes. However, one member of the board, Secretary of the Interior Harold L. Ickes, stubbornly and vehemently opposed, and stopped, the sale. Ickes subsequently told the Germans that the deal fell through "because your Hitler is preparing for war." The decision turned out to be politically correct, since ships like the *Hindenburg*, which had large swastikas on its vertical fins, had become symbolic of Nazi Germany.

The tragedy of the *Hindenburg* marked the end of the era of zeppelin travel. Airplanes were being developed, and though they carried fewer passengers and less freight, they were much faster. It was hoped that someday airplanes might even carry passengers across the ocean.

—F.M.W. and C.O.M.

THE LIMA SOCCER RIOT

More than 45,000 soccer fans were jammed into National Stadium in Lima, Peru, for a pre-Olympics qualifying match between Peru and Argentina. The great majority of spectators were Peruvians who passionately wanted their team to garner a place in the upcoming soccer finals in Tokyo. The unbridled enthusiasm of the crowd was short-lived, however, as the soccer match turned into one of the most violent and bizarre events in sports history.

When: March 24, 1964.

Where: Lima, Peru.

The Loss: 328 persons killed and more than 500 injured.

The Disaster: Argentina led 1–0, but with less than five minutes to play, Peruvian winger Lobaton scored to tie the game. However, the Uruguayan referee, Angel Eduardo Payos, nullified the goal because of rough play by the Peruvians. While the crowd booed its disapproval, a well-known fan, Matias Rojas, raced onto the playing field. Nicknamed "the Bomb," Rojas headed straight for the referee but was apprehended by police.

As the fans watched Rojas being arrested and dragged away, they became more incensed. Then Payos ordered the game suspended, claiming, with understandable justification, that police protection on the field was inadequate. The crazed crowd surged onto the field while the police hustled Payos and the players to safety. Before long, mounted police appeared and began herding the rioters toward the exits, many of which were, unfortunately, locked. Tear-gas grenades were fired by the police, while the Peruvian soccer fans responded by throwing stones and bottles and setting part of the stadium on fire.

As the fans surged toward the locked exits, many were trampled to death or suffocated as hundreds of bodies were pressed together in an attempt to escape. People at the front of the pack screamed at the others to turn back but the warnings went unheeded. One injured man held his eighteen-month-old daughter over his head to protect her, but he dropped her after someone tripped him and he lost his balance.

The child, like many others, was crushed against one of the iron exit doors. The dead and injured seemed to be everywhere, often lying on top of one another.

After the exit gates were finally opened, the riot continued in the streets for another three hours. The mob broke storefront windows, wrecked buses and cars, and set fire to a tire factory. Demonstrators marched to the National Palace demanding an end to police brutality and the declaration of a tie in the match with Argentina. Neither demand was met.

As the tragic day came to an end, makeshift morgues were set up on the lawns of nearby hospitals. Panicked relatives of the victims poured into hospitals trying to learn the fate of their loved ones. While most of the victims had been trampled to death, at least four persons were shot by police bullets.

Aftermath: The trouble continued the next day when another mob broke into the stadium and stole trophies from the practice rooms. A student demonstration called for the ouster of the entire Peruvian cabinet. The government responded by declaring a state of emergency throughout Peru and suspended certain constitutional rights for a period of thirty days, until an investigation of the riot could be completed. The president of Peru proclaimed that the country would observe a seven-day period of mourning for the victims. In addition, the government paid for the funerals of the victims and provided monetary compensation to their families.

Three days after the tragedy, the police arrested fifty people who had taken part in the riots. Some were charged with inciting violence; others were charged with robbing the victims as they lay dead or injured on the field. In its final analysis of the riot, the government unconvincingly claimed it had been caused by "left-wing extremists."

As for the sports outcome—Argentina went on to the Olympics in Tokyo but the team lost both of its matches.

—D.W.

TANGSHAN: MODERN HISTORY'S MOST DEVASTATING EARTHQUAKE

On the night of July 27, 1976, a million people in the flourishing but heavily polluted northern Chinese industrial and mining center of Tangshan quietly went to bed. By morning a quarter of them were dead and their city was rubble. What destroyed Tangshan was one of the most devastating earthquakes in recorded history. Several hours before daybreak, lightning flashed ominously across the sky, then the ground began vibrating with small but rapid ripples. Almost immediately, the earth started wrenching itself through a sequence of violent motions, while simultaneously jolting up and down. Just ten seconds of this chaotic movement leveled Tangshan. By daybreak a pall of dust covered the ruined city and the screams of the trapped and injured filled the air.

When: Tuesday, July 28, 1976, 3:42 A.M.

Where: Tangshan in northeastern China.

The Loss: The official death toll is 242,419, including one out of every eight people in Tangshan itself; unofficial estimates run as high as 800,000. Sixteen percent of the victims were killed instantly by falling beams, bricks, walls, and other objects. Another 30 to 40 percent suffocated to death in the dust caused by the original earthquake and by a second one at 6:45 P.M. Another 20 to 30 percent of the victims died of thirst, hunger, or exhaustion before help could reach them. More than 160,000 people were seriously injured and several hundred thousand more received minor injuries. More than 90 percent of Tangshan's 680,000 buildings were badly damaged or destroyed; more than a hundred bridges collapsed; and more than 300 reservoirs were damaged. Every basic city service was ruined.

The Disaster: The modern world has felt earthquakes registering higher on the Richter scale than the Tangshan quake's 7.8. None, however, has hit such a heavily populated region and done so much damage to life and property. There is, in fact, no human scale on which to measure the devastation that this earthquake wrought. Even the two atomic bombs dropped on Japan during World War II destroyed fewer buildings and killed fewer people. Tangshan's earthquake rocked a region inhabited by 15 million people that encompasses Tangshan, Beijing, and Tianjing. Severe jolts were felt as much as a hundred miles away in Beijing. Australian premier Gough Whitlam, who happened to be in nearby Tianjing during the quake, described seeing his nine-story hotel "split down the middle."

A crucial reason for the severity of Tangshan's quake was the region's unusual geology. The quake's hypocenter was directly under Tangshan, whose naturally unstable land was honeycombed with coal mines. When the first tremor hit this fragile formation, it generated a medley of violent motions. The surface not only palpitated up and down, it twisted wildly—after starting to lurch from east to south, it switched to lurch in the opposite direction, then changed ninety degrees to reel from east to north, and finally, in a direction opposite that. A man who happened to be exercising in a park described feeling as if he were in a giant sieve being sifted. Throughout the city, people who were outside were knocked off their feet and could only watch helplessly as buildings collapsed around them.

Although the first tremor lasted less than ten seconds, it was long enough to bring down more than 93 percent of Tangshan's residential buildings and more than three-quarters of its industrial buildings. As many as 80 percent of its residents were buried in rubble. Since the quake also knocked out electrical power, the city was left in darkness and rescue efforts were impossible until dawn a few hours later. Amazingly, several hundred thousand people dug themselves out and turned their attention to helping others. After daybreak, rescue work began in earnest. New crises quickly presented themselves, however. So complete was the city's destruction that food, water, medical supplies, and other necessities were unobtainable. Further, the transportation system had collapsed. All the railways and roads leading out of Tangshan were closed down and even telephone communication with the outside world was cut off for six hours. In fact, it was twelve hours before the central government authorities learned—from a coal miner, Li Yulin, who had driven six hours in an ambulance to reach Beijing—that Tangshan had been leveled.

Once the central government in Beijing got word of Tangshan's devastation, it mobilized a national relief effort and sent more than 100,000 troops, 20,000 medical workers, and 30,000 technical relief workers to Tangshan. During the first two days, the massive convergence of relief workers on the city caused a monumental traffic jam on the city's crippled roads. Meanwhile, a second quake—a 7.1—had hit the city fifteen hours after the first. This quake brought down more buildings and raised a new pall of dust that suffocated thousands of people still trapped under debris from the first quake. Fortunately, the absence of natural gas lines in Tangshan kept fire from becoming a serious problem.

In the days that followed, hot, rainy weather aggravated Tangshan's mounting health problems. Disposing of human and animal corpses was a massive undertaking and broken sewage lines made things even worse. As flies, mosquitoes, and bacteria proliferated, increasing numbers of people suffered from dysentery, influenza, typhoid fever, and encephalitis—all health problems that would last for a year.

Aftermath: The long-term costs in human suffering were staggering. In addition to the huge loss of life, the quake left a legacy of massive social dislocation: in Tangshan at least 7,000 entire families were wiped out, more than 4,000 children lost both their parents, about 15,000 married people lost their spouses, and thousands of old people were left without families to care for them. The earthquake also left most of the nation morbidly afraid of earthquakes.

Before Tangshan, China had a long history of devastating earthquakes. In 1556, for example, an earthquake in central China reportedly killed more than 800,000 people. Although traditional Chinese belief sees such natural disasters as mandated by heaven, China's government began fostering research into earthquake prediction after the devastating Xingtai quake of 1966. This research paid off in early 1975 with the successful prediction of a 7.3 quake in Haicheng that saved many lives. This was hailed as the world's first scientifically predicted major earthquake. Chinese scientists did not, however, predict the quake that hit Tangshan a year later. After 1976, the Chinese government began instituting stricter earthquake-resistant building standards—particularly around Tangshan, whose vulnerability to seismic activity had not previously been appreciated. The government also poured money into retrofitting older structures.

Although a case was made for abandoning Tangshan as an urban center and distributing its residents and industries elsewhere, the decision to rebuild the city on its original site was made just two months after the earthquake. The rebuilding plans called for cleaner industries, seismically safe structures, broader and straighter roads, and arrangements in the infrastructure to make it possible to respond more quickly to future disasters. By 1985 more than 95 percent of Tangshan's original surviving residents were resettled in the city. By 1995 the population was up to 1.55 million people and Tangshan ranked twenty-third among China's 460 urban centers in the value of its agricultural and industrial production.

According to Chinese tradition, a terrible disaster presages the end of a dynasty or the death of a leader. In fact, China's "Great Helmsman," Mao Zedong, died only six weeks after the Tangshan earthquake.

—R.K.R.

THE COLLISION OF THE JUMBO JETS

The trio of air traffic controllers at Tenerife's Los Rodeos Airport had their hands full that fateful Sunday afternoon in 1977. The single runway and adjacent taxiways were jammed with aircraft, many of which had been diverted from nearby Las Palmas on Grand Canary Island because a bomb had exploded in a passenger terminal and there was a possibility of a second bomb. Matters were complicated by a steadily worsening fog and an airport control tower that had no ground radar to track runway traffic in bad weather. When the crew of a KLM jumbo jet apparently misunderstood instructions from the tower and began an unauthorized takeoff, the fates of hundreds of people were sealed. In the worst disaster in the history of air travel, the KLM aircraft collided with a Pan American 747 that was still on the runway.

When: At 5:07 P.M. on Sunday, March 27, 1977.

Where: On the runway at Los Rodeos Airport, Tenerife, Canary Islands.

The Loss: 583 passengers killed; many of the 61 survivors severely burned and injured; two multi-million-dollar 747s destroyed.

The Disaster: Among the many aircraft diverted to Los Rodeos were KLM flight 4805 from Amsterdam and Pan Am flight 736 from Los Angeles and New York. KLM's Boeing 747 with 248 aboard arrived at 1:38 P.M. and was directed to park at the far end of the runway. Shortly after 2:15 P.M. the Pan Am jumbo jet arrived and was ordered to the same area. As the KLM and Pan Am jets and nine other aircraft awaited clearance for takeoff, the fog rolled in. By 5:00 P.M. pilots could see no more than 1,600 feet down the two-mile runway.

Under such circumstances, there is little margin for error in facilitating the takeoff in swift succession of two 747s. With the taxiway in front of the Los Rodeos terminal blocked to planes the size of the 747s, the control tower instructed the KLM and Pan Am jumbos to backtrack down the runway. KLM 4805 was to backtrack the entire length of the runway, make a 180-degree turn, and wait for further instructions. Pan Am 1736 was to follow and park on the third taxiway to the left. At this point there apparently occurred the first in a series of errors or misunderstandings; the Pan Am jet proceeded toward the fourth taxiway to the left. Although the air traffic controllers apparently thought the Pan Am jet was near taxiway three, rather than heading for number four, they did know it was still on the runway. They would not clear the KLM for takeoff until Pan Am reported clear. The control tower tape reveals the fateful misunderstanding that ensued:

KLM COPILOT: WE ARE NOW AT TAKEOFF.
TOWER TO KLM: OK. STAND BY FOR TAKEOFF CLEARANCE. I WILL CALL YOU.
PAN AM COPILOT: CLIPPER 1736.
TOWER: PAPA ALPHA 1736, REPORT RUNWAY CLEARED.
PAN AM: WE'LL REPORT RUNWAY CLEARED.
CONTROLLER: OK. THANK YOU.

These were the final words exchanged before the KLM 747 attempted to take off. Possibly the KLM captain, premier pilot fifty-one-year-old Jacob Veldhuizen van Zanten, failed to hear the controller's instruction to stand by; possibly van Zanten missed part of Pan Am's message. At any rate, van Zanten, responding as if the

Pan Am jet had already left the runway, released the brakes on his 747 and began his takeoff run.

In the seconds preceding the collision, the Pan Am pilots, still on the runway, saw the KLM's lights in the fog. At first they thought the KLM was merely standing at the end of the runway. Too late they realized that the massive aircraft was bearing down on them. Quickly the Pan Am crew boosted their engines and attempted to swerve to the left. With only seconds to react, the KLM pilot pulled up the nose of his 747 in a desperate effort to clear the Pan Am jet, but time had already run out.

The KLM smashed the Pan Am at midship, shearing the top off, destroying the first-class lounge, and starting a fire. After a second in the air, the KLM returned to the ground and bounced down the runway. Some 500 yards beyond the Pan Am 747, it exploded, killing all 248 on board. Of the passengers and crew on board the Pan Am jumbo, 335 eventually died, while 61 survived.

Heavy fog patches and dense clouds made visibility so bad that the control tower heard explosions but could not see any fire. When fire trucks headed out at top speed, the firemen felt heat radiation before they could actually see any flames. As they fought one fire, they saw a bright light farther away—through a clearing in the fog. At first, the firemen believed the second fire was part of the same plane that had broken off. Upon further inspection, however, they discovered that a second plane was also on fire. It took aproximately eleven hours to extinguish the fires.

Aftermath: The official investigation of the collision was issued at the end of 1978. While it mentioned a lot of contributing factors to the accident—bad weather, poor radio transmissions, language difficulties—the report placed the fundamental cause of the crash on the KLM captain. The captain of the Dutch aircraft had taken off without official clearance. He did not obey the "stand by for takeoff" from the tower. And he did not interrupt takeoff when Pan Am reported that it was still on the runway.

Recordings of communications aboard the KLM flight showed that the KLM captain was not paying strict attention to his job. Or, as the report stated: "The captain seemed a little absent from all that was heard in the cockpit." When the captain was advised by the copilot that they did not have clearance to take off, the captain told the copilot to ask again for clearance, but while the copilot followed orders, the captain opened the throttle and started to take off. In addition, the KLM flight engineer asked the captain if the Pan Am plane was clear of the runway. The captain didn't understand the question, so the engineer asked again, "Is he not clear, that Pan American?" This time the captain gave an emphatic "Yes." Both the copilot and the engineer stopped their objections. Thirteen seconds later, the plane crash occurred.

Also noted in the report was the fact that the KLM captain was under stress because he was concerned about flight time limitations on the KLM crew. Dutch laws were very strict on how may hours KLM employees were allowed to fly in one month, and some employees were close to exceeding the limits. The captain had no power to extend duty time, and breaking the rules could mean fines and imprisonment. The captain, however, was advised that if he departed before a certain time, no laws would be broken.

—S.Fi. and C.O.M.

THE POISON CLOUD OF BHOPAL

Shortly after midnight on a quiet Indian Sunday, a chill wind swept through Bhopal from the northwest, pushing a heavy white cloud whose vapors swirled and oozed through more than twenty square miles of crowded residences. Within minutes, hundreds of thousands of persons were gasping and sputtering as their lungs burned and filled with fluid. With their eyes searing, they blindly tumbled into the streets vomiting and retching. Uncertain which way to run, thousands stampeded wildly, screaming and wailing, stumbling over each other until many dropped from exhaustion, dying where they fell. The lucky few with vehicles took off at breakneck speed, with little regard for those on foot. When police vans rolled into this hell with loudspeakers blaring—"Poisonous gas is spreading! Run for your lives!"—history's worst industrial accident reached its chaotic climax.

When: Monday, December 3, 1984, from 12:45 to 2:30 A.M.

Where: Bhopal, central India.

The Loss: It is estimated that between 6,500 and 16,000 lives had been lost through 1994. Another 20,000 persons were permanently disabled, with more than 200,000 more suffering minor injuries.

The Disaster: When Union Carbide built a modern pesticide plant on the northern outskirts of Bhopal in 1969, its arrival was such a boon to the capital of the impoverished state of Madhya Pradesh that environmental concerns such as its location upwind of populated areas went unnoticed. The plant brought hundreds of jobs to Bhopal, but by the 1980s, competition from cheaper rival pesticides had made it unprofitable. It was also becoming dangerous, thanks to its basic design flaws, cost-cutting measures, and poor worker morale. In 1982 a report of American inspectors on the plant's hazardous conditions was ignored. Two years later, Raj Kumar Keswani was also ignored when he published a series of newspaper articles with unambiguous titles such as "Bhopal on the Mouth of a Volcano."

On the evening of December 2, 1984, plant workers spotted something leaking from a storage tank of methyl isocyanate (MIC) —a highly toxic and volatile pesticide component that reacts violently with water. That same evening a new supervisor told an inexperienced worker to flush out a pipe used to filter MIC. The worker then connected a water hose to the pipe near the leaky valve and left it on. The tank's pressure and temperature began rising abnormally, but leaky valves and unreliable instruments were too routine for anyone to be alarmed. Around 11:30 P.M., workers smelled MIC leaking. Unperturbed, the plant supervisor waited until after a postmidnight tea break to begin searching for the leak. Meanwhile, water seeping into the MIC tank had started a runaway chain reaction that pushed the tank to near its bursting point. By 12:40 A.M., escaping gas was choking workers. When they finally initiated safety measures, it was too late, and poisonous gas was soon spewing into the atmosphere. Helpless to stop it, the terrified workers evacuated the plant— taking care to flee upwind. The only employee injured that night was the supervisor, who broke his leg while climbing a fence on his way out.

Meanwhile, people downwind were dying before the plant even sounded an alarm. Over the next hour and a half, forty tons of MIC and other deadly chemicals wafted through Bhopal. Many of the city's 900,000 residents slept in structures offering no protection, and hundreds—particularly the frail and elderly— were asphyxiated in their sleep. Thousands of others awakened violently, with their eyes and lungs searing. Feeling as though they were burning up from inside, they vomited and excreted uncontrollably as fluids filled their lungs and choked them. Blinded, weakened, terrified, and in agonizing pain, tens of thousands of people ran outdoors and rushed about madly, sucking in ever more poison. Many ran for miles until they dropped, to drown in their own fluids or be trampled.

Residents of upper-story quarters in well-sealed buildings generally survived; others got through the nightmare by lying still and covering themselves—an effective measure that Union Carbide never bothered advising residents of Bhopal to follow. After ravaging the shantytowns ringing the plant, the toxic cloud moved to the railway station, where it killed dozens of people instantly and left 200 unconscious and another 600 lying helpless in their own excreta. Even amid this nightmare, several railway workers remained at their stations to warn away incoming trains. The cloud did some of its deadliest work as much as four miles from the plant and was still killing as it continued south.

Around 2:00 A.M., victims began descending on Bhopal's five hospitals. Twenty thousand people crowded into the hospital nearest the plant. Hospital workers packed several patients into each bed, crowded others on floor mats, and stuffed still more into tents outside. Medical personnel quickly gave up keeping records in order to treat as many victims as possible. Handicapped by lack of information about what type of chemical poisoning they were fighting, they concentrated on symptomatic relief. With victims dying every minute, bodies were piled up like cordwood.

By dawn, human and animal bodies littered the city, vegetation was blackened, and vultures circled overhead. Fear of epidemics made disposal of bodies imperative. Officials had time to do little more than photograph the dead and separate Muslims—who were to be buried— from Hindus, who were to be burned. All day, scores of huge funeral pyres ringed the city. In several places, unconscious victims awakened just in time to avoid being burned alive.

Meanwhile, no one could explain why Bhopal's people had never been told how to respond to an emergency or why an alarm was not sounded the moment the disaster became imminent.

Aftermath: Soon after the vultures, American lawyers descended on Bhopal to sign up victims whom they could represent against Union Carbide. The company, meanwhile, was quick to claim that its Bhopal operation met the same safety standards as the rest of its facilities— including a similar pesticide plant in West Virginia. The truth, however, was soon shown to be otherwise, so Union Carbide tried shifting blame to Indian government policies and local mismanagement. It also suggested that sabotage had occurred. After an American court refused to hear a class-action suit, legal issues were left to be settled within India. Nearly five years of legal wrangling resulted in the government of India's accepting $470 million from Union Carbide in full settlement for all claims. This agreement satisfied few, however, and became an issue in the national elections in November 1989. The victorious government of V. P. Singh promised to begin paying interim benefits to all those able to prove they were in the vicinity of the accident when it occurred. Documentation, however, proved to be a nightmare. Those hardest hit by the disaster were the poor; many of them had fled Bhopal afterward. Even those still in Bhopal's shantytowns were difficult to locate and monitor. In any case, the claims courts to determine eligibility were not set up until 1992 and were soon overwhelmed by more than 600,000 claims. Many claims were clearly fraudulent, and bribery and corruption permeated the entire process. By the end of 1994, only $102 million had been distributed. The average death benefit was $3,840. Other victims began receiving $6 a month for three years.

A decade after the disaster, the legal case remained unresolved. Bhopal's hospitals still overflow with patients suffering from brain damage, loss of motor control, and chronic nervous disorders, and unknown thousands suffer from mental depression brought on by the nightmare of December 1984 and the helplessness they have felt ever since.

—R.K.R.

THE *CHALLENGER* CATASTROPHE

Launch pad 39-B held a twelve-story-high Atlas rocket to which were attached a huge external fuel tank, twin 149-foot rocket boosters, and the space shuttle *Challenger*. It was a chilly morning in Florida as the shuttle's seven-person crew awaited the last of the countdown that would signal the rocket's solid-fuel engines to fire up and provide the million pounds plus of thrust needed to pierce through the atmosphere and take the flight into Earth orbit. The flight was to last for a week, but barely seventy-three seconds had elapsed before the *Challenger* became a sky-borne inferno.

When: Tuesday, January 28, 1986, 11:38 A.M.
Where: Cape Canaveral, Florida.
The Loss: The entire crew (Mission Commander Dick Scobee, Mission Pilot Michael J. Smith, Ellison S. Onizuka, Judith A. Resnick, Gregory B. Jarvis, Ronald E. McNair, and Christa McAuliffe); the space shuttle *Challenger*; and the *Challenger*'s cargo: a communications satellite and the Spartan-Halley Observatory.
The Disaster: The *Challenger*'s most recent flight had concluded with a successful landing on November 6, 1985. There were ten weeks in which to ready the craft and its next crew for a return to space, the *Challenger*'s next mission originally being scheduled for January 22, 1986.

Nineteen eighty-six was intended to be a banner year for NASA. It planned to launch fifteen missions during the year, six more than it had in 1985. The *Challenger*'s next mission was to be its tenth and the twenty-fifth shuttle flight overall. This was to be the mission that would symbolize the craft's safety and would likewise demonstrate its multiple-launch capabilities.

Mission 51 LI was unique in yet another way; it was to carry Christa McAuliffe into space. McAuliffe, a thirty-seven-year-old science teacher at Concord (New Hampshire) High School, was to be the first ordinary citizen to experience space travel.

After ten intense weeks of preparation and repeatedly scrubbed takeoffs, the crew, the support staffs on the ground, and the Atlas rocket engines were ready to be fired up, each prepared to do its part in sending a human payload to the clouds and beyond. The Florida air was cold on the winter morning when the *Challenger* lifted skyward on its tenth mission. It was the coldest-ever weather in the history of shuttle launches. That didn't stop the final countdown; not this time. The mission had already been postponed four times: twice because of postponements of the shuttle flight scheduled before it; once because weather conditions were judged to be unacceptable; once because of a faulty hatch door.

The seven astronauts took up their positions in the *Challenger* at 9:07 A.M. on January 28, 1986. Two hours and four minutes later they braced themselves as the *Challenger*'s three main engines engaged. Six seconds later, the twin booster rockets blasted off. Black smoke surged out from the bottom section of the right booster at eight seconds into liftoff. The smoke dissipated a dozen seconds later; the computerized sensors detected no trouble and issued no warning.

At fifty-nine seconds after liftoff, the craft reached its maximum dynamic pressure—the highest intensity of vibrations from its engines combined with the stress of gravity-defying momentum—plus the pressures of heavy, shifting winds and wind resistance.

A second small burst of black smoke quickly reappeared from the lower right booster. An O-ring (including both a primary and a backup seal) had ruptured. The *Challenger* was traveling at nearly 2,000 miles an hour as flames flew from the ruptured seals and set off a series of explosions that detonated in a chain reaction that climaxed when the main fuel tank of hydrogen split open and burst, less than seventy-four seconds into the flight. The resulting, awesome fireball ravaged man and machine as shards of melting metal and those aboard Mission 51 LI were scattershot into the air some ten miles above the Earth. The craft and crew then plummeted down to the sea, about seven miles beyond the Florida coastline. A shocked Mission Control immediately ordered air and sea rescue teams into action. There was, however, no possibility of rescue.

Aftermath: After getting word of the catastrophe, President Ronald Reagan canceled the State of the Union address he had prepared to deliver that evening. Vice President George Bush was immediately dispatched to the Cape to meet with, among others, the families of crew members who had gathered to witness the launch.

Pieces of the ill-fated rocket were recovered from the Atlantic from January 29 through March 7, 1986. NASA announced, on April 19, that they had found the remains of the crew. They were flown to Dover Air Force Base on April 29, where they were released to the astronauts' families. The rest of the search was officially called to a halt on August 28.

A thirteen-member Presidential Commission, headed by former secretary of state William Rogers, was appointed to investigate the cause of the disaster and issue recommendations on how such a tragedy could be avoided in the future.

The commission's 256-page report, released on June 9, 1986, affixed blame to the defects in the faulty O-ring seals. It discovered that NASA, as well as Morton Thiokol (the manufacturer of the booster rockets), had not "fully understood the mechanism by which the joint sealing action took place."

Temperature played the key and ultimately fatal role in the short duration of this mission. Though the ambient temperature at the time of takeoff was thirty-six degrees Fahrenheit, it was only an approximate twenty-eight degrees Fahrenheit in the shaded area around the right booster rocket's seal. The coldest it had ever previously been at launch time was fifty-three degrees Fahrenheit. Investigators revealed that warnings concerning seal failures caused by cold weather had been issued years before the first shuttle ever took flight. Morton Thiokol had failed to correct the defect, and NASA had minimized the defect's potential for harm, stupefyingly citing it as being "acceptable."

The scandal surrounding the calamity went on for months as the shuttle program was suspended, NASA's director was fired, and its hierarchy was shaken up. Senate hearings and lawsuits ensued for months. Work was eventually begun on a replacement craft.

A consensus of opinion for the central and overriding cause of the *Challenger* catastrophe has been reached in the years that have elapsed since the event took place. The blame has been affixed to "pressure"—not hydraulic or some other mechanically induced pressure, but human pressure. NASA was in a rush to demonstrate the shuttle's practicality and to secure (if not expand) its congressionally allotted budget. Spacecraft manufacturers were under pressure to keep their costs down and, thus, their profits high. Everyone involved had deadlines to meet. In the frenzy of budgeting, building, and blasting off, warnings had been ignored, safety factors had been overlooked, and haste had been rewarded.

The hardest truth to accept was that the crew would not have had to perish. The shuttle's abort system, responsible for ensuring crew survival in event of disaster, was designed to be operative only in case of main engine failure. No such system had been provided to function in case one or both of the solid-fuel rocket boosters failed during the first two minutes of the flight. Though the Mercury, Gemini, and Apollo missions were all equipped with launch-escape systems, the shuttle was not. The reason it wasn't, according to NASA, was that booster failure after launch was considered highly improbable.
—**R.N.K.**

THE CHERNOBYL MELTDOWN

By the time radiation levels 20 percent above normal were detected in Sweden, the world's worst nuclear accident was already two days old. For days the international community demanded answers but instead received silence followed later by only a tersely worded Soviet reply.

When: Saturday, April 26, 1986, at 1:23:58 A.M.
Where: Reactor Number Four; Chernobyl Nuclear Power Facility, northern Ukraine; at Chernobyl, 62 miles (100 kilometers) northwest of the Ukrainian capital, Kyiv (formerly Kiev); on the Pripyat River (which empties into the largest river in Ukraine, the Dnepr).
The Loss: Nearby cities were abandoned and an exclusion zone formed around the area; more than 335,000 people displaced from their homes; dangerous radiation levels for at least a hundred years; incidents of birth defects, various cancers, and radiation-related diseases—especially among children; total loss of Reactor Number Four; extensive ecological and agricultural devastation; local economies shattered; fallout spread worldwide; cleanup estimated at $358 billion. Total number of deaths is unknown.

The Disaster: From the beginning, the Chernobyl nuclear facility was slated to be the Soviet Union's nuclear showcase. The plant was located on the outskirts of the previously little-known town of Chernobyl ("Chornobyl" in Ukrainian). Two and a half miles to the northwest was the workers' community of Pripyat.

Chernobyl, one of nineteen RBMK, or "water-cooled, graphite-moderated," reactor plants, had four massive reactors that produced nearly 17 percent of the nation's total power. Each RBMK unit, or reactor, contained about 2,000 tons of nuclear material. They could be easily serviced without costly shutdowns and could produce weapons-grade plutonium rather than waste. Despite the catastrophe that occurred at Reactor Four, RBMKs have a demonstrated history of reliability and safety as long as they are carefully managed.

Unfortunately, Chernobyl-style reactors also have several design flaws and are most vulnerable at low power. Perhaps the greatest flaw, however, was the human factor. Undertraining, bad management, and a politically torn Soviet government removed from its people made for a tragedy ready to happen.

On Friday, April 25, 1986, the people of Chernobyl and Pripyat prepared for the coming weekend unaware of a series of tests scheduled to start at Reactor Four. These tests were ordered by incompetent managers who, knowing little about how reactors work, pressed their staff to proceed because they wanted to see how far the reactor could be pushed. As part of these tests, critical reactor systems and backups were completely disabled. By 1:00 A.M. the next day the reactor was powered down.

Within the next twenty-three minutes numerous thunderous explosions simultaneously destroyed system after system. Only when it was too late did the managers on duty decide not to ignore the signs of impending disaster. Attempts to stabilize the reactor proved futile—it was out of control.

Plant foreman Valery Perevozchenko, while trying to get back to the control room, witnessed a strange and terrifying sight. Two thousand reactor core lid cubes, each weighing 770 pounds (350 kilograms), were dancing about wildly as a result of explosions in the fuel channels beneath them.

Finally, at 1:23:58 A.M., tragedy struck. Two massive explosions blew away the building's roof and sides and ejected thousands of tons of radioactive material. A plume of radioactive material extended skyward 36,000 feet (11 kilometers). All around, the smell of ozone filled the air.

A radioactive cloud quickly spread over northern Ukraine and Belarus and across Europe, and was even slightly measurable in North America. Within the remains of the shattered core a fierce radioactive graphite fire burned out of control. Flames leaped higher than a hundred feet (thirty meters) and temperatures soared above 4,532 degrees Fahrenheit (2,500 degrees centigrade). Unable to use water on this fire because it would further ignite the graphite, firefighters had to throw sand. As surrounding asphalt melted and burned, firefighters found their boots sticking in

this quickly forming, intensely radioactive quagmire. Two workers inside the plant died quick but terrible deaths from the intense radiation.

In an act of unparalleled heroism, Aleksandr Lelechenko, deputy chief of the electrical section, believing the reactor was still intact, tried three times to restart reactor cooling systems. To do this he went, unprotected, through piles of radioactive debris measuring 5,000 to 15,000 roentgens and through knee deep radioactive water, thus sparing his younger coworkers this deadly task. Regular plant radiation levels measure about three roentgens. His total exposure was 2,500 rads—enough to kill five people instantly. After receiving first aid, Lelechenko rushed back and helped for several more hours. He later died a horrible, agonizing death in Kyiv.

Deadly radiation poisoning spread quickly among both firefighters and the people of the surrounding communities. More than 15,000 people were reported to have died in Kyiv hospitals. Thirty-one workers who were at Reactor Four died within two weeks. The morning of the accident, a man sunning himself outside ran back inside and proudly showed off a tan he acquired in only several minutes. Unaware that this was a "nuclear tan," he started vomiting and went into convulsions within an hour. Like countless others, he later died.

Authorities, arguing over the seriousness of the accident, were slow to react. In surrounding communities people unwittingly wiped ever-accumulating radioactive dust from furniture. Most windows were still open. Spectators watched an eerie cloud of reddish radioactive mist, described as a strange growing flower, spread over the reactor and into surrounding neighborhoods. Finally, more than thirty-six hours later, evacuations began and firefighters were reinforced by hundreds of helicopters dropping a concrete mix in an attempt to smother the fire and contain radiation. Unfortunately, the very helicopters sent in to help were kicking up and spreading radioactive dust.

A nineteen-mile (thirty-kilometer) exclusion zone was implemented. Nearby towns were completely abandoned. One hundred and thirty-five thousand people were evacuated, followed by 200,000 more later. A 1.5-mile (2.4-kilometer) dike was built to prevent radioactive groundwater contamination of the Pripyat River, but it ultimately failed. The reactor suffered a total core meltdown and continued to burn for nine days. England, which had experience with fighting graphite fires, offered help but was rebuffed by a confused Soviet government bent on covering up this catastrophe.

Radiation was so intense that cleanup workers, lowered to the roof by helicopter, could work only one-minute shifts. Most of these workers, including the pilots, later died within a year of radiation-related diseases. As Soviet president Mikhail Gorbachev later began learning the details and extent of the accident that had been kept from him, he vowed to bring those responsible to justice.

Aftermath: Viktor Bryukhanov and five others were later convicted of complicity in causing this tragedy. Over time the toll of those affected is expected to grow to 4 million. Birth defects among people and animals living in surrounding areas have increased at an alarming rate. Among livestock tragic birth defects are especially evident. Horses are born with eight deformed legs, pigs with no eyes, and eggs often contain several yolks. Tragically, many of the people of these regions returned to their homes because they did not believe in the invisible threat of radiation. Soldiers protecting surrounding areas often sat around without their shirts, ignorant of radioactivity in the area. As far away as Italy, meat was found to be tainted with radiation. Thyroid cancer continues to pose a serious health risk, especially among children. The reactor itself was finally encased in a concrete sarcophagus, but it has repeatedly cracked and released radioactive gases.

Fortunately the lessons of Chernobyl were learned in the West long ago and without any such catastrophe. In a final twist of irony, not only does Chernobyl continue to be used but a tourist company has started booking tours of Chernobyl at twenty-five dollars a person.

—M.E.R.

9 UNUSUAL DISASTERS

1. THE SAINT PIERRE SNAKE INVASION
Volcanic activity on the "bald mountain" towering over Saint Pierre, Martinique, was usually so inconsequential that no one took seriously the fresh steaming ventholes and earth tremors during April 1902. By early May, however, ash began to rain down continuously, and the nauseating stench of sulfur filled the air. Their homes on the mountainside made uninhabitable, more than a hundred fer-de-lance snakes slithered down and invaded the mulatto quarter of Saint Pierre. The six-foot-long serpents killed fifty people and 200 animals before they were finally destroyed by the town's giant street cats. But the annihilation had only begun. On May 5 a landslide of boiling mud spilled into the sea, followed by a tsunami that killed hundreds; and three days later, on May 8, Mount Pelée finally exploded, sending a murderous avalanche of white-hot lava straight toward the town. Within three minutes Saint Pierre was completely obliterated. Of its 36,000 population, there were only three survivors.

2. THE SHILOH BAPTIST CHURCH PANIC
Two thousand people, mostly African-Americans, jammed into the Shiloh Baptist Church in Birmingham, Alabama, on September 19, 1902, to hear an address by Booker T. Washington. The brick church was new. A steep flight of stairs, enclosed in brick, led from the entrance doors to the church proper. After Washington's speech, there was an altercation over an unoccupied seat, and the word *fight* was misunderstood as *fire*. The congregation rose as if on cue and stampeded for the stairs. Those who reached them first were pushed from behind and fell. Others fell on top of them until the entrance was completely blocked by a pile of screaming humanity ten feet high. Efforts by Washington and the churchmen down front to induce calm were fruitless, and they stood by helplessly while their brothers and sisters, mostly the latter, were trampled or suffocated to death. There was no fire—nor even a real fight—but 115 persons died.

3. THE GREAT BOSTON MOLASSES FLOOD
On January 15, 1919, the workers and residents of Boston's North End, mostly Irish and Italian, were out enjoying the noontime sun of an unseasonably warm day. Suddenly, with only a low rumble of warning, the huge cast-iron tank of the Purity Distilling Company burst open and a great wave of raw black molasses, two stories high, poured down Commercial Street and oozed into the adjacent waterfront area. Neither pedestrians nor horse-drawn wagons

General devastation following the 1919 Boston molasses flood.

could outrun it. More than 2 million gallons of molasses, originally destined for rum, engulfed scores of people—21 men, women, and children died of drowning or suffocation, while another 150 fifty were injured. Buildings crumbled, and an elevated train track collapsed. Those horses not completely swallowed up were so trapped in the goo they had to be shot by the police. Sightseers who came to see the chaos couldn't help but walk in the molasses. On their way home they spread the sticky substance throughout the city. Boston smelled of molasses for a week, and the harbor ran brown until summer.

4. THE PITTSBURGH GASOMETER EXPLOSION

A huge cylindrical gasometer—the largest in the world at that time—located in the heart of the industrial center of Pittsburgh, Pennsylvania, developed a leak. On the morning of November 14, 1927, repairmen set out to look for it—with an open-flame lamp. At about ten o'clock they apparently found the leak. The tank, containing 5 million cubic feet of natural gas, rose in the air like a balloon and exploded. Chunks of metal, some weighing more than one hundred pounds, were scattered great distances, and the combined effects of air pressure and fire left a square mile of devastation. Twenty-eight people were killed and hundreds were injured.

5. THE GILLINGHAM FIRE "DEMONSTRATION"

Every year the firemen of Gillingham, in Kent, England, would construct a makeshift "house" out of wood and canvas for the popular fire-fighting demonstration at the annual Gillingham Park fete. Every year, too, a few local boys were selected from many aspirants to take part in the charade. On July 11, 1929, nine boys—aged ten to fourteen—and six firemen, costumed as if for a wedding party, climbed to the third floor of the "house." The plan was to light a smoke fire on the first floor, rescue the "wedding party" with ropes and ladders, and then set the empty house ablaze to demonstrate the use of the fire hoses. By some error, the real fire was lit first. The spectators, assuming the bodies they saw burning were dummies, cheered and clapped, while the firemen outside directed streams of water on what they knew to be a real catastrophe. All fifteen persons inside the house died.

6. THE EMPIRE STATE BUILDING CRASH

On Saturday morning, July 28, 1945, Bill Smith, a veteran army pilot, took off in a B-25 light bomber from Bedford, Massachusetts, headed for Newark, New Jersey. A copilot and a young sailor hitching a ride were also aboard. Fog made visibility poor. About an hour later, people on the streets of midtown Manhattan became aware of the rapidly increasing roar of a plane and watched with horror as a bomber suddenly appeared out of the clouds, dodged between skyscrapers, and then plunged into the side of the Empire State Building. Pieces of plane and building fell like hail. A gaping hole was gouged in the seventy-ninth floor. The landing gear strut and its forty-seven-inch wheel hurtled through seven walls and came out on the floor below at the opposite side of the building, and an engine shot through an elevator shaft, severing the cables and sending the car plummeting to the basement. When the plane's fuel tank exploded, six floors were engulfed in flame, and burning gasoline streamed down the sides of the building. Fortunately, it was a Saturday and few offices were open; only ten persons in the building—plus the three occupants of the plane—died. A fourteenth died later of injuries. Had the crash occurred on a weekday, 25,000 people would have been in the building.

7. THE TEXAS CITY CHAIN REACTION EXPLOSIONS

On April 15, 1947, the French freighter *Grandcamp* docked at Texas City, Texas, and took on some 1,400 tons of ammonium nitrate fertilizer. That night a fire broke out in the hold of the ship. By dawn, thick black smoke had port authorities worried because the Monsanto chemical plant was only 700 feet away. As men stood on the dock watching, tugboats prepared to tow the freighter out to sea. Suddenly a ball of fire enveloped the ship. For many it was the last thing they ever saw. A great wall of flame radiated outward from the wreckage, and within minutes the Monsanto plant exploded, killing and maiming hundreds of workers and any spectators who had survived the initial blast. Most of the business district was devastated, and fires raged along the waterfront, where huge tanks of butane gas stood imperiled. Shortly after midnight a second freighter—also carrying nitrates—exploded, and the whole sequence began again. More than 500 died, and another 1,000 were badly injured.

8. THE AL BASRAH MASS POISONING

In September 1971 a huge shipment of seed grain arrived in the Iraqi port of Al Basrah from Mexico. The 22,000 tons of barley and 73,000 tons of wheat had been chemically treated with methylmercury, a fungicide, and were sprayed a bright pink to indicate their lethal coating. Clear warnings were printed on the bags—but only in Spanish. The treated grain was accidentally distributed to about 200,000 Iraqi people. The Iraqi government, embarrassed at its criminal negligence or for other reasons, hushed up the story, and it was not until two years later that American newsman Ed Hughes came up with evidence that 6,530 hospital cases of mercury poisoning were attributable to the unsavory affair. Officials would admit to only 459 deaths, but it was estimated that 45,000 people were poisoned, many of them suffering such permanent effects as blindness and brain damage.

9. THE LAKE NYOS POISON CLOUD
In August 1984, naturally formed carbon dioxide gas spewed out of tiny Lake Monoun in the West African nation of Cameroon, asphyxiating thirty-seven people. Scientists considered the event a tragic oddity, but it turned out to be an unsuspected prelude to an even worse disaster when nearby Lake Nyos exploded in August 1986. This time the poisonous cloud rushed down a river valley at forty-five miles per hour, killing people as far as fifteen miles (twenty-five kilometers) downstream from the lake. The final death toll was more than 1,700.

—N.C.S.

HUMAN DISASTER

ADOLF HITLER

BIRTH
Adolf Hitler was born April 20, 1889, at Brannau am Inn, Austria-Hungary, a town on the border between Austria and Bavaria. His father, Alois, was born out of wedlock and had borne the last name of Schicklgruber (his mother's maiden name) until he succeeded in having it changed to Hitler 1876. The name Hitler may be Czech in origin. The Hitlers, however, were German speaking.

Alois, a self-made man, once a shoemaker's apprentice, worked his way into civil service as a customs officer. He had two hobbies—beekeeping and womanizing. After his second wife died, he married their children's nursemaid, Klara Pîlzl, a young country girl twenty-three years younger than he, who was pregnant by him. The baby died. Adolf was born four years later. He had five brothers and sisters, of which only one, Paula, survived childhood.

CHILDHOOD
Hitler's mother was frail and gentle, his father paunchy and formidable. In *Mein Kampf* Hitler wrote only a little about them. In fact, he devoted only seventeen pages to his childhood, much of it propaganda about his precocious leadership, historical insights, oratorical gifts, and German patriotism.

Adolf's sister Paula said Adolf "challenged my father to extreme harshness" and "got his sound thrashing every day." Certainly there was a contest of wills between father and son. Hitler said, "My father did not deviate from his 'never,' and I opposed him even more vehemently with my 'oh, yes.'" Thereafter, according to one biographer, Charles Bracelen Flood, Hitler had "the classic desire of a whipped child: the need for revenge, the still unformulated search for an enemy to punish."

After his father retired at age sixty from the Hapsburg customs service, the family moved from Lambach, a small town of 1,700, to the outskirts of Linz, capital of upper Austria. In Linz Adolf met August Kubizek, who was his friend from the age of fifteen to nineteen. Kubizek described Hitler's "eternal guerrilla warfare with his teachers." The teachers' reports about him bear that out. His early promise in the Lambach Benedictine monastery school, where he won all As, seemed to have withered. His French and German teacher said he knew "the gaunt, pale-faced youth pretty well. He had definite talents, though in a narrow field. But he lacked discipline, being notoriously cantankerous, willful, arrogant, and irascible. . . . Moreover, he was lazy; otherwise, with his fine intelligence he would have done much better. . . . He demanded of his fellow students . . . their unqualified subservience, fancying himself in the role of a leader." Sometime during this time, Adolf contracted encephalitis, which may have affected his personality and ability to learn. Some Hitler experts have speculated that he had a learning disorder. If he did, it did not prevent him from learning the anti-Slavic and antisocialist ideology and glorification of German culture pounded into the class by the history teacher, Dr. Leopold Pîtsch.

With his only good grade in drawing, Hitler decided he wanted to be an artist. His father was against it. He suggested that Adolf become a civil servant like himself, partly for the security of it. Hitler's response was: "No powers in the world will move me to be a civil servant."

Alois died of a pleural hemorrhage in the street when he was sixty-five. Adolf was only thirteen, but his father's pension and savings continued to support the family after he was gone.

After leaving school at age sixteen, Hitler stayed in Linz with his mother, not doing much except dreaming about being an artist, affecting an ivory-tipped black cane, and reading books on art, history, and the military. He liked in particular American cowboy stories by German author Karl May, who had never visited America. Hitler's mother indulged him, cooking for him and fussing over him. So perhaps he fitted Freud's description of what lies at the core of a successful man: "A man who has been the indisputable favorite of his mother keeps for life the feeling of a conqueror, that confidence of success that often induces real success." Kubizek's portrait of Hitler would bear this out—he said that he experienced delusions of grandeur, planning "gigantic projects" that were "expounded to the last detail," like rebuilding the entire city of Linz.

Yet, in spite of his authoritarian father and adoring mother, and in spite of his grandiose dreams, nothing in Hitler's childhood seems to foreshadow his heinous later life. His art was dull and normal, with no sign of insanity in it. Yes, he had flashes of paranoia—he thought the Austrian government was planning a program of "slow extermination of everything German." But so did many others. And almost every child harbors unrealistic dreams of greatness.

Nonetheless, psychologists have sought to explain him at least partially. Erich Fromm points to Hitler's high school failure as spurring him into withdrawal into a fantasy world. Fromm also says that Hitler could be classified as a narcissistic personality type, experiencing only himself as real. All perhaps true, all not enough.

CAREER

On October 22, 1907, Hitler learned that his mother was dying of breast cancer. He nursed her until she died on December 21. Klara Hitler's doctor later said, "In all my forty-odd years of practice I had never seen a young man so broken by grief and bowed down by suffering as young Adolf Hitler was on that day."

When he was nineteen, Hitler went to Vienna to apply to the General School of Painting at the Academy of Fine Arts, thinking it would be a "cinch to pass." To his surprise, he was not admitted—his drawings were too lifeless. "When I received my rejection, it struck me as a bolt from the blue," he said. He then thought of becoming an architect, a "master builder," but couldn't get into school because he had not finished his secondary education.

In Vienna, Hitler became a self-confessed oddball, living among loners and losers. He later said, "I owe it to that period that I grew tough, and I am still capable of being tough."

At the end of February 1908, August Kubizek came to study music at the conservatory in Vienna and they shared a room. Hitler pretended to be going to classes, then told August of his rejection by the academy. August recounted his view of his friend's mental state: "Altogether in those early days in Vienna, I had the impression that Adolf had become unbalanced. . . . Choking with his catalog of hates, he would pour his fury over everything, against mankind in general who did not understand him, who did not appreciate him and by whom he was persecuted."

Later that year, Hitler tried to get into the academy again, but failed. On November 20 he moved out of his room, without telling August

where he was going. He began a truly marginal life, reading in public libraries, living in cheap rooms. When he ran out of money in mid-September 1909, he skipped out on his rent. All that his parents had left him was gone. He started sleeping in coffeehouses, on park benches, in flophouses.

He hit rock bottom one cold night in December 1909. He had no overcoat, only a dirty checked blue suit, and stood freezing in a line of homeless, waiting for free shelter for one night in the Obdachlosenheim, a huge building for housing the poorest Viennese.

Two months later he was living at the Männerheim, a higher-level shelter, where he had a cubicle with a bed. He wrote to his aunt Johanna, who sent him some money with which he bought art supplies, and went into business with Reinhold Hanisch, another down-and-outer. Hitler painted watercolor postcards of street scenes, and Hanisch sold them to tourists in bars. Then Hitler started also painting larger watercolors and oils for frame makers—frames sold better when there was something in them. Only six months after going into partnership with Hanisch, he had the man arrested for cheating him of his share of a sale. After that, Hitler sold his own artwork.

He and several others who were the "intellectuals" of the Männerheim hung out in the reading room. He would quietly paint there until he disagreed with something, then he would jump to his feet, go into a harangue, and finally return to painting.

He understood what it was to be déclassé. He later wrote, "I do not know which it was that appalled me most at the time: the economic misery of those who were then my companions, their crude customs and morals, or the low level of their intellectual culture." They spoke of Marxism, and it horrified him. "Are such men worthy of belonging to a great people?"

He solidified his ideas in Vienna, which was saturated with anti-Semitism. He saw Austria as a repulsive "mixture of Czechs, Poles, Hungarians, Ruthenians, Serbs, and Croates, and everywhere the perennial bacteria poisoning humanity . . . Jews and more Jews." He associated Jews with prostitution, white slavery, modernism in art, and anti-German press criticism. August Kubizek remembers walking by a synagogue with Hitler, "This shouldn't be here," Hitler said.

He did not read critically but instead took from his reading what he needed to reinforce and build his own ideas of the world. He read *Ostara*, a magazine published by a defrocked monk that pushed the idea of a superior Aryan race needing to guard itself against the genes of dark-complexioned ape-men. One finds echoes of this attitude in *Mein Kampf* where Hitler talks of "the nightmare vision of the seduction of hundreds of thousands of girls by repulsive crooked-legged Jew bastards." He viewed Marxist theory as a "weapon of decomposition" with plans for the "enslavement or extermination of all non-Jewish people."

As a standee, he attended performances of Wagnerian opera. It fitted in with his mythology of a heroic Germany of the past. He liked its bigger-than-life drama and sense of power. In almost every way, Wagner fitted in with Hitler's idea of the artist as romantic genius. As a youth, Hitler had seen *Rienzi*, based on the life of a Roman dictator who had been of the common folk and wanted to bring back the greatness of ancient Rome. Transported, he had said that he would have such a mission and would lead his people out of bondage.

In 1913 he moved to Munich, but he was called back to Austria for military service in 1914—only to be declared unfit as "too weak." It was just as well. The Austro-Hungarian army, which served the Hapsburg regime he hated, had, he thought, the intention of achieving "the gradual Slavization of the German element."

When World War I broke out, Hitler volunteered for the German army. An enlisted man who helped train Hitler said that on the second day of training, he saw Hitler looking at his rifle "with delight, as a woman looks at her jewelry." Hitler served in the front lines as headquarters runner. His regiment served almost four years in the front lines and took part in thirty-six major battles. Hitler later said that he "passionately loved soldiering" and that World War I was "the greatest and most unforgettable time" of his "earthly existence." He voiced none of the repugnance toward war that so many other World War I soldiers expressed. With praise from his commanding officers, he received the Iron Cross, second class (December 1914), and Iron Cross, first class (1918), and wore the latter for the rest of his life.

Gassed in 1918, Hitler was in the hospital when the war ended. When he heard of Germany's defeat, he cried—for the first time since his mother's death eleven years before. It was "the greatest villainy of the century." He speculated that there had been a Jewish international plot to destroy Germany, whose conspirators hoped for a "Jewish world empire." Hitler's interest in politics began about then.

He remained in the army until 1920, and joined the German Workers' Party (later the Nazi Party) in Munich in 1919 as an army agent. That year he found out that he "could make a good speech" that could hypnotize the masses. After leaving the army, he stayed in the party, in charge of propaganda, striving to win "Marxist-infected" workers to the cause of a greater Germany. Ironically, during the war he had learned something about propaganda by studying British pamphlets dropped from planes to encourage British prisoners of war.

He was arrogant, and not everyone liked him,

but when other party members tried to restrict him, he offered to resign, and they gave in—after all, he had great ability to organize publicity and get money. In accordance with what he had learned about propaganda, his speeches were simple, featuring the struggle between good and evil. He spoke against the Versailles Treaty, demanding that Germany get back colonies, glory, and economic power. He spoke against those whom he called traitors—Jews, socialists and liberals, pacifists, democrats. He spoke about murdering Jews.

The solution to everything, to his mind, was not democracy, which had failed with the degenerate Weimar Republic, but national dictatorship to remilitarize the nation and "cleanse" it of its internal enemies. By 1923 he had become the center of a cult of leadership, considered above criticism—the dictator of the Nazi Party.

In November of that year, with 600 Brownshirts, he tried to seize power in the Beer Hall Putsch. He jumped on the table in the hall, crowded with 3,000 people, with pistol drawn and fired a shot into the ceiling. "The National Revolution has broken out!" he shouted. Not everyone agreed. Germans wanted stability, not revolution against what Hitler called the "November Criminals" (German government). No big-time politicians backed his attempt to seize power. Hitler fled and was later arrested at the house of a friend. He was sentenced to a five-year term in prison, of which he served nine months. During that time he wrote the first volume of *Mein Kampf*. In this book he claimed that biological laws had created three kinds of "races": "creators of culture" (Aryans), "bearers of culture" (Japanese, among others), "destroyers of culture" (Jews). He also said that the basic unit of mankind was *Volk* ("folk"), that the greatest good was to preserve the German *Volk*, and that the incarnation of *Volk* was the Fuhrer. He believed that the Aryan "master race" had three enemies—Marxists, Jews, and Slavs. The greatest threat was Marxism (including social democracy and Communism), which he saw as controlled by Jews.

> Through clever and constant application of propaganda, people can be made to see paradise as hell, and also the other way round, to consider the most wretched sort of life as possible.
>
> Adolf Hitler,
> *Mein Kampf*, 1925–26
>
> Success is the sole earthly judge of right or wrong.
> Adolf Hitler,
> *Mein Kampf*, 1925–26

In 1925, out of prison, he put the Nazi Party back together. By 1929, Germany in disarray, he formed a coalition with industrialists and businessmen who wanted to establish a right-wing, anti-working-class government. With their money he propagandized the lower middle class and unemployed. As always, he used people who thought they were using him.

He did not become a German citizen until 1932.

In January 1933, Hitler became chancellor under Hindenburg, then an old man. By late March the Nazis had "legal" powers of dictatorship. By the end of 1933, the Nazi Party was the only legal political group in Germany and Hitler was already sole dictator in all but name. Hindenburg died in 1934, and the offices of president (which Hindenburg had held) and chancellor were joined, with Hitler holding both—in a plebiscite 90 percent of voters approved the Hitler regime.

His first ambition was reunion of the German peoples. He planned to conquer the Ukraine and European Russia—then to colonize those regions with "pure-blooded" Aryans. He would deport or enslave the Slavs, educating them only enough "to understand our highway signs." Then with Japan, Italy, and perhaps Great Britain as allies, he would make Germany the greatest power in the world.

On March 7, 1937, the German military occupied the demilitarized zone of the Rhineland. There were only weak protests from France and Great Britain. "I go the way that Providence dictates with the assurance of a sleepwalker," he said. In that year Germany hosted the Olympic Games, soft-pedaling anti-Semitism. He felt driven by destiny. Next Germany took Austria—the conquest was accelerating.

Before unleashing the invasion of Russia (June 27, 1941), he said, "I feel as if I am pushing open the door to a dark room never seen before without knowing what lies behind it." Perhaps he had an intimation of the downfall that lay before him. At the end of 1942, facing defeat, he shrank from reality, refused to visit cities that had been bombed, and wouldn't read reports of failures. After the disastrous rout at Stalingrad in January 1943, he stopped making public speeches.

On July 20, 1944, military leaders tried to assassinate him. They met in Hitler's headquarters in Wolfschanze (Wolf's Lair), East Prussia. Claus Schenk von Stauffenberg, chief of staff of the 600,000-man army guarding the home front, put a briefcase under the table near Hitler and left to take a telephone call that had been arranged beforehand. The briefcase exploded. It killed two staff members. It also blew the seat out of Hitler's pants, split his coat, and ruptured his eardrums. Von Stauffenberg was shot that day. Hitler put the conspirators on trial and killed about 5,000 people who he claimed had been involved in plotting his death.

Adolf Hitler.

Was Hitler crazy? Adleff H. Schwaab claims that Hitler did indeed become mentally ill, that his hysterical speeches at first were just tactical, but later they became part of his delusional system—he became incapable of distinguishing between reality and fantasy.

If he was crazy, though, he was crazy like a fox. He excelled as a grand manipulator. In foreign policy he was opportunistic, following objectives outlined in *Mein Kampf*, exploiting the weaknesses of others. He spoke no foreign language yet was able to bamboozle world leaders.

He didn't like routine, perhaps still seeing himself as an unfettered artist. He rarely worked—his teachers had been right in saying that he was lazy. He rarely listened. He preferred to work with one person at a time. He demanded that all documents he had to read be less than a page long, yet he was the only one allowed to make important decisions. He delegated lesser authority to his subordinates, but they had overlapping spheres that allowed him to control them.

Hitler's personal life was meager. After leaving prison in 1928, he lived on the Obersalzberg, near Berchtesgaden, with his half sister Angela Raubal and her two daughters. He was devoted to Geli, one of the daughters, but his possessiveness drove her away. He was furious when he found out she had made love with his chauffeur and would not let her go to Vienna to have her voice trained. She committed suicide in September 1931. He was grief stricken. Her room was kept as she had left it.

Eva Braun, a shop assistant, became his mistress, but he kept her out of the public eye and felt that marrying her would get in the way of his career. She was a warm-hearted blonde, but she was not too smart. According to entries in her diary, Hitler treated her badly. She tried suicide twice.

Many other women, even the socially powerful, admired him—the light blue burning eyes, the famous mustache and lock of hair that fell over his forehead, the oratory. Women by the thousands became hysterical during his speeches. He liked to have beautiful women around, provided that they were not intellectual—he disliked intellectual women.

Some said he was impotent. Putzi Hanfstaengl, a companion of his, said that he was—that his "abounding nervous energy" got no sexual release. "In the sexual no-man's land in which he lived, he only once nearly found the woman [Geli] and never even the man who might have given him relief. . . . My wife summed him up very quickly, 'Putzi,' she said, 'I tell you, he is a neuter.' " Erich Fromm guessed that "his sexual desires were largely voyeuristic, anal-sadistic with the inferior type of women, and masochistic with admired women."

Certainly Hitler was not very sensual. He didn't care much about clothing or food—he didn't smoke, didn't drink alcohol or tea or coffee. All that simplicity, and all that excess.

TOLL OF DESTRUCTION
Historian Alan Bullock claimed that the Holocaust was unique because "mass murder became not an instrument but an end in itself." The first concentration camps were established in 1933 for opponents of the Nazis. In that same year, Germany began the policy of sterilizing the "hereditarily sick," and the medical killing by injection or carbon monoxide gas of "life unworthy of life." Christian Worth of the SS Criminal Police designed the first Nazi gas chamber, disguised as a shower room.

On April 1, 1933, Hitler initiated a nationwide boycott of Jews to ruin them economically. On April 7, 1933, a law to restore civil service contained the "Aryan paragraph" that effectively made Jews second-class citizens. They were barred from work as officials in government, even as teachers or streetcar conductors. Four of ten Jewish lawyers were disbarred, and the rest faced disaster because they could not present a case before a Nazi judge or jury. No Jew was allowed to have cultural influence. On September 15, 1935, Germany enacted the Nuremberg Laws, in which Jews lost their rights as citizens.

When war broke out, those suspected as enemies, including clergy—Catholic and Protestant—were put into concentration camps without trial. In 1941 Hitler said that the war was ideological, all rules off, with civilians subject to summary execution and reprisals.

Hitler's major objective—the invasion of the Soviet Union through Operation "Barbarossa"—began in June 1941. His purpose: to provide Lebensraum ("living space") for Aryans and destroy the Soviet state, which he saw as "Jewish-controlled" and the center of the Communist "bacillus." With that invasion, 3,000 Blackshirts (SS) started murdering Jews en masse. Example (from a report by the SS): "In Kiev the Jewish population was invited by poster to present themselves for resettlement. Although initially we had only counted on 5,000–6,000 Jews reporting, more than 30,000 Jews appeared; by a remarkably efficient piece of organization, they were led to believe the resettlement story until shortly before their execution." The Nazis shot all 30,000. In other instances, Nazis took Jews to the countryside, stripped them, forced them to dig their own graves, then shot them. Nazi killers massacred half a million Jews in the last five months of 1941. They tried to cover up the evidence by digging up the bodies, burning them on oil-soaked grids, and grinding their bones in special machines.

Hitler took desperate risks—with other people's lives. He so believed the Russian campaign would be a quick success that he did not provide his soldiers with winter clothes and equipment. It was a disaster. By the beginning of 1945, German army dead, wounded, and missing numbered 8.3 million.

As he took more and more territory, Hitler had more and more Jews to consider. In January 1942, at the Wannsee Conference, Hitler's men honed plans for the "Final Solution of the Jewish Question." Memo: "Around eleven million Jews come into consideration for this final solution of the European Jewish question. . . . In the process of carrying out the final solution, Europe will be combed through from west to east." How many Jews actually were killed during the Hitler regime? Perhaps 7 million, at least 5 million. The horror was exacerbated by the machinelike methods of killing adopted by the Nazis.

The death toll from war and genocide: some estimate 50 million dead, many more millions injured. And of course there was the resulting moral, economic, social, and cultural destruction. It was a horrifying destruction that the world would never forget.

THE END
Late in April 1945, the Soviets were within hours of taking Hitler's bunker. Suffering from nervous exhaustion, perhaps insane, he planned suicide. About midnight on the night of April 28–29 he married Eva Braun. After the ceremony, the Hitlers and their entourage drank champagne. Hitler then dictated his political

testament, in which he justified his career and appointed successors. He gave his picture of Frederick the Great, which had always hung on the wall of his office, to Hans Baur, a pilot. He said to Baur, "I want my epitaph to be, 'He was the victim of his generals.' "

The Hitlers went into a room. A shot rang out. "Right on target!" said Helmut, son of Joseph Goebbels, Hitler's propagandist.

The bodies were put in a trench, soaked in gasoline, and set on fire. Reported aide Otto Günsche, who was in charge of taking care of the bodies: "Suddenly, as the flames shot up, all the men present, without any prior consultation, raised their arms in a Nazi salute."

The Thousand-Year Reich had lasted twelve years and three months.

—A.E.

FOOTNOTE PERSON

"TYPHOID MARY" MALLON

In the palatial Long Island summer home rented by New York City banker William Henry Warren in the year 1906, the recently hired cook worked over a special hot-weather menu. An icy-cold Nantucket cucumber soup would be appropriate, she thought. Perhaps lobster thermidor served with steamed rice and cold champagne. Or a dish of Grand Central oysters baked in their shells. After all, wasn't this Oyster Bay?

The guests who ate that summer dinner relished every mouthful. But ten days later six of them, sick and feverish, were admitted to a New York hospital. They had contracted a highly contagious disease: typhoid fever. Local health authorities investigated but were unable to find a cause for the illnesses. (It later turned out that it was the cook's dessert that made them sick: ice cream with fresh, sliced peaches.)

Shortly afterward the owner of the summer home, George Thompson, hired Dr. George Soper, a sanitary engineer for the New York City department of health, to solve the case. Thompson feared that the typhoid outbreak would scare away potential renters, and he needed the highly respected Soper, who was also an epidemiologist, to get to the bottom of the mystery. Soper may not have had the brilliant analytical faculties of a Sherlock Holmes, but he did question, test, and finally deduce that the culprit responsible for the minor epidemic at Oyster Bay was the hired cook, a Miss Mary Mallon.

Mary had changed jobs by then. In fact, she had completely disappeared. While attempting to track her down, Soper discovered that she changed jobs frequently. And wherever she had worked, a case of typhoid was soon reported. After an extensive door-to-door search, he finally cornered her in March 1907. He explained that as far as the Department of Health could determine, she was probably the first known typhoid carrier in the United States. He pointed out the importance of unrecognized cases and begged her to submit to a physical examination and tests. Brandishing a large carving fork, she chased him out of the building and slammed

the door after him. For the New York Health Department, this was only the beginning of thirty years of cat-and-mouse games with Mary Mallon.

The city, determined to apprehend this public menace, sent Dr. S. Josephine Baker, three police officers, and an ambulance to Mary Mallon's living quarters. Mallon was home and even opened the door. After realizing who the visitors were, she slammed the door in their faces and escaped out the back door. After an extensive search, police found her hiding in a nearby house. Kicking and screaming, she was placed in the ambulance, and Dr. Baker had to sit on her to prevent another escape. "It was like being in a cage with an angry lion," Baker later said. Mallon was placed in an isolation ward at Willard Parker Hospital, where she was subjected to countless tests. These proved that she was indeed a typhoid carrier.

Before her detention in 1907, she had been the cause of at least seven outbreaks involving twenty-six cases of the fever. She had probably been infecting people since 1900 when she worked as a cook for a family in Mamaroneck, New York; a houseguest at the home came down with typhoid. In 1902 Mallon worked, again as a cook, in the summer home of a New York attorney, J. Coleman Drayton. Seven members of Drayton's household were sick within weeks of Mallon's arrival. Instead of running away, her usual reaction after an outbreak, Mallon stayed to nurse the victims. For her dedication, Drayton gave her a fifty-dollar bonus, thus rewarding the very person who was responsible for the misery. Mallon jumped from job to job until George Soper caught up with her.

A few years earlier, a number of German bacteriologists had found that "intestinal carriers" such as Mary were prolonged spreaders of the disease. Untreated, the typhoid organism is capable of surviving indefinitely in a carrier's intestines. Typhoid germs also settle in the gallbladder, and it was suggested that removal of this organ might cure her. Mary Mallon was a stubborn woman. Since she felt perfectly well, she refused to have the operation. Finally she was transferred to Riverside Hospital on North

"Typhoid Mary" Mallon.

Brother Island and given an ultimatum. Either she would cooperate with the doctors or she would spend the rest of her life in the hospital. Mary promptly hired a lawyer and for the next few years engaged in court battles that failed to bring about a solution. Tired of the prolonged hassle, and determined to put an end to the case, the city health officials agreed that Mary could have her freedom if she gave up cooking or handling any food. She also promised that she would report to the Health Department every ninety days.

It was 1910 when Mary Mallon gained her release. By then various newspapers had picked up the story, and she had been labeled "Typhoid Mary." Reporters sought interviews, but she refused to see anyone. She wouldn't allow herself to be photographed, and she cut herself off from all her friends. Taking a new identity, she disappeared once again. For five years she evaded the health authorities. She also broke her promise and continued to work in the kitchens of clubs, hotels, restaurants, and private homes.

A final confrontation came in 1915, when the Sloane Hospital for Women reported an out-break of typhoid. Twenty-five nurses and attendants were ill, and two employees had died. When Dr. Soper was called in, he discovered that the elusive Mary Mallon had been employed in the hospital kitchen. Police were put on her trail. She was found working in a suburban home, was arrested, and then was returned to North Brother Island.

During the subsequent years of her confinement, she continued to refuse treatment. Physicians called her "the human culture tube" because her system was so heavily infested with typhoid bacteria. Fifty-three original cases and three deaths were attributed to her, though she herself was immune to the disease. In her later years she became a lab technician at the hospital and, though restricted to its grounds, appeared to have "settled in."

On November 11, 1938, Mary Mallon died of a paralytic stroke at Riverside Hospital, North Brother Island, New York. She was seventy years old. Nine persons, who would not identify themselves, attended the Mass held for her at Saint Luke's Catholic Church. She is buried in Saint Raymond's Cemetery in the Bronx.

—E.Bi. and C.O.M.

ARMAGEDDON OUTA HERE— THE END OF THE WORLD

NOVEMBER 13, 1900—THE BROTHERS AND SISTERS OF RED DEATH
In czarist Russia a district called Kargopol (about 400 miles from Saint Petersburg) contained a 200-year-old sect that called itself the Brothers and Sisters of Red Death. They shared some provocative ideas. Marriage was forbidden but sexual intercourse was allowed, providing the sinners immediately submitted themselves to suffocation with a large red cushion. Believing that the world was due to end November 13 (November 1 Old Style), 862 members thought it would please God if they sacrificed themselves by being burned to death. When news of this plan reached Saint Petersburg, troops were rushed to Kargopol. They were too late. More than a hundred members had already perished. When the appointed day passed without catastrophe, the sect disbanded.

OCTOBER 1908—LEE T. SPANGLER
Remembering a prediction he had made after coming out of a trance at the age of twelve, Lee T. Spangler announced that the world would end in a rain of fire during October of 1908. Spangler, a grocery store owner from York, Pennsylvania, convinced a number of people with his prophecy. However, the only thing that fell on York in October was a light rain, on the last day of the month.

1910—THE PRESS
In 1910 some scientists made the announcement that the world would pass through the tail of Halley's comet. The press began to print dire predictions about poisonous gases asphyxiating all life on Earth. In Sydney, Australia, people were warned to remain indoors on the day that the earth would be enveloped in the tail of the comet.

DECEMBER 17, 1919—ALBERT PORTA
Born in Italy, Albert Porta emigrated to the United States in 1875. An expert seismographer and meteorologist, Porta settled in San Francisco and published regular weather forecasts in a small Italian newspaper. Owing to his accurate predictions of several earthquakes, he began to receive worldwide attention. Therefore, people sat up and took notice when he announced that on December 17, 1919, there would occur a conjunction of six planets. This would result in a magnetic current that would pierce the sun, cause great explosions of flaming gas, and eventually engulf the earth. There was widespread alarm. Weather stations were besieged with calls, and a statement was issued that said that while there would be such a planetary conjunction, it would not be dangerous. As December 17 approached, suicides and hysteria were reported throughout the world. The fatal day arrived and all the planets aligned, but the world still remained. Porta returned to predicting the weather.

FEBRUARY 13, 1925, AND OCTOBER 10, 1932—ROBERT REIDT
A young Los Angeles, California, girl named Margaret Rowan announced that the archangel Gabriel had told her that the end of the world would take place at midnight on Friday, February 13, 1925. This intelligence was seized upon by Robert Reidt, a Freeport, Long Island, housepainter. He immediately placed large advertisements in New York newspapers summoning the faithful to join him on a hilltop at the hour of doom. His followers—all dressed in white muslin robes—gathered on the hilltop and waited, and exactly at midnight they threw up their hands and chanted, "Gabriel! Gabriel! Gabriel!" Nothing happened. Reidt announced that the hour of doom was to be on Pacific rather than Eastern Standard time, so there were

three hours yet to wait. When nothing happened at 3:00 A.M., Reidt turned on the press, blaming the news photographers' flashbulbs for the failure. Seven years later, after Reidt had immersed himself in the Book of Revelation, he came up with a revised doomsday date. Quoting from the Second Epistle of Peter, Reidt thundered, "Before the year is out 'the heavens shall pass away with a great noise, the elements shall melt with fervent heat, the earth also and the works that are therein shall be burned up.' " Joined by his revived followers, Reidt awaited October 10, 1932, which was to be the day of disintegration. But the target day came and went without noise, heat, or burning. Reidt got the message and permanently retired from doomsdaying.

APRIL 25, 1943, AND APRIL 25, 2038—NOSTRADAMUS
The famous French prophet and astrologer Nostradamus (1503–66) predicted that the world would end when Easter fell on April 25. So far this has happened in 1666, 1734, 1886, and 1943. It will occur again in 2038.

SEPTEMBER 21, 1945—REVEREND CHARLES LONG
It was the middle of the night in 1938 when Reverend Long was mysteriously awakened in his Pasadena, California, home. At the foot of his bed he saw a blackboard on which a ghostly hand wrote 1945. A voice later whispered that the world would end at 5:33 P.M. on September 21 of that year. Reverend Long felt duty-bound to spread the news about the coming destruction. He wrote a 70,000-word tract outlining how, on the fatal day, the earth would be vaporized and all human beings would be turned into ectoplasm. He mailed copies to the world's major leaders. Long also rented the Pasadena Civic Auditorium, where his son held meetings during which he urged members of the audience to repent and be baptized. Together they impressed a number of people and developed a following. Seven days before doomsday the Longs and their followers gave up food, drink, and sleep—presumably forever. They sang and prayed fervently during the last hours, but nothing happened. The group eventually disbanded.

JANUARY 9, 1954—AGNES GRACE CARLSON
The Children of Light was a Canadian religious sect based at a farm near Keremeos, about thirty miles from Vancouver. Their leader, Mrs. Agnes Grace Carlson, announced on December 26, 1953, that the end of the world would come the following January 9. She collected thirty-five faithful converts, including eight children, in a farmhouse and awaited the final day. They passed their seventeen-day vigil by singing

hymns and sitting in awed silence while Mrs. Carlson sought inspiration. Meanwhile, the local school had obtained summonses under the School Attendance Act, and when the local sheriff called to serve them, the farmhouse congregation quickly dispersed.

MAY 24, 1954—ITALIAN PROVERB
An Italian adage that "Rome and the world are safe, so long as the Colosseum stands" brought mass hysteria to Italy in 1954. On May 18, engineers were alarmed when huge cracks appeared in the 1,800-year-old amphitheater. Someone suggested it was a "sign" and set the day of destruction for Monday, May 24. Thousands besieged the Vatican, hoping that the pope would absolve them from their sins. Despite a sharp rebuke from a Vatican prelate, who added, "The world will see Tuesday and more Tuesdays to come," thousands appeared in Saint Peter's Square on May 24. The prelate was proved right, and builders were sent to repair the Colosseum.

JUNE 28, 1954—HECTOR COX
For many years cobbler Hector Cox had been one of London's best-known and most colorful talkers at the famous Speaker's Corner in Hyde Park. His main topics were the truths he had discovered in the Egyptian Book of the Dead. On Sunday, June 27, he startled his audience by announcing that the world would end within twenty-four hours. For Cox, his prophecy proved right; the following day he was found dead. Police ruled out foul play, although a knife had been plunged into his heart.

DECEMBER 20, 1954—DR. CHARLES LAUGHEAD
Forty-four-year-old Dr. Charles Laughead, a Michigan State College physician, was a much-respected, down-to-earth professional man. It was a surprise to all who knew him when he suddenly became a doomsday prophet. This transformation was largely due to the influence of medium Dorothy Martin. Dr. Laughead claimed that with Mrs. Martin's help, he had had communications with a cosmic civilization. These voices told him that there would be worldwide upheaval. America's Atlantic Coast would submerge and France, England, and Russia would become big seas. The date set for these events was December 20, 1954. As the time approached, Dr. Laughead and his followers held all-night sessions with Mrs. Martin. They learned from cosmic voices that a spaceship would land and pick them up, and they would be saved. Everyone anxiously awaited the ship, but in vain. The next morning, Dr. Laughead announced to the press that "God had stopped it all." The doctor's relatives tried to have him committed to a mental institution, but

a court ruled that even though he had "unusual ideas" he was not mentally ill.

JULY 14, 1960—ELIO BIANCO
The Community of the White Mountain was a forty-member-strong sect led by Elio Bianco, a forty-six-year-old Italian pediatrician. He claimed that in 1958 his sister Wilma, since deceased, had warned him that at exactly 1:45 P.M. on July 14, 1960, an accidental thermonuclear explosion of the secret American "E" bomb would destroy the world. Bianco kindly informed the press and then, with the help of his forty followers, proceeded to build a fifteen-room ark 7,000 feet up Mont Blanc. The appointed hour came and passed safely. At 1:58 P.M. Dr. Bianco issued a statement: "Anyone can make a mistake. Be happy that I have. Our faith has not collapsed because of that." Bianco was later charged by police with spreading false reports.

FEBRUARY 2, 1962—HINDU ASTROLOGERS
For the first time in four centuries, eight planets were due to line up in a spectacular planetary conjunction as they entered the House of Capricorn. This was to happen on February 2, 1962, between 12:05 and 12:15 P.M. Indian astrologers regarded this as a terrible portent signifying the end of the world. Although Prime Minister Jawaharlal Nehru described the whole affair as "a matter of laughter," throughout the whole subcontinent millions gathered in nonstop prayer meetings in hopes of calming the anger of the gods. In one marathon invoking Chandi Path, the goddess of power, one and one-half tons of pure butter and thousands of marigolds were burned. The Hindu liturgy was intoned 4.8 million times by a relay of 250 priests. U Nu, the prime minister of Burma, released 3 bullocks, 3 pigs, 9 goats, 60 hens, 60 ducks, 120 doves, 120 fish, and 218 crabs in the hope of averting the evil forces. Millions waited, and when the hour of doom passed they all gave thanks that their prayers had been answered.

DECEMBER 25, 1967—ANDERS JENSEN
On the *David Frost Show*, in front of millions of TV viewers, Anders Jensen, the Danish leader of the Disciples of Orthon, predicted Christmas Day would mark the Apocalypse. The sect chose a field near Copenhagen to build an underground bunker with a twenty-ton lead roof to see them through the danger period. Fifty disciples spent Christmas Day underground. The expected nuclear explosion failed to happen. One by one the disciples reappeared from their shelter and were applauded by delighted sightseers. Jensen said, "We expected to see ash covering the ground, a red glow in the sky, and everything destroyed. It's all a bit disappointing, but we are confident there is a

simple explanation." The disciples later sold the bunker at a profit.

FEBRUARY 20 AND MARCH 17, 1969— MARIA STAFFLER

Self-appointed "popess" Maria Staffler told her subjects that the world would suffer a disaster on February 20, 1969. She invited the faithful to follow her to the safety of a mountaintop. When only a few showed up, Staffler shrewdly moved the date to March 17. On that day a few more of the faithful appeared and waited with Staffler inside a specially built hut. When nothing catastrophic happened, the people became restless. They were told, "Wait for one hour." The hour passed, and still all was peaceful. This time everyone left and the hut was demolished.

1970—TRUE LIGHT CHURCH OF CHRIST

Based on Bible interpretation and study, the leaders of the True Light Church of Christ in Charlotte, North Carolina, prophesied that the world would end in 1970. They adhered to the traditional belief that the world would end 6,000 years from the time of creation. They placed creation at 4000 B.C. and reasoned that thirty years were lost from the first century of the Christian calendar. In anticipation of the end, seventeen True Lights resigned their jobs. The members were shocked and surprised when their prediction failed to come true. However, they said that the failure of this prophecy did not cause them to doubt other church doctrine.

SEPTEMBER 1975—VIOLA WALKER

In September of 1975, Mrs. Viola Walker of Grannis, Arkansas—then sixty-seven years old—announced to her relatives that she had received a message from God. The Second Coming and the end of the world were close at hand. Exactly twenty-one kinfolk joined Mrs. Walker in a vigil that took place in a three-bedroom house. They stopped paying bills and took their children out of school. The vigil lasted ten months and was not brought to an end until July 16, 1976, when two deputy marshals went to the house. Everyone was evicted because the bank had foreclosed on the vigil house's mortgage. A spokesman for the group said that they would now continue the vigil in their hearts and that their faith was not shaken.

OCTOBER 23, 1976—GEORGE KING

One day in 1954, taxi driver George King was drying dishes in his Maida Vale flat in London when he suddenly received a message from Mars that the world would end twenty-two years hence. Fortunately, King and his followers, organized as the Aetherius Society, were able to avert the catastrophe by concentrating 700 hours of prayer energy into a prayer book and releasing it in forty-eight minutes on the appointed day.

DECEMBER 1982—JOHN R. GRIBBIN AND STEPHEN PLAGEMANN

In 1974 astronomers John R. Gribbin and Stephen Plagemann predicted worldwide catastrophe caused by a planetary alignment they called "the Jupiter Effect." A rare lineup of several planets on one side of the sun was supposed to exert an additional gravitational pull that would cause massive destruction on Earth. Southern California was to be the focal point, with the astronomers predicting that "the San Andreas fault will be subjected to the most massive earthquake known in the populated regions of the Earth in this century. . . . Los Angeles will be destroyed." Accompanying cataclysms would include disruptions in the earth's upper atmosphere, severe climate changes, and volcanic activity around the globe.

No earthquake destroyed Los Angeles in December 1982, though there was a reported increase in "end of the world" parties throughout California. A few years later Gribbin insisted that there was indeed an increase in seismic activity during the planetary alignment, though the increase was so small as to be unnoticeable by all but experts. He failed to mention that the "rare planetary alignment" actually occurs every 179 years. Gribbin and Plagemann have gone on to predict that May 2000 will see an even greater lineup of planets and an accompanying greater catastrophe.

MAY 1990—ELIZABETH CLARE PROPHET

Elizabeth Clare Prophet, leader of the Montana-based Church Universal and Triumphant, declared that a Soviet nuclear war would erupt sometime in May of 1990. In preparation, Prophet's followers had been building enormous underground bunkers on the church's thirty-five-acre ranch forty miles south of Yellowstone National Park. National park officials and local residents grew alarmed, especially when ex–church members claimed that huge caches of weapons were also being stored in the underground havens. A toxic spill of 30,000 gallons of heating fuel from the bunkers didn't help matters much.

The fall of the Berlin Wall and the collapse of Communism in Eastern Europe in 1989 did not sway Ms. Prophet from her prediction, but as May 1990 came closer, the predictions became much less specific about what actually would happen that month. May 1990 passed without any sign of total nuclear war, and Prophet later claimed that she never predicted a specific date, simply a period of possible danger.

Though Prophet's prophecy was apparently

wrong on every particular, the failure of Doomsday did not cause any mass exodus from the
church. Prophet insists that the period of
apocalyptic danger has still not passed; membership has remained steady; and the bunkers and
weapons caches are still maintained.

OCTOBER 28, 1992—LEE JANG-RIM

On October 28, 1992, the capital of South Korea
virtually closed down and the streets were
filled with riot police and ambulances as religious cultists awaited "the Rapture" that would
bring them to heaven and signal the end of the
world. Cult minister Lee Jang-rim of South
Korea's Dami Mission was the first to predict a
doomsday of October 28, and other groups soon
spread the idea throughout Korea. Twenty thousand people around the world eventually were
caught up in the hysteria, many of them in the
Korean communities of the United States. Four
of Lee's followers in Seoul committed suicide
in preparation for the Rapture, and in Los
Angeles one of the believers died after a forty-
day fast.

One thousand people gathered at the mission's main temple in Seoul on October 28,
awaiting the midnight deadline. Fearing mass
suicides, 1,500 riot police and more than 200
plainclothes detectives surrounded the building, closing off exits to the roof and barring
the windows. A closed-circuit TV monitor
displayed the followers inside, weeping, shouting, and listening to hymns played on a steel
guitar.

Midnight came and passed. Ten minutes after
Doomsday, a teenage boy poked his head out of
a window and shouted "Nothing's happening!"
to the police below. By morning the disappointed doom-watchers had all gone home.

Leader Lee Jang-rim was convicted on fraud
charges a few months later. With the $4.4
million he had personally collected from his
followers, Lee had bought large amounts of
bonds that would mature well after the October
28 "End of the World." Wherever he expected
his followers to be, Lee himself planned to be
around to enjoy his long-term investments.

NOVEMBER 14 AND NOVEMBER 24, 1993— MARINA TSVYGUN

It all started when Yuri Krivonogov, who had
researched mind-altering drugs at the Institute
of Cybernetics in Kyyiv, Ukraine, convinced
journalist Marina Tsvygun that she was really
Maria Devi Khristos—the Second Coming of
Jesus Christ. Tsvygun left her husband and son,
dressed in white robes, and, in early 1990,
began preaching that Judgment Day would
come on November 24, 1993, a date that she
later moved up to November 14. Tsvygun
eventually attracted more than 2,000 followers,
some of whom jumped onstage at the Bolshoi

Theater and the Grand Kremlin Palace opera
house to spread their message. Tsvygun claimed
that she would die in Kyyiv's Saint Sophia
Square and be resurrected three days later. She
and her followers broke into the Cathedral of
Saint Sophia and began celebrating around the
altar. They were arrested. When the world did
not end on November 14, Tsvygun reverted
to her earlier prediction. On November 24
Tsvygun did not die and she did not resurrect.
She was, however, charged with "hooliganism,"
and Krivonogov was forced to face outstanding
charges of extortion.

SEPTEMBER 1994—HAROLD CAMPING

In 1992 religious broadcaster Harold Camping
revealed the secret he had been keeping for
more than twenty years: the world would end in
September 1994. Basing his prediction on a
complex set of calculations, he spread the
warning on his nightly talk show, which aired
on forty radio stations. At first he said the end
would come between September 15 and September 27, but when September 28 unexpectedly
dawned, Camping urged his listeners to wait
until October 2. When that day, too, passed,
Camping admitted that he may have miscalculated his biblical data.

1997—CHET SNOW

In the mid-1980s, hypnotherapist Chet Snow
began putting subjects into "future-life progressions" on the assumption that if "past-life
regressions" can work, the opposite concept can
work as well. In his initial study, Snow was
alarmed to find that very few of his subjects had
"future memories" of the twenty-first century,
though most had very vivid visions of life in the
twenty-third century and beyond. Only a small
percentage "recalled" anything in the near
future, and those who did had visions of
disturbing similarity: massive weather changes,
destruction of cities, complete cultural breakdown, and a massive die-off of the human
population. Most of the subjects attributed this
apocalypse to natural catastrophes, as opposed
to nuclear war.

Snow is proud of his study's prophetic track
record. In the mid-eighties, his subjects envisioned a worldwide recession, a young American president, war in the Persian Gulf, and
even fighting on the Temple Mount. Many of
Snow's followers have bought property in
remote locations that they have "seen" as safe
from the upcoming catastrophes that threaten
the globe.

Perhaps what is most disturbing about these
future-life progressions is not their similarity
but the date on which they all seem to agree. All
of Snow's subjects—believers and skeptics
alike—foresaw the same date for the beginning
of this catastrophic period: the year 1997.

1998—PROPHETS

Christ died in the 1,998th week of his life, according to some prophets, who have chosen this year as the fateful one.

1999—CRISWELL

Criswell, a psychic prophet, claimed that a black rainbow (a magnetic disturbance) will suck the oxygen off the Earth in 1999. Then the planet will race into the sun, incinerating everyone and everything.

MAY 5, 2000—RICHARD KIENINGER

In 1963 a Chicago engineer named Richard Kieninger, using the pseudonym Eklal Kueshana, published a book called *The Ultimate Frontier*. In it he described a childhood visit from a mystery man known as Dr. White who brought him an ice cream cone and informed Kieninger that he was a former Egyptian pharaoh who had been chosen to form a new society. Kieninger saved his money and in 1973 bought a 320-acre ranch in the cornfields of northeastern Illinois. There he and a small group of devoted followers began building the town of Stelle, where they would live until the destruction of life on Earth, which Kieninger predicted would take place on May 5, 2000. The Stelle group, which grew to about 200 people, would survive by hovering above the turmoil in lighter-than-air vehicles and would then form a new city in the Pacific Ocean. In 1975 Kieninger was expelled from Stelle after charges of womanizing. The community continued but eventually disavowed Kieninger's prediction. Kieninger himself moved to Texas and founded another town, Adelphi, outside of Dallas.

APRIL 14, 2126—HARVARD-SMITHSONIAN CENTER FOR ASTROPHYSICS

Scientists at the Harvard-Smithsonian Center for Astrophysics claim that a six-mile-wide comet is destined for earthly collision on April 14, 2126. The comet's collision will not be as spectacular as the collision of Shoemaker-Levy with Jupiter, but it will be as big as the collision that scientists agree wiped dinosaurs off the face of the earth.

Comet Swift-Tuttle, named after its Civil War–era discoverers, passes by Earth on a regular course, much like Halley's comet. Yet the comet's next go-round will bring it much closer to the heat of our sun, which will possibly throw it just the slightest bit off track—and directly into Earth's path. If so, it will hit the atmosphere at 100 times the velocity of a speeding bullet and with the explosive force of 100 million tons of TNT. The impact could cause entire continents to burst into flame and a tidal wave three miles high.

Though other scientists disagree with the Harvard-Smithsonian's prediction, all astronomers agree that a collision with a comet or a massive asteroid is a very real possibility for our planet in the near future. The fossil record shows this happens every 10 to 30 million years. And we're now about 10 million years overdue.

—A.T., J.B., T.E., and D.W.

Chapter 4

CRIME

Major Strasser has been shot. Round up the usual suspects.
Julius J. Epstein, Philip G. Epstein,
and Howard Koch, *Casablanca*, 1942

CRIMES OF THE CENTURY

SACCO AND VANZETTI

The Crime: On April 15, 1920, a paymaster and a security guard were shot to death by two robbers while delivering $15,776.51, the weekly payroll of the Slater and Morrill shoe factory in South Braintree, Massachusetts. The assailants escaped in a waiting getaway car. Thus began the story of a violent but unremarkable robbery on that spring day. Far more serious were the police and judicial crimes that followed and, indeed, echoed down through the century with lingering suspicions and unanswered questions.

The Investigation: Police were already investigating a recent similar robbery in Bridgewater, and a man named Mike Boda was under suspicion. On May 5 police were alerted that Boda had come back to a garage to pick up a car he'd left. Police turned their interest to two other men who had been with him—Nicola Sacco and Bartolomeo Vanzetti. Both men were carrying guns and, unskilled in English, gave police what were considered evasive and suspicious answers to their questions.

They may have given evasive answers because they were both active anarchists at a time when suspicion and hostility ran wild against foreigners, and especially against anarchists and "Reds." The police chief's statement at the time of the arrests reflects perfectly the prevailing attitudes: "In my own mind, I believe that the men who committed this atrocious crime knew no God and had no regard for human life. Anarchists fit the bill and Sacco and Vanzetti were anarchists."

Although the two men were, indeed, active in the anarchist movement, they were both workingmen. Sacco, a family man, worked at a shoe factory, where he was trusted enough to serve occasionally as night watchman; Vanzetti, more of a loner, had held a number of jobs and was working at that time as a peddler of fish.

The "evidence" against the men was enough to cause police and prosecutors to stop looking for the South Braintree malefactors: Sacco and Vanzetti were foreigners and anarchists, they had fled to Mexico to avoid serving in the army during World War I, and they had both been armed when they were arrested. That was apparently enough.

At this point the frame-up started. Although some eyewitnesses identified them, others did not, and the ones who didn't were never disclosed to the defense. Rather than viewing a lineup, witnesses were asked to look at the two men crouched down as though in the act of shooting.

Vanzetti was tried for the earlier Bridgewater robbery and, in a trial where the evidence against him was practically nonexistent, he was convicted even though he produced sixteen witnesses who said he had been peddling eels on the streets of Boston at the time of the robbery. Unfortunately for Vanzetti, all sixteen were Italians and, in the atmosphere of the time, their testimony counted for little.

The Trial: On May 31, 1921, the two men went on trial in Dedham, Massachusetts, before Judge Webster Thayer. To one crony Thayer bragged, "I'll show them and get those guys hanged." To law professor J. P. Richardson, he blustered, "Did you see what I did with those anarchist bastards the other day?"

The atmosphere outside the courtroom at the beginning of the trial was not any friendlier. A newspaper reporter called them "a couple of wops in a jam who believed that property was theft."

Again, Vanzetti had an alibi of a day of selling fish. Sacco had an even better story: he had been to see the Italian Consulate in Boston that day, intending to obtain permission to return to

Nicola Sacco (right) and Bartolomeo Vanzetti (middle) handcuffed to a jail guard and to each other.

Italy to visit his ailing mother. A clerk remembered him because he brought an identity photo much too large. Obviously, prosecutor Frederick Katzenbach maintained, the clerk was mistaken—Sacco had gone on some other day and brought the large photo so he would be remembered.

Ballistics, then an infant science, apparently indicated that one of the bullets that killed the paymaster had come from Sacco's gun. The prosecution expert said of this bullet, "My opinion is that it is consistent with being fired by that pistol." Later, he signed an affidavit stating that, while it could have come from Sacco's pistol, it could equally have been fired by some other gun.

A cap, said to be Sacco's and supposedly found at the crime scene, was produced. Prosecutors pointed out a distinctive tear in it from being hung up on a nail in his workplace. Later the cap would be revealed to have probably been picked up the night before the crime, and the tear was produced by a detective looking for markings.

There was precious little evidence, and what there was, investigations over the years have shown, was manufactured. After five hours of

deliberation, the jury found the two men guilty. Seven years later, on April 29, 1927, Judge Thayer passed a sentence of death by electrocution on the two men.

The Aftermath: During the trial, the Sacco and Vanzetti Defense Committee, run by Italian anarchists and a few liberals, raised money and did their best to publicize the plight of the two men. But it was after the trial, in the years leading up to the execution, that the world became much more aware of the case.

Foreign governments tried to intercede, with Soviet Russia and Fascist Italy in curious accord. Albert Einstein, writer Thomas Mann, author John Dos Passos, poet Edna St. Vincent Millay, novelist Katherine Anne Porter, and violinist Fritz Kreisler were only a few of the famous people who spoke out for fairness. Even Alfred Dreyfus, another victim of injustice, joined their ranks. In an article in the *Atlantic Monthly*, Professor Felix Frankfurter, a future justice of the U.S. Supreme Court, attacked Thayer and the trial.

Some who have studied the case believe that all of the outsiders who criticized Judge Thayer may actually have done more harm than good.

Thayer was a stubborn man, unwilling to let anybody tell him how to administer justice in his courtroom. Even so-called supporters of the men had agendas of their own. When Katherine Anne Porter said she hoped they could keep the two men alive, leftist Rosa Baron snapped, "Alive—what for? They are no earthly good to us alive."

At a few minutes after midnight on August 22–23, 1927, Sacco and Vanzetti went to their deaths. As he was strapped into the electric chair, Sacco cried out in Italian, "Long live anarchy!" Vanzetti, after saying good-bye to loved ones, uttered these words: "I have never committed a crime but sometimes sin. I am innocent of all crime, not only of this, but all."

Several books have been written since then, combing through the evidence, minutely examining the trial, and searching for rare wisps of new information. Some of the books found the men totally innocent; one bolstered the verdict of guilty. Writer Francis Russell in *Tragedy at Dedham* made a plausible case that points to the guilt of Sacco and the innocence of Vanzetti. But William Young and David E. Kaiser, in their book *Postmortem, New Evidence in the Case of Sacco and Vanzetti*, argue that both men were completely innocent.

In 1977 Governor Michael Dukakis of Massachusetts handed Nicola Sacco's grandson Spencer Sacco a public proclamation that enumerated the various miscarriages of justice, criticized Judge Thayer, and pointed out that new evidence gathered over the years would have acted in favor of the two men. Republican senators attacked Dukakis for besmirching the state's legal system, and leading Democrats voted against the proclamation, or abstained.

We are left, all these years later, with the question that cannot be answered with certainty: did the two men commit robbery and murder as charged?

I am so convinced to be right that if you execute me two times, and if I could be reborn those other two times, I would live again to do what I have already.
                                    Nicola Sacco, 1927

If it had not been for this thing, I might have lived out my life talking at street corners to scorning men. I might have died unmarked, unknown, a failure. Now we are not a failure. This is our career and our triumph. Never in our full life could we hope to do such work for tolerance, for justice, for man's understanding of man, as now we do by accident.

Our words—our lives—our pain: nothing! The taking of our lives—lives of a good shoemaker and a poor fish peddler—all! That last moment belongs to us—that agony is our triumph.
                                    Bartolomeo Vanzetti, letter to his son,
                                    April 9, 1927

What is certain, and about which there is little disagreement, is that both men went to their deaths without anything like a fair trial.
                                                              —R.W.S.

LEOPOLD AND LOEB

The Crime: The murder victim was fourteen-year-old Bobby Franks, son of a wealthy Chicago family. His body was found on May 22, 1924, stuffed in a drainpipe in a marshy area on the outskirts of Chicago. All of his clothes had been removed and identification of the body was difficult because hydrochloric acid had been poured over his face. He died from repeated blows to the head with a blunt object.

The Investigation: A pair of eyeglasses found near the body gave police a big break very early in the case. The frames were custom-made, and the manufacturer knew of only three customers in the Chicago area who had purchased them. The investigation led to nineteen-year-old Nathan Leopold, son of a wealthy business tycoon, who not only lived in the same neighborhood as the victim but also admitted that the eyeglasses belonged to him. He had lost them, he said, while bird-watching in the same area where the victim was found. Detectives subsequently learned that Leopold's best friend was eighteen-year-old Richard Loeb, who for days had been hanging around police and newspaper reporters—trying to help them solve the crime.

At first it seemed unthinkable that the two friends could be the murderers. Both were from very affluent families and were considered geniuses. Loeb was the youngest student ever to graduate from the University of Michigan. Leopold was the youngest student ever to graduate from the University of Chicago, was pursuing a law degree, and was a recognized ornithologist. And the victim, Bobby Franks, was a distant relative of Loeb's. What possible motive could lead such gifted, wealthy young men to commit such a crime?

Police interrogated the suspects separately and their alibis conflicted. Leopold said that on the day of the murder he and Loeb were out driving around in his family's car and had picked up two girls. Loeb said he was home alone. Despite other conflicting facts in their statements, police behaved as if the men were guests rather than suspects. They were even treated to an expensive dinner at a nearby hotel. Then another piece of damaging evidence turned up.

The murderers had typed up a ransom note and sent it to the victim's family, but before the money was to be delivered, Bobby Franks's body was discovered. The ransom note, however, had been written on a typewriter with a defective *t*. Two investigative reporters from the *Chicago Daily News*, Al Goldstein and Jim

Mulroy, set out to link the typewriter to the suspects. After locating some old school papers typed up by Leopold, the reporters took the papers to a typewriter expert, who compared them with the ransom note. The note and the school papers had been composed on the same typewriter.

Information from the Leopold's family chauffeur further sealed the boys' fate. The chauffeur said that the Leopold family car was in the garage during the entire day of the murder, thus contradicting Nathan Leopold's claim that he and Loeb had been driving around. Further, said the chauffeur, on the day after the murder he saw Leopold and Loeb trying to wash red stains from the carpet of a rental car. The young men said they were merely trying to clean up some red wine they had spilled. The police then located the rental car, and employees at the car company identified Leopold as the person who had rented the automobile.

When confronted with the mounting evidence, Loeb confessed, then Leopold. They had planned the murder for months. The victim had been chosen almost at random as the murderers drove the rented car around the area surrounding Harvard Preparatory School. Once Bobby Franks was in the car, his head was bashed in with a chisel (neither Leopold nor Loeb would admit to inflicting the fatal blows, but it was later believed that Loeb killed the boy while Leopold drove the car). Then they ate a five-course meal at a restaurant while they waited for darkness. After dark they drove the body to the drainpipe at a predetermined site, stripped the body of clothing, and poured acid over the young boy's face. They buried the murder weapon and the boy's shoes and jewelry. At Loeb's house they burned the victim's clothing. Finally, they called Bobby Franks's father, told him of the kidnapping, and said that a ransom note would be delivered. The next day they tried to clean the blood stains from the rental car and broke apart the typewriter used for the ransom note and tossed it into a lagoon.

As police dug into the young men's backgrounds, they learned that Leopold had an obsessive fascination with the "superman" theories of German philosopher Friedrich Nietzsche. He fantasized that Loeb was "king" and he was the "slave." He would later say of Loeb: "I felt myself less than the dust beneath his feet. . . . I'm jealous of the food and drink he takes because I cannot come as close to him as does his food and drink." And Loeb, it was discovered, fantasized about being the world's greatest detective, or a master criminal capable of committing the perfect crime. The two young geniuses, however, had committed far less than a perfect crime. The body, which they believed would never be discovered, was found in less than twenty-four hours, and the two killers were apprehended a mere ten days after the murder. The crime had no real motive; it was an intellectual exercise. Leopold and Loeb were called "the thrill killers" by the press.

The Trial: Clarence Darrow, the country's most noted criminal lawyer, was hired to represent Leopold and Loeb. He pleaded the boys guilty, since a not-guilty plea would have meant a trial by jury. The guilty plea put the verdict into the hands of Judge John R. Caverly. It was one of the most publicized cases in U.S. history. One newspaper offered to broadcast the trial over its radio station. Another newspaper offered to hire Sigmund Freud to psychoanalyze the young men. The judge rejected both offers.

The trial lasted thirty-three days, and Darrow's strategy was evident from the start. He didn't claim that the boys were insane but that they were emotionally, or mentally, deficient. While they came from wealthy families, both boys had miserable childhoods, had committed numerous petty crimes, had never developed an adequate set of moral standards. They oftentimes could not tell the difference between fantasy and reality. A parade of psychologists testified before the judge. Testimony about the sexual activities of Leopold and Loeb (they were believed to be sexual partners) was handled with great delicacy. Judge Caverly asked the lawyers to approach the bench to discuss sexual matters and ordered all women out of the courtroom.

Darrow was brilliant and eloquent. His case was really an assault against the death penalty, which was allowed in Illinois. His summation was passionate: "Your Honor, if a boy of eighteen and a boy of nineteen should be hanged in violation of the law that places boys in reformatories instead of prisons—then we are turning our faces backward toward the barbarism which once possessed the world. Your Honor stands between the past and the future. . . ." When Darrow finished, twelve hours later, Judge Caverly was in tears.

Nathan Leopold and Richard Loeb each received a sentence of ninety-nine years for kidnapping and life imprisonment for murder. The judge said he chose imprisonment over death because of the ages of the defendants.

The Aftermath: The convicted murderers were sent to Stateville Prison in Joliet, Illinois. Newspaper reporters continued to follow their stories for many years and claimed that while in prison, Leopold and Loeb received preferential treatment. Allegedly, they were allowed unlimited phone calls, were given special meals, and were permitted to visit each other in private.

Richard Loeb was stabbed to death in the prison's shower on January 28, 1936, by another inmate. The other inmate claimed self-defense, saying that Loeb had tried to molest him; he was acquitted.

Nathan Leopold was a model prisoner. He

worked in the prison library, tutored other prisoners, and took part in medical experiments to test antimalarial drugs. His sentence was reduced and in 1958 he was paroled, after serving almost thirty-four years. Leopold wrote an autobiography, *Life Plus Ninety-Nine Years*, and moved to Puerto Rico, where he worked in medical research, taught mathematics, and raised money for church missions. He died of a heart attack in 1971 at the age of sixty-six.

Clarence Darrow had a tough time collecting his fee from the Loeb and Leopold families. While his asking price was $200,000, he compromised at $100,000. It is believed that, after repeated requests, Darrow received a total of $40,000.

Cub reporters Al Goldstein and Jim Mulroy, who doggedly investigated and reported the crime, received a Pulitzer Prize in 1925.

—C.O.M.

THE SAINT VALENTINE'S DAY MASSACRE
The Crime: For Chicago gangster Bugs Moran, Saint Valentine's Day, 1929, was a lucky day—that morning he dodged a bullet, or rather dozens of bullets, meant to rub him out.

The night before, a hijacker had phoned Moran offering him a truckload of whisky from Detroit at the rock-bottom price of fifty-seven dollars a case. Moran jumped at the deal, telling the caller to deliver it the next day to the S-M-C Cartage Company warehouse at 2122 North Clark Street. Waiting to unload the booze in the warehouse that icy morning were six members of Moran's gang and an optometrist, Reinhardt Schweimmer, who got his thrills by hanging out with gangsters.

At 10:30 three men wearing police uniforms burst in, guns in their hands, and disarmed the seven men, lining them up against the wall. They were followed by two men in suits. For Moran's gang it probably seemed to be business as usual, with crooked cops barging in to put the squeeze on them.

Then the shooting started. The men in suits opened fire with machine guns.

Seven men lay in a widening pool of blood— six dead, and one still clinging to life, as observers outside saw the uniformed "cops" pretend to march the men in suits out at gunpoint and drive off in their black Cadillac, fitted out like a police raid car. The charade had worked; the massacre had been swift and bloody.

But it had failed in its prime objective. Bugs Moran had not been inside. Albert Weishank, a

Some of the victims of the 1929 Saint Valentine's Day Massacre.

gang member who resembled Moran, had walked into the warehouse that morning dressed in the style of overcoat and fedora his boss usually wore. Lookouts posted in an apartment across the street, mistaking him for Moran, had telephoned the killing crew with the go-ahead.

Just as the bogus cops were entering the building, Moran and two other gang members rounded the corner. They pulled back and hid.

The Investigation: Although there seemed to be little doubt that Al Capone had ordered and planned the killings, Chicago police were hampered by two stumbling blocks.

First was the embarrassing fact that few people had any problem believing that the killers could, in fact, have been cops involved in Moran's bootlegging enterprise who were angered over some double cross.

The second problem was that nobody was talking. Even Frank Gusenberg, the one Moran man who made it barely alive to the hospital, spat out his dying words to detectives pleading with him to name his assassins: "I ain't no copper."

Al Capone, when the shooting occurred, was planning a party in his luxurious mansion on Palm Island off the coast of Florida. The Miami winter season was at its peak and he had invited more than a hundred guests.

The police started routinely, collecting physical evidence at the bloody crime scene and canvassing the area for anyone who had seen anything.

There was also the matter of rounding up "the usual suspects" for questioning. Bugs Moran himself had an opinion on who had planned the massacre. "Only Capone kills like that," he said. On Palm Island, New York Post sportswriter Jack Kofoed approached his host and said, "Al, I feel silly asking you this, but my boss wants me to. Al, did you have anything to do with it?" Al's answer was classic Capone: "Jack," he said with a grin, "the only man who kills like this is Bugs Moran."

Under the direction of Chief of Detectives John Egan, crime scene investigators recovered seventy empty .45-caliber machine-gun cartridges and fourteen spent bullets of the same caliber. Forensic ballistics was a fledgling science and Chicago did not have a sophisticated enough crime lab to do the tests that could match a spent cartridge or bullet with the gun that fired it. Because of this case, wealthy Chicagoans came up with the money to equip a state-of-the-art lab, to be located at Northwestern University, the first of its kind in the country and the model for many others, including the FBI lab.

Detectives interviewed a Mrs. Doody, the landlady of the apartment building across the street, who told of three men who rented a room with a view of the warehouse. The men rarely left their room, spending their time sitting at the window staring down at the warehouse. On the morning of the massacre they disappeared. These men, police theorized, had been the lookouts who had given the mistaken word that Bugs Moran was in the building and the hit could go forward.

Bugs Moran, perhaps planning his own retribution, would not give police the name of the hijacker who had called him the night before the killings, saying only that he was someone he had trusted.

The Cadillac turned up in a garage behind a house on the North Side when the fire department responded to a fire. The car had been partially demolished by an acetylene torch, which firemen believed had set the garage on fire. The engine number led police to a dealer who said he sold the car to a "James Morton" of Los Angeles, a name that could never be traced; the garage had been rented to a "Frank Rogers," another apparently made-up name.

In December of 1929 police in Saint Joseph, Michigan, arrested a man named Fred "Killer" Burke for shooting a policeman. In his home was a machine gun that, when tested in the crime lab back in Chicago, turned out to be one of the weapons used in the massacre. Michigan authorities refused to hand Burke over to Illinois, preferring to try him for the murder of the cop.

Although the investigation continued for years and focused on lots of suspects, Fred Burke—and, of course, gangster kingpin Al Capone—are the only men who can be blamed with any degree of certainty.

The Trial: There was, of course, no trial. Al Capone, although one of the most notorious criminals in history, was jailed only twice— once on a minor gun possession charge, and once on federal income tax evasion charges. Although he became fabulously wealthy distributing bootleg liquor during Prohibition, authorities were never able to charge him with more serious crimes because they couldn't come up with enough solid evidence or witnesses who were willing to talk.

Everybody knew Al Capone supplied most of the city's illegal booze, but influential Chicagoans didn't seem to care. As Capone put it, "When I sell liquor, it's bootlegging. When my patrons serve it on silver trays on Lake Shore Drive, it's hospitality."

The Aftermath: Soon after the massacre, the IRS came up with serious charges of tax evasion against Capone. It was the only way prosecutors could nail him. His excuse, given with a straight face and widely quoted, was, "I didn't know you paid taxes on illegal earnings." Sentenced to eleven years in 1931, he was released after eight years and allowed to spend his remaining time at his sumptuous Palm Island hideaway, a pathetic lunatic in advanced stages of syphilis. He died in 1947, at the age of forty-eight.

Bugs Moran lived on that February morning but lost to Al Capone his hold over the North Side bootlegging business. He turned to robbing banks and spent most of his remaining years in prison.

The Saint Valentine's Day Massacre so captured the imaginations of writers and filmmakers that it has been depicted repeatedly. Unfortunately for Chicago, Al Capone is often, to this day, the first name that comes to mind when people think of the Windy City.

—R.W.S.

THE LINDBERGH KIDNAPPING

The Crime: Following his legendary transatlantic flight in 1927, Colonel Charles A. Lindbergh became one of the world's most celebrated heroes. Largely as a refuge from the public glare, Lindbergh and his wife, Anne, built a palatial weekend home in Hopewell, New Jersey. The two-story Normanesque mansion was situated in an isolated spot, off a narrow, unpaved country lane at the end of a mile-long driveway; yet its location was widely reported by the press. By February 1932 the Lindberghs, with their twenty-month-old son Charles Jr., had been spending weekends there for several

A detective examines the ladder purportedly used by a kidnapper to enter the nursery at the home of Charles Lindbergh in Hopewell, New Jersey.

months, although a few details of construction, such as the warped—and, hence, unclosable—shutters on the second-floor nursery's corner window, remained unfinished.

On the evening of Tuesday, February 29, 1932, owing to a scheduling mix-up, the famed aviator missed a speaking engagement in New York City and, unexpectedly, drove out through a late-winter storm to join his wife and child in their country home. Shortly after 10:00 P.M. their English nurse went up to the nursery to check on the baby, who had been tucked in early with a cold. She found the corner window wide open and the four-poster crib empty. On top of the radiator lay a white envelope; opened in the presence of police a few hours later, it contained a crudely worded note demanding $50,000 in ransom. There were several other clues: footprints were found beneath the nursery window, and a chisel and a roughly made wooden ladder would shortly be discovered nearby.

The Investigation: Lindbergh immediately notified the New Jersey state police, who set up roadblocks on all major arteries leading into Newark, Trenton, and New York. The founding director of the state police, Colonel H. Norman Schwarzkopf, soon arrived to oversee investigation of the crime, the news of which had spread like wildfire. Before the night was out, an army of reporters had descended on the house, and by daybreak the site had turned completely chaotic, with hundreds of journalists and curious spectators trampling about in the surrounding underbrush, effectively destroying any additional evidence.

In the days that followed, the scene became even more surreal. Twenty additional phone lines were laid into the house, which was transformed into a command post populated by a strange mélange of police, reporters, family friends, and various bizarre characters who had insinuated themselves into the proceedings. A notorious con man named Mickey Rosner, for example, much to the dismay of the police, gained the family's trust with claims that he could find the child through his underworld connections. For much of the first week he and two other thugs took over the house's living room, smoking cigars, treating Mrs. Lindbergh like a waitress, and loudly accusing family friends of complicity in the crime. Al Capone, convicted of tax evasion a few months before, even got into the act, offering to track down the kidnappers in return for a pardon. The Lindberghs would receive several hundred thousand letters—including some 12,000 from people who claimed that their dreams held the key to the crime.

From the beginning, police focused on the fact that this was the first weekday night that the baby had spent at the home—an indication, they

Vendors selling souvenir miniature ladders outside the trial of Bruno Hauptmann for the murder of the Lindbergh baby.

thought, of an inside job. Early suspicions centered on the nurse's Norwegian boyfriend, who was quickly exonerated. Then, on March 8, a retired school principal named John I. Condon published an open letter in a local paper, offering $1,000 of his own money in addition to the ransom. He was contacted by the kidnapper the next day, and three nights later he met a man calling himself "John" in a nearby cemetery. John's manner made Condon suspect that the baby was already dead; however, Lindbergh insisted that the ransom be paid without police involvement. Condon—himself not averse to his new-found importance—was contacted again, and on the night of April 2, Lindbergh drove Condon to a cemetery in the East Bronx, where "Graveyard John" and another man were waiting. Condon turned over $50,000 in return for a letter with instructions stating that the baby could be found in a boat near Elizabeth Island, just off Cape Cod. Lindbergh's desperate air search, however, revealed that he had been cruelly tricked. The following month the decomposed body of Charles Lindbergh Jr. was found in the woods a few miles from the Lindbergh home; the toddler had been killed by a blow to the head some two months earlier.

The investigation now centered on household servants of Mrs. Lindbergh's family; a maid, repeatedly questioned, was actually driven to suicide. As the months passed, however, various leads drifted into dead ends, and the case gradually receded from the front pages. Then, after more than two years, police got a lucky break. On September 15, 1934, a man bought gas with a twenty-dollar gold certificate, which should already have been redeemed for standard bank notes, since the country had gone off the gold standard a few months earlier. The wary gas station manager took down his license number; the certificate's serial number revealed

it to be part of the ransom. Bruno Richard Hauptmann, a thirty-six-year-old German immigrant, was arrested five days later.

The Trial: A circuslike atmosphere prevailed at the trial, which began in Flemington, New Jersey, on January 2, 1935, and was satirically described by H. L. Mencken as "the most important event since the Resurrection." Regular spectators ranged from socialites and movie stars to famous writers and Mafia kingpins. Many brought picnic lunches, which they consumed noisily, often hooting and cheering. The prosecution was led by David T. Wilentz, a smart young lawyer trying his first criminal case. Hauptmann's attorney was "Big Ed" Reilly, an alcoholic, slightly over-the-hill showman; his retainer was being paid by the Hearst organization, in the hope that he could boost newspaper sales by injecting some dramatic flair into what was widely considered an open-and-shut case.

While Lindbergh was initially the center of attention, he was quickly eclipsed in the popular mind by the accused killer. Hauptmann, whose defense fund was run by Nazi sympathizers, would indeed have made a perfect SS poster boy; at first his handsome Aryan features won many hearts, and one female juror even developed a crush. As the trial progressed, however, his snarling, smirking demeanor turned almost everyone against him. His claim that the ransom money had been given to him by a former business partner named Isidor Fisch, who had recently died after returning to Germany, was punctured by Wilentz's cross-examination.

The evidence against Hauptmann was compelling. He had a criminal record in Germany. The wooden ladder found at the crime scene was matched with floorboards in his attic; his handwriting was linked to the ransom notes; and several eyewitnesses, including Condon, identified him as the man who had negotiated the ransom and received the money, some $14,000 of which police had found in his garage. He was convicted of first-degree murder and sentenced to death. Governor Harold Hoffman of New Jersey, a political rival of Wilentz who was hoping to discover evidence of prosecutorial malfeasance, then launched his own investigation; when it turned up nothing, he finally offered to delay or even commute Hauptmann's sentence in return for an admission of guilt. Hauptmann refused, and on April 3, 1936, still proclaiming his innocence, he went to the electric chair.

The Aftermath: The decades following the trial have seen considerable debate concerning Hauptmann's innocence or guilt. Various alternative scenarios of the crime have been advanced, ranging from the outlandish to the vaguely plausible. One of the earliest and most sordid was presented by the German Nazi tabloid press, which claimed, not surprisingly, that the crime had been committed by Jews. Another theory suggested that the kidnapping was arranged by cronies of Al Capone in order to effect the notorious gangster's freedom.

Perhaps the most thorough revisionist account is presented by Anthony Scaduto in his book *Scapegoat: The Lonesome Death of Bruno Richard Hauptmann* (1976). Scaduto questions the reliability of the prosecution's handwriting experts, demonstrates that the defense failed to call witnesses who could have buttressed Hauptmann's claims that Fisch had given him the money, casts some doubt on the eyewitness testimony, and presents a credible case that the incriminating plank linking Hauptmann to the ladder was planted by a police captain who had earlier inquired if it were possible to counterfeit fingerprints—presumably Hauptmann's. According to Scaduto, the real culprit may have been Paul H. Wendel, a disbarred attorney who had known connections to Isidor Fisch, and who confessed to the crime. Scaduto does acknowledge that Wendel later repudiated his confession, which he claimed had been coerced after he himself had been kidnapped.

Joyce Milton, in her painstakingly detailed biography of the Lindberghs, *Loss of Eden* (1993), presents a compelling case for Hauptmann's guilt. She claims that, while police and prosecutors may well have violated Hauptmann's rights and broken laws governing rules of evidence, most if not all discrepancies can easily be explained without recourse to fanciful alternative theories. The evidence against Hauptmann, according to Milton, was very solid, and the forensic work quite advanced for its time. She also argues convincingly that Wendel's kidnapping and brutally coerced confession were arranged by none other than New Jersey governor Hoffman himself, in the hope of destroying his hated rival's political career. Under the Lindbergh Law, which was passed in 1932 and expanded the FBI's jurisdiction in kidnapping investigations, a detective named Ellis Parker (see page 128) and his son were indeed convicted of abducting Wendel.

It is unlikely, however, that the mystery surrounding the Lindbergh case will ever be completely resolved. Perhaps the most poignant—if not necessarily the most convincing—case for Hauptmann's innocence has been made by his widow, Anna, who, up until her own death in 1994, repeatedly claimed—as she had on the witness stand—that Hauptmann had been framed, and that her husband had been with her on the night of February 29, 1932.

—E.H.B.

THE MANSON KILLINGS

The Crime: The killings that occurred in Los Angeles on the night of August 8, 1969, live in the annals of grisly crime as perhaps the most horrifying and fascinating of the century.

For Steve Parent, an eighteen-year-old student who had come to 10050 Cielo Drive in Benedict Canyon to visit his nineteen-year-old buddy, caretaker William Garretson, the night, and his life, ended early. As he was driving his car off the estate, Tex Watson, a tall, scruffy young man with a Texas accent, stepped in front of his white Rambler, revolver drawn.

"Please don't hurt me," Parent pleaded. "I won't say anything." Watson shot him four times at point-blank range. Garretson, in a small house in one corner of the large property, heard nothing of what then happened in the big house.

In the house, large and luxurious, were Sharon Tate, twenty-six, eight months pregnant and the wife of Roman Polanski, director of high-quality horror films such as *Rosemary's Baby*. She and Polanski shared the big house with another couple, Abigail Folger, the twenty-five-year-old heiress to the coffee fortune, and her boyfriend, Voytek Frykowski, thirty-two, a Polish-born would-be writer and film producer. Also with them that night was Jay Sebring, thirty-five, hairstylist to the rich and famous.

Sharon Tate was clean and sober that night, but the others had ingested various drugs. Sebring was known to supply his rich clients with more than a good haircut—he was also a drug dealer.

Watson crept around the house, peering in windows. He then ordered his companions, Susan Atkins, Patricia Krenwinkel, and Linda Kasabian, to follow him in. Kasabian refused to go in, and was left outside as a lookout.

Frykowski was asleep on the sofa. Drawing his gun, Watson ordered, "Get up."

Frykowski wanted to know who he was. "I'm the Devil," Watson replied. "I'm here to do the Devil's business."

Watson sent the two girls to check out the rest of the house. Atkins found Abigail Folger in a bedroom. Putting a knife to her throat and assuring her she wouldn't get hurt if she followed orders, Atkins brought Folger into the living room.

Krenwinkel took over and Atkins, the more aggressive, burst into the room occupied by Sharon Tate and Jay Sebring. "Hurry," she said, "they need you in the living room. Something terrible has happened." Tate and Sebring rushed into the living room.

Watson ordered everybody onto the floor on their stomachs so he could tie them up. "I can't," Tate cried. "Can't you see I'm pregnant."

"Be reasonable, for Christ's sake," Sebring pleaded. "The woman'll hurt herself."

"Don't talk to me about Christ," Watson replied, and shot Sebring. He then tied a rope around Sebring's neck and looped it around the two women's necks as well. He tossed it over a beam and yanked on it, forcing them to their feet.

Frykowski, who had been tied up with a towel, was working his way free. In the struggle that ensued, Frykowski was stabbed by Atkins. Watson hit him with the pistol, but Frykowski managed to bolt. As he ran, Watson shot him twice.

Then it was Folger's turn. Even with Watson and Krenwinkel stabbing at her repeatedly she managed to run out toward the pool. They caught her and stabbed her over and over in a frenzy.

As all this happened, Tate was working free of the noose. Watson and Atkins plunged a bayonet into the pregnant woman's stomach. Over and over they stabbed her.

Using Tate's blood, the killers wrote "Pig" on a door, and fled.

Two nights later, on August 10, two more victims, in a house in the Silver Lake district, faced a crew of frenzied killers. Rosemary LaBianca, thirty-eight, and her husband Leno, forty-four, were suddenly confronted by an intruder armed with a gun—a short, skinny man with a bushy beard. This was Charles Manson. He tied them up with some ornamental leather thongs he had around his neck.

Tex Watson then appeared and stabbed Leno LaBianca, leaving the knife in his throat. In the bedroom, Patricia Krenwinkel and another female member of the group, Leslie Van Houten, were stabbing Rosemary LaBianca. They stabbed her forty-one times, including thirteen wounds made after the woman was dead.

With the fresh blood of their victims, the killers scrawled "Rise" and "Healter [sic] Skelter" on the walls. On Leno LaBianca's stomach, Watson scratched "war" with a carving fork.

The Investigation: It took police a while to connect the Cielo Drive murders with the killings of Leno and Rosemary LaBianca. The first break in the case came in a classic manner. A young woman named Susan Atkins, who also called herself Sadie Mae Glutz, was in jail on a minor charge. Another prisoner, Virginia Graham, heard Atkins bragging about what she knew of the murders of Tate and the others. Graham told police the man they wanted to talk to was Charles Manson.

Manson, thirty-four; Tex Watson, twenty-three; Susan Atkins, twenty-one; and Patricia Krenwinkel, twenty-one, were arrested. Linda Kasabian, twenty, the young woman who balked at going into the house on Cielo Drive, was granted immunity for her testimony, and, bit by bit, disturbing information started to come out about Charles Manson and his "family."

Atkins also confessed, pouring out her story to a grand jury. In March 1970, after a short meeting with Charles Manson, she retracted her confession.

The Trial: One of the longest (ten months), most costly, and most bizarre trials in California history started on June 15, 1970. It would end on March 29, 1971, and during that time America and the world would follow its unpredictable ins and outs and come away sickened and frightened at the revealing picture of society that would emerge.

Manson, the out-of-wedlock son of a teenage prostitute, was an almost illiterate ex-convict who had spent most of his life behind bars. As the trial progressed, it would emerge that this tiny man—he stood five-two—with an uncanny sense of street psychology and a gift of weaving verbal webs had collected around him a group of lost young souls. From the Haight-Ashbury neighborhood of San Francisco and the streets of Berkeley, he led his band of sad cases south to the dilapidated and abandoned Spahn Movie Ranch near Los Angeles.

There, on a diet of drugs, unlimited sex (the lion's share going to the guru himself), and rock music, he spun out his fantasy of Helter Skelter. The words were taken from the Beatles' "White Album" and, in Manson's twisted psyche, stood for the coming race war he was sure he could bring about. If he could get blacks to subdue their white "enemies," then he could step in when they found themselves incapable of governing themselves.

Mixed into this witch's brew was his desire to be famous in the music world. Two of his followers tortured and murdered Gary Hinman, someone on the periphery of the business that Manson thought should have been more helpful. Also angered at Gary Melcher, son of Doris Day and a player in the music world, Manson ordered his followers to brutally murder the residents of the house at 10050 Cielo, where Melcher had once lived. This would show Melcher how powerful he, Manson, was and get him the break he wanted in the music world—and, at the same time, bring on Helter Skelter.

How those two things could occur at the same time was clear only to Manson. His method of choosing the LaBiancas as his second set of victims was equally insane. They lived next door, Manson told his followers, to some people he'd once taken LSD with and who were rude to him. He'd show them—he'd kill their next-door neighbors!

After ten months of observing bizarre courtroom antics, the jury finally returned a verdict of guilty. Death was the sentence, but before it could be carried out the Supreme Court declared the death penalty unconstitutional.

The Aftermath: Interest in the Manson killings has risen and fallen since 1969, with special attention being paid in 1994, the twenty-fifth anniversary of the horror. At that time Charles Manson, Tex Watson, Susan Atkins, Patricia Krenwinkel, and Leslie Van Houten were all serving life sentences. All three of the women now claimed to denounce Manson. Linda Kasabian was a mother of four and believed to be living on the East Coast.

Watson declared himself a "born-again" Christian; he married and fathered three children during conjugal visits. Lynette "Squeaky" Fromme, who took over leadership of the family when Manson was jailed, tried to assassinate President Gerald Ford on September 5, 1975. She is in a federal prison in Marianna, Florida. Sandra Good, one of Manson's most loyal followers, did time on a lesser charge and lives in Hanford, California, to be near Charlie.

Before sending his followers to incite Helter Skelter, Manson wrote a song, "Look at Your Game, Girl." Nobody in the music business would touch it then, but now it appears on a Guns N' Roses album, The Spaghetti Incident? Manson's share of royalties goes to Bartek Frykowski, son of Voytek. The first check was for $72,000.

Will Manson ever get out of prison? The parole board has turned him down eight times. But the man himself has said, "At my will, I walk your streets and am right out there among you."
—R.W.S.

THE SIMPSON-GOLDMAN MURDERS
The Crime: Orenthal James Simpson, known by his more familiar name of O. J. Simpson, became one of America's most popular sports heroes in the late 1960s and the 1970s. His popularity stemmed as much from his charming personality as it did from his athletic ability on the football field. Simpson first achieved fame as a running back at the University of Southern California. In 1968 he won the Heisman Trophy, emblematic of college football's top player. He continued to achieve individual success in the professional ranks. In 1973, while playing for the Buffalo Bills, Simpson became the first National Football League (NFL) running back to gain more than 2,000 yards in one season. He was eventually elected to pro football's Hall of Fame.

But what seemed to separate Simpson from other sports stars during that same era was his image. The sixties and seventies were a time of tremendous and tumultuous changes in American race relations and that was often reflected on the athletic field. There was heavyweight champion Cassius Clay becoming Muhammad Ali and adopting the Islamic religion. Basketball star Lew Alcindor made a similar religious conversion and became Kareem Abdul-Jabbar. In 1968, during a victory ceremony at the Mexico City Olympics, two African-American athletes raised their arms and clenched their fists in a Black Power salute.

O. J. Simpson took part in none of this. If he was anything, he was noncontroversial. He was good looking. He was smooth. He seemed to be unassuming.

O. J. Simpson and his ex-wife, Nicole Brown Simpson, October 19, 1993.

Simpson was a black sports star who white America could adore, and executives on Madison Avenue took note of that. In what may have been his greatest success, Simpson became the spokesman for Hertz Rent-A-Car. After Simpson retired from professional football in 1979, his popularity continued. He earned success as a character actor appearing in such popular hit films as The Naked Gun, and he was a football analyst on NFL broadcasts.

The only scar came in 1989 when Simpson pleaded no contest to beating his wife, a stunning blond-haired woman, Nicole Brown Simpson. She was Simpson's second wife, and eleven years younger than he. But even then Simpson's image emerged virtually unscathed.

Simpson played down the incident and the public was willing to brush it aside as well. It would turn out that there was a side of O. J. Simpson that no one knew.

In the late hours of Sunday night, June 12, 1994, Simpson's now ex-wife Nicole and an acquaintance of hers, Ronald Goldman, were brutally stabbed to death in front of Nicole Brown Simpson's condominium in west Los Angeles. Later, investigators would call it an "overkill," a crime of rage.

The Investigation: Police were called to the murder scene just past midnight on June 13, and within a few hours their attention was focused on Nicole Brown Simpson's former husband, O. J. Simpson. Detectives discovered a bloody right-hand glove at Simpson's nearby Brentwood estate that matched a left-hand glove found at the murder scene. As detectives continued their investigation, they found a trail of small blood drops leading away from the murder scene and a similar trail leading into O. J. Simpson's house—blood drops that matched O. J. Simpson's blood type.

As police continued their search, more and

more signs pointed toward Simpson as a jealous ex-husband who went over the edge and brutally murdered his wife. The pristine public image appeared to be a facade. It turned out that the Simpsons' marriage was volatile and full of violent incidents.

Police revealed a frightening 911 emergency call placed by Nicole Brown Simpson on October 25, 1993, less than eight months before the murders took place. "He's fucking going nuts," Nicole Brown Simpson told a police dispatcher.

The day of the murders Simpson attended an afternoon dance recital for his daughter, Sydney. Also there were Nicole Brown Simpson; her parents, Louis and Juditha Brown; her sister Denise Brown; and the Simpsons' other child, Justin. There was no indication of trouble—in fact, Simpson gave a polite kiss to Denise Brown after the recital ended. The Brown family, without O. J. Simpson, went from the recital to a popular west-side restaurant, Mezzaluna, to celebrate Sydney's performance.

It was at Mezzaluna that Ronald Goldman's life became entangled in the murder mystery. Goldman, a good-looking twenty-five-year-old who hoped to become a model or actor, worked as a waiter at Mezzaluna and knew Nicole Brown Simpson from her frequent visits there. After dinner Nicole Simpson's mother apparently dropped her glasses outside the restaurant, a fact she discovered only when she returned home. When Nicole Brown Simpson phoned the restaurant, Ronald Goldman agreed to return them to Nicole at her condominium.

As for O. J. Simpson, while the Brown family was at Mezzaluna, he was at McDonald's with Kato Kaelin, who lived in a guest house at the Simpson estate. Kaelin and Simpson returned to the Simpson home at around 9:45 P.M., and for the next hour and fifteen minutes no one saw O. J. Simpson.

Simpson was scheduled to take an 11:52 P.M. flight to Chicago that night and had ordered a limousine to take him to the airport at around 11:00 P.M. But when limo driver Alan Park arrived at 10:40 P.M., there was no answer at Simpson's house. Park saw a black person enter Simpson's home just before 11:00 P.M., and shortly thereafter O. J. Simpson emerged, saying he had been sleeping.

The morning after the murders, Simpson returned from Chicago after being contacted by police, but because of his celebrity status he was allowed to remain free as the investigation continued. Every day more and more evidence seemed to point to Simpson. On Thursday, four days after the killings, Simpson and his children attended Nicole Brown Simpson's funeral.

The next day, Friday, police decided to make an arrest. But Simpson, along with Al Cowlings, his childhood friend and teammate at USC and with the Buffalo Bills, disappeared and Simpson was declared a fugitive. Police finally located Simpson and Cowlings in a white Ford Bronco, and a slow-speed chase ensued along Los Angeles freeways. Cowlings contacted police on a cellular phone and said he was taking Simpson back to his house.

For more than an hour dozens of police cars traveled in front of and behind the Bronco as Cowlings drove Simpson home. The entire chase was broadcast live on television across the United States.

When it was over, Simpson, who was carrying his passport and almost $9,000 in cash, was arrested and booked into the Los Angeles County jail as prisoner number BK4013970061794.

The Trial: Officially it was called *The People of the State of California* v. *Orenthal James Simpson*, and probably no trial has ever received so much attention. The first task for the court was to select a jury, and that proved to be an incredibly long and arduous task. Hundreds of prospective jurors were called in and given a 77-page questionnaire asking questions that included their experience with domestic violence, their personal feelings about Simpson, their knowledge of the case, and even their favorite TV shows and magazines.

Each prospective juror was then individually questioned by Judge Lance Ito and by the lawyers for both sides. The process took several months. It was almost like a human chess game with each side supposedly having its preferences. The prosecution preferred well-educated jurors who were white, while the defense wanted less-educated people who were black. Each side hired jury consultants to observe the way prospective jurors were answering questions.

It was decided that the jurors would be sequestered throughout the case at a Los Angeles hotel. All their actions, including phone calls to family members, would be monitored.

The jury that was eventually selected was predominately African-American. The judge decided before the case began to also select a large group of twelve alternate jurors who could be used as replacements in case any of the regular jurors had to be dismissed. It proved to be a wise move as the comings and goings of the jurors became a sideshow.

Ten jurors were dismissed in the first five months of the case and there was concern that the judge would run out of jurors, forcing a mistrial to be declared. There were various reasons for the dismissals. Some jurors were proved to have given false statements on their questionnaires, another was thought to be writing a book, another got stressed out by the pressure and had to be hospitalized. There was also a dispute between some of the black jurors and some of the white jurors.

The opening statements began on January 24, 1995, more than six months after the crime. The prosecution claimed Simpson was a football hero who had two very different sides. The defense claimed Simpson was a wonderful man who could not have killed. The prosecution portrayed Simpson as a control addict who could not deal with the fact that he no longer held sway over his former wife. Jurors were told of disturbing incidents in the years prior to the killings where Simpson would spy on his ex-wife and stalk her. Prosecutor Christopher Darden told the jurors that this was "a story as old as mankind."

Simpson assembled a high-priced team of well-known attorneys. They became known as the "Dream Team." It was led by Johnnie Cochran, a highly respected and charismatic black Los Angeles lawyer. He was assisted by Robert Shapiro and by F. Lee Bailey, a Boston-based lawyer who gained fame in the 1960s and had represented such famous clients as Dr. Sam Sheppard (who had been found guilty of the murder of his wife after ferocious pretrial publicity and whose conviction was overturned thanks to Bailey), Albert DeSalvo (the Boston Strangler), and Patricia Hearst (kidnapped newspaper heiress turned outlaw).

In his opening statement, Cochran said the blood evidence against Simpson was "contaminated, compromised, and corrupted." But the key suggestion by the defense was that Simpson was set up and framed by corrupt Los Angeles police. One policeman took center stage in the defense conspiracy theory—detective Mark Fuhrman. The defense, backed by audiotapes, argued that Fuhrman was a racist who didn't like the fact that O. J. Simpson was married to a white woman. Simpson's attorneys claimed that Fuhrman took a glove found at the murder scene and planted it at Simpson's estate to implicate him.

The defense also claimed that blood found at the murder scene and in Simpson's Bronco and on the infamous glove was planted by other policemen involved in a conspiracy with Fuhrman. Or perhaps the police had mixed up some of the blood samples at the crime lab.

They also suggested that the killings might have been a drug hit by murderers hired by a Colombian drug cartel. However, they were unable to produce any hard evidence to support their conspiracy theories.

The prosecution offered some emotional testimony. Denise Brown, a sister of Nicole, cried on the stand as she told how Simpson once threw her and her sister out of his house in a temper tantrum. The centerpiece of the prosecution's case, however, was the blood evidence, specifically DNA test results that matched blood found at the murder scene and Simpson's estate with the defendant and the two victims. The jury was told that in some instances the odds that another individual might have the same blood characteristics were several billion to one.

The prosecution made one memorable and perhaps fatal error. They asked Simpson to try on the gloves that were recovered at the murder site and at his house. Simpson stood in front of the jury box and pulled them on, but they didn't seem to fit. The prosecution accused Simpson of faking, but the damage had been done.

The defense was never able to come up with a believable alibi for Simpson. For months Simpson had stated that he was asleep at the time of the murders. But when phone records revealed that he had placed a call from his car phone at the time, his lawyers argued that he had actually been practicing golf in his yard.

In his closing argument, Johnnie Cochran tried to shift the focus from Simpson to Mark Fuhrman and the police. He also repeatedly reminded jurors of the glove demonstration, telling them over and over again, "If it doesn't fit, you must acquit."

In a city where the police and the criminal justice system had repeatedly mistreated minorities, would a jury composed largely of African Americans convict one of black America's biggest sports heroes? On October 3, 1995, after less than four hours of deliberation, the jury of nine blacks, two whites, and one Latino pronounced O. J. Simpson not guilty.

—S.F.

GREAT DETECTIVES AND THEIR MOST FAMOUS CASES

RAYMOND SCHINDLER AND THE SMITH CASE (1911)
The Crime: In New Jersey's Asbury Park, in early 1911, ten-year-old Marie Smith went to school one morning and didn't return. Her body was found the following afternoon in some bushes. She had been smashed over the head with a heavy object, sexually assaulted, and strangled with her own stocking. There were no clues, no murder weapon, no footprints.

Enter the Detective: At twenty-three, prospecting for gold in northern California, Raymond C. Schindler lost his small grubstake. He arrived penniless in San Francisco on April 19, 1906, the day after the great earthquake. Eventually he found work with an insurance company, investigating damage done by the earthquake. Schindler was so thorough in his research that he was later appointed to a federal team investigating the corrupt practices of San Francisco city government. When this investigation was brought to a successful close, the head of the team opened his own detective agency and asked Schindler to head the New York office. Two years later, Schindler formed his own agency.

A large, muscular man, Schindler was wildly creative and utterly thorough, a combination that quickly earned him an international reputation. The Marie Smith case, one of Schindler's earliest, is still considered a work of art.

The Chase: The search for the child's attacker led to the home of Thomas Williams, a black man who neighbors said "had been in trouble before." Williams's only alibi: "I stopped to drink from a bottle of whiskey I had with me and I fell asleep." The public cried for vengeance, but the case was too pat for Sheriff Clarence Hatrick. Secretly, lest the citizens outraged with Williams become uncontrollable, Hatrick hired Schindler to investigate.

Posing as a credit-company investigator, Schindler quietly compiled information about the Smiths' neighbors; he eliminated all but one of them as suspects. He would have dismissed a young German, Frank Heideman, as a suspect too, except that Heideman had been in the United States for only two years. Schindler left nothing to chance. In checking with German authorities, he discovered that Heideman had been arrested for child molesting. When the charges were dismissed, Heideman had immediately sailed for the United States.

Schindler also planted one of his men as a prisoner in the cell with the accused Williams. Several days of conversation between the two men convinced the black investigator that Williams was innocent. With no evidence, Schindler's only hope was somehow to trick Heideman into confessing to murder. For this, Schindler masterminded a plot worthy of Arthur Conan Doyle himself.

The Hound of the Baskervilles provided inspiration for an outlandish plan, but it backfired on Schindler. The florist who employed Heideman, and owned the house where he boarded, kept a large dog. Schindler's strategy was to cause the dog to howl all night until Heideman broke. Schindler's detectives threw rocks at the dog for a week, but Heideman didn't break; he moved to New York to get away from the howling dog and enjoy a night's sleep. Or so he told his friends.

Schindler's men followed Heideman to Manhattan. He ate every meal at the same German restaurant, always at the same table and at about the same time. On Schindler's staff was a young man named Neimeister who hailed from the same region of Germany as Heideman. Schindler instructed Neimeister to frequent the restaurant until Heideman engaged him in conversation.

Neimeister took his meals a few tables away from the suspect. Several days passed. Then Neimeister casually pulled a German newspaper from his pocket. Heideman looked up. "You read German?"

"Why not?" replied Neimeister. "I come from Germany. Would you like to look at my paper?"

A conversation ensued, and their friendship quickly developed. One afternoon Heideman asked his friend, "Don't you have to work for a living?" From the beginning, Neimeister had been coached to the answer to this question. "Not me," he replied. "I'm one of the fortunate ones. My father died and left everything to me."

Schindler next arranged for Neimeister to withdraw money from a dummy bank account in Heideman's presence. When they entered the bank, a bank officer, well rehearsed by Schindler, greeted the supposed wealthy German heir. Neimeister wrote a check for several thousand dollars and held it so that Heideman could readily see the amount. The bank officer cashed the check himself and returned with two fistfuls of cash. Heideman was impressed.

At Heideman's suggestion, the two men became roommates, but Heideman confided nothing to Neimeister about the murder. Schindler stepped up the pace.

He asked a producer friend for "the worst horror picture you have on hand." The producer offered a French film about a little girl who is attacked by a sex maniac and must fight for her life. Schindler arranged with a theater for a one-time showing of the silent horror film. During their after-dinner stroll, Neimeister and Heideman passed the theater and Neimeister suggested they stop in to relax and watch a show. Halfway through the film, Heideman jumped out of his seat in a sweat, saying, "I can't stand any more of this." He returned to their room alone, but he said nothing more.

Next, from his bag of tricks, Schindler pulled a German newspaper, a fake edition printed by a publisher friend containing a short piece about a man named Heideman who had worked for a florist in Asbury Park and then disappeared. Neimeister remarked that here was a story about a man with the same name as his roommate's. Heideman read it. "That's me, I worked two weeks in Asbury Park, but I couldn't stay there after that horrible murder. Good thing they caught the murderer."

The next scenario was just that; Schindler composed a one-act play starring Neimeister and carefully rehearsed the actors, except for Heideman. Following the script, Neimeister suggested to Heideman that they take a ride in Neimeister's automobile. Traveling down a predetermined, deserted road, the actor-detective suddenly told Heideman he thought a tire was going flat. When he got out to inspect the faulty tire, a Schindler man dressed as a tramp appeared and asked for a ride. Neimeister refused. The tramp became surly and pulled a knife. Then Neimeister drew a pistol from his pocket and fired a blank shot at his assailant, who fell "dead" on cue. The young German heir then leaped into the car and raced back to their rooming house, pleading with Heideman not to tell anyone what had happened.

Schindler's encore took place the following morning, with the aid of another forged German newspaper with a short article on the murdered tramp. Neimeister read it first, then handed it nervously to Heideman, who assured him his secret was safe.

To force Heideman's hand, Schindler hastily rewrote the script to include a steamship ticket to Germany for Neimeister, who left the ticket lying in a conspicuous place. Heideman was alarmed at seeing it. "What's that?" he asked. "You aren't leaving me, are you?"

"Yes, I am," said Neimeister. "I'm going back to Germany, where they'll never find me." Heideman suggested they go together, but Neimeister said, "You saw me kill a man. Suppose we had a falling out and you decided to squeal on me?"

Heideman answered slowly, "Listen, if you had a hold on me like I have on you, then would you take me along?"

Neimeister had waited a long time for just such a nibble; now feigning reluctance, he quizzed Heideman, waiting patiently for the hook to set. Finally, an exasperated Heideman blurted out, "Would it make any difference if I told you I had killed that little girl in Asbury?" The hook was set. Heideman began to flop and sputter. He said he had been overcome by sexual desire. He said he had killed the little girl and hidden her body. He said, "They've arrested another man. They'll never get me." But Neimeister remained adamant. He went to bed, leaving his fish on the line, churning the water.

The Solution: Secretly, Neimeister notified Schindler, who in turn notified the Asbury Park police. The next morning, with a crowd of officials concealed in an adjoining room, Neimeister landed his catch, who talked at length about Marie Smith's murder. When the police stepped out and arrested him, he claimed he had concocted the wild story merely to win the confidence of his friend.

Williams was released from jail. Heideman pleaded innocent, but his confession before the law officers persuaded the jury to find him guilty of murder. He died in the electric chair.
—G.K.

ELLIS PARKER AND THE PICKLED CORPSE CASE (1920)

The Crime: When on October 5, 1920, a sixty-year-old bank runner disappeared with a pouch containing $70,000 in cash and another $30,000 in negotiable securities, it was assumed he had absconded. Investigation showed that although considered to be a prim husband, David Paul of Camden, New Jersey, was quite a wild lover and had taken part in numerous orgies at a cottage some distance outside of town. His sex-oriented friends insisted they had not seen him the night before his disappearance. Then eleven days later Paul's body was found in a shallow grave in a weeded area. He had been shot through the head. Mysteriously, while the ground around the corpse was bone-dry, Paul's overcoat and clothing were sopping wet. The only explanation the police could come up with was that possibly his murderer hadn't been sure whether the bullet had killed him and had therefore "drowned" him in a nearby stream, Bread and Cheese Run. He had been dead, however, according to an autopsy, for only forty-eight to seventy-two hours. Thus either he had absconded with the money and was later killed for it, or he had been kidnapped at the start but kept alive by his abductor for eight or nine days before being eliminated.

Enter the Detective: Ellis Parker was a five-foot-six-inch, soft-spoken, blue-eyed, gentle-looking man who could have passed for a small-town grocer or almost anything but what he was—the chief of detectives of Burlington County, New Jersey. Known as the "county detective with a worldwide reputation," Parker was noted for his ability as a crime solver, and other jurisdictions, especially other sheriffs, in the state often called on him for aid. Parker firmly believed that the logical interpretation of facts was almost always the correct one. So far as alibis were concerned, he was convinced that most criminals fabricate an alibi before they commit a crime; therefore, he automatically suspected any person with an alibi. He once nailed a soldier for the murder of a fellow GI at Fort Dix, even though there were more than a hundred likely suspects. Only one man could provide an alibi for the time the crime was committed. It was illogical for someone to remember what he was doing three months earlier, so the soldier with that alibi headed Parker's suspect list. The shrewd detective soon found incriminating evidence against the murderer and got a confession.

The Chase: Two things about the Paul case struck Parker as illogical. One was that the killer or killers had apparently kept the victim alive for eight or nine days. If they were going to kill him, logic demanded that they do it immediately. The second illogical fact was that the dead man's clothing had been soaking wet. Parker concluded that these two perplexing facts must somehow be related. The more he thought about the case, the more he felt that Paul had been killed at once, regardless of medical findings. Parker would instantly have realized the reason for the victim's wet clothing if Camden County had been his own bailiwick. He would have known about the water in Bread and Cheese

Run. As it was, he did not guess the solution until he happened to discover that tanning factories lay upstream. At this point he filled a bottle with water and took it to a chemist for analysis. Bread and Cheese Run, he discovered, contained a high percentage of tannic acid. And tannic acid is an excellent preservative. A body submerged in this stream would undergo virtually no decomposition in ten days and would therefore appear to be that of a person dead only a very short time.

The Solution: Once Parker had determined that Paul was killed close to the time of his disappearance, he reexamined alibis. The fact that the killer or killers knew about the chemical properties of the stream meant they were locals. Who had been questioned about the case who didn't have an alibi for the time Paul disappeared, but did have one for the "false" period of his murder?

The answer was Frank James and Raymond Schuck, the two men who shared an orgy cottage with Paul. James, a salesman, had been in Detroit for five days at a convention, but that merely proved he couldn't have murdered Paul on the day that he allegedly was killed. Schuck was in the same boat; he had conveniently gone to visit friends downstate during that supposedly critical period. Parker found that while the two men had not spent any large sums of money recently, Schuck, a married man, had given a girlfriend who frequented the cottage an expensive fur coat the day after Paul's disappearance.

Separately, Parker broke the two men down, first building up their confidence and then shattering their useless alibis. Each confessed, meanwhile insisting that the other had done the actual killing. Most of the stolen money was found buried in a Camden cemetery in the grave of Schuck's mother. Both men were executed.

Parker managed to carve out an illustrious record in four decades of detective work, during which he solved about 350 crimes, including 118 out of the 124 murder cases submitted to him. Yet he ended up a tragic figure. When news of the Lindbergh kidnapping broke in 1932, Parker was insulted because the law officials who had leaned on him so much in the past failed to contact him. Parker brooded about the case, and after the arrest of Bruno Hauptmann he became convinced that the real culprit was Paul Wendel, a Trenton, New Jersey, man. Parker virtually kidnapped Wendel and held him captive in various hideaways in Brooklyn and New Jersey until he extracted a so-called confession. In court Wendel effectively repudiated this "confession," and Parker faced a federal charge of abduction. He was sent to prison for six years and died at the penitentiary in Lewisburg, Pennsylvania, before he had finished half his sentence.

—C.S.

EDWARD HEINRICH AND THE MAIL TRAIN MURDERS (1923)

The Crime: On October 11, 1923, a Southern Pacific mail train, its coaches filled with passengers, was moving slowly through a tunnel in the Siskiyou Mountains in southern Oregon when two men armed with shotguns climbed over the tender (the car behind the engine) and ordered the engineer and fireman to stop as soon as the engine and tender cleared the tunnel. The trainmen could do nothing but comply. They pulled to a halt as the third car, which carried the mail, was also partially clear of the tunnel. As the railroaders watched, immobile in the stare of the shotguns, a man emerged from the woods holding a bulky package, which he placed against the side of the mail car. Running back to a detonator, this third man set off an explosion. The mail car was enveloped in flames. In fact, the charge was so great that the robbers could not even approach the mail car. Their attempt to rob it was therefore a failure; furthermore, they had incinerated the lone clerk inside.

Before the trio could leave, a brakeman who had heard the explosion came running forward through the tunnel. Perhaps out of frustration, perhaps to prevent identification, the bandits shot down the three railroaders in cold blood, bringing the death toll to four, and fled.

Enter the Detective: Immediately after the tragedy, county lawmen, railroad police, postal detectives, and other authorities descended on the scene. They found a detonating device equipped with batteries. Nearby were a revolver and a well-worn and greasy pair of blue denim overalls, as well as some shoe covers made out of burlap soaked in creosote, evidently intended to be worn by the bandits to throw bloodhounds off their scent. It appeared that the criminals had used some alternative false-scent tactic, because posses utilizing canine trackers were stopped cold. After several weeks all the investigators had come up with was a mechanic from a garage some miles away who, not surprisingly, worked in grease. The grime on his clothes appeared to be similar to the grease found on the overalls. He was questioned at length, but he kept insisting he was innocent. Then someone finally suggested, "Let's see if that fellow Heinrich in Berkeley can help us."

Edward Oscar Heinrich at forty-two was a private investigator and handwriting expert who lectured at the University of California on scientific methods of criminal detection. He had already aided police all over the country in hundreds of cases, among them the Fatty Arbuckle manslaughter scandal, and he was commonly known as the "Edison of crime detection." To call him a private detective was indeed a put-down. He was, rolled into one, a geologist, a physicist, a biochemist, a handwriting expert, and an authority on papers and inks. According to Heinrich, the scene of a criminal act always contains many clues, and it is up to the scientific investigator to find and interpret those clues correctly.

The Chase: The first thing Heinrich did was to make a microscopic examination of the overalls and their "contents," such as the dried grease stains and lint from the pockets. He then ordered the mechanic released. "The stains are not auto grease. They're pitch from fir trees. The man you are looking for," he told awed detectives, "is a left-handed lumberjack who's worked the logging camps of the Pacific Northwest. He's thin, has light brown hair, rolls his own cigarettes, is fussy about his appearance. He's five feet ten inches and is in his early twenties."

None of this was guesswork. Heinrich had found everything out during his laboratory tests. He readily identified the stains as pitch from fir trees, and in the pockets he found bits of Douglas fir needles, common to the forests of the Pacific Northwest. The pockets on the left side of the overalls were worn more than those on the right, and the garment was habitually buttoned from the left side. Hence, the man was left-handed. In the hem of a pocket were two or three fingernail trimmings, carefully cut, indicating that the man was fussy about his appearance. On one button the scientists found a single light brown hair. It indicated the man's coloring, of course; but even more important, through special techniques Heinrich had devised, he was able to compute the man's age by the thickness and character of this single hair.

Heinrich had a final clue, which other investigators had totally overlooked. Wedged at the bottom of the narrow pencil pocket was a small wad of paper, apparently accidentally jammed down by a pencil and washed with the garment several times. The printing on the slip had been blurred past all legibility, but by treating the paper with iodine vapor, Heinrich succeeded in identifying it as registered mail receipt number 263-L, issued at Eugene, Oregon.

The Solution: Heinrich's work was now completed, and postal and other detectives took over. They found that the mail receipt had been obtained by Roy D'Autremont of Eugene when he sent fifty dollars to his brother in Lakewood, New Mexico. Authorities located Roy's father in Eugene. It turned out that the elder D'Autremont was worried about his twin sons, Roy and Ray, and another son, Hugh, who had disappeared on October 11, the date of the train holdup. Left-handed Roy fit all the characteristics Heinrich had cited. What followed was one of the most intensive manhunts in American history. Over the next three years and four months, half a million dollars was spent search-

ing for the trio. Circulars were printed in a hundred languages and mailed to police departments around the world. Records of the wanted men's teeth, eyeglass prescriptions, and medical history were supplied to dentists, oculists, and doctors. Finally, in March 1927, Hugh was captured in Manila in the Philippines, and a month later the twins were found in Steubenville, Ohio, working in a steel mill under assumed names. Faced with Heinrich's evidence, the three brothers pleaded guilty and were sentenced to life imprisonment.

Edward Heinrich went back to his laboratory. By the time of his death in 1953 he was credited with having solved 2,000 major and minor mysteries for the police, when they had been baffled by what they considered a lack of clues.
                                                              —C.S.

MAXIMILIAN LANGSNER AND THE MURDERER'S MIND (1928)

The Crime: On the evening of July 8, 1928, the Royal Canadian Mounted Police received a panicky telephone call from Dr. Harley Heaslip, who reported a mass murder on a farm some five miles outside of Mannville, Alberta, where the wealthy Booher family lived, along with their hired hands. "Half of them have been murdered," Heaslip said. Constable Fred Olsen went to the scene immediately and found the body of Mrs. Rose Booher slumped over the dining room table. She had been shot in the back of the head. In the kitchen lay the body of her elder son, Fred, shot three times in the face. An inspection of the bunkhouse and barn turned up two more corpses, hired hands who could conceivably have heard the first shots and seen the killer. Since Mrs. Booher had been killed while picking stems from a batch of strawberries, she was obviously the first victim, for she would hardly have gone on hulling strawberries if she had heard her son being murdered in the next room. Clearly, Fred had heard the shot and had come to the door to investigate. There the killer had shot him. Then the killer had marched outside and eliminated the two hired hands so that they could never tell what, if anything, they had heard or seen.

Henry Booher and his younger son, Vernon, had spent the afternoon working separately on different parts of the farm, and the two daughters in the family had been in town. Neither of the two male Boohers had paid any attention to the shots because they were common in the country, especially just then when foxes were on the prowl.

Enter the Detective: The police, under Inspector James Hancock, head of the Bureau of Criminal Investigation at Edmonton, and Detective Jim Leslie, arrived the next day to take charge of the case. Nothing had been stolen, and judging by what Mrs. Booher had been doing at the time of the crime, it was also clear the murderer was neither a stranger nor an intruder. Indeed, the fact that the killer had hunted out the men in the barn and bunkhouse confirmed this. The murder weapon was not found, but it was identified as a .303 Lee-Enfield rifle, and such a weapon had been reported stolen from the home of a neighboring farmer, Charles Stevanson. The killer obviously knew his way about the Stevanson home as well, since the weapon was always hidden in a closet. Everything pointed back to the surviving Boohers. But which one? Henry Booher appeared totally crushed by the tragedy; however, Vernon seemed strangely unmoved. Police inquiries unearthed the fact that Vernon had recently expressed hatred for his mother because she had broken up his romance with a local girl. Although Vernon was taken into custody, he refused to make a statement, and without the murder weapon the police had no case.

With the investigation still stymied after several weeks of legwork, Inspector Hancock did a strange thing for a professional policeman. He risked public ridicule by bringing in a Vienna-born mind reader who was then demonstrating his art in Vancouver. Maximilian Langsner had studied psychology with Freud in Vienna and later had gone to India, where he researched the way yogis attempted to control the mind. According to Langsner, the human mind, under stress, produced signals that another trained mind can learn to pick up. Newspaper accounts of his career told of the aid he had given European police in solving crimes. For instance, he had assisted the Berlin police in the recovery of some stolen jewels. To do this he had sat facing the suspect for some time, until he got a "signal" telling him where the jewels were hidden. Following Langsner's instructions, the police found the loot, and the thief confessed. Remarkably, Langsner had recently duplicated this feat in a similar case in Vancouver.

The Chase: Langsner, a dapper little man of thirty-five who resembled screen actor Adolphe Menjou, arrived in Edmonton a few days later. After being briefed, he was taken by the inspector to confront Vernon Booher. Following a quick, silent meeting with the prisoner, Langsner told Hancock, "The rifle is unimportant. He is guilty. He admitted it to me."

Hancock reminded Langsner that this was not proof and added that if they could locate the Enfield, they would probably get a confession. Langsner placed a chair outside the suspect's cell and sat there staring at twenty-one-year-old Vernon Booher. He explained to Hancock that the prisoner would know he wanted to determine where the rifle was and so would start thinking of it, thus giving off the proper impulses. Finally, after a five-hour period during which Booher alternately sat quietly and screamed at the mentalist, Langsner left the cell block. He had his information.

The Solution: Langsner sketched a farmhouse, a number of bushes, and some trees. Then he sketched more bushes some 500 yards from the house and said the rifle was buried there. The building Langsner described was white with red shutters—the Booher place. When Langsner and the officers went to the farm, they quickly located the bushes the mind reader had sketched. Within moments the .303 Enfield was found buried under the soft sod. Brought to the scene and confronted with the crime, Vernon Booher broke down and confessed, as his tearful father and sisters watched. He had meant to shoot only his mother, but when his brother Fred rushed into the house, Vernon knew he had to kill him too. Vernon expressed remorse only for the death of his brother. He shrugged off the murder of the handymen as merely part of a necessary cover-up.

Vernon Booher—the man who, according to Langsner, could not "escape his own thoughts"—was hung for quadruple murder on April 26, 1929. As for Maximilian Langsner, whose work in the case was fully reported in the newspapers of the time thanks to a grateful Inspector Hancock, he left Vancouver shortly thereafter to spend the next several years conducting psychic research among the Eskimos. The little Austrian was last heard of in 1939, as he prepared to launch a tour of the Middle East.
—C.S.

TAMEGORO IKII AND THE BANK POISONING MASSACRE (1948)

The Crime: The doors of the Teikoku Bank in the bustling Shiina-machi district of Tokyo, Japan, were about to close at 3:30 P.M. on January 26, 1948, when a thin, distinguished-looking man wearing a loose-fitting white coat with an official-looking armband bearing the word *Sanitation* on it pushed inside. At his urgent request he was ushered into the office of the acting bank manager, Takejiro Yoshida. Once there he explained that he was a civilian doctor attached to General Douglas MacArthur's staff and that he had been sent to immunize the bank's employees against amoebic dysentery, which had become rife in the area.

The bank officer had no objection. In postwar Tokyo the drastic shortage of food had resulted in numerous cases of food poisoning; in fact, Yoshida's superior had gone home early that day with an upset stomach. Then, too, civilians were used to following the orders of the occupying powers. At the time, MacArthur was often referred to as Shogun MacArthur.

The "doctor" told the entire staff plus Yoshida to bring their teacups, which he filled with a liquid he said offered better immunization than an injection. He said some of them might find their throats irritated for a moment, and for them he had a second liquid to relieve the discomfort. He instructed everyone to drink quickly, since he had many other places to visit and was pressed for time. As they drank, many were overcome with excruciating pain and dropped to the floor. Only Yoshida, two other men, and one woman would survive.

The bogus doctor stepped over the bodies and went to the tills, picking up 164,400 yen and an uncashed check for 17,405 yen, or a total of just over $500, in exchange for a dozen lives.

Enter the Detective: At forty-three, Tamegoro Ikii was one of Tokyo's crack investigators, having solved his share of murder and robbery cases. When several weeks of inquiry by teams of investigators turned up only dead ends, Ikii was ordered to drop his other assignments and concentrate on the poison-in-the-teacup affair.

The Chase: At first all that the police could discover about the worst crime committed in postwar Japan was that it had been preceded by two apparent "rehearsals" at other banks. During one the murderer had given the bank manager a card that identified him as Dr. Shigeru Matsui. (He had presented a card imprinted with a different name to the bank official in the fatal robbery, but he had reappropriated it.) These earlier guinea pigs had drunk the proffered liquid and suffered no ill effects. The doctor left, promising that a military health team would check up on the bank later, but none did. Since no crime was apparent, however, no one reported the incident.

The exchange of calling cards has an important meaning in Japan, and custom calls for each party to retain cards so received. When the police tracked down the real Dr. Matsui, he said he had had 100 such cards printed and had only four left. He had exchanged about fifty and given the rest to patients. Because he could not remember which patients, the police questioned all of them. Ikii was convinced the solution lay in the fifty calling cards Dr. Matsui had exchanged with businessmen, fellow doctors, and other acquaintances. He questioned and requestioned the recipients, and surreptitiously checked the financial condition of each of them. That led eventually to the most likely suspect in Ikii's view, an artist of some renown whom the doctor had met on a ferry. Fifty-six-year-old Sadamichi Hirasawa, who lived on the Japanese island of Hokkaido, had been interrogated earlier and dropped as a suspect because he was so quiet and mild-mannered. However, Ikii discovered that the artist had actually been in Tokyo at the time of the crime, and further check of his movements showed that he could have been at the Teikoku Bank at the crucial moment. Ikii also discovered that Hirasawa

needed money badly, and that shortly after the robbery 44,500 yen had been deposited in his bank account. Ikii was by then convinced that Hirasawa was his man, because he felt the plot was not only ingenious but also so bizarre that it would take an artist's mind to conceive it. No one else on the suspect list qualified.

The Solution: Although ordered by his superiors to drop the artist as a suspect, Ikii persisted. He believed no murderer could conceal the facts without telling little lies. Hirasawa claimed the money he deposited in the bank came from one of his artistic benefactors—the patronage system was still much in use in Japan—but Ikii learned that actually this man had died two months earlier. During his meetings with the suspect, Ikii treated him with the utmost respect and even asked him for an autographed photo of himself. Hirasawa said he had none, which Ikii knew had to be another lie; all artists used photographs to promote their careers. Before escorting the suspect to a restaurant, the officer phoned the hostess there and asked her to have photos taken as he and his guest said good-bye. But in one the artist dropped his gaze and in the other he distorted his face, so the survivors of the massacre could not identify Hirasawa from the pictures.

Finally the detective caught Hirasawa in a lie that all of the other investigators had overlooked. He had said he no longer had Dr. Matsui's card because the card had been in the pocket of an overcoat that had been stolen in a Tokyo restaurant the previous day. Ikii pounced on that, charging the artist with a string of deceptions, the supposed theft of the garment being the capping one. No one in Tokyo, he pointed out, wore an overcoat in the steamy month of May.

The artist eventually cracked and made a full confession. He also admitted that the so-called rehearsals had been tries at the real thing but his mixture of potassium cyanide had been too weak to kill. At his trial Hirasawa retracted his confession, saying the police had not allowed him to sleep until he made a statement. In a Japan mindful of democratic reforms, the defendant's charge was taken seriously, even though few crimes had enraged the public as much as the mass poisoning. Defense leagues were organized for the artist, and they pointed out that some of the survivors were shaky in their identification of Hirasawa. Nonetheless, the artist was found guilty and sentenced to be hung. Many Japanese, however, fought against any resumption of the death penalty. As a result the case dragged on as the courts rejected no less than twenty-four appeals. In time Hirasawa became the oldest person on death row anywhere in the world. He eventually died of pneumonia on May 10, 1987, at the age of ninety-five. While many people fought to prevent the execution of Hirasawa, many others lionized Officer Ikii. When he retired in 1964, he held the rank of inspector and was often hailed in the streets as a celebrity.

—C.S.

UNSOLVED MURDERS

THE HALL-MILLS CASE (1922)

The Crime: On the afternoon of September 16, 1922, a young couple strolling in De Russey's Lane near New Brunswick, New Jersey, stumbled across the bodies of a man and a woman. The man, dressed in a suit and a clerical collar, had been shot once in the head. The woman, who wore a blue polka-dot dress, lay beside him. There was a triangle of bullet holes in her forehead. Her throat had been cut and her tongue, larynx, and trachea had been neatly excised.

The man was identified as the Reverend Edward Wheeler Hall, aged forty-one, rector of Saint John the Evangelist, a fashionable Episcopal church in New Brunswick. The woman was Mrs. Eleanor Mills, thirty-four, wife of the sexton in the Reverend Mr. Hall's church and a member of the church choir. There was speculation that the murderer took her tongue, larynx, and trachea because she was a singer.

The bodies were carefully arranged under a crab apple tree. The woman's head was cradled in the man's arm and her dress was smoothed out and properly extended down past her knees. The minister's eyeglasses were still on and one of his calling cards was propped against his shoe.

Scattered around the bodies were a number of torrid love letters written by Mrs. Mills and addressed to the clergyman. "I know there are girls with more shapely bodies, but I do not care what they have," read one. "I have the greatest of all blessings, the deep, true, and eternal love of a noble man. My heart is his, my life is his, all that I have is his . . . I am his forever."

The Investigation: Because of the intimate relationship between the victims, suspicion naturally focused on their families. But the investigation was, according to one observer, "shot through from beginning to end with incompetent bungling." First of all, the victims were from Middlesex County but the bodies were found just over the county line in Somerset County. As government officials battled over which county had jurisdiction over the case, the crime scene was neglected. The police did not cordon off the scene and curious onlookers trampled over the land, picking up key pieces of evidence.

The police, desperate to solve the crime, arrested Clifford Hayes, a nineteen-year-old friend of the couple who had discovered the bodies. Unable to build a case around Hayes or come up with a credible motive, the police released him after a few days in custody. Suspicion once again focused on the victims' families, primarily on Mrs. Hall and her brothers, but a five-day grand jury hearing failed to charge anyone with the murders. No suspects were indicted during the next four years, and had it not been for the prodding of the *New York Daily Mirror*, the case might have been closed.

In July 1926 the Hearst paper printed a petition for the annulment of the marriage between Arthur S. Riehl and Louise Geist—a former maid at Reverend Hall's residence. In his petition, Mr. Riehl stated that his wife of ten months had withheld from him the following information: On the night of the murder, Miss Geist had informed Mrs. Hall that her husband and Mrs. Mills were planning to elope. The Halls' chauffeur then drove Mrs. Hall and her brother Willie, who lived with them, to De Russey's Lane. Louise Geist was paid $5,000 to be quiet.

The Reverend Edward Hall (far left) and his mistress, Eleanor Mills (standing in white), were found murdered on September 16, 1922.

Although this story was later denied by both Miss Geist and the Halls' chauffeur, other witnesses came forth and the *Mirror* continued to run front-page articles about the unsolved murder. Under public pressure, Governor A. Harry Moore ordered the case reopened.

Finally, on July 28, the clergyman's widow, the former Frances Noel Stevens, was accused of committing the double murder. The staid daughter of a socially prominent family, she had been seven years older than her philandering husband. Charged with her were her two brothers, Willie and Henry Stevens. Willie, swarthy and bushy-haired, was an eccentric who could find nothing better to do than hang around the firehouse. Henry was prim and respectable, the model of a country-club gentleman. Also arrested—but held over for a separate trial— was their cousin, Henry Carpender, a distinguished New York stockbroker.

Clues: The prosecution faced an uphill battle. Most of the scant evidence collected in 1922 was missing and key witnesses had moved out of the area. Sworn affidavits of grand-jury witnesses, as well as the transcribed testimony given in the grand jury, had mysteriously vanished.

Also missing was a .32-caliber gun that police believed to be the murder weapon. Autopsy reports confirmed that the victims had been killed with a .32-caliber pistol, and cartridge shells had been found at the murder scene. Mrs. Hall's brother Willie, thought to be mentally deficient, owned a .32-caliber pistol. Back in 1922 police had located the gun but discovered that the gun wouldn't shoot because the firing pin had been filed down. Prior to the trial, the gun couldn't be found and neither could the mechanic who had filed the firing pin.

Even the crab apple tree had disappeared. Over the years, souvenir hunters had literally ripped it apart.

The Trial: Opened on November 3 in the Somerset County Courthouse in rural Somerville and lasting a month, the trial fueled the tabloid headlines every day. Justice Charles W. Parker, of the state supreme court, presided. He was assisted by a local justice named Frank A. Cleary.

The special prosecutor was Alexander Simpson, an ambitious state senator who made up in melodramatics what he lacked in solid evidence. Early in the trial he established the torrid relationship between the clergyman and the choir singer by calling to the stand the dead woman's sixteen-year-old daughter, Charlotte, a flapper who reveled in the limelight. She identified the love letters of the Reverend Mr. Hall and Mrs. Mills, which Mrs. Mills had stored in a crocheted bag in her living room. One of the minister's letters addressed his lover

as "Darling wonder heart" and went on to say: "I just want to crush you for two hours. I want to see you Friday night alone by our road, where we can let out, unrestrained, that universe of joy and happiness that will be ours."

Prosecutor Simpson presented one of the Reverend Mr. Hall's calling cards, found at the scene of the murder, and experts identified the fingerprints on it as those of Willie Stevens. But the prints were later proved to have been fraudulently superimposed.

Then came the most sensational moment of the trial. Simpson called Mrs. Jane Gibson, who claimed to be an eyewitness to the murders. Because she owned a pig farm near the lovers' lane, she had been dubbed "the Pig Woman" in the press. On the first day of the trial she had collapsed of what was diagnosed as a severe stomach ailment and had had to be hospitalized. When she testified on November 18, she was carried into court on a stretcher and put on a hospital bed in front of the judge.

On the night of the murders, she said, while she was looking for a thief who had been stealing her corn, she heard several people having an argument. First one woman demanded, "Explain these letters." Then there were the sounds of a scuffle. Finally a shot and the voices of two women: "One said, 'Oh, Henry,' easy, very easy; and the other began to scream, scream, scream so loud, 'Oh my, oh my, oh my.' So terrible loud . . . that woman was screaming, screaming, trying to run away or something; screaming, screaming, and I just about got my foot in the stirrup [of the saddle on her mule] when bang! bang! bang!—three quick shots."

From her stretcher she identified Mrs. Hall, the Stevens brothers, and Henry Carpender as the people she had seen. The dramatic testimony of the Pig Woman was, however, interrupted by her elderly mother, who intermittently cried out, "She's a liar. She's a liar."

The defense was headed by Robert H. McCarter, a former state attorney general and a leading light of the New Jersey bar. He was assisted by attorney Clarence Case, who had little trouble pointing out the many contradictions in Mrs. Gibson's account. He even showed that Mrs. Gibson was confused about her own names and marriages.

Surprisingly, the defense's star witness was "Crazy Willie" Stevens, whom the prosecution had vowed to tear apart if he took the stand. However, when Alexander Simpson interrogated Stevens, "the idiot" answered in a calm, coherent manner. He even injected a bit of humor when he corrected Simpson's mispronunciation of a word.

The trial was not going well for the prosecution. Willie Stevens had turned out to be an intelligent, believable witness. Prior to his testimony, his brother Henry Stevens stated that

The Pig Woman, Jane Gibson, is rolled into court to testify in the Hall-Mills case.

he was fishing miles away on the night of the murders; three witnesses corroborated his account. When Mrs. Hall, the third defendant, was questioned, she vehemently denied any involvement in the crime. And Willie Stevens's testimony agreed with his sister's account of their movements on the night of the murders.

The closing arguments matched each other in vituperation. The defense intimated that many others could have committed the crime—even the Pig Woman herself!—while Simpson called Mrs. Hall "a Messalina," "a Lucretia Borgia," and "a Bloody Mary."

On December 3, 1926, after five hours' deliberation, the jury found all three defendants not guilty. The charges against Carpender were subsequently dropped. Governor A. Harry Moore summed up popular sentiment when he said: "I think the state has gone far enough. It's prosecution, not persecution, we want."

Unanswered Questions: The entire case remains a mystery owing to the initial bungled investigation. The only undisputed fact is that the victims were shot to death. In addition, it is generally believed that their adulterous affair was the reason they were killed.

From time to time, new theories about the case emerge, the most prominent claiming that the Ku Klux Klan was behind the crime. Powerful in rural New Jersey at the time of the murders, the Klan was known to take action against "sins of morality," and the Hall-Mills relationship was far from secret.

—P.H.

THE ZODIAC KILLER (1966–?)

The Crime: Officially, the bizarre but deadly Zodiac case started on December 20, 1968, with the murder of two high-school sweethearts, David Faraday, seventeen, and Bettilou Jensen, sixteen, who were parked on a lonely road outside Vallejo, California, northeast of San Francisco. The boy was shot in the car; the girl was gunned down by five shots when she tried to run away. The killer was never found. The following July 4 the killer shot another young couple in a nearby park; the girl died, but the boy survived despite four bullet wounds. The killer had temporarily blinded him with a flashlight, so his description of the assailant was very sketchy. A short while later the Vallejo police got an anonymous phone call. A man said, "I just shot the two kids at the public park.

With a .9mm automatic. I also killed those two kids Christmas."

On August 1, 1969, the Vallejo newspaper and two San Francisco dailies got letters from the killer, each with a note and one-third of a cryptogram—an odd series of letters and signs offering no easy interpretation. The killer's signature was a circle divided by a cross, his symbol for the zodiac. In subsequent letters he started off: "This is Zodiac speaking."

The Investigation: While newspapers printed "Zodiac's" taunting letters and promises of more violence, police pressed their hunt. In addition *San Francisco Chronicle* reporter Paul Avery discovered that the handwriting in a letter written by the murderer of college coed Cheri Jo Bates in 1966 matched that of Zodiac.

Clues: It took days to crack Zodiac's cryptogram, mainly because his spelling was wretched (perhaps deliberately so). The code was finally broken not by police but by two amateur cryptographers, high-school teacher Donald Harden and his wife, Bettye, in the nearby town of Salinas. Zodiac's message was, to say the least, chilling: "I like killing people because it is more fun than killing wild game in the forrest because man is the moat dangerus anamal of all to kill something gives me the most thrilling expeerence. The best part of it ia thae when I die I will be reborn in paradice and all the I have killed will become my slaves. I will not give you my name because you will trs to sloi down or stop my collecting of slaves for my afterlife."

In September 1969, Zodiac, wearing a square mask resembling a medieval executioner's hood, captured two college students picnicking near Lake Berryessa and tied them up. He stabbed the boy six times and gave the girl a total of twenty-four knife wounds in the form of a bloody cross. The girl, Cecelia Shepard, died, but the boy, Bryan Hartnell, survived. A few weeks later, on a foggy Saturday night in the heart of San Francisco, Zodiac killed a cab driver named Paul Stine, a twenty-nine-year-old doctoral student at San Francisco State University. Two teenagers witnessed the crime from a nearby window and phoned in a report and detailed physical description to a police operator. However, the operator made a crucial mistake, issuing a bulletin that described the suspect as a black male rather than as a white man with short, brown (perhaps reddish) hair, twenty-five to thirty years old, five feet eight inches tall, wearing a dark jacket and thick glasses. In the minutes following the murder, two policemen in a patrol car stopped a heavy-set white man who was lumbering toward the Presidio and asked him if he had noticed anyone suspicious. The man replied that he had seen someone with a gun running east on Washington Street. The prowl car roared off;

had the officers looked more closely, however, they might have noticed that the man had with him a shirt soaked in blood. A few days later the *Chronicle* received a piece of that bloodied shirt as well as a letter from the killer revealing that, in fact, the heavyset man had been none other than Zodiac himself.

Unanswered Questions: For the next several years, Zodiac played a number game. When the police credited him with five murders, he claimed seven. When they upped their figure to six, he raised it to seventeen. Eventually, Zodiac claimed more than thirty murders, and San Francisco police insisted there hadn't been that many corpses. However, in 1975 Sonoma County sheriff Don Striepeke came up with a computer study of murder records filed in the state attorney general's office that indicated that forty murders in five western states could be linked to one killer—possibly Zodiac—because of the similarity in technique. In Washington State a symbol of two rectangles connected by a line—formed by twigs and with two stones within one of the rectangles—was found by some girls' bodies. Striepeke established that the symbol was a form of witchcraft in England, and that it was once put on the hearth of homes of deceased persons in order to facilitate the journey of the dead to the afterlife (a voyage with which Zodiac was most certainly concerned).

At least the sheriff's numbers matched Zodiac's fairly well, for in one of his last letters, written in 1974, Zodiac claimed thirty-seven murders. There was one more letter after that, but it proved to be a fake. What happened to Zodiac? Was he out of commission, perhaps dead? Or was he simply killing more and writing less? Sheriff Striepeke at one point came up with the theory that the mass killer was leaving—over several western states—a trail of bodies that when traced on a map formed the letter Z.

In all, police checked more than 2,500 possible suspects. Perhaps the most likely was a strange young man who could be placed in the vicinity of all six confirmed Zodiac killings. He fit the physical description exactly, was intelligent, was a hunter and gun collector, and often mentioned to family and friends that "humans were the most dangerous game of all." On the day of the Lake Berryessa attacks in 1969, his sister-in-law had spotted a bloody knife on the seat of his car. Two months later she noticed a sheet of paper with drawings of strange symbols and characters. Other oddities followed, and the family finally notified the police, who immediately searched the trailer in Santa Rosa where the man lived. They found, among other things, a freezer packed with animal innards and mutilated rodents, suggesting that the suspect was perhaps a bit unbalanced, but no evidence actually linking the man to the Zodiac killings. His fingerprints did not match those collected from Paul Stine's taxi, so police let him go. In 1975 he was convicted of child molestation and spent three years in an institution for the criminally insane, giving responses during psychiatric exams that were disturbingly consistent with those that Zodiac could likely have given. Police investigations also revealed that in the past he had boasted to friends that he was the killer. Dave Toschi, a long-time Zodiac investigator for the San Francisco police, said in 1978, "My gut feeling is that he is the man." There was, however, no hard evidence, and the prime suspect in the Zodiac killings died in 1992.

—E.H.B. and C.S.

WAS SHE MURDERED?

MARILYN MONROE

Victim: The sex symbol of a generation, Marilyn Monroe began her life as Norma Jeane Mortenson on June 1, 1926. She never knew her father; her mother was institutionalized when Marilyn was seven. At age sixteen, after a childhood spent in foster homes, Marilyn married a neighbor named Jim Dougherty, whom she called "Daddy," but the marriage quickly foundered. In the early fifties she broke into movies, rising to stardom in such classics as *Gentlemen Prefer Blondes* (1953) and *Some Like It Hot* (1959). Her emotional life, however, remained profoundly unsettled; Marilyn developed a severe addiction to sleeping pills and other tranquilizers, enduring failed marriages to baseball great Joe DiMaggio and playwright Arthur Miller, as well as having affairs with a number of notable men, ranging from Frank Sinatra to John and Robert Kennedy.

Her Death: On Saturday, August 4, 1962, Monroe puttered around her newly purchased Spanish-style home in the exclusive Brentwood area of Los Angeles. She chatted by the swimming pool with her friend and press agent Patricia Newcomb, who had been her overnight houseguest. Her psychiatrist, Dr. Ralph Greenson, stopped by and spoke privately with her at about five in the afternoon. Miss Newcomb left about 6:00 P.M. and Dr. Greenson departed about thirty minutes later. Neighbors also reported having seen Bobby Kennedy at the house late that day. Marilyn received a number of phone calls—including one from her friend Peter Lawford, who was married to John and Robert Kennedy's sister, Pat, inviting Monroe to dinner that evening. Marilyn declined. At about 7:45 Lawford called again, hoping to persuade her to change her mind, but the man who had introduced Marilyn to the Kennedys some eight years earlier was shocked and frightened by what he now heard. Thick-voiced, Marilyn told him in heavily slurred, almost inaudible speech, "Say goodbye to Pat, say good-bye to Jack, and say good-bye to yourself, because you're a nice guy." Frantic, Lawford called a friend, who warned him to stay clear because he was "the presi-

dent's brother-in-law." Lawford then called Mickey Rudin, Marilyn's attorney, who in turn obtained assurances from her housekeeper, Eunice Murray, that the star was in no danger. Lawford did not, however, go to check on Marilyn personally, a dereliction for which he would reproach himself for the rest of his life.

At 4:25 A.M. the Los Angeles Police Department received a call from Dr. Hyman Engelberg, Marilyn's personal physician, who reported that he had pronounced the star dead at 3:40 A.M.

Official Version: The Los Angeles police report stated that Mrs. Murray awoke about 3:30 A.M. and noticed that a light was still on in Marilyn's bedroom. After knocking on the door and getting no response, Mrs. Murray went to the bedroom window and saw Marilyn lying naked on her bed. Sensing something was wrong, she called Dr. Greenson, the psychiatrist, who told her to call Dr. Engelberg also. Greenson entered the bedroom at approximately 3:40 and found Marilyn's body. Dr. Engelberg arrived shortly thereafter and pronounced her dead.

The subsequent coroner's report, issued by Los Angeles deputy medical examiner Dr. Thomas Noguchi, gave the cause of death as "acute barbiturate poisoning, ingestion of overdose." The toxicologist's report, prepared by R. J. Abernathy of the Los Angeles County Coroner's Office, recorded 4.5 milligrams of barbiturates in the blood and 13 milligrams in the liver.

Dr. Greenson stated that Marilyn had been despondent recently, particularly on Saturday. Also, Dr. Engelberg noted that he had given her a prescription for fifty Nembutals (a barbiturate) a couple of days earlier. Police found the Nembutal vial among fifteen other prescription bottles next to her bed, with only three capsules left in it.

An unofficial investigation, conducted to ascertain whether the overdose was accidental or intentional, revealed that Marilyn had attempted suicide previously as a means of getting attention but that she had always called someone to rescue her. In this case, Dr. Greenson noted on discovering her body that she had the telephone receiver in her hand. The investigators concluded that she had repeated

port showed barbiturates only in the blood and liver. Dr. Sidney Weinberg, a noted forensic pathologist, has stated, "There is no way Marilyn Monroe could have orally taken the drugs she allegedly took without some of them being present in her [digestive] system."

The official ingestion theory falls short on other points as well. The suicide investigation team estimated "that she took one gulp [of the alleged forty-seven Nembutals] within—let's say—a period of seconds." Dr. Engelberg's statement that he had given her a prescription for fifty Nembutal capsules was incorrect. Pharmacy records show that the prescription was for only twenty-five Nembutals. And, though no one admitted moving her, Marilyn's body was neatly stretched out with no signs of the convulsions normally associated with such a death.

What all this suggests, as Dr. Weinberg and other pathologists have concluded, is the possibility that Marilyn Monroe died of an injected overdose of barbiturates. However, no syringe was found in her house, and she was never known to have given herself an injection. The only recent injections she had had were of various drugs given to her by Dr. Engelberg over the previous month and a half. The coroner's report stated there were no injection marks on her body; the bill Dr. Engelberg filed against her estate, however, states that he had given her an injection the day before she died. The mark from that injection should have been easily detected.

Another discrepancy is the time of death, given in police and coroner reports as Sunday, 3:40 A.M. However, when Engelberg arrived it was obvious to him that rigor mortis had set in and that Marilyn had been dead for three to six hours. Death probably came in the late hours of Saturday night, a likelihood borne out by statements of her agent, who claims to have been informed of her death before midnight.

The motive for suicide, or even for a faked suicide, rests on Dr. Greenson's comment that Marilyn had seemed despondent on Saturday. But Eunice Murray, Peter Lawford, press agent Pat Newcomb, and Joe DiMaggio Jr. all reported that she seemed happy and positive when they talked to her. Despite problems on her current picture, Marilyn was receiving more offers of movies than she could possibly handle. Financially, she was well off; she had just purchased her first house and was busy decorating it.

She was, however, having problems with her love life. It has long been widely believed that Monroe was involved in an affair with Attorney General Robert Kennedy and that she earlier had also had one with President John Kennedy. Fred Lawrence Guiles, in Legend: The Life and Death of Marilyn Monroe (1984), for example, argues that the star had grown infatuated with Bobby Kennedy. For several weeks, possibly a

Marilyn Monroe (shown here with Peter Lawford) performed a sexy rendition of "Happy Birthday" at President John F. Kennedy's birthday celebration.

her past pattern but had been overcome by the effect of the drugs before she could call anyone to help her.

Theories and Unanswered Questions: Since Monroe's death, various theories have been advanced. All are quite critical of the official version, which has by now been widely discredited. A number of investigators have asserted that she did not commit suicide but was murdered. They point to inconsistencies and contradictions in the statements made by the various people involved and in the official reports of the police and coroner.

The center of the controversy is the Los Angeles County coroner's report. It gives the cause of death as ingestion of barbiturates, but when the coroner examined the stomach and duodenum on that Sunday morning, he found no trace of pills. In fact, the stomach contained nothing but an ounce of brownish liquid. An analysis for refractile crystals, which should have been left as a residue of the barbiturates, came back negative. The coroner noted that the small intestine appeared normal. In other words, the digestive system showed no signs of ingestion of barbiturates. The toxicologist's re-

month, before her death, Robert Kennedy had attempted to break off the affair, but Marilyn had persistently tried to reach him at the Justice Department. A few days before her death Marilyn had told a friend, writer Robert Slatzer, "If he [Robert Kennedy] keeps avoiding me, I might just call a press conference and tell them about it . . . and my future plans." In his biography of Marilyn, Slatzer asserts that Bobby had surreptitiously visited her on the day before she died, flying down to Los Angeles from San Francisco, where he was officially supposed to be, and spending the night at Peter Lawford's home in Santa Monica.

The Kennedy connection is a confusing and sensitive one. It is widely believed that Marilyn's phone had been tapped both by Robert Kennedy and by his enemy, Teamster boss Jimmy Hoffa. Monroe's telephone records were mysteriously confiscated two days after she died. The Los Angeles police and coroner are widely suspected of conducting a cover-up. Sergeant Jack Clemmons, who was the first police officer to arrive at Marilyn's house the night of her death, later stated, "She was murdered by needle injection by someone she knew and probably trusted. I have no doubt of it. This was the cover-up crime of the century— a matter of [Los Angeles chief of police] Bill Parker and other officials . . . protecting a famous political family of the East who had good reason to shut Monroe's mouth." Deputy Coroner Lionel Grandison, who signed Marilyn's death certificate, later stated, "The whole thing was organized to hide the truth. An original autopsy file vanished, a scrawled note that Marilyn Monroe wrote and which did not speak of suicide also vanished, and so did the first [Sergeant Clemmons's] police report. I was told to sign the official report—or I'd find myself in a position I couldn't get out of."

It is also interesting to note that two key witnesses were not available for questioning after Marilyn's death. Mrs. Murray moved out of her apartment the next day, leaving no forwarding address. She later reported that she had come into some money and taken an extended trip to Europe. Pat Newcomb, Marilyn's press agent, had an argument with reporters Sunday when the body was discovered, and was fired from her job with the agency for which she worked. She immediately accepted an invitation to visit the Kennedy compound at Hyannisport, after which she also took a long European vacation. When she returned, she went to work for the Justice Department as an aide to Bobby Kennedy.

In Marilyn: The Last Take (1993), Peter H. Brown and Patte B. Barnham contend that Monroe was killed by agents of Bobby Kennedy to cover up their affair, which RFK had broken off that summer.

James Spada, in a 1991 book, claims that Marilyn had a long affair with John Kennedy

and a briefer but more profound one with Robert, who became alarmed at her dependency on him and, realizing that both he and his brother had become extremely vulnerable, brutally ended the relationship. Spada says that Monroe's home was bugged and quotes one source as stating that, on a tape recorded by Bernard Spindel, a surveillance expert, on the day Monroe died, "you could hear Marilyn and [Bobby] Kennedy . . . `arguing . . . about why Kennedy was not going to marry her." Spindel's tapes were seized during a 1966 raid on his home by the New York district attorney and were never recovered. Spada quotes a private detective who claims that, immediately following Monroe's death, Lawford had asked him to go to the house to help Lawford remove evidence linking the star with the Kennedy brothers. He contends that Kennedy and Lawford were involved in a cover-up of the "Kennedy connection" following Monroe's death, but that neither was involved in her murder.

In his book Who Killed Marilyn? (1976), Tony Sciacca presents a number of murder theories. One is that Kennedy loyalists in either the Justice Department or the CIA— possibly through Mafia connections—killed the star with a lethal dose of injected barbiturates in order to protect the Kennedy brothers from the threat of scandal. Sciacca strenuously argues that Robert Kennedy was not involved in any way. Another theory claims that rightist groups within the CIA killed Marilyn in an attempt to expose her affair with Robert Kennedy and frame both Kennedy brothers. After their plot failed, they decided on more drastic measures against the Kennedys, which eventually led to the assassinations in Dallas and Los Angeles.

A number of writers, including Norman Mailer, relate other, sometimes bizarre, theories. One claims that Jimmy Hoffa and the Teamsters were involved in an effort to discredit or blackmail Robert Kennedy. A second says that Cuban agents murdered Monroe as a reprisal against the Kennedys for the CIA-initiated Mafia contract that was put out on Fidel Castro. Yet another outlandish theory attributes her death to Communist conspirators who sought to ruin the Kennedy brothers by linking them to murder.

Donald Spoto, in his thoroughly researched Marilyn Monroe: The Biography (1993), presents a very different—and highly credible— scenario. Spoto, who, unlike any other writer on the subject, had access to Monroe's personal papers, radically downplays the supposed "Kennedy connection," claiming that Monroe and Joe DiMaggio had renewed intimate relations in 1961, with the troubled star finding deep solace in the constancy of the baseball legend's love. On the last weekend in July 1962, Spoto contends, the two vacationed with the Lawfords in Lake

Tahoe and decided to remarry two weeks hence; upon returning to Los Angeles, Monroe was fitted for a wedding gown. It is therefore impossible that Monroe, who believed herself on the threshold of the happiness that had so long eluded her, would have committed suicide. Nor was she murdered by the Kennedys or by anyone else. Spoto casts Dr. Greenson as the unwitting villain, claiming that, on that fateful Saturday, the psychiatrist ordered Mrs. Murray to give Monroe an enema of chloral hydrate, a sleep-inducing drug that, when combined with the Nembutal prescribed by Monroe's physician, Dr. Engelberg, produces a highly toxic—and usually fatal—reaction. In this view, Marilyn Monroe's death was neither a murder nor a suicide but a tragic accident; her funeral service, on August 8, 1962, occurred on the very day that she was to have been remarried.

—R.J.F. and E.H.B.

ASSASSINATIONS

ARCHDUKE FRANZ FERDINAND

The Victim: Born in Graz on December 18, 1863, Franz Ferdinand, heir to the throne of the Austro-Hungarian Empire, grew up as an insignificant archduke. However, he suddenly became important after the suicide of his cousin, Crown Prince Rudolf, and the death of his own father, Archduke Karl Ludwig, put him next in line to the throne of his uncle, Emperor Franz Joseph. On July 1, 1900, Franz Ferdinand married Countess Sophie Chotek, but because the emperor considered the Choteks commoners unworthy of marrying into the Hapsburg family, Franz Ferdinand first had to renounce the right of succession to the throne of his children and all future generations.

Franz Ferdinand was an ardent hunter who killed more than 250,000 animals, including 6,000 stags. He refused to use a repeater rifle or a telescopic sight because he considered them unsporting. On the other hand, because he was under doctor's orders to avoid excess exertion, he usually waited in one position and allowed a large staff to drive the animals in front of him.

On October 6, 1908, Emperor Franz Joseph annexed Bosnia-Herzegovina. In 1914 Franz Ferdinand, as inspector general of the Armed Forces of the Empire, announced that he would visit Bosnia and its capital, Sarajevo, in order to oversee military maneuvers. Franz Ferdinand was warned that a trip to Sarajevo would be dangerous because Serbian nationalists might try to kill him, especially as his visit was planned for Saint Vitus's Day, the greatest of Serbian festivals. However, he viewed assassination as an occupational hazard and dismissed the warnings. "Worries and precautions cripple life," he once said. "Fear is always one of the most damaging things." Another time he stated, "We are all constantly in danger of death. One must simply trust in God." His wife, Sophie, insisted on accompanying him. She believed that no one would shoot at her husband if she, a woman, was by his side. Both of them wore amulets and holy relics to protect them against misfortune.

The Date: June 28, 1914.
The Event: Franz Ferdinand and his party arrived in Sarajevo by train after the completion of the military maneuvers. His program for the day, which was published in detail in all the local newspapers, called for a motorcade along the Appel Quay, the city's main thoroughfare, a visit to the town hall, a tour of a new museum, and lunch at the governor's mansion with Feldzeugmeister Oskar Potiorek, the emperor's abrasively arrogant representative in Bosnia. The motorcade consisted of seven cars. Franz Ferdinand, dressed in the full uniform of a cavalry general, was seated in the third car, an open-topped right-hand-drive Graf und Stift. Sophie was beside him. Across from him, seated on fold-down seats, were Potiorek and the owner of the car, Count Franz Harrach.

Potiorek, despite repeated warnings from military intelligence and others, refused to believe that Franz Ferdinand's life was in danger. Consequently, the entire motorcade route was protected by only 120 policemen. In fact, six assassins, all of them young Bosnians armed with pistols and bombs, were mingling with the crowd along a 350-yard stretch of the Appel Quay. The cars proceeded at a pace of about ten to twelve miles per hour. When Franz Ferdinand's car reached the first conspirator, Muhamed Mehmedbašić, he froze and did nothing. The second would-be assassin, Vaso Čubrilović, also failed to act, as did Cvetko Popović.

The fourth conspirator was nineteen-year-old Nedeljko Čabrinović. Earlier in the day Čabrinović had dressed in his best clothes and visited a professional photographer, posing for a formal portrait with a bomb hidden in his jacket pocket. As the motorcade passed by, Čabrinović asked a policeman which car the archduke was in. Then he knocked the safety cap off his bomb and threw the bomb at Franz Ferdinand. Harrach's chauffeur, hearing the safety cap pop off, instinctively accelerated. The bomb bounced off the back hood of the car and exploded in the street, injuring at least a dozen people, including Potiorek's adjutant,

Colonel Erik Merizzi, who, having been seated in the car behind the archduke, received a head injury and was rushed to a hospital. The passengers of the first two cars had no idea what had happened and continued on to the town hall. Franz Ferdinand, on the other hand, realized that an attempt had been made to kill him. He ordered the chauffeur to stop and told Count Harrach to go back and make sure no one was injured.

Meanwhile the fifth conspirator, nineteen-year-old Gavrilo Princip, the instigator of the plot, was unsure of what was going on. Unusually short, he could not see over the crowd. Noting that a car had stopped in front of him, but unable to see who was in it, Princip assumed that the assassination attempt had succeeded. He turned the other way and saw Čabrinović in police custody. When he turned back, the car started to move again, and he recognized Sophie and realized that she and the archduke had survived. Confused, Princip wandered a bit and then, deciding to try again when the motorcade returned from the town hall, he positioned himself in front of Moritz Schiller's delicatessen, where the motorcade was scheduled to turn on its way to the museum.

Despite the close call on Appel Quay, the organizers went ahead with the planned program in the open air on the steps of the town hall. The mayor of Sarajevo, Fehim Curčić Effendi, had no idea an assassination attempt had taken place and stood up to give his welcoming speech. Suddenly the gravity of the situation struck Franz Ferdinand, who burst out: "To hell with your speech! I have come to visit Sarajevo and am greeted by bombs. It is outrageous!" Then he composed himself and said, "Very well, now go on with your speech." The bewildered mayor went ahead with his prepared text, which included the words, "All the citizens of Sarajevo, overwhelmed with happiness, greet Your Highnesses' most illustrious visit with the utmost enthusiasm."

Franz Ferdinand decided to go ahead with the rest of the day's schedule, with one exception: he wanted to visit the injured Colonel Merizzi in the hospital before visiting the museum. This meant that instead of turning right in front of Moritz Schiller's delicatessen, the motorcade would continue back up Appel Quay the way it had come. Incredibly, no added security precautions were taken except that Count Harrach insisted on standing on the running board of the car in order to shield the archduke from one side.

The motorcade passed by a sixth conspirator, Trifko Grabéz, who for the second time that day watched Franz Ferdinand go by without doing anything. Apparently no one bothered to tell the chauffeurs about the changed itinerary, and the first car turned right at the delicatessen as planned. Harrach's chauffeur followed it.

Potiorek realized the mistake and ordered him to stop. The chauffeur came to a complete halt in front of the delicatessen. Princip, who was standing on the sidewalk, found himself a mere five feet away from his intended victim with a clear shot, since Harrach was on the opposite side of the car. Princip pulled out his revolver, but hesitated when he saw Sophie. Then he turned his head away and pulled the trigger twice. Despite the fact that he hadn't aimed, his first shot hit Sophie and the second struck Franz Ferdinand in the neck. Harrach grabbed the archduke and asked, "Is Your Imperial Highness in great pain?" "It is nothing," replied Franz Ferdinand. He repeated this six or seven times, each time more faintly, until he lost consciousness. Both Franz Ferdinand and his wife died within minutes.

The Assassin: Gavrilo Princip, born July 13, 1894, was the son of a poor Serbian farmer in the Krajina region of northeast Bosnia. In 1910 a Serbian law student named Bogdan Žerajić tried to assassinate General Potiorek's predecessor as governor, Feldzeugmeister Maryan Varešanin, while Varešanin was visiting Sarajevo. The attempt failed. Žerajić committed suicide and was buried in an unmarked grave. Gavrilo Princip, like many young Bosnian Serbs, began visiting Žerajić's grave. One night, after a long

Gavrilo Princip seized by police after he assassinated Archduke Franz Ferdinand in Sarajevo on June 28, 1914. The incident touched off World War I.

vigil, he vowed to follow Žerajić's example and to avenge his death. In 1912, while studying in Belgrade, the Serb capital, Princip tried to join the Serbian army, but he was rejected for being too small and weak. Two years later he read in a German newspaper that Archduke Franz Ferdinand was planning a visit to Bosnia. Princip proposed to Čabrinović that they assassinate the archduke. They added Grabéz to their plot. A few weeks later, Grabéz was granted an audience with Major Vojin Tankosić, the same Serbian commander who had rejected Princip's attempt to enlist in the army. Tankosić ordered a follower to instruct the conspirators in the use of pistols. Numerous others were made aware of the plot.

After the assassination both Princip and Čabrinović swallowed cyanide on the spot, but they succeeded only in making themselves sick. The "trial of Gavrilo Princip and his associates" began on October 12 and included twenty-five defendants. Sixteen of them were convicted of murder or complicity in murder. Mehmedbašić escaped to Montenegro. The other five assassins were all under the age of twenty at the time of the killing and thus were exempt from execution. However, Princip, Čabrinović, and Grabéz all died of tuberculosis, Princip on April 28, 1918, the others in 1916. At his trial Princip stated, "I do not feel like a criminal because I put away the one who was doing evil." His only regret was that he had killed Sophie when he had meant to kill Potiorek.

Aftermath: Back in Vienna, Franz Ferdinand's death made little impression. He was little known and no one imagined that his assassination would affect their daily lives. However, despite no evidence of official Serbian involvement in the conspiracy, Austria-Hungary used the incident as an excuse to declare war on Serbia on July 28, 1914. The Russian czar supported Serbia; Germany backed up Austria and declared war on Russia and then on France. When German troops crossed into Belgium, Great Britain declared war on Germany. On August 6, despite the fact that Franz Ferdinand himself had consistently warned against war with Serbia and Russia, Austria declared war on Russia, and World War I had begun. Princip never imagined that his act would lead to such consequences, but, in fact, six months after his death, the Hapsburg dynasty collapsed and never rose again.

—D.W.

LEON TROTSKY

The Victim: Leon Trotsky (Lev Davidovich Bronstein), cofounder of the Bolshevik movement, organizer of the Red Army, leading opponent of Soviet dictator Joseph Stalin, was twice arrested in his youth for revolutionary activities and exiled to Siberia. Both times he escaped. He returned to Russia in 1917 and was one of the leaders of the October Revolution. Following the death of Lenin in 1924, Trotsky lost the struggle for power to Stalin, who expelled him from the Communist Party in 1927 and from the Soviet Union in 1929. Trotsky was granted asylum in Turkey and then moved to France and Norway. After he published the anti-Stalinist book The Revolution Betrayed, the Norwegian government yielded to Soviet pressure and expelled Trotsky, who settled in Mexico. From Mexico City and then from his fortified villa in Coyoacán, Trotsky intensified his war of words against Stalin with such works as Stalin's Crime, The Real Situation in Russia, and The Stalinist School of Falsification. George Bernard Shaw said of Trotsky's writing, "When he cuts off his opponent's head, he holds it up to show that there are no brains in it." In 1940 Trotsky was preparing an "antibiography" called Stalin.

> It was the supreme expression of the mediocrity of the apparatus that Stalin himself rose to his position.
>
> Leon Trotsky, My Life, 1924

The Date: August 20, 1940.

The Event: Back in Russia, Trotsky and other "heretics" were convicted in absentia and Stalin sent his secret police, the GPU, to hunt down his exiled opponents and kill them. In 1938 Stalin's agents murdered Trotsky's thirty-two-year-old son, Lev Sedov, in Paris. On May 24, 1940, the painter David Alfaro Siqueiros led a twenty-man assault on Trotsky's villa. They lured some of the guards away with women posing as prostitutes and overpowered the rest. They set up a machine gun outside Trotsky's bedroom and opened fire with seventy-three bullets. They also threw two incendiary bombs, one of which hit the bedroom door of Trotsky's grandson Seva. Incredibly, neither Trotsky nor his wife, Natalya, nor anyone else was killed or seriously injured.

Three months later Trotsky was feeding his pet rabbits in the late afternoon when he was approached by a nervous young man wearing a hat and carrying a bulky overcoat. This man had weaseled his way into Trotsky's entourage by becoming the lover of Sylvia Agelof, an American whom the Trotskys respected. When he first met Agelof he presented himself as Jacques Mornard, a French journalist. When he and Agelof traveled to the United States and then on to Mexico, he used the alias Frank Jacson.

The twenty-six-year-old Jacson had visited the villa four times in the previous two weeks. When he joined Trotsky by the rabbit hutch this day, he asked him to look over an article that he (Jacson) had written. The two men retired to Trotsky's study, where Trotsky sat down at a table that he used as a desk and began reading the manuscript. Trotsky kept two loaded guns in the room: a Colt .38 automatic inside a drawer and a .25 automatic that served as a paperweight on his table. Underneath the table was a switch that could be pressed to activate an alarm.

While Trotsky read, Jacson laid his overcoat on the table in a way that made it difficult to reach the switch. Inside the coat were a dagger, a revolver, and a short-handled Alpine ice pick. Hoping that he could kill Trotsky in silence and then escape, Jacson, at the last moment, decided to use the ice pick. He later confessed: "I took the *piolet* out of my raincoat pocket, took it in my fist and, closing my eyes, I gave him a tremendous blow on the head."

Had Jacson not closed his eyes, he might have gotten away with his crime. But he struck the side of Trotsky's head instead of the crown of his skull. Jacson, in his excitement, also used the flattened end of the ice pick instead of the sharp, pointed end. Jacson tried to strike again, but the sixty-year-old Trotsky jumped up from his chair, grabbed Jacson's hand, and bit it. As the two men grappled, Trotsky let out a scream that, in Jacson's words, "I will never forget as long as I live. His scream was . . . very long, infinitely long, and it still seems to me as if that scream were piercing my brain." This scream attracted Natalya Trotsky and three guards. Trotsky staggered outside and lay down while his wife tried to tend to his wound. "Natasha, I love you," he said. "Promise that everyone who comes to see you is first searched. You must take Seva away from all this. You know, while I was in there, I knew—I sensed what he wanted to do." Twenty-six hours later, Trotsky died at a nearby hospital.

The Assassin: While Trotsky was waiting for an ambulance, he heard Jacson continuing to struggle and ordered his guards not to kill him. "He must be made to talk," said Trotsky. It was a simple order but one that proved hard to follow. In the hospital and then in prison, Jacson claimed that he was really Jacques Mornard Vandendreschd, a Belgian born in Teheran. But his story was riddled with obvious lies. A team of Mexican psychologists interviewed him six hours a day for six months. At their first meeting he announced, "You are not going to get anything out of me." He was right. The 1,359-page final report concluded that he was probably a Spaniard who had been trained in the Soviet Union. In 1943 he was finally brought to trial, convicted, and sentenced to twenty years in prison. Still he refused to talk.

Finally, in September 1950, ten years after the assassination of Trotsky, one of the psycholo-gists, Dr. Alfonso Quiroz Cuaron, took a copy of Jacson-Mornard's fingerprints to the Madrid police and learned that they matched those of Jaime Ramón Mercader del Rio Hernandez, who had been arrested as a Communist organizer in Barcelona on June 12, 1935. Photographs in the police file left no doubt that Mercader and Jacson-Mornard were one and the same.

Mercader had been released from prison in July 1936, following a general amnesty for political prisoners. He was given the rank of lieutenant in the Republican army. While fighting against Franco in the Spanish Civil War, he was recruited into Soviet intelligence by Colonel Naum Kotov (Leonid Eitingon), who was, by some accounts, the lover of his mother, a Cuban Communist named Caridad Mercader del Rio. It was Kotov and Caridad who were waiting in a getaway car when Mercader attacked Trotsky.

Mercader turned out to be a model prisoner in Mexico. He joined a program to teach illiterate prisoners to read, worked as an electrical engineer, and was eventually placed in charge of the prison electrical system. He was given his own large room and was even allowed to have a mistress. After serving his term, he was released from prison on May 6, 1960. He flew to Prague, where he became a journalist, and then he lived for fifteen years in Moscow, where he was awarded the Order of the Soviet Union. He died in Havana, Cuba, on October 18, 1978.

—D.W.

MAHATMA GANDHI

The Victim: Mohandas Karamchand Gandhi, religious and political leader and apostle of nonviolence, was born in Aorbandar, India, on October 2, 1869. Gandhi was educated in London and practiced law in India before moving to South Africa in 1893. There he led a nonviolent movement against racially discrimi-nating laws. He returned to India in January 1915 and began campaigning for political inde-pendence from Great Britain. Sticking to nonvio-lent tactics, Gandhi became the most famous and most respected person in India. He was known to his followers as Mahatma ("great soul" in Sanskrit) Gandhi. When the British finally granted independence to India on Au-gust 15, 1947, they split the country into Muslim Pakistan and Hindu India. Gandhi opposed this partition, urging all parties to live in harmony. As beloved as Gandhi was, he was not without his enemies.

Following the partition, an ethnic cleansing occurred in which Muslims sought refuge in Pakistan and Hindus and Sikhs fled to India. These population shifts were accompanied by rape, torture, and murder on both sides. Hindu nationalists, outraged by Muslim atrocities,

Mohandas K. Gandhi at a Muslim shrine in New Delhi, three days before his assassination in 1948.

were furious when Gandhi urged Hindus not to retaliate. On January 12, 1948, the Indian government announced it would withhold £44 million owed to the Pakistani government. Gandhi considered this unjust and announced that he would protest the decision by fasting until death. Three days later Prime Minister Jawaharlal Nehru reversed the decision.

The Date: January 30, 1948.

The Event: On January 20, 1948, five days after Nehru's reversal, Gandhi held his usual daily prayer service at 5:00 P.M. outside Birla House in Delhi. Behind the audience, neighborhood children were playing on the lawn. A mother, Sulochana Devi, came to fetch her son and noticed a young man set fire to something on the ground and then rush away to stand by her. The object exploded and the young man was quickly apprehended. The services continued as if nothing had happened.

The bomber turned out to be twenty-year-old Madan Lal Pahwa, a Punjabi Hindu refugee whose father had been seriously injured by a Moslem mob. When police searched him they found that he was also carrying a live hand grenade.

Despite this violent incident, the police made no serious attempt to safeguard Gandhi's life. Nor did they pursue obvious leads regarding a conspiracy. The seventy-eight-year-old Gandhi, who had survived at least three previous assassination attempts, was philosophical. "Do not be angry with the youth," he said of Madan Lal Pahwa. "He did not know that he was doing wrong. . . . We should try to win him over and convert him to right thinking and doing." A few days later, he remarked, "There is nothing I would like more than to meet a shower of bullets with a smile on my face."

On January 30 Gandhi stayed too long in conversation with Sardar Patel, India's deputy prime minister, and was late for five o'clock services. "I hate being late," he noted. "Those who are late are punished."

Gandhi emerged from his room and, leaning on the shoulders of his grandnieces Abha and Manu, headed into the garden of Birla House toward the prayer ground. The congregation opened a path to let him through. Suddenly a man in a khaki tunic rushed forward, bowed briefly, and shot Gandhi three times—once in the abdomen and twice in the chest. Gandhi muttered "Hai Ram! Hai Ram!" and then collapsed and died. The assassin was seized immediately.

The Assassins: Nathuram Godse was thirty-seven when he killed Mahatma Gandhi. For the previous four years he had been editor of a Marathi-language daily newspaper, *Hindu Rashra*, in Poona. Although as a student Godse had followed Gandhi's teachings, he was soon attracted to the extreme Hindu nationalist views of the Hindu Mahasabha, for a time the second-largest political party in India, and to its charismatic president, Vinayak Savarkar. Despite Godse's denials, it soon became clear that he had not acted alone but in concert with several others. Within two weeks police had arrested the following seven coconspirators in addition to Madan Lal Pahwa:

• Narayan Apte, a former teacher at the American Mission High School. The managing director of Godse's newspaper, Apte was the "brains" of the conspiracy.
• Vishnu Karkare, another Gandhi supporter turned Savarkarite. Karkare gave up ownership of a tea house to devote himself full-time to local politics in Ahmednagar.
• Gopal Godse, Nathuram's younger brother.
• Digambar Badge, a bookseller and arms dealer who supplied weapons for the January 20 assassination attempt.
• Shankar Kistayya, Badge's servant.
• Dattatraya Parchure, a doctor who helped procure the revolver that Nathuram Godse used to kill Gandhi.
• Vinayak Savarkar, who was considered such a

hero by Godse and Apte that his picture appeared on the front page of their newspaper every day. Before independence Savarkar spent twenty-seven years in prison for "conspiracy to wage war against the King Emperor." Twice he was implicated in assassinations of British officials.

The trial of the eight alleged conspirators began at the Red Fort in Delhi on May 27, 1948. The prosecution called 149 witnesses and translated all testimony into six languages to satisfy the needs of all the participants in the case. The defense attorneys insisted that Godse had acted alone and that the incidents of January 20 and January 30 were unrelated. In the words of Apte, "As a person of the stature of Mahatma Gandhi was assassinated, the police thought that there must have been a conspiracy, that it could not have been the act of one or two ordinary men."

Unfortunately for Apte and the others, one of the accused turned approver, which is to say he agreed to testify for the prosecution in exchange for a pardon. In testimony lasting nine days, Badge related how all of the accused, save Savarkar and Parchure, had gathered in a hotel room on January 20, before proceeding to Birla House to kill Gandhi. The plan called for Madan Lal Pahwa to cause a diversion by setting off an explosion. During the confusion that followed, Karkare, Gopal and Nathuram Godse, and Shankar Kistayya would throw hand grenades at Gandhi, and Badge would shoot him. However, there was no confusion. As soon as Madan Lal Pahwa was arrested, the others escaped without using their weapons. Badge immediately withdrew from the plot and took Kistayya with him. He also disposed of most of the remaining weapons, forcing the remaining four conspirators to go to great lengths to acquire an extra revolver for their second and ultimately successful attempt.

Given an opportunity to make a statement at the trial, Nathuram Godse spent five hours reading a ninety-three-page thesis. He accused Gandhi of developing a "subjective mentality" and of doing "whatever would please the Mohammedans." He believed that Gandhi's practice of nonviolence would lead to "the emasculation of the Hindu community." Nevertheless, he added, "my respect for the Mahatma was deep and deathless. It therefore gave me no pleasure to kill him."

On February 10, 1949, Nathuram Godse and Apte were sentenced to death. Karkare, Gopal Godse, Parchure, and Madan Lal Pahwa were sentenced to life imprisonment, while Shankar Kistayya received seven years' "rigorous imprisonment." Savarkar was acquitted. On appeal, Parchure and Kistayya were also acquitted.

Like Gandhi, Nathuram Godse faced death without fear. "The time before birth and after death," he wrote, "is the real permanent state of man, and this intermediate period is a separate journey." He read voluminously in prison. The last book he read, right up until the day before his execution, was a treatise on Albert Einstein's theory of relativity. Apte, meanwhile, wrote a book entitled *Principles of Successful Administration*.

On the night before their execution, two men were caught sneaking into the prison. They were not supporters trying to free their comrades but rather reporters looking for an exclusive interview.

On the morning of November 15, 1949, Godse and Apte were led to the scaffold to be hung. From the gallows Godse thanked his jailers for their kind treatment and asked forgiveness for any inconvenience he and Apte might have caused them. After Godse and Apte were hung, their bodies were cremated and their ashes and bones were secretly thrown into a shallow river. Enthusiastic young supporters later recovered the bones and distributed them to their friends.
—D.W.

PATRICE LUMUMBA

The Victim: Patrice Hémery Lumumba, prime minister of the Congo, was seemingly destined to become one of the great Pan-African statesmen of the twentieth century, but his meteoric rise to power was cut short after little more than two months in office. Yet Lumumba served long enough to antagonize everybody from the United Nations and the Central Intelligence Agency to the twisted political foes in his own country, leaving his death shrouded in mystery.

Lumumba, a member of the Batelela tribe, was born on July 2, 1925, in the village of Onalua in the Kansai province of the Belgian Congo. He was educated in Protestant and Roman Catholic schools and went on to an unspectacular career in the Congolese civil service, winding up as the assistant postmaster of Stanleyville before being found guilty of embezzlement in 1956. Lumumba served one year in prison for his crime. Although active in trade unionism as early as 1955, he threw himself into politics upon release from jail, and helped found the Movement National Congolese (MNC) in 1958. The group's primary aim was independence for the Congo from Belgium. Embracing a style of militant nationalism that alarmed Western leaders, Lumumba nevertheless grew increasingly popular among the Congolese, so much so that he was imprisoned for inciting an anti-Belgian riot that left thirty dead in Stanleyville in 1959.

Still, Lumumba was released from prison in order to attend an independence conference in Brussels in 1960, and it was there that he emerged as the Congo's dominant politician.

Calling for a strong unitary state, his party won a substantial minority of seats in the first general election in May 1960, and Lumumba was asked in June to form a government as prime minister, with profederalist rival Joseph Kasavubu installed as president. But the alliance between the two foes proved fragile. The Congo gained its independence on June 30, 1960, but a wholesale army mutiny five days later turned the country upside down. The rich mining province of Katanga declared itself independent behind provincial president Moise Tshombe—who was backed by European business leaders and the Belgian government—and other secessionist movements quickly followed. Lumumba sought help from the United Nations to oust the Belgians from Katanga and reunify the country, but when that plan proved ineffective, he turned to the Soviet Union for aid. Soon Russian and Czech "technicians" began pouring into the country, terrifying the United States, which feared the USSR's gaining a Cold War foothold in Africa. In fact, Lumumba was regarded as so powerful and dangerous that the CIA ordered his assassination and began training operatives to carry out the task. Lumumba, meanwhile, had no desire to become a pawn of the East or the West. "We are not Communists, Catholics, Socialists," he once declared. "We are African nationalists." Toward that end, he called for all independent African states to meet in Leopoldville to support his suppression of the Katanganese secessionists.

By September Lumumba and Kasavubu had openly broken and were seeking to oust one another from office. The army, led by Joseph Mobutu, intervened and deposed them both—although Kasavubu was later reinstated—condemning Lumumba to house arrest. For two months Lumumba and his family lived as prisoners in their own home, with two rings of armed security personnel surrounding the estate: United Nations peacekeeping forces on the inside to protect the prime minister, Congolese army forces on the outside to keep him from escaping. Lumumba did manage to get free on November 27. Wriggling through a small band of supporters, he headed toward Stanleyville, where he hoped to reestablish his government. Yet Lumumba's willingness to make political speeches at villages along the way made him easy to find, and he was recaptured by Kasavubu's forces on December 2 while attempting to cross the Kwilu River at Sankuru.

The Date: January 17, 1961.

The Event: No one but the perpetrators knows for sure who killed Patrice Lumumba, or exactly how he died. For that matter, even the date of his death is in dispute. But this much is known: approximately six weeks after being returned to Leopoldville by Mobutu's soldiers, Lumumba and two aides—cabinet minister Maurice Mpolo

and senate vice president Joseph Okito—were reported dead. The executions, which followed weeks of cruel and sadistic torture at the hands of the army, probably occurred on the night of January 17, when all three were flown to Katanga for imprisonment. They were reportedly attacked and beaten by Katanganese army troops as they disembarked, already bloodied and in handcuffs, from a DC-4 Air Congo plane, then dumped into the back of a jeep and driven to a farmhouse two and a half miles away. All three were then shot to death sometime during the night, although numerous accounts indicate that Lumumba was first stabbed in the chest with a bayonet. In obvious agony, he was finished off with a single bullet to the head by a Belgian mercenary at the scene. The bodies were probably stored for a short time in a refrigerator at the nearby Union Miniere installation, then either buried in an unmarked grave or dissolved in a vat of sulfuric acid at the Jadotville copper plant.

Confirmation of Lumumba's death was difficult to secure. The Congolese government insisted for several days afterward that all three men were alive, prompting one U.S. government official to warn that Lumumba should not be mistreated for fear of stirring up pro-Lumumba sympathizers, and the United Nations kept up demands to visit the prisoners well into February. But rumors of Lumumba's death began trickling out as early as January 23. In response to growing international pressure, the local Katanganese government reported that the prisoners had escaped on February 10, initially offering a reward for their return, then admitting three days later that they were dead.

What's amazing is that Lumumba was not killed earlier. In addition to the many Congolese arrests and plots he sidestepped while prime minister, he was a prime target of the CIA. According to a 1975 Senate investigation of covert CIA activities, Lumumba was one of five foreign leaders—Fidel Castro of Cuba, Ngo Dinh Diem of South Vietnam, Rafael Leonidas Trujillo of the Dominican Republic, and General Rene Schneider of Chile were the others—targeted for death, and there was "reasonable inference" to believe President Dwight Eisenhower authorized the assassination attempts. CIA director Allen Dulles issued the order for Lumumba's death, according to the investigation.

The plan was to introduce a deadly bacterium into Lumumba's toothpaste, since CIA plotters deduced that the prime minister was vain and took great pride in his teeth. But despite the training of two operatives and the disguising of their features through plastic surgery, the plot failed because the agents could find no means by which to slip the toxic toothpaste into Lumumba's hands. Before a second plan could be hatched, Lumumba was dead.

—D.W.C.

JOHN F. KENNEDY

The Victim: The murder in Dallas, Texas, of John Fitzgerald Kennedy, the thirty-fifth president of the United States, proved to be one of the most profound acts of the twentieth century. The youngest man ever elected to the White House, Kennedy, winner of the 1960 presidential election at the age of forty-three, embodied a new American era after decades of aged leaders. His good looks, reforming, liberal policies; and commitment to civil rights and youth inspired a new vision—the so-called Camelot—that stood in stark contrast to more than half a century of isolationism, economic depression, and war.

Not surprisingly, Kennedy's death has been difficult for millions of Americans to comprehend. An entire generation was cut adrift when he died, and the lack of a clear, concise explanation of who killed him and why has left many searching for hidden plots and villains. And there are many theories: the Mafia, J. Edgar Hoover, the FBI, the CIA, pro-Castro Cuban forces, anti-Castro Cubans, right-wing warmongers, the U.S. military-industrial establishment. Hundreds of books have been published on the Kennedy assassination and the conspiracies that supposedly brought it about, but there is little in the way of hard evidence and the debate continues to rage today. The thought that Lee Harvey Oswald, a troubled drifter with no clear agenda, could have killed Kennedy all by himself—as the Warren Commission that investigated the assassination concluded in 1964—fails to satisfy. "You want to add something weightier to Oswald," wrote historian William Manchester. "It would invest the president's death with meaning, endowing him with martyrdom. A conspiracy would, of course, do the job nicely." But not even the ongoing declassification of the complete House Select Committee on Assassinations files is expected to provide any real answers. "There's no smoking gun in there," said G. Robert Blakey, the committee's chief counsel.

In 1963 Kennedy was visiting Texas with an eye toward the 1964 election. The Democrats had lost Texas in 1960, and a split within the local party organization made it necessary for the president to heal the rift in person if a united front was to be presented the following year. Planning for the trip began in April 1963, and a one-day stopover was initially considered. But the trip was extended to two days—including a presidential motorcade through downtown Dallas—when the itinerary was officially announced in October 1963. Four days before the president arrived, the exact route of his motorcade was printed in Dallas newspapers.

The Date: November 22, 1963.

The Event: The presidential party, which included Kennedy's wife, Jacqueline, arrived at

November 22, 1963: President Kennedy arrives at the airport in Dallas, accompanied by his wife, Jacqueline, and Texas governor John Connally.

Dallas's Love Field under a clearing sky. The president took time to shake hands with the spectators gathered at the airport, and the crowd seemed amiable and receptive. Kennedy had been apprehensive about the trip, and made a prophetic remark earlier in the day. "If anybody really wanted to shoot the president it is not a very difficult job," he said. "All one has to do is get on a high building some day with a telescopic rifle and there is nothing anyone can do to defend against such an attempt."

The Secret Service lined up the automobiles for the upcoming parade and marked each car with a slip of paper bearing its number in the motorcade. Kennedy was supposed to ride in the 1961 Lincoln Continental limousine bearing the number 7, but a mix-up left his car second in line, preceded only by a 1963 Ford sedan carrying Dallas police chief Jesse Curry and other local officials. A Secret Service car followed directly behind the president's, but the press vehicle—which was normally placed ahead of the president's in order to facilitate photo coverage of the event—was lined up last (fourteenth). For this reason, photographers in that vehicle were unable to provide any footage or photos of the assassination when it took place.

The president's limousine was not outfitted with the usual protective bubble top because the weather was nice and Kennedy had asked that it be left off. The president sat in the right rear seat with his wife on his left, while Texas governor John B. Connally occupied the jump seat directly in front of him. Connally's wife, Nellie, sat in the jump seat in front of the First Lady. A Secret Service agent sat with driver William Greer up front. The parade proceeded from Love Field through the central part of Dallas. The entourage, destined for the Trade Mart, where Kennedy was scheduled to speak, was nearing the end of its trek when it turned off Houston Street, practically coming to a halt as it negotiated a tight, 120-degree turn left onto Elm Street. The motorcade entered Dealey Plaza, passing directly in front of the Texas School Book Depository building.

Mrs. Connally turned to the Kennedys and said, "Mr. President, you can't say that Dallas doesn't love you."

Suddenly gunshots echoed through the plaza. Kennedy, who was waving to the crowd with his right hand, reached for his throat with clenched fists, his elbows pointing to either side of the street. Apparently he had been struck in the back. Mrs. Kennedy leaned forward, aware that something was horribly wrong. "My God, I'm hit!" Kennedy reportedly said. Greer slowed the limousine almost to a standstill and turned to see what was the matter. Connally also turned to look over his right shoulder, but then a second bullet struck Kennedy, ripping through the right front section of his head, sending up a red mist of blood and bone and brain tissue. Connally was also hit, wounded in the chest, the right wrist, and the left thigh. "My God, they are going to kill us all!" the Texas Governor exclaimed, and fell over into his wife's lap.

The entire attack lasted between six and eight seconds. As the president slumped down into the seat, Mrs. Kennedy turned to her right and scrambled across the trunk of the limousine as Secret Service agent Clint Hill climbed on board. With Hill clinging to the rear of the car, the limousine sped down Elm Street and proceeded directly to Parkland Memorial Hospital four miles away. They arrived at 12:36 P.M.

At the hospital, Connally struggled to his feet to make way for the president—then collapsed. A Secret Service agent removed his coat and covered Kennedy's head. The president was placed on a stretcher and rushed inside to trauma room 1, where a hastily assembled team of surgeons struggled to save his life. But most conceded he was too badly wounded from the start. "My first thought was, 'My God, he is dead,' " remembered Dr. Paul Peters, one of the dozen or so doctors in the room. ". . . A considerable portion of the skull, of the brain, was gone. It looked like a wound we could not salvage."

Nevertheless, a tracheotomy was performed,

whereby a hole was made in Kennedy's throat and a breathing tube was inserted, and external chest massage was performed in the hope of sparking a pulse. But after thirty minutes the doctors conceded that Kennedy was too far gone. In fact, he was so badly wounded that they never even turned him over to look for wounds in his back. A Catholic priest came in and delivered the last rites, and the president was declared dead at 1:00 P.M. As a final act, Mrs. Kennedy slipped the ring off her finger and placed it on the president's finger.

Meanwhile, chaos reigned back at Dealey Plaza. Although some bystanders followed two uniformed police officers, who had been flanking the presidential limousine, up a grassy knoll facing the motorcade in search of the gunman, most witnesses identified the shots as coming from the upper southeast corner of the Texas School Book Depository building. Howard Brennan, a construction worker who was standing directly across the street from the depository, said he looked up moments before the limousines passed and saw "an unsmiling and calm" white man looking out of the sixth-floor window. After the first shot rang out, Brennan said he looked up again and saw the same man, now bearing a rifle. Unable to cry out, Brennan dove to the ground as shots and screams filled the air, then looked up at the window one last time. "To my amazement, the man still stood there," he said. ". . . He didn't appear to be rushed. There was no particular emotion visible on his face except for a slight smirk . . . a look of satisfaction."

Within fifteen minutes of the assassination, Dallas police broadcast the first description of the suspect: a white male, approximately thirty years old, slender build, height five feet ten inches, weight 165 pounds. Meanwhile, Lee Harvey Oswald, a clerk at the depository, slipped out the front door of the building on Elm Street, instructed an NBC newsman where to find a telephone, then boarded a downtown bus. When pandemonium made the streets impassable, Oswald hopped off the bus and walked two blocks to the Greyhound bus station and took a taxi back to his rooming house.

At about 1:15 P.M., Oswald was walking hurriedly along Tenth Street when he was confronted by patrolman J. D. Tippit. Oswald seemed to match the suspect's description that had been broadcast four times in the last thirty minutes, but Tippit, a ten-year veteran, was so unsure he didn't even draw his gun. Oswald did, however, whipping a revolver from the waistband of his pants and shooting Tippit dead. At least a half dozen people saw either the murder of the officer or Oswald fleeing with a gun in his hands, and the noose quickly tightened. Panicked, Oswald ducked into the Texas Theater on Jefferson Avenue without stopping to buy a ticket, prompting a cashier to

Lee Harvey Oswald, the accused assassin of John F. Kennedy, is shot to death on live television by Jack Ruby.

alert the police. Within minutes squad cars sealed the theater's exits, and officers turned up the lights inside to scrutinize the patrons. Oswald, asked to stand, said, "Well, it is all over now," then punched a policeman and attempted to fire his gun again before being subdued. As he was carried out past an angry mob of more than 200 people, Oswald shouted, "I protest this police brutality!"

Held for two days at the Dallas police headquarters, Oswald was being transferred to the city jail on the morning of November 25, 1963, when local nightclub owner Jack Ruby stepped out of a crowd in the basement of the police building and shot Oswald at point-blank range. "You killed my president, you rat!" screamed Ruby. Rushed by ambulance to Parkland Hospital—ironically, where Kennedy had been treated forty-eight hours earlier—Oswald died shortly thereafter.

The Alleged Assassin: Lee Harvey Oswald was born on October 18, 1939, in New Orleans, the victim of a broken home who spent part of his childhood in foster homes. A moody, troubled youth, Oswald enlisted in the U.S. Marines at the age of seventeen, yet found himself increasingly swayed by Marxist ideology and writings. He proved to be a good marksman, earning the title of sharpshooter, the marines' second-highest level. Oswald was posted to a U.S. airbase in Japan and worked with the U-2 spyplane program, but was given a hardship discharge in 1959 because of his mother's health. Back home, Oswald grew restless and emigrated to the Soviet Union that same year. He applied for citizenship but was refused, prompting him to attempt suicide by slashing his wrists in a bathtub in Moscow on October 21, 1959. Saved by blood transfusions, Oswald continued to press for asylum, offering the Soviets information regarding strategic military

installations and codes gathered while in the marines. But the KGB was firm. Two psychiatrists found Oswald "mentally unstable," and KGB officer Yuri Nosenko said he "made us feel he should be avoided at all costs."

Still, Oswald's suicide attempt made him a loose cannon in the eyes of the Soviets, who were reluctant to have an American tourist die in their country. In addition, the recent Eisenhower-Krushchev summit made for a slight thaw in the Cold War. Oswald was granted asylum and sent to work in a transistor radio factory in Minsk. He lived in the Soviet Union for two and one-half years, marrying Marina Pruskova on April 30, 1961, then returned to the United States with his wife and baby daughter on June 13, 1962. Oswald, whose discharge from the marines had been changed from "hardship" to "dishonorable," nevertheless received a loan from the U.S. State Department and settled in New Orleans, where he quickly gained notoriety as a political agitator.

By late 1962 Oswald had become a member of the "Fair Play for Cuba" committee in New Orleans, a pro-Castro organization that listed its address as 544 Camp Street. That same office building was also known as 531 Lafayette Street—the entrance around the corner—and was rented to Guy Bannister, a known conduit for money, arms, and munitions for CIA counterinsurgency forces. Bannister's primary focus at the time was a second invasion of Cuba, a direct violation of the executive order given by President Kennedy. Bannister's close friend and consultant was David Ferrie, a former Eastern Airlines pilot who was then a CIA operative running guns to Cuba. Ferrie was also connected to Carlos Marcello, the godfather of the New Orleans Mafia. Ferrie and Oswald seem to have been in the Civil Air Patrol at the same time in 1955—even though Ferrie was suspended that year for giving unauthorized political lectures to cadets—and at least one photograph appears to show the two together. Six witnesses also place the two men in the patrol at the same time.

In 1963 Oswald, once again fed up with the United States, apparently traveled to Mexico City by bus and visited both the Cuban and Soviet embassies, seeking visas to both countries. Rebuffed, he was met there by two CIA agents, who were told by their station chief, E. Howard Hunt, to "baby-sit" Oswald. He then returned to the United States and resettled in Dallas. Moody and frustrated, Oswald turned his attention to looking for work. Marina was pregnant with the couple's second child, but Oswald was unable to find employment until a neighbor suggested to Marina that he apply at the Texas School Book Depository. In fact, that neighbor, Ruth Hyde Paine, telephoned the depository for him to arrange an interview.

Oswald was hired on October 16, 1963, filling book orders at the salary of $1.25 an hour.

On the morning of November 22, 1963, Oswald left for work without waking his wife. He placed $170 in cash—probably all of their savings—on the bureau, along with his wedding ring. Driven to work by a neighbor, Buell Frazier, Oswald carried a brown package measuring approximately four feet in length close to his side. When asked what was in the box, he replied, "Curtain rods." At the book depository, Oswald was observed several times peering down from the windows onto Dealey Plaza, and later asked coworker James Jarman why crowds were gathering outside. Told that the president's motorcade was due to pass by in a couple of hours, Oswald said simply, "Oh, I see."

The Aftermath: What happened in the minutes, hours, days, and weeks following the assassination of President Kennedy has had as great an impact on America as the assassination itself. Did some massive conspiracy and cover-up surge to life? Were all of the botched investigations, interviews, inconsistencies, and inaccuracies just coincidental? Was the White House involved? The CIA? The FBI? The Mafia? Or did Oswald, acting out of frustration, anger, and self-pity, simply kill the president single-handedly, thereby orphaning an entire nation?

The first official act came on November 29, when President Lyndon Johnson appointed a blue-ribbon panel to investigate the Kennedy assassination. A Gallup poll taken one week after the assassination showed that only 29 percent of Americans believed Oswald acted alone, and Johnson hoped that the so-called Warren Commission (named after its chairman, Earl Warren, chief justice of the Supreme Court) would clear the air. Likening the growing public suspicion of a conspiracy to war, Johnson granted the commission almost unlimited power in return for a report that would close the book on Kennedy for good. Of the six other members, two were ranking senators (John Sherman Cooper and Richard Russell), two were senior House members (Hale Boggs and Gerald Ford), and attorney John J. McCloy was the former director of the World Bank. The most curious member, however, was Allen Dulles, the CIA's former spymaster who had been ousted by Kennedy. Sloppy and seemingly disinterested in the investigation, Dulles's inclusion has long been a vital clue to conspiracy theorists, who believe he spent more time covering up facts than seeking out the truth.

Still, the Warren Commission conducted a massive investigation that resulted in an 888-page report, which was submitted to Johnson on September 24, 1964. After more than 27,000 interviews and 3,000 investigative reports, the Warren Commission concluded that one man, Lee Harvey Oswald, acted alone in murdering John F. Kennedy and that there was no conspiracy of any kind behind the crime. The commission placed Oswald on the sixth floor of the Texas School Book Depository—where a 6.5mm bolt-action, clip-fed, 1938 Mannlicher-Carcano rifle, belonging to Oswald and bearing his palm print, was later found—and stated that he fired the three shots necessary to kill the president. According to the official hypothesis, the first shot struck Kennedy in the back and exited through his throat, hitting Connally twice before settling in his thigh. The second shot went astray, striking the curb near a bystander, James T. Tague, spraying his foot and cheek with fragments of cement and lead. The third shot shattered the right front side of Kennedy's head.

The Warren Commission report was challenged from the moment it was released, predominantly in two areas—bullet trajectory and time lapse. The assertion that one bullet struck Kennedy and Connally a total of four times—and then was found in near-pristine condition on Connally's stretcher in the hospital—defied logic, and it was promptly dubbed the "magic bullet" theory. If, for instance, Oswald was firing from the sixth floor of the building, the angle of trajectory would be seventeen degrees, forty-three minutes, thirty seconds, in a downward direction. That bullet apparently entered Kennedy's back, five and one-half inches down from his collar line—yet the only other wound on the president's body was a small slit in his throat. The Warren Commission theorized that this slit was caused by the exit of the bullet that continued on to strike Connally. But since the bullet struck no bone in Kennedy's body that might have deflected its trajectory upward, how did it change course? And could that same bullet have been powerful enough to pass through Connally's body and wrist before lodging in his thigh? And still not be badly mangled?

As for the time factor, an 8mm home movie shot by Abraham Zapruder has become the single most important—and unforgettable—piece of evidence in the Kennedy assassination investigation. Perched atop a block of granite seventy-two feet from the middle of Elm Street, Zapruder filmed Kennedy's limousine as it passed by, recording the president's reaction as he was hit by bullets. The Zapruder film was purchased immediately after the assassination by *Life* magazine but was never released in its full form by the Time-Life Corporation. The only two official copies were made by the Secret Service and the FBI. But in 1967 New Orleans district attorney Jim Garrison subpoenaed the Zapruder film as evidence in the trial of New Orleans businessman Clay Shaw, who was accused of conspiracy in the assassination of Kennedy. Garrison obtained the film, copied it, and thus became the source of the film for many researchers and investigators.

A careful frame-by-frame analysis of Zapruder's film reveals that ten frames passed between the last moment before Kennedy was hit and the second Connally was struck. Since Zapruder's camera operated at 18.3 frames per second, that represents an apparent time value of .546488 seconds—just over half a second. Meanwhile, a bullet fired from the Oswald weapon and passing through the neck of Kennedy, as the Warren Commission claimed, would move at a speed of 1,772 feet to 1,779 feet per second. Based on that formula, the bullet would have had to pause in midair for approximately one-half second between leaving Kennedy's body and entering Connally's.

Special Agent Robert A. Frazier of the FBI testified as the firearms expert before the Warren Commission. He stated that the bolt action of the Italian rifle took at least 2.3 seconds, according to tests run by expert riflemen. Therefore, he concluded, it is impossible that the weapon was fired twice within the half-second time slot.

Such analyses fanned the flames of conspiracy and gave rise to the persistent notion that two or more shooters were stationed throughout Dealey Plaza, catching the presidential limousine in a hail of gunfire. But author Gerald Posner, writing in his 1993 book, *Case Closed*, believes the Warren Commission to be correct. Posner cites a computer program, created by a firm named Failure Analysis Associates, that he claims verifies the "magic bullet" theory. It shows that the bullet grazed Kennedy's vertebra and tumbled end over end after it exited the president's throat. As for the pristine condition, the fact that the bullet never hit a hard object (such as the bones in Connally's wrist) at full speed would have allowed the bullet to keep its shape. Posner fails to inform his readers that Failure Analysis prepared its computer analysis for a 1992 mock trial of Lee Harvey Oswald staged by the American Bar Association. In fact, they prepared two analyses, one for the prosecution and one for the defense. They did so not to re-create the assassination, but to support the positions of each side. The analysis that Posner cites is merely the one created to support the prosecution.

The time lapse is even trickier, but Posner believes Kennedy was actually hit a split second or two earlier than first believed. Suffering a condition known as Thorburn's position—whereby a blow to the spinal column instantaneously forces the victim's arms up and out—Kennedy may have been reacting to the first bullet when his hands were supposedly going for his throat. As a result, the president could actually have been hit as much as 3.5 seconds before Connally, more than enough time for Oswald to recock the gun and fire again.

Yet the magic bullet and the time lapse are just two of the Warren Commission inconsistencies seized upon by conspiracy theorists over the years. Unable to accept the conclusion that a lone nut killed the president with a very lucky shot, they have proposed other scenarios. For instance:

• The Mafia ordered Kennedy's assassination as payback for his brutal crackdown on organized crime. Oswald, Ruby, Ferrie, and Bannister all had connections to New Orleans bosses, and Oswald insisted he was a "patsy" from the minute he was arrested. Ruby's murder of Oswald also appears to be a classic Mafia "hit."
• The CIA ordered Kennedy's assassination in order to keep him from going too "soft" on Communism and/or pulling out of the burgeoning war in Vietnam.
• The KGB ordered Kennedy's assassination as payback for the Cuban Missile Crisis and because he was an avowed foe of Communism. Oswald certainly had Marxist sympathies, but would the Soviet secret police allow such a lunatic to carry out their dirty work?
• The Cubans (pro-Castro or anti-Castro, take your pick) ordered Kennedy's assassination either as payback for the failed Bay of Pigs invasion or as payback for failing to authorize a second Bay of Pigs invasion.
• Other theories range from a Secret Service agent accidentally shooting Kennedy while reaching for his gun in response to Oswald's gunfire, to Oswald himself hitting the president by accident while actually attempting to kill Connally.

In fact, Kennedy conspiracies have become an industry unto themselves. A convention is held each year in Dallas to swap theories and sell gruesome memorabilia, such as Oswald's coroner's tag, Ruby's gun, and bootleg autopsy photos, and a magazine, the *Grassy Knoll Gazette*, exists as a clearinghouse for wild theories. In 1992 Oliver Stone's emotional and misleading film, *JFK*, touched off a whole new wave of conspiracy mania, even though his apparent conclusion—that Oswald was framed by a cabal of military-industrial hard-liners that included Lyndon Johnson and the whole Joint Chiefs of Staff—is rejected by even the most dedicated theorists as far-fetched.

Still, the endless debate over who shot Kennedy and why led the U.S. government to reopen the investigation in the late 1970s. After two years of hearings and testimony, the House Select Committee on Assassinations issued its final report in 1978, announcing only that there was a "ninety-five percent" chance that four shots had been fired at Kennedy. But no new names and no new evidence were presented, and no new conclusions were reached; in effect, the 1978 committee vindicated the work of the Warren Commission fourteen years before. In

1992 three pathologists who examined Kennedy's body immediately after the assassination came forward to refute theories that the president had been hit by gunfire from the front. All three agreed he had been struck from behind.

The same conclusions were reached by Posner, whose *Case Closed* was released to coincide with the thirtieth anniversary of Kennedy's assassination. Praised for its calm, level-headed approach to the murder and its ensuing investigation, Posner's book dispels many conspiracy theories, inconsistencies, and inaccuracies of the last three decades, often shedding light on evidence (Oswald's fingerprints on his rifle) or witnesses (the man who suffered a seizure moments before the president's motorcade passed by) that had been "missing" for all these years. Naturally, Posner's book prompted a gut reaction on all levels. Although the mass media fell over each other in their attempts to praise *Case Closed*, Posner has also been accused of being guilty of using tactics he criticizes when used by others: misquoting witnesses, ignoring evidence that doesn't fit his theory, and even claiming to have interviewed people who say they never spoke with him.

It's doubtful the full truth about the assassination of John F. Kennedy will ever be known. Why was the name and home telephone number of FBI agent James Hosty found in Oswald's phone book when he was arrested? Why was the president's brain missing when his body was returned to Bethesda Naval Hospital for an autopsy? Why was Jack Ruby allowed to attend Oswald's press conference at the Dallas police headquarters on November 22, even though he was not a newsman and admitted carrying a gun? Why did so many of the employees at the Texas School Book Depository change their testimony as to when and where they had last seen Oswald before the assassination? On and on the questions go, some defying easy answers, others not. But the only real truth was expressed by Robert F. Kennedy in 1964, when he turned down an invitation to testify about his brother to the Warren Commission. "I don't care what they do," he told an aide. "It's not going to bring him back."

—D.W.C., B.C., and R.R.

MALCOLM X

The Victim: Malcolm X, one of the most powerful and controversial leaders of the black civil rights movement of the 1960s, was a gifted orator. Malcolm spent more than a decade as the voice of the Nation of Islam religious sect under its leader, Elijah Muhammad, advocating a strict program of black supremacy and self-reliance. But his growing popularity and provocative statements led to his exile from the group on December 1, 1963. Following a pilgrimage to Mecca, Malcolm broke completely with the Nation of Islam on March 8, 1964, by establishing the Organization of Afro-American Unity (OAAU), an orthodox Muslim sect with more mainstream views on violence and black-white relations.

But the rift between the two groups quickly turned vicious. Malcolm's house in Queens, New York, was firebombed on February 13, 1965—an act widely attributed to followers of the Black Muslims—and he was hounded by death threats the last two weeks of his life. An attempt to poison Malcolm also reportedly occurred while he was in Egypt in August 1964. Yet Malcolm's growing tolerance led him to publicly "pardon" the Black Muslims in a conversation with his biographer-friend, Alex Haley, the night before he was killed. "The more I keep thinking about this thing, the things that have been happening lately, I'm not sure at all it's the Muslims," Malcolm said. "I know what they can do, and what they can't, and they can't do some of the stuff recently going on."

The son of a Baptist preacher turned black nationalist, Malcolm Little was born in Omaha, Nebraska, on May 19, 1925. After the family moved to Lansing, Michigan, his father was murdered—possibly by white vigilantes—and his mother suffered a mental breakdown, leaving the eight Little children wards of the state. Despite excelling in school, Malcolm drifted into a life of street crime and drugs, adopting the persona of "Detroit Red," and was convicted of burglary and sentenced to ten years in prison at the age of twenty. It was there that Malcolm discovered the religion of Islam, and he emerged from prison angry and educated enough to take on the world. He dropped his "slave" surname and replaced it with an X to signify his lost African heritage, and quickly became a top recruiter and speaker for the Chicago-based Nation of Islam. Malcolm's motto was "By any means necessary," and his platform provided a menacing contrast to Dr. Martin Luther King's more popular nonviolent approach. "We're not Americans," he said in 1964. "We're Africans who happen to be in America. We were kidnapped and brought here against our will from Africa. We didn't land on Plymouth Rock—the rock landed on us."

As Elijah Muhammad's chief missionary and protégé, Malcolm crisscrossed the country, opening temples and rounding up new members. "My hobby," he said, "is stirring up Negroes." But his growing stature threatened almost everybody. Whites regarded Malcolm as a troublemaker bent on revolution, prompting both the FBI and the CIA to place him under surveillance, while most blacks still preferred King's pacifist approach. Even the Black Muslims viewed his newfound celebrity and power base with alarm. But Malcolm wasn't comfortable with the Nation of Islam either; specifically, reports of Elijah Muhammad's infidelity caused him to reassess the entire church. When Malcolm gloated over the assassination of John F. Kennedy to reporters on December 1, 1963—defying Elijah Muhammad's orders not to comment on the murder—the die was cast. Muhammad suspended his chief minister for ninety days, prompting Malcolm to bolt the Nation of Islam and form his own church.

But while Malcolm's OAAU extended a peace offering to whites, it infuriated the Black Muslims, who saw it as direct competition. Although it is doubtful Muhammad ever directly ordered the assassination of Malcolm, many church elders began plotting ways to be rid of him, and the final year of Malcolm's life was haunted by violence and fear. He kept loaded automatic guns in his home, changed his unlisted telephone number repeatedly, and even lived apart from his wife and four daughters in order to protect them. He was unable to get life insurance, and he expected to die soon. "To come right down to it," Malcolm wrote in his autobiography, ". . . it [is] just about impossible for me to die of old age."

The Date: February 21, 1965.

The Event: Malcolm X's speech at the Audubon Ballroom in Harlem that Sunday afternoon would continue to spread his vision of the OAAU, an organization that was still evolving from its strict Islamic roots into a more practical sect. The Audubon had been a vital part of the black community for decades, and Malcolm had spoken to a crowd of 600 there less than a week before. Still, tension within the black community was extremely high, and a heavy security force was on hand at the Audubon. Malcolm was so concerned that he initially refused to let his wife, Betty Shabazz,

The body of Malcolm X is taken away by police after he was shot to death at a rally in New York City.

and his children attend the speech, but later he relented.

Malcolm was edgy as he took the stage around 3:00 P.M. The scheduled warm-up speakers failed to show—forcing an OAAU deputy to fill in—and Malcolm looked drawn and tired as he stood behind the lectern and greeted the packed ballroom with the customary Islamic words, "As-salaam alaikum" (Peace be unto you). The room responded, "Wa-alaikum salaam" (And unto you be peace). Just then a disturbance broke out somewhere in the crowd as one man called to another, "Get your hands out of my pocket!" Angry words were exchanged, and several of Malcolm's bodyguards moved to break up the fight. Malcolm himself stepped forward and raised his hand. "Hold it!" he shouted, "Hold it! . . . Let's cool it, brothers."

Suddenly a crude smoke bomb was detonated at the rear of the auditorium. As the crowd began to stir, a black man stepped forward with a sawed-off shotgun and blasted buckshot into Malcolm's chest, sending him crashing into a pile of folding chairs. A second shotgun blast ripped the lectern in half. Two other black men rushed the stage and began firing bullets into his prone body. In all, Malcolm was hit sixteen times. The three men then turned and quickly joined the crowd rushing for the exits.

"They are killing my husband!" shrieked Betty Shabazz, who fought through the panic to reach her fallen husband. Friends and followers quickly surrounded him, and Gene Roberts, an undercover police officer who had infiltrated the OAAU, tried in vain to resuscitate Malcolm's graying body. But the damage was too great. Carried by stretcher out of the ballroom and rushed across the street to the Columbia Presbyterian Medical Center, Malcolm X was declared dead shortly thereafter.

Meanwhile, the assailants fled. Although at least two apparently got away, bodyguard Reuben X Francis shot wildly, wounding one man, Talmadge Hayer, in the thigh. Stumbling as he fell out of the building, Hayer was seized by the crowd and severely beaten. Only the intervention of three New York police officers saved Hayer, who was arrested and taken to Bellevue Hospital for treatment. Press accounts also reported that a second man was beaten by the crowd and later arrested, and Jimmy Breslin wrote in the *New York Herald Tribune* that the man had been taken to the Wadsworth Avenue precinct. But the New York Police Department denied ever making a second arrest, and the newspaper dropped the story from its later editions.

Malcolm X's body was put on display at the Unity Funeral Home in Harlem on February 22, 1965. Despite bomb threats and the objections of orthodox Muslims, who argued that the body should be buried before the setting of the second sun, an estimated 30,000 people visited the funeral home. Malcolm's funeral was held amid tight security on February 27, with more than 1,000 people wedging themselves into the Faith Temple Church and another 3,000 waiting outside. Actor Ossie Davis spoke, calling Malcolm X "our own black shining Prince." After the performance of Islamic rites, Malcolm was taken to Ferncliff Cemetery in Westchester County to be buried under the name El-Hajj Malik El-Shabazz, his full Muslim name. Rather than allow white grave diggers to cover their fallen hero, mourners, many of them dressed in their best suits and ties, scooped earth over the coffin with their bare hands.

The Alleged Assassins: The investigation into the assassination of Malcolm X was as complicated as it was confusing. Black hostility toward the police department made it difficult to track down leads and suspects, and fears of Black Muslim reprisals against informants only made the situation worse. In addition, detectives and prosecutors either ignored or overlooked evidence that might have helped. Still, three men were arrested and charged with the murder: Talmadge Hayer, Norman 3X Butler, and Thomas 15X Johnson. The trial got under way on January 21, 1966, and all three were convicted on March 11, 1966. They were sentenced to life imprisonment on April 14, 1966, with no chance of parole until 1991.

Talmadge Hayer (a.k.a. Thomas Hayer and/or Thomas Hagan) was the only man to confess to the murder of Malcolm X. Arrested at the scene of the crime carrying a .45-caliber cartridge that matched the murder weapon, Hayer's fingerprint was also found on a piece of flammable film from which the smoke bomb had been made and which was recovered at the back of the ballroom. Hayer acted as his own lawyer and admitted to the crime in court on February 28, 1965. But he also testified that the other two defendants were not involved. Hayer stated that he and four accomplices—whom he refused to name—had been hired to do the job. Hayer said that he was not a Black Muslim and said that the man who hired him was not a Black Muslim either.

Years later, Hayer was serving time at New York's Attica Prison when the bloody 1971 inmate revolt took place. As the resident Muslim minister, he played a pivotal role by using his influence to protect the prison guards who were taken hostage.

Butler, a known and admitted Black Muslim, was also a member of the "Fruit of Islam" elite security force. But on the morning of the assassination, Butler had been treated by a doctor for superficial thrombophlebitis, which resulted in the bandaging of his right leg and the prescription of oral medication. Although some witnesses testified that Butler was stationed at one of the exits in the ballroom, others dis-

agreed. Either way, how could a man with a heavily bandaged leg have hoped to make a getaway?

Johnson, a known Black Muslim, was a companion of Butler's and both were arrested in January 1965 for an assault on a Black Muslim defector. The prosecution accused Johnson of being the man wielding the shotgun in Malcolm X's murder. But Johnson said he stayed home that day and denied ever handling a shotgun. In addition, Johnson's lawyer argued that both he and Butler were well known as Black Muslims by the OAAU and would never have been allowed inside the ballroom.

In 1977 Hayer broke his silence and identified his coconspirators as Muslims from the Nation of Islam Mosque number 25 in Newark, New Jersey. According to Hayer, Benjamin X Thomas (a.k.a. Ben Thompson), Leon X Davis, William X Bradley, and Wilbur X Kinley had participated in the killing with him, not Butler and Johnson. As a result, the two men were paroled in 1985. A model prisoner, Hayer earned two college degrees and is now in a New York City work-release program.

But the debate over who authorized Malcolm X's assassination continues. At the time of the murder, Elijah Muhammad denied any knowledge, stating his "shock and surprise" in an interview with a Chicago radio station. According to some reports, Betty Shabazz removed a list of five potential assassins from her husband's coat pocket as he lay on the Audubon Ballroom stage, but she has never made the list public. In 1994 she did accuse Nation of Islam leader Louis Farrakhan of complicity in Malcolm's murder, saying "Nobody kept it a secret. It was a badge of honor. Everybody talked about it, yes." Farrakhan, chief minister of the Nation of Islam's Boston mosque in 1965, once stated that Malcolm X was "worthy of death." But he denies any involvement in the assassination, and filed a $4.4 billion lawsuit against the *New York Post* in 1994 for printing Shabazz's accusations.

> I, for one, believe that if you give people a thorough understanding of what confronts them and the basic causes that produce it, they'll create their own program; and when the people create a program, you get action.
>
> Malcolm X

Theories that the U.S. government authorized or participated in Malcolm X's assassination fail to hold up under scrutiny. Although the FBI feared he would form an alliance with Martin Luther King, and the CIA was troubled by his relationships with foreign leaders such as Fidel Castro, there is no evidence to suggest either ordered his death, nor was the New York City

Police Department involved. In fact, the FBI warned Malcolm of threats against his life and promised to provide witnesses if he wished to take the Black Muslims to court. The police, meanwhile, offered round-the-clock protection, which Malcolm turned down.

The Legacy: As with most martyrs, Malcolm X is more popular in death than he ever was in life. His maxims of self-reliance, self-respect, and economic empowerment continue to hit home with American blacks, and his violent urgency has attracted scores of new followers, especially in the wake of the 1992 Los Angeles riots. Spike Lee's popular and controversial 1992 film, *Malcolm X*, also triggered a wave of Malcolm mania, and rap groups, artists, and politicians now invoke his words at will. A quarter century after Malcolm X's death, the X symbol adorns everything from baseball caps to lunch boxes. "There's something in Malcolm which touches the core of younger people," said Howard Dodson of the Schomburg Center for Research in Black Culture, in an interview with *Newsweek* magazine. "He was willing to stand up, to talk straight. Malcolm was a man— a real man." Yet it's clear that society is struggling with the correct way to honor that man.

—D.W.C.

MARTIN LUTHER KING JR.

The Victim: Martin Luther King Jr., black Baptist minister from Alabama who spearheaded the civil rights movement from the mid-1950s until his death in 1968 at the age of thirty-nine, organized the Southern Christian Leadership Conference (SCLC) and gained recognition as an advocate of the Gandhian principle of nonviolent resistance. Through his efforts, national attention was focused on the plight of blacks, resulting in the passage of the 1964 Civil Rights Act and the 1965 Voting Rights Act. In 1964 King was awarded the Nobel Peace Prize. At the time of his assassination, he was planning a Poor People's March on Washington.

The Date: April 4, 1968.

The Event: Beginning in February 1968, Memphis, Tennessee, became the scene of a controversial strike by the city's 1,300 sanitation personnel. As the result of a large-scale disturbance, instigated in part by undercover law-enforcement infiltrators, one youth was killed and 238 persons were arrested. King was invited to Memphis in April to help the strike proceed in a more peaceful manner.

On April 3 King checked into the Lorraine Motel, room 306. That evening he was to speak at the Mason Street Temple. Late in the after-

noon, Memphis was struck by strong winds and rain. King felt that his speech should be given by Ralph Abernathy, his associate. If the weather kept the crowds away, reporters would have an excellent opportunity to make journalistic stabs at King's speaking to an empty house. When Abernathy arrived at the Mason Street Temple, however, more than 2,000 people greeted him and strong support was obvious. The group wanted to hear Martin Luther King. King complied with a speech that contained a passage bordering on prophecy.

Well, I don't know what will happen now. We've got some difficult days ahead. [But] I've been to the mountain top. I won't mind. Like anybody, I'd like to live a long life. Longevity has its place but I'm not concerned about that now. I just want to do God's will, and He's allowed me to go up to the mountain. And I've looked over. And I've seen the Promised Land. I may not get there with you, but I want you to know tonight that we as a people will get to the Promised Land. So I'm happy tonight. I'm not worried about anything. I'm not fearing any man. Mine eyes have seen the glory of the coming of the Lord.

King spent April 4 in his motel room in Memphis. As evening approached, he and his associates were preparing   dinner engagement. King stepped out onto the balcony overlooking a parking lot and started a short conversation with Rev. Jesse Jackson, who, with their mutual friend the musician Ben Branch, was standing in the lot.

"You remember Ben?" Jackson asked. "Oh, yeah. He's my man. Be sure to play 'Precious Lord' and play it real pretty," King replied. Solomon Jones, King's chauffeur, called to him that it was chilly and advised him to wear his topcoat. King agreed. As he straightened up to leave, a single shot rang out. King was thrown violently backward, and his necktie was ripped completely off his shirt. He was bleeding profusely as shocked associates and staff members ran to his aid. The bullet had struck King in the right side of the jaw, entered his neck, and severed his spinal cord.

Within fifteen minutes an ambulance arrived and carried the stricken leader to Saint Joseph's Hospital, where he was pronounced dead at 7:05 P.M., an hour and four minutes after the shooting.

The Alleged Assassin: The first lead was the discovery of a zippered satchel, a bedspread, and a cardboard case containing a .30/06-caliber Remington Gamemaster rifle, model 760, with a 2 × 7 telescopic sight. The parcels had been hastily deposited in front of Guy Canipe's Amusement Company. "He sure burned leather," declared Canipe about a man on foot. Two of

Moments after Martin Luther King was assassinated, his aides point out where the fatal shot came from.

Canipe's customers, Bernell Finley and Julius Graham, had also seen the man run past and drop the items, but no one could give a clear description to Shelby County Deputy Sheriff Judson Ghormley of the Memphis police.

In the rooming house next door to Canipe's business, tenants were perplexed by the man from room 5B, who had locked himself in the floor's only bathroom. He had registered that morning as John Willard and had bypassed more expensive rooms to choose a location fifteen feet down the hall from the bathroom. The fatal shot had apparently traveled from the bathroom window some 210 feet, across to the balcony of room 306.

Two tenants at the rooming house, Willie Anschutz and Charles Stephens, claimed to have seen Willard going around the corner at the end of the hall and down the stairs shortly after the shot was fired, but no one was able to give a positive identification and Stephens was admittedly very drunk that afternoon. The most detailed description of the supposed killer was given by Canipe, who said he had been "a white man, a little under six feet, pretty well dressed, dark-headed, no hat, and wearing a dark suit." In addition, not one but two white Mustangs had pulled away from the amusement store after the murder, and they had been going in opposite directions. Lieuten-

ant Rufus Bradshaw called in a report that one of the cars had been spotted and was being chased, but police following Bradshaw's directions found nothing. The lieutenant later stated that he had gotten his information from a young motorist of doubtful credibility.

Next the police turned their attention to the items left behind at the Canipe establishment. In the small canvas satchel they found some clothes, a pair of pliers, and a newspaper headlined "King Challenges Court Restraint. Vows to March." The pliers were traced to the Romage Hardware Store in Los Angeles, and laundry marks on the clothes led to a cleaners two blocks away. Police were thus able to come up with a name: Eric Starvo Galt. Meanwhile, in Atlanta, Georgia, an abandoned white Mustang registered in the name of E. Galt was found.

Police next discovered that Galt had been taking dancing lessons and attending a bartending school while living at the Saint Francis Hotel in Los Angeles. The bartending school was able to provide a picture of Galt, and the picture was identified as that of James Earl Ray.

No fingerprints had been found in Willard's room or the bathroom, not even on the doorknobs. Only a single fingerprint on a map in the Mustang had been discovered, and one print was also reportedly found on the rifle itself. The unusual scarcity of fingerprints was added to two other puzzles. Clothes found in the satchel and in the trunk of the Mustang were of different sizes. Also, despite the fact that Ray was a nonsmoker, the motel room and the floor of the Mustang were littered with Viceroy butts. These facts suggest the possibility that it was not Ray—or at least not Ray alone—who occupied the room and drove the car.

Suspecting that Ray had left the country, authorities began to examine passport information. In Canada the Royal Mounted Police discovered that Ray had obtained passports in the names of at least three other men: Paul Edward Bridgeman, Toronto policeman George Ramon Sneyd, and Eric St. Vincent Galt (who signed his middle name so that it appeared to be "Starvo").

Ray was finally arrested on June 8 in London's Heathrow Airport. In attempting to board a British European Airways flight for Brussels, he had accidentally shown two passports, one for George Ramon Sneyd and a second for George Ramon Sneya. While questioning him about the dual passports, security officers routinely searched him and discovered a loaded .38-caliber pistol. Ray stayed calm until Scotland Yard official Thomas Butler told him that he knew his true identity and that he was wanted for murder. At that point Ray laid his head on his hands and wept.

A question that continues to dog the Ray case is that of money. Ray had spent $2,000 for the Mustang, undergone plastic surgery, attended bartending school and dancing lessons in Los Angeles, and lavishly entertained a Canadian woman who reported that he had told her, "There's plenty more where that came from." Yet Ray was a prison escapee with no money of his own. The only benefactor he might have had was his brother Jerry, a manual laborer unable to finance the costly pursuits Ray indulged in.

In spite of these discrepancies, law enforcement officials continue to maintain that there was no conspiracy in the murder of Dr. King. When news reports exposed FBI activities concerned with King, the U.S. Justice Department began an internal probe to determine the validity of accusations of a cover-up. It revealed no evidence that the FBI had been involved in the assassination. Not surprisingly, a second investigation, headed by the FBI itself, also failed to unearth evidence of conspiracy or FBI involvement.

Nonetheless, a retired FBI agent from the Atlanta office (who was working there at the time of the killing) had told the press that there were deep anti-King feelings within the FBI and that one agent literally jumped for joy when he learned of King's assassination. Furthermore, he alleged that his superiors washed out leads suggesting conspiracy.

Memphis police detective Ed Reddit stated that he was pulled off the King detail immediately prior to the assassination after suggesting a plan to seal off a four-block area in Memphis in the event a shot was fired. He was told to remove himself from the case, and when he refused, he was placed under "virtual house arrest" and was not allowed to continue in his duties that day.

Years later revelations were made regarding the FBI's illegal harassment of Martin Luther King. The FBI admitted that not only had it wiretapped King's home, but it had sent Mrs. Coretta King letters implying that her husband was seeing numerous other women. It even sent King a letter that intimated that he should commit suicide prior to the scheduled awarding of the Nobel Peace Prize in 1964. The letter read in part: "King—there is only one thing left for you to do. You know what it is. You have just thirty-four days in which to do it. It has definite practical significance. You are done. There is but one way out."

J. Edgar Hoover's feelings about Dr. King were well known. He had called King "the most notorious liar in the country" and had berated his selection as the Nobel Peace Prize recipient. He was obsessed with ferreting out the details of King's sex life and had himself authorized many of the illegal harassments that plagued King before his death. Hoover was also responsible for a news story that had attacked King for his initial choice of a white-owned hotel in Memphis, and which had caused him to change his reservations to the Lorraine Motel, where the assassination took place. Then-senator Walter Mondale described the FBI activities in the King matter as "a mad map to the destruction of American democracy."

James Earl Ray was one of seven children of George Ellis Ray and Lucille Maher. Ray's mother became an alcoholic and died in 1961. Although Ray and his brothers reported their father dead also, George—who had changed his last name to Rayns—was still alive. Because he had been out of touch with his son for some time, he could give little information to the authorities. But he did say that if James had killed King, "he couldn't have planned it alone; he wasn't smart enough for that."

Ray dropped out of school in the tenth grade and worked at menial jobs until 1946, when he joined the U.S. Army. On December 23, 1948, he was discharged for "ineptness and lack of adaptability to military service." Thereafter he was arrested for a series of armed robberies, served three years for forgery, and was involved in other small-time smuggling and burglary activities. When he escaped from Missouri State Prison at Jefferson City on April 23, 1967, he was not regarded as much of a criminal. His "wanted" poster offered the minimum reward of fifty dollars and displayed the wrong set of fingerprints. After his incarceration for the King murder, Ray managed to escape from prison again on June 10, 1977. He eluded a massive manhunt until June 13, when he was recaptured and returned to jail.

In his book *Who Killed Martin Luther King?* (1992), Ray spells out in considerable detail his version of the assassination. He claims that he was a patsy, set up by a mysterious figure known as Raoul, who first contacted him in Toronto in 1967, after Ray had escaped from prison, about a year before King was killed. Raoul, Ray claims, lured him into a smuggling scheme in both Canada and Mexico; over the next year, Raoul gave him money, met him at various points throughout the country, had him buy a white Mustang and the Remington .30/06 rifle that apparently was used to kill King, and, finally, ordered him to meet up in Memphis on April 3 to further an alleged gunrunning scheme. On the afternoon of April 4, Ray claims, Raoul disappeared—with the rifle—just before the shooting, supposedly to meet with underworld connections. Ray contends that he later heard on the car radio that King had been assassinated and that police were looking for a man in a white Mustang; that was when he decided to flee. He also claims that he had no help in escaping, but did so on his own, and, further, that he was coerced by his lawyer, Percy Foreman, into pleading guilty.

There is considerable circumstantial evidence to suggest that Ray did not act on his own. He had neither the resources nor the contacts to supply himself with passports, money, and weaponry. The bullet recovered from Dr. King's body has never been scientifically linked with the alleged murder weapon. And Ray's motive in the killing, had he acted alone, is also unclear. It wasn't James Earl Ray who had publicly denounced Dr. King, and it wasn't Ray who had the resources necessary to travel 20,000 miles and spend a vast amount of money to evade capture. But it was Ray who pleaded guilty to the crime and was sentenced to ninety-nine years in prison.

In the late 1970s the House Select Committee on Assassinations (HSCA) conducted an investigation into the King assassination. It concluded that while Ray had fired the fatal bullet, there was a "likelihood" of a conspiracy based in right-wing racist circles in Saint Louis. Russell Byers, a figure in the Saint Louis underworld, had told an FBI informant in 1974 that John Kaufman, another Saint Louis underworld figure, had invited him to the home of John Sutherland, a wealthy Saint Louis attorney, Civil War buff, and organizer of the local White Citizens Council. In his den, which was crammed with Civil War memorabilia, including a large rug in the design of a Confederate flag, Sutherland, decked out in the uniform of a Confederate colonel, offered Byers $50,000 to

have Martin Luther King killed. While Byers did nothing, the HSCA concluded that this was in all probability a standing offer—of which, for several reasons, James Earl Ray could well have been aware. One of Kaufman's friends, a Dr. Hugh Maxey, was the physician at Missouri State Prison, where Ray was serving time. Russell Byers's brother-in-law, a fellow inmate of Ray's, worked under Dr. Maxey in the prison hospital. And Ray's brother and sister owned and operated a tavern in Saint Louis that was located across the street from the local George Wallace campaign headquarters and was a favorite hangout for underworld types and the right-wing lunatic fringe. Sutherland, meanwhile, was the Saint Louis area's leading Wallace supporter.

The HSCA's conclusion that "no federal, state, or local agency was involved" in the assassination, as well as the HSCA's overall methods of investigation, have come under serious scrutiny, most notably by Philip H. Melanson, professor of political science at the University of Massachusetts. In *The Murkin Conspiracy* (1989), Melanson contends that both the FBI and the HSCA investigations were seriously flawed. "A close examination of the fingerprint, ballistics, and eyewitness evidence," he writes, "reveals . . . gaps and inconsistencies . . . clearly biased toward establishing Ray's guilt."

Melanson suggests that merely because the FBI may not have killed King doesn't mean that no other federal agency was involved. He cites such documents as a May 1965 CIA internal memo that states that an informant "feels that somewhere in the negro movement . . . there must be a negro leader who is 'clean' and who could step into the vacuum and chaos if Martin Luther King were either exposed or assassinated." Melanson speculates that the assassination may well have been the work of a cabal within the CIA and/or U.S. military intelligence, whose motives would have been rooted less in classic racism than in the widely held perception that King, who had recently begun to speak out against the Vietnam War, was serving— wittingly or unwittingly—as a conduit for pro-Hanoi propaganda.

Ray's own story concerning Raoul, says Melanson, is entirely consistent with the methods of a sophisticated covert operations handler experienced in "tradecraft." Following up on an earlier investigation by a Canadian journalist, Melanson succeeded in identifying a shadowy character named Jules Ricco Kimble, whose movements during the critical months leading up to the assassination coincide with the dates and places of Ray's alleged meetings with Raoul. Melanson also provides a thorough critique of the celebrated "fat man" who mysteriously appeared at Ray's rooming house in Toronto while Ray was on the lam after the assassination, bearing an envelope for the fugitive, and who police claimed was merely a Good Samaritan returning an envelope Ray had inadvertently left in a phone booth. Melanson tracked down and questioned the "fat man," who seemed to be in great fear for his life, and who told Melanson that the contents of the envelope he had found made clear that Ray had had accomplices. Melanson, who believes that Ray is keeping quiet out of fear for his life, argues that while Ray may well have killed King, he did not act alone. "The best evidence," he concludes, "suggests that Ray was an unexceptional criminal who had exceptionally clever help."

Arthur Murtagh, a former agent in the FBI's Atlanta office, who is stricken by guilt over his role in the bureau's harassment of King, believes that Ray was, in fact, framed. Noting that Raoul's behavior was consistent with standard FBI procedures, he told a *Los Angeles Times* reporter that he thinks that "Raoul was feeding [Ray] the rifle and . . . making sure . . . that his fingerprints were on [it]. . . . Raoul or some other operative was probably involved in the shooting that killed King."

In the 1990s the King assassination and the question of Ray's guilt once again became front-page news. On April 4, 1993, the twenty-fifth anniversary of the assassination, HBO aired a $3 million production entitled *Guilt or Innocence: The Trial of James Earl Ray.* The unscripted mock trial was filmed in a Memphis courtroom, with real attorneys questioning real witnesses; Ray testified and was cross-examined via a satellite hookup from prison, and was visible on a television monitor in the courtroom throughout the trial. The jury found Ray innocent.

Since then the case has taken several bizarre new turns. Betty Spates, a black woman who in April 1968 was working at Jim's Grill, a diner on the ground floor of the flophouse where Ray was staying, came forward with an astounding story that was published in 1994 by the *Los Angeles Times.* She says that she was having an affair with Lloyd Jowers, the owner of Jim's Grill, and that she came into the diner on the afternoon of April 4, thinking that she might catch him with another woman. What she saw, however, was Jowers coming in from the bushy field out back, the field from which three witnesses have claimed the fatal shot may have been fired, with mud on his pants, carrying a rifle, with a look of terror on his face. Spates, then seventeen, entangled in a web of love, conflicting loyalties, and fear, says that she tried to block the image from her mind for twenty-six years, until William Pepper, Ray's newest attorney, finally succeeded in getting her to tell her story.

For his part, Jowers claims that, at the behest of a friend, he did indeed hire a gunman to kill King, and that gunman was not James Earl Ray. Jowers told ABC's *Prime Time Live* that he would provide all the details in return for a promise of immunity from prosecution. Law enforcement officials have scorned his request. The friend in question, however, has been identified as Frank Liberto, a local produce supplier with ties to the New Orleans Mafia, who has since died. Interestingly, back in 1968, a witness named John McFerren had told the FBI that he had overheard a telephone conversation Liberto was having in his store just a few hours before King was shot. "Kill the S.O.B. on the balcony and get the job done," Liberto allegedly said, unaware that McFerren was within earshot. "Don't come out here. Go to New Orleans and get your money. You know my brother."

Pepper claims that Jowers, rather than hire a hit man, probably killed King himself in order to keep the $10,000 he would allegedly have paid for the contract. After the murder, police found fresh footprints in the field behind Jim's Grill. Incredibly, however, the next day city officials ordered the field cleared and the bushes cut down, destroying any potential additional evidence. Jowers, meanwhile, has moved, reportedly to the Ozarks, to escape the media. Investigators maintain that McFerren's testimony had been investigated in 1968, and that the conversation was found to be "unrelated" to the King murder.

In any case, Ray's attempts to gain a trial continue. In April 1994 a Tennessee judge named Joseph Brown, citing the overwhelming historical importance of the case, granted Ray a hearing to present evidence showing why he could not have killed King. In September 1994, however, the Tennessee Court of Criminal Appeals overturned Brown's ruling and denied Ray the hearing. Ray's lawyers have filed an appeal.

Ironically, King's old friends and colleagues, many of whom have always been convinced that the FBI was involved in the assassination, have joined with Ray in requesting a full and public hearing. Jesse Jackson wrote the forward to Ray's book; Rev. James Lawson, who had invited King to visit Memphis during that fatal week in April 1968, conducted Ray's 1978 wedding ceremony in prison and has started a fund for Ray's defense. And in December 1994 Joseph Lowery, president of the SCLC, formally requested the Justice Department to investigate the new information that has emerged concerning a possible conspiracy. If the hearing Ray has requested finally takes place, says his lawyer Pepper, "we are going to walk the . . . nation . . . through the assassination of Martin Luther King and establish James Earl Ray's actual innocence." Even should that occur, however, it is unlikely that the many conflicting theories about the King assassination will ever be resolved into a single, clear view of the events of April 4, 1968, in Memphis, Tennessee.

—B.C., R.R., and E.H.B.

ROBERT KENNEDY

The Victim: Robert Francis Kennedy, U.S. senator from New York and candidate for the Democratic nomination in the 1968 presidential election, had been overshadowed by his older brother, former president John F. Kennedy, for much of his political career. But "Bobby" Kennedy came into his own in the late 1960s. His frank, liberal agenda tackled many of the tough issues of the day—the Vietnam War, urban decay, racism, the Middle East, unemployment, and, above all, human rights—and the massive crowds that came out to support him during the campaign treated him like a pop star. Kennedy was young (forty-four), handsome, talented, and smart, and he revived the vision of Camelot that had seemingly died five years earlier with his brother.

Yet Kennedy was not a lock for the Democratic nomination, let alone the presidency. President Lyndon Johnson's surprising decision not to run for reelection in 1968 had thrown the primary wide open, and Kennedy found himself pitted against a number of tough candidates, including Vice President Hubert Humphrey and Senator Eugene McCarthy. In fact, Kennedy had recently been defeated in the Oregon primary and was licking his wounds as he prepared for the California primary on June 4. He campaigned furiously, at one point collapsing from exhaustion, and mounted such a hysterical, demagogic campaign that adoring crowds tore at his clothing. Yet there was a dark side too. Death threats were a regular part of Kennedy's campaign, and someone threw a rock at him during a motorcade appearance. But Kennedy pressed on, and found strength in California's misery. Staring at a sea of black faces on a drive through downtrodden south-central Los Angeles, Kennedy told an aide, "If I don't win, these people are not going to trust another white politician for a long time."
The Date: June 5, 1968.
The Event: By the late evening of June 4, Kennedy held a 3 percent lead over McCarthy, and the 174 delegates he'd captured brought the nomination within striking distance. Positively buoyant in his victory speech at the Ambassador Hotel in Los Angeles, Kennedy thanked everybody from ex officio bodyguards Rafer Johnson and Roosevelt Grier to Hispanic activist Cesar Chavez, then set his sights squarely on the upcoming Democratic convention. "On to Chicago!" he declared, before stepping down from the podium and moving toward the pantry area of the kitchen at the rear of the ballroom.

Kennedy was headed toward the Colonial Room, which served as the pressroom that evening, and he used the kitchen in order to avoid larger crowds waiting outside. As he walked along, Kennedy's right hand was firmly grasped by Carl Uecker, the Ambassador Hotel's maître d', but he freed himself twice to shake

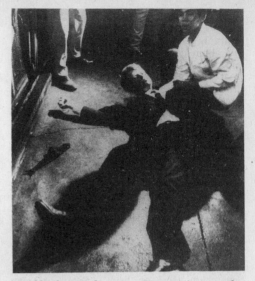

Hotel kitchen employee Juan Romero tries to comfort a dying Senator Robert Kennedy after the presidential candidate was shot in Los Angeles.

hands with a pair of hotel employees—Juan Romero and Jesus Perez. Uecker regained his grasp on the senator's hand each time, however, and they continued through the narrow passageway, followed closely by a local armed private security guard, Thane Eugene Cesar. Others in the entourage included Kennedy's wife, Ethel, author George Plimpton, newscaster Roger Mudd, Grier, and Johnson.

Suddenly a small wiry man named Sirhan B. Sirhan stepped forward from the crowd in the kitchen toward Kennedy. His eyes were glazed. Sirhan raised a small, .22-caliber Iver Johnson pistol and fired at Kennedy. Then he fired again. By this time Uecker, momentarily stunned, lunged for Sirhan and slammed the hand holding the gun against a steam table to his left. Other hands reached in from all directions, grabbing portions of Sirhan's clothes and body. Johnson, a former Olympic decathlon champion, and Grier, a lineman for the Los Angeles Rams, tackled Sirhan, slamming him to the floor. "I put my hand under the hammer so the gun wouldn't go off, then I wrenched it away from Sirhan," Grier said. "I don't remember his size. All I know is he seemed to have a lot of strength."

As Kennedy lay on the floor mortally wounded, Juan Romero moved closer and slipped a rosary into his hand. Sobs, screams, and echoes of "Noooo" filled the hotel. Kennedy motioned Romero closer, then whispered something in his ear. "Is everyone all right?" Kennedy asked. Three bullets had struck the senator. Two entered in the region of one armpit—within inches of each other—and a third, the fatal bullet, entered the right mastoid (the side of the head behind the right ear).

In addition, five others—Paul Schrade, Elizabeth Evan, Ira Goldstein, Irwin Stroll, and William Weisel—were struck by bullets, with Schrade suffering a cracked skull when he was hit in the head. Two bullets were later recovered from the counter divider of the pantry doors at the entrance, and another was removed from the door frame of the door at the back of the stage.

Kennedy was rushed by ambulance to the nearby Good Samaritan Hospital, but the damage was too great. He died in the early-morning hours of June 5, 1968, without regaining consciousness. Kennedy was buried alongside his martyred brother at Arlington National Cemetery outside Washington, D.C.; his funeral was a dark, somber affair. Former astronaut John Glenn, a close friend, held the U.S. flag at the service, and the live television coverage of the event was some of the most moving in broadcast history. Kennedy's grave bears an epitaph from the Greek poet Aeschylus: "In our sleep, pain which cannot forget falls drop by drop upon the heart until, in our own despair, against our will, comes wisdom through the awful grace of God."

Sirhan, carrying car keys but no identification, was whisked away by police; he refused to give his name. Only when his flabbergasted brothers saw his face on television the next morning and notified police did Sirhan's identity become known. The Los Angeles Police Department (LAPD) formed a special investigative task force called Special Unit Senator to work the case, and Sirhan was found guilty on April 17, 1969, of murdering Kennedy.

The Assassin: Sirhan Bishara Sirhan was born on March 19, 1944, in Jordan. His family emigrated to the United States when he was thirteen years old, settling in Pasadena, California, and Sirhan spent an unremarkable adolescence there. In fact, nothing about his life indicates he was a killer in the making. What might motivate the twenty-six-year-old Arab to fire shots at the senator is the question that troubles investigators to this day.

The most widely accepted theory is that Sirhan, born in territory later occupied by Israel, was angered by Kennedy's pro-Israeli politics. The Sirhan family spent nine years as starving refugees in Israeli-occupied land prior to emigrating to the United States, and Sirhan witnessed the death of his own brother when he was run over by an Israeli truck. Israel's victory in the Six-Day War also troubled him. At his trial, Sirhan left no doubt that he bore scars from his youth. "The Jews kicked us out of our homes," he said, and scribbling found in notebooks recovered from Sirhan's apartment seem to indicate a wild, growing anger. As a result,

Kennedy's endorsement of a plan to sell fighter jets to Israel is seen by many experts as the catalyst to violence. "Sirhan's motive," said retired FBI agent Amadee O. Richards, "was easily understood."

But there are flaws in that theory. For starters, Kennedy was not the only presidential candidate advocating support for Israel—others included McCarthy and Humphrey for the Democrats and Richard Nixon among the Republicans, and President Lyndon Johnson was perhaps the most visible pro-Israeli politician of them all. In addition, Sirhan's "smoking-gun" notebooks failed to include a single mention of Israel, Palestine, Zionism, occupation, genocide, or any of the popular buzzwords associated with the Middle Eastern politics of the late 1960s. The only exception is an entry that states, "Robert F. Kennedy must be assassinated before 5 June 68," the one-year anniversary of the start of the Six-Day War. But some dispute that association, believing June 5 refers to the end of the California primary.

Another theory is that Sirhan was brainwashed into killing Kennedy. According to his mother, Sirhan fell into strange company about eight months prior to the assassination, and began keeping late hours and acting abnormally. In addition, most experts agree that he was in an altered mental state at the time of the assassination. But if Sirhan was under hypnosis, was it powerful enough to make him a murderer? If so, who was programming his mind?

Some believe Sirhan underwent self-hypnosis in order to prepare himself for the murder. It is known that he practiced mind-control techniques at home, mesmerizing himself with lighted candles and a mirror, but there is no evidence to link this with a preplanned assassination. Others lay vague blame on anti-Israeli groups or friends experimenting with hypnosis.

Yet the most popular—if far-fetched—scenario is the "Manchurian Candidate" theory, whereby Sirhan was a programmed assassin prepared to kill Kennedy, then forget he'd done it. *The Manchurian Candidate* was a 1959 bestselling novel that centered on an American prisoner of war programmed by the North Koreans to kill the president of the United States. It was later made into a hit film starring Frank Sinatra and Laurence Harvey. Wild accusations claim to link Sirhan's hypnosis to U.S. intelligence, but most assassination experts reject the notion out of hand. "A crackpot theory," said Dr. Bernard Diamond, the chief psychiatrist for Sirhan's defense team.

Still, there is a great deal of evidence to suggest that Sirhan did not act alone, even though the amateurish investigation into Kennedy's death and the sloppy prosecution have blurred the facts. Not surprisingly, conspiracy theorists have chipped away at the assassination for more than a quarter century, convinced that such high-level bungling is evidence of a cover-up. Various alleged culprits include the Mafia, J. Edgar Hoover, the Teamsters, Jimmy Hoffa, the CIA, pro-Castro supporters, the Shah of Iran, southern racist groups, Richard Nixon backers, and hard-line cold warriors, but no strong links have been established to any of them. The most likely scenario is that, anxious to avoid the controversy and confusion surrounding John F. Kennedy's assassination in 1963, officials investigating Robert Kennedy's murder simply acted too hastily in pursuit of a tidy conviction. Once they did, evidence that might have cast doubt on Sirhan's guilt or possible accomplices was either lost or destroyed.

Nevertheless, several facts surrounding the Robert Kennedy assassination and its ensuing investigation are bizarre enough to warrant attention. For instance:

One, Sirhan's gun was not the only one fired on the night of June 4, 1968. In all, ten bullets were recovered from the crime scene, even though Sirhan's gun held only eight bullets and he had no time to reload. Dr. Thomas Noguchi, the Los Angeles County coroner who performed the autopsy on Kennedy, listed the cause of death as a "gunshot wound of right mastoid, penetrating brain," and testified that the bullets were fired from a position "very, very close" to the senator. He went on to estimate that the muzzle of the gun was only "two or three inches" from Kennedy's right ear, and performed tests using a gun and pig ears to double-check his findings. Yet every single eyewitness placed Sirhan in front of Kennedy and several feet away from him.

What's more, two distinctly different types of bullets were recovered from the victims. A bullet removed from the abdomen of William Weisel bore different rifling marks (the pattern left on the bullet by the gun muzzle) from a bullet that entered through Kennedy's armpit and lodged in his neck, and several top criminologists agreed that different guns were used. Yet this theory was never proven con-clusively for the simple reason that Sirhan's gun was never test-fired, a stunning oversight of standard police procedure. Furthermore, Sirhan's gun was mislabeled by police at the time of the trial, resulting in a different gun's being introduced as the murder weapon— although tests were never performed on that gun either.

A seven-member panel was finally convened in 1976 to study the bullet/gun controversy, but could find no evidence of a second gun. The most plausible answer is that Thane Eugene Cesar, the security guard standing directly behind Kennedy, fired his gun during the assassination, perhaps hitting the candidate in the process. A right-winger who reportedly hated Kennedy, Cesar also owned a .22-caliber pistol around the time of the killing. But Cesar always denied shooting Kennedy, and the LAPD failed to examine his pistol on June 5, 1968. The gun was later stolen.

Two, a woman wearing a polka-dot dress was seen with Sirhan in the pantry area by numer-ous witnesses just prior to the assassination. Some speculate she was Sirhan's "baby-sitter" or control while under hypnosis. This same woman left before Kennedy entered the room, and appeared to match the description of a woman seen leaving the hotel around the time of the murder who said, "We shot him!" Yet the police could find no such woman, and were humiliated when Sandra Serrano, a twenty-year-old Kennedy campaign worker, went on national television and told of seeing the woman. The police treated Serrano more like a suspect than a witness, however, badgering and interrogating her mercilessly until she was no longer sure of the facts. "It's too messed up," she told a police investigator, following a grueling lie detector test. "Even I can't remem-ber what happened anymore."

The police eventually produced a woman by the name of Cathy Fulmer, but Serrano did not identify her as the one she had seen. Fulmer was found dead in a motel room several days after Sirhan was convicted.

Three, Sirhan's trial brought virtually none of these inconsistencies to light, even though they might have dramatically altered the outcome. In what proved to be an astounding strategic error, Sirhan's attorneys chose not to challenge any of the prosecution's supposed "facts," relying in-stead on the defense of impaired judgment (that is, hypnosis), which the jury quickly dismissed. Sirhan was found guilty and sentenced to life imprisonment, for which he is still being held at a California state prison, having been denied parole on nine occasions as of July 1995.

Despite the buzz over conspiracies and cover-ups swirling around Kennedy's assassination, at least one man has been exonerated. Khalid Khawar, a freelance photographer who was standing next to Kennedy at the time of the murder, was identified as his true assassin in a story printed by The Globe tabloid newspaper in 1989. Khawar sued The Globe and was awarded $1.1 million by a Santa Monica, California, superior court judge, who ruled that the newspaper had failed to test whether the story was accurate. "I'm thankful I can now be recognized as Robert Kennedy's admirer and not his murderer," Khawar said.

The Aftermath: Although bits and pieces of the Robert Kennedy assassination case have been reopened over the years, a full review has never been granted, despite the lobbying of celebrities such as author Norman Mailer and historian Arthur Schlesinger Jr. The LAPD files themselves—sealed for almost two decades— were finally turned over to the California State

Archives and opened to the general public in 1988, but they raised far more questions than they answered. Few believe those questions will ever be addressed.

Kennedy's legacy continues to grow by leaps and bounds. He was an inspiration to President Bill Clinton, who dedicated a joint Robert Kennedy–Martin Luther King peace memorial in Indianapolis in 1994. Several of Kennedy's children have also entered politics, including son Joseph Kennedy II (a congressman from Boston) and daughter Kerry Kennedy Cuomo, the executive director of the Robert F. Kennedy Memorial Center for Human Rights. "Yes, I do think the country would be different today had he lived," she wrote in People magazine. ". . . He would be horrified by what he would see today—crack, violence, children having children—and I can only imagine some of these issues might have been addressed with a little more vigor."

—D.W.C.

OLOF PALME

The Victim: Olof Palme, prime minister of Sweden, was a charismatic and controversial leader. Palme first worked as a journalist specializing in boxing and theater. When he changed careers, he explained, "I naturally opted for something that combined both—politics." Palme caused a sensation in 1968 when, while serving as minister of education and religious affairs, he marched in a demonstration against U.S. involvement in the Vietnam War. He also spoke out against the Soviet invasion of Czechoslovakia. After Palme, at age forty-two, was sworn in as prime minister on October 14, 1969, U.S. president Richard Nixon was so piqued he refused to accept the credentials of the Swedish ambassador-designate for almost two years. In fact, Palme was not completely anti-American: in 1948 he graduated from Kenyon College in Gambier, Ohio, and then spent several months hitchhiking around the United States. Palme was voted out of office in 1976, but returned as prime minister in 1982, and was serving his fourth term when he was assassinated.

The Date: February 28, 1986.

The Event: Palme prided himself on the fact that he could walk the streets of Stockholm unguarded and he mocked the tight security precautions used to protect other world leaders. On the night of February 28, 1986, he informed SÄPO, the Swedish Security Police, that he planned a quiet evening at home and he dismissed his bodyguards. When Mårten, one of Palme's three sons, called to invite Palme and his wife, Lisbet, to a movie, the prime minister didn't bother to tell SÄPO.

Instead, the Palmes took the subway to the Sveavägen, Stockholm's main thoroughfare, and joined Mårten and his girlfriend, Ingrid Klering, at the Grand Cinema, which was showing The Brothers Mozart, a new Swedish comedy. They stood in line like everyone else, but when they reached the ticket booth, the show was sold out. The cashier recognized her nation's leader and found four tickets that had been reserved but not picked up.

Two hours later Olof and Lisbet Palme left the theater, said good-bye to their son and his girlfriend, and began walking back up Sveavägen. Six minutes later, at 11:21 P.M., they reached the intersection of Tunnelgatan, a pedestrian street since renamed Olof Palme Street. Lisbet Palme, walking ahead of her husband, heard a loud bang. She turned around to ask Olof if it was a firecracker and discovered a man in a dark coat with a cap pulled over his forehead. He had just shot the prime minister through the back with a Smith & Wesson .357 Magnum revolver. The assassin fired a second time, grazing Lisbet Palme's fur coat, and then escaped up Tunnelgatan, disappearing in the maze of streets nearby. Olof Palme fell to the pavement and was dead within a matter of minutes.

The Investigation: It had been almost two hundred years since Sweden's last political assassination—the killing of King Gustav III at a masquerade ball in 1792—and the police authorities were simply unprepared for such a shocking event. Trains leaving the nearby Central Station were not halted until 12:40 A.M.—seventy-nine minutes after Palme was shot. The order to watch roads out of the city was not given until ten minutes after that, and the nation's airports weren't shut down until 2:05 A.M. Police allowed mourners to cover the sidewalk with red roses, the symbol of Palme's Social Democratic Party, thus obscuring a potentially important source of physical evidence. The two bullets were found not by the police but by ordinary citizens many hours after the shooting. Investigators then announced that the copper-tipped bullets were unusual, maybe even handmade. But journalists were able to buy boxes of them at a store only two blocks from police headquarters.

On March 12 police arrested Åke Viktor Gunnarsson, a thirty-three-year-old follower of the European Workers' Party (EAP), a right-wing group founded by American fanatic Lyndon H. LaRouche. The EAP considered Olof Palme "the devil of devils" and distributed bumper stickers bearing the slogan "A new Palme is born every day: wear a condom." It soon developed that the evidence against Gunnarsson was weak, at best. One witness had been shown a photograph of Gunnarsson before identifying him in a lineup. Powder marks found on Gunnarsson's clothes were different from those found on Palme. Within a week, Public Prosecutor K. G. Svensson released the suspect. In May police arrested Gunnarsson again, and again he was released.

By now a 140-man task force was investigating the crime. The focus shifted to foreign terrorist groups, especially the Kurdish Workers' Party (PKK), a Marxist organization campaigning for an independent Kurdistan. On June 20, 1984, a PKK assassin had murdered a party defector by shooting him in the back of the head in a public square in Uppsala. On November 2, 1985, another PKK defector was shot in the back of the head in public, this time in Stockholm. The assassin, Nuri Candemir, was sentenced to life imprisonment two days before Olof Palme was murdered. On January 20, 1987, police arrested thirteen PKK members and claimed that four of them were suspects in the Palme killing. Their alleged motive was revenge for the Swedish government's refusal to grant a residence permit to the leader of the PKK. A week later all of the detainees were released for lack of evidence. At that point Hans Holmer, Stockholm's police commissioner, was removed from the case. He later wrote a book defending his PKK theory.

The final arrest in the Palme case came on December 14, 1988. The suspect was Christer Pettersson, a forty-one-year-old loner whose front door bore the sign (in English) "Go to Hell." By the time of his arrest, Pettersson had racked up sixty-three convictions, including one for bayoneting a man to death on a Stockholm street while he was high on LSD. In 1977 Pettersson had been falsely accused of killing his own father. He celebrated his release from jail by buying drugs from a pusher and then stabbing him with a bayonet.

On June 5, 1989, Pettersson was put on trial for killing Olof Palme. The evidence against him proved pathetically weak and the case seemed to hinge on the testimony of Lisbet Palme. Unfortunately, the victim's widow imposed a number of conditions before she would testify. She insisted that no tape recorders be allowed in the courtroom and that the closed-circuit television used to transmit the proceedings to journalists in another room be shut down. The court also agreed to remove Pettersson from the courtroom while she testified. It also came out that the lineup at which Mrs. Palme identified Pettersson included only Pettersson, who was an unhealthy alcoholic, and eleven brawny policemen.

Although the prosecution was never able to produce a murder weapon or a motive, on June 27 Pettersson was found guilty by majority verdict. The six lay jurors voted guilty, while the two judges on the panel voted not guilty. Three and a half months later a higher court voted 7–0 to overturn the verdict. Back on the streets again, Pettersson told reporters, "I have been guilty of a lot of things. I never thought I would be in a situation where I could honestly say I was innocent." This time he celebrated his release by drinking Swedish Explorer vodka and Bailey's Irish Cream.

Lisbet Palme's credibility as a witness was so badly damaged that it appears unlikely that anyone will ever again be charged with the murder of Olof Palme unless the murder weapon is found or the murderer confesses. Still, as recently as 1995, a twenty-two-member team of police investigators was continuing to work on the case.

One of the more intriguing theories still unresolved is that Palme's assassination was related to his role as a mediator in the Iran-Iraq War at a time when Swedish companies were involved in arming the Iranians. The Iraqis were naturally upset by this turn of events, while the Iranians protested when Palme stopped the arms shipments twenty-four days before he was killed. In January 1987 Carl-Fredrik Algernon, the inspector of war matériel, the man in charge of weapons export control, "fell" in front of a subway train and was killed six days before he was due to testify before a special prosecutor in the arms-to-Iran case.

—D.W.

CHICO MENDES

The Victim: Francisco "Chico" Mendes Filho, labor leader and environmentalist, was born on a rubber estate near Xapuri in the state of Acre in the westernmost corner of Brazil. Mendes was the son of poor rubber tappers and began working at the age of nine. When he was eighteen a left-wing revolutionary named Euclides Fernando Távora taught him to read and also taught him about the importance of trade unions, as well as how to find the Voice of America, Radio Moscow, and the BBC World Service on the radio. When cattle ranchers began arriving in the area in the 1970s, Mendes joined the Confederation of Agricultural Workers. In 1980 he founded a rural workers' union in Xapuri and became its president. Using tactics of nonviolent civil disobedience, Mendes and his followers successfully prevented the burning and clearing of millions of acres of forest. He helped organize the First National Rubber Tappers' Congress and convinced the Brazilian government to establish "extractive reserves" in which only renewable resources, such as rubber and Brazil nuts, could be exploited. Eventually Mendes's work attracted the attention of international environmentalists, who flew him to Miami and Washington, D.C., where he successfully lobbied the Inter-American Development Bank to stop funding a major road into the forest that had been promoted by the cattle ranchers. In 1987 Mendes was awarded the United Nations

Global 500 Prize as well as a medal from the Society for a Better World in New York.

The Date: December 22, 1988.

The Event: Chico Mendes's international fame made little impression on the people of Acre, where the cattle ranchers considered him nothing more than a particularly troublesome obstacle on their path to profits. In 1984 the ranchers founded the Rural Democratic Union (UDR), a right-wing lobby group that attracted 230,000 members across Brazil. In Acre, as in many other parts of the country, the ranchers used hired gunmen, *pistoleiros*, to drive tens of thousands of tappers out of the forest. One especially violent family of ranchers was that of Darly Alves da Silva, who had moved to Xapuri in 1974 from the state of Paraná and bought a 10,000-acre ranch. Alves lived with his wife, three mistresses, and thirty children.

One of the less pleasant traditions of rural Brazil is the *anúncio*, in which a person receives an anonymous threat that he or she will be killed. The advance warning serves as a method of psychological torture. On the night of May 24, 1988, Chico Mendes, who had survived previous assassination attempts, was *anunciado*. He was told that he would not live out the year.

The confrontation between the rubber tappers and the ranchers was transformed into a personal struggle between Chico Mendes and Darly Alves and his sons. The Pastoral Commission for the Land, a group supportive of Mendes and the rubber tappers, hired a lawyer, Genésio Natividade, to dig up dirt on the Alveses' past. He discovered that Darly Alves and his brother Alvarinho were wanted for a murder that had been committed fifteen years earlier in Paraná. On September 26 a warrant for their arrest was forwarded to Mauro Spósito, the state superintendent of the Federal Police in Acre. The next day Mendes and Natividade spotted Darly Alves drinking a beer in the plaza in front of Federal Police headquarters. They called the police, who did nothing. It was another sixteen days before the warrant was sent on to Xapuri, where Darly Alves's brother worked as a clerk at the police station. Not surprisingly, when, another six days after that, the police finally got around to visiting the Alveses' ranch, Darly and Alvarinho had already gone into hiding.

The following month Mendes sent off a series of letters and telexes to the judge of Xapuri, the governor of Acre, the superintendent of the Federal Police, and others warning that Darly and Alvarinho Alves were plotting to kill him. No action was taken.

On December 6 *O Rio Branco*, the ranchers' newspaper, owned by UDR president João Branco, announced that "a 200-megaton bomb will be exploded and there will be nationwide repercussions. Important people may be harmed when this is done." With the end of the year fast approaching, Mendes knew that his own end was also near. "I don't want flowers on my grave," he wrote, "because I know they'll have been pulled up from the forest. . . . Good-bye, it was a pleasure. I am going to Xapuri to a meeting with death, from which I am certain no one can free me. I am not a fatalist, just a realist. I have already denounced those who want to kill me and no steps have been taken."

He told the *Jornal do Brasil*, "If an angel from heaven were to descend and guarantee that my death would strengthen our struggle, it would even be worth it, but experience teaches us the opposite. Thus I want to live. Public gestures and a well-attended funeral will not save Amazônia. I want to live." Still, on December 15, the night of his forty-fourth birthday, he told a friend, "I don't think I'm going to live until Christmas."

One week later, on December 22, Mendes was playing dominoes with two bodyguards when his wife, Ilzamar, began serving dinner. Mendes told them to start without him: he wanted to take a shower in the bathhouse in the backyard. He grabbed a towel and started to the back door. "It's so dark out there, they could get me," he said. He went and got a flashlight, opened the door, began to step outside—and was blasted in the chest by a .20-gauge shotgun. He staggered back into the kitchen and collapsed on the floor. "Damn," he said, "they got me." Ilzamar rushed out into the street, screaming, "They've killed Chico!" The policemen sitting in front of their station a few yards away did not move.

The Assassins: According to a report compiled by Americas Watch, between 1964 and 1989, 1,566 farm workers, church people, and other activists involved in land disputes were killed in Brazil. Only seventeen trials were conducted and only eight convictions were achieved. Clearly the men who shot Chico Mendes had little reason to believe they would suffer any consequences because of their crime. But they had failed to take into account Mendes's international celebrity. His death made the front page of the *New York Times*. Within forty-eight hours a media army had descended on Xapuri.

Embarrassed government authorities immediately launched an investigation, headed by Romeu Tuma, the director general of the Federal Police, who arrived in Xapuri along with sixty police armed with submachine guns. On December 26 Darci Alves Pereira, Darly's twenty-one-year-old son, turned himself in and confessed to shooting Chico Mendes. He even showed police the thicket where he had hidden in ambush. Darci claimed he had acted alone, but no one believed him. For one thing, the thicket was littered with cigarette butts. Darci told police he didn't smoke. Eventually Tuma also pressed charges against Darly Alves and Darly's nephew, Jardeir Pereira. Pereira was never found, but in December 1990, two years after the Chico

Mendes murder, Darly and his son Darci were finally brought to trial. They were both found guilty and sentenced to nineteen years in prison. In March 1992 Darly's conviction was overturned for lack of evidence; however, he was kept in prison pending a trial for the 1973 murder in Paraná. Life in prison was not harsh for father and son. They had their own refrigerator, freezer, stove, and color television, as well as overnight visiting rights with women. However, when it became apparent that Darly would soon be transferred to a more serious prison in Paraná, he and Darci escaped. It was the fifth successful escape from the prison in two months. Darly and Darci Alves are still at large.

It seems likely that the conspiracy to kill Chico Mendes actually went beyond the Alves family. The most revealing piece of evidence concerns four reporters and one photographer from *O Rio Branco*, the ranchers' newspaper that had predicted the "200-megaton" explosion. They arrived in Xapuri one and a half hours after the murder and took photos of Mendes's body, which they later sold to the wire services. In the next day's paper the reporters bragged about their scoop and described the way they had covered the 150 kilometers (90 miles) between their office and Xapuri in ninety minutes despite stopping once to change a flat tire and once to drink a beer. The problem was that it was actually a three-hour drive at best, in the dry season in daylight. The reporters had allegedly done it at night, in the rainy season.

The Aftermath: The assassination of Chico Mendes focused attention on the destruction of Amazônia. The Brazilian government abolished tax benefits that made it profitable to cut down the forest and turn it into pastureland. They also established a 2.4-million-acre extractive reserve in Acre, allowing 3,000 families to make their living gathering wild rubber and Brazil nuts. However, throughout Brazil ranchers and their allies continued to kill labor organizers and their allies.

—D.W.

TERRORIST ACTS

TEL AVIV AIRPORT SHOOTINGS
Date: May 30, 1972
The Attack: Three young Japanese men boarded Air France flight 132 in Paris bound for Rome and then Tel Aviv's Lod International Airport. They passed routinely through police security checks, including metal detectors. Their checked luggage was subjected to a metal detector before being stowed. No problems were detected. The flight was uneventful.

The men deplaned in Tel Aviv along with 116 other passengers and waited patiently for their luggage. When it arrived they took from their suitcases three assault rifles, each supplied with twelve aluminum magazines holding thirty cartridges each, and several hand grenades, each designed to scatter shrapnel when they exploded. The attackers opened fire and began to throw grenades into the thick of the crowd.

Authorities later estimated that between 250 and 300 people were in the luggage area when the carnage started. "The passenger's hall," said one airport worker, "looked like a battlefield after a brief but very savage clash, with bodies lying everywhere."

One gunman was killed accidentally by gunfire from one of his compatriots, another died from the blast of a grenade, either a suicide or an accident, and one was captured after he ran outside and started shooting at two airplanes on the runway.

The Popular Front for the Liberation of Palestine (PFLP), a guerrilla group that specialized in hijackings, claimed responsibility for the attack. It was in retaliation, they said, for the May 9, 1972, deaths of two Palestinian hijackers at Lod. They went on to say that the attackers were members of the "Patrick Arguello Squad," named after a South American member of the Front who was killed in an attempt to hijack an El Al airliner in 1970. The attack, the statement said, was also to mark the fifth anniversary of the Arab-Israeli war, and the attackers had been told to kill as many people as possible—Israelis, of course, but whoever happened to be there.

Of the twenty-seven killed and sixty-nine wounded, most were Catholic pilgrims from Puerto Rico.

Although the PFLP claimed responsibility, it soon became clear that the actual attackers were members of Sekigun, the Japanese Red Army, a group who hired themselves out as hijackers and terrorists.

The Reckoning: King Hussein of Jordan condemned the attack; in Lebanon a government statement denounced "any action . . . which aims to harm innocent civilians." Dr. Aziz Sidky, the prime minister of Egypt, however, said that the Lod attack had "unveiled the truth behind imperialist propaganda which boasted of Israeli might. . . . Three machine guns did what they have done. Where then was Israeli might?"

With the other two attackers dead, Kozo Okamoto, the one terrorist who survived, faced the Israeli authorities alone.

As he began to reply to his interrogators' questions, a picture became clear of how and why the attack had occurred and exactly who was responsible.

The Japanese Red Army was founded in the late 1960s. Its foremost leader was a woman named Fusako Shigenobu, who proved to be one of the fiercest of terrorists. The group's goal: world revolution against imperialists, and especially against Israel. Shigenobu planned the attack at Lod and personally handed over the weaponry to be used. Her philosophy was summed up in her own words: "We in the Red Army declare anew our preparedness to fight hand-in-hand with the Palestinians . . . to defeat the Israeli enemy . . . and imperialists throughout the world."

Okamoto himself was ready to speak out in defending their actions.

"The Arab world," he said, "lacks spiritual fervor, so we felt that through this attempt we could perhaps stir up the Arab world."

The attack and Okamoto's trial focused attention on the Japanese Red Army, one of the most bloodthirsty of terrorist groups. It was learned that earlier in 1972, they had eliminated fourteen of their own members, whose mangled and tortured bodies were found in a spa in the mountains above Tokyo. Some had apparently been buried alive.

"My profession," Okamoto said in a rambling speech at his trial, "is war . . . and war involves slaughtering and destruction. We cannot limit warfare to destruction of buildings. We believe slaughtering of human bodies is inevitable."

In an eerily poetic defense of his actions, Okamoto mused, "We three soldiers, after we die, want to become three stars of Orion. When we were young we were told that if we died we became stars in the sky. The revolution will go on and there will be many more stars."

In a more prosaic vein, Okamoto revealed that he had begun his murderous odyssey in Tokyo in February 1972, and had made stops in Montreal, New York, and Paris. Then he flew to Lebanon, where he joined his terrorist companions, and where they received training in throwing grenades and firing automatic weapons.

Although, according to Israeli law, the death penalty could have been imposed on Okamoto, his defense counsel, Max Kreitzman, urged against it because it would "make a hero" out of a man who had killed so many. Okamoto was sentenced to life in prison.

The PFLP made several attempts to get him out, including him on the list of prisoners they demanded to be released in return for the Israeli hostages taken at the 1972 Olympics.

Ghassan Kanafani, a spokesman for the PFLP, had bragged about the group's responsibility for the airport slaughter; a month later, he was killed by ten pounds of explosives hidden under the hood of his car. With him was his seventeen-year-old niece, another innocent victim of terrorism.

The Japanese government turned over large sums of money to the wounded and the families of those who died in the Lod attack. Fusako Shigenobu went on to plan and execute other terrorist acts. In July of 1973 a Japanese jumbo jet was hijacked and destroyed apparently to punish Japan for having paid the compensation.

At the end of the 1970s the Japanese Red Army formally renounced violence as a means of achieving political change, and little has been heard of them since.

—R.W.S.

BLACK SEPTEMBER INVADES OLYMPICS
Date: September 5, 1972
The Attack: Shortly before dawn eight men climbed the fence surrounding the Olympic Village in Munich, which was temporary home to 12,000 people—athletes, coaches, and support staff for the Games of the XX Olympiad. They were hooded and heavily armed with automatic weapons and grenades, and they had a very specific target.

They burst into the block housing the Israeli national contingent, forcing their way into a dormitory where twelve athletes and coaches lay sleeping. One man, wrestler Gad Tzabari, escaped in the ensuing confusion by jumping through a window, two athletes who resisted were shot dead on the spot, and the remaining nine were seized as hostages.

On notes dropped out of windows, the terrorists identified themselves as the dreaded Black September organization. They made their demands clear: in return for the lives of their hostages, they wanted the release of 200 Arab prisoners held in Israeli custody; they insisted on an airliner to be supplied by the West German government to fly the "commandos" and the captives to an Arab capital other than Amman or Beirut; and they demanded helicopters to ferry

A hooded terrorist appears on a balcony of the Olympic Village in Munich after taking hostage members of the Israeli Olympic team.

the group to Fürstenfeldbruck Airport, where the airliner would be waiting for them.

The deadline: noon. If their conditions were not met by then they threatened to shoot one hostage every two hours until they were.

An emergency staff was hurriedly set up to handle the situation. Hans-Dietrich Genscher, the federal minister of the interior, was joined by the premier of Bavaria, Bruno Merk, and Manfred Schreiber, Munich's chief of police. Federal chancellor Willy Brandt rushed to the city to take personal charge of negotiations with the terrorists.

Police began to make preparations for what they hoped would not be a bloody confrontation. Large numbers of officers in armored cars surrounded the block where the hostages were held, but it was decided that no attempt could be made to rescue them because the terrorists had threatened to murder them if any such attempt were made. Mark Spitz, a Jewish-American dental student who had just won seven gold medals for swimming, a feat never before achieved, was flown out of Munich for fear that he might be a particular target for further terrorist attacks.

As the day passed and negotiations dragged on, the deadline was extended to 1:00 P.M., and then three, five, and eight o'clock.

Chancellor Brandt went on West German television to announce that a large ransom had been offered to the terrorists, along with a promise that they would be allowed to leave Germany, in return for the safe release of the hostages. Another offer was made that prominent West German politicians and police officials would take the places of the Israeli hostages. The terrorists' reaction to both offers: no deal. They insisted on acceptance of their original demands.

The Black September group was told that their demands were being met, and at 8:30 that night two helicopters landed at the Olympic Village with the promise that they would take the terrorists and their captives to the military airfield at Fürstenfeldbruck, where a Lufthansa jet would be waiting for them.

The Arabs and their Israeli captives were moved by bus from the dormitory to the waiting helicopters, and then flown to the airfield. So far everything had gone smoothly. That was to end suddenly in a bloody encounter no one wanted.

German police marksmen opened fire in the almost total darkness that engulfed the airfield. One terrorist, still inside one of the helicopters, pulled the pin on a grenade. The helicopter burned fiercely, killing everyone inside and lighting up the tarmac. Other terrorists immediately opened fire with their automatic weapons on their bound and blindfolded captives. All nine Israeli athletes were killed, along with a German police officer and five terrorists. The remaining three terrorists were captured. One of the helicopter pilots, although seriously wounded, escaped with his life by falling flat on the tarmac and lying still.

The Reckoning: The horror at the airfield was compounded by a communications blunder that has never been fully explained: an official announcement was made on TV and radio shortly after midnight that after a gun battle, all the hostages were safe.

This misinformation was greeted with relief and jubilation in Israel and around the world, and went on to appear in morning editions of papers worldwide. At 3:00 A.M., however, Schreiber and Merk held a news conference in Munich at which the awful truth was finally revealed.

It was also announced that the decision for German sharpshooters to try to kill the terrorists had been made only after Brandt failed to obtain an assurance from Egyptian prime minister Dr. Aziz Sidky that the airliner would be allowed to land in Cairo and that the hostages would be immediately released. This, Brandt said, combined with the fact that the Israeli government had refused to release the 200 prisoners they held, left only the option of direct action.

As more information became available, it was learned that three of the terrorists, including their leader, had held jobs inside the Olympic Village. Investigators also came to believe that the attack had been masterminded by Ali Hassan Salameh, also known as Abu Hassan and "the Red Prince," a senior security aide to Yasir Arafat, head of the Palestinian Fatah. Salameh would top the Israeli Mossad's hit list for most of the 1970s, until he was finally killed by a car bomb in 1979.

More than 80,000 people crowded the Olympic Stadium on September 6 for a solemn memorial. The Arab countries and the Soviet Union stayed away. The games continued twenty-four hours later, but the entire Israeli Olympic contingent withdrew and returned home with their fallen comrades.

The only Arab leader who publicly and unequivocally condemned the attack was Jordan's King Hussein. He referred to the attackers as "sick people who come out of the sewer," and went on to say that "the vast majority of Arabs oppose the crime . . . with all their hearts."

—R.W.S.

THE RAID ON ENTEBBE
Date: July 4, 1976
The Attack: It was one of the boldest commando raids in modern history, which turned a potential terrorist tragedy into a stunning triumph for the free world. On June 27, 1976, four Arab and German terrorists belonging to the Popular Front for the Liberation of Palestine (PFLP) hijacked an Air France jetliner with 258 passengers and crew

members en route to Paris from Tel Aviv. The hijackers' leader, German Wilfred Böse, ordered the jet's captain to fly to Benghazi, Libya, and then on to the Entebbe Airport in Uganda, where they landed on the morning of June 28 and were joined by three more accomplices.

Uganda's dictator, the tyrannical Idi Amin, was an avowed enemy of Israel and a friend to the Palestinian terrorists. He welcomed the hijackers with open arms while professing to the West that he was helpless to free the hostages. Meanwhile Amin, dressed in full military uniform and cowboy hat, regularly visited the hostages, who were kept in an abandoned passenger lounge. He assured them they would be well taken care of.

The hijackers demanded the release of fifty-three Palestinian "freedom fighters," most of them being held prisoner in Israel and four other countries, in exchange for the hostages. If their demands were not met in two days the hostages would suffer "severe and heavy penalties."

In the tense days that followed, the hijackers gradually released more than half of the hostages, until only 106 remained captive at the airport, most of them Jews. With only hours left before the extended deadline of July 4, the Israeli government, fearing for the lives of its citizens and adamantly opposed to negotiating with terrorists, put into action a daring rescue mission. A force of Israeli paratroops led by Commander Yonatan Netanyahu left the country in three Hercules C-130 cargo planes early on July 3 and flew 3,000 circuitous miles to Uganda. The thirty-year-old Netanyahu had come to Israel from the United States at the age of two. His group had rehearsed for four days, relying on information from a variety of sources—outdated blueprints of the Entebbe Airport from the Israeli firm that had originally built it (the airport had since been expanded), El Al pilots, Pentagon satellite photos, and even Israeli agents who managed to pass vital information out of Entebbe.

The members of "Operation Jonathan" landed at the Entebbe Airport under cover of darkness shortly after midnight. The Ugandans were thrown into confusion by a limousine the Israelis had brought along that resembled the one Amin rode in. As for the terrorists, they were completely taken by surprise, as were the hostages. When the Israelis stormed the lounge, the hostages thought they were the terrorists come to kill them. "We heard submachine guns, rockets, detonations—you name it," recalled hostage Uzi Davidson later. "The stuff was flying in all directions for something like ten minutes." All seven of the hijackers were killed in the fierce fighting, along with three unfortunate hostages who stood up at the wrong time and were mistaken by the Israelis for the enemy. When the firing ceased, one soldier told a group of hostages in Hebrew, "Comrades, we came to take you home."

In minutes, hostages and their rescuers were racing for the airport runway, some riding in jeeps and others running for their lives in their underclothes and bare feet. By now the Ugandan troops were on the offensive and attacked the scattered Israelis. The paratroops killed at least twenty Ugandans in the fighting and destroyed eleven Soviet-made MiG fighter jets on the runway. The Israelis suffered only one casualty—the brave commander of their mission. As Yonatan Netanyahu led his men to the transports he was killed by a shot in the back by a Ugandan sniper in a control tower.

Moments later the freed hostages and their rescuers were in the air, headed for Nairobi, Kenya, and safety. The astonishing rescue raid had taken fifty-three minutes. En route to Israel, the freed hostages wept and prayed, while one woman repeatedly cried "Ness! Ness!" (A miracle! A miracle!).

The Reckoning: The homecoming for the victors of Entebbe and their charges was a national celebration for Israel. That it had happened on the bicentennial of the United States made it all the more significant. B'nai B'rith president David Bromberg saw it as a birthday gift to the world—"The Eleventh Commandment: thou shalt not bow down to terrorism."

Unfortunately, one more hostage was added to the list of three who would not share in the celebration. Dora Bloch, an Israeli woman in her seventies, had choked on some food while being held captive and was taken to a hospital in the Ugandan capital of Kampala shortly before the raid began. Forgotten and left behind in the frantic rescue mission, she was later pulled from her hospital bed by Amin's henchmen and murdered in an ugly and senseless retaliation. Amin later told an old Israeli colleague on the phone that he had cut his ties with the Palestinians because the hijackers "only brought problems for me."

But Amin's problems would only grow worse. The embarrassment he suffered at Entebbe would be a contributing factor in his overthrow by the Tanzanians in 1979. He escaped to Saudi Arabia, where he remains today.

On the other hand, the raid boosted the previously floundering government of Prime Minister Yitzhak Rabin. Israel regained much of the international status it had lost after the Yom Kippur War three years earlier. The Entebbe raid was immortalized in books and feature-length films.
—S.A.O.

BOLOGNA TRAIN STATION
Date: August 1, 1980
The Attack: Crowds, composed of international tourists and locals alike, filled the massive stone railway terminal in Bologna, Italy, on a sweltering Saturday morning. The building offered not only transit facilities for those entering and leaving this city (renowned for its

leftist politics, its medical services, its cuisine, and the oldest university in Europe) but comfort as well; its air-conditioned waiting rooms and restaurant offered respite from the ninety-degree temperatures being recorded outside.

The scene in another important city building was especially heated. There, in a courtroom, a judge was handing down indictments to eight terrorists charged with having bombed a train in 1974, an incident that resulted in the loss of a dozen lives.

Approximately an hour and a half after the indictments were rendered, conditions within the terminal suddenly became explosively hot. A bomb, equal to about ninety pounds of dynamite, was detonated in the corner of a second-class waiting room. Building supports tumbled over as walls blew out and the roof lifted. When the roof followed its momentary rise with a shuddering collapse, an entire wing of the building was destroyed. The falling roof flattened two waiting rooms and the restaurant. It crushed a train platform and struck four cars of an express train that was standing idle when the bomb went off. Witnesses reported hearing a tremendous roar and seeing a bolt of intense flames snake instantaneously through the building. A mushroom-shaped cloud soon billowed above the horrific rubble of stone, timber, steel, flesh, and bones. Eighty-five people, some of whom were dismembered, perished in the blast. Two hundred and seventy others were wounded, including several seated in the stationary train. The bomb left yet another indication of its power: a crater four feet in circumference and eight inches deep.

Volunteer rescuers immediately began to search for victims, using their bare hands to pick through the rubble until cranes and bulldozers arrived on the scene. Phone calls to the police came in soon thereafter by parties claiming to be responsible for the disaster. The claim taken most seriously was that of a neofascist organization known as the Armed Revolutionary Nuclei. They attributed their motivation for their terrorist act to their need to "honor Mario Tuti"—one of their leaders who had been indicted that day on charges connected to the bombing in Milan six years before.

Reaction, from politicians and the public and the police, was swift and purposeful. Italy's president and premier arrived in Bologna to inspect the situation. The premier addressed Parliament a day later and compared the sinister forces responsible with those who had ruled and ruined Italy during World War II. While the premier spoke, work stoppages and demonstrations erupted all over the nation to protest the fascist threat. Ten thousand people in Bologna staged a rally in condemnation of the terrorists as well as to honor the victims. The police launched one of the most thorough investigations ever conducted in Europe.

The Reckoning: By the end of August 1980, police had arrested more than twenty suspects. Their continuing investigation followed up leads that implicated various suspects and such clandestine and/or criminal groups as the Mafia, international smugglers dealing in weapons and drugs, a Masonic lodge, and escaped Nazis hiding in South America. There were reports that linked elements in the Italian secret service, the Vatican Bank, government officials, and executives in the Italian media, manufacturing, and service industries. The hunt for the culprits who financed, planned, and carried out the bombing extended beyond Italy's borders to France, England, Germany, Switzerland, Monaco, Venezuela, Paraguay, and Argentina.

The manhunt eventually led to the arrest, in London, of the bomb-planting terrorists on September 12, 1981. Defendants, including General Pietro Musumeci (a former deputy chief of the military intelligence service), General Giuseppe Belmonte (assistant to General Musumeci), Licio Gelli (grand master of the outlawed P-2 Masonic Lodge), and Stefano Delle Chiaie (one of Italy's leading neofascists), were finally brought to trial on January 19, 1987.

Of the original twenty defendants, thirteen were found guilty. Subsequent appeals of the verdicts dragged through the courts for years. On July 19, 1990, an appeals court set aside the conviction of Gelli and canceled the life sentences of four neofascists. The two generals were judged guilty of slander and were given a term of three years' imprisonment.

Italy's left-wing newspapers decried the legal proceedings as an outrageous injustice, but the verdicts have remained unchanged. Secret reports allege that the bombings had taken place in order to shake up the nation and cause confusion while the two generals involved staged a military coup.

A panel inscribed with the names of the eighty-five victims of the bombing now hangs in the rebuilt second-class waiting room of Bologna's train station. Even this most solemn element in the saga of the bombing has generated controversy. Vittorio Mussolini, eldest son of dictator Benito Mussolini, objected to the memorial panel's description of the bombing as a "fascist act." On December 4, 1990, a Bologna judge ruled that Mussolini was legally entitled to sue the city's mayor and the Italian Railway for describing it as such.

—R.N.K.

BEIRUT: THE ATTACK ON U.S. MARINES
Date: October 23, 1983
The Attack: On June 6, 1982, the Israeli army invaded southern Lebanon, driving the forces of the Palestine Liberation Organization all the way to Beirut. When 800 U.S. Marines, along with French and Italian forces, first went ashore in Lebanon on August 25, they were welcomed

as neutral peacekeepers. But President Ronald Reagan and his advisors appeared befuddled by the multisided civil war in Lebanon. Accustomed to the simple good guy–bad guy outlook of the Cold War, the Reagan administration abandoned its neutrality and supported the Christian government. Good will toward the Americans quickly soured among the Muslim and Druse communities.

It was a beautiful Sunday morning in the war-torn city of Beirut, Lebanon. Most of the U.S. Marines stationed at the American headquarters near Beirut International Airport were still asleep in their barracks at 6:20 A.M. when a yellow-painted Mercedes truck drove toward the south gate of the compound from the direction of the airport parking lot. The sergeant on guard duty was eyeing the truck suspiciously when the driver, without warning, gunned the motor and crashed through a sand-bag barrier into the compound's interior courtyard. Another marine on the scene later recalled that the driver was smiling as he drove straight for the four-story concrete building that contained a chapel, gymnasium, and barracks.

A few seconds later the driver threw a switch in the truck, setting off 12,000 pounds of explosives. Driver, truck, and everything in their path were blown to smithereens. The explosion left a crater thirty feet deep and forty feet across. The concrete building crumbled like a house of cards. Sleeping marines were thrown out of their beds, some hurled through windows to their deaths. Inside the building men screamed with pain and horror as they were suddenly trapped between concrete and steel girders. Human arms and legs hung from trees and lay in the rubble of the blast. "I haven't seen carnage like this since Vietnam," said marine major Robert Jordan, who was sleeping a half mile away from the blast, where the door to his hut was torn off from the impact.

"I was sleeping, then suddenly I saw fire and stuff coming down all around me," said a sailor closer to the target. "It was like a big nightmare."

The nightmare was not over. A few minutes after the first explosion, a second suicide driver rammed his vehicle into the French army headquarters in Beirut a few miles away. Fifty-eight French soldiers were killed.

The death toll at the American headquarters was much higher. In the final count 241 marines and sailors died and nearly a hundred were wounded. It was the worst attack on American forces since the Vietnam War had ended.

A few hours later the Agence France Press in Beirut received an anonymous telephone call claiming the attack was made by the Islamic Jihad. The Jihad had been a relatively unknown name in the shadowy world of Middle East terrorists. It would become all too well known in the months and years ahead. This pro-Iranian Lebanese fundamentalist group was utterly ruth-less in its bloody mission to drive the United States and other national peacekeeping forces out of Lebanon. They claimed responsibility for a similar suicide truck bombing of the U.S. Embassy in Beirut six months earlier in which forty-nine people had been killed, sixteen of them Americans.

The Reckoning: The initial reaction of President Ronald Reagan to the Beirut bombing was one of unyielding commitment: "We are more determined than ever that they cannot drive us from that vital and strategic area—and for that matter, any other part." But these bold words were not supported by the American public, who saw no reason why young Americans should die in Lebanon for a peace that warring religious factions obviously did not want. In retaliation the battleship *New Jersey* and Israeli jets shelled known terrorist centers, but no further offensive was mounted against a shadowy enemy that vanished in the desert landscape.

Faced with growing opposition at home and abroad, the Multi-National Forces (MNF), consisting of troops from the United States, Italy, Britain, and France, withdrew from Lebanon in February 1984.

The Long Commission, a panel convened by the Department of Defense, investigated the bombing and came to the conclusion that slack security was partly responsible for the tragedy. However, it added that even if the suicide truck had been intercepted outside the compound, the explosion would have taken many lives. The commission also pointed the finger of guilt at Syria and Iran, who had provided money and access to the terrorists. Fourteen terrorists were named as being behind the plot. To date, none has been brought to justice.

The frustration and anger of the American public over what many believed was a senseless tragedy was typified by the comment of Lance Corporal Nick Mattola: "What was our mission? I'll tell you what our mission was. A lot of people died for nothing and then we left."

The attack was a fatal reminder to the West that a fanatic who is willing to sacrifice his life for his cause can accomplish almost any act of terror. As a direct result of the Beirut attack, special barricades were erected in front of the White House in Washington. Other government buildings were reinforced with concrete pylons to withstand explosives.

Such measures did not end the Jihad reign of terror. On December 12, 1983, they bombed eight locations in Kuwait, including the American and French Embassies. In January 1984 they claimed responsibility for the assassination of Dr. Malcolm Kerr, president of the American University in Beirut. Since then the Jihad has been involved in the kidnapping of numerous Westerners, including diplomats and journalists. But it was the ruthless attack on the marine headquarters in October 1983 that most weakened the resolve of the West to intercede in the Middle East in the name of peace.

In 1990 John Knippel, who lost a son in the bombing, helped plant a cedar of Lebanon at Arlington National Cemetery, where his son and twenty-five other marines who died that day lay buried. "That cedar tree from Lebanon provides a sense of continuation . . . , " said Knippel. "It connects the families with the soil of where their sons died."

—S.A.O.

AIR INDIA

Date: June 22–23, 1985

The Attack: Air India flight 182, a Boeing 747, took off from Toronto, Canada, with 329 people (including its crew) and headed for London's Heathrow Airport, where it was scheduled to make a stopover before going on to Bombay, India. The jumbo jet was only eight years old and had recently gotten a major servicing. A veteran pilot was in command. Weather conditions were good.

As the Air India plane cruised over the Atlantic at an altitude of 31,000 feet, a Canadian Pacific jet (also bound for Bombay and carrying 374 passengers) made a scheduled stopover landing at Narita International Airport in Tokyo, Japan. Its passengers safely disembarked, but a terrorist's bomb exploded as its cargo was being off-loaded. Two baggage handlers were killed by the blast. An investigation eventually established a connection between what happened at Narita and what was about to take place off the shores of Ireland.

One hour after the bomb went off in Tokyo, no indication of any trouble was yet apparent as the Air India flight entered Irish airspace. The captain of flight 182 made contact with air traffic controllers at Shannon Airport at 8:03 A.M. Approximately ten minutes later, however, the plane's image on the controllers' radar screens dimmed. It disappeared a little more than a minute after that, and though no Mayday distress signal was heard to be coming from flight 182, an order was issued for an immediate search and rescue mission.

Planes, ships, and helicopters from the Irish Navy, the Royal Navy, the Royal Air Force, and the U.S. Air Force were dispatched to the location where flight 182 was estimated to have been when electronic contact with it was lost. A four-and-a-half-mile-long oil slick, floating approximately 120 miles from the Irish shore and the city of Cork, was observed by spotters.

More evidence of the disaster quickly became apparent as pieces of jet wreckage and uninflated life rafts came into view. Bodies without life jackets, sighted as they bobbed in the waters of the Irish Sea, were retrieved. Bits of the aircraft and the remains of more of its passengers lay scattered across five square miles of open water. Most of the jumbo jet, however, including its black boxes, had sunk 6,000 feet and come to rest on the ocean floor. It had taken only an instant for Air India flight 182 to become the first jumbo jet ever to be blasted out of the sky by a terrorist's bomb. The bomb claimed the lives of all those on board.

Aftermath: A salvage operation, financed by Canada (which claimed 290 of the victims as citizens), was mounted to collect more wreckage. While the details of how the jet was destroyed and precisely who had brought about its destruction remained to be answered, there was little doubt that Sikh extremists were behind the calamity.

In June 1984, just a year before 182's final flight, the Indian army had attacked Sikh nationalists who had gathered at the Golden Temple of Amritsar in the Sikh-dominated region of Punjab. Twelve hundred people were massacred in the attack, including the former president of the Sikh Student Federation, which subsequently promised to avenge the killings.

Violence had chronically erupted between Hindus and Sikhs pressing for an independent homeland. More than 2,500 lives had been lost in the conflict between 1980 and 1985. Sikh nationalism had spread from the Punjab to the Sikh community in Canada, which numbered more than 200,000.

Aside from the Sikhs' Canadian base, reports indicate that Pakistan was financing Sikh extremists and that two such agents had attended a mercenary training camp in Alabama. The FBI was hunting for these men, whom they suspected of plotting the murder of Indian prime minister Rajiv Gandhi.

Governments around the world took part in examining the web of clandestine Sikh operations. The Canadian Royal Mounted Police, the Canadian Aviation Safety Board, the Accidents Investigation Branch of the British Department of Transport, the American National Transportation Safety Board, and security agencies of Ireland, France, Japan, and India cooperated, competed, and conflicted in the search for answers.

Flight 182's black boxes (the flight data recorder and the cockpit recorder) were recovered in July of 1985. They revealed little in the way of explaining how the plane was sabotaged. All the evidence pointed to Sikh extremists, specifically a pair of terrorists known as Lal (a.k.a. Manjit) Singh and Ammand Singh—men who had allegedly been trained at the mercenary camp in Alabama and who had plotted an assassination attempt on Rajiv Gandhi.

The Reckoning: All the evidence, however, was circumstantial, and Canada could not prosecute the two suspects. A third Sikh, Inderjit Singh Reyat, was eventually apprehended, prosecuted, and convicted of manslaughter for his participation in the Narita Airport bombing—an act of terrorism with which the other two are strongly suspected of having been connected.

In 1992, seven years after the crime, Manjit Singh was arrested in India and confessed to his complicity in the bombing of Air India flight 182. Ammand Singh, and anyone else who may have been involved, has apparently disappeared in the Sikh underground.

—R.N.K.

PAN AM FLIGHT 103

Date: December 21, 1988

The Attack: Pan Am flight 103 originally began as a 727 "feeder" flight from Frankfurt to London, where U.S.-bound passengers then switched to a 747 (the *Clipper*) before heading on to New York City. Among those who boarded in London were many Americans returning home for the holidays. Thirty-five students were flying back to the States after participating in Syracuse University's overseas study program. There were American soldiers on leave from military bases in Germany. Four of the passengers were employees of the State Department. Three were children. According to some sources, nineteen of the passengers worked for the CIA.

Flight 103 was scheduled to take off at 6:00 P.M. but was running twenty-five minutes late by the time it taxied away from Heathrow Airport's Terminal 3 and took to the air carrying 243 passengers and 16 crew members. The trip was expected to last seven and a half hours. Less than an hour later, while soaring some 31,000 feet above Scotland and carrying seventy-five tons of fuel, the jet blasted apart into six sections, and the splintered remains of craft, travelers, and cargo plummeted to earth across an area about forty miles wide in and around Lockerbie, population 3,000. One section hit a gas station, creating a 20-foot-wide, 30-foot-deep crater and a fireball that rose some 300 feet in the air. Structures were demolished and ablaze all over the town, and eleven people on the ground were killed.

An investigation, considered to be unprecedented in its scope and resources, was quickly initiated. An ad hoc organization, called the Joint Intelligence Group, was established near the crash site to coordinate an international effort to determine the cause of the crash of flight 103—be it mechanical or human error, or a catastrophe attributable to an act of God or to saboteurs.

The investigation's preliminary steps were enormous in themselves. Forest, farmland, towns, and villages covering a fourteen-mile-wide swath of Scotland were combed in a search for evidence. More than 10,000 pounds of scrap, rubble, and remains were collected, assembled, x-rayed, and cataloged. There were pieces of human bodies, bits of documents, shards of metal, strips of cloth, and twisted machine parts, which investigators examined in high-tech detail for clues. Police, military, overt and covert security agencies—local, national, and international—all took part in the hunt for the cause of the deadly explosion and then ultimately for the culprits responsible for plotting and staging the destruction of Pan Am 103. Among these agencies were Britain's Scotland Yard and military intelligence bureaus MI5 and MI6; West Germany's Bundeskriminalamt; Israel's Mossad; SÄPO from Sweden; intelligence officers from Cyprus; France's secret services; and America's FBI and CIA.

Investigation quickly revealed that a chronology of warnings pointing to the possibility of an act of aviation terrorism had immediately preceded the act itself. West Germany, dealing with the case of bomb-making Palestinian radicals belonging to Ahmed Jibril's Popular Front for the Liberation of Palestine–General Command (PFLP-GC), issued theirs at an international conference during the first week of November 1988. The second warning, dated November 18, came from an aviation security bulletin. A British alert, directed to their own carriers, came on November 22. The American FAA delivered theirs on December 9, followed—on December 19, just two days before the bombing—by a warning released by the British Ministry of Transport.

The Reckoning: Analysis of crash wreckage led to the discovery that flight 103 was brought down by a plastic explosive called Semex, which had been hidden inside a combination radio–tape cassette player. The player was thought to have been placed in luggage that was loaded in Frankfurt and ticketed for the through flight to New York.

Investigators spoke with 16,000 people, traveling to places as diverse as Finland, Japan, Malta, and the suburbs of Detroit, to piece together the many traces of information. There were strong indications that pointed to the complicity of East Germany's Stasi secret police, and to figures operating in Lebanon, Syria, Iraq, Iran, and Libya. By the spring of 1989, U.S. intelligence agencies had become increasingly convinced that the terrorist act had been ordered by the Iranian Revolutionary Guard, had had bomb technology expertise supplied by a shadowy Palestinian splinter group called the Arab Organization of May 15, and had been executed by the PFLP-GC.

On July 3, 1987, the U.S. Navy cruiser *Vincennes* had mistaken an Iranian Air Bus passenger liner for an F-14 fighter and shot it down, killing 290 people. The U.S. government had refused to apologize for the disaster. In 1988, two weeks before the Pan Am disaster, Yassir Arafat had announced the PLO's recognition of Israel . . . thereby kindling the anger of Arab extremists.

Despite claims made alleging that Iran had commissioned the crime as retaliation for the downing of the Air Bus, investigators ignored the politically sensitive Iranian and Syrian connections and focused their attention on Libya. At the end of 1993, Libyans Abdel Bassit Ali Megrahi and Lamen Khalifa Fhimah were accused of having smuggled a bomb-laden suitcase aboard a plane that flew from Malta to Frankfurt, where the suitcase was reloaded onto Pan Am flight 103. These two men were given safe haven in Libya by dictator Colonel Muammar Gadhafi. The United Nations Security Council, at the behest of Great Britain and the United States, ordered sanctions against Libya in order to force Gadhafi to allow the two suspects to be extradited to either Great Britain or the United States for trial. Travel and diplomatic sanctions, including the cutting off of Libya's air links with the international community and a ban on arm sales, have not succeeded. In March 1995 the FBI stepped up pressure on Libya by putting the two men on its Most Wanted List.

—R.N.K.

THE WORLD TRADE CENTER

Date: February 26, 1993

The Attack: It was a frosty February morning when a rented, yellow 1990 Ford Econoline van entered the Holland Tunnel—which runs beneath the Hudson River between Jersey City, New Jersey, and New York, New York—and headed for the World Trade Center. The van drove down a ramp that led to the second-level parking garage below the Vista Hotel and parked. Located in lower Manhattan, close by the Wall Street financial district, the twin towers of the Trade Center have more than 100 floors each . . . qualifying them as the second-tallest building in the world. More than 100,000 people a day visit or work in the sixteen-acre complex, of which the towers are only a part. The configuration of structures numbers seven different buildings, including the twenty-two floors of the Vista Hotel. There is also a four-level underground parking garage, several levels of subbasements, a PATH station, and, below that, a network of railway tubes through which trains speed commuters into and out of New York City.

After parking the van, one of the men flicked a lighter, reached into the van's rear cargo area, and put flame to four fuses. Then the pair got out and disappeared. The four twenty-foot-long fuses, each embedded in surgical tubing, led first to four charges of gunpowder affixed to four canisters of nitroglycerin. The nitro was packed alongside three cylinders of compressed hydrogen, which were in contact with 1,500 pounds of newspapers, paper bags, and rags soaked in nitric acid and urea, which, in paste form, filled four cardboard boxes. The fuses ran

from the gunpowder charges through the other components and ended in the boxes. The lighter's fire set off a chain reaction that set off the gunpowder, which combusted the nitroglycerin, which ignited the hydrogen, which, in turn, prompted the detonation of the incendiary paste. The surgical tubing encasing the fuse line served to retard the speed of the fire's advance, allowing about twenty minutes to elapse from start to ultimate explosion.

The Aftermath: The bomb went off with a concusive blast force that traveled at a speed of 5,000 miles per second. It ricocheted off the base of Tower One and created a crater measuring 200 feet by 150 feet, reaching a depth of 100 feet and extending upward from its detonation location on the B-2 parking level through the B-1 level and to the floor of the Vista Hotel. A steel cross-brace, twelve feet long and weighing 14,000 pounds, was launched more than seventy-five feet. Expanding gas, emanating from the bomb, created a cyclone with 1,500 pounds of pressure per square centimeter. Two hundred and twenty-six parked cars were pulverized and cement blocks were reduced to powder. Two hundred thousand linear feet of plaster cracked, and smoke rose a quarter of a mile high from the subbasements through the skyscrapers via elevator shafts.

The pandemonium and destruction caused by smoke, fire, falling floors, crashing ceilings, crumbling walls, rocketing shards of glass, by office furniture and the computers, typewriters, copiers, and adding machines that went racing through the air like a deluge of meteorites, resulted in a casualty count that numbered six fatalities and more than 1,000 people injured. Seventeen traumatized kindergarten students, visiting the World Trade Center from a public school in Brooklyn, were among the thousands of survivors.

Wilfredo Mercado, a thirty-seven-year-old man working in the truck delivery depot for the Windows on the World restaurant, was napping in his chair in a room situated on parking level B-1 and was not among the fortunate. He is believed to have been the first of the six who died that day. The explosion blew him out of the room and hurled him to his death. He was upside down and still somehow seated when his body was discovered several days later. He was five stories deeper into the earth than he had been while napping. He was also buried beneath twelve feet of cement. The other five victims were found within two hours of the bombing. A forty-five-year-old salesman, John DiGiovanni of Valley Stream, New York, was crushed as he exited his car in the underground garage.

Four employees of the Port Authority, the agency that operates the World Trade Center, were spending their lunch hour in a subterranean cafeteria when the bomb went off. The blast caused massive external and internal injuries that killed the pregnant, thirty-five-year-old Monica Smith and the seven-month fetus she was carrying. Forty-seven-year-old Bill Macko was blown apart. Sixty-one-year-old Robert Kirkpatrick, with only six months left before retirement, died of a fractured skull when struck by an overhead pipe propelled by the blast. Forty-eight-year-old Stephen Knapp, a veteran of the Vietnam War, was doomed by a bombardment of shrapnel composed of shattered concrete.

The bomb also set off a chain reaction among law-enforcement organizations. Word went from the Port Authority Police to the New York Police Department to a number of federal agencies, three of which led the collective quest to identify and capture those involved with the catastrophe. The FBI went to an immediate Code Red and deployed its Anti-Terrorist Task Force to work jointly with New York police on the crime. The CIA urgently set its Counter-Terrorism Department into high gear. The Federal Bureau of Alcohol, Tobacco, and Firearms activated its regional on-call unit of veteran specialists, the National Response Team, to investigate the trails of evidence connected to the explosives used in the bombing.

Once it was established that the explosion was not accidental but the result of terrorism, the New York Police Department was required to allow the FBI to take charge of the investigation. Among the terrorist groups initially suspected were cells of violent radicals drawn from guerrilla organizations associated with Russia, the warring factions in the former Yugoslavia, and terrorists based in Palestine, Iran, Iraq, and/or Libya.

Investigators, sifting through the rubble at the spot where the bomb detonated, found a scrap of metal bearing the letters AGL. The letters, it was discovered, identified the metal as part of a hydrogen gas tank that AGL Welding had delivered to a New Jersey storage locker—the very one that was later proved to be where the bomb was built. Another piece of metal debris, identified as part of a chassis, bore a serial number that investigators were able to trace as having come from a Ryder Trucks rental van. A check with the Ryder agency was enlightening. Not only had the terrorists rented their van from Ryder but they had also reported it as being stolen. Compounding their mistake, the terrorists had actually reappeared at the rental agency seeking to have their deposit refunded after the van had been blown up in the bombing.

The Reckoning: The 1993–94 trial of Mohammad Salameh, Ahmad Ajaj, Nidal Ayyad, and Mahmud Abouhalima—the first of the terrorists apprehended—began in the federal court located in Manhattan's Foley Square. The first two of the accused men faced ten charges each; the latter two faced nine counts apiece. The total of thirty-eight charges included conspiracy, explosive destruction of property, interstate transportation of explosives, assault on a federal officer, and use of a destructive device during a violent crime.

Federal District Judge Kevin Duffy presided over a five-month-long trial in which federal prosecutors presented 1,003 exhibits, called 207 witnesses to the stand, and compiled more than 10,000 pages of trial transcript. Lawyers were hired and fired by the defendants, none of whom testified in his own behalf. Only one of the accused called on supporting witnesses. Defense attorneys, however, intensely cross-examined government witnesses and argued that all the evidence was circumstantial, that no one saw the bomb being made or saw it delivered to the site of its detonation.

A jury of eight women and four men spent just over four days in deliberation, and returned with guilty-on-all-charges verdicts against each of the four. Judge Duffy handed down his sentences on May 4, 1994. The terrorists were each given terms of 240 years' imprisonment. The number of years was based on the combined life expectancies of the four men (a cumulative 180 years), plus an extra 30 years for each.

The World Trade Center bombing is believed to have been only one part of an even more massive undertaking. The four men convicted in the case belonged to a militant, underground Islamic cell led by the blind Egyptian sheikh Omar Abdel Rahman. The cell's overall membership included fifteen others. Authorities allege that this larger group was behind the Trade Center destruction and that it also hatched a conspiracy to destroy the United Nations building, New York's Federal Plaza, and the Lincoln and Holland Tunnels. Their trial, in which a government informant who worked as the sheikh's bodyguard testified as the prosecution's star witness, began in February 1995. The trial of Ramzi Yousef, the alleged bomb maker, was scheduled for the fall of 1995. The capture in Jordan of Eyad Najim in August 1995 meant that there was only one known suspect outstanding: Abdul Yasin.

—R.N.K.

THE OKLAHOMA CITY BOMBING

Date: April 19, 1995

The Attack: Shortly before 9:00 A.M. on the morning of Wednesday, April 19, a rented Ryder truck pulled up to the curb in front of the nine-story Alfred P. Murrah Federal Building in downtown Oklahoma City. Inside the building, some 500 federal employees, as well as several hundred visitors, were beginning the day's business. Inside the truck was a two-ton homemade bomb, made of fuel oil and ammonium nitrate fertilizer. At 9:04 A.M. the bomb exploded, blowing away the front half of the building; the thunderous blast, which was felt thirty miles away, sent an orange fireball and black smoke soaring into the blue Midwest sky, hurling shards of glass over a five-block radius and sending a shock wave of horror through the entire country.

In addition to the Federal Building, which was turned into a twisted mass of concrete, steel, and shredded human bodies, a number of surrounding structures, including a Y.M.C.A. center and Saint Joseph's Cathedral, were heavily damaged. Downtown Oklahoma City was a nightmare scene of urban carnage. A swarm of firemen, police, nurses, priests, frantic relatives, and rescuers began to dig through the bloodied rubble, where screams and groans told them that many victims, though buried, were still alive. Doctors and paramedics quickly set up nearby triage stations. By early afternoon, National Guard units, FBI counterterrorist teams, and forensic specialists had arrived on the scene, along with heavy cranes and backhoes, which began working through the debris. An urban rescue team arrived from Phoenix with special cameras and listening devices to search for survivors. Over the next several days, a number of victims were pulled alive from the wreckage, but the bombing's tragic toll soon became clear: 168 people were dead, including some 20 infants from the building's second-floor day care center, and several hundred more were wounded, in the worst terrorist attack in U.S. history. The final death toll was 169.

The Reckoning: In the hours following the blast, comparisons were quickly drawn with the 1993 bombing of New York's World Trade Center, and reports circulated of several men of Middle Eastern complexion walking away from the scene of the blast. On Friday, however, authorities announced the arrest of Timothy McVeigh, a twenty-six-year-old gun enthusiast and former soldier, who had, in fact, been picked up on minor traffic and weapons charges a few hours after the explosion. Authorities would also detain the brothers James and Terry Nichols, as well as McVeigh's army buddy Michael Fortier, who agreed to turn state's witness; it soon became grotesquely clear that the horror in the heartland was as American as apple pie.

The bombing occurred on the second anniversary of the deadly raid by federal agents of the Branch Davidian religious sect's compound in Waco, Texas, an event that had become a

rallying point for right-wing extremists. The suspects, it was discovered, had links to several of the self-styled citizen militias that in recent years had sprung up from Florida to Idaho, united by a love of guns, a loathing of government, and, in many cases, a fervent belief in outlandish conspiracies—that the United States, for example, is being taken over by a "world government" working through the United Nations. While long known to federal agents, these groups had largely been ignored by the media or dismissed as "boys with toys" who liked to dress like real soldiers, eat beans, and romp in the woods on weekends. All the militia groups denied any connection with the bombing; however, to many Americans they seemed rather less harmless than before, lending a newly lethal edge to the right-wing paranoics and their quixotic struggle—in the tradition, they believed, of Paul Revere and Patrick Henry—against unseen, far-off forces. April 19, it was noted, was also the date on which were fired the first shots of the American Revolution.

Within a few days, the tragedy had come to be enmeshed in the spiteful rhetoric of an increasingly fractured American body politic. President Clinton quickly condemned the bombing, which, he said, had been carried out in a climate of hatred fostered by irresponsible right-wing radio talk shows. Right-wing radio extremist Rush Limbaugh protested that the president was playing politics with the disaster. For his part, G. Gordon Liddy, the former Watergate conspirator turned talk show host, generously offered advice to listeners on the best ways to shoot federal agents.

The authorities, meanwhile, doggedly pursued their investigation, with more than 1,000 FBI agents working on the case. They felt sure that McVeigh was part of a wider conspiracy— he had, for example, telephoned a neo-Nazi group shortly after renting the fatal truck—but the search for solid evidence of a full conspiracy continued to prove frustrating. Using information suppled by Fortier, Terry Nichols was charged as an accomplice. Another man, believed to have been with McVeigh when he rented the tuck, was the focus of an intense manhunt; he turned out to be an innocent bystander. Wherever the investigation may lead, however, the bombing in Oklahoma City brought home to Americans the deadly reality of terrorism.

—E.H.B.

NOTEWORTHY TRIALS

THE MONKEY TRIAL
On an afternoon in May 1925, two entrepreneurs sat scheming in a drugstore in Dayton, Tennessee. George Rappelyea and F. E. Robinson

pored over a notice in the *Chattanooga Times*, placed by a little-known New York organization called the American Civil Liberties Union (ACLU). The notice sought a biology teacher willing to be the defendant in a case to test a new Tennessee law, the Butler Act. The Butler Act forbade the teaching in the public schools of any theory that claimed that human beings had evolved from lower forms of animal life.

To Rappelyea and Robinson, a test case of the Butler Act looked like a heaven-sent opportunity for the sleepy village of Dayton. Pitting Fundamentalist Christians against the proponents of the modern, scientific approach to creation, it would bring reporters, famous lawyers, experts on science and religion, and flocks of spectators—all with money to spend in Dayton's shops and boardinghouses. With the help of one willing biology teacher, they could put Dayton, Tennessee, on the map.

Dates: July 10–21, 1925.
Defendant: John T. Scopes was not a teacher of biology. He coached football and basketball at Dayton's Central High School, where he also taught math, physics, and chemistry. But when the actual biology teacher refused to get involved, Scopes agreed to help build the ACLU's case. Rappelyea and Robinson arranged for him to tutor three high-school boys, making sure that the subject of evolution came under thorough discussion. Then Robinson, chairman of the Dayton School Board, arranged to have Scopes arrested. John Scopes, a soft-spoken young man with a bent for scientific inquiry, suddenly found himself at the vortex of a national maelstrom.

Charges: Scopes was charged with teaching "a certain theory or theories which deny the story of the divine creation of man taught in the Bible, and teach instead that man has descended from a lower order of animals." Such teaching was in flagrant violation of the Butler Act. If convicted, Scopes could be fined $100.

Named for its creator, legislator John Washington Butler, the Butler Act was intended to protect the Christian children of Tennessee from the growing menace of agnosticism. As Butler put it, "The Bible is the foundation upon which our American government is built. . . . The evolutionist who denies the Biblical story of creation . . . cannot be a Christian. It makes Jesus Christ a fakir, robs the Christian of his hope, and undermines the foundation of our government."

Christian Fundamentalists, with their interpretation of the Bible as literal truth, were a strong political force in Tennessee. While many legislators privately questioned the wisdom of the Butler Act and feared it would make their state a laughingstock, few dared to offer public opposition. The Butler Act sailed through the legislature almost unchallenged. When Governor Austin Peay signed it into law on March 21, 1925, he remarked off the record that he never expected to see the law enforced.

The Prosecution's Case: From the first, the issue was not to determine whether Scopes had taught evolution. Clearly and deliberately, he had broken the law. But the ACLU wanted to test whether the Butler Act was constitutional. The prosecution set out to defend the law itself, to show that it protected the right of Christians to raise their children with the belief that the Bible was the only truth. Leading the prosecution was the venerable William Jennings Bryan.

A brilliant speaker, Bryan was sometimes called "the golden-tongued orator." He had had a long and notable career as lawyer, lecturer, and statesman. Three times he was the Democratic presidential candidate. He served as secretary of state under Woodrow Wilson. He was a pacifist in the years before World War I, and a vocal champion of woman suffrage. He was also a devout Christian with an unshakable conviction that the Bible should be interpreted literally.

The prosecution sought to prove that the theory of evolution was in direct conflict with the tenets of Christianity. At home and at church, Scopes's students learned that God created the earth and all its creatures in six days. Yet Scopes told them that human beings had evolved from lower life-forms over uncountable millions of years. The teaching of this scientific theory sabotaged the students' Christian beliefs, in violation of their constitutional right to freedom of religion.

All the ills from which America suffers can be traced back to the teaching of evolution. It would be better to destroy every other book ever written, and save just the first three verses of Genesis.
William Jennings Bryan, 1923

I do not consider it an insult, but rather a compliment to be called an agnostic. I do not pretend to know where many ignorant men are sure—that is all that agnosticism means.
Clarence Darrow, Scopes trial, Dayton, Tennessee, July 13, 1925

The Defense's Case: Marshaled by the ACLU, Scopes's defense lawyers set out to prove that there was no conflict between Christianity and the theory of evolution. The defense sought to show that millions of people found evolution compatible with their Christian beliefs. It was purely a matter of personal interpretation. Each individual was free to listen and to learn, to weigh and decide as he or she saw fit.

Heading the defense team was the renowned Chicago attorney Clarence Darrow, who had volunteered his services free of charge. Like Bryan, Darrow had had a long and illustrious career. He upheld the rights of labor organizers and expounded radical ideas on criminal

Clarence Darrow (left) and William Jennings Bryan during a break in the 1925 Scopes trial concerning the teaching of evolution in public schools.

psychology. Darrow was an avowed agnostic to whom Christian Fundamentalism was anathema. Like Bryan, he was a gifted speaker, passionately committed to his own idea of justice.

As Rappelyea and Robinson had hoped, the trial made Dayton famous. Each day telegraph operators tapped out the latest developments for newspapers across the country. Radio station WGN, based in Chicago, broadcast the proceedings over the air waves; never before had a trial been aired live for a radio audience.

People poured into Dayton. Despite the stifling July heat, spectators packed the courthouse and spilled onto the lawn. Photographers clambered onto chairs to snap pictures over the heads of the crowd. Vendors hawked ice cream, pop, and souvenirs. The theory of evolution suggested that humans had descended from the apes, so many of these mementos took the form of monkeys. There were stuffed toy monkeys, monkey rings, and umbrellas with grinning monkey-head handles. The trial in Dayton, Tennessee, came to be known as the Monkey Trial.

For the first several days of the trial, the lawyers argued over technical points of law. The crowd grew restless, and some people drifted away. Then, on July 21, Darrow stunned the courtroom by calling Bryan himself to the stand. The two men faced each other for the final confrontation that had been unfolding throughout the trial.

No longer were John Scopes and the Butler Act on trial. Darrow's razor-sharp questioning was a direct assault on Fundamentalism, on the belief system that Bryan held dear. Mercilessly, Darrow exposed the Bible's inconsistencies one after another. If God created only two people, Adam and Eve, whom did their son Cain marry? Bryan said he didn't know—he would let the agnostics look for her. Did Bryan believe that God made snakes crawl on their belly because a serpent tempted Eve? How did snakes move about before that time—on the tips of their tails? Did Bryan truly believe that God created the earth in six days? Well, Bryan admitted, perhaps the days at that time were not really twenty-four hours long.

After an hour and a half, Bryan was exhausted and beaten. He had been unable to counter

Darrow's arguments, and his deeply held beliefs had become the object of public ridicule. Five days after the trial, Bryan died in his sleep, apparently of a heart attack.

After Bryan's testimony, both sides conceded that the trial had gone on long enough. The judge asked the jury to reach its verdict.

The Verdict and Its Aftermath: The jury (twelve men, ten of them farmers) deliberated for nine minutes. To the satisfaction of both sides, it brought in a guilty verdict. Darrow had hoped Scopes would be found guilty so that the case could be appealed, perhaps to the U.S. Supreme Court. It did reach the supreme court of Tennessee a year later, and Scopes's conviction was overturned on a legal technicality. The Butler Act remained on the books until 1967, unchallenged and unenforced.

John Scopes left Central High to pursue further studies in science. He shunned publicity, but he always clung to his belief in the power of ideas. In 1960, in a rare interview, a reporter asked him why the battle for academic freedom continued to rage. "Well," Scopes replied, "people just don't change that quickly."
—D.A.K.

THE NUREMBERG WAR CRIMES TRIALS

Just as *Watergate* would, nearly a quarter of a century later, the single word *Nuremberg* came to designate much more than a location. For the World War II generation, *Nuremberg* stood for nearly indescribable evil and the attempt to hold the evildoers accountable for their actions through the judicial process.

The Bavarian city in which the trials of Nazi leaders were held in 1945 and 1946 had been Nazi Party headquarters during the 1930s, and it had been the site of massive rallies (documented in Leni Riefenstahl's film *The Triumph of the Will*) featuring displays of the finest of Aryan youth and spellbinding speeches by the führer. Nuremberg had also lent its name to a series of anti-Semitic laws, the opening salvo of Adolf Hitler's "final solution."

It was with a degree of poetic justice, therefore, that the victors over Nazism in World War II chose Nuremberg for the holding of the International Military Tribunal—the official name for the trials of 1945 to 1946. But that official name would soon be supplanted throughout the war-weary world by the simple "Nuremberg" as the all-encompassing descriptive term for civilization's attempt to deal with the barbarism of Hitler and his subordinates.
Dates: November 19, 1945–October 1, 1946.
Defendants: The indictment—as drawn up by the United States, Great Britain, France, and the Soviet Union—included twenty-four top Nazis. Not included were Adolf Hitler, Joseph Goebbels, and Heinrich Himmler, who had killed themselves as the war drew to a close.

Martin Bormann, although reportedly killed by an Allied mortar shell, was tried in absentia. Gustav Krupp, though indicted, was declared unfit to stand trial because of advanced senility. Robert Ley, also indicted, hanged himself before the trial.

Among those actually in the dock during the 1945–46 Nuremberg trials, the most prominent was Hermann Göring, Luftwaffe chief and Hitler's second in command. Also on trial was Rudolf Hess, next in line behind Göring until he was imprisoned following a bizarre flight to England in 1941. Others included Joachim von Ribbentrop (foreign minister), Hans Frank (governor-general of occupied Poland), Albert Speer (director of raw material and labor utilization during the war and chief Nazi architect), Baldur von Schirach (leader of Hitler Youth), Julius Streicher (virulent anti-Semite who led Nazi attacks on Jews in the 1930s), Wilhelm Keitel (armed forces chief of staff), Alfred Jodl (chief of Wehrmacht operations staff), Karl Doenitz (admiral who commanded U-boat operations), Hans Fritzsche (radio and newspaper propagandist), Erich Raeder (commander in chief of the navy), Ernst Kaltenbrunner (administrator in charge of the concentration camp system and program for exterminating Jews), Franz von Papen (chancellor of Germany in 1932 who smoothed the way for Hitler's assumption of power), and Alfred Rosenberg (leader in the looting and destruction of Eastern Europe, including the mass killing of millions of Jews).

Charges: The defendants faced a four-count indictment, drawn up in London in August 1945: (1) conspiracy to turn Germany from a peaceful nation into a perpetrator of aggressive war, (2) violation of Germany's international treaty obligations, (3) commission of war crimes—murder; torture; enslavement; destruction of cities, towns, and villages—and (4) commission of crimes against humanity—the deportation and genocide of Jews and other groups in Europe.

The trial began on November 19 with the reading of the indictment, a tedious activity that took two days to complete. The defendants were then called on to plead. All pleas were entered as "Not guilty," although several Nazis offered their own versions: Jodl—"I have a clear conscience before God and my people"; Göring—disappointed that he was not permitted to make a speech—"Not guilty in the sense of the indictment"; and Hess—apparently out of his mind—simply "Nein."

The Prosecution's Case: The prosecution began its case on the afternoon of November 21, with the opening statement of chief American prosecutor (and associate justice of the U.S. Supreme Court) Robert H. Jackson. It proved to be the high point of the Nuremberg trials for both

Jackson and the Allied prosecution team. He began by stating the necessity of holding the trials:

The privilege of opening the first trial in history for crimes against the peace of the world imposes a grave responsibility. The wrongs which we seek to condemn and punish have been so calculated, so malignant, and so devastating, that civilization cannot tolerate their being ignored, because it cannot survive their being repeated. That four great nations, flushed with victory and stung with injury, stay the hand of vengeance and voluntarily submit their captive enemies to the judgment of the law is one of the most significant tributes that power has ever paid to reason.

He went on to deal with the thorny issue of "victor's justice"—that the winners in the war were taking advantage of their conquest of Germany to punish Nazi leaders. He noted that there really was no alternative, but he also pointed out how essential it was to accord fairness to the accused:

Unfortunately, the nature of these crimes is such that both prosecution and judgment must be by victor nations over vanquished foes. The worldwide scope of the aggressions carried out by these men has left but few neutrals. . . . We must never forget that the record on which we judge these defendants is the record on which history will judge us tomorrow. To pass these defendants a poisoned chalice is to put it to our lips as well. We must summon such detachment and intellectual integrity to our task that this trial will commend itself to posterity as fulfilling humanity's aspirations to do justice. . . .

If these men are the first war leaders of a defeated nation to be prosecuted in the name of the law, they are also the first to be given a chance to plead for their lives in the name of the law.

Jackson concluded by drawing a clear line of distinction between these criminal leaders and the German people as a whole. Only the former were on trial at Nuremberg. In fact, Jackson made it sound as though the prosecution regarded ordinary Germans as Nazi victims, too:

If the German populace had willingly accepted the Nazi program, no storm troopers would have been needed in the early days of the party and there would have been no need for concentration camps or the Gestapo. . . . The German, no less than the non-German world, has accounts to settle with these defendants.

From the high eloquence of Jackson's opening statement the prosecution case quickly descended to a much lower level. The plan was to overwhelm the tribunal with documents that would show, in their own words, how the Nazi leaders conducted a conspiracy to take over Germany, conquer Europe, enslave and brutalize subject populations, and eliminate Jews. The problem was that Jackson's subordinates glutted the court with more documents than the judges could readily assimilate, failed to make enough copies of the documents available to the defense attorneys, and supplied the documents only in English. The problem was resolved by having the prosecution read each document into the record, allowing for instantaneous access and translation. While solving the problem of too few copies of English-only documents, this procedure slowed the Nuremberg trials to a crawl.

Moments of real drama were rare. Of those that did occur, surely the strangest was the revelation of Rudolf Hess's false amnesia. Hess claimed that he could remember nothing of his Nazi past, and when he wasn't asking permission to leave the courtroom to relieve his stomach cramps, he ignored the proceedings by reading paperback novels. Finally, Jackson urged that Hess be given amnesia-alleviating medications. Hess then addressed the court:

I would like to make the following declaration before the Tribunal, . . . Henceforth my memory will again respond to the outside world. The reasons for simulating loss of memory were of a tactical nature. . . . I also simulated loss of memory in consultation with my officially appointed defense counsel. He has, therefore, represented me in good faith.

Hess's confession produced one of the few outbursts of laughter at the Nuremberg trials.

Two notable moments in the prosecution's case revolved around films. The prosecution showed a documentary called *The Nazi Plan* to support the first two counts of the indictment. The film reviewed the defendants' roles in the Nazi takeover of Germany and the launching of World War II. To the surprise of many in the courtroom, Göring and his cohorts loved it. The former Luftwaffe chief and Reichsmarschall reveled in seeing himself "in the good old times." Ribbentrop upon seeing the führer could not restrain himself: "Can't you just feel Hitler's tremendous personality? For us it was the most fearfully stimulating thing that has ever happened in our lifetime." Hess predicted Germany would rise again.

The second film was a good deal more sobering. It was a compilation of concentration camp footage as shot by Allied forces who liberated the grotesquely emaciated survivors, buried the mounds of skeletons, and revealed to the world the existence of gas chambers, crematoria, and other ghastly remnants of the Holocaust. The film shocked courtroom viewers; even the Nazis could not watch. Only Streicher seemed to enjoy the sight of stacked Jewish corpses, nodding his head in approval. The judges left in silence as the film ended, not even bothering to announce adjournment. That night, in their cells, nearly all the defendants denied knowledge of or responsibility for such horrors.

But the prosecutors had the documents, and they concluded their case with overwhelming evidence that the defendants had perpetrated a host of crimes against humanity. In just one of many examples, they cited Hans Frank in December 1941:

As far as the Jews are concerned, I want to tell you quite frankly that they must be done away with one way or another. . . . This war would be only a partial success if the whole lot of Jewry would survive it, while we would have shed our last blood to save Europe. . . . We must annihilate Jews, wherever it is possible, in order to maintain the structure of the Reich as a whole.

The Defense's Case: Ignorance and denial were the cornerstones of the defense case. The professional soldiers, like Doenitz and Keitel, maintained that they were merely following orders. Others attempted to blame everything on Hitler, claiming that they knew nothing of the evils with which they were now being charged. Göring insisted that both he and Hitler had known nothing of the extermination camps—it had all been Himmler's fault.

Göring, however, was eager to accept responsibility for the Nazi takeover of Germany and the conquests that had preceded the outbreak of war in 1939. Aware that he was almost certainly going to receive the death penalty, Göring wanted to portray himself as the unrepentant national hero of the German people. "It is correct," he boasted, "that I have done everything which was at all within my personal power to strengthen the National Socialist movement, to increase it, and have worked increasingly to bring it to power as the one and only authority." Almost singlehandedly, Göring furnished all the evidence necessary to convict himself and many of his Nazi cohorts on the first two counts of the indictment.

The Verdict and Its Aftermath: Four judges—one each from the United States, Great Britain, France, and the Soviet Union—rendered the verdict in the Nuremberg trials. They sentenced eleven of the defendants to be hanged, three to life imprisonment, and four to briefer prison terms. The judges acquitted three of the defendants. Göring, one of the eleven to be hanged, cheated the gallows by swallowing cyanide shortly before his scheduled execution. By 1966 only Rudolf Hess remained incarcerated. The United States, Great Britain, and France were willing to see him released, but the Soviet Union—convinced that Hess's flight to England in 1941 had been intended to bring the British into an anti-Soviet alliance—insisted that Hess

"drink his cup of retribution to the last drop." From 1966 to his suicide at age ninety-three on August 17, 1987, Rudolf Hess was the sole occupant in Germany's Spandau Prison.

—J.L.K.

ADOLF EICHMANN

On a May evening in 1960, a thin, balding man of fifty-four clambered from a bus in a suburb of Buenos Aires. Suddenly three men seized him and hurried him into a waiting car. They drove to a rented house, where they tied him to a bed. After nine days, the prisoner was bundled onto an El-Al plane destined for Israel.

The captive put up almost no resistance. He readily admitted that he was a former Nazi who had been living under an assumed name. For years the Israeli secret police and private "Nazi hunters" had been searching for him. To thousands of survivors of the Nazi concentration camps, and to millions of people whose loved ones perished in the Holocaust, this man symbolized the most profound evil of which human beings were capable. The man kidnapped on that spring evening in Argentina was the notorious Adolf Eichmann.

Dates: April 11–August 14, 1961.

Defendant: Adolf Eichmann was born in Solingen, Germany, on March 19, 1906, and grew up in the picture-postcard town of Linz, Austria. As a young man he was swept up by the passionate rhetoric of the rising Nazi Party. With fierce devotion he served Adolf Hitler throughout the Second World War, heading the Nazi bureau known as IVA 4B, which dealt with "Jewish affairs."

Eichmann was captured when Germany fell to the Allies in 1945. But he escaped from prison and eventually made his way through Switzerland and Italy to Argentina. There he lived in virtual poverty with his wife and children, in a house without electricity or running water. His capture in 1960 ripped him from his obscurity. Adolf Eichmann became the focus of one of the most celebrated trials in history. After centuries of persecution, it was the first time that the Jewish people were able to bring an oppressor to justice.

Charges: Eichmann was tried in the district court of Jerusalem under a 1950 Israeli law, the Nazis and Nazi Collaborators Punishment Act. Hatred of Eichmann was so intense that he had to be protected in the courtroom by a bulletproof glass cage and two armed guards. He was indicted on fifteen counts—four counts of "crimes against the Jewish people," seven counts of "crimes against humanity," one count of "war crimes," and three counts of belonging to groups declared criminal organizations by the 1946 International Military Tribunal at Nuremberg. These organizations were the SS, the SAID, and the Gestapo. Among other things, the

Former Gestapo officer Adolf Eichmann, standing inside a bulletproof enclosure, listens to an Israeli judge condemn him to death.

indictment specified that Eichmann had arranged to transport millions of Jews to concentration camps; that he had ordered the involuntary sterilization of Jewish and Gypsy women; that he had confiscated Jewish-owned property and turned it over to the German government; that he had caused the deaths of thousands of non-Jewish Gypsies, Poles, Slovenes, and Hungarians; and that he had ordered the gassing of millions of Jews in such concentration camps as Auschwitz and Treblinka. Eichmann was charged with participating in the newly identified crime of genocide—the systematic attempt to annihilate an entire race of people from the face of the earth.

The Prosecution's Case: Led by Israel's attorney general, Gideon Hausner, the prosecution amassed papers from the archives of various ministries of the Third Reich: from the offices of the German security police; from war-crime commissions in Poland, France, Holland, Denmark, and Belgium; and from the vast records of the Nuremberg trials. In addition, the prosecution showed films of the concentration camps. They also brought 113 witnesses to the stand, ninety of them men and women who had survived the camps. One by one, each witness told a wrenching personal story of brutality and horror, spreading the Holocaust before the

world like an immense, bloodstained tapestry. Some of the witnesses described mass shootings, the sadistic killing of babies, and other scenes so cruel and evil that they feared they would not be believed. Much of this unspeakable cruelty, the prosecution contended, had been orchestrated by the man in the bulletproof defendant's box, Adolf Eichmann.

The Defense's Case: As the lawyer for his defense, Eichmann chose Dr. Robert Servatius of West Germany. The defense attempted to show that Eichmann acted only from a sense of duty to his superiors, that he was "only a cog." As Servatius put it, he had committed acts "for which you are decorated if you win and go to the gallows if you lose." Yes, Eichmann had arranged for Jews to be sent to detention camps in Eastern Europe. But he was a glorified railway official, "concerned strictly with timetables and technical transport problems." He personally had never killed anyone. The real guilt, the defense argued, lay with the high-ranking Nazi officials who gave Eichmann his orders.

Eichmann took the witness stand on June 20, six weeks into the trial, and was questioned by the defense until July 7. The prosecution cross-examined him for nearly two more weeks. Then the three judges handling the trial questioned him for another two and a half days. Over all this time, Eichmann remained composed, steadfastly maintaining that he was "not guilty in the sense of the indictment." In his final statement before the court, he declared, "I am not the monster I am made out to be. I am the victim of a fallacy. It is my profound conviction that I must suffer for the acts of others."

On August 14 the long trial finally came to a close. For nearly four months, Adolf Eichmann awaited the court's final decision.

The Verdict and Its Aftermath: The court reconvened on December 11, 1961. For two days the three judges read the court's sprawling pronouncement, a document of 244 sections. Eichmann was convicted on all fifteen counts of the charges against him. The court found him guilty of crimes "with the intent to destroy the Jewish people," of participating in deliberate acts of genocide. He was also held responsible for crimes against such non-Jewish peoples as the Gypsies and Poles. Each of the first twelve counts of his conviction carried the death penalty.

As Eichmann's execution date drew nearer, Israel's president Itzak Ben Zvi received a flood of letters. Many applauded the court's decision. But hundreds of organizations and individuals, including some prominent Jewish leaders from around the world, wrote to plead for clemency. Some people agreed with Eichmann's own argument that he could not be blamed for obeying orders. Others feared that Eichmann's death would free the German people from a sense of guilt that they deserved to carry with them. Some letters insisted that hanging was too good for Eichmann, and suggested a variety of torments that might be more suitable.

On May 29, 1962, Ben Zvi rejected Eichmann's own plea for mercy, a four-page, handwritten letter in which he restated the arguments he had raised during the trial. Just after midnight on the night of May 31, Eichmann was led to the gallows. Witnesses reported that he went to his death bravely, without flinching or protesting.

A Protestant minister sat with Eichmann during his final hours and offered to read him passages from the Bible. Eichmann refused to hear the Holy Scripture. Yet his last words suggest that he believed in an afterlife, where perhaps he would face his ultimate judgment. "After a short while, gentlemen, we shall all meet again," he said. "Such is the fate of all men. Long live Germany, long live Argentina, long live Austria. I shall not forget them." The following morning, Eichmann's body was cremated and his ashes were dumped into the Mediterranean.

—D.A.K.

CASES OF TERRIBLE INJUSTICE

LEO FRANK

The Crime: Early on the morning of Sunday, April 27, 1913, Newt Lee, a night watchman at a pencil factory in Atlanta, Georgia, discovered the bound and bloodied body of a thirteen-year-old employee named Mary Phagan in the factory basement. A noose was around her neck, and she had deep gashes on her head. She had been sexually assaulted and murdered after collecting her pay the previous day. The murder outraged the city. Local papers, such as William Randolph Hearst's *Atlanta Georgian*, trumpeted lurid headlines and called for quick and severe justice. The public's grief contained an almost religious fervor; the death in an urban factory of the little girl from the country town of Marietta crystallized the sufferings and resentment of many lower-class southern whites. Some ten thousand mourners viewed her body at the morgue, and more than one thousand attended her funeral. Lee himself, a black man, became the first principal suspect. He was arrested, imprisoned, and beaten by police, who were, however, obliged to concede that they had no real evidence against him. Spurred on by a rabid media, the constabulary quickly sought out another culprit.

The Accused: Attention soon focused on the factory's supervisor, a twenty-nine-year-old Jewish man named Leo Frank, who had moved to Atlanta from New York in 1907 in order to manage his uncle's pencil factory. He had married a girl from a distinguished Atlanta Jewish family in 1911, and by 1913 he had become a prominent citizen. On the day of the murder, Frank had given Phagan her pay, and it was reported that when police first told him of the crime, he had acted nervous. Frank was in fact not a good-humored man, nor was he a handsome one. He was, however, wealthy, Jewish, and a northerner—the perfect scapegoat for populist and Christian Fundamentalist ha-

tred, particularly when the police disclosed after his arrest that he had also frequented a local bordello and indulged in the "perverted" practice of oral sex—an act which, in the good state of Georgia, was itself then punishable by death.

The press and police knew they had their man. The southern populist leader and editorialist Tom Watson noted, as evidence of Frank's guilt, his "satyr eyes . . . protruding sensual lips, and . . . animal jaw." Local papers called

In 1913, Leo Frank, a Jew who was a supervisor at an Atlanta pencil factory, was falsely accused of murdering a thirteen-year-old girl.

him simply "the strangler" or "the monster"; when details of the crime were not forthcoming, reporters did not hesitate to invent them. Such antics notwithstanding, it soon became clear to those close to the case that the evidence against Frank was highly problematic. Unfortunately for the accused, however, the prosecutor, Hugh Mason Dorsey, was an ambitious man who had early on made forceful public statements concerning Frank's guilt; should he opt not to pursue the case, he would appear to have "sold out to the Jews" and would thus effectively nip in the bud a promising political career. (He was later elected governor of Georgia.) Ignoring evidence that his leading witness, a black factory janitor named Jim Conley, was quite possibly the actual murderer, Dorsey proceeded to trial, which began in late July. Conley testified that Frank had confessed to the murder and even tried to force him to burn the body in the incinerator. Defense lawyers were unable to shake Conley's testimony. Although Frank testified that Conley was lying, on September 26, 1913, the jury brought in a verdict of guilty, setting off hearty celebrations in the streets of Atlanta, which intensified to near fever pitch when Judge Leonard Roan sentenced Frank to death.

The rest of the nation, however, did not share in the local glee. Over the next eighteen months, more than 100,000 letters arrived protesting the verdict. A petition to similar effect garnered a million signatures. Appeals in state courts were unsuccessful, and in April 1915 the U.S. Supreme Court also denied Frank a new trial. In June, convinced of Frank's innocence and stating that he would rather live in fear of his life than endure a guilty conscience, John Slaton, the outgoing governor of Georgia, despite receiving more than a thousand death threats, courageously commuted Frank's sentence to life imprisonment. A few days later the governor's mansion was attacked by an angry mob, and Slaton, along with his family, was forced to flee the state. On July 17 a fellow prisoner slashed Frank's throat, almost killing him.

Outraged that Slaton had subverted southern justice, Tom Watson proclaimed that "the next Jew who does what Frank did is going to get exactly what we give to Negro rapists." Inspired by Watson's rhetoric, about twenty-five members of a recently formed vigilante group calling themselves the Knights of Mary Phagan attacked Milledgeville Prison Farm, where Frank was imprisoned, on the night of August 16, 1915. They abducted the luckless man, drove him back to Marietta, and, the next morning, hung him from an oak tree. The lynchers, who

A proud lynch mob displays the body of Leo Frank.

included a sheriff and a former judge, made no attempt to hide their identity, but none was ever prosecuted. The group then adapted a more venerable name, the Knights of the Ku Klux Klan; thus resuscitated, the Klan initiated a reign of terror that would last for another five decades. A snapshot of Frank's gently swinging corpse, meanwhile, became a popular postcard, long sold for a nickel in local drugstores.

The Truth: Beset by an uneasy conscience, Judge Roan had informed Governor Slaton that Jim Conley had repeatedly confessed having committed the murder to his attorney (a fact that had not, however, prevented the jurist from sentencing Frank to death). In 1982 a black man named Alonzo Mann, a fourteen-year-old office boy at the time of the killing, confirmed this version, stating that he had seen Jim Conley, who had died in 1962, carrying Phagan's body down to the basement, and had kept silent because Conley had threatened to kill him. On March 11, 1986, the Georgia Board of Pardons reluctantly issued Leo Frank a posthumous pardon, although their statement refused to acknowledge his innocence.

—E.H.B.

JAMES MONTGOMERY

On November 15, 1923, in Waukegan, Illinois, a sixty-two-year-old mentally deranged shoelace peddler, a white woman named Mamie Snow, claimed that she had been raped by James Montgomery, a thirty-year-old black man. Montgomery was a war veteran and a skilled factory worker who owned two houses, one of which he rented out. He had never been arrested before— but he had had one previous run-in with the Waukegan police. Earlier that year the police had ransacked his home, allegedly searching for bootleg liquor. Montgomery threatened to sue but agreed to accept $600 compensation instead. When Montgomery was arrested for rape, the local Ku Klux Klan threatened his lawyer, who then declined to present his planned defense. The trial lasted twenty minutes and Montgomery was sentenced to life imprisonment.

While in prison Montgomery was taught to read and write by the notorious murderer Nathan Leopold. In 1946 other prisoners brought Montgomery's plight to the attention of Luis Kutner, a well-known attorney and civil rights activist. After ten nights of rummaging through papers stored in the basement of Waukegan's Victory Memorial Hospital, Kutner found the original report on Mamie Snow's medical examination. It showed that she had not been raped. In fact, she was a virgin. Then Kutner broke into the headquarters of the local Ku Klux Klan and found an old document that detailed the plot to frame Montgomery. After working on Montgomery's case for more than three years, Kutner presented his evidence in court, and on

August 10, 1949, after spending more than twenty-five years in prison for a crime that never occurred, James Montgomery was finally allowed to go free. He died on July 9, 1962.

—R.J.F.

STEPHEN DENNISON

On September 9, 1925, sixteen-year-old Stephen Dennison was walking along Route 22 near Salem, New York, on his way to look for work. He was starved and he desperately needed a cigarette—his two-pack-a-day habit had begun when he was fifteen. Noticing a roadside stand that he knew was owned by Nellie Hill, he approached; but the canvas-covered stand was closed. On impulse, Dennison cut through the canvas and stole three boxes of chocolates, a pack of cigarettes, and some chocolate marshmallow bars—total value, five dollars.

When Salem undersheriff A. M. Alexander and five police officers caught up with Dennison in Clarence Priest's barn, the boy surrendered immediately. On advice of his court-appointed attorney, Herbert Van Kirk, Dennison pleaded guilty, received a ten-year suspended sentence, and was placed on probation for one year, provided he report to Methodist minister Claude Winch once a month.

Dennison failed to report as instructed and, on August 14, 1926, was confined to the Elmira State Reformatory for parole violation. Through a "tragic error," he was classified as a low-grade moron and transferred in 1927 to the Institution for Male Defective Delinquents in Napanoch. Over the years, Dennison broke a number of minor rules, and extra time was added to his sentence.

In March 1936, without prior notice or judicial review, Dennison was sent to Dannemora State Hospital for the Criminally Insane, where, forgotten and ignored, he remained for the next twenty-four years, until his half brother, George, obtained his release on December 16, 1960. Dennison's sole possessions at the time of his incarceration were returned to him—two pennies.

Dennison sued the state of New York for damages. New York State Court of Claims judge Richard S. Heller, in making a $115,000 award to Dennison, said, "No sum of money would be adequate to compensate the claimant for the injustices he suffered and the scars he obviously bears."

Last known to be working as a janitor in Glens Falls, New York, Dennison never received any of the $115,000 awarded to him.

—J.E.E.

JULIUS KRAUSE

In 1931, at the age of eighteen, Julius Krause and another man were arrested, convicted, and imprisoned for the robbery and murder of a store clerk in Ohio. Four years later, just before he died, the other man told prison officials that Krause was innocent and that his real accomplice in the murder was a man named Curtis Kuermerle. However, the police did nothing about this deathbed confession. After nine years in prison, Krause, while working as a trustee at the Ohio State Fair, escaped, found Kuermerle, persuaded him to confess, and turned himself and Kuermerle in to the authorities. Even though Kuermerle was convicted for the same murder that Krause supposedly had committed, the courts refused to review Krause's case, and he spent another eleven years in prison. Finally Jane Lausche, the governor's wife, for whom Krause worked as a gardener and driver, championed Krause's case to her husband. The governor refused to pardon Krause, but he did commute his sentence to time served and Krause was released in 1951.

—R.J.F.

THE "SCOTTSBORO BOYS"

The "Crime": On March 25, 1931, seven disheveled white youths entered a railroad stationmaster's office in a small town in northern Alabama and claimed that, while riding as hobos on a Memphis-bound freight, they had been attacked and thrown off the train by a band of young blacks. The stationmaster phoned up the rail line to the sheriff in Paint Rock, who deputized "every man who owned a gun" and gave orders to "round up every Negro on the train." In different railcars, deputies found nine black youths, aged twelve to twenty, as well as two young white women—Victoria Price, nineteen, and Ruby Bates, seventeen. The women claimed that they had been gang-raped by twelve black men, including those found aboard, who were jailed in the nearby town of Scottsboro.

The alleged crime immediately set off a furor, touching on the deepest guilts and fears of the white South—guilt rooted in the antebellum experience, when white plantation owners had raped black slave women as a matter of course, and fears rooted in the widely held white assumption that, given the opportunity, black men would do the same. The local press had convicted the so-called Scottsboro Boys by nightfall; the next morning's headline in a local paper read simply, "Nine negro men rape two white women." The "crime," opined one typical editor, was a "wholesale debauching of society . . . that savored of the jungle." Many Alabamans favored lynching; others, however, counseled prudence, noting that this was an opportunity for the kinder, gentler new South to show its new face, and arguing that the blacks should "be tried first" and only then executed. Trial was set for a mere two weeks hence.

The Accused: Charlie Weems, twenty; Clarence Norris, Haywood Patterson, and Andy Wright, nineteen; Olin Montgomery, seventeen and virtually blind; Willie Roberson, seventeen and syphilitic, virtually incapable of having sex; Ozzie Powell, sixteen; Eugene Williams, thirteen; and Roy Wright, Andy's brother, twelve, were charged with rape. Over the next six years, they would be subjected to a nightmare series of trials and would together serve more than one hundred years in jail.

At the first trial in Scottsboro, where the youths were defended by a lawyer who was regularly drunk by 9:00 A.M., the defendants' poorly managed testimony was often contradictory. The two "victims," meanwhile, were presented as virtuous southern belles who had been cruelly attacked by a band of "sex-mad savages." Victoria Price did most of the talking, recounting in detail how she and Bates had been threatened at knifepoint, beaten, and brutally raped six times each. Dr. R. R. Bridges and another physician, however, who had examined the women the day of the alleged crime, testified that neither bore any signs of violent treatment and that, while the women's vaginas did contain semen, it was "non-motile," or inactive, meaning that intercourse could not have taken place as recently as they had claimed. Nonetheless, after only three days, all nine youths were found guilty, and all but twelve-year-old Roy Wright were sentenced to death in the electric chair.

The Truth: Much to the surprise of Alabama officials, who were basking in the warm glow of their own civil rectitude—had they not, after all, prevented a lynching?—the verdicts were met with worldwide indignation. Thousands of letters arrived protesting the boys' innocence, including missives from such notables as John Dos Passos, Thomas Mann, and Albert Einstein. In Harlem, 300,000 blacks and whites marched in protest under banners bearing the slogan, "The Scottsboro Boys shall not die." The American Communist Party, seeing an opportunity to condemn "capitalist justice," vied with the National Association for the Advancement of Colored People (NAACP) to represent the youths in the appeal process. In November 1931 the U.S. Supreme Court ruled that the presiding judge's disdain for the defense had denied the youths due process, and overturned the convictions.

A second trial was scheduled; this time, however, the defense would be conducted by a crack legal team headed by Samuel Liebowitz, a noted criminal attorney from New York, who had been retained by the Communist Party's International Labor Defense wing (ILD). He obtained a change of venue to Decatur, Alabama. At the trial of Patterson, the first of the nine youths to be retried, the evidence presented heavily favored the defense. Dr. Bridges again testified that, in his opinion, the women had not been raped; a second doctor told Judge James Edward Horton in chambers that he knew the women were lying, but if he testified for the youths he'd "never be able to go back into Jackson County." Victoria Price was revealed to have spent time in jail for adultery and fornication, and to possess a rather considerable reputation as a woman of dubious morals. Liebowitz crowned his defense with two surprise witnesses: Lester Carter, a young white man who testified that he and a friend had had sex with the two "victims" the day before the "crime"; and Ruby Bates herself, who now corroborated Carter's testimony and testified that she and Price, fearful of being arrested for vagrancy, had fabricated the entire story. In response, the fire-and-brimstone prosecutor could only claim that Carter and Bates had been bribed and demand that justice not "be bought with Jew money from New York."

The all-white (and, presumably, all-Christian) jury again voted unanimously to convict on the first ballot. Judge Horton, however, noting the likelihood of perjured testimony, threw out the verdict, ordered a new trial, and then, under pressure from the Alabama attorney general, withdrew from the case. Patterson's third trial was presided over by Judge William W. Callahan, seventy, who disallowed testimony relating to Price's sexual activity the day before the alleged crime and told the jury that any sexual intercourse between a black man and a white woman constituted rape. First Patterson was again found guilty, and then Norris, but the U.S. Supreme Court once more overturned the convictions. The years 1936 and 1937 brought the final round of trials: Patterson was sentenced to seventy-five years, Andy Wright to ninety-nine years, Weems to seventy-five years, Powell to twenty years for assaulting a sheriff while in prison; Norris was again given a death sentence (which was later commuted to life imprisonment). Further appeals were denied. Charges against Williams, Montgomery, Roberson, and Roy Wright were dropped.

The five convicted men would each serve between six and thirteen additional years in prison. Charlie Weems was paroled in 1943. Norris and Andy Wright, released the following year, left Montgomery in violation of their parole and were reincarcerated for two years and four years, respectively. In 1948 Haywood Patterson escaped from prison and went north to Detroit. Andy Wright, the last of the nine to be released, was paroled in 1950, the same year Patterson, still a fugitive, was arrested by the FBI; the governor of Michigan, however, refused to extradite Patterson to Alabama. He was convicted of manslaughter the following year and died in a Michigan prison in 1952. In 1959 Roy Wright, who had been twelve years old when he began doing prison time, murdered his wife in a jealous fit and then committed suicide.

In 1976 NBC aired a docudrama on the Scottsboro case; Bates and Price sued the network, claiming that they had been unfairly cast as villains and, therefore, slandered. The suit was dismissed. Bates died later that year; Price would meet her maker in 1982.

In 1976 Clarence Norris, the only surviving "Scottsboro Boy," was officially exonerated; returning to Alabama to accept his pardon from Governor George Wallace, he was, as he wrote in his autobiography, Last of the Scottsboro Boys, "treated as a king." (The next year, however, the Alabama state legislature would reject a bill awarding him $10,000 as compensation for his twenty years in prison.) Questioned by reporters at the time of his pardon, Norris wept, thinking, he said, "of those eight other boys who grew to manhood in the penitentiary." Asked if he was bitter, he replied that he was not. "They had said I was a nobody, a dog, but I stood up and told the truth," he said. "I'm just so glad to be free." Norris succumbed to Alzheimer's disease in 1989 at the age of seventy-six.

—E.H.B.

JAMES RICHARDSON

The Crime: It was gruesome. On October 25, 1967, the seven children of James and Annie Mae Richardson suddenly began foaming at the mouth and writhing in pain. Six of the seven died within a couple of hours; the seventh, Diane, lived until the following morning. Those who went quickest were spared the agony of prolonged suffering.

It didn't take the authorities long to figure out the cause of death: poisoning by ingestion of parathion—a lethal agricultural insecticide. When De Soto County (Florida) sheriff Frank Cline went to the Richardson home, he was struck by the presence of a bitter metallic smell. "I smelled that poison. I smelled it twenty-five foot from the house. . . . I knew right away that it was parathion." The smell emanated from the lunch the Richardson kids had eaten that day: rice, beans, and grits all laced with insecticide. Cline searched the apartment and the shed behind the building but couldn't find the source of the poison that somehow had found its way into the lunch and from there into the bodies of the Richardson children.

While their children were dying, the Richardsons were picking fruit in a citrus grove about fourteen miles away. A neighbor, Betsy Reese, had come over to heat up and serve the meal that Annie Mae had prepared earlier. By the time the Richardsons could be located and brought to the hospital, six of their children had died. Richardson told reporters he didn't know why his children had died. "The sheriff better find out," he said. "That's his job."

The next morning, Betsy Reese reported that she had found a bag of parathion—enough poison to wipe out a city—in the shed behind the Richardson apartment. State prosecutor Frank Schaub thereupon charged James Richardson with premeditated murder.

The Accused: James Richardson was poor, black, and almost completely illiterate. He supported his family by working the citrus groves around Arcadia, Florida. He had fathered many children, four with Annie Mae. Two of his children from a previous marriage had died, one of dehydration and the other of an infection. James and Annie Mae were inseparable and to all appearances loving parents.

On the night before the children were poisoned, an insurance salesman had come, uninvited, to the Richardson home. He and James discussed a life insurance policy for the entire Richardson family, a policy that would pay $1,000 upon the death of any of them; the policy also provided a double indemnity payment in the event of sudden death. But James Richardson could not pay the $3.20 premium, and the salesman departed, leaving his card with figures scribbled on the back.

At Richardson's May 1968 trial, prosecutor Schaub insisted that the lure of collecting $14,000 had motivated the impoverished fruit picker to commit the most heinous mass murder in Florida history. No matter that there had never been a valid policy because no premium had been paid; Richardson, Schaub asserted, "understood that he was insured." Schaub also claimed that three convicts had heard Richardson confess while he was in prison. The state presented no evidence that linked James Richardson to the mysterious sack of parathion in the shed nor any evidence that he had put the insecticide into his children's lunch. Yet the jury of eleven men and one woman—all white—needed just eighty-five minutes to reach its verdict: guilty of first-degree murder with no recommendation for mercy. James Richardson would die in the electric chair.

The Truth: On April 25, 1989—nearly twenty-one years after he was sentenced to die—James Richardson walked out of the De Soto County courthouse a free man. His conviction had been thrown out. It had been obtained in the first place, according to special prosecutor Janet Reno, with the "knowing use of perjury." Reno obtained a sworn statement from one of the three convicts who had testified about Richardson's supposed confession that the convict had perjured himself. Her assistant accused Sheriff Cline of having made a deal with the three inmates whereby they would testify against Richardson in exchange for reduced sentences. Reno also blasted the prosecution and state investigators for suppressing evidence and for ignoring the obvious possibility that the real murderer was Betsy Reese.

Reese, it seems, was on parole at the time the Richardson children were poisoned, for having shot and killed her second husband. She was also suspected of having killed her first spouse, with poison. Her third husband, perhaps fearing what she might have in mind for him, had recently abandoned Betsy for another woman. And who was the other woman? James Richardson's cousin. In late 1986, Reese—suffering from early Alzheimer's and confined to a nursing home—confessed. A nursing home employee who suspected Reese was the murderer asked: "Did you kill those kids, Betsy?" "Yeah, I did that," Reese responded.

Not everyone was convinced that James Richardson had been subjected to one of the worst injustices in American history, however. When Richardson's lawyers sued Frank Schaub for $35 million, the state of Florida hired former U.S. attorney Robert Merkle as an expert witness to help defend him. Merkle claimed that Betsy Reese might not have put poison in the food of the Richardson children because parathion was also found in flour and other items kept in a locked refrigerator. Merkle also denied that Richardson's three former cellmates had cut a deal to testify against him. Meanwhile, James Richardson—who divorced Annie Mae and married an English teacher—remained unemployed and waiting for a promised movie deal about his life.

—J.L.K.

20 UNDERWORLD NICKNAMES

1. FRANK "THE DASHER" ABBANDANDO
A prolific hit man for Murder, Inc.—organized crime's enforcement arm in the 1930s—and with some fifty killings to his credit, Frank Abbandando once approached a longshoreman on whom there was a "contract." Abbandando fired directly into his victim's face, only to have the weapon misfire. The chagrined executioner dashed off, circling the block so fast that he came up behind his slowly pursuing target, and this time Abbandando managed to shoot him dead, picking up his moniker in the process.

2. TONY "JOE BATTERS" ACCARDO
Until his death in 1992, tough Tony Accardo, a Chicago syndicate boss since the 1930s, was still called Joe Batters, harkening back to his earlier days of proficiency with a baseball bat when he was one of Al Capone's most dedicated sluggers. He was also known as "Big Tuna" after he was photographed with a 400-pound tuna.

3. JOSEPH "HA HA" AIUPPA
An old-time Capone muscle man, Joseph Aiuppa, operating from a prison cell, was still

in 1995 the Mafia boss of Cicero, Illinois, and—according to some law-enforcement officials—the top man in the Chicago mob. Because he is a notorious scowler not given to smiling, he is called Ha Ha.

4. ISRAEL "ICEPICK WILLIE" ALDERMAN
This Minneapolis gangster liked to brag about the grotesque murder method that earned him his nickname. Israel Alderman (also known as Little Auldie and Izzy Lump Lump) ran a second-story speakeasy where he claimed to have committed eleven murders. In each case he deftly pressed an icepick through his victim's eardrum into the brain; his quick technique made it appear that the dead man had merely slumped in a drunken heap on the bar. Icepick Willie would laughingly chide the corpse as he dragged it to a back room, where he dumped the body down a coal chute leading to a truck in the alley below.

5. LOUIS "PRETTY" AMBERG
Louis Amberg, the underworld terror of Brooklyn from the 1920s to 1935—when he was finally rubbed out—was called Pretty because he may well have been the ugliest gangster who ever lived. Immortalized by Damon Runyon in several stories as the gangster who stuffed his victims into laundry bags, Amberg was approached when he was twenty by Ringling Brothers Circus, who wanted him to appear as the missing link. Pretty turned the job down but often bragged about the offer afterward.

6. MICHAEL "UMBRELLA MIKE" BOYLE
Business agent of the mob-dominated electrical workers union in Chicago in the 1920s, Michael J. Boyle gained the title of Umbrella Mike because of his practice of standing at a bar on certain days of the week with an unfurled umbrella. Building contractors deposited cash levies into this receptacle and then magically were not beset by labor difficulties.

7. LOUIS "LEPKE" BUCHALTER
Louis Buchalter—who died in the electric chair in 1944—was the head of Murder, Inc. He was better known as Lepke, a form of "Lepkeleh." This was the affectionate Yiddish diminutive, meaning "Little Louis," that his mother had used. Affectionate, Lepke was not. As one associate once said, "Lep loves to hurt people."

8. "SCARFACE" AL CAPONE
Al Capone claimed that the huge scar on his cheek was from a World War I wound suffered while fighting with the Lost Battalion in France, but actually he was never in the service. He had been knifed while working as a bouncer in a Brooklyn saloon-brothel by a hoodlum named Frank Galluccio during a dispute over a woman.

"Scarface" Al Capone.

Capone once visited the editorial offices of Hearst's *Chicago American* and convinced that paper to stop referring to him as Scarface.

9. VINCENT "MAD DOG" COLL
Vincent "Mad Dog" Coll was feared by police and rival gangsters alike in the early 1930s because of his utter disregard for human life. Once he shot down several children at play while trying to get an underworld foe. When he was trapped in a phone booth and riddled with bullets in 1932, no one cried over his death, and police made little effort to solve the crime.

10. JOSEPH "JOE ADONIS" DOTO
Racket boss Joseph Doto adopted the name Joe Adonis because he considered his looks the equal of Aphrodite's famous lover.

11. CHARLES "PRETTY BOY" FLOYD
Public enemy Charles Arthur Floyd hated his nickname, which was used by prostitutes of the Midwest whorehouses he patronized, and in fact he killed at least two gangsters for repeatedly calling him Pretty Boy. When he was shot down by FBI agents in 1934, he refused to identify himself as Pretty Boy Floyd and with his dying breath snarled, "I'm Charles Arthur Floyd!"

12. CHARLIE "MONKEY FACE" GENKER

For several decades after the turn of the century a mainstay of the Chicago brothel world, Charlie "Monkey Face" Genker achieved his moniker not simply for a countenance lacking in beauty but also for his actions while employed by Mike "de Pike" Heitler (a piker because he ran a fifty-cent house). Monkey Face matched the bounciness of his jungle cousins by scampering up doors and peeking over the transoms to get the girls and their customers to speed things up.

13. JAKE "GREASY THUMB" GUZIK

A longtime devoted aide to Al Capone, Jake Guzik continued until his death in 1956 to be the payoff man to the politicians and police for the Chicago mob. He often complained that he handled so much money he could not get the inky grease off his thumb. This explanation of the "Greasy Thumb" sobriquet was such an embarrassment to the police that they concocted their own story, maintaining that Jake had once worked as a waiter and gained his nickname because he constantly stuck his thumb in the soup bowls.

14. "GOLF BAG" SAM HUNT

Notorious Capone mob enforcer "Golf Bag" Sam Hunt was so called because he lugged automatic weapons about in his golf bag to conceal them when on murder missions.

15. ALVIN "CREEPY" KARPIS

Bank robber Alvin Karpis was tabbed "Creepy" by fellow prison inmates in the 1920s because of his sallow, dour-faced looks. By the time he became public enemy number 1 in 1935, Karpis's face had become even creepier, thanks to a botched plastic-surgery job that was supposed to alter his appearance.

16. GEORGE "MACHINE GUN" KELLY

Somehow a blundering bootlegger named George R. Kelly became the feared public enemy Machine Gun Kelly of the 1930s. His criminally ambitious wife, Kathryn, forced him to practice with the machine gun she gave him as a birthday present, while she built up his reputation with other criminals. However, Kelly was not a murderer, nor did he ever fire his weapon in anger with intent to kill.

17. CHARLES "LUCKY" LUCIANO

Charles Luciano earned his "Lucky" when he was taken for a ride and came back alive, although a knife wound gave him a permanently drooping right eye. Luciano told many stories over the years about the identity of his abductors—two different criminal gangs were mentioned as well as the police, who were trying to find out about an impending drug shipment, but the most likely version is that he was tortured and mutilated by the family of a cop whose daughter he had seduced. Luciano parlayed his misfortune into a public-relations coup, since he was the one and only underworld figure lucky enough to return alive after being taken for a ride.

18. THOMAS "BUTTERFINGERS" MORAN

The acknowledged king of the pickpockets of the twentieth century, Thomas "Butterfingers" Moran picked his first pocket during the 1905 San Francisco earthquake and his last in 1970 at seventy-eight, some 50,000 pockets in all. He could, other practitioners acknowledged rather jealously, "slide in and out of a pocket like pure butter."

19. LESTER "BABY FACE" NELSON

The most pathological public enemy of the 1930s, Lester Gillis considered his own name nonmacho and came up with "Big George" Nelson instead—a ridiculous alias considering the fact that he was just five feet four inches tall. He was called Baby Face Nelson behind his back and by the press, which constantly enraged him.

20. BENJAMIN "BUGSY" SIEGEL

Alternately the most charming and the most vicious of all syndicate killers, Benjamin Siegel could thus be described as being "bugs." However, no one called him Bugsy to his face, since it caused him to fly into a murderous rage. His mistress, Virginia Hall, likewise clobbered newsmen who called her man by this offensive sobriquet.

—C.S.

GREAT THEFTS

THE *MONA LISA*

On the morning of August 21, 1911, a short, gentle man with dark hair and a thick mustache nonchalantly walked empty-handed into the Louvre, cruised through its massive galleries (225 in all), and headed straight for the lady who, with her mysterious and alluring smile, has intrigued the art world ever since she was painted by Leonardo da Vinci's hands in the first decade of the sixteenth century.

Soon the man stood directly in front of the lady, alone with the precious *La Gioconda*, also known as the *Mona Lisa*. He removed her from the four wall hooks, concealed her in the darkness of his white smock, and, within twenty minutes, walked through a door leading to the outside of the museum. He had escaped with the world's most famous painting. As easy as that.

That same morning, Louis Beroud, a painter, set his easel in the Salon Carre in front of the Mona Lisa's empty space, a spot he knew all too well, having painted La Gioconda many times before. He was about to begin painting a portrait of his model primping and powdering, using the Mona Lisa's protective glass case as her mirror. Suddenly Beroud noticed something was terribly wrong. He looked at the empty space, her space, and quickly asked a guard, "Where is La Gioconda?"

Copies of portraits such as the Mona Lisa were often made in the photography room within the museum, and the guard replied that that was where she was. However, after three hours of waiting, Beroud's suspicions and impatience grew and he asked the guard to search out the painting. Minutes later the guard returned, empty-handed, with the startling announcement that the Mona Lisa was gone.

Within hours Parisians and the rest of the world were amazed that someone would actually steal one of the greatest symbols of the high Renaissance. Certainly the thief wouldn't plan on selling the masterpiece (in 1911 the Mona Lisa was estimated to be worth five million dollars; today it is priceless), for fear of getting caught, and it was believed that even the most demanding of art collectors wouldn't purchase the original Mona Lisa for fear of the same. For these reasons French police ruled out professional art thieves.

The public quickly painted their own theories. Some believed the theft was that of a joker who hid the work inside the Louvre, and it was just a matter of time before someone would happen upon it. Patriots of France believed the Germans stole the painting in a plot to humiliate France politically. Whatever the case, Parisians refused to believe the Mona Lisa's absence was forever.

It took a week for investigators to search thoroughly the five miles of corridors in the museum, since the guards believed nobody could have escaped with the 38¼-by-21-inch panel on which da Vinci painted Madonna Lisa del Gioconda.

Finding the gilt frame thrown on top of the staircase the thief used for his escape, investigators were at once convinced the Mona Lisa was stolen. The Louvre's priceless prize had been lifted.

As months passed, Parisians feared that the portrait, which was commissioned by Francis I of France, who paid da Vinci 4,000 gold florins for the masterpiece and then hung it in his bathroom, would never be seen again.

For the next two years investigators hunted, searched, and followed empty clues. The Mona Lisa was nowhere to be found.

But on November 29, 1913, Alfredo Geri, a wealthy Italian art dealer, received a letter addressed from Paris. Geri read the letter carefully, shocked at its contents. The writer, who called himself "Leonard," said he had the Mona Lisa and that, for a price, he would return the lady to the country where she belonged, Italy. Although Geri was skeptical of what the writer had to say, it was too intriguing not to follow up on "Leonard" to see if he spoke the truth. Inviting "Leonard" to Florence to allow him to inspect the painting, Geri couldn't help wondering if he was wasting his time on some lunatic who enjoyed joking at the missing Mona Lisa's expense.

On December 10, 1913, Geri, along with Giovanni Poggi, director of the Uffizi Gallery in Florence, received their answer. "Leonard" led the two men to the Tripoli-Italia Hotel. It was there on the third floor that "Leonard" removed from under the bed a hat, a pair of pliers, a smock, paintbrushes, plastering tools, and finally an object wrapped in red silk. He placed the object on the bed as Geri and Poggi stood in wide-eyed anticipation. Silence. And suddenly the Mona Lisa was before them. Poggi immediately examined it and concluded that it was, indeed, the original da Vinci.

Covering the Mona Lisa with the red silk, the three men took the painting to the Uffizi Gallery for a short stay, where thousands toured the gallery for a glimpse of La Gioconda, until she was later returned to the Louvre. She was unharmed, except for two tiny scratches that were apparently made when the thief rolled the Mona Lisa into his tool box.

Before La Gioconda was safely home again, however, police surrounded the hotel room where "Leonard" waited to accept his reward for returning the Mona Lisa. Instead, he was surprised to find authorities arresting him.

Soon the world learned that "Leonard" was really Vincenzo Peruggia, an Italian born in the small village of Dumenza, in northern Italy.

When Peruggia was taken to jail, inspectors asked the inevitable question: Why did he take the Mona Lisa? At his trial, while hundreds packed the courtroom in Florence on June 14, 1914, Peruggia explained that he stole the Mona Lisa because he wanted to set right the path of Italy, and to seek vengeance on Napoléon Bonaparte.

A housepainter by trade, Peruggia told the art world that he first laid his eyes on the Mona Lisa in 1908 and then in 1909 when he was employed at the Louvre. He said her alluring smile compelled him to steal her away from France and return her to Italy, where she belonged.

However, prosecutors said Peruggia had previously been arrested in Mâcon, France, for attempted robbery and illegal possession of firearms. With his prior convictions it was difficult for Peruggia to prove his patriotic motives.

In fact, police found Peruggia's diary, which contained the names of several art dealers and collectors in the United States and Italy, such as Andrew Carnegie, J. P. Morgan, and Alfredo Geri. The list was made ten months prior to the theft, which led prosecutors to believe that Peruggia planned to sell the painting.

When asked how he justified selling *La Gioconda* if he loved her so much, Peruggia replied that he needed to escape her haunting smile—a smile, Peruggia went on to say, that he stared at every night in his small room, while falling in love with her.

Although the prosecution asked for a three-year sentence, Peruggia was sentenced to one year and fifteen days. He served only seven months.

Moving back to his hometown, Peruggia married, served in the Italian army during World War I, then moved to Paris, opening a hardware store. He died in 1927, still considering himself one of Italy's greatest heroes.

—R.S.S.

THE BRINKS ROBBERY

Regarded to this day as "the almost perfect crime," the Great Brinks Robbery took place on a winter's night in 1950. It was an act, however, that had been two years in the making. Designed as if it were a top-secret military mission and choreographed like an intricate ballet, the Brinks Robbery was also cast, costumed, and rehearsed as if it were a grandly staged play set to open on Broadway.

Eleven men worked together to perpetrate the theft of more than $2 million in cash, coin, money orders, and securities from the Brinks Armored Car depot in Boston, Massachusetts. Their vision and their execution of this daring heist were so spectacular that even taciturn, grim-jawed law-enforcement officials were prompted to exclaim publicly what a remarkable job the gang of thieves had done. Not only had they dared to strike a nearly unthinkable target, they also came within a few days of outlasting the statute of limitations and getting away with what many have termed the crime of the century.

It all began when Tony Pino, a Boston area con, happened to discover that the Brinks depot was a much less secure building than one would ordinarily imagine such a place to be. Inspired by its vulnerability and the prodigious amount of money held within it, Pino enlisted a bar owner named Big Joe McGinnis to help him assemble a group of nine other men for the venture. While all the men had criminal backgrounds, three men were picked especially for their particular skills—two were expert getaway drivers; one was a master locksmith. Pino's master plan called for long-term preparations.

For eighteen successive months, the gang watched the depot. Their surveillance was a round-the-clock operation. Logs of shipment arrivals and departures were kept and studied so that the thieves could ascertain the times when the depot would be holding its maximum amount of money.

The gang systematically entered the depot to remove, one by one, five locks that secured doors between the outside of the building and the location where the money was kept. They made keys for the five locks and then replaced them before anyone discovered what was going on. They burglarized the American District Telegraphy Company's offices in order to steal and study the file holding the Brinks alarm system's schematics, then returned it without anyone's realizing it was missing.

As thorough as the gang's labors were, Pino insisted on even more intricate preparations. His exacting standards called for a team of seven men actually to enter the depot and steal the money. The seven were chosen for their physical similarities: each was about five feet ten inches tall and weighed between 170 and 180 pounds. Each was allotted an identical wardrobe for the robbery—matching Navy pea coats, gloves, rubber-soled shoes, and Halloween masks.

Rehearsals for the robbery were held repeatedly to ensure that no mistakes would be made when the crime was committed for real. Pino eventually settled on the date of January 17, 1950, as the time to strike. The team of seven thieves entered the building just prior to 7:00 P.M. While they made their way into the depot, treading quietly up its stairs and down its hallways, passing through the five locked doors to which they held keys, one of their compatriots stood on a nearby rooftop and monitored the streets, using binoculars and a telescope, for any sign of police and/or guards. While these eight men did their work, two others waited for them in a getaway truck parked nearby. McGinnis, the eleventh, would join them later.

The team of seven reached the Brinks counting room at 7:10 P.M. A locked, wire-mesh door, to which they had no key, stood between them and six Brinks employees—the head cashier and five guards. Only one of the guards was carrying his weapon, the others had them stored in the close-by gun rack. The thieves announced their intention to rob the Brinks vault and ordered the wire-mesh door to be opened. The armed guard heeded their command without drawing his gun. The robbers entered and directed the Brinks men to lie facedown on the floor with their arms behind their backs. Three of the thieves then went to work binding the men and securing their mouths shut with adhesive tape while the other four began collecting the loot in a bucket-brigade manner.

One thief would pull the booty off a shelf and dump it into a canvas bag held open by another thief. Once a bag was filled, its holder would pass it to another and he to another. Fourteen canvas sacks, weighing a total of 1,200 pounds, were filled and dragged away from the scene by 7:27 P.M. Less than a half hour had elapsed since the thieves had begun their work.

After stashing the loot in the back of the truck, they all took off with what amounted, at that time, to the biggest cash haul in the history of American crime. Their take added up to $1,218,211.29 in cash and coin, $1,557,183.33 in checks and money orders.

The truck was driven to the home of one of the gang members in a Boston suburb. McGinnis joined them there to help count the loot—it would be his job to destroy the negotiable securities and $90,000 in new bills that they suspected of being marked. Agreeing to leave the money where they stashed it until attention sure to be generated by the heist had died down, the men departed and resumed the lives they had been leading prior to January 17, 1950.

Most of them, along with scores of other Boston-area men with prison records, were questioned by local and state police as well as by the FBI. Each was released after being questioned, and a month later they all re-grouped at the house where they had secreted the money and split the take into individual shares of about $100,000 per man. One of them, named "Specs" O'Keefe, left $90,000 of his share with another gang member to hold for him, as he was headed to jail after being convicted of another, unrelated crime.

The law-enforcement agencies investigated intensely, but Pino's precisely laid and executed plans caused them to wind up with only three pieces of negligible evidence: a cap whose label had been removed, and two pieces of cotton string.

The culprits, who had pledged to stay out of trouble for six years (the length of the statute of limitations), went unapprehended as months and then years passed. Their downfall started when O'Keefe began worrying about the likelihood of ever receiving his share. Afraid that O'Keefe would turn against them, an assassin named Trigger Burke was hired to kill him. Burke went after O'Keefe with a machine gun, and its bullets hit their intended target in the arm and chest. O'Keefe, however, survived his wounds and Burke was caught by the police. O'Keefe, agreeing to testify against the others in return for leniency, implicated his partners, and eight of the thieves were captured, convicted, and given sentences of life imprisonment. The robbery, which resulted in a loss of more than $2 million, wound up costing the FBI $25 million to investigate, and only a small portion of the stolen funds was ever recovered.

—R.N.K.

> What is robbing a bank compared with founding a bank?
>
> Bertolt Brecht, *Dreigroschenoper* (Threepenny Opera), 1928

> Thieves respect property; they merely wish the property to become their property that they may more perfectly respect it.
>
> G. K. Chesterton, *The Man Who Was Thursday*, 1908

THE GREAT TRAIN ROBBERY

Keeping to its secret, unpublished schedule, a Royal Mail train carrying seventy-five postal workers and $7.3 million left Glasgow, Scotland, for London, England, on August 8, 1963. It was carrying mail and surplus cash from banks in Scotland and northern England on an all-night run when a gang of men intent on relieving it of its precious cargo went to work in the English countryside. They methodically cut telephone lines in the vicinity of Cheddington, thirty-six miles northwest of London. They also tampered with the railway signals, faking a yellow light so that the train's engineer would respond by slowing down, and faking a red light that directed him to stop the train completely. The diesel engine, pulling twelve cars behind it, came to a stop in the dark at 3:00 A.M. Fifteen men, all of them masked and several of them armed, then ambushed the mail train. They immediately uncoupled the diesel and the two cars directly behind it from the rest of the train. These two cars, as they had been told, held money and not mail. They also knew that the seventy-five postal workers, all unarmed, were at work in the rear cars.

After the uncoupling, the ambushers handcuffed the coengineer and slugged the engineer so as to force him to drive the shortened train for about a mile up the track toward the bridge by Sears Crossing. Waiting beneath that bridge were a couple of Land Rovers and a truck painted so as to appear to be a military vehicle. With fast-paced efficiency, the gang off-loaded 120 sacks of loot, totaling two tons, into the Land Rovers and the truck.

While the thieves worked, the seventy-five postal workers left behind had yet to realize what was taking place. Most figured that the engine had broken down. But as time passed, some exited their coaches and discovered that the first two cars and the engine were gone. As the thieves drove away with their stolen property, the postal workers ran off to search for a phone to contact the police—only to discover that they couldn't get through. Forty-five minutes passed from the time the train had been stopped until the police were finally alerted to the situation. Meanwhile, dawn was nearly breaking as the thieves, driving with lights dimmed, approached the rural hideout they had previously set up at a five-acre property called Leatherslade Farm.

Once inside the farmhouse, the money was counted up, and the robbers reveled in celebration of the huge haul they had brought in. Their plan was to remain at Leatherslade Farm for several days while waiting for the expected furor over the robbery to die down. They had all agreed to maintain strict vigilance about leaving clues and evidence at Leatherslade so as not to compromise their security. Gloves were to be worn at all times and a clean-up worker had been designated to eliminate any sign that the farmhouse had been occupied by the criminals once they had departed.

They changed their plan of remaining at the farm when they heard a radio broadcast that reported that the police intended to search every place within a thirty-mile radius of the looted train. Leatherslade was twenty-six miles from the scene of the crime. The gang split up, its members returning to their families or to sanctuaries provided by friends. However, they had not been as meticulous after the robbery as they had been during it. Fingerprints were left everywhere and the worker who was supposed to ensure its cleanliness never did the job.

The gang's leaders, fearful of having left evidence in their wake, made a hasty decision to return to the farm and burn it down. The idea was just as quickly aborted, however, after the thieves tuned in to a police radio transmission concerning a herdsman who had seen the men at the farm and was tipping the police to the fact.

Leatherslade Farm was soon being combed by detectives, who found fingerprints all over the place. While police pursued the trails of those to whom the prints belonged, Scotland Yard began an exhaustive search for the money.

A dozen of the train robbers were apprehended over the following few months and were brought to trial. After sixty-seven days in court, all were found guilty on April 16, 1964. Seven of them received thirty-year sentences for their roles in the crime. Two robbers were given twenty-five-year terms. A tenth member of the

Notorious train robber and escapee Ronald Biggs poses with his son Michael in Rio de Janeiro in December 1993. Michael is wearing one of the T-shirts his father sells to tourists who also pay to have lunch with him.

gang was handed down a twenty-four-year sentence, and an eleventh thief was sent away for twenty years; the twelfth received three years in jail. Three men involved in the Great Train Robbery were never caught.

The saga didn't end with these convictions, however. Gang leader Charles Wilson escaped from Green Prison in August 1964, and wasn't caught until July of 1968, when authorities nabbed him in Montreal, Canada. He was released from prison in 1979, and was murdered gangland style in 1990 in Marbella, Spain.

Another gang member, Ronald Biggs, also escaped: he broke out of Wandsworth Prison on July 8, 1965. Biggs, who remains a free man, now lives in Brazil, where he has waged a constant battle against extradition and has become a minor celebrity. He is the only apprehended gang member who still has a prison term to face.

The rest of the surviving men caught were released by the mid-seventies; a few had died while in custody. Only about a tenth of the money was ever recouped despite huge rewards offered for information leading to the discovery of its whereabouts.

—R.N.K.

16 STUPID THIEVES
(AND 3 DISHONORABLE MENTIONS)

1. JUST REWARDS

Every night Mrs. Hollis Sharpe of Los Angeles took her miniature poodle, Jonathan, out for a walk so that he could do his duty. A responsible and considerate citizen, Mrs. Sharpe always brought with her a newspaper and plastic bag to clean up after Jonathan. "You have to think of

your neighbors," she explained. On the night of November 13, 1974, Jonathan had finished his business and Mrs. Sharpe was walking home with the bag in her right hand when a mugger attacked her from behind, shoved her to the ground, grabbed her plastic bag, jumped into a car, and drove off with the spoils of his crime.

Mrs. Sharpe suffered a broken arm but remained good-humored about the incident. "I only wish there had been a little more in the bag," she said.

2. SELF-INFLICTED CAPITAL PUNISHMENT
On August 7, 1975, John Anthony Gibbs, described by witnesses as "very nervous," entered a restaurant in Newport, Rhode Island, flashed a gun, and demanded cash. After collecting $400, he put the money in a bag and tried to stuff the bag into his shirt pocket. Unfortunately, he was holding his gun in the same hand as the bag. The gun went off under his chin and Gibbs, twenty-two, was killed instantly.

3. A MINOR DETAIL
Edward McAlea put on a stocking mask, burst into a jewelry store in Liverpool, and pointed a revolver at the three men inside. "This is a stickup," he said. "Get down." None of them did, since all of them noticed the red plastic stopper in the muzzle of McAlea's toy gun. After a brief scuffle, McAlea escaped, but not before he had pulled off his mask. The jeweler recognized him as a customer from the day before, and McAlea was apprehended.

4. WHO WAS THAT MASKED MAN?
Clive Bunyan ran into a store in Cayton, near Scarborough, England, and forced the shop assistant to give him the £157 in the till. Then he made his getaway on his motorbike. To hide his identity, Bunyan had worn his full-face crash helmet as a mask. It was a smooth and successful heist, except for one detail. He had forgotten that across his helmet, in inch-high letters, were the words "Clive Bunyan—Driver." Bunyan was arrested and ordered to pay for his crime by doing 200 hours of community service.

5. THE WORST LAWYER
Twenty-five-year-old Marshall George Cummings Jr. of Tulsa, Oklahoma, was charged with attempted robbery in connection with a purse snatching at a shopping center on October 14, 1976. During the trial the following January, Cummings chose to act as his own attorney. While cross-examining the victim, Cummings asked, "Did you get a good look at my face when I took your purse?" Cummings later decided to turn over his defense to a public defender, but it was too late. He was convicted and sentenced to ten years in prison.

6. BELATED COVER-UP
Gregory Lee Cornwell had everything in order when he planned to rob the Continental Bank in Prospect Park, Pennsylvania, in 1978: a car for the getaway, a ski mask to conceal his identity, an army knapsack for the money, and a sawed-off shotgun to show he was serious. On August 23 he parked his car in front of the bank and went inside. Displaying his shotgun, he threw the knapsack on the counter and demanded money. Then he put on his mask. Although he managed to leave the bank with $8,100, Cornwell was apprehended quickly and was easily identified.

7. CHECKING OUT
Eighteen-year-old Charles A. Meriweather broke into a home in northwest Baltimore on the night of November 22–23, 1978, raped the woman who lived there, and then ransacked the house. When he discovered that she had only $11.50 in cash, he asked her, "How do you pay your bills?"

She replied, "By check," and he ordered her to write out a check for thirty dollars. Then he changed his mind and upped it to fifty dollars.

"Who shall I make it out to?" asked the woman, a thirty-four-year-old government employee.

"Charles A. Meriweather," said Charles A. Meriweather, adding, "It better not bounce or I'll be back."

Meriweather was arrested several hours later.

8. THE WELD-PLANNED ROBBERY
On the night of August 23–24, 1980, a well-organized gang of thieves began their raid on the safe of the leisure-center office in Chichester, Sussex, by stealing a speedboat. To avoid making loud noise they used water skis to paddle across a lake, then picked up their equipment and paddled on to the office. However, what they thought were cutting tools turned out to be welding gear, and they soon managed to seal the safe completely shut. The next morning it took the office staff an hour to hammer and chisel the safe open again.

9. BURGLARY BY THE NUMBER
Terry Johnson had no trouble identifying the two men who burglarized her Chicago apartment at 2:30 A.M. on August 17, 1981. All she had to do was write down the number of the police badge that one of them was wearing and the identity number on the fender of their squad car. The two officers—Stephen Webster, thirty-three, and Tyrone Pickens, thirty-two—had actually committed the crime in full uniform, while on duty, using police department tools.

10. A PETTY THIEF
Things didn't work out quite the way Clay Weaver had planned on the night of February 16,

1982. The nineteen-year-old entered Hutchinson's Fine Foods in West Valley City, Utah, at 9:00 P.M., intending to rob the store. He waved a gun at the clerk, who laughed because she thought it was a toy. The gun was quite small, but it was in fact real—a two-bullet derringer. Weaver cocked the gun, but the bullets dribbled out onto the counter. Weaver then fled but got into an argument with his accomplice, Gary Hendrikson, who pushed Weaver away and drove off without him. Finally he was chased down and hauled back to Hutchinson's by two store employees who happened to be members of the high-school wrestling team. Weaver later confessed to fourteen other robberies he had miraculously managed to commit.

11. DOUBLE-SEXED FORGER
Houston pawnbroker Ted Kipperman knew something was wrong when a man entered his store on April 8, 1982, and attempted to cash a $789 tax-refund check, claiming his name was "Earnestine and Robert Hayes." Noting that the check was made out to two parties, Kipperman asked the customer for identification, whereupon the man produced an ID card with the name "Earnestine and Robert Hayes." He explained that his mother had expected twins. When only one child showed up, she gave him both names. Kipperman took the stolen check and the makeshift ID and then told the man that the police had just come by looking for the check, which caused the would-be customer to flee. Kipperman located the real Earnestine and Robert Hayes, a couple who lived in southeastern Houston, and gave them back their tax-refund check.

12. BIG MOUTH
Dennis Newton was on trial for armed robbery in Oklahoma City. Assistant District Attorney Larry Jones asked one of the witnesses, the supervisor of the store that had been robbed, to identify the robber. When she pointed to the defendant, Newton jumped to his feet, accused the witness of lying, and said, "I should have blown your – – – – head off!" After a moment of stunned silence, he added, "If I'd been the one that was there." On November 1, 1985, Newton was sentenced to thirty years in prison.

13. PENNYWISE, DOLLAR DUMB
On January 6, 1990, David Posman lured an armored car driver away from his truck in Providence, Rhode Island. Posman knocked him on the head with a bottle, then ran back to the truck and grabbed four thirty-pound bags of loot and staggered away. The weight of the bags greatly slowed his escape and police had little trouble capturing him in a nearby parking garage. The bags all contained pennies.

14. SAFE AT LAST
On the night of June 12, 1991, John Meacham, Joseph Plante, and Joe Laattsch were burgling a soon-to-be demolished bank building in West Covina, California, when Meacham came upon an empty vault. He called over his accomplices and invited them inside to check out the acoustics. Then he closed the vault door so they could appreciate the full effect. Unfortunately, the door locked. Meacham spent forty minutes trying to open it, without success. Finally he called the fire department, who called the police. After seven hours, a concrete sawing firm was able to free the locked-up robbers, after which they were transported to another building they couldn't get out of.

15. MOST PHOTOGENIC
Vernon Brooks, thirty-four, thought he was being a clever thief when he robbed a Radio Shack in Raleigh, North Carolina, on July 9, 1992. Before leaving the store, he disconnected the video surveillance camera and took it with him. However, he forgot to take the recorder to which the camera had been connected. Police found a perfect full-face shot of Brooks on the tape and had little difficulty identifying him. After he was released from jail, Brooks was again captured on film by a surveillance camera, this time while robbing a grocery store.

16. TOO HEAVY TO HEIST
In the early-morning hours of April 8, 1993, twenty-one-year-old Michael Foster and a seventeen-year-old companion broke into a tavern in Monroe County, Wisconsin, and hauled away a seven-foot-tall electronic dart machine. They managed to load the enormous game into the back of their pickup truck, but the machine was so heavy that when they tried to drive away, the truck sank into the mud in the tavern's parking lot. Unable to extract it, Foster and his friend decided they needed a tow. So they called the local sheriff's department, who towed the truck—and arrested them.

DISHONORABLE MENTION

1. STUPID DRUG DEALER
Alfred Acree Jr. was sitting in a van in Charles City, Virginia, on April 7, 1993, with three friends and at least thirty small bags of cocaine. When sheriff's deputies surrounded the van, Acree raced into a dark, wooded area by the side of the road. He weaved in and out of the trees in an attempt to evade his pursuers. He thought he had done a pretty good job—and was amazed when the deputies caught him (and found $800 worth of cocaine in his pockets). What Acree had forgotten was that he was wearing L.A. Tech sneakers that sent out a red

light every time they struck the ground. While Acree was tiring himself zigzagging through the forest, the sheriffs were calmly following the blinking red lights.

2. STUPID TERRORIST
In early 1994 an Islamic fundamentalist group in Jordan launched a terrorist campaign that included attacks against secular sites such as video stores and supermarkets that sold liquor. During the late morning of February 1, Eid Saleh al Jahaleen entered the Salwa Cinema in the city of Zarqa. The cinema was showing soft-core pornographic films from Turkey. Jahaleen, who was apparently paid fifty dollars to plant a bomb, had never seen soft-core porn and became entranced. When the bomb went off, he was still in his seat. Jahaleen lost both legs in the explosion.

3. STUPID MURDERER
In 1981 Gerald Voyles was one of three people charged with shooting two men, wrapping their bodies in wire fencing, weighting them with concrete blocks, and dumping them in a pond. Voyles's accomplices were finally arrested in 1993 and a $3,000 reward was offered for information leading to Voyles's capture. On March 7, 1995, Voyles walked up to the information window at the Polk County jail in Florida, gave his name, and tried to collect the award. He did not get the money, but he was arrested immediately.

—D.W.

FORGERS

THOMAS JAMES WISE
The entry for Thomas James Wise in *The Dictionary of National Biography* published in London for the years 1931 to 1940 begins "Book collector, bibliographer, editor, and forger."

When asked on his deathbed to finally confess to everything he had done, he replied, "It's all too complicated to go into now."

It started simply enough, with a young man working in London in the "essential oils" business. With every spare pound, he indulged his passion for collecting rare English literature. For many years he didn't make enough at his job to buy what he wanted, so, early on, he began his career as a forger.

He started by buying incomplete copies of rare books and filling them out with pages he stole from copies in the British Museum, later forging copies of pamphlets no one had ever heard of until he, as an increasingly trusted expert, listed them in a bibliography.

Eventually he was betrayed by discrepancies in typeface and by the fact that the paper in certain of the forged items contained traces of esparto grass, which was not used in paper making until years later.

When he was found out in 1934, he blamed the phony pamphlets on deceased bibliophiles, and when that didn't work he retreated into obstinate silence. He died, embittered and disgraced, in 1937.

JEAN DE SPERATI
Jean de Sperati (1884–1957) has been called the best forger of rare stamps of the twentieth century, but of course it is more accurate to refer to him as the best of those who didn't get away with it. The best forgers are the ones who never get caught.

Actually, de Sperati worked in a murky area of legality, because he apparently always sold his forgeries as fakes. The problem came because he signed them on the back only in faint, soft pencil, probably knowing that some of his customers would erase his name and the stamps would enter the philatelic marketplace as genuine.

The master faker fell afoul of the law in an oddly similar way to the art forger Elmyr de Hory. De Sperati was caught trying to smuggle a batch of his stamps out of France during World War II, which broke the law against the exportation of capital from the country. To acquit himself of this serious charge and be convicted only of the lesser offense of forgery, he produced identical fakes for the authorities.

At seventy, with his eyesight failing, he sold his stock of bogus stamps and all his trade secrets to the British Philatelic Association. His "genuine fakes" have, ever since, brought relatively high prices at auction.

HANS VAN MEERGEREN
In an ironic twist of fate, Hans Van Meergeren had to confess to being an art forger in order to save his life.

Born in 1889, Van Meergeren was a painter whose work was, at best, mediocre until he hit upon the idea of perpetrating one of the most audacious and successful art frauds ever. He began to forge the work of the great Dutch painter Vermeer (1632–75).

His first knock-off Vermeer, *Christ at Emmaus*, sold for $250,000. During World War II Van Meergeren painted and sold five more "Vermeers," one to Nazi bigwig Hermann Göring, for $265,000.

Brought up on charges of collaboration after the war, he was accused of selling a Dutch "national treasure," the bogus painting he'd palmed off on Göring. The sentence, if he was found guilty, was death by firing squad.

If the authorities supplied him with paints and canvas, he could, he claimed, create another "Vermeer" in his jail cell. He succeeded in convincing the judge he was only a lowly, if immensely talented, art forger. The sentence, instead of death, was a year in jail.

He died of a heart attack at age fifty-seven, before he could begin to serve his sentence.

ELMYR DE HORY

One of the greatest and most prolific art forgers of all time, Elmyr de Hory was not only a master counterfeiter of great paintings but also a deft con man.

Born into a wealthy Hungarian Jewish family in 1906, and schooled as an artist, he fled when the Nazis confiscated his family's property at the beginning of World War II. He found himself in Paris, scraping to make a living with his paintings.

He began to copy Picasso, Gauguin, Matisse, Chagall, Cezanne, Modigliani, Dufy, Braque, and others. As a member of a formerly wealthy family, he was able to pass them off as genuine.

As skilled and clever as he was, an incredibly inept mistake finally brought him down. In 1968 two large "Matisse" paintings were offered for sale before the paint was completely dry. His French art dealers went to prison, and de Hory, by then in Spain, spent two months in jail as a vagrant.

His forging days were over, but he continued to paint. Largely because of Clifford Irving's biography of de Hory, Fake, his "paintings in the manner of" famous artists began to sell on their own.

Faced with the lingering legal repercussions of his earlier forgeries, he committed suicide in 1979.

THE VINLAND MAP

In this almost successful forgery, the question "whodunit?" will probably never be answered.

Historians and cartographers were thrilled when a map was discovered that seemed to lend indisputable credence to the idea that the Vikings sailed to the New World before Columbus. Several map experts argued that words written on the map, the style of the map, and other details strongly argued for its authenticity.

There was even a crowning touch that must have been very difficult to achieve. The map had been discovered by Laurence Witten, an antiquarian book dealer from New Haven, Connecticut. It was bound between an authentic thirteenth-century document and an authentic fifteenth-century document, and wormholes through all three matched perfectly, making its

forger perhaps the only one in history who employed bookworms as accomplices.

Yale University acquired the map in 1959, and in 1972 it was turned over to McCrone Associates of Chicago, a company that specializes in scientific testing of suspected art and other forgeries.

A microscopic examination of the map showed that its black ink lines had a faint yellow border along their length. This was to be expected, as ink from the period often "bled" beyond its edges with this sort of yellow discoloration. Close scrutiny of the yellow, however, revealed that it contained a chemical not available before 1917.

CLIFFORD IRVING

In 1971 Clifford Irving was a freelance writer living amid the expatriate community on the Spanish island of Ibiza. He got to know a world-class art forger, Elmyr de Hory, and wrote a book, Fake, about him.

An idea for a lucrative literary forgery of his own hatched in Irving's mind. With his wife, Edith, and a writer friend, Richard Suskind, Irving began to create what was one of the most cleverly convoluted literary scams ever, an "authorized biography of Howard Hughes."

Hughes was trying to buy into the Las Vegas gambling world. A hand-written letter authorizing a representative to speak for him was published in Newsweek and Life and Irving sat down to learn to forge the eccentric recluse's handwriting. He created a letter in which Hughes explained why he had chosen him to be his biographer.

McGraw-Hill fell for the con to the tune of $850,000, to be paid to Hughes through Irving in the form of checks made out to H. R. Hughes. Meanwhile, Irving's wife, Edith, obtained a passport in the name of Helga R. Hughes and began to deposit the publisher's checks in Zurich.

The book, through more phony letters from Hughes, changed into an "as told to" autobiography, with Irving putting it all down on paper. Irving and Suskind did painstaking research to make the manuscript seem authentic.

Hughes then categorically denied that he had had any contact with Clifford Irving, and his lawyers obtained an injunction against the book's publication. The courts became involved and Irving, his wife, Edith, and Suskind were sent to prison.

HITLER'S DIARIES

In April 1983 the German magazine Stern called it "the journalistic scoop of the post–World War II era," and indeed it would have been if the sixty-two volumes of Adolf Hitler's handwritten diaries had proved to be genuine.

Stern's investigative reporter, Gerd Heideman, told hair-raising stories of his dealings with so-called documents dealer Konrad Kujau that included clandestine meetings with former Nazi officials, mysterious payoffs to East German officials, and high-speed encounters where sacks of cash were flung from one car to another.

Stern's high-ranking brass took the bait and tossed aside normal journalistic safeguards almost completely. They believed Heideman when he said the diaries had been rescued by farmers when a plane carrying Hitler's personal effects crashed near Dresden in the final days of the war. Although the diaries contained glaring historical inaccuracies, Stern handed over a total of almost $4 million to get their hands on them.

What they bought was the handiwork of one Konrad Kujau, an anti-Semitic collector and forger of Nazi memorabilia, including other Hitler documents and paintings by the dictator. Although a bad painter, Hitler had been prolific, and people were willing to pay handsome prices for his authentic art—and, of course, fakes created by Kujau.

Relying on genuine handwriting samples and the massive number of biographies of Hitler, Kujau penned the diaries and handed them on to Heideman.

Finally, when tests were done on the paper, it was revealed that it contained polyester fibers and other postwar materials.

Heideman and Kujau went on trial. It was not proved that Heideman actually knew the diaries were fakes. On July 8, 1985, he was convicted of embezzling some of Stern's money, and Kujau was convicted of being the creator of the most expensive forgery of the century.

—R.W.S.

THE REAL PEOPLE BEHIND 8 NOTABLE SUPREME COURT CASES

1. HIRABAYASHI v. THE UNITED STATES (1943)

Five months after Japanese forces dropped their first bombs on Pearl Harbor (then an American possession), the U.S. government made an appalling decision: it ordered the army to round up all persons of Japanese ancestry then living on the West Coast. The entire Japanese population was abruptly shipped off to internment camps on the cruel and baseless assumption that each man, woman, and child was a potential threat to U.S. security.

One of the victims was American-born Quaker Gordon Hirabayashi, a former Boy Scout, then a senior at the University of Washington. Accompanied by his lawyer, Hirabayashi appeared at the FBI office in Seattle in May 1942. Threatened with evacuation to a detention camp, which was the ultimate fate of more than 120,000 Americans of Japanese descent, Hirabayashi had refused to register for this openly racially inspired banishment, claiming "the privileges of a citizen" under the Constitution. Also, he had defied the curfew order to stay indoors until his case was dealt with. Hirabayashi was jailed for five months before being tried for refusing to register and breaking curfew. The irate government prosecutor summoned Hirabayashi's parents as witnesses. Taken from the internment camp where they were being held, they were jailed for two weeks before their son's trial. The prosecutor hoped their Japanese accent would remind the trial jurors of how recently the couple had been citizens of the enemy's land. The judge chimed in with his opinion that military law supersedes the Constitution. The obedient ju-rors quickly returned with "guilty" verdicts on both charges and Hirabayashi was sentenced to jail, having been denied release on bail for the three months before his appeal to the Supreme Court would be decided. The Court admitted that the internment orders were racially motivated and that the curfew sat on the edge of constitutionality, but upheld Hirabayashi's conviction anyway.

Members of President Franklin D. Roosevelt's Cabinet declared the Constitution was nothing more than "a piece of paper" and added that "a Jap's a Jap." But even the head of the FBI, J. Edgar Hoover, thought the army was "getting a bit hysterical."

Although Japan surrendered in 1945, the internment of Japanese Americans continued. One more year passed before the last internment camp closed. Many of the prisoners, reluctant to return to the areas from which they'd been expelled, never returned to their home states.

Forty years passed before the ugly affair would again rear its head. Inspired by a new generation of civil-rights activists and the antiwar protesters of the sixties, Japanese Americans discarded the tradition of their ancestors that obliged them to keep their pain hidden. In 1981 the internment issue was brought forward. A congressional review resulted in the decision to pay $20,000 to each internee still surviving. The government neither offered an apology nor acknowledged misconduct in Hirabayashi's case, so he pressed to have his criminal convictions overturned in court.

Not until 1987 did an appellate court decide that the original internment order was racist and based on prejudice rather than military necessity. Only then was Hirabayashi's name fully cleared. Gordon Hirabayashi, the unjustly harassed college student, went on to become a college professor. He retired as a sociology professor at the University of Alberta in Edmonton, Canada.

2. *BROWN v. BOARD OF EDUCATION* (1954)

Oliver Brown, a thirty-five-year-old African-American welder of boxcars, was tossed up by history to give his name to the momentous Supreme Court decision ending racial discrimination in public schools. A responsible, religious man, Brown resided in his own home in Topeka, Kansas, with his wife and three daughters. Disgusted by a state rule that required seven-year-old Linda to leave home at 7:30 A.M., cross dangerous railroad tracks, and frequently endure cold, rain, or snow while waiting for the bus that would deliver her to her depressing segregated school by 9:00 A.M., Oliver Brown was ripe for protest when the National Association for the Advancement of Colored People (NAACP) took up his case. On a September morning, Brown took little Linda's hand and led her up the steps of an all-white school situated only three and a half blocks from his house. Together father and daughter entered the school principal's office to enroll Linda in the third grade. Not unexpectedly, Oliver Brown's attempt to register Linda failed and Linda was denied entrance. Simultaneously, a black mother was anguished because her musically gifted daughter was barred from a white school nearby and made to attend a black school that offered none of the music classes available in the school for the white children.

Grouped with similar cases from South Carolina, Virginia, and Delaware, the Brown suit came before the court of Chief Justice Earl Warren. The Court's epic decision declared that segregated schools deprived black citizens of equal protection of the law under the Fourteenth Amendment to the Constitution (states may not make or enforce laws that restrict the rights of citizens of the United States). The decision broke the back of school systems that deliberately separated black children from their white peers and lighted the way to desegregation of hospitals, parks, public facilities, and voting places. Brown, who believed God approved of his participation in the case, died in 1961. Linda, later the divorced mother of two, remained in Topeka, where her own children attended public school. She and fifteen other parents fought to get the case reopened in 1979 because of the slow pace of desegregation. Linda was a grandmother when, in 1994, the school board of Topeka was finally forced to submit a workable plan for ending racial imbalances.

3. *MAPP v. OHIO* (1961)

In 1957 Dollree Mapp, a beautiful black divorcée in her late twenties and a onetime companion of ex–light heavyweight champion Archie Moore, was spending the afternoon at home in her two-family house in Shaker Heights, Ohio when a police sergeant rang her doorbell. The sergeant, acting on an anonymous and unspecific telephone tip, and without a search warrant, made a forced entry into the Mapp home. Exploring the premises, the officer uncovered pornographic literature. Convicted under state law of illegal possession of lewd material, Mapp appealed to the Supreme Court. In a landmark decision, the Court ruled that all states must henceforth abide by federal law as spelled out in the Fourth Amendment to the Constitution, which not only forbids "unreasonable searches and seizures," but also denies the use of evidence so obtained. Dollree Mapp was freed. Nine years after her victory, police in Long Island again entered Ms. Mapp's home. This time, armed with a search warrant, they uncovered a cache of illegal drugs and stolen goods. In 1971 Mapp was convicted of criminal possession of heroin and dealt a sentence of twenty years to life. Determined to be free, she studied law in prison and retained a well-respected attorney for her appeal. Dollree Mapp was released from prison in 1981.

4. *GIDEON v. WAINWRIGHT* (1963)

In 1962 Clarence Earl Gideon, an obscure felon convicted after a one-day trial and confined to a Florida state prison for an alleged burglary, applied his pencil to lined sheets of paper and carefully printed a petition to the Supreme Court. Declaring he was too poor to employ counsel, Gideon wrote, "I requested the Florida court to appoint me an attorney, and they refused." Gideon, a tall, skinny, gray-haired man in his fifties with three previous felonies on his record, was a loner; his prison file recorded no name on his mailing or visiting lists. Nonetheless, Gideon yearned for freedom. Aware that poverty had prevented him from hiring counsel, Gideon maintained that no indigent should be denied the constitutional right to due process. To its credit, the Supreme Court plucked Gideon's crude petition from the mass of mail it receives daily and saw merit in his cause. Abe Fortas, who was later to sit on the bench himself, was Gideon's court-appointed counsel (Louie L. Wainwright, as director of the Florida Division of Corrections, was named defendant), and Gideon's conviction was reversed. Attorney General Robert F. Kennedy declared that Gideon's letter changed the course of American history by establishing the rights of indigents to be provided free legal representation (court appointed) in serious criminal cases. Upon his release, Gideon, the father of three by a previous marriage, remarried and went to work in a gas station in Fort Lauderdale, Florida. He died in 1972 at age sixty-one.

5. MIRANDA v. ARIZONA (1966)

In 1963 Ernesto Miranda, aged twenty-two, unemployed and undereducated, was arrested for stealing eight dollars from a bank employee in Phoenix, Arizona. A year later Miranda was picked out of a police lineup by a young girl who accused him of kidnapping and rape. Despite Miranda's initial denial of guilt, two hours spent with police interrogators persuaded him to sign a confession. However, the Arizona police neglected to advise Miranda of his Fifth Amendment right against self-incrimination. The case moved to the Supreme Court to determine whether the Fifth Amendment, ratified in 1791, extended to "custodial interrogation." Chief Justice Earl Warren held for the Court that a suspect must be warned prior to interrogation of his right to remain silent, as any statement made may be used against him, just as he must also be advised of his right to have an attorney at his side if he so requests. The decision, unpopular with outraged citizens who contend it handicaps arresting officers and coddles criminals, is still on wobbly ground.

Although Miranda was the victor in the original case, he was retried when his former common-law wife testified he had confessed the disputed rape to her. This time Miranda was convicted and sentenced to a twenty-to-thirty-year term in Arizona State Prison. In 1972 he was paroled. A brief three years later he got into a fight over a card game and was stabbed to death in a Phoenix skid-row bar. The murder suspects were duly advised of their rights under the Miranda ruling.

6. REED v. REED (1971)

In 1967 Sally Reed, a Boise, Idaho, housewife, separated from Cecil Reed, fought to gain equal legal standing with her husband. At stake was the property of their adopted minor son Skip, an apparent suicide. The Idaho court automatically ruled that Skip's modest property was to go to his father, thereby following laws laid down in the days of slavery when the husband was viewed as possessor of all earthly goods, including his wife. The spoils in Reed v. Reed were a clarinet, a savings account, and Skip's clothing—assets totaling $801.22. The court's decision did not sit well with Sally Reed, who promptly hired a lawyer, Allen Derr. The astounded Derr, who initially thought he had taken on a simple case, found himself before the Supreme Court.

An unlikely feminist, Sally Reed had sought the protection of the Fourteenth Amendment to the Constitution, which declares that all citizens are entitled to equal protection under the law. In a unanimous decision in Sally Reed's favor, the Supreme Court, for the first time, applied the equal protection clause to women.

7. ROE v. WADE (1973)

Abortion.

Possibly no other social issue has so divided the American public in recent decades. At dispute: Does a woman have the right to total control over her body, or, as right-to-life advocates insist, is the fetus a living human being from the moment of conception (or, as still others contend, after quickening, when the movement of the fetus is felt in the mother's womb)?

Norma McCorvey, already the mother of two, claimed she was a rape victim and later said she was a consensual partner (at age twenty-one) to the activity that brought about her third pregnancy. After working as a low-paid waitress and housepainter, she agreed to lend her case history, as "Jane Roe," to abortion-rights advocates because, she said, she needed the money. Indeed, a goodly sum did subsequently come her way as the result of personal appearances and speeches.

McCorvey and her attorneys, Sarah Weddington and Linda Coffee, brought the case against Henry Wade, the Dallas, Texas, district attorney, because at that time Texas law did not allow abortions. The plaintiff argued that under the Ninth and Fourteenth Amendments, a U.S. citizen has the right to determine the course of his or her own life. The defendant argued that "Jane Roe" had made her choice prior to becoming pregnant, and that she had chosen to live in Texas.

In 1973, a seven-to-two Supreme Court decision made abortion legal in the United States. Too late for McCorvey: she bore her baby and gave it up for adoption. McCorvey went on to become a marketing director for a Dallas, Texas, women's clinic. In August 1995 McCorvey publicly announced her opposition to abortion after the first trimester.

8. UNIVERSITY OF CALIFORNIA v. BAKKE (1978)

An unpredictable twist to the Brown v. Board of Education drama occurred in 1978, when the Supreme Court was confronted with the case of Regents of the University of California v. Bakke. The university medical school, in its determination to comply with President John F. Kennedy's call for "affirmative action" in the treatment of minorities, allocated 10 places out of 100 in each new class for "disadvantaged students," a category in which the university included African Americans, Chicanos, American Indians, and Asian Americans. Blond, blue-eyed Allan Bakke, aged thirty-three, of Norwegian origin, was an aerospace engineer, a former Vietnam marine commander, married, father of three, and unmistakably white. Eager to become a doctor, he applied for admission to the medical school at Davis in 1973 and again in 1974, and both times he was rejected. Upon learning he had been passed over in favor of applicants of other races—although his grade average exceeded that of certain "disadvantaged students" who were accepted—Bakke sued the university, claiming "reverse discrimination." The case was heard in the California Supreme Court, and Bakke won. The university then carried the suit to the U.S. Supreme Court, which in 1978 ruled for Bakke. After an initially frosty reception by much of the student body, Bakke, despite his fifteen-year absence from academic studies, completed his medical studies in 1982. He went on to become an anesthesiologist in Minnesota.

—S.W.

17 UNUSUAL LAWSUITS

1. THE KABOTCHNICKS SPEAK ONLY TO GOD
The elite status of the Cabot family of New England is summarized in the old ditty

And this is good old Boston,
The home of the bean and the cod,
Where the Lowells talk to the Cabots
And the Cabots talk only to God.

In August 1923 the Cabots received a bit of a jolt when Harry and Myrtle Kabotchnick of Philadelphia filed a petition to have their last name changed to Cabot. Immediate objections were raised by several prominent members of the Cabot family as well as by the Pennsylvania Society of the Order of Founders and Patriots of America. However, Judge Charles Young Audenried ruled in favor of the Kabotchnicks, and a new branch was grafted onto the Cabot family tree.

2. A CABLE CAR NAMED DESIRE
The case of Gloria Sykes caused a sensation in San Francisco throughout the month of April 1970. A devout Lutheran and college graduate from Dearborn Heights, Michigan, the twenty-three-year-old Sykes had been in San Francisco only two weeks when, in September 1964, she was involved in a cable car accident. The Hyde Street cable car lost its grip and plunged backward, throwing Sykes against a pole. She suffered two black eyes and several bruises, but worst of all, claimed her lawyer, she was transformed into a nymphomaniac. Although she had had sex back in Michigan, she became insatiable after the accident and once engaged in sexual intercourse fifty times in five days. This inconvenience caused her to sue the Municipal Railway for $500,000 for physical and emotional injuries. The jury of eight women and four men was basically sympathetic and awarded Sykes a judgment for $50,000.

3. SUING A FOREIGN PRINCE
In 1971 Gerald Mayo filed suit in Pennsylvania at a U.S. district court against Satan and his servants, claiming they had placed obstacles in his path that had caused his downfall. On December 3 Mayo's complaint was denied on the grounds that the defendant did not reside in Pennsylvania.

4. SHARPER THAN A SERPENT'S TOOTH IS A THANKLESS CHILD
In April 1978 twenty-four-year-old Tom Hansen of Boulder, Colorado, sued his parents, Richard and Shirley, for "parental malpractice." Young Hansen claimed that his parents had done such a bad job of rearing him that he would be forced to seek psychiatric care for the rest of his life. He asked $250,000 in medical expenses and $100,000 in punitive damages. In explaining his reasons for filing the suit, Hansen said it was an alternative to his desire to kill his father: "I felt like killing my father for a long time. I guess I found a more appropriate way of dealing with it." The suit was subsequently dismissed by the district court and later by the Colorado Court of Appeals.

5. STANDING UP FOR THE STOOD UP
Tom Horsley, a forty-one-year-old accountant from Campbell, California, was quite upset in May 1978 when his date for the night, thirty-one-year-old waitress Alyn Chesselet of San Francisco, failed to show up. He was so upset, in fact, that he sued her for "breach of oral contract." His lawyer explained that Mr. Horsley was "not the type of man to take standing up lying down." Horsley asked for $38 in compensation: $17 for time lost at his hourly wage of $8.50, $17 in travel expenses, and $4 in court costs. Chesselet, in her defense, said she had attempted to call Horsley about her change in plans, which was due to having to work an extra shift, but he had already left his office. Judge Richard P. Figone ruled against Horsley, who remained philosophical. "I feel good about the whole thing," he said. "It raised people's consciousness about this problem. . . . There's too much of this thing, broken dates. It shows people are not sincere."

6. PREMATURE DETHRONEMENT
When Julie Wullschleger was chosen Miss Arlington (Texas) of 1978, she was told that her

reign as beauty queen would last for twelve months. Thus it came as a rude shock when she learned that she would be dethroned two and one-half months early because the 1979 pageant had been rescheduled in order to give the new Miss Arlington time to prepare for the all-important Miss Texas pageant. Wullschleger, who was also the reigning Miss Miracle Whip, claimed that her career as a model was being harmed, so she sued the city of Arlington for $10,000 in actual losses and $50,000 in punitive damages. District court judge H. M. Lattimore ruled against Wullschleger, saying: "The possible injuries to [Miss Wullschleger] do not overbalance the injury to [the city] if the injunction is upheld."

7. THE WANDERING BELLY BUTTON

Virginia O'Hare, forty-two, of Poughkeepsie, New York, filed a malpractice suit against plastic surgeon Howard Bellin after her navel ended up two inches off center following surgery in November 1974 to give her "a flat, sexy belly." Dr. Bellin had previously performed successful operations on O'Hare's nose and eyelids. Bellin argued that O'Hare's navel (which was later returned to its proper position by another plastic surgeon) had been misplaced by only a half inch, which he called "not cosmetically unacceptable." In May 1979 a state supreme court jury awarded O'Hare $854,219, including $100,000 for pain and suffering, $4,219 for the corrective surgery, and $750,000 for loss of earnings. Not surprisingly, Dr. Bellin appealed the verdict, but he later agreed to pay Mrs. O'Hare $200,000.

8. THE POORLY TRAINED SPY

Maria del Carmen y Ruiz was married to one of Fidel Castro's intelligence chiefs when, in 1964, she was approached by the CIA in Cuba and asked to be a spy. She worked diligently at her new job, but in January 1969 she was caught by Cuban counterintelligence agents and sentenced to twenty years in prison. After serving eight and one-half years, she became the first convicted American spy to be released from Cuban custody. In May 1980 Ruiz, now remarried and known as Carmen Mackowski, sued the CIA for inadequate training. She also charged that the CIA had misled her into believing that if she was detected, they would arrange for her immediate release. U.S. District Court judge Dickinson Debevoise of Trenton, New Jersey, ruled in favor of the CIA because, as one newspaper put it, federal judges "do not have authority to intervene in CIA employment matters that might result in the release of intelligence information."

9. X-RATED SHRUBBERY

In September 1980 in La Jolla, California, the "Grand Old Man of Divorce Law," John T. Holt,

and his wife, Phyllis, filed suit against their neighbors, William and Helen Hawkins, claiming that the Hawkinses had trimmed their hedges into obscene shapes. The Holts named twenty other neighbors as coconspirators. They asked $250,000 in punitive damages and demanded removal of trees and hedges that had been shaped "to resemble phallic symbols." The case was finally dismissed in January 1982.

10. THE MUMMY'S CURSE

Police officer George E. La Brash, fifty-six, suffered a stroke on September 23, 1979, while guarding the 3,300-year-old golden mask of King Tutankhamun when it was on display in San Francisco. La Brash claimed that he was a victim of the famous curse of King Tut, which had allegedly caused the sudden death of numerous people involved in the 1923 discovery of Tut's tomb. For this reason he contended that the stroke was job related and that he was entitled to $18,400 in disability pay for the eight months of his recuperation. On February 9, 1982, superior court judge Richard P. Figone denied La Brash's claim.

11. LACK OF FORESIGHT

In 1982 Charles Wayne Brown of Newton, Iowa, was struck in the right eye by a golf ball stroked by car salesman Bill Samuelson. The accident caused permanent damage to Brown's eye. Brown sued Samuelson for failing to yell "fore" before he hit the ball. The case was dismissed in 1984.

12. L-A-W-S-U-I-T

The two finalists in a contest to decide who would represent Los Altos School in the 1987 Ventura County, California, spelling bee were Steven Chen, thirteen, and Victor Wang, twelve. Victor spelled *horsy* h-o-r-s-y, while Steven spelled it h-o-r-s-e-y. Contest officials ruled that Steven's spelling was incorrect and advanced Victor to the county finals. But when Steven went home, he found both spellings in his dictionary and returned to the school to lodge a protest. It turned out that the officials had used an inadequate dictionary, so it was decided that both boys could advance. At the county finals, Steven defeated defending champion Gavin McDonald, thirteen, and advanced to the National Spelling Bee. Gavin's father sued the county event's sponsor, the *Ventura County Star—Free Press*, charging mental distress, and asked for $2 million in damages. He claimed that Steven Chen should not have been allowed to compete because each school was allowed only one entrant. A superior court judge and a state court of appeals dismissed the suit, stating that the major reason Gavin McDonald lost the Ventura County Spelling Bee was not that the contest was poorly run but that he had misspelled *iridescent*.

13. NERDS NOT ALLOWED

Two cases filed in Los Angeles challenged the right of fashionable nightclubs to deny entrance to would-be patrons because they are not stylishly dressed. In the first case, settled in 1990, Kenneth Lipton, an attorney specializing in dog-bite cases, was barred from entering the Mayan nightclub because a doorman judged his turquoise shirt and baggy olive pants to be "not cool." Owners of the club were forced to pay Lipton and three companions $1,112 in damages. The following year, the California State Department of Alcoholic Beverage Control won its suit against Vertigo, another trendy club that refused admittance to those people they claimed had no fashion sense. Administrative law judge Milford Maron ruled that Vertigo would lose its license if it continued to exclude customers based on a discriminatory dress code and the whim of doormen. Vertigo's owners chose to close the club in December 1992.

14. FALSE PREGNANCY

"World's Oldest Newspaper Carrier, 101, Quits Because She's Pregnant," read the headline in a 1990 edition of the Sun, a supermarket tabloid. The accompanying article, complete with a photograph of the sexually active senior, told the story of a newspaper carrier in Stirling, Australia, who had to give up her job when a millionaire on her route impregnated her. The story was totally false. Stirling, Australia, didn't even exist. But, as it turned out, the photo was of a real, living person—Nellie Mitchell, who had delivered the Arkansas Gazette for fifty years. Mitchell wasn't really 101 years old—she was only 96, young enough to be humiliated when friends and neighbors asked her when her baby was due. Mitchell sued the Sun, charging invasion of privacy and extreme emotional distress. John Vader, the editor of the Sun, admitted in court that he had chosen the picture of Mitchell because he assumed she was dead. Dead people cannot sue. A jury awarded Mitchell $850,000 in punitive damages and $650,000 in compensatory damages.

15. A HARD CASE

On the surface, Plaster Caster v. Cohen was just another lawsuit concerning disputed property. What made the case unusual was the nature of the property.

In 1966 Cynthia Albritton was, in her own words, "a teen-age virgin dying to meet rock stars." She was also a student at the University of Illinois. When her art teacher gave her an assignment to make a plaster cast of "something hard," she got an idea. She began approaching visiting rock groups and asking if she could make plaster casts of their penises. She had no problem finding girlfriends to help her prepare her models. At first she used plaster of paris, then a combination of tinfoil and hot wax, before settling on an alginate product used for tooth and jaw molds. Her project gained underground notoriety and she changed her name to Cynthia Plaster Caster. In 1970 her home in Los Angeles was burglarized, so she gave twenty-three of her rock members to music publisher Herb Cohen for safekeeping. Cohen refused to return them, claiming they were a payoff for a business debt owed him by Frank Zappa, who had employed Plaster Caster. In 1991 Plaster Caster filed suit against Cohen, who countersued. Two years later a Los Angeles superior court ruled in favor of Cynthia Plaster Caster, who regained control of her "babies," including Jimi Hendrix, Anthony Newley, Eric Burdon, and Eddie Brigati.

16. ROTTHUAHUAS

Canella, a rottweiler living in Key Largo, Florida, was in heat and her owner, Kevin Foley, had plans to mate her with "an acceptable male" and then sell the litter. But before he could do so, a neighboring Chihuahua named Rocky sneaked onto Foley's property and engaged Canella. Rocky and Canella were caught in the act, both by Foley, who snapped a photo of the incident, and by an animal control officer who happened to be passing by and stopped to watch the unusual coupling. A month later Foley learned that Canella was pregnant. He terminated the pregnancy by hysterectomy and sued Rocky's owner, Dayami Diaz. On November 1, 1993, Monroe County judge Reagan Ptomey ruled in favor of Foley and ordered Diaz to pay him $2,567.50.

17. BANK ROBBER SUES BANK

On May 25, 1992, Asmil Dinsio Sr., his brother, his son, his nephew, and a friend who specialized in safecracking tried to break into the United Carolina Bank in Charlotte, North Carolina. They were stopped immediately because the FBI had received a tip about the heist and had been trailing the Dinsios for days. Caught red-handed, the gang members pleaded guilty. Federal sentencing guidelines allowed U.S. District Court judge Robert Potter to take into account, when determining the robbers' sentences, the amount of money the bank might have lost if the robbery had been successful. He gave Asmil Dinsio Sr. and his brother James the maximum sentence—forty-six months in prison. Languishing in jail with nothing better to do, Asmil sued United Carolina Bank, claiming they had inflated the potential loss figures in an attempt to punish him. The case is still pending.

—D.W.

QUOTEBOOK: CRIME

BREAKING THE LAW

There are two kinds of crime: those committed by people who are caught and convicted, and those committed by people who are not. Which category a particular crime falls into is directly related to the wealth, power, and prestige of the criminal. The former category includes such crimes as purse snatching, mugging, armed robbery, and breaking and entering. The latter category includes war atrocities, embezzlement, most political actions, and budget appropriations.

Dick Gregory, Dick Gregory's Political Primer, 1972

When the law contradicts what most people regard as moral and proper, they will break the law—whether the law is enacted in the name of a noble ideal . . . or in the naked interest of one group at the expense of another. Only fear of punishment, not a sense of justice and morality, will lead people to obey the law.

Milton Friedman and Rose Friedman, Free to Choose, 1980

Deeds of violence in our society are performed largely by those trying to establish their self-esteem, to defend their self-esteem, to defend their self-image, and to demonstrate that they, too, are significant. . . . Violence arises not out of superfluity of power but out of powerlessness.

Rollo May, Power and Innocence, 1972

SEX CRIMES

Prostitution is really the only crime in the penal law where two people are doing a thing mutually agreed upon and yet only one, the female partner, is subject to arrest.

Kate Millett, The Prostitution Papers, 1971

[Rape] is the only crime in which the victim becomes the accused.

Freda Adler, Sisters in Crime, 1975

POLICE

The police and so forth only exist insofar as they can demonstrate their authority. They say they're here to preserve order, but in fact they'd go absolutely mad if all the criminals of the world went on strike for a month. They'd be on their knees begging for a crime. That's the only existence they have.

William S. Burroughs, in The Guardian, 1969

I have never seen a situation so dismal that a policeman couldn't make it worse.

Brendan Behan

LAWYERS

We all know that the law is the most powerful of schools for the imagination. No poet ever interpreted nature as freely as a lawyer interprets the truth.

Jean Giraudoux, The Trojan War Will Not Take Place, 1935

PRISON

Half the people in prison should never be there at all, although the other half should never be let out.

James Anderton, chief constable of Greater Manchester, quoted in John Mortimer's In Character, 1983

The same skills needed to be a successful criminal are needed to survive in prison.

Robert Chesshyre, "This Is Your Life," Observer, August 9, 1981

America has the longest prison sentences in the West, yet the only condition long sentences demonstrably cure is heterosexuality.

Bruce Jackson, New York Times, September 12, 1968

Chapter 5

WAR

THE 10 DEADLIEST WARS OF THE TWENTIETH CENTURY

1. WORLD WAR II, 1939–45

The Second World War was the deadliest of all armed conflicts of the twentieth or any other century. No other war has even come close—not by tens of millions of deaths. The generally accepted figure for total war deaths immediately following the war was 30 million, but the research of recent decades has pushed the final toll beyond 40 million to as high as 55 million.

Well over half of the total deaths from all causes—combat, disease, massacre, and so forth—came on the eastern front, the Russo-German conflict of 1941–45. In fact, if the struggle between Hitler and Stalin were treated as a separate conflict—distinct from World War II—it would rank as the bloodiest war of the century (and in all history), with World War I coming in second, and all the other campaigns of the rest of World War II placing third on this dolorous list.

The Soviet Union alone, according to official Soviet sources, lost 20 million dead from all causes (recent Russian counts run as high as 26 million dead). Military fatalities alone numbered 13.6 million, including 3.5 million who died in prisoner-of-war (POW) camps.

Though the United States had 407,318 military dead (including 292,131 killed in combat) in World War II, a toll exceeded in American history only by the 623,026 dead of the Civil War, America's losses were insignificant compared with those of half a dozen other nations. In all, eleven countries suffered more battle and nonbattle deaths than did the United States: the Soviet Union, 20 million; Poland, 6.3 million, including 5.7 million civilians (3 million of whom were Jews); China, 4.2 million, including 2 million civilians; Germany, 4 million, including 780,000 civilians; Japan, 3.2 million, including 700,000 civilians; Yugoslavia, 1.5 million, including 1.2 million civilians; France, 595,000; Italy, 530,000; Romania, 500,000; Great Britain, 495,000; and Hungary, 490,000. The total Allied military dead, in and out of combat, was at least 15.8 million; the Axis military toll surpassed 7.1 million.

Shattered more catastrophically than any nation was the Jewish population of Europe. Of the Continent's 8.9 million Jews, nearly 6 million died in the Holocaust.

2. WORLD WAR I, 1914–18

Unlike World War II, the Great War was much more a killer of soldiers than of civilians. There were no large-scale extermination campaigns against ethnic groups, except for that carried out by the Ottoman Turks, who killed as many as 1.5 million Armenians in 1915, and there was only limited aerial bombardment. The British naval blockade of Germany did result in some 760,000 deaths, and the worldwide Spanish flu pandemic beginning in the last year of the war killed an estimated 30 million (more deaths than World War I accounted for). But it was largely the soldiers stuck miserably in the trenches who suffered in the "War to End All Wars."

As in World War II, it was the Russian peasant soldiers who were sacrificed in the greatest numbers for the Allied cause, accounting for 1,700,000 dead. Almost a generation of Frenchmen, 1,366,000, died in the trenches of the western front and elsewhere. Britain and the British Empire counted 908,000 dead. Italy lost 462,000 dead along its Alpine battlefront. Though American involvement was probably decisive in 1918, United States deaths were a rather modest 116,708, including 53,513 combat dead (although the toll was the third highest in U.S. history after the Civil War and World War II). Even Romania (336,000 deaths) and Serbia (125,000) lost more.

Of the Central Powers, Germany counted the highest fatal military toll, 1,809,000. The Austro-Hungarian Empire lost 1,290,000; Ottoman Turkey, 325,000; Bulgaria, 76,000. The total Central Powers military deaths were 3.5

million, with 8.4 million wounded out of 22,850,000 mobilized. The Allied military toll was 5.1 million dead and 12.8 million wounded out of 42.2 million mobilized, for a combined military casualty toll of 8.6 million dead and 21.2 million wounded. Civilian deaths for the Allied nations were about 3 million; those for the Central Powers, about 3.5 million.

3. SINO-JAPANESE WAR, 1937–45

The conflict between China and Japan merged into World War II after Pearl Harbor, but for nearly four and a half years China, already weakened by three decades of revolution and civil war, bore alone the brunt of the Rising Sun's imperialist ambitions. China's Nationalist government reported the losses of its regular forces as 1,319,958 killed in action (KIA), 1,761,335 wounded in action (WIA), and 130,116 missing in action (MIA). The Chinese Communists, who had been fighting the Nationalists before the Japanese invasion and then turned their guns on the foreign foe, admitted to 500,000 dead. Non-Communist Chinese guerrillas may have lost another 400,000 dead. Including deaths from disease, Chinese military fatalities may have approached 3 million.

Losses for the Chinese civilian population are difficult to gauge. Estimates range from a low of 2 million to a high of 10 million, when one includes deaths caused by flooding and famine directly attributable to the war.

Japan and its puppet Chinese and satellite Manchurian allies admitted to battle casualties of 960,000 killed and wounded and 280,000 missing or captured. A fair estimate of Japanese military deaths from battle and disease would be at least 500,000.

4. CHINESE CIVIL WAR, 1927–37 and 1945–49

The two Chinese civil wars were really just one extended conflict interrupted by the Japanese invasion and World War II. Even while the competing Nationalists and Communists were

battling the Japanese invaders, they often fought one another just as energetically.

The first contest to decide who would rule postimperial China culminated in the famous Long March of 1934–35, when the Communists fought their way 6,000 miles to a safe haven in the north at a cost of 81,000 casualties. By the time the Japanese threat in 1937 had at least momentarily diverted Chinese attention away from killing each other, probably 1,275,000 soldiers on both sides had died. Civilian deaths numbered in the millions, with noncombatant fatalities reckoned as high as 1 million alone in the year-long (1933–34) Fifth Extermination Campaign waged by Chiang Kai-shek's forces against the Communist soviets (base areas).

The defeat of Japan in 1945 allowed a full-scale resumption of the civil war in 1946. By the time Mao Zedong's armies had chased Chiang's forces out of China to a refuge on Taiwan in December 1949, the People's Liberation Army had lost 1,522,500 killed or wounded. Nationalist losses from June 1946 to the end of 1949 amounted to 2,020,000 killed or wounded and 4,118,000 missing or captured. Total battle deaths for both sides were at least 1.2 million. As always, nobody bothered to count the massive civilian toll.

5. RUSSIAN CIVIL WAR, 1918–21

The war between the Red and the White armies following the culmination of the Russian Revolution in October 1917 added immensely to the miseries of a Russia already reeling from the staggering losses of World War I. Battle deaths in the civil war were appalling enough. Leon Trotsky's Red Army alone recorded 701,847 battle deaths from 1918 to 1920 in campaigns against the counter-revolutionary White forces and another 237,908 deaths in suppressing a series of peasant and anarchist uprisings against Lenin's revolutionary regime from 1920 to 1921. The White Russian armies must have suffered at least as many combat casualties.

WHEN THE UNITED STATES INVADED RUSSIA

The Cold War did not begin in the 1950s but in 1918, when U.S. troops invaded Russia with the aim of unseating the Communists. Actually, it wasn't a cold war. It became quite heated.

Early that year—with the end of World War I still months off—several of the Allied nations sent troops into Russia. Britain and France's principal motive was to pressure Moscow back into the war against Germany, with whom the Soviets had just established a separate peace. Japan took part in the invasion out of territorial greed. And the United States went in to keep an eye on Japan, to protect vital ammunition and supply depots, and to secure northern Soviet ports against the German forces. Or so the United States maintained.

Just before the invasion, civil war had broken out

in Russia between the ruling Bolsheviks, or Reds, and the counterrevolutionary Whites. Although the Whites failed to capture Moscow, they did secure much of the country. The real reason for America's intervention was to help the Whites topple the Communists.

In August and September 1918, the United States landed 4,500 troops at Archangel, on the White Sea, and 8,000 at Vladivostok, in eastern Siberia. After Germany surrendered in November 1918, there was no longer a valid reason for the Allies to remain in Russia, but they were in no hurry to decamp. American troops engaged the Bolsheviks in battle and backed the Whites in their ultimately thwarted campaign. It wasn't until April 1920 that the last U.S. soldiers returned home.

However, the greatest killing machines of the civil war were operated by famine, disease, and the security forces of the opposing sides. The notorious Soviet Cheka probably executed 500,000 people; White security police killed a similar number. Chaos and anarchy added immeasurably to the toll. No one knows the final figures; the highest estimate claims as many as 16 million dead, including lives lost to famine from 1921 to 1922.

Russians were not the only nationality to die in the civil war. Some 13,000 Czech POWs from World War I died in eastern Russia and Siberia while fighting for the White cause. The World War I Allies—Britain, France, Japan, and the United States—sent troops to northern Russia and Siberia to retrieve supplies sent to the fallen czar and to support the Whites. Britain suffered 1,073 casualties in the intervention, including 307 KIA. The United States lost 144 KIA and 100 dead from other causes, with 305 WIA, in northern Russia; the casualties in Siberia were 35 KIA and 52 WIA. Japan's 74,000 troops in Siberia lost at least 700 killed.

The Red Army victory in 1921 hardly ended the killing. Repression under Lenin turned to mass slaughter under Stalin, resulting in as many as 13 million deaths owing to collectivization and famine from 1930 to 1932 and more than 7 million deaths in the purges of 1934 to 1938.

6. VIETNAM WAR, 1957–75

The second Indochina war was a tragedy in terms of lives lost for the United States, but a calamity for the Vietnamese. There are 58,153 names etched onto the Vietnam Veterans Memorial in Washington, D.C., including those of 47,357 American servicemen who died in combat and 10,796 who died in nonhostile situations. Another 303,678 were wounded, 153,303 of whom were hospitalized. America's longest war was also America's fourth-deadliest conflict, after the Civil War, World War II, and World War I. But the sacrifice was small when set next to that of the Vietnamese.

The ARVN (Army of the Republic of Vietnam) and the militia forces of South Vietnam lost 254,257 dead and 783,602 wounded. The Viet Cong, the National Liberation Front, and the North Vietnamese lost, according to the official count, more than 1 million dead. Though the infamous "body count" may have been inflated by as much as one-third, the toll of Communist soldiers still could not have been much less than 700,000.

Vietnamese civilians suffered almost as grievously, with an estimated 522,000 noncombatants killed in South Vietnam and 65,000 slain by the U.S. bombing in North Vietnam. Another 1.2 million civilians were injured north and south.

In addition to as many as 2 million Vietnamese and nearly 60,000 Americans claimed by the war, the so-called Free World contingents sent to aid South Vietnam lost 5,575 dead, including 4,687 South Koreans, 494 Australians, and 351 Thais.

The toll in Indochina extended beyond Vietnam. Concurrent and often intermixed civil wars in Laos, 1959–75, and Cambodia, 1970–75, added 250,000 dead in Laos and as many as 600,000 dead in Cambodia to the cost of war in Southeast Asia.

7. KOREAN WAR, 1950–53

The "Korean Police Action" was the United Nations' first military action of consequence and by far its deadliest. It also devastated the Korean Peninsula, north and south. The northern invaders lost 214,899 KIA, 303,685 WIA, and 101,680 MIA. Their Chinese allies lost 401,401 KIA, 486,995 WIA, and 21,211 MIA. Another 400,000 Chinese and North Korean soldiers died of disease. As many as 1 million North Korean civilians may have succumbed to bullets, bombs, disease, and famine.

The Republic of Korea army lost 46,812 KIA, 159,727 WIA, and 66,436 MIA. Noncombatants made up by far the greatest percentage of casualties in the south, with South Korean deaths in and out of battle, civilian and military, totaling 415,004 and the wounded or injured numbering 428,568.

The United States in its first hot confrontation in the forty-five-year-long Cold War with Communism lost 33,629 KIA, 20,617 nonbattle dead, 103,284 WIA, and 10,218 missing or captured, making Korea the fifth-bloodiest of the ten major U.S. wars.

The other fourteen nations that dispatched armed units to serve with the United Nations command defending South Korea lost a total of 3,194 KIA, 11,297 WIA, and 2,769 MIA or POWs. Great Britain absorbed the heaviest casualties of this group—710 KIA, 2,278 WIA, and 2,029 MIA or POWs. Turkey recorded 717 KIA, 2,246 WIA, and 386 MIA or POWs.

8. CAMBODIAN CIVIL WARS, 1970–75, 1978–91

For more than a decade while neighboring Vietnam and Laos were convulsed by violence, Cambodia, though used as a sanctuary by the Viet Cong, remained an oasis of peace in Indochina. But when war finally came to Cambodia no nation in Southeast Asia, or hardly on Earth, suffered such shocking atrocities.

When Prince Norodom Sihanouk's neutralist government was overthrown in March 1970 and a Khmer Republic was established by General Lon Nol, the incipient Communist Khmer Rouge guerrilla movement expanded vastly and, with full-scale Viet Cong and North Vietnamese support, began an armed uprising. Despite massive U.S. bombing, the Khmer Rouge achieved victory on April 17, 1975. Lon

Nol's defeated army admitted to 50,000 killed and 200,000 wounded. Communist and civilian losses pushed the total number of violent deaths up to 250,000, but the grand total from disease and all other war-related causes was nearer 600,000.

The end of the first civil war only heralded the beginning of the real killing. Pol Pot's revolutionary regime proceeded to carry out an Indochinese holocaust in a frenzied attempt to create a new classless society. In eighteen months at least 1 million and perhaps as many as 2 million Cambodians were executed, worked to death, or starved to death in the "killing fields" of Cambodia (see page 270).

Border skirmishes with Vietnam in 1977 brought on a full-scale Vietnamese invasion on December 25, 1978. The invaders quickly swept the Khmer Rouge out of Phnom Penh and set up a puppet Cambodian government, but then the Vietnamese became bogged down in the same kind of guerrilla war that they had employed so successfully against the French and the Americans when the Khmer Rouge and two non-Communist factions retreated to border areas and continued insurgent warfare. Vietnam pulled out in September 1989 after losing 25,300 dead and 55,000 wounded in Cambodia. The rival Cambodian armies fought on until October 1991, when all factions agreed to a cease-fire and UN-supervised elections. At least another 200,000 Cambodians died in this second civil war and in the long resistance to the Vietnamese. Even the elections of 1993 and the formation of a coalition government did not entirely end the killing, as the disgruntled Khmer Rouge refused to disband and continued low-intensity warfare.

9. AFGHAN CIVIL WAR, 1978–92
When the Afghan monarchy was toppled in April 1978 by a coup carried out by the Marxist Khalq Party, Afghanistan became the last nation to fall to Communism forcefully. Islamic fundamentalists and other anti-Communist rebels immediately launched a guerrilla campaign from the harsh mountains of the Central Asia nation. As Marxist factions bickered bloodily with one another in Kabul, the Soviet Union in December 1979 launched an invasion to secure Afghanistan as a client state.

The cities fell rapidly but the countryside remained defiant. Afghanistan became the Soviet Union's Vietnam War (as well as the last war in its history), sapping the strength of the Red Army and contributing to the eventual collapse of the empire created by Lenin.

By the time the last Soviet soldiers were withdrawn in February 1989, 14,454 Soviet military personnel had died in Afghanistan, including 11,381 in combat. The puppet Afghan Communist government was expected to fall rapidly to the Western-armed mujahedin rebels, but the guerrillas fought among themselves as much as against the government army and did not complete their conquest of Kabul until April 1992. By then, fourteen years of civil war and nine years of Soviet intervention had left Afghanistan a devastated nation. Some 1.3 million Afghan soldiers and civilians had died from battle, disease, and starvation, and 3.5 million were refugees. The guerrilla victors almost immediately fell to fighting one another and Kabul was still racked by violence two years later.

10. MEXICAN REVOLUTION, 1910–20
The bloodiest of all Latin American revolutions was really a series of four major civil wars linked by numerous minor rebellions, uprisings, and coups. But the deadly decade has always been treated as a tumultuous whole. The longest and fiercest of the integral civil wars of the revolution was the 1914 to 1920 conflict between the Conventionist forces of Pancho Villa and Emiliano Zapata and the Constitutionalist armies of President Venustiano Carranza. About 200,000 died in the battles and massacres of this civil war, including Zapata, betrayed by one of his own generals and killed in 1919. At least 1 million Mexicans died in and out of battle as a result of their revolution.

Also killed were more than 230 Americans, mostly civilians, on both sides of the border. U.S. Marines lost nineteen dead in seizing Vera Cruz in 1914, and more than thirty American soldiers died in General "Black Jack" Pershing's 1916 march into Mexico in pursuit of Pancho Villa following his deadly raid on Columbus, New Mexico.

—M.D.C.

BATTLES

TSUSHIMA, 1905

On October 9, 1904, during the Russo-Japanese War, Czar Nicholas II of Russia ordered his "invincible" forty-five-ship Baltic Fleet to sail

18,000 miles around the world and attack Japan. Steaming into the North Sea, the Russian armada scored its first victory. Russian sailors spotted "Japanese torpedo boats" on the misty horizon, opened fire, and sank one and damaged several others. Unfortunately, the boats turned out to be English trawlers.

The fleet proceeded on around Africa, stopping at a small island off the coast of Madagascar. Russian commander Admiral Zinovi Rozhdestvenski ordered mechanical repairs on the ships, which had been plagued by boiler and engine problems. However, he departed as quickly as possible in order to avoid another Russian naval squadron ordered to join his ships at Madagascar. The squadron on its way to link up with Rozhdestvenski, under the command of Rear Admiral Nebogatoff, was composed of ships so old that it was jokingly called "the sink-by-themselves class."

Traveling 4,500 miles from Madagascar, the fleet again dropped anchor at Cam Ranh, on the coast of French Indochina (Vietnam). There the admiral received explicit orders to wait for Nebogatoff. Once the two squadrons were joined, Rozhdestvenski decided to push straight north through the Tsushima Strait, which separates Korea and Japan, to Vladivostok, the only Russian port left in Asia.

Admiral Heihachiro Togo guessed the Russian plan and was waiting with the entire Japanese fleet in the narrow Tsushima Strait. The Russians sailed into the trap on May 27, 1905. At noon the two fleets made contact, and Togo successfully crossed in front of the advancing Russian ships, unleashing a savage broadside. Twenty minutes after the battle had begun, Rozhdestvenski watched his *Ossliabya* go down, the first steam battleship in history to be sunk by gunfire. For the rest of the day, the better-trained Japanese sailors on their faster, better-constructed ships hammered away at the Russians. The Russian flagship foundered, then three more battleships followed it to the bottom. At sunset, as the Russians fled north, the *Borodino*, beautifully silhouetted against the setting sun, was hit by a single shell in its ammunition magazine. It exploded and sank within seconds.

That night Togo sent his torpedo boats after the remnants of the Russian fleet. By the next morning the twelve remaining Russian ships found themselves encircled by the Japanese. They promptly surrendered. Of the entire Russian fleet, only three ships managed to escape to Vladivostok; the rest had been sunk or captured. The Japanese had lost only three small torpedo boats. About 590 Japanese sailors were wounded and 117 killed. The Russians lost more than 5,917 wounded or captured and 4,830 killed.

Tsushima was the first major naval battle to occur since 1827. Prior to 1905 no naval battle had been spread out over such a large area— 150 miles. In addition, the prolonged refusal of the Russian fleet to surrender had an impact on navies around the world. Before Tsushima, it was not dishonorable to surren-

der after a courageous battle had been waged. After Tsushima, a fight-to-the-finish mentality emerged.

Tsushima ended the Russo-Japanese War. Peace negotiations were presided over by President Theodore Roosevelt, who for his efforts won the Nobel Peace Prize. While the terms of the peace treaty gave Japan most of what the country had asked for, many Japanese officials were not satisfied. The war had left the country on the verge of bankruptcy, and the Japanese had hoped for greater compensations to make up for their losses.

For Russia, Tsushima brought international humiliation, and revolution at home. The battle made Japan a major naval and world power, thereby dispelling the then popular belief in the inferiority of the "Oriental race."

—R.J.F. and C.O.M.

TANNENBERG, 1914

Wanting to help his hard-pressed French allies, Czar Nicholas II of Russia ordered an immediate offensive against Germany in August 1914, at the outbreak of World War I. Unfortunately, the Russian army had only begun mobilizing and was unprepared for this premature attack.

The Russian objective was East Prussia, which was to be attacked from the west and from Russian Poland to the south. The southern army was commanded by General Alexander Samsonov, who had never before commanded an army in combat. Samsonov marched his ill-prepared Second (Warsaw) Army north to the frontier and, on August 22, invaded Germany near the village of Tannenberg.

At this point German generals Paul von Hindenburg and Erich Ludendorff wheeled their entire army from northeast Prussia to the south. They concentrated their forces on both Russian flanks while allowing the enemy center to bulge forward. The Germans were aided by the Russian practice of sending radio messages uncoded. German intelligence knew the location of Russian units better than Samsonov did. By August 24 even Samsonov realized something was wrong on his flanks and slowed his advance. But his superior, General Yakov Zhilinsky, ordered him to quit "acting the coward and resume the offensive."

On August 26 the Germans counterattacked with an assault on the Russian east flank, which was routed, giving the Germans an open road into the Russian rear. During the next two days, German attacks also wiped out the Russian west flank. With both flanks crushed, the overextended Russian center was caught in the mouth of the German army, with the jaws slamming shut behind it. The Russian

Second Army disintegrated. Retreat was impossible because the Germans had formed a line across the Russian rear. Having lost any semblance of control over his army, the despondent Samsonov walked off into the woods and shot himself. The Germans had won a total victory.

Military historians have long speculated about whether the devastation of the Second Army could have been prevented, or lessened, if General Samsonov had had a better relationship with his military equal, General Pavel Rennenkampf. Rennenkampf, in charge of the First (Vilna) Army, was part of the Russian offensive and had entered East Prussia ahead of Samsonov. Hatred between the two generals dated to the Russo-Japanese War of 1904. That same year the two rivals had slugged it out, in front of their staff officers, on the platform of a railway station at Mukden. When Samsonov was being crushed by the German army at Tannenberg, he sent out repeated messages for the First Army to come to his aid. But Rennenkampf never arrived. A high-ranking German officer would later say, "If the battle of Waterloo was won on the playing fields of Eton, the battle of Tannenberg was won on a railway platform at Mukden."

The Germans named the battle after a small village called Tannenberg, even though the village had not played an important role in the battle. The German officers chose the name because in 1410 the Order of the Teutonic Knights had suffered a resounding defeat at Tannenberg in a battle with an army of Poles, Bohemians, Lithuanians, and Russians. Some five hundred years later, that loss was avenged.

Russian losses were 92,000 captured and 30,000 killed or missing. German casualties were 13,000 killed or wounded. Tannenberg ensured the eventual defeat of Russia and precipitated the Russian Revolution. Thus Czar Nicholas II paid for his rash decision with his throne and his life. The German victory was offset by their defeat at the Battle of the Marne, in France, at about the same time.

—R.J.F. and C.O.M.

against each other, over a 125-mile area. The scale of the combat was equaled by the scale of casualties. In seven days, each side, the Allies and the Germans, lost more than a half million men. At that time it was the bloodiest battle in history.

The Schlieffen Plan, devised by General Helmuth von Moltke's predecessor as Germany's chief of staff, called for France's conquest by a quick "blitzkrieg" thrust through neutral Belgium, outflanking the strong French border fortifications. The westward strike was then, after capturing Paris, to swing south and east like a giant scythe to crush the main French forces from the rear in Alsace-Lorraine.

Von Moltke modified the plan, with disastrous results. He sharply limited the attack potential of his First and Second Armies—the spearhead—by reassigning five corps for new drives on the Alsace-Lorraine and Russian fronts. His decision violated von Schlieffen's basic strategy, which strongly advised against pursuing a simultaneous two-front war.

Von Moltke was, for many reasons, an odd choice for Germany's chief of staff. At sixty-six he should have been retired from active duty, but he was held in high regard by the kaiser, partly because he was the nephew of Colonel-General Helmuth von Moltke, one of Germany's most revered soldiers. But the chief of staff was not popular among his men. He was overweight and in poor physical condition and often fell off his horse during maneuvers. Nonetheless, the aging general was confident that his planned invasion of France would work.

In initial action, sixty-six-year-old General Alexander von Kluck, the aggressive but brash First Army commander, had already moved his entire force north of the Marne River, fifteen miles from Paris, to the Ourcq River, attacking Marshal Michel Maunoury's French Sixth Army. The unexpected attack caused Maunoury to request reinforcement troops from Paris, about thirty miles away. Since the number of troops needed could not be transported solely by rail, it was necessary to use taxicabs. Rounded up throughout the streets of Paris, approximately 1,200 taxis carried thousands of French soldiers to the battlefield.

THE MARNE, 1914

The Marne, one of the most decisive battles of World War I, pitted more than 2 million soldiers

Despite receiving von Moltke's orders to hold in abeyance his attack on Paris, von Kluck continued to advance because he believed that the supreme commander did not understand the real situation. But von Kluck's extended

A German victim of the Battle of the Marne.

assault opened a twenty-five-mile gap between his and General Karl von Bülow's Second Army, on his left flank. When von Moltke intercepted a radio message giving news of the separation, he sent his intelligence chief, Lieutenant Colonel Richard Hentsch, forward on September 8 to review the situation. Hentsch possessed oral authority to act in von Moltke's name if necessary, since von Moltke's headquarters were located in Luxembourg, more than a hundred miles from the front.

As Hentsch reached the Second Army's command post, he was informed of a night assault by Franchet d'Esperey's French Fifth Army, which had turned back von Bülow's right flank. Fearing an immediate envelopment, Hentsch ordered a withdrawal, to which a weary von Bülow readily agreed. The retreat left von Kluck's flank highly vulnerable, although the First Army was itself in good position and attacking well. Hentsch arrived at First Army headquarters while von Kluck was at the front, conferred with the general's chief of staff, and strongly advised a similar withdrawal. Upon Hentsch's return to Luxembourg with his full report, von Moltke ordered a general retreat of not only the First and Second Armies but the Third as well, pulling back to the Aisne River.

For the French, a "miracle" at the Marne had taken place—the German threat to Paris was over. But General Joseph Joffre's forces were too exhausted to follow up their great moral victory, and the German armies gained valuable time to dig in. Their primary tactics subsequently changed from rapid mobility to static entrenchment, initiating the bloody months of the next four years. The "fixed position" of trench warfare, protected by machine gun, barbed wire, and a new invention called the tank, became the accepted plan for battle.

—W.K. and C.O.M.

VERDUN, 1916

German field marshal Erich von Falkenhyn believed he could win World War I by "bleeding France white" in a long battle of attrition. His strategy would be tested against the French fortress of Verdun, on the river Meuse.

An attack on Verdun was a direct assault on French national pride. Considered impregnable, Verdun was a chain of twenty forts built under layers of concrete and armor plate, with artillery mounted in automatic turrets. The forts were dug into formidable natural defenses, the rough hills above the Meuse. One ridge bore an ancient but prophetic name: Mort-Homme (Dead Man).

Falkenhyn believed he couldn't lose. If Verdun fell, the blow to morale could force France out of the war. In any case, French prestige would demand the commitment of scarce reserves in a defensive battle à outrance— to the final limit.

At dawn on February 21, 1916, a huge Krupp cannon fired a shell that traveled twenty miles and blew off a corner of Verdun's cathedral. This was the opening shot of a day-long German barrage from more than 1,200 guns, the first use of artillery on such a massive scale. In another first, Falkenhyn launched air-to-ground strikes using 166 airplanes, 14 balloons, and 3 zeppelins. He intended to fight a limited ground offensive, after the French had been thoroughly hammered by bombs and artillery.

At first Falkenhyn's strategy seemed to work. On February 25 German infantry took Fort Douamont, Verdun's strongest position. France panicked. Just as Falkenhyn had predicted, every available French unit was rushed to Verdun.

But Verdun's commander, General Henri Petain, was one of the few leaders on either side who understood modern warfare. In another first, Petain used motor transport to supply Verdun. Down a narrow road known as Voie Sacre (Sacred Way) roared 1,700 trucks a day. To protect his scarce human reserves, Petain used the Sacred Way to rotate battle-weary troops out of Verdun and fresh units in. Petain also brought in every heavy gun he could scrape up, neutralizing the German artillery advantage and bringing Falkenhyn's guns under ceaseless counterbattery fire.

Falkenhyn quickly lost control of his "limited" offensive. During the first week each side lost 25,000 men. Attrition is a two-edged sword, Falkenhyn soon learned, and battles can attain a terrible momentum beyond the control of human commanders. Verdun became a slaughterhouse for both sides. "One eats, one drinks beside the dead . . . ," wrote Georges Duhamel, French poet and doctor who served at Verdun. "One laughs and sings in the company of corpses." In addition to its other firsts, Verdun was a test lab for two hellish new weapons: flamethrowers and poison gas.

In December, after ten months of daily combat, the Germans were forced back to their starting line. Neither side had gained a clear strategic or tactical advantage. Each had lost about 350,000 men, mainly owing to the new tactic of endless artillery duels.

As horrendous as those losses were, the long-term effects of Verdun were worse. The fortress held, convincing the French to turn their nation into a sort of super-Verdun: in the years after World War I, France would nearly bankrupt itself building the "impregnable" Maginot Line. But in the German trenches at Verdun was a young officer named Heinz Guderian, who took a different lesson from the battle. In 1940 Guderian would lead his tanks around the Maginot Line, and in a matter of days France would fall to Nazi Germany.

—M.S.S.

JUTLAND, 1916

Since the beginning of World War I, the German High Seas Fleet had not ventured out to challenge the numerically superior British Grand Fleet, which maintained a stranglehold blockade on Germany. In 1916 command of the German fleet was given to Admiral Reinhard Scheer, an aggressive officer who wanted to end the stalemate by battling the British and destroying the blockade.

On May 31, German admiral Franz von Hipper led a squadron north from Germany along the Danish Jutland Peninsula, while Scheer followed fifty miles behind with the main German fleet. The German force consisted of ninety-nine ships, including twenty-two battleships. British intelligence, having broken the German naval code, informed Admiral Sir John Jellicoe of the German foray.

Realizing the Germans could not be allowed freedom in the North Sea, Jellicoe put to sea the same morning. From Scotland he steamed eastward with the main fleet, while a smaller squadron under Admiral Sir David Beatty paralleled his course seventy miles to the south. The British fleet was composed of 148 ships, including 28 battleships.

At 3:30 P.M., the squadrons of Beatty and von Hipper made contact. Von Hipper turned south, luring Beatty toward the main German fleet. When Beatty saw the main enemy fleet dead ahead, he turned and ran for Jellicoe's aid. The combined German fleets pursued. At 5:30 the Germans sighted Jellicoe's battleships on the horizon. Both navies plunged forward and cleared for action. The British battle-wagons fired first and set von Hipper's flagship, the Lützow, aflame. The Germans returned fire, and the British Invincible sank in three minutes.

At dusk Jellicoe crossed the German rear, thereby blocking the German route home. Afraid of losing his ships too quickly, Jellicoe ordered them to avoid further combat. But at midnight Scheer attacked the British rear, and after four hours of confused night battle, the Germans broke through and escaped to Germany. With the Germans back in harbor, the British steamed homeward, picking up survivors along the way.

> *Jellicoe was the only man on either side who could lose the war in an afternoon.*
> Winston Churchill, referring to Admiral Sir John Jellicoe, who commanded the British fleet at the Battle of Jutland

Six thousand ninety-seven British sailors were killed and 2,551 Germans. Both sides had lost six major ships; however, the British had lost twice as much tonnage. Although scoring a technical victory, the German fleet never again came forth to fight a major battle. The British navy's pride was hurt, but it still dominated the North Sea and continued the blockade for the rest of the war.

—R.J.F.

THE SOMME, 1916

General Joseph Joffre, commander of the French army, firmly believed the war on the western front would be won by a decisive breakthrough, even though two years of trench warfare had demonstrated this to be suicidal idiocy. In 1916 Joffre planned a grand offensive employing British and French troops. The British commander, General Sir Douglas Haig, also dreaming of a breakthrough, agreed to the plan.

The strategy called for a French attack along a ten-mile front south of the Somme River in France, while the major attack would be launched by the British along a fifteen-mile front north of the river. On June 24, 1916, the Allied artillery began a seven-day barrage of the German lines, expending 1,627,824 shells. Hidden away in their forty-foot-deep bunkers, the Germans were alerted to the impending attack by the long bombardment. Young corporal Adolf Hitler waited with enthusiasm, while other Germans erected banners taunting, "Come on, British pigs; we're ready for you."

On July 1 the shelling stopped, and at 7:28 A.M.—a warm Saturday morning—the Allies attacked. The Germans scrambled out of their dugouts to man their machine guns. The British soldiers, carrying sixty-six pounds of equipment each, lumbered forward in dense waves, only to be caught in the German barbed wire and massacred by machine gunners. That first day, the British lost 57,450 men, including 19,240 dead, and gained a mere 1,000 yards. Their casualties were two per yard along the sixteen-mile battle line. In one day three times as many British soldiers met their death as in the two and a half years of the Boer War. The French did only slightly better.

For the next ten weeks, the Germans coordinated a strong defense, while the Allies continued their futile frontal attacks, thus causing 10,000 casualties a day. Haig admonished his men to attack "without intermission." By September 15 Haig, in a desperate mood, decided to use his secret weapon—the tank. Eighteen British tanks (another thirty-one broke down on the way to the front) rolled into the German lines. However, there were too few to endanger seriously the German position (see page 235).

For another two months the battle dragged on. Torrential rains came. Soldiers drowned in trenches, and the wounded fell down and disappeared in the mud. Finally this battle of attrition simply petered out on November 19. The Allies had won a strip of land thirty miles long and seven miles wide at its widest point. The cost was more than 200,000 French casualties, 415,690 British, and 434,500 German.

The Somme—the bloodiest battle in all history—had merely rearranged the trench lines. Its architect, Joffre, was ordered to retire, for his grand design left more than a million men dead or wounded and achieved nothing.

—R.J.F.

AIR BATTLE OF BRITAIN, 1940

Reichsmarschall Hermann Göring's aerial assault on England—given the code name Operation Adler (Eagle)—began in July 1940, to clear the way for Hitler's immediate land invasion of the British Isles. Göring's timetable called for a Royal Air Force (RAF) defeat in four days. He commanded three Luftflotten (air fleets) based in northern France, the Low Countries, and Norway. Overall, the Luftwaffe had 2,800 aircraft, mostly Messerschmitt fighters and Heinkel bombers. Göring's counterpart in Britain, Air Marshal Sir Hugh Dowding, opposed the attack with almost 1,200 aircraft; 80 percent of the 700 in Fighter Command were combat-ready Spitfires and Hurricanes. In addition, the RAF also used 500 long-range bombers to carry out raids against Continental targets.

Strategically, Göring concentrated on the RAF's southeast airfields, commanded by Air Vice Marshal Keith Park. Dowding responded by giving Park the option to offer only limited aircraft commitment, supported by radar, against the German airmen.

The British radar stations on the cliffs and bluffs of coastal England allowed Park to "see" incoming bombing "boxes" at substantial distances. The sophisticated early-warning system permitted great efficiency in the use of Fighter Command aircraft. Its flyers, guided by precise vector information on enemy strength and location, were able to strike quickly and often by surprise, without wasting valuable time and fuel on airborne defensive patrols.

Nevertheless, Göring's continual strikes, delivered throughout August, reduced Fighter

Command's resistance to the point of near collapse. Then, on August 24, the British received an unexpected assist. Luftwaffe bombers mistakenly bombed London, and the RAF immediately countered with a night raid on the Berlin suburb of Ruhleben. The retaliation infuriated Hitler, who had promised the German people Berlin would never be touched. Hitler now concentrated air attacks on London, abandoning his original plan to destroy the RAF. The decision was a major tactical blunder that gave British Fighter Command enough time to recover.

After the strategy change, Göring unleashed a massive daylight blow on London on September 7, followed by fifty-seven straight days of bombing. London was under siege. Day and night the bombing continued. Many Londoners fled to public shelters created underground in the subway stations. They dragged food and blankets with them; the government provided first-aid supplies and toilets. In order to sustain some degree of normalcy, they provided their own amusements by organizing games and community sing-alongs. At one subway station near London's theater district, professional entertainers such as Laurence Olivier and Vivien Leigh performed.

Prime Minister Winston Churchill, who had easy access to an underground air-raid shelter, preferred to walk the streets as the bombs fell. His valet, afraid that Churchill would be killed, sometimes hid his shoes in an effort to stop the prime minister from wandering around. An angry Churchill responded: "I'll have you know that as a child my nursemaid could never prevent me from taking a walk in the Green Park when I wanted to do so. And, as a man, Adolf Hitler certainly won't."

For a while it seemed as if the bombs were hitting only the poorer sections of the city, and the more affluent districts were escaping unharmed. Those who lived in the devastated sections, particularly the East End, became angry and resentful. The upper class appeared immune to the attack, while the poor couldn't get the government to mount an adequate relief effort.

Then German planes dropped a number of bombs directly over the fashionable districts of London. One landed in the courtyard of Buckingham Palace, endangering the lives of the royal family. The incident helped dispel public anger and became symbolic of the fact that rich and poor alike were suffering from the relentless aerial attack.

> I'm glad we've been bombed. It makes me feel I can look the East End in the face.
> Queen Elizabeth, the Queen Mother, to a policeman, September 13, 1940

On October 12 Hitler canceled Operation Sea Lion, the code name for his planned land invasion of the British Isles. When the air battle was finally over, on November 2, the Germans had failed to destroy the Royal Air Force. The Luftwaffe lost 1,789 aircraft. In addition, German planes had dropped countless bombs on seventy fake airfields, skillfully designed by the British. The RAF lost 915 aircraft, and 481 of its 1,434 pilots were killed, wounded, or missing. In a speech to Parliament, Winston Churchill paid tribute to the RAF pilots: "Never in the field of human conflict was so much owed by so many to so few."

—W.K. and C.O.M.

PURSUIT OF THE *BISMARCK*, 1941

With the European continent in Nazi hands, the Atlantic convoys were Britain's lifeline. These convoys were already under constant German U-boat attacks when the Germans planned to unleash yet another threat—the battleship *Bismarck*. Launched in 1939, the 53,546-ton *Bismarck* was the largest, most powerful ship afloat, secretly exceeding the size limitations set by international treaty. If it were loose in the Atlantic, its radar-controlled fifteen-inch guns could sink whole convoys.

On May 21, 1941, a British reconnaissance plane spotted and photographed two German ships hidden in a Norwegian fjord. They were the *Bismarck* and its companion, the cruiser *Prinz Eugen*. The British navy was alerted, but it was too late. The *Bismarck* had bolted for the open seas on the same day. Admiral Sir John Tovey, commander of the British fleet, ordered all available ships to hunt it down.

On May 23 the scouting cruiser *Norfolk* spotted the two German raiders heading south between Greenland and Iceland. The British sped the battleships *Hood* and *Prince of Wales* to intercept them. On the twenty-fourth, at 5:53 A.M., the British battleships located and fired on the *Bismarck*. In turn, the *Bismarck* shot a salvo into the *Hood*, which exploded and sank into the icy Arctic waters in six minutes. Of the *Hood*'s 1,419 men, only 3 survived. The *Prince of Wales* was hit eight times but managed to limp away to safety. The *Bismarck* had been hit twice; one shell had punctured its fuel tanks and caused a severe oil leakage of about 1,000 tons.

With insufficient fuel, the *Bismarck* was forced to head toward the French port of Brest for repairs. But on May 26 fifteen planes from the British aircraft carrier *Ark Royal* plowed two torpedoes into the *Bismarck*, destroying its rudder and steering gear. Out of control, the ship sailed in circles; it was finally located 400 miles west of Brest.

At nine the next morning, the British battleships *Rodney* and *King George V*, with two cruisers, began bombarding their prey. The crippled *Bismarck* fought back, but by 10:15 its guns were silent and its decks ablaze. A British cruiser delivered the death blow, sending two torpedoes into the lifeless hulk. Amid explosions, the *Bismarck* rolled over and slid beneath the waves, with more than 2,000 Germans aboard. One hundred fifteen of the crewmen were rescued.

The British had destroyed the deadliest ship in existence and proved that they were capable of keeping the sea-lanes open to beleaguered Britain.

—R.J.F.

STALINGRAD, 1942–43

Assuming direct command of the German armies, Adolf Hitler planned an attack on the industrial and transportation center of Stalingrad on the Volga River in southern Russia. The German Army Group B, with the Sixth Army spearheading, attacked eastward from the Donets River basin on June 22, 1942.

At first the German blitzkrieg appeared to be a complete success. After reaching the outskirts of Stalingrad (now Volgograd), the Luftwaffe pounded the city, killing 40,000 people, most of them civilians. Never before had there been such a deadly air raid. On August 24 General Friedrich von Paulus's Sixth Army began its ground assault. But it took them a month of house-to-house fighting to gain the center of the city, after suffering heavy casualties. Soviet soldiers and civilians—constantly exchanging the admonition "Comrade, kill your German," desperately defended the rubble heap that Stalingrad had become.

By November 12 most of the city had fallen and the Volga had been reached. However, the German position was tenuous. Stalingrad was at the eastern apex of a German salient, with the north and south flanks of this protrusion weakly guarded by unreliable Romanian, Italian, and Hungarian troops. Russian general Georgi Zhukov secretly concentrated a million soldiers against these flanks while the Germans were storming Stalingrad. The German army had stuck its tongue into a meat grinder.

On November 19 the Russian armies struck the north and south flanks of the salient, at a point that was defended not by the German army but by the Romanians. By the twenty-third the Soviet pincers had met, surrounding the 300,000-man German Sixth Army in Stalingrad. Von Paulus asked permission to fight his way back to the German lines, but Hitler replied, "Where the German soldier sets his foot, there he remains." Ranting "I won't leave the Volga," Hitler approved Göring's plan to supply the besieged Germans by air. However, the German Luftwaffe failed miserably. The Sixth Army required an absolute minimum of 300 tons of supplies a day; the Luftwaffe was able to deliver an average of only 100 tons, while losing 490 planes and 1,000 air crewmen.

Meanwhile the Russian ring was squeezing the Sixth Army to death. Dying of starvation, the Germans ate horses, cats, dogs, and rats, as the temperature dropped to thirty below zero. Through December and January, the Germans stubbornly resisted the attacks from all directions. Hitler ordered them to fight to the death. On January 30 Hitler promoted von Paulus to field marshal because no field marshal in German history had ever surrendered. Three days later von Paulus and 91,000 German soldiers surrendered. With their surrender, the myth of Nazi invincibility was destroyed.

Stalingrad cost the Germans 600,000 men and the Russians 400,000. The loss of weaponry and men weakened the German army so badly that it never regained the offensive on the eastern front. The Soviets now turned to the attack, which didn't end until they had reached Berlin. Of the 107,800 prisoners of war taken by the Red Army at Stalingrad, only 6,000 survived to return to Germany after the war.

—R.J.F.

LEYTE GULF, 1944

The largest naval action in history, the Battle of Leyte Gulf saw an amazing number of blunders on both sides.

In October 1944 American general Douglas MacArthur kept a famous promise and returned to the Philippines with an army. His assault was protected by Admiral Thomas Kincaid's Seventh Fleet and the Third Fleet under Admiral William "Bull" Halsey.

Despite overwhelming odds, the commander of the Japanese Combined Fleet, Admiral Suemo Toyoda, believed he could destroy the Seventh Fleet and stop the landings.

Toyoda divided his fleet into three strike forces. Northern Force, under Vice Admiral Jisaburo Ozawa, was simply live bait. Toyoda knew that Halsey's aircraft carriers provided the only air cover for the Leyte invasion. Ozawa's mission: lure Halsey far to the north. Ozawa's carriers held only 116 airplanes. Facing Halsey, with 12 carriers and more than 1,000 aircraft, Ozawa himself predicted the "total destruction" of Northern Force.

The strongest punch was Center Force, led by Vice Admiral Taeko Kurita. Kurita had more than forty vessels, including the world's largest battleships, *Yamato* and *Musashi*. A weak Southern Force, under Vice Admiral Shoji

Nishimura, consisted of two battleships and a handful of cruisers and destroyers.

While Northern Force decoyed Halsey, Center and Southern Forces would crush the Seventh Fleet between them, then attack the helpless transports in Leyte Gulf. Code-named Sho (Victory), the plan depended on coordination and surprise.

Surprise was lost immediately. On October 23, 1944, Center Force was spotted by American submarines. The subs sank two cruisers and alerted Halsey. On October 24 Halsey's planes hit Center Force with more than 250 attacks. The huge new battleship *Musashi* went to the bottom, though it took seventeen bombs and nineteen torpedoes to sink it.

Kurita retreated to wait for darkness. Halsey assumed—wrongly—that he was out of the fight for good. Later on October 24, Halsey made another wrong guess: that Ozawa's carriers were the biggest Japanese threat (though in all fairness, Halsey had to assume this). As Toyoda hoped, Halsey ran north at flank speed to attack Northern Force. In his third bad guess of the day, Halsey believed Kincaid's Seventh Fleet was covering the northern entrances to Leyte Gulf. Kincaid assumed the same about Halsey. Not a single patrol boat was left in the area. The door to Leyte Gulf stood wide open, and the Sho plan could still work.

Out of touch with Kurita, Nishimura decided to attack alone. On the night of October 24, his ships crept up Surigao Strait, hoping to surprise the Seventh Fleet. But Kincaid had been tracking Southern Force. Nishimura sailed right into a trap; the Seventh Fleet sank or crippled all of his ships. Surigao Strait was the most successful single action in U.S. Navy history.

Other, weaker American forces would pay for it. At dawn on October 25, Center Force passed undetected through the northern approaches to the gulf. Dead ahead, Kurita thought he saw Bull Halsey's fleet of carriers and battleships.

Halsey was 300 miles away, ravaging Ozawa. What Kurita saw was Taffy Three, a command of thirteen tiny ships: six escort carriers (converted merchant ships carrying only twenty-eight planes), three destroyers, and four destroyer escorts. Their biggest weapons were five-inch guns; Kurita's *Yamato* boasted eighteen-inch guns capable of throwing a 3,000-pound shell more than twenty miles.

Leyte Gulf would see the first use of Japanese suicide pilots, the kamikaze, but Taffy Three showed that the Japanese had no monopoly on suicidal bravery. Outnumbered and outgunned, Taffy Three aggressively attacked Kurita's battlewagons—the equivalent of a toy poodle attacking a timber wolf. The destroyer *Johnston* was hit with three fourteen-inch shells, which a crewman compared to "a puppy being smacked by a truck." Burning and nearly dead in the water, *Johnston* kept firing.

Ducking in and out of a storm, laying smoke, Taffy Three completely bamboozled Kurita, who thought he was under attack by a much stronger force.

Incredibly, the bluff worked. Just when he could have forced his way into Leyte Gulf, Kurita ordered a retreat.

Throughout the action, Taffy Three had sent uncoded messages screaming for help. These messages reached Admiral Chester Nimitz, overall American naval commander in Hawaii. Nimitz sent a coded message to Halsey: "WHERE IS TASK FORCE 34 RR THE WORLD WONDERS." The last three words were part of the code, nonsense "padding" to confuse enemy code breakers.

Halsey mistook the message for a personal insult. Leaving his carriers to finish Ozawa, a fuming Halsey led his battleships south. They arrived too late. While Taffy Three faced overwhelming odds, America's mightiest warships spent the day racing to and fro without firing a shot.

Both sides made mistakes at Leyte Gulf, but the Japanese made more and bigger mistakes. The United States lost three light carriers, two destroyers, and one destroyer escort, with 3,000 casualties. The Japanese navy was virtually knocked out of the war, losing four carriers, three battleships, ten cruisers, nine destroyers, and 10,000 lives.

—M.S.S.

INCHON, 1950

The Korean War began on June 25, 1950, when the North Korean People's Army (NKPA) launched a surprise attack. By September the U.S. Eighth Army and its United Nations allies had almost been run out of Korea. The Allies were pinned into a small defensive sector, the Pusan Perimeter, with the NKPA in front and the Sea of Japan behind.

> War, undertaken for justifiable purposes, such as to punish aggression in Korea, has often had the principal results of wrecking the country intended to be saved and spreading death and destruction among an innocent civilian population.
> Robert A. Taft, A Foreign Policy for Americans, 1951

At his Tokyo headquarters, General Douglas MacArthur devised a counterstrike, Operation Chromite. The plan horrified his superiors and his subordinates alike: an amphibious landing at the South Korean port of Inchon.

"Make up a list of amphibious 'don'ts,' " said one navy officer, "and you have an exact description of the Inchon operation." Inchon's thirty-foot tides were among the fiercest and fastest in the world. At low tide the harbor was a morass of mud flats. Troops who hit the beach in the morning would be stranded for twelve hours, until the next high tide.

Inchon's shallow Flying Fish Channel was cluttered with reefs and dominated by North Korean artillery on Wolmi-do (Moontip Island). Mainland beaches were blocked by high concrete seawalls. Finally, unlike the remote islands MacArthur had assaulted in World War II, Inchon was a city; an attacker could be ground to pieces in house-to-house fighting.

All the "don'ts" simply guaranteed surprise, MacArthur insisted. By landing 150 miles behind the NKPA, he would cut its lines of supply and communication. His sudden appearance would draw the NKPA to Inchon, allowing Allied forces to escape from the Pusan Perimeter. He would then link up with the Eighth Army, destroy the NKPA, and end the war. MacArthur won a faint approval from the high command.

The wrong war, at the wrong place, at the wrong time and with the wrong enemy.
General Omar Bradley

The fortress island of Wolmi-do would be attacked first, at dawn. Morning tide allowed less than two hours for the landing, which was designated Green Beach. On the evening tide, with little daylight remaining, landings would take place at Red Beach, north of Inchon, and Blue Beach to the south. Marine units would lead the assaults, with support from the U.S. Army's Seventh Infantry Division and South Korean troops. On September 13 ships and aircraft began an intensive two-day bombardment.

On September 15, with MacArthur watching from the cruiser *Mount McKinley*, the Marines stormed Wolmi-do at 6:33 A.M. An hour and a half later, the island surrendered. Not one American had been killed.

At 5:30 P.M., the landings on Red and Blue Beaches began and the lack of preparation for Inchon became apparent. Boats landed in the wrong places. United Nations forces were hit by friendly fire. On Blue Beach, the landing ships grounded on mud flats, forcing troops to wade 300 yards through the knee-deep muck.

The marines attacking Red Beach had to fight their way inland and take several heavily defended objectives. One was the Asaki Brewery, the capture of which promised an epic beer bust. By midnight all objectives had been secured. The brewery turned out to be another kind of bust; preinvasion shelling and bombing had broken every last bottle of beer.

Tactically, Inchon was the stunning victory MacArthur had predicted. Landing more than

13,000 troops, the United Nations lost 22 killed and 174 wounded. NKPA casualties were estimated at 1,350 killed, wounded, or captured. Less than a month after Inchon, MacArthur had shattered the NKPA and sent it fleeing north.

MacArthur failed, however, in his strategic objective, a quick end to the war. This was probably inevitable, since he was seeking a military solution to the political problem of a divided Korea. The war would drag on for three years and end as it had begun: with two Koreas threatening each other across the thirty-eighth parallel.

I fired him because he wouldn't respect the authority of the President. That's the answer to that. I didn't fire him because he was a dumb son of a bitch, although he was, but that's not against the law for generals. If it was, half to three quarters of them would be in jail.
Harry S. Truman, on his dismissal of General MacArthur as commander in chief of U.S. forces in Korea, 1951, quoted in *Plain Speaking: An Oral Biography of Harry S. Truman*, by Merle Miller, 1974

—M.S.S.

DIEN BIEN PHU, 1954

French forces first attacked Vietnam in 1847. By 1954 the French had been governing Indochina for more than seventy years. The Battle of Dien Bien Phu climaxed nine years of fighting without decisive efforts or results. The French government was too preoccupied with other problems to be overly concerned with a war in a small Asian country far from home. French soldiers in Indochina were tired, battle weary, and had long since forgotten what they were fighting for. But the Vietminh had no such feelings or doubts. They were fighting for their homes, their rice paddies, and the right to live their lives without foreign interference.

General Henri Navarre, French commander in Indochina, was appointed to his command in May 1953 for the sole purpose of finding a way for France to get out of an embarrassing and costly situation. Until his takeover, French losses had exceeded 70,000 lives and $10 billion.

Because Navarre had absorbed the logic of the Western military, he sought a purely military solution. He chose to establish a garrison in the valley of Dien Bien Phu, 180 miles west of Hanoi, by the Laotian border. It would serve as a baited trap to entice the forces under General Vo Nguyen Giap out into the open where they would, Navarre thought, be destroyed by the superior fighting ability of the French.

The strategy was doomed to failure. French intelligence estimates of Vietminh logistics were either misinterpreted, disbelieved, or ignored. The French seriously doubted that the Vietminh could keep its army supplied, over an extended period of time, with food, weapons, and ammunition. But the Vietminh were more than up to the challenge. While some trucks were used, a vast amount of supplies was transported via a "bicycle and back" corps. More than 250,000 porters moved supplies six hundred miles over rugged terrain from the Chinese border to the battleground. A single bicycle could carry more than 400 pounds of food and ammunition. It is estimated that before the battle ended, more than 8,000 tons of supplies had been transported from China to Dien Bien Phu.

The French concentration proved to be an easy, visible target for Vietminh mortars, whereas the garrison artillery found itself shooting blindly at invisible targets in the surrounding terrain. When defeat seemed inevitable, the French government asked the United States and Great Britain to conduct air strikes against the Vietminh; both countries refused to become involved. On May 7, 1954, the garrison fell after bloody hand-to-hand combat, and the 6,500 survivors were taken prisoner. Less than half of them survived.

Though the battle was relatively minor, fought with a mixed force of no more than 15,000 French army regulars, mercenaries, Foreign Legionnaires, T'ai tribesmen, and West Africans—and seventy-five air force and navy planes—it was nonetheless decisive. It heralded France's ultimate loss of its colonial empire in Asia. It also gave the Vietminh a distinct advantage in negotiating a peace settlement; the French defeat occurred one day before peace negotiations were scheduled to begin in Geneva.

—F.M.W. and C.O.M.

TET OFFENSIVE, 1968

> The United States has broken the second rule of war. That is, don't go fighting with your land army on the mainland of Asia. Rule One is don't march on Moscow.
>
> Viscount Bernard Law Montgomery of Alamein, "Of American Policy in Vietnam," July 1968

Throughout 1967 General William Westmoreland sent American troops rampaging through South Vietnam in massive "search and destroy" operations. Using unreliable body counts as an infallible indicator of success, the American military announced that the war was being won. The deputy commander in Vietnam, General Bruce Palmer, declared, "The Vietcong

has been defeated from Da Nang all the way down in the populated areas." On NBC's *Today* show, Vice President Hubert Humphrey concurred, saying, "We are on the offensive. Territory is being gained. We are making steady progress."

> Vietnam was the first war ever fought without any censorship. Without censorship, things can get terribly confused in the public mind.
>
> William C. Westmoreland, *Time*, April 5, 1982

The Communists had suffered from the gargantuan American military buildup in Vietnam, but they were not defeated. For even as the Americans declared eventual victory, Communist general Vo Nguyen Giap, the mastermind of Dien Bien Phu, was readying his forces for a grand offensive in early 1968. Hoping for a complete military victory, Giap was nevertheless prepared to settle for a psychological defeat of South Vietnam and the United States.

Both sides agreed to a truce for the beginning of the Tet (lunar new year) festival. However, on the second day, Giap launched simultaneous assaults on five of South Vietnam's six major cities, thirty-six of forty-four provincial capitals, and numerous other towns and military installations, including twenty-three airstrips. One-half of the South Vietnamese Army was on leave. Enjoying the holidays, the South Vietnamese soldiers were taken completely by surprise. North Vietnamese and Vietcong units drove into the city of Hue. Assassination squads with death lists initiated a reign of terror. Communist forces infiltrated and attacked Saigon, where American marines beat off an attack on the U.S. Embassy by nineteen Viet Cong in civilian clothing, and South Vietnamese troops battled on the lawns of the presidential palace.

Gradually, after savage fighting, the Americans and South Vietnamese pushed the Communists out of Saigon, Hue, and the other cities. The spontaneous uprising of urban Vietnamese, which Communist military leaders had counted on, had failed to materialize. From a strictly military point of view, the Communists had gained little and had lost thousands of their best soldiers. The U.S. Army quickly proclaimed victory, claiming 60,000 Communist soldiers killed to only 2,600 Americans and South Vietnamese. Indeed, the Viet Cong had been reduced to a weakened junior partner to the North Vietnamese Army, which, by June 1968, outnumbered the Viet Cong in South Vietnam.

However, in the United States the Johnson administration had been dealt a fatal blow in an election year. Lyndon Johnson's "credibility gap" had become a "credibility canyon." Off the screen, TV anchorman Walter Cronkite expressed the feelings of most Americans when he asked, "What the hell is going on? I thought we were winning the war!" One month after the Tet Offensive, Lyndon Johnson halted the bombing of most of North Vietnam, called for the opening of peace negotiations, and announced that he would not run for reelection. Giap had won his psychological victory, which ultimately led to the Communist takeover of South Vietnam.

> You will kill ten of our men, and we will kill one of yours, and in the end it will be you who tire of it.
> Ho Chi Minh

—R.J.F.

EYEWITNESS TO WORLD WAR II

PEARL HARBOR

When: December 7, 1941

How: During the years preceding World War II, U.S. relations with Japan had grown increasingly strained. When in 1931 Japan began moving into Manchuria, presumably to stop the spread of Communism, the United States took Chiang Kai-shek for an ally; the League of Nations called for withdrawal of Japanese troops and a withholding of recognition by member countries of the new puppet state. As a result, Japan pulled out of the League. The Japanese continued their buildup in Manchuria, and the uneasy stalemate with the United States continued throughout the thirties. Diplomacy between the two countries broke down in 1941, when President Franklin Roosevelt refused to meet with the Japanese emperor, and the United States insisted Japan clear out of Indochina and China altogether. By then Japan had already become a member of the Axis by signing the Tripartite Pact with Germany and Italy in September 1940.

Throughout 1941 the United States inched closer and closer toward war. After the 1940 presidential election, during which both candidates, incumbent Roosevelt and Republican Wendell Willkie, promised peace, Roosevelt pushed through the Lend-Lease Act in March 1941. This act officially acknowledged the already existing policy of supplying Britain with war materials. Roosevelt also ordered convoys to protect the Atlantic Ocean, and made speeches stating that "the war is approaching the brink of the Western Hemisphere itself. It is coming very close to home."

Meanwhile, during 1940, Colonel William Friedman, army cryptanalyst, and his assistant Harry Lawrence Clark had successfully created a machine that broke the most secret diplomatic code of the Japanese. Given the name "Magic," the code breaker was the first to intercept messages showing that—but not where—Japan planned an attack. On Saturday, December 6, 1941, Mrs. Dorothy Edgen, a new employee in the Office of Navy Intelligence, attempted to inform her superiors that a message showed Honolulu as a target. However, the officers in charge said the message could wait until Monday.

On Sunday, less than three hours before the attack, General George C. Marshall, army chief of staff, received an intercepted message that indicated that an attack in the Pacific was imminent. Marshall sent messages of warning to Manila, the Panama Canal Zone, and San Francisco. But atmospheric conditions prevented the relay to Fort Shafter near Pearl Harbor. The chief of traffic operations sent the message by commercial facilities and the warning arrived in Honolulu ten hours later.

At 6:30 A.M. Honolulu time, the crew of the supply ship *Antares* spotted a small half-submerged submarine. They shot at it and hit its conning tower. The sub dropped below the surface and an oil slick appeared in its place. The *Antares* radioed news of the encounter to naval headquarters at Pearl Harbor, but it did not receive a request for more information until 7:37.

At 7:55 A.M. the first bomb hit Pearl Harbor. Minutes later the USS *Oklahoma* was hit by five torpedoes, the *West Virginia* by six, the *California* by two, the *Utah* by two, and the *Detroit*, *Raleigh*, and *Helena* by one each.

Men who had never fired automatic weapons manned them and shot down enemy aircraft. American prisoners at Hickam and Wheeler fields were released to fight.

> Praise the Lord and pass the ammunition!
> Howell Maurice Forgy, U.S. naval lieutenant,
> December 7, 1941

By 10:00 A.M. eighteen ships were sunk, beached, or badly damaged, including the battleships *Arizona*, *Oklahoma*, *West Virginia*, *California*, *Tennessee*, *Maryland*, *Pennsylvania*, and *Nevada*; the target ship *Utah*; destroyers *Downes*, *Shaw*, and *Cassin*; the minelayer *Oglala*; cruisers *Helena*, *Honolulu*, and *Raleigh*; the seaplane tender *Curtiss*; and the repair ship *Vestal*. In addition, 188 planes were destroyed and 159 were damaged.

Casualties included 2,008 sailors killed, 710 wounded; 218 soldiers killed, 346 wounded; 109 marines killed, 89 wounded; 68 civilians killed, 35 wounded.

The Americans shot down twenty-nine Japanese planes, exploded one large and six midget submarines, and killed fifty-five airmen, nine submarine crewmen, and an undetermined number of other submarine crew members.

> I fear that we have only awakened a sleeping giant, and his reaction will be terrible.
>
> Yamamoto Isoroku, Japanese admiral

A scare swept the United States that the Japanese might follow through and attack the West Coast. However, it soon became clear that the attack forces were traveling west. On December 8 Japanese aircraft attacked the Philippines. Two days later, two British battleships were sunk by Japanese torpedo bombers off the coast of Malaya. On December 25 Hong Kong fell to the Japanese.

Pearl Harbor ensured U.S. entry into the war. Indeed, Roosevelt was accused by some critics of deliberately ignoring foreknowledge of the attack to precipitate U.S. entry into the war. Clare Boothe Luce commented, "He lied the American people into war because he could not lead them into it." On the other hand, pro-Roosevelt thinkers maintain that the President was merely preparing the nation for the inevitable.

Eyewitness Report: Commander Mitsuo Fuchida, who led the first wave of 183 planes to attack Pearl Harbor, later wrote: "We flew through and over the thick clouds which were at 2,000 meters, up to where the day was ready to dawn. And the clouds began to brighten below us. At 0700 I figured that we should reach Oahu in less than an hour. But flying over the clouds we could not see the surface of the water, and, consequently, had no check on our drift. I switched on the radio direction-finder to tune in the Honolulu radio station and soon picked up some light music. I found the exact direction from which the broadcast was coming and corrected our course, which had been 5 degrees off. I was wondering how to get below the clouds after reaching Oahu. If the island was

After the Japanese attack on Pearl Harbor, a small boat goes to the rescue of seamen on the burning USS West Virginia.

covered by thick clouds like those below us, the level bombing would be difficult, and we had not yet had reports from the reconnaissance planes. In tuning the radio a little finer, I heard, along with the music, what seemed to be a weather report. Holding my breath, I adjusted the dial and listened intently when I heard it come through a second time, slowly and distinctly: 'Averaging partly cloudy with clouds mostly over the mountains . . . visibility good. Wind north, ten knots.' What a windfall for us!" Nearly an hour later, Fuchida gave the Japanese word for tiger, signaling that a full surprise had been accomplished: "Tora! Tora! Tora!"

James Cory was a marine private on board the *Arizona* when a Japanese bomb detonated the ship's forward magazines. His account is taken from *Remember Pearl Harbor: Eyewitness Accounts of U.S. Military Men and Women*, edited by Robert S. La Forte and Ronald E. Marcello. "The bombs struck forward—forward of us. . . . And immediately you could feel them penetrating the decks, and then there was this big 'Whoosh!' Now it wasn't a 'Bang!' It wasn't a 'Boom!' It was a 'Whoosh!' You could hear the bombs whistling down and feel them hit and penetrate, and then this 'Whoosh.' It was all very rapid, almost simultaneous. . . . Major Alan Shapley [commander of the ship's marine detachment and officer in charge of the fire control station] gave the order: 'Abandon Ship! Let's get below!' I waited until six men got through that hatch. I was right beside it, and I wanted to be the first out; but I forced myself to wait until some other men had gone first. I was so confused that I wanted to run. Fear had now taken hold, but not to the point to destroy discipline. I went down the proper ladders until I got to the searchlight platform, and then I said: 'To hell with traffic rules! I'm going down this ladder!' I remembered not to touch the hot ladder rails as I raced down that ladder, facing aft, onto the quarterdeck. There were bodies of men. I'd seen this from above, but it didn't register clearly until I got down on the quarterdeck. These people were zombies, in essence. They were burned completely white. Their skin was just as white as if you'd taken a bucket of whitewash and painted them white. Their hair was burned off; their eyebrows were burned off; the pitiful remnants of their uniforms in their crotch was a charred remnant; and the insoles of their shoes were about the only things that were left on these bodies. They were moving like robots. Their arms were out, held away from their bodies, and they were stumping along the decks. These were burned men!"

Ed Sheehan, an ironworker at Pearl Harbor, recalled in his book *Days of '41*: "When the second-wave planes came in, they appeared as if from out of nowhere, even soundless at first. They darted like angry birds at the *Nevada*,

hitting her again and again. From a distance she seemed to shiver and shrug, but miraculously kept moving. Moments later racking detonations came from the nearby dry-dock area. Concussions followed, pulsing blasts of warm wind. I wanted desperately to hide, to crawl under something, anything, but there was no place to go. I realized that those last hits must have been made on the *Pennsylvania, Cassin,* or *Downes*— perhaps all three. A crane moving beside the dry dock stopped. Flames leaped out of the big sunken basin and smoke whorled up. I thought for a moment about the chief doing his Christmas cards there, only the night before. I kept moving toward the dry dock. I didn't want to go, but could think of nothing else to do. Then the destroyer *Shaw* was hit, out on the floating dry dock. The eruption was monstrous, appalling.

"The ship appeared to disintegrate into a million pieces, becoming a gargantuan fireball. The blast sent scraps twisting and flying in all directions, for thousands of feet, in great slow-motion arcs trailing streamers of smoke. I was probably a quarter of a mile away, yet one of the pieces fell at my feet. I picked it up, a curl of steel ripped clean and shiny, handball-sized. I thought of keeping it as a souvenir; it would have made a conversation-piece as a paperweight. Then I threw it away."

—W.G.

D-DAY

When: June 6, 1944
How: In early 1942 Dwight David "Ike" Eisenhower was a freshly minted brigadier general, the protégé of army chief of staff General George C. Marshall. Eisenhower had never been in combat, and in fact had never led any military formation larger than a battalion. Even so, in the untested Eisenhower, Marshall perceived the command personality necessary for World War II's most delicate and important assignment.

No one else could match Eisenhower's gift for cajoling powerful and frequently antagonistic Allied leaders into forgetting their personal agendas and pulling together to pursue a common objective. The high and mighty sometimes underestimated Ike's unobtrusive, impartial intellect, but they usually found themselves doing exactly what he asked of them.

Named chief of the War Plans Division by Marshall, Eisenhower struggled to hew a feasible scheme for the liberation of Europe out of a mountain of preliminary British/American staff work. The problem was to somehow shepherd an Allied armada across the notoriously unpredictable English Channel, over the deadly beachheads of Normandy, and deep into the interior of Hitler's "Fortress Europe."

The cross-channel invasion would be the largest, most complex, and most difficult military operation of all time. To have any hope of success, the invasion plan had to garner the whole-hearted support not only of President Roosevelt and the War Department but also of the skeptical British prime minister Winston Churchill; the headstrong, hypersensitive Charles de Gaulle, head of the French Committee of National Liberation; and the embattled Soviet leader Josef Stalin, who continuously harangued the English and Americans to immediately, and at all costs, open a second front in Europe.

Not only did Eisenhower face seemingly insoluble political obstacles, but also the invasion force's operational effectiveness depended on its surviving the exceptionally formidable German coastal defenses, which had been personally organized and lethally refined by Field Marshal Erwin Rommel, Hitler's finest field commander.

Rommel had bluntly informed the führer that Germany's only hope for a tolerable end to the war lay in fending off an Allied attack while it was still at sea, or failing that, in pinning the invaders down and crushing them on the beachhead with an overwhelming counterattack by armored Panzer units. If the Allies gained a foothold on the Continent, Rommel warned, Germany was doomed.

Preoccupied with his invasion of Russia, Hitler grudgingly agreed, and beginning in March 1942, slave labor transformed the entire coastline of Nazi-occupied Europe into a 1,200-mile-long death trap of naval and land mines, barbed wire, tank traps, machine-gun pillboxes, trench networks, and artillery emplacements.

As many as 50,000 losses had been predicted for the invading Allies during the first few hours after landing on the beaches of Europe. And yet, despite its myriad terrors and difficulties, the invasion of Nazi-occupied Europe had to be undertaken. The alternative, accepting a totalitarian Europe under Hitler and/or a victorious Stalin, was too nightmarish in its implications for the survival of democracy elsewhere in the world.

Eisenhower's plan, with modifications proposed by British Twenty-first Army commander General Bernard Law Montgomery, was agreed on by the Allies on January 15, 1944. Eisenhower was elevated to the rank of four-star general and designated Supreme Commander, Allied Expeditionary Forces.

Code-named Overlord, the actual invasion was preceded by an elaborate campaign of deception, which cut rail transport to Normandy from the air and guilefully convinced the German High Command that General George S. Patton would be spearheading Allied landings in the Pas de Calais region.

Rommel correctly predicted the real invasion would land in Normandy at the Seine bight, on the Cotentin Peninsula near Cherbourg. But Hitler mulishly disagreed, as did Rommel's fawning superior, Field Marshal Gerd von Rundstedt, on the grounds that the invasion fleet would be certain to take the shortest possible route to its target.

On the basis of Hitler's misplaced self-confidence, German infantry divisions were stationed in two rows between the Somme River and the Schelde Estuary, and also in the Boulogne/Calais area, which was further defended by heavy batteries protected by concrete or armor.

In the vicinity of the five Normandy beaches, where the invasion was actually headed, the German mobile reaction force consisted of one understrength infantry division and a random scattering of service units. An inflexible German command structure of sixty divisions in France all but guaranteed that Rommel wouldn't be able to call for Luftwaffe and Panzer support when he needed it urgently.

As it happened, Rommel wasn't present when the fateful day came. Clinging to the Pas de Calais delusion, von Rundstedt failed to react to the invasion in time. Upon being informed by an aide that the führer was still asleep when the invaders started coming ashore, von Rundstedt cravenly hesitated to notify Hitler of the landings until the next day. By then the die was cast.

The Allied invasion armada of 150,000 men, borne on 5,300 ships and landing craft, departed from their English staging areas on June 3, 1944, anticipating a landing on June 5. But the weather deteriorated on the fourth, and choppy seas in the Channel forced Eisenhower to postpone the invasion. On June 5 the Supreme Commander's chief meteorologist, RAF Group Captain J.M. Stagg, informed Eisenhower that he thought the weather might clear on the sixth.

The whole fate of the operation descended on Eisenhower's shoulders at that moment. He said to his generals, "I am quite positive that the order [not to postpone] must be given. I don't like it, but there it is. I don't see how we can do anything else." The greatest invasion in world history was on. Eisenhower quietly jotted a statement taking sole personal responsibility for the operation, in case his decision to proceed resulted in disaster.

The landing sites were "softened up" by 10,500 Allied airplanes flying 14,000 combat sorties. The Germans had fewer than 500 planes nearby and were quickly knocked out of the skies, but not before a handful of German fighter pilots managed strafing runs during the early stages of the landings.

Allied ships off-loaded assault troops into landing ships for tanks (LSTs) eleven miles from the shore. Hundreds of soldiers who made it to shore were seasick, off course, and disoriented.

Many landing craft sank or were grounded on sandbars before dropping their ramps. The troops inside jumped into deep water wearing an average seventy pounds of equipment. Many soldiers drowned. Others, wounded or exhausted, were unable to outcrawl the swiftly rising tide and drowned within ten yards of the beach.

Thirty-two Duplex Drive amphibious tanks were launched 5,000 yards from the beach. Twenty-seven of them promptly sank in heavy seas, with the loss of almost all their crew members. Forty out of seventy-two boats carrying artillery pieces capsized.

There were five invasion beachheads—Utah, Omaha, Gold, Juno, and Sword—covering a front of about sixty miles. The assault began with the wind-scattered and disorganized landing of 13,000 paratroopers. The American Eighty-second Airborne Division's drop zone was near Sainte-Mère-Église, astride the N-13 road to Cherbourg. The Eighty-second was on the left wing of the invasion force and screened the left flank of the U.S. Fourth Infantry Division's landing site at Utah Beach.

The 101st Airborne Division landed to the south of the Eighty-second, at nearby Sainte Marie du Mont. After regrouping, the paratroopers secured vital roadways and villages, allowing the Fourth Division to move inland from Utah Beach. Although hampered by poor visibility and delivered to the wrong sector, the Fourth overcame comparatively light German resistance and quickly linked up with the paratroopers.

At Omaha Beach, between Saint-Laurent-sur-Mer and Colleville-sur-Mer, American riflemen from the U.S. First and Twenty-ninth Infantry Divisions faced the fiercest fighting of the day. All but a few of the first-wave invaders landed a mile south of their objective. Pinned down behind a seawall by prelaid, intersecting German lanes of machine-gun, artillery, and mortar fire, and despite suffering heavy losses, the Americans advanced, pressing the attack inland over a 200-yard-wide beach and heavily fortified bluffs defended in depth and commanded by 88mm coastal artillery pieces.

During this, the heaviest fighting of the Omaha landings, three companies of the American Second Ranger Battalion scaled the sheer 100-foot cliffs of Pointe du Hoc on the west side of Omaha Beach on ropes. Their mission was to destroy a battery of 155mm guns that dominated the seaborne approaches to Omaha. The surviving Rangers who made it to the top discovered that the Germans had removed the guns to protect them from aerial bombardment.

At roughly the same time, 7,000 British "Red Devils" of the Sixth Airborne Division were landing east of the British Third Division at Sword Beach near Ouistreham, seizing the critical road juncture to Caen in the face of stiff German resistance. The British secured their beaches by 10:00 P.M. and repulsed the only counterattack of the invasion by German armor. British paratroopers further secured vital bridges inland, to the east.

The Canadian Third Division took Juno Beach, protecting the right flank of the British Fiftieth Division landing on Gold Beach, near Arromanches, outside of Bayeux. The Canadians faced bitter fighting but attained their village objectives and linked up with the British by midmorning.

All that day and night, the Allies poured ashore: 35,250 at Utah Beach, 34,250 at Omaha Beach, 20,000 paratroopers, 83,115 in the British and Canadian sectors. The casualties were high, estimated at 10,274, including 2,132 killed in action. Even so, the landings were successful beyond the wildest dreams of their planners.

By D-Day plus eleven, exactly 487,653 men and 89,728 vehicles had landed on the continent. The Allies now held the initiative, and despite the fierce German resistance they soon encountered in the hedgerow country beyond the beachheads, they would not be dislodged. As Rommel had predicted, the Third Reich's days were numbered. Upon his return to the beaches two decades later, ex-president Dwight Eisenhower explained, "The thing that pulled this out was the bravery and courage and the initiative of the American GI."

Eyewitness Reports: One week shy of her fifteenth birthday, Anne Frank wrote a diary entry describing how she and her family, huddled by a clandestine radio in their Amsterdam hiding place, breathlessly listened to the news of the invasion. "This is the day!" she exulted. "I have the feeling friends are approaching."

At 1:10 A.M. Private First Class Robert Murphy, eighteen, a pathfinder with the Eighty-second Airborne, jumped out of a C-47 300 feet above Sainte-Mère-Église burdened with a Thompson submachine gun, 300 rounds of .45 ammunition, and a 40-pound radar unit. Murphy and his fellow pathfinders began setting up the radar beacons and signal lights that would soon guide hundreds of airplanes and thousands of paratroopers onto their drop zones.

In his excitement upon landing on enemy territory, while extricating himself from his parachute harness, Murphy inadvertently cut away his ammunition belt. All he had left was the twenty rounds in his Thompson's magazine.

Murphy saw the sky fill with 1,800 more parachutes. His was the only drop zone where men landed where they should have. Some paratroopers were shot while still in the air. Others fell into the open locks of the Merderet River at high tide and drowned in four feet of water, helplessly tangled in their chutes.

First Lieutenant Jack Isaacs, a platoon leader with the Eighty-second, parachuted through an antiaircraft barrage unharmed, but winds blew him seven miles off course from his intended landing spot—the village of Sainte-Mère-Église. Private John Steele's parachute was blown into the village, and settled onto the steeple of the local church. Hit in the heel, Steele played dead for two hours before the Germans cut him down and took him prisoner.

Battalion commander Lieutenant Colonel Edward Krause gathered his paratroopers and headed an assault against the German garrison at Sainte-Mère-Église and put them to flight. He took the American flag his unit had raised over Naples, Italy, from his pocket, went to the town hall, and ran up the colors. The trees all around the village square were festooned with dead paratroopers.

By 4:30 A.M. all Allied paratroopers and glider-borne support troops were on the ground. And almost all of them were lost, having been so widely scattered over Normandy that they wandered around in the dark in squad-sized pickup units, trying to make contact with each other by clicking small metal recognition devices called crickets.

At 6:30 A.M. the Fourth Infantry Division splashed ashore at Utah Beach, on the west flank of the invasion. Fifty-six-year-old brigadier general Theodore Roosevelt, the son of the twenty-sixth president, landed with the first wave (the only general to go ashore with the troops that day) and studied his maps, ignoring German small-arms fire. When Roosevelt consulted with Colonel James Van Fleet, the commander of the Eighth Regiment, the two men discovered they were a mile south of their objective. Roosevelt remarked, or so the story goes, "We'll start the war from right here." Seeing that the Fourth had caught the enemy at a weak point, Van Fleet ordered his unit to lead the way and push straight ahead.

Engineers and demolitions specialists set about exploding Rommel's beach obstacles, clearing eight fifty-yard gaps. Sherman tanks roared through them and turned inland. The Fourth followed in their wake, collecting paratroopers as it went, and establishing an aid station in a nearby farmhouse.

At the foot of the Pointe du Hoc promontory, twenty-three-year-old sergeant William Petty, whose nickname was L-Rod, was among the Rangers attempting to fire rockets carrying grappling hooks to the top of the cliff. Allied ships had bombarded German positions up above with the equivalent of ten kilotons of high explosives, but still the Germans directed withering automatic and mortar fire on the elite American assault unit huddled at the base of the cliffs.

Grappling hooks started to catch in the cliff face, and the Rangers began the murderous climb toward their objective. Germans were rolling "potato masher" percussion grenades down onto the Rangers.

Trucks outfitted with fire ladders advanced on the promontory, but only one of them could get enough traction in the sandy soil to approach closely. Sergeant William Stivison took an M-2 .50-caliber machine gun up the ladder and precariously sprayed German positions from his swaying, dipping perch.

L-Rod Petty was about forty feet up the face when he started to fall backward. At first he thought his rope had been cut, but then he realized the grappling hook at the upper end must be slipping in loose soil. Sergeant Billy McHugh, climbing on an adjacent rope, offered Petty a few words of advice. "L-Rod," McHugh said, "you're going the wrong way . . . you're supposed to be going up, like I am."

"Comic," thought Petty, as he slipped to the bottom of the hill. Unharmed, he found another rope and ascended again.

On top of the hill, Rangers stared dumbfounded at empty gun emplacements. Then First Sergeant Leonard Lomell and Staff Sergeant Jack Kuhn discovered tire tracks in a dirt road that led to a camouflaged emplacement fifty feet away, hidden under some trees. There were five enormous guns pointing at Utah Beach, guarded by about eighty Germans. Lomell and Kuhn crept up to the guns and used thermite grenades to melt their breeches and traversing mechanisms.

Their retreat was covered by an enormous explosion. Other Rangers had located and destroyed an enormous German ammo dump nearby.

Meanwhile, it was murder on Omaha Beach. The first company of the Twenty-ninth Infantry to splash ashore took more than 90 percent casualties. German artillery and mortars opened up on the Twenty-ninth's assault boats from 300 yards out. Nineteen-year-old sergeant Bob Slaughter watched one of the boats get raked with heavy machine-gun fire, sparks flying off its steel ramp. "Man, this is it. We're going to catch hell," Slaughter said to no one in particular.

The coxswain of Slaughter's LST panicked and tried to drop his ramp prematurely, intending to discharge the riflemen with deep water underfoot, obliging them to swim for it. Willard Norfleet, Slaughter's platoon sergeant, cocked his .45 automatic and held it to the sailor's head all the rest of the way in. Slaughter was among the first to disembark. Six feet five inches tall, he was up to his chest in the surf. Corpses floated all around him. Slaughter and his fellow riflemen somehow made it to the seawall. There Brigadier General Norman J. Cota and Slaughter's regimental commander, Colonel Charles Canham, rallied the men who sought shelter against the heavy fire by striding around unprotected and cursing at them.

THE DUMMY D-DAY

The invasion of Normandy on June 6, 1944, owed much of its success to a remarkable practical joke.

As the Allies geared up for D-Day, they knew it would be impossible to conceal their invasion plans from the Germans. But they could mislead them as to the time and place of the offensive. In the spring of 1944, German surveillance cameras photographed widespread "covert" military operations in southeastern England—bustling army bases half hidden in the woods, large-scale movements of jeeps and tanks, and an oil refinery under construction at Dover, across the English Channel from Calais, France. The Germans also monitored "secret" radio transmissions concerning new troop concentrations near Dover. It all added up to a single unmistakable conclusion: The Allies would invade Europe through Calais, probably in late July.

But the Nazis were mistaken. The oil refinery was made of old sewage pipes and canvas, built by movie-set designers. The combat vehicles were inflatable rubber, the military bases were dummies, the radio messages were fake—and the real invasion was planned not for Calais in late July but for Normandy in early June.

Nor did the deception cease once the invasion was under way. While Allied troops were storming the beaches at Normandy, two decoy fleets accompanied by British air squadrons were crossing the Channel toward Calais. The decoy ships carried electronic devices that amplified and returned the pulses of the Germans' radar equipment, and the squadrons overhead released strips of metal foil. Both maneuvers gave the illusion on Nazi radar screens of a massive air and sea attack. Meanwhile, scores of dummy paratroopers—equipped with recordings of gunfire and soldiers' cries—were dropped on the beach south of Calais. The elaborate ruse lured Hitler into spreading his troops dangerously thin, and the Allies got their foothold in Europe. Even after D-Day, the führer remained convinced that the *real* invasion was still planned for late July. By the time he got it straight, Germany was on the road to defeat.

Rubber tanks at an Allied base near Dover and faked radio transmissions tricked the Nazis into thinking the D-Day invasion would come at Calais in July rather than Normandy in June.

"Colonel Canham," shouted a battalion commander from the cover of a nearby pillbox, "if you don't get out of the open and take cover, you're going to get killed!"

"Get your goddamned ass out of that goddamned pillbox and get your men off this goddamned beach!" Canham replied.

Sergeant Perry Bonner charged up the bluff and discovered a trail. Slaughter and several other men followed him and met several American GIs escorting a long column of surrendering German prisoners. The Twenty-ninth started to move inland, the enemy fire weakening at last.

East of Sword Beach, just after midnight on the morning of June 6, elements of the British Sixth Airborne under Major John Howard and Lieutenant Danny Brotheridge assaulted and took the heavily defended and vital Benouville Bridge. The French later renamed the site Pegasus Bridge, in honor of the Sixth's insignia and the heroism of men like Brotheridge, who, according to historian Stephen Ambrose, may have been the first Allied soldier killed by the Germans on D-Day.

Lieutenant Colonel Terence Otway's Ninth Parachute Battalion—or, rather, 150 of the 750 who had jumped with him—destroyed the German battery at Merville, assaulting a German force three times the size of its own. Half of Otway's 150 paratroopers were killed or wounded in the attack and the remaining 600 were scattered in the dark.

At Juno Beach, the Canadian Third Infantry Division, a tough outfit of miners, fishermen, and lumberjacks, had the misfortune of landing ten minutes behind schedule. Bouncing back from a B-17 strike and naval bombardment, German gunners decimated the Canadians, who took casualties of almost 50 percent. But by 6:00 P.M. the Canadians had penetrated three miles inland, farther than any other Allied unit. They linked up with the British who had landed on Gold Beach.

On the eastern flank of the invasion, at Sword Beach, thirty-two-year-old brigadier Simon Christopher Fraser (Baron Lovat) led a mixed force of French, English, and Scottish commandos from the British Third Infantry Division ashore in the traditional manner, behind Pipe Major Bill Millin in full regalia. Millin was playing a somewhat nervous rendition of "Highland Laddie."

Fraser's commandos rushed a colony of seaside villas at Ouistreham, running up against a casino the Germans had transformed into a fortress. The fortunes of war were not with the Germans, and the commandos overran them, turning inland. On reaching open country, Fraser's unit effected an emotional linkup with the paratroopers of the Sixth British Airborne Division.

A young French girl ran up to Pipe Major Millin and asked for a song. He studied her black hair and brown eyes and played her a rendition of "Nut Brown Maiden." Guillaume Mercader, a twenty-nine-year-old Résistant, broke out a French flag with the Cross of Lorraine and carried it openly, welcoming the liberators. Possession of the flag would have been enough to have gotten him executed the day before. "It was a strong moment," he murmured fifty years later, remembering June 6, 1944, as vividly as if it were yesterday.

—M.C.S.

THE FIREBOMBING OF DRESDEN

When: February 13–15, 1945
How: During the closing days of World War II, the medieval eastern German city of Dresden— the seventh largest town in the Reich—had somehow managed to keep itself free of the Hitler regime's bristling defense industries. Internationally celebrated for its exquisite china and ornate baroque architecture, Dresden was often described as Florence on the Elbe River.

Its citizens had another nickname for their home: Germany's Safest Air-Raid Shelter. They trusted in the rumor that Allied planners had chosen Dresden to become Germany's postwar capital on the basis of its cultural value and lack of military significance.

Dresden, the wishful thinking ran, would no doubt be spared the kind of aerial bombardment that had by then obliterated most other German cities of comparable size. This faith in Dresden's demilitarized status was so pervasive that the city had been all but stripped of its antiaircraft batteries. Fighters at a nearby Luftwaffe base had long been grounded for lack of fuel. The city was literally defenseless.

In February of 1945, Dresden was dangerously overcrowded, its usual population of about 630,000 swollen by more than a million refugees, fleeing before the advancing Red Army. The Russians were just forty miles away, closing in from the east.

Most of the city's wartime inhabitants were noncombatants: women and children, the old and war-wounded, allied prisoners of war, and slave laborers conscripted from Nazi-occupied Europe.

But on the night of February 13, just after ten o'clock, the Pathfinders, preceding the first wave of 244 RAF Lancaster bombers, appeared over Dresden, dropping "primary green" marker flares just west of the railway tracks that encircled the city, at the juncture where they met the bend of the Elbe River.

The incendiary bombs of the first wave fell wide of their illuminated aiming point. A great number of houses and public buildings near the city's center were hit. Most Dresdeners had never experienced an air raid before, and many ventured from the safety of their homes to help their neighbors put out fires. Such altruism frequently proved fatal.

Eyewitness Reports: Fifteen-year-old Annemarie Waehmann was in a public ward of the Friedrichstadt Hospital complex when the bombs started falling. All ambulatory patients sought refuge in the cellar. She remembers: "There was a crashing and thundering, whistling and howling. The walls trembled, swayed by the impact of the bombs. How long it lasted, don't ask me. . . . It seemed to be hours. . . . Then some of the doctors screamed, 'Everyone out of the cellar, the whole building is going to collapse!' From a certain distance the doctors watched the collapse of the houses, and as soon as there was a few seconds respite in between collapsing masses of debris, they shouted 'Come on, two or three people, out!' and a few [of us] shot outside. At the second 'Come on' I too ran for my life into the next building. Did all of them get out? How many didn't manage? I don't know. Everyone was in such a panic that all we wanted was to save our naked lives."

The 529 Lancasters of the second wave hit the already burning city with more incendiaries and high explosives at 1:22 A.M., February 14. The resultant firestorm closed off most escape avenues to clear ground and greedily consumed all the oxygen in its path. The ancient city was rapidly transformed into a vast open-air crematorium. Fire and rescue services stood helpless before such a conflagration.

Flight Sergeant Peter De Wesselow, an RAF "bomb aimer" who had studied in Germany before the war, recalled his feelings on the night he dropped his cargo of firebombs during the second wave, as reported in Alexander McKee's *Dresden 1945: The Devil's Tinderbox* (1984): "Dresden was one experience among many for us. At briefing we were told it was a communications center for the Russian front. I think we knew, and were probably told, that [the mission] was to help, and still more, impress the Russians with the power of bomber command. . . . My main memory is coming down for a better view. I couldn't identify the aiming point, which is why I came down to 5,000 feet . . . just above the blast range of our 4,000 pound bombs. . . . The city was distinctly lit up. I saw people in the streets. I saw a dog rushing across the road and felt sorry for it (is that absurd?). The uniqueness of Dresden to me was coming down . . . so I saw much more; it was more intimate. All these raids were pretty horrifying, though. We went to Dresden with the usual sinking feeling of personal fear, suppressed by busying ourselves with our technical tasks, in the usual ignorance of why our masters chose this target and briefed on the matter only so far as it was relevant to destroying what they wanted to destroy."

Twenty-four-year-old Margret Freyer took refuge from the second wave of RAF bombers with one man and forty-one other women in a cellar on Ferdinandstrasse. She had soaked two handkerchiefs in water before descending into the improvised bomb shelter. When the shelter filled with smoke, she clapped the wet handkerchiefs over her nose and mouth and, clawing her way to freedom, emerged, the only survivor.

"Because of flying sparks and the firestorm I couldn't see anything at first. A witches' cauldron was waiting for me out there: no street, only rubble nearly a meter high, glass, girders, stones, craters. . . . Someone behind me called out, 'Take off your coat, it's started to burn!' In the pervading extreme heat I hadn't even noticed. . . .

"Suddenly I fall into a big hole—a bomb crater about six meters wide and two meters deep, and I end up down there lying on top of three women. I shake them by their clothes and scream at them, telling them that they must get out of here—but they don't move any more. . . . I seemed to have lost all emotional feeling. To my left, I suddenly see a woman. . . . She carries a bundle in her arms. It is a baby. She runs, she falls, and the child flies in an arc into the fire. It's only my eyes which take this in; I myself feel nothing. Why? What for? I don't know, I just stumble on. The firestorm is incredible, there are cries for help and screams from somewhere, but all around is one big inferno. . . . Suddenly I saw people again right in front of me. . . . Then—to my utter horror and amazement—I see how . . . they simply seem to let themselves drop to the ground. I had a feeling they were being shot, but my mind could not understand what was really happening. Today, I know that these unfortunate people were the victims of lack of oxygen. They fainted, and then burnt to cinders."

Hugo Eichhorn was north of the city in the neighboring town of Heller that night, commanding an SS engineer unit that supplied many of the rescue teams who would excavate the charred rubble of Dresden in the days ahead.

"As we had no shelters, my soldiers were taking cover in trenches which had been dug in the parade ground. My adjutant and I stood on the barrack square and watched the bombing through binoculars. We just had to stand there as the whole city with 650,000 inhabitants and at least as many refugees went up in flames and died. . . . Because of the fire storm, at first it was possible to give help only at the periphery of the fire. Advancing into the cellars eventually we were met with the most gruesome sights . . . whole groups of people, dead in cellars without surface wounds, their lungs torn by blast. And other cellars full of water and drowned people. How many were there? Figures can only be approximate. I reckon there could have been 300,000, perhaps as many as 400,000 killed."

Other accounts estimating the dead range from the most conservative, at 35,000, to the most often-quoted figure of 135,000. Because of the vast numbers of refugees in the streets and the hygienic urgency of disposing of corpses as quickly as possible, an accurate body count will never be known.

There was more horror yet to come. On the following day, February 15, 400 B-17 Flying Fortresses of the U.S. Eighth Air Force appeared and renewed the assault, dropping 782 more tons of incendiaries on top of the RAF's 3,000 tons. But by that time the major damage had been inflicted, and the B-17s were bombing rubble. About 1,600 acres of the medieval city center had vanished in rolling waves of flame, which had reached temperatures as high as 1,800 degrees. Apes, elephants, bears, and ostriches escaped from the city zoo and, terrified, bolted surreally into the streets, where molten asphalt flowed like a black river.

In the wake of the departing B-17s, American P-51 Mustang fighters swooped onto stunned and disoriented survivors of the raid at treetop level, strafing everything that moved with .50-caliber machine-gun fire.

Novelist Kurt Vonnegut, then a 106th Infantry Division POW put to work by the Germans excavating survivors from the rubble, was one of the targets of the American strafing attack. In *Slaughterhouse Five*, his fictional account of the Dresden raid, Vonnegut noted that the only reason the Mustangs failed to kill him and many of his fellow American prisoners was that the plentiful rubble afforded them such excellent cover. Dazed and confused civilians moving about in nearby open meadows were less fortunate.

Apologists for the attack later marshaled a list of rationales for targeting Dresden. The most frequently cited objective of the bombardment was to make it difficult for the German army to bring up reinforcements to oppose the advancing Russian troops.

Wartime documents since released by the British government seem to indicate that Winston Churchill ordered the raid to conciliate Soviet leader Josef Stalin. But Churchill, belatedly appalled by the after-action reports of tens of thousands of civilians burned alive on his order, later wondered aloud in a Cabinet meeting whether it was right to "bomb German cities simply in order to increase the terror."

Fifty years after the raid, many military analysts have concluded that destroying an undefended and militarily insignificant city like Dresden, so late in the war (peace was less than three months away), made no tactical or strategic sense at all. The firebombing of Dresden could only be explained as an act of vengeance.

In 1995, at a ceremony commemorating the fiftieth anniversary of the Allied bombing of Dresden, representatives of Britain, the United States, and Germany laid wreaths in a silent ceremony before a memorial stone at Heidefriedhof Cemetery. Dresden's landmark baroque Church of Our Lady, which for fifty years had been left a bombed-out ruin as a reminder of the horrors of war, will be rebuilt as a symbol of the city's rise from the ashes.

—M.C.S.

HIROSHIMA

When: August 6, 1945
How: The dropping of "Little Boy," scientists' nickname for the 9,000-pound, ten-foot-long, twenty-eight-inch-round uranium bomb encasing the equivalent of 13,500 tons of TNT, which had been achieved at a cost of $2 billion over a two-and-one-half-year period, was the most controversial decision ever made in military history. It was named the atom bomb because it involves splitting an atomic nucleus by bombarding it with neutrons, which sets off a chain reaction of fission that releases enormous quantities of energy, infinitesimal matter bursting into infinite power. The first atom bomb fell on Hiroshima on August 6, 1945. Immediately it turned Japan's eighth major city, with a population of 300,000, into what one writer called "the world's largest guinea pig." No warning had been given, other than the half million leaflets that had shimmered down from the skies like so much confetti two days earlier. These warned, "Your city will be obliterated unless your Government surrenders."

Already by the summer of 1945 Japan's great urban centers of Tokyo-Yokohama and Osaka-Kobe had endured "conventional" destruction by saturation and carpet bombings to an unimaginable degree. B-29s fire-bombed these cities daily—weather permitting—and had incinerated 100 square miles of habitation, gutted or razed 2 million buildings, devastated and rendered homeless 13 million people. In one massive, all-night raid by 1,000 planes, 74,000 people were killed or wounded. Hiroshima, however, a city of minor military significance and until then quite undamaged (the Japanese conjectured that Americans were saving it as a residential sector, if and when they won the war), was wiped from the map by one plane discharging a single bomb.

That morning of August 6, a B-29 Superfortress from the 509th Composite Group of the Air Force, the *Enola Gay*—so named for the mother of the young southern pilot who commanded the plane, Paul Tibbets Jr.—set off from the tiny Pacific atoll of Tinian, which had been captured from the Japanese a year earlier. Flying at a speed of 285 miles per hour and a height of 32,000 feet, its target was Aioi Bridge in the heart of downtown Hiroshima. The bomb, inscribed with nasty remarks about the emperor, exploded in the air 600 yards above Shima Surgical Hospital 300 yards off its intended target (the bridge was damaged but remained standing; the hospital and its patients were vaporized).

There was a *pika*, a blinding flash of pink, blue, red, or yellow light—none of the survivors ever agreed on the color—brighter than 1,000 suns but coming from a fireball only 110 yards in diameter. In that split second the hypocenter or point of impact reached a heat of 3,000 degrees centigrade. Within a 1,000-yard radius, granite buildings melted, steel and stone bridges burned, and so did the rivers below them. Roof tiles boiled and people evaporated, leaving their shadows "photographed" like X-ray negatives on walls and pavements.

In a matter of seconds, four square miles of central Hiroshima were turned into rubble. Every clock and watch stopped at exactly the same time: 8:15 A.M. Because of ionization, the choking air filled with a sickish sweet "electric smell." The bright blue, sunlit sky turned darkly yellow, and a churning cloud of smoke spurted upward for 50,000 feet. From a distance it looked like a gigantic mushroom, but to the escaping *Enola Gay* crew the shape was more that of a grotesque question mark. They heard Captain Robert Lewis, the co-pilot, exclaim as he saw it rolling in the air, "My God, look at that sonofabitch go!" (In notes he penned later, he wrote that his initial response was a more sober, "My God, what have we done?") The cloud rose so high its heat condensed water vapor. In minutes "black rain," sticky, pebble-sized drops of wet radioactive dust, dripped down over Hiroshima, staining the skin of the survivors with red blotches.

Within an hour or so, 70,000 Japanese had died. So did twenty-two American men and women who were prisoners of war. A twenty-third, a young soldier surviving the explosion, was dragged from the rubble of the detention camp and slaughtered by angry Japanese. The population still able to walk wandered about the smoking ruins in a bewildered daze, unable to find their loved ones, incapable of orienting themselves, as all landmarks had vanished. Amazingly, the survivors felt little pain. It was as if the greater terror of the unknown canceled the lesser horror of suffering. Most of the walking wounded were naked, their clothes having been burned or blown off, but among the

Hours after the atomic bomb exploded over Hiroshima on August 6, 1945, victims search for first aid in the southern part of the city.

sizzled bodies it was impossible to tell men from women. Those who had been wearing white were less scarred than others, since dark colors absorbed, rather than deflected, thermonuclear light. Friends did not recognize each other because some had lost their faces. Others had "imprints" of their nose or ears outlined on their cheeks. Those who reached out to help the more severely disabled drew back their hands only to find they were holding gobbets of charred flesh. Wounds smoked when dipped in water.

In time another 130,000 Japanese would slowly die from thermal burns and radiation sickness. This, one of the most horrifying side effects of atomic bombing, manifested itself capriciously among persons who had been badly injured and whose wounds had healed to keloid scars, as well as among others who apparently had originally escaped unharmed. The symptoms, erratic and sudden as they might be, were unmistakable—loss of hair, sudden and immobilizing weakness, vomiting, diarrhea, fever on the coldest days, chills at the height of summer, boils, blood spots under the skin, and a massive drop in white-corpuscle blood count. Most terrible to the people of Hiroshima was the biological aftereffect: an

extraordinary number of birth defects and genetic mutations were found in infants born to mothers who lived through the bombing. For the first time in history, as one correspondent wrote, not only had innocent people been killed but the as-yet-unborn were maimed.

Although it was Americans who dropped it, the atom bomb was the product of many people past and present pooling knowledge from all over the world. From Wilhelm Roentgen's 1895 discovery of the negative electricity of X rays, the Curies' discovery of radium, and Albert Einstein's 1905 theory that mass and energy are one, to Ernest Rutherford's establishing in England how radioactivity works and the "look" of an atom, history steadily delivered piece after piece of the atomic bomb's jigsaw puzzle. In Japan, physicist Sakae Shimizu studied gamma-ray scattering and radioactive decay. His counterpart in the USSR, Pyotr Leonidovich Kapitsa, inquired into the properties of radioactivity. The Italian Enrico Fermi produced the first chain reaction in uranium; the German Otto Hahn uncovered nuclear fission; the Dane Niels Bohr produced "heavy water" as a booster to radioactivity and thereby sped "the chain reaction in natural uranium under slow neutron bombardment"; and the American Ernest Lawrence separated isotopes in thermal diffusion. Fascism and Nazism in Europe drove many of the most distinguished atomic scientists in the world to the United States and it was there that the know-how, means, method, and money all crystallized the reality. It began in October 1938, when Einstein wrote to President Franklin Roosevelt about the possibility of creating a fission bomb of superlatively destructive power. "This requires action," Roosevelt said to an aide.

The theory behind the possibility turned from probability into likelihood. After the establishment of the supersecret Manhattan Project, first at Oak Ridge, Tennessee, and then at Los Alamos, New Mexico, in 1943, where a team of foreign and American scientists worked with breathtaking speed and cooperation, the implications for the future began to rise like unwelcome specters. Niels Bohr, the Nobel Prize winner and one of the brightest luminaries working at Los Alamos, worried as early as February 1944 about the political implications of the bomb and the tensions it would create between the superpowers. "A weapon of unparalleled power is being created. Unless, indeed, some international agreement about the control of the use of the new active materials (uranium, plutonium, etc.) can be obtained, any temporary advantage, however great, may be outweighed by a perpetual menace to human society," he wrote to both Churchill, who said, "I do not agree," and Roosevelt, who answered, "The suggestion is not accepted."

Meanwhile, Klaus Fuchs, another refugee at Los Alamos, convinced that no one country, however benevolent, should be the sole possessor of the means of destroying the entire Earth, passed the bomb's secrets to the Soviet Union. In April 1945 Einstein himself had second thoughts about what he had started. Again he wrote to Roosevelt, asking for extreme caution in the use of the bomb, but Roosevelt died and the letter lay on his desk. By June 1945 the German James Franck, the Hungarian Leo Szilard, and fifty-seven other top-ranking scientists petitioned from New Mexico, stating that "if the United States releases this means of indiscriminate destruction upon mankind, she will sacrifice public support throughout the world and precipitate the race for armaments." Robert Oppenheimer, in charge of the Manhattan Project's scientists, said, "When you see something that is technically sweet, you go ahead and do it." His coworker Arthur Compton, on the other hand, wanted a nonmilitary demonstration to "warn" and "impress" the Japanese before actually using the bomb.

The government in Washington argued back and forth. Secretary of War Henry Stimson and some of the members of the Joint Chiefs of Staff insisted that it would save 100,000 American lives and that dropping it by surprise on a "combined military and residential target would produce maximum psychological shock." (These were the same reasons Hitler had given for the attack on Rotterdam.) General George Marshall wanted the Soviets to join the war against Japan and to save the bomb for use at some possible future date against the Soviets. General Dwight Eisenhower felt that the Japanese were already beaten, that acceptable warfare could finish off the job and bring about surrender. He said, in short, that the bomb was completely unnecessary and would rouse world condemnation.

Throughout the discussions and disputations, as Arthur Compton would later say, "It seemed a foregone conclusion that the bomb would be used." The final decision was up to President Harry Truman. When John Toland, author of The Rising Sun, asked him if he had done any soul-searching before making his decision, Truman replied, "Hell, no. I made it like that," and he snapped his fingers in the air. To Truman the bomb was just "another powerful weapon in the arsenal of righteousness." On July 24, 1945, from Potsdam, he ordered the bomb sent to the Air Force. On July 26 it was in Tinian. On the twenty-seventh the Japanese were informed for the first time of the Potsdam ultimatum threatening "utter devastation or unconditional surrender." In any event, the Japanese were already suing for peace through the Soviets, who were not yet at war with them. Still, the bomb fell, ushering in a troubled new era in world history.

Eyewitness Report: Dr. Michihiko Hachiya, director of the Hiroshima Communications Hospital, was wounded in the bombing of Hiroshima while at his home 1,860 yards from the hypocenter at Aioi Bridge. His hospital was one mile away from the intended center of destruction. Eighty of Hiroshima's 190 doctors were killed in the bombing, and Hachiya was the only one to keep a day-by-day record of his experiences from August 6 to September 30, 1945. This document, unique in the annals of atom-bomb literature for its first-hand, technical, and perceptive information, was first serialized in a small medical magazine for circulation among doctors and staff tending postal, telegraph, and telephone employees of the Communications Ministry. In 1955 the manuscript was translated and published in the United States under the title Hiroshima Diary: The Journal of a Japanese Physician. Following are excerpts from Hachiya's entries for that first day: "We stood in the street, uncertain and afraid, until a house across from us began to sway and then with a rending motion fell almost at our feet. Our own house began to sway, and in a minute it, too, collapsed in a cloud of dust. Other buildings caved in or toppled. Fires sprang up and, whipped by a vicious wind, began to spread.

232

WAR

"It finally dawned on us that we could not stay there in the street, so we turned our steps towards the hospital. Our home was gone; we were wounded and needed treatment; and after all, it was my duty to be with my staff. This latter was an irrational thought—what good could I be to anyone, hurt as I was.

"We started out, but after twenty or thirty steps I had to stop. My breath became short, my heart pounded, and my legs gave way under me. An overpowering thirst seized me and I begged Yaeko-san [his wife] to find me some water. But there was no water to be found. . . .

"I was still naked, and although I did not feel the least bit of shame, I was disturbed to realize that modesty had deserted me. . . .

"I paused to rest. Gradually things around me came into focus. There were the shadowy forms of people, some of whom looked like walking ghosts. Others moved as though in pain, like scarecrows, their arms held out from their bodies with forearms and hands dangling. These people puzzled me until I suddenly realized that they had been burned and were holding their arms out to prevent the painful friction of raw surfaces rubbing together. A naked woman carrying a naked baby came into view. I averted my gaze. Perhaps they had been in the bath. But then I saw a naked man, and it occurred to me that, like myself, some strange thing had deprived them of their clothes. An old woman lay near me with an expression of suffering on her face, but she made no sound. Indeed one thing was common to everyone I saw—complete silence. . . .

"The streets were deserted except for the dead. Some looked as if they had been frozen by death while in the full action of flight; others lay sprawled as though some giant had flung them to their death from a great height.

"Hiroshima was no longer a city, but a burnt-over prairie. To the east and to the west everything was flattened. The distant mountains seemed nearer than I could ever remember. How small Hiroshima was with its houses gone. . . .

"Between the Red Cross Hospital and the center of the city I saw nothing that wasn't burned to a crisp: Streetcars were standing and inside were dozens of bodies, blackened beyond recognition. I saw fire reservoirs filled to the brim with dead people who looked as though they had been boiled alive. In one reservoir I saw one man, horribly burned, crouching beside another man who was dead. He was drinking bloodstained water out of the reservoir. In one reservoir there were so many dead people there wasn't enough room for them to fall over. They must have died sitting in the water. . . .

"What a weak and fragile thing man is before the forces of destruction. After the pika the entire population had been reduced to a common level of physical and mental weakness. Those who were able walked silently towards the suburbs and distant hills, their spirits broken, their initiative gone. When asked whence they had come, they pointed to the city and said, 'That way'; and when asked where they were going, pointed away from the city and said, 'This way.' They were so broken and confused that they behaved like automatons. . . .

"A spiritless people had forsaken a destroyed city; the way and the means were of no importance. Some had followed the railways, some as if by instinct had chosen footpaths and paddy fields, whereas others found themselves shuffling along dry river beds. Each to his separate course for no better reason than the presence of another in the lead.

"As the day ended I might as well have been suspended in time, for we had no clocks and no calendars."

In 1995, as Japan prepared to mark the fiftieth anniversary of the end of World War II, its citizens debated the emotional issue of Japanese wartime aggression and atrocities. Nobel Prize–winning novelist Kenzaburo Oe called on Japan to apologize for starting the war and the United States to apologize for using the atomic bomb.

Minoru Omuta, director of the Hiroshima Peace Culture Center, remembered watching the mushroom cloud and thinking "it looked beautiful in a strange way." He wondered if "fifty years isn't long enough to agree on a common history."

—F.B.

THE ORIGINAL PROFESSIONS OF 16 NAZI LEADERS

1. Martin Bormann (1900?–45), deputy chief of Nazi party: farm estate manager.
2. Sepp Dietrich (1892–1966), commander of the Sixth SS Panzer Army: butcher's apprentice.
3. Adolf Eichmann (1906–62), head of the Jewish office of the Gestapo: traveling salesman for the Vacuum Oil Company of Austria.
4. Hans Frank (1900–46), Nazi commissioner of justice and governor-general of occupied Poland: industrial lawyer and law professor.
5. Wilhelm Frick (1877–1946), Nazi minister of interior: Bavarian police officer and informer for Hitler.
6. Walther Funk (1890–1960), Reichsbank president: financial newspaper editor.

7. Joseph Goebbels (1897–1945), Nazi propaganda minister: bank clerk, bookkeeper, tutor, floorman on Cologne stock exchange, playwright, poet.

8. Hermann Göring (1893–1946), air force minister and president of war economy council: World War I fighter ace, piloted air taxis for Sweden's Svenska Lufttrafik airline.

9. Rudolf Hess (1894–1987), deputy chief of Nazi party: business wholesaler and exporter, German army officer.

10. Reinhard Heydrich (1904–42), deputy chief of Gestapo: unemployed German navy intelligence officer who had been court-martialed and cashiered for having an affair with a teenage girl.

11. Heinrich Himmler (1900–45), commander of SS and Gestapo: salesman for a fertilizer company and chicken farmer.

12. Adolf Hitler (1889–1945), führer of Third Reich: architect's draftsman, commercial artist, German army corporal.

13. Rudolf Höss (1900–47), commandant of Auschwitz: German army sergeant, murderer, ex-convict, farm laborer.

14. Joachim von Ribbentrop (1893–1946), Nazi minister of foreign affairs: wine and spirits importer, freelance journalist.

15. Ernst Röhm (1887–1943), Nazi commander of SA (Storm Troopers): German army officer.

16. Alfred Rosenberg (1893–1946), Nazi commissioner of occupied Eastern Europe: artist, architect, journalist.

—R.J.F.

WEAPONS

MACHINE GUN

Description: The machine gun is a rifled gun that mechanically ejects empty shells, reloads, and fires itself when the operator presses a triggering mechanism. It fires a rapid, continuous stream of bullets, which are automatically fed into it by a belt, clip, or magazine.

Origin: In 1881 Hiram Maxim, an American electrical engineer, attended the Paris Exposition, where an American friend told him, "If you wish to make a pile of money, invent something that will enable these Europeans to cut each other's throats with greater facility." Following this wise counsel, Maxim moved to London and began designing an automatic rapid-fire gun. In 1883 Maxim patented the first completely automatic machine gun.

Years before, after firing a rifle and receiving a severely bruised shoulder from the gun's recoil, Maxim had decided this energy could be used for better purposes than injuring the shooter's shoulder. In his London workshop, he devised a gun that used the recoil energy of each bullet fired to eject the empty cartridge, load a new bullet, and release the firing pin. Since the recoil from each shell loaded and discharged the next shell, the gun fired continuously and automatically while the operator pressed the trigger. To supply the gun with ammunition, Maxim constructed a mechanism that fed the gun a canvas belt loaded with 250 cartridges. Also, he invented a water jacket, holding seven pints of liquid, to cool the gun while firing. The first true machine gun, the Maxim gun weighed 40 pounds and fired 600 rounds a minute.

After Maxim gave a demonstration of his new weapon for the Prince of Wales (later King Edward VII), British army officers, and War Office officials, the British government purchased the Maxim gun, which was then manufactured by the Vickers factory and supplied to the army in 1888.

First Notable Use: At the Battle of Omdurman in the Sudan, in 1898, British general Horatio Kitchener employed Maxim machine guns for the first time in a large-scale conflict. At Omdurman, Kitchener formed his battle line parallel to the nearby Nile River and stationed twenty Maxim guns in the front ranks.

On September 2, 1898, tens of thousands of Sudanese dervish cavalrymen charged the British line, but in minutes the machine guns cut down the attacking men and their horses. The Sudanese launched repeated attacks, only to be slaughtered by the hail of bullets from the Maxim guns. The continuous use of the Maxim guns caused the water in their cooling systems to boil and evaporate, forcing the machine gunners to stop firing. Soldiers quickly ran down to the Nile and brought back fresh water. After pouring the cool water into the guns' water jackets, the machine gunners renewed their work.

At the end of the day, a young British lieutenant named Winston Churchill noted that in front of the Maxim machine guns there were "20,000 men, who strewed the ground in heaps and swathes."

Weapon Today: Since the Battle of Omdurman, the machine gun has been greatly improved. The supreme reign of the machine gun came during World War I, when its victims were counted in the millions. In World War II the emergence of tanks and airplanes supplanted the singular importance of the machine gun. However, it was adapted for use in tanks and airplanes. Since World War II the machine gun has lost its place in aerial combat to guided missiles, but in new lightweight forms it remains an important weapon of the infantryman. Outside of warfare, the Thompson or tommy gun gained fame in the 1920s because of its widespread use by American gangsters. In the 1970s it gained popularity with terrorist groups involved in urban guerrilla warfare and hijacking, and in the 1980s with urban drug gangs.

—R.J.F.

POISON GASES

Description: The poison gases used as weapons of mass destruction in modern warfare are grouped according to their gross physiological effects. Following are the main categories of such weapons:

• Lung irritants, which attack the respiratory tract, particularly lung tissue, and often cause death by pulmonary edema. Often used during World War I, examples of lung irritant gases include chlorine, chloropicrin, phosgene, and diphosgene.
• Vesicants, which produce blisters (or vesicles) on all exposed body surfaces, but especially on the mucous membrane and the cornea of the eye. The main example of a vesicant is mustard gas (by far the most deadly and widely feared chemical weapon of World War I) or any of its analogues, such as nitrogen mustard gases.
• Lacrimators, or tear gases, which cause intense eye irritation and copious tears. Mostly harmless to troops equipped with gas masks, "CS gas" has often been employed all around the world for crowd control and against barricaded or fortified human targets. Examples of lacrimators include diphenylchloroarsine, diphenylchanoarsine, and diphenylaminechloroarsine.
• Sternutators, which cause physical discomfort, such as nausea, sneezing, vomiting, or incontinence. These are organoarsenic compounds, and examples include diphenylchanoarsine and diphenylaminechloroarsine.
• Blood gases, such as cyanogen chloride or hydrogen cyanide, enter the bloodstream and lethally block oxygen circulation. Under its trade name of Zyklon-B, the Nazis used hydrogen cyanide to kill millions in the gas chambers of World War II death camps.
• Psychochemicals, which are used to disorient, demoralize, and confuse the enemy. The hallucinogenic LSD is one of these.
• Nerve gas, first synthesized by Gerhard

Schroeder in 1936 as the German organic chemist was attempting to synthesize a new insecticide. (Many commercial insecticides are still essentially watered-down nerve gases.) Nerve gases are among the most toxic substances known; they are organophosphorus compounds that kill by blocking the action of a crucial enzyme called acetylcholinesterase.

This enzyme breaks down and removes acetylcholine, which transmits nerve signals to the respiratory and digestive systems. If nerve gases prevent the enzyme from breaking down acetylcholine after it causes the synapse to fire, the muscles will be continually stimulated, causing paralysis, convulsions, and death.

Deployed as vapors, nerve gases will kill very rapidly if inhaled. In the form of colorless, tasteless liquids, they are topical, seeping imperceptibly through the dermal tissue without surface damage or sensation, and rapidly causing death almost immediately after entering the bloodstream.

The best-known nerve gases are sarin (which was used in a terrorist attack against Japanese commuters in March 1995), trilon 46, tabun, soman, and the most deadly of all, the comparatively new VX. Unlike its older predecessors, VX evaporates very slowly and can "deny an area" to an enemy, contaminating it for days.

The Nazis had tons of the newly developed nerve gases stockpiled in warehouses at the end of World War II, but they were never unleashed against the Allies, probably for fear of retaliation in kind. In fact, the Allies had no such retaliatory capability.

There was, however, one striking use of nerve gas by a prominent German in the closing days of the war. In his memoirs, Nazi economic minister Albert Speer recounts how he borrowed a special grenade filled with tabun, intending to introduce the deadly nerve gas into the führer's bunker to kill Hitler and everyone around him.

To Speer's unhappy surprise, the ventilation shaft he chose to gain access to the bunker's air supply turned out to have been recently retrofitted with iron bars and new air filters, foiling the nerve-gas assassination plot.

Origin: Poison gases have been used in warfare since the Spartans burned wood treated with sulfur and pitch to create toxic clouds of sulfur dioxide. Artillery shells were modified to deliver poison gases by both sides during the American Civil War and may actually have seen limited service.

First Notable Use: A giant step for inhumanity was taken by the Germans on April 22, 1915, when they released 168 tons of highly toxic chlorine gas near the Ypres salient in Belgium. Two days later they released more. Drifting over the Allied positions, the light green gas was said to have produced 15,000 casualties, of whom 5,000 were killed. Some of the dead were Germans, killed by their own chemical weapon when the wind reversed direction.

After 1915 both sides, issuing masks to filter out enemy toxins, actively employed poison gas. The Germans used most of it (mustard, chlorine, and phosgene) on the Russian front, where there were 56,000 deaths and 419,430 casualties. In the West, 8,109 British soldiers died and 180,607 were stricken. Eight thousand Frenchmen died under gas and 182,000 were gas casualties. U.S. losses to gas numbered 1,462 killed and 71,345 casualties. German deaths numbered 9,000, with 191,000 casualties. All in all, about 125,000 metric tons of poisonous gases were used in World War I, accounting for about 1.3 million total gas casualties.

Weapons Today: After World War I, widespread moral repugnance against chemical warfare culminated in a resolution at the Geneva Convention of 1925, outlawing the use of poison gas (and poisoned bullets) on the battlefield.

The only Western country to have used it since (at least on the battlefield) was Italy, which employed mustard gas in the Ethiopian war of 1935 to 1936. Germany used hydrogen cyanide extensively in its murder camps but not in the field. Japan employed poison gases in its invasion of China in 1936.

Both Great Britain and the United States seriously contemplated using poison gas in World War II: the United States against fanatically defended Japanese island strongholds, and the British to counter an expected amphibious invasion by the Germans.

These contingencies never took place, but both the United States and Great Britain engaged in extensive and hazardous testing programs, subjecting tens of thousands of military "volunteers" and convicts to poisonous gases and corrosive ointments. Some test subjects were apparently killed by their exposure to various experimental toxins.

The United States used nonlethal tear gas and emetics against Viet Cong tunnels in Vietnam, and poison gas has occasionally been used in post-Vietnam conflicts by the Vietnamese themselves for "ethnic cleansing" against indigenous Hmong, Rhade, and Meo tribesmen, and also against Chinese, Cambodians, and Laotians during border disputes in the seventies and eighties.

Egypt used poison gas artillery shells against Yemen between 1963 and 1967. The Soviet Union is accused of having employed toxic chemicals and biological agents against mujahedin guerrillas in Afghanistan in the late seventies and early eighties. This charge has never been satisfactorily proved.

Saddam Hussein used poisonous gas and nerve gas extensively (mustard and phosgene) against Iranian troops in the Iran-Iraq war, and gassed defenseless Kurdish civilians between 1982 and 1989. Iraqi radio crowed that Hussein had a special insecticide for every kind of insect. His use of chemical warfare probably turned the military tide for Iraq, staving off a certain defeat and compelling the Iranians to come to the bargaining table.

The indifference of world opinion to Hussein's chemical genocide against the Kurds is believed to have given Hussein encouragement for his subsequent invasion of Kuwait. Some Gulf War veterans maintain that poison gas was used against them in the desert, and there is some evidence to support their belief.

Although universally condemned and widely banned by treaty and agreement, chemical warfare troops and caches of chemical weapons are still maintained by fifteen militarily significant nations just in case. The principal U.S. reserves are held at Johnson Island in the Pacific and are said to be undergoing disposal, as is the widely scattered and extensive chemical warfare arsenal of the former Soviet Union.
—M.C.S.

TANK

Description: Since its introduction into the language during World War I, the term *tank* has been applied to any military armored vehicle equipped with an internal combustion engine, caterpillar treads, and onboard armaments, such as machine guns, rockets, or cannons.

In the eighty years since it first lumbered onto the twentieth-century battlefield, the tank, along with the airplane and the submarine, has become one of the most versatile, deadly, and highly evolved weapons of mechanized warfare.

Origin: Tanks were first fielded by the British, who shipped the original armored juggernauts to France in crates that had been marked as "water tanks" to misdirect the enemy. Hence the name. The modern term is Main Battle Tank, or MBT.

The British tank of 1917 was a desperate response to the inability of unprotected infantrymen to maneuver or gain ground without suffering terrifying losses inflicted by that other modern terror weapon, the machine gun.

The vulnerability of men out in the open facing entrenched defenders was a problem as ancient as armed conflict itself. Homer's fabled Trojan horse was the faint glimmering of the tank idea, a primitive attempt to remain alive long enough to engage the enemy on his own ground. Roman legionnaires assaulting walled fortified positions took the first steps toward armored warfare when they huddled together under their upraised shields in a marching formation called the testudo, or tortoise. Thus shielded en masse, the Romans enjoyed a modicum of protection from arrows, stones, or boiling oil being dropped onto them from parapets.

Although Guido da Vigevano in 1300, and Leonardo da Vinci in 1500, designed what were recognizably armored combat vehicles, the first modern, motorized tank was invented by E. L. de la Mole of North Adelaide, Australia, in 1912. De la Mole sent his designs to the British War Office, where they were expertly filed and ignored by seasoned bureaucrats.

Unaware of de la Mole's invention, Colonel Ernest Swinton of the British Royal Engineers virtually reinvented the modern tank on his own during the early years of World War I. Swinton's brainstorm came after reading an article on American agricultural tractors.

Swinton remembered his ancient military history and armored the Yankee tractor in the hope of ending trench warfare in Europe—a striking example of beating a plowshare back into a sword. Swinton's primitive tank impressed the British War Office, which assigned Lieutenant W. G. Wilson to further refine the invention.

Working at Foster's Engineering Works in Lincoln, England, Wilson constructed the Mark 1, the first tank used in battle. First tested in January 1916, the Mark 1 was box shaped, with two movable guns protruding from its sides and six machine guns. Manned by a crew of eight, it weighed twenty-six tons and was propelled by a six-cylinder, 105-horsepower engine, and ran at a maximum speed of four miles per hour.

First Use: By the summer of 1916, the British had already lost an entire generation of young men, and their offensive on the Somme was fast becoming the bloodiest and most useless battle in history. Hundreds of thousands of lives had been sacrificed to no military advantage whatsoever.

The lines of both sides were static and unyielding. The only hope for an end to the stalemate was that either the Allies or the Central Powers would be bled white, defeated by sheer attrition. Commanders on both sides feared mass mutiny in the trenches.

British general Sir Douglas Haig ordered the newly arrived Mark 1 tanks into battle in September 1916. Forty-nine tanks rumbled toward the German positions, but thirty-one broke down before reaching their jump-off point.

The remaining eighteen tanks were strung out along a five-mile front and, after a three-day artillery barrage, were ordered into action on September 15, 1916.

Just before dawn the mammoth, noisy Mark 1s chugged off into no-man's-land, disappear-ing into the fog and smoke, and trundled toward the German lines.

Hearing strange metallic noises, German soldiers peeked from their trenches and were confronted with what must have looked like mechanical dinosaurs advancing upon them from the mists of no-man's-land. Even more alarming, bullets bounced off the monsters.

When the Mark 1s opened fire, the terrified Germans panicked and bolted for the rear. The tanks crossed the enemy trenches in pursuit, but began to run low on fuel. Three tanks reached the village of Fers, where they rolled down the streets demolishing German fortifications, causing the terror-stricken Germans to flee for their lives.

Even though they had penetrated seven miles behind the German trenches, the British tanks failed to break the enemy line because of fuel shortages and mechanical failures. They also failed to exploit the initiative they had gained, because they had no way to communicate with each other, and were thus unable to act in concert.

Weapon Today: After the tank's promising debut in World War I, visionary commanders of World War II, such as Heinz Guderian of Germany and George S. Patton of the United States, realized the tank was the twentieth-century equivalent of yesteryear's heavy cavalry.

Intelligently used as an armored spearhead, tanks could provide fast mobile reconnaissance, or punch through and bypass enemy strongholds, suddenly appearing in the enemy's rear to raise havoc with his lines of communication and supply.

Blitzkrieg warfare was born when the tank came into its own, utilized in deadly coordination with front-line tactical aviation and mechanized artillery and infantry.

The collapse of the supposedly impregnable French defenses before the lightning-fast onslaught of armored German Panzer units caused American armor general George S. Patton to remark: "Fortified positions like the Maginot line are monuments to nothing but human stupidity."

Ex-cavalryman Patton practiced what he preached, using his tanks to demonstrate that flexibility and mobility were the new way to win wars.

Tanks have retained their preeminence in ground warfare, seeing service in almost every conflict since 1945. They were not extensively used by either side in Vietnam, but the masterful Israeli use of armor, in coordination with the superlative Israeli tactical air force, handily defeated a much larger invading Arab force in the 1967 Arab-Israeli War.

In the Gulf War, Saddam Hussein's tanks were dug into fixed defensive positions facing the Allies, their potential wasted by being miscast as static artillery batteries. The dug-in Iraqi tanks failed to offer any meaningful support to Saddam's infantry and proved little or no impediment to the Allies, who simply swept around them.

The Allied air forces pounced on and made mincemeat of the stationary Iraqi tanks, while the Allied armor columns, decisively employed by General H. Norman Schwarzkopf in his "statue of liberty play," outflanked and overwhelmed the incompetently commanded Iraqi forces. The result was the most one-sided defeat in modern military history. Iraq is said to have lost at least 3,700 of its 4,200 Main Battle Tanks in the war.

In the countries of Egypt, Jordan, Syria, and Israel, there are now more than 15,000 tanks, while Russia has 45,000 and the United States 10,000.

The most recent U.S. Main Battle Tank, the M1A2 Abrams, is more reminiscent of a modern fighter jet than the steel-plated tractors of 1916. Heavily armored, the sixty-eight-ton Abrams MBT is powered by a 1,500-horsepower Textron-Lycoming engine that can be fueled with diesel fuel, aviation gasoline, or, in a pinch, even kerosene.

Capable of off-road speeds of up to forty miles per hour, the M1A2 is equipped with satellite inertial navigation systems, laser rangefinders, thermal target acquisition imaging, all-weather night vision, and blow-off panels incorporated into its high-tech composite armor to allow its crew to survive in the event of a direct hit. Widely regarded as the finest Main Battle Tank in the world, the Abrams is expected to see service with the U.S. armed forces and America's allies for at least the next twenty years.

—M.C.S. and R.J.F.

GUIDED MISSILE

Description: The guided missile is a pre-programmed and/or remote-controlled rocket that carries high-explosive, nuclear, or chemical/biological payloads. The most common classification of guided missiles is based on the place of launching and the position of the target. The different types, therefore, are air-to-surface missiles (ASM), surface-to-air missiles (SAM), surface-to-surface missiles (SSM), and air-to-air missiles (AAM).

Origin: The Chinese invented unguided missiles, or rockets, and employed them for rituals and in warfare as early as 1200 A.D. Rockets began to figure in European conflicts by around 1400 A.D.

In Europe they were used almost exclusively for signaling at first, notably in ship-to-shore, or ship-to-ship communications at sea. When,

sometime in the late 1500s, British naval gunners discovered the propensity of potassium chlorate to explode on impact, the first crude surface-to-surface explosive warheads made their appearance.

Impact-explosive rockets began seeing service as siege weapons and incendiaries throughout Europe in the next two centuries, essentially being chemical improvements over the flaming arrow or the Greek fire-spewing catapults of the Dark Ages.

These unguided ballistic missiles were the same rockets whose "red glare" so impressed national-anthem author Francis Scott Key when he witnessed them in action during the British rocket bombardment of Fort McHenry, outside of Baltimore, during the War of 1812.

The first effective guided missile to be used as a weapon was the German V-2. The research program that developed the V-2 had its beginnings with the experiments of a clique of hobbyists, who started a private German rocket club in 1927.

In 1937 the club members were recruited by the rapidly expanding German army to establish a military rocket research program. This new missile project was headed by Dr. Walter Dornberger and his nineteen-year-old assistant and collaborator, Wernher von Braun.

Throughout the 1930s, Dornberger and von Braun developed a series of rockets, constantly improving the propulsion and guidance systems.

During the early years of World War II, German missile researchers designed and built the A-4, later renamed the V-2, at the German rocket center at Peenemünde. They were sometimes assisted by slave laborers, who had been pressed into service from concentration camps by the SS.

Though his dream was to send rockets into space, von Braun energetically worked on the V-2 project, inventing an ingenious robot pilot mechanism that guided the V-2 to a target nearly 200 miles away with a high degree of accuracy. It was also von Braun who concocted the V-2 rocket's propellant fuel—a combination of nine tons of alcohol and liquid oxygen.

As the V-2 was nearing completion in March 1943, work was suspended by Hitler because in a dream he had envisioned that the V-2 would never strike England. Six months later, Dornberger and von Braun persuaded Hitler to let them continue with the V-2. But as soon as they resumed work, the British launched Operation Crossbow, bombing the Peenemünde research station and further delaying the project.

Finally, in the late summer of 1944, the V-2 was ready for launching. A surface-to-surface missile, the V-2 was forty-six feet long and five feet in diameter and weighed fourteen tons.

First Use: On September 8, 1944, a mobile launcher carrying the first V-2 pulled into an open field in Holland. Carloads of German army officers, Nazi officials, and scientists were on hand to witness the takeoff, and with it, the birth, of a terrible new weapon of war.

The V-2 successfully lunged into space, sprouting a flaming yellowish red tail. Five minutes and twenty seconds later, a British radar operator picked up an object flying faster than the speed of sound and inbound for London.

Less than five seconds after that sighting, the V-2 plowed into a residential square of houses. The 2,200-pound warhead exploded, completely destroying an entire city block.

Weapon Today: Since the first V-2, the guided missile has evolved into the most sophisticated and important strategic weapon in the arsenal of modern nations. The high speed of the rocket (especially when fired from a stealthy nuclear sub) severely limits an enemy's reaction time. That, plus the horrifying assortment of nuclear, biological, and chemical warheads available, adds to the guided missile's terrifying potential as a first-strike weapon.

Unlike a manned bomber, a rocket cannot be recalled once launched, only destroyed. Today, thanks to the incredibly complex computerized missile defense networks in the United States and other countries, the question remains whether or not ICBMs with the capacity for global destruction can truly be said to be completely subject to human command and control.

Further, the real defensive capability of particle-ray or laser-beam firing anti–intercontinental ballistic missile weapons systems stationed in outer space (as envisioned by the Reagan administration in its so-called Star Wars defense program) has yet to be validated.

Probably the most famous missile defense system deriving from so-called Star Wars defense technology is the Patriot, which saw service against Iraqi SCUD missiles in the Gulf War. It now appears that the Patriot's claimed success rate against the SCUDS was greatly exaggerated by the Pentagon. (See page 548.)

By 1995 the United States possessed 1,054 land-based and 656 submarine-based intercontinental missiles with nuclear warheads, while Russia had 1,549 land and 842 submarine missiles.

The newest American missile is the extremely accurate Tomahawk cruise missile, which can follow terrain features at treetop level and can be outfitted with either conventional high-explosive or nuclear/biological/ chemical warheads.

Tomahawks were used with almost pinpoint accuracy during the Gulf War, when Special Forces operators on the ground "splashed" the target with homing beams from a handheld laser target designator. The result was a guided missile that can literally fly a ton of high explosives through the door or window of choice.

—M.C.S. and R.J.F.

NAPALM

Description: Napalm is a flammable gel that is sprayed from flamethrowers or encased in incendiary bombs. Chemically, napalm is an aluminum soap composed of organic hydrocarbon acids that thicken gasoline. Napalm is also the name given to the gasoline thus thickened. The word *napalm* derives from two of its principal components, naphthenic acid and palmitic acid.

Origin: At the beginning of World War II, Great Britain developed an effective incendiary substance by mixing rubber and gasoline. However, after Japan seized the world's major rubber-producing regions, the Allies were forced to invent a new incendiary weapon. In the United States this task was assigned to researchers at Harvard University, the Arthur D. Little Corporation, and Nuodex Products Company.

Working together, the scientists from Harvard and the private sector investigated a multitude of hydrocarbon acids. After more than a year of study, they came up with a formula for napalm, consisting of 25 percent oleic acids, 25 percent naphthenic acids derived from crude oil, and 50 percent palmitic acids derived from coconut oil.

They then mixed napalm with aviation gasoline to produce an incendiary jelly. The U.S. Army was greatly pleased with napalm because it was inexpensive and easy to manufacture. Initial tests showed that napalm burned at a much higher temperature (5,000 degrees Fahrenheit), and for a much longer time, than any other incendiary composition then in use.

Furthermore, it was discovered that napalm adhered to whatever it struck until it completely burned out. This property made it a highly effective means of killing enemy personnel or clearing brush from around one's position to create a high-visibility "kill zone" for infantry weapons.

The U.S. Army Chemical Warfare Service constructed a large napalm bomb. This bomb was dropped from a relatively low flight altitude; at a few hundred feet above the ground, it burst open and scattered hundreds of smaller napalm bombs over a wide area.

First Notable Use: Outside of its use in flamethrowers, the first major employment of napalm occurred on the night of March 9–10, 1945.

After high-explosive bombs failed to demolish Japanese cities, General Curtis LeMay decided to use napalm bombs against them. On March 9, without notifying Washington, LeMay ordered 333 B-29 bombers to attack Tokyo with napalm. That evening the B-29s took off from the islands of Guam, Tinian, and Saipan and headed north for Tokyo.

Before midnight, air-raid sirens blared in Tokyo, but the city's residents, who had become accustomed to the nightly visits of B-29s, paid little attention to the warning. At 12:15 A.M. on March 10, two B-29s flew over Tokyo and dropped their napalm payloads, which created a flaming X, marking the center of the city. Guided by the X, three formations of bombers flew over and unloaded 1,900 tons of napalm bombs on Tokyo.

Tokyo's crowded wooden buildings erupted into flames, and strong winds spread the conflagration through central Tokyo out toward the suburbs. The resultant firestorm lasted for days, reaching temperatures of 1,800 degrees Fahrenheit and totally destroying fifteen square miles of Tokyo. A quarter of the city was burned to the ground, and a million people were left homeless. More than 80,000 charred corpses, reduced to half their normal size by the searing heat, littered the ruins.

Weapon Today: Napalm continues to be used all over the world today, especially for counterinsurgency purposes, where it is often employed against troops dug into hills, caves, and bunkers.

In the Vietnam War, the United States used napalm (renamed "incendergel") extensively against an elusive, hit-and-run guerrilla enemy that conventional ground forces were often unable to see. Napalm was often dropped onto areas where it was suspected the enemy might be.

Napalm was configured in aerial munitions and flamethrowers carried on the backs of infantrymen, and spewed from specially modified Armored Personnel Carriers known as Zippo Tracks.

U.S. troops referred to napalm as a "waste the area weapon," and used it under authority at the company level to "sanitize" suspected enemy troop concentrations and hostile hamlets. Horror stories about the indiscriminate use of napalm abounded, and campus recruiters for the Dow Chemical Company, which manufactured napalm for the military, often found themselves compared to the German chemical company, I. G. Farben, that had supplied Zyklon-B poison gas to the Nazi extermination camps.

Humanitarian concerns voiced by the antiwar movement were countered by the military's assertion that napalm sucks oxygen out of the air so rapidly that enemy troops caught in its path die from being suffocated rather than from being burned to death. If so, argued napalm opponents, then by the military's own logic, napalm was a chemical weapon and thus prohibited from U.S. military use by treaty and custom.

Still, the famous 1972 Associated Press photograph of a naked nine-year-old girl terribly burned by napalm after an accidental bombing of her village probably did more to turn public opinion against the use of the incendiary than any amount of pro and con rhetoric.

In 1972, and again in 1974, the United Nations General Assembly passed resolutions condemning the use of napalm and other incendiary weapons. The United States and the Soviet Union both abstained from the vote. Huge stockpiles of napalm were said to have been left behind after the 1975 American pullout from Vietnam and to have been used by the Vietnamese in their own battles with Cambodia.

Napalm was extensively employed against Iraqi defenses during the Gulf War, both to ignite trenches filled with crude oil placed in the path of advancing allied armor by the Iraqis, and as an antipersonnel weapon.

Napalm has recently been dropped from the U.S. inventory and replaced by the even more horrifying FAE, or fuel air explosive, bombs. As the name implies, the U.S. GBU-28 FAE superbomb is an airburst weapon that covers an area 1,000 feet long with blast pressures of 200 pounds per square inch (psi). Humans can withstand only 40 psi.

According to a CIA report on FAEs: "The pressure effect of FAEs approaches those produced by low-yield nuclear weapons at short ranges. The effect of an FAE explosion within confined spaces is immense. Those at the fringes are likely to suffer many internal . . . injuries, including burst eardrums, crushed inner-ear organs, severe concussions, ruptured lungs and internal organs, and possible blindness."

—M.C.S and R.J.F.

Terrified Vietnamese children flee down a road after a napalm attack on June 8, 1972.

ATOMIC BOMBS

An optimist, in the atomic age, is a person who thinks the future is uncertain.

> Russel Crouse and Howard Lindsay, *State of the Union*, 1948

The dangers of atomic war are overrated. It would be hard on little, concentrated countries like England. In the United States we have lots of space.

> Robert Rutherford McCormick, *Chicago Tribune*, February 23, 1950

Following a nuclear attack on the United States, the United States Postal Service plans to distribute Emergency Change of Address Cards.

> Federal Emergency Management Agency, Executive Order 11490, 1969

Description: The term *atomic bomb* is loosely applied to all nuclear weapons whose power is based on fission, fusion, or both.

The theory of nuclear fission was proposed in 1938 from work done by German physicists, and was proved feasible by Enrico Fermi on December 2, 1942, when he created the first controlled, self-sustaining nuclear chain reaction in his experimental reactor, housed in a squash court under the stands of an abandoned football stadium in the heart of Chicago.

The implications of Fermi's work were these: If you could get a lot of uranium atoms to split up at once, the neutrons given off when the atoms came apart (the process called fission) could split more atoms in turn. In a lump the right size and shape—a "critical mass"—every neutron produced would have a good probability of hitting and splitting another nucleus.

The resultant chain reaction can lead to an atomic explosion. An atomic bomb, then, is engineered to produce the rapid fissioning of a combination of selected materials to induce such an explosion caused by the massive energy released by reactions involving atomic nuclei.

The hydrogen bomb, or H-bomb, differs from a conventional atomic bomb in that light atomic nuclei of hydrogen are joined together in an uncontrolled nuclear *fusion* reaction that is literally apt to be a thousand times more powerful than an atomic bomb. An atomic bomb in its own right produces a *fission* reaction about a million times as powerful as a bomb of the same size deriving its explosive power from high explosives like TNT.

A hybrid type of nuclear weapon is the neutron bomb, a small hydrogen bomb. A nuclear explosion releases energy force in the form of nuclear radiation, thermal radiation (heat), and blast. Nuclear radiation, which includes alpha, beta, and gamma radiation as well as neutrons, can be increased relative to the other forces by modifying the weapon's design parameters.

The first peacetime atomic bomb test, in the atmosphere over Bikini Atoll in the Marshall Islands, July 1, 1946.

Neutron bombs are often called ERs, or enhanced radiation weapons, because the number of neutrons they emit is apt to be between six and ten times as great as in a conventional nuclear weapon of the same explosive force.

Neutrons, or uncharged particles, travel through matter until they are slowed or stopped, usually by collision with light atoms. Human bodies are largely water, and water contains the lightest atom, hydrogen.

Buildings or other man-made structures, on the other hand, have a higher proportion of heavier atoms and are therefore less prone to alteration from encounters with neutrons. Neutron bombs are specifically intended to be more damaging to living things than to structures.

First Notable Use: See page 229, "Hiroshima."

Weapons Today: The principal technical requirement for developing nuclear weapons is the possession of an adequate amount of either plutonium or highly enriched uranium.

A basic fission nuclear weapon (or atomic bomb) needs ten kilograms of weapons-grade plutonium or about ten times as much highly enriched uranium. Unlike uranium, plutonium does not occur in nature; it has to be produced in a nuclear reactor. Then it has to be separated from other elements in a special plutonium reprocessing facility.

Natural uranium is U-238, which contains

about .7 percent of the U-235 isotope. For any hope of sustaining the nuclear chain reaction called for in a nuclear weapon, uranium must be enriched to about 90 percent U-235 by gaseous diffusion in a uranium enrichment plant or a nuclear reactor.

The basic engineering task in creating a nuclear weapon is to bring subcritical masses of either plutonium or highly enriched uranium together in such a way as to optimize the fission process.

As a result, almost all the International Atomic Energy Agency's (IAEA) nonnuclear proliferation efforts are devoted to keeping tabs on the uranium fuel that comes into nuclear power plants and the plutonium-containing waste that comes out of them. The great nightmare of Third World nuclear proliferation is that countries such as Iraq, Iran, or North Korea will, in effect, reproduce the U.S. Manhattan Project, which invented the A-bomb in the 1940s.

In other words, outlaw regimes will simply build a secret, dedicated, bomb-building complex and refuse to allow IAEA inspectors to see it. Building an atomic bomb, once the most closely guarded secret in the world, now offers few challenges to any reasonably talented physi-

cist, as long as he owns a personal computer and the requisite fissionable material.

H-bombs, or fusion nuclear weapons, present a more difficult design problem. Temperatures of tens of millions of degrees must be reached in order for fusion to occur. Unlike the atomic bomb's fission reaction, which stops when the pieces of uranium or plutonium fueling the device scatter in the explosion, the H-bomb's fusion reaction has no theoretical limit.

France, Great Britain, and China each have strategic and tactical nuclear arsenals. Israel reportedly possesses about 100 nuclear weapons. India, South Africa, and Pakistan probably have the capability to manufacture nuclear weapons. Iran, Iraq, and North Korea are currently moving to procure them, either by manufacturing them or by purchasing them. Huge quantities of the world's known supplies of weapons-grade plutonium and uranium are presently unaccounted for by the IAEA.

The yield, or explosive force, of nuclear weapons is commonly reckoned in kilotons or megatons. A kiloton is equal to the explosive force of 1 thousand tons of TNT; a megaton is equal to 1 million tons of TNT. A one-megaton groundburst would cover about 775 square miles with 500 rem (roentgen equivalent in man, or the dose that will cause about the same amount of injury as one roentgen of X-ray exposure) or more of nuclear fallout, enough to kill about half the exposed population with radiation sickness.

In terms of explosive force, heat radiation would cause third-degree burns on all unprotected persons at a distance of up to five miles from a one-megaton explosion. A one-megaton explosion would produce an overpressure of air of about ten pounds per square inch and winds from 300 to 600 miles an hour at a distance of about two miles from the blast, destroying concrete structures. Most people not vaporized by the intense heat of the explosion at ground zero could expect death from radiation sickness, or a delayed demise from leukemia or cancer.

Today the yield of nuclear weapons ranges from .01 to 1.0 megatons for the small sixty-four-pound "backpack nukes" or SADMS in the arsenals of both the United States and the former USSR to the Soviet Super H-bombs of the early sixties, which were 60 megatons.

The first atom bomb dropped on Hiroshima in 1945 had a yield of thirteen-and-a-half kilotons, and killed about 100,000 people within the first week after the explosion. An additional 100,000 Hiroshima victims died in the succeeding five years of illnesses and cancers thought to have been caused by nuclear radiation.

Most hydrogen weapons in the nuclear arsenals of the United States and the former Soviet Union are mounted on ICBMs (intercontinental ballistic missiles) carrying up to twelve MIRVs (multiple individually targeted reentry vehi-

The original caption to this photo, released by the Joint Army-Navy Task Force, read, "Two pretty nurses from the Navy hospital ship Benevolence *sunbathe after a swim in Bikini Lagoon, declared free of radioactivity 48 hours after the atom test." The lagoon was the site of Bikini's second atom bomb test, and, in fact, dangerous levels of radiation were still being registered on the atoll decades later.*

cles, or independently targeted warheads), with each warhead in the twenty-megaton range. A single twenty-megaton bomb is estimated to be capable of destroying everything within a ten-mile radius of the blast.

At the beginning of the 1990s, the United States and the USSR had about 50,000 nuclear warheads between them, about half strategic (ICBMs) and half tactical ("battlefield nukes"—SADMs, low-yield artillery shells, and neutron bombs).

The breakup of the Soviet Union and the Strategic Arms Reduction Talks treaties and other agreements are expected to result in a reduction in force to about 3,000 nuclear warheads apiece for the United States and Russia by the turn of the century.

That is, assuming that Russia can regain control of the nuclear warheads deployed in breakaway former Soviet republics, such as Ukraine and Kazakhstan. The threat of nuclear warfare has by no means ended with the Cold War. It has simply shifted from an unthinkable conflict involving superpowers to the strong likelihood that the world will soon be forced to come to terms with an outlaw regime suddenly in possession of a small but formidable nuclear capability.
—M.C.S.

AK-47

Description: The AK-47 is an automatic/semiautomatic assault rifle that measures less than a yard long, weighs less than ten pounds when unloaded, and has a rate of fire of up to 600 rounds per minute. A curved, banana-shaped magazine (holding 30 or 100 rounds) feeds 7.62mm shells into the barrel. The rifle offers an optional folding stock that allows the weapon to be more easily concealed.

Origin: Russian weapons designer Mikhail Kalashnikov was a teenage soldier in the Soviet army when, in 1941, he was wounded in battle against the Nazis. It was during his recovery that he began to develop a new infantry rifle. His first prototype submachine gun was produced in 1942 and underwent modifications until 1947, when it was formally introduced. The Soviets began mass-producing it in 1949. A further upgrade, which called for the use of machined rather than stamped steel, made the rifle more durable, and it was officially adopted for use by the Soviet military in 1951.

The AK-47 is considered to be extremely rugged and reliable. It can be dropped in water or buried in dirt and still function without jamming. Its effectiveness, cost, and suitability to multiple applications created a worldwide demand for the weapon. The former Communist bloc nations of East Germany, Poland, Bulgaria,

Romania, Hungary, and Yugoslavia, as well as North Korea and the People's Republic of China, were allowed to manufacture the Avtomat-Kalashnikova (19)47. Finland and Israel both developed and manufactured their own versions.

Weapon Today: The AK-47 came along too late for use in World War II but it has played a prominent role in conflicts all over the globe. It was the weapon of choice for the People's Liberation Army to quell prodemocracy protesters when they shot up Beijing's Tiananmen Square on the night of June 3–4, 1989.

AK-47s are the signature weapons of Somalia's warlords and Afghanistan's mujahedin. Its fire has been heard in Beirut and Port-Au-Prince, in Jerusalem and Johannesburg. The street gangs of America's inner cities, soldiers in Croatia, drug lords in Colombia, mercenaries in Africa and Central America, terrorists from Sri Lanka to Sudan, pirates operating in the Sea of Java, and even tribal warriors in the highlands of primitive Papua New Guinea all use AK-47s or knockoff versions of it.

Black market prices vary from nation to nation. An AK-47 can sell for up to $1,000 in Washington, D.C.; for less than $100 in Thailand and Honduras; for $50 in Pakistan; and for $8 in South Africa. More than 55 million of them have been built since the weapon was first introduced, making it the most popular armament in history.
—R.N.K.

BIOLOGICAL WARFARE AGENTS

Description: Biological warfare is the attempt to introduce incapacitating illness into the ranks of one's enemy by deliberately spreading disease-producing microorganisms in their midst. These organisms can be delivered by rocket, artillery shells, airburst bombs, or human agents.

"Good" military microorganisms (suitable for use as weapons) are selected from the enormous pool of known viruses and bacteria and then genetically engineered, or customized, on the basis of the following criteria:

• Virulence: the damage produced by the infection. It must be severe enough to overburden enemy health-care resources but not necessarily be permanent or fatal.
• Infectivity: the size of dose needed to spread a continuing infection must be small enough to be effectively delivered.
• Stability: the organism must be stable enough to be delivered to its "host" (the victim) in an active or infectious condition.
• Natural immunity: the target population must be previously uninfected by the organism to ensure there is no natural resistance to it already present when introduced.

• Availability of vaccines: vaccines must be available within one's own ranks but not commonly available to the enemy, so as to eliminate the danger of "backlash" infection to friendly troops or populations.
• Ease of therapy: the strain must resist commonly available cures, such as antibiotics. Epidemicity, or ease of interhost contagion, must also be low, since the objective is to neutralize a given population and not to start a worldwide epidemic.

Biological warfare is very much a weapon of mass destruction, and disturbingly, it offers real advantages for potential use by Third World terrorists, unscrupulous individuals, or rogue governments. A biological warfare capability is far cheaper than either chemical or nuclear weaponry. In effect, all that is required is one microbiologist and one laboratory.

The facilities necessary to manufacture biowar agents are far less conspicuous than chemical or nuclear facilities, and they can be effectively "covered," or represented as legitimate civilian research establishments. Biowar agents are 160 times as deadly as toxic chemicals of the same weight. They are easily smuggled and easily released. Finally, biowar agents are difficult if not impossible to track back to their point of origin.

The real problem for the defender is detecting the biological cloud in time to take prophylactic action, and since the human senses cannot themselves detect invading microorganisms, some form of air sampling is the only (and inadequate) defense. Biowar agents can therefore be unleashed secretly and deniably, and the target populace will be too confused and uncertain of the source of infection to retaliate effectively.

Origin: Biological warfare was a frequent occurrence in antiquity. Dead animals were tossed into wells to contaminate the water sources of besieged cities. Rotten carcasses were hurled over walls via catapult to sicken besieged defenders on putrid meat. During the French and Indian War, Sir Jeffrey Amherst created a devastating smallpox epidemic among several Indian tribes by deliberately distributing blankets formerly used by infected British soldiers.

First Notable Use: The actual use of these agents in the twentieth century is, understandably, a matter of extreme secrecy and controversy. However, one known accidental biowar outbreak took place in 1979 at Compound 19, a military microbiology center outside of Sverdlosk, in the former Soviet Union. An accidental release of an anthrax strain from Compound 19 infected hundreds in the Sverdlosk area and took sixty-eight lives.

Complicating the efforts of doctors to save victims of the virus, the KGB promptly appeared on the scene and confiscated all medical and autopsy records associated with the incident. Russian president Boris Yeltsin later publicly admitted that the tragedy was linked to "our military developments."

Weapons Today: Lethal biowar agents with a military potential include smallpox, plague, melliodosis, anthrax, Lhassa fever, assorted botulisms, and *Coxiella burnetii*, or Q fever. This last has the distinction of being perhaps the most infective, since one-fifth of an ounce, properly distributed, would be sufficient to infect the entire world population (though, thankfully, the mortality rate from Q fever is only about one percent).

By 1990 ten nations, including the United States and the former Soviet Union, were known to have biological warfare capability. The 1972 Biological Warfare Convention, signed by more than a hundred nations, bans production or use of biological weapons. The loophole in the agreement is that research for defending against these weapons is completely permissible, which more or less implies the same knowledge necessary for their offensive use.

The Pentagon is said to have spent more than 1 billion dollars on biological warfare research since the end of World War II, more than 500 million dollars of it since 1984. The official position, however, is that the United States has neither biological weapons nor any research efforts under way to produce them.

—M.C.S.

AERIAL BOMBINGS OF
THE MAINLAND UNITED STATES

COMIC OPERA BOMBING

An aerial bombing occurred inside the United States on November 12, 1926, in Williamson County, Illinois. It was not a foreign power that initiated the raid but a bootlegging gang of farmboys led by Carl, Earl, and Bernie Shelton. Their air strike was against a rival gang headed by Charlie Birger.

Originally the two gangs had worked together,

but once they quarreled over protection money, the war was on.

The target of the Sheltons' outrageous air raid was Birger's stronghold, Shady Rest, a roadhouse built of foot-thick logs. For $1,000 and a stolen car, they hired a World War I biplane and a barnstormer pilot. Blackie Armes of the Shelton gang climbed aboard with three dynamite bombs, and the pilot took off. While the plane made a pass over Shady Rest, Blackie desperately tried to light the fuses, finally succeeded, then threw the bombs over the side. Two were duds. The third exploded beside a cockfighting pit. It destroyed some bleachers and killed a bulldog and a caged eagle.

The pilot flew Blackie back to the field and landed. When he saw the armed and angry Shelton gang waiting, he forced Blackie out of the plane with a .38 pistol, then roared off.

To retaliate for the failed attack, a Birger gang member drove to the nearest landing field and shot up what he thought was the offending plane, then set it on fire. It was the wrong plane.
—The Eds.

"FRIENDLY" FIRE

David Cosson was twelve years old on the night of August 10, 1944, a night he still relives in terror. The Cosson family lived only a mile and a half from Eglin Air Force Base, Florida, where pilots were given a crash training course before being sent to the front. The Cossons were accustomed to the flares that lit up the sky as if it were midday and to the sounds of the bombs landing in the range a few miles away.

On this night, however, either the bomber pilot mistook the farmhouse for a target, or the bomb release mechanism failed, and the whole load of bombs landed on the Cosson farm. David Cosson's father, uncle, and two cousins were killed and he was paralyzed. He remembers his cousin Wallace Cosson, who was down the road visiting his grandmother, loading the bodies of the family into a truck and racing to town.

A nurse looked into the pickup and said, "Take them to the funeral home, they'll all be dead soon anyway." But an officer from Eglin, who was standing nearby, threatened to take over the hospital by martial law. Soon military vehicles were driving the victims to the Eglin Hospital, thirty miles away. But for four of them it was too late.

The Cosson family had no life or medical insurance. Cosson's mother, who also survived, was awarded $259. In 1946 Congress awarded the family $30,000, including $6,000 for David. A few years later Congress gave David another $15,000, but the government never turned it over because a county judge feared a lump-sum payment would be used up too quickly and because David wouldn't sign a waiver releasing the government from further responsibility.

Disabled, in and out of hospitals, David was forced to go on welfare. Family members kept the case alive, and finally, in 1980, President Jimmy Carter signed a bill that provided Cosson $18,000 a year. "You don't ever get over it," Cosson says, "I don't. I live with it every day."

The Army Air Corps never had a formal hearing on the events of that night, but an army nurse told the family a few years later that the pilot had a complete breakdown after the incident and was confined to a hospital.

PAPER BALLOONS

In World War II only six people died from enemy action on the mainland United States. The Reverend Archie Mitchell and his pregnant wife, Elsie, accompanied a group of children on a picnic on Gearhart Mountain in Oregon on May 5, 1945. The children came upon a shiny object. One of them reached out to touch the object, detonating a bomb that killed all the children as well as Elsie Mitchell. The device was part of a Japanese plan to attack the West Coast of the United States with incendiary devices and fragmentation bombs attached to large paper balloons.

More than 6,000 of these balloons were constructed by Japanese schoolchildren and then launched into the jet stream toward the United States. Only 350 of these bombs, constructed of paper and controlled by primitive guidance systems, landed in America. Of those that landed, most either failed to detonate or landed in remote areas and did little damage. Only the six people killed in Oregon became victims of one of the last desperate attempts by the Japanese military, just three months before the United States detonated atomic bombs over Hiroshima and Nagasaki. One of the balloons did hit the main transmission lines in Hanford, Washington, where the plutonium for the Nagasaki bomb was being produced, shutting off production for three days.

The intention of the Japanese military was to cause forest fires and instill panic in the American population. American officials, however, to keep Japan from knowing that their plan was in any way successful, forbade journalists to cover the story, and no mention was made of the bombs or the casualties for forty years. Only recently has the story been revived, when it was learned that another wave of balloons was planned, this time carrying plague, anthrax, and nerve gases. Saturation bombing of the balloon-making facility and the detonation of the atomic bombs halted the bombing and ended the war before more balloons could be launched.

As a result of the secrecy and news blackout surrounding this story, as well as the size and shape of the balloons, the balloon bombing was a source of some of the first and most reliable eyewitness accounts of UFOs in the United States and Canada.

MOVE

The aftermath of a controversial police raid left eleven people dead and fifty-three homes and two city blocks of Philadelphia burned to the ground. Two hundred forty people were made homeless. Thirteen members of a cultlike group called Move had barricaded themselves inside their house in a previously quiet neighborhood. Move members, using bullhorns to shout their demands, refused to surrender unless other members of Move, who were in prison for murder, were released.

The Move members were well armed and their house had a concrete bunker on its roof and another bunker dug into its basement. On May 13, 1985, the police, tiring of negotiating with Conrad Africa, Move's "defense minister,"

decided to toss a knapsack filled with plastic explosives onto the roof bunker. This decision was made knowing that there were at least four children in the house and that the explosion could touch off a fire that could spread to neighboring houses.

But the police had miscalculated the devastation that would follow. The explosive charge caused the roof to collapse and a firestorm to start. At first police refused to allow firefighters in, hoping that the fire would force Move to surrender. After firefighters were called in, they at first refused to fight the fire, saying that they were firemen not infantrymen. By the time a plan to fight the blaze was put into effect, it was too late. Two Move members survived—Ramona Africa and thirteen-year-old Michael Ward.

W. Wilson Goode, mayor of Philadelphia, watching the scene from his office, took full responsibility and pledged that the city would immediately rebuild all the damaged houses. Although the fire cost the city of Philadelphia $27 million in lawsuits, legal fees, and rebuilding costs, and although commissions spent years studying the conduct that led to the bombing, no action was ever taken against any public figure.

—D.C.

SPIES

WORLD WAR I

COLONEL ALFRED REDL
Austro-Hungarian, worked for Russia
To the cold-eyed men who ran agents for the Okhrana, the czar's intelligence service, Colonel Alfred Victor Redl was the catch of a lifetime.

The rising star of the Austro-Hungarian Empire's General Staff, Redl was well known to the Russians as the genius who had single-handedly remade the lackluster Austrian foreign intelligence and internal security apparatus in his own tireless, efficient image.

It was the resourceful, meticulous Redl who had pioneered the use of hidden cameras for covert surveillance, and who had first bugged interrogation rooms with gramophone disks. It was Redl who had introduced the use of clandestinely gathered fingerprints to entrap a long roster of enemy agents, most of them Russian.

Even more distressing from the Russian point of view, it was Redl who had personally negotiated an intelligence-sharing pact with the hated and feared Germans.

These and other startling tradecraft innovations made Colonel Redl's Austrian Evidenzbureau one of the most formidable counterintelligence services in pre–World War I Europe.

The fastidious young colonel, recipient of the Emperor's Medal of Supreme Satisfaction, was plainly being groomed for high command, perhaps even for the top post of chief of staff. Apparently well off, universally liked and respected, Redl seemed almost too good to be true. And so he was.

A self-made man from the lower middle class, Colonel Redl was unable to reconcile his army officer's pay with an irresistible appetite for life's finer things: shiny Daimler limousines, closets crammed with custom-tailored uniforms and civilian clothes, champagne parties, and luxury apartments.

The colonel carefully concealed his homosexuality from his superiors, and yet he lavished an allowance more generous than his own official income on a young lieutenant, whom he introduced to people as his nephew.

It was Redl's turn-of-the-century susceptibility to sexual blackmail that the Russians discovered and used against him, turning the Austrian spy chief into a "defector in place." The Russians sweetened the bitter pill of coercion by paying Redl frequently and well. He was an excellent investment.

From 1903 to 1913, Redl served his Russian handlers as tirelessly as he had served his emperor, diverting suspicion from Russian agents in Austria and betraying Austrian spies sent abroad to spy on the Russians. Careful to maintain his invaluable reputation as the top Austrian spy catcher, the Russians sometimes permitted him to arrest agents they deemed expendable.

Redl's most damaging betrayal by far was the selling of Plan III to the Russians. Plan III was the painstakingly drafted Austrian contingency plan for invading the buffer state of Serbia. The Russians lost no time in passing Plan III to their Serbian allies, with the result that when the inevitable war finally came, Redl's treachery cost his Austrian countrymen more than a half million casualties and decisively contributed to the collapse of the Austro-Hungarian Empire.

After ten years as a double agent, Redl was snared by operatives of Major Maximilian Ronge, the successor he himself had handpicked and trained. Redl, who certainly should have known better, was apprehended after picking up his payoff money from a post office box known to be a Russian "dead drop."

Ironically, Ronge was able to incriminate his former chief and mentor by comparing the writing on Redl's post office box application with a still top secret forty-page monograph on counterintelligence that Redl had penned in his own hand.

By the time Austria entered the war, the man destined to be remembered as one of history's greatest traitors was already dead. Cornered, Redl had revealed the whereabouts of a cache of secret documents to his captors, and in return, he had asked to be left alone with a revolver with one bullet in the chamber, invoking the traditional prerogative of disgraced officers.

His betrayal was so cataclysmic that his superiors informed a shocked emperor that Redl had killed himself in a fit of depression caused by overwork and insomnia.

—M.C.S.

CAPTAIN FRANZ VON RINTELEN
German, worked for Germany

In 1915 the peacetime United States vacillated between its official neutrality toward a still entirely European conflict and its desire to sell war materiel to both the Allies and the Central Powers. Nobody paid much attention to an aristocratic German naval captain named Franz von Rintelen as he disembarked from a transatlantic passenger ship to begin his new duty assignment in New York City.

Rintelen, posing as a businessman, entered the country as an "illegal," operating without the protection a diplomatic cover would have afforded him. Thanks to his father's extensive American banking connections, von Rintelen was fluent both in English and in the language of commerce. His family background and sailor's knowledge of ships and harbor facilities had influenced his superiors in German intelligence to select him for his highly sensitive mission.

Von Rintelen had been ordered to sabotage American ships carrying food, clothing, and munitions, and to otherwise divert crucially needed American resources from reaching the French and British by any means he could devise.

Von Rintelen's first move was to establish contact with Franz von Papen, the German military attaché who doubled as control officer for all clandestine German intelligence operations in the United States.

Von Papen was more diplomat than soldier and not particularly gifted at either calling. He practiced a low-risk, plausibly deniable brand of economic warfare. Before von Rintelen's arrival, the attaché's favorite tactic had been to back-order vast quantities of American war supplies and then do everything he could to tie up the production of the corporations he did business with. He had also founded an American-managed but German-owned business concern called the Bridgeport Projectile Company.

Von Papen used Bridgeport as a front for ordering gunpowder, which he then hoarded or destroyed, denying it to the Allies. Under von Papen's control, Bridgeport aggressively competed for munitions contracts, which it predictably failed to fulfill.

Von Rintelen was more of a man of action than von Papen, the cautious political animal, and almost from their first meeting, the two spies clashed. Acting on his own brief, Captain von Rintelen recruited a German-sympathizing technician and began seeding the holds of American freighters with time-delayed incendiary devices.

One such weapon was an ordinary-looking pipe divided by a copper partition into watertight compartments, with one space filled with sulfuric acid and the other containing picric acid. The sulfuric acid ate through the copper at a predictable rate, allowing the saboteur to plant the bomb and be safe onshore when the mixture came together and the device ignited in the hold of some unlucky ship at sea.

Another improvised saboteur's tool was a bomb triggered by the revolutions of a ship's screws. In both cases the saboteur's objective was not to sink ships and take lives but rather to force the ship's crew to fight a fire belowdecks by frantically throwing the precious munitions from the hold into the sea.

Grudgingly taking a leaf from von Papen's book, von Rintelen also founded an espionage front company. His concern, E. V. Gibbons, was able to obtain lucrative munitions contracts from the Allies, which not only expanded von Rintelen's sabotage opportunities but also legitimized his ersatz corporation with sizable revenues.

Von Rintelen took advantage of his heady success as a war profiteer to found a new union on the waterfront, the Labor's National Peace

Council, which was responsible for numerous strikes throughout the United States.

Unimpressed, von Papen suspected von Rintelen of exaggerating or even lying outright about the tonnage of Allied supplies he had allegedly damaged or destroyed. He investigated the shipping records of 1915 and concluded that they failed to corroborate his rival's reported successes.

Dispatching a telegram to Berlin demanding von Rintelen's recall, von Papen portrayed the naval officer as a liar and a loose cannon, one who might very well compromise the entire German intelligence mission in America.

This coded telegram was deciphered by British Naval Intelligence with suspicious ease, suggesting that von Papen may have deliberately used a cipher he knew was being read by the Allies.

If it was indeed von Papen's intention to have von Rintelen captured, he achieved it. The British, waiting at Southampton for von Rintelen, marched him off a neutral Dutch ship when it put in at the British port on its way to the Continent.

Von Rintelen was interned in England until the United States entered the war, and he was then shipped to the federal penitentiary in Atlanta, Georgia, where he was imprisoned for three years.

In 1920 he returned to Germany a forgotten man; still cursing von Papen for his capture, he moved to England, where he died in 1949. The duplicitous von Papen became chancellor of Germany and later Adolf Hitler's puppet foreign minister. Von Papen was sentenced to death at the Nuremberg war crimes tribunal for waging aggressive war and crimes against humanity, but his death sentence was commuted to a prison term, and he died a free man in 1969.

—M.C.S.

WORLD WAR II

MATHILDE CARRÉ
French, worked for France and Germany

All of Paris was abuzz when, on January 8, 1949, newspaper headlines throughout the city announced that the Fourteenth Criminal Court had handed down its decision in the Carré case. The defendant was celebrated for her beauty, and the press was breathlessly calling her "the Mata Hari of World War II."

"The Cat"—Micheline Mathilde Carré—had been convicted of collaborating with the Germans. It was the finding of the court that Carré had exploited the trust reposed in her by the leaders of the wartime resistance movement (exploiting her considerable sex appeal as well), to betray at least thirty-five key members of the Free French Underground to the Germans.

Educated at the Sorbonne during the 1930s, Carré had been living in Algeria, listlessly teaching school to augment her army officer husband's meager income, when the war broke out. She was a petite brunette with flawless white teeth, sensuous green eyes, and, as one smitten biographer put it, "marvelously expressive legs."

Her husband was killed in action in the early days of the war, and Carré volunteered to go to Paris for nurse's training. "Now life will begin!" she exulted. She indulged in a brief shipboard fling with a young French paratrooper on the journey.

Arriving in the City of Light, she wrote in her diary, "It is unimaginable that the Boches can conquer Paris. In Paris, I am happy, I am in heaven! And I shall do my part to see that hell doesn't win a victory over heaven!" But the unimaginable did indeed happen, and the triumphant Germans paraded down the Champs-Elysées.

Carré's medical unit fled, setting up aid stations in Beauvais and then in Toulon. Reliable and hardworking, she was assigned to establish a reception center for French troops who had become separated from their units. It was at the reception center that she met Roman Czerniawski, a Polish officer of the General Staff who had been serving as a liaison with the defeated French army.

Czerniawski ("Armand" to Carré, who soon became his lover), had been captured by the Germans and had escaped. He was determined to set up an espionage and resistance cell, which he called Interallié.

Because Armand was wanted by the Germans, he used Carré for contact work, effectively making the unit's entire complement of agents known to her. It was Armand who nicknamed Carré "the Cat," in tribute to her feline grace. One wonders if it ever occurred to him that cats always land on their feet.

Carré was an effective field agent, and soon Interallié boasted a network of Free French officers in both occupied and unoccupied France. Carré personally identified and pinpointed the size and disposition of Luftwaffe and SS Panzer units near Bordeaux. Later, through her flirtation with an unsuspecting Luftwaffe supply officer, she was able to confirm that the Germans had given up their plans to attack Gibraltar.

Based on these and other successes, an intelligence professional from the Deuxième, Lieutenant Colonel Paul Achard, was detailed to head up Interallié. Achard was in contact with the British Special Operations Executive (SOE) in London, and through them, the Free French high command under Charles de Gaulle.

Renamed "Valenty" by the British, Carré's resistance group specialized in gathering information from amorous German officers with the help of the Cat and another hastily recruited female agent named Renée Borni, code name "Violette."

To Carré's chagrin, Violette also commenced a love affair with Armand. She also promptly got Carré's beloved Armand apprehended by the Germans.

Violette, as it turned out, was a double agent being run by a German sergeant named Hugo Bleicher of the Abwehr, Admiral Wilhelm Canaris's counterintelligence service. Bleicher had Carré yanked off the streets on the way to a rendezvous and detained in an Abwehr villa that had been confiscated from a French movie star.

Rather than using torture, Bleicher employed a combination of psychological pressure and his personal charm to turn Carré against her former comrades.

Willingly or not, the Cat became the German's mistress. For the next two months, with Bleicher and an armed squad of German troops at her heels, Carré exposed virtually every member of her Résistance organization. She made one significant exception, though, stubbornly refusing to betray the whereabouts of Colonel Achard.

Even so, Interallié's vital communication links with London had been disrupted by the arrests, and it was decided that Carré, still a trusted member of the cell, would accompany Résistance leader Pierre De Vomecourt on a clandestine mission to London. Bleicher was ecstatic at the thought of infiltrating a mole into the supersecret British SOE and eagerly arranged for the pair of them to slip out of occupied France unmolested.

But British counterintelligence, MI5, deftly put the pieces together and unmasked Carré as a traitor, arresting her in July 1942. She remained in British custody until the end of the war.

Despite her treachery, her old commander, Lieutenant Colonel Paul Achard, spoke up for her at her postwar trial, testifying that "Madame Carré performed remarkable services for the French Army. During the years she worked for us, she was able to deliver to us many of the German Army's plans of campaign." The judge was unimpressed and sentenced the Cat to death.

She coolly told him, "I await the verdict without fear. But I can't help remembering that while the death sentence is asked for me in this court, Hugo Bleicher is living free in Hamburg."

A few months later the president of the French Republic commuted Carré's sentence to life imprisonment. She was released in 1954 and is believed to have died in 1970.

—M.C.S.

KLAUS FUCHS
German, worked for Russia

Although the Soviet Union fought on the side of the Allies in World War II, neither Franklin Roosevelt nor Winston Churchill could stomach the thought of sharing atomic weapons research with the tyrannical, unstable Josef Stalin.

An utterly ruthless paranoid whose appetite for mass murder surpassed even Hitler's, Stalin simply couldn't be trusted with a strategic weapon of mass destruction.

Motivated by anti-Nazi fervor, German-born physicist Klaus Fuchs secretly appointed himself the USSR's key informant on the bomb's development. He felt that since the Soviet Union was bearing the brunt of the war against the Nazis, it was morally entitled to any weapon in the Allied arsenal.

Despite being a known member of the Communist Party, in 1941 the talented Fuchs was cleared by British security and hired to work on the English nuclear research program. Fuchs promptly contacted Moscow and offered Stalin's GRU, the military intelligence agency, his services as the first atom-age spy.

Nuclear research had become too costly for the embattled British, and so Fuchs was spirited out of England in 1943, and after a stint at Columbia University, where it is believed he met the American Communist courier he knew as "Raymond," he arrived at a highly secured facility in the desert outside of Los Alamos, New Mexico.

The Allied nuclear weapons research effort being conducted there was code-named the Manhattan Project. Under the direction of the brilliant Dr. Robert Oppenheimer, an international team of Allied physicists and engineers was feverishly racing against their Nazi counterparts to invent a workable atom bomb. Or so Fuchs and everyone else at Los Alamos believed at the time.

Allied intelligence didn't comprehend that Hitler's virulent anti-Semitism had cost Germany the services of her most capable physicists, many of them Jews who had been hounded out of their university posts or murdered in concentration camps. Hitler had raved that physics was a "Jewish science," and German nuclear research was therefore at a standstill.

Enjoying the full confidence of Dr. Oppenheimer, Fuchs was privy to all vital aspects of the bomb—design, construction, components, detonating devices, and test results. Technical data amassed by Fuchs were passed to "Raymond" (later identified as Harry Gold) in Santa Fe, and relayed from there to the Kremlin.

When President Harry Truman finally revealed the existence of the atom bomb to Josef Stalin at the Potsdam Conference, the president was astounded at the Soviet leader's lack of reaction. Stalin privately gloated over the consternation the Americans and the British were hard-pressed to hide.

Thanks to Klaus Fuchs and company, Stalin knew all about the scientific breakthrough in New Mexico. Fuchs's treachery had saved the

Soviets literally billions of dollars in research and development costs. Even if they could have mustered the financial resources, it would conservatively have taken the Soviets several years to do the theoretical work on their own.

As Stalin attended the conference to discuss the peace settlement in Europe and the continuing war against Japan, a team of Soviet scientists, working from microfilmed diagrams and notes supplied by Fuchs, was hurriedly constructing a Soviet A-bomb.

Even before the Red bomb was successfully tested, the defection of a GRU cipher clerk named Igor Gouzenko from the Soviet embassy in Ottawa confirmed everyone's worst fears.

Gouzenko revealed to Royal Canadian Mounted Police counterintelligence that the Soviets had stolen the plans for the A-bomb. Fuchs, who had moved to England in June 1946, was subsequently arrested while working at the British nuclear research center at Harwell after the FBI, acting on Gouzenko's information, alerted the British to the probable identity of the traitor in their midst. The Cold War era of nuclear terror and its byproduct, the doctrine of mutually assured destruction, was loosed on the world. The arms race was on. Suddenly wary of Soviet nuclear muscle, the Allies were

Atom spy Klaus Fuchs relaxes in his East German office at the Institute of Nuclear Physics in 1965, six years after his release from a British prison.

helpless against Soviet imperialism in the Baltic States and Eastern Europe.

The fear and suspicion caused by the revelations of nuclear spy rings operating in the United States and Great Britain turned inward and festered, ushering in a wave of American political repression under the auspices of political opportunists such as Senator Joseph McCarthy and other unscrupulous members of the House Un-American Activities Committee.

Eventually Gouzenko's information led directly or indirectly to the capture not only of Fuchs but of the other operatives of the Russian spy ring as well: Alfred Nunn May, David Greenglass, Harry Gold, and both Julius and Ethel Rosenberg. The Rosenbergs were executed in the electric chair amid great international furor after what amounted to an American show trial.

Fuchs, the real culprit, spent ten years of his fourteen-year maximum sentence in a British prison, and after his release he left the country and continued his nuclear research in East Germany. He died in 1988.

The penetration of Los Alamos by Fuchs and his GRU handlers is still celebrated in the former Soviet Union as the crowning achievement of Russian intelligence. Since the collapse of the Soviet Union, it has been rumored that the retired Soviet spymasters, now old men, may yet choose to reveal the involvement of other counterparts of Klaus Fuchs—nuclear traitors at Los Alamos who were never unmasked.

—M.C.S.

JUAN PUJOL
Spanish, worked for Great Britain

During World War II, Juan Pujol was a citizen of the neutral country of Spain, a man with no background in intelligence, with no special position or connections—yet he managed to make himself perhaps the most effective double agent of the entire war. A strong antifascist and an incurable romantic, Pujol was motivated by Hitler's conquests to offer his services as a spy to the British embassy in Madrid. Turned down, he succeeded in getting the Abwehr to hire him as a German agent. He received cash and invisible ink from his new employers, then moved to Lisbon, where he pretended that he had gone to London, had set up a spy network, and was dispatching his reports to Portugal through a courier who flew for KLM Airlines. Despite hilarious errors in his reports (Pujol had little knowledge of England, since he had never been there), the Germans eagerly devoured his made-up information. Given his success, British secret service was only too happy to accept his renewed offer to work as an Allied agent. After flying to London, Pujol was given the code name "Garbo" and assigned to work with Tomas Harris, his MI5 case officer. Together they established an elaborate network of fictitious spies; the Germans were so convinced, they sent Pujol assessments of the strengths and weaknesses of each false agent. The deception was intricate: at one point the Germans received messages from the nonexistent subagents that Pujol had been arrested. Trembling in fear for their star spy, the Nazis soon got word that he had been released—MI5 even sent official documents from the Home Office apologizing for the arrest. But the greatest hoax came with D-Day, the invasion of France on June 6, 1944. Through carefully orchestrated reports, Pujol and Harris helped convince the Germans that the Allied landing at Normandy was a feint; for invaluable days after the invasion, Hitler himself ordered troops held back to meet the imagined second assault in the Pas de Calais region. Despite the obvious falsity of the information, Berlin never caught on. Pujol was even awarded an Iron Cross. The British gave him a medal as well, and helped him to relocate to South America, out of fear of retribution from vengeful Nazis. There he lived under an assumed name, his secret kept by all for another forty years.

—T.J.S.

COLD WAR

Let us not be deceived—we are today in the midst of a cold war.

Bernard M. Baruch, Speech, Columbia, South Carolina, April 16, 1947; ghostwritten by Herbert Bayard Swope

COLONEL RUDOLF ABEL
Russian, worked for Russia
Colonel Rudolf Ivanovich Abel of the KGB was the model of a Soviet illegal *rezident*, a career intelligence professional who operated outside of diplomatic channels, clandestinely running agents in a foreign country.

The colonel's real name remains as mysterious as the true nature of his activities in the United States. Most sources agree that "Abel" was Russian born and spent time in England as a boy. He was fluent in English, German, Polish, and Yiddish. He was a talented painter and photographer, a competent jeweler, and a proficient ham radio operator. In short, he was a man who never lacked for cover identities.

During World War II, radio enthusiast Abel served in Soviet signals intelligence and is said to have penetrated an Abwehr (German counterintelligence) headquarters as a chauffeur. At the end of the war the highly decorated KGB colonel "submarined," or went under deep cover, insinuating himself into a displaced persons camp in Germany, assuming the name Andrew Kayotis.

Abel/Kayotis applied for and was granted permission to enter Canada in 1947, and once in Canada, he illegally crossed the border into the United States. In the United States Abel activated his carefully constructed American "legend," or cover identity, posing as Emil R. Goldfus, painter and photographer.

Abel communicated directly with Moscow on the ham radio set in his artist's studio, relaying masses of data with specialized high-speed mathematical ciphers of his own design. Although Abel has often been characterized as the head of the American atomic spy cell, he never made a deal or boasted of his professional triumphs in captivity. Thus red-faced American counterintelligence officers were never able to reliably determine what Abel had really been up to all those years.

Perhaps the best guess is that he had been sent to the United States to rebuild the espionage organization "blown" by defecting cipher clerk Igor Gouzenko. (See entry on Klaus Fuchs.) Then too, he might merely have been lying fallow until an American traitor important or productive enough to be worthy of the colonel's agent-handling talents presented himself.

Mostly from confiscated vacation photographs, Abel/Goldfus is known to have traveled widely in America, presumably familiarizing himself with the country and customs. In 1950 it is believed he settled comfortably into the post of KGB *rezident* in New York, and again, speculation would have it that he functioned as the overseer for the entire KGB North American, Mexican, and Central American networks.

Abel enjoyed acting out the artist's aversion to routine to explain his frequent and sporadic absences. He was popular in bohemian circles, a gentlemanly, companionable man who enjoyed good food and wine and the company of other artists.

Cartoonist Jules Feiffer knew Abel in New York and commented that Abel impressed him as a man who had been on the bum at one point in his life, a man who had lived through a rough time. As it happened, Abel's most trying years were before him.

When Abel was arrested in 1957, J. Edgar Hoover's FBI spin doctors concocted a comic-book account of how the "master spy" had mistakenly handed a newspaper boy a hollow nickel full of microfilm, thus bringing the vigilant G-men down on his neck the moment the patriotic tyke raced for a telephone. As usual, the truth was far more prosaic.

Abel had been turned in by a KGB defector named Reino Hayhanen, a drunken, erratic, womanizing assistant dumped on the *rezident* by Moscow center. Abel lost patience with Hayhanen and complained to his superiors in hopes of having Hayhanen replaced.

Fearing the consequences of bungling his New York assignment, Hayhanen defected in Paris. He made a beeline for the American embassy's resident CIA man and sold Abel out in exchange for sanctuary in the United States.

After his arrest, Abel admitted only that he was a Russian who had entered the country illegally; then he clammed up. His possession of espionage tools (including his radio equipment and the famous hollowed-out nickel full of microfilm) was enough to get him convicted of espionage and sentenced to die in the electric chair.

Abel's sentence was later commuted to thirty years, but he remained behind bars for only five years, until 1962, when the Americans traded him for the shot-down CIA contract employee, U-2 pilot Francis Gary Powers, being held in the Soviet Union. (See section on Francis Gary Powers.) CIA director Allen Dulles admiringly said of Abel that he wished the CIA had several men like him in Moscow.

Abel returned home to Moscow, startled to discover he had become a glamorous public figure in his absence. He was awarded the Order of Lenin and is believed to have semiretired, as an emeritus instructor at the KGB's Felix Dzherzhinski training school, until his death in 1971.

—M.C.S.

ALDRICH AMES
American, worked for Soviet Union

For nine of the thirty-one years he worked at the Central Intelligence Agency, Aldrich Hazen Ames (born in 1941 in the all-American town of River Falls, Wisconsin) lived a double life resembling the plot of a John Le Carré novel. A second-generation CIA officer, Ames was head of counterintelligence for the Soviet/East European Division of the CIA. But he was also a mole, or deep-penetration Russian agent. He peddled every agency secret he could lay his hands on to the KGB. He was one of the most destructive turncoats in the history of American espionage.

Ames's treachery is said to have led directly to the execution of ten or more Russians on the CIA/FBI payroll. One such agent was GRU general Dmitri Polyakov, code-named "Top Hat," who had spied for the CIA since 1961. The legendary Top Hat was the most important and productive Soviet "asset" the agency ever had.

Despite the untold damage he caused, there were major differences between the sloppy, lackluster "Rick" Ames and his stealthy counterparts in espionage fiction.

The first was his astoundingly brazen lifestyle. Ames was twice reprimanded for drinking (he liked vodka). He spent the $2.5 million plus that the Russians paid him with an utter disregard for appearances, recklessly spending way over his annual CIA salary of $69,000. He bought a $540,000 house in pricey Arlington, Virginia, for cash, and spent a further $99,000 on home improvements, again paying cash. The house was filled with signed impressionist prints, expensive computers, watches, and stereo equipment. Ames drove a flashy new red Jaguar (price:

$40,000). His shrewish Colombian-born second wife, Maria del Rosario Casas Dupuy, drove a more sedate Honda Accord but bought herself two apartments and a farm outside of Bogota, as well as a lavish collection of jewelry. The Ameses had three bank accounts in Switzerland, one in Italy, and eight in the United States. About a million dollars of their ill-gotten money is still unaccounted for.

Ames had met Rosario while she was a Colombian consular official in Mexico, and, on the rebound from a costly divorce from another CIA employee, he had recruited Rosario as an agency informant. Ames was given a slap-on-the-wrist reprimand for using agency safe houses for sexual liaisons with Rosario. In 1986 he flunked a lie detector question about his personal finances. In 1991 he again made the polygraph needle quiver when he was asked if he had ever worked for the Soviet Union. Incredibly, nothing was done to follow up on any of these glaring danger signals.

Ames's treachery began in 1985. One night at a Washington cocktail party, he calmly introduced himself to a KGB officer and sold the Russian a list of American agents, pocketing $9,000 in cash. Suddenly intelligence information coming from the Soviet Union simply dried up as the Russians arrested agent after agent.

Owing to a spectacular series of espionage arrests by the FBI that year (including the bungled attempt to apprehend Edward Lee Howard, a rogue CIA officer who outsmarted his FBI pursuers and safely escaped to Moscow), much of the damage Ames did was initially ascribed to other sources.

Despite warnings from the IRS that Ames was banking large sums of cash, he avoided serious scrutiny until 1992, when he was observed meeting with a Soviet contact during an unauthorized and unreported trip he made to Caracas, Venezuela.

The FBI started investigating him in 1993, bugging his home and personal computer and sifting through his garbage. It didn't take long for them to amass definitive evidence of Ames's guilt, including letters from his Russian handlers and a note he had written them on a Post-it pad, listing intelligence "dead drops" and contact procedures. There was also a picture of a Russian dacha (country house) and a note telling Ames that this building and the land around it was now his for all time. The FBI found large quantities of highly classified documents in Ames's possession, including thousands on high-density computer disks. Incredibly, Ames was arrested one day before he was scheduled to leave for a new CIA assignment—Moscow, where he was to confer on the narcotics trade in Russia with officers of the Sluzhba Vneshnei Razvedki (the Russian foreign intelligence service and successor to the KGB).

Convicted of espionage and income tax evasion, Ames received a life sentence. Rosario Ames received a sentence of sixty-three months in prison as part of a plea bargain whereby Ames helped reveal to intelligence authorities the scope of his betrayal in the hope that his wife could one day be reunited with their son.

Interviewed after his conviction, Ames downplayed the seriousness of what he had done: "I do not believe our nation's interests have been noticeably damaged by my acts, or for that matter those of the Soviet Union or Russia noticeably aided. I had come to dissent from the decades-long shift to the extreme right in our political spectrum and from our national security and foreign policies. Second, I had come to believe that the espionage business, as carried on by the CIA and a few other agencies, is a self-serving sham, carried out by careerist bureaucrats who have managed to deceive several generations of American policy makers and the public about the necessity and value of their work."

Meanwhile, it is believed that other moles, perhaps even more dangerous than Ames, are presently embedded within the U.S. intelligence community.

—M.C.S.

THE CAMBRIDGE FIVE
British, worked for Soviet Union

The most successful known spy ring in modern times was never really a ring at all. The five members knew each other, knew of each other's espionage work, some of them perhaps even slept together, but the thing that united them as spies was that they had all been recruited by the Soviets when they attended Cambridge University in the 1930s, or shortly after. They were Guy Burgess, Donald Maclean, Anthony Blunt, John Cairncross, and Harold Philby (better known by his nickname Kim). Dubbed the "Magnificent Five" by Soviet intelligence, they began working for the Communists during the idealistic days of the depression; the bulk of their work was done during World War II, when they penetrated the British foreign office and intelligence services. Kim Philby, the son of explorer Harry St. John Philby (see p. 305), was the first, the most damaging, and ultimately the most famous of the five; he was recruited in Austria in 1934 and later joined the Special Operations Executive after the outbreak of war. Back at Cambridge, student Guy Burgess acted as the principal recruiter for the other members of the group. A flamboyant history student, a devoted Marxist, and openly homosexual, he developed a passionate relationship with Anthony Blunt (an outstanding art history scholar) and also recruited John Cairncross and Scotsman Donald Maclean (who may also have been involved with Blunt). By 1935 the five were all Soviet agents. All took government posts, and with the eruption of war in 1939 they rapidly moved into ever more sensitive positions in the Foreign Office, MI6 (the foreign intelligence service), and MI5 (the domestic counterintelligence unit). Throughout the war, these five funneled to their Soviet controllers critical information that the Churchill government was holding back from its ally. Kim Philby was so successful in his double life that he was considered for the post of "C"—chief of British intelligence. After the war, Blunt went into semiretirement, but Cairncross continued to report from the Treasury Department, Burgess from the Foreign Office, Maclean from a diplomatic committee coordinating nuclear research with the Americans, and Philby from his post as intelligence liaison with Washington. In 1951 things came to an abrupt halt: the Americans had earlier deciphered a Soviet message that identified a member of the British diplomatic delegation as a spy code-named "Homer." A British investigation gradually led to Maclean. Acting on a warning from Philby, Maclean and Burgess both fled to the Soviet Union; though Blunt carefully cleaned out Burgess's apartment, he failed to detect notes from Cairncross, who was subsequently interrogated and forced to resign from the Treasury but was not publicly identified as a spy by the embarrassed government. Blunt received similar treatment. Philby was suspected but was officially cleared in 1955—only to be uncovered as the famed "Third Man" in 1963, when he defected to the Soviet Union, where he was made a general in the KGB, given superficial chores, and forgotten. Despite tremendous public interest in the scandal, Blunt would not be publicly named as the "Fourth Man" until 1979, nor Cairncross as the "Fifth Man" until 1991.

—T.J.S.

COLONEL RYSZARD J. KUKLINSKI
Polish, worked for United States

Between 1970 and 1981, the CIA received detailed information on more than 200 of the most advanced Soviet weapons systems, on the location and defenses of the Warsaw Pact's secret command centers, on the Soviet battle plans in the event of a war in Europe, and on the martial-law crackdown on the Solidarity movement in Poland. It even took possession of documents intended for Polish army chief Wojciech Jaruzelski before they reached Jaruzelski's own desk. The source: Colonel Ryszard J. Kuklinski, head of Poland's Department I for Strategic Defense Planning, and liaison with the Red Army. Kuklinski's father had been a Polish patriot who was arrested, tortured, and killed by the Gestapo during the German occupation. After World War II, Kuklinski joined the Polish army, but he came to see the Soviets as simply another foreign oppressor. The use of the Polish army to put down worker unrest in Gdansk and other cities in 1970 drove him to contact the CIA and offer his services. The documents he sent were so valuable, a special unit was established by the army to analyze them. In fact, his material was so voluminous, most unit members assumed it flowed from multiple sources (they were never told where the papers came from). In 1981 the Soviets warned the Polish army that they intended to invade to put down Solidarity unless the Poles themselves acted. Kuklinski stepped up his dispatch of classified documents as Jaruzelski planned to announce martial law. One day in November 1981, Kuklinski attended a meeting of high-ranking Soviet and Polish officers; there the Russians announced that they had detected a high-placed mole inside the Warsaw Pact high command. Feigning shock with the others, Kuklinski left and quickly arranged a daring escape to the West with CIA help. Today he lives in secret in the United States. He was convicted of treason in absentia—a ruling left standing by the post-Communist government he had so eagerly hoped for.

—T.J.S.

JONATHAN JAY POLLARD
American, worked for Israel
Jonathan Jay Pollard is less remarkable for the damage he did to America's security than for the fact that he worked for Israel, a close ally of the United States. The alarming case of an American Jew spying on his native country for the Jewish state provoked strong and contradictory reactions from the U.S. government, the Israeli leadership, and the American Jewish community.

Pollard joined the naval intelligence in 1979. In 1984 he was hired by the new Anti-Terrorism Alert Center in the Threat Analysis Division of the Naval Investigative Service. Pollard moved from watch officer to research specialist, with access to secret information on terrorist threats in the Caribbean and the United States. Thanks to the center's honor system, however, he could obtain intelligence documents on virtually any part of the globe. In June 1984 Pollard—long outspoken in his support of Israel—made contact with the Israeli embassy in Washington. The chief Israeli foreign intelligence agency, Mossad, had a standing policy against running agents in the United States out of the embassy, but Pollard was picked up by Lakam, the unit responsible for scientific and technical intelligence and for protecting Israel's nuclear program. Pollard's case was personally overseen by legendary Israeli spy Rafi Eitan, who assigned air force colonel Aviem Sella as Pollard's contact. For the next year, Sella told the American what information was needed; every week or two, Pollard would carry a suitcase full of documents to the apartment of an Israeli embassy secretary for copying.

Pollard later claimed he was driven by his commitment to Israel, yet he was paid handsomely for his work—tens of thousands of dollars in cash and gifts. In addition, in 1981—long before working for Israel—he had made contact with South Africa, hoping to spy for them. His action was detected, but the navy let him off with a slap on the wrist. In any event, his activities lasted barely a year. In November 1985, fellow navy intelligence officers detected his unusual requests for documents. Together with his wife, Anne Henderson Pollard, he was quickly arrested. Pollard was sentenced to life in prison; despite an Israeli plea for clemency, President Bill Clinton affirmed the sentence on March 23, 1994.

—T.J.S.

FRANCIS GARY POWERS
American, worked for United States
One of the greatest technical achievements in the history of espionage combined with a brave, hapless young pilot to produce what was perhaps the most painful public embarrassment in U.S. diplomatic history.

The technical achievement was the U-2 spy plane, essentially a glider with a jet engine, and the finest aerial photography platform of its day. The aircraft was a highly classified masterpiece: sleek, fast, flimsily built, and incomparably capable of prolonged flight at hitherto impossible altitudes.

As a CIA official put it, "What ciphers were in the 1940s, photography was in the 1950s." The U-2 had been designed in conditions of maximum secrecy to provide the kind of hard military intelligence the United States found nearly impossible to get from the closed society of the Soviet Union in the days before satellite reconnaissance: flawless, razor-sharp photo intelligence.

Known as the "black lady of espionage" to the despairing Russian Air Defense Command, the U-2 was capable of staying in the air for ten hours at an altitude of 70,000 feet (later 80,000 feet), a ceiling no Soviet missile or aircraft was thought capable of matching. That is, until CIA contract pilot Francis Gary Powers was shot out of the sky by one of the new, improved, Soviet surface-to-air missiles (the SAM-2) on May 1, 1960.

Powers, a former air force fighter pilot who had been flying covert intelligence missions for the CIA for more than four years at the time of the incident, was making three times what he had been paid in uniform, and was the senior pilot of the small pool of U-2 jockeys at his home base in Turkey. Some of the pilots he flew with regarded the missions as milk runs.

Powers's assignment was to take off from Peshawar, Pakistan, get some photos of the Soviet missile works at Tyuratam, and land in Bodo, Norway, having overflown 3,800 miles of the Soviet Union.

He was knocked out of the air by what was probably a near miss by a SAM outside of the town of Sverdlosk. Powers didn't trust the ejection seat or the auto-destruct buttons the CIA had installed, suspecting that they might have been designed to kill the pilot automatically when he attempted to use them. Neither did he elect to use the suicide needle covered with shellfish toxin hidden in a silver dollar in one of his pockets. He bailed out and took his chances.

As he told one of the KGB men who came riding up on a bicycle to take him into custody, "I wanted to live."

Russian Premier Nikita Khrushchev, delighted at having a pretext to pull out of a forthcoming and politically hazardous summit conference in Paris, gleefully allowed the United States to spin cock-and-bull cover stories about off-course weather airplanes for five days before he announced that the U-2 pilot had survived. The Russians had the wreckage, the film, and a living CIA pilot to back up their story.

The United States was humiliated, and President Dwight D. Eisenhower was forced to admit publicly not only the overflights but that he had lied about making them. In fact he had not even known about the mission. He told advisors that he could imagine nothing more calculated to throw the American people into a war frenzy than the Soviets' flying the same kind of mission over American air space.

Powers spent twenty-one months in Moscow's Lubyanka Prison before being traded for Soviet master spy Rudolf Abel in 1962. He returned to the United States reviled as a coward by some, celebrated as a hero by others. In 1965 the CIA awarded him the Intelligence Star, its highest decoration. In 1970 he wrote a best-selling autobiography, very much against CIA wishes.

Powers soon discovered that his years of flying for the CIA would not count toward his retirement from the Air Force, so he took employment with Rockwell. In 1977 Powers was killed while flying a traffic helicopter for a Los Angeles television station.

Nikita Khrushchev may have scored a propaganda victory abroad with the fallout from the U-2 incident, but he was discredited at home with Communist hard-liners. He had been urging them to trust the Eisenhower administration, but the downing of Powers's aircraft put an end to any such possibility. Soon after the Cuban Missile Crisis (in which U-2s again played a decisive role), Khrushchev was ousted from power for engaging in "hare-brained schemes" on the world stage.

Just before his death, a wistful Dwight Eisenhower mused, "I had longed to give the world a gift of lasting peace. Instead, all I accomplished was contributing to a stalemate."

—M.C.S.

ETHEL AND JULIUS ROSENBERG
American, worked for Soviet Union

"I was part of Stalin's circle when he mentioned the Rosenbergs with warmth," said Nikita Khrushchev. "I heard from both Stalin and Molotov . . . that the Rosenbergs provided very significant help in accelerating the production of our atom bomb." Perhaps no criminal case in American history has aroused greater controversy than that of Ethel and Julius Rosenberg, the only Americans executed for espionage during peacetime. Though many still proclaim the Rosenbergs' innocence, recent evidence leaves little doubt that Julius, at least, was indeed the center of a spy ring that smuggled information out of the Manhattan Project at Los Alamos, New Mexico, to the Soviet Union. The source of the information was a technician at Los Alamos named David Greenglass—Ethel's brother. Like his sister and her husband, Greenglass was a devoted Communist; working for ideological reasons, he smuggled drawings and other bits of information to Santa Fe and on to New York through a courier named Harry Gold; there Julius (and perhaps Ethel) directed the material to a Soviet controller. The operation began in the early 1940s and continued for several years. The defection of a clerk from the Soviet embassy in Canada, however, led the FBI to Gold, Greenglass, and the Rosenbergs, along with such other atomic spies as Klaus Fuchs and Alfred Nunn May. The federal agents, however, were even more concerned about an industrial espionage ring that Julius was still working with; the FBI tried to use the charges in the atomic-secrets case—especially the charges against Ethel, who might indeed have been largely innocent—to get him to talk. Julius refused to give up his fellow agents. At the

Ten-year-old Michael Rosenberg tries to comfort his six-year-old brother, Robert, after paying a final visit to their parents, convicted spies Julius and Ethel Rosenberg.

Rosenbergs' trial, Greenglass testified against his sister and brother-in-law, earning them both convictions. In a sentencing procedure that involved several irregularities (Judge Irving Kaufman engaged in improper ex parte communication with the prosecutor, then refused to hear his sentencing recommendations in open court, since the prosecutor had only asked for prison sentences), the Rosenbergs were both condemned to death. Despite a flurry of appeals by left-wing sympathizers convinced of the Rosenbergs' innocence, the couple were sent to the electric chair in New York on June 19, 1953.

—T.J.S.

THE WALKER SPY RING
American, worked for Soviet Union

One of the most damaging spy rings in American history operated undetected for seventeen years before an aggrieved former spouse brought it to the attention of the FBI in 1984. Led by John A. Walker Jr., this small group of friends and relatives allowed Soviet intelligence almost completely to penetrate U.S. naval communications from the Vietnam War into the Reagan military buildup. The stakes were enormous: if war had broken out, one secretary of the navy commented, the Walker intelligence would have given the Soviets an advantage equal to the Allies' decoding of the German Enigma transmissions during World War II.

Unlike the Communist spies of an earlier era, Walker was driven by money rather than ideology when he walked into the Soviet Embassy in Washington in 1968. He was a navy radioman with access to the service's secret communications and codes. His value was immediately recognized in Moscow—the KGB, in fact, seems to have muscled out the GRU (military intelligence), which would normally have handled such a spy. The agency dictated elaborate procedures for his drops, involving multiple signals—such as soda bottles (later cans) left at various roadside locations—and tortuous, roundabout routes. At least once a year he met with his handlers in Vienna—again after taking painstaking measures to prevent anyone from following him. The Soviets gave him a specially designed device to pass along the outside of his ship's cryptographic machine, to record its internal

construction. An extraordinary unit was established in Moscow to analyze his priceless intelligence: here, just as the Soviet Union was expanding its navy from a collection of coastal ships to a truly oceangoing fleet, was a complete portrait of the operations of the largest and finest navy in the world. As the Pentagon spent tens of billions of dollars to make its submarines silent and undetectable, the Kremlin had a thorough record of their deployment and movements.

Over the next decade and a half, Walker would be paid hundreds of thousands of dollars for his remarkable intelligence. By the time he neared retirement from the navy, he had grown accustomed to a lavish, free-spending lifestyle. To keep the money flowing, he recruited a fellow radioman, Chief Petty Officer Jerry Whitworth. Though the KGB was furious with Walker for his freelance recruiting, it was pleased with the quality of the material Whitworth passed along from his posts on aircraft carriers and ashore. Soon the new spy also became addicted to a life filled with luxuries. Yet misgivings nagged him; eventually he began to turn over less and less information, and Walker turned to his brother, Commander Arthur Walker, and then his son, Seaman Michael Walker. Soon they, too, were handing over secret documents and codes for delivery to the KGB.

Despite some suspicions aroused by the greedy spies' lavish living, it took John Walker's estranged and alcoholic wife, Barbara, to lead the FBI to the sixteen-year-old ring. After failing to extort money out of her spy ex-husband, she called the agency in November 1984. Her first interview left an agent thoroughly unimpressed, but a routine review of his report three months later led to an investigation. In May 1985 a massive trailing and stakeout operation led to John Walker's arrest at a motel in Rockville, Maryland, after a foiled drop. In the trials that followed, Walker received a 30-year sentence; his son Michael was given 25 years, thanks to his father's cooperation; John's brother Arthur received three life sentences (running concurrently) plus 40 years; and Jerry Whitworth was hit with a 365-year sentence—making him eligible for parole in 2046, when he turns 106—presumably still with a guilty conscience.

—T.J.S.

THE MYSTERIOUS MATA HARI

One of her lovers had a typically French plan for her last-minute escape from the firing squad: Mata Hari, the most notorious spy since Delilah and the most accomplished mistress since La Pompadour, was to wear only a long fur coat on the morning of her execution. As soon as the

rifles were raised, she would throw open her fur, and *certainement*, no red-blooded male would be able to fire upon her glorious body.

Actually this was not the most bizarre of the many ruses designed to save history's most celebrated spy and courtesan. As she waited calmly in her prison cell, demanding the luxuries she considered necessities, Mata Hari's lovers plotted incessantly. One playboy aviator volunteered to buzz Saint Lazare Prison and strafe his beloved's firing squad. Edouard Clunet, Mata's brilliant lawyer, decided to spring a technicality on her unsuspecting jailers at the last moment—under French law no woman can be executed if pregnant, and he, her seventy-five-year-old lover, would claim that Mata Hari was carrying his child.

Most dramatic of all was the scheme attributed to Pierre Mortissac, a wealthy Spanish playboy who had squandered all his sizable fortune trying to win Mata Hari's love. Mortissac, who had lifted his plan directly from the opera *Tosca*, allegedly intended to bribe the firing squad to use blank cartridges and his lover would fall "dead" at the first mock volley. Late at night he and his confederates would spirit her live body from a grave dug especially shallow so that she wouldn't suffocate in her coffin. Later Mortissac, having failed to rescue the woman he loved, was said to have joined an order of Trappist monks at Miraflores in northern Spain, a miniature portrait of Mata Hari hanging in a locket around his neck. Several English and French newspapers reported that Mortissac died during the Spanish Civil War while single-handedly defending the monastery from assault by General Franco's troops.

Strange as it may seem, Mata Hari was an innocent, even drab, Dutch housewife before becoming a spy. Behind the façade provided by the pseudonym "Mata Hari" was the rather prosaic Margaretha Geertruida Zelle. The future spy was born on August 7, 1876, in a small town in Holland, her religious parents enrolling her in a Catholic convent when she was only fourteen. But while on vacation in The Hague four years later, she met Captain Rudolph MacLeod, a handsome Scot who served in the Colonial Army in the Dutch East Indies. Though more than twice her age—he was over forty—this drunken roué somehow appealed to Margaretha. He married her, but even prior to taking her to Java, he revealed his essentially brutal nature. Before their first child, Norman, was born, Margaretha suffered verbal abuse and beatings at MacLeod's hands. He threatened her with a loaded revolver on one occasion and he betrayed her with other women.

While in Java, Margaretha studied the Vedas and other Oriental books describing the joys of sensual love, becoming adept in the ancient arts they taught. More important, those years in Java introduced her to the suggestive ritual dances that the Javanese *bayas* performed in the Hindu temples. A new personality was already emerging as she practiced her own interpretations of these Indonesian dances.

The transformation became complete when her children were mistakenly poisoned by a

Mata Hari.

nurse who was trying to kill MacLeod. Her daughter, Non, survived, but Norman died. Margaretha later claimed that she strangled this servant, but in any event, the death of her son marked the emergence of a new woman. Even the fact that her daughter survived did not temper her hatred for MacLeod, whom she felt was responsible for the death of their infant son. After MacLeod disappeared with Non, Margaretha moved to Paris and began the career that was to make her life a legend.

Margaretha made her dancing debut at a chic Parisian salon. Adorned with an authentic Eastern headdress and breastplate, she swirled her multicolored veils, then feverishly tore them from her body, prostrating herself before the altar of the god Siva. For her second dance, she wore the veil of Javanese maidens and danced with an "enchanted" passionflower. Reviewers praised her performance as "intelligent, natural and refined," predicting that she would rival the great Isadora Duncan.

Soon her stage name and photographs were a common sight in Paris newspapers. The photographs reveal a voluptuously attractive woman possessing an animal sensuality that transcends her every defect. Mata Hari knew how to "move a long, thin and proud body as Paris had never seen one moved before," the French writer Colette once observed. The photos, of course, were taken when she began her performances, before she shed her diaphanous coverings. The only part of herself she didn't expose was her breasts, which she claimed were disfigured by her husband, and she kept them covered with jeweled breastplates barely affixed to her body. (The doctor who examined her in prison found no disfigurement, only small breasts and discolored nipples.) Some of her dances were graceful, others frankly lewd, but all were immensely popular.

Mata Hari's exotic charms captivated the most sophisticated of cities and finally all of Europe. She followed the career path of many French courtesans of the day, combining a stage career with sexual liaisons with wealthy and powerful men. Men vied for her favors, and she always obliged—but never for less than $7,500 a night, she once bragged. Said to be numbered among her countless lovers were Jules Cambon, chief of the French Ministry of Foreign Affairs; French minister of war Adolphe-Pierre Messimy; and extraparliamentary Dutch prime minister Pieter Cort van der Linden. But her favors always came high, whether she demanded cash, fabulous jewelry, or luxurious apartments on the Champs-Elysées—and once her noble or millionaire lovers went broke, she abandoned them without a second thought. She enjoyed sex so much that she was often observed "relaxing" in Parisian brothels.

There was one lover, however, for whom "she would have gone through fire"—Vladimir de Masloff, a captain in the First Russian Imperial Regiment. He proposed but they did not marry because his noble family would disapprove and she was in need of substantial funds.

Upon her return from The Hague to Paris in 1915, she packed up her belongings, selling her thoroughbred horses. Such was her reputation for excess that a story circulated that rather than sell her favorite horse, Vichnou, to a new master, she thrust a gold stiletto into its heart. In fact, she did sell the horse.

Approached by the Germans to become a spy, Mata Hari accepted 20,000 francs from them as compensation for the furs that had been confiscated by the Germans at the outset of World War I. She was given the code number "H. 21," a series issued only to prewar agents, but in fact she never contacted the Germans with information, and she threw the invisible ink that they had given her into the North Sea.

Mata Hari was detained by the British in 1915 on suspicion of espionage, but there was no evidence that she was guilty of spying for the Germans. She was accused of informing the Germans of the development of the British "land ship," or tank, but in fact that information came from a British prisoner of war. It appears that, rather, she was merely one of the nearly 30,000 people detained by the British as "alien enemies and dangerous persons" during the hysteria of the war.

Nevertheless, suspicions about her activities followed her back to France. Captain Georges Ladoux, head of the French espionage bureau,

approached Mata Hari about performing "a great service for France"—working as a double agent. A gambler and risk taker by nature, she accepted the assignment. Ladoux later claimed that the idea of counterespionage came from her, though other details of his story were riddled with inaccuracies. He later denied having hired her and actually fostered suspicions about her working for the Germans.

Oblivious to Ladoux's change of heart, Mata Hari checked into the Élysée Palace Hotel in Paris. As usual, she was experiencing financial difficulties and hoped for a million francs from an assignment to Belgium. Ladoux, meanwhile, informed the French police of the whereabouts of the notorious Margaretha Zelle, a.k.a. Mata Hari, whom Scotland Yard suspected of being AF44—a notorious German spy. The police entered her room, finding her eating breakfast and in poor health, and informed her that she was being placed under arrest.

On July 24, 1917, Mata Hari was brought before a court-martial on charges of espionage. Her image—that of a mysterious, sensuous courtesan involved with men at the highest level of politics—did nothing to help her case. But neither did Ladoux, who distorted the evidence against her to strengthen his case that she was an agent for Germany. In fact, the prosecution's entire case rested on doctored telegrams supplied by Ladoux. Further, the press and the public were barred from the courtroom. Denied the right to call key witnesses, the defense attorney, Edouard Clunet, relied on a defense that was at best a dubious one—that a woman who possessed such a beautiful body might be revered and spared an awful punishment. This strategy failed— the tribunal unanimously sentenced her to death.

Mata Hari was able to enjoy her confinement in cell number 12 at Saint Lazare as much as the drab surroundings permitted. She was given wine with her meals and was permitted cigarettes and books. Even in those final hours in prison she entertained her young doctor and the two incredulous nuns who watched over her. At the nuns' insistence, she performed one of her famous dances, then slept soundly after being given a sedative.

At 4:00 A.M. on October 15, 1917, Mata Hari was awakened and prepared for the firing squad. As all the fantastic plans for her escape failed one by one, her confidence in her invincibility was shaken. Clunet tried his maternity ploy, but when the doctor came to examine her, Mata Hari realized the futility of the scheme and refused an examination. As for the fur-coat plan, its absurdity was so apparent that even Mata Hari had never considered it more than a morale-building joke. She asked permission to write three last letters. One was to her daughter, Non, from whom she asked forgiveness. But hope still prevailed as Mata Hari drank the traditional last glass of rum prescribed by law for all prisoners sentenced to death.

She was taken out into the chill morning to the rifle range at Vincennes. She faced her firing squad as the death warrant was read, refusing a blindfold and also convincing her captors that there was no need to tie her wrists. As the firing squad took aim, she smiled and blew kisses to the pastor and Clunet; she even waved to the nuns. The volley of shots rang out, and she fell motionless to the ground. A sergeant delivered the coup de grâce, a bullet to the temple. As no one claimed the body, it was sent, following the funeral, to the University of Paris Medical School for dissection—an ignominious end for this beautiful courtesan who became known, unjustly, as it turns out, as one of the most notorious spies of World War I.

—R.H. and L.C.

COURTS-MARTIAL

BILLY MITCHELL SPEAKS OUT

Battling with his military bosses in September 1925, Brigadier General Billy Mitchell used a fearsome new weapon: the press conference. He accused his superiors of "incompetency, criminal negligence, and almost treasonable administration of the national defense."

Mitchell had joined the army as a private. In 1906, three years after the Wright brothers' first flight, Mitchell predicted that future wars would be air wars, whereupon he took flying lessons at his own expense.

During World War I, Mitchell became a general at thirty-six while commanding the army's infant Air Service. He urged paratroop drops behind enemy lines and strategic bombing of German cities. The brass thought Mitchell was crazy.

After the war he pushed for an independent U.S. Air Force. When the navy said battleships were "unsinkable," Mitchell led the bombers that sank them in public demonstrations during 1921 and 1923. He told the navy that its ships were "sitting ducks," and predicted enemy aircraft would someday attack the biggest sitting duck of all—the Pacific Fleet at Pearl Harbor, Hawaii.

Mitchell did not spare his own, denouncing the army for neglecting aviation and sending pilots up in "flaming coffins."

Having told Mitchell to shut up on numerous occasions, by 1925 the army had reduced him to colonel, banished him to a minor command, and given his beloved Air Service to an army engineer. The navy tried public relations. To prove a commitment to aviation, in 1925 the navy sent three fighter planes from California to Hawaii and launched the dirigible Shenandoah on a tour of state fairs in the Midwest.

Of the three fighters, two crashed and the third disappeared. The Shenandoah broke apart in flight, killing thirteen.

Mitchell was disgusted. On September 5, 1925, he summoned the press and accused the navy of sacrificing lives for publicity. "The bodies of my former companions in the air molder under the soil in America and Asia, Europe and Africa . . . a great many sent there by official stupidity." As Mitchell expected, he was summoned before a general court-martial.

Mitchell was charged with violating the ninety-sixth Article of War, a catchall that punished any "conduct of a nature to bring discredit upon the military service." He was tried by thirteen officers, not a single one of whom had ever been in an airplane. The court included Major General Douglas MacArthur, who called this trial one of the most distasteful orders he ever received. The widow of the Shenandoah's captain, Mrs. Zachary Landsdowne, testified that the military had clumsily tried to influence her testimony. Defense witnesses included famed aviators Eddie Rickenbacker, Carl Spaatz, and "Hap" Arnold.

On December 17, 1925, the court took just three hours to find Mitchell guilty. He was suspended from rank, command, and duty, with forfeiture of all pay and allowances for five years.

Mitchell's prophecies about air power were uncannily accurate, though he died in 1936, before they were proven in World War II. The army and navy continued to neglect air power, entering that war with obsolete aircraft like the aptly named Brewster "Buffalo." In 1942 American pilots bombed Tokyo with B-25 medium bombers, called "Mitchells." In 1947 the United States finally created an independent air force. Mitchell's son tried to clear his name in 1958, but the secretary of the air force upheld the 1925 conviction.

—M.S.S.

THE PORT CHICAGO FIFTY

On July 17, 1944, all clocks stopped at 10:19 P.M. in Port Chicago.

The small northern California town owed its existence to a U.S. Navy munitions depot. On July 17 the cargo ship E. A. Bryan was taking on 5,000 tons of ordnance. Down in the stifling

hold, the work was backbreaking and dangerous. Greased 500-pound bombs slid down
ramps. Ammunition crates hung from overhead
cranes. The Mark 47 depth charges being loaded
were filled with TPX, an explosive more unstable than TNT.

Port Chicago's loaders were black seamen
straight from boot camp. Neither the sailors nor
their white officers had received any training in
handling explosives. The rule was not safety,
but speed, first.

At 10:19, with a blast heard fifty miles away,
the *Bryan* exploded. In the worst stateside
disaster of World War II, more than 320 people
were killed, two-thirds of them black sailors,
and 390 were injured. Only fifty-one bodies
were intact enough for positive identification.

The survivors were traumatized. Recognizing
this, the navy awarded thirty-day leaves to
white sailors. Black personnel were denied
leave and put to work cleaning up; fifty years
later, one would recall "pulling decapitated
bodies out of the water." The lopsided treatment was typical. With more than 100,000 black
enlisted men, the navy had commissioned its
first black officers only a few months before the
Port Chicago explosion.

On August 8 the loaders were ordered back to
work. Two hundred and fifty-eight men refused.
On the docks, safety still came last and untrained officers were still in charge. Some of the
258 volunteered for any other job, including
combat; and they would obey any order except
an order to load ammunition.

The Twelfth Naval District commander, Admiral C. W. Wright, had praised his black sailors
for their courage during the July 17 explosion.
Now he threatened to put them in front of a
firing squad. By refusing to load ammunition,
Wright said, they were committing mutiny. In
wartime, mutiny was punishable by death.

The men were stunned. Like most Americans,
they believed mutiny occurred when rebellious
sailors took over a ship. Their act was simply a
work stoppage, the military equivalent of a
wildcat strike.

Not quite. The navy law was so elastic that
almost any refusal to obey an order could be
construed as mutiny.

Two hundred and eight men offered to go
back to work. Fifty refused and were summoned
to the largest mutiny trial in navy history.

The court-martial, open to the public, began
September 14, 1944, before seven white navy
officers. One member of the public who attended was Thurgood Marshall, later the first
black justice of the Supreme Court. A National
Association for the Advancement of Colored
People (NAACP) attorney in 1944, Marshall
turned the court-martial into a forum on navy
racial prejudice.

The fifty defendants shared five lawyers. The
defense team put up a lively fight, showing that

the navy definitions of mutiny were ambiguous.
To disprove conspiracy (an essential element of
mutiny), defense lawyers had each sailor testify
that he had refused to work "of his own
initiative."

On October 24 the court deliberated for eighty
minutes and returned fifty sentences of guilty.
Each defendant was given fifteen years in
prison and a dishonorable discharge.

Navy secretary James Forrestal ordered the
court to reconvene. Thurgood Marshall had
filed an appeal, insisting "there is no set rule as
to what is mutiny." He had also noted twenty-
three instances of hearsay evidence during the
trial. Nonetheless, the court stood by its original
verdicts.

The Port Chicago court-martial, and other
racial incidents, accelerated desegregation in
the navy. In February 1946 the Navy Department ordered: "Negro personnel . . . shall be
eligible for all types of assignments, in all
ratings, in all facilities and all ships." The other
military services remained segregated until
1948.

The navy quietly reduced the sentences of the
Port Chicago Fifty to sixteen months' hard labor
and returned the men to duty. Honorable dis-
charges were promised if they stayed out of
trouble. However, the mutiny conviction stayed
on their service records forever.

In January 1994 a California congressional
delegation asked Secretary of the Navy John
Dalton to overturn the convictions. He refused,
finding no evidence that the 1944 court-martial
was tainted by racial prejudice.

On July 17, 1994, the fiftieth anniversary of
the explosion, a monument was dedicated to
the black and white sailors who died at Port
Chicago.

—M.S.S.

EDDIE SLOVIK REFUSES TO FIGHT

Eddie Slovik was far from an ideal soldier when
he was drafted into the U.S. Army in January
1944. A small, frail young man, Slovik had a
prison record, suffered from a debilitating bone
condition in both legs, and was married to a
disabled woman who was pregnant. In addition, he hated guns and couldn't stomach the
thought of killing any living thing. A year after
entering the army, Slovik, the reluctant draftee,
would become the only American soldier executed for desertion of military duty since the
Civil War.

Born in Detroit, Michigan, Slovik grew up in
a poor neighborhood, and from the age of ten he
was involved in a host of petty crimes. When he
was eighteen, Slovik was sent to prison for
stealing candy, cigarettes, gum, and some
change from a drugstore where he worked; the

Private Eddie Slovik, the only American to be executed for desertion in World War II.

total amount of money and goods stolen came to $59.60.

Out on parole, he and a few friends stole a car, which they smashed up, and Slovik, who turned himself in, went back to prison. There he was befriended by a prison supervisor who trained him to be a wood finisher. According to the supervisor, Slovik was a hardworking, trustworthy man who never caused any trouble.

Once out of prison, Slovik got a good job and married a loving bookkeeper who was a victim of infantile paralysis. Just as he seemed to have his life turned around, Slovik received a notice from the army—his 4-F status (resulting from his physical condition and prison record) had been changed to 1-A. Apparently the U.S. Army, desperate for soldiers, had significantly lowered its standards for new recruits.

Slovik landed on Omaha Beach in France in August 1944. He and eleven other soldiers were ordered to make their way to Elbeuf, about eighty miles outside of Paris, and join up with G Company of the 109th Infantry, 28th Division. Before reaching their destination, the soldiers fell under heavy gunfire and took cover in foxholes. The next morning Slovik and another soldier, John F. Tankey, became lost from their unit. The two privates subsequently linked up with a Canadian provost unit and remained with the unit for six weeks. The Canadians praised the two Americans, since they were resourceful at foraging. Slovik became known as "a damn good guy" and a good cook, partly

because of the tasty potato pancakes he frequently served.

Since Tankey had written a letter to the 109th explaining what had happened to him and Slovik, no disciplinary action was taken against them in October, when they finally caught up with the 109th near Elsenborn, Belgium. Shortly thereafter, their unit was engaged in battle; Tankey was hit by shrapnel, Slovik retreated to safety.

Sickened by war and death, Slovik decided to take action. Since the day he joined the army, he had been trying to get out. Repeated efforts to get a discharge, on the grounds that his wife was solely dependent on him, failed. He told his buddies that he could never fire a rifle; he wrote to his wife, telling her how desperate he had become. Finally, he approached the commander of G Company and told him that he was scared and nervous and wanted to be assigned to a rear area, away from combat. The request was refused and Slovik disappeared.

The next morning Slovik turned himself in, handed over a written confession, and was thrown in the stockade. He was offered a deal: return to the front line and the confession would be destroyed; there would be no court-martial proceedings. Slovik said no. He figured that a court-martial would find him guilty and he would be put in jail until the war was over. He preferred jail to being killed and he wasn't afraid of being in prison again.

The court-martial took less than two hours. All nine men on the court were noncombatant officers; the defense counsel was not formally trained as a lawyer. When Slovik was given the opportunity to defend himself, he replied, "I will remain silent." He was found guilty of desertion to avoid hazardous duty and was sentenced to be shot to death.

Military procedure required that before the sentence was carried out, it had to be subjected to several military reviews. One of the reviews turned up Slovik's previous criminal record, which ruined his chances of getting clemency. As one colonel would later say, "From Slovik's record, the world wasn't going to lose much."

Recognizing that he might be executed, Slovik wrote a long letter to General Dwight Eisenhower. He explained his situation, begged for his life, and said that he wanted "to continue to be a good soldier." Eisenhower, however, was never given the letter, and after being advised on the Slovik case, the Supreme Commander of the Allied forces signed a formal execution order. One last review board failed to save Slovik and on January 31, 1945, he was taken to a place near Sainte Marie aux Mines in France to face a firing squad.

Private Eddie Slovik was tied to a wooden post and a black hood was put over his head. He asked someone to tell the twelve marksmen to aim well so he wouldn't suffer. Then he said:

"They're not shooting me for deserting the United States Army. Thousands of guys have done that. They just need to make an example out of somebody and I'm it because I'm an ex-con. I used to steal things when I was a kid, and that's what they're shooting me for." The execution command was given and all of the bullets hit Slovik's body, but none hit his heart. Since he was still breathing, the soldiers reloaded. Before the second volley, Slovik was pronounced dead; he was twenty-four years old. He was buried in a nearby military cemetery reserved for murderers and rapists. In 1987 Slovik's body was exhumed and flown to Detroit for reburial.

Approximately 40,000 American soldiers deserted during World War II. Of those, 2,864 were brought before a court-martial. Forty-nine were sentenced to death. Only one soldier was executed.

—C.O.M.

THE MY LAI MASSACRE

The objective of the American military mission was clear: search and destroy the My Lai hamlet of Son My village in the Quang Ngai Province of South Vietnam. What wasn't clear was what to do with any civilians who might be encountered at My Lai. On March 16, 1968, Charlie Company, a unit of the U.S. Eleventh Light Infantry Brigade, was ordered into combat by Captain Ernest Medina. The 150 soldiers, led by Lieutenant William Calley, stormed into the hamlet, and four hours later more than 500 civilians—unarmed old men, women, and children—were dead. Charlie Company had not encountered a single enemy soldier; only three weapons were confiscated. The only American casualty was a soldier who had shot himself in the foot. It was a massacre that would haunt the conscience of the U.S. Army and the American people.

The average age of the soldiers in Charlie Company was twenty; they had been in South Vietnam for three months. Trained in Hawaii, the unit was considered one of the best in the army, even winning a coveted "company of the month" award. William Calley, aged twenty-four, was not particularly popular with the men he led. Small in stature, he was considered nervous and excitable and too gung ho—always trying to impress his superiors. Captain Medina ridiculed Calley, calling him Lieutenant Shithead in front of the troops.

When the soldiers in Charlie Company pushed into the hamlet, they expected to be locked into fierce combat with a Viet Cong battalion believed to be at My Lai. For three months the American unit had been in no major battles but had suffered a lot of casualties from snipers, mines, and booby traps. The soldiers were ready to prove themselves, ready to exact revenge on the enemy.

Charlie Company met no resistance; there were no Viet Cong soldiers at My Lai. Calley then ordered the slaughter of the civilians. People were rounded up into ditches and machine-gunned. They lay five feet deep in the ditches; any survivors trying to escape were immediately shot. When Calley spotted a baby crawling away from a ditch, he grabbed it, threw it back into the ditch, and opened fire. Some of the dead were mutilated by having "C Company" carved into their chests; some were disemboweled. One GI would later say: "You didn't have to look for people to kill, they were just there. I cut their throats, cut off their hands, cut out their tongues, scalped them. I did it. A lot of people were doing it and I just followed. I just lost all sense of direction."

Women were repeatedly raped, then shot; the GIs referred to themselves as "double veterans." One soldier put the muzzle of his rifle into a woman's vagina and pulled the trigger. Another soldier ordered a group of women to strip so he could rape them; when some refused, he killed them all. When Calley saw a soldier holding a gun to the head of a small child whose mother had been ordered to perform oral sex, Calley ordered the soldier to pull up his trousers and get back to winning the war against Communism.

Flying above the slaughter was helicopter pilot Hugh Thompson. Sickened by what he was witnessing, Thompson set down his aircraft and began to rescue the Vietnamese survivors. He ordered his machine gunner to open fire on any American soldiers who continued to shoot the villagers. In one ditch Thompson pulled out a three-year-old child, almost smothered in blood, but not injured. After he radioed for help from other helicopters, an enraged Thompson reported to his section leader and in graphic detail told what he had seen. Soon afterward, Charlie Company was ordered to stop killing civilians.

Cover-up of the massacre began immediately. Reports on the My Lai operation stated that it was a stunning combat victory against a Viet Cong stronghold. Stars and Stripes, the army newspaper, ran a feature story applauding the courage of the American soldiers who had risked their lives. Even General William Westmoreland sent a personal congratulatory note to Charlie Company. An initial investigation into My Lai was swift and definitive: My Lai was a combat operation in which twenty civilians had accidentally been killed.

Too many soldiers knew what had really happened at My Lai. One of them was Ronald Ridenhour, a Vietnam veteran who was not at My Lai but had heard about the operation from several of his friends who had served in Charlie Company. A year after My Lai, Ridenhour wrote

Slaughtered women and children on the road leading out of My Lai, March 16, 1968.

a letter about the atrocity and sent it to his congressman, Morris Udall. He also sent a copy of the letter to thirty other prominent government officials, including President Richard Nixon. Reaction to the letter was quick, and Westmoreland ordered an immediate inquiry.

Two separate investigations uncovered the horror of My Lai. The soldiers of Charlie Company were extensively interviewed. An army photographer, who had been at My Lai, produced pictures of the carnage. In addition, it was learned that hundreds of civilians had also been killed by other army units, at My Khe and Co Luy. Details of the investigations were leaked to the press, and an interview with William Calley, by freelance reporter Seymour Hersch, put My Lai on the front pages of American newspapers.

Eighty soldiers were initially under investigation for the My Lai massacre. Twenty-five officers and enlisted men, including Lieutenant William Calley and his superior officer Captain Ernest Medina, were eventually charged with crimes. Only six cases were ever tried. In some cases the evidence was overwhelming; some of the defendants admitted to killing the civilians. But only one soldier, William Calley, was found guilty of murder.

The court-martial of Lieutenant Calley began on November 17, 1970. For more than four months, witness after witness came forward to testify before a six-officer jury; all six officers had been in combat and five had served in Vietnam. Calley's defense was straightforward— he had simply followed orders given to him by Captain Medina. As he testified: "I was ordered to go in there and destroy the enemy. That was my job that day. That was the mission I was given. I did not sit down and think in terms of men, women, and children. They were all classified the same."

Did Captain Medina, at a briefing given the day before My Lai, explicitly order Charlie Company to kill any civilians encountered? Testimony at the court-martial failed to answer the question. Some soldiers said Medina made it clear that the villagers should be killed; other soldiers disagreed. Yet another group claimed that Medina didn't exactly say that civilians should die, but he implied it.

When the prosecutor made his final summation to the jury, he quoted what Abraham Lincoln said to the troops he commanded during the Civil War: "Men who take up arms against one another in public do not cease on this account to be moral human beings, responsible to one another and to God." The jury found Calley guilty of murdering twenty-two civilians at My Lai and sentenced him to life imprisonment.

After Calley had served three days in prison, President Nixon ordered that he be taken to Fort Benning, Georgia, to be held under house arrest. Sequestered in a comfortable apartment, Calley was allowed to have pets, entertain guests, and cook his own meals.

Many Americans thought the Calley verdict was unjust. Some believed he was a scapegoat used to mask enormous blunders made by the U.S. Army. Others felt he was a hero, fighting a battle against Communism. Protests were staged on his behalf. A record, "The Battle

Hymn of Lieutenant Calley," became a hit. Thousands of telegrams in support of Calley poured into the White House; a World War II veteran gathered up his combat medals, including two Purple Hearts, and sent them to the president. Women wrote romantic letters to him, and one sympathizer bought Calley a Mercedes. The legislatures of several states passed resolutions asking for clemency for Calley.

Calley's life sentence was subsequently reduced to twenty years, then reduced again to ten years. In 1974 he was paroled after serving three years under house arrest.

—C.O.M.

GENOCIDE

THE ARMENIAN GENOCIDE

Background: The cradle of civilization, the Euphrates River, became a mass grave in the summer of 1915. Turkish army officers began insisting on burials, though not out of respect for the dead. Their reasoning was purely practical; the thousands of corpses in the river were jamming the mills downstream.

Armenians had settled in Asia Minor around the sixth century B.C. In the fourth century A.D., Armenia was the first nation to adopt Christianity as its official religion. At around the same time, an alphabet and a language developed, giving Armenians a strong national identity. The rise of Turkey's Ottoman Empire put Christian Armenia firmly under Islamic rule.

In 1828 Armenia was divided between the Ottoman and Russian Empires. By the late nineteenth century, the Ottoman Empire was tottering under the corrupt rule of Sultan Abdul Hamid. The European powers were itching to make a land grab; France held 60 percent of Ottoman debt, and Russia threatened to annex Ottoman Armenia under the pretext of Christian fellowship. Needing a distraction, Abdul Hamid decided to pit his troublesome ethnic minorities against each other.

In 1894, with official encouragement, Kurds began attacking Armenian villages in the eastern provinces. Government troops went in, but observers reported that the army stood by and watched as Kurds killed Armenians. A British diplomat wrote, "Armenians were absolutely hunted like wild animals."

The massacres continued for two years and killed 200,000 to 500,000 people. When Abdul Hamid was overthrown in the "Young Turk" revolution of 1909, Armenians briefly enjoyed full citizenship.

By 1910 the Young Turks had been replaced by hard-line nationalists. These leaders dreamed of a new Ottoman Empire populated by Turkish Muslims; they were not inclined to accommodate ethnic or religious minorities. In 1914 Turkey sided with Austria and Hungary in World War I.

When the Turks learned that Russian Armenians were fighting against them, they declared open season on their Armenian countrymen. As Turkish troops marched to the front, they stripped Armenian provinces of food, gang-raped women, and randomly killed thousands.

Some Armenians refused to be victims. The citizens of Van fortified their town and put up a fierce defense. This resistance provided justification for the government to solve its Armenian problem once and for all.

In January 1915 all Armenian soldiers and police were disarmed and put to work at hard labor. Soon they were taken to remote areas and killed. Armenian priests, educators, and civic leaders received the same treatment. With the defenders and the leadership eliminated, the government announced that all Armenians would be deported. The deportation would be supervised by the army and a "Special Organization" (S.O.). The S.O. consisted of criminals and convicts, armed and trained by the government. Apparently in accordance with a plan and a strict timetable, the deportations began on April 24, 1915.

The euphemism of "deportation" fooled no one. In July 1915 the German ambassador wrote that the Turks were "exterminating the Armenian race in the Ottoman Empire."

The Killing: By August thousands of corpses lay piled along the deportation routes. Hundreds more hung from trees and telegraph poles. In some deportee columns, more than a hundred Armenians a day died from murder, starvation, and disease.

Enraged by the rebellious city of Van, the

Turkish army turned on neighboring villages and slaughtered 24,000 Armenians in three days. The town of Zov also fought back. When Zov fell, survivors were herded into straw-filled horse stables, soaked with kerosene, and burned alive.

Other trouble spots marked for special consideration were the towns of Bitlis and Mus. In Bitlis 4,500 men were rounded up and put to work digging ditches, which became their graves. In both towns, entire Armenian families committed suicide together rather than face the Turks.

The wave of blood engulfed the whole nation. Before 1915 thousands of Armenians had lived in the district of Erzurum. When the Russian army reached the area in January 1916, only twenty-two could be found. The young men of Sivas were slaughtered with axes. In the towns of Perkemig and Ulas, 400 children between the ages of two and six were killed. Older children were poisoned or bayoneted; infants were thrown against walls.

The deportations followed a pattern. Influential Armenians and able-bodied men were killed first. The deportees consisted only of women, children, and the elderly. Rape, torture, robbery, and killing were encouraged; anyone attempting to help the Armenians was severely punished. In June, at the infamous Kemakh Gorge, 10,000 Armenian women, children, and old men were pushed off cliffs.

The government spared a few members of each group, mainly old people, to show the world that deportations were being carried out. The survivors were detained in camps that were breeding grounds for cholera and typhus. At the Islahiye camp, 600 were buried each day, yet piles of corpses always awaited burial. The end of the line was a forced march into the deserts of Syria and Mesopotamia.

Incredibly, the government believed it could keep the massacres secret. This was impossible: in Van, 4,000 Armenians lived under the protection of American missionaries. Eyewitness reports were written. Some of the most detailed reports came from the German embassy, despite the alliance between Germany and Turkey. The Allies warned the Turkish government that it would be held accountable for the genocide.

Though they were enemies, German diplomats helped their British, French, and American counterparts in protecting Armenians. Protestant and Catholic missionaries also joined forces. Some Turks and Kurds risked their lives to hide Armenian friends.

Toll of Destruction: It is impossible to know for certain, but probably between 1.2 million and 1.5 million died. In some districts, the entire Armenian population vanished. Before World War I there were 1,845,000 Armenians in the Ottoman Empire. Two hundred fifty thousand escaped to Russia. As many as 200,000, primar-

ily young women and girls, were kidnapped by Turkish and Kurdish villagers during the forced march to Syria. Only 400,000 made it all the way.

Aftermath: The Allies blustered about "the martyred Armenian people," but did nothing. Defeat in World War I shattered the Ottoman Empire, and its government fled,

During 1919 a new government collected evidence of the deportations and massacres. A show trial of the missing leaders was held to assuage consciences. The invisible defendants were sentenced to death in absentia. In July 1923 Turkey signed a treaty with the United States, Britain, and France. No one mentioned Armenia.

Twenty years later, another leader was asked how his government expected to get away with a policy of official genocide. Knowing that the world can have a short memory, Adolf Hitler replied: "Who still speaks of the extermination of the Armenians?" To this day, the Turkish government still insists that no genocide took place and that the Armenian deaths were due to fighting and disease.

—M.S.S.

THE STALINIST PURGES

Of all the treasures a State can possess, the human lives of its citizens are for us the most precious.
                                                Joseph Stalin

I have known Stalin for thirty years. Stalin won't rest until he has butchered all of us, beginning with the unweaned baby and ending with the blind great-grandmother.
        Budu Mdivani, former premier of Soviet Georgia,
            shortly before he was shot on Stalin's orders

Background: Joseph Stalin's genocidal rampage during the 1930s is known as "the Great Purge." There were actually three purges. The first was a deliberate famine in the Ukraine from 1930 to 1932. Next came the decimation of the state leadership between 1935 and 1938, and finally the mass arrests and killings of ordinary citizens in 1937 and 1938.

Stalin needed tons of food for his urban industrial work force. The USSR's breadbasket, the Ukraine, was tilled by two largely non-Communist groups: the kulaks (prosperous independent farmers) and the muzhiks (peasant farmers). In 1929 Stalin ordered all farmland surrendered to the state. When his order was ignored, Stalin decided to set an example. On December 29, 1929, he ordered: "Liquidate the kulaks as a class."

Stalin's secret police, the NKVD, swept into the Ukraine accompanied by armed gangs. All *kulak* property, even winter clothing, was confiscated. Those who protested were shot or clubbed to death. With nothing but the clothes on their backs, *kulak* families were shipped to work camps in Siberia or the Arctic north.

The *muzhiks* fought back. NKVD men were dismembered with scythes and skewered on pitchforks. *Muzhiks* burned their own property and smashed farm equipment before they could be stolen by the state. Livestock was butchered and eaten in wild community feasts.

Stalin sent in the Red Army, who attacked their rural comrades with tanks and flamethrowers. This bred even fiercer resistance, and by the summer of 1932 the Ukraine was in a state of open warfare. What Stalin could not accomplish with tanks was finally done by pen and paper. In July 1932 he ordered the Ukraine to produce impossibly large grain quotas. Government agents visited every farm to collect the crops.

Stalin created the largest man-made famine in world history. While millions of people starved in the Ukraine, 5 million tons of wheat were exported in 1931. Tons of eggs, butter, and meat were also sold for export, and tons more rotted in warehouses.

With the Ukraine subjugated, Stalin turned to his party. He had many enemies and imagined even more. He needed only a pretext to make a clean sweep. It was provided on December 1, 1934, in Leningrad.

At Communist Party headquarters, the usual guards were mysteriously absent from the office of Leningrad's party boss, Sergei Kirov. Kirov was a popular figure often mentioned as Stalin's successor. A shot rang out. Stalin wept at the funeral and decreed that Kirov's name would be immortalized by a state ballet troupe.

Thousands of innocent Leningraders were implicated in the assassination and shipped to work camps. More than a hundred political leaders and army officers were shot. In a decree of April 7, 1935, Stalin extended adult penalties, including death, down to children of twelve. Between August 1936 and March 1938, dozens of party leaders were prosecuted in show trials, then killed.

The man who assassinated Kirov, Leonid Nikolayev, had close contacts in the NKVD. This indicates the true assassin, since NKVD boss Genrikh Yagoda allowed nothing to happen without Stalin's approval.

Next Stalin purged his purgers. Beginning in the fall of 1936, Yagoda and about 3,000 NKVD agents were killed. Yagoda was replaced by the murderous bureaucrat Nikolai Yezhov.

Out on the horizons of his paranoia, Stalin saw one more enemy: the Red Army. He had a special hatred for its chief of staff, the brilliant Mikhail Tukhachevsky. In 1920, twenty-seven-year-old Tukhachevsky had stopped the Polish army when it tried to annex the Ukraine. He had

later invaded Poland, unfortunately with a glory-seeking commander on his left flank. That commander, Joseph Stalin, had charged ahead and uncovered the flank, allowing the Poles to slam the Red Army back across its border.

Tukhachevsky was arrested on trumped-up charges of spying for Germany. Most of the army leadership followed him to prison or a death sentence. The Red Army was decapitated.

Then the last phase of the purge began, when Stalin turned on his citizens. In one year, arrests for "counterrevolutionary crimes" increased tenfold. Police and NKVD agents who didn't arrest enough people were arrested themselves.

Family members were encouraged to report each other. One man in Odessa denounced 230 people. An observer estimated that in the average city office, every fifth person was an informer. In the country, among semiliterate workers with no interest in politics, 1.5 million were arrested for subversive activities.

Between 1937 and 1938 Yezhov sent 383 lists to Stalin, containing thousands of names. A typical list read:

> *Comrade Stalin,*
> I am sending for your approval four lists of people to be tried by the Military Collegium:
> List No. 1 (General)
> List No. 2 (Former military personnel)
> List No. 3 (Former personnel of the NKVD)
> List No. 4 (Wives of enemies of the people)
> I request sanction to convict all in the first degree.
> *Yezhov*

"In the first degree" was the code for "shooting." On December 12, 1937, Stalin worked late and approved 3,167 death sentences. Then he went to the movies.

Since every person arrested had to name "accomplices," the proceedings became a sort of pyramid scheme trading in human lives instead of money. By 1938 at least 5 percent of the entire population of the USSR was under arrest.

The Killing: During the famine in the Ukraine, thousands starved to death every day. People ate rats, worms, boiled shoe leather, and bark from trees. Cannibalism occurred. The famine was worse than that of 1921 to 1922 in the Ukraine, and during that time a report noted: "Children who die are not taken to the cemetery, but are kept for food."

Many Ukrainians were shipped to the gulag, an acronym in Russian for "chief administration of corrective labor camps." These camps were located in Siberia or the Arctic north. The farthest northern camp, Magadan, was so cold that even guard dogs froze to death. So did thousands of starving, half-naked prisoners. Thousands more were worked to death. Logging sleds were normally pulled by a tractor or team of horses; in the camps they were pulled by prisoners, in teams of five men or seven women.

Of the millions arrested for political subversion, many died before their mock trials. In Moscow's Butyrka Prison, 140 men were crammed into cells built for 24. The dead had no place to fall.

After arrest came interrogation. The favorite method was called the conveyor: a prisoner was kept awake for days, with fresh interrogators taking turns every few hours. When Stalin ordered the NKVD to hurry the confessions, new techniques were adopted: water tortures, drilling into healthy teeth, and stuffing prisoners into crates swarming with insects.

One of the most effective methods was torturing a wife or child in front of the prisoner. A party notable named Rossior stood up to several days of NKVD torture. He finally confessed when his sixteen-year-old daughter was raped in front of him.

After confession and a quick trial, the accused was led into a cell and shot in the back of the neck with a pistol. Records from the city of Vinnitsa show that this was not very reliable. Of 9,432 executed, 6,360 needed two shots in the head; 78 needed three; and 2 hardy souls required four bullets.

Toll of Destruction: The actual number of deaths is unknown—the Soviet government accounted for dead livestock more accurately than dead people. One estimate for 1930 to 1938 was 20 million dead. The Russian scholar Roy Medvedev believed 40 million to be more accurate, while Aleksandr Solzhenitsyn estimated 60 million.

The suppression and famine left about 13 million dead from 1930 to 1932. More than 6 million were killed or died in the labor camps, while 7 million starved.

During the purges of 1934 to 1938, between 7 and 9 million died. About a million were executed; according to Soviet documents declassified in the 1980s, as many as 230,000 Russians were shot by their government in one year. The rest died of overwork, exposure, starvation, or disease in the gulags. By 1938 more than 125 camps held more than 8 million people.

The Red Army lost 35,000 officers, from field marshals down to junior captains and lieutenants. From 1937 to 1938, Stalin killed more Russian officers than Hitler's soldiers did in all of World War II.

Aftermath: The purges ended suddenly in 1938, apparently because Stalin was satisfied that the spirit of the nation was crushed.

On June 22, 1941, in history's largest land attack, Hitler invaded the Soviet Union on a thousand-mile front. The Red Army crumpled; officers who had survived the purge were incapable of taking any initiative. By October,

Panzer units prowled the outskirts of Moscow. Stalin narrowly averted disaster in World War II by drafting almost every man, woman, and child in the USSR.

Stalin's successor, Nikita Khrushchev, said that one day in 1951 he heard Stalin muttering: "I'm finished. I trust no one, not even myself." Stalin was planning yet another great purge when he died on March 2, 1953.

—M.S.S.

THE HOLOCAUST

The broad mass of a nation . . . will more easily fall victim to a big lie than to a small one.
                                   Adolf Hitler, Mein Kampf, 1923

Background: Millions of words have been written about Adolf Hitler's extermination of several million innocent people. The world still wonders: Why?

The world had plenty of warning. In his 1923 political statement *Mein Kampf*, Hitler made two promises: to destroy Communism and to erase the Jews from Europe.

On January 30, 1933, within the existing democratic processes, Hitler became chancellor of Germany. By the late 1930s, his Nazi government had stripped Jews of their legal rights. Jews could not work in most professions, could not visit movie theaters or public swimming pools. The names of Jews who died fighting for Germany in World War I were erased from war memorials.

Jews were officially encouraged to leave Germany. In one of history's oddest partnerships, the Nazi government worked with Zionist organizations to send Jews to Palestine—after the Jews had surrendered all liquid assets to the Third Reich. About 170,000 Jews escaped this way.

Many countries refused Jewish refugees. With large populations of both Jews and immigrants, the United States seemed a likely haven. It was not. One reason was the Great Depression; Americans did not want more immigrants while they were still fighting for jobs.

An uglier reason was an ingrained American anti-Semitism. America was willing to take the occasional celebrity refugee such as Albert Einstein or Thomas Mann, but in general the tired, the poor, and the huddled masses of Jews escaping Hitler were not welcome.

The world knew what was happening. Some European Jewish organizations appealed for an international boycott of Germany. When the International Olympic Committee threatened to move the 1936 Olympics out of Berlin, Hitler temporarily eased up. After the mad rampage of Kristallnacht, "the Night of Broken Glass," in

1938, President Franklin D. Roosevelt withdrew the American ambassador.

But in general the world ignored Germany's internal policies. Those policies included four "protective custody" camps on German soil: Dachau, Sachsenhausen, Buchenwald, and the women's camp at Lichtenburg. Here citizens "detrimental to the interests of the nation" were held indefinitely: homosexuals, Jehovah's Witnesses, and beggars. In June 1937 the first 1,500 Jews were sent to these camps.

Some undesirables, such as the mentally retarded, were turned over to the "rest homes" of the T4 program. Those in the know called T4 by its real name: the euthanasia program. At first patients were poisoned or starved. These methods were inefficient, and the T4 program began experimenting with gas chambers.

On January 21, 1939, Hitler told the Czech foreign minister: "We are going to destroy the Jews. . . . The day of reckoning has come." Nine days later he told the German Parliament: "If the Jewish international financiers . . . [involve] the nations in another war . . . it will be the end of the Jews in Europe."

On September 1, 1939, Hitler began "another war" by invading Poland. The eastern part of the country was turned into a human dumping ground, where Germany began building "labor camps": Belzec, Sobibor, Majdanek, Chelmno, Treblinka, and Auschwitz.

The fate of Europe's Jews was sealed. Some historians make much of the fact that Hitler left no written orders for their extermination. The obvious answer is that he didn't need to; in a 1942 diary entry Joseph Goebbels wrote: "The deportation of the Jews . . . is a pretty barbarous business—one would not wish to go into details—and there are not many Jews left. The Führer is the moving spirit of this radical solution both in word and deed."

Nazi Germany was a hive of fiercely competing and overlapping bureaucracies, but the genocide had a fairly clear chain of command.

Before the death camps were ready, the men who rounded up and killed Jews belonged to Special Action Squads (Einsatzgruppen). These units reported directly to Reinhard Heydrich, chief of the Reich Security Main Office (RSHA). Hitler called him "the man with an iron heart."

Heydrich reported to the Reichsführer-SS, Heinrich Himmler. From a tiny group of personal bodyguards of Hitler, the SS grew into a state within a state. It furnished personnel for the first concentration camp, Dachau, and all the camps that followed.

A warren of SS and RSHA bureaucracies appeared as numbers on organization charts. One of these, Department IV-B-4, was the Office of Jewish Affairs. It was managed by a hustling bureaucrat named Adolf Eichmann.

On June 22, 1941, Hitler invaded Russia. Millions of Jews were suddenly added to those already in Nazi-occupied nations. As chief of economic planning, Reichsmarschall Hermann Göring directed Heydrich to prepare a detailed plan for "the final solution to which we aspire."

In January 1942 Heydrich called Eichmann and others to a conference to discuss Göring's order. The minutes of the Wannsee Conference never mentioned gas chambers. Jews would be deported east, to work at hard labor until they dropped. But since the surviving Jews would be tough and might form a "new cell from which the Jewish race could again develop," the survivors had to be "treated accordingly."

Eichmann began searching for the most efficient way to kill en masse. In late 1941 he used a new method on 1,000 Jews and Russian prisoners of war at Auschwitz: a fuming rat poison called Zyklon-B.

By early 1943 Auschwitz held four large gas chambers and four crematoria to dispose of the evidence. Both the technical and administrative machinery were in place for a "final solution."

The Killing: The first mass killings were shootings in Poland and Russia. During two days in September 1941, near the Ukrainian capital of Kyyiv, the Einsatzgruppen shot between 30,000 and 34,000 Russian Jews at a ravine called Babi Yar. A German civil engineer witnessed the massacre:

"The people who got off the trucks, men, women, and children of every age, had to undress on orders from an SS man. . . . The completely naked people walked down [into] the pit. . . . They lay down in front of the dead and wounded; some stroked those who were still living and murmured what seemed to be words of comfort. Then I heard a series of shots."

From Minsk, Nazi commissar Wilhelm Kube reported that his "subhumans" were blue-eyed "blondies." Kube had an eye for this sort of thing; when he received 7,000 German Jews to kill along with those of Minsk, Kube spotted two girls with "Aryan features." Kube had 3,000 Russian Jews shot but spared all the Germans. This earned him a visit from a furious Heydrich, who personally supervised the shooting of the 7,000 Germans, plus 3,000 more Russian Jews. (Kube's weakness for "blondies" eventually did him in; one of them replaced his nightly hot-water bottle with an antipersonnel mine.)

Shooting was not always necessary. Thousands of Jews died from starvation and disease in the ghettos of Warsaw, Libau, Vilna, and other cities. Once the death camps were operating, "clearing" the ghettos became a priority.

Jews fated for the camps first received orders for "deportation to the East." Assembling at railroad stations, they were crammed into freight cars with no food, water, or sanitation.

At Treblinka, Chelmno, and the other camps, death was ritualized. Those who looked strong were selected for work. At Auschwitz, some

After liberating the concentration camp at Buchenwald, United States Third Army military police force German civilians from nearby Weimar to view a truckload of victims from the camp.

were chosen for Dr. Josef Mengele's hideous medical experiments. The ones judged unfit to work were marched to a "hygiene station."

Women and girls had their hair cut. (The SS sold the hair.) The new arrivals then stripped and jammed into a room with one square foot allotted per person.

Josef Clare was an SS medical orderly at Auschwitz: "It was like a beehive. They came into the gas chamber, and when they were ready . . . the gas was fed into the chimney. Then there was a buzzing; hmmm, hmmm, hmmm. The tone got quieter and quieter, until you couldn't hear anything more. That was a gruesome death."

The gassing could take up to thirty minutes. With more victims waiting, the bodies were immediately hauled out: "blue, wet with sweat and urine, the legs covered with feces and menstrual blood."

Those who were not gassed were worked to death on a starvation diet. Workers wore thin rags in subzero weather. Frostbite became necrosis; noses, fingers, and toes rotted off. The workday was punctuated with random torture or shootings.

Death in the camps could come in a thousand hellishly inventive ways. According to German journalist Heiner Lichtenstein, a female SS guard at Auschwitz "set dogs on pregnant prisoners, who . . . had the unborn child torn from their bodies and eaten."

Toll of Destruction: Some historians believe that 40 million European civilians died between 1939 and 1945, many the result of Nazi genocide. This is double the number of combined military and civilian deaths in World War I; in something of a throwback to the Middle Ages, World War II saw the casual killing of noncombatants on a mass scale. Poland alone lost 5.5 million civilians, or roughly 1 million for each year of German occupation.

For Jews, the commonly accepted figure is 6 million dead. This was about 67 percent of Europe's prewar Jewish population. Though Jews were the main target, the Nazis also killed thousands of other "undesirables." With 500,000 massacred, Gypsies almost disappeared as a distinct ethnic group.

Throughout the war, Germany's mindless

racial policies also doomed thousands of its own soldiers. German soldiers often died because the trains they depended on for food and ammunition were carrying defenseless civilians to the gas chambers.

Aftermath: The Allies convened the Nuremberg Trials in November 1945 (see page 179). Some were beyond the reach of justice: Reinhard Heydrich had been killed by the Czech underground. Heinrich Himmler and Hermann Göring committed suicide. Ten top Nazis were hanged.

Other trials judged 1,500 people who had been concentration camp staff, Gestapo, or SS. Four hundred and twenty were hanged and twenty-nine reprieved. The rest were given prison sentences.

Adolf Eichmann escaped to Argentina, where he was nabbed in 1960 by the Israeli secret service. He was hanged in Jerusalem in 1962 (see page 181). Like Eichmann, an estimated 20,000 Nazis fled to other countries after the war. Some are still at large today.

The war Adolf Hitler had started in 1939 left 50 million dead and millions more wounded. Other millions were homeless, starved, and diseased. Europe lay in ruins. Shortly before he blew his brains out on April 30, 1945, Hitler dictated a last testament. He blamed everything—the war, Germany's defeat, the destruction of Europe—on the Jews.

—M.S.S.

Although we know that God is merciful, please God, do not have mercy for those people who created this place. Remember the nocturnal procession of children, of more children, and more children, so frightened, so quiet, so beautiful. If we could simply look at one, our hearts would break. But it did not break the hearts of the murderers.

Eli Wiesel in Oswiecim, Poland, ceremonies commemorating the fiftieth anniversary of the liberation of the Auschwitz-Birkenau death camp, January 26, 1995

THE CHINESE COMMUNIST MASSACRES

Background: Modern China, under the control of Mao Zedong, provides two of the most striking and lethal examples of modern genocide. Two great movements of Mao's China—the Great Leap Forward (1957–58) and the Cultural Revolution (1966–69)—were responsible directly and indirectly for millions of deaths.

The Great Leap Forward and the Cultural Revolution stemmed from Mao's dissatisfaction with the slow pace of change from the decadent old ways, and from his anger and frustration with the millions of Chinese who just didn't seem properly enthused by or indoctrinated with the new order of communism. What was absolutely necessary, Mao came to believe, was a total and very rapid overthrow of all the established old ways. The hardy, the strong, and especially the young capable of becoming members of the new order because they had no links to the old—these would survive.

The Killing: In the Great Leap Forward, a number of stumbling blocks had to be rooted out quickly: the peasants' love of their individual plots of land; the emergence of an "intellectual" class enamored of their own status to the detriment of the revolution; and the near impossibility, at least in Mao's opinion, of effectively communizing the cities.

Everywhere Mao looked he saw cracks in the structure of the new order. In spite of the land reform program, more and more "rich" and middle-level peasants were emerging, and a new class of educated managers formed within the party a conservative element that Mao feared would cling to their own status quo and not push for the final and complete transition to perfect communism.

Although not as drastic in his removal of people from cities as Pol Pot was later to be, Mao began to force the population into the countryside, far from their homes.

In a land where tradition and respect for old people and ancient ways was strong, Mao sought to uproot and destroy every conventional pattern of work, thought, and behavior.

Imported technology was violently put aside and the people who knew how to make a technological economy work had a hoe shoved in their hands. Trained doctors were ignored and the famous "barefoot doctors" dispensed herbs and roots.

The Great Leap Forward, as we know today, was a great leap into a mammoth pit of economic and agricultural failure and death on a horrifying scale. Mao resigned his position as chairman of the republic in 1958 and licked his wounds, plotting what was to be his next nationwide upheaval in the name of achieving perfect communism.

The Cultural Revolution began in 1966. If the revolutionary political goals of the Cultural Revolution sound similar to those of the Great Leap Forward, the methods were now to be much more a purge of unwanted elements of society and government than a massive relocation of the population.

The central problem, as Mao saw it, was that there had developed a new elite more interested in their own power and status than in completing the transformation to full communism. Totally untrained and very young political ideologues took over highly technical jobs on the assumption that their political ardor would see them through.

Mao's infamous Red Guards were made up mostly of the very young, many still in their teens. They had been indoctrinated in an extreme form of communism approved by Mao himself and sent out into the society as a sort of powerful, bullying thought-police. Their rallying cries were "fight self-interest, establish the public interest" and the anti-intellectual "better red than well read."

Their targets were rural cadres who had made too much of an accommodation with the peasants, or who had simply been in their jobs too long and were too powerful; low-ranking functionaries whose loyalty was to their boss rather than Mao; peasants with kinship ties to village leaders; and any peasant with an economic stake in the status quo.

These rambunctious groups of Red Guards were sent to locations far from their own homes so they would have no personal connections to the people whose lives they disrupted.

To read the accounts of the violence of this period is to enter a kind of Alice in Wonderland world of conflict and counterconflict. Red Guards pulled people from their homes and workplaces, attacking, torturing, and killing anyone who fell under suspicion, for the slightest reason, of being antirevolutionary. Foreign diplomats reported that they saw elderly people beaten to death on the streets or in trains.

The Red Guards, far from being effectively controlled, even by Mao, became a many-headed monster, clashing murderously with workers and peasant groups and with army units. They even fought viciously among themselves. Who was the "real" and who the "false," only masking bourgeois ideals behind the façade of revolutionary fervor? Gunfire resounded through the land as more and more Chinese were killed in local clashes. In Canton, for example, the East Wind group entered into a vicious and deadly battle with the Red Flag group. In the midst of this homicidal chaos countless personal feuds were permanently settled.

Mao, who had sown the seeds of the Red Guard, eventually authorized military units to wipe out groups of recalcitrant Red Guards. Blood flowed across the huge land, with more and more brutal clashes.

A more recent incident of mass killing in China took place at Beijing's Tiananmen Square on June 4, 1989. Going beyond what authorities were ready to accept in demonstrations for democracy and against repression, crowds of Chinese thronged the huge square bordering on the legendary Forbidden City.

Tanks rolled in, and the night was punctuated with the deadly crackle of machine guns.

Toll of Destruction: The death rate in China soared during the years of the Great Leap Forward, and it is estimated that a total of 20 million people may have died of starvation and disease between 1957 and 1962. Although no accurate figures exist on just how many deaths the Cultural Revolution caused, the number is far smaller than the millions who starved in the agricultural disaster of the Great Leap Forward.

Tiananmen Square is another matter. Western estimates put the figure of deaths at a thousand or more, with many more wounded. What sets it apart is that it was so concentrated in time and, because of modern communication technology, so visible to the rest of the world, a world that saw images of a nation that wants to enter the modern economic and political world in the act of shooting down hundreds of peaceful protesters.

Aftermath: The Great Leap Forward, and even the Cultural Revolution, has begun to fade into history in a nation that is so populous it can sustain millions of deaths.

Chinese president Jiang Zemin said in 1993 that judgments about the 1989 massacre should be left to "history" as well, and that the world must remember that it is "not an easy job to manage a country of 1.2 billion people."

The question in China is, "Can it happen again?" The answer is nobody really knows. The economy is looser now, people can watch foreign TV, listen to rock music, read sexy novels, and travel abroad. They can make lots of money if their entrepreneurial skills haven't been totally deadened. But the government still has totalitarian power, the army still has its guns, and the shadow of Tiananmen Square remains a chilling factor in Chinese life.

—R.W.S.

THE KHMER ROUGE

Background: The man known as Pol Pot who ruled his native Cambodia from 1975 to 1979 holds a position of dark and murderous distinction: no other ruler in post–World War II history has slain more of his own people. Although his butchery is well documented by international observers, he has never been brought to justice and, in fact, his shadowy and threatening presence continues to influence the course of his nation's development.

A pudgy, ever-smiling man known to his followers as "Brother No. 1," he has an obscure background. He is believed to have been born on May 19, 1928, but it may have been 1925. There is even some question as to his true identity, although reliable sources say his real name is Saloth (or Salot) Sar.

"I am the son of a peasant," Pol Pot said in an

interview with the Vietnam News Agency in July 1976. He went on to claim, "I stayed in a Buddhist monastery . . . for six years, two of which I spent as a monk."

He became active in the anti-French resistance in Indochina and fought under Ho Chi Minh; in 1946 he was accepted as a member of the clandestine Communist Party. He went to Paris to study radio electronics at the École Française de Radio-Electricité and joined the Marxist-Leninist Khmer Students' Association.

Pol Pot was not a good student. "As I spent most of my time in radical activities," he said in the 1976 interview, "I did not attend many classes." His scholarship was cut short, and he was sent home. Some observers believe that the seeds of his anti-intellectualism, which was to be expressed in such a murderous way later, were planted at this time.

Through the 1960s and early 1970s he rose in the ranks of the party, taking the nom de guerre of Pol Pot and retiring to the jungles of Cambodia to become a shadowy figure of mystery leading his deadly fighting force in harassing the government. William Shawcross, in his book *Sideshow: Kissinger, Nixon, and the Destruction of Cambodia*, states that the 1970 bombings and invasion of Cambodia by American and South Vietnamese forces was largely responsible for the growing strength of the Khmer Rouge.

Starting with a 4,000-man force, his army grew to more than 70,000. Pol Pot's murder machine took over the country on April 17, 1975.

The Killing: Then began one of the most murderous and the most bizarre periods in history. Pol Pot began to drive Phnom Penh's population of 2 million from the city, including 20,000 sick and wounded hospital patients, forcing everyone to march far into the countryside.

Pol Pot, influenced by his admiration for Mao Zedong's Great Leap Forward and Cultural Revolution in China, was trying to wrench Cambodia past all intermediate steps and into a pure communist society in record time.

Even those who survived the violent uprooting of their lives and the long forced marches to the rural areas had to begin brutally difficult new lives. They died by the thousands of rampant disease and starvation.

"Darkness cloaked the machinelike maneuvers of the Khmer Rouge," wrote Nayan Chanda in the *Far Eastern Economic Review*. "The black, pyjama-clad figures marched into Phnom Penh . . . drove the population out of the city . . . and closed the country's borders. As far as the outside world was concerned Cambodia became a non-country."

The horror of what happened in the next four years in that closed noncountry, although well documented later, still defies the imagination.

The skulls of victims of the Khmer Rouge displayed in a pile after being dug up from a mass grave.

The reason, if that word can be used, for driving the population out of Phnom Penh is summed up in a statement by one of Pol Pot's assistants: "From now on, if people want to eat, they should go out and work in the rice paddies. . . . Cities are evil. . . . That is why we shall do away with cities." Only in rural areas far from their homes, where they had no roots or property, could people be turned into the ideal new communists.

As Anthony Paul, in *Murder of a Gentle Land*, put it, Pol Pot "had resolved to annul the past and obliterate the present. . . . The looting of stores and homes, not to acquire but to destroy valuables; the demolition of buildings; the desecration of temples; the smashing of automobiles, medical equipment, and other products of foreign technology—all seemed like madness. Yet . . . all it did was purposeful, consistent and logical."

At a time when thousands of Cambodians were dying, working themselves to exhaustion and illness, suffering torture and death for the slightest disagreement with Pol Pot, the government announced a new constitution that described democratic Kampuchea (the new name of the country) in Utopian terms as "a nation of workers and peasants" where "unemployment does not exist and the standard of living of the people is guaranteed."

Family life had been virtually destroyed and children were urged to spy on their parents, watching for the slightest deviation from Pol Pot's gospel. These same children worked in factories and fields from the age of five. The offspring of "undesirables" were reportedly buried alive. Workers toiled sixteen hours a day and those who complained or fell by the wayside were executed.

Of the country's 500 doctors, only a few survived, allowed to dispense only herbs and roots. To be certain that no intellectuals remained to question the regime, anyone who could speak French was murdered, and in one of the most grotesque actions of the Pol Pot years, anyone who wore eyeglasses was executed.

The Khmer Rouge were so intent on obliterating all signs of modern culture and returning to the traditional ways of the ancient Khmer Empire that they ordered the destruction of existing irrigation systems and the construction of new canals based on the lines found on an old map. Unfortunately, the "canals" on the antique map turned out to be longitude and latitude lines. Water was diverted away from crops, and even more suffering developed.

Not only were dissidents and slackers killed, but Pol Pot also instigated a mammoth program of murderous ethnic cleansing: 100,000 ethnic Vietnamese, 225,000 ethnic Chinese, 100,000 Muslims, and 12,000 Thais were killed. At the beginning of Pol Pot's reign there were 2,680 Buddhist monks in Cambodia—in the end, 70 survived.

Pol Pot was driven from control of Cambodia in January 1979 by insurgents backed by Vietnamese forces.

Toll of Destruction: Although estimates vary, the total number of deaths is always expressed in the millions. Some say it was at least a million, others make an educated guess at between 1 and 2 million. No one will ever know for sure.

Aftermath: Far from having been brought to justice for his deeds, Pol Pot spent much of the 1980s in Thailand and to this day continues to live and command his well-equipped army of 10,000 on the Thai-Cambodian border. He is propped up with money, guns, and sanctuary by corrupt military commanders and businessmen from across the border in Thailand who reap enormous profits from the gems and logging in the stretches of western Cambodia under Pol Pot's control.

In the border villages the people refer to him as a *peesat*, a ghost. They know he is there, some must have seen him, but no one admits it openly. Mystery surrounds the man, as it has for much of his life, and he understands the power that grows from that because of the fear it inspires.

"He's out there," said David P. Chandler, whose 1992 book is considered the definitive biography of Pol Pot, "but a lot of people seem to want to forget that. . . . If Cambodia were full of diamonds or uranium, somebody would have done something about him long ago. But it's not. It's Cambodia, so nobody gives a hoot."

Although the Khmer Rouge announced that Pol Pot had retired in 1985, Chandler doesn't believe it. "The Khmer Rouge system does not allow for peaceful replacement. Pol Pot is there for life."

He's there, living in comfort with his second wife (his first went insane) and his young daughter, commanding his army, and growing richer daily. U.N. researchers estimated that by 1995 his Khmer Rouge was operating again in about 25 percent of Cambodia.

—R.W.S.

THE RWANDAN MASSACRES

Background: The massacre of Tutsis by Hutus in Rwanda and Burundi has its genesis in the colonial past. Germans had first colonized the area in the nineteenth century. It was then conquered by Belgians, who controlled Rwanda from World War I until 1962. Both the Germans and the Belgians backed the Tutsi minority over the Hutu majority. The Hutus overthrew the Tutsi-led government in 1966, after a seven-year civil war. In that war, between 20,000 and 100,000 Tutsis were killed and 150,000 were driven into exile. These exiles formed the RPF (Rwandanese Patriotic Front) under former defense minister Yoweri Museveni and invaded Rwanda from Uganda in 1990. The Hutus, fearing the return of Tutsi rule, began the wholesale massacre of Tutsis.

Although the violence has been reported as ethnic or tribal in nature, the Hutu and Tutsi share a common language and history. In fact, the characteristics, the class divisions, and even the names used to separate Hutu from Tutsi are the creation of the colonialists. When they arrived in Rwanda, the Germans and Belgians found a feudal society based on the division of cattle ownership (Tutsi) and farming (Hutu), divisions that the two groups had accepted as the status quo. They even share a common religion, Catholicism, although many of the massacres took place in churches where great numbers of people had sought sanctuary.

The massacre began on April 6, 1994, after a plane carrying the president of Rwanda, Juvenal Habyarimana, and the president of Burundi, Cyprien Ntaryamira, was shot down. Both presidents were Hutus. Hutu nationalist fanatics in Rwanda spread hysteria, using radio broadcasts to exhort Hutus to "fill the half-empty graves." Conservative estimates of the violence put the death toll at more than 500,000, with more than 2 million refugees out of a total population of 8 million.

While the American and European nations wrung their hands, dozens of countries, among them most of the former Soviet republics, rushed to provide both sides with weapons at bargain prices. To intensify the tribal nature of the violence and, it is thought, to conserve expensive ammunition, much of the killing was done with machetes, leaving thousands of corpses of people who had been hacked to death. The radio broadcasts made a point of saying that all infants and children must be killed.

Before his death, Habyarimana, fearing a coup, had organized the Interahamwe (those who kill as one), a fanatically nationalist Hutu militia, to carry out his orders. At the same time, under pressure from Western aid donors, Habyarimana was forced to negotiate with the RPF and allow a transitional government to be formed. Secretly, however, he and Theoneste Bagorosa, the head of the army, had already begun to unleash the terror of the Interahamwe. The chronology of events and the efficiency with which the administrative infrastructure carried out the massacres both indicate that the massacres were planned and executed by a small group close to the president. Hours after Habyarimana's death, the horror began.

The Killing: Using a special code of markings that had been created during a "census" undertaken in February 1994, and the "ethnic" identity cards introduced by the Belgians, the militia began the killing, turning the capital of Kigali into a grid of death. Lists of people to be killed were circulated, targeting all born of Tutsi fathers, regardless of whether their mothers were Hutus. Individual Hutus were also marked for death, including the supporters of democracy, opposition politicians, and those involved in the human-rights movement. The 500,000 Tutsi deaths occurred in the space of only ten weeks, turning the whole country into a wasteland of devastation.

Early intervention by the United Nations could have saved the thousands of Tutsis who had huddled in churches, schools, and stadiums, where they were killed. Belgian and French paratroopers were sent in only to evacuate all foreigners who wished to leave. Very few Rwandans were evacuated, not even those who had worked for UN agencies, embassies, or nongovernmental organizations. Intervention did not take place largely because the United States, still shaken by events in Somalia, refused to commit to action in a region of no strategic interest. Only the French sent troops, although the French acted largely out of their own strategic and economic interests, and they did nothing to stop the root causes of the killing.

While the Interahamwe were trying to kill every Tutsi in Rwanda, the RPF was winning the war, and soon the Hutus joined the Tutsis on the road to exile. The instigators of the massacres survived the war and soon took over the refugee camps and commandeered the humanitarian aid, stockpiling the provisions for a counterrevolution. Soon thousands more, both Hutu and Tutsi, were dying of dysentery and cholera, diseases that do not discriminate among their victims.

Aftermath: While the RPF government includes Hutus and claims it has no interest in reprisals, many refugees remain too afraid to return. The deployment of human-rights workers and the efficient and equitable distribution of humanitarian aid are needed to facilitate a climate of return. The United Nations, however, is stalled on the issue of what constitutes genocide and whether to hold war-crimes trials.

The situation in Rwanda is a grisly addendum to the history of European involvement in Africa. The vacuum left by the end of the Cold War has been filled with corruption, greed, and violence.

—D.C.

PEACE LOVERS

Violence never settles anything right: apart from injuring your own soul, it injures the best cause. It lingers on long after the object of hate has disappeared from the scene to plague the lives of those who have employed it against their foes.
Obafemi Awolowo

What we now need to discover in the social realm is the moral equivalent of war: something heroic that will speak to men as universally as war does, and yet will be as compatible with their spiritual selves as war has proved itself to be incompatible.
William James, The Varieties of Religious Experience, 1902

I'd rather see America save her soul than her face.
Norman Thomas, to antiwar demonstrators, Washington, D.C., November 27, 1965

It is better to win the peace and to lose the war.
Bob Marley

Sometime they'll give a war and nobody will come.
Carl Sandburg, The People, Yes, 1936

Join the Army, see the world, meet interesting people— and kill them.
Antiwar slogan, 1972

Nonviolence is a flop. The only bigger flop is violence.
Joan Baez, Observer, 1967

Peace, n: in international affairs, a period of cheating between two periods of fighting.
Ambrose Bierce, The Devil's Dictionary, 1911

JANE ADDAMS (1860–1935)
Jane Addams was a social reformer, political activist, and pacifist. Reacting to the poverty she saw around her, she cofounded Hull House in Chicago in 1889. She believed that only through international cooperation in the eco-

nomic, political, and social spheres and with the establishment of a lasting peace could nations begin to devote their resources to the basic needs of their citizens. In 1909 she became the first woman president of the National Conference of Charities and Corrections. At the same time, she was active in the suffrage movement and was the vice president of the National American Women Suffrage Alliance.

During World War I, however, she aroused hostility by speaking out against American involvement. In 1915 she became the chairwoman of the Women's Peace Party and president of the first Women's Peace Congress at The Hague. She traveled throughout Europe seeking to mediate a peaceful settlement, and after the war she worked for a just peace.

In 1920 she became a founding member of the American Civil Liberties Union. The Daughters of the American Revolution once called her the "most dangerous woman in America." She shared the Nobel Peace Prize in 1931.

VINOBA BHAVE (1895–1982)

Vinoba Bhave was one of the principal spiritual heirs of Mohandas Gandhi. He preached renunciation of worldly goods, especially land, as the best way to achieve the aims of nonviolent Indian revolution. He was born into a Brahman family and, unlike Gandhi, was a brilliant student. He was on his way to a secular career when a spiritual transformation caused him to abandon that path. He became an ascetic and lifelong celibate.

In 1916 Bhave traveled to Gandhi's ashram at Sabarmati. Too shy to approach him directly, he wrote a letter asking for admittance. He was to become a tireless supporter of Gandhi. In 1921 he was sent to Sevagram to build a second ashram, which was later to become Gandhi's headquarters. "He is one of the ashram's rare pearls," said Gandhi, "one of those who have come not to be blessed but to bless, not to receive but to give."

He was a vigorous proponent of home industries, especially the spinning and weaving of cotton, a crucial part of the program for Indian self-sufficiency. He also worked for the end of the caste system, and during the 1920s he organized campaigns by untouchables to gain entry into Hindu temples. Brahman priests beat him so severely that he was left deaf in one ear.

Gandhi chose him as one of the leaders of the satyagraha against British rule, for which he was jailed six times. He spent his years in jail proselytizing his fellow prisoners, speaking of the coming independence and of the Bhagavad Gita.

But his years of greatest activity began after Gandhi's assassination. Hearing of turmoil in Hyderabad between landless peasants and brutal landlords, he set off on foot to the area, converting thousands along the way to ahimsa (nonviolence), including both armed guerrillas

and landlords. From this movement sprang Bhoodan yajna (land-gift sacrifice). "I have come to loot you with love," he would say. "Consider me as one of your sons, and give me my share of land, so I may give it to the landless." In three years he collected more than 4 million acres. When the movement seemed to falter in the mid-fifties—much of the donated land was of no agricultural value—Bhave began to preach gramdan (village gift), a larger concept involving the parceling out of an entire village's land among all its inhabitants.

Bhave retired from the world in the 1960s to live permanently in his ashram at Paunar. He ate nothing but curds and unrefined sugar during most of his life, and usually weighed less than a hundred pounds. In 1982 he suffered a heart attack and, seeing his death approaching, refused all food and medical aid. He died a week later.

CORBETT BISHOP (1906–61)

Corbett Bishop was an American bookseller and a legendary pacifist absolutist. He firmly believed that conscription was slavery and that war was contrary to Christ's teaching. He was sentenced to prison for violating the draft law during World War II. While in prison he refused to cooperate in any way with the authorities. He would not move, feed, or clean himself while in the government's custody. He had to be carried in and out of court by the FBI and force-fed by his jailers. He went a total of 426 days without voluntarily taking food or water. "The authorities have the power to seize my body; that is all they can do. My spirit will be free," he said.

He won his own release from prison five months after being returned for parole violations. He continued to pursue his resistance free from personal hostility or resentment.

HELDER PESSOA CAMARA (b. 1909)

Helder Pessoa Camara, archbishop of Olinda and Recife, impoverished areas of Brazil, is a frail, diminutive man dedicated to Liberation Theology, a philosophy that preaches revolution as a way to achieve social justice. Perched between an often repressive government and an equally conservative Catholic hierarchy, Camara has maintained his position in the face of constant opposition. "My vocation," he says, "is to argue, argue, argue for moral pressure upon the lords."

During the first session of the Second Vatican Council, in 1962, he prepared a sermon criticizing the council for not dealing with urgent social issues. The sermon was censored and translations were ordered destroyed. On the eve of the second session, Camara issued an open letter to the prelates urging them to forego honorifics, luxuries, and privileges that create distance between them and working-class Catholics.

In early 1970 he gave a speech denouncing political torture in Brazil and participated in a report called "Black Book: Terror and Torture in

Brazil." Soon his influence was limited by the government's barring of his voice and message from newspapers, television, and radio.

"For three centuries," Camara pointed out, "the church has accepted the ethic of slavery and acquiesced in the social order—really the social disorder—that keeps millions of human creatures living in sub-human conditions." In 1970 he was nominated for the Nobel Peace Prize and was awarded the Martin Luther King Prize. He feels that his cause in Brazil has much in common with the nonviolent civil-rights struggle initiated by King. "The violence of the peaceful" is how he explains the passive resistance of Gandhi and King. "There is the primary violence ... which is the injustice that exists everywhere.... I call injustice violence because, in fact, misery kills more than the most bloody war."

CESAR CHAVEZ (1927–93)
Cesar Chavez rose from total poverty to become a major force in improving the conditions of farmworkers as well as Mexican Americans and Latinos in the United States. After losing their farm during the depression, the Chavez family moved to San Jose, California, to pick carrots, cotton, and other crops. In the 1950s Cesar Chavez met Saul Alinsky, who was organizing Mexican Americans into a political bloc. Chavez joined Alinsky's Community Service Organization and played a key role in registering Mexican Americans to vote.

Chavez left the Community Service Organization in 1962 and formed the National Farm Workers Association, which later became the United Farm Workers Union. In 1965 Chavez began his famous "La Huelga" strike against table-grape growers in the San Joaquin Valley. By 1968, 17 million Americans had stopped buying grapes because of the boycott. In 1970 the growers conceded defeat and signed an agreement that granted farmworkers the right to collective bargaining.

Chavez was a shy man who adhered to a lifestyle that was almost monastic. He was a strict vegetarian and often fasted to draw attention to his cause. He did not own a house or a car, and his income never rose above $1,000 a month. While the power of Chavez's union has faded, the gains his UFW made have led to improved working conditions for all farmworkers. He believed that "we must respect all human life, in the cities, in the fields, and in Vietnam. Nonviolence is the only weapon that is compassionate and recognizes each man's value."

ALBERT EINSTEIN (1879–1955)
Albert Einstein first achieved prominence as a pacifist in 1914, when he was one of only four German intellectuals to sign the *Manifesto to Europeans* protesting Germany's involvement in World War I. His pacifism was rooted in the

belief that militarism is a direct threat to intellectual freedom, which he considered the foundation of civilization. War is therefore an assault on the natural laws of the universe, laws that he spent his life defining.

> My pacifism is not based on any intellectual theory but on a deep antipathy to every form of cruelty and hatred.
> Albert Einstein, attributed, 1914

After the complete failure of the manifesto, Einstein and a small group of pacifists organized the Bund Nues Vaterland (New Fatherland League) to press for peace and to establish a supranational organization to make future wars impossible. The League was suppressed in 1916. Subsequently he became involved in the League of Nations by sitting on the Committee of Intellectual Cooperation, the precursor to UNESCO. His membership in the committee was clouded by both the anti-German and the anti-Semitic feelings prevalent at the time.

Beginning in 1928 Einstein began to promote direct war resistance. "People," he wrote, "should assume the solemn and unconditional obligation not to participate in any war, for any reason." However, the rise of fascism in Germany, while confirming his distaste for militarism and nationalism, forced him to grapple with a new reality. In 1933 he began his tenure at the Institute for Advanced Studies at Princeton, and soon after stated his belief that the nations of western Europe had no alternative except to defeat German aggression. This led him to write to President Franklin Roosevelt about the possibility of developing an atomic bomb. Einstein, however, was not involved in the Manhattan Project and was shocked and revolted when the atomic bomb was dropped on Hiroshima in the last days of the war. The fact that his genius for defining universal physical laws could be used for such destructive purposes caused Einstein to redouble his efforts for peace. Along with other prominent scientists, he organized the Emergency Committee of Atomic Scientists in 1946. The virulence of Cold War rhetoric led to the collapse of the committee in 1948.

In the 1950s Einstein was America's preeminent scientist and he used his fame to challenge the official orthodoxy of the time. He opposed McCarthyism and championed resistance and individual noncooperation. In the last months of his life, he involved himself with Bertrand Russell's direct appeal for the abolition of war. This Einstein-Russell declaration, issued on July 9, 1955, was the last document he signed. In it he stated, "We are speaking ... not as members of this or that nation, continent or creed but as human beings ... whose continued existence is in doubt. People have to learn to think in a new way. We have to learn to ask ourselves, not what steps can be taken to give military victory to whatever group we prefer, for there are no longer such steps; the question we have to ask ourselves is: What steps can be taken to prevent a military contest of which the issue must be disastrous."

MOHANDAS KARAMCHAND GANDHI (1869–1948)

> *Means are not to be distinguished from ends. If violent means are used, there will be bad results.*
> Mohandas K. Gandhi

> *It is better to be violent, if there is violence in our hearts, than to put on a cloak of nonviolence to cover impotence.*
> Mohandas K. Gandhi, *Non-Violence in Peace and War,* 1948

> *A nonviolent revolution is not a program of seizure of power. It is a program of transformation of relationships, ending in a peaceful transfer of power.*
> Mohandas K. Gandhi, *Non-Violence in Peace and War,* 1948

Charlie Chaplin meets with Mahatma Gandhi in London, September 29, 1931.

Mohandas Gandhi was born into a merchant caste family. His father and grandfather had been prime ministers in the native system of government under British rule. He was sent to school in London to study law, where he was a mediocre student plagued by extreme fear and shyness.

He returned to India and began to practice law. His career was cut short when he was too shy to present a brief in a minor case. He was subsequently offered a job representing a Muslim client in a lawsuit in the Natal province of South Africa. The insults he received and the abuses he witnessed there forced him to confront and transcend his fears. He became a spokesman for the Indian community, moved to Johannesburg in 1903, and set up a newspaper, *Indian Opinion.* Increasingly restrictive legislation led to a public mass declaration of refusal to obey the law, to which Gandhi soon applied the names satyagraha (truth force) and ahimsa (nonviolence). He was jailed three times in 1908 and 1909, the last time at hard labor. A satyagraha of 2,000 Indian coal and sugar workers led to the Indians Relief Act of 1914, after which Gandhi felt free to return to India.

Arriving in Bombay in 1915, Gandhi at the age of forty-five was a national hero and given the title "Mahatma" (Great Soul) by Rabindranath Tagore. He started an ashram in Ahmedabad, where he continued to train a core of disciplined workers. In 1917 he led a strike of millworkers and a peasant strike in Kheda. In 1919 he called for a one-day work stoppage, which led to the killing of 379 unarmed civilians in Amritsar. In 1920, after a violent incident perpetrated by his followers, Gandhi was arrested, tried, and sentenced to six years in prison.

He was released in 1924 because of ill health and devoted himself to his Constructive Program, including khaddar (homespun cloth), Hindu-Muslim unity, and the eradication of untouchability. He called for complete independence by 1929 and when it was not granted began another satyagraha. In 1930 he marched 240 miles to the sea, where he broke the salt laws and launched a wave of protest resulting in the jailing of more than 60,000 men and women. In 1931 he negotiated a pact with the viceroy ending protests over the salt laws. He was again jailed in 1931 and vowed to "fast unto death" against separating untouchables from caste Hindus in the electoral roles. He was released in 1933.

After a few years of concentrating on social and economic issues, Gandhi again took up the issue of independence with the advent of World War II, launching a series of satyagrahas in 1940 against Britain's refusal to let Indians make a choice regarding participation in the war. He declared the Quit India campaign in 1942, for which he was again jailed.

As independence drew near, Muslim nationalism led by M. A. Jinnah threatened Indian unity. In 1947 Gandhi walked through many villages in East Bengal to quell Hindu-Muslim violence. He halted similar riots in Calcutta with a three-day fast. Failing to prevent the partition of India and Pakistan, he struggled to overcome the fears and violence that had been unleashed among the citizens and, in the fall of 1947, moved to Delhi. He was assassinated by a Hindu nationalist in 1948. "I object to violence," he once said, "because when it appears to do good, the good is only temporary; the evil it does is permanent."

DICK GREGORY (b. 1932)

Dick Gregory is an American comedian, activist, and social critic. He grew up in poverty in Saint Louis, Missouri, where he shined shoes in a pool hall where the white customers would rub his head for good luck. He became a track star in college but left without earning his degree. He drifted to Chicago, where he was fired from his post office job for flipping letters to Mississippi in the "overseas" slot.

After a few more years of drifting, he became a prominent stand-up comedian, the first black comedian to cross from race-based material to social commentary. When a documentary on urban life that Gregory participated in was refused airtime in eight southern cities, he quipped, "I wouldn't mind paying my income taxes if I knew it was going to a friendly country."

In the 1960s Dick Gregory campaigned for civil rights and marched and fasted in protest of the Vietnam War. He believed that fasting creates a rallying point where "all the honest, ethical forces can gather." In 1968 he ran for president with the Peace and Freedom Party. He also wrote two autobiographies, *From the Back of the Bus* and *Nigger: An Autobiography*.

In 1991 Gregory was arrested three times while protesting U.S. involvement in the Gulf War. He has said, "I believe any time you muster an army together that's willing to die for what's right, you frighten the death out of armies that are willing to kill for what's wrong."

TOYOHIKO KAGAWA (1888–1960)

Toyohiko Kagawa was a world-famous author, labor leader, social activist, and pacifist. He was the author of more than a hundred books, which include novels, poems, and Christian and pacifist writings. Born into a wealthy Buddhist family, he converted to Christianity, gave away his possessions, and went to live in Kobe's notorious Shinkawa slums. He lived there for fourteen years, working with the poor and writing *The Psychology of Poverty*, which brought the plight of the slum dwellers to official attention.

In 1912 Kagawa turned to labor organizing, founding the first labor union in Japan among the shipyard workers. He organized the Labor Federation in 1918. From 1919 on he took an active part in the cause of universal suffrage, social reform in general, and the improvement of labor conditions.

He spoke out against Japan's war with China in 1936, and was jailed for his pacifism in 1940. "The way to stop war," he said, "is by cooperative movements." With that spirit, he launched nineteen churches, seventeen schools, six cooperative societies, an ex-prisoners' home, an employment agency, a social research bureau, and two monthly periodicals.

ABDUL GHAFFER KHAN (1890–1988)

Abdul Khan's nonviolent leadership during India's freedom struggle earned him the title "the Frontier Gandhi." He was a Muslim Pashtun from the North-West Frontier Province of Pakistan, an area known for its fierce warriors. But after eighty years of activism, thirty of them spent in jail, Khan became known as one of the greatest exponents of nonviolence in the world.

In 1930 he founded the Servants of God, a nonviolent "army" of Pashtuns. The Red Shirts, as they were called, faced some of the most bitter repression of the Indian freedom struggle and provided the strongest resistance to British rule. Khan's Red Shirts also challenged the prevailing myths about nonviolence: that it can be followed only by those who are gentle, that it cannot work against ruthless repression, and that nonviolence has no place in Islam.

Because the Pashtun homeland included the strategically important Khyber Pass, the British were determined to hold the area at any cost. The British jailed or deported Pashtuns by the thousands, bombed their villages, and murdered thousands more, yet the Pashtun territory was never fully subjugated.

It was within the context of this violence, despair, and tyranny that Abdul Khan's work was done. Moved by the poverty and ignorance of his people, in 1912 Khan opened several Islamic schools and helped educate villagers in hygiene and agricultural methods. In 1919 he became active in Gandhi's first civil disobedience movement (satyagraha) against the Rowlatt Acts. He was arrested and served six months in prison. Freed when martial law was lifted, he resumed his reform work and was again jailed and ordered to discontinue his reform activity. He refused and was jailed for three years, much of it spent in solitary confinement.

In the 1920s and 1930s Khan and his Pashtuns became an integral part of Gandhi's satyagraha against the salt laws. The nonviolence of the Pashtuns surprised both the British and the Indians. The India League reported, "That nonviolence still remains the rigidly observed rule of the nationalist movement in an area where arms are readily available is a tribute to the sincerity with which the creed has been embraced."

Khan was at heart a religious man, a reformer rather than a politician, who always preferred village work to political life. Nevertheless, in 1934 he was again arrested and sentenced to two years in prison. After his release he was banned from his province and settled with Gandhi at his ashram. Khan served another three-year prison term during the Quit India movement of 1942. After the partition of India and Pakistan in 1947, a move he resisted, he was jailed by the Moslem League for supporting a Pashtun state. His sentence was extended twice. During Pakistan's first eighteen years of independence, Khan spent fifteen in jail. When freed, he continued to speak out for Pashtun independence, and faced prison again in 1958 and 1961.

In 1962 Khan was selected by Amnesty International as prisoner of the year. It said in its statement, "Nonviolence has its martyrs. One of them, Abdul Ghaffer Khan . . . symbolizes the suffering of upwards of a million people all over the world who are in prison for their conscience. Despite appeals, the old man still lies in jail." He was seventy-two.

He was jailed in 1975 and again in 1983, at the age of ninety-three. He died on January 20, 1988. Abdul Ghaffer Khan supported the pro-Soviet government in Afghanistan, claiming Muslims were more free there than in Pakistan. When he was buried in Afghanistan, terrorist bombs killed seventeen people at the funeral.

MARTIN LUTHER KING JR. (1929–68)

When Rosa Parks refused to take her place in the back of the bus in Montgomery, Alabama, in 1955, Martin Luther King was the twenty-six-year-old pastor of the Dexter Avenue Baptist Church. Her arrest sparked a 382-day bus boycott and Martin Luther King's leadership brought the civil-rights movement to national attention. This movement, stressed King, was founded on Christian ideals and Gandhian strategy. Both his ideals and his strategy were to be constantly tested for the rest of his life.

King was arrested twenty times; he was stabbed and assaulted, and his house was firebombed. In 1963 he led the protest in Birmingham, Alabama, in which police used dogs and high-pressure fire hoses on peaceful demonstrators. When he was arrested as a result of the demonstration, he wrote his "Letter from a Birmingham Jail," which became a manifesto calling for a "Negro Revolution" to be waged in a nonviolent but persistent fashion. Three months later his "I Have a Dream" speech during the March on Washington galvanized both black and white support for the movement and increased his worldwide prominence.

Martin Luther King on his way to a jail cell at police headquarters in Montgomery, Alabama, September 3, 1958.

In 1964 King won the Nobel Peace Prize and used it to accelerate the fight against all forms of racism and to attack the poverty that institutionalized it. He went on to lead the Selma-Montgomery march in 1965 and the Mississippi march in 1966. King's Southern Christian Leadership Conference (SCLC) also launched its first major effort outside the South, the Fair Housing march in Chicago, which he called the most frightening of his life. He also expanded his role by speaking out against the Vietnam War, drawing harsh criticism from many who previously supported him.

In the last years of his life, King's thinking became more pessimistic and radical. His early belief that discrimination could be eradicated by political reform was shattered by the realization that racism was endemic to American society. While he remained committed to nonviolence, his plans became more obstructive. He was assassinated in 1968, in Memphis, Tennessee, where he had been invited to help sanitation workers on strike achieve their goals peaceably. (See page 155.)

JOHN LENNON (1940–80)

John Lennon's peace activism was as personal, quixotic, and troubled as the man himself. By the time of his first "bed-in," to celebrate his marriage to Yoko Ono in 1969, he had already been through rock and roll stardom, the Maharishi's ashram, LSD, and the political fallout from his song "Revolution." The bed-in lasted a week and its intention was to protest all the suffering and violence in the world. John and Yoko stayed in bed, giving interviews ten hours a day, saying in one interview, "They know how to play the game of violence. But they don't know how to handle humor, and peaceful humor—and that's our message really."

In 1969, denied entry into the United States by immigration officials, John and Yoko staged another bed-in in Montreal. On the last night of the event, John taught everyone in the room the new song he had written. It was "Give Peace a Chance." The backup singers included Dick Gregory, Timothy Leary, Tommy Smothers, a rabbi, a priest, and the Canadian chapter of the Radna Krishna Temple. In October 1969, in New York during a Vietnam Moratorium Day protest, "Give Peace a Chance" became an antiwar anthem. Pete Seeger began to sing it at another Moratorium Day protest in Washington, D.C., and he was joined by nearly half a million protesters.

In 1971 John and Yoko began living in New York. Through their music and their involvement with peace activists such as Jerry Rubin, they sought to make a contribution to the peace movement. Their efforts were thwarted by a cynical press, the left's confusion over using the tactics of violence or nonviolence, and their own frequent lapses into rhetorical excess. Yet through it all Lennon was able to maintain his commitment to nonviolence.

After the Vietnam War, John and Yoko retreated into creating a harmonious private life. "I like it to be known," said Lennon, "that yes, I looked after the baby and I made bread and I was a househusband and I am proud of it. It's the wave of the future and I'm glad to be in the forefront of that, too."

By 1980 John and Yoko were recording again and *Double Fantasy*, an album that celebrated love and family life, was released in November. A month later John Lennon was shot to death in front of his apartment building by Mark David Chapman, a fan who had been stalking him.

ABRAHAM JOHN MUSTE (1885–1967)

A. J. Muste was an ordained minister, a Trotskyist, labor organizer, war resister, pacifist, and civil-rights activist. According to Muste, economic inequality is a primary cause of war. Thus his conversion to pacifism in World War I led him into a career of radical activism. By the late 1920s he had become so involved in the struggles of the American labor movement that he temporarily traded his pacifism for Trotskyism, becoming one of the founders of the Workers Party of the United States. However, returning from a conference in 1936, he was reconverted to pacifism after having a religious experience in the church of Saint Sulpice in Paris. After the outbreak of World War II, he became executive secretary of the Fellowship of Reconciliation (FOR), maintaining that military action against fascists only fed the forces of brutality; he advocated instead a redistribution of the world's resources.

After U.S. atomic bombs were used against Japan, Muste called for America to disarm unilaterally. He renewed his commitment to the War Resister League and the Committee for Nonviolent Action. He was jailed for refusing to pay income taxes (as a war resister), defying civil-defense laws, encouraging attempts to halt nuclear testing, and trespassing on federal property.

Because he saw an intimate connection between aggression in foreign policy and racism in domestic action, A. J. Muste also championed civil rights and was an organizer and mentor for both the Congress of Racial Equality and the Southern Christian Leadership Conference. As the Vietnam War intensified, Muste appealed to civil-rights activists to join the peace movement, acting as a major influence on Martin Luther King's deepening resistance to the war. In 1967 he went to North Vietnam with a small group of peace activists and brought back an offer from Ho Chi Minh to President Lyndon Johnson to talk about peace. Less than three weeks later, Muste developed an aneurysm and died, in February of 1967. His death notice in an antiwar newsletter read, "In lieu of flowers, friends are requested to get out and work for peace, for human rights, for a better world."

GEORG FRIEDRICH NICOLAI (1874–1964)

A handsome, prosperous, and renowned cardiologist and consulting physician to the German empress, Georg Nicolai was the son-in-law of an armaments manufacturer and the only German intellectual to actively oppose World War I. Reacting to the infamous *Manifesto to the Civilized World*, in which ninety-three leading German intellectuals defended the invasion of neutral Belgium, Nicolai wrote *Manifesto to Europeans* and tried to convince Albert Einstein and two others to sign it. In this countermanifesto, Nicolai condemned war as a catastrophic attack on the universal nature of civilization and went on to predict that the war would have no victor, only victims, and to predict that the outcome of the war would become the source of other wars. Only one man, an old friend, was willing to sign, and the *Manifesto to Europeans* remained unpublished until it became the introduction to Nicolai's *The Biology of War*.

Nicolai, disillusioned by his fellow scientists' lack of commitment to the pursuit of truth, went on to deliver a series of lectures, "War as a Biological Factor in Human Evolution." While there was no basis for legal action, the German Reich reacted by transferring Nicolai to a small garrison town, where he was assigned as an assistant to a unit for contagious diseases. It was at Graudenz, in 1915, that he wrote *The Biology of War*, a diatribe against war not only on moral and humanist grounds but also as a biological and evolutionary catastrophe, stating, "The morality of the future must be compatible with the evolutionary interests of the species."

In a country that considered war a means of spreading its notion of civilization, this view was heresy. In order to control Nicolai, the authorities transferred him to even more remote garrisons, drafted him involuntarily into the military, and suppressed his writings and political views. Nicolai, however, as a former professor and member of the German upper classes, fought every move with un-Prussian-like stubbornness and insubordination. He managed to smuggle his book to Switzerland, where it finally appeared in 1917. This resulted in Nicolai's court-martial on charges of violating the German Articles of War. The military judges, fearing to create a martyr, let him off with a fine. But *The Biology of War* became an international sensation and overnight placed Nicolai in a position of moral and intellectual leadership among pacifists everywhere. A series of transfers and courts-martial ensued, during which time Nicolai refused to bear arms, as a conscientious objector under the Geneva Convention. Threatened with imprisonment, he went into hiding. Soon afterward he made a daring and unlikely escape as the navigator of a small airplane piloted by a member of the Spartacists. They landed in Denmark and caused another international sensation. The German government declared him insane in absentia. In 1918 Nicolai returned to Germany and attempted to take part in the efforts to found a German Republic. He wrote and lectured and was one of the leaders of the delegation sent to Bern to represent Germany at the conference that planned the League of Nations. But his old academic enemies branded him a deserter, and when he tried to resume his medical lectures he was confronted by a mob of rioting nationalist students. He was expelled from the university and found not one defender except Einstein. Nicolai finally accepted an offer to teach at the Argentine University of Cordoba and, except for brief visits, never returned to Germany.

The second part of his career was spent in Argentina, and later in Chile, where he became revered as a teacher and a thinker. He wrote numerous books and essays dealing with ethics and their relation to science, with epistemology, relativity, dialectics, the psychoanalytic method, and socioeconomic problems. The moral sense, he wrote, is not a rational system of thought but a poorly developed instinct inherited from human ancestors. "He who understands what it means to be human is ipso facto objectively moral."

JEANETTE RANKIN (1880–1973)

Jeanette Rankin's pacifism originated in connection with the suffragist movements in Washington and Montana. Writers such as Minnie J. Reynolds and Benjamin Kidd led her to the conclusion that women were the primary source of power for all future peace movements.

After helping women to win the vote in Montana, Rankin became the first woman elected to the House of Representatives in 1916. Within four days of assuming her seat, she voted against U.S. entry into World War I. Later, in 1941, while serving a second term in the House, she became the only congressional opponent of entry into World War II. Rankin always remained true to her pacifist ideal: she objected to the use of American military force anywhere in the world, except for the defense of the continental United States.

After World War II, Jeanette Rankin became a consistent critic of the Cold War, including the Korean and Vietnam conflicts. As the war in Indochina intensified, she gave serious consideration, at the age of eighty-eight, to running for a third term in Congress. Her final protest was at the head of the Jeanette Rankin Brigade, organized in 1967.

OSCAR ROMERO (1917–80)

When the shy, soft-spoken Oscar Romero was appointed archbishop of San Salvador, neither the military government nor the Catholic activist movement expected him to do more than administer church affairs. However, after the murder of a Jesuit friend, he denounced political violence and called for social change, including the redistribution of wealth, land reform, and justice and equality for the poor. His stance brought him a huge following and made him important enemies.

When dictator Carlos Humberto Romero (no relation) was overthrown in 1979, Archbishop Romero gave his qualified support to the new junta. But he soon grew disillusioned with its inability to carry out promised reforms and began to accuse them of continued repression. He wrote an open letter to President Jimmy Carter, begging him not to send military aid to the junta. "We are fed up with weapons and bullets," he said. Nevertheless, a House subcommittee approved the Carter administration's request for military aid for the junta.

Archbishop Romero began to read lists of the disappeared or killed from the pulpit during Sunday mass. Soon after, seventy-two sticks of dynamite were discovered in the cathedral moments before he was to celebrate mass. A month later, a right-wing group blew up the transmitter that carried his sermons throughout the country. Romero recorded his sermons and passed out the cassettes. "If the defense of human rights is subversive," he said, "then I am subversive."

On the morning of March 24, 1980, Archbishop Romero celebrated mass in the chapel of the Hospital of Divine Providence. As he was elevating the host, a man in civilian clothes stepped out of the shadows and shot Romero from close range. Although Roberto D'Aubuisson, head of the right-wing death squads, was believed to have ordered the assassination of Archbishop Romero, no one was ever tried or convicted, and D'Aubuisson danced at President Ronald Reagan's inaugural ball. A few days before his death, speaking at a retreat, Romero said, "If they kill me I will rise again in the Salvadoran people."

BERTRAND RUSSELL (1872–1970)

Although Bertrand Russell claimed that his conversion to pacifism came as the result of a mystical experience, he was also a pragmatist, for whom peace was essential, while the means of obtaining and preserving it were negotiable. Russell was horrified by the outbreak of World War I and he campaigned in favor of peace negotiations while devoting himself to the No-Conscription Fellowship.

Between world wars Russell joined numerous peace organizations and sought to lay the foundations of a more peaceful world through his writing. He examined power, freedom, and organization, attempting to find the root causes of war. His work in ethics, including *Conquest of Happiness*, was directed toward ending conflict by enlarging people's views and objectives to

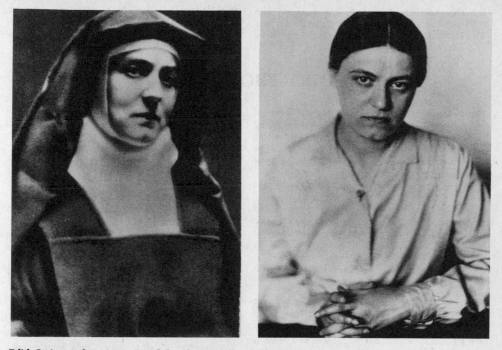

Edith Stein was born into a Jewish family in Breslau, Germany. She converted to Catholicism and became a Carmelite nun. However, she was arrested by the Nazis and died in a gas chamber at Auschwitz.

encompass unselfish ends. He also sought to develop an educational system that would promote peace.

The outbreak of World War II found Russell's pacifism overcome by his perception of the evils of Nazism. By mid-1940 he was speaking out in favor of the Allied war effort. The use of the atomic bomb, however, convinced him that war was again unthinkable and for the rest of his life he worked to combat the threat of war. Together with Albert Einstein, he issued an appeal that led to a series of conferences of atomic scientists from both sides of the Cold War to discuss the problems caused by the nuclear age. The first of these conferences was held at Pugwash, Nova Scotia, in 1957.

Toward the end of his life, Russell came to view the dangers of U.S. militarism and economic imperialism to be as threatening as Communism and vehemently opposed the Vietnam War. He viewed the task of turning the world back from the brink of nuclear destruction as the most important of his life.

EDITH STEIN (1891–1942)

The Gestapo came for Sister Teresa Benedicta of the Cross at the Carmelite convent in Echt, the Netherlands, on August 2, 1942. She and her sister Rosa were given five minutes to pack. They died in Auschwitz on August 9. "Come,"

she said to her sister, "we are going for our people." In those words rest a paradox, a mystery, a tragedy, and a controversy.

Sister Teresa was born Edith Stein in Breslau. She studied philosophy at universities in Breslau and Göttingen, under renowned phenomenologist Edmund Husserl. Yet, after reading a biography of Teresa of Avila, she decided to convert to Catholicism, over the objections of her family. For the next eight years she taught in a convent school at Speyer, where she acquired a reputation for piety and asceticism. During this time she wrote *Finite and Eternal Being*, attempting to reconcile phenomenology with Christian theology. She was also a popular lecturer on women's significance in contemporary life.

In 1934, after the Nazis banned Jews from academic posts, she entered a Carmelite convent in Cologne, taking the name Sister Benedicta of the Cross. In 1938 she was sent to Echt in the Netherlands. She attempted to transfer to a convent in Switzerland and safety, then refused when the convent would not also accept her sister Rosa.

She was beatified, the first step toward being declared a saint, by Pope John Paul II in 1987. The Pope's move was controversial with both Catholics and Jews. Her words, "Come, we are going for our people," were taken to refer to her

Jewish origin; and therefore, it was argued, she could not be a Christian martyr if she died a Jew. The Catholic hierarchy was especially sensitive to this issue because of long-standing criticism that it did not do enough to stop the Holocaust.

—D.C.

QUOTEBOOK: WAR

War is, after all, the universal perversion. We are all tainted: if we cannot experience our perversion at first hand we spend our time reading war stories, the pornography of war; or seeing war films, the blue films of war; or titillating our senses with the imagination of great deeds, the masturbation of war.

John Rae, The Custard Boys, 1960

I discovered to my amazement that average men and women were delighted at the prospect of war. I had fondly imagined what most pacifists contended, that wars were forced upon a reluctant population by despotic and Machiavellian governments.

Bertrand Russell, 1967

All wars are popular for the first thirty days.

Arthur Schlesinger Jr.

They wrote in the old days that it is sweet and fitting to die for one's country. But in modern war there is nothing sweet or fitting in your dying. You will die like a dog for no good reason.

Ernest Hemingway, Notes on the Next War

This war, like the next war, is a war to end war.

David Lloyd George, referring to the popular opinion that World War I would be the last major war, 1916

Yes; quaint and curious war is!
You shoot a fellow down
You'd treat if met where any bar is,
Or help to half-a-crown.

Thomas Hardy, "Man He Killed," 1909

In wartime, the degree of patriotism is directly proportional to distance from the front.

Philip Caputo, "War Torn," New York Times Magazine, February 24, 1991

All wars are wars among thieves who are too cowardly to fight and who therefore induce the young manhood of the whole world to do the fighting for them.

Emma Goldman, "Address to the Jury," Mother Earth, July 1917

When the rich wage war it is the poor who die.

Jean-Paul Sartre, The Devil and the Good Lord, 1951

The draft is white people sending black people to fight yellow people to protect the country they stole from red people.

Gerome Ragni and James Rado, Hair, 1967

War is not an adventure. It is a disease. It is like typhus.

Antoine de Saint-Exupéry, Flight to Arras, 1942

Wars, conflict, it's all business. One murder makes a villain. Millions a hero. Numbers sanctify.

Charlie Chaplin, Monsieur Verdoux, 1947

We must remember that in time of war what is said on the enemy's side of the front is always propaganda and what is said on our side of the front is truth and righteousness, the cause of humanity and a crusade for peace. Is it necessary for us at the height of our power to stoop to such self-deceiving nonsense?

Walter Lippmann, 1966

Madam, I am the civilization they are fighting to defend.

Heathcote William Garood, British classical scholar, replying to criticism that he was not fighting to defend civilization during World War I, 1918

Chapter 6

ANIMALS

NOTEWORTHY ANIMALS

THE DOLPHIN PILOT

He was a fourteen-foot Risso's dolphin who for more than two decades guided steamships off New Zealand through perilous waters into safe harbor. He was the first dolphin in history whose life was protected by a special government proclamation or law.

Pelorus Jack, named for Pelorus Sound, became renowned in 1888 when he expertly piloted steamships through a six-mile stretch of the rough, swirling waters of Cook Strait between New Zealand's two main islands. He gained the love of both sailors and passengers who watched him playfully leaping through the waves toward their vessel. Often he would scratch his back against the ship's hull and then swiftly glide out in front and pilot the steamer into the dangerous French Pass. After getting one ship safely through, the dolphin would immediately leave to wait for another vessel.

Passengers aboard the ships described the dolphin as beakless and silvery white, with eyes that looked "almost human." He always traveled alone and cut through the waves with the greatest of ease. When two ships needed his services at the same time, Pelorus Jack always chose the faster steamship.

In 1903 a drunken sailor on the SS *Penguin* tried to shoot Pelorus Jack with a rifle. Luckily, the shot missed. Jack didn't show up again for two weeks, but then he came back, apparently no worse for the experience. However, he never again accompanied the *Penguin*, which was wrecked in 1909 in Cook Strait; seventy-five people were killed.

In September 1904 the government of New Zealand passed a law to protect Pelorus Jack, carrying a fine of 5 to 100 pounds for anyone who did him harm. Jack had become an international celebrity. A movie was made about him. His picture was featured on postcards. He inspired numerous songs. A chocolate bar was named after him. Sightseers, including Mark Twain and Rudyard Kipling, came great distances to see him, and when they saw him bounding toward them, someone would always shout, "Here comes Pelorus Jack!"

In 1912 Pelorus Jack disappeared. A local newspaper printed a tentative obituary, concluding, "If he is dead, more's the pity; if he has been slaughtered, more's the shame." Pelorus Jack was never seen again.

Incidentally, no one will ever know, but he may have been a she.

THE BLOODHOUND DETECTIVE

Born in 1899, Nick Carter, named after the fictional detective, had a career that most detectives, both fictional and real, would envy. Known as the "finest tracking dog in the world," the bloodhound was involved in more than 600 investigations that resulted in criminal convictions. In one year alone, Nick solved 126 cases out of 161—a 78 percent conviction rate.

Nick's owner was Captain Volney G. Mullikin of Lexington, Kentucky, who bred and trained bloodhounds for the specific purpose of tracking down criminals. While Nick and his owner worked primarily in Kentucky, they were often called upon to help solve cases in nearby states.

Nick's incredible sense of smell helped to capture all manner of criminals—murderers, robbers, arsonists. In addition, he worked on missing-persons investigations. The relentless tracker pursued his prey through all kinds of weather, over mountains and across valleys, through swamps and heavy undergrowth. No matter how many times the trail was lost, Nick refused to quit and persevered until he again picked up the scent. In one instance, Nick had to travel fifty miles before catching three men who had robbed a post office safe. Winding their way through hilly areas, the men kept wading through creeks and streams. Nick lost the scent three times but eventually caught up with the robbers.

Two of Nick's cases are frequently cited in stories about the bloodhound detective. One involved an arsonist who burned down a henhouse. Although the criminal was apprehended less than a mile away, the trail was 105 hours old when Nick began his search. His ability to follow such a cold trail set an "oldest trail" record that was to last for more than twenty-five years. In another case, Nick set a record for solving a crime involving the shortest trail, one that measured only ten feet. This time the culprit was a crazed mother who planned to kill her three children. After using rope to tie them up in the chicken coop, the Kentucky woman left to sharpen an axe that she planned to use as a weapon. A neighbor discovered the children, and the murders were prevented, but the children were terrified of pointing the finger at their mother. Nick, called in by the police, sniffed at the ropes and promptly walked ten feet to where the mother was standing. She immediately confessed and was later committed to a mental institution.

Little is known about Nick Carter's retirement years or when he died. However, he did enjoy celebrity status and fans often showed up at a crime scene to cheer him on. In addition, he and his fellow bloodhound detective, Iva Belle, produced a litter of nine puppies, all of them trained to hunt down criminals.

—C.O.M.

THE COUNTING HORSE

The talk of the town in 1904 in Berlin, Germany, was a mathematical genius—Clever Hans, the horse who could count. Not only could he count from one to a hundred, but he could also solve arithmetic problems, tap out the alphabet, answer yes or no questions by nodding, and locate nearby objects. When tapping out an answer, Clever Hans used his right foot. When finished, the horse switched to his left foot for a single tap. The big question was whether the horse was a truly intelligent animal, capable of independent thinking, or whether Clever Hans was a clever hoax.

The man who owned Clever Hans was Wilhelm von Osten, a German mathematics teacher. He welcomed investigations of the horse's abilities and never charged admission to the horse's theatrical demonstrations. It all seemed so believable that Clever Hans began to get an enormous amount of publicity, and his picture appeared on postcards and liquor labels.

A special commission of respected Germans, some of them scientists, was organized to find out the real facts about the horse. Von Osten, sixty-five at the time, was extremely cooperative with the members of the commission. The final report of the commission stated that there was no evidence of trickery or fraud, but the

Clever Hans, the calculating horse, with his trainer, Wilhelm von Osten.

commission had no idea how smart the horse was or how he was able to count.

A subsequent investigation was conducted by Oskar Pfungst of the Psychological Institute at the University of Berlin. He believed that Clever Hans was trained, on purpose or accidentally, to respond to body cues, intentional or unintentional. He devised a series of experiments to prove his hypothesis, and he watched von Osten as much as he watched the horse. In addition, more than forty other persons, including Pfungst, worked with the horse during the course of the experiments.

Pfungst concluded that when the questioner knew the answer to a problem, Clever Hans was almost always correct; when the questioner didn't know the answer, the horse was usually wrong. When Clever Hans could actually see the questioner, he was usually correct; when the horse couldn't see the questioner, he was usually wrong.

Pfungst also noted that when Clever Hans was wrong, he always overtapped and never undertapped. Pfungst believed that when the questioner gave a body cue—such as leaning forward to observe the horse's hoof—Clever Hans would begin to tap; the body cue was the signal for the horse to begin tapping. When the horse tapped the final tap of the correct answer, the questioner inadvertently straightened up— the cue for the horse to stop tapping. The second cue, the body straightening up, was the reason the horse always overtapped, never undertapped, when he made an error.

What did Pfungst really prove? That Clever Hans wasn't able to independently solve math problems. The horse was able to learn from a cue given by one person and transfer that learning when working with another person. Pfungst never claimed that any kind of fraud was taking place. The cues were "unconscious," and Pfungst was never able to explain how a variety of those unconscious cues, given by dozens of different people, could produce the same answers from Clever Hans. In addition, Pfungst never adequately tested his leaning forward and leaning back theory.

Pfungst's conclusions were published in 1907 and the bottom line was clear—Clever Hans was not a mathematical genius. Von Osten was devastated by the report and he and Clever Hans went into seclusion. He became so distraught that he blamed his misfortunes more on the horse than on Pfungst, wishing that "Hans would spend the rest of his life pulling hearses."

When von Osten died in 1909, Clever Hans was given to horse trainer Karl Krall, who was also experimenting with the idea that horses were capable of independent thinking. Krall hoped that Clever Hans would be able to teach what he knew to Krall's other horses, but when that idea failed, Clever Hans faded into obscurity. Unfortunately, lost in the hoax controversy

was the fact that Clever Hans was an extraordinary animal with an uncanny ability to learn.
—C.O.M.

For further reading: *Feral Children and Clever Animals*, by Douglas Keith Candland. New York: Oxford University Press, 1993.

THE CHAMPAWAT TIGER

For centuries, stories of man-eating tigers have been the stuff of legends—the kind of stories big brothers tell little brothers to ensure sleepless nights. However, in the mountains of Asia, these legends have all too often come true.

Of all known man-eaters, the most prolific was the tigress of Champawat. Her nefarious career began in the early twentieth century in Nepal, where she was credited with 200 deaths over a four-year period. Continuously hounded by hunters and angry villagers, the tigress crossed the border into India sometime in 1907. Establishing her home in the hill country around Naini Tal, the Champawat tiger killed another 236 people within four years.

Although many attempts were made to destroy the man-eater, she continued her rampage until she was finally brought down in 1911 by the famous hunter and tiger killer, Jim Corbett. Corbett was responsible for destroying at least a dozen man-eating tigers, who had killed approximately 1,500 people among them. This latest killer was brought to his attention when he heard of the death of a woman in the village of Pali. When Corbett arrived, he discovered that the villagers had refused to leave their homes for five days. Corbett tracked the animal to nearby Champawat, where it had already made its 436th kill. When Corbett found the tiger it was eating a human leg. With a small army of 298 volunteers, Corbett trailed his quarry to a narrow gorge. Corbett fired four shots, hitting the animal twice. One of the shots proved fatal, finally bringing an end to the tigress's reign of terror. The villagers chopped up the body into little pieces and distributed them to their children to wear as lockets.
—K.A.R.

THE PIGEON HERO OF WORLD WAR I

On October 4, 1918, American soldiers fighting in the Argonne Forest in France found themselves not only surrounded and shelled by the Germans but also under attack by their own army. For days the soldiers, part of the Seventy-seventh Division of the U.S. Army, had been fighting off German soldiers. Under the command of Major Charles W. Whittlesey, the Americans had suffered many casualties and had almost run out of rations and medical supplies. Faced with the additional "friendly fire" that kept growing heavier, Whittlesey penned a note to his superiors at division headquarters at Rampont: "We are along the road parallel 276.4. Our own artillery is dropping a barrage directly on us. For Heaven's sake, stop it!"

The only way to get the message to headquarters, about twenty-five miles away, was via carrier pigeon. Whittlesey had six pigeons. As he sent them up, one by one, they were killed by German marksmen. The final pigeon to be sent up was Cher Ami (dear friend), the message encased in a capsule tied to his leg.

As soon as Cher Ami was released, he made a few wide circles and then landed on the branch of a nearby tree, where he leisurely began to preen his feathers. Whittlesey and the unit's pigeon handler, Sergeant Richards, shouted and waved their hands in an effort to motivate Cher Ami. They even tossed stones at the pigeon, but nothing worked. Finally, Richards, dodging enemy fire, climbed the tree and shook the branch that held Cher Ami. The pigeon took off.

Cher Ami had not been flying for long when he was shot and fell to the ground. Back in the air a few minutes later, the pigeon was hit again but continued to make his way "home" to Rampont. By the time Cher Ami arrived at his destination, he had lost one eye, a leg, and had been shot in the breast. But the message was still attached to his shattered leg and the bombing of Americans, by Americans, stopped.

For his heroism, Cher Ami received the Distinguished Service Medal from the United States and the Croix de Guerre from France. After recuperating, the pigeon was sent to Washington, D.C., to be cared for by the U.S. Signal Corps. When the famous pigeon died in 1919, he was put on display at the Smithsonian Institution.

—C.O.M.

THE LOYAL DOG

Every morning Hachi, a white Akita dog, accompanied his master, Eisaburo Ueno, to the Shibuya railroad station in Tokyo. Ueno, a professor of agriculture at Tokyo University, returned on an evening train and Hachi was always there to greet him. However, one day in 1925 Professor Ueno suffered a heart attack at school and died.

> A dog is the only thing on earth that loves you more than you love yourself.
>
> Josh Billings,
> The Complete Works of Josh Billings, 1919

For the rest of his life—another ten years—Hachi returned every evening to the train station, where he patiently waited for his master. When the professor didn't arrive, the dog sadly went home. Even though he was eventually abandoned by the professor's family, Hachi never failed to meet the evening trains,

and he became a familiar sight to Japanese travelers. When Hachi died he was at Shibuya station, still hopeful that the professor was on the next train.

Today a statue of Hachi sits outside of Shibuya station and passersby put wreaths around the statue's neck and leave small gifts. In 1987 Japanese filmmakers made a feature-length movie about Hachi to honor the dog that has become a national symbol of loyalty and devotion.

—C.O.M.

RIN TIN TIN

On September 15, 1918, during the last days of World War I, a group of American servicemen in Lorraine, France, stumbled upon a German shepherd and her litter of puppies in the bombed-out remains of an abandoned war-dog station. One of the GIs, Lee Duncan, adopted two of the puppies and brought them home to California. One of the dogs died en route, but the other, named Rin Tin Tin, after a good-luck doll carried by many French soldiers, became one of the most well known movie stars of his day.

Rin Tin Tin starred in some of the most popular silent movies of the 1920s for Warner Brothers. His films included Where the North Begins, Clash of the Wolves, and Dogs of the Regiment. His first "talkie" was Frozen River, released in 1929, in which "Rinty" barked his few lines. Darryl F. Zanuck, later the head of

An autographed photo of the real Rin Tin Tin.

Twentieth Century Fox, wrote many of Rinty's scripts and credited the dog with much of his own success. Rin Tin Tin did all of his own stunts, which included such feats as leaping through closed windows (made of candy), opening locked doors, and pulling the correct levers (in their proper order) to close the locks of a dam. The hardworking canine also starred in his own radio series. He had at his disposal a valet, a chef, and a chauffeur, as well as his own car.

The original Rin Tin Tin died on August 10, 1932, while being cradled by Duncan and his neighbor, actress Jean Harlow. Rin Tin Tin's son and namesake made feature films throughout the 1930s and also starred in popular adventure serials such as *The Wolf Dog* and *The Adventures of Rex and Rinty*. Another of Rinty's descendents made a film in 1947, while a fourth Rin Tin Tin starred in a popular television series in the 1950s and 1960s.

—K.A.R.

THE POOCH POW
Judy, a pedigree pointer, was born in Shanghai, China, in 1936. She escaped from the Shanghai Dog Kennels before she was six months old and found refuge with a shopkeeper. Japanese sailors, however, ransacked the shop, beat the shopkeeper, and kicked the dog savagely. A young girl found her and returned the pup to the kennel.

British sailors adopted her and she became the mascot of Royal Navy gunships that patrolled the Yangtze River. The dog's instinctual pointing and barking served as an alarm to alert her mates to the threats of both river pirates and enemy aircraft. She once inadvertently went overboard and was saved from drowning by her fellow crew members.

Judy went on to serve on the HMS *Grasshopper* and saw action in the Malay-Singapore campaign. When Singapore fell to the Japanese, the *Grasshopper* tried to sail off for Java but fell victim to enemy aircraft that bombed the ship on February 14, 1942. Judy and the rest of the crew survived the attack and found refuge on an uninhabited island. Once again, the dog faced death along with her human companions but managed to avoid such fate when she discovered a freshwater spring.

The survivors were eventually captured by the Japanese and brought to a prisoner-of-war camp on Sumatra. It was here that Judy became attached to the man who would become her best friend, Leading Aircraftsman Frank Williams.

When the inmates were transferred to a camp in Singapore, Judy was to be left behind. Her companions, however, were as loyal to her as she was to them and Williams managed to successfully smuggle her along in a sack. But the ship taking them to Singapore was torpedoed on June 26, 1944. Five hundred of the 700 prisoners were killed and Judy was separated from Williams. Miraculously, they were reunited three days later.

Transferred to yet another POW camp in central Sumatra, Judy faced death again when the camp's commandant ordered her to be killed. Once more the dog was saved by going into hiding. Two days later the camp was liberated.

Judy was taken to England after Japan's surrender and was awarded the Dickin Medal for her heroism and bravery during war. She had not only confronted death and managed to survive six times but had also given birth to nine puppies during her years of internment. She is the only dog ever to have been officially registered as a prisoner of war. Judy died in February 1950 and is buried in Nachingwea, Tanzania.

—R.N.K.

For further reading: *The Judy Story: The Dog with Six Lives*, by E. Varley. London: Souvenir Press, 1973.

THE DOG HERO OF WORLD WAR II
Chips, a husky-collie-shepherd mix, was a sentry with the U.S. Army Third Infantry Division. One of the first war dogs to be sent overseas in World War II, he arrived in Sicily in July 1943 after several months in North Africa. It was in Italy that he performed a heroic feat. One night he broke away from his handler, Private John Rowell, and attacked an enemy machine gun pillbox. Despite being shot twice, Chips actually seized one man and forced four more to surrender. The army awarded him the Purple Heart and Silver Star. Later, officials took these honors away because they were "contrary to Army policy." To make up for it, his company presented him unofficially with a battle star and campaign ribbons. Chips was discharged from the army on December 10, 1945, and returned to his owner, Edward Wrens of Pleasantville, New York.

—A.E.

THE FIRST ANIMALNAUT
On November 3, 1957, the first living creature to orbit the earth was launched into space by the Soviet Union. The two-year-old female dog aboard *Sputnik II* was named Laika and she was a mix of Pomeranian, Samoyed, and sheepdog. One of the main purposes of the mission was to study the effects of space travel on a live animal in order to prepare for sending human beings into space.

Laika was hooked up to feeding devices that she had been trained to use when a bell rang. The dog's vital signs were constantly monitored and the results transmitted to Earth. Soviet scientists issued periodic reports that Laika was in good physical shape and adapting well to weightlessness.

In 1957, Laika became the first space traveler. Here she is seen just before being sealed into Sputnik II and launched into space, where she died of oxygen starvation after seven days.

Animal lovers around the world were skeptical about Laika's chances for survival. Animal rights groups were flooded with letters and phone calls, pressing them to act on Laika's behalf. One group in the United Kingdom called for a moment of silence every day in honor of Laika. And a German newspaper wrote: "For a few days, black and white, democrats and communists, republicans and royalists in all countries, islands, and continents have one feeling, one language, one direction . . . our feeling of compassion for this little living being twirling helplessly over our heads."

The Soviets never planned to bring Laika back to Earth, since a recovery system for doing so had not yet been invented. Confined in a small space and surrounded by numerous technical instruments, the dog circled the earth for a week and died when her oxygen supply ran out. The Soviet scientist who was her trainer made the official announcement of her death, claiming that she was "comfortable to the end" and died "painlessly."

—C.O.M.

THE BIRD WHO LOVED TO TALK AND TALK . . .
Sparkie was a budgerigar, or "budgie," a type of parakeet that originally came from Australia. Owned by Mrs. Mattie Williams of Newcastle, England, Sparkie had a vocabulary of 531 words and could speak 354 sentences. His first words were "Pretty Sparkie," appropriate for a handsome bird with a green back, bright yellow head, and peacock blue tail.

Sparkie first gained widespread attention after winning a bird-talking contest in 1958 that was sponsored by the British Broadcasting Corporation (BBC). He easily out-chattered the other contestants and quickly moved on to a lucrative advertising contract that called for

him to sell bird seed on television. Sparkie also had a hit record that taught other budgies how to speak. His professional career was so successful that he had to open his own bank account and sign up for his own income tax number.

Sparkie probably had a competitive edge over the other budgies, since his owner was an English teacher. But Mrs. Williams was convinced that the bird was able to do more than just mimic words and sentences. He could construct his own sentences, and his first original creation was "Mama, put your bells back." Sparkie also recognized his owner's friends and relatives and was able to greet them by name. In addition, he loved to recite nursery rhymes; among his favorites were "Little Jack Horner" and "Mary Had a Little Lamb."

Sparkie's reputation stemmed from his versatility as much as from his vocabulary. There have been other birds who had a greater vocabulary. Most notable is a female African grey parrot named Prudle, also of Great Britain, who won twelve consecutive titles as "best talking parrot-like bird" at the annual National Cage and Aviary Bird Show in London. Prudle, who retired, undefeated, from competition in 1977, was able to speak 800 words.

Sparkie died on December 4, 1962. His last words were "I love Mama . . . Sparkie." News of his demise was covered by newspapers around the world. His owner had him stuffed, put on his favorite perch, and placed in the Hancock Museum in Newcastle.

—C.O.M.

THE SENSUAL LION
If a ninety-year-old man should suddenly find himself in complete control of a harem of seven beautiful young maidens, what results could be expected? When a Mexican circus went bankrupt, the owner could no longer afford to feed his animals, so he gave one elderly male lion to the southern California wildlife preserve called Lion Country Safari, on February 13, 1971.

Frasier, the scrawny, scruffy lion, was clearly past his prime. He was bleary-eyed, suffered from arthritis and rheumatism, and even had trouble walking. He was in his early twenties, even though most male lions do not live past age fifteen. He was nursed back to health and then introduced into a pride consisting of seven young females. Putting Frasier in with the females was a joke. Previously, the hard-to-please lionesses had spurned at least five young, virile males; one would-be lover was badly mauled. But now the unexpected happened.

The morning after Frasier was turned loose, the lionesses were found basking placidly in the sun, and a very tired but happy Frasier was lying on his back, paws in the air. He had obviously been a most phenomenal pussycat during the night. In the days that followed, whenever this lady-killer was hungry, the adoring young fe-

Frasier the sensual lion (with tongue hanging out), relaxing with members of his satisfied harem.

males fetched his food. (Frasier was toothless and had to be fed ground meat.) A lioness took her place on each side of his overaged bones when he decided to take a walk. His great success as a lover—he sired twenty-two cubs in sixteen months—made him a national sex symbol. His exploits attracted national attention, and Frasier T-shirts, watches, and caps were marketed with such favorable results that attendance at Lion Country Safari took a tremendous leap. Frasier was named Father of the Year in a congressional resolution.

His amorous activities finally took their toll. He died in his sleep on July 13, 1972, and was buried at the Laguna Hills, California, preserve. They had inserted him into the pride as a joke, but the old cat took the challenge seriously. The results proved once again that the art of making love knows neither time nor season.

—N.J.M.R.

THE TALKING GORILLA

Man's dream of being able to communicate with animals is an ancient one. The idea that a member of the ape family might prove capable of being taught to comprehend and speak English dates back at least to the seventeenth century. The English diarist Samuel Pepys made an entry on August 24, 1661, that documents his encounter with a baboon. Pepys wrote, "It already understands much English, and I am of the mind it might be taught to speak or make signs."

A gorilla named Koko, born at the San Francisco Zoo on July 4, 1971, 310 years after Pepys's speculation, has proved that a great ape can indeed be taught to use language. In 1972 a graduate student in developmental psychology named Francine Patterson initiated the gorilla's incredible education. Patterson began teaching her American Sign Language, and the physi-

cally imposing female (five feet four inches tall and weighing 290 pounds) quickly showed herself to be an adept student.

Patterson and her assistants began by teaching Koko the signs for *food, drink,* and *more.* Eventually Koko was able to transfer concepts. For example, she was taught that *dirty* referred to feces, but soon she applied it to people and events as well. She also chose her own meaning for certain signs, such as *good* to mean "yes" and *lip* to mean "woman." She learned to make jokes, and once she was interviewed on television.

Koko has been learning for more than two decades, a span of time during which she has mastered about 900 different signs and become the subject of the longest uninterrupted study in interspecies communication ever conducted.

In order to discover whether or not Koko can pass on her acquired language skills, the researchers working with Koko at California's Woodside Gorilla Foundation embarked on a search for a suitable mate for her in 1983. Koko was shown videotapes of several prospective suitors. Only Bongo, a gorilla kept in an Italian zoo, elicited a positive response from the discerning Koko. Bongo's keepers, however, doomed the possibility of a relationship by refusing to part with him. Koko remained disinterested in all other likely mates until being introduced, in 1994, to Ndume, a twelve-year-old from the Chicago Zoo. They were quickly attracted to each other.

Critics of Patterson's experiments with Koko grumble that the gorilla has never learned grammar or how to ask a question. Nonetheless, there is no doubt that Koko and other gorillas can *answer* questions, usually with one-word signs.

—R.N.K.

THE WAYWARD WHALE

When a forty-ton humpback whale took a wrong turn at San Francisco in October 1985, he became a worldwide celebrity. West of California, the Pacific humpback migration swings right toward Hawaii, but Humphrey, as newspapers dubbed him, turned left. Trailed by Coast Guard vessels and hundreds of private craft, he swam under the Golden Gate Bridge and through the busy shipping lanes of San Francisco Bay to spend twenty-five days wandering the Sacramento–San Joaquin River delta. In that maze of narrow waterways, the levee-ringed islands often lie lower than the freshwater shallows. Humphrey's sunburned back towered above the cars and pickup trucks of spectators lining the levee roads.

An endangered species, Pacific humpbacks numbered about 1,200 at the time. Whale experts still have no ready explanation for Humphrey's unprecedented odyssey. To lure him seaward, the experts played recorded whale songs under water. Finally, in Shag Slough, seventy-five miles inland and twenty miles from Sacramento, he reversed his forty-foot length and headed back the way he had come. He hesitated long and hard at the clanking Rio Vista drawbridge but eventually reached the ocean.

In ensuing years Humphrey was regularly spotted during the annual whale migration—until in 1990 he entered San Francisco Bay again and beached himself on the mud flats near Candlestick Park. Out of water a whale's own weight will cause it to suffocate. Although rescuers coaxed Humphrey back to the open sea, he has not been sighted since October 1990, and researchers assume he no longer survives.

—J.F.K.

THE WHITE BUFFALO

On August 20, 1994, a female white buffalo was born on the farm of Dave and Valerie Heider in Janesville, Wisconsin. The Heiders were delighted with this oddity but went on with their daily lives. However, as word of the birth got out, Native Americans began appearing from hundreds of miles away to pay homage and leave sacred offerings. As the crowds grew, the Heiders started reading about American Indian legends and myths to try to understand what was happening to them.

The tribes living on the Great Plains consid-ered the white buffalo to be sacred. The Cheyenne, Mandan, Arapaho, and Pawnee all accorded it special powers, which their medicine men invoked during prayer and healing rituals. Warrior chiefs, believing the white buffalo capable of protecting them from enemies, wore robes fashioned from its coat into battle.

Several centuries ago, when more than 60 million bison ranged across the North American continent from Mexico to Canada, from what is now Pennsylvania to beyond the Rocky Mountains, a white buffalo was extremely rare. It is believed that only one in about 5 million births resulted in the delivery of a white calf. By the 1880s, because of the almost complete destruction of the bison herds, the chances of a white buffalo being born became infinitesimal. So when the Heider's white calf was born, it was not surprising that they named her Miracle.

According to Sioux Indian cosmology, White Buffalo Woman would come some day to bring peace and prosperity and to unify the nations of the four colors—black, red, yellow, and white. The Plains Indians believe that the spirit of White Buffalo Woman lives in Miracle. She turned black in January 1995, red in June, and yellow in November of that year. In spring 1996, she returned to a silvery white.

—R.N.K. and D.W.

11 EXTINCT ANIMALS LOST IN THE TWENTIETH CENTURY

1. QUELILI (GUADELUPE CARACARA)

A large brown hawk, the quelili flourished on the Pacific island of Guadelupe, 140 miles (224 kilometers) off the coast of Baja California and 180 miles (290 kilometers) southwest of San Diego, California. A ruthless bird of prey, it ran afoul of local goatherders who accused the quelili of attacking newborn and baby goats. Using rifles and poison, the goatherders had almost eliminated the quelili by the 1860s. Once word of its scarcity got out, collectors moved in to finish the job.

In 1897 an adventurer named Harry Drent captured four quelili and put them on display in a large cage in San Diego. He turned down opportunities to sell them, insisting that he be paid $150 per bird. There were no takers at such an exorbitant price and the four quelili died within a month.

Later that year a fisherman brought a quelili to San Diego and also tried to sell it for $150. Again there were no takers. Disgusted, the fisherman killed the bird, cut off its wings and threw its body into the ocean. Some boys found the body and brought it to taxidermist Frank Holzner, who already owned two of Drent's deceased quelilis. Holzner tracked down the fisherman, bought the wings, reconstructed the rare bird, and displayed it in his store as "the Last Guadelupe Eagle." Two weeks later the store burned down.

In fact there was still one more flock of quelili left on the island—but not for long. On the afternoon of December 1, 1900, Rollo Beck, an ornithologist and collector, spotted eleven quelili flying toward him. Mistakenly believing them to be abundant, he shot, killed, and "secured" nine of them. The other two were never seen again.

2. PASSENGER PIGEON

In 1813 passenger pigeons were so numerous that naturalist John James Audubon calculated that a single flock in Kentucky contained 1.1 billion birds. In 1850 there were estimated to be 9 billion passenger pigeons in North America, and as late as 1876 a colony twenty-eight miles long and more than three miles wide was reported in Michigan. Yet a mere thirty-five years later, there was only one passenger pigeon still alive.

Humans had been killing and eating passenger pigeons for centuries, but in the 1870s shooting and trapping pigeons became an obsession among hunters. Millions of baby pigeons were sent to market to serve the public taste for squab. Their elders were trapped and used as targets in shooting contests, while still others were killed just for the sake of "sport," although until the very end, passenger pigeons were so plentiful and so easy to kill, it is hard to imagine what satisfaction hunters gained in bringing them down.

By the mid-1880s it was clear that the passenger pigeon was endangered, but the hunters paid little attention. In the 1890s a few states enacted laws to protect the birds, but it was too little, too late. The last wild passenger pigeon was shot to death by a young boy near Sargents in Pike County, Ohio, on March 24, 1900. Its stuffed skin is now preserved in the Ohio State Museum.

There were still a few passenger pigeons living in zoos, but by 1909 even their number was down to three—two males and a female, Martha, residing at the Cincinnati Zoo. One of the males died in April 1909. The remaining couple built a nest and Martha laid some eggs, but all the eggs proved infertile. When the male died on July 10, 1910, the survival of the species that once filled the skies for days on end was doomed. Zoo officials offered a reward to anyone who could find a mate for Martha, but none could be found. Martha herself was found dead at 1:00 P.M. on September 1, 1914. Her body was packed into 300 pounds of ice and shipped to the Smithsonian Institution, where it was examined, stuffed, mounted, and put on permanent display.

3. CAROLINA PARAKEET
The only member of the parrot family native to the United States, the green, yellow, and orange Carolina parakeet was once common in the deciduous forests of the East and the South. Trappers captured the birds and sold them to be used as caged pets, but their downfall came when settlers cut down the forests and planted fruit orchards and fields of grain. The Carolina parakeets took a liking to apple and pear seeds and corn, destroying the crops before they could ripen. The farmers, their livelihood threatened, shot as many parakeets as they could. This turned out to be quite easy. Over the centuries the Carolina parakeets had developed an effective defense against predators: whenever one of their number was wounded, they would gather around him until the enemy fled. But what was effective against other animals proved suicidal with human hunters, who fired away at will at the gathering horde.

The last Carolina parakeet in the wild was probably a female killed near Orlando, Florida, on December 4, 1913. Before long, the only Carolina parakeets left were Lady Jane and Incas, an elderly couple who were cagemates for more than thirty years at the Cincinnati Zoo, the home of Martha, the last passenger pigeon. Lady Jane died in the late summer of 1917.

Incas pined away gradually, dying in the company of his keepers on February 21, 1918. Like Martha, Incas was supposed to be shipped to the Smithsonian Institution, but his body disappeared en route and was never recovered.

4. BARBARY LION
The Barbary lion once roamed all of the forested areas of North Africa. They became famous when they were trapped, shipped to Rome, and put to work in the arena eating Christian martyrs and serving as victims for gladiators. Over the centuries their habitat was destroyed by humans and the forests turned to deserts. By the twentieth century the Barbary lion could be found only in the wild woodlands of the Atlas Mountains in Morocco. The last one was shot to death in 1922.

5. HEATH HEN
A relative of the prairie chicken, the heath hen was so common in the open lands of New England that servants often refused employment unless they were promised that they would not have to eat heath hen more than a few times a week. But many factors worked against the harmless fowl, including overhunting and the introduction of cats and other domestic animals. Worst of all was the transformation of their prairie habitat into farmland. By 1830 the heath hen was extinct on the mainland United States and survived only on the island of Martha's Vineyard in Massachusetts. Even there the population had fallen to about fifty when, in 1908, a 1,600-acre reservation was established for their protection. By 1915 the heath hen population had grown to 2,000 and their revival appeared to be an environmental success story.

However, in the summer of 1916 a brush fire destroyed much of the heath hens' breeding area. Then came a brutal winter and an invasion of goshawks. In 1925 special wardens were hired to protect the heath hens against poachers and cats, 120 of which were killed (the cats, not the poachers). It was no use. By 1927 there were only thirteen heath hens left, by 1928 only two, and by 1930 only one. The last survivor became a tourist attraction and was almost run over by a car. He finally died, at age eight, on March 11, 1932.

6. TOOLACHE (GREY'S WALLABY)
One of the fastest and most beautiful members of the kangaroo family, the toolache was doomed by these very characteristics. Fur traders killed them for their pelts, and hunters pursued them for the challenge. In addition, during the early part of the twentieth century, the Australian government offered sixpence for any dead marsupial, so in times of economic hardship, even the swift toolache was a tempting target for poor Australians. By 1923 the only remaining wild toolache were a group of four-

teen living on Konetta Sheep Run ranch near the town of Robe. A well-meaning campaign to save the toolache by capturing them and moving them to a sanctuary on Kangaroo Island turned to disaster when several of the toolache ran themselves to death trying to escape their protectors. News of the toolache's endangered status attracted hunters to the sheep ranch; they shot to death as many as they could find. The last wild toolache died about 1940 and the last captive one passed on a few years later in the Adelaide Zoo.

7. WAKE ISLAND RAIL
A small, flightless bird, the Wake Island rail lived a peaceful existence, without enemies, until World War II when Japanese soldiers occupied the island. As the war moved to its climax, the Japanese garrison on Wake Island was cut off from supplies and the soldiers began to starve. One by one the defenseless birds were killed and eaten until none remained.

8. CARIBBEAN MONK SEAL
The Caribbean monk seal was the first New World animal to be sighted by Christopher Columbus and his crew in 1492. They were eight feet long and weighed about 400 pounds. Because they were slow moving and unsuspicious, they were easy to kill, and because they were fur bearing, people wanted to kill them. By 1850 the Caribbean monk seal was already scarce. The last significant population of 200 lived on the Triangle Keys off the Yucatan Peninsula. In 1911 a group of Mexican fishermen slaughtered all of them. A small colony was sighted in 1952 on Serranilla Bank in Jamaican waters, but they were never seen again.

9. PALESTINIAN PAINTED FROG
This tiny frog probably holds the record for shortest time between discovery and extinction. It lived on the swampy shore of Hula Lake on the Israeli-Syrian border. Two tadpoles were discovered in 1940 and put in a terrarium, where one of them ate the other one. In 1955 another specimen was captured by collector M. Costa, who observed and recorded its habits until it died. By 1956 an Israeli land-reclamation project had destroyed the painted frog's habitat and it disappeared forever.

10. MEXICAN SILVER GRIZZLY
The largest animal native to Mexico, the silver grizzly measured six feet from nose to tail and weighed up to 700 pounds. At one time they ranged as far north as the United States from California to Texas, but by the 1930s so many of them had been shot, poisoned, and trapped that they existed only in the remote Sierra del Nido in the state of Chihuahua. By 1960 only thirty silver grizzlies remained. In 1961 local ranchers, using poisons supplied by the U.S. Department of the Interior, began a campaign to finish off the great beast. In 1964 they succeeded.

11. EASTERN COUGAR (EASTERN PUMA)
The elusive eastern cougar has a checkered history as an extinct species. It once ranged from eastern Canada to the Carolinas, but because it preyed on livestock, several states offered bounties for killing them. In 1946 the cougar was declared extinct. Sightings continued to be made, however, particularly in New Brunswick and Virginia. In June 1973 the U.S. Department of the Interior upgraded the eastern cougar's status from "extinct" to "endangered." By 1990, however, it was considered extinct once again. Nonetheless, sightings have persisted at a rate of 200 a year. According to John Lutz of the Eastern Puma Research Network, "An Eastern cougar is like a U.F.O. with four feet. Hundreds of people report seeing them, but the authorities' position continues to be that they don't exist."

—D.W.

For further reading: The Doomsday Book of Animals, by David Day. New York: Viking Press, 1981. And Extinct Birds, by Errol Fuller. New York: Facts on File Publications, 1987.

9 LARGE ANIMALS DISCOVERED IN THE TWENTIETH CENTURY

In 1812 the "Father of Paleontology," Baron Georges Cuvier, rashly pronounced that "there is little hope of discovering new species" of large animals and that naturalists should concentrate on extinct fauna. In 1819 the American tapir was discovered, and since then a long list of "new" animals have disproved Cuvier's dictum. Even within the present century rather astounding zoological finds have been announced, and the fact remains that other animals are probably out there waiting to be "found" by modern scientists.

1. OKAPI
By saving a group of Congolese Pygmies from a German showman who wanted to take them to the 1900 Paris Exhibition, Sir Harry Johnston immediately gained their trust. He then began hearing stories about the okapi, a mule-sized animal with zebra stripes. In 1901 Sir Harry

sent a whole skin, two skulls, and a detailed description of the okapi to London, and it was found that the okapi had a close relationship to the giraffe. In 1919 the first live okapis were brought out of the Congo River basin, and in 1941 the Stanleyville Zoo witnessed the first birth of an okapi in captivity. The okapis, striking in appearance, became rare but popular attractions at the larger, more progressive zoological parks of the world.

2. MOUNTAIN NYALA
First discovered in the high mountains of southern Ethiopia in 1910, the misnamed mountain nyala is actually more closely related to the kudu than the nyala. The male has gently twisting horns almost four feet long and can weigh up to 450 pounds. The coat is a majestic grayish brown with white vertical stripes on the back. After the mountain nyala was first described by Richard Lydekker, the eminent British naturalist, it was ruthlessly hunted by field biologists and trophy seekers through some of the most inhospitable terrain in existence. The mountain nyala lives at heights above 9,000 feet, where the sun burns hotly in the day and the night temperatures fall to freezing. Its existence is presently threatened by illegal hunting as well as destruction of its habitat by loggers and ranchers.

3. PYGMY HIPPOPOTAMUS
Karl Hagenbeck, a famous German animal dealer, established a zoological garden near Hamburg that was the prototype of the modern open-air zoo. In 1909 Hagenbeck sent German explorer Hans Schomburgk to Liberia to check on rumors about a "giant black pig." After two years of jungle pursuit, Schomburgk finally spotted the animal thirty feet in front of him. It was big, shiny, and black, but the animal clearly was related to the hippopotamus, not the pig. Unable to catch it, he went home to Hamburg empty-handed. In 1912 Hans Schomburgk returned to Liberia, and to the dismay of his critics, he came back with five live pygmy hippos. A full-grown pygmy hippopotamus weighs only about 400 pounds, one-tenth the weight of the full-grown common hippopotamus.

4. KOMODO DRAGON
These giant monitor lizards are named for the rugged volcanic island of Komodo, part of the Lesser Sunda Islands of Indonesia. Unknown to science until 1912, the Komodo dragon can be as long as twelve feet and weigh more than 350 pounds. The discovery of the giant lizard was made by an airman who landed on Komodo Island and brought back incredible stories of monstrous dragons eating goats and pigs, and even attacking horses. At first no one believed him, but then the stories were confirmed by Major P. A. Ouwens, director of the Buitenzorg

Botanical Gardens in Java, who offered skins and photographs as proof. Soon live specimens were caught and exhibited. The world's largest living lizard is now a popular zoo exhibit.

5. CONGO PEACOCK
Some animal discoveries are made in museums. In 1913 the New York Zoological Society sent an unsuccessful expedition to the Congo in an attempt to bring back a live okapi. Instead, one of the team's members, Dr. James P. Chapin, brought back some native headdresses with curious, long, reddish brown feathers striped with black. None of the experts could identify them. In 1934 Chapin, on another of his frequent visits to the Congo, noticed similar feathers on two stuffed birds at the Tervueren Museum. They were labeled "Young Indian Peacocks," but Chapin immediately knew that was not what they were. As it turned out, a mining company in the Congo had donated them to the museum and called them "Indian peacocks," but Chapin soon discovered that they were a new species. The following year he flew down to the Congo and brought back seven birds. Chapin confirmed them as the first new bird genus discovered in forty years. They were not peacocks, after all, but pheasants. The Congo peacock is now commonly found in European and North American zoos.

6. KOUPREY
The kouprey is a large wild ox that was found along the Mekong River in Cambodia and Laos and has been the source of much controversy. It first came to the attention of Western scientists in 1936 when it showed up as a hunting trophy in the home of a French veterinarian. The following year the director of the Paris Vincennes Zoo, Professor Achille Urbain, went to northern Cambodia and reported that a new wild ox, unlike the gaur and the banteng, was to be seen in Cambodia. Other naturalists felt he was wrong and suggested that the kouprey might be just a hybrid of the gaur and the banteng. Finally, in 1961 a detailed anatomical study of the kouprey proved it to be so different from the area's other wild oxen that it might belong in a new genus, although many scientists continue to insist that it is not. Urbain's 1937 discovery was upheld. The Vietnam War was responsible for the death of many koupreys. A 1975 New York Zoological Society expedition was unable to capture any, although they did see a herd of fifty. It is feared that the kouprey might now be extinct.

7. BLACK-FACED LION TAMARIN MONKEY
Brazilian scientists found the black-faced lion tamarin monkey in June 1990 on the island of Superagui, along Brazil's heavily populated Atlantic coast, where less than 5 percent of the country's original Atlantic forest still remains. The amazing discovery led biologist Dr. Russell

Mittermeier, president of Conservation International, to say, "It's almost like finding a major new species in a suburb of Los Angeles." The monkey has a lionlike head and a gold coat. Its face, forearms, and tail are black. Prior to its discovery, there were only three known species of the lion tamarin monkey. It is estimated that fewer than two dozen of the new primate species exist. In 1992, two years after this species' discovery, another new species of monkey, the Maues marmoset, was found in Brazil—this time in a remote part of the Amazon rain forest. First spotted near the Maues River, a tributary of the Amazon, by Swiss biologist Marco Schwarz, the tiny monkey has a pink koala-like face and faint zebralike stripes.

8. SAO LA

According to British biologist John MacKinnon, who discovered the sao la in May 1992, the mammal "appears to be a cow that lives the life of a goat." Skulls, horns, and skins of the sao la were found by MacKinnon in the Vu Quang Nature Reserve, a pristine 150,000-acre rain forest in northwestern Vietnam near the Laotian border, during an expedition sponsored by the World Wildlife Fund. Known to the local Vietnamese as a "forest goat," the sao la—also called the Vu Quang ox—weighs about 220 pounds. Smaller than a cow but larger than a goat, the mammal has a dark brown shiny coat with white markings on its face. It has daggerlike straight horns about twenty inches long and two-toed concave hooves that enable it to maneuver through slippery and rugged mountain areas. While the animal had occasionally been spotted, trapped, and eaten by local hunters, scientists did not get to see a live example of the new species until June 1994, when a four-month-old female calf was captured. Unfortunately, the calf, and another adolescent sao la that was subsequently captured, died in October 1994; both died from an infection of the digestive system. MacKinnon estimates that only a few hundred sao las still exist, and the Vietnamese government has outlawed hunting or trapping the animal. However, the enormous publicity surrounding the discovery of the sao la caused numerous scientists and reporters to travel to Vietnam in search of the animal. Some television crews reportedly offered a huge bounty to local farmers to entice them to capture a sao la; four more sao las were found in 1994, but all eventually died. Environmentalists fear that the sao la could become extinct—a victim of its own popularity.

9. GIANT MUNTJAC DEER

Muntjacs, or barking deer, are a common food in Vietnam. But in April 1994, the World Wildlife Fund and the Vietnamese Ministry of Forestry announced that a new species of the mammal—the giant muntjac deer—was discovered in Vu Quang Nature Reserve, the same rain forest where the sao la had been found two years earlier. One and a half times larger than other muntjacs, the deer weighs about a hundred pounds and has eight-inch antlers that are bowed inward. It has a reddish coat and large canine teeth. While the initial identification of the giant muntjac was made from skulls and skins, a live animal was captured in Laos by a team of researchers working for the Wildlife Conservation Society. It is expected that other new species of animals will be found in the Vu Quang Nature Reserve, which miraculously escaped bombing and herbicide spraying during the Vietnam War. British biologist John MacKinnon calls the area "a corner of the world unknown to modern science" and "a biological gold mine."

—L.Co. and C.O.M.

10 ANIMALS TRIED FOR CRIMES

There has been a long and shocking tradition of punishing, excommunicating, and killing animals for real or supposed crimes. In medieval times, animals were even put on the rack to extort confessions of guilt. Cases have been recorded and documented involving such unlikely creatures as flies, locusts, snakes, mosquitoes, caterpillars, eels, snails, beetles, grasshoppers, dolphins, and most larger mammals. In seventeenth-century Russia, a goat was banished to Siberia. The belief that animals are morally culpable is happily out of fashion—but not completely, for even now, in the twentieth century, these travesties and comedies still occur.

1. TOO MUCH MONKEY BUSINESS

In 1905 the law against public cigarette smoking was violated in South Bend, Indiana. A showman's chimpanzee puffed tobacco in front of a crowd and was hauled before the court, where he was convicted and fined.

2. THE CRUEL DEATH OF "FIVE-TON MARY"

There are ancient records of the hangings of bulls and oxen, but there is only one known case of the hanging of an elephant—it happened in Erwin, Tennessee, on September 23, 1916. The Sparks Circus was stationed in Kingsport, Tennessee, when Mary, a veteran circus elephant, was being ridden to water by an inexperienced trainer, Walter Eldridge. On the way, Mary spotted a watermelon rind and headed for this snack. When Eldridge jerked hard on her head with a spear-tipped stick, Mary let out a loud trumpet, reached behind her with her trunk, and yanked the trainer off her back. Mary dashed Eldridge against a soft-drink stand and then walked over and stepped on his head. A Kingsport resident came running and fired five pistol shots into the huge animal. Mary groaned and shook but didn't die—in fact, she performed in that night's show. The next day the circus moved to Erwin, where "authorities" (no one is sure who) decreed that Mary should die on the gallows, to the great sorrow of her friends in the circus. She was taken to the Clinchfield railroad yards, where a large crowd was gathered. A chain was slung around her neck, and a 100-ton derrick hoisted her five feet into the air. The chain broke. The next chain held, and Mary died quickly. The grave for her five-ton corpse was dug with a steam shovel.

3. THE ELITIST RACEHORSE
Champion racehorse Minoru, owned by King Edward VII of England, reached the peak of his career on May 26, 1909, when he won the derby at Epsom Downs. For his retirement, Minoru was sent to a stud farm in Russia, but the 1917 Russian Revolution put a quick end to Minoru's tranquil life. The Bolsheviks, out to destroy all symbols of wealth and privilege, raided the stables and farms of the elite and killed any horses they could find. Because Minoru was truly an elitist horse, he was paraded through town, put on trial, found guilty of crimes against the proletariat, and beheaded.

4. CANINE CONVICT NO. C2559
Pep, a male Labrador retriever in Pike County, Pennsylvania, belonged to neighbors of Governor and Mrs. Gifford Pinchot. In 1924 Pep, a friendly dog, unaccountably went wild one hot summer day and killed Mrs. Pinchot's cat. An enraged Governor Pinchot presided over an immediate hearing and then a trial. Poor Pep had no legal counsel, and the evidence against him was damning. Pinchot sentenced him to life imprisonment. The no-doubt bewildered beast was taken to the state penitentiary in Philadelphia. The warden, also bewildered, wondered whether he should assign the mutt an ID number like the rest of the cons. Tradition won out, and Pep became No. C2559. The story has a happy ending: Pep's fellow inmates lavished him with affection, and he was allowed to switch cellmates at will. The prisoners were building a new penitentiary in Graterford, Pennsylvania, and every morning the enthusiastic dog boarded the bus for work upon hearing his number called. When the prison was completed, Pep was one of the first to move in. In 1930, after six years in prison (forty-two dog years), Pep died of old age.

5. A HOOF FOR A HOOF
The Wild West custom of killing a horse responsible for the death of a human was reenacted by a group of Chicago gangsters in 1924. When the infamous Nails Morton died in Lincoln Park after being thrown from a riding horse, his buddies in Dion O'Banion's gang sought revenge. They kidnapped the animal from its stable at gunpoint and took it to the scene of the crime, where they solemnly executed it.

6. IT'S A DOG'S LIFE
In 1933 four dogs in McGraw, New York, were prosecuted to the full extent of the law for biting six-year-old Joyce Hammond. In a full hearing before an audience of 150 people, their lawyer failed to save them from execution by the county veterinarian. Proclaimed Justice A. P. McGraw: "I know the value of a good dog. But this is a serious case. . . . The dogs are criminals of the worst kind."

7. MONKEYING AROUND
Makao, a young cercopithecoid monkey, escaped from his master's apartment in Paris and wandered into an empty studio nearby. He bit into a tube of lipstick, destroyed some expensive knickknacks, and "stole" a box that was later recovered—empty. The victims of Makao's pranks filed a complaint stating that the box had contained a valuable ring. The monkey's owner contended that his pet could not possibly have opened such a box. On January 23, 1962, Makao was ordered to appear in court, where he deftly opened a series of boxes. His defense ruined, Makao's master was held liable for full damages.

8. THE RISING COST OF AIR TRAVEL
At Tripoli in 1963, seventy-five carrier pigeons received the death sentence. A gang of smugglers had trained the birds to carry bank notes from Italy, Greece, and Egypt into Libya. The court ordered the pigeons to be killed because "they were too well trained and dangerous to be let loose." The humans were merely fined.

9. LAST-MINUTE ESCAPE
On September 30, 1982, Tucker, a 140-pound bull mastiff, ran into a neighbor's yard and attacked the neighbor's black miniature poodle, Bonnie. Tucker's owner, Eric Leonard, freed the poodle from Tucker's mouth, but the poodle had suffered critical injuries and died. A district court in Augusta, Maine, ruled that Tucker was a danger to other dogs and should be killed by intravenous injection. Leonard appealed to the Maine Supreme Court but it upheld the lower court's ruling. In 1984, as Tucker awaited

execution in an animal shelter, someone entered the shelter and stole the dog. What happened to Tucker is unknown.

10. DEATH-ROW DOG

The long arm of the law almost took the life of a 110-pound Akita named Taro, who got into trouble on Christmas Day of 1990. Owned by Lonnie and Sandy Lehrer of Hayworth, New Jersey, Taro injured the Lehrers' ten-year-old niece, but how the injury occurred was in dispute. Police and doctors who inspected the injury said the dog bit the girl's lower lip. The Lehrers said the child provoked the dog and that while protecting himself, Taro scratched her lip. Taro had never before hurt a human being, but he had been in three dogfights and had killed a dog during one of the fights. A panel of local authorities ruled that Taro fell under the state's vicious-dog law and sentenced the Akita to death. A three-year legal nightmare ensued as the Lehrers fought their way through municipal court, superior court, a state appeals court, and finally the New Jersey Supreme Court. While the legal battle raged on, Taro remained on death row at Bergen County Jail in Hackensack, where he was kept in a climate-controlled cell and was allowed two exercise walks a day. By the time his execution day neared, the dog had become an international celebrity. Animal rights activist and former actress Brigitte Bardot pleaded for clemency; a businessman from Kenya raised money to save the dog. Thousands of animal lovers wrote to the Lehrers and offered to adopt the dog. Even the dog's jailers and the assemblyman behind the vicious-dog law interceded on behalf of Taro. But when the courts failed to free the dog, the final verdict fell to Governor Christine Todd Whitman. Although the governor didn't exactly pardon the Akita, she agreed to release him on three conditions: Taro would be exiled from New Jersey; Taro must have new owners; Taro's new owners, or the Lehrers, must assume all financial liability for the dog's future actions. The Lehrers agreed, and the dog was released in February 1994, after spending three years in jail. The Lehrers subsequently found a new home for Taro in Pleasantville, New York. When all the costs of the canine death-row case were added up, the total exceeded $100,000.

—A.W. and C.O.M.

THE WOLF CHILDREN

"Two children live in a wolf's lair—Bishop's amazing story—Girl who barked—Ate with mouth in dish!"

So ran the front-page story in the *Westminster Gazette*, a London newspaper, on October 22, 1926—but was it a hoax? It began in India in October 1920 with the Reverend J. A. L. Singh, a missionary who ran the Orphanage of Midnapore, sixty-five miles west of Calcutta. He often combed the jungle for natives to capture and convert, and on one of these outings, he heard of the *manush-bagha* (man-beasts)—ghosts who haunted the jungle near the Santal village of Godamuri (Ghorarbandha). Terrified natives asked Singh to exorcise the demons.

What he found, he wrote in his diary, was "a white-ant mound as high as a two-story building," inhabited by a wolf family. While watching them leave through holes at the base of the mound, Singh and his party saw the "ghosts"—two pale creatures running on all fours behind the animals. Some days later, on October 17, Singh's men returned, killed the mother wolf with bows and arrows, and dug out the mound. Inside were two wild children curled up with the wolf cubs, baring their teeth and resisting capture. With makeshift nets, Singh separated them; he carried them to the orphanage in bamboo cages.

The girls, who were not sisters, were estimated to be three years old and five or six years old. Had the children been abandoned by their parents, or had they been stolen by the she-wolf for food, and then raised instead with her cubs? Had she nursed them? Since the girls were not sisters, the wolf had evidently repeated the experiment.

Singh and his wife named the girls Kamala and Amala. Attempts were immediately begun to civilize them: they were made to wear loincloths, which they tried to tear off. They growled, bared their teeth, and would eat only with the orphanage dogs, who accepted them as their own. They refused all vegetable food, and ate only milk, raw meat, mice and cockroaches that they caught, or dirt and pebbles. Singh built them a cage, in which they huddled during the day, avoiding the light. They became animated only at night, pacing and howling continuously. They showed liveliness only when they were taken outside, when eating raw meat, or after dark. Slowly and steadily, Mrs. Singh made efforts to "humanize" them, but the results were minimal.

Almost a year after their capture, both girls fell ill with dysentery and worms. Kamala recovered, but after two weeks Amala died. Singh said that two tears fell from Kamala's eyes, and she was severely withdrawn and distraught for weeks after the death.

Kamala slowly recovered, and in the next eight years she responded bit by bit to Mrs.

Kamala the Wolf Child lapping her food, circa 1925.

Singh's attention. She learned to stand on her knees, and then to walk upright, to drink from a glass, to speak about thirty words, and even to run simple errands. For all this, her closest relationships were with the orphanage animals, especially a hyena cub, which Reverend Singh had brought for her to play with.

The Singhs fed Kamala a mixed diet, with very little raw meat, and this may have severely weakened her health. In the last two years of her life, she was increasingly sick. Because of her ill health, Reverend Singh declined an offer to display her on tour in America. On November 13, 1929, she died at the age of fourteen or fifteen.

Despite decades of controversy and academic argument, it appears that Singh's diary account of Kamala and Amala's stay in the orphanage was not a hoax. However, what remains a mystery is how he found them. More than fifty years later, author Charles Maclean tracked down a witness, Lasa Marandi, who confirmed that Singh was present when the children were removed from the ant hill. However, Singh himself often told reporters and others that Santal tribesmen had found the children and taken them to him. Singh may have made up this version to keep from his mission superiors the fact that he was out hunting and raiding villages for converts, or he may have made up the first version to enhance his role in the discovery. It is this uncertainty that led critics to claim that Kamala and Amala had not been raised by a wolf mother, but that they were autistic children whom villagers were trying to get rid of. There is, however, no evidence to support this critique and the wolf girls of Midnapore remain the best-recorded case of children who were raised by animals.

—A.W.

For further reading: *The Wolf Children*, by Charles Maclean. New York: Hill and Wang, 1977.

QUOTEBOOK: ANIMALS

The great pleasure of a dog is that you may make a fool of yourself with him and not only will he not scold you, he will make a fool of himself too.

Samuel Butler,
The Notebooks of Samuel Butler, 1912

Cats seem to go on the principle that it never does any harm to ask for what you want.

Joseph Wood Krutch,
"February," *The Twelve Seasons*, 1949

Man is the only animal that can remain on friendly terms with the victims he intends to eat until he eats them.

Samuel Butler,
The Notebooks of Samuel Butler, 1912

Ants are so much like human beings as to be an embarrassment. They farm fungi, raise aphids as livestock, launch armies into war, use chemical sprays to alarm and confuse enemies, capture slaves, engage in child labor, exchange information ceaselessly. They do everything but watch television.

Lewis Thomas,
The Lives of a Cell, 1974

Chapter 7

TRAVEL AND TRANSPORTATION

WHO REALLY DISCOVERED THE NORTH POLE?

Polar exploration is at once the cleanest and most isolated way of having a bad time which has been devised.

Apsley Cherry-Gerrard, *The Worst Journey in the World*, 1922

THE EXPLOIT

For centuries men had striven to reach the North Pole, first as a means of finding a trade route to the Orient and later as an end in itself. During the 1800s, expeditions of Englishmen, Norwegians, Americans, and Italians inched closer and closer to the unmarked point where lines of latitude and longitude meet at ninety degrees north. By the turn of the century, means of travel had improved to such an extent that feeling was high that the Pole would be reached soon. And indeed discovery of the North Pole was claimed in 1909—by two different men.

THE CONTENDERS AND THEIR STORIES

FREDERICK COOK

Responding to a newspaper ad, twenty-six-year-old New York–born Dr. Frederick Cook applied for a position as surgeon on an Arctic expedition in 1891. The expedition's leader, U.S. Navy lieutenant Robert Peary, hired him, and the two men became friends during the next two years on the Greenland glaciers. Peary praised Cook for his skills both as a doctor and as an explorer.

After leaving Peary in 1892, Cook explored Greenland in 1893 and 1894 and then returned to New York to practice medicine. But by 1897 he was off on an Antarctic expedition. For his role in this expedition, he was knighted by the king of Belgium. In 1901 he rejoined Peary in Greenland.

Cook continued to seek out challenges. In 1906 he claimed to have scaled Mount McKinley in Alaska. He subsequently wrote a book entitled *To the Top of the Continent* in which he described his feat.

Cook then took on the most important challenge of his career—the attainment of the North Pole.

Telling the press he was going on a hunting trip, Cook sailed to Annoatok in northern Greenland in August 1908. On February 19, 1909, he crossed over the ice to Ellesmere Island and traveled on to Axel Heiberg Island with 11 sleds, 103 huskies, and 10 Eskimos. From this point on, the last uncontested fact is that Cook and two Eskimos, Itukusuk and Aapilaq, set out northward onto the polar ice cap. According to Cook, his party—often hindered by blizzards and ice floes—headed straight north.

On April 21 Cook calculated by means of a sextant that he was but a few miles from the North Pole. When he arrived at the pole that day, Cook remarked, "What a cheerless spot to have aroused the ambitions of man for so many ages." In his diary entry for the day, he wrote, "We were the only pulsating creatures in a dead world of ice." After two days at the Pole, Cook headed south, but drifting ice forced him westward. He reached North Devon Island and spent the winter there. The next spring he returned to his Greenland base, after a fourteen-month absence.

On his voyage home, Cook first reached Copenhagen and told of his achievement. The world press proclaimed him the conqueror of the North Pole. Two days later, however, a cable arrived from Peary in Greenland stating that he had discovered the North Pole. The controversy had begun.

ROBERT PEARY

Robert Peary was a self-centered, domineering man with one ambition—to be the first human at the North Pole. Born in Cresson, Pennsylvania, on May 6, 1856, Peary joined the U.S. Navy at the age of thirty and went to the Arctic on a leave of absence in 1891. For the next two decades, he studied the Eskimos' methods of travel and explored the Arctic. In 1892 he crossed Greenland and proved for the first time that it was an island.

Believing that he would be as famous as Christopher Columbus if he discovered the Pole, Peary devoted his life and eight toes lost to frostbite to working toward this goal. Despite the fact that Peary brought his wife to Greenland to live, he enjoyed several Eskimo "wives," who bore him children. Cook also engaged in the Eskimo custom of wife sharing.

After numerous exploratory expeditions, Peary tried to attain the North Pole in 1906, but bad weather stopped him. When his sled dogs began cannibalizing each other and his men were forced to eat all but one of the remaining dogs, Peary turned back.

Two years later he tried again. Traveling into the Arctic, he established his base camp at Cape Columbia on Ellesmere Island in September 1908. With 23 men—including 17 Eskimos—19 sleds, and 133 dogs, Peary set out for the Pole on February 22, 1909. As supplies were used up, one sled after another was sent back to the base. By April 1, after traveling 300 miles and with another 33 to go, Peary, Matt Henson—an African-American who was Peary's constant companion—and four Eskimos, Egingwah, Ooqueah, Ootha, and Seegloo, were left to finish the journey.

On April 6 Peary calculated his position as latitude eighty-nine degrees fifty-seven minutes north—only three miles from the pole. Exhausted as they were, he and his five companions pushed on. He wrote in his diary that day, "The pole at last! My dream and goal of twenty years. Mine at last!" Peary planted five flags: the American flag, the U.S. Navy banner, the flag of the Daughters of the American Revolution, the Red Cross flag, and the flag of his college fraternity, Delta Kappa Epsilon. Then he buried a bottle—which has never been found—containing a message claiming the North Pole for the United States.

Frederick Cook's supporters erect a welcoming arch in his honor in New York City, 1909.

After one night at the pole, Peary sped back to his camp, anxious to let the world know of his victory. He reached his base camp and sailed for home on April 27. He cabled his wife, "Have made good at last. I have the old pole." He later wrote, "I knew that we were going back to civilization with the last of the great adventure stories."

When he heard of Cook's claim, Peary was enraged, believing Cook was trying to cheat him out of his lifelong dream.

THE CONTROVERSY

PRO-COOK

After studying Cook's journal, Roald Amundsen, the Norwegian Arctic explorer and discoverer of the South Pole, was convinced that Cook had discovered the Pole before Peary. Cook had been in the Arctic for fourteen months, and his journal records how each day was spent and includes astronomical calculations and geographic observations. Cook's supporters assert that since he had spent more than a year in the Arctic wastes, there was no reason why he should not have headed for and reached the North Pole. In 1909 Cook published an account of his exploits, *My Attainment of the Pole*. The book so graphically describes the Arctic territory and journey that only a very imaginative liar could have faked it. A 1909 poll conducted by the *Pittsburgh Press* revealed that 96 percent of the respondents believed Cook had attained the Pole, while only 24 percent believed Peary had made it.

Cook's supporters argue that the jealous and vindictive Peary and his proponents did everything in their power to discredit Cook. Having given Peary extensive favorable coverage for twenty years, the partisan press attacked Cook while uncritically heralding Peary as the hero of the Pole. Meanwhile, the National Geographic Society, the U.S. Navy, and the U.S. government—all biased inasmuch as they had all spent fortunes financing Peary's expeditions—dismissed Cook as a liar without having any real evidence against him. Cook's claim suffered most because of Peary's newspaper popularity and the conniving of Peary's powerful official backers. Some Cook advocates claim that Peary's supporters, in order to destroy Cook's reputation, also fabricated the story that Cook had not really climbed to the top of Mount McKinley.

Did Peary even discover the Pole? His only witnesses were Henson, his loyal comrade, and four Eskimos, who were never interviewed. Cook's adherents claim that Peary lied about arriving at the Pole because he desperately wanted the glory of being its discoverer and was paranoically afraid that Cook would rob him of his dream. Peary recorded mileage based on dogsled speeds twice as fast as proven possible. If correct, some of Peary's calculations indicate that he was far off course and might have missed the Pole completely. Landmarks Peary described later proved nonexistent, and most of his charts were discarded by the Navy in 1926 because they were totally inaccurate.

PRO-PEARY

Peary's reputation as a twenty-year veteran of Arctic exploration is impressive. The National Geographic Society and many other scientific bodies supported his claim. And in 1911 the U.S. Congress formally gave Peary recognition for having reached the North Pole.

Peary's exhaustive scientific and astronomical observations are further proof of his accomplishment. His book *The North Pole* is a dry yet thoroughly convincing diary of his well-planned assault on the pole.

Peary was convinced Cook's claim was fraudulent. He claimed that he had talked to Cook's two Eskimo companions and that both of them swore that Cook had journeyed a short distance north, then swerved west and south. In 1918 Donald MacMillan reported that he too had been told by the two Eskimos that Cook had not come within 500 miles of the pole; however, MacMillan had been a member of the Peary expedition.

In his report to the University of Copenhagen—the authority on the Arctic—Cook included no scientific or astronomical observations. The university therefore concluded that he had no proof that he had discovered the Pole. And when he did release some of his data, it contradicted known scientific facts concerning Arctic astronomy.

Later, when other Arctic explorers tried to retrace Cook's path, they found none of the landmarks described in his journal and book.

The most damaging evidence against Cook concerns Mount McKinley, not the North Pole. In 1909 Cook's companion at McKinley, Edward Barrille, swore in an affidavit that Cook had never reached the summit. A 1913 expedition which reached the top of Mount McKinley proved that Cook had climbed a lesser peak, which they named Fake Peak in his honor. Since *To the Top of the Continent* was therefore a fantastically well-written hoax, Cook's book and claim of discovering the Pole are considered by many to be similar hoaxes.

THE CONTINUING CONTROVERSY

Robert Peary died on February 20, 1920, and Frederick Cook died on August 5, 1940, but

Robert Peary with his huskies.

the North Pole controversy outlived them. In 1984 CBS aired a made-for-TV movie, *Race for the Pole*, starring Richard Chamberlain as Cook and Rod Steiger as Peary. The movie portrayed Cook as a martyred hero and Peary as a lying villain. This was too much for Peary's family, who decided to release, for the first time, Peary's diary and all of his papers, assuming that these documents would bolster their ancestor's claim. The National Geographic Society, Peary's long-time advocate, hired Arctic explorer Wally Herbert to analyze the diary and papers. Herbert surprised both the Peary family and the National Geographic Society, however, by concluding, in a September 1988 article, that Peary had *not* reached the Pole. Exasperated, the National Geographic Society commissioned another study, this one headed by Thomas Davies of the Navigation Foundation.

Davies's report, released in December 1989, declared that Peary *had* reached the Pole. Herbert had stated that the movement of the ice had carried Peary west of his goal; the Navigation Foundation declared that this drift was counteracted by later drift to the east. Their main evidence in support of Peary was the length of shadows on Peary's photographs, which they claimed proved that his final camp was no more than five miles from the Pole. The report also pointed out that Peary's unusually high speeds during his final dash to the Pole had been matched by other explorers.

Unfortunately for Peary supporters, the Navigation Foundation report was brutally attacked at a 1991 symposium sponsored by the U.S. Naval Institute. For example, Herbert explained that when other explorers with dog teams had reached Peary's alleged speed of twenty-six miles a day, it had always been done on smooth ice, not on Arctic Ocean pack ice. It was also pointed out that Peary kept detailed records of his positions on all his journeys—except the voyage to the Pole. In

fact, he sent back his two most competent observers, Captain Robert Bartlett and Ross Marvin, and made the final dash with only Henson and the Eskimos, none of whom was scientifically trained. It was shown that the shadow evidence was inconclusive and that there were no records to prove the alleged counteracting ice shift to the east.

An interesting sidelight to the controversy concerns Matthew Henson. In a 1910 article in the *Boston American*, Henson recalled the famous day of April 6, 1909:

" 'Well, Mr. Peary,' I spoke up, cheerfully enough, 'we are now at the Pole, are we not?'

" 'I do not suppose that we can swear that we are exactly at the Pole,' was his evasive answer."

Henson concluded that Peary had intended to leave him behind a few miles short of the Pole so as not to have to share the glory, but that Peary had miscalculated and reached their goal before the separation had taken place. More skeptical historians have interpreted Peary's disappointment and his subsequent coolness toward Henson as evidence that Peary knew that he had not reached the Pole at all.

On the whole, it is a good bet that neither Peary nor Cook reached the North Pole.

OTHER CLAIMANTS

Since the validity of both Cook's and Peary's claims is questionable, some historians propose that another American, Richard Byrd, first reached the North Pole. In 1926 Byrd shipped his three-engined German Fokker to Spitsbergen Island in the Arctic Ocean. From there he took off on May 9 and tried to fly his plane over the North Pole, returning to Spitsbergen the same day. Using instruments not yet invented in Cook and Peary's time, Byrd claimed that he had reached the North Pole, although anti-Byrd literature has cast strong doubt on his claim. The Russian Otto Schmidt may have been the first to set foot at the Pole, in 1936, after having set up a scientific observation station. The first uncontested surface attainment of the North Pole was achieved on April 18, 1968, by a four-man snowmobile expedition led by American Ralph Plaisted. On April 22, 1994, Börge Ousland of Norway became the first person to reach the Pole alone and unaided by either dogs or air-dropped supplies. Ousland was so concerned with lessening the weight of his 275-pound sledge load that he trimmed the bristles on his toothbrush and cut off the margins on the two books he brought with him—the New Testament and Herman Hesse's *Narcissus and Goldmund*.

—R.J.F. and R.W.G.

GREAT EXPLORERS

*One does not discover new lands without consenting
to lose sight of the shore for a very long time.*
        André Gide, *The Counterfeiters*, 1926

*We shall not cease from exploration
And the end of all our exploring
Will be to arrive where we started
And know the place for the first time.*
        T. S. Eliot, *Little Gidding*, 1942

*One of the main troubles about going to Europe is that
no one wants to hear about your trip when you get
back home. Your friends and relatives are rife with
jealousy, and are not only sorry that you went to
Europe, but deeply regret that you came back.*
        Art Buchwald, *Vogue*, April 1, 1954

THE SOURCES OF
THE GREAT RIVERS

In 1895, on an expedition into the Takla Makan
Desert of central Asia, Swedish explorer Sven
Hedin and his men ran out of water and nearly
perished before Hedin stumbled upon a pool of
water in a dry riverbed. This fortuitous discovery spared Hedin for what was perhaps his
greatest adventure—the search for the sources
of the Brahmaputra and Indus Rivers. A genuine claimant to the title of the last great
European explorer of Asia, Hedin was a brazen
risk taker who craved physical challenge: "The
adventure, the conquest of an unknown country, and the struggle against the impossible,
have a fascination which draws me with irresistible force." Hedin also seemed driven by an
obsession to be the first European to set foot on
a particular spot.

Born in Stockholm on February 19, 1865,
Hedin began early on to prepare himself for the
role of explorer and adventurer; as a young child
he toughened himself by rolling in the snow and
sleeping by an open window even during the
harsh Swedish winters. After receiving his doctorate from the University of Halle in Germany,
he obtained financial backing from King Oscar II
of Sweden for his foray into the Takla Makan, the
nearly ill-fated expedition that he made despite
the previous loss of sight in one eye.

In 1906 he encountered an obstacle that he
found "more difficult to surmount than the
Himalayas"—the British government, which
denied him access to Tibet through India.
Successfully outwitting the authorities, he entered Tibet and, disdaining the company of
fellow Europeans, commissioned three Tibetans, whom he dubbed "the Three Musketeers,"
to accompany him. Crossing the craggy mountain range that stretched for 1,000 miles along

the northern watershed of the Indus, the party
followed a tributary of the Brahmaputra River,
making the arduous ascent into "a world of
gigantic peaks, black but covered with perpetual snow." At an altitude of 15,958 feet, Hedin
gazed down on the glacier that formed the
source of the Brahmaputra.

On September 10, 1907, acting on information
from a Tibetan monk, Hedin and a party of five
men followed the three main affluents of the
Indus River until they came upon several small
springs. On a limestone terrace were three small
cairns and a small niche containing clay offerings and stones incised with prayers and sacred
symbols. Hedin, who pocketed the image of the
Buddha as a souvenir, wrote, "I had the joy of
being the first white man to penetrate to the
sources of the Brahmaputra and the Indus." The
price of greatness came cheaply enough—the
combined monies paid to his Tibetan guides for
both expeditions totaled seventy-seven dollars.

Hedin's achievements as an explorer were
overshadowed by his controversial political
views. His apparent Nazi sympathies (he was
the only foreigner to accept Hitler's invitation to
speak in the main stadium during the 1936
Berlin Olympics) cost him his membership in
the Royal Geographic Society. He died on
November 26, 1952, in the end denied the
approbation that he had sought all his life.
        —L.C.

THE SOUTH POLE

With a tremendous ability to learn and adapt,
Norwegian Roald Amundsen (1872–1928) became the most professional and successful of
polar explorers. He was the first man to sail the
Northwest Passage above the North American
continent and the first to reach the South Pole.
Through a combination of Laplander, Eskimo,
and Nordic skills and technology, he became
the consummate explorer of the ice lands and
ice seas.

The son of a wealthy ship captain, he decided
at the age of fifteen to become a polar explorer
after reading the accounts of Sir John Franklin,
who had died stranded in the Arctic. He
immersed himself in this profession by training
himself as a cross-country skier and a ship's
captain, studying magnetism in Germany and
cold-weather survival techniques in Lapland,
and serving on a seal-hunting boat in the Arctic
Ocean. Then he spent his inheritance on a
herring fishing boat named *Gjöa*. In 1903 he left
Oslo, Norway, aboard the *Gjöa*, a paraffin-
powered motorized sailing boat, to sail the
Northwest Passage and to reach the North

Magnetic Pole, which had been attained only once before, in 1831. Having borrowed every kroner possible, his inspiring comment to his men as they cleared the Norwegian coast was, "Well, boys, we're clear of the creditors now!"

For two years he and his crew of six fought storms, reefs, and engine-room fires as they traversed the waterways of the Canadian Arctic. For two winters they lived with Netsilik Eskimos, who taught them about igloo building, dog handling, and loose-fitting caribou-fur clothing, which they wore layered, from parkas to underwear.

At Boothia Peninsula, Amundsen disembarked with his Norwegian army buddy, Sergeant Peder Risvedt. The two men, with dogsleds and skis, set out in search of the North Magnetic Pole. When the food they had brought failed to keep up the strength of their dogs, Amundsen fed them his excess Eskimo clothing, which the dogs devoured. Risvedt commented on this, stating, "The menu of the polar dog is comprehensive. I think I can manage many dishes, but I don't think I could have managed your [Amundsen's] old underpants." When the companions arrived at where the magnetic pole had been discovered in 1831, they found that it had moved. Thus they proved that the magnetic poles are migratory. They searched for the new location but missed it by thirty miles. After three years they completed their journey, sailing into Nome, Alaska, and on to San Francisco.

Amundsen's next challenge was to be the first man to reach the North Pole. However, in 1909 it was reported that Robert Peary and Matthew Henson had beaten him there. He quickly changed his goal to the South Pole, informing his backers of the change in plans only after he had sailed. At the same time, Sir Robert Scott left England with the same objective. A British-Norwegian race to the South Pole had begun.

Amundsen had become the most skilled and well-organized polar traveler of all time. He and his four men dashed across the Antarctic landscape on skis and with Eskimo dogsleds. Compared with other expeditions, especially Scott's, which had men on snowshoes pulling sleds, the Norwegians moved at an incredible speed of up to thirty miles a day. They left food deposits behind at regular intervals, and as dogs died they fed them to the remaining dogs. On December 14, 1911, at 3:00 P.M., Amundsen reached the South Pole. Sixteen thousand miles from home, they took pictures of themselves around the Norwegian flag and celebrated with extra rations of seal meat. A month later, Scott and his expedition would arrive to find the Norwegian flag already at the South Pole, and on their return all would perish.

Owing to excellent planning, Amundsen's return trip was uneventful. Coming down from the 10,000-foot-high central plateau, they had an exhilarating eleven-mile downhill ski that dropped them 4,500 feet. Healthy and in great morale, they returned to their ship having covered 1,400 miles.

Amundsen would go on to sail the Northwest Passage from the Atlantic to the Pacific above the Asian continent and to be the first man to reach both Poles (he had finally made it over the North Pole by dirigible in 1926). He died at the age of fifty-seven in an airplane crash in the Arctic while on a mission to save another explorer whose dirigible had gone down near the North Pole.

—R.J.F.

THE TERRIBLE JOURNEY

Douglas Mawson (1882–1958) died at the age of seventy-six, a retired college president, after a productive life. However, forty-five years earlier he had contemplated suicide as he hung by a dogsled harness fourteen feet over the edge of a crevasse's blue-black abyss. Starved, in physical agony, and alone for more than a month in the Antarctic, he had thought, "It would be but the work of a moment to slip from the harness, then all the pain and toil would be over."

That 1913 incident was not the first time that Mawson had hung so precariously in a crevasse. Mawson, an Australian scientist, had joined an expedition to the Antarctic in September 1908. In December 1908 he fell into a crevasse and was pulled up by his companions. Mawson thrived on the adventure and was, with Professor Edgeworth David, one of the first men to reach the South Magnetic Pole, a few months into the expedition. One day in camp while working with some photographic plates in his tent, Mawson heard David ask from outside if he was busy. Mawson called back that he was indeed busy. Almost apologetically, David replied, "I am so sorry to disturb you, Mawson, but I am down a crevasse and I really don't think I can hold on much longer."

In January 1912 Mawson returned to Antarctica with his own scientific expedition. He established a base camp at Commonwealth Bay, where winds blew an average 64 miles per hour, sometimes gusting as high as 200 miles per hour (for comparison, a strong hurricane is 140 miles per hour). On November 10, 1912, after a breakfast of penguin egg omelette, Mawson left his base camp to map an unknown region with two companions, Belgrave Ninnis, a twenty-three-year-old British lieutenant, and Xavier Mertz, a twenty-eight-year-old Swiss lawyer and mountaineer. Ninnis subsequently suffered snow blindness, which Mawson successfully treated by placing zinc-cocaine tablets under his eyelids. Then 316 miles from their camp, Ninnis suddenly and silently disappeared. A search revealed an eleven-foot hole through which Ninnis had fallen to his death in a seemingly bottomless crevasse. With him went most of their food, all their dog food, and their tent.

With only ten days' food rations, they were at least thirty-four days from base. They crossed glaciers and ice sheets, feeding their dogs old mittens and leather strips. Then as the dogs died, Mawson and Mertz ate them. The last animal died on December 25 and was served for Christmas dinner. However, the dog meat was diseased and Mertz was stricken with dysentery. With Mertz progressively unable to travel and with the food supply dwindling, both men's chances of survival were bleak. On January 7, 1913, Mertz fell asleep and never awoke.

Suffering stomach cramps himself, Mawson struggled on alone. The soles of his boots came off, his toenails were loose and festered underneath, his hair fell out in clumps, and boils erupted all over his body. Ten days after Mertz died, Mawson fell into a crevasse. Unlike his 1908 fall, this time he had to pull himself up. With superhuman effort he overcame the desire to lie in his sleeping bag and wait for death. For a month he trekked on, covering a mere mile or two a day. Near the end of January, he found a cache of food that had been left for him by searchers.

Finally, on February 8, Mawson reached Commonwealth Bay, only to see his supply ship sailing away. Fortunately, five volunteers had stayed behind in the hope that the long-overdue expedition would eventually return. Mawson endured nine months of Antarctic winter before another ship could come to take him home.

Returning to Australia, Mawson was hailed as a hero and knighted. Fourteen years later he led an uneventful expedition to Antarctica, after which he settled into the regular routine of a peaceful academic life.

—R.J.F.

THE ANTARCTIC RESCUE MISSION

A great, bossy bear of a man, Ernest Shackleton (1874–1922) was considered by another Antarctic explorer, Sir Robert Scott, to be a weakling, lacking in stamina. Despite his demonstrations and appearance of strength and energy, Shackleton was indeed physically flawed, which led to an early grave for this courageous man.

Born in Ireland and raised in England, Shackleton attended Dulwich College. He was not a good student, and left to join the merchant marine at age sixteen. Seeking fame, he joined Scott's Antarctic Expedition of 1901–1903. Scott, a Royal Navy officer, considered this merchant marine officer not equal to his other regular navy cohorts who had been chosen to

set up a base camp. However, when Scott chose Dr. Edward Wilson to accompany him to the South Pole, Wilson convinced Scott to include Shackleton.

The team failed to reach the South Pole, largely because of scurvy. According to Scott, Shackleton slowed the expedition and forced it to turn back; in fact, all three were aching from scurvy. Scott blamed Shackleton for their failure.

Back in Great Britain, Shackleton became secretary of the Scottish Geographical Society, unsuccessfully ran for Parliament, and married a wealthy women six years his senior. After a highly successful fund-raising campaign, he had raised enough money to launch his own South Pole expedition in 1907. Using Manchurian ponies to pull the sledges, his expedition came within ninety-seven miles of the Pole before being forced back by starvation. By the time they returned to base they had eaten all their ponies.

This exploit made him a national celebrity. In August 1914, just as World War I erupted, Shackleton set out again for Antarctica in his ship the *Endurance*. Anchoring in the Antarctic Weddell Sea in December, the ship became trapped in ice. For the next ten months, through the winter gloom, the men listened as the ice slowly crushed their ship—their lifeline home.

A month before the *Endurance* finally sank, Shackleton rallied his men and set off in the ship's boats. By dragging their boats onto fast-moving ice floes, after four months they reached Elephant Island just off the Antarctic coastline, south of Argentina. Taking only five companions in an open boat, Shackleton set out across the open Antarctic sea in the agonizing cold and wet. He was sailing to South Georgia Island, which lay 800 miles to the north, where there was a whaling ship station. During the hellish voyage, a freak gigantic wave nearly capsized them. After sixteen days at sea, they shipwrecked on the southern rocky shore of South Georgia. Unfortunately, the whaling station was on the island's north side across a snowy mountain range. Proceeding on with only two companions, Shackleton, in twenty-four hours without sleep, traversed glaciers, climbed mountains, and plunged down icy waterfalls before he finally reached help.

Shackleton quickly rescued his companions on the south shore of South Georgia. Next he went to the rescue of those left on Elephant Island, not knowing whether they were still alive, but three ships failed to reach them. Finally Shackleton, aboard a Chilean steamboat, arrived to find all twenty-two had survived. They had lived under two upturned lifeboats for three and a half months. They all returned home to England.

Shackleton spent fifteen years trying to prove that, despite what Scott had believed, he was constitutionally fit for Antarctic exploration.

Ernest Shackleton's ship, the **Endurance,** *being crushed by ice floes, 1915.*

So, regardless of a heart murmur, he led his fourth expedition to the Antarctic in 1922. Reaching his jumping off base at South Georgia Island, he suffered a coronary thrombosis and died at the age of forty-eight. When the Uruguayan government was making arrangements to return his body, his wife sent word to bury him on South Georgia Island, near the whaling station, where he belonged.

—R.J.F.

THE EMPTY QUARTER

An Englishman who knew the Arabian deserts well, T. E. Lawrence, "Lawrence of Arabia," had written of the Rub'al Khali, "Only an airship could cross it."

Two other Englishmen, Bertram Thomas and Harry St. John Philby, each sought to prove Lawrence wrong. Both were determined to cross the last great area of Arabia to defy the explorer. The Rub'al Khali, or Empty Quarter, as it had come to be known, was 250,000 square miles of waterless, sandy desert that made up most of the southern half of the Arabian Peninsula. Not only were the physical hazards of the land threatening to explorers, but the bedouin tribes who dwelled there strongly resented intrusion by the Europeans.

The goal of crossing this desolate land in the early winter ignited a race between Thomas and Philby, who had both started their careers as British officials in the Middle East; Thomas had become adviser to the sultan of Muscat and Oman, while Philby converted to Islam and became adviser to Saudi king Ibn-Saud. Philby's advice to Ibn-Saud not to join the fighting in World War II resulted in the explorer's arrest by the British government. His son, Kim, was one of the notorious Cambridge spies.

In October of 1930 Thomas set out on camelback from the southeastern coastal city of Dhufar with a party of ragged bedouin from the north. Under the constant danger of attack by raiders, the expedition traveled north across the coastal plain and through the grassy foothills of the Qara Mountains.

At the well of Shanna, some 330 miles from Thomas's goal of Doha on the Qatar Peninsula, he reduced his party to thirteen men, thirteen fast camels, and five pack camels carrying rations for thirty days.

Owing to foul water, the small caravan survived on camel milk until they reached Samam, where the water was sweet. Moving on, they finally rested at Banajan before heading north again. Their spirits rose as they neared Qatar, where they spotted local herdsmen. Thomas was thrilled as he gazed upon the bare walls of the fort at Doha. He had made it. For the first time in history, the Empty Quarter had been crossed by a European.

Despite Thomas's success, Philby remained obsessed with conquering the Rub'al Khali himself. Since Thomas had traveled south to north, Philby set out to cross the Empty Quarter from north to south.

On January 7, 1932, Philby departed from the wells of Dulaiqiya, west of the peninsula of Qatar. His party of nineteen men headed southwest toward the Jabrin Oasis.

Philby had always been intrigued by the legendary presence of the ruins of Ubar, an ancient city in the middle of the great desert. But all he found were several large craters near the site of Al Hadida, probably the result of a giant meteor.

Disappointed but determined, Philby led his party south to Naifa, then Shanna, where his men rebelled, leaving him with a reduced team. This he led westward across the arid Empty Quarter, paralleling Thomas's route.

On March 11, 1932, after 575 miles of dry desert, Philby arrived at the oasis of Sulaiyil. The local villagers could not believe that he'd come across the desert—no stranger ever had before. Though Thomas had made it first, Philby had crossed the much more difficult western region of the desert.

—J.L.

THE GRAND VALLEY

On April 9, 1907, American Richard Archbold was born into enormous wealth, the grandson of John D. Archbold, one of the founders and the president of the Standard Oil Company (now the Exxon Corporation).

Inherited wealth and a Columbia University education afforded Richard the means to become a mammalogist and explorer. As an associate of the American Museum of Natural History, he made many expeditions on its behalf, most notably, three to Dutch New Guinea.

In 1938, for his third expedition—conducted in cooperation with the Dutch East Indies government—he purchased and employed the use of a navy long-range PBY Catalina flying boat, which he named the Guba—the most air- and seaworthy aircraft in existence at the time.

It was Archbold's objective to explore what was New Guinea's least-known large area, the northern slopes of the eastern Nassau Range.

His plan was to fly scientists from Hollandia directly to Lake Habbema, provided a water landing was feasible, and then concentrate on the stretch of land lying between Mount Wilhelmina and the Idenburg River.

During the flight from Hollandia, the Guba flew over an unmapped valley of the Baliem River about fifteen miles east of Lake Habbema. Archbold was certain his party of white men were the first to penetrate this unknown and isolated forty-mile-long, ten-mile-wide domain. He named the territory the Grand Valley and estimated its population, a linguistic group known as the Dani, at approximately 60,000.

After establishing a base camp at the Idenburg River, Archbold's next objective was to gain access by air to Lake Habbema, where he intended to set up another camp from which he could explore the nearby Grand Valley on foot.

Since the minimum depth required for landing the Guba was five feet, ropes of that exact length were dropped from the air, with weights attached to one end and floats to the other. If the floats remained above water, landing was out of the question. Fortunately, the floats disappeared instantly upon hitting the water. The Guba landed, placing Archbold and company on the mountaintop Lake Habbema in little-known New Guinea. The natives, who proved friendly and accommodating, were awed by the large, noisy bird that had swooped down onto the lake.

Meanwhile, as a security measure, a party led by Dutch lieutenant V. J. Arcken set out from the Idenburg camp to cut a track to Lake Habbema that could be used as an escape route should the Guba not be able to take off from the lake once it had landed.

After the plane was unloaded, a trial takeoff was attempted. Within a minute the Guba rose above the water, made a wide circle around the lake, and came back down.

Once the region at Lake Habbema had been explored, the expedition, including Dutch soldiers commanded by Captain C. G. J. Teerink, set out to cross the Grand Valley.

The entire expedition lasted fourteen months and produced a body of important scientific work on their discovery of and encounter with the people of the previously unknown Dani tribe, as well as mapping the area. An article and pictures of the expedition appeared in National Geographic and stirred further interest in the region. Archbold, who never married, died on August 1, 1976, at the age of sixty-nine.

—J.L.

KON-TIKI

Probably the definitive adventurer of the late 1940s, Thor Heyerdahl, born October 6, 1914, in Larvik, Norway, thought of himself as simply someone who loved nature and the wilderness.

In 1936 he convinced his wife, Liv, to accompany him to the South Pacific island of

Fatu Hiva in French Polynesia, where they would live off the land for a year with no concessions other than a machete and a metal cooking pot.

While on Fatu Hiva, Heyerdahl became fascinated with the notion that people of primitive cultures could have migrated across the sea long before the Europeans did. He learned from the local islanders that the pale god known as Tiki had led their ancestors to the Marquesas Islands from what Heyerdahl believed was South America, specifically Peru.

To prove his theory that a voyage across the vast seas from the Americas to Polynesia was possible centuries earlier, he employed the help of an engineer friend and built a raft he supposed was similar to the kind used by the pre-Inca natives to flee across the Pacific to Polynesia. He christened the raft Kon-Tiki, in honor of the pale, bearded god of the Polynesians. It was forty-five feet long and made of nine huge balsa logs and bamboo. As in the time of the Incas, no nails or wire hawsers were used; the logs were bound together with rope. A small bamboo cabin was built on the deck to house the processed army rations, fresh fruit, fishing gear, kerosene stove, and a wireless used to report weather conditions.

Like Noah in the Bible, Heyerdahl had his own scoffers—academics who questioned how balsa wood could stay afloat more than a few hundred miles without becoming waterlogged and sinking.

With unrelenting determination, Heyerdahl assembled a crew of six, including himself, his engineer, two skilled wireless operators, an experienced sailor, and a Swedish ethnologist, all sincerely interested in Heyerdahl's migration theory.

On April 28, 1947, Heyerdahl and company were towed out of the harbor at Callao, Peru, and the Kon-Tiki was set adrift.

Constantly followed by sharks, whales, and rare deep-sea fish, the remarkably engineered raft served to carry the six long-bearded sailors across 4,300 miles of open ocean, rising and falling between wave crests as buoyantly as a cork.

After nearly a hundred days, the trade wind and the current carried the raft past the Polynesian islands of Puka Puka and Angatau. On day 101 it drifted toward the dangerous Takume and Raroia Reefs, where the crew held on for dear life as the breakers hurled the crude craft into the Raroia coral atoll, where it finally ran aground, cabin smashed, mast broken like a matchstick. Wave upon wave pulled them over the reef until, jubilant, the crew was able to wade their way to a palm-covered island. Heyerdahl was so overwhelmed, he sank to his knees and thrust his fingers into the dry warm sand. He'd proven that a balsa-wood raft could cross the Pacific Ocean.

His popular account of the extraordinary voyage, Kon-Tiki, was published in 1948 and his documentary film of the same name won an Academy Award in 1951.

—J.L.

THE MARIANA TRENCH

Jacques Piccard could never have conquered the Mariana Trench in 1960 if not for his father, Auguste, a Swiss scientist who designed and constructed the bathyscaphe, a free-floating "deep-sea ship" that consisted of two major parts, a cabin and a float. The cabin, a steel sphere weighing ten tons, was built to withstand the crushing pressures of the deep ocean. The portholes were made of a newly developed, shatterproof plastic called Plexiglas. After a number of experiments, Auguste decided to use common gasoline as the buoyant material in the float portion of the vessel.

The bathyscaphe was made to dive by loading it with ballast, tons of steel or iron shot contained in cylindrical silos. To descend, gasoline was emptied from the float. To ascend, the iron shot was released in appropriate amounts.

After father and son had made more than fifty descents using the most advanced of Auguste's bathyscaphes, the Trieste, they sold it to the U.S. Navy and Jacques teamed up with scientists, engineers, and naval officers to make additional descents, including a 23,000-foot dive off the coast of Guam.

All of his record-breaking dives were just a dress rehearsal for the big one, the deepest known spot on Earth—the floor of the Challenger Deep of the Mariana Trench, a huge crescent-shaped gorge on the bottom of the western Pacific Ocean, 100 miles wide and 400 miles long. The navy scientist in charge of the expedition longed for his explorers to return with the news of living creatures seven miles under the sea on the bottom of the trench.

On January 23, 1960, the Trieste was towed 200 miles from Guam, where Piccard and Donald Walsh, a twenty-eight-year-old Annapolis lieutenant and experienced submariner, were sealed inside the steel sphere. They began their historic descent at 8:23 A.M.

Wide-eyed and munching on American Hershey bars, the two men slowly descended through various degrees of blackness until, three hours later, they were at the virgin depth of 29,150 feet, as deep under the sea as Mount Everest is high above it.

At 35,500 feet, they sighted the bottom of the trench. Its floor was light and clear, covered with snuff-colored ooze. Piccard was thrilled when he spotted an inch-long red shrimp and an ivory-colored, foot-long flatfish, thus proving that there were creatures that spent their lives under the tremendous pressure of these ocean depths.

After spending twenty minutes photographing the wonder of their surroundings and unrolling their U. S. and Swiss flags, the two men released ten tons of the bathyscaphe's shotgun pellets, lightening its weight so they could start upward.

At 4:57 P.M., after eight and one half hours under water, Piccard and Walsh reached the surface. The navy flew them to Washington, where President Dwight Eisenhower personally presented them with awards and commended them on their outstanding contribution to the United States and to science in the field of oceanographic research.

—J.L.

FIRST SURFACE CROSSING OF THE ARCTIC

Born on October 24, 1934, Wally Herbert is an Englishman who has spent much of his life exploring the remote corners of the earth. The son of a Royal Navy captain, Herbert enlisted in the British army and weathered his first overseas years in the extreme heat of the Suez Canal, where he was based from 1953 to 1955. After his military stint, he spent almost another year traveling alone through the Middle East. Before that year was over, he accepted a position with the Falkland Islands Survey, a job that took him to the British base at Hope Bay, Antarctica, where he spent the next three years mapping the frozen continent.

In 1960 Herbert joined an expedition that was bound for the opposite end of the planet: Lapland, Spitzbergen, and Greenland. Once this adventure had concluded, he reversed direction once again by joining the New Zealand Expedition to Antarctica, for which he served as director of mapping. Wally Herbert's mapping team charted more than 26,000 square miles of the forbidding mountains known as the Queen

Maud Range. In 1962 he followed another explorer's map, instead of creating a new one, as he retraced Roald Amundsen's route to the South Pole.

This adventure spurred him to envision a journey that no one else had ever made. With backing provided by the Royal Geographic Society, Herbert planned and prepared to cross the Arctic from one end to the other. He spent 1967 training for this epic journey by dogsledding 1,400 miles from Greenland to Canada across frozen sea. His Trans-Arctic Expedition began on February 21, 1968, in Point Barrow, Alaska. Along with three other men (each driving a dog team), he set off on the journey's first leg, which would take them to the North Pole. Supplies were air-dropped to the explorers to sustain them for the nearly fourteen months it took to complete the leg.

After wiring Queen Elizabeth that they had reached the Pole, they took off for their final destination of Spitzbergen. Though this leg was much shorter than the one they had completed, it posed much more hardship. Summer was approaching and the ice floes began melting beneath them as they made forced marches to the south.

Herbert's brushes with death in the far north hardly deterred his urge to return. He went back to Greenland and Canada's Arctic territories to film the native culture of the region during the early 1970s. From 1978 to 1982, Herbert coursed the entire circumference of Greenland (the world's largest island) by dogsled and kayak. After completing that remarkable trip, he took two years off to research and write a book in which he argued that the legendary Arctic explorer, Robert Peary, had not been the first man to reach the North Pole. Herbert wrote that Peary had faked his claim and had never, in fact, reached the Pole at any time.

In 1987, he once again traversed the Arctic—from the upper reaches of Greenland, across the snowfields of Ellesmere Island, and all the way up to the North Pole—with a movie camera, intent on capturing more of its mystery, mayhem, and beauty and bringing it back on film for the rest of the world to behold.

—R.N.K.

FOOTNOTE PERSON

ALEXANDRA DAVID-NEEL
(1868–1969)

Alexandra David-Neel spent many years in Tibet and was the first European—much less the first European woman—to visit various parts of that mysterious land. Some of the hardships and hazards she faced were unbeliev-

ably difficult, yet she never hesitated to push on. Her heroic adventures were fully documented in a number of books and articles she published in French and English.

Alexandra David was born on October 24, 1868, in Paris to French parents of moderate income. She spent an unhappy childhood, often ran away from home, and came to detest her mother. As a young person Alexandra dreamed of traveling to faraway places. Although she was devoted to her father, she left home as soon as possible to make her way in life.

Alexandra was influenced by Oriental art, the Stoicism of Epictetus, and ambition. She became completely self-disciplined. All of her life she was capable of denying herself diversions or physical pleasure.

Only five feet tall, she steeled her body to withstand the rigors of the hard life. Photographs of her in the 1890s reveal a face with a quizzical but determined countenance. In the last decade of the nineteenth century, she became a renowned opera performer, traveling to Hanoi, Athens, and Tunis with various touring opera companies. She eventually tired of the theater and turned, in 1903, to journalism in order to support herself. Her articles, generally on Eastern topics, were published in the magazines of England and France. But always her main goal was to explore the lands of central Asia.

Against her better judgment, she married in 1904. Her husband was Philippe-François Neel (1861–1941), a distant cousin, who was a representative of the French government in Tunis. Their relationship was far from traditional; Alexandra stated more than once that marriage and the role of wife and mother were repressive and threatening to her independence. Sex was evidently repugnant to her, and she adamantly refused to consider bearing children. Most of the time the couple lived apart, while still professing love for one another. Philippe Neel provided his wife with money to carry out her explorations even when she remained in Tibet for fourteen years.

From 1903 to 1911, Alexandra David-Neel lived in London and Paris while studying and writing, only occasionally going to Tunisia to see Philippe. Nevertheless, Philippe acquiesced to her desires to travel in the Far East and, as he had earlier promised, paid for her passage to India in August 1911. In India she slowly made a break with the European life and customs she had known and began to become the Orientalist she was at heart. A European Buddhist in Asia, she was something of a novelty, though highly respected for her intimate knowledge of Buddhist doctrines. She was granted a private audience with the spiritual ruler of Tibet, the Dalai Lama, who was then living in exile in Darjeeling after fleeing Lhasa when the Chinese invaded Tibet in February 1910. She was the first European woman to have ever been so privileged. At the urging of the Dalai Lama, David-Neel began learning the Tibetan language. Before long she was speaking it as though it were her native tongue.

She visited many sacred and secluded monasteries. At one monastery she was given—as an attendant—a Sikkimese boy of fifteen named

Alexandra David-Neel.

Yongden. Throughout her years of journeying in northern India, China, and Tibet, Yongden accompanied and aided her. He remained with her until his death in France in 1955.

From her travels in and around Sikkim, David-Neel became familiar with Tibetan life and religion. But she wanted more. She desired to know the secrets of Tibet and to experience the Tibetan way of life. But the only way to penetrate the consciousness of the people, she discovered, was to undergo the training for the priesthood.

For two years Alexandra David-Neel lived as a hermit in a cave on top of a 13,000-foot mountain. The hardships of cold, hunger, and isolation exhilarated her. There were days without food or warmth, but she never complained. When she emerged in 1916, it was with the blessing of the holy men of Tibet. No one could recall a woman ever undergoing such an experience in order to understand a way of life.

There was still another important accomplishment ahead. The forbidden city of Lhasa had never been seen by a white woman. The only way to get there was to journey through China and approach the city from the north, over the Himalayan Mountains.

Alexandra David-Neel and Yongden began the arduous task and spent nearly a year journeying to Lhasa. They had to travel disguised as a Tibetan peasant woman and her Buddhist monk son. In many situations they encountered, to have been discovered would have meant certain death. But they were saved time and again by Alexandra's intimate knowledge of the Tibetan people, their language and customs. Along the way they faced waist-deep snow, bitter cold, and dangerous crossings of mountain ridges and passes up to 20,000 feet.

On one memorable occasion, exhausted after struggling nineteen hours straight over a high, snow-covered mountain pass, Yongden found that his flint and steel were wet and would not light a fire. Realizing they could not last the night, Yongden called on Alexandra to try the ancient art of *thumo reskiung*, bringing on internal warmth through willpower. She had learned the basics of this feat years before when, like a Tibetan monk, she had been able to dry wet sheets wrapped around her as she sat exposed to the cold.

Even in such a desperate situation, she kept her head. Instead of concentrating on warming herself, she wisely concentrated on drying out the flint and steel and some tinder. By the time Yongden returned from searching for fuel, she had a fire going.

Besides the trials of the uncharted mountains, Alexandra and Yongden had to contend with possible attacks from bandits, who were very active in the area at the time. There was scant law enforcement in western China, and many travelers had been murdered. Although she carried a pistol and was prepared to use it, they encountered no violence along the way.

Upon arrival in Lhasa—in 1923, when she was fifty-five years old—Alexandra David-Neel remained disguised and undetected. After several months' residence, she and Yongden returned to India. Arriving in Europe after a fourteen-year absence, she wrote *My Journey to Lhasa*, published in 1927.

For ten years she remained in Europe and wrote continuously. By the mid-1930s the urge to travel took her back to Tibet. In 1944 the Japanese invasion forced her to join other refugees fleeing on foot. She was seventy-six years old. Her husband had died in 1941, and the war prevented her from further exploration. She returned to France to live and write.

During her lifetime Alexandra David-Neel was awarded many honors, including membership in the French Legion of Honor and a Gold Medal from the Geographical Society of Paris. Her importance lies not only in her explorations but also in her writings. She wrote dozens of books and articles, and much of what is known of modern central Asia, as well as Tibetan Buddhism, is derived from her observations.

Alexandra David-Neel was not an easy person to get along with. She demanded of others the same standards she placed on herself. At times she could be rude, arrogant, and insulting. There is no reason to believe she mellowed in old age. When she died peacefully on September 8, 1969, seven weeks shy of her 101st birthday, she had the satisfaction of knowing that few people had lived so long and enjoyed life so much. No other Western woman ever traveled to and explored so many places where Europeans had never ventured before.

—L.H.C.

FOOTNOTE PERSON

OTA BENGA (1883–1916)

"A dwarfy, black specimen of sad-eyed humanity" is how one newspaper reporter described him, but to thousands of patrons at the Bronx Zoo, he was the most incredible creature that they had ever seen. How Ota Benga, a Congolese Pygmy, came to reside in a cage at the zoo's monkey house is a tale as tragic as it is bizarre.

Benga was born in what was then the Belgian Congo. When he was about twenty, his village was attacked by a rival tribe and his wife was killed. Benga was taken into slavery by his enemies and brought to a slave market in Baschilele. Here he was bought for a pound of salt and a bolt of cloth by a white missionary and explorer, Samuel Phillips Verner. Verner's saving of Benga was more than an act of charity. He had been hired by organizers of the Saint

Louis World's Fair of 1904 to bring back African Pygmies to appear in the anthropological wing of the fair.

Benga, without home or family, agreed to go to the United States with Verner and expressed his gratitude to his benefactor by encouraging four other Pygmies to join him on the voyage. The Pygmies, along with various other indigenous people, including representatives of fifty North American tribes, were put on display in their natural habitat. Probably the most famous "savage" in the exhibition was vanquished Apache chief Geronimo, who was billed as a "Human Tyger." Geronimo took a liking to Benga and gave him one of his polished arrowheads. The University of Man, as the display was called, was more a carnival sideshow than a serious anthropological exhibit, but there was far worse to come for Benga.

When the fair ended, Benga returned to Africa with Verner, remarried, and toured much of Africa with his benefactor. The Pygmy had difficulty explaining to his people why he had gone to America, so Verner illustrated by allowing Benga to put him in a wooden pen, seated in a rocking chair, listening to Edison records on a phonograph. The other pygmies got the idea.

When Benga's second wife died of snakebite, he pleaded with Verner to take him back to America. The pair arrived in New York City in August 1906. Verner, who was pursuing various other projects, left Benga in the "satisfactory hands" of William Temple Hornaday, director of the Bronx Zoological Gardens. Hornaday made the incredible decision to exhibit the four-foot-eleven-inch-tall Pygmy in a cage with a parrot and an orangutan. Benga seemed content in his new home, and while the public gawked, he slept in a hammock, wove mats, and practiced his skills with a bow and arrow. Hornaday had bones scattered in the cage to remind patrons, if they didn't get the point from Benga's sharpened teeth, that he was a cannibal.

Members of New York's black community and leading clergymen were mortified. "Instead of making a beast of this little fellow we should be putting him in school for the development of such powers as God gave him," said the Reverend R. S. MacArthur of Calvary Baptist Church. Hornaday, however, insisted that Benga was perfectly free to leave the cage whenever he chose to.

Finally, public pressure grew so great that Hornaday was forced to release his star attraction at the monkey house. But Benga, having nowhere else to go, remained at the zoo, helping the keepers with their chores and strolling around in a white suit and canvas shoes. He was as much a curiosity as before and crowds followed him wherever he went. One day a crowd cornered him and someone asked him how he liked America. "Me no like America," Benga replied, "me like St. Louis." Another time, a mob so cruelly teased him that he resorted to his bow and arrow and wounded one of his tormentors before fleeing back to the monkey house.

Soon after, Benga left the Bronx Zoo for good. Verner, who was reduced to working as a ticket taker on the New York subway, was in no position to look after his former prodigy. Benga was admitted to the Howard Colored Orphan Asylum in Brooklyn as a ward of the state. He found a certain peace there, playing baseball on the asylum team and slowly improving his English. Benga even spent a semester at the Baptist Seminary in Lynchburg, Virginia. Virginia, with its warmer climate and rich vegetation, reminded Benga of his homeland and he moved there permanently in January 1910.

Benga worked odd jobs in Lynchburg and spent the rest of his time smoking *bangi*

Ota Benga, the man who lived in a cage in the Bronx zoo.

(marijuana) and leading a band of local children into the woods, where he taught them to hunt and fish. They listened in awe to his stories of Africa and of his days at the equally exotic Bronx Zoo. Their parents seemed to accept the little black man and called him Otto Bingo.

But Benga, alone and abandoned by his friend Verner, now longed for the homeland he had given up. Realizing he could never afford the steamship ticket that would take him back to Africa, he became more and more bitter and depressed. One day, he stole a revolver and, on March 21, 1916, singing a Pygmy chant, put a bullet through his heart. He was buried in an unmarked grave in a Lynchburg cemetery. When the news reached his former keeper, William Hornaday, he commented, "Evidently, he felt that he would rather die than work for a living." Samuel Verner was more sympathetic about his prodigy's sad end. "Between the impossible conditions of Ota Benga's own land and those which he could not surmount in ours, the homeless pygmy found no abiding peace."

—S.A.O.

THE CONQUEST OF EVEREST

Question: *Why do you want to climb Mount Everest?*
Answer: *Because it's there.*

George Leigh Mallory, in the *New York Times*,
March 18, 1923

Back in 1749 the Survey of India discovered, among the Himalayas, what it called Peak XV, an enormous pyramid upon which rested three giant ridges and three wide faces. Through various computations over the next hundred years, the Survey measured it at 29,002 feet, making it the highest mountain known to man. (In 1955, its official height was computed at 29,028 feet.)

Although, in 1856, Peak XV was officially named after the former surveyor general of the area, Sir George Everest, the Nepalese chose to call it Chomolungma, while the Tibetans referred to it as Chha-mo-lung-ma. Both names translated into "Goddess Mother of the World."

George Mallory, a respected name among adventurous Englishmen, was involved in the first three British expeditions to Everest in 1921, 1922, and 1924. During the final stages of his 1924 climb, Mallory employed the use of oxygen apparatus and, from among his climbing party, chose Sandy Irvine as his assault partner because Irvine knew how to repair the appliances if anything went wrong.

Setting out from Camp 6 on the morning of June 8, the two men headed straight for the summit. Sometime later another member of the expedition scanned the ridge and spotted two dots moving slowly toward the top of the peak. Something was wrong. Mallory and Irvine had apparently fallen five hours behind their timetable, and a storm was brewing. Their comrade's apprehension was well founded. The two men were never heard from again. There was much speculation as to their fate. Had they split up, had their oxygen failed them, had they been caught in the storm, fallen, or just run out of time and energy and frozen to death? And no one would ever know the answer to whether or not Mallory or Irvine had made it to the summit. Only the mountain itself knew.

No expeditions of any note attempted Everest for nine years after the loss of Mallory and Irvine. During the following twenty years there were several, among them six British and two Swiss. The mountain also began attracting amateurs whose determination and faith were their strongest assets. Englishman Maurice Wilson in 1934, Canadian Earl Denman in 1947, and a Dane, Klavs Becker-Larsen in 1951. These men had one thing in common, the audacity to make a solo and clandestine attempt at the mountain. Although none of them succeeded, Larsen fared the best. Wilson's body was discovered by a British reconnaissance team the year after his attempt.

In 1951, four years after Nepal had finally opened its borders to outsiders, Edmund Hillary, a native New Zealander, entered the picture. Born in 1919, Hillary didn't see his first mountain until the age of sixteen on a school field trip. He dropped out of college after two years and went to work as a beekeeper for his father, developing his enthusiasm for climbing in the Southern Alps on South Island, New Zealand.

In 1951, after going to Nepal and climbing Mukut Parbat (23,760 feet), Hillary was invited to join a British reconnaissance expedition on Mount Everest, where he and his comrades climbed various faces of the mountain to determine the best approach. By 1953 thirteen expeditions had attempted Everest and failed to reach the summit. Fifteen men had died along the way. That year, Colonel John Hunt of the British army invited Hillary on a full-scale Everest expedition to be conducted from the Southeast Ridge on the Nepal side. Among the several accompanying Sherpa guides and porters was Tenzing Norgay, a native of Nepal and a very able climber.

Tenzing had spent his youth herding yaks in the nearby mountains and dreaming about Everest. Thus far he had participated in seven different expeditions—three of them before World War II by the northern route.

With plenty of army rations, Colonel Hunt's expedition departed from Kathmandu on March 10, 1953. Each climber was allowed three pairs of gloves, silk, down, and windproof cotton. Worn on top of one another, they were amazingly flexible. Hunt and some of his men had tested the tents, clothes, and other items under extreme conditions in Switzerland and were pleased with the results. Nearly eight tons of supplies were hauled by porters to the advance base camp at the foot of the Lhotse Face. On May 23 the party made a difficult climb to Camp 7, halfway up the Lhotse Face.

As soon as Camp 8 was established at the South Col, four assault teams were assigned to set out every twenty-four hours. It was Hillary and Tenzing's job to set up a Camp 9 somewhere near 28,000 feet. From there the two men would make their attempt at the summit. Hunt was certain that Tenzing and Hillary would work splendidly together. They were different physical types: Hillary tall with long legs, Tenzing short but powerful. Since Tenzing had actually attempted the peak several times before, Hunt thought it fair to give him this special chance.

One of the other teams attempted the first assault against the South Summit. From there they spotted the final ridge. It looked narrow and menacing, with cornices edging it and masses of overhanging snow. They concluded that making it over the ridge and getting back to the South Summit would take them until 6:00 P.M., in which case they'd be out of oxygen. They wisely decided to turn back. The weather became brutal, so all the men stayed in camp, biding their time.

On the morning of May 28, the wind eased enough to encourage Hillary's assault. First a support party left camp, and the assault team followed an hour later.

When the two groups rejoined, Tenzing found a tent site and the support party unloaded their supplies before heading back, leaving Hillary and Tenzing all alone. With their axes the two men carved out a level strip where they could spend the night. They pitched their tent on the world's highest campsite, 28,200 feet, where the bone-chilling cold made it difficult to sleep.

In the morning they had a breakfast of sardines, with plenty of lemonade to prevent dehydration. Hillary thawed his frozen boots over the Primus flame until he could slip them on, then he and Tenzing began their trudge up the Southeast Ridge, a broad, mixed rock and snow ridge that led them to the South Summit. There Hillary was delighted to discover that the snow was hard and safe. An hour more of climbing brought them to the feared rock step, (later named the Hillary Step), a forty-foot-high smooth wall that cut across the ridge.

Discouraged, Hillary noticed a cornice to the right of the step, not completely flush with the rock, which formed a narrow gap between the two. He squeezed himself into it, facing the rock while digging the heels of his crampons behind him.

With a great deal of effort, using his shoulders, knees, and elbows, he hoisted himself upward, eventually making it to the top. He planted himself firmly, then pulled Tenzing up beside him. Victory wasn't far off and the tired men were suddenly energized.

By half-past eleven they stood where no one had stood before, the very top. Overwhelmed with a sense of relief and exhilaration, they shook hands, then threw their arms around each other. They had reached the earth's highest point.

A devout Buddhist, Tenzing dug a hole in the snow and buried offerings to the gods. Hillary removed a crucifix that Hunt had given him with the instruction to push it into the snow if they made it to the summit. Hillary pulled out a

Tenzing Norgay and Edmund Hillary at Thyang-boche Monastery after their successful climb to the highest spot on Earth.

camera and took pictures of Tenzing, though Tenzing was unable to take any of Hillary.

Overhead, Tenzing held the flags of the United Nations, Great Britain, Nepal, and India. After fifteen minutes on the summit, the men began their descent. The rest of the party was awaiting them on the col. After wolfing down some hot soup and oxygen, Hillary's first words were, "Well, we've knocked the bastard off!"

In London, on June 2, 1953, the newly crowned Elizabeth II knighted Edmund Hillary for conquering Everest. By August Hillary had married and was knee-deep in a personal-appearance tour, lecturing across Europe and the United States. On May 10, 1990, Hillary's son, Peter, reached the peak of Everest.

Tenzing also attained worldwide recognition after climbing Everest. In London he was awarded the George Cross for his achievement, and, along with Hillary, he was honored by the king and queen of Nepal. Not comfortable with the celebrity that came with his feat, he settled for becoming the director of field training at the Himalayan Mountaineering Institute in Darjeeling.

In 1978 Italian Reinhold Messner became the first person to climb Everest without oxygen and in 1980 he was the first person to climb it solo.

—J.L.

11 UNUSUAL JOURNEYS

Adventure is the result of poor planning.
        Colonel Blatchford Snell

An adventure is only an inconvenience rightly considered. An inconvenience is only an adventure wrongly considered.

    G. K. Chesterton, *All Things Considered*, 1908, "On Running After One's Hat"

1. OVERLAND FROM PARIS TO NEW YORK

Parisian Harry De Windt's plan had been to find a route for railroad service between Paris and New York. After a failed attempt at this trek in 1896, De Windt set out again in December of 1901. His route took him through Europe and Asia and across almost the whole of Siberia, a distance of more than 11,000 miles; by the time he had reached the Bering Strait he noted that he had employed the labors of 808 horses, 887 reindeer, and 114 dogs.

When De Windt arrived at East Cape, the easternmost point in Asia, he was forced to stay for a month with the Chukchi people until a ship arrived that could take him across the Bering Strait. The remainder of the journey, down through Alaska and the Pacific coast to San Francisco and then across country to New York, was far less arduous. De Windt arrived in New York on August 25, 1902, having covered a total distance of 18,494 miles. His journey, however, had been for naught—by the time he had passed through the crushing ice hazards of the Bering Strait he realized the impossibility of his dream.

2. CRAWLING FROM TEXAS TO WASHINGTON

Many people have made use of odd and sometimes peculiar methods in order to get to Washington, D.C., but perhaps none was as basically strange as that of Hans Mullikin; the logger and sometime Baptist minister crawled the entire distance from his home in Marshall, Texas, to the gates of the White House, a journey that took him two and a half years and ended on November 23, 1978.

Mullikin's was not a continuous journey; in the winters he returned home to work to finance the odyssey. His mode of crawl travel was to go a certain distance on his knees (equipped with goalie kneepads donated by the Dallas Blackhawks hockey team), then jog back to his car and bring it up to his stopping point—repeating this process over and over.

His avowed purpose, said Mullikin, was to "show America that we need to get on our knees and repent." He had hoped to meet with President Jimmy Carter but this could not be arranged. "A lot of people," said Mullikin, smiling, "tell me I'm crazy."

3. BACKWARD WALK FROM SANTA MONICA TO ISTANBUL

On April 15, 1931, a thirty-six-year-old man named Plennie L. Wingo set out from his home in Santa Monica, California, on a journey to Istanbul, Turkey. What made the journey unusual was his intention of walking the entire distance backward.

His basic technical problem—that of seeing where he was going as well as where he had been—was solved when he saw advertised a pair of sunglasses fitted with rearview mirrors. His route, which took him across the United States and much of Europe, covered a distance of more than 8,000 miles and took more than eighteen months to complete. Wingo had hoped to walk backward around the world but was barred from entering Pakistan because of a civil war then in progress.

Wingo's dream was to gain recognition by this unusual feat, and this he accomplished; he is listed in the *Guinness Book of Records* and is the subject of an exhibit in the Ripley's Believe It or Not Museum in San Francisco.

4. A JOURNEY THROUGH "UNIMPORTANT NATIONS"

Travel writer John Sack, apparently having decided that the popular destinations of the

George Schilling tried to walk around the world while pushing a seven-foot globe that also served as his tent.

world's tourists had received too much attention, decided to visit countries that were so small or obscure that most travelers bypassed them.

Sack's purposefully odd journey took him first to Lundy—a small country in the Bristol Channel off England—thence to Sark, another island in the Channel, and at the time of Sack's visit, the only feudal state in all of Europe, presided over by the dame of Sark, a lady named Sybil Hathaway, who collected the annual taxes in chickens. Next came Andorra, the tiny country between France and Spain given its independence by Charlemagne in 784; Sack noted that its principal industries then appeared to be tobacco, tourism, and smuggling. After a brief stop in Monaco—too popular to hold Sack's interest for long—he continued through tiny Lichtenstein and San Marino to the S.M.O.M.—short for the Sovereign Military Order of Malta. This country can be found in the center of Rome and is approximately the size of half a football field; it had diplomatic relations with several countries and its population, at the time of Sack's visit, was two persons.

Sack's next stop was Athos, and it was only an accident of birth that allowed him to visit; no females are allowed in this monastic land, a rule that includes not only people but all other fauna. Other countries visited included Sharja, on the Persian Gulf; Swat, near Afghanistan; Amb, in the center of Pakistan; and Punial and Sikkim, both in the Himalayas.

A collection of Sack's articles on these countries was published in 1959 under the title *Report from Practically Nowhere*; it is not known whether the book caused an upsurge in tourism.

5. WALKS AROUND THE WORLD

In 1970 brothers David and John Kunst of Minnesota began a journey in which the two planned to walk completely around the world. They walked across much of the United States and Europe and passed through Monaco, where they were received by Princess Grace. Their journey was tragically interrupted in Afghanistan, when they were set upon by bandits who murdered John and left David for dead.

After taking his brother's body back to Minnesota, David returned and continued the journey, this time with brother Peter accompanying him for much of the distance. The walk, which was intended to raise money for UNICEF, took Kunst more than four years to complete, averaging about 40 miles a day and covering 14,450 miles.

Nearly ten years later, in 1983, Steven Newman, twenty-eight, set out on a similar journey, beginning at his home in Bethel, Ohio. His journey, like Kunst's, took four years and is the only authenticated solo walk around the world. Newman traveled through Northern Ireland, crossing the Channel to Belgium, then down

through France, Spain, Algeria, and Morocco, through Italy and Turkey, across Asia to Thailand and Australia, and finally back to the United States.

Many stalwarts have attempted the feat of walking around the world—Hungarian Alexandre Kelemen, Belgian Jan de Vautrieul (who had lost an arm and a leg in wartime), and American Joseph Mikulec, among others, but their successes have not been verified.

6. BOWING FOR BUDDHA

Following the Buddhist tradition for a particular kind of religious journey known as a bowing pilgrimage, two American Buddhist monks—Hung Ju and Hung Yo—set out in 1973 to make such a pilgrimage from San Francisco to Seattle, in the cause of world peace. After every third step of the 1,100-mile journey, each made a bow; this was not, however, a simple nod of the head but a bow in which the monk went to his knees and brought his forehead down almost to the pavement. The pilgrimage began in October 1973 and ended in August 1974.

A similar journey was undertaken by two other American Buddhist monks in 1977. Heng Chau and Heng Sure set out from Los Angeles for a Buddhist monastery located near Ukiah, California. This journey, like the earlier one, included the bowing with full prostration every third step, and took several months to complete.

7. AROUND THE WORLD ON A BET

In 1958 three latter-day Phileas Foggs—cousins Bertrand and Marc d'Oultremont, and Abel Armand, Belgian counts all—set off on a round-the-world journey to win a bet made with their friend Dino Vastapane, the stakes being the expenses of the journey. To make things a bit more difficult, Vastapane allowed them only thirty days rather than Fogg's eighty—and they had to win certain "points" at each stop by acquiring various items, ranging from a button from a flight attendant's jacket (easy) to an Alcatraz prison uniform (almost impossible) to a skull from the Parisian catacombs (completely impossible). Vastapane's challenges were difficult, but not insurmountable, and the three counts won their bet when they returned to Belgium with literally only minutes to spare.

8. AFRICA TO GREENLAND

Born in Togo in Africa, Tété-Michel Kpomassie learned in a French-run school of the wonders of the outside world, and Greenland and its Eskimos exercised a strange fascination on the young man. At the age of sixteen, in 1950, he ran away from home and spent six years making his way to Greenland, where he lived a fish-out-of-water existence among the inhabitants for a dozen years. Kpomassie traveled across the country to Baffin Bay, and eventually left to settle in France, where his writings have earned him literary awards.

9. AMPHIBIAN JOURNEY ACROSS THE ATLANTIC

In 1950 Australian Ben Carlin, with his wife, Elinore, set out from Montreal in an amphibious jeep; the craft took to the water off Nova Scotia and crossed the entire Atlantic Ocean, making landfall at the Canary Islands after a stop in the Azores. The Carlins continued their journey by land, eventually stopping in England and going to Malmo, Sweden. Carlin tried to interest British auto manufacturers in his heavily modified vehicle, but there were no takers.

10. A JOURNEY AROUND INDIA

In 1969 a strange bequest from one of its former residents allowed the forty villagers of a tiny Bengali town to tour their country; most had never been more than a few miles from their birthplace, and the landowner who left the bequest explained that she wanted her towns-people to see that India was "very big and very beautiful." The 9,300-mile trip took seven months and is the subject of a book—*Third-Class Ticket*—by Canadian author Heather Wood.

11. FROM PEKING TO PARIS BY AUTOMOBILE

Those who recall the 1965 Tony Curtis–Jack Lemmon film *The Great Race* may wonder if the notion of a car race through various countries is just the fantasy of a screen-writer; in fact such races actually did take place, and one of the earliest was from Peking (now Beijing), China, to Paris, France—a 10,000-mile journey.

The race was suggested first in the French newspaper *Le Matin*, and more than two dozen drivers applied—but when a large money deposit was required, the field narrowed down to five. Of these vehicles, three were French, ranging from six to ten horse-power; one was Dutch, with a fifteen-horsepower engine; and the last was Italian and boasted forty horsepower.

The cars were shipped by boat to Peking and, in June 1907, the overland journey began. Prince Scipione Borghese, owner of the Italian car, had set up elaborate preparations, but the going was extremely difficult, the roads often only mud paths, and sometimes not even that. It was actually a relief to the travelers to encounter the Gobi Desert, for its flat bleakness was ideal for the vehicles. The autos progressed through Siberia and Russia, encountering rough terrain and officials eager for bribes.

Sixty days after departing Peking, Prince Borghese arrived in Paris; the rest of the "race" contestants staggered in three weeks later. If the contest actually proved little, it probably caught the popular imagination and paved the way for more general acceptance of the horse-less carriage.

—T.A.W.

FOOTNOTE PERSON

JOHN HOWARD GRIFFIN (1920–1980)

One of the most vivid personal accounts of the experience of being black in America, *Black Like Me*, was written by a white man, John Howard Griffin. In November 1959 Griffin went to a New Orleans doctor who administered the drug Oxsoralen, which makes skin turn a dark brown upon exposure to the ultraviolet rays of the sun or a sun lamp. Used in conjunction with a vegetable dye, it allowed Griffin to "pass" for black and find out firsthand the prejudice Negroes had to endure.

"As a Southerner," said Griffin, who was born in Dallas, Texas, on June 16, 1920, "I became increasingly tormented by the similarity of our racist attitudes and rationalizations to those I had encountered in Nazi Germany. I began to do studies dealing with the problems and patterns of racism. In 1959, convinced that we were making little progress in resolving the terrible tragedy of racism in America—a tragedy for the white racist as well as for the Negro (and other) victim groups—I had myself medically transformed into a Negro and lived in the states of Louisiana, Mississippi, Alabama, and Georgia.

"I wanted to test whether we really judge men as human or whether we draw up an indictment against a whole group. I kept my name and changed nothing but my pigment."

On assignment from *Sepia* magazine, Griffin worked shining shoes in New Orleans and then hitchhiked, walked, and rode buses through the South for four weeks. He discovered to his dismay the extent and intensity of racial hatred that existed.

On one bus ride to Hattiesburg, Mississippi, he was not allowed to get off at a rest stop with the white passengers. In another incident, this time on a New Orleans city bus, the driver refused to let Griffin out at his requested stop and drove on for eight more blocks before opening the door.

Whenever Griffin managed to hitch rides with whites, they seemed always to turn the

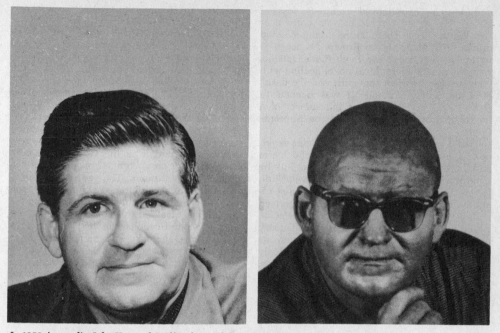

In 1959, journalist John Howard Griffin changed the color of his skin and traveled in the American South as a black man.

conversation toward one general subject—the sexual appetites, preferences, and private parts of blacks. His questioners wanted to know if all the sexual myths about blacks were true and if he had ever had or wanted a white woman. One driver even went so far as to ask Griffin to expose himself because he had never seen a black man completely naked.

Later Griffin was told to "move on" in a public park, was not allowed access to restaurants and rest rooms, had his change thrown on the floor when he tried to purchase a bus ticket, and was given what he called the "hate stare" whenever he came in contact with whites. In general, he learned the daily indignities that blacks had to suffer and it made him sick at heart.

Black Like Me was compiled from Griffin's notes and *Sepia* articles and was well received critically when it was published in 1961. A second edition was published in 1977 with a new epilogue by the author. Altogether, the book has sold more than 12 million copies, and has been translated into fourteen languages. In 1964 it was made into a movie. The book was not popular with some of Griffin's neighbors in Mansfield, Texas; in fact, they hung him in effigy.

Black Like Me was a remarkable project, but Griffin was a remarkable man. When he was fifteen years old he came across a magazine ad

for a boarding school in France. He wrote to the headmaster asking for admission and offering to work in exchange for tuition, since he had no money. He was accepted, and in 1936 he went to France to study at the Lycée Descartes in Tours. He graduated in 1938 and went on to study psychiatry, working as an assistant in an asylum. He worked on experiments using Gregorian chants to treat the insane, and his research led him to pursue a career in musicology.

At the outbreak of World War II, Griffin joined the Défense Passive, a French resistance organization. He helped evacuate Austrian and German Jewish refugees fleeing the Nazis, disguising some of them as mental patients by wrapping them in straitjackets and sending them away in the asylum ambulance. He was almost caught by the Gestapo but eventually returned safely to America. Once home, he enlisted in the U.S. Army Air Corps and was stationed in the South Pacific. During his tour of duty he studied the ethnology and anthropology of the people of the islands around him. In combat, Griffin suffered severe head wounds in a bomb explosion. Presumed dead by medics, he was rescued by a burial crew. As a result of his injuries, he began to lose his eyesight in 1946.

Even though partially blind, Griffin resumed his musical studies in France at the Abbey of Solesmes in Sarthe. After earning a *certificat* d'études, he experienced complete loss of vision. He settled on his parents' farm near Fort Worth, Texas. There, at the urging of noted drama critic John Mason Brown, he began to write. His first book, *The Devil Rides Outside*, was a semiautobiographical novel dealing with "the struggle between the spirit and the flesh" of a monastery student. It was banned in Detroit and in 1957 it was the subject of a landmark obscenity hearing in the Supreme Court.

Griffin was married in 1953. He later developed spinal malaria and lost the use of one arm and both of his legs for two years. But he continued to write, and his second novel, *Nuni*, was completed in 1956. *Nuni* was again semiautobiographical, the story of an American college professor who crash-lands on a Pacific island inhabited by a primitive tribe. In January of 1957, as he was walking unaided from his workshop to the farmhouse, Griffin suddenly regained his vision after ten years of blindness. Upon seeing his wife and two children for the first time (he later had two more children), he said, "They are more beautiful than I ever expected. . . . I am astonished, stunned, and thankful."

Shortly afterward, Griffin undertook the *Black Like Me* project. Less than a year later he began to suffer bone deterioration and tumors. By 1970 he had undergone seventy operations. But in the interim he worked, lectured, taught, and wrote to correct the racial situation that had so affected him during his weeks as a black man. In 1964 he predicted the "massive and deep bloodshed" that was to come in the black uprisings that soon erupted in cities and towns across the country.

Toward the end of his life, Griffin spent nine years working on an official biography of the famous Trappist monk, Thomas Merton. However, his failing health forced him to give up the project before he was able to complete it. By the time of his death on September 9, 1980, of diabetes complications, he had managed to publish several books and numerous shorter works. In one of the last of these he wrote, "I write not because I understand anything and want to expose, but because I understand nothing. . . . I write to seek understanding."

—J.N.

AUTOMOTIVE FIRSTS

1900—National Automobile Show: The first National Automobile Show was held in Madison Square Garden, New York City, in November. Sponsored by the Automobile Club of America, the show featured more than forty automakers exhibiting more than 300 cars. Over the week that the show ran, attendance averaged 6,000 people a day.

1900—Steering Wheel: The first steering wheel was used on the Packard Model C, then built by the Ohio Automobile Company. Before this time, automobiles were steered by tillers, much like boats. Visitors to the National Automobile Show referred to the new steering wheel as "that foreign thing." In defense of its innovation, Packard stated, "In machines that are designed to travel in excess of twenty miles an hour," a steering wheel was an absolute necessity.

1900—Presidential Passenger: William McKinley became the first U.S. president to ride in an automobile.

1901—Statewide Laws: Connecticut became the first of the United States to enact uniform, statewide motor vehicle laws.

1901—Registration: New York passed the first state law requiring registration for automobiles, collecting $954 in fees.

1901—Cheap Oil: A major oil discovery in Beaumont, Texas, pushed oil prices down to around five cents a barrel for the first time. The resulting drop in gas prices made gasoline-powered cars the most practical form of automotive transportation and foreshadowed the eventual death of alternative power sources such as electricity and steam.

1901—Speedometer: The 1901 curved-dash Oldsmobile was the first model equipped with a speedometer.

1902—Eight-Cylinder Engine: The first eight-cylinder engine, a 7.2-liter racing engine, was produced by Charron, Girardot, and Voight in Paris.

1903—Six-Cylinder Engine: The first six-cylinder engine was built by the Spyker company in the Netherlands. The 8.7-liter motor was developed especially for racing.

1903—Land Speed Record: The first land speed record was set at Daytona Beach, Florida, by Alexander Winton in his Winton automobile. His speed was 68.189 miles per hour. The record was broken a few months later by William K. Vanderbilt, Jr., who reached 92.307 miles per hour in a Mercedes. Vanderbilt had also been the first man officially to drive a mile a minute racing his Mercedes on a road outside of Paris in 1902.

1903—Truck Race: On May 20 the first commercial-vehicle (truck) race was held in New York City. Thirteen vehicles were entered—seven heavy trucks and six delivery wagons. The race, sponsored by the Automobile Club of America, publicized the virtues of motorized trucks and sent sales soaring. As a result, the American trucking industry grew up as a way to bring goods—especially perishable farm produce—to market quickly and less expensively.

1903—Speed Limit: In England the world's first speed limit was set at twenty miles per hour.

1904—100 Miles Per Hour: Louis Rigolly drove a Gobron-Brillié to a world-record speed of 103.55 miles per hour at Ostend, Belgium, becoming the first man to exceed 100 miles per hour.

1905—Drag Race: The first drag race was held at Ormond Beach in Florida. A Stanley Steamer outran two Mercedes and a Napier.

1905—Stolen Car: The first car was reported stolen in Saint Louis.

1906—Grand Prix Race: The first Grand Prix, run near Le Mans in France, was won by Ferenc Szisz, driving a ninety-horsepower Renault at an average speed of sixty-five miles per hour for 770 miles.

1907—Parkway: The first parkway, Vanderbilt Motor Parkway, opened on Long Island. The privately owned toll road was conceived and financed by millionaire sportsman and auto enthusiast William K. Vanderbilt Jr. It was originally intended as a venue for the running of the Vanderbilt Cup Races. Ground was broken on June 6, and costs for the sixty-mile parkway eventually reached a total of $2 million.

1908—Interchangeable Parts: Cadillac cars were the first to use interchangeable parts. Three Cadillacs were shipped to England and completely disassembled. The parts were then intermixed and the cars reassembled. The interchangeability concept revolutionized automotive manufacturing techniques by making it possible to produce parts ahead of time and reduce the need to hand-build each automobile individually.

1908—Model T: The first Ford Model T was introduced. Henry Ford's low-priced, mass-produced car made it possible for the general public to own cars, taking automobile ownership out of the exclusive hands of the rich.

1908—Safety Feature: An inventor named John O'Leary developed one of the first vehicle safety features. He patented a device that was mounted on the front fender and deployed a large net meant to scoop unwary pedestrians out of the way before they could be run over.

1908—Cross-Country Family Trip: The first family transcontinental trip was made in a Packard. Jacob Murdoch traveled from Pasadena, California, to New York City with his two teenage daughters, his ten-year-old son, and 1,200 pounds of supplies. The trip took twenty-five days. Packard printed a publicity booklet about the trip entitled *A Family Tour from Ocean to Ocean.*

1908—Concrete Pavement: The first mile of concrete pavement was laid on Woodward Avenue in Detroit at a cost of $13,534.59.

1909—U.S. Racing Championship: The first national racing championship series was sponsored by the American Automobile Association. All of the races were run on public roads except for three events that took place at the newly completed Indianapolis Motor Speedway.

1909—All-Woman Cross-Country Trip: Alice Huyler Ramsey, twenty-two, and three female friends drove from New York to San Francisco, becoming the first all-woman team to cross the United States by automobile. The 4,200-mile trip took fifty-two days, with a total driving time of thirty-five days.

1909—White House Car: President Taft ordered the first official White House car, a White Steamer. Taft, a large man, was so impressed with the roominess of the White that he continued to use the steam vehicles throughout his term and bought others for his personal use after he left office. Other well-known personalities who preferred White Steamers included John D. Rockefeller and Buffalo Bill Cody.

1910—Drunk Driving Law: New York State passed the first drinking-and-driving laws.

1911—Self-Starter: Charles Kettering of Dayton Engineering Laboratories Company (Delco) installed the first self-starter in a Cadillac. The starter replaced the need for strenuous—often dangerous—hand cranking, making it easier for most people, especially women, to drive.

1911—Indianapolis 500: The first Indianapolis 500 was run on May 30. It was won by Ray Harroun in a Mormon Wasp. Harroun's car also sported a previously unknown feature—a rearview mirror. His was the only car in the race that had no riding mechanic on board to tell him if another car was about to overtake him, so he improvised.

1911—Windshield Wiper: The earliest practical wiper was the invention of Prince Henry of Prussia, who fitted it to the windshield of the Benz automobile he drove from Hamburg to London in July 1911. This device was operated by hand, as was the first windshield wiper to be manufactured for sale a year later. Automatic wipers were developed in America in 1916 as standard equipment on the Willys Knight touring car.

1912—Center Lines: The first white lines were painted down the center of roads in Redlands, California.

1913—Moving Assembly Line: In August the first moving production line was installed at Ford's Highland Park, Michigan, assembly plant. A tow rope was hooked to a Model T chassis, pulling it past the workers. By the end of the year, the assembly line was motorized. The use of the line increased Model T production from 7½ to 146 cars per hour.

1913—Gas Station: Gulf opened the first drive-in gas station in Pittsburgh.

1913—Intoxicated Indy Winner: Jules Goux set the record among Indy 500 drivers for drinking the most alcohol while participating in the race. He drank six pints of champagne during his pit stops and went on to win.

1914—Transcontinental Road: Work began on the Lincoln Highway. Proposed by Carl Graham Fisher, the highway was the first transcontinental road, stretching from New York City to San Francisco.

1914—Stop Sign: The first stop sign was put up in Detroit.

1914—Safety Tests: The Dodge Brothers Company performed some of the first auto crash and safety tests. John Dodge took one of the first cars his firm built and drove it straight into a brick wall at twenty miles per hour. He also tested the safety of the cars' tires by throwing them off the top of a four-story building.

1914—Key Starters: Interstate produced the first cars to be started with keys.

1914—Electric Traffic Signals: The first electric signal for controlling cross streams of traffic was installed at the intersection of 105th Street and Euclid Avenue in Cleveland, Ohio, on August 5, 1914. Erected by the American Traffic Signal Company, it consisted of red and green lights surmounting a fifteen-foot-high standard and a warning buzzer to alert drivers when the lights were about to change. An amber warning light was added by African-American inventor Garrett Morgan, who patented his invention in 1923 and sold it to General Electric for $40,000. Racial prejudice had interfered with the sales and marketing of one of his earlier inventions—the gas mask—despite the fact that he had personally demonstrated its worth by rescuing workers trapped in a smoky tunnel. The masks were a hit until buyers learned that the manufacturer was black; even his posing as a Canadian Indian did not help. When sales slumped, he turned his efforts to the traffic light and eventually to the equal-rights movement.

1916—Federal Funding for Road Building: Woodrow Wilson signed the Federal Aid Road Act, providing the first federal money for building roads.

1919—Power Brakes: European automaker Hispano-Suiza introduced the first power brakes. The servo-assisted four-wheel brakes were hailed as the most efficient system ever developed.

1919—State Gas Tax: Oregon passed the first state gasoline tax.

1921—Drive-In Restaurant: J. G. Kirby's Pig Stand, the first drive-in restaurant, opened in Dallas.

1921—Adjustable Seat: Hudson introduced the first adjustable front seat on both Hudson and Essex models.

1921—Highway: The first highway designed for the free flow of traffic without intersections was begun in Berlin in 1909, but with the delays occasioned by World War I, it was not completed until 1921. The Avus Autobahn extended for six and one-fourth miles from Grunewald to Wannsee, with dual carriageways, each twenty-six feet wide, and a grassed-over central reservation of the same width. Cross traffic was carried on ten ferroconcrete flyovers spanning the autobahn. The Italians pioneered with the first freeway connecting two cities when the Milan to Varese autostrada was opened in 1924, and a year later America had its first freeway with the completion of the fifteen-and-a-half-mile Bronx River Parkway.

> *Thanks to the interstate highway system, it is now possible to travel across the country from coast to coast without seeing anything.*
> Charles Kuralt, *On the Road*, 1985

1922—Shopping Mall: National Department Stores opened the first suburban shopping mall near Saint Louis.

1922—Police Car: The Denver police department took delivery of the first car designed especially for police work. The car, called a bandit-chaser, used a Cadillac engine and chassis equipped with a special body. Built with a reinforced frame and bulletproof steel, the car had no top or doors. It was equipped with a gun rack, two rifles, two searchlights, and a machine gun mounted on the hood. The rear seats were slightly raised so the officers in the back could shoot over the heads of those in front.

1923—Twenty-Four-Hour Race: The first twenty-four-hour race for production vehicles was held at Le Mans. The event, conceived by Charles Faroux and George Durand, was won by A. Lagache and R. Leonard in a French-built Chenard-Walcker.

1923—Recall: The 1923 air-cooled Chevrolet became the first model subjected to a recall.

1924—Quick-Drying Paint: DuPont introduced a new paint called duco lacquer that dried by evaporation and cut automotive drying time from thirty days to two hours. Initially available only in blue, the new paint was first introduced on the 1924 Oakland.

1925—100 Miles Per Hour in a Race: At Indianapolis, Peter DePaolo became the first person to break the 100-miles-per-hour average in a race. His speed averaged 101.13 miles an hour.

1926—Safety Glass: Stutz introduced the first safety glass. To prevent shattering, the windows had wire embedded in the glass.

1927—Auto-Styling Studio: Harley Earl formed General Motors's Art and Colour Department, Detroit's first auto-styling studio. His goal was to design new automotive models completely within the company, rather than using outside consultants or letting the work of the engineering department drive the look of the car, as was normally done. The first car the Art and Colour Department designed was the 1927 LaSalle.

1929—Car Radio: The first car radios were sold by Motorola for aftermarket installation. The radios were developed by Paul Galvin and Bill Lear, later the founder of Lear Jet.

1930—V-16 Engine: Cadillac introduced the first V-16 automobile engine. The overhead-valve, 452-cubic-inch engine developed 165 horsepower and reached a top speed of ninety miles an hour. The V-16 was available in thirty-three different models, submodels, and trim variations, ranging in price from $5,350 to $8,750.

1932—Fender Skirts: The first fender skirts appeared on the 1932 Graham Blue Streak Eight. Designed by Ames Northrup, the skirts would become a nearly universal design element within a few years.

1932—Federal Gas Tax: The U.S. government levied the world's first national gasoline tax.

1933—Drive-In Theater: The first drive-in movie theater opened in Camden, New Jersey. By the fifties there were more than 4,000 drive-ins around the United States, much to the joy of teenagers everywhere.

1935—Autoworkers Union: The United Automobile Workers union was formed in August. That fall the union instituted a series of work stoppages and strikes at various auto plants. After several intense, often bloody, confrontations with the major automotive companies, the UAW received bargaining rights with General Motors and Chrysler in 1937. Ford Motor Company held out longer but finally officially recognized the union in April 1941.

1935—Chain Restaurant: The first franchised chain restaurant opened when Howard Johnson contracted with a friend to open an identical version of his already-successful restaurant on Cape Cod. Within a year, thirty-nine more Howard Johnson franchises had opened. In 1940 the company received the franchise to provide food service for the newly opened Pennsylvania Turnpike. By 1941 more than 150 Howard Johnson restaurants stretched along the roads from Florida to New England.

1935—Parking Meter: Carlton Magee, editor of Oklahoma City's *Daily News*, was chairman of the local Traffic Committee when he conceived

Three weeks after the world's first parking meters were installed on the streets of Oklahoma City, in 1935, a resident tries out the new invention.

the idea of parking meters and formed the Dual Parking Meter Company to manufacture them. The name signified the meters' dual purpose of regulation and revenue. On July 16, 1935, when the first 150 meters went into operation on one side of a busy shopping street, the parking spaces on the opposite side were rapidly filled. But much to their surprise, the store owners on that side found that they were doing far less business then the store owners on the metered side. People who had to pay to park made their purchases quickly and left, leaving the space to another shopper. After three days the meterless store owners petitioned the Traffic Committee for parking meters on their side of the street.

1937—Automatic Transmission: Oldsmobile offered the first fully automatic transmission, called the Hydra-Matic. The transmission used four speeds and added fifty-seven dollars to the price of the car. By the late forties and fifties, the Hydra-Matic was also used by Cadillac and Pontiac, as well as by independent automakers such as Nash, Hudson, and Kaiser-Frazer.

1939—Air-Conditioning: Nash offered the first automotive air-conditioning as an option. Dubbed the Weather-Eye, the highly innovative option was a combination heating-and-ventilation system.

1939—Flashing Turn Signals: Buick introduced the first flashing electric turn signals. The signals were installed on the rear of the car as part of the trunk emblem.

1940—Modern Long-Distance Road: The first modern U.S. long-distance road, the Pennsylvania Turnpike, opened on October 1.

1942—National Speed Limit: On January 1 the manufacture of civilian cars and trucks was frozen for the duration of World War II. The next day the Automotive Council for War Production was formed as the auto industry switched all of its manufacturing facilities to the production of war matériel. Tires and gas were rationed by March. The first national speed limit, set at thirty-five miles per hour, was established as well. In January 1943 a ban on driving for pleasure was put into place.

1946—Fiberglass Body: The first fiberglass-bodied car, the Stout 46, was introduced. Also known as Project Y, the car was designed by William B. Stout, who built it in partnership with Kaiser-Frazer. The project died because the car was thought to be too radical and too expensive—it was estimated that a production version would cost $10,000 to build. The prototype car is owned today by the Detroit Historical Museum.

1948—Electric Windows: British Daimler introduced the first electric windows.

1948—Tail Fins: Cadillac put the first tail fins on its cars. Inspired by the design of the Lockheed P-38 fighter plane, fins became the most well known styling feature of cars of the fifties, and every major automaker incorporated them into the designs of their vehicles.

1949—Padded Instrument Panel: Chrysler offered the first padded instrument panel.

1950—Dream Car: In January Nash-Kelvinator unveiled the NX1 Surview car, the first "idea" or "dream" car. These special, one-of-a-kind vehicles were built by the auto companies for display at auto shows around the country. Often wildly futuristic, they were meant to show the public possible features and designs for later models. The styling of the NX1 was later modified for the small Nash Metropolitan. Late in 1950 Chrysler debuted its dream-car program with the Plymouth XX500 and General Motors displayed its dramatic LeSabre.

1952—Holiday Inn: The first Holiday Inn was opened after its founder, Kemmon Wilson, found himself extremely dissatisfied with the accommodations he found on a long car trip. Holiday Inn eventually became the world's largest motel chain.

1953—Mass-Produced Plastic Body: The Chevrolet Corvette became the first plastic-bodied car to be built in quantity.

1955—Bucket Seats: Bucket seats were offered for the first time on Corvettes and Thunderbirds.

> The automobile changed our dress, manners, social customs, vacation habits, the shape of our cities, consumer purchasing patterns, common tastes and positions of intercourse.
> John Ketas, The Insolent Chariots, 1958

1956—Record Player: Chrysler offered the first in-dash record player as an option. The Highway Hi-Fi played special 16⅔ RPM records.

1956—Safety Package: Ford introduced the first optional safety package for its cars. Consisting of lap seat belts, a padded dash, sun visors, a deep-dish steering wheel, and safety door latches, the package was a commercial failure. Very few were sold, and Ford withdrew it as an option after one model year.

1958—Japanese Export to U.S.: Datsun exported its first cars to the United States. Total

American sales for the year reached only eighty-three units.

1959—Swivel Seats: Chrysler offered the first swivel front seats. The seats turned automatically toward the outside when the door was opened. A possibly apocryphal story holds that the option was discontinued when the wife of a top Chrysler executive found herself in an extremely awkward position. The couple were on their way to a party one hot summer night and the well-dressed lady had been cooling her legs by raising her skirt and enjoying the blowing of the air-conditioning. Unfortunately, when they arrived at their destination, the unwitting valet opened the passenger door too quickly and . . .

1959—Import Success: For the first time, imported cars accounted for more than 10 percent of sales to the American market.

1960—Toyota Sold in U.S.: Toyota sold its first cars to customers in the States. Toyota Tiara models were exported to the United States beginning in June, and the company had opened sixty-five American dealerships by the end of the year.

1960—Anti-Pollution Law: California became the first state to pass legislation requiring all cars to install special equipment to limit exhaust pollution. Following California's lead, Congress passed the Clean Air Act in 1963 and the Motor Vehicle Air Pollution Control Act in 1965. The Air Quality Act of 1967 gave the federal government the power to set clean-air standards for all states.

1961—V-6 Engine in U.S.: In September the first U.S. V-6 engine was offered by Buick for its 1962 models. The 198-cubic-inch, 135-horsepower engines were available in the Buick Special Standard series only, but by the end of the model year, more than 59,200 V-6–equipped cars had been sold.

> Americans are broad-minded people. They'll accept the fact that a person can be an alcoholic, a dope fiend, a wife beater, and even a newspaperman, but if a man doesn't drive, there is something wrong with him.
>
>   Art Buchwald, *How Much Is That in Dollars?*,
>   1961

1962—Seat-Belt Requirement: Wisconsin passed the first law requiring all cars sold there to have seat belts installed. Before that time, seat belts were available only as an option—often at extra cost.

1963—150 Miles Per Hour at Indy: Parnelli Jones became the first driver to break 150 miles per hour at the Indianapolis 500.

1963—National Safety Law for Government Vehicles: The U.S. Congress passed the first national safety law in the world. It required all automobiles purchased by the federal government to be equipped with seventeen safety items, including lap belts, dual brake systems, outside rearview mirrors, padded instrument panels and sun visors, and backup lights.

1966—National Safety Law for All Vehicles: The National Traffic and Motor Vehicle Safety Act became law in the wake of Ralph Nader's book, *Unsafe at Any Speed*, which exposed safety problems in domestic automobiles. The act mandated equipment such as head restraints, energy-absorbing steering columns, penetration-resistant windshields, better door locks, side-impact beams, and safety belts.

1969—1 Million Imported Cars: Registrations of imported cars topped the 1-million mark in the United States for the first time this year, with sales of all imports totaling 1,061,617. Also in 1969, Toyota became the first Japanese carmaker to exceed 100,000 deliveries to the States in one year.

1971—Tape Player: Chrysler offered the first in-dash stereo cassette tape player/recorder, complete with a microphone.

1974—Airbag: One of the most important safety devices developed for automobiles, the airbag was first fitted to the Mercury cars of Allstate Insurance's company fleet. Later in 1974 they were made available to private motorists when Oldsmobile offered them as an optional extra on their Delta 88, Delta 88 Royale, Eighty-Eight, and Toronado models.

1974—55 Miles Per Hour Law: The 55-miles-per-hour national speed limit was imposed in the United States, the first time since World War II that the government had instituted such a regulation.

1977—200 Miles Per Hour at Indy: Tom Sneva became the first driver to break 200 miles per hour at the Indianapolis 500.

1982—Foreign-Owned Factory in North America: Honda opened the first "transplant"— a foreign-owned automotive plant operating in North America. The Japanese automaker assembled 100 Honda Accords a week at its Marysville, Ohio, assembly plant.

1983—U.S.-Japan Joint Venture: On December 22 the Federal Trade Commission approved a joint venture between General Motors and

Toyota to build cars in California—the first such venture between American and Japanese automakers.

1984—Seat-Belt Law: On July 12 New York became the first state to require drivers, front-seat passengers, and children under the age of ten to wear seat belts.

1987—CD Player: The 1987 Lincoln Town Car was the first American car to offer a factory-installed CD player as an option.

1991—One-Price Policy: In March the Ford Motor Company attempted to simplify vehicle pricing strategies by testing a new program in three sales regions. All Ford Escort LX models with manual transmissions were sold for the same price, no matter what the body style. For the first time, every dealer sold cars under a unified pricing structure. The program went nationwide in March 1992, and another one-price policy was put in place for the 1993 Ford Thunderbird and Mercury Cougar.

1993—Personal Security Package: The firm of O'Gara, Hess and Eisenhardt Armoring Co. introduced an innovative "personal security vehicle," the PSV2. Designed to combat terrorist attacks, assassination attempts, and car-jackings, the special package could be added to most production sedans and small trucks. It featured lightweight armor, tires that could run when flat, an intercom system, a dual-battery system, tamper-proof doors, and a self-sealing foam fuel tank. The PSV2 added $40,000 to $70,000 to the cost of an automobile.

—K.A.R.

AUTO BIOGRAPHIES

ROLLS-ROYCE

A charming Rolls-Royce legend says that the color of the radiator emblem was changed from red to black when Henry Royce died. In fact, Royce himself ordered the change shortly before his death in 1933. The red emblem, he believed, clashed with the paint colors on some Rolls-Royces. And Royce was determined that nothing on his cars would be inharmonious.

That attention to detail allowed Rolls-Royce to become known as the best car in the world. The marque has always been associated with the rich and famous. India's seventh nizam of Hyderabad owned one with a body cast of solid silver. William Randolph Hearst owned two, complete with bars, tables, and rolltop desks. Beatle John Lennon decorated his Rolls with a psychedelic paint job. (Royce would not have approved.) Rolls-Royces have been bullet-proofed, equipped with bathtubs, and built to accept the wheelchairs of their owners.

Exotic cars are only part of the story. During World War I, Rolls-Royce armored cars motored to glory in Arabia under the command of T. E. Lawrence. Lawrence wrote of his amazement at Rolls-Royce durability. Burdened with three tons of armor plate, his vehicles ran on and on with a bare minimum of maintenance. Some of those same armored cars would harass the Germans again in World War II, a war that Rolls-Royce aircraft engines helped win; the Merlin engine powered such legendary aircraft as the Spitfire and the P-51 Mustang.

The Rolls-Royce story began in 1904, when Frederick Henry Royce bought a used car. Royce was the product of dire poverty; problems stemming from childhood malnutrition would plague him all his life. But he was mechanically talented and had an awesome capacity for work. By 1904 Royce was a successful engineer with his own company. He needed a car, but his used French Decauville disappointed him. Characteristically, Royce decided to build a better car. The first Royce rolled out for its road test on April Fool's Day, 1904.

A customized Rolls-Royce.

Charles J. Rolls came from a well-to-do family. A childhood infatuation with machines stayed with him into adulthood, and Rolls fell in love at his first glance of an automobile. He grew into a daredevil who raced motorcycles and cars and flew balloons. With his friend Claude Johnson, Rolls became the distributor for several makes of car.

Through the car-fanatic grapevine, Rolls heard about a fellow named Royce, whose homemade auto outperformed many manufactured products. Royce and Johnson were impressed enough first to sell Royce's cars, then to go into business with him. The Rolls-Royce company was formed in March 1906.

Their first cars were four-seaters with a top speed of thirty miles per hour from a two-cylinder, ten-horsepower engine. Cylinders and horsepower doubled in the next model, a fact advertised in its name: the Long 20. The new company was a success; demand exceeded production even in 1906, when production was only forty cars. In the beginning, Royce built the cars and Rolls often raced them.

Rolls's daredeviltry finally got the better of him. After Wilbur Wright took him for a ride in an airplane, Rolls had to have an aircraft of his own. He bought a Wright-designed plane in which he crashed and died in 1910. The tragedy left a mark on Henry Royce. Though he would design some of the world's best aircraft engines, Royce never flew in an airplane.

Royce and Claude Johnson were left to run Rolls-Royce alone. Johnson's forte was administration. The engineering had to come from Royce, and he almost worked himself to death. After a serious mental breakdown, Royce moved to a villa in the south of France. He continued to run Rolls-Royce by mail, sending his employees letters filled with engineering specifications and design data.

This correspondence was bound into a volume called "the bible" by company executives. "The bible" is still used as a reference today, and decisions often turn on "whether or not Henry Royce would have done it." Royce built cars with quality first, never mind the cost. In practical terms, this meant that a finely machined 32-pound brake drum began as a 106-pound hunk of forged metal. Years before stress analysis was common in car factories, Rolls-Royce employees were using magnifying glasses to search for hidden flaws in metal.

The Rolls-Royce family tree contains such famous names as the 1905 Grey Ghost, the Silver Ghost built from 1906 to 1925 and considered by many the best Rolls ever made, and the Phantoms of the 1920s and 1930s. Many Rolls-Royces wore custom bodies ("bespoke bodywork") by designers such as Kellner of Paris. The tradition continued with the Silver Wraiths, Silver Dawns, Silver Clouds, Silver Shadows, down to the Camarques and Corniches of the present.

Today Rolls-Royce turns out about twenty cars per week that feature the best hand-fitted bodywork in the world. A Rolls-Royce representative still travels each year to select personally the walnut trees that will eventually grace the cars' dashboards. The leather interior still requires eight full cowhides. Henry Royce would approve, and would no doubt quote his favorite proverb: "The quality will be appreciated long after the price is forgotten."

FORD MODEL T

Henry Ford's Model T was the first "people's car." More than merely a car, the Model T was a cultural phenomenon. People wrote songs and made up jokes about it. They called it the Universal Car, the flivver, and, most often, the Tin Lizzie. Accessory manufacturers turned out more than 5,000 gadgets that could convert the T into a racing car, a farm tractor, or (by attaching a belt to the rear axle) a sawmill.

"I am going to democratize the automobile," Ford declared, "and when I'm through, everybody will be able to afford one and about everybody will have one." Introduced in 1908 at $850, the price dropped every year of production until it hit $290 in 1923. Ford sold 15.8 million Model Ts between 1908 and 1927. That production record was finally and fittingly broken by another "people's car"—the Volkswagen Beetle.

Henry Ford never intended simply to build a cheap car. He wanted to build a good car as inexpensively as possible. The Model T offered a four-cylinder twenty-horsepower motor, a revolutionary planetary transmission, and a high-riding body of vanadium steel with four sturdy wheels.

The Tin Lizzie opened the vast rural and small-town market, where the automobile had been unaffordable. In 1908 half of the American population lived on farms or in towns of less than 2,500 people. To farmers, Henry Ford, a

A sporty couple in their 1920 Ford Model T Runabout.

farm boy himself, offered an automobile that could outperform a team of horses. It was also so simple that any shade-tree mechanic could repair it.

Though often credited with the feat, Henry Ford did not invent the moving assembly line (Ransom E. Olds did). His genius lay in the way he improved the idea. Ford's economic philosophy was to cut costs by building only one model and by developing creative new production techniques. This philosophy lay behind his famous remark that the customer could have a Model T in any color he wanted, as long as it was black. From 1908 to 1913, the Model T could also be had in red, green, blue, or gray. Then Ford discovered that the paint that dried fastest—and kept his assembly lines moving—was japanned black enamel.

Ford passed on his savings to the consumer in lower prices, which boosted sales, which increased production and lowered prices still further. Americans admired Henry Ford as a businessman who passed on his profits to the buyer (through lower prices) and to the worker (by doubling his employees' wages to five dollars a day in 1914).

The automaker was a contradictory man. He was a rabid anti-Semite but one of the few bosses of his day who hired black workers and paid them the same wages as whites. He was an avowed pacifist who made millions from defense contracts. He said, "History is more or less bunk," yet left behind Greenfield Village, in Dearborn, Michigan, so future generations could see how people lived in preindustrial America. As he grew older, Ford increasingly yearned for that rural America—an America he largely helped destroy with all those Model Ts. Ford's refusal to improve the Model T eventu-

ally doomed the Tin Lizzie. In 1909 he proclaimed that there would be "no new models, no new motors, no new bodies, and no new colors." During the 1920s Ford nominally retired and his son Edsel became president of the company. Their relationship was complex and unhappy. Edsel showed brilliance in automotive design and styling, but he was not the man to stand up to old Henry or his personal thug, Harry Bennett. Edsel once had a Model T modified with an up-to-date body. He thought Henry would come around and agree to change the outdated design. When Henry saw the car, he picked up a hammer and began smashing it, while furiously ordering Edsel never to touch the Model T again.

Meanwhile, a man named Alfred P. Sloan had gathered several struggling carmakers into a corporation named General Motors. Sloan believed that while the Model T had brought basic transportation to America, people were ready for style and comfort along with the basics. Sloan aimed his Chevrolet directly at Ford's market, offering different colors and fresh styling each year.

Henry Ford bowed to the inevitable in 1927 and killed the Model T. But the old flivver would be remembered affectionately by millions of Americans; for many it was their very first car. Celebrity Model T owners included the Nobel Prize–winning novelist Sinclair Lewis, Charles Lindbergh, Babe Ruth, and even the Mexican bandit Pancho Villa. You could drive a Tin Lizzie anywhere—across streambeds, up steps, or down the rutted cow paths that served as roads in rural America during the early 1900s. You could count on a Model T. According to a popular joke, one Model T owner asked to be buried with his Tin Lizzie because "the darned thing pulled me out of every hole I ever got into, and it ought to pull me out of that one."

HENRY FORD'S SOYBEAN FIXATION

Henry Ford is best known as the man who put America on wheels. But his greatest obsession was not the automobile. It was soybeans.

Actually, Ford was big on all vegetables, but he worshipped the soybean with a feeling akin to reverence. To him it was the cure for all of mankind's woes, as rich in manufacturing applications as in dietary value. In the 1930s the Ford Motor Company built three processing plants in Michigan, where soybean oil was extracted and made into automobile paint and plastic fittings for Ford cars—gearshift knobs, horn buttons, distributor housings, and switch handles. Indeed, Ford dreamed of someday making sleek cars and beautiful furniture entirely from soybeans.

At the peak of Ford's soybean mania, his company was growing more than fifty varieties of the plant on 8,000 acres and buying an additional 500,000 bushels yearly from Michigan farmers. Meanwhile, the

industrialist spoke constantly about the ancient Oriental staple. No meal was served in his home without soybeans or their derivatives on the table, and a pitcher of cold soybean milk was always in the refrigerator for parched guests. Once Ford appeared at a convention dressed in a suit and matching tie woven of soy-derived fabric. At the 1934 Century of Progress Fair in Chicago, his company served a sixteen-course soybean dinner, featuring puree of soybean, soybean croquettes with green soybeans, soybean coffee, and soybean cookies.

Ford's agricultural obsessions did not end with the soybean. His researchers fiddled with cornstalks, cantaloupe seeds, and milkweed, all grown in abundance on company-owned property. But of all the fruits of nature, none drove him bananas so completely as the soybean.

—The Eds.

VOLKSWAGEN BEETLE

Known to millions of devoted owners as the Bug or the Beetle, the Volkswagen earned a different sort of nickname from Henry Ford II: "a little shit box." On a March 1948 trip to Germany, Ford was offered the entire VW factory—free. He turned it down. Grandson of the man who invented the Model T, Ford knew what Americans wanted. And he knew they would never buy the VW.

By 1972, when Beetle number 15,007,034 puttered off the main assembly line in Wolfsburg, Germany, Volkswagen had broken the total production record for Model T's. In its own modest way, the Beetle revolutionized the car industry, becoming the first true world car. Dependable as a crowbar and almost as indestructible, the Beetle was cheap to buy and operate. Its air-cooled engine ignored temperature extremes, and the VW's light weight and tough torsion-bar suspension let it travel roads that could destroy larger but lesser cars.

In April 1933 Adolf Hitler met with a self-educated engineer named Ferdinand Porsche. Hitler wanted a car for every German. A "people's car"—a *Volkswagen*. He was talking to the right man. Like his idols Thomas Edison and Henry Ford, Porsche believed in spreading technology to rich and poor alike. On January 17, 1934, Porsche sent a Volkswagen design to Hitler. A few months later, he was summoned to a secret meeting with Hitler at Berlin's Kaiserhof Hotel.

In about fifteen minutes, Adolf Hitler changed automotive history. Germany would build the "people's car" in a new automobile plant—the world's biggest. Then der Fuehrer dropped the real bombshell. The Volkswagen must sell for 1,000 Reichsmarks (about $250)—the price of a medium-sized German motorcycle. Hitler directed Porsche to start work immediately, with help from the Reich Motor Industries Organization (RMIO).

But the RMIO—Mercedes-Benz, Opel, and others—wanted their executives in charge, not Porsche. The RMIO ordered Porsche to build three running prototypes in ten months, which they knew was impossible. Porsche missed the deadline. The RMIO gleefully notified Hitler, then waited for the thunderbolts to fall.

Which they did . . . right on the heads of the RMIO. Exact events are unknown, but the archives of Daimler-Benz contain a bland 1935 letter saying German carmakers "decided to build the Volkswagen as a common effort." Porsche soon had all the help he needed.

The 1,000-mark price ceiling was still impossible. To cut costs, Porsche had designed a two-cylinder VW engine. When it failed, he delegated the engine design to an employee, Franz Reimspeiss. In forty-eight hours, Reimspeiss drew up a four-cylinder, horizontally opposed engine. Coworkers joked about "the Rolls-

Ulrich Csernak of Wermelskirchen, Germany, mowing his VW Bug, 1972.

Royce engine," for its perceived cost. But the four-cylinder proved cheaper to mass-produce than a two-cylinder. Reimspeiss's basic 1934 design powers every Beetle ever built, right down to the present.

On May 26, 1938, Hitler laid the cornerstone for the world's largest auto assembly plant under one roof, near an old estate called Wolfsburg. The car was renamed to credit the Nazi regime: "the Strength-Through-Joy Motor Car." Strength Through Joy (Kraft-durch-Freude, in German, or KdF) was the Nazi version of bread and circuses—a program that rewarded workers with free vacations and the like, to distract them from such minor inconveniences as the Gestapo.

Every German could own a KdF car, through a radical government savings plan: workers would have five marks per week deducted from their pay and deposited in a special KdF-car bank account. This scheme collected more than $68 million . . . which disappeared. (The savers didn't forget. After a 1961 legal decision, Volkswagen offered them either a 100-mark refund or a discount of 600 marks on a new VW.)

In 1939 the VW began a unique six-year proving test called World War II. Porsche designed two military models, the Kubelwagen (bucket-car) and the amphibious Schwimmwagen. Volkswagens were often the only cars running on the Russian front, where winter temperatures dropped to minus forty degrees Fahrenheit. In the blistering African desert, Field Marshal Erwin Rommel bamboozled the British by disguising his VWs as tanks.

During World War II, bombing destroyed two-thirds of the Wolfsburg plant, killing 73 workers and injuring 160. However, Volkswagen production never stopped.

When Germany surrendered in 1945, Porsche was briefly arrested as a war criminal, then left alone to pursue another dream: a two-seat, rear-engine sports car. He died, aged seventy-five, on New Year's Day 1951—two months after driving a black Porsche 356 from Stuttgart to Paris in seven hours.

Porsche lived long enough to see more than 50,000 of his "people's cars" produced, largely through the efforts of Heinrich Nordhoff (1899–1968). The American-trained Nordhoff, formerly an Opel executive, became manager of Volkswagen in 1948. He cut production time from 400 to 100 hours and insisted on higher-quality materials for the VW. Like Porsche, Nordhoff didn't want a cheaper car; he wanted a better car.

By 1953 Volkswagen produced nearly half of West Germany's total car production. On August 5, 1955—just ten years after World War II—the millionth VW was produced. In 1974 the last German Beetle rolled down the Wolfsburg assembly line. But the Bug is harder to kill than Count Dracula: VW plants in Mexico and Brazil produced more than 100,000 Beetles in 1994, bringing total production over sixty years to more than 21 million.

Today automotive engineers spend millions of computer-aided dollars trying to reproduce the Beetle's phenomenal success. But the secret of that success was revealed in a 1956 *Popular Mechanics* article by Arthur Railton: "The Volkswagen sells because it is, more than anything else, an honest car. It doesn't pretend to be anything it is not."

TRABANT

How many workers does it take to build a Trabant?

Two. One to fold and one to paste.

How can you double the value of a Trabant?

Fill it up.

If the Trabant had two tailpipes, according to a worker on the Trabant assembly line, it would make a fine wheelbarrow.

The East German Trabant inspired many jokes, mainly from its owners, during a thirty-two-year production run. Though rooted in the truth that the Trabant was cranky and obsolete, the jokes also expressed the perverse pride East Germans felt for "der Trabi."

"The Trabi was a lot like East Germany," said actor Wolfgang Stumph. Stumph costarred with a heroic blue Trabant in a 1991 German movie, *Go Trabi Go.* "It was far from perfect, but somehow it worked. You had to improvise every day to keep it going. It was small and smelly and broke down a lot, but it was what we had."

Like a motorcycle, the Trabi's two-stroke engine was lubricated by mixing oil with the gasoline. To East Germans fleeing westward in late 1989, this burning mixture produced "the smell of freedom." West Germans were more

The much-maligned Trabant gained a little respect in 1989 when it carried tens of thousands of East Germans to the West before the final fall of Communism.

unkind. "Trabi-German" became a pejorative for the stereotypical East German, and the Trabant was dubbed "the little stinker."

The Trabant's noisy twenty-six-horsepower engine produced as much pollution as thirty large Mercedes-Benzes—probably the only comparison that will ever be made between Mercedes and Trabant. The Trabant lacked carpeting, a glove box, or even a fuel gauge. The rear windows were glued shut. Its sole passenger comfort was a primitive heater, in which a fan simply blew hot engine air into the interior—along with "the smell of freedom."

All this might imply that the Trabant was undesirable. Far from it. The average Trabant owner waited as long as eighteen years to take delivery of a car. The price equated to a year's salary, and black-market Trabis sold for double that amount.

The East German government began Trabant production in 1959, shortly after the Soviet Union launched the first artificial satellite, *Sputnik*. *Trabant* is the German equivalent of *sputnik*, meaning either "satellite" or "fellow traveler."

The car was built in a dim, sooty old Horch auto plant in Zwickau. Workers often pushed Trabis down the antique assembly line, and almost all assembly was done with common hand tools such as pliers and screwdrivers.

Like its West German cousin, the VW Beetle, the Trabant was designed as a people's car, with simplicity and economy foremost. The Trabi designers succeeded with a vengeance.

Suspension was straight out of the 1930s, using single transverse springs front and rear. The front-wheel-drive transmission was a four-speed manual, controlled by a clunky steering-column shifter.

The 600-cc, air-cooled, two-cylinder engine was a pre–World War II design. Valve adjustment was never required because the engine had no valves. This power plant could wheeze from zero to sixty miles per hour in a little more than thirty seconds, with an eventual top speed of sixty-six miles per hour.

The Trabi stopped as leisurely as it accelerated. Road-testing a Trabant in 1990, *Car and Driver* reported: "The engine provides no braking effect at all. Nor do the brakes."

Overall length was 140 inches, comparable to the smallest subcompacts. Trabis came in three colors (blue, white, or gray) and two body styles: the wildly misnamed Limousine sedan and the Universal, a station wagon.

From 1959 to 1990, 150,000 Trabis per year were built. As these figures imply, construction was unhurried. "The government had a slogan, 'Socialism will last forever,' " said a machinist in the Trabant plant. "That made us think, 'Why do we have to worry or hurry? Because if we don't do it today, we could always do it tomorrow.' "

For the Trabi, "tomorrow" came in early 1991. The newly reunified Germany passed strict tax laws to get rid of polluting cars. The last Trabant was built in April of that year.

The Trabi is dead, but not gone. Even junked Trabants pose grave environmental dangers. The Trabant body was made of Duroplast, a mix of phenol plastic and cotton matting, which releases dioxins when burned. Dead Trabants are occasionally ground up and spread on snowy roads in winter. In 1993 the rock group U2 recycled old Trabis by using them as stage props on a world tour.

For its contribution to democracy by bringing thousands of East Germans across collapsing Communist borders, *Car and Driver* named the Trabant the "1990 Import Car of the Year."

Rock star, movie star, and the conveyance that carried its fellow citizens "in from the cold" to a new life of freedom.

Maybe "der Trabi" had the last laugh after all.

DATSUN 510

The Datsun 510 was a Trojan horse. The plain exterior fooled American auto executives, who dismissed it as just another Japanese econobox. But auto engineers saw through the disguise. The 510 had an overhead-cam engine, four-wheel independent suspension, and front disc brakes. The Japanese had built an inexpensive family sedan with the heart of a sports car.

When the 510 reached the United States in 1967, the import market was dominated by Volkswagen, selling 25,000 Beetles per month. Nissan was selling only 33,000 Datsuns per year.

The 510 alone accounted for 100,000 sold during its first year on the market.

Within five years, VW lost a quarter of its U.S. market to the Japanese, and America's complacent "big three" carmakers were suddenly faced with serious competition. Much of the credit for Japan's conquest of automotive America belongs to the 510.

Not bad, for a car Nissan did not want to build. The Datsun 510 has a secret history, one that proves that Japanese car companies can be just as hidebound and shortsighted as their American counterparts. According to Yutaka Katayama, the Nissan employee who fought for a decade to get the 510 built, his bosses behaved "as timidly as those in a government bureaucracy."

Maybe it was corporate genetics. In 1911, three cautious financiers pooled their resources and bought a car company, Kwaishinsa Motor Car Works. The financiers were Mr. K. Den, Mr. R. Aoyama, and Mr. A. Takeuchi. In 1925 they renamed the company, using their initials—D.A.T. When they built a new family car in 1931, they christened it *Dat* (which means fast rabbit in Japanese), and since the car was their baby, or son, it became Datson. Then they realized that in Japanese, son also translates as "loss"—not a great connotation for a new company, especially one headed by financiers. The car's name was changed to Datsun.

In 1933 DAT Motors became Nissan Motor Company. Datsun was a success, and by 1935 Datsuns were being exported. In 1938 Japan's military dictatorship restricted civilian car production, and Nissan began making army trucks.

After World War II Nissan slowly rebuilt, again copying other cars (the Datsun copied the British Austin) while designing its own vehicles. By 1957 the Datsun 110 sedan and 120 pickup truck were in production. The Datsun 310 was exported to North America in 1958.

Enter Yutaka Katayama, Nissan's American representative on the West Coast. Daily witnessing the thundering metal flood on California freeways, Katayama knew that Datsuns had one glaring fault in the American market—they were underpowered. Katayama began relentlessly pushing for a larger engine.

His Tokyo bosses ignored him. Nissan executives did not believe in "export models." If a car was good enough for the Japanese home market, it was good enough for any country in the world. Katayama argued, sometimes with the president of Nissan himself, that their company would never become a world-class competitor until it built a world-class car.

He got nowhere until Nissan hired a former government official named Keiichi Matsumura. As a newcomer from a high position, Matsumura owed nothing to Nissan company politics. He was too powerful, and too independent, to be intimidated by the "bureaucrats" who had frustrated Katayama. Hoping to increase Datsun export sales, Matsumura frequently visited Katayama in the United States and listened to his ideas.

With Matsumura's backing, Katayama got the engine size increased from 1400 to 1600 cc.

Even more important, the new engine would go in a new car, the kind of car Katayama had always wanted: a sports sedan, like the BMW 1600, which embodied the best automotive engineering, but built with Japanese mass-production techniques to keep the price in reach of anyone.

One of his American friends said that, while waiting for his first 510 shipment, Katayama was "more like an expectant mother than an auto executive." The first car off the transport ship was a white 510 with a red interior; Katayama jumped in and personally drove it to the Nissan parking facility.

Almost immediately, 510 sales moved Nissan to third place among imported cars. Dealers could not keep the 510 in stock, especially on the West Coast. Motor Trend magazine raved in April 1968: "Reliable, comfortable, maneuverable, and economical to run—a true fun car . . . [It] certainly seemed to be engineered for U.S. roads and drivers, and we definitely began to get the feeling that we were driving a much bigger car." Motor Trend pointed out that the 510 cost "less than a dollar a pound."

The 510 soon proved that the label "sports sedan" was not just advertising hype. In the hands of drivers like Pete Brock, modified 510 sedans burned up the race circuits. In the 1972 American Road Race of Champions, competing in B-sedan class against BMW and other more expensive makes, the 510 won first, second, third, and fifth places.

Not long after the 510 went on sale, Katayama began receiving inquiries from Volkswagen dealers who wanted to sell Datsuns. A year after the 510 reached America, for the first time in two decades Volkswagen's share of the American market did not increase. By the late 1960s, the Japanese had been selling cars in the United States for more than a decade. And with the Datsun 510, there was no doubt that the Japanese had arrived.

—M.S.S.

12 CARS WITH UNUSUAL NAMES

1. CAR WITHOUT A NAME
T. S. Fauntleroy, H. R. Averill, and E. H. Lowe of Chicago formed an automotive firm in 1909. As the start of production neared, they still had not settled on a name for the new vehicle and began to call it "the Car Without A Name." The designation stuck until 1910, when the three men decided to change it to F. A. L., using their initials. The F. A. L. was built until 1914, and the company estimated total production at 65,000 units, although the figures were probably exaggerated.

2. MYSTERY CAR
Dubbed "the Mystery Car," this one-of-a-kind vehicle was exhibited at the Auditorium Hotel during the 1925 Chicago Automobile Show. The five-passenger touring model was priced at around $500, according to the sign on its windshield. Not only was the car a mystery, but the builder was as well. The American Motorist said that the man behind the venture was reportedly "one of the most spectacular merchandising geniuses in the country, a man who has been strangely silent." He was never

identified, and the car never entered regular production.

3. BEN HUR
Produced between 1917 and 1918 in Willoughby, Ohio, the Ben Hur was built by fledgling automaker L. L. Allen. He chose the name because it sounded far more dramatic than "the Allen." Approximately forty cars were produced before the company entered receivership in May 1918.

4. DOLLY MADISON
As a tribute to the late U.S. First Lady, the Madison Motor Company of Anderson, Indiana, named their first cars "Dolly Madison" in 1915. Unfortunately, they didn't do enough research—President Madison's wife spelled her name "Dolley." The firm's later cars were called "Madison" and were produced until 1919.

5. AVERAGE MAN'S RUNABOUT
George Adam of Hiawatha, Kansas, produced the Average Man's Runabout for only one year—1906. Apparently its name was sadly apt, as the car had nothing remarkable about it. The public wanted its cars to serve as status symbols, and very few of the cars were produced during their short production run.

6. MILLIONAIRE'S CAR
Officially named the Orson, the Millionaire's Car—as it was more popularly known—was built in Springfield, Massachusetts, in 1911. The company was backed by 100 of the most prominent bankers in New York City, who were to take delivery of the first 100 vehicles built. Unfortunately, financial mismanagement and expensive lawsuits killed the company within two years.

7. SEVEN LITTLE BUFFALOES
William Andrew DeSchaum of Buffalo, New York, began production of a car under his own name in 1908. However, sales were extremely poor. DeSchaum decided that a name change to the more whimsical Seven Little Buffaloes might help. It didn't. Production ended in 1909.

8. PICKLE
The Pickle, named for its inventor, Fred Pickle, was a one-of-a-kind car built in Greenville, Michigan, in 1906. The unusual-looking car used ordinary bicycle wheels and a small three-and-a-half horsepower engine.

9. BIG BROWN LUVERNE
The Luverne auto was built in Luverne, Minnesota, from 1904 through 1916. Its most popular model was the Big Brown Luverne. An exceptionally large car with a 130-inch wheelbase, the model featured a distinctive solid silver radiator, many coats of "Luverne brown" paint, and special upholstery of—according to the sales literature—"Old Spanish brown leather with all hair filling."

10. AMERICAN CHOCOLATE
William Walter owned the American Chocolate Machinery Company in New York City. In 1902 he decided to expand his business into automotive production by building cars in his factory. While he called his car the Walter, much of the public knew it as the sweeter-sounding American Chocolate. Production was relatively successful and continued until 1909.

11. GRUBB
William I. Grubb produced steam cars in Pottstown, Pennsylvania, between 1901 and 1902. Known both as the Grubb and the Light Steamer, only two examples were assembled.

12. ECK
James Eck of Reading, Pennsylvania, built steam-powered vehicles under the model name of Boss from 1897 to 1909. Production was rather haphazard over the years, and a total of only twenty-two cars was manufactured.

—K.A.R.

HARLEY-DAVIDSON

After World War II, the United States was basking in the glow of military victory. The economy was strong and Americans were getting down to the business of starting families. Almost everyone was desperate to get back to normal, traditional life—*almost* everyone. On July 4, 1947, 3,000 motorcycle enthusiasts gathered in the small town of Hollister, California, for a day of track and hill-climbing races. Among that group was an outlaw gang element who got drunk and fought with the locals and the police. The rioting lasted until the following morning. Present that day was a photographer from the *San Francisco Chronicle* who had gone to Hollister to cover the races. He snapped a picture of a slovenly, pot-bellied biker, his eyes glazed, holding a beer bottle in each hand and leaning back in the seat of a powerful motorcycle. The motorcycle was a Harley-Davidson.

The *Chronicle* photograph appeared on the cover of *Life* magazine, which warned its readers of a frightening threat to decent society. A film based on the Hollister incident was released in 1954. The film, *The Wild One,* starred Marlon Brando as the leader of a motorcycle gang. Although the film portrayed a rival gang and its leader, played by Lee Marvin, as gross and evil, Brando's character was so appealing that motorcycle gangs became a positive symbol for disaffected young people. The Harley-Davidson itself became a symbol both of the free and independent spirit of the open road and of the dangerously violent flip side of the American dream.

The Harley-Davidson Company was founded in 1903 by William S. Harley and Arthur Davidson. They were later joined in the enterprise by Arthur's brothers Walter and William. Aunt Janet Davidson did the painting for the first motorcycles, which were built in a shed behind the Davidson family home by the Davidson boys' father.

The earliest Harley-Davidsons were built by Harley and the Davidsons in their spare time. By 1906, however, the company had grown to six full-time employees and production had risen to a total of fifty for the year. Business began to blossom when Walter Davidson won an endurance run sponsored by the Federation of American Motorcyclists in 1908. The Harley-Davidson's excellent showing, combined with a great deal of favorable press coverage, sent sales soaring, and the company began to expand its markets in the U.S. and overseas.

With the advent of World War II, Harley-Davidson turned its attention to the production of the WL model for the American, Canadian, and British military. These extremely sturdy bikes were the company's sole product during the war, and the surplus was sold to the public when peace was declared.

After Harley-Davidson returned to full-capacity peacetime production in 1947, it brought out the Panhead—a replacement for its 1936 Knucklehead—featuring the redesigned Evolution engine. However, for the first time the company was facing strong competition from overseas as lighter, cheaper British bikes hit American shores. Harley-Davidson's primary American competitor, Indian, was unable to survive the new competition and closed down in August 1953.

Another foreign threat faced Harley-Davidson

with the growing popularity of Japanese motorcycles. By the mid-1960s Harley-Davidson's domestic market share had shrunk significantly. The company was bought out by the American Machine and Foundry Company in 1969. Management changes and production increases led to problems with product quality and worker dissatisfaction.

Harley sales remained strong, particularly with the introduction of the best-selling FX Super Glide in 1981. However, the Japanese continued to cut into Harley-Davidson's market share, and AMF began to lose interest in running the company. Harley chairman Vaughn Beals, along with twelve other executives, purchased the company in a leveraged buyout in 1981. At the same time, the firm convinced the government to levy extra tariffs on Japanese imports.

By 1983 Harley made a profit after losing $25 million the year before. However, Citicorp, which had financed the management buyout, refused to advance Harley-Davidson any additional funds. Other lenders were reluctant to take on an account in which Citicorp placed so little faith, and Harley-Davidson's lawyers began to put together bankruptcy plans. Fortunately, at the eleventh hour, Heller Financial Corporation came through for Harley, loaning the firm $49.5 million. This new financing, together with management's aggressive improvements, brought the company back from the brink of disaster. Market share rebounded, and by 1987 the company was in excellent shape and asked the government to remove the tariffs on Japanese motorcycles a year ahead of schedule.

As for the Hell's Angels, the quintessential outlaw gang of Harley owners formed in 1948, in 1993 they went to court, not for the usual reasons—to defend themselves against criminal charges—but to sue Marvel Comics for damaging the club's "goodwill" by issuing a comic book titled *Hell's Angel*. In 1996, Harley-Davidson, Inc., went to court as well, demanding that it be allowed to trademark the powerful rumbling sound made by the Harley's V-twin engines.

—K.A.R. and D.W.

EYEWITNESS TO HISTORY

THE WRIGHT BROTHERS AT KITTY HAWK

When: December 17, 1903

How: On a gray, bone-chilling Thursday in December 1903, a 745-pound wheelless biplane nicknamed the *Flyer* perched precariously on a

dolly that was set on a wooden monorail anchored in the sand dunes near Kitty Hawk, North Carolina. The aircraft's twelve-horsepower motor roared, the wind whistled through the wire bracing, and the angry surf rumbled as Orville Wright lay face down in a hip cradle set in the middle of the forty-foot-long lower wing. His brother Wilbur released the restraining cable,

Wilbur Wright watches his brother Orville take the first flight in history. It took place at Kill Devil Hill near Kitty Hawk, North Carolina, on December 17, 1903, and lasted twelve seconds.

and the plane moved slowly forward into the twenty-seven-mile-per-hour wind.

Wilbur Wright ran alongside, holding the right wing tip to steady the aircraft. Near the end of the runway, the *Flyer* rose smoothly into the air and climbed steadily to about ten feet above the sand. It flew erratically for several seconds, rising and falling, then made a nose-dive toward the ground, slapped sharply against the sand, and skidded to a halt. The flight, the first by a powered aircraft, had lasted a mere twelve seconds and traveled only about 120 feet. But as the Wright brothers recognized, it was the "first in the history of the world in which a machine carrying a man had raised itself by its own power into the air in free flight, had sailed forward on a level course without reduction of speed, and had finally landed without being wrecked."

The Wrights made three more flights that morning before the *Flyer* was damaged by a sudden gust of wind. The final flight was 852 feet in length and lasted fifty-nine seconds.

Orville, thirty-two, and Wilbur, thirty-six, were not engineers; in fact, they were high-school dropouts. The brothers owned a bicycle shop in Dayton, Ohio, when in 1899 they began their methodical survey of existing aviation literature—little more than a confusing collection of rumors and untested theories. Then, over the next four years, they developed and tested their own theories. Inspired by German engineer Otto Lilienthal's success in glider flying, Wilbur Wright concluded that the secret to flight lay in developing airworthy rigid wings. Once a person could learn to balance and soar in the air on man-made wings, it would be easy to add a motor and propeller to complete the flying machine.

The Wrights conducted thousands of experiments on each part of the airplane, including testing scale models of more than 200 wing formations in a wind tunnel they built themselves. For three consecutive autumns they tested their theories by building and flying gliders at Kitty Hawk, selected for its ideal wind conditions and treeless sand dunes.

The brothers worked as a team, although the severe, silent Wilbur was the dominant partner and a more brilliant theoretician than Orville. Their debates were often heated, according to the recollections of Charles Taylor, the man they hired in 1901 to run the bicycle shop. "One morning following the worst argument I ever heard, Orv came in and said he'd guess he'd been wrong, and they ought to do it Will's way. A few minutes later Will came in and said he'd been thinking it over and perhaps Orv was right. First thing I knew they were arguing it all over again, only this time they had switched ideas."

The Wrights' historic flight was largely ignored by the world outside Kitty Hawk, not, as is commonly believed, because of press apathy but because of Wilbur's attempts to keep technical details secret until the Wrights could market the plane. After signing contracts in 1908 with both the U.S. Army and a French commercial concern, the Wright brothers gave public demonstrations of their airplane and astounded a skeptical world. René Gasnier, a French aviator who witnessed one of Wilbur Wright's flights in France, exclaimed: "Compared with the Wrights, we are as children." Wilbur died of typhoid fever in 1912 but Orville continued his research until his death in 1948.

Eyewitness Report: One of the five spectators at the Wright brothers' first flight was John T. Daniels, a patrolman with the Kill Devil Hills U.S. Life Saving Service (now the Coast Guard). It was Daniels who took the famous photograph of the first flight—even though he had never used a camera before. Daniels remembered watching the Wrights during their first visit to Kitty Hawk and recounted his impressions in an interview for the September 17, 1927, *Colliers:*

"We couldn't help thinkin' they were just a pair of poor nuts. We'd watch them from the windows of our station. They'd stand on the beach for hours at a time just looking at the gulls flying, soaring, dipping. They would watch the gannets and imitate the movements of their wings with their arms and hands. They could imitate every movement of the wings of those gannets; we thought they were crazy, but we just had to admire the way they could move their arms this way and that and bend their elbows and wrist bones up and down and every which a way."

Then Daniels described the actual flight.

"Wilbur and Orville walked off from us and stood close together on the beach, talking low to each other for some time. After a while they shook hands, and we couldn't help notice how they held on to each other's hand, sort o' like they hated to let go; like two folks parting who weren't sure they'd ever see each other again.

> The airplane stays up because it doesn't have the time to fall.
> Orville Wright, explaining the principles of powered flight; attributed, 1903

"Wilbur came over to us and told us not to look sad, but to laugh and hollo and clap our hands and try to cheer Orville up when he started.

"We tried to shout and hollo, but it was mighty weak shouting, with no heart in it. . . .

"Orville climbed into the machine, the engine was started up, and we helped steady it down the monorail until it got underway. The thing went off with a rush and left the rail as pretty as you please, going straight out into the air maybe 120 feet, when one of its wings tilted and caught in the sand, and the thing stopped. I like to think about that first airplane the way it tailed off in the air at Kill Devil Hills that morning, as pretty as any bird you ever laid your eyes on. I don't think I ever saw a prettier sight in my life."

—B.B.

FAMOUS AIRPLANES AND FLIGHTS

SPIRIT OF ST. LOUIS (1927)

In May 1919 New York hotelier Raymond Orteig offered a $25,000 prize for the first nonstop flight from New York to Paris. In June 1919 British pilots John Alcock and Arthur Brown made the first nonstop flight across the Atlantic Ocean, but they took the shortest route, from Newfoundland to Ireland. New York to Paris was nearly twice as far as Newfoundland to Ireland, about 3,600 miles. The load of fuel required for such a long flight meant that the first problem was simply getting off the ground. The top French fighter ace of World War I, René Fonck, tried for the Orteig Prize in September 1926. He crashed on takeoff, killing two crewmen. In April 1927 Noel Davis and Stanton Wooster also died trying to take off for Paris.

While famous pilots were trying for the Orteig Prize and dying, an unknown twenty-five-year-old flier approached the American Tobacco Company. He not only would fly from New York to Paris, he offered to fly alone. In return for financial backing, he would name his aircraft for American Tobacco's most famous product: Lucky Strike cigarettes.

The company refused, with visions of the name "Lucky Strike" in flames on a runway. The young pilot's résumé probably didn't impress the tobacco executives either. He had dropped out of college to take flying lessons. Starting at the bottom of aviation as a barnstormer and wing walker, he was currently flying mail from Saint Louis to Chicago. He also flew fighters in the Air Corps Reserve. Like all hotshot pilots, he had a nickname: "Slim." After a near-fatal parachute jump, his buddies came up with a new name for Charles Augustus Lindbergh Jr.: "Lucky Lindy."

Lindbergh wanted to fly the Atlantic in the hottest aircraft of 1927, a Bellanca monoplane. The Wright-Bellanca Company was as skeptical as American Tobacco; a solo Atlantic flight was a harebrained, suicidal stunt. Besides, wealthy aviation fan Charles Levine had already purchased a Bellanca and hired an experienced pilot for a run at the Orteig Prize.

Time was running out. In addition to Levine, famous aviator Richard E. Byrd had announced his intention to take the Orteig Prize with a three-man crew.

Lindbergh finally won sponsorship from a

Charles Lindbergh arrives in Paris after his epic solo flight across the Atlantic, May 21, 1927.

newspaper, the *St. Louis Globe-Democrat*, and a few businessmen promoting their city as an aviation center. His financiers provided a name for the unbuilt aircraft: *Spirit of St. Louis*.

The young, unknown Lindbergh approached another group of young unknowns, the Ryan Aircraft Company of San Diego, California. Ryan's M-1 had debuted in 1926, a clean, high-wing monoplane in an era of biplanes cluttered with bracing wires. The M-1 was followed by the nearly identical M-2.

Ryan had some problems with their wing design. The problems were solved by an anonymous, self-educated engineer in Los Angeles. He cut the wing's weight by 200 pounds (and he wouldn't always be anonymous; his name was Jack Northrop, and more than half a century later his company would build the B-2 Stealth bomber). Ryan's planes were small and agile, just twenty-seven feet nine inches long, with a thirty-six-foot wingspan. The planes hauled mail on the far-flung western routes, which spoke well for their reliability.

On February 25, 1927, Lindbergh arrived in San Diego with a $1,000 down payment. At drafting table and workbench, he labored beside Ryan workers to modify an M-2 for a very long trip.

The wingspan was lengthened ten feet to make room for fuel. The fuselage was extended two feet, the engine moved forward, the cockpit moved back, and a massive fuel tank installed in front of the pilot. The new tank eliminated the windshield.

Lindbergh figured he didn't need a windshield; there wasn't much to see over the Atlantic, and nothing he could hit. For takeoff and landing he had side windows. A small periscope was built into the instrument panel, allowing some forward vision.

The instrument panel had plenty of room. It held only a drift sight, a turn-slip indicator, and two compasses. To save weight, Lindbergh

refused to carry a radio. A standard M-2 had a takeoff weight of 3,300 pounds. With the extra fuel, Lindbergh calculated he would take off at a lumbering 5,250 pounds. Every extra ounce had to go; even the pilot's seat was replaced with a lightweight wicker chair.

The one and only Ryan model NYP—"New York to Paris"—was built in two months and cost about $6,000. On May 10 Lindbergh left for New York. He set new coast-to-coast records on the way, which were overshadowed by the latest Orteig Prize fatalities. Perhaps hoping to reverse fate along with the route, French pilots Charles Nungesser and François Coli—both World War I fighter aces—had left Paris for New York on May 8. They were missing somewhere over the Atlantic. When reporters heard that Lindbergh was flying to Paris solo, they dubbed him "the Flyin' Fool."

On the rainy morning of May 20, 1927, the *Spirit of St. Louis* took on 451 gallons of fuel at Roosevelt Field, New York. Its wheels sank deep into the mud. Obsessed with weight, Lindbergh refused a last-minute offer of $1,000 to carry a few letters for a wealthy stamp collector.

At 7:52 A.M. the *Spirit of St. Louis* clawed its way into the air, barely clearing the runway. Plane and pilot saw their last land over Nova Scotia, where they were battered by a sleet storm.

Lindbergh struggled to stay awake. He dozed once and awoke in a sideways dive, one wing pointed straight down. Another catnap ended with his wheels skimming the North Atlantic.

After thirty-three hours, twenty-nine minutes, and thirty-three seconds, the *Spirit of St. Louis* landed at Le Bourget field about six miles outside Paris. The throng of people that came to greet him caused the largest traffic jam in the history of France; the people broke police lines to get near the plane. Charles Lindbergh was the ninety-second person to fly the Atlantic, but the first to do it alone. He received 3.5 million letters, 100,000 telegrams, and an offer of $1 million if he would allow a movie company to film his wedding. An intensely private man, Lindbergh was unprepared for the public frenzy that enveloped him.

> *In the spring of '27 something bright and alien flashed across the sky. A young Minnesotan who seemed to have nothing to do with his generation did a heroic thing, and for a moment people set down their glasses in country clubs and speakeasies and thought of their old best dreams.*
>
> F. Scott Fitzgerald on Charles Lindbergh

Back home, man and machine went on a brief goodwill tour. Then Lindbergh took the *Spirit of St. Louis* on its last flight, to the Smithsonian Institution.

The machine could rest in eternal honor, but not the man. Lindbergh's future held the 1932 kidnapping and murder of his infant son (see page 120), and a European sojourn during which he accepted medals from Nazi Germany. He became the spokesman for America First, a far-right isolationist group with a nasty streak of anti-Semitism.

After Pearl Harbor, his services were refused by President Franklin Roosevelt, who called Lindbergh a traitor. Lindbergh eventually served with distinction in the Pacific. After the war he and his wife moved to Hawaii, where Lindbergh died on August 26, 1974.

In 1976 the *Spirit of St. Louis* took one last trip. It was moved via flatbed truck, at a maximum speed of ten miles per hour, to the Smithsonian's new National Air and Space Museum. According to Walter J. Boyne, curator of aeronautics: "We had one offer from a passerby to take it off our hands if we were going to junk it. We weren't." Boyne found the aircraft "in surprisingly good condition, with no rot or rust, and with the fabric still usable." Today, when nonstop Atlantic travel means a routine eight-hour flight, the *Spirit of St. Louis* remains one of the Smithsonian's most popular attractions.

> I have seen the science I worshipped, and the aircraft I loved, destroying the civilization I expected them to serve.
>
> Charles A. Lindbergh, *Time*, May 26, 1967

CHINA CLIPPER (1935–46)

> There are only two emotions in a plane: boredom and terror.
>
> Orson Welles

The elegant *China Clipper* was born as a flying mail truck. In 1935 Pan American Airways acquired a new seaplane, the Martin M-130. Only three were built. Pan Am christened them *Hawaii Clipper*, *Philippine Clipper*, and *China Clipper*.

On November 22, 1935, the original *China Clipper* left San Francisco with 110,865 letters. It landed at Honolulu, Midway Island, Wake Island, Guam, and finally Manila, flying 8,210 miles in fifty-nine hours and forty-eight minutes. The aircraft later lived up to its name by adding stops in Macao and Hong Kong.

After Pan Am had proven the route with mail and cargo, passenger service began in October 1936. A ticket from San Francisco to Manila cost $799, more than a new Ford.

By 1939 Pan Am needed larger planes. Boeing had built one example of a mammoth bomber, the XB-15, with a wingspan half a city block long (152 feet). The wing was so large that a crewman could walk inside, during flight, and repair an engine.

At Pan Am's request, this wing design was grafted onto a massive but graceful 100-foot fuselage. Four 1,600-horsepower engines allowed a cruising speed of 186 miles per hour, and "sea wings" on the fuselage improved stability in the water. The sea wings also carried 750 gallons of fuel, supplementing the 600-gallon wing tanks.

Boeing prosaically designated the aircraft Model B-314, but it became universally known as the Clipper. A total of twelve were built, including the Atlantic Clippers. The new aircraft increased Pan Am's cargo capacity by 500 percent over the M-130. Clippers hauled mail, movies, trees, prescriptions, fresh fruit packed in dry ice, machine parts, wedding gowns for brides across the Pacific, and thousands of other items.

The 314 could carry seventy-four people, and Pan Am invested more than $5 million in Clipper passenger service. At the desolate interim stops—Midway, Wake, and Guam— luxury hotels were built. On Midway, where drinking water had to be shipped in, the tired flier's bath was heated by solar power and windmills. On Wake Island, coral reefs were dynamited to provide landing room. Each stop boasted an ultramodern communications facility, where every Clipper was tracked continuously across the Pacific.

Passengers were greeted by an eight-man crew of two pilots, two engineers, and four stewards. The Clipper borrowed both the language and the elegance of the posh cruise lines. "Decks" were plushly carpeted in a color known as tango rust, and passengers slept in "staterooms." The ultimate Clipper accommodation was the deluxe aft suite, available for $1,140 one way to Hong Kong.

During the long first leg from San Francisco to Honolulu, passengers were called in shifts to a formal dinner. The tablecloth was snow-white linen, the silver of finest sterling. A typical menu featured hearts-of-lettuce salad, soup, steak with new potatoes and string beans, and several dessert choices.

The Clipper's heyday was brief but glorious. Claire Boothe Luce wrote of a swim on Wake Island, sheltered by the massive aircraft: "On the underside of the wing, just above my head, they have painted a great American flag . . . The clear water casts its reflection on the flag, making it seem to wave silkily. The young Secretary paddles out into this Star-Spangled grotto. He looks up at the banner that covers him. He makes no comment. Is one required?"

As Luce implied, the star-spangled Clipper may have seemed like a flying statement about America's transpacific empire. But those "great American flags" served a more practical purpose between 1939 and 1941: they warned fighter pilots that Clippers were American, and therefore neutral, aircraft. Neutrality and normal Clipper service both ended on December 7, 1941. Most of the Clippers were drafted by the U.S. military. World War II helped kill flying boats like the Clipper; the war built airports even in the most remote parts of the world.

On April 9, 1946, the *American Clipper* arrived in San Francisco from Honolulu for the last time. A new land-based plane, the Lockheed Constellation, left Hawaii with the Clipper and landed in California four hours sooner. Pan Am's Clipper flight cost $278 to fly one way from Hawaii to California. Carrying more passengers, the "Connie" cut the price to $195.

Pan Am saw the handwriting on the fuselage, and it did not say China Clipper. The airline sold all the Pacific Clippers during 1946. None ever flew again. After rotting in storage at San Diego's Lindbergh Field, in 1951 the magnificent airplanes were sold as scrap metal.

The Clippers deserved a better aloha.

SPRUCE GOOSE (1947)

Though Howard Hughes loathed the name, his most famous aircraft will always be known as the Spruce Goose. Built mostly of birch, the mammoth seaplane cost more than $25 million and made one flight of about one minute. Since the Goose consumed $18 million of government funds, that flight cost American taxpayers about $300,000 per second. (Hughes spent $7.5 million of his own money.)

It was the largest airplane ever built. The Lockheed C-5 and Boeing 747 are longer than its 218.5 feet, though not by much. Its 320-foot wingspan is nearly a hundred feet longer than that of a 747, and it was powered by eight 3,000-horsepower engines.

The *Goose* was born of desperation in World War II. Its official name was HK-1, for "Hughes-Kaiser, Design 1." By 1942 Henry J. Kaiser's shipyards had cut the build time of a cargo vessel from 355 days to 48. But German submarines were still sinking ships even faster than Kaiser could build them.

Kaiser came up with a solution: a sort of flying Liberty Ship that could carry 750 people or 50 tons of cargo. Aircraft companies were not enthusiastic. When Kaiser pitched his idea to the owner of Hughes Aircraft, Howard Hughes responded: "You're crazy." Hughes was an aviator of some talent. In 1938 he broke Wiley Post's record for an around-the-world flight. As president of TWA, he influenced the design of the innovative Lockheed Constellation.

Kaiser, a master salesman, talked him into a deal. Hughes would design the monster seaplanes and build the prototype, Kaiser would put them into production at his shipyards.

They won a contract, with the first prototype to be delivered in 1943 for $9.8 million. Facing wartime metal shortages, the military insisted that the HK-1 be built of "non-critical materials," meaning wood.

Construction began in autumn 1942 at Hughes Aircraft in Culver City, California. To house the wooden plane, Hughes built the world's largest wooden building, measuring 750 feet long, 250 feet wide, and 100 feet high.

By mid-1943, radar and sonar had reduced the submarine threat. At Hughes Aircraft, HK-1 managers reported only to Howard Hughes—if and when they could find him. Workers took blueprints to Hughes's house, late at night, for approval. Six million dollars had been spent with very little to show for it.

The chaos led the government, in February 1944, to try to cancel the HK-1. Hughes went to Washington and lobbied. The government finally agreed to pay him $18 million for a single prototype. At this point $13 million was already spent, and the first HK-1 was less than half finished.

When World War II ended, the HK-1 was still a pile of unassembled parts. In June 1946 it was moved to Long Beach harbor for final assembly and testing. The move took two days, a fleet of trucks, and $80,000.

In 1947 Hughes was called before a congressional committee investigating his wartime contracts. Many questions were asked about the $25 million flying boat that had never flown. With Kaiser gone, the aircraft was renamed the H-4 *Hercules*. During the hearings it was also called "a flying lumberyard" and "a white elephant." To prove a point to his congressional tormentors, Hughes became obsessed with flying it.

On November 2, 1947, Hughes took the aircraft out for taxi tests in Long Beach harbor. On his last run of the day, to the surprise of reporters and VIPs on shore, the huge airplane lifted into the air. The Spruce Goose had finally flown, albeit at an altitude of no more than 70 feet. Hughes ordered design changes to upgrade the craft for commercial use. A climate-controlled hangar costing $1.75 million was built in Long Beach, but Hughes gradually lost interest in his big toy.

The Spruce Goose was hidden in its hangar for more than thirty years. Hughes died on April 5, 1976, without a will. A probate court ordered Hughes's executors to get rid of the Spruce Goose and its $1 million annual maintenance costs.

The Goose was nearly scrapped, but it was saved at the last minute as a tourist attraction. Appropriately enough, the Goose would be displayed under the world's largest clear-span aluminum dome in Long Beach Harbor.

The aircraft had to move only 600 yards to its new home, but the short trip turned into a huge engineering project. After thirty-three years, the storage hangar had settled nearly twelve feet into the water. Workers took two months to cut off the doors with blowtorches and remove part of the roof to clear a path for the eight-story tail.

On October 29, 1980, the Spruce Goose once again floated into Long Beach harbor, scene of its only flight. It served as a Long Beach tourist attraction until 1993, when it was sold and moved to Oregon.

CONCORDE (1976)

Concorde is great. It gives you three extra hours to find your luggage.

            Bob Hope, to reporters at Heathrow Airport

"Passengers for Air France flight 085 are requested to proceed to the departure gate." On January 21, 1976, at Paris's de Gaulle Airport, this ordinary message announced an extraordinary flight. One hundred passengers boarded a droop-nosed, delta-winged aircraft called the Concorde. They would fly 6,000 miles in seven hours and twenty-six minutes, in the world's first commercial supersonic flight.

It was the dawn of a new era, but an era that didn't quite turn out as expected.

In the 1950s the sonic boom became a common sound as jet fighters broke the sound barrier (Mach 1, or about 700 miles per hour). With this sort of progress, a supersonic transport (SST) for passenger travel seemed right around the corner.

The United States and the Soviet Union announced SST programs. In 1962 the British and French governments agreed to cooperate on an SST. Britain would build the forward fuselage and the tail and do most of the work on the new Olympus 593 engines. France was responsible for wings, controls, and rear passenger cabin.

Disagreements occurred. In 1964 England's Labour government briefly withdrew from the project. But on December 11, 1967, the prototype Concorde (number 001) was rolled out in Toulouse, France. Its needlelike fuselage was more than 203 feet long but only about as wide as the old DC-3. The four engines each provided 38,000 pounds of thrust, for a cruising speed of approximately Mach 2 (about 1,350 miles per hour). The engines were carried beneath the delta wings, which spanned eighty-three feet.

The Concorde's most remarkable feature was its drooping nose. With the pilot thirty-five feet above the ground, the nose section "drooped" to allow visibility on takeoff and landing. In flight, the nose hydraulically lifted for streamlining.

Amid the celebrations at Toulouse, trouble was brewing. Earlier in 1967 a military supersonic flight in England had brought 4,000 noise complaints (though a seventy-three-year-old London man, deaf since 1954, apparently had his hearing restored by the sonic booms). Environmentalists warned that the SST might damage the atmosphere above and people below.

The American SST was planned as a joint commercial venture with government backing. Congress looked at the escalating cost of the Concorde and saw a money pit for taxpayers. Despite intense aerospace lobbying, Congress killed the SST. Events would prove Congress exactly right.

The USSR was determined to fly an SST first. The Tupolev Tu-144 looked suspiciously like a certain droop-nosed European aircraft—so much so that it was dubbed "Concordski" in the West. Not having to worry much about citizen complaints, the Soviet government achieved its goal. The Tu-144 was the world's first SST to fly, on December 31, 1968. The Concorde's turn came on March 2, 1969, when 001 flew for the first time.

On September 13, 1970, the Concorde made its first landing at London's Heathrow Airport. Residents complained about the noise. By this time thousands of people around the world were organizing against SSTs. Some hated the noise, some worried about the environment, and a few simply resented the Concorde as a plaything for the wealthy.

Airlines had taken options to buy more than seventy Concordes. Throughout the 1970s, those options were dropped. Environmental concerns had less influence than the fact that the aircraft was just not economically feasible. The $65 million Concorde carried only 118 passengers. The Boeing 747 cost $21 million and carried three times the passengers, with much lower operating costs. In the end, only British Airways and Air France used the Concorde.

During the 1973 Paris Air Show, a Tu-144 crashed into a Paris suburb. Its crew of six, and eight people on the ground, were killed. Aeroflot used the SST on its Moscow-Kazakhstan route until 1978, when the Tu-144 was grounded.

The Concorde, by comparison, has been in continuous service since 1976. On May 21, 1977, a Concorde flew from New York to Paris to celebrate the fiftieth anniversary of Lindbergh's flight. Lindbergh had crossed the Atlantic in thirty-three and a half hours. The Concorde made the same trip in three.

Today the Concorde still flies into New York's Kennedy Airport. Since the Concorde outruns the time zones, passengers arrive in New York more than an hour before their London departure time. Its cruising altitude, at twice the height of Mount Everest, occasionally allows a glimpse of the earth's curvature below.

In the final analysis, the Concorde was a great technological success but an economic and social failure.

GOSSAMER ALBATROSS (1979)

The *Gossamer Albatross* is one of several unique aircraft designed and built by Dr. Paul

MacReady of Pasadena, California (see *Solar Challenger*). Like Lindbergh's *Spirit of St. Louis*, the *Gossamer Albatross* was designed to win a prize.

A British industrialist, Henry Kremer, was fascinated by human-powered flight. In 1959 Kremer offered 50,000 British pounds (about $95,000) for the first human-powered flight around a one-and-one-quarter-mile, figure-eight course. Kremer offered twice that amount for the first human-powered flight across the English Channel.

Human-powered flight is not as easy as it might seem, when turning is required, as in the Kremer Prize course. At the slow speeds generated by a human, control in a turn is very difficult, and stalling (stopping dead in the air) is always imminent.

MacReady designed and built the *Gossamer Condor* for the Kremer Prize figure-eight course. Like its descendant, the *Gossamer Albatross*, the *Condor* was powered by a human pumping bicycle pedals. On August 23, 1977, the *Gossamer Condor* won the Kremer Prize for human flight around a measured course. At the controls was a young bicycle racer and hang glider enthusiast named Bryan Allen, who had neither a pilot's license nor any aeronautical training.

MacReady began planning his assault on the Kremer Prize for a crossing of the English Channel. As before, MacReady designed an aircraft that was built by himself and his son Parker. The "fuselage" of the new *Gossamer Albatross* was a plastic bag around a bicycle frame. For maximum lift, its wingspan was ninety-three feet ten inches—about the same as a Boeing 737, though the *Albatross* was considerably lighter at seventy pounds. The aircraft was built of thin aluminum tubing braced with stainless-steel wires. Its skin was clear Mylar, allowing emergency repairs with a high-tech material normally used to wrap sandwiches.

Like the fragile aircraft, the human "engine" needed careful preparation. The English Channel is about twenty miles across. Bryan Allen calculated that he could reach a top speed of ten miles per hour, so he would be pedaling for at least two hours. Allen rode a bicycle as much as possible to build up his endurance. In his spare time he rode a static exercise bike. By the summer of 1979, Allen believed he could stay in the air for more than four hours if necessary.

At 7:00 A.M. on June 13, 1979, Allen pedaled the *Gossamer Albatross* into the air from Kent, England. Cruising sixteen feet above the Atlantic, he landed almost three hours later in Cap Gris-Nez, France.

MacReady donated the *Gossamer Albatross* to England's Science Museum. The aircraft is often on loan to the Smithsonian's National Air and Space Museum, where the *Gossamer Condor* is on permanent display.

SOLAR CHALLENGER (1980)

By 1980 several aircraft had flown using solar batteries for power. Dr. Paul MacReady (see *Gossamer Albatross*) believed he could go one step further and build an airplane that would fly on energy drawn directly from the sun.

Unlike MacReady's human-powered craft, this design would have to carry a power source: 16,128 solar cells, each measuring three-quarters by one-half inch, with a thickness of .013 inch. The cells would power a three-horsepower electric motor attached to a seven-foot variable-pitch propeller.

Weight was a critical factor. Knowing the fixed weight of his components, MacReady saved weight in the one variable area: the pilot. Already tiny, Janice Brown dieted until she weighed only ninety-nine pounds. MacReady built a test model, the *Gossamer Penguin*. With banks of solar cells towering above a huge wing, the *Penguin* looked like a cross between a high-school science project and an invading spacecraft. On August 7, 1980, Brown flew the *Gossamer Penguin* for two miles at Edwards Air Force Base in the California desert.

This was the first sustained flight using pure solar power, but MacReady wanted to do better. He built a new craft, *Solar Challenger*. The solar cells were buried in the wing and horizontal stabilizer, for a much cleaner design. MacReady had to solve one unprecedented design problem: ensuring that the tail's shadow did not fall across the solar cells in the forty-seven-foot wing.

On November 6, 1980, the new design was ready for its first flight. Takeoff imposed stringent conditions: *Solar Challenger* had to face the wind for lift, with the sun high and directly behind, beaming into the solar cells.

With the cells charged, Brown switched on the electric motor. *Solar Challenger* soared to sixty feet and stayed aloft for two minutes, fifty seconds. On December 6 it flew for eighteen miles between Tucson and Phoenix, Arizona, finally being grounded by a heavy rainstorm. MacReady made constant improvements. The original straight wing became banana-shaped, the better to catch the sun's rays. *Solar Challenger* eventually reached an altitude of 14,300 feet and stayed in the air for more than eight hours.

MacReady took it to Europe, where he waited a month for sunny weather. On July 7, 1981, with twenty-eight-year-old Stephen Ptacek at the controls, the *Solar Challenger* took off from an airfield near Paris. Cruising at thirty-seven miles per hour, Ptacek climbed to 12,000 feet. Five hours and twenty-five minutes later, *Solar Challenger* touched down at an RAF base in Kent, England. A solar-powered craft had crossed the English Channel, its only trouble being the turbulence kicked up by an escorting helicopter.

Solar Challenger was donated to the Science Museum of Virginia, though it is often on loan to the Smithsonian Institution's National Air and Space Museum.

—M.S.S.

GREAT ARCHAEOLOGICAL DISCOVERIES

PALACE OF KNOSSOS

Year: 1900
Location: Near Heraklion on the island of Crete
Discoverer: Arthur Evans
Findings: Arthur Evans came to Crete with the intention of tracing the origins of Mycenaean art. Jewels from this culture had shown microscopic hieroglyphs similar to symbols scratched on seal stones indigenous to the island. Evans was extremely nearsighted, a condition that enabled him to study minuscule markings at very close range. Intrigued, however, by the imposing mound of Kephala, a few miles from Heraklion, he began to excavate instead. Before Evans had finished, twenty-five years later, he had resurrected one of the great marvels of antiquity—the palace of Knossos, center of the Minoan civilization.

The one-fifth-acre excavation became a lifelong project. Evans used his vast personal fortune, nearly $1,263,600—to finance the dig. During his excavation he found suggestions of the ancient Greek legend of Theseus and the half-man, half-bull Minotaur. Wall frescoes of bullfighting scenes came into view. Shields covered with hides were dug up. Ceremonial chambers appointed with bull horns and other bull-worshipping vessels were found. The palace itself was a huge labrinyth of narrow passageways and interconnected apartments, a maze through which Theseus, after slaying the fearsome creature, might well have wandered, guided by the slender thread given him by King Minos's daughter, Ariadne. The sprawling ruin contained not only a throne room but also an immense wine and oil storage area with a capacity of more than 80,000 gallons.

In the restorative work, Arthur Evans faced an unusual dilemma. The palace of Knossos had crumbled around 1389 B.C., succumbing to one of the catastrophic earthquakes that devastate Crete three or four times each century. Much of the original limestone used for walls and columns had disintegrated from rain and sun. Timber beams and ceilings had likewise vanished. Evans's solution—the use of reinforced concrete to replace the missing members—made him a controversial figure. Some of his critics derisively said that he had produced a "concrete Crete." They further claimed that his inclination to re-create, employing his vivid imagination, made it virtually impossible to tell which portions of the restored Knossos were of genuine Minoan design.

His detractors cannot, however, overlook his discovery of three syllabic scripts written in two distinct hieroglyphic forms, which he christened Linear A and Linear B. Linear A, the earlier version, remained undeciphered decades later. Linear B was solved by the shrewd deductions of Michael Ventris in 1952. Ventris proved to his skeptical colleagues that the markings were an early version of the Greek language. His conclusion, a direct consequence of Evans's work, showed that spoken Greek had been used by the ancient Cretans at least 600 years before the time of Homer.

—W.K.

RUINS OF MACHU PICCHU

Year: 1911
Location: Peru
Discoverer: Hiram Bingham
Findings: In 1911 Yale University sent a small archaeological expedition, led by Professor Hiram Bingham, to a portion of the Urubamba Valley in Peru called the Unknown Zone. A mule trail had been cut through the area to make it accessible for the first time.

On the sixth day out of Cuzco, a poor plantation owner, for the sum of fifty cents, offered to lead the curious Bingham and a Peruvian soldier through the jungle toward the magnificent precipices at nearby Machu Picchu.

They used a shaky bridge of four logs to cross some roaring rapids, then traipsed through more jungle and made their way up a precipitous slope, where an Indian family led them farther along a path of crude ladders of vines and tree trunks, all fastened to the face of a precipice. Eventually, on a very narrow ridge of the Andes, 7,000 feet above the sea, Bingham got his fifty cents' worth, his first glimpse of a spectacular, 2,000-year-old city built by the Incas.

He believed he'd discovered the largest and most important ruins in the whole of South America since the Spanish conquest. He also believed he'd found the famous Sanctuary of Vilcabamba.

He brought in workmen who cleared away the foliage and exposed signs of nearly 200 edifices expertly made of white granite. Because the architecture was exclusively Peruvian, it indicated that the city must never have been invaded or even found by the Spanish Conquistadors.

Convinced he wanted to excavate and map the ruins in detail, he persuaded Yale University and *National Geographic* magazine to back him on a second expedition the following year.

Once the excavation was under way, it was evident that this city, set on a mountaintop, was one of refuge, better defended by nature than any other part of the Andes.

Its most impressive structure was the Sacred Plaza in the center of the town, which included the Chief Temple, the extraordinary Temple of the Three Windows, and the elevated Intihuatana stone or sundial. Amazingly, neither cement nor mortar was used in any of the masonry.

One-room houses were built on terraces along the steep sloping hillsides. Part of the city was divided into various "clan" or family groups, eight or ten houses surrounded by a wall with only one entrance, a gateway with an inside locking device.

Stairways were everywhere, connecting the agricultural terraces and providing access to otherwise difficult-to-reach locations.

Burials of the dead had been meticulously recorded on the caves that entombed them. Most skeletons were found in sitting positions with their knees drawn up under their chins.

The water supply was routed through very narrow channels, called *azequias*, which connected with a series of fountains and basins located on the principal stairway of the city. Bingham speculated that one reason the city had eventually been deserted was perhaps that a radical change in climate had caused a scarcity of water.

Except for Cuzco, it has been determined that Machu Picchu has more edifices and is larger than any other ruin discovered in Peru. What was most significant about it was that the Conquistadors never found it and occupied it. Remaining unaltered and whole, it represents a fine picture of an Inca town circa the fifteenth century A.D.

Although Bingham was quite certain he'd stumbled upon the city of Vilcabamba, he was proven wrong in 1964 when an American expedition found Vilcabamba, not among the mountains of the Andes but in the steamy jungle of the Amazonia.

—J.L.

UR

Year: 1922
Location: 9 miles west of Nasiriya, Iraq, on the river Euphrates, 200 miles from the Persian Gulf
Discoverer: Charles Leonard Woolley
Findings: The world's earliest known dig was

made at Ur by Nabonidus, a sixth-century-B.C. king of Babylonia. An avid collector of old inscriptions, with a recorded passion for restoration, he rebuilt the Mesopotamian city's ruined ziggurat, or tower.

Leonard Woolley originally trained for the ministry but was diverted into archaeology by Dr. W. A. Spooner (of "spoonerism" fame). After World War I, Woolley began explorations in the Euphrates-Tigris Delta, hoping to make an important find of a biblical nature. His success was almost immediate. Working with the consummate skill and patience for which he became noted, Woolley discovered Sumerian temple ruins dating back to 2600 B.C. Encouraged, he selected a new site at the great mound of Tell el-Muqayyar, a sixty-foot-high ziggurat known to conceal Ur of the Chaldees, because of prior excavations done in 1854 by J. E. Taylor, the British consul at Basra. In 1929 Woolley stirred worldwide interest with a melodramatic telegram, sent to London: WE HAVE FOUND THE FLOOD!

Deep down in the forty-foot shaft sunk into the mound, Woolley had discovered a stratified layer of river clay almost ten feet thick. The deposit, he reasoned, could have come only from a flood of immense dimensions, a disaster of such magnitude that it had without doubt given substance to the Genesis legend of Noah and the ark.

The discovery, revealing as it was, was not Woolley's greatest triumph at Ur. In 1926, excavating in the area known to be the royal cemetery, Woolley uncovered Ur's most shocking secret: gruesome proof that the priests of the fortieth-century-B.C. kingdom had practiced mass murder and human sacrifice. Laid out in precise rows, the remains of both royalty and commoner lay where the bodies had fallen after being struck down from behind, killed so that they might accompany their dead ruler into the next world.

The discoveries at Ur established the ancient Sumerians, previously known only as myth or legend, as historical reality, the ancestors of a Babylonia yet to be. Woolley's lucid accounts of his Ur excavations, published between 1928 and 1938, were eagerly read by the general public.

—W.K.

TOMB OF TUTANKHAMEN

Year: 1922
Location: Luxor, Egypt, in the Valley of the Kings
Discoverer: Howard Carter
Findings:

AT LAST HAVE MADE WONDERFUL DISCOVERY IN VALLEY; A MAGNIFICENT TOMB WITH SEALS INTACT; RECOVERED SAME FOR YOUR ARRIVAL; CONGRATULATIONS

This telegram, sent by Howard Carter to his sponsor, Lord Carnarvon, on November 6, 1922, electrified the world. Searching amid rubble heaps left by dozens of archaeologists over a span of a hundred years, Carter had finally tried one last desperate dig. His area: a small triangle of rocky debris bounded by the tombs of Ramses II, Merneptah, and Ramses VI. Almost by chance, his native laborers cleared away three feet of earth beneath an innocuous workman's hut erected centuries before, and found the first of sixteen steps cut steeply down into the bedrock. The hidden entry led to a blocked-up, sealed door bearing the special mark that identified the tomb as a royal necropolis. With admirable restraint, Carter went no further. Filling the stairway with rubble again, to prevent looting, he posted a guard and awaited Carnarvon's arrival three weeks later.

On November 25, with Carnarvon present, Carter pulled down the sealed door. Beyond it he found another rubble-filled passageway thirty feet long and a second sealed door. Again the barricade was torn away—to reveal a sight that rendered him speechless. By the flickering light of his candle, he saw strangely shaped animal figures and statues and a jumbled mass of objects—all glinting of gold. As his eyes became accustomed to the dim light, gilded couches, gold-plated chariots, and hundreds of other spectacular treasures, strewn haphazardly about the chamber, appeared. They had found the burial place of the boy-king Tutankhamen.

The news went out immediately. For two months, Carter's team photographed, cataloged, and packed the items for shipment to Cairo. With great care, Carter treated the thirty-two-centuries-old objects to preserve them against further decay, as the press reported his every move from tents hastily pitched at the site.

On February 17, with the antechamber now cleared, Carter and Carnarvon broke through into the next sealed room, the burial chamber itself. The sight was unbelievable. The entire room—except for a fifteen-inch space at each side—was filled by a huge golden shrine ten feet nine inches wide, sixteen feet six inches long, and nine feet high. Carter opened the folding (but not sealed) doors at the shrine's east end. A second set of doors confronted him, these bolted and sealed. At last Carter's search had reached the ultimate, a point beyond which grave robbers had not been able to penetrate. An undefiled mummy still lay concealed within the shrine.

Lord Carnarvon did not live to marvel at what was to come next; he died just two months later, in 1923, from an insect bite. Despite a series of delays imposed by the Egyptian government, Carter continued the discoveries through the winter season of 1925–27. The tremendous shrine proved to be actually four shrines, one inside the other, Chinese box–fashion. And inside the innermost was the sarcophagus, a large, yellow quartzite block with a rose granite lid that weighed well over a half ton.

The climax was yet to come. Before the sarcophagus lid could be raised, the shrine had to be taken apart and removed from the room. Its transfer from the burial chamber took eighty-four days of struggle—almost a full day for each of its component parts, all of them heavy, hard to handle, and very fragile. Ironically, Carter discovered that while the artisan craftsmanship used to build the shrine had been superb, the assembly laborers had left a good deal to be desired. Ignoring the markings that indicated the proper assembly sequence, the workers had put the shrine together backward, with the doors facing east instead of west and the side panels reversed. And they had pounded reluctant joinings into position with heavy hammer blows, leaving noticeable dents.

The opening of the sarcophagus gave the final surprise. An outer anthropoid coffin concealed a second, and the second a third. The innermost coffin was the most amazing find of all: a solid gold case six feet one and three-quarters inches long and nearly one-quarter inch thick, worth a princely sum. Within the final coffin lay the goal of the dig—the mummy of King Tut. On Tut's face was a twenty-two-and-one-half-pound solid gold burial mask measuring twenty-one and one-quarter inches from top to bottom. Carter soon learned that the king's embalmers had erred in seeking to preserve the corpse for the ages. They had poured a tarlike unguent between the gold coffin and the wooden (middle) coffin as well as over the wrapped mummy. During the centuries a chemical reaction had carbonized the bones and tissues beyond any hope of salvage.

The mummy's bindings hid 143 pieces of jewelry, which joined the treasures already found. Eventually a total of 5,220 items were cataloged. Tut's body was returned to the tomb, where it rests today. The valuable treasures, however, are on display at the Cairo Museum. On rare occasions the Egyptian authorities permit exhibitions of them outside the country.

King Tut himself was probably insignificant, dying around 1323 B.C. at the age of about nineteen. But the riches found in his tomb gave the world its first glimpse of a complete funerary assemblage for an Egyptian pharaoh, objects previously described in religious texts and contemporary writings.

Opening the tomb gave rise to a press-inspired "pharaoh's curse." Carnarvon had died almost immediately, and allegedly a score of other individuals were struck down because of their involvement with dismantling the shrine. The legend is false. Of the ten principal diggers at Tutankhamen's tomb, two were alive forty years later and another five lived an average of twenty years beyond its opening.

Howard Carter emerging with a box of relics from King Tutankhamen's tomb.

However, the tomb itself was the victim of a curse—tourists. By 1991 3,000 visitors a day were entering the tomb and stirring up the dust on the walls. Their sweat released salt that clung to the walls and their breath released organisms that remained trapped inside the tomb. The tourists brought with them bacteria and fungi that damaged the contents of the tomb, leading the Egyptian Antiquities Organization to declare the area closed.

—W.K.

PERSEPOLIS

Year: 1932
Location: 32 miles northeast of Shiraz, Iran, and 150 miles due east of the Persian Gulf
Discoverer: Ernst Herzfeld
Findings: When a monumental staircase emerged from the rubble of centuries, Ernst Herzfeld saw that Persepolis would exceed his wildest dreams. Herzfeld, director of the Oriental Institute at the University of Chicago, came to the site in 1924 at the request of the Iranian government. He found Persepolis in ruins, much

as Alexander the Great had left it after a night of feasting and sacking in 330 B.C. Now windblown dust and ash filled the summer palace of the Achaemenid kings, obscuring all but a few standing columns. For generations, desert nomads, leery of the huge winged stone beasts atop the columns, had avoided the region. By 1932 Herzfeld had surveyed the site and located the outline of the first of many palaces. He cleared the spacious *apadana* (audience hall) with its thirty-six columns rising to a height of sixty-five feet. But the room lay well above the surrounding terrace. Herzfeld searched for stairs—and under twenty-six feet of debris he found them.

What he saw must have taken his breath away. Each of two staircases bore magnificent six-foot-high carvings—a thousand linear feet of carvings. They told the story of a New Year's Day festival in Persepolis, with the founder, Darius I, receiving delegations from an empire that reached from the Danube to the Indus.

The Persian New Year coincided with the spring equinox, and the high breezy plateau Darius chose for Persepolis suited the season. He began construction in about 520 B.C. His son Xerxes added the Hall of One Hundred Columns and the eighty-square-foot public gatehouse, called "All Lands," beyond which was the *apadana*, or audience hall, that had been built by Darius. Other structures included a harem and a royal treasury. Artaxerxes I, son of Xerxes, completed the monument some sixty years after it was begun.

Herzfeld's excavations and those of his successor, Erich Schmidt, continued until 1939. They found underground channels that suggested the whole complex had been built to a master plan. Fallen columns, their capitals heavy with palm, papyrus, and animal-head motifs, had once supported soaring roofs of painted cedar. Varying decorative styles evidenced artisans from all over the world. Many of the designs, originally embellished with gold and jewel-like colors, depicted the god Ahuramazda, whose earthly representative was Zoroaster. Additional inscriptions in old Persian laid down the duty of the king: to embrace the truth, shun the lie, and perfect the arts of horsemanship and archery.

The destruction of Persepolis inspired Handel's oratorio "Alexander's Feast." To recover some of the greatness, Herzfeld and Schmidt sifted the earth, recovering beads, gold, bronze, pottery, jewelry, clay tablets, tools. They unearthed two more staircases, these leading from the valley floor to the terrace, a 1,500-by-900-foot area hewed out of rock. Each staircase had 111 steps of polished gray limestone. Midway up, the flights reversed direction, so that they came together at the top. The steps were wide and the risers shallow, allowing horses and chariots to ascend.

In the 1940s the Iranian government undertook further excavations. Later, restoration work was led by scholars from the Italian Institute for the Middle and Far East. Parts of the monument were rebuilt, while other parts remain as first unearthed, a forest of massive gates and columns.

—J.F.K.

SUTTON HOO SHIP

Year: 1939
Location: At Sutton Hoo, near Woodbridge, England, and the river Deben
Discoverers: C. W. Phillips and others
Findings: The curiosity of a Suffolk woman, Edith Pretty, led to the greatest find ever located on English soil. Intrigued by eleven strange mounds on her property, she hired Basil Brown, a part-time employee at the Ipswich Museum, to investigate. In May 1939, some months after he began, he opened a long trench on the largest mound. Almost at once he saw a pattern of rusty iron clench bolts in the sand, easily recognizable as the outline of a boat. No wood remained, having long since decayed, but an impression, like a photographic negative, could still be seen.

Brown correctly assumed that the long barrow hid the remains of a huge buried ship.

Britain's Ministry of Works took over, calling in C. W. Phillips and a professional archaeological team. In late July they began to excavate at the mound's midpoint, searching for a burial chamber. Gold and silver jewelry and trappings appeared in such magnificent abundance that the elated team realized they had uncovered a royal burial site.

The treasures found included a solid-gold purse filled with Merovingian gold coins, a belt studded with more than 4,000 garnets, and a fourteen-ounce gold buckle for a royal shoulder belt. The Viking-style burial also produced a Swedish battle helmet of gilt bronze, a sword and shield embossed with gold, a huge Byzantine silver dish, nine smaller bowls, and many other precious objects, in an excellent state of preservation.

The discoveries added considerably to knowledge about the cultural achievement of the Anglo-Saxons in the period just before East Anglia converted to Christianity. Not only was a very high level of craftsmanship shown, but the mixture of Byzantine, Scandinavian, and central European styles indicated a much wider interchange through commerce than had been previously suspected. The site also closely verified the burial ceremonies afforded to the fallen warriors in the epic *Beowulf*, where they are laid to rest with many treasures and ornaments from distant lands.

No body was found. The Sutton Hoo ship-burial was a cenotaph, a memorial for a person whose body is buried elsewhere. Its mix of pagan and Christian aspects pointed to Raedwald, a seventh-century East Anglian king, as the ruler being honored. Raedwald, who died around 624 A.D., was a Christian convert who held on to some of his pagan beliefs.

The treasure was removed just before World War II began. No further digging was done until the mid-1960s, when British Museum experts reopened the site to study the ship with new scientific techniques. Some damage had occurred, chiefly caused by the use of the mounds as an obstacle course for British army tank commanders during the war. These studies established the ship's length as eighty-nine feet and its width as fifteen feet, and revealed sides tapering in to a sharp point at each end. There being neither a proper keel nor a sail, the ship relied on thirty-eight oars for its propulsion.

To settle the question of who owned the valuables—the crown or Edith Pretty—a coroner's inquest was called, more than a millennium after the event. The jury ruled in favor of Mrs. Pretty, giving her a treasure valued in six figures. She promptly donated it all to the British Museum, where it can be seen today.

—W.K.

CAVES OF LASCAUX

Year: 1940
Location: Dordogne region of France near Montignac
Discoverer: Marcel Ravidat
Findings: When Marcel Ravidat, a seventeen-year-old garage apprentice, and a group of friends followed his dog, Robot, through a narrow, bramble-covered opening on a lazy autumn afternoon, he did not imagine he was about to discover one of the greatest prehistoric sites. On that day, September 8, 1940, Ravidat and his friends were not prepared to enter the cave. They agreed to meet the next Sunday to explore their discovery. Ravidat, however, could not wait. Four days later, with different friends, Marsal, Agnel, and Coencas, he returned. Ravidat entered the cave and slid down a kind of well that opened on a large chamber, whose importance he did not recognize because he had only a box of kitchen matches. His friends soon joined him, but having no way to explore further, they climbed back, swearing each other to secrecy.

The next day they returned with a lamp. They reached the chamber and began to explore, following a narrow corridor. It was here, raising his lamp to the walls, that Ravidat saw, in the dull glow of the lamp, faint lines in different colors. Slowly examining the walls, he and his friends discovered several large animal figures. Excitedly, they began to run around the cave, going from discovery to discovery. According to Ravidat, "Our joy was indescribable. A band of savages doing a war dance could not have done better."

A few days later, no longer being able to contain their excitement, they told their old schoolmaster, Monsieur Léon Laval. After descending into the cave and visiting all the chambers, Laval rushed to notify the renowned French prehistorian, the Abbé Henri Breuil. Soon visitors and archaeologists were rushing to visit the caves.

The initial excitement was forgotten during the German occupation and visitors became rare. After the war the entrance chamber and staircase were rebuilt, and trenches were dug for electricity. The cave welcomed the public on Bastille Day, July 14, 1948.

The drawings date from the Palaeolithic period and appear to be the work of the same group of people over a relatively short time. Carbon dating fixed the age of the paintings at more than 14,000 years old. The cave itself is about 100 meters (328 feet) long. The different areas of the cave are known as the Rotunda, the Axial Gallery, the Passage, the Apse, the Shaft, the Nave, and the Chamber of the Felines. They contain monumental groups of animal figures, painted in red and black. The compositions include bison, bovines, horses, ibexes, felines, rhinoceroses, reindeer, a "unicorn," and some smaller stags. There are also geometric signs, the meanings of which remain a mystery.

On the walls of the Shaft is depicted a scene, a rare occurrence in Palaeolithic art. A rhinoceros stands to the left of a man, one of the very few human figures, who appears to have been thrown by a bison. A spear has been drawn across the bison's body and it stands with its entrails pouring out.

The paintings were not the only discoveries. Lying on the floor were pieces of flint and bone tools, including sixteen spears, pierced and unpierced shells from beaches, and the bones of reindeer. They also found the remains of painting pigments and of lamps. These were probably fueled by grease, tallow, or oil.

The caves of Lascaux do not seem to have been a permanent habitation, there being little evidence of long-term use. Archaeologists believe they were used for ritual purposes by bands of hunter-gatherers. Many think the rituals involved "sympathetic magic." The hunters drew the animal they wished to catch. Such an interpretation suggests that it was the act of painting that was the focus of the ritual.

However, from the bone remains found at Lascaux and elsewhere, it seems that reindeer provided most of the animal diet, although they are not frequently depicted, while the animals they painted, bison, aurochs, and horses, were not the most common food animals. This leads other archaeologists to conclude that the sites were of more religious significance, and they point to the thousands of children's footprints preserved in the clay floors as evidence of ritual dances.

After World War II Lascaux became a popular site for tourists. More than 1,500 people a day visited the caves and its paintings. In 1955 it was noticed that the paintings were beginning to suffer from the carbon dioxide of exhaled breath and the moisture visitors brought with them. In 1962 a green mold was beginning to form on the walls, and the caves had to be closed to visitors. What had survived 14,000 years of obscurity barely survived twenty years of discovery.

While the caves are of unsurpassed historical interest, it is the artistry of these primitive paintings that continues to astonish those who have seen them. The sureness of the strokes, without erasure or alteration, is evidence that these were master painters who were adept at using a kind of perspective, as well as being able to utilize the irregularity of the walls as elements in their designs. Their art is "primitive" only in age, not in intention. When Picasso saw Lascaux he exclaimed, "We have invented nothing!"

In 1994 spelunker Jean-Marie Chauvet and two friends discovered another treasure trove of Paleolithic art in a huge cave in the Ardeche

Gorge northwest of Avignon, France. Art authorities believe the Chauvet cave may be as important as the Lascaux caves.

—D.C.

QUMRAN AND THE DEAD SEA SCROLLS

Year: 1947–55
Location: Hills at northwest corner of the Dead Sea, Jordan
Discoverers: Elazar L. Sukenik, G. Lankester Harding, and Father Roland de Vaux
Findings: The circumstances surrounding the actual discovery of the Dead Sea Scrolls are shrouded in mystery, with variant, retold stories. Allegedly, Muhammed Adh-Dhib, a member of the Ta'amireh bedouin who perennially scavenged the wastes in the Judaean desert, located the first scrolls in the spring of 1947. While pursuing an errant sheep or goat, he threw some stones into an opening in a cliffside cave. When he heard a shattering sound, he climbed inside and found a cache of tightly sealed clay jars.

Three of the battered leather manuscripts packed inside the jars were removed and taken to "Kando," an Assyrian Christian cobbler from Bethlehem, also doing business as a go-between dealer in the illicit antiquities market. These scrolls came to the attention of Elazar L. Sukenik, an archaeology professor at Hebrew University. Sensing their immense value, Sukenik braved the dangers of the Jewish-Arab war then raging in Palestine to purchase the scrolls for Israel.

Kando, meanwhile, had looted the cave of another four scrolls, along with the largest fragments he could remove. The cobbler found a second buyer, the Syrian cleric Athanasius Yeshue Samuel, metropolitan at the Monastery of Saint Mark in Jerusalem. In 1948 Athanasius learned that the scrolls for which he had reluctantly paid twenty-four pounds were authentic biblical manuscripts at least 1,000 years older than any other known. Ultimately, in 1954, after placing a blind advertisement in the *Wall Street Journal*, the churchman sold the four scrolls to the Israeli government for $250,000.

Dating the scrolls accurately became an immediate problem. Challenges from critics who doubted their authenticity were swept away in 1951 by Lankester Harding and Father Roland de Vaux, who headed a trial excavation at Qumran, an ancient ruin just a half mile south of Cave I. (The eleven caves in which scrolls were discovered are numbered I through XI.) By pure luck, the first room worked yielded pottery fragments that perfectly matched the unidentified pottery pieces found scattered in Cave I. In the same immediate area, the team discovered a coin bearing a date corresponding to 10 A.D. Some 500 coins of nearly continuous dating, which spread over two centuries, further pinpointed the years. Analysis of the Qumran dig proved that the site had been occupied by an ascetic sect called the Essenes up to 68 A.D., when the Romans had totally destroyed the commune. Warned somehow of the approaching disaster, the sect had concealed its most prized possession—the library of scrolls—in the nearby marl caves, where they remained undisturbed for 1,879 years.

Cave I—the original discovery—yielded the only complete scrolls discovered to date: the great scroll of Isaiah, unrolling to a length of seven and one-half yards. Cave II produced an unusual two-strip copper scroll enumerating the hiding places of many precious treasures. Cave IV proved to be the most prolific of all, containing thousands of additional fragments, enough to keep scholars busy for years.

Most of the scrolls are from the Old Testament, and the remainder comprise biblical apocrypha or secular works. Every book of the Hebrew Bible except Esther is represented. There are nearly complete versions of biblical books in both Hebrew and Aramaic, as well as poetry, almanacs, and calendars. The scrolls, while explaining many obscure passages and gaps in the Bible, suggest no radical theological changes in the Old Testament in use today. The sectarian manuscripts identified the Essene leader as the Teacher of Righteousness, founder of the world's first-known monastery. Among the apocryphal scrolls are the Book of Tobit, written in the original Aramaic, a work seen previously only in a Greek translation, and a new narration called The War between the Children of Light and the Children of Darkness.

In 1953 the Jordanian government awarded exclusive translation rights to a small group of scholars known as the Israel Antiquities Authority, although, at the time, none of the scholars was Israeli. As the decades wore on, other scholars became impatient with the group's leisurely pace of work. The Authority's monopoly was finally broken in 1991. First Martin Abegg of Hebrew Union College in Cincinnati used a computer program to reconstruct the texts of the scrolls from a privately printed index to the manuscripts. Then the Huntington Library in San Marino, California, released a complete photographic set of the scrolls comprising 3,000 negatives.

Along with the breaking of the physical monopoly of the scrolls came challenges to the established theory of their origin. Some scholars believe that the remains at Qumran were not left by the Essene sect but rather that the Dead Sea Scrolls represent a mainstream library hidden during the Jewish uprising against the Romans.

In addition, some scholars point to evidence, such as Arabic and Byzantine coins and third-century A.D. lamps, that indicate that the caves were used long after the scrolls were hidden.

—W.K. and D.W.

XIAN

Year: 1974
Location: Near the city of Xian in central China, in the ancient kingdom of Qin
Findings: In March of 1974, farmers in central China, while digging a well, struck a terra cotta head. Digging deeper, they unearthed a life-size figure of a soldier. Archaeologists arrived and began to uncover figure after figure, still arranged in military formation twenty feet underground. Soon the dimensions of the terra cotta army reached enormous proportions. More than 7,500 soldiers have been discovered and the excavations will not be complete for years.

Archaeologists and historians are astounded not only by the number of figures but also by their artistry. Each head is uniquely modeled, with lifelike expressions. Furthermore, each detail is perfectly reproduced. There are different kinds of armor, footwear, and weapons. The weapons are authentic and, because they were coated with a special oil, still sharp after being buried for 2,200 years. There are also war chariots drawn by magnificent terra cotta horses of unsurpassed power and artistry.

The Xian warriors were not cast from molds but individually modeled. Heads, arms, and torsos were fashioned separately, then joined with clay strips. The hollow heads and torsos rest on solid clay legs. Head and body were roughcast, then coated with a thinner layer on which were carved facial details, types of dress, and armor. Warriors and horses were originally painted bright colors, most of which have faded from being so long underground. More than 10,000 weapons have been unearthed, including bows and crossbows as well as spears, swords, and broadswords. It is thought that the artists created a portrait of each soldier in the imperial guard so that they could continue to guard the emperor after his death. The soldiers probably made excellent models. They would have known that past kings had their guards and concubines interred with them. The lives of these soldiers were therefore spared, while their visages and expressions were immortalized by the Xian artists.

This army was meant to protect the remains of the first emperor of China, Qin Shi Huang Di. After ending the 200 years of bloodshed known as the Warring States period, he was the first to unify China under one rule in 221 B.C., and at once he set about utilizing its vast resources for imperial ends. Huang Di began the building of the Great Wall and immediately undertook the building of palaces and a mausoleum. Men numbering 500,000 were conscripted to build the wall, and another 1.5 million to construct palaces and tombs. He built more than 1,500 miles of roads and dug canals to link major waterways. Many canals and irrigation systems built during his reign are still in use.

The four pits that comprise this vast terra cotta army cover 500 acres and are deployed to protect the as-yet unexcavated imperial mausoleum, which rests under a mound fifteen stories high. It is thought that the emperor attempted to create an ideal imperial city as his tomb, a city guarded by its own terra cotta army.

Si-ma Qien, China's first great historian, writing about 100 B.C., describes how workmen dug through three subterranean streams and poured molten copper for the outer foundations. The tomb was filled with palaces, as well as reproductions of the country's main rivers in quicksilver, which, by mechanical means, was made to flow into a miniature ocean.

In life the emperor sent numerous expeditions in search of the "Fountain of Youth" and so feared assassination that he rarely slept two nights in the same bed. Yet, from the beginning of his reign, he made the world's most lavish preparations for his own death and burial.

—D.C.

An antique is something that's been useless so long it's still in pretty good condition.
Franklin P. Jones, *Saturday Evening Post*,
February 21, 1956

The advantage of being married to an archaeologist is that the older one grows the more interested he becomes.
Agatha Christie, *Murder in Mesopotamia*, 1936

Chapter 8

SKY AND SPACE

BIZARRE WEATHER

HIGHEST TEMPERATURE
On September 13, 1922, the temperature in Azizia, Libya, reached 136.4 degrees Fahrenheit (58 degrees centigrade)—in the shade.

LOWEST TEMPERATURE
On August 24, 1960, the thermometer at Vostok, Antarctica, registered −126.9 degrees Fahrenheit (−88.3 degrees centigrade). Vostok also holds the record for consistently cold weather. To reach an optimum temperature of 65 degrees Fahrenheit, Vostok would require 48,800 "heating degree days" a year. By comparison, Fairbanks, Alaska, needs only 14,300.

EXTREME TEMPERATURES
Temperatures in Verkhoyansk, Russia, have ranged from 93.5 degrees Fahrenheit down to −89.7 degrees Fahrenheit, a variance of 183.2 degrees Fahrenheit.

SUDDEN TEMPERATURE RISE
On February 21, 1918, the temperature in Granville, North Dakota, rose eighty-three degrees in twelve hours—from −33 degrees Fahrenheit in the early morning to 50 degrees Fahrenheit in the late afternoon.

SUDDEN TEMPERATURE DROP
On December 24, 1924, the temperature in Fairfield, Montana, fell eighty-four degrees in twelve hours, from 63 degrees Fahrenheit at noon to −21 degrees Fahrenheit at midnight. In one twenty-four-hour period on January 23–24, 1916, the temperature in Browning, Montana, dropped a hundred degrees, from 44 degrees Fahrenheit to −56 degrees Fahrenheit.

GREATEST TEMPERATURE FLUCTUATION
The most bizarre temperature change in history occurred at Spearfish, South Dakota, on January 22, 1943. At 7:30 A.M. the thermometer read −4 degrees Fahrenheit. However, by 7:32 A.M. the temperature had risen forty-nine degrees in two

minutes to 45 degrees Fahrenheit. By 9:00 A.M. the temperature had drifted up to 54 degrees Fahrenheit. Then suddenly it began to plunge—fifty-eight degrees in twenty-seven minutes—until, at 9:27 A.M., it had returned to −4 degrees Fahrenheit.

LONGEST HOT SPELL
Marble Bar, Western Australia, experienced 160 consecutive days of 100-degree-Fahrenheit temperatures from October 31, 1923, to April 7, 1924.

MOST RAIN IN ONE MINUTE
The most rain ever recorded in one minute was 1.5 inches at Barot on the Caribbean island of Guadeloupe on November 26, 1970.

FASTEST FOOT OF RAIN
Holt, Missouri, received twelve inches of rain in forty-two minutes on June 22, 1947.

THE RAINIEST DAY
On March 16, 1952, 73.62 inches of rain—more than six feet—fell at Cilaos on Réunion Island east of Madagascar. Another 24 inches fell during the twenty-four hours surrounding March 16.

MOST RAIN IN FIFTEEN DAYS
Cherrapunji, Assam, India, received 189 inches of rain between June 24 and July 8, 1931. Back in 1861, Cherrapunji received 366.14 inches of rain in one month and 905.12 inches for the calendar year.

POINT RAINFALL
An extreme case of localized rainfall occurred on the night of August 2, 1966, one and a half miles northeast of Greenfield, New Hampshire. Robert H. Stanley reported that rain began to fall at 7:00 P.M., reaching great intensity from 7:45 P.M. until 10:15 P.M. When he awoke the next morning, Mr. Stanley found that his rain gauge had filled to the 5.75-inch mark. How-

ever, Stanley's neighbor three-tenths of a mile away had collected only one-half inch in his rain gauge. Walking around the area, Stanley discovered that the heavy rainfall was limited to no more than one-half mile in any direction.

Another strange case of point rainfall took place on November 11, 1958, in the backyard of Mrs. R. Babington of Alexandria, Louisiana. Although there were no clouds in the sky, a misty drizzle fell over an area of 100 square feet for two and a half hours. Mrs. Babington called a local reporter, who confirmed the phenomenon. The Shreveport weather bureau suggested the moisture had been formed by condensation from a nearby air conditioner, but their theory was never proved.

NO RAIN
The driest place on Earth is Arica, Chile, in the Atacama Desert. No rain fell there for more than fourteen years, between October 1903 and December 1917. Over a fifty-nine-year period, Arica averaged three-hundredths of an inch of rain a year.

HEAVY SNOWFALL
On April 5 and 6, 1969, sixty-eight inches of snow fell on Bessans, France, in only nineteen hours.

SNOWIEST DAY
The largest snowfall in a twenty-four-hour period was 75.8 inches—more than six feet—recorded at Silver Lake, Colorado, on April 14–15, 1921.

SNOWIEST SEASON
Paradise Ranger Station on Mount Rainier in Washington State recorded 1,122 inches of snow in 1971–72. Their average is 582 inches.

CURIOUS PRECIPITATION AT THE EMPIRE STATE BUILDING
While rain was falling on the street in front of the Empire State Building on November 3, 1958, guards near the top of the building were making snowballs.

SNOW IN MIAMI
At 6:10 A.M. on January 19, 1977, West Palm Beach, Florida, reported its first snowfall ever. By 8:30 A.M. snow was falling in Fort Lauderdale, the farthest south that snow had ever been reported in Florida. The snow continued south to Miami, and some even fell in Homestead, twenty-four miles south of Miami International Airport. The cold wave was so unusual that heat lamps had to be brought out to protect the iguanas at Miami's Crandon Park Zoo.

CHAMPION HURRICANE
Hurricane John, which flourished in August and September of 1994, was notable for two reasons. It lasted for all or part of thirty-one days, making it the longest-lived tropical storm on record. It also crossed over the international date line twice, changing its name from Hurricane John to Typhoon John and back to Hurricane John.

—D.W.

21 THINGS THAT FELL FROM THE SKY

1. MONEY
On October 8, 1976, a light plane buzzed the Piazza Venezia in Rome and dropped 500-lire, 1,000-lire, and 10,000-lire bank notes on the startled people below. The mad bomber was not found.

2. GOLDEN RAIN
When yellow-colored globules fell over suburban Sydney, Australia, in late 1971, the minister for health in New South Wales, Arnold Jago, blamed it on the excreta of bees, consisting mostly of undigested pollen. However, there were no reports of vast hordes of bees in the area, and no explanation was given as to why they would choose to excrete en masse over Sydney.

3. A 3,902-POUND STONE
The largest meteorite fall in recorded history occurred on March 8, 1976, near the Chinese city of Jilin. Many of the 100 stones that were

found weighed more than 200 pounds; the largest, which landed in the Chinchu commune, weighed 3,902 pounds. It is, by more than 1,000 pounds, the largest stony meteorite ever recovered.

4. THE LARGEST METEORITE
The largest known iron meteorite, weighing sixty-six tons, crashed to Earth in late 1920, landing on a farm in the Hoba district west of Grootfontein in northern Namibia. It has since been declared a national monument and is visited by more than 20,000 tourists a year. A minor international incident occurred in 1989 when thirty-six Malaysian soldiers serving in a U.N. peacekeeping force tried to cut pieces from the boulder for souvenirs.

5. SOOT
A fine blanket of soot landed on a Cranford park on the edge of London's Heathrow Airport in 1969, greatly annoying the local park keepers.

Members of the Chinese Academy of Sciences examine the hole made by the 3,902-pound meteorite that landed in Jilin Province on March 8, 1976.

The official report of the Greater London Council stated that the "soot" was composed of spores of a black microfungus, *Pithomyces chartarum*, found only in New Zealand.

6. HUMAN WASTE
On Sunday, October 18, 1992, Gerri and Leroy Cinnamon of Woodinville, Washington, were watching a football game on TV in their den with Gerri's parents when something crashed through the roof of their living room. "I expected to see Superman soar through the hole," said Leroy. Instead they found several baseball-sized chunks of greenish ice. As it melted it began to smell bad. Two days later the Federal Aviation Administration confirmed that the Cinnamons' roof had been damaged by frozen human waste from a leaky United Airlines sewage system. "It's a good thing none of us was killed," reflected Leroy. "What would you put on the tombstone?"

Unfortunately, falls of waste blobs are not uncommon. On April 23, 1978, for example, a twenty-five-pound chunk landed in an unused school building in Ripley, Tennessee. Other attacks have occurred in Denver and Chicago. And then there's the story of the unfortunate Kentucky farmer who took a big lick of a flying Popsicle before he discovered what it was.

7. FIVE HUNDRED BIRDS
About 500 dead and dying blackbirds and pigeons landed on the streets of San Luis Obispo, California, over a period of several hours in late November 1977. No local spraying had occurred, and no explanation was offered.

8. WHITE FIBROUS BLOBS
Blobs of white material up to twenty feet in length descended over the San Francisco Bay area in California on October 11, 1977. Pilots in San Jose encountered them as high as 4,000 feet. Migrating spiders were blamed, although no spiders were recovered.

9. LUMINOUS GREEN SNOW
In April 1953 glowing green snow was encountered near Mount Shasta, California. Mr. and Mrs. Milton Moyer reported that their hands itched after touching it and that "a blistered, itching rash" formed on their hands, arms, and faces. The Atomic Energy Commission denied any connection between the snow and recent A-bomb tests in nearby Nevada.

10. MYSTERIOUS DOCUMENTS
The July 25, 1973, edition of the *Albany* (New York) *Times Union* reported the unusual case of Bob Hill. Hill, the owner of radio station WHRL of North Greenbush, New York, was taking out the station garbage at 4:15 P.M. when he noticed "twirling specks" falling from a distance higher than the station's 300-foot transmitter. He followed two of the white objects until they landed in a hay field. The objects turned out to be two sets of formulas and accompanying graphs that apparently explained "normalized extinction" and the "incomplete Davis-Greenstein orientation." No explanation has been made public.

11. BEANS
Rancher Salvador Targino of João Pessoa, Brazil, reported a rain of small beans on his property in Paraíba State in early 1971. Local agricultural authorities speculated that a storm had swept up a pile of beans in West Africa and dropped them in northeastern Brazil. Targino boiled some of the beans, but he said they were too tough to eat.

12. SILVER COINS
Several thousand rubles' worth of silver coins fell in the Gorki region of the USSR on June 17, 1940. The official explanation was that a landslide had uncovered a hidden treasure, which was picked up by a tornado, which dropped it on Gorki. No explanation was given for the fact that the coins were not accompanied by any debris.

13. MUSHROOM-SHAPED THINGS
Traffic at Mexico City Airport was halted temporarily on the morning of July 30, 1963, when thousands of grayish, mushroom-shaped things floated to the ground out of a cloudless sky. Hundreds of witnesses described these objects variously as "giant cobwebs," "balls of cotton," and "foam." They disintegrated rapidly after landing.

14. HUMAN BODY

Mary C. Fuller was sitting in her parked car with her eight-month-old son on Monday morning, September 25, 1978, in San Diego, California, when a human body crashed through the windshield. The body had been thrown from a Pacific Southwest Airlines jetliner, which had exploded after being hit by a small plane in one of the worst air disasters in United States history. Mother and son suffered minor lacerations.

15. FISH

About 150 perchlike silver fish dropped from the sky during a tropical storm near Killarney Station in Australia's Northern Territory in February 1974. Fish-falls are common enough that an official explanation has been developed to cover most of them. It is theorized that whirlwinds create a waterspout effect, sucking up water and fish, carrying them for great distances, and then dropping them somewhere else.

16. ICE CHUNKS

In February of 1965 a fifty-pound mass of ice plunged through the roof of the Phillips Petroleum plant in Woods Cross, Utah. And in his book *Strangest of All*, Frank Edwards reports the case of a carpenter working on a roof in Kempten—near Düsseldorf, Germany—who was struck and killed in 1951 by an icicle six feet long and six inches around that shot down from the sky.

17. PEACHES

On July 12, 1961, unripe peaches were scattered over a small portion of Shreveport, Louisiana, from a cloudy sky.

18. DEADLY WHITE POWDER

On Saturday, July 10, 1976, the citizens of Seveso, Italy, were startled by a sudden loud whistling sound coming from the direction of the nearby ICMESA chemical factory. The sound was followed by a thick, gray cloud, which rolled toward the town and dropped a mist of white dust that settled on everything and smelled horrible. It was nine days before the people of Seveso learned that the white dust contained dioxin, a deadly poison far more dangerous than arsenic or strychnine. It took another five days for the company to suggest that the area be evacuated. By then it was too late. The effects of dioxin poisoning had already begun. The area was finally evacuated, surrounded by barbed wire, and declared a contaminated zone. Thousands of birds and hundreds of exposed animals were killed, ugly black pustules formed on the skin of young children, and older people began to die of liver ailments. In 1975 only three babies were born with birth defects in the Seveso area. In 1978 the number rose to fifty-three. Reports released in 1989 and 1993 revealed increased rates of cardiovascular deaths and elevated risk for several forms of cancer.

19. NONDAIRY CREAMER

White powder of a more innocuous kind began falling on the small town of Chester, South Carolina, in 1969—shortly after the Borden company started production of a corn syrup–based nondairy creamer in its local plant. Whenever the plant's exhaust vents clogged, the creamer spewed into the air and landed on people's homes and cars. Although basically harmless, the powder would mix with dew and rain and cause a sticky mess. Said homeowner Grace Dover, "It gets on your windows and you can't see out. It looks like you haven't washed your windows for a hundred years." In 1991 Borden paid a $4,000 fine for releasing Cremora beyond plant boundaries. By that time the company had already taken steps to reduce the low-fat rain.

20. SPACE JUNK

In September 1962 a metal object about six inches in diameter and weighing twenty-one pounds crashed into the intersection of North Eighth and Park Streets in Manitowoc, Wisconsin, and burrowed several inches into the ground. The object was later identified as part of *Sputnik IV*, which had been launched by the USSR on May 15, 1960. On July 11, 1979, *Skylab*, the seventy-seven-ton U.S. space station, fell out of orbit over the south Indian Ocean and Western Australia. The largest piece of debris to reach land was a one-ton tank. There is so much space junk still in the sky that one U.S. satellite, known as *Solar Max*, was hit by two hundred pieces of litter and had to be repaired by shuttle astronauts.

21. HAY

A great cloud of hay drifted over the town of Devizes in England at teatime on July 3, 1977. As soon as the cloud reached the center of town, it all fell to Earth in handful-sized lumps. The sky was otherwise clear and cloudless with a slight breeze. The temperature was twenty-six degrees centigrade.

—D.W.

TUNGUSKA FIREBALL OF 1908

During the first moments of dawn on June 30, 1908, a falling star flashed into sight over western China. It came to Earth in a desolate region of peat bogs and pine forests near the

Podkamennaya (Stony) Tunguska River in central Siberia, exploding above the ground with the force of 2,000 Hiroshima bombs.

Awed witnesses of what was later to be called the Tunguska fireball reported a blinding light and a series of deafening thunderclaps audible at a distance of 500 miles. It was, in the words of author and planetarium director Roy A. Gallant, "the most devastating assault on our planet in the history of civilization."

That night luminous clouds veiled northern Europe. A bright, diffused white and yellow glow lit Berlin, Copenhagen, London, and Königsberg with an intensity sufficient to permit photography. Ships could be seen for miles out at sea. Scientists attributed the unusual "northern lights" to solar flares, for news of the great Siberian explosion was long delayed.

The devastation caused by the Tunguska fireball, photographed almost twenty years later in 1927.

Not until 1927, after war and revolution had swept Russia, did a scientist, Russian meteorite specialist Leonid A. Kulik, attempt to reach the blast site. His first obstacle was finding a guide to lead him into the area. The local Tungus people believed that the fireball had been a punishment sent by Ogdy, their god of fire. They considered the region enchanted and refused to enter it. Finally Kulik induced a Tungus named Ilya Petrov to be his guide by giving him cloth, building materials, and two sacks of flour. After hiking more than sixty miles, Kulik reached the summit of Mount Shakharma. What he saw staggered the imagination even of a man who had expected a giant meteorite fall.

To a radius of twelve miles from the epicenter of the explosion, the pine forest was leveled and blackened. Uprooted trees lay parallel to one another, their tops pointed away from the blast. At a five-mile radius the wrecked forest showed evidence of an instantaneous incineration from above. At the center of the devastated area, Kulik found a mysterious island of upright trees, blackened and stripped of bark and branches, resembling a forest of telegraph poles. There was no sign of the giant meteorite Kulik had expected to discover. Indeed, to this day no remnant of a meteorite has been found.

Eyewitnesses to the explosion related tales of horror to Kulik. Thousands of reindeer had been instantly reduced to ash. The nomadic herdsmen were thrown as much as thirty-five feet through the air. One old man died of shock, others lay unconscious for two days.

War and politics restricted further scientific investigation until 1958, and foreign scientists were not permitted to visit the area until 1989.

Several exotic theories have been advanced to account for the Tunguska fireball, and these have kept pace with developments in science. In the 1930s a Russian engineer turned author, Aleksandr Kazantsev, suggested that the Siberian explosion had actually been the nuclear pyre of an alien spaceship trying to land.

Other explanations include collision with an antimatter meteorite or a "black hole." When particles of antimatter and ordinary matter meet, they annihilate one another in a reaction 1,000 times more efficient than that of a hydrogen bomb. This theory holds that a fast-moving black hole struck Earth, producing an effect akin to a nuclear explosion. It then passed through like a bullet, its speed virtually undiminished.

The current prevailing theory is that a stony meteorite, a piece of comet Encke 100 feet in diameter, exploded six miles above Earth, leading to "catastrophic fragmentation." Astronomers believe that Tunguska-like collisions occur every 300 years or so. One thing is certain, if the next such collision were to hit an urban area, rather than a remote region, the loss of life would dwarf that of any other disaster in history.

—L.B.W. and D.W.

WERNHER VON BRAUN

Basic research is what I am doing when I don't know what I am doing.

Wernher von Braun

From German weapons specialist to champion of the American space program and celebrity— this is the remarkable trajectory of the career of Wernher von Braun. Von Braun was one of the German scientists who, following the collapse of the Third Reich, were brought to America under the secret Overcast mission. The fact that many of these scientists, von Braun among them, had been members of the Nazi Party and may have participated in war crimes was overlooked by the U.S. government in its zeal to exploit their knowledge of weapons technology.

His Nazi affiliation effectively suppressed, von Braun rose to become one of the most important figures in the U.S. space program, a powerful proponent for manned space exploration.

Born on March 23, 1912, in Wirsitz, Germany, von Braun demonstrated an early childhood aptitude for rocket science. As a young boy, he hypothesized that he could make his red wagon "fly" by attaching rockets to the sides and igniting them. The rockets sent the wagon shooting down the street, the experiment ending in a fiery explosion. This early penchant for toys that "go bang" led the scientific wunderkind to study engineering at the technological institutes of Berlin and Zurich, Switzerland. In 1930 the eighteen-year-old student read an article on travel to the Moon that fired his imagination for space travel. filling him with "a romantic urge to soar through the heavens and actually explore the mysterious universe!"

Inspired by the work of Goddard and other pioneers in rocket science, von Braun began conducting his own experiments, receiving his B.S. in engineering in 1932. The German military was not unaware of the potential for this field of science, which could provide state-of-the-art weaponry not prohibited by the Treaty of Versailles. The fledgling rocket program was transferred to the military, and von Braun, then only twenty years old, was made chief of the station at Kummersdorf. In 1934, the year after Hitler came to power, von Braun received his doctorate in physics from the University of Berlin. Hitler poured vast sums of money into the German rocket program, and by 1938 von Braun's team at Peenemünde had developed a successful prototype of what was to become the deadly V-2 missile, which was capable of carrying a ton of explosives as far as 190 miles. Some 3,600 of these dreaded missiles were fired on London in 1944. In an interview for the *New Yorker*, von Braun expressed a "genuine regret that our missile, born of idealism . . . had joined in the business of killing. We had designed it to blaze the trail to other planets, not to destroy our own." Yet a colleague recalls that von Braun and his team toasted their triumph with champagne following the first bombing.

In 1945, with the Nazi regime collapsing, von Braun and his colleagues concluded that their best chance for survival lay not with the advancing Russian troops, but with the Americans. They eluded the SS, hiding out at various Bavarian resorts, until they could arrange for a surrender to American troops. At first skeptical of von Braun, who seemed too young to be the inventor of the V-2, the Americans quickly realized that they had stumbled upon a veritable mother lode of scientific knowledge. Operation Overcast, later called Paperclip, gathered up these former enemy scientists and whisked them to the United States, where they were set to work on the U.S. rocket program.

Project Paperclip specifically prohibited the use of war criminals and persons with ties to the Nazi Party, yet the initial security report on von Braun, issued in 1947, indicated that he was an SS officer. While no evidence was found to suggest that he was an ardent Nazi (in fact, he was arrested briefly by the SS for allegedly sabotaging the rocket program), he was classified as a potential security risk. This report, along with those on other German scientists with dubious backgrounds, was suppressed. A new report on von Braun was issued, suggesting that his Nazi affiliation was simply a matter of expediency and that he "may not" constitute a security threat to the United States. This second report paved the way for von Braun to remain in the United States and obtain American citizenship. It also allowed the U.S. government to continue to exploit scientific expertise that was considered invaluable to the Cold War struggle.

> Don't say that he's hypocritical,
> Say rather that he's apolitical,
> "Once the rockets are up, who cares where they come down?
> That's not my department," says Wernher von Braun.
>
> Tom Lehrer, "Wernher von Braun," 1965

Wernher von Braun (right) shares an amusing moment with a German general.

Having been "rehabilitated," von Braun became the linchpin in the U.S. space program. In the 1950s, while at Huntsville, Alabama, he was instrumental in the development of the Redstone ballistic missile and the Jupiter intermediate-range ballistic missile, both early stages of the *Explorer*, America's first satellite launch, and the *Pioneer* satellite. In 1960 von Braun became the director of NASA's George C. Marshall Flight Center, which developed the Saturn booster rockets that sent the manned Apollo capsules into space. By 1969 von Braun had realized his lifelong dream of landing a man on the Moon. For his contributions to the

U.S. space program, the former winner of the German Knight's Cross was awarded the National Medal of Science in 1975.

Von Braun's celebrity extended beyond the confines of the space program. He authored several books, collaborated on a series of articles for *Colliers* magazine, and, unable to resist the lure of Hollywood, served as technical adviser on several Walt Disney films on space flight. (He may even have served as the inspiration for Professor Ludwig von Drake, the Disney cartoon character who looked like a duck but spoke with a German accent.)

Von Braun continued to enjoy his lifelong love of diving, sailing, and other outdoor activities until the mid-1970s, when his health began to fail. He died on June 16, 1977, in Alexandria, Virginia, embracing death as an opportunity to "observe and learn and finally know what comes after all those beautiful things we experience during our lives on Earth."

—L.C.

NOTABLE SPACE MISSIONS

SPACE PROBES

1957: *SPUTNIK I*
Dates: Launched: October 4, 1957
Country: Soviet Union
Accomplishments: *Sputnik I* was the first man-made object to orbit the Earth. Its launch by the Soviet Union single-handedly opened up the frontier of outer space and began the U.S.-Soviet "space race." *Sputnik* was launched from the Baikonur cosmodrome in Kazhakhstan by an R.7 ICBM (NATO code word SS-6 Sapwood, also known as A-1 in the West). At just 184.3 pounds (83.6 kilograms), *Sputnik* was nothing more than a spiderlike 22.8-inch (58-centimeter) metal sphere with four long external antennas. It orbited the Earth every 96.2 minutes. It contained no scientific instruments except for chemical batteries and a two-frequency (20.005 and 40.002 MHz) transmitter. *Sputnik* reached an elliptical orbit of 141 miles (227 kilometers) by 585 miles (941 kilometers). Signal variations in its transmissions allowed tracking stations to infer information on the Earth's ionosphere and temperatures encountered by *Sputnik*. *Sputnik*'s transmissions ended after twenty-one days. On January 4, 1958, it burned up in the Earth's atmosphere, its reentry path providing additional upper-atmospheric data.
Sidelights: *Sputnik I*, whose name literally means "traveler," was launched much to the disbelief and shock of the world. Yet just two years prior to its launch, rumors that the Soviets were going to launch an artificial Earth satellite had spread throughout the West. Five months prior to its launch the Soviets boldly announced *Sputnik*'s transmission frequencies. Critics who claimed the launch was faked were silenced by the launch of an even larger *Sputnik II* only a month later, which contained a dog (see page 287).

1959: *LUNA 3*
Dates: Launched: October 4, 1959
Country: Soviet Union

Accomplishments: *Luna 3* was the third in a series of Luna spacecraft that were part of the Soviet Union's ambitious early lunar program. *Luna 3* weighed 957 pounds (434 kilograms), almost half a ton. *Luna 3* was placed into a 15.8-day barycentric orbit and became the first spacecraft to photograph the Moon's far side. After stabilizing its orbit about 3,853 miles (6,200 kilometers) above the lunar surface, the spacecraft began photographing the side of the Moon that is hidden from view from Earth. *Luna 3* used a primitive but ingenious imaging system that actually photographed the Moon, processed the film in an onboard automated laboratory, then digitally scanned the pictures and radioed back the information for reconstruction into images back on Earth.
Sidelights: *Luna 3* was larger than either of its Luna predecessors. The last of the Soviet Union's "direct ascent," or impact, missions, *Luna 3* hit the Moon after its orbit started to decay in April of 1960. Unlike the battery-powered *Lunas* 1 and 2, *Luna 3* used solar power for the first time. *Luna 3* was known in the former Soviet Union as the Automatic Interplanetary Station.

1960: *TIROS 1*
Dates: Launched: April 1, 1960
            Mission duration: 89 days
Country: United States
Accomplishments: *TIROS 1* was the first in a series of extremely successful meteorological satellites that provided the first global cloud-cover pictures. The TIROS satellites, now in a fifth generation configuration, continue to operate to this day. The original TIROS-series satellites were the cornerstone of an effort by NASA (National Aeronautics and Space Administration), ESSA (U.S. Environmental Science Services Administration), and NOAA (National Oceanic and Atmospheric Administration) to produce twenty-four-hour television infrared global weather monitoring.

Future TIROS satellites expanded upon *TIROS 1*'s success, except for *TIROS 5*, whose infrared imaging system failed. The ground-breaking *TIROS 1* satellite alone transmitted a whopping 22,950 pictures in its eighty-nine-day life span.

Sidelights: The name TIROS is actually an acronym for Television Infrared Observation Satellite. The original TIROS-series satellites were simply numbered *TIROS* 1 through 10 and were stubby cylinders covered in solar cells. The U.S. Weather Bureau handled analysis and distribution of TIROS data.

When the ESSA took control, it redesignated the program. The first two spacecraft managed by the ESSA were called *ESSA 1* and *2*. However, from *ESSA 3* on these TIROS spacecraft were also called TOS (TIROS Operational Satellites). When project management was taken over by the NOAA, the spacecraft were once again redesignated. The first of these was known as *ITOS 1* (for Improved TIROS Operational System). Afterward, all spacecraft carried a dual designation with the name NOAA added. The first of this third series was called *ITOS-A/NOAA 1*. When management finally reverted back to NASA, the spacecraft were redesignated TIROS-N. Improvements in spacecraft design resulted in the TIROS satellites' being redesignated one last time to Advanced TIROS-N.

1966: *LUNA 9*
Dates: Launched: January 31, 1966
                 Landed on Moon: February 3, 1966
Country: Soviet Union
Accomplishments: *Luna 9* was the first spacecraft to soft-land on the Moon. *Luna 9* was actually a modular spacecraft system. It was composed of an orbiter and a three-part lunar-lander system. *Luna 9* had a combined weight of 3,391 pounds (1,538 kilograms).

When it was 5,157 miles (8,300 kilometers) above the Moon's surface, *Luna 9*'s lander separated from the orbiter. During its descent it ejected unnecessary equipment, a ground probe and its spherical 221-pound (100-kilogram) main payload probe. Protected by shock absorbers during landing, this 24-inch (60-centimeter) landing sphere then opened by deploying four petal-like protective covers on its top half.

Using facsimile panoramic television cameras, *Luna 9* provided the first-ever pictures from the surface of the Moon. The spacecraft was able to monitor conditions on the lunar surface and perform three special television sessions. Three days later, on February 6, 1966, *Luna 9*'s batteries ran out and ended this historic mission.

Sidelights: After the successful *Luna 3* mission in 1959–60, the Soviet lunar space program appeared to go into a three-year hiatus. Apparently this break was used to work on development of a new generation of lunar craft capable of soft landings rather than impacting (hard landings). Beginning with a pre–*Luna 4* unannounced (and unnumbered) Luna launch on January 4, 1963, the Soviet Union embarked on an ambitious program to be the first to soft-land a spacecraft on the Moon. These missions used a new heavy-lift A-2e booster capable of carrying larger payloads.

Seven Luna missions in a row failed for one reason or another. Three years after the first attempt, however, *Luna 9* successfully soft-landed on the Moon. Ever cautious and guarded about their program, especially in the face of so many failures, the Soviet Union announced details of *Luna 9*'s spectacular space "first" to the West only after the fact.

1972: *PIONEER 10*
Dates: Launched: March 2, 1972
                 Encountered asteroid belt: July 15, 1972
                 Encountered Jupiter: December 3, 1973
                 Exited solar system (crossed heliopause): 1994
Country: United States
Accomplishments: This plucky little 570-pound spacecraft was originally intended to fly by Jupiter, transmit pictures of the Jovian giant and its major moons, and then swing out of the solar system. It was also supposed to prove the feasibility of outer solar system exploration. It far exceeded these goals.

Pioneer 10's first major "first" was the crossing of the treacherous debris-laden asteroid belt on July 15, 1972. In 1973 *Pioneer 10* flew within 81,000 miles of Jupiter and became the first spacecraft to visit the gas giant and the first to an outer planet. *Pioneer 10* took some 300 pictures of Jupiter and its moons and mapped Jupiter's radiation belts for the first time.

By June 13, 1983, *Pioneer 10* crossed the orbit of Neptune, another first. Unfortunately, the outer planets were all in the wrong positions for Pioneer to photograph. In 1994 *Pioneer 10* crossed the heliopause, or edge of the heliosphere (the Sun's atmosphere). Plunging into interstellar space, *Pioneer 10* became the first man-made object actually to leave the solar system. *Pioneer 10* continues to function, though its imaging system is shut down.

Sidelights: *Pioneer 10*, also known as *Pioneer F*, is actually the first probe of a dual-probe mission. Its sister spacecraft, *Pioneer 11* (*Pioneer G*), was launched just over a year later, on April 6, 1973, and not only encountered Jupiter but also became the first spacecraft to visit Saturn.

Amazingly, *Pioneer 10* carried no cameras. Instead, NASA scientists used its imaging photopolarimeter to measure narrow-band light levels in order to reconstruct digital pictures.

Launched in 1972, *Pioneer 10* continues to work to this day. Originally designed to survive only long enough to reach Jupiter, its power isn't expected to run out until 1998. At its present speed it will fly by the star Aldebaran (16 parsecs or 52.16 light-years away) in the year 8,001,972. On board the tiny nine-foot-diameter spacecraft is a plaque (a similar one is carried by *Pioneer* 11) that contains diagrammed information about our solar system as well as scale drawings of a man and a woman. It is hoped that if there is intelligent life outside our solar system this plaque will serve as a greeting.

1973: *MARINER 10*
Dates: Launched: November 3, 1973
                Planetary encounters:
                    Venus: February 5, 1974
                    Mercury: March 29, 1974
                              September 21, 1974
                              March 16, 1975
                Shut down: March 24, 1975
Country: United States
Accomplishments: *Mariner 10* was the first spacecraft to visit more than one planetary body. Shortly after launch its cameras took some of the best available pictures of the northern highland regions of the Moon. As it swung into the inner solar system it flew by Venus and televised the first and best pictures (even to this day) of Venus's clouds. Using Venus's gravity to propel itself toward Mercury, *Mariner 10* became the first spacecraft to pioneer the use of a gravitationally assisted trajectory.

Placed into an orbit around the Sun, *Mariner 10* flew by Mercury a total of three times and imaged nearly half the planet. It found a planet that appeared cratered and moonlike at first glance. Mercury, *Mariner 10* would reveal, was actually very different from the Moon. *Mariner 10* found not only craters but also massive faults, compressional and lava-flooded features, a large earthlike iron core, a weak magnetic field, and even a thin trace atmosphere. It is the only spacecraft, to date, to visit Mercury.
Sidelights: Although *Mariner 10* was the first spacecraft to use a gravity-assist trajectory to slingshot itself from one planet to another, the concept was not new. The origin of the idea dates back to the 1920s, but its use was resisted because it appeared to violate the law of conservation of energy. Finally used by *Mariner 10*, it worked so well that future missions, such as the Voyager mission and the current Galileo mission to Jupiter, would have been nearly impossible without this technique.

Even though it had already exceeded its original mission goals, *Mariner 10* could have flown additional Mercury flybys but it ran out of attitude-control gas and had to be shut down.

1975: *VENERAS 9 and 10*
Dates: Launched:
                    Venera 9: June 8, 1975
                    Venera 10: June 14, 1975
                Landed on Venus:
                    Venera 9: October 22, 1975
                    Venera 10: October 25, 1975
Country: Soviet Union

Accomplishments: To ensure success, both the United States and the Soviet Union began building and flying spacecraft in pairs. *Veneras* 9 and 10 were considered a dual-probe mission. In this case each probe itself was also a dual probe consisting of an orbiter and a lander. The *Venera* orbiters made observations of Venus's turbulent atmosphere and the landers attempted to land and survive the hellish surface conditions and radio back data before being melted and crushed.

Each lander was provided with floodlights, which proved unnecessary because they found that the surface was surprisingly well lit in spite of Venus's dense permanent cloud cover. The *Venera* 9 lander was the first to reach the surface. It transmitted data, as well as the first-ever panoramic television pictures of the surface, within 115 minutes of landing. The pictures revealed an active planet with an apparently young yellowish brown surface and a hazy yellow sky.
Sidelights: A large number of unsuccessful and partially successful Soviet spacecraft paved the way for the highly successful *Venera* 9/10 dual mission. The first spacecraft to land on Venus, or for that matter the first ever to reach the surface of another planet, was *Venera* 3. It impacted on the Venusian surface on February 27, 1966. Unfortunately, *Venera* 3 ceased data transmission just before entering Venus's scalding atmosphere.

Venera 7 touched down on Venusian soil on December 15, 1970, and was the first to transmit data (for twenty-three minutes) from the hot Venusian surface, but it landed on the night side and took no pictures. It reported temperatures of 475 degrees Celsius, enough to melt lead, and an atmospheric surface pressure more than ninety times that of Earth—equivalent to the crushing pressure at the bottom of Earth's deepest ocean.

Venera 8 made the first day-side landing but provided no pictures from the surface. Additionally, two Kosmos missions (*Kosmos 359* and *482*) failed while still in Earth orbit and never reached Venus.

On the heels of these missions came the *Venera* 9/10 dual mission. In order to survive the tortuous Venusian surface conditions, their landers were reinforced and provided with a special internal cooling system. Their tremendous success opened the door for three more highly successful dual-probe missions, which also managed to use radar to penetrate Venus's permanent cloud deck and provide the first global maps of Venus.

1975: *VIKINGS 1 and 2*
Dates:
        Launched: Viking 1: August 20, 1975
                        Viking 2: September 9, 1975
        Soft landing   Viking 1: July 20, 1976
        on Mars: Viking 2: September 3, 1976

Final transmissions:

Viking 1:   Orbiter: August 7, 1980
              Lander: November 13, 1983
Viking 2:   Orbiter: July 25, 1978
              Lander: April 12, 1980

Country: United States

Accomplishments: Viking was a dual-probe mission. Launched separately, both Viking 1 and Viking 2 actually consisted of two parts: an orbiter and a lander. Fully fueled, the massive Viking orbiters weighed 5,125 pounds each, and the landers 2,353 pounds each. Each orbiter was powered by four large solar panel arrays. Using vidicon cameras, the pictures provided by the two Viking orbiters constitute the highest-resolution global coverage of Mars ever taken to this day—more than 55,000 pictures covering 97 percent of the Martian surface.

Lander 1 soft-landed on Mars in the equatorial region Chryse Planitia. Twenty-five seconds after touchdown it began transmitting the first-ever live pictures from the surface of Mars. Each picture took nineteen minutes to reach Earth. Viking Lander 2 landed in September in the northern plains area of Utopia Planitia.

Combined, the two landers provided more than 5,000 pictures of the surface. They supplied daily weather reports, soil analysis, and science results that indicated that Mars was a much more dynamic planet than previously anticipated. They found water on Mars in the form of ground fogs, frozen subsurface permafrost, surface frosts (clearly visible in winter pictures), and vast frozen deposits of ice in the northern polar cap. In the past Mars was probably a much warmer earthlike world with a thick atmosphere and standing oceans. Biology experiments on both landers proved inconclusive, leaving unanswered the questions Does microbial life presently exist on Mars, and, Did the planet sustain primitive life in the past?

Sidelights: NASA's Viking mission was preceded by three pairs of dual Mariner missions, of which only Mariners 3 and 8 were lost. The Soviet Union launched more than half a dozen missions toward Mars—with only partial success. Several Soviet pre-Viking attempts to place landers on Mars also failed. The Viking Lander 1, originally intended to set down on July 4, 1976, the Bicentennial of the United States, had to delay landing until July 20, 1976, so that a suitable landing site could be chosen. All four Viking spacecraft exceeded their six-month intended life spans by many years.

1976: KEY HOLE

Dates: Launch of KH 11: December 19, 1976
           Program exposed: March 1978

Country: United States

Accomplishments: The Key Hole spacecraft are military reconnaissance satellites (or "spy satellites"). They represent some of the most sophisticated Earth-orbiting imaging satellites available.

Key Hole satellites were born out of a line of short-life-span spy satellites that date back to 1959. They belonged to two basic classes: "recoverable," which took high-resolution pictures from orbit, then ejected recoverable canisters of film, or "search-and-find," which were directed toward specific targets and radioed pictures back.

The Key Hole, or KH, series developed from the giant "Big Bird" satellites that evolved from a merging of early recoverable and search-and-find satellites. Though the program is still cloaked in secrecy, it is estimated that KH satellites operate from high-altitude polar orbits, are about 64 feet (21.3 meters) long, weigh some 30,000 pounds (13,605 kilograms), and have demonstrated lifetimes of more than a year. They reputedly have the ability to resolve objects less than a foot across from more than a hundred miles away. Using infrared imaging, they can supposedly track past events by their residual heat signatures.

Sidelights: KH satellites, also known as Code 1010 or Project 1010, are classified U.S. DOD (Department of Defense) programs. What little is known has been revealed only as the result of a security breach that occurred in the CIA. In March 1978 a former CIA clerk named William P. Kampiles sold a KH 11 manual to the Soviet Union. The manual cost the Soviets $3,000 and detailed the physical characteristics, capabilities, and limitations of the U.S. KH 11 and Rhyolite military satellites. Kampiles's arrest resulted in a highly publicized spy trial that exposed many details of this extremely classified program. Kampiles was sentenced to forty years in prison, and the satellite programs were adjusted to maintain their military integrity.

1977: VOYAGERS 1 and 2

Dates:

Launched:

    Voyager 1:   September 5, 1977
    Voyager 2:   August 20, 1977

Planetary encounters:

    Voyager 1:   Jupiter: March 5, 1979
                  Saturn: November 12, 1980
    Voyager 2:   Jupiter: July 9, 1979
                  Saturn: August 25, 1981
                  Uranus: January 24, 1986
                  Neptune: August 25, 1989

Country: United States

Accomplishments: Voyagers 1 and 2 dazzled the world for more than a decade with spectacular pictures of the outer planets. The incredible odyssey of Voyagers 1 and 2 through the outer solar system and beyond remains an unequaled accomplishment to this day.

Among the nearly countless discoveries and observations by these two intrepid NASA spacecraft were rings around Jupiter, Uranus, and Neptune; numerous new moons; active volcanism on Io; spoke features in Saturn's rings; ring clumping at Neptune; fierce 1,500-mile-per-hour winds on Neptune, the strongest in the solar system; Neptune's Great Dark Spot, a massive Earth-sized storm similar to Jupiter's Great Red Spot; imaging of exotic Miranda; and ice geysers on Triton. Combined, the *Voyagers* took nearly 80,000 pictures.

Both *Voyagers* continue monitoring their environments as they plunge out of the solar system toward interstellar space. On February 14, 1990, *Voyager* 1's cameras were turned on one last time and took sixty pictures looking back from more than 4 billion miles out. Once assembled, the pictures provided a haunting mosaic image (called the Family Portrait) of our Sun and its tiny planets—mere specks nearly lost in the eternal glare of the Sun.

Sidelights: *Voyager* followed in the footsteps of *Pioneers* 10 and 11, which proved the viability of exploring the outer solar system. They participated in what NASA called the Grand Tour: a rare opportunity to visit the outer planets because of a fortuitous alignment. This alignment, though not a straight line, would allow a spacecraft to use each planet's gravity to "swing" from one planet to the next. Both *Voyagers* carried plaques similar to those on board the *Pioneers*, but these also contained pictures and recorded messages from Earth.

Voyager 1, which visited Jupiter and Saturn, was originally slated to continue on toward Pluto. This option was scrapped in favor of a closer approach to Saturn's mysterious cloud-covered moon, Titan. Unfortunately, the closer flyby proved a great disappointment because Titan's clouds were too thick for any surface features to be visible.

MANNED FLIGHTS

Space—the final frontier. . . . These are the voyages of the starship Enterprise. Its five-year mission: to explore strange new worlds, to seek out new life and new civilizations, to boldly go where no man has gone before.

Gene Roddenberry,
introduction to *Star Trek*, 1966

1961: VOSTOK 1
Dates: Launched: April 12, 1961
                    Recovered: April 12, 1961
Crew: Lt. Yuri Gagarin
Country: Soviet Union
Accomplishments: As a result of the Cold War, the United States and the Soviet Union were

locked in a "space race." The successful launch of *Sputnik* in 1957 made the Soviet Union the first nation to launch a man-made object into space. Launches of more *Sputniks* (the second one containing a dog) began a heated race between the two superpowers to become the first to put a man into orbit.

At 9:07 A.M. (Moscow time) the Soviet Union's *Vostok* 1 lifted off from the Baikonur cosmodrome approximately twelve miles north of Tyuratam, Kazhakhstan, in Central Asia, carrying Lieutenant Yuri A. Gagarin. His primitive 10,419-pound (4,725-kilogram) one-man capsule was lofted into low Earth orbit by a derivative Sputnik A-1 booster—a modified ICBM launcher.

The *Vostok* 1 capsule actually consisted of two basic modules: an 8.46-foot-diameter (2.58 meters) spherical manned capsule supported by a large equipment module below it. After completing a single orbit, the manned capsule separated from this equipment module by firing explosive bolts at 10:45 A.M. (Moscow time). Ten minutes later *Vostok* 1 reentered Earth's atmosphere at 18,000 miles per hour and landed in a plowed field near the village of Smelovaka near Saratov, Russia, and was greeted by a woman, a girl, and a cow. Yuri Gagarin became the first man in space. News of his successful 108-minute flight rocked the world and ushered in the era of manned space flight.

Sidelights: Five previous unmanned Vostok flights had been flown between May 15, 1960,

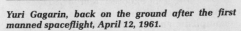

Yuri Gagarin, back on the ground after the first manned spaceflight, April 12, 1961.

and March 25, 1961, under the name *Korable Sputnik*, prior to Gagarin's historic flight. They carried mannequins, dogs, and biological experiments. These early trial missions proved Vostok craft could fly up to seventeen orbits. Gagarin made only one full 89.1-minute orbit.

During reentry *Vostok* (also known as Swallow) was designed to blow its hatch at an altitude of 4.3 miles (7 kilometers) and eject the cosmonaut. The two would then land separately by parachute. Gagarin, however, opted against this bail-out technique and landed in his capsule. His landing, however, was so rough that the five *Vostok* cosmonauts that followed him all used the ejection technique.

1964: *VOSKHOD 1*
Dates: Launched: October 12, 1964
Recovered: October 13, 1964
Crew: Konstantin Feoktistov
Comdr. Vladimir Komarov
Dr. Boris Yegorov
Country: Soviet Union
Accomplishments: The Voskhod series of flights were a bridge between the earlier Vostok series and the later Soyuz program. The Voskhod spacecraft were launched on heavy-lift modified A-2 ICBM boosters. The use of this more powerful launcher allowed payload weight to be increased from 10,419 pounds to 11,729 pounds (4,725 kilograms to 5,320 kilograms).

The Voskhod spacecraft itself was nothing more than a modified Vostok spacecraft. The ejection seat assembly was removed from the interior of the manned capsule so as to accommodate up to three cosmonauts. Retrorockets were added in order to cushion the final part of the landing descent.

Doctor of Medicine Boris Yegorov, Commander Vladimir Komarov, and engineer and spacecraft designer Konstantin Feoktistov flew in *Voskhod 1*. *Voskhod 1* marked the first flight of a multiman crew on board a spacecraft. With Feoktistov on board, it was also the first time that the designer of a spacecraft had flown aboard his own craft. Another Voskhod first was the presence of Yegorov—the first medical doctor in space. The three cosmonauts made sixteen orbits and spent twenty-four hours seventeen minutes in space. Their mission was televised live.
Sidelights: *Voskhod 1*, a.k.a. Ruby, was actually the second Voskhod craft to be launched. The first, simply called *Kosmos 47*, was launched six days before on October 6, 1964. It flew in an orbit that was nearly identical to the orbit *Voskhod 1* would fly. This unmanned mission was probably a flight test of the new Voskhod systems and A-2 launcher.

Voskhod 1 also holds the distinction of being the first mission ever to have a crew that did not wear bulky space suits. The space saved made it easier to accommodate the third cosmonaut.

This daring practice continued intermittently until the *Soyuz 11* disaster.

1965: *VOSKHOD 2*
Dates: Launched: March 18, 1965
Recovered: March 19, 1965
Crew: Col. Pavel Belyayev
Lt. Col. Aleksei Leonov
Country: Soviet Union
Accomplishments: Where *Voskhod 1* proved the viability of a multiman mission, *Voskhod 2* added further milestones by showing what such a crew could accomplish. Instead of flying with a full complement of three cosmonauts, only two cosmonauts manned *Voskhod 2*. This change allowed the wearing of space suits and the addition of an inflatable airlock that, during launch, occupied the space normally filled by a third cosmonaut.

Once in orbit the airlock was inflated and deployed. Leonov entered the pressurized airlock while Belyayev remained in the capsule. Ten minutes after the airlock was depressurized, Leonov exited the airlock into space. He was attached only by telephone and telemetry cables. A backpack supplied his oxygen. This EVA, or "extravehicular activity," provided the Soviets with a spectacular "first": the first-ever space walk from an orbiting spacecraft. The EVA was televised live.
Sidelights: *Voskhod 2* was also known as Diamond. Like *Voskhod 1*, it was also preceded by an unmanned test vehicle. *Kosmos 57*, the prototype for *Voskhod 2*, was launched on February 22, 1965. Unfortunately, *Kosmos 57* exploded in orbit. This failure caused a month's delay while the Soviets evaluated the disaster prior to *Voskhod 2*'s launch.

Because of a failure in *Voskhod 2*'s attitude-control systems, the cosmonauts had the opportunity to prove their craft could be brought back in an emergency. After flying one extra orbit the cosmonauts successfully brought *Voskhod 2* back manually. *Voskhod 2* landed 746 miles (1,200 kilometers) northeast of Moscow in a remote snowy region hundreds of miles from its target zone. Damage to *Voskhod*'s antenna during reentry interrupted communications and delayed recovery of craft and crew.

1968: *APOLLO 8*
Dates: Launched: December 21, 1968, 7:51 A.M. EST
Splashdown: December 27, 1968
Crew: USAF Col. Frank Borman (commander)
Navy Capt. James A. Lovell Jr. (command module pilot)
USAF Lt. Col. William Anders (lunar module pilot)
Country: United States
Accomplishments: *Apollo 8* was the third manned Apollo mission. It was the first to use

the massive, thundering Saturn V launch vehicle, one of the most powerful rockets ever built. *Apollo 8* represented a tremendous leap in man's conquest of space: the first manned flight to another world.

Flying within 70 miles (112.6 kilometers) of the lunar surface, *Apollo 8* entered a 69-mile (111-kilometer) lunar orbit. As the astronauts orbited the Moon for the first time ever they broadcast live television pictures of the dramatic and lonely lunar panoramas below them. *Apollo 8* orbited the Moon ten times in twenty hours six minutes. Returning to Earth, *Apollo 8* jettisoned its service module. The gumdrop-shaped command module containing the three astronauts entered Earth's atmosphere at 24,243 miles (39,010 kilometers) per hour. The spacecraft splashed down in the Pacific Ocean and was recovered by the aircraft carrier USS *Yorktown*. Total mission time was 147 hours 0 minutes 11 seconds.

Sidelights: Because of the perception at NASA that the Soviets were on the brink of sending cosmonauts on a circumlunar flight mission, it was decided that *Apollo 8*'s test flight would become a lunar orbiting mission. After *Apollo 8* was launched there was some concern at Mission Control. Shortly after passing through the Earth's protective Van Allen radiation belt and out through the magnetosphere, Commander Frank Borman became ill. Fortunately, he quickly recovered and the mission continued.

The *Apollo 8* spacecraft, or CSM-103 (its mission designation), went into orbit around the Moon early on December 24, 1968. On Christmas Eve the world was moved by stirring readings of extracts from the Book of Genesis by the astronauts broadcast live from lunar orbit.

1969: *SOYUZ 4 and 5*
Dates:
  Soyuz 4:   Launched: January 14, 1969
             Recovered: January 17, 1969
  Soyuz 5:   Launched: January 15, 1969
             Recovered: January 18, 1969
Crew:
  Soyuz 4:   Col. Vladimir Shatalov
  Soyuz 5:   Yevgeny Khrunov
             Boris Volynov
             Aleksei Yeliseyev
Country: Soviet Union
Accomplishments: *Soyuz 4* was launched at 10:39 A.M. (Moscow time) on January 14, 1969. *Soyuz 4* was originally manned by a single cosmonaut, Colonel Vladimir Shatalov. *Soyuz 5* was launched one day after *Soyuz 4* and was manned by three cosmonauts. *Soyuz 5* joined *Soyuz 4* in orbit and the two spacecraft performed the first docking of two spacecraft in orbit. Another Soviet first, the first-ever transfer of crew from spacecraft to spacecraft, took place after the docking. Yeliseyev and Khrunov transferred, via space walk, from their *Soyuz 5* craft

to *Soyuz 4* to join their comrade Shatalov for the return to Earth. Volynov returned in *Soyuz 5*.

The two spacecraft remained docked for a total of four hours thirty-five minutes. The spacecraft were recovered about twenty-five miles (forty kilometers) northwest of Karaganda, Kazhakhstan.

Sidelights: *Soyuz* incorporated a whole new advanced design over previous program craft. *Soyuz 4* and *5* were preceded by seven Kosmos test craft and three Soyuz spacecraft. Two of these spacecraft, *Kosmos 186* and *188*, actually performed a docking before *Soyuz 4* and *5*. They docked in October of 1967. Though they performed a successful docking, these automated Soyuz-class craft were unmanned.

Soyuz 4 was the first manned launch by the Soviets in winter. Previously, the Soviets were concerned that landing in freezing winter conditions could put the crew at risk of exposure. Both *Soyuz 4* and *5*, however, were retrofitted for a contingency ocean landing if needed. *Soyuz 4* completed forty-eight orbits around the Earth and logged a total mission elapsed time of seventy-one hours fourteen minutes; *Soyuz 5* stayed in orbit a day longer.

1969: *APOLLO 11*
Dates: Launched: July 16, 1969, 9:32 A.M.
             EDT
             Moon landing: July 20, 1969,
             4:17:43 P.M. EDT
             First footstep on the Moon: July 20,
             1969, 10:56:20 P.M. EDT
             Splashdown: July 24, 1969, 12:51 P.M.
             PDT
Crew: Neil Armstrong (commander)
             USAF Lt. Col. Michael Collins (command module pilot)
             USAF Col. Edwin Aldrin Jr. (lunar module pilot)
Country: United States
Accomplishments: As *Apollo 11*'s 7.5-million-pound-thrust F-1 Saturn V engines roared to life, it rose on a pillar of flame on a historic mission to land a man on the Moon and return him safely home. Four days later a stunned world, the largest TV viewing audience in history, watched with riveted attention as the lunar module *Eagle* descended toward the surface of the Moon.

At 4:17:43 P.M. EDT, July 20, 1969, *Eagle* touched down in the Sea of Tranquility and the astronauts calmly announced, "Houston, Tranquility base here. The *Eagle* has landed." At 10:56:20 P.M. EDT, Neil Armstrong placed his left foot on lunar soil and became the first human being ever to set foot on another world. Twenty minutes later Aldrin joined him outside. They deployed scientific instruments and collected 48.5 pounds (22 kilograms) of moon rock and samples in two hours, thirty-one minutes, and forty seconds of total EVA time.

EYEWITNESS TO HISTORY: THE FIRST MOON WALK

When: July 1969

How: It began at 9:32 A.M. eastern daylight time, on July 16, 1969, when three astronauts—Neil Armstrong, Michael Collins, and Edwin Aldrin—lifted off from Launch Complex 39 at Cape Kennedy (Cape Canaveral), Florida, in *Apollo 11*, powered by a 364-foot-tall Saturn V rocket. They were on their way to the Moon, where man would set foot for the first time. After a temporary parking period 115 miles above the earth to check instruments, the spacecraft started on its journey, traveling at a speed of 24,300 miles per hour. When they were thirty-four hours into the flight, the astronauts began broadcasting to the world a live color-television special of what they were doing. More than 500 million people were watching. The three said they were impressed by the sight of the earth receding, and Aldrin added, "The view is out of this world."

As they neared the Moon's surface, the propulsion system was fired; engine burn brought the spacecraft's velocity down from 6,500 miles per hour to 3,700 miles per hour and put it into an elliptical orbit around the Moon. It was 1:22 P.M. eastern daylight time, July 19. They had traveled 244,930 miles in a little more than three days. They went twice around the Moon, then re-ignited the propulsion system to put the craft into a roughly circular orbit between sixty-two miles and seventy-five miles above the surface. Armstrong said, "It looks very much like the pictures but like the difference between watching a real football game and one on TV. There's no substitute for actually being here." While the *Apollo* was on the far side of the Moon, they undocked the *Eagle*, the lunar module, from the *Columbia*, the command module. Armstrong and Aldrin, who would walk on the Moon while Collins piloted the *Columbia*, crawled through the pressurized tunnel between the two modules and opened connective hatches to enter the *Eagle*. When they came around to the near side of the Moon, NASA experts in Houston asked via radio, "How does it look?" "*Eagle* has wings," answered Armstrong. The lunar module was free from the *Columbia*.

The *Eagle* went into an extremely elliptical orbit, with a perilune of about 50,000 feet above the surface. From that near point, it began to sink downward until it was about 7,600 feet above the surface and 26,000 feet away from the planned touchdown point in the Sea of Tranquility northwest of Moltke Crater. When still about 500 feet up, Armstrong and Aldrin looked down at the Moon's surface to decide on the best place to land. Shortly after, the two took over the controls, running the *Eagle* on semiautomatic. Then, because a program alarm showed the onboard computer to be overloaded, the astronauts, with the help of Houston, brought the *Eagle* down with instruments and visual landmarks. It was a tense moment, and the *Eagle* was heading toward a rocky crater, a poor place to land. Armstrong burned the engines for another seventy seconds in order to reach another landing site about four miles away. Aldrin, in the last moments, said, "Forward, forward, good. Forty feet. Picking up some dust. . . . Drifting to the right. . . . Contact light. OK. Engine stop!" They had landed. Armstrong looked down, he said later, to see a sheet of moon dirt being blown by the rocket exhaust. He shut off the engine and reported, "Tranquility base here. The *Eagle* has landed." He seemed to be calm. However,

his heart was beating at 156 beats per minute, twice its usual rate. It was 4:17:43 P.M. eastern daylight time, July 20, 1969.

The two were supposed to spend eight hours checking the *Eagle* out, eating, and resting, but they were anxious to leave the *Eagle* and explore the Moon, certainly too excited to rest, so Houston agreed that they could skip the rest period. It took them three hours to put on their equipment, including the awkward life-support-system backpacks. It was six and one-half hours after landing before they had depressurized the cabin and were ready to open the hatch. Slowly Armstrong went down the nine-rung ladder. When he reached the second rung, he let down a television camera. On home viewing screens all over Earth the image of his heavy-booted foot appeared. Then his foot—encased in a size 9½ B boot—landed on the surface. It was 10:56:20 P.M. He stopped to say his now-famous words, "That's one small step for [a] man, one giant leap for mankind."

He began describing the material on which he was walking: "The surface appears to be very, very fine-grain, like powder. . . . I can kick it loosely with my toes. Like powdered charcoal. I can see footprints of my boots in the small, fine particles. . . . No trouble to walk around." Aldrin, who had stayed in the capsule, said, "Is it OK to come out?" and received permission to do so. "I want to back up and partly close the hatches, making sure to lock it on my way out," he said. "Good thought," answered Armstrong. "That's our home for the next couple of hours. We want to take care of it," said Aldrin. The two men bounded with a "kangaroo hop," finding it far easier to maneuver than experts had predicted.

Armstrong showed viewers the plaque that he placed at the landing site: "Here men from the planet Earth first set foot upon the Moon July, 1969 A.D. We came in peace for all mankind."

Edwin Aldrin Jr., the second man to walk on the moon, as photographed by his commander, Neil Armstrong, the first man to set foot on the moon.

It was signed by the astronauts and by U.S. President Richard Nixon. The two put up a metallic American flag, which would never wave on the windless Moon.

During the next two and one-half hours, Armstrong and Aldrin checked the *Eagle* for landing damage, studied the depression made by its footpads, practiced running and walking, and collected data. Armstrong picked up about fifty pounds of rock and soil samples, which were put first into sealed bags, then into aluminum boxes. Later a NASA official was to say that they were "worth more than all the gold in Fort Knox." The rocks were amazingly old, some dated before any that had ever been found on Earth. The men set up three instrument systems: a solar-wind-composition detector, a seismic detector, and a laser reflector. Armstrong tried to take some core samples of subsurface materials but had trouble: "I could get the first coring device down about the first two inches without much of a problem and then I would pound it in about as hard as I could do it. The second one took two hands on the hammer, and I was putting pretty good dents in the top of the extension rod. And it just wouldn't go much more than—I think the total depth might have been about eight inches or nine inches. But even there, it . . . didn't seem to want to stand up straight, and it would dig some sort of a hole, but it wouldn't just penetrate in a way that would support it . . . if that makes any sense at all. It didn't really to me." They talked about the crater, their footprints, which went only one-eighth-inch deep, and the tiny glass balls in the soil that made it slippery.

After the two and one-half hours were up, they returned to the module. Their walk on the Moon was over. Behind them they left "junk"—cameras, backpacks, tools, and some footprints that would probably, in that airless place, remain forever. It had been a strange adventure, described almost prosaically by the two awed men—the triumph of technology and the fulfillment of a dream that was almost as old as humankind.

Eyewitness report: Once they landed on the Moon, Armstrong and Aldrin gazed out at the satellite on which they would soon walk and then they radioed Earth descriptions of what they saw: "[There is a] level plain cratered with a fairly large number of craters of the five-to-fifty variety. And some ridges, small, twenty feet to thirty feet high, I would guess. And literally thousands of little one- and two-foot craters around the area. We see angular blocks out several hundred feet in front of us that are probably two feet in size and have angular edges. There is a hill in view just about on the ground track ahead of us. Difficult to estimate, but might be half a mile or a mile. . . .

"I'd say the color of the local surface is very comparable to that we observed from orbit at this Sun angle—about ten degrees Sun angle or that nature. It's pretty much without color. It's gray, more like an ashen gray, as you look out ninety degrees to the Sun. Some of the surface rocks in close here that have been fractured or disturbed by the rocket engine plume are coated with this light gray on the outside. But where they've been broken, they display a dark, very dark, gray interior and it looks like it could be country basalt."

—A.E.

Overhead, Michael Collins maintained a solitary vigil in the command module *Columbia* as he orbited the Moon, conducting scientific experiments, taking pictures, and waiting for the safe return of the *Eagle*. *Columbia* made thirty revolutions around the Moon in 59.5 hours. The *Eagle* safely redocked with *Columbia* after a total stay time on the Moon of twenty-one hours, thirty-six minutes, twenty-one seconds.

As Armstrong and Aldrin rejoined Collins in the command module *Columbia*, they jettisoned *Eagle* and headed home. *Apollo 11*'s historic mission ended when it splashed down in the Pacific. *Columbia* was recovered by the USS *Hornet* just southwest of Hawaii and the three astronauts were given a much-deserved heroes' welcome.

Sidelights: As the lunar module descended toward the lunar surface, a computer alarm sounded a possible problem. Responding calmly the astronauts managed to override it. With fuel running dangerously low, the astronauts found their original landing site too rough and took manual control. They maneuvered the *Eagle* horizontally out of harm's way to smoother ground, landing with barely thirty seconds of fuel remaining.

> This is the greatest week in the history of the world since the creation.
>
> Richard Nixon, greeting astronauts
> on the USS *Hornet*, July 24, 1969

As the world watched breathlessly, Armstrong stepped down and announced, "That's one small step for [a] man, one giant leap for mankind." The article *a* was missing from the original voice transmission and transcript but was later added.

—M.E.R.

SPACE SHUTTLE AND SPACE STATIONS

1971: *SALYUT 1*
Dates:

Salyut 1:	Launched:	April 19, 1971
	Reentry:	October 11, 1971

Soyuz 10:	Launched:	April 23, 1971
	Recovered:	April 24, 1971
Soyuz 11:	Launched:	June 6, 1971
	Recovered:	June 29, 1971

Country: Soviet Union
Crew:
Soyuz 10: Col. Vladimir Shatalov
Aleksei Yeliseyev (flight engineer)
Nikolai Rukavishnikov (systems specialist)
Soyuz 11: Comdr. Georgi Dobrovolky
Viktor Patsayev (research engineer)
Vladislav Volkov (flight engineer)

Accomplishments: Salyut 1 was the first prototype space station ever to be placed into orbit. It opened the door to what would become fourteen productive years in the life of a total of seven Salyut space stations. Salyut 1 was made up of four connected cylinders of various diameters ranging from 6.56 feet (2 meters) to 13.6 feet (4.15 meters). Its overall length was about 47.3 feet (14.4 meters) and it weighed 40,344 pounds (18,300 kilograms). Salyut 1 had 3,532 cubic feet of habitable room and could host up to five cosmonauts.

This first space station was used primarily as an observing platform to gather information on earth resources, meteorology, astronomy, and space medicine (especially the effects of prolonged weightlessness). The Soyuz 11 cosmonauts conducted various studies onboard Salyut 1 and set a new space endurance record of twenty-three days.

Sidelights: Salyut 1 (a.k.a. Salute) was visited by Soyuz 10 in April 1971. Because of the Soviet policy of secrecy at the time, little is known as to exactly what happened. Probably the three cosmonauts, though experienced veterans, were not able to gain entry into Salyut 1. Because of the hasty predawn landing of Soyuz 10 after the failed Salyut 1 boarding, it is widely accepted that whatever the problem was, it was probably on board Soyuz 10.

Later in June, however, Soyuz 11 successfully docked with Salyut 1. Twenty-three days later tragedy struck when, after the undocking sequence on their way home, a valve malfunctioned. As the crew valiantly tried to solve the problem, all their air leaked out. Ground recovery crews later found Soyuz 11's landing capsule—its three cosmonauts dead from suffocation.

1981: STS-1 COLUMBIA
Dates: Launched: April 12, 1981
Landed: April 14, 1981
Crew: Comdr. Robert Crippen
Capt. John Young
Country: United States
Accomplishments: America's space shuttle program represented the world's first reusable spacecraft system, providing regular access to space. The shuttles would also become the first spacecraft capable not only of launching other

smaller spacecraft but also of repairing in flight, or even retrieving previously spaceborne craft.

Problems with the complex jigsawlike thermal tile protection system delayed the first flight of the space shuttle Columbia. Additionally, a computer problem caused the first flight to be aborted on April 10, 1981. Two days later the successful launch of Columbia, and its safe landing two days after that on the dry lake bed at Edwards Air Force Base, California, heralded a new era of space flight and the first flight of a space shuttle. "What a way to come to California!" exclaimed an excited astronaut Crippen over Columbia's radio.

It was the first time an American spacecraft landed on land. It also marked the first time any manned spacecraft used solid rockets (the shuttle's SRBs, or Solid Rocket Boosters). Total mission elapsed time was fifty-four hours twenty minutes fifty-three seconds.

Sidelights: Officially the space shuttle program is known as the Space Transportation System (STS). The first shuttle was actually the Space Shuttle Orbiter Enterprise, named after the famous starship in the Star Trek TV series. It was a drop-test vehicle that was released from a Boeing 747 in midflight. Enterprise made five successful free-flight tests prior to Columbia's history-making maiden flight into space.

Columbia's first flight was marred by the discovery that an overpressure wave created by the SRBs caused extensive loss of and damage to its protective thermal tiles. Modifications of the launch pad's water sound-suppression system solved this problem for later flights.

1987: SOYUZ TM-4/MIR
Dates:
Launched: Mir: February 19, 1986
Soyuz TM-4: December 21, 1987
Crew:
Mir: Comdr. Yuri Romanenko
Aleksandr Aleksandrov
Soyuz TM-4: Comdr. Vladimir Titov
Musakhi Manarov
Anatoli Levchenko
Country: Soviet Union
Accomplishments: On February 5, 1987, Yuri Romanenko and Aleksandr Leveykin arrived at the Mir space station aboard Soyuz TM-2. The two performed several Mir maintenance-related space walks and rectified onboard power shortages. This crew played host to two additional crews. The first visiting crew arrived aboard Soyuz TM-3. It consisted of Aleksandr Viktorenko (commander), Aleksandr Aleksandrov (flight engineer), and Mohammad Al Faris (the first Syrian cosmonaut).

On July 30 this crew was to return home onboard the docked TM-2 craft, but when original Mir crewman Leveykin fell ill it was decided he would return home. TM-3 cosmonaut Aleksandrov remained onboard Mir with original Mir crewman Romanenko.

On December 21, 1987, Soyuz TM-4 was launched. Onboard were Commander Vladimir Titov and flight engineer Musakhi Manarov, who would replace Romanenko and Aleksandrov. The third crewman, researcher Anatoli Levchenko, unlike the other cosmonauts, was a test pilot with the Soviet shuttle program who was onboard in order to log flight experience. On December 29, 1987, Romanenko, Aleksandrov, and Levchenko returned to Earth. Titov and Manarov remained behind on Mir.

With these continuing Mir/Soyuz missions, the Soviets continued to set new space-endurance records. To this day Russia (the inheritor of the former Soviet Union's space program) continues to conduct medical experiments in long-duration space missions. With the close of the Soyuz TM-4/Mir mission the cosmonauts had logged a variety of endurance records: Romanenko 326 days and Aleksandrov 160 days. Romanenko's cumulative logged space time was an incredible 430 days in space.

Sidelights: Mir, which means "peace," is a space station similar to the Salyut in design. It orbits around the Earth every 90.9 minutes. It is used for materials-processing research, astrophysics, earth resources, and long-duration space mission medical research. It also has a large five-port docking module on the forward end and one extra port on the aft, or back, end. Thus a total of six space vehicles can be docked at any one time at Mir.

—M.E.R.

THE SOLAR SYSTEM AND BEYOND

THE SOLAR SYSTEM

Since first looking skyward toward the heavens, human beings have tried to understand all that was around them. Of primary concern were the Sun, the Moon, comets, and planets—the main members of our solar system. They were part of ancient belief systems and later we would grow to know them as neighbors in our cosmic backyard.

Statistics:
Diameter (Sun to outer edge of Oort cloud): approximately 9.3 trillion miles (15 trillion kilometers)
Number of planets: 9 known
Names of planets (closest to farthest from Sun): Mercury, Venus, Earth, Mars, (the asteroid belt), Jupiter, Saturn, Uranus, Neptune, Pluto
Total number of moons of planets: 63 known
Distance from galactic center: approximately 30,000 light-years, within the local group of stars, in the Orion arm of the Milky Way galaxy
Speed around galactic center: 155 miles (250 kilometers) per second
Period of revolution around galactic center: 200 million years
Closest star: Proxima Centauri (Alpha Centauri-C): 4.22 light-years

Before 1900: The early Greeks believed in a "geocentric" (Earth-centered) universe. For millennia many proposed models tried to explain observable events in the sky. After Copernicus died in 1543, his heliocentric (Sun-centered) view prevailed.

In 1610 Galileo's observations of Jupiter and its moons conclusively demonstrated the basic principles of celestial mechanics. Astronomers finally began turning to new principles (physics, motion, and gravity), as laid down by such scientific luminaries as Isaac Newton and Johannes Kepler, which revealed the solar system as we know it today. Additionally, the discovery of Uranus in 1781 and Neptune in 1846 expanded the borders of our known solar system.

After 1900: The ninth and last planet in our solar system, Pluto, was discovered in 1930. With exponential advances in observational technologies over the last century, membership in the solar system has grown to include more than 5,700 asteroids, some 900 comets, the Kuiper belt just beyond the orbit of Pluto, the spherical Oort cloud, and the heliopause (the end of the Sun's atmosphere) at the dark and frigid outer edge. Beyond lies the cold void of interstellar space.

The solar system formed 4.6 billion years ago. Dust and gases from a previous generation of stars spun up into a disc of material called the solar nebula. The Sun ignited and material collected into orbiting clumps known as protoplanets. As they cooled they shed their massive primordial atmospheres and were pummeled by a billion-year rain of asteroidal debris called the early bombardment phase. Most of the large craters we see on other planets and moons are a result of this violent time. In the outer solar system a wandering star or planet disrupted Neptune and tipped Uranus over on its side.

In about 5 billion years the Sun will deplete its hydrogen and burn helium, becoming a red giant. Its surface will expand out to the orbit of Mars, consuming the inner solar system. Its helium gone, it will release its outer shell of gas, leaving behind a tiny white dwarf star no bigger than the Earth. Eventually this remnant star will burn itself out, leaving a dead, cold stellar corpse and ending the life of the solar system as we know it.

At present we have found only indirect evidence of other solar systems. New telescopes and recent technologies hold the promise of revealing planets around other stars. Current observations seem to indicate that solar systems may be common. If so, then we may not be alone.

THE SUN

The Sun is a star located at the center of our solar system. For this reason it appears larger than any other star visible in the night sky. Without the Sun life on Earth would be impossible.

The Sun's gravitational force is so great that it governs the motion of the Earth as well as all other bodies in the solar system. The Sun is so big that its interior could hold 1.3 million Earths.

Statistics:

Diameter (equatorial): 864,950 miles (1.4 million kilometers), or 109 times the Earth's diameter

Mass: 2.19×10^{27} tons (332,000 times the mass of Earth)

Composition: primarily gases—hydrogen, some helium, and other trace elements.

Rotation around axis (variable): 25 days at equator

Revolution around the center of our galaxy: 225 million years

Distance from center of galaxy: 30,000 light-years

Before 1900: The Sun has understandably been the center of worship for many cultures of the past. Incredibly, the idea that the Sun was the center of the solar system dates back to the time of the ancient Greeks, who believed the Sun was a burning rock two feet across. This heliocentric concept lost credence for more than 1,500 years, before gaining acceptance again—backed, this time, by scientific observations.

In the seventeenth century the first proper measurements of the Sun were made. Sunspots, which appear as dark splotches on the Sun, were discovered by Galileo. William Herschel believed sunspots were holes to a supposedly cooler interior that might be inhabited. By 1666 a revolution occurred in the study of the Sun when Isaac Newton split sunlight by passing it through a prism.

After 1900: By the 1950s the Sun and its various cycles were fairly well understood. The Sun has no permanent surface features and so is always changing. At the center of the solar interior lies the core at which burns the nuclear engine that drives the Sun. Temperatures at the core average an incredible 15 million Kelvin (27

million degrees Fahrenheit). The Sun consumes 11.023 billion pounds (5 billion kilograms) per second to produce its energy. Unlike the nuclear reactors commonly used in the twentieth century, which use nuclear fission (splitting the atom), the Sun "burns" cleanly by using nuclear fusion (the fusing of atoms into more complex ones—releasing energy in the process). It is for the reason of clean burning that scientists around the world are trying to develop fusion energy reactors.

As the Sun fuses hydrogen into helium, the energy released takes nearly 20,000 years to rise to the surface. By the time it reaches the Sun's fiery surface, it becomes the sunlight we are familiar with and takes only 8.5 minutes more to travel to Earth. It could be said that the sunbeams that warm and nourish our planet are some 20,000 years old.

The surface of the Sun is seething with activity. The bright visible part of the Sun is called the photosphere. Though it appears smooth, satellite pictures have revealed it to be a mottled fine-grained patchwork of cells called granules. These granules are formed from the powerful turbulent convective motion of searing hot gases that rise to the surface from the interior. Temperatures there average about 5,760 Kelvin (10,891 degrees Fahrenheit).

Sunspots, even the smallest of which can dwarf our Earth, appear as dark irregularly shaped splotches on the surface. They are actually cold areas that are the result of immense magnetic storms.

Solar flares, many thousands of miles across, stream out from the surface in titanic fiery eruptions that reach 50,000 degrees centigrade. These eruptions can make for brilliant displays of light, called auroras, at the Earth's poles. During eclipses, when the Sun is temporarily blocked by the Moon, many of these features become readily visible. Astronomers use specially equipped telescopes and spacecraft to regularly study these solar activities. In the 1970s NASA's *Skylab* space station continually monitored the Sun. Among the many things studied was the Sun's eleven-year sunspot cycle.

The equivalent of a solar atmosphere exists above the photosphere and is called the chromosphere. Beyond that lies the corona, which extends out millions of miles farther. Temperatures, for reasons once not fully understood, increase in the corona and can easily top 10 million Kelvin. Scientists now know, through modern X-ray observations, that this temperature increase is the result of changes that occur in an extremely thin transition zone.

Farther out, beyond the corona, flows the solar wind—and temperatures drop dramatically. The solar wind ends well outside the orbit of even the farthest planets, Neptune and Pluto, at what is known as the heliopause. Only four unmanned spacecraft have ventured beyond this point and into the cold void of interstellar space.

All stars, including the Sun, are classified by type on what astronomers call the H-R (Hertzsprung-Russell) diagram. The Sun is a class G2V star: an average second-generation yellow dwarf star born of the dust and debris of a previous generation of stars.

Main sequence stars like the Sun have a life expectancy of 10 to 12 billion years. Our Sun is about 4.6 billion years old now. Its nuclear furnace should continue to fuse hydrogen into helium for at least another 5 billion years.

MERCURY

The innermost planet in the solar system, Mercury is a scarred, sunbaked, pockmarked world that is one of the five original classic planets that have been observed since the dawn of civilization. Unlike any other planet, however, Mercury's close proximity to the Sun has made it an elusive object to observe—even by twentieth-century standards.

Statistics:

Mean distance from Sun: 36 million miles (57.9 million kilometers)

Diameter (equatorial): 3,031 miles (4,878 kilometers)

Rotation (Mercurian day): 58.65 Earth days

Revolution (Mercurian year): 87.97 Earth days

Before 1900: Mercury appropriately derives its name from the elusive Roman messenger to the gods. Its name aptly describes its sun-elusive nature and seeming ability to appear and disappear unpredictably and at will. Because it is the closest to the Sun, it can be viewed with the naked eye only within an hour of sunrise or sunset—and then only if it is in the right position.

As astronomers turned their attention to discovering the true nature of the planet, they found their work difficult at best. It is said that Copernicus complained that in all his life he never was able to view it successfully.

As their telescopes turned toward Mercury, one of the first things astronomers such as Galileo looked for was phases—which they predicted should be visible for any planet inside the Earth's orbit. What astronomers actually found, however, was not just phases but hints of strange markings, including dark spots. Giovanni Schiaparelli and others believed there was strong evidence of a cloudy atmosphere and oceans because these markings sometimes appeared to be obscured.

The planet's rotational period was also poorly known, and because of this Schiaparelli announced in 1889 that Mercury's rotation (length of Mercurian day) was not twenty-four hours but was locked to its period of revolution at eighty-eight days. This remained the accepted school of thought well into the twentieth century.

After 1900: Mercury remained largely a mystery for some time and had even been confused with a purported other inner planet called Vulcan, which never really existed. By 1965 radio astronomy had progressed sufficiently that it was possible to bounce radar signals even as far as Mercury and then receive and interpret the echoes. The results of even these first primitive "radar pictures" completely changed our view of this, the second-smallest planet in the solar system.

First to go was the Schiaparellian notion of a tidally sun-locked rotational period. Instead Mercury's period of rotation was found to be roughly in two-thirds resonance with its period of revolution. It is this very peculiarity that misled astronomers in the past by causing the same side to be turned toward Earth during prime viewing times. This resonance, however, is not completely perfect and new features do eventually start slowly coming into view after about seven years.

But, whether optical or radar, even the best images were very fuzzy and indistinct, lost in the glare of the Sun, and lacking any true detail except for hints of cratering.

Most of the knowledge that has been gleaned of the solar system's innermost planet came from NASA's *Mariner 10* mission. Launched in 1973, *Mariner 10* whisked by Venus and then flew by Mercury three times, managing to image less than half of its surface.

The results of the *Mariner 10* mission forever shattered our view of this tiny elusive world. Images returned by this plucky spacecraft revealed a barren, sunswept rocky surface that had been battered in its past. Appearing moonlike, Mercury is covered by both craters and smooth plains akin to lunar maria.

It also appears to be covered by porous, fine-grained soil. Mercury suffered a violent early history of heavy bombardment and subsequent volcanism that resulted in the formation of a unique system of gently rolling intercrater plains. Giant impact basins have shattered its surface and a global system of titanic compressive stress fractures have torn open its crust.

Unlike that of the other terrestrial planets, Mercury's atmosphere is mostly derived from the rarefied solar wind that flows past the planet. This extremely tenuous atmosphere is made up mostly of atomic helium (98 percent) and hydrogen (approximately 2 percent) and is less than a million-millionth the surface pressure of Earth's atmosphere. Though its surface appears moonlike, Mercury's interior seems to be more like Earth's than any other planet. It even has a magnetic field, an iron core, and an overall density close to Earth's.

Though Mercury is forever being bathed in the searing heat of the Sun, 1994 radar observations confirmed the existence of ice locked in low-lying permanently shaded polar areas. Astronomers who had theorized about the possibility of the existence of such ices were often criticized by their peers, who said that finding ice on Mercury was like finding snowballs in hell. The implication for possible future bases on the Moon is great. These same scientists believe that similar water ice may be locked up in vast permanently shaded areas of our own moon and could provide an incredible resource to space travelers in the future.

VENUS

Commonly known as the evening or morning star, Venus is actually the brightest planet that can be seen from Earth. Venus is named after the Roman goddess of love. It is the second planet from the Sun and has often been called Earth's twin. It can easily be seen as a very bright "star" several hours before sunrise or for several hours after sunset. It is the closest planet to the Earth. Strangely, Venus rotates very slowly on its axis in the direction opposite that of other planets. An observer on its hostile and foreboding surface would see the Sun appear to rise in the west and set in the east.

Statistics:
Mean distance from Sun: 67.2 million miles (108.2 million kilometers)
Diameter (equatorial): 7,521 miles (12,104 kilometers)
Rotation (Venusian day): 243.01 Earth days, retrograde
Revolution around the Sun (Venusian year): 224.7 Earth days

Before 1900: Unlike any other terrestrial planet, Venus has truly been shrouded in mystery—its surface hidden behind a permanent veil of thick clouds. Viewed with a telescope, Venus can be seen to go through phases because of its location inside Earth's orbit. However, no hint of the surface is visible. Historically, this led to a great deal of imaginative speculation as to what Venus was like. Wild theories sprang up about great earthlike alien civilizations that lived in a steaming primeval jungle world beneath a vast cloudy canopy. The theories were often romantic or exotic tales of a Venus teeming with life and adventure for intrepid future space explorers.

After 1900: Well into the twentieth century life on Venus was simply considered a given. Edgar Rice Burroughs, author of the wildly popular Mars and Tarzan books, wrote a series of fictional books about Venus as well. He envisioned a hot world covered by mile-high trees populated by largely arboreal beings. Hollywood added to the myths about Venus by often portraying it as a world populated by a predominantly female society. After all, they reasoned, Venus is named for a goddess.

Venus didn't give up its secrets easily. It was only with the advent of sophisticated modern spacecraft that could actually visit the planet that earthlings unraveled their twin world's many mysteries, and discovered new ones in the process.

By the 1960s these romantic visions of Venus began quickly crumbling away. Blurry early Earth-based radar images hinted at a cratered rocky surface. Astronomer Carl Sagan predicted that the clouds on Venus caused the planet's atmosphere to retain heat, in what he termed "the greenhouse effect."

In 1962 NASA's Mariner 2 spacecraft flew by Venus and became the first spacecraft in history to visit another world. Several dozen American and Soviet spacecraft followed. Of these, the Soviet's Venera 9 actually landed and successfully transmitted two photographs of the surface.

In 1978 the American Pioneer-Venus spacecraft, armed with impact probes, successfully reached Venus. Amazingly, one of these probes survived its crash through the crushing Venusian atmosphere and continued to radio information for an additional hour.

In the 1980s a number of Soviet Venera orbiters and landers visited Venus. The orbiters used cloud-penetrating radar that could be bounced off the surface to assemble blurry first-ever global maps of the Venusian surface. These maps were later improved upon by NASA's Magellan mission, which in 1990 systematically radar-mapped the Venusian surface in exquisitely fine detail. Magellan plummeted to a fiery death in October 1994 and ended the most successful mission in the history of the American space program.

The picture of the real Venus that has emerged is of a world covered by thousands of volcanoes: thirty times more than Earth. The surface is torn by some of the most dramatic landforms in the solar system, including vast lava fields extending hundreds of miles, extensively cracked and fractured elevated plains, and mountains more than seven miles high. Temperatures on the surface exceed half the melting point of most rocks and are hot enough to melt lead. The surface pressure is a crushing ninety times that of Earth's. Its atmosphere is mostly carbon dioxide (a "greenhouse gas"), and the clouds that forever shroud Venus's face contain highly corrosive sulfuric acid. Probes that have landed on Venus have never been able to survive more than a few hours because of these hellish conditions.

In spite of all this, Venus is actually very earthlike. If one were able to grind up Venus and Earth and compare them, one would find that the two planets are nearly identical in composition; they vary only in elemental distribution. The water on Venus, for example, is bound up in Venusian minerals. In size and density the two are also nearly identical.

Indeed, Venus may at one time have been very earthlike. Scientists are especially interested in Venus as a twin world because something happened to it to cause it, at some point, to evolve into the Dante's *Inferno* we know now, while Earth evolved to the lush world teeming with life with which we are so familiar. Are ozone depletion and the greenhouse effect a cause for concern here on Earth? Venus may hold the answers.

EARTH
The third planet from the Sun, Earth is a virtual oasis in a universe filled with harsh environments. It is the only planet known to harbor life. Evidence of other possible solar systems, and water and organics in comets and asteroids (suspected to have seeded life on Earth), hint that life may be widespread throughout the cosmos.

Statistics:
Mean distance from Sun: 93 million miles (149.6 million kilometers)
Diameter (equatorial): 7,926 miles (12,755 kilometers)
Period of rotation: 23 hours, 56 minutes
Period of revolution: 365.26 days
Life: More than 1 million known described species
Moons: 1 (the Moon)

Before 1900: Earth is a planet like any other visited with space probes. Perception of our world as such, however, is fairly recent. Many ancient religions centered around a "mother Earth." It was generally accepted that the earth was flat, until great thinkers and men of science, such as Copernicus and Galileo, challenged these long-held beliefs and redefined our understanding of the Earth and the universe around it. As beliefs changed, understanding of the world we live in expanded, especially through exploration and colonization of new lands. Humankind also learned to harness many of Earth's vast resources, such as timber and a variety of plants, animals, and metals.

After 1900: By the twentieth century humans had explored most of the Earth. Then, in 1969, astronauts landed on the Moon and our perception of Earth was forever changed. For the first time we saw the Earth from the vantage of another world. Earth, our home, was a fragile, tiny life-sustaining world.

Born in a swirling solar nebula, Earth and the other planets of our solar system formed about 4.6 billion years ago. Like all other planets, Earth

was pummeled by meteoric material early in its history. Because of erosion by wind and water, craters are not the dominant landform on Earth as on other worlds. More-recent craters, such as Barringer Crater in Arizona, are still visible. Earth is also protected from such space debris by its atmosphere, which also shields its surface from dangerous solar radiation—making life possible.

Life on Earth followed the development of oceans but was limited to various single-celled microbes. The first extensive fossil evidence of life occurs in the late Cryptozoic (or Precambrian) era, some 650 million years ago, when an explosion of diverse ocean life occurred. With the evolution of fish came amphibians, followed by dinosaurs and mammals.

Cyclic changes, such as ice ages, have helped shape the Earth. The Earth's bombardment history also defined many of its climatic and evolutionary eras. The age of dinosaurs ended 65 million years ago when an asteroid hit the Earth. The impact triggered global environmental changes that ultimately spelled the demise not only of the dinosaurs but of 75 percent of all life.

Stripped of the oceans that cover 75 percent of its surface, the Earth can be seen to be made up of continents defined by massive tectonic plates. The Earth was once dominated by a single continent, Pangaea, which began breaking up into the continents we know now during the age of dinosaurs. Giant ridge systems, such as the Mid-Atlantic Ridge, produce "fresh land," as evidenced by sea-floor spreading. In other areas, great subduction zones, like the Mariana Trench in the Pacific, swallow ancient land for reprocessing in the Earth's interior. In the Himalayas, continental plates have collided, forming the tallest mountains on Earth. A zone of highly active faults and volcanoes also circumscribes the Pacific basin in what is known as the ring of fire. All these processes,

Earth from space.

known collectively as plate tectonics, are responsible for the slow, ever-present movement of the Earth's continents and for changes to its crust. In the 1960s the notion of continental drift and plate tectonics finally became developed and accepted.

The Earth's four seasons are the result of a 23.44-degree axial tilt. Vast deserts, tropical jungles, forests, volcanic island and mountain chains, are typical of the incredible biological and geological diversity evident on Earth: diversity that exists on no other known planet.

THE MOON

The Moon is planet Earth's only natural satellite. It is well over a fourth the size of the Earth. As such, the Moon has had a profound influence on the Earth and its many life-forms.

Statistics:
Mean distance from Earth: 238,851.25 miles (384,400 kilometers)
Diameter (equatorial): 1,080 miles (1,738 kilometers)
Period of rotation and revolution (sidereal): 27.32 days
(Note: the Moon always keeps the same face toward Earth)

Before 1900: Second only to the Sun, the Moon dominates the Earth's sky. It is the closest celestial body to the Earth and is responsible for Earth's tides. It has been worshipped since antiquity. Its cyclic phases caused it to be associated with the cycle of life. The ability to predict such apparent "cataclysms" as eclipses was used effectively by ancients to maintain power and influence over the populace. As people became more enlightened by science, their imaginations began broaching the idea of possibly flying to the Moon. Writers such as Jules Verne, H. G. Wells, and Edgar Rice Burroughs spun fantastic tales of travel to the Moon.

After 1900: During the Cold War both the United States and the former Soviet Union engaged in a space race to get to the Moon. Both countries embarked upon ambitious programs that resulted in phenomenal technological leaps. The spin-offs and their applications in our daily life continue to benefit us.

The Moon has been visited by a virtual armada of international unmanned spacecraft that came both before and after NASA's manned Apollo program. On July 20, 1969, American Apollo astronaut Neil Armstrong set foot on the lunar surface and became the first human ever to touch another world. Between 1969 and 1972 Apollo astronauts returned with a total of 842 pounds (382 kilograms) of lunar material. Most of the knowledge we have about the Moon has been gleaned from Apollo.

The Moon's early history was so violent that few traces remain. As its surface cooled it was heavily bombarded and its enormous basins were formed by colossal catastrophic asteroidal impacts. Lunar craters range from a fraction of an inch deep to hundreds of miles across.

About 4 billion years ago this bombardment ended and heat generated by radioactive elements in its interior caused lava to rise and flood these basins. On the Moon's near side, 700 million years of lava flooding formed the now familiar dark areas Galileo called "maria." This volcanism may have continued on a small scale until as recently as 1 billion years ago.

The Moon's origin, however, still remains a mystery. Did an errant Mars-sized asteroid strike the Earth cataclysmically, throwing off material that coalesced into the Moon, or did it simply form together with the Earth? Was the Moon a wanderer captured by Earth's gravity, or was it somehow torn from the Earth? Are there lunar polar ice lakes? Perhaps new data from missions such as NASA's Clementine and Galileo missions will answer these and other mysteries.

MARS

Probably no single celestial object has captured the imagination more than Mars. Also known as the red planet, it is the fourth planet from the Sun and second-closest planet to the Earth. Observed since before antiquity, Mars's reddish color is probably responsible for its being named after the Roman god of war.

Statistics:
Mean distance from Sun: 141.6 million miles (227.9 million kilometers)
Diameter (equatorial): 4,219 miles (6,790 kilometers)
Average period of rotation: 24 hours, 37 minutes
Average period of revolution: 686.98 days
Moons: 2 (Deimos [terror] and Phobos [fear])

Before 1900: The love affair with Mars began when the first telescopic observations revealed seasonally varying polar caps and green regions. The prevalent interpretations were that Mars was covered by a rust-colored sandy desert and green areas of vegetation that spread and shrank with the seasons. Tantalizing notions of life on Mars saturated both the public and the scientific psyche.

In 1877 Giovanni Schiaparelli produced a map of Mars that showed sharp connecting lines that Father Pietro Angelo Secchi in Rome called "canali" (Italian for "grooves"). The term was quickly embraced but became transposed as "canals." Percival Lowell claimed he saw four times more canals than anyone else had and interpreted them as desperate attempts by an advanced Martian civilization at irrigating their dying world. Others said they saw no canals. So was born one of the greatest and most colorful debates in astronomy.

In 1877 Asaph Hall discovered Mars's two moons. Slight orbital peculiarities and their small size and dimness later sparked debates over whether they were artificial satellites placed into orbit by Martians. In 1898 H. G. Wells published *War of the Worlds*, which imparted a new sensationalism to the popular imagination.

After 1900: By 1938 Orson Welles's Mercury Theatre radio broadcast of *War of the Worlds* resulted in mass panic by people who believed a Martian invasion force had landed on Earth. Mars became associated with "little green men" and "flying saucers." It was, therefore, with wide-eyed amazement that in 1965 scientists viewed the first close-up pictures of Mars taken by NASA's *Mariner 4*. They revealed a desolate, cratered planet. Gone were the civilizations, vegetation, and canals.

Mars, however, was not quite the dead world these first twenty-two pictures revealed. Future missions established Mars as a fascinating, dynamic world. Inconclusive results from NASA's Viking landers also left open the possibility of primitive microbial life.

The canals and green areas were found to be optical effects resulting from shifting sands caused by the seasonal winds that dominate Mars. Global summer dust storms lasting months sometimes completely smother Mars. Its polar caps are mostly carbon dioxide ice. Water, however, has been found to exist in ground fogs, frosts, the northern remnant summer polar cap, and probably in a layer of subsurface permafrost.

The sheer enormity of Martian features is staggering, considering Mars is about half the size of Earth. The surface is a mix of vast sandy and boulder-strewn deserts, hundreds of miles of dunes near the north pole, ancient riverbeds, floodplains, immense flat impact basins, and laminated polar ice fields. A massive northern volcanic plateau contains some of the largest volcanoes anywhere in the solar system.

Mars's magnificent towering volcanoes and immense system of canyons are the largest in the solar system. The volcano Olympus Mons is an incredible 16.7 miles (27 kilometers) high and, at three times its height, dwarfs Earth's Mount Everest. Incomparable Valles Marineris, a canyon system created by a combination of erosion and faulting, is more than 3,000 miles (4,800 kilometers) long. Nearly 4.5 miles (7 kilometers) deep, Valles Marineris is so enormous that Earth's Grand Canyon could easily fit into one of its small tributaries!

Temperatures on Mars range from 71.6 degrees Fahrenheit (22 degrees centigrade) to minus 193 degrees Fahrenheit (minus 125 degrees centigrade). More than 2 billion years ago Mars may have had standing oceans and a warmer, thicker atmosphere. These oceans dried up about a billion years ago. This ocean period is long enough for primitive sea life to have evolved. Will future astronauts landing on Mars find fossil evidence of such life? Whatever the findings, the ramifications for us here on Earth could be of incalculable significance.

ASTEROID BELT

The asteroid belt is a region between Mars and Jupiter that contains objects known as main belt asteroids. An asteroid is any one of numerous minor planetary bodies, usually chunks of free-floating rocky space debris. Sometimes asteroids get "bumped" out of the asteroid belt and hit planets as meteorites. The larger ones, like the type that hit the Earth and killed the dinosaurs, can pose a deadly hazard.

Statistics:
Asteroid belt's mean distances from Sun:
Inner edge of main belt: 204.6 million miles (329.1 million kilometers)

The first panoramic view of Mars, taken by Viking Lander 1 *in July 1976.*

Outer edge of main belt: 334.8 million miles (538.5 million kilometers)

Statistics on some prominent main belt asteroids:

Name	Diameter (mi.)	(km.)	Period of rotation (hours)	Period of revolution (years)
Ceres	302.8	487	9.078	4.60
Pallas	167.3	269	7.811	4.61
Vesta	163.5	263	5.342	3.63
Juno	83.3	134	7.21	4.36

Before 1900: Though asteroids are very faint, some main belt asteroids are the size of small planets and are bright enough to be seen with the naked eye. Ceres was the first asteroid to be discovered. First observed on January 1, 1801, by Giovanni Piazzi, Ceres is the largest known asteroid. Pallas, Juno, and Vesta were discovered in 1802, 1804, and 1807, respectively. Collectively these are the four largest known asteroids. All four reside in the asteroid belt. In all, more than 430 asteroids were discovered during the 1800s.

After 1900: As technology improved, the number of asteroids discovered increased exponentially to more than 5,700 by 1995. Astronomers now calculate that their total population probably exceeds 30,000. These objects come in sizes ranging from less than twenty-one yards to hundreds of miles. One of the smallest known asteroids, 1991 BA (its discovery designation), is barely seven yards across.

Asteroids are usually classified by orbital type or color (which can also indicate their composition). Asteroids can be made up of any combination of carbon, nickel, iron, other various metals, rock, and even organics. To date no asteroid is known to have an atmosphere, and their surface temperatures average a bitter minus 99.4 degrees Fahrenheit (minus 73 degrees centigrade).

The first truly detailed pictures of asteroids were obtained by NASA's *Galileo* spacecraft when it traversed the asteroid belt en route to Jupiter. It provided crisp digital pictures of 951 Gaspra (in 1991) and 243 Ida (in 1993). NASA also made a striking discovery: 243 Ida has a small moon (Dactyl) that measures about a mile across. It is the first natural satellite to be discovered around an asteroid.

Asteroids are also important to our understanding of the early history of our solar system. Two main theories exist for the origin of the asteroid belt: a planet formed, then broke up, or the material for a planet was there but never formed and became a belt of rocky debris. Like comets, asteroids provide us a direct look at material that dates back to the solar system in its infancy.

Most asteroids populate the asteroid belt; those that get knocked out exist in highly irregular orbits. One very select class of asteroids known as NEAs (near-Earth asteroids) cross the earth's orbit. In 1994 asteroid 1994XM1 passed within 106,000 miles of Earth—over Russia.

The economic potential inherent in mining such readily accessible asteroids for scarce resources is tremendous. Unfortunately, such objects pose a potentially devastating threat. It was presumably such an Earth crosser that slammed into our planet 65 million years ago and caused cataclysmic environmental changes that resulted in the extinction of 75 percent of all life on Earth—including the dinosaurs.

In 1994 humans got a rare look at the sheer destructive capacity of a planetary impact. Comet Shoemaker-Levy 9 broke into twenty-one chunks and hit Jupiter. The ensuing explosions, millions of megatons each, ripped holes in even this gargantuan planet.

A global network of astronomers continue to monitor the skies in the event one of these cold, dark objects is ever found to be heading our way.

JUPITER

The fifth planet from the Sun, Jupiter is the largest planet in the solar system. It orbits beyond the outer edge of the asteroid belt. Its gravitational influence on objects in the solar system (especially in the asteroid belt) is second only to the Sun's.

Statistics:

Mean distance from Sun: 483.6 million miles (778.3 million kilometers)

Diameter (equatorial): 88,729 miles (142,796 kilometers)

Period of rotation: 9 hours, 55 minutes

Period of revolution: 11.8 years

Moons: 16

Names of moons (listed closest to farthest from Jupiter): Metis, Adrastea, Amalthea, Thebe, Io, Europa, Ganymede, Callisto, Leda, Himalia, Lysithea, Elara, Ananke, Carme, Pasiphae, and Sinope.

Rings: 2 very thin faint rings surrounded by an even fainter halo of material

Distance of rings from Jupiter's cloud tops:

Inner edge of inner ring: 0 miles (at cloud tops)

Outer edge of outer ring: 35,734 miles (57,508 kilometers)

Before 1900: Jupiter is 318 times more massive than the Earth and more than ten times Earth's diameter. An enormous sphere of turbulent swirling gases that is rotationally flattened at the poles, Jupiter's colorful cloud bands have now been observed for more than 300 years.

Jupiter was of great importance to astronomers such as Galileo. He discovered the four largest of Jupiter's moons (Io, Europa, Ganymede, and Callisto) and so demonstrated that the Earth was not the center of the universe. Newton then used orbital observations of these Galilean moons to do the first-ever calculations of Jupiter's mass and density.

Jupiter's most striking feature, the Great Red Spot, is an enormous hurricane-like storm that dwarfs the Earth. It was first observed in 1664 and has been raging for possibly a million years.

After 1900: Jupiter emits more energy than it receives and is now considered to be a "brown dwarf"—a star that lacked sufficient mass to ignite a nuclear fire. Most of what is known of this denizen of the outer solar system has been learned from the four NASA spacecraft that have visited it, the last being *Voyager 2* in 1979. Among their many findings is the serendipitous discovery that Jupiter has two very faint dusty rings.

Of Jupiter's fascinating collection of moons, the Galilean satellites are the most intriguing. Innermost of the four is tiny Io. Its interior heated by a tidal tug-of-war, erupting volcanoes and molten sulfur lava lakes cover its surface. This was the first time active volcanism was discovered outside the earth.

Next out is Europa, which, like Io, has also been tidally heated. Constantly being resurfaced by a labyrinthine network of global cracks and ridges, its thin, brittle icy crust covers a warmer, possibly oceanic, interior of liquid water. Because of these conditions, scientists suspect that primitive microbes may have evolved there. No direct evidence exists yet.

Beyond Europa lies Ganymede—largest moon in the solar system. Its 1,635-mile (2,631-kilometer) radius makes it bigger than either Mercury or Pluto. Made up of rock and ice, its surface has been contorted by a twisting sinuous system of grooves.

Outermost of the Galilean moons is battered Callisto—the most heavily cratered object in the solar system. Callisto is a dead frozen world where no geologic activity has occurred except the recording of its brutal bombardment history in the form of endless numbers of craters. A gigantic multiringed basin, the result of a violent ancient impact, is its prominent feature.

After a tortuous six-year journey, NASA's *Galileo* spacecraft arrived at Jupiter in December 1995 in order to provide long-term monitoring of the Jovian system. *Galileo* also released a drop probe into Jupiter's turbulent atmosphere that was crushed several hours later by Jupiter's massive gravity. *Galileo* is currently collecting data that will be analyzed for years to come.

SATURN

Graced with an extensive and exquisite set of rings, Saturn is unquestionably the most stunning planet in the solar system. The sixth planet from the Sun, Saturn is one of four planets known to have rings. Like Jupiter, it is a gas giant that plays host to a diverse array of moons.

Statistics:
Mean distance from Sun: 888.2 million miles (1,429 million kilometers)
Diameter (equatorial): 74,975 miles (120,660 kilometers)
Distance of rings from Saturn's cloud tops:
Inner edge (innermost ring): 4,147.2 miles (6,670 kilometers)
Outermost edge (outermost ring): 260,934.7 miles (419,670 kilometers)
Period of rotation: 10 hours, 40 minutes
Period of revolution: 29.46 years
Moons: 20
Names of moons (listed closest to farthest from Saturn): Pan, Atlas, Prometheus, 1995-S3, Pandora, 1995-S4, Epimethius, Janus, Mimas, Enceladus, Tethys, Telesto, Calypso, Dione, Helene, Rhea, Titan, Hyperion, Iapetus, and Phoebe.

Before 1900: Second only to gargantuan Jupiter in size, Saturn is among the brightest night-sky objects. Saturn's spectacular rings had to await the invention of the telescope to be discovered. When Galileo first saw them in 1610 with his crude telescope he concluded that Saturn was actually composed of three objects.

Two years later the rings disappeared. Because Saturn is inclined twenty-nine degrees, its rings go through a fifteen-year viewing cycle. They can be viewed from Earth as fully open or, as in 1612, be nearly invisible when seen edge on. Six years later Galileo was even more confused by their return and concluded that they were some sort of "appendages." It wasn't until 1659, four years after he also discovered Saturn's moon Titan, that Christian Huygens correctly identified Saturn's mysterious "appendages" as rings.

After 1900: Most of the knowledge we have about Saturn comes from the three NASA spacecraft that have visited it: *Pioneer 11* (1979), *Voyager 1* (1980), and *Voyager 2* (1981).

Saturn is ninety-five times more massive than Earth and nearly ten times its diameter. It is composed mainly of hydrogen and helium gases that surround a bizarre liquid-metallic hydrogen-helium mantle and an icy silicate core. Its poles are flattened owing to rapid rotation around its axis. The frigid minus 178 degrees centigrade temperature of its atmosphere causes Saturn's clouds to appear as hazy yellow and faint light-brown bands that are much blander than Jupiter's.

Storms regularly disrupt its placid atmosphere and appear as white oval spots hundreds of miles across. On rare occasions Saturn's atmosphere is torn by massive storms that are thousands of miles across. The last two such storms, in 1933 and 1990, appeared as spectacular white global eruptions that spanned the entire planet and lasted for months.

Saturn's rings are made up of seven main rings and a gap called the Cassini Division. Each of these rings actually comprises thousands more tiny thin rings that are made up of minute icy particles of dust. Saturn's rings are fairly young, about 100 million years old, and will fully collapse within the next 100 million years.

Saturn plays host to a strange assortment of enigmatic moons. Until 1980 only half of its twenty moons were known. Most notable among these geologically fascinating objects is Titan. Titan has a radius of 1,600 miles (2,575 kilometers) and is the only moon with an atmosphere so thick it conceals the surface. Titan is of special interest because it resembles our Earth when it was in its primordial infancy.

Studies of the complex Saturn system continue. Two new moons, temporarily named 1995-S3 and 1995-S4, were discovered in photos by the Hubble Space Telescope in May 1995. Future missions, such as NASA's *Cassini* probe, will orbit Saturn. By providing comprehensive long-term monitoring of Saturn's atmosphere, scientists hope to better understand Earth's weather systems. *Cassini* will even drop a lander probe through Titan's clouds, for the first time exposing this mysterious world to scientific scrutiny.

URANUS

Uranus is the seventh planet from the Sun. Third-largest planet in the solar system, it was the first to be discovered in a calculated effort to find a planet. Since its discovery, little had been learned about this mysterious gas giant until a flyby mission in 1986 revealed a world even more enigmatic than previously suspected.

Statistics:

Mean distance from Sun: 1,786 million miles (2,875 million kilometers)

Diameter (equatorial): 31,763 miles (51,118 kilometers)

Average period of rotation: 16.8 hours

Average period of revolution: 84.07 years

Moons: 15

Names of moons (listed closest to farthest from Uranus): Cordelia, Ophelia, Bianca, Cressida, Desdemona, Juliet, Portia, Rosalind, Belinda, Puck, Miranda, Ariel, Umbriel, Titania, and Oberon.

Rings: 11

Distance of rings from Uranian cloud tops:

Inner edge of inner ring: 6,835 miles (11,000 kilometers)

Outer edge of outer ring: 16,031 miles (25,800 kilometers)

Before 1900: Faintly visible to the naked eye, Uranus has been mistaken for a star in the past and appears on star charts as early as 1690. Because the Titius-Bode law correctly predicted planetary positions, astronomers found that it might also predict the orbit of a planet beyond Saturn.

As a result of a systematic telescopic survey, William Herschel discovered Uranus on March 13, 1781. For sixty years the planet had three names, until "Uranus," a mythological name, eventually became accepted. In 1787 Herschel also discovered two moons, Titania and Oberon. In 1851 William Lassell discovered Ariel and Umbriel.

Until the late twentieth century little was known about this mysterious planet except that it was curiously tipped over (97.9 degrees) on its side. Its rotational axis lies in what is the equatorial plane for most planets. Uranus's north and south poles gradually alternate facing the Sun. Uranus's moons rotate about its vertically tipped equator.

After 1900: Discovered in 1948, Uranus's moon Miranda was the fifth and last moon discovered until *Voyager 2* reached this distant world on January 25, 1986. Its first close-up pictures proved surprisingly disappointing. NASA scientists noted, "Uranus looks like a fuzzy green tennis ball." Uranus showed none of the extensive brilliant banded cloud structures visible on Jupiter and Saturn. Extensive digital image processing, however, did reveal the dynamic and turbulent nature of its atmosphere.

Uranus has a rocky Earth-sized core bathed in a scalding ocean of water and dissolved ammonia probably 6,200 miles (10,000 kilometers) deep. Its atmosphere is primarily made up of hydrogen and helium, with traces of methane, ammonia, and water vapor.

The sunlit side of Uranus's atmosphere is shrouded in a type of photochemical acetylene-ethane "smog." Extending thousands of miles beyond its ever-hazy atmosphere is a mysterious ultraviolet sheen astronomers call "electroglow." Uranus also has a magnetic field (15 percent weaker than Earth's), which, rather than being oriented about its axis like that of other planets, is tilted up toward the vertical (fifty-five degrees)—away from the side-lying Uranian axis.

Voyager discovered ten additional moons. Of Uranus's fifteen charcoal-dark icy moons, probably the most interesting is Miranda. Its surface is an odd patchwork of widely varied terrains. Smooth plains, winding valleys, and battered cratered areas appear to be slapped together somehow. Astronomers theorize that an object had smashed into Miranda and shattered it. The larger pieces, still hot, managed to come together and re-form the moon as we know it today.

Using star occultations, scientists discovered nine rings around Uranus prior to *Voyager's* arrival. *Voyager* discovered two more, bringing the total to eleven. Unlike the brilliant icy rings that circle Saturn, Uranus's rings are composed of dark boulder-sized chunks. They are so dark that they reflect only 2 percent of the sunlight that falls on them.

NASA hopes to launch a dual-probe Uranus-Neptune orbiter mission in the early twenty-first century to further explore this strange yet beautiful planetary system.

NEPTUNE

Neptune is the fourth-largest planet in the solar system. A Jovian gas giant that is the eighth planet from the Sun, it is located in the bitter-cold outer reaches of our solar system. This blue behemoth is so far from the Sun that it is visible from Earth only through a telescope. Neptune was discovered as a result of extensive mathematical calculations and careful observations.

Statistics:
Mean distance from Sun: 2,799 million miles (4,504 million kilometers)
Diameter (equatorial): 30,775 miles (49,528 kilometers)
Period of rotation: 16 hours, 6 minutes
Period of revolution: 164.82 years
Moons: 8
Names of moons (listed closest to farthest from Neptune): Naiad, Thalassa, Despina, Galatea, Larissa, Proteus, Triton, and Nereid.
Rings: 5
Distance of rings from Neptune's cloud tops:
Innermost ring: 9,613 miles (16,236 kilometers)
Outermost ring: 23,613 miles (38,236 kilometers)

Before 1900: Observations of Uranus revealed perturbations in its orbit that strongly suggested another planet's influence. In 1841 John Couch Adams (1819–92) concluded that the irregularities in Uranus's orbit were due to an unknown object whose orbit was outside Uranus's. He predicted an orbit and position for this unknown planet.

Coincidentally, French astronomer Urbain Leverrier (1811–77) presented the results of his own calculations just a few months after Adams. Leverrier managed to convince the Prussian Observatory in Berlin to search for the planet. Johann Galle (1812–1910) and student Heinrich d'Arrest (1822–75) then used Leverrier's predictions and, on September 23, 1846, after only one hour of searching, discovered Neptune.

All four shared the discovery and it was Leverrier who named the planet "Neptune," after the Roman god of the sea (because of its prominent blue color). Several weeks after Neptune's discovery, English astronomer William Lassell (1799–1880) discovered Neptune's retrograde orbiting moon Triton.

In January 1613, 233 years before Neptune was "officially" discovered, Galileo had already observed it. It is clearly marked on his charts. Unfortunately, he did not realize he had inadvertently plotted a planet. Additionally, on October 2, 1846, Lassell noted what he thought was a ring around Neptune. Long forgotten, rings were rediscovered nearly 140 years later.

After 1900: Neptune's second moon, Nereid, was not discovered until 1949. Little else was known about Neptune until NASA's *Voyager 2* arrived in 1989. Star occultation observations, similar to those that resulted in the discovery of rings around Uranus, had met with limited success. The observations could only be explained by Neptune's having partial rings or "ring arcs." *Voyager* confirmed complete rings that turned out only to appear as arcs because they are composed of bright clumps and fainter connecting portions.

Neptune's magnetic field was found to be strangely tipped away from its rotational axis toward its equatorial plane by minus forty-seven degrees. Neptune's clouds turned out to be the most turbulent of any planet's in the solar system. They are whipped by torrential winds of 1,500 miles (2,400 kilometers) an hour.

Voyager also discovered a fierce Earth-sized storm, the Great Dark Spot. It resembles Jupiter's Great Red Spot, spins counterclockwise, and moves westward at an incredible 745 miles (1,200 kilometers) per hour.

Voyager also detected six more moons. While observing the largest moon, Triton, it found that the moon not only had a thin atmosphere (1/70,000th of Earth's) but also had active geyserlike ice volcanoes. This is the only place other than Earth, besides Jupiter's moon Io, that is known to have active volcanism. Triton's peculiar pink and blue surface also undergoes seasonal variations and is covered by curious so-called cantaloupe terrain and a receding ice cap. Triton's surface is one of the coldest ever observed: a frigid minus 391 degrees Fahrenheit (minus 235 degrees centigrade).

Because Triton orbits in a direction opposite Neptune's spin, it is spiraling in toward Neptune. In 10 to 100 million years Neptune's gravity will rip it apart, forming a spectacular ring that will rival its dim present-day rings.

PLUTO

Pluto is the ninth and smallest planet in the solar system. It is a dark frigid world that is 1,600 times too faint to be seen from Earth with the naked eye. It is the only planet in our solar system not visited by a spacecraft.

Statistics:
Mean distance from Sun: 3,666 million miles (5,900 million kilometers)
Diameter (equatorial; approximate): 1,429 miles (2,300 kilometers)
Period of rotation: 6.39 days, retrograde
Period of revolution: 248.6 years
Moons: 1 (Charon)
Rings: None known

Before 1900: Though Pluto was discovered in the twentieth century, the search for this tiny remote world began much sooner. With the successful discovery of Neptune in 1846, scientists began looking for an even more distant planet. The perturbations in Uranus's and Neptune's orbits could not be accounted for and many astronomers felt confident that further searches would result in the additional discovery of a massive dark planet that orbited at the very edge of our solar system. This planet was often referred to as Planet X, the name coined by Percival Lowell (1855–1916).

After 1900: The search for Planet X was legitimized by Lowell and fellow Bostonian William Pickering (1858–1938). Both published several sets of predictions between 1915 and 1919. Searches at both the Lowell (Arizona) and Mount Wilson (southern California) Observatories turned up nothing.

In 1929 a search program, founded by Lowell before his death in 1916, was instituted at the Lowell Observatory to systematically survey the sky in a search for the phantom planet. On February 18, 1930, Lowell astronomer Clyde W. Tombaugh (b. 1906) used a blink comparator and discovered this extremely faint world. Pluto was named in honor of Percival Lowell, whose initials are the first two letters in its name, and after the Greek god of the underworld. Because Pluto turned out to be nearly 100 times smaller than indicated by the perturbations of Uranus and Neptune, its discovery was more a product of Tombaugh's continual perseverance and keen observations than of predictive calculations.

Pluto rotates on its side, as does Uranus. Its axis of rotation is tilted off the vertical by 122 degrees, thus giving Pluto extreme seasons. Pluto's orbit is inclined seventeen degrees off the ecliptic plane—more than any other planet's. Its orbit is also the most eccentric, or elongated, bringing it inside the orbit of Neptune at times. Pluto has been inside the orbit of Neptune since 1979, temporarily making Neptune the most distant planet in the solar system. Pluto will move back beyond Neptune in March 1999. Because of this highly irregular orbit, many astronomers have suggested that Pluto may actually be an errant Neptunian satellite.

In 1978 James Christy and Robert Harrington discovered Pluto's only moon, Charon. With a diameter of approximately 746 miles (1,200 kilometers) Charon is the largest moon in proportion to the size of its host planet. The orbits of Pluto and Charon are gravitationally locked so that both always keep the same face toward each other. Detailed observations have revealed that because Charon orbits barely 12,500 miles (20,000 kilometers) from Pluto's surface, Pluto and Charon may share a tenuous atmosphere. Pluto is predominantly covered by methane ice. Charon is covered by mostly water ice. Both seem to have rocky cores. Why their surfaces are so different is not clearly understood.

NASA hopes one day to launch a mission to this, the only truly unexplored planet in our solar system. Until then, one can only imagine what the frozen barren surface of this ever-remote world and its moon are like. Charon probably appears enormous, a dark lonely sentinel that dominates Pluto's sky. In the dim Plutonian day the distant Sun appears almost as tiny as any other of the stars that splash across its sky.

COMETS AND METEORS

Comets and meteors often produce spectacular displays in the night sky, making them the subject of much awe and mystery. Comets were historically considered harbingers of misfortune. There are about 900 known comets, and only recently have they been properly understood.

Definitions:
Comet: meteoric object that contains volatile ices
Meteor: "shooting star"; a meteoroid that enters a planet's atmosphere and appears as a bright flash
Meteor shower: meteors that appear to originate simultaneously from a single source
Fireball: very large fiery meteor
Meteorite: meteor or fireball that lands on a planet
Meteoroid: minor planetary/cometary debris that crosses planetary orbits
Swarms: groups of meteoroids
Statistics:
Orbits (comets and meteoroids): highly elliptical; vary widely
Size:
Meteoroids: microscopic to tens of miles
Comets: Nucleus: .5 to 12 miles
Tail: up to 93.2 million miles
Period of revolution:
Short-period comets: less than 200 years
Long-period comets: more than 200 years
Meteoroids: varies widely

Before 1900: Probably no celestial event is as spectacular as the appearance of a comet. Historically comets were not greeted with the fanfare and scientific inquisitiveness they receive now. Past superstitions have linked comets to disasters and historic events. It is theorized that the Christmas star, often described as having a tail, was actually a comet.

Once thought to be one-time objects, Edmund Halley proved that comets are periodic objects. He correctly predicted the return of a comet in 1758 to 1759 and it was named in his honor. Later studies showed that Halley's comet had been observed as early as 240 B.C. by the Chinese.

A dramatic rash of meteoric hits in the mid-1700s caused scientists to begin to investigate their origins. By the 1860s Giovanni Schiaparelli (1835–1910) had correctly deduced that most meteoroids are debris left behind from comets. Some rarer meteoroids owe their origins to more exotic sources such as the asteroid belt and even Mars. Almost ten tons of meteoric material rains down on the Earth every day—mostly as very fine dust.

After 1900: In 1910 one of the most spectacular sightings of a comet occurred when the Earth actually passed through the tail of Halley's comet. Panic gripped many parts of the world and entrepreneurs took advantage and sold gas masks and comet pills. The comet was so prominent in the sky that it was visible even in broad daylight and produced numerous meteor showers. Unfortunately, the 1986 return of Halley's comet was dismal at best. The most spectacular comet since Halley's 1910 appearance occurred with little fanfare when comet West ("Milkman's comet") made an unexpectedly dazzling appearance in predawn skies in 1976.

Comets are, for the most part, "dirty snowballs" made up of water ice and rock, with traces of methane and ammonia. Remnants of the solar system's formation, comets come from two regions that lie beyond the orbit of Pluto: the Oort cloud and the Kuiper belt.

Two comets have been visited by spacecraft so far. In 1985 America's *International Cometary Explorer* flew through the tail of comet Giacobini-Zinner. In 1986 an international armada of five spacecraft visited Halley's comet. Europe's *Giotto* probe actually flew through the comet's coma (or atmosphere) to within 373 miles (600 kilometers) of the eleven-mile-long (eighteen-kilometers), peanut-shaped nucleus and photographed it. Its dramatic pictures revealed a dark surface and magnificent streams or "jets" of dust and gas shooting off the surface from geyserlike vents.

Often comets, like meteoroids, can hit planets. On June 30, 1908, a piece of comet Encke entered the Earth's atmosphere and exploded in the air over a remote area of Siberia in what is now known as the Tunguska fireball. The violent thunderous explosion devastated the countryside and could be heard more than 500 miles away (see page 351). More recently, comet Shoemaker-Levy 9 broke into twenty-one pieces that hit Jupiter in 1994. Each fragment blasted massive holes in the Jovian giant's atmosphere that bested, in force, the world's total nuclear arsenal by thousands of times. It is suspected that such an occurrence, 65 million years ago by an asteroid or comet, killed more than 75 percent of all life on Earth—including the dinosaurs.

COSMOLOGY

The field of cosmology arose out of a need to understand the world around us. The modern definition of what the universe is would be: the totality of all matter, energy, and space. Cosmology seeks to explain the origin and structure of the observed universe.

Statistics:
Width of known universe (radius): approximately 17.8 billion light-years
Age of universe: 10 to 20 billion years
Age of solar system: 4.6 billion years

Before 1900: Early Chinese astronomers defined a universe of limited size. Taoists, several thousand years ago, subscribed to the concept of "empty infinite space." Early theories of an Earth-centered universe gave way to the Copernican heliocentric (Sun-centered) universe in the sixteenth century. By the late eighteenth century William Herschel endorsed the notion of an "island universe" in infinite space.

After 1900: Until Edwin Hubble's work in the early twentieth century, it was not realized that other distant galaxies existed beyond our own Milky Way galaxy. His landmark work revealed the universe as we know it today. Hubble discovered that the spectrum of light from an object moving away from an observer was redshifted (or moved over into the red part of the spectrum). Conversely, he found that objects moving toward an observer were blueshifted. Coupled with Einstein's general theory of relativity in 1915, a more accurate view of the universe began to emerge.

> *My own suspicion is that the universe is not only queerer than we suppose, but queerer than we can suppose.*
>   J. B. S. Haldane, "On Being the Right Size,"
>   *Possible Worlds and Other Essays,* 1927

Many new theories arose. Prominent among them is the steady state theory (proposed by Fred Hoyle et al.) and the big bang theory (term dubbed by George Gamow). The steady state theory puts aside all questions of beginning and end by assuming an infinite universe where matter is constantly being created. The big bang theory assumes a closed system. All matter exploded from a single primordial fireball (cosmic egg). Some believe that if this explosion was not powerful enough, then the universe will collapse in on itself (big crunch) and reexplode in 80 billion years (oscillating universe). Big bang theorists found support in redshifted galaxies and in the discovery of remnant uniform background radiation, believed to be the signature of the big bang itself.

Recent discoveries, however, have sent astronomers scrambling. The distribution of galaxies, galactic superclusters, and the uniform background radiation are all proving to be not so uniform. Additionally, not all galaxies are red shifted, as predicted by the big bang theory. Black holes, the largest as immense as 40 million suns, are being found in the centers of many galaxies. Quasars, some of the most distant and oldest members of the universe, are proving to be neither. The search for enough dark matter continues. For the big bang to work it would have to be 99 percent dark matter.

In 1994 a startling new paradox arose when studies of Cepheid Variables, a type of pulsating star whose brightness and rhythm are directly linked to its size, showed the universe to be only half as old as the oldest stars and galaxies it contains. New theories, such as NASA astronomer Marian Rudnyk's "multiple big bang theory" may supersede past theories by combining elements of past ideas to fit new observations. In a multiple big bang universe the universe would be infinite and matter would tend to clump randomly, or "bubble" (much as boiling water does), each primordial clump exploding at different times—and the matter from each would interact. Quasars would not, in this model, be driven by ravenous black holes but by black holes that have consumed so much material that they are now coughing it up.

The struggle to define the exact nature and origin of the universe has often led to new discoveries. One of the fundamental principles that evolved from many of these observations is that stars have a life cycle. They are born. They live. They die.

All stars, including our sun, are classified by type on what astronomers call the H-R (Hertzsprung-Russell) diagram. After billions of years, a typical star will run out of hydrogen and begin fusing helium and swell into an enormous red giant star. As helium runs out it will turn to heavier elements and begin collapsing into a tiny white dwarf—finally burning itself out into a cold, dark cinder. When stars die, new stars eventually form in their place. Such a fate awaits our solar system.

There are many stars both bigger and smaller than the Sun. The red giant Betelgeuse, for example, is 490 light-years from Earth and is so immense that, by volume, it is 27 million times bigger than our sun. These larger stars, such as blue or red supergiants, live much differently. Because they are so massive, gravity begins to take over as the star ages and turns to heavier, less efficient nuclear fuels. Such stars can tear themselves apart in cataclysmic asymmetrical thermonuclear explosions called supernovas that leave behind bizarre enigmatic objects. Supernovas can be detected by an enormous coincidental burst of neutrinos and can outshine their host galaxy. The famous Crab Nebula is the remnant of such an explosion. Buried within the gas-and-dust nebula is usually a neutron star, a tiny object so dense that a teaspoon of its material can easily weigh a thousand tons.

Pulsars (a type of neutron star) spin extremely fast, their beam of streaming radio energy sweeping by an observer much like the light from a lighthouse. The timing of a pulsar's spin is so regular that in 1994 the minute wobble in pulsar PSR B1257+12 (a star so small and dense that it is smaller than the size of the city of Los Angeles) resulted in the discovery of three planets around it. Because of the nature of their parent star, it is doubtful there is any life on these planets.

In 1996, a new type of pulsar that shakes was discovered. Scorpius X-1 beams X-rays that vibrate at an unexpected 1,130 times per second. The result of violent surface bursts barely the size of a throw rug, each explosion releases the equivalent of billions of nuclear weapons a second.

Other stars continue to collapse and become black holes, bizarre objects dominated by runaway gravity. Once trapped in a black hole's gravitational death grip, not even light can escape. Anything pulled within its event horizon, or edge, ultimately gets crushed down to the subatomic level and swallowed up by the singularity at the center. Einstein's theory of relativity predicted such objects. Cygnus X-1, the first black hole to be discovered, was found because it was cannibalizing its companion star HDE226868.

Increasingly, there is evidence that galaxies, including our own Milky Way, contain supermassive black holes at their center. Black holes may also drive quasars—quasi-stellar objects that shine with the brightness of a million galaxies and are considered the oldest, most-distant known objects. Quasars and Cepheid Variables are among the objects that are routinely used to determine the size and age of the universe.

Much about the larger structures in the universe still remains not fully understood. Cosmic strings, defects in the fabric of space, were created during the early evolutionary stages of the universe's development. If the "threads" discovered within the structure of our Milky Way galaxy in 1986 turn out to be such "cosmic strings," then they may provide answers to many puzzles, such as the evolution and formation of galaxies. Such discoveries may also hold clues to the nature of galactic superclusters, the viability of the existence of dark matter and missing mass, the "great wall" (a continuous sheet of galactic clusters—the largest known structure in the universe), "elephant trunks" (huge stalagmite-like towers of cold, dark gas), and other mysterious phenomena that continue to puzzle scientists.

—M.E.R.

Can we actually "know" the universe? My God, it's hard enough finding your way around in Chinatown.

Woody Allen, *Getting Even*, 1966

COMMUNICATION

TWENTIETH-CENTURY WORDS

I used to think I was poor. Then they told me I wasn't poor, I was needy. They told me it was self-defeating to think of myself as needy, I was deprived. Then they told me underprivileged was overused. I was disadvantaged. I still don't have a dime. But I have a great vocabulary.

Jules Feiffer,
cartoon in the *Village Voice*, 1965

Acid Rain (revised early 1970s) n.: Precipitation containing relatively high concentrations of acid-forming chemical pollutants released into the atmosphere from industrial emissions that are harmful to the environment. Passed from a technical term into everyday usage in the 1980s when environmental concerns became a public issue.

Aerobics (late 1960s) n., **aerobic** adj.: A form of physical, sustained exercise designed to stimulate and strengthen the heart and lungs to improve the body's utilization of oxygen. Coined by U.S. Air Force major Kenneth Cooper, who developed a fitness program for astronauts. Became a popular fitness craze in the early 1980s when it was rhythmically combined with music to create an exercise routine.

Ageism (1969) n.: Discrimination or prejudice against individuals based on their age; particularly applied to the middle-aged or elderly. Coined by Dr. Robert Butler, a specialist in geriatric medicine in Washington, D.C.

AIDS (Acquired Immunodeficiency Syndrome) (1980) n.: A disease of the immune system characterized by increased susceptibility to opportunistic infections. Caused by a retrovirus (HIV, HTLV) transmitted primarily through blood or blood products into a body via sexual contact, contaminated hypodermic needles, or transfusion. It can also be transmitted through other bodily fluids. A death from AIDS was recorded as early as 1959. The disease, which primarily manifested itself among male homosexuals, drug users, and hemophiliacs, reached epidemic proportions in the United States in 1984 and was referred to in as the scourge of the decade.

Allergy (1906) n.: An abnormal reaction or hypersensitivity of the body to a previously encountered allergen introduced by inhalation, ingestion, injection, or skin contact. Coined by Clemens von Pirquet.

Astronaut (late 1920s) n.: A person engaged in or trained for spaceflight.

Baby Boom (1940s) n.: A period reflecting a sharp increase in the birthrate, primarily exemplified by the generation of U.S. babies born after World War II up until 1965. Members of this generation, called baby-boomers, are considered so numerically significant that advertisers, businesses, and politicians specifically cater to the needs, desires, ideals, and mores of this group.

Bag Lady (c. 1972) n.: A homeless woman who lives and sleeps on city streets or in public places and carries all of her personal belongings in shopping bags. Earliest reference noted in New York City, but the phenomenon and term spread throughout the United States and United Kingdom by the mid-1980s. The term later evolved into the inclusive "bag person" and "bag people."

Barrette (1901) n.: A clasp for holding a woman's or a girl's hair in place. Taken from the French for "a little bar or rod."

Beatnik (mid-1950s) n.: A member of the beat generation that came of age after World War II who rejected or avoided social standards and conventions of the day. The writings of Jack Kerouac, Allen Ginsberg, Gregory Corso,

Lawrence Ferlinghetti, and William Burroughs illustrate the beliefs and ideologies of the group.

Bebop (mid-1940s) n.: Jazz term probably derived from the nonsense syllables of scat singing.

Bikini (1946) n.: A scanty, revealing two-piece bathing suit for women or a pair of bathing trunks for men. Coined in honor of the Marshall Islands atoll in the Pacific Ocean where atomic bomb tests were conducted in July 1946.

Bimbo (early 1920s) n.: A slang term to describe an attractive but unintelligent young woman. A derivative of the Italian word *bambino* (baby) combined with some possible influence from *dumbo*. Originally associated with women of loose morals but more recently applied to women willing to disclose particulars of their affairs with rich, famous, or socially prominent men, ruining their careers and reputations. Can also refer to a disreputable, contemptible man.

Biodegradable (1963) adj.: The spontaneous decomposition of matter through the action of

Micheline Bernardini of Paris models the first bikini on July 11, 1946. The tiny swimsuit was named in honor of Bikini Atoll, site of atomic testing ten days earlier.

biological agents, most notably bacteria, which prevents the material from becoming an environmental hazard.

Birth Control (1914) n.: Deliberate control or prevention of conception through artificial or natural means. The term was publicized by Margaret Sanger, who opened the first U.S. birth control clinic in 1916.

Black Hole (1969) n.: An astronomical term describing a theoretical massive hole in space created by the gravitational force of a star collapsing on itself. The resultant gravitational field is so intense that no electromagnetic radiation, including light, can escape.

Black Market (1931) n., **black-market** v.: A place, or the act, of illegally buying and selling goods in violation of legal price controls and rationing.

Blimp (c. 1916) n.: A small, nonrigid airship or dirigible, especially one used chiefly for observation.

Blitzkrieg (1939) n.: German for "lightning war." A warfare maneuver characterized by an overwhelming attack utilizing ground and air forces.

Blue-Collar (late 1940s) adj.: Of or pertaining to wage-earning workers who wear work clothes or other specialized clothing on the job, such as mechanics, longshoremen, and miners.

Blurb (1907) n., v.: A brief advertisement or announcement, especially a laudatory one. To advertise or praise in the manner of a blurb. Allegedly coined by artist Gelett Burgess.

Boondocks (1944) n.: A remote rural area, an uninhabited wild region overgrown with dense natural vegetation, a backwoods or backcountry area. Taken from the Tagalog *bundok*, meaning "mountain," and subsequently pluralized in English. A slang derivative is "the boonies." First used by U.S. soldiers stationed in the Philippines during World War II.

Boondoggle (late 1920s) n., v.: Work of little or no value done merely to keep or look busy; to deceive or attempt to deceive. Coined by American scoutmaster R. H. Link to describe a product of simple manual skill made typically by a camper or a scout.

Bra (mid-1930s) n.: An abbreviation of *brassiere*, a woman's undergarment for supporting the breasts.

Brainwashing (1950) n.: Any method of controlled systematic indoctrination based on repetition or confusion, used to change attitudes or alter beliefs. Originated in totalitarian countries, especially through the use of torture, drugs, or psychological-stress techniques.

Briefcase (1926) n.: A flat, rectangular case with a handle, often of leather, for carrying books, papers, etc.

Brinkmanship (1956) n.: The technique or practice of maneuvering a dangerous situation to the limits of tolerance or safety in order to secure the greatest advantage.

Broadcast (1922) n., v.: A program transmitted from a radio or television station. To transmit a program from a radio or television station.

Bromide (1910) n.: A person whose thoughts and conversation are conventional and commonplace. Also, a commonplace saying or trite remark.

Bustier (late 1970s) n.: Derived from the French for "bodice." A woman's close-fitting, sleeveless, often strapless top, often elasticized, usually having boning or facing to give it shape. Popularized by the rock star Madonna in the early 1980s.

Call Girl (mid-1930s) n.: A female prostitute with whom an appointment can be made by telephone, or who is available to be called on at a brothel.

Camcorder (1982) n.: A portable videotape camera with built-in synchronized sound-recording capabilities that can produce recorded videocassettes, and in some cases can also play them back. Camera and video recorder. Prototypes were initially developed by Japanese companies in the early 1980s.

Camouflage (1917) n., adj., v.: The act, means, or result of obscuring or concealing an object, normally associated with the military as a device or stratagem to deceive an enemy, as by painting or screening objects so that they are lost to view in the background, or by making up objects that have from a distance the appearance of fortifications, guns, roads, etc. Also clothing and fabric made with a mottled design, usually in shades of green and brown. Derived from the French camoufler, meaning "to disguise," which is related to camoflet, meaning "smoke blown in someone's face as a practical joke."

Canned Laughter (1952) n.: A separate sound track of prerecorded laughter that is dubbed onto radio or television shows to create the impression of a live audience, or to enhance or feign audience responses. Also known as a laugh track.

Car Pool (early 1940s) n., **carpool** v.: An arrangement among a group of automobile owners by which each in turn drives the others or their children to and from a designated place.

Cassette (1959) n.: A small cartridge containing magnetic tape used for recording or playing back audio or video performances. More recent developments contain programs for computer games.

CAT Scan (mid-1970s) n.: A noninvasive medical diagnostic examination using computerized axial tomography, which creates a series of cross-sectional X-ray images of the whole body or any given area or part. The technique was developed by two researchers working independently of each other—Godfrey Hounsfield, of EMI's Central Research Laboratories in Great Britain, and Allan Cormack, a physics professor at Tufts University. CAT scanning is instrumental in reducing the need of exploratory surgery.

Catch-22 (1961) n.: A phrase and concept based on American novelist Joseph Heller's eponymous book, exemplifying a frustrating situation in which one is trapped by contradictory regulations or conditions. Any illogical or paradoxical problem or situation.

CD-ROM (1988) n.: An abbreviation for "compact disc read-only memory." A compact disc that contains or can have voluminous amounts of digitized read-only data recorded on it, including text, images, and sound.

Chain Reaction (1926) n.: A series of events in which each event is the result of the one preceding and the cause of the one following. In physics, a self-sustaining reaction in which the fission of nuclei of one generation produces particles that cause the fission of at least an equal number of nuclei of the succeeding generation.

Chairlift (late 1930s) n.: A motor-driven cable device featuring suspended chairs used to convey passengers up the side of a slope, most notably for skiing.

Charisma (1947) n.: Derived from the Greek word meaning "the gift of grace." A strong personal appeal, quality, or magnetism that gives an individual influence or authority over large numbers of people. It can contain a sexual element but more often is derived from an individual's power, abilities, office, function, or position.

Cheeseburger (mid-1930s) n.: A hamburger cooked with a slice of cheese on top of it.

Child Abuse (1972) n.: The deliberate maltreatment of children by physical, sexual, psychological, or verbal abuse, perpetrated by an adult.

Cineplex (1987) n.: A cinema complex that offers a choice of several movie screens and auditoriums.

Clone (altered early 1970s) n., v.: A person or thing that duplicates, imitates, or closely resembles another in appearance, function, performance, or style. To produce a copy or imitation.

Collage (1919) n., v.: A technique of composing a work of art by pasting various materials (newspaper clippings, parts of photographs, theater tickets, fabric, wallpaper, etc.) that are not normally associated with each other onto a single surface; or a film that presents a series of seemingly unrelated scenes or images or shifts from one scene or image to another suddenly and without transition. Taken from the French *colle*, meaning "paste," "glue."

Colorize (altered early 1980s) v.: To add color to a black-and-white film using a computerized program called a Colorizer. The process generated considerable controversy in the 1980s, prompting critics to argue that classic black-and-white films are works of art not to be tampered with. The Colorizer was registered as a trademark in the mid-1980s.

Comic Book (1940s) n.: A magazine featuring one or more comic strips, sometimes in a serialized format.

Comic Strip (c. 1920) n.: A sequence of drawings, either in color or black and white, relating a comic incident, adventure, or mystery story, etc., often serialized, typically having dialogue printed in balloons, and usually printed as a horizontal strip in daily newspapers and in an uninterrupted block or longer sequence of such strips in Sunday newspapers and in comic books.

Compact Disc (CD) (1980) n.: An optical disk, approximately 5 inches in diameter, containing digitally encoded data or music, which is scanned by a laser beam, decoded, and transmitted to a playback system, computer monitor, or television set. CD technology was invented by Philips for audio recording in the late 1970s and produces a finer sound quality than conventional phonograph records.

Concentration Camp (1900) n.: A guarded compound for the detention or imprisonment of aliens, members of ethnic minorities, political opponents, etc., especially any of the camps established by the Nazis prior to and during World War II for the confinement and persecution of prisoners.

Condo (1962) n.: An abbreviation of *condominium*. An apartment house, office building, or other multiple-unit complex, the units of which are individually owned, each owner receiving a recordable deed to the individual unit purchased, including the right to sell, mortgage, etc., that unit, but sharing in joint ownership any common grounds, passageways, etc.

Cosmic Ray (1915) n.: A physics term defining radiation of high penetrating power that originates in outer space and consists partly of high-energy atomic nuclei. Coined by U.S. physicist Robert Millikan.

Couch Potato (1976) n.: Slang terminology for a person whose leisure time is spent passively watching television or videos. Coined by Californian Tom Iacino after seeing a Robert Armstrong cartoon depicting a "boob tuber" (a person who watches inordinate amounts of TV) drawn as a potato.

Counterculture (late 1950s) n.: The culture and lifestyle of people, particularly the young, who reject or oppose the dominant values and behavior of conventional society. Most notably applied to the hippie generation in the United States in the late 1960s and popularized by the concept Theodore Roszak put forth in his 1969 book *The Making of a Counter-Culture*.

Counterinsurgency (1962) n., adj.: A program or an act of combating guerrilla warfare and subversion, or pertaining to or designed for those purposes.

Crack (1988) n.: Slang for purified, potent crystalline pellets of cocaine that are heated and smoked through a small glass pipe. Its potency and highly addictive quality frequently force its users to a life of crime to support their habit. The word has been compounded to form such terms as *crack head* (a crack user) and *crack house* (a place where crack is sold).

Crooner (1930s) n.: A person who sings in an evenly modulated, slightly exaggerated manner with a soft and soothing voice.

Cryonics (1962) n.: The process of deep-freezing human bodies immediately after death for preservation and possible revival in the future. Also known as cryopreservation.

Cursor (altered 1950s) n.: A distinctive, movable symbol on a computer screen that indicates where the next character will appear or where the next action will take effect, controlled by the movement of a mouse or keyboard commands. Derived from the Latin for "runner." First applied to computer technology by John Lentz of IBM.

Cybernetics (1948) n.: A term introduced by Norbert Wiener to describe the study of human control functions and of mechanical and electronic systems designed to replace them, involving the application of statistical mechanics to communication engineering.

Cyberspace (1984) n.: The world of data created and shared by the millions of computers and people connected by online communications. The term was created by William Gibson in his novel *Neuromancer*.

Database (c. 1970) n., adj.: Any comprehensive collection of information organized for convenient access, generally applied to the inputting, sorting, and retrieval of information managed by a computer software package.

Deniability (altered 1973) n.: The ability to deny something, as knowledge of or connection with an illegal or improper activity. Most notably and commonly associated with political scandals such as Watergate (1972–74) and the Iran-Contra affair (1986). In the political sense, the term seems to have originated in CIA jargon, where it was sometimes used in the phrase "plausible deniability," but its popularization is attributed to an article written by Shana Alexander for *Newsweek* magazine commenting on the Watergate scandal.

Desegregate (1950s) v.: To eliminate racial segregation (as in schools or other public or common arenas).

Desertification (mid-1970s) n.: An ecological term describing the process of rapid depletion of plant life and loss of topsoil, usually caused by a combination of drought and the over-exploitation of grasses and other vegetation by people. Recognized as a global environmental problem in the mid-1980s, but more popularly championed as an environmental cause by the Green movement in the late 1980s. Also known as desertization.

Détente (c. 1908) n.: An easing of tensions achieved through negotiations or agreements. Commonly applied to political relations between countries, where it gained its specific modern use by such diplomats as Henry Kissinger. From the French word meaning "relaxation of tension."

Disco (late 1960s) n., adj., v.: A style of popular music for dancing, recorded with complex electronic instrumentation, featuring simple, repetitive lyrics accentuated by a heavy, pulsat-

ing, rhythmic beat. An abbreviation of *disco-theque*, a nightclub for dancing to live or recorded music and often featuring sophisticated sound systems, elaborate lighting, and other effects.

Disinformation (1966) n.: The deliberate dissemination of inaccurate, distorted, or false information to confuse and undermine the business, military, or espionage operations of one's opponents.

Docudrama (1960) n.: A dramatized documentary designed to inform and entertain television audiences; often presented in such a style to intensify the sense of authenticity. Gained wide popularity as a fashionable form of entertainment in the late 1970s.

Documentary (1914) n.: A film, radio, or television program based on or re-creating an actual event, era, life story, etc., that purports to be factually accurate and contains no fictional elements. The term was first used by director Edward Sheriff but did not catch on until 1926 when John Grierson used it in a review of Robert Flaherty's *Moana*.

Downsize (1970s) v., adj.: To design or manufacture a smaller version or type; or to reduce in number or cutback, especially of a workforce.

Drive-By (c. 1986) n., adj.: A criminal activity, usually a shooting, perpetrated from a moving vehicle (drive-by shooting). Associated with teenage gang activities and initiation rites, but originally witnessed as gangster activity associated with organized crime in the 1920s and 1930s.

Duplex (1920s) n.: A house or apartment building containing two separate entrances and living quarters for its occupants.

Ecology (altered 1960s) n.: The branch of biology dealing with the relations and interactions between organisms and their environment. More recently transformed from a scientific study to a political cause advocating conservation of the environment, as embodied by the ecology movement of the 1970s. Aldous Huxley predicted a concern with and a concentrated study of the subject in his paper "The Politics of Ecology" in 1963.

Electronics (1910) n.: The science dealing with the development and application of devices and systems involving the flow of electrons in a vacuum, in gaseous media, and in semiconductors.

Espresso (1940s) n.: A strong coffee prepared by forcing live steam under pressure, or boiling water, through ground dark-roast coffee beans.

Fallout (late 1940s) n.: An unexpected or incidental effect, outcome, or product accompanying an activity, statement, or decision. Originally applied to the radioactive refuse of a nuclear bomb explosion. In broader terms, can incorporate physical, psychological, or emotional trauma, etc.

Fax (early 1940s) n., v.: Abbreviation of facsimile. Facsimile telegraphy is a system that allows documents to be scanned, digitized, and transmitted to remote destinations using a telephone network. The first successful transmission took place in 1925 and its subsequent applications were utilized by newspaper publishers and the military in World War II.

Fiberglass (late 1930s) n.: A material consisting of extremely fine filaments of glass that are combined in yarn and woven into fabrics, used in masses as a thermal and acoustical insulator, or embedded in various resins to make boat hulls, fishing rods, etc.

Floozy (c. 1911) n.: Slang terminology used to describe a gaudily dressed woman of questionable morals, especially a prostitute.

Fosbury Flop (1969) n.: Sports term describing a style of high jumping in which the jumper approaches the bar backward and stretches out faceup, landing on his or her back. Originated by the U.S. jumper Dick Fosbury, winner of the Olympic gold medal in 1968.

Freeway (late 1920s) n.: A toll-free express highway with no intersections, usually having traffic routed on and off by means of a cloverleaf.

Gaffe (1909) n.: A social blunder or faux pas. Taken from a specialized use of the French word *gaffe*, signifying an iron hook with a handle used to land a large fish.

Gas Station (late 1910s) n.: A place equipped for servicing automobiles by selling gasoline, oil, and auto parts, and by making repairs. Also known as a service station.

Gay (altered early 1900s) n., adj.: A homosexual; indicating or supporting homosexual interests or issues. Adjectival use noted as early as the turn of the century, with more common usage applied during World War II, where it was derived from the slang term *geycats*. Wider usage began in the early 1970s, where it predominantly described male homosexuals.

Genocide (1940s) n.: The deliberate and systematic extermination of a national, racial, political, or cultural group. Originally used to describe the atrocities perpetrated by the Nazis against the Jews and Gypsies during World War II.

Gentrification (late 1960s) n.: The buying and renovation of property for commercial and residential use in deteriorated urban neighborhoods by upper- or middle-income persons, thus improving property values but often displacing low-income families and small businesses. First used by town planners and became a notable trend through the 1980s.

Gigolo (1922) n.: A man living off the earnings or gifts of a woman, especially a younger man supported by an older woman in return for his sexual favors and companionship, or a male professional dancing partner or escort. The masculine equivalent of the French word *gigolette*, meaning female prostitute or a woman who frequents public dance halls. Both terms were derived from the Middle French word *giguer*, meaning "to frolic."

Glitch (1962) n., v.: Slang terminology describing a defect, malfunction, error, or problem. Possibly derived from the Yiddish *glitsh* meaning "a slip." First used by U.S. space programmers to describe unpredictable behavior from electronic instruments or complete crashes of computer systems.

Gobbledygook (1940s) n.: Language characterized by circumlocution and jargon, usually difficult to understand. Also known as gibberish, double-talk, mumbo jumbo.

Gofer (1960s) n.: A corruption of *go for*; originally identified with persons at television, film, and radio studios, or in theaters or record companies, who were solely employed to run errands, to "go for."

Googol (1938) n.: The number 1 followed by 100 zeros. It was coined by nine-year-old Milton Sirotta and made popular in 1940 by his uncle, mathematician Edward Kasner, in *Mathematics and the Imagination*. A googolplex is a googol number of googols.

Greenhouse Effect (1920s) n.: An atmospheric heating phenomenon caused by shortwave solar radiation being readily transmitted inward through the earth's atmosphere but longer-wavelength heat radiation being less readily transmitted outward because of increases in carbon dioxide, contributing to global warming.

Gridlock (late 1970s) n., adj., v.: A complete and extended stoppage of traffic that is interlocked at a road junction and cannot move in any direction; to be incapable of any movement. Any situation in which nothing can move or proceed in any direction.

Groupie (late 1960s) n.: An ardent fan of a celebrity or of a particular activity, usually a female teenager. Most notably applied to persons who follow rock musicians and groups on tour attempting to gain personal access to them. The word gained universal currency when *Rolling Stone* magazine ran an entire "groupie" issue in early 1969.

Guesstimate (1920s) n., v.: A rough estimate; to estimate without substantial basis in facts or statistics. A combination of *guess* and *estimate*.

Gung Ho (1942) adj.: Wholeheartedly enthusiastic, eager, loyal, zealous. Introduced as a training slogan by U.S. marine officer Evans F. Carlson during World War II. Derived from the Chinese word *gonghe*, meaning "work together," which is shortened from *Zhongguo Gongye Hezuo She*, the name of the Chinese Industrial Cooperative Society.

Hacker (1960) n.: A person who enjoys computing for its own sake rather than for its applications. A microcomputer enthusiast who attempts to gain unauthorized access to proprietary computer systems.

Heavy Metal (1964) n., adj.: A style of loud, vigorous rock music characterized by the use of heavily amplified instruments, a strong (usually fast) beat, intense or spectacular performance, and often a clashing harsh musical style. A later development of "hard" rock music.

High Five (1966) n., v.: A gesture of greeting, good-fellowship, or triumph in which one person slaps the upraised palm of the hand against that of another, often exhibited at sporting events by players and spectators. University of Louisville basketball player Derek Smith claimed to have coined the phrase. Formed by compounding *five* (as in fingers) with *high* (over the head).

Hip-Hop (late 1970s) n., adj., v.: A street subculture that originated in New York City that combines rap music, break dancing, and graffiti art with distinctive codes of dress and speech. Formed by combining *hip* (cool) with *hop* (dance), and popularly adopted after disc jockey and rapper Lovebug Starsky formed the chant "To the hip hop, hip hop, don't stop that body rock."

Hippie or **Hippy** (1966) n.: A member of the late 1960s counterculture who sought spontaneity, direct personal relations expressing love, and expanded consciousness, often expressed externally in the wearing of casual, folksy clothing (used garments, beads, headbands, sandals, flowers, etc.). Descended directly from the word *hip*, a black coinage of the 1930s.

Homeboy (late 1960s) n.: Slang term for close friend or fellow gang member. The female equivalent is *home girl*. A generic pluralization is *homies*.

Honcho (late 1940s) n., v.: Derived from the Japanese *hancho* (squad leader). A boss, leader, chief, or senior figure. To organize, supervise, or be the leader of any major project or organization.

Hormone (1905) n.: Any of various internally secreted compounds, formed in endocrine glands, that affect the functions of specific receptive organs or tissues when transported to them by the body fluid, such as insulin, thyroxin, and estrogen. Coined by William Bayless and Ernest Starling.

Hot Rod (early 1940s) n., v.: Slang term for an automobile specially built or altered for fast acceleration and increased speed; to drive very fast.

Humongous (late 1960s) adj.: A slang term used to describe something extraordinarily large. Considered a combination of *huge* and *monstrous*.

Hunk (altered 1940s) n.: A slang term used to describe a sexually attractive, ruggedly masculine young male with a well-developed physique. Popularized in tabloid journalism in the 1980s in response to gender-derogatory words used to describe women.

Hydroponics (1929) n.: The cultivation of plants by placing the roots in liquid nutrient solutions rather than in soil; soilless growth of plants.

Hype (altered 1969) n., v.: To intensify or create interest in via advertising, promotion, or publicity by ingenious, flamboyant, questionable, or exaggerated claims, methods, etc. An abbreviation of *hyperbole*. Also derived from *hypodermic* (needle) (to be hyped up: high on drugs) and *hype* as the giving of short change, as in any form of confidence trick or deception.

Icon (altered 1967) n.: In computer parlance, a small symbolic graphic featured on a computer screen representing an application or function, used to facilitate the running of a program. A development in computer manufacturing to make computers more user-friendly.

Infomercial (early 1980s) n.: A television or video commercial presented in the form of a short, informative documentary. A combination of "informational" and "commercial." Usually featuring celebrity spokespersons and entrepreneurs.

Iron Curtain (1940s) n.: A barrier to understanding and the exchange of information and ideas created by ideological, political, and military hostility of one country toward another, exemplified by the Soviet Union and its allies. Used by Winston Churchill in 1946 to describe the line of demarcation between Western Europe and the Soviet zone of influence.

Isotope (1913) n.: A chemical term describing any of two or more forms of a chemical element, having the same number of protons in the nucleus, or the same atomic number, but having different numbers of neutrons in the nucleus, or different atomic weights. There are 275 isotopes of the eighty-one stable elements, in addition to more than 800 radioactive isotopes. Coined by English chemist Frederick Soddy.

Jacuzzi (1966) n.: A trademark brand name for a whirlpool bath device and related products.

Jaywalk (1917) v.: To cross a street at a place other than a regular crossing or in a heedless manner, as diagonally or against a traffic light.

Jazz (1909) n., adj., v.: Music originating in New Orleans and subsequently developing through various increasingly complex styles, generally marked by intricate, propulsive rhythms, polyphonic ensemble playing, improvisatory, virtuosic solos, melodic freedom, and a harmonic idiom ranging from simple diatonicism through chromaticism to atonality. To excite, enliven, or accelerate. Sometimes believed to be a derivation of the vulgar Creole word meaning "to copulate," or from the black patois meaning "to excite."

Jeep (1941) n.: A trademark name for a small, rugged military motor vehicle having four-wheel drive and a quarter-ton capacity. An alteration of the abbreviation *G.P.V.* (general purpose vehicle). Also, the name of Eugene the Jeep, an animal featured in the Popeye comic strip.

Jet Lag (1969) n., adj.: A temporary disruption of the body's normal biological rhythms resulting from high-speed air travel through several time zones, causing exhaustion and disorientation.

Jet Set (mid-1950s) n., adj.: Wealthy persons of a fashionable social set who travel frequently by jetliner to parties, resorts, and social functions seeking a succession of expensive pleasures.

Jogging (1948) n.: A popular form of exercise in which participants run at a leisurely gentle pace, physically exerting themselves between running and walking.

Jukebox (1906) n.: A coin-operated phonograph, typically in a gaudy, illuminated cabinet, having a variety of records that can be selected by push button.

Junk Bond (mid-1970s) n.: A financial term describing any corporate bond with a low rating and a high yield, often involving high risk, issued by a company seeking to raise a large amount of capital quickly. Junk is a dismissive reference to rubbish, something worthless. Debt incurred through the issuing of junk bonds is known as junk debt.

Junk Food (mid-1970s) n.: Any food containing a high caloric content but possessing little nutritional value, such as potato chips, candies, and fast food.

Junk Mail (late 1950s) n.: Unsolicited commercial mail, usually of an advertising nature.

Kamikaze (1945) n., adj.: A member of a special corps in the Japanese air force during World War II charged with the intentionally suicidal mission of crashing an aircraft laden with explosives into an enemy target, especially American or Allied warships. More recently used to describe a person or thing that behaves in a wildly reckless or destructive manner. Taken from the Japanese word meaning "divine wind."

Karate (1955) n.: A style of martial art developed in Japan in which practitioners defend themselves without the use of weapons by striking sensitive areas on an attacker's body with the hands, elbows, feet, or knees. Taken from the Japanese word meaning "empty hand."

Kinky (1959) adj.: Slang term describing unconventional, bizarre, or eccentric preferences or behavior, usually with a sexual overtone. The description gained popularity with the television series *The Avengers*, whose female star, Honor Blackman, was regularly outfitted in "kinky" costumes. Her musical collaboration with her costar, Patrick Macnee, on the pop song "Kinky Boots" further propelled widespread use of the term.

Landfill (1970s) n.: Land that is built up from deposits of solid refuse in layers covered by soil to create (in some instances) more usable land.

Laptop (early 1980s) n., adj.: A portable, lightweight, battery-operated microcomputer small enough to balance on a user's lap. First marketed in the United States in the early 1980s.

Laser (1960) n.: An acronym of light(wave) amplification by stimulated emission of radiation. A device that produces a nearly parallel, nearly monochromatic, coherent beam of light by exciting atoms to a higher energy level and causing them to radiate their energy in phase.

Laugh Track (c. 1962) n.: See Canned Laughter.

Leisure Suit (1970s) n.: A man's casual suit, consisting of trousers and a matching jacket styled like a shirt, often made in pastel colors and often from synthetic materials.

Lifestyle (1929) n., adj.: The habits, attitudes, tastes, moral standards, economic level, etc., that together constitute the mode of living of an individual or group. A quality advertisers and marketers attempted to identify and cater to in merchandising campaigns during the 1980s.

Liposuction (early 1980s) n.: A cosmetic surgical procedure to withdraw excess fat from local areas under the skin by means of a small incision and vacuum suctioning through a tube or cannula. The technique was developed to remove unwanted fat that is diet and exercise resistant or in people who are diet and exercise resistant.

Lowbrow (c. 1906) n., adj.: A person who is uneducated or uninterested or uninvolved in intellectual activities or pursuits; of, pertaining to, or proper to a lowbrow.

Lyme Disease (1975) n.: A pathological term used to describe an acute inflammatory disease caused by a tick-borne spirochete, *Borrelia burgdorferi*, characterized by recurrent episodes of decreasing severity in which joint swelling, fever, and rash occur, sometimes with cardiac or nervous system complications. Taken from the name of the town (Lyme) in Connecticut where the first outbreak occurred.

Macho (altered late 1960s) n., adj.: Taken from the Spanish meaning "masculine." Having or characterizing qualities considered manly or virile, especially when manifested in an aggressive, assertive, self-conscious, or dominating way. Used by feminists to criticize male posturing.

Magic Realism (1943) n.: A style of painting and literature in which fantastic or imaginary and often unsettling images or events are depicted in a sharply detailed, realistic manner. Taken from the German *magischer Realismus*, originally coined by Franz Roh in 1925. Exemplified by the works of Charles Shuler, Edward Hopper, Jorge Luis Borges, Gabriel García Marquez, Günter Grass, Italo Calvino, and Salman Rushdie.

Mammogram (1930s) n.: An X-ray photograph of a breast used for the detection of tumors.

Marginalize (mid-1970s) v.: To place in a position of marginal importance, influence, or

power. Became a social buzzword of the 1980s taken up by special-interest groups to focus public attention on their causes.

Media (1920s) n., adj.: A collective noun covering a variety of forms of communication: print, radio, and television.

Meltdown (1955) n.: The melting of a significant portion of a nuclear-reactor core resulting from inadequate cooling of the fuel elements. A condition that could lead to the escape of radiation, or cause a nuclear explosion. Also applied to a disastrous and uncontrolled event with far-reaching repercussions. Per nuclear physics, associated with the Three Mile Island incident and Chernobyl accident, and in the financial sense applied to the U.S. stock market crash of October 1987.

Meter Maid (1950s) n.: A female police or traffic-control officer responsible for issuing tickets for parking violations, in some cases to vehicles whose time allotment has expired on coin-operated parking meters.

Microwave (1931) n., adj., v.: An electromagnetic wave of extremely high frequency that can be applied to many uses, most commonly to cooking in a microwave oven.

Minimalism (1965) n.: A major art movement, first described by Robert Wolheim, that promoted clarity and simplicity while rejecting the ornamentation and emotional self-expressionism of abstract expressionism. Its influence later extended to architecture, design, dance, theater, and music.

Miniseries (1973) n.: A television program or film broadcast in parts as a dramatization of a literary work or treating a particular theme.

Miniskirt (1965) n., adj.: A very short skirt or dress ending several inches above the knee. Compounded from *miniature* and *skirt*.

Monetarism (1963) n.: An economic theory, epitomized by the teachings of Milton Freeman and his colleagues of the "Chicago school" of economists, purporting that changes in the money supply determine the direction of a nation's economy, thus affecting inflation, interest rates, and unemployment. It directly opposes Keynesian economic theory.

Moonlight (altered 1957) v.: To work at an additional job after one's regular, full-time employment, as at night.

Motel (1925) n.: A combination of *motor* and *hotel*. A hotel providing travelers with lodging and free parking facilities, typically a roadside hotel having rooms adjacent to an outside parking area, or an urban hotel offering parking within the building.

Ms. (1952) n.: A title of respect prefixed to a woman's name that does not denote her marital status. Popularized by the feminist movement of the 1970s and the title of one of the movement's leading magazines.

Nacho (late 1940s) n.: A snack or appetizer consisting of tortilla chips topped with cheese, jalapeño peppers, and spices, then broiled. The Tex-Mex dish is credited to Ignacio Anaya ("Nacho" being a diminutive form of Ignacio), a Mexican chef who worked in the border area of Piedras Negras. Its pluralization may have been a misinterpretation of the possessive "Nacho's." The word may also be borrowed from the Mexican-Spanish adjective meaning "flat-nosed."

Nanosecond (1959) n.: One-billionth of a second.

Nerd (1950) n: A slang term describing a stupid, irritating, ineffectual, or unattractive person, or an intelligent but single-minded individual obsessed with a nonsocial hobby or pursuit.

Neutrino (1933) n.: Physics term describing any of the massless or nearly massless electrically neutral leptons. There is a distinct kind of neutrino associated with each of the massive leptons. Coined by physicist Enrico Fermi.

Ninja (1964) n., adj.: A Japanese warrior trained in ninjutsu, the martial art of stealth and invisibility, which was developed in feudal times in Japan for covert purposes ranging from espionage to sabotage and assassination. This segment of martial arts gained popularity in the late 1980s owing to the commercial success of the children's television series *Teenage Mutant Ninja Turtles*. From the Japanese word formed from nin, meaning "stealth" or "to endure," and ja, meaning "person."

Nylon (1938) n.: Any of a class of thermoplastic polyamides capable of extrusion when molten into fibers, sheets, etc., of extreme toughness, strength, and elasticity, synthesized by the interaction of a dicarboxylic acid with a diamine, used especially for yarns, fabrics, brush bristles, and ladies' stockings. Coined as a generic by the DuPont Chemical Company.

Outreach (c. 1968) n., adj.: The deliberate act of extending government or social services and benefits to a wider section of the population, particularly in those areas where disinterest or underuse of such programs was previously noted.

Outtake (c. 1960) n.: A segment of film or videotape edited out of the final version because of a technical error.

Ozone Layer (1951) n.: Meteorological term describing the layer of the upper atmosphere where most atmospheric ozone is concentrated, located between eight and forty miles above the earth's surface, with a maximum ozone concentration occurring at an altitude of about twelve miles. Also known as the ozone shield or ozonosphere, it protects the earth from the effects of excessive ultraviolet radiation.

Page-Turner (1974) n.: A book, often a bestseller, that is so exciting or gripping that the reader is compelled to read it very rapidly.

Palimony (1978) n.: A form of alimony awarded to one of the partners in a romantic relationship after the breakup of that relationship following a long period of living together unmarried. The term was coined when film star Lee Marvin was sued by his ex-girlfriend Michelle Triola Marvin, who claimed that she had abandoned her own career to support him.

Pantyhose (1960s) n.: A one-piece, skintight garment worn by women, combining panties and stockings.

Paparazzo (pl. **Paparazzi**) (1968) n.: A freelance photographer who specializes in taking candid pictures of celebrities to be sold for publication. Taken from the Italian surname of a character in Federico Fellini's film *La Dolce Vita* (1959), after the name of a hotel keeper in George Gissing's novel *By the Ionian Sea* (1901), read by Fellini at the time the movie was being filmed.

Paramedic (mid-1950s) n., adj.: A person who is trained to assist a physician or to give first aid or other health care in the absence of a physician, often as part of a police, rescue, or firefighting squad, para meaning similar to but not an exact copy. In military parlance, a doctor (medic) in the paratroops who parachutes into remote areas to give medical care.

Paranoid (c. 1904) n., adj.: Of, like, or suffering from paranoia (1805–15), a mental disorder characterized by systematized delusions and the projection of personal conflicts that are ascribed to the supposed hostility of others, sometimes progressing to disturbances of consciousness and aggressive acts believed to be performed in self-defense or as a mission.

Phony (1900) n., adj.: Not real or genuine; fake, counterfeit, false; insincere, deceitful, affected, pretentious. A person or thing possessing these qualities. Derived from the Irish Gaelic *fawney*, a slang term for "finger ring," referring to a confidence game in which a brass ring is sold as a gold one.

Photo Opportunity (1976) n.: In media jargon, a brief, organized, usually carefully staged opportunity for the media to take photographs of a public, political, or celebrity figure. It allows for the encapsulation of an event destined to make an impact on newspaper front pages or on television. Often abbreviated as "photo op."

Plasma (1900) n.: Anatomical and physiological term describing the liquid part of blood or lymph, as distinguished from the suspended elements. Coined by U.S. chemist Irving Langmuir when he was nineteen years old.

Plea Bargain (1969) n., v.: A process whereby a defendant and/or his lawyer bargain with the court to plead guilty to a lesser charge rather than risk conviction for a graver crime, in order to avoid a protracted trial or in exchange for the defendant's cooperation as a witness.

Pooper-Scooper (1972) n., adj.: A small shovel or scooping device specifically designed to clean up pet excrement from streets, sidewalks, or other public places. Of or pertaining to laws, city ordinances, etc., that require a person to use a pooper-scooper.

Premenstrual Syndrome (1980s) n.: Also known as PMS. A pathological description of a complex of physical and emotional changes, including depression, irritability, appetite change, bloating and water retention, breast soreness, and changes in muscular coordination, one or more of which may be experienced by a woman in the several days prior to the onset of her menstrual flow.

Prequel (1973) n.: A literary, dramatic, or film work that prefigures a later work by portraying the same characters at a younger age. Developed after the success of the original work that created the characters' popularity. A prequel may also be the only means of capitalizing on a success where the creator has unwittingly killed off the protagonist in the original story. The word was created by combining pre (meaning previously) with (se)quel.

Privatize (1940s) v.: To transfer from government or public control or ownership to private enterprise.

Psychedelic (1956) adj.: Of or noting a mental state characterized by a profound sense of intensified sensory perception, sometimes accompanied by severe perceptual distortion and hallucinations and by extreme feelings of either euphoria or despair. Coined by Humphrey Osmond, who along with Aldous Huxley was among the first nonmedical experimenters to use hallucinogenic drugs such as LSD and to experience their mind-expanding effects. The term is derived from two Greek words: psyche (mind) and delos (manifest, evident).

Psychoanalysis (c. 1906) n.: A systematic structure of theories concerning the relation of conscious and unconscious psychological processes; a technical procedure for investigating unconscious mental processes and for treating psychoneuroses.

Pulsar (1968) n.: An astronomical term describing one of several hundred known celestial objects, generally believed to be rapidly rotating neutron stars that emit pulses of radiation with a high degree of regularity. A contraction of pulsating star.

Punk Rock (late 1960s) n., adj.: A form of rock and roll music, which peaked in the late 1970s, characterized by loud, assaultive music and abusive or violent protest lyrics. Punk rockers, performers and followers of this type of music, were distinguished by extremes of dress (ripped clothes and harshly spiked hair) and socially defiant behavior.

Put-Down (1962) n.: A disparaging, belittling, or snubbing remark or act intended to humiliate or embarrass someone.

Quark (1961) n.: A physics term proposing that all subatomic particles are composed of combinations of fundamental particles known as quarks, which are distinguished by flavors (up, down, strange, charm, bottom or beauty, and top or truth) and colors (red, blue, and green). U.S. (Cal Tech) physicist Murray Gell-Mann coined the word after reading James Joyce's novel Finnegans Wake, which mentions "E quark croak," "G Quark curd," and "Three quarks for Master Mark." Other theories claim that there may be as many as eighteen quarks altogether.

Quasar (1964) n.: Astronomical term describing any one of over a thousand known extragalactic objects, starlike in appearance and having spectra with characteristically large redshifts, that are thought to be the most distant and most luminous objects in the universe.

Quirk (c. 1960) n.: An unpredictable, eccentric, or bizarre action, behavior, mannerism, or personality.

Radar (1940s) n.: An acronym for radio detecting and ranging. An electronic term to describe a device for determining the presence and location of an object by measuring the time for the echo of a radio wave to return from it and the direction from which it returns.

Rap Music (1970s) n.: A style of popular music in which an insistent, recurring beat provides the background and counterpoint for rapid, slangy, sometimes improvised, and often boastful rhyming patter glibly intoned by a vocalist or vocalists.

Raunchy (altered c. 1967) adj.: This word's meaning was expanded to include sexual overtones such as sexy, provocative, lecherous, vulgar, smutty, crude, and obscene.

Rayon (1920s) n.: A regenerated, semisynthetic textile filament made from cellulose, cotton linters, or wood chips by treating these with caustic soda and carbon disulfide and passing the resultant viscose solution through spinnerettes.

Roadie (c. 1969) n.: A slang term used to describe a member of a road crew for a traveling group of musicians or other entertainers, whose work includes maintaining and setting up performance equipment. A combination of road (as in "on the road") with ie (analogous to "groupie").

Robot (1923) n.: A machine that resembles a human and does mechanical, routine tasks on command. Derived from the Czech word robota, meaning "work," "toil," "compulsory labor," and robotnik, meaning "a peasant owing such labor." Coined by Karel Capek in his 1921 play R. U. R. (which stands for Rossum's Universal Robots).

Rock and Roll (1950s) n., adj., v.: A style of popular music that derives in part from blues and folk music and is marked by a heavily accented beat and a simple, repetitive phrase structure; of or pertaining to this music; to dance to or play this music.

Salesclerk (1920s) n.: A person who sells goods in a store.

Scam (c. 1963) n., v.: A confidence game or other fraudulent scheme designed to make a quick profit, to cheat, swindle, or defraud by use of a scam.

Scuba (early 1950s) n., v.: Acronym for self-contained underwater breathing apparatus. A portable breathing device for free-swimming divers, consisting of a mouthpiece joined by hoses to one or two tanks of compressed air that are strapped on the back. To dive with such a device.

Serial Killer (1960s) n.: A multiple murderer who kills a series of victims (usually of a similar type and using a similar method) over an extended period of time.

Sexism (c. 1965) n.: Attitudes and behavior manifested in discrimination, prejudice, or devaluation against a person, usually a woman, based on traditional stereotypes of sexual roles.

Significant Other (1950s) n.: A sociological term to describe a spouse or cohabiting lover, or any other individual who greatly influences one's behavior and self-esteem.

Simulcast (1940s) n., v.: A program broadcast simultaneously on radio and television, or on more than one channel or station, or in several languages, or from a live event. A combination of simultaneous broadcast.

Sitcom (1964) n.: A comedy drama, especially a television series made up of distinct episodes about the same group of characters. A contraction of situation comedy.

Sit-In (1960) n.: An organized passive public protest where the demonstrators occupy and refuse to leave the premises.

Skateboard (1964) n., v.: A sport and recreational device consisting of a short, oblong board made of various materials mounted on four rollerskate-type wheels on which a person balances himself while maintaining a forward motion or performing elaborate tricks. Developed by California surfers as an alternative to surfboarding when weather conditions prohibited them from going into the ocean.

Skinny-Dip (c. 1966) n., v.: A swim in the nude, or to swim in the nude.

Slalom (1921) n., v.: A skiing term describing a downhill race over a winding, zigzagging course marked by poles and gates. Also applied to any twisting and turning course to test the maneuverability of cars, boats, skateboards, etc. Derived from the Norwegian word slalam, meaning "sloping track."

Slam Dunk (mid-1970s) n., **slam-dunk** v.: A basketball term describing a particularly forceful overhand shot made by leaping up and dramatically slamming the ball down through the hoop.

Sleaze (late 1960s) n.: A slang term to describe a contemptible, vulgar, shabby, or slovenly person, or the quality of seediness, sordidness, dilapidation, or squalor. A person can also be referred to as a sleazebag.

Smog (1905) n., v.: Smoke or other atmospheric pollutants combined with fog in an unhealthy or irritating mixture. A combination of smoke and fog. The term was first used by H. A. Des Voeux to describe the condition over British towns.

Michael Jordan performing a slam dunk.

Snafu (early 1940s) n., adj., v.: An acronym for situation normal: *all fucked* (or *fouled*) *up*. A badly confused or ridiculously muddled situation; in disorder, out of control, chaotic; to throw into disorder.

Snorkel (1944) n.: A hard rubber or plastic breathing tube used by a swimmer while moving facedown at or just below the surface of the water. Derived from the German word *Schnorchel,* meaning "air intake." Originally applied to a submarine airshaft that ventilated diesel-engine exhaust fumes and foul air out above the water's surface and provided air intake.

Snowmobile (1967) n., v.: A motorized track vehicle with a revolving tread in the rear and steerable skis in the front upon which a person sits to travel over snow.

Software (1960) n., adj.: Computer term for programs used to direct the operation of a computer, as well as documentation giving instructions on how to use them.

Sound Bite (mid-1970s) n.: A brief, pithy, striking remark or statement excerpted from an audiotaped or videotaped interview, speech, etc., to be used in a broadcast news story. *Bite* implies the idea of a snatch of soundtrack taken from a longer whole and includes undertones of the high-tech description of units of information (bytes).

Speed Bump (1970s) n.: A rounded ridge built crosswise into the pavement of a road or driveway to force vehicles to reduce their speed.

Spin Doctor (1984) n.: Political slang for a press agent or senior political spokesperson employed to promote favorable news coverage of a political candidate or event. *Spin* refers to the positive or negative slant extrapolated from information, and *doctor* figuratively refers to the act of patching up or mending.

Spin-Off (late 1940s) n., adj.: Any product that is an adaptation, outgrowth, or development of another similar product; a secondary or incidental product or effect derived from technological development in a somewhat unrelated area.

Stagflation (1960s) n.: An inflationary period accompanied by rising unemployment and lack of growth in consumer demand and business activity. A combination of *stagnation* and *inflation*.

Station Wagon (late 1920s) n.: An automobile with one or more rows of folding or removable seats behind the driver and no luggage compartment but an area behind the seats into which suitcases, parcels, etc., can be loaded through a tailgate.

Steroids (1936) n.: A biochemical term describing any of a large group of fat-soluble organic compounds, as the sterols, bile acids, and sex hormones, most of which have specific physiological action. A combination of *sterol* and *-oid*.

Stonewall (1964) n., adj., v.: The act of intentionally evading, resisting, blocking, or filibustering, from the idea of erecting a stone wall against all opposition, and from the nickname of U.S. general Thomas "Stonewall" Jackson.

Stretch Marks (c. 1960) n.: Horizontal lines occurring typically on the abdomen or thighs and caused by the stretching of the skin resulting from pregnancy or obesity.

Suffragette (c. 1906) n.: A female advocating women's rights to vote, especially in a political election. A combination of *suffrage* and the feminine diminutive *ette*. Originally a term of derision used by opponents of women's suffrage. Early advocates called themselves *suffragists*.

Superconductivity (1911) n.: A physics term to describe the phenomenon of almost perfect conductivity shown by certain substances at temperatures approaching absolute zero. The recent discovery of materials that are superconductive at temperatures hundreds of degrees above absolute zero raises the possibility of revolutionary developments in the production and transmission of electrical energy.

Supernova (1920s) n.: An astronomical term describing the explosion of a star during which its luminosity increases by as much as twenty magnitudes and most of the star's mass is blown away at very high velocity, sometimes leaving behind a dense core.

Surrogate Mother (1975) n.: A medical term describing a woman who voluntarily agrees (usually for payment) to carry to term an embryo conceived by a couple and transferred to her uterus, or to be inseminated with the man's sperm and either donate the embryo for transfer to the woman's uterus or carry it to term. The practice has generated heated moral and legal debates after incidents arose where the surrogate mother was reluctant or refused to relinquish the baby, insisting that a mother-child bond had been established in utero, resulting in court battles to determine child custody.

Sweatsuit (1930s) n.: A set of garments made of soft absorbent fabric consisting of sweatpants and a sweatshirt, commonly worn during athletic activity for warmth or to induce sweating.

Synthesizer (altered 1969) n.: Any of various electronic, sometimes portable, consoles or modules, usually computerized, for creating, modifying, and combining tones or reproducing the sounds of musical instruments by controlling voltage patterns, operated by means of keyboards, joysticks, sliders, or knobs. An industry standard version was developed by U.S. engineer Robert A. Moog, who registered his name as a trademark for the Moog synthesizer.

Tabloid (c. 1906) n., adj.: A newspaper-type publication that concentrates on publishing sensational and lurid news, usually heavily illustrated.

Tax Shelter (1961) n.: Any financial arrangement, such as an investment, charitable donation, allowance, etc., that results in a reduction or elimination of taxes due.

Tearjerker (1920s) n.: A pathetically dramatic, excessively sentimental story, play, film, etc., so emotionally overwrought that it "jerks" the tears from one's eyes.

Technocrat (1930) n.: A proponent, adherent, or supporter of theories and movements advocating control of industrial resources, reform of financial institutions, and reorganization of the social system, based on the findings of technologists and engineers.

Teenage (1920s) adj.: Of, pertaining to, or characteristic of a person in his or her teenage years, from thirteen through nineteen.

Telethon (1949) n.: A television broadcast, lasting several hours, sometimes featuring celebrities and entertainment and usually commercial-free, devised to solicit monetary support for a charitable cause.

Television (c. 1907) n.: The broadcasting of a still or moving image via radio waves to receivers that project a view of the image on a picture tube, more commonly known as a television or TV set.

Theme Park (1960) n.: An amusement park in which landscaping, buildings, and attractions are based on one or more specific themes.

Think Tank (1950s) n.: A research institute or organization employed to solve complex problems or predict or plan future developments.

Third World (1956) n., adj.: The underdeveloped nations of the world, especially those with widespread poverty. The term was coined by French diplomat Georges Balandier and referred specifically to the twenty-nine African and Asian nations that met at the Bandung Conference in April 1955.

Tokenism (1962) n.: The practice, policy, or legislation of demonstrating only minimal compliance with rules, laws, or public pressure to offer opportunities to minorities equal to those of the majority.

Toyboy (early 1980s) n.: British slang describing an attractive young man who is "kept" as a lover by an older person.

Transistor (late 1940s) n.: An electronics term for a semiconductor device that amplifies, oscillates, or switches the flow of current between two terminals by varying the current or voltage between one of the terminals and a third: although much smaller in size than a vacuum tube, it performs similar functions without requiring current to heat a cathode.

Tsunami (1904) n.: An unusually large sea wave produced by an earthquake below the sea or an undersea volcanic eruption. Also known as a seismic sea wave. Taken from the Japanese meaning "harbor wave."

Tutu (1910) n.: A short, full skirt, usually made of several layers of tarlatan or tulle, worn by ballerinas. From the French word for "ballet skirt," generally accepted to be a childish alteration of cucu, a diminutive of cul, meaning "anus," "rear end," "bottom," which a tutu covers.

Underachiever (late 1940s) n.: A student who performs less well in school than would be expected on the basis of abilities indicated by intelligence and aptitude tests; a person or thing that performs below expectations.

Unisex (1968) adj.: Pertaining to, characterized by, or designed for a style of dress, appearance, or facilities that are equally applicable to either sex.

Uptight (c. 1965) adj.: Slang for tense, nervous, jittery, annoyed, angry, suffering emotional instability to a varying degree, or stiffly conventional in manner or attitudes.

User-Friendly (1979) adj.: Easy to use, operate, and understand and designed with the needs of a novice in mind. Initially coined by Harlan Crowder to describe the ease, or lack thereof, with which the lay user could operate a computer system, but now used in other contexts outside computing.

VCR (1971) n.: An abbreviation of videocassette recorder, an electronic apparatus capable of recording television programs or other signals onto videocassettes and playing them back through a television receiver.

Video (1930s) n.: The elements of television, as in a program or script, pertaining to the transmission or reception of the image, as distinguished from an audio portion.

Virtual Reality (1985) n.: A realistic simulation of an environment through high-speed, three-dimensional computer graphics created using interactive software and hardware. Also known as VR.

Walkman (1979) n.: A trademark brand name for a small, portable, battery-operated stereo cassette player, radio, or combination cassette player and radio used with headphones. So named because it can be used while walking, cycling, or participating in a number of activities.

Wanderlust (1902) n.: A strong, innate desire or fondness to rove or travel about. Comes from the German words *wandern* (to wander) and *Lust* (desire).

Wheeler-Dealer (early 1950s) n.: A shrewd bargainer or one who operates dynamically for his or her own profit or benefit.

Whistle-Blower (c. 1970) n.: A person who informs (usually via the press) on another person or entity (company, organization, government), revealing duplicity, corruption, wrongdoing, incompetence, or mismanagement, thus publicly disclosing the situation.

White-Collar (1920s) adj.: Of or belonging to or pertaining to the ranks of office and professional workers whose jobs generally do not involve manual labor or the wearing of a uniform or work clothes.

Whodunit (c. 1930) n.: A narrative dealing with a murder or a series of murders and the detection of the criminal. A jocular formation from the question "Who done it?"

Wholefood (1960) n., adj.: A British term describing food with little or no refining or processing and containing no artificial additives or preservatives; health, natural, or organic food.

Wimp (c. 1920) n., v.: A weak, ineffectual, timid, or cowardly person, taken from the cartoon character Wellington Wimpy in the Popeye comics. To be or act like a wimp.

Workaholic (c. 1968) n., adj.: A person who works compulsively at the expense of other pursuits; addicted to working.

WYSIWYG (1982) adj.: An acronym for *what you see is what you get*. In computerese, a slogan indicating that what appears on the terminal screen exactly replicates the eventual printout.

Yuppie (1982) n., adj.: An acronym for young, urban (or upwardly mobile) professional. A young, ambitious, well-educated city dweller who has a professional career and an affluent lifestyle.

PRIMARY SOURCES:

Neologisms: New Words Since 1960, by Jonathon Green. London: Bloomsbury Publishing Limited, 1991.

Oxford Dictionary of New Words, compiled by Sara Tulloch. Oxford: Oxford University Press, 1991.

Random House Unabridged Dictionary, edited by Stuart Berg Flexner. New York: Random House, 1993.

DOUBLESPEAK

That's not a lie, it's a terminological inexactitude.
            Alexander Haig, TV interview, 1983

The Committee on Public Doublespeak of the National Council of Teachers of English began giving Doublespeak awards in 1974. The awards are a "tribute" to public figures who use language that is "grossly deceptive, evasive, euphemistic, confusing, or self-contradictory."

COLONEL DAVID H. E. OPFER, USAF (1974)

After a bombing raid, Colonel David Opfer, a press officer in Cambodia, complained to reporters, "You always write it's bombing, bombing, bombing. It's not bombing. It's air support."

RON ZIEGLER (1974)

When asked whether a certain batch of Watergate tapes was still intact, a question that would seem to have required a simple answer of yes or no, Ron Ziegler, President Nixon's press secretary, gave the following ninety-nine-word reply: "I would feel that most of the conversations that took place in those areas of the White House that did have the recording system would in almost their entirety be in existence, but the special prosecutor, the court, and, I think, the American people are sufficiently familiar with the recording system to know where the recording devices existed and to know the situation in terms of the recording process, but I feel, although the process has not been undertaken yet in preparation of the material to abide by the court decision, really, what the answer to that question is."

YASSER ARAFAT (1975)

Apparently a believer in the philosophy that "love is hate" and "war is peace," Yasser Arafat, the leader of the Palestine Liberation Organization, stated, "We do not want to destroy any people. It is precisely because we have been advocating coexistence that we have shed so much blood."

THE QUAKER OATS COMPANY (1978)

Quaker Oats's Aunt Jemima frozen Jumbo Blueberry Waffles were advertised as being made with "Real Blueberry Buds and Other Natural Flavors." On the back of the package, however, the following ingredients were listed in small type: "Blueberry Buds (sugar, vegetable stearine [a release agent], blueberry solids with other natural flavors), salt, sodium carboxymethyl cellulose [a thickening agent], silicon dioxide [a flow agent], citric acid, modified soy protein, artificial flavor, artificial coloring, maltol."

THE NUCLEAR POWER INDUSTRY (1979)

Following the accident at Three Mile Island, the nuclear power industry came up with an extraordinary array of euphemisms to downplay the dangers of nuclear accidents. An explosion became "energetic disassembly" and a fire "rapid oxidation." The word accident was taboo and was replaced with "event," "incident," "abnormal evolution," "normal aberration," or "plant transient." The phrase "plutonium contamination" was another no-no. In its place came the phrases "plutonium infiltration" or "plutonium has taken up residence."

A. J. SPANO (1979)

In an attempt to downplay Denver's air-pollution problem, Colorado state representative A. J. Spano introduced a bill to change the wording of the state's air-quality scale. Spano suggested that the level of pollution that the federal government called "hazardous" be called "poor" instead. "Dangerous" was to become "acceptable," and "very unhealthful" was to become "fair." The bill, which passed the House Transportation Committee, changed "unhealthful" to "good" and "moderate" to "very good."

GENERAL JOÃO BAPTISTA FIGUEIREDO (1979)

Upon being elected president of Brazil, Figueiredo told reporters, "I intend to open this country up to democracy, and anyone who is against that, I will jail, I will crush."

JIMMY CARTER (1980)

President Carter referred to the failed military rescue of the American hostages in Iran as an "incomplete success."

NEW JERSEY DIVISION OF GAMING ENFORCEMENT (1980)

In an official report concerning participants in organized crime, the New Jersey Division of Gaming Enforcement avoided the terms mob, syndicate, Mafia, and Cosa Nostra, and instead referred to a "member of a career offender cartel."

NUCLEAR REGULATORY COMMISSION (1980)

In a report to Congress on the subject of safety at nuclear power plants, the NRC displayed an unusual method of counting accidents, which they of course referred to as "events." The commission enumerated 400 such accidents, including two "abnormal occurrences." One of these "abnormal occurrences" turned out to be accidents at nineteen different reactors. Because the nineteen accidents were caused by the same design problem, they were counted only once. Another "abnormal occurrence" occurred so frequently that it was called a "normally expected occurrence."

U.S. DEPARTMENT OF AGRICULTURE (1981)

The USDA attempted to classify catsup as a vegetable so that it could be counted as one of the two vegetables required as part of the school lunch program. The department also reclassified chickens that had been chilled to twenty-eight degrees Fahrenheit from "frozen" to "deep chilled" so that they could be sold as fresh chickens.

ALEXANDER HAIG (1981)

Former secretary of state Alexander Haig was well known for his bizarre use of the English language, peppering his speech with such phrases as "careful caution," "saddle myself with a statistical fence," "definitizing an answer," "caveat my response," and "epitemologicallywise." What won Haig the Doublespeak Award was a series of statements he made to congressional committees following the murder of three American nuns and a religious lay worker in El Salvador. The four women were shot in the head, and three of them were raped. Testifying before the House Foreign Affairs Committee, Haig said, "I'd like to suggest to you that some of the investigations would lead one to believe that perhaps the vehicle that the nuns were riding in may have tried to run a roadblock, or may accidentally have been perceived to have been doing so, and there'd been an exchange of fire and then perhaps those who inflicted the casualties sought to cover it up. And this could have been at a very low level of both competence and motivation in the context of the issue itself. But the facts on this are not clear for anyone to draw a definitive conclusion."

The next day, before the Senate Foreign Relations Committee, Haig was asked to clarify his previous statement. Was he suggesting that the nuns might have run a roadblock? "You mean that they tried to violate . . . ? Not at all, no, not at all. My heavens! The dear nuns who raised me in my parochial schooling would forever isolate me from their affections and respect." When he used the phrase "exchange of fire," did he mean to imply that the nuns had fired guns at people, asked Senator Claiborne Pell. Haig replied, "I haven't met any pistol-packing nuns in my day, Senator. What I meant was that if one fellow starts shooting, then the next thing you know they all panic."

REPUBLICAN NATIONAL COMMITTEE (1982)

The Republican National Committee produced a TV commercial crediting President Ronald Reagan for a cost-of-living hike in Social Security benefits. The commercial portrayed a friendly postman delivering Social Security checks. President Reagan "promised that raise," says the postman, "and he kept his promise in spite of those sticks-in-the-mud who tried to keep him from doing what we elected him to do." In fact, the cost-of-living increases had been provided automatically by a law passed six years before Reagan took office. Indeed, it was Reagan who tried three times to roll back or delay the increases, although he was overruled by Congress. A Republican official, quoted in the *Chicago Tribune*, called the commercial "inoffensive," adding, "Since when is a commercial supposed to be accurate?"

OFFICE OF MANAGEMENT AND BUDGET (1983)

OMB officials referred to a four-cents-a-gallon increase in the federal gasoline tax as a "user fee" so as not to use the word *tax*.

U.S. DEPARTMENT OF STATE (1984)

The State Department announced that the word *killing* would no longer be used in its annual reports on human rights around the world. Instead, *killing* would be replaced with the phrase "unlawful or arbitrary deprivation of life."

CENTRAL INTELLIGENCE AGENCY (1984)

When the CIA hired mercenaries to carry out raids in Nicaragua, the agency referred to their warriors not as mercenaries but as "unilaterally controlled Latino assets."

CASPAR WEINBERGER (1984)

As U.S. secretary of defense, Caspar Weinberger denied that movements of American troops in Lebanon constituted a retreat. "Nothing has changed," he said. "We are not leaving Lebanon. The marines are being deployed two or three miles to the west." "Two or three miles to the west" happened to be off of Lebanese soil and onto ships in the Mediterranean Sea.

U.S. AIR FORCE (1986)

When a cruise missile crashed, the air force announced that it had actually "impacted with the ground prematurely" and that the test was "terminated five minutes earlier than planned."

NATIONAL AERONAUTICS AND SPACE ADMINISTRATION (1986)

NASA officials called the *Challenger* space shuttle explosion an "anomaly," the bodies of the astronauts "recovered components," and their coffins "crew transfer containers."

U.S. DEPARTMENT OF DEFENSE (1986)

In a triumph of bureaucratic obfuscation, a Department of Defense manual referred to a hammer as a "manually powered fastener-driving impact device," a steel nut as a "hexiform rotatable surface compression unit," and a tent as a "frame-supported tension structure."

> What are we to make of terms like "nuclear exchange," "escalation," "nuclear yield," "counterforce," "megatons," or of "the window of vulnerability" or (ostensibly much better) "window of opportunity"? Quite simply, these words provide a way of talking about nuclear weapons without really talking about them. In them we find nothing about millions of human beings being incinerated or literally melted, nothing about billions of corpses. Rather, the weapons come to seem ordinary and manageable or even mildly pleasant: a "nuclear exchange" sounds something like mutual gift-giving.
>
> Robert Jay Lifton,
> *Indefensible Weapons*, 1982

OLIVER NORTH (1987)

In testimony before Congress, Oliver North would not admit that he had "destroyed" certain documents. Rather, the documents were "non-log" and kept "out of the system so that outside knowledge would not necessarily be derived from having the documents themselves." In referring to a fake chronology of events that he helped construct, North could not bring himself to say that the chronology was false, only that it was "a different version from the facts."

ORRIN HATCH (1988)

U.S. senator Orrin Hatch said that "capital punishment is our society's recognition of the sanctity of human life."

DAN QUAYLE (1988)

While a candidate for vice president, Quayle defended his vote against establishing a cabinet-level position for the Veterans Administration by describing the vote as a "youthful indiscretion." The vote had actually been cast only one month earlier.

ROGER TAYLOR (1988)

The mayor of Elliot Lake, Ontario, Roger Taylor said he had no objection to a permanent dump for radioactive wastes being located near his town, because it was not a dump. "It's a containment initiative."

MARLIN FITZWATER (1988)

After a U.S. Navy fighter fired two missiles at an Iranian passenger jet, presidential spokesperson Marlin Fitzwater declared, "At this point I will not confirm any part of the incident." He did say that President Reagan had been informed "soon after the incident happened." Which incident was he talking about? "The incident that I'm not confirming."

U.S. DEPARTMENT OF TRANSPORTATION (1989)

Anhydrous ammonia, which can kill or cause injury in an accidental spill, is not classified as a "poison gas" by the Department of Transportation—it is an "inhalation hazard."

GEORGE BUSH (1989)

When he campaigned for president in 1988, Bush promised "no net loss of wetlands." After his inauguration, he clarified his pledge to mean no net loss of wetlands except "where there is a high proportion of land which is wetlands"; in other words, those areas most in need of protection, such as the Alaskan tundra and the Florida Everglades.

U.S. AIRLINE INDUSTRY (1989)

Aircraft engines do not "explode." Accidents such as that which brought down United's flight 232 in Iowa result from what the industry called "uncontained engine failure."

U.S. ARMY (1990)

Two female army officers who fought in Panama were denied the Combat Infantryman's Badge because they were not designated infantry by their military occupational specialty. Others who fought alongside them were given the badge. An army official said, "We have a combat exclusion policy for women, but that doesn't mean women are excluded from combat."

U.S. SUPREME COURT (1990)

In a 1990 ruling, a person stopped by the police, questioned, and asked to show identification is simply engaged in a "consensual encounter."

U.S. SUPREME COURT (1991)

The Eighth Amendment to the Constitution of the United States prohibits cruel and unusual punishments. In 1991 the Supreme Court ruled that a sentence of life in prison without possibility of parole for the possession of 672 grams of cocaine might be cruel, but it was not unusual. In other words, as long as a punishment is imposed often enough, it is not unconstitutional.

NEWT GINGRICH AND GOPAC (1991)

GOPAC, a conservative Republican group headed by Representative Newt Gingrich, published a booklet entitled *Language: A Key Mechanism of Control*, designed to be used by Republican candidates for office. The booklet includes sixty-nine positive words to be used to "help define your campaign and your vision," and sixty-four negative words to "define our opponents." The positive list included "environment, peace, freedom, fair, flag, we/us/our, moral, family, children, truth, hard-working, reformer, and candid." The negative list included "traitors, betray, sick, lie, liberal, radical, corruption, permissive attitude, they/them, anti-flag, anti-family, anti-job, unionized, bureaucracy, and impose."

DAVID MACK (1991)

During the conflict with Iraq, the Bush administration was caught between wanting to convince the American people that U.S. soldiers were fighting for democracy and not wanting to offend the governments of Kuwait, Saudi Arabia, Syria, and Egypt, which were not democratic. So, instead of using the dreaded D-word, Deputy Assistant Secretary of State David Mack called on Kuwait to "maximize internal political participation in accordance with all traditional institutions."

TED STEVENS (1991)

When the U.S. Senate voted itself a $23,000 pay raise, Senator Ted Stevens of Alaska declared that it was not a pay raise but, rather, "a pay equalization concept."

DAVID WHIPPLE (1991)

Commenting on the testimony of CIA agents before Congress, David Whipple, a former CIA agent and head of the Association of Former Intelligence Officers, said, "The whole question of lying to congress—you could call it a lie, but for us, that's keeping cover."

THE WALL STREET JOURNAL (1993)

According to an editorial in the *Wall Street Journal*, Senator Robert Packwood of Oregon didn't lie during his reelection campaign when he denied there was a press investigation into allegations against him of sexual harassment. He was just being "factually flexible in the heat of a campaign."

GEORGE BUSH (1993)

Before leaving office, President Bush pardoned six government officials for crimes they had committed relating to the Iran-Contra affair. Bush called the six "patriots" and claimed their convictions were the result of a "criminalization of policy differences." The crimes they committed included destroying evidence and lying to a grand jury and to Congress.

BILL CLINTON (1993)

Trying to raise taxes without saying so, President Clinton announced that his proposed health care plan would be partially financed by a "wage-based premium"—in other words, a tax. This recalled the Reagan administration's successful attempt to avoid using the T-word by creating the term *revenue enhancement*.

—D.W.

WIT AND WISDOM

WOODY ALLEN

Born Allan Konigsberg in Brooklyn on December 1, 1935, Allen began writing quips for gossip columnists at age fifteen. After graduating from high school, he landed a job writing for Sid Caesar's classic television comedy series *Your Show of Shows*. In 1961 he branched out from writing to stand-up comedy. He also wrote plays and screenplays before directing his first film, *Take the Money and Run*, in 1969. As his filmmaking skills improved, Allen gained a loyal international audience that stuck with him through his ugly custody battle with Mia Farrow (see page 444).

Woody Allen, 1965.

It seemed the world was divided into good and bad people. The good ones slept better . . . while the bad ones seemed to enjoy the waking hours much more.
                                           Side Effects, 1981

Don't listen to what your schoolteachers tell you. Don't pay attention to that. Just see what they look like and that's how you know what life is really going to be like.
                                   Crimes and Misdemeanors, 1990

[Intellectuals] are like the Mafia. They only kill their own.
                                       Stardust Memories, 1980

Sun is bad for you. Everything our parents told us was good is bad. Sun, milk, red meat, college.
                                            Annie Hall, 1977

The prettiest [girls] are almost always the most boring, and that is why some people feel there is no God.
                                       "The Early Essays," 1973

Sex alleviates tension and love causes it.
                        A Midsummer Night's Sex Comedy, 1982

Nothing sexier than a lapsed Catholic.
                                                 Alice, 1990

Love is deep; sex is only a few inches.
Bullets Over Broadway, 1994

I thought of that old joke, you know, this guy goes to a psychiatrist and says, "Doc, my brother's crazy. He thinks he's a chicken." And the doctor says, "Why don't you turn him in?" And the guy says, "I would but I need the eggs." Well, I guess that's pretty much how I feel about relationships. You know, they're totally irrational and crazy and absurd . . . but I guess we keep going through it because most of us need the eggs.
Annie Hall, 1977

To you, I'm an atheist . . . to God I'm the loyal opposition.
Stardust Memories, 1980

I don't want to achieve immortality through my work, I want to achieve it through not dying.

Someone once asked me if my dream was to live on in the hearts of my people, and I said I would like to live on in my apartment. And that's really what I would prefer.
1987

There's this old joke. Two elderly women are in a Catskills Mountain resort and one of 'em says: "Boy, the food at this place is really terrible." The other one says, "Yeah, I know, and such small portions." Well, that's essentially how I feel about life. Full of loneliness and misery and suffering and unhappiness, and it's all over much too quickly.
Annie Hall, 1977
—D.W.

ALBERT EINSTEIN

Although Albert Einstein is known as the greatest scientist of the twentieth century, he was not one to isolate himself from political issues. He was an active pacifist and turned down an offer to become the first president of Israel. (For more on Einstein, see pages 275 and 554.)

God is subtle but he is not malicious.
Remark at Princeton, 1921

When you are courting a nice girl an hour seems like a second. When you sit on a red-hot cinder a second seems like an hour. That's relativity.
News Chronicle, March 14, 1949

If my theory of relativity is proved successful Germany will claim me as a German and France will declare I am a citizen of the whole world. Should my theory

Albert Einstein on his seventy-second birthday.

prove untrue, France will say I'm a German and Germany will say I am a Jew.
Quoted in *News Review*, May 8, 1947

As far as the laws of mathematics refer to reality, they are not certain, and as far as they are certain, they do not refer to reality.
1930

I am convinced that He [God] does not play dice. [Sometimes quoted as "God does not play dice with the universe."]
Letter to Max Born, December 4, 1926

The hardest thing in the world to understand is income tax.
Attributed, 1930

Common sense is the collection of prejudices acquired by age eighteen.

Nationalism is an infantile disease. It is the measles of mankind.
To George Sylvester Viereck, 1921

When I examine myself and my methods of thought, I come close to the conclusion that the gift of fantasy has meant more to me than my talent for absorbing positive knowledge.

I never think of the future. It comes soon enough.
In an interview, December 1930

Imagination is more important than knowledge.
                                              On Science

If one purges Judaism of the Prophets and Christianity as Jesus Christ taught it of all subsequent additions, especially those of priests, one is left with a teaching which is capable of curing all the social ills of humanity.
                              The World As I See It, 1934

The pursuit of knowledge for its own sake, an almost fanatical love of justice and the desire for personal independence—these are the features of the Jewish tradition which make me thank my stars that I belong to it.
                              The World As I See It, 1934

The true value of a human being is determined by the measure and the sense in which he has attained liberation from the self.
                                  My World-Picture, 1934

Never do anything against conscience even if the state demands it.
                                  Quoted in Virgil Hinshaw,
                Albert Einstein: Philosopher Scientist, 1949
                                                  —D.W.

W. C. Fields clearing the course of obstacles.

W. C. FIELDS

Born William Claude Dukenfield in Philadelphia on January 29, 1880, Fields was already earning his living as a juggler at age fifteen. He became a successful magician and vaudeville performer and even performed for King Edward VII at Buckingham Palace in 1913. Fields made his first film, *Pool Sharks*, two years later. Over the next twenty-eight years he perfected two roles: the small-time gambler and con man, and the bumbling, henpecked husband. A heavy drinker, Fields died on Christmas—a day he always claimed to hate—in 1946.

The government fixes it so that you have a choice of: 1. starving to death by having an income so low that you do not have to pay a tax, or: 2. having an income high enough to pay a tax—and then starving to death after you've paid it.

Never try to impress a woman. Because if you do she'll expect you to keep up to the standard for the rest of your life. And the pace, my friends, is devastating.

Women are like elephants to me. I like to look at them, but I wouldn't want to own one.

If at first you don't succeed, try, try again. Then quit. No use being a damn fool about it.

There is no question as to whether whiskey or the dog is man's best friend. When two kindred souls get together for a friendly session, do they sit there and pet dogs?

There is no such thing as a tough child. If you parboil them first for seven hours, they always come out tender.

Ah! What symmetrical digits. Soft as the fuzz on a baby's arm.
                                  My Little Chickadee, 1940

All Englishmen talk as if they've got a bushel of plums stuck in their throats and then after swallowing them got constipated from the pits.

Drown in a vat of liquor? Death, where is thy sting?
                        Never Give a Sucker an Even Break, 1941

I've been asked if I ever get the d.t.'s. I don't know. It's hard to tell where Hollywood ends and the d.t.'s begin.

I never drink water. That's the stuff that rusts pipes.

Once during Prohibition, I was forced to live for days on nothing but food and water.

My dear old grandfather Litcock said, just before they sprung the trap, you can't cheat an honest man, never give a sucker an even break or smarten up a chump.
                        You Can't Cheat an Honest Man, 1939

She drove me to drink. That's the one thing I'm indebted to her for.
                        Never Give a Sucker an Even Break, 1941

For reasons I have never understood, Alexandria, Virginia, is screamingly funny to Washingtonians, while the great city of Oakland never fails to get a chuckle out of San Franciscans. And Bismarck, North Dakota, is funny anywhere in the United States.

I am free of all prejudice. I hate everyone equally.

—D.W.

WILSON MIZNER

Little known to the public at large, Wilson Mizner (1876–1933) was one of the great wits of modern times. Mizner was a jack-of-all-trades: Klondike gold seeker, Florida realtor, Broadway playwright, Hollywood screenwriter, Atlantic gambler, as well as prizefight manager. Here is a capsule of Miznerisms.

ONE-LINERS

If you steal from one author, it's plagiarism; if you steal from many, it's research.

I respect faith, but doubt is what gets you an education.

Treat a whore like a lady and a lady like a whore.

Be nice to people on your way up because you'll meet them on your way down.

Life's a tough proposition, and the first hundred years are the hardest.

A good listener is not only popular everywhere, but after a while he gets to know something.

A drama critic is a person who surprises the playwright by informing him what he meant.

I am a stylist, and the most beautiful sentence I have ever heard is, "Have one on the house."

I've had several years in Hollywood and I still think the movie heroes are in the audience.

A fellow who is always declaring he's no fool usually has his suspicions.

Many a live wire would be a dead one except for his connections.

The gent who wakes up and finds himself a success hasn't been asleep.

Some of the greatest love affairs I've known involved one actor, unassisted.

Insanity is considered a ground for divorce, though by the very same token it's the shortest mental detour to marriage.

DESCRIPTIONS OF PEOPLE

He'd steal a hot stove and come back for the smoke.

You're a mouse studying to be a rat.

You sparkle with larceny.

To a conceited movie producer: "A demitasse cup would fit over your head like a sunbonnet."

On a cocky man who went through bankruptcy and was cockier than ever: "Failure has gone to his head."

On a very thin man: "He's a trellis for varicose veins."

On the owner of a major movie studio: "He's the

only man I ever knew who had rubber pockets so he could steal soup."

Two signs he posted for guests when he was manager of the Hotel Rand, New York, 1907:

"No opium-smoking in the elevators."

"Carry out your own dead."

On Hollywood: "It's a trip through a sewer in a glass-bottomed boat."

During a game of draw poker, his opponent took out his wallet and threw it on the table announcing, "I call you." Mizner glanced at the wallet, pulled off his right shoe, placed it on the table, and said, "If we're playing for leather—I raise."

For a while he was married to Myra Moor Yerkes, the second-richest woman in America, who owned a $2 million art collection. One day, in need of money, he took a version of The Last Supper off her wall and sold it. When his wife saw the empty frame, she cried out, "Bill, what happened to the masterpiece I had in the living room—The Last Supper?" Replied Mizner, "Some masterpiece. I got only fifty dollars a plate."

Mizner once managed Stanley Ketchel, the middleweight boxing champion. In London in October 1910, Mizner received a telephone call notifying him that a jealous rancher husband had shot and killed Ketchel. Said Mizner: "Tell them to start counting ten over him, and he'll get up."

On his deathbed, as Mizner came out of a coma, a priest tried to comfort him, and Mizner waved the priest away: "Why should I talk to you? I've just been talking to your boss."

—I.W.

DOROTHY PARKER

Born in New Jersey in 1893, Dorothy Parker died in New York in 1967. In between she wrote critical pieces for Vogue, Vanity Fair, and The New Yorker; published four books of light verse and collections of short stories such as the memorable Big Blonde; and collaborated on several Broadway plays and a number of screenplays. Politically, she was an activist, pro–Sacco and Vanzetti, anti-Franco from the start. Yet what has survived most of Dorothy Parker is the legend of her rapier wit. Her cleverness and bright cracks were publicized by Franklin P. Adams in the "Conning Tower" column and by Alexander Woollcott, Robert Benchley, and George S. Kaufman of the Algonquin Round Table, that informal group that gathered in New York to engage in quotable conversation. This sweet little lady with the sharp tongue—Woollcott called her a cross between Little Nell and Lady Macbeth—will be remembered always for such witticisms as the following:

"If all the girls who attended the Yale prom were laid end to end—I wouldn't be a bit surprised."

A review of Katharine Hepburn starring in a Broadway play: *"She runs the gamut of emotions from A to B."*

Suggesting an epitaph for her own gravestone: *"Excuse my dust."*

Asked to use the word *horticulture* in a sentence: *"You can lead a horticulture, but you can't make her think."*

On a London actress who had broken a leg: *"How terrible. She must have done it sliding down a barrister."*

"A girl's best friend is her mutter."

"Wit has truth in it. Wisecracking is simply calisthenics with words."

"I bet you could get into the subway without using anybody's name."

Telegram to a friend who went to the country to have a baby: *"Congratulations, we all knew you had it in you."*

On hearing President Calvin Coolidge had died: *"Why, I never even knew that he was alive."*

"The only ism Hollywood believes in is plagiarism."

On hearing that Clare Boothe Luce was always kind to her inferiors: *"And where does she find them?"*

On a drunk who kept insisting he was talented: *"Look at him, a rhinestone in the rough."*

"I was the toast of two continents: Greenland and Australia."

Reviewing A. A. Milne's *The House at Pooh Corner* and his use of such coy words as *hummy* in her column "Constant Reader": *"Tonstant Weader fwowed up."*

On Oscar Wilde and her own wit:
If, with the literate, I am
Impelled to try an epigram,
I never seek to take the credit;
We all assume that Oscar said it.

Lonely in her office, yearning for the company of the opposite sex, she went out and printed one word on her door: MEN.

By the time you swear you're his,
 Shivering and sighing,
And he vows his passion is
 Infinite, undying—
Lady, make a note of this:
 One of you is lying.

Men seldom make passes
At girls who wear glasses.

"Salary is no object; I want only to keep body and soul apart."

"Most good women are hidden treasures who are only safe because nobody looks for them."

Of Margot Asquith's four-volume autobiography:

"The affair between Margot Asquith and Margot Asquith will live as one of the prettiest love stories in all literature."

Reviewing two plays, each containing a character based on her, one by George Oppenheimer and the other by Ruth Gordon: *"I wanted to write my autobiography but now I'm afraid to. George Oppenheimer and Ruth Gordon would sue me for plagiarism."*

After a quarrel with one of her handsome young lovers, John McClain: *"Yes, his body went to his head."*

Of her second husband: *"Oh, don't worry about Alan. Alan will always land on somebody's feet."*

—I.W.

WILL ROGERS

Will Rogers was born on November 4, 1879, on his parents' ranch near Oologah in what is now Oklahoma. He was part Cherokee. He worked as a cowboy in Texas and Argentina and then began performing in Wild West shows and circuses. His specialty was rope tricks. He also appeared on vaudeville stages and in the movies. In 1922 Rogers made his first radio broadcast. Throughout the twenties and early thirties he entertained Americans not just with his folksy humor but with an incisive political wisdom that would have earned him many enemies if he had expressed himself with anger rather than disguising his observations in jokes. An avid fan of airplanes, Rogers, in 1927, was

Will Rogers.

the first civilian to fly across the United States with mail pilots. On August 15, 1935, he was killed in a plane crash while flying in Alaska with the famous pilot Wiley Post. Poet Carl Sandburg called Rogers "one of those individuals we as Americans could call without embarrassment a great man."

Did you read how many thousands (not hundreds) but thousands of students just graduated all over the country in law? Going to take an awful lot of crime to support that bunch.
Newspaper column, June 15, 1931

It always will seem funny to us United Staters that we are about the only ones that really know how to do everything right. I don't know how a lot of these other Nations have existed as long as they have till we could get some of our people around and show 'em really how to be Pure and Good like us.
More Letters of a Self-Made Diplomat, February 27, 1932

Every invention during our lifetime has been just to save time, and time is the only commodity that every American, both rich and poor, has plenty of. Half our life is spent trying to find something to do with the time we have rushed through life trying to save. Two hundred years from now history will record: "America, a nation that flourished from 1900 to 1942, conceived many odd inventions for getting somewhere, but could think of nothing to do when they got there."
Newspaper column, April 28, 1930

My ancestors dident come over on the Mayflower, but they met 'em at the boat.

Lord, the money we do spend on Government. And it's not a bit better government than we got for one-third the money twenty years ago.
Newspaper column, March 27, 1932

Any audience who would gather to hear a politician speak wouldn't know a good speech if they heard one.
Radio broadcast, April 27, 1930

Never blame a legislative body for not doing something. When they do nothing, that don't hurt anybody. It's when they do something is when they become dangerous.
Newspaper column, November 22, 1929

In this country people don't vote for; they vote against.
Radio broadcast, June 9, 1935

I have found out that when newspapers knock a man a lot, there is sure to be a lot of good in him.
Newspaper column, April 15, 1923

I honestly believe there is people so excited over this election that they think the President has something to do with running this country.
Newspaper column, October 30, 1932

Washington, D.C., papers say: "Congress is deadlocked and can't act." I think that is the greatest blessing that could befall this country.
Newspaper column, January 27, 1924

You see they have two of these bodies—Senate and Congress . . . in case one passes a good bill, why the other can see it in time, and kill it.
Newspaper column, June 8, 1924

A tax paid on the day you buy is not as tough as asking you for it the next year when you are broke.
Newspaper column, September 7, 1931

The income tax has made more liars out of the American people than golf has.
Newspaper column, April 8, 1923

There's no income tax in Russia, but there's no income.
Radio broadcast, April 7, 1935

Why don't somebody print the truth about our present economic situation? We spent six years of wild buying on credit (everything under the sun, whether we needed it or not) and now we are having to pay for 'em under Mr. Hoover, and we are howling like a pet coon.
P.S. This would be a great world to dance in if we didn't have to pay the fiddler.
Newspaper column, June 27, 1930

Nations are just like individuals. Loan them money and you lose their friendship.
Newspaper column, January 11, 1925

You know you can be killed just as dead in an unjustified war, as you can in one protecting your own home.
Newspaper column, May 26, 1929

People talk peace, but men give their life's work to war. It won't stop till there is as much brains and scientific study put to aid peace as there is to promote war.
Newspaper column, May 31, 1929

Well, the [disarmament] conference met today and appointed a commission to meet tomorrow and appoint a delegation who will eventually appoint a subcommittee to draw up ways and means of finding out what to start with first.
Newspaper column, January 28, 1930

What spoiled China was somebody saving their History. The minute you teach a man he is backed up by Tradition, why, you spoil him for real work the rest of his life.
More Letters of a Self-Made Diplomat, April 2, 1932

[Women] first showed us their calves. Well that looked fairly promising, and we seemed enough shocked to add spice to our views. But when they just practically overnight yanked another foot off their apparel and we woke up one morning with thousands of knees staring

us in the face, why there is where I will always think they overstepped and took in too much territory.
Newspaper column, April 20, 1930

But if you want to have a good time, I don't care where you live, just load in your kids, and take some congenial friends, and just start out. You would be surprised what there is to see in this great Country within 200 miles of where any of us live. I don't care what State or what town.
Newspaper column, August 31, 1930

It's not what you pay a man but what he costs you that counts.
Newspaper column, March 22, 1925

Cities are like gentlemen, they are born, not made. You are either a city, or you are not. Size has nothing to do with it. New York is "yokel" but San Francisco is "city" at heart.
Newspaper column, April 30, 1934

I know how proud Christopher Columbus must have felt when he heard they had named Columbus, Ohio, after him.
Newspaper column, February 16, 1930

I see where Mr. Hoover got a great welcome in Nicaragua. No wonder. I guess he and Lindbergh were about the only Americans they ever saw that weren't marines.
Newspaper column, November 28, 1928

Ireland treats you more like a friend than a tourist.
Newspaper column, September 8, 1926

Now rumor travels faster, but it don't stay put as long as truth.
Newspaper column, March 9, 1924

Everybody is ignorant, only on different subjects.
Newspaper column, August 31, 1924

A fanatic is always the fellow that is on the opposite side.
Radio broadcast, June 8, 1930

The best doctor in the world is a veterinarian. He can't ask his patients what is the matter—he's got to just know.
The Autobiography of Will Rogers, 1949

Politics has got so expensive that it takes lots of money to even get beat with.
Newspaper column, June 28, 1931

Will you please tell me what you do with all the vice presidents a bank has? I guess that's to get you more discouraged before you can see the president. Why, the United States is the biggest business institution in the world and they only have one vice president and nobody has ever found anything for him to do.
Speech, International Bankers Association, 1922

Communism is like prohibition, it's a good idea but it won't work.
Autobiography, November 1927

Hunt out and talk about the good that is in the other fellow's church, not the bad, and you will do away with all this religious hatred you hear so much of nowadays.
Newspaper column, March 11, 1923
—D.W.

GEORGE BERNARD SHAW

George Bernard Shaw was born in Dublin, Ireland, on July 26, 1856, and moved to London in 1876. By 1884 he was an active socialist, not to mention a teetotaler, vegetarian, and non-smoker. For the next few years he struggled along as a journalist, lecturer, and (using the pseudonym Cornetto di Basso) music critic. Shaw's first produced play was *Widowers' Houses*, which appeared in 1892. Among his most famous works were *Mrs. Warren's Profession, Man and Superman, Major Barbara,* and *Pygmalion.* He was awarded the Nobel Prize in 1925. From age forty on, Shaw was much sought out by interviewers. He took advantage of his celebrity to spread his political ideas and ideals, but no matter how harshly he criticized people, they continued to be charmed by him. Shaw died on November 2, 1950, after falling while pruning a tree in his garden. He was ninety-four years old.

Do not do unto others as you would that they should do unto you. Their tastes may not be the same.
"Maxims for Revolutionists," *Man and Superman,* 1903

He who can, does. He who cannot, teaches.
"Maxims for Revolutionists," *Man and Superman,* 1903

George Bernard Shaw on his ninetieth birthday.

[Dancing is] a perpendicular expression of a horizontal desire.

Except during the nine months before he draws his first breath, no man manages his affairs as well as a tree does.
"Maxims for Revolutionists," Man and Superman, 1903

We laugh at the haughty American nation because it makes the Negro clean its boots and then proves the moral and physical inferiority of the Negro by the fact that he is a shoeblack, but we ourselves throw the whole drudgery of creation on one sex, and then imply that no female of any womanliness or delicacy would initiate any effort in that direction. There are no limits to male hypocrisy in this matter.
Man and Superman, 1903

Marriage is popular because it combines the maximum of temptation with the maximum of opportunity.
"Maxims for Revolutionists," Man and Superman, 1903

ELLIE: Why do women always want other women's husbands?
CAPTAIN SHOTOVER: Why do horse-thieves prefer a horse that is broken in to one that is wild?
Heartbreak House, Act II, 1919

The sex relation is not a personal relation. It can be irresistibly desired and rapturously consummated between persons who could not endure one another for a day in any other relation.
Letter to Frank Harris

The politician who once had to learn to flatter Kings has now to learn how to fascinate, amuse, coax, humbug, frighten, or otherwise strike the fancy of the electorate.
"The Revolutionist's Handbook and Pocket Companion," Man and Superman, 1903

Any person under the age of thirty, who, having any knowledge of the existing social order, is not a revolutionist, is an inferior. And yet revolutionists have never lightened the burden of tyranny: they have only shifted it to another shoulder.
"The Revolutionist's Handbook and Pocket Companion," Man and Superman, 1903

Democracy substitutes election by the incompetent many for appointment by the corrupt few.
"Maxims for Revolutionists," Man and Superman, 1903

He knows nothing and he thinks he knows everything. That points clearly to a political career.
Major Barbara, Act III, 1905

You'll never have a quiet world till you knock the patriotism out of the human race.
O'Flaherty, V.C., 1915

Revolutionary movements attract those who are not good for established institutions as well as those who are too good for them.
Preface to Androcles and the Lion, 1916

An election is a moral horror, as bad as a battle except for the blood: a mud bath for every soul concerned in it.
Preface to Back to Methuselah, Part II, 1920

The only man who had a proper understanding of Parliament was old Guy Fawkes.
On the Rocks, Act II, 1933

Unless the highest court can be set in motion by the humblest individual, justice is a mockery.
Geneva, Act II, 1938

A government which robs Peter to pay Paul can always depend on the support of Paul.
Everybody's Political What's What, 1944

The man with toothache thinks everyone happy whose teeth are sound. The poverty stricken man makes the same mistake about the rich man.
"Maxims for Revolutionists," Man and Superman, 1903

MENDOZA: I am a brigand, I live by robbing the rich.
TANNER: I am a gentleman: I live by robbing the poor.
Man and Superman, Act III, 1903

In an ugly and unhappy world the richest man can purchase nothing but ugliness and unhappiness.
"Maxims for Revolutionists," Man and Superman, 1903

Englishmen never will be slaves: they are free to do whatever the Government and public opinion allow them to do.
Man and Superman, Act III, 1903

Assassination is the extreme form of censorship.
"The Rejected Statement,"
The Shewing Up of Blanco Posnet, 1917

You use a glass mirror to see your face: you use works of art to see your soul.
Back to Methuselah, Part V, 1920

A drama critic is a man who leaves no turn unstoned.
The New York Times, November 5, 1950

Beware of the man whose god is in the skies.
"Maxims for Revolutionists," Man and Superman, 1903

If you go to Heaven without being naturally qualified for it, you will not enjoy yourself there.
Man and Superman, Act III, 1903

Hell is the home of honour, duty, justice, and the rest of the seven deadly virtues.
> Man and Superman, Act III, 1903

Heaven, as conventionally conceived, is a place so inane, so dull, so useless, so miserable, that nobody has ever ventured to describe a whole day in heaven, though plenty of people have described a day at the seaside.
> Preface to Misalliance, 1910

All great truths begin as blasphemies.
> Annajanska, 1917

I have the utmost respect for the magnificent discoveries which we owe to science. But any fool can make a discovery. Every baby has to discover more in the first years of its life than Roger Bacon ever discovered in his laboratory.
> Preface to Back to Methuselah, 1920

Mark Twain and I are in very much the same position. We have to put things in such a way as to make people, who would otherwise hang us, believe that we are joking.
> Table Talk, 1924

When two people are under the influence of the most violent, most insane, most delusive, and most transient of passions, they are required to swear that they will remain in that excited, abnormal, and exhausting condition continuously until death do them part.
> Preface to Getting Married, 1908

Old men are dangerous; it doesn't matter to them what is going to happen to the world.
> Heartbreak House, 1920

I have always despised Adam because he had to be tempted by the woman, as she was by the serpent, before he could be induced to pluck the apple from the tree of knowledge. I should have swallowed every apple on the tree the moment the owner's back was turned.
> Quoted by Hesketh Pearson, 1942

The liar's punishment is not in the least that he is not believed, but that he cannot believe anyone else.
> The Quintessence of Ibsenism, Chapter 4, 1891

The fickleness of the women I love is only equaled by the infernal constancy of the women who love me.
> The Philanderer, Act II, 1893

Lack of money is the root of all evil.
> Man and Superman, 1903
> —D.W.

MAE WEST

Mae West (August 17, 1892–November 22, 1980) was born in Brooklyn. She began acting

Mae West confronted society with an early challenge to its notions about female sexuality.

at age eight and debuted on Broadway at nineteen. She was a successful vaudeville and nightclub performer and also wrote and produced plays, including Sex (1926), which earned her a ten-day jail term. She got one day off for good behavior. She made her movie debut in 1932 and starred in several successful films over the next eight years. She even appeared once with W. C. Fields—in My Little Chickadee (1940). As a strong woman, proud of her sexuality, Mae West presented a shocking contrast to other screen actresses of the period and she served as a primary target for the era's censors. Some of the lines that made her famous were written for her, but most were her own creations.

Hatcheck Girl: Goodness, what lovely diamonds.
Maudie Triplett: Goodness had nothing to do with it, dearie.
> Night After Night, 1932

In one of her stage shows, West was told that ten men were waiting to meet her at home. She replied: "I'm tired, send one of them home."

It takes two to get one in trouble.
> She Done Him Wrong, 1933

Referring to *I'm No Angel* (1933): "*I wrote the story myself. It's all about a girl who lost her reputation but never missed it.*"

Asked what kind of a character she was playing in the film *I'm No Angel*, West replied: "*She's the kind of girl who climbed the ladder of success, wrong by wrong.*"

In a spot where the script of *I'm No Angel* called for her to look bored, Miss West turned to her maid and ad-libbed: "*Peel me a grape, Beulah.*"

A man in the house is worth two in the street.
                Belle of the Nineties, 1934

It is better to be looked over than overlooked.
                Belle of the Nineties, 1934

Between two evils, I always pick the one I never tried before.
                Klondike Annie, 1936

A man's kiss is his signature.
                My Little Chickadee, 1940

I play no favorites. There's something about every man. A man may be short, dumpy, and rapidly getting bald—but if he has fire, women will like him.

Whenever a guy starts boasting to me about his family tree, I seem to smell a strong sniff of sap rising.

The score never interested me, only the game.

It's not the men in my life that counts—it's the life in my men.

Is that a gun in your pocket, or are you just glad to see me?

Gentlemen may prefer blondes—but who says that blondes prefer gentlemen?

Women with "pasts" interest men because men hope that history will repeat itself.

The curve is more powerful than the sword.

When I'm good, I'm very, very good, but when I'm bad, I'm better.
                I'm No Angel, 1933

I used to be Snow White . . . but I drifted.

Brains are an asset to the woman in love who's smart enough to hide 'em.

Marriage is a great institution, but I'm not ready for an institution yet.

Every man I meet wants to protect me. I can't figure out what from.
                My Little Chickadee, 1940

I generally avoid temptation . . . unless I can't resist it.
                My Little Chickadee, 1940
                —D.W.

Years ago, I tried to top everybody, but I don't anymore. I realized it was killing conversation. When you're always trying for a topper you aren't really listening. It ruins communication.
Groucho Marx, The Groucho Phile, 1976

FOOTNOTE PERSON

JAMES KILROY
(1902–62)

Everybody knew the man by name. American servicemen in World War II had carried his name to remote corners of the world. He was Kilroy, whose name GIs scrawled almost everywhere they went in the catchphrase "Kilroy Was Here."

Was there really a Kilroy?

Well, one fall evening in the late 1940s, James J. Kilroy, a forty-seven-year-old shipyard worker from Halifax, Massachusetts, was trying to figure out how to scrape up enough money to buy Christmas presents for his nine children. No matter how hard or how long a day a man might work, there never seemed to be enough

money around at Christmas when there were nine children in the house.

"We'll be pinching pennies again this Christmas, Margaret," Kilroy remarked to his wife that evening. They were sipping cocoa and listening to the kitchen radio after the children had been put to bed. "We'll only be able to come up with one small gift for each of the children. Money's tight."

Then over the radio came the coaxing voice of an announcer with still another commercial. "Are you Kilroy?" the radio voice asked. "If you are the man responsible for the slogan 'Kilroy Was Here,' and can prove it, we have a wonderful prize waiting for you."

Both Kilroys beamed when they heard the announcement. That "wonderful prize" might be cold cash. And with Christmas so close at hand, it certainly would come in handy. At least, Jim and Margaret thought, the prize would be "something sensible." Alas, that was not the case in this contest, sponsored by the Transit Company of America.

James Kilroy is dead now. He died in 1962. His widow resides in Plympton, a town only a few miles from Halifax. "My Jim," she recalled, "was too old for the Second World War. And he was too young for the First World War. But he was very proud of the tribute our American servicemen paid him when they adopted his 'Kilroy Was Here' slogan as their very own."

After the broadcast that night, she remembered, Kilroy sat down and penned a letter to the Transit Company of America, proving he indeed was the Kilroy who was "here."

"Jim was a checker at the Fore River Shipyard in Quincy, just south of Boston," says Mrs. Kilroy. "He started to work there in 1941 shortly before Pearl Harbor. His job was to go around and count the number of holes a riveter had filled. The riveters were on piece work and got paid so much for each rivet. After he had counted the rivets, he'd put a check mark in chalk, so the rivets wouldn't be counted twice.

"Now, some riveters would wait until the checker went off duty and erase the last mark. Another checker would come through and count the rivets a second time, and the riveters would get paid twice. Just as he was going off duty one day, Jim heard his boss ask a riveter if Kilroy had been by checking rivets. The riveter said no. When Jim heard that, he got angry because he had just checked those particular rivets. He took some chalk, went over to where the two men were standing, and wrote 'Kilroy Was Here' in big letters over the rivets. That was the start of it. After that, every time he checked the rivets, he scrawled 'Kilroy Was Here' in big letters next to the check mark."

Ordinarily, the rivets and chalk marks would have been covered up by paint. But there was a war on, and ships were leaving the Quincy yard so fast there wasn't time enough to paint them. And so they arrived at their destinations with the now mysterious inscriptions still on them.

Kilroy's prize in that Transit Company contest turned out to be a two-ton trolley car. It was twenty-five feet long and seven feet high. Exactly what the Transit Company of America figured Kilroy or anybody else was supposed to do with a vintage trolley—it had been built in 1910—must remain a moot point.

Jim Kilroy, however, was not about to be overwhelmed by a mere streetcar. He gathered his children around him. When Peggy, fifteen; James, thirteen; Mary Ann, twelve; Robert, ten; Ellen, nine; Ann, six; Kathleen, four; Larry, three; and Judy, six months, were all together,

he asked them: "How would you like Santa Claus to bring you a trolley car for Christmas?" They were overjoyed. After all, what child wouldn't want a real trolley car for Christmas?

On December 23 the old trolley was loaded aboard a seventy-five-ton low-bed trailer to be lugged over the road to Halifax. That king-size truck may not have looked much like a sleigh as it grunted and groaned its way out of the Boston Elevated trolley yard in Everett, about thirty-five miles from Halifax, but to the Kilroys, it was just that.

The trolley was escorted by a crew of nine men, and their assignment was to make certain it didn't get caught under any low bridge or in any street lights during the long, slow trip to Halifax. The first day, the trolley traveled about twenty miles. It was just about halfway home. That night it was parked in a vacant lot in the town of Canton. Overnight, tiny flakes of snow drifted slowly down from the sky. A few at first. Then more and more of them. By daybreak it was a blizzard. It was going to be a white Christmas after all.

White Christmases may be what most people want, but at the Kilroys' in Halifax, a couple of nervous parents did a lot of fingernail nibbling. To them it seemed the entire family was destined to endure a gloomy Christmas thanks to all that white stuff outside. With so much of it on the ground, how was Santa going to be able to make his special Christmas delivery at their house?

During the afternoon the snow stopped. And in the evening, a crowd of neighbors and friends, and even the local Board of Selectmen, were on hand to welcome the trolley—if it ever showed up. It didn't. After a reasonable wait in the snow, everybody went home.

The Kilroy children hung their stockings by the fireplace with care and headed up to bed. The older ones prayed the trolley would be there in the morning. The younger ones knew it would be there. Such is the power of Santa.

Christmas morning dawned. Like children all over, the children were up early that day at the Kilroy home. In fact they were all dressed and out in the backyard playing when their parents awoke. In the yard, amid all that snow, was the bright orange trolley. It was parked by the side of the house, and though it lacked tracks, the vintage vehicle was destined to make countless journeys to wonderlands even modern-day trolleys, with all their complex gadgets, have never been privileged to visit. There may have been a blizzard that Christmas Eve. But Saint Nick was not about to disappoint those nine Kilroy children. Chalked on the ceiling of the trolley was the message "Santa Was Here."

Source: Reprinted with permission from the NRTA Journal. Copyright 1976 by the National Retired Teachers Association.

QUOTEBOOK: COMMUNICATION

The root function of language is to control the universe by describing it.

James Baldwin, *Notes of a Native Son*, 1955

Swearing was invented as a compromise between running away and fighting.

Finley Peter Dunne

Cut out all those exclamation marks. An exclamation mark is like laughing at your own joke.

F. Scott Fitzgerald, quoted by Sheila Graham and Gerald Frank, *Beloved Infidel*

A period is a stop sign. A semicolon is a rolling stop sign; a comma is merely an amber light.

Andrew J. Offutt, in *Writer's Digest*, July 1978

The medium is the message. This is merely to say that the personal and social consequences of any medium . . . result from the new scale that is introduced into our affairs by each extension of ourselves or by any new technology.

Marshall McLuhan, *Understanding Media*, 1964

One picture is worth ten thousand words.

Frederick R. Barnard, *Printers' Ink*, March 10, 1927

Chapter 10

MOVIES

MOVIE FIRSTS

1900—Scriptwriter: The movies were just five years old when the new century dawned. Most of them were actualities. Then the American Mutoscope and Biograph Company hired New York journalist Roy McCardell to write ten scenarios a week at fifteen dollars each—about twice the weekly wage of a store clerk. As the films ran only ninety seconds, a full script could be written on a single sheet of paper. McCardell completed his first week's assignment in a single afternoon.

1900—Talking Films: Everyone knows that the first talkie was *The Jazz Singer* in 1927. Or was it? Talkies had a long history by then, starting with a program of short films premiered at the Paris Exposition on June 8, 1900. Presented by Clement Maurice of the Gaumont Company, they were synchronized with disks played on an amplified record player. A highlight of the program was Sarah Bernhardt, doyenne of French theater, in the duel scene from *Hamlet*— and yes, she played the Prince of Denmark.

1900—Woman Director: Like many successful businesswomen before the era of equal opportunity, Alice Guy started out as a secretary. It was her good fortune to be hired by Leon Gaumont, one of France's pioneer producers in the 1890s. Alice stopped pounding the typewriter keys one day to tell Gaumont that his films were all too much of a "muchness"—what they lacked was originality. Gaumont's response was if she was so smart, why didn't she direct a movie herself? She jumped at the chance and made a delightful fantasy called *La Fée aux Choux*, in which young lovers strolling in the countryside encounter a fairy in a cabbage patch and are presented with a child—their firstborn.

1903—Western: Just about every reference book on the movies records the fact that *The Great Train Robbery* was the first to tell a story and the first western. Wrong on both counts. It was copyrighted by the Edison Company on December 1, 1903. Six weeks earlier two westerns had been copyrighted by the American Mutoscope and Biograph Company (who had been making dramatic films since 1900). One was *Kit Carson*, the other *The Pioneer*, but as the former was shot first, on September 8, 1903, it takes pride of place. Directed by Wallace McCutchen, it was filmed in the Adirondack Mountains of New York State—about as far from the real West as it is possible to get in the continental United States— and at twenty-one minutes' running time was the longest dramatic movie made at that date.

1906—Feature Film: In 1906 the average length of a film was five to ten minutes— American and European producers did not believe that the semiliterate audiences of the nickelodeons could follow a story line for longer than that. But the Australians thought differently. The world's first full-length feature, running for more than an hour, was premiered on December 24 at the Athenaeum Hall in Melbourne, Victoria. Made for $2,250, Charles Tait's *The Story of the Kelly Gang* was an epic drama about the Australian bushranger Ned Kelly. But nobody knows the name of the star. He was an unidentified Canadian from a theatrical touring company who walked off the set shortly before the film was completed. The movie was finished with a stand-in playing the remaining scenes in long-shot.

1906—Film Score: It was the Italians who pioneered the composition of music specially for films, a practice that did not become widespread elsewhere until the 1920s. The first film composer was Romolo Bacchioni, who scored two Cines productions of 1906, *Malio dell'Oro* and *Pierrot Innamorato*. It was not until ten years later that the first American film score was composed by Victor Herbert for *The Fall of a Nation*, forgotten sequel to the D. W. Griffith classic *The Birth of a Nation*.

1906—Cartoon Film: A popular act at the vaudeville halls in the early years of the century was the lightning cartoonist who drew cartoons of the famous and infamous on a blackboard. One such was an Englishman in New York named J. Stuart Blackton. Although there had been a number of short films of lightning cartoonists at work from the earliest days of filmmaking, Blackton took the technique a stage further. The artist's drawing took on a life of its own, the still pictures magically starting to move. In *Humorous Phases of Funny Faces*, the world's first animated film, Blackton depicted a top-hatted gent with a large "ceegar" blowing smoke into the face of a demure Gibson girl. She reacts as any young woman of New York would do today—with horror and disgust.

1906—Newsreel: The idea of a weekly film series depicting the news has generally been credited to the Pathé brothers of Paris in 1908. In fact, two years earlier an English producer named Will G. Barker had presented a regular newsreel at the Empire Theater in London's Leicester Square. And this one was daily, just like the television news that would supersede—and eventually kill off—the movie newsreel. Or almost daily. Barker's *Day by Day* lived up to its title except on the days when London's pea-soup fogs prevented filming.

1906—Purpose-Built Movie Theater: The earliest movie theaters were the converted stores with hard wooden benches and a bedsheet for a screen that came to be known as nickelodeons. In America, where many moviegoers were illiterate immigrants, these survived until World War I and gave the movies a down-market image as entertainment fit only for the poor. In Europe it was different. As early as 1906 the first purpose-built, luxury cinema was opened on the boulevard Montmartre in Paris. The Omnia Pathé, which opened on December 1 of that year with a film called *Le Pendu*, was also the first with a raked floor so that everyone could see above the heads in front. The price of a ticket was double the price of the storefront movie theaters but the Paris bourgeoisie were prepared to pay the extra to sit in comfort. Other luxury theaters followed and two years later *Film d'Art* began to attract the intelligentsia into the new palaces of art and entertainment.

1908—Flashback: How to show an episode that took place before the main action of the story? There were so few movies that told a proper story before 1906 that the need had never arisen. But in the Lubin production *A Yiddisher Boy*, it was crucial to the narrative that the hero had been involved in a boyhood street fight twenty-five years earlier. And so the flashback was born.

1908—Color Movie: George Albert Smith's *A Visit to the Seaside* was an evocative documentary depicting a summer's day at Brighton, the elegant resort on England's south coast. It showed children paddling in the sea and eating ice cream, a performance by the White Coons Pierrot troupe, a pretty girl falling out of a boat, and the band of the magnificent kilted Cameron Highlanders playing the pipes and drums. And there was a very daring scene that caused many a stout matron in the audience to clap a hand across her children's eyes—of men peeping through the back of the bathing machines as the lady bathers disrobed. Shot in the new Kinemacolor process for the Urban Trading Company, it was the world's first commercially produced movie in natural colors.

1909—Stars: The "star system" began to emerge when producers realized that audiences would go to see a film simply because it featured one of the anonymous five-dollar-a-day players they had seen and liked in a previous role. But even before they took the momentous step of billing the names of leading players—who promptly fulfilled their worst expectations by demanding ten dollars a day—the word *star* had appeared in print to connote the new heroes and heroines of the silver screen. Surprisingly, it was coined by the august *New York Times*, a paper little read by the patrons of the five-cent nickelodeons, and headed a letter from a Brooklyn reader published on March 11, 1909, with the title "Moving Pictures 'Stars.' "

1911—Hollywood Studio: The Centaur Company specialized in westerns—all of them shot in New Jersey. Their leading director, Al Christie, wanted to head west to real sagebrush country in California. Centaur's owner, David Horsley, figured Florida would be better, but agreed to abide by a heads-or-tails decision. Christie tossed and won. He toured southern California looking for a cheap enough building to rent for a studio and eventually found a derelict roadhouse in a small town a few miles from Los Angeles. The tumbledown shack was only forty dollars a month, and what if it was on a dusty road heading nowhere in particular? At least the name of the road would look good on the studio letterhead even if nobody had ever heard of it: Sunset Boulevard.

1911—Backlighting by Reflectors: One rule of the pioneer cameraman was never face the camera to the sun. But one day on set D. W. Griffith's cameraman Billy Bitzer playfully turned his camera on Mary Pickford and Owen Moore as they sat at a shiny-topped table with the sun behind them. Instead of the couple's appearing in silhouette, as he expected, Bitzer found that he had obtained a beautifully lit shot with the two artists' faces bathed in

radiance—suitably, since they were in love—
the effect of the sun's rays reflected from the
tabletop. He devised a system by which one
mirror would reflect the sun into another,
which could then be beamed to the back of a
performer's head. Bitzer employed this technique for the first time in *Enoch Arden*, which
opens with a superbly backlit shot of the
villagers bidding the sailors goodbye.

1911—Cinema Organ: The earliest cinema
music was played on tinkling pianos in shabby
nickelodeons. As the movies began to appeal to
a more sophisticated audience, something more
ambitious was needed. In 1911 the first cinema
organs were produced by the Wurlitzer Company of North Tonawanda, New York. The
"Mighty Wurlitzer" was built to the design of an
immigrant from Liverpool, England, named
Robert Hope-Jones. While the organs prospered,
he did not. Exasperated by the expense of his
constant improvements in design, Hope-Jones's
employers locked him out of the organ factory.
In total despair the brilliant inventor killed
himself.

1911—Double Bill: Australia was the first
country in the world to make full-length feature
films (see 1906) and in 1911 it had the highest
output of features in the world. On May 15 of
that year Australia pioneered again when for
the first time not just one but two features were
shown on the same program. The theater was
the Glacarium in Melbourne and the double bill
consisted of an Australian main picture, *The
Lost Chord*, and an Italian supporting feature,
The Fall of Troy.

1912—Serial: In America in 1912 producers
and exhibitors were still uncertain that audiences had the attention span to sit through a full-
length feature, despite the fact that films of an
hour or even an hour and a half were proving
successful in Europe and Australia. The Edison
Company came up with a new idea—a long story
told in weekly ten-minute episodes. Their first
serial was called *What Happened to Mary*, a
twelve-parter that starred Mary Fuller as a found-
ling seeking her lost inheritance. Unlike the racy
cliff-hanger serials that followed, it was a sentimental melodrama catering to the taste of an unsophisticated audience. Some of the exhibitors
were equally unsophisticated. When the picture
opened in the small town of Haddington in Scotland, the local cinema manager put up a large
poster proclaiming in foot-high letters WHAT
HAPPENED TO MARY TWICE NIGHTLY.

1912—Full Frontal Male Nudity: It was in the
Italian feature *Dante's Inferno* that male geni-
talia were first revealed on screen, albeit fleet-
ingly. Well over half a century was to pass
before any leading players exposed themselves,

*Alan Bates and Oliver Reed nude wrestling in the
1969 production of* Women in Love.

when Alan Bates and Oliver Reed wrestled in
the nude in Ken Russell's 1969 movie *Women in
Love*.

1913—Native American Cast: *Hiawatha* was
the first of only four full-length features with an
all-Native American cast. Its 150 performers,
drawn from various tribes, included leading
lady Soongoot as Minnehaha. None has been
made since 1930, when Chief Yellow Robe of
the Ojibwa tribe starred in a Canadian-U.S.
coproduction titled *The Silver Enemy*, a picture
also notable for the fact that only four members
of a cast of several hundred had ever seen a
movie.

1913—Camera Dolly: The first time a mobile
camera was used on a feature film was when
cameraman Nikolai Kozlovski of Moscow's
State Film Studios executed a tracking shot in
the opening reel of Yevgeny Bauer's *The Twilight of a Woman's Soul*. It was not until two
years later that the camera dolly arrived in the
United States, but cameraman William F. Adler
advanced the technique by using one for
forward and backward tracking shots and another for sideways movement when he shot
The Second-in-Command in 1915. Camera mobility could also be achieved without a dolly.
When the celebrated German director F. W.
Murnau wanted to depict Emil Jannings's
drunken view of the wedding in his 1924
classic *The Last Laugh*, he mounted his cameraman on roller skates.

1914—Feature Film Directed by a Woman: Lois Weber became the first American woman director in 1907 when she started to make primitive "talkie" shorts for Gaumont Talking Pictures in New York. Seven years later she pioneered again, as the first woman in the world to direct a full-length feature, the Rex production of The Merchant of Venice. If anything needed speech it was Shakespeare, but this one was a silent picture.

1914—All-Color Feature Film: The 1935 production Becky Sharp may have been the first three-color feature film (see 1935), but at least forty full-length features in color had been made earlier. The earliest of all was the one-hour-and-forty-minute Kinemacolor production The World, the Flesh and the Devil, which opened at the Holborn Empire in London on April 9, 1914, billed as "A £10,000 Picture Play in Actual Colours" in "four parts and 120 scenes." Directed by F. Martin Thornton, it starred Frank Esmond and Stella St. Audrie. According to the critics the color was great, the direction and acting execrable.

1914—Movie Make-Up: In the primitive movies of the pre-1910 period, even interior scenes were shot in natural light—with ceilingless rooms built on outdoor stages. It was not until artificial lighting became widespread and the movies moved indoors that makeup became necessary for the performers. It soon became apparent, however, that stage makeup would not answer well enough. The orthochromatic film stock used was insensitive to the red end of the spectrum, so that freckles and skin blemishes registered as black, pink cheeks a murky gray, and skin tones a deathly white. In order to create the impression of a natural skin tone on screen, a heavy application of yellow makeup became necessary. First to address this problem with a makeup designed specifically for the screen was Polish immigrant Max Factor, who moved to Hollywood in 1914 and introduced his Supreme Greasepaint—custom-made for the movies.

1914—Book of the Film: Selig-Polyscope's 1913 The Adventures of Kathlyn, starring the daring athlete Kathlyn Williams, was the first of the cliff-hanger serials, with audiences left in an agony of suspense at the end of each of the twenty-seven episodes until the last one. It was also the first film to be "novelized," when best-selling novelist Harold McGrath took Gilson Willets's original scenario and turned it into a fast-paced thriller with a generous dollop of sex. Published in Indianapolis in 1914, the book had a lurid full-color cover showing a resolute Kathlyn, having spurned the attentions of an Oriental potentate, being dragged away to a nameless fate by two turbaned members of an ethnic minority. The stills from the film that illustrated the spicy text were somewhat more decorous.

1915—Camera Cranes: The use of camera cranes was pioneered by cameraman William F. Adler for the elevated shots he needed on Metro's Francis X. Bushman starrer The Second-in-Command, and independently by Allan Dwan, who constructed a rather more ambitious elevator on tracks for filming scenes during the Babylonian sequence of D. W. Griffith's epic Intolerance. The 115-foot-high structure enabled Griffith to secure a parabolic shot, commencing at the ramparts of the palace and descending forward over a sea of extras to ground level and a close shot of the leading players. It was one of the more spectacular effects in early filmmaking.

1915—Nude Star: Hedy Lamarr is famous as the first leading lady to appear on screen in the altogether. Except that she wasn't. Nearly twenty years before Lamarr's notorious Extase, Audrey Munson had bared her all in George Foster Platt's Inspiration. In the film Munson played an inexperienced country girl who is hired as a "life model" by a sculptor with whom she falls in love. The film created a storm of controversy, some considering the nude scenes "artistic" and "educational," others condemning them as depraved. None of this discomforted Audrey Munson, who appeared once more as nature intended in her next film, meaningfully titled Purity.

1916—All-Black Cast: Jersey City sees few world premieres, but on July 14, 1916, it had the distinction of hosting the opening of the first all-black feature film. Produced by the Frederick Douglass Film Company, the six-reel The Colored American Winning His Suit had a cast made up of "young men and women of the race from the best families in New Jersey." The advantage of employing these scions of middle-class black families was that they did not require payment. In later years the professional artistes who performed in black movies were probably the worst paid in the industry. White director Edgar G. Ulmer recalled paying the fifty black chorus girls in his 1939 Moon over Harlem twenty-five cents a day each. The shooting schedule was four days and the girls had to pay their car fares from Harlem to the studio in Jersey out of the one dollar they earned for a week's work.

1916—Star Autobiography: The star system began to emerge only about 1912, but it was barely four years later that the first of many thousands of movie-star autobiographies made its appearance in the bookshops. Published by Doran of New York, Pearl White's Just Me was a lively and wholly unreliable account of her rise as the queen of the silent serials.

1917—Continuity Girl: Sarah Y. Mason had no intention of becoming a continuity girl, because no such profession existed in 1917 when she was invited to Hollywood by Douglas Fairbanks. He had seen her in a high-school play and thought she had star quality. She was cast in Fairbanks's next movie, *Arizona*, but found that performing on the amateur stage and playing in a major motion picture presented quite different demands. Reluctantly, Fairbanks released her, but she was still determined to make the grade in Hollywood. Explaining that she was an experienced stenographer, she persuaded Allan Dwan, director of *Arizona*, to let her stay on to take notes of each scene so that continuity mistakes could be avoided. She also checked for anachronisms, notorious in period films in the silent era. So much money was saved by avoiding costly retakes that the studio hired her permanently and other studios soon followed suit by appointing their own continuity girls.

1919—Gay Movie: In the permissive atmosphere following the collapse of society in Germany immediately after World War I, the government abolished film censorship. During the eighteen months before it was reimposed, a rash of sex films exploded onto German theater screens. Most were about rape, prostitution, and adultery, but one was notable as the first motion picture in the world with an overtly homosexual theme. Directed by Richard Oswald, *Anders als die Anderen* starred Conrad Veidt and Reinhold Schunzel as star-crossed male lovers in the Bohemian world of contemporary Berlin. No other film about male homosexuality was made anywhere in the world before World War II.

1922—Sound-on-Film Drama: Although numerous attempts had been made to produce films with sound synchronized from phonograph records, no real progress was made toward a technically proficient system until the Tri-Ergon process of recording audio directly onto film was developed in Germany by Joseph Engl, Joseph Masolle, and Hans Vogt. On September 17, 1922, they presented their first "talkie" before an invited audience of 1,000 at Berlin's prestigious Alhambra Kino. Titled *The Arsonist*, it had a cast of three, with Erwin Baron playing seven of the nine roles. But talkies failed to find favor in Germany because critics objected to what they saw as a contradiction of the true art of the motion picture—mime. They also feared—probably justifiably—that German films would cease to have an international audience. Eventually the Tri-Ergon process was acquired by American movie mogul William Fox, who used it to make the first sound newsreels—Fox Movietone—and the first sound-on-film feature movies.

1922—Banned Star: By the early 1920s Hollywood had established a reputation for moral license that had the mothers of the nation calling for government action. To stave off federal interference, the studios formed their own self-regulating body and appointed former postmaster general Will H. Hays to head what was formally titled the Motion Picture Producers and Distributors of America but was better known as the "Hays Office." Hays's brief was to clean up Hollywood and he needed a dramatic gesture to show he meant business. One of his first acts was to slap a banning order on comedian Roscoe "Fatty" Arbuckle, then the highest-paid star in the world. Six days earlier Arbuckle had been acquitted of the manslaughter of "good-time girl" Virginia Rappe during a drunken party. Arbuckle may have been innocent in the eyes of the law, but he had transgressed against the moral code of Middle America and for that he paid with his career. Apart from a few roles in short films in the early 1930s, he never worked again. (See page 434.)

1922—3-D Feature Film: Any quiz show that allows *Bwana Devil* (1952) as the correct answer to the question "What was the first full-length feature in 3-D?" is thirty years out. The first was Nat Deverich's melodrama *Power of Love*, produced in an anaglyphic process developed by Harry K. Fairall and premiered at the Ambassador Hotel Theater, Los Angeles, on September 27, 1922. It starred Terry O'Neil as a young sea captain in the California of the 1840s, with Barbara Bedford as his love interest.

1923—Wide-Screen Movie: "A wide screen just makes a bad film twice as bad," quipped Sam Goldwyn. Filoteo Alberini would have been unlikely to agree. He devised the first wide-screen process, Panoramico Alberini, as early as 1914, but had to wait another nine years to see it used in a feature film—and then only for a single sequence in Enrico Guazzoni's *Il Sacco di Roma*.

1923—Freeze-Frame: Abel Gance is remembered chiefly for his epic *Napoléon* of 1926. Three years earlier he had made a vast, sprawling melodrama about life on the railroad, *La Roue*. In its original version it ran for eight hours and thirty-two minutes, the longest film ever made at that date (he was to do a nine-hour cut of *Napoléon*). *La Roue* was also notable for the first use of the freeze-frame device, employed by Gance at the end of the movie to heighten the dramatic intensity of the death of the old railwayman Sisif.

1925—Back Projection: Back projection is the technique by which outdoor scenes can be shot in the studio by placing the performers against a back-projected filmed background. It was first used by special-effects maestro Willis O'Brien for a single scene of *The Lost World*, an early precursor of *Jurassic Park* about twentieth-century adventurers encountering dinosaurs in unexplored territory.

1926—In-Flight Movie: *The Lost World* scored another first on April 16, 1926, when it became the first motion picture to be shown in an airplane. This was aboard a scheduled Imperial Airways flight from London to Paris, then a three- to four-hour flight that allowed ample time for watching a full-length feature.

1927—Footprints Outside Grauman's Chinese Theater: The bestowal of an Oscar may be Hollywood's greatest accolade, but being invited to impress your footprints into the paving outside Grauman's Chinese Theater must run a fairly close second. The first pair belonged to Norma Talmadge and the date was May 18, 1927, but is it true that she happened to step on the wet cement by accident, thereby giving Sid Grauman a great idea for publicizing his new theater? Like most Hollywood legends, it is more fun to believe it than not.

1927—Feature-Length Talkie: *The Jazz Singer* was not supposed to be a talkie—Sam Warner's intention was to have synchronized songs and sound effects but no speech. It was Al Jolson's own idea to ad-lib a few lines to introduce the first song, which he did with the now immortal words: "Wait a minute. Wait a minute. You ain't heard nothing yet!" Most people have assumed that this was a clever allusion to the fact that nobody had ever heard words spoken from the screen before (they had—see 1900). In fact it was a catchphrase Jolson was accustomed to using in his stage act. There were only two talking sequences, the first of 60 words, the second of 294. In the latter Eugenie Besserer as Jolson's screen mother spoke thirteen words and disapproving father Warner Oland said just one—"Stop!" Happily, Sam Warner liked the ad-libbing enough to keep it in when the film premiered at the Warner Theater on October 6, 1927. The rest was history.

> Moving pictures need sound as much as Beethoven symphonies need lyrics.
> Charlie Chaplin, 1928

1928—All-Talking Feature: Once Sam Warner had been convinced that talking did not spoil an audience's enjoyment of a film, he could not have enough of it. Warner Brothers' *The Lights*

The Jazz Singer, *starring Al Jolson, was* not *the first talking film.*

of New York, starring Helene Costello, was so determinedly a talkie that the dialogue continued nonstop from opening credits to end titles. Warner's trumpeted "100% Talking!" *Variety* responded "100% Crude."

1928—Artificial Sound Effects: *The Lights of New York* (see above) may have been crude, but Warner Brothers was groping its way forward in a new and untried medium. One new problem that had to be confronted was how to create sound effects. The first one needed for *The Lights of New York* was of a train in motion. This was achieved with a small cylinder and piston mounted on a flat board, together with a nine-inch length of copper tubing set in an upright position. By turning a crank and blowing into the tube, the operator could simulate the sound of a mighty express train. After this success Warner Brothers established its own library of prerecorded sound effects, starting with just five—the gurgle of water, the squeak of a new pair of shoes, a train whistle, an automobile, and the crash of breaking glass. Within three years it had grown into 1 million feet of film.

1928—Hit Song from a Movie: None of the songs from *The Jazz Singer* (see 1927) was a hit, even though the film was. But with his next movie, Al Jolson struck gold in Tin Pan Alley. "Sonny Boy," which he sang in *The Singing Fool*, was the swooning, sentimental lyric for which Jolson will always be remembered. Composed by Buddy De Sylva, Lew Brown, and Ray Henderson, it swept America in those heady, optimistic, and affluent days just before the Wall Street crash and the onset of the Great Depression. Within nine months of the film's release, the song had sold two million disks and 1.25 million pieces of sheet music.

1929—Dubbing: When the talkies arrived, stars with a foreign accent were in trouble unless they happened to be Greta Garbo. Suave Hungarian leading man Paul Lukas had arrived in Hollywood in 1928 and was an immediate success in some of the last silent pictures to be made by the major studios. But when he was cast as a stockbroker in *The Wolf of Wall Street*, the front office got cold feet. Lukas was playing an American, and not many Wall Street wolves sound as if they have just arrived from Budapest. So for the first time one actor was seen on screen and another actor's voice was heard emanating from his mouth—for the record, the voice was that of one Lawford Davidson. Happily, Hollywood woke up to the fact that America, the melting pot, has more accents than any other country on Earth and for the next thirty years Lukas was able to play leading roles in his natural voice.

1929—Subtitled Movie: The coming of the talkies was a crisis for European filmmakers. Few films could make a profit in the domestic market—even then big bucks meant American distribution. The solution was subtitles and it created a new career opportunity for Herman G. Weinberg, a German immigrant who had settled in New York. He wrote the titles for the first subtitled movie released in the United States, *Two Hearts in Waltztime*. And during the next forty years he was to subtitle a record 450 foreign-language movies.

1929—All-Color Talkie: Warner Brothers had pioneered the first part-talking feature (see 1927) and the first all-talking feature (see 1928). Now they kept ahead of the game with the first all-talking feature in glorious Technicolor—albeit the somewhat somber-hued two-color version of Technicolor. Alan Crosland's *On with the Show* starred Betty Compson and Joe E. Brown in a story of backstage life on Broadway, which was premiered at the Winter Garden in New York on May 28, 1929. *Variety* opined that the color gave the picture "its leading topic of notice," but added "flesh coloring at times too prominent due to make-up."

1929—Unscheduled News Event on Sound Film: Fox *Movietone* pioneered the sound newsreel in 1928 and a year later secured the first sound scoop. On October 24, 1929, Prince Humbert of Italy was due to pay tribute to the Italian war dead at the Tomb of the Unknown Warrior in Rome. Permission to film the solemn occasion was withheld, but *Movietone* cameraman Jack Connelly concealed himself behind the tomb in an effort to secure forbidden pictures. He had just been discovered by the *polizia* when a shot rang out. Connelly kept the camera running as the cops scattered, and secured the only footage of the attempted assassination of Prince Humbert.

1930—Call of Nature Depicted on Film: Before stark reality invaded the cinema screen it was often remarked that no one ever seemed to feel the call of nature. Not until 1930 was anyone seen to relieve himself in a feature and it was the uninhibited French and the earthy Russians who led the way. In Luis Buñuel's *L'Age d'Or* a woman is depicted squatting on the lavatory, though precisely what bodily function she is performing is unclear. There was no room for doubt, though, in Alexander Dovzhenko's *Earth*. Like many Soviet pictures of the Stalinist era, it was about tractors and when one of them runs out of water a peasant does what a peasant has to do—urinates into the radiator.

1930—Multiplex Theater: Long before the present expansion of cinemas with multiple auditoriums, the Regal Twins in Manchester, England, was offering its patrons a choice of simultaneous programs. It was another twenty-five years, though, before Burnaby Theater in Burnaby, British Columbia, became the first triplex, with the first quad following in 1966 in Kansas City, Missouri. (For the world's largest multiplex, see Movie Records, page 427.)

> The legitimate theatre is in a panic . . . [with] talking pictures . . . all their seats at the same price. . . . Get it? The rich man stands in line with the poor.
>
> Lloyd Lewis, *New Republic*, 1929

1931—Lesbian Movie: Just as the first gay male movie came from Germany (see 1919), so did the first film about love between women. *Mädchen in Uniform* starred Dorothea Wieck as an insecure teenage girl in a repressive Prussian boarding school who forms a passionate attachment to a kind and beautiful teacher, played by Hertha Thiele. Two years later the same two

The first cinema portrayal of lesbian love came in the 1931 German film, Mädchen in Uniform.

actresses were reunited in another story of forbidden love entitled *Anna and Elizabeth*.

1931—360-Degree Pan in a Dramatic Film: Panning shots are almost as old as film, dating back to a German comedy short of 1896, and the first 360-degree pan followed not long after in a 1901 actuality shot by Edwin S. Porter from the Electric Tower at the Pan American Exposition. The idea of using a circular pan for dramatic effect, though, did not emerge for another thirty years. First to use it was James Whale in his classic *Frankenstein*, with Boris Karloff.

1931—Sound Flashback: In *City Streets* director Rouben Mamoulian employed a new technique to portray memories by synchronizing speech and sounds from the past with an image of the present. Dialogue heard earlier in the film was repeated over a huge close-up of Sylvia Sidney's tear-stained face as she recalls voices of those she has loved.

1932—Annual Film Festival: Venice, like most other holiday resorts, was badly hit by the depression. In order to attract visitors, the city fathers decided to hold a film festival as part of the Venice Biennale. A total of eighteen films from Germany, Britain, France, Italy, and the United States were unspooled at the Hotel Excelsior between August 6 and 21, 1932. Unusual for the time, three of them had been directed by women. No awards were made, but the public were invited to vote for their favorites. The venture was so successful that it was repeated two years later and then became an annual event.

1933—Drive-In Theater: Richard Hollingshead opened the first drive-in on a ten-acre site on Wilson Boulevard at Camden, New Jersey. The Camden Automobile Theater, which had accommodations for 400 autos, opened on June 6, 1933, with Adolphe Menjou in *Wife Beware*. Curiously, the idea did not really catch on until the advent of TV, with the number of drive-ins in the United States mushrooming from barely a thousand in 1949 to a peak of more than 4,000 in 1958. Was it parents staying home to watch *I Love Lucy* that drove the kids out to the drive-ins?

1933—Sex on Screen: The Czech film *Extase*, which first brought Hedy Lamarr to the notice of Hollywood, is famous for being the first movie in which the leading lady appeared in the nude, which it wasn't (see 1915). But it was the first theatrically released film in which the sex act was depicted. Hedy Lamarr, then known as Hedwig Kiesler, is a young bride who flies from her impotent husband, runs naked through the woods, bathes in a lake, and then encounters a young engineer. They repair to a hut, where she is fulfilled as a woman. Needless to say this sequence was not seen in the version released in America.

1934—Precredit Sequence: Nowadays it is not uncommon for a film to run five or even ten minutes before the titles and credits come up. The idea of having a sequence before the credits was completely new when Ben Hecht and Charles MacArthur decided they needed a device to point up the symbolism of the story in *Crime without Passion*. The opening shot was an extreme close-up of the barrel of a gun. The gun fires and drops of blood are seen falling to the floor. The three Furies of Greek mythology ascend from the puddle of blood in flowing robes and fly over a modern metropolis inciting various crimes of passion. One of the Furies sweeps her arm across the face of a skyscraper, shattering the window glass. The broken fragments of glass form the words of the main title, *Crime without Passion*.

1934—Hollywood Censorship: Hollywood had been attempting to censor itself ever since 1922, when the studios set up the Motion Picture Producers and Distributors of America to regulate the industry, averting the government regulation urged by outraged moralists. The problem about self-regulation in the twenties was that it was largely voluntary; those with innocuous scripts were happy enough to submit them to the MPPDA in advance, while others simply ignored the requirement. It was only in 1934 that the Production Code Administration Office was set up and penalties imposed for evasion. Every film had to have a seal of approval, the first being granted to Fox on July 11 for John Ford's production *The World Moves On*, saga of a Louisiana family starring Madeleine Carroll and Franchot Tone.

1935—Film with Stereophonic Sound: In 1932 French director Abel Gance, pioneer of the freeze-frame (see 1923), and his partner, André Debrie, patented a system for reproducing a sound track stereophonically. In 1935 they presented a reedited version of Gance's silent classic *Napoléon* at the Paramount Cinema in Paris, with added dialogue sequences and sound effects in stereophonic sound. The Gance-Debrie system worked well enough for speech, but the first successful stereo process for film music was Fantasound, developed by RCA and employed in 1941 to record the Philadelphia Orchestra's accompaniment of Disney's 1941 animated feature *Fantasia*.

1935—Film in Three-Color Technicolor: It was a pity that the first use of "three-strip" Technicolor, the progenitor of most color processes used today, was not for a more distinguished picture than Rouben Mamoulian's *Becky Sharp*, a lackluster adaptation of the Thackeray classic *Vanity Fair*. With a miscast Miriam Hopkins as the scheming Becky, it was not only the acting and the direction that were found wanting by the critics. The uneven color also failed to find favor, *Liberty* magazine remarking that the actors looked like "boiled salmon tipped in mayonnaise." Pat Nixon, future First Lady of the United States, had a walk-on part in the film.

1940—Overlapping Dialogue: The convention that one actor waits for another to finish speaking before responding works well enough in the legitimate theater, since realism is seldom a high priority. Early films borrowed most of the stage conventions, but as techniques grew more sophisticated with the coming of sound, audiences began to demand a more natural style of acting. The first use of overlapping dialogue is usually attributed to Orson Welles in his highly innovative *Citizen Kane* of 1941. But it was actually introduced a year earlier in the wild and witty Cary Grant–Rosalind Russell comedy *His Girl Friday*. The director responsible for this breakthrough in naturalistic performances was Howard Hawks.

1941—First Camerawoman: A small and select band of camerawomen had been shooting short films ever since the Brazilian Rosina Cianelli became the first of her profession in 1909. Breaking into feature films took a lot longer. It was not until 1941 that a woman was hired to shoot a full-length feature, and even then Soviet camerawoman Tamara Lobova shared the camera credit for *Suvorov* with her husband, Anatoli Golovnya. It was another five years before a woman achieved solo camera credit—also a Russian, Galina Pushkova, for *Songs of Abay*.

1944—Combined Live-Action–Animation Film: Walt Disney had pioneered the use of live actors in combination with animated characters with his *Alice* series in the early 1920s, but a full-length feature employing the difficult technique had to await a special need. It came from the U.S. State Department. When America entered World War II, it was crucial that the Latin American countries, many of them with strong cultural ties to Germany, be dissuaded from lending active support to the Nazis. Washington's secret weapon—or at least one of them—proved to be Donald Duck. He was cast opposite Aurora Miranda, sister of Carmen, in Disney's *The Three Caballeros*, an engaging piece of escapism set chiefly in idealized Mexican and Brazilian locales. Whether encouraged by the goodwill overtures of Ambassador Duck or not, Brazil became the only country south of the Rio Grande to declare war on the Axis.

1945—Woman Executive Producer: Women had produced movies since the pioneer days before World War I, but these were either line producers (experienced producers who work on a particular film supervising most facets of production as well as the work of the production manager) or, like Mary Pickford, women who owned their own production outfits. Real power in Hollywood lay with the heads of the major studios and—one rung below them—the executive producers in charge of a production slate. The first woman to join this select company was Virginia Van Upp, hired by Columbia in January 1945 to oversee twelve to fourteen big-budget productions a year. The line producers responsible to her for the individual films were all men.

1947—Helicopter Aerial Shots: Shooting from the air was limited before the advent of the helicopter. Conventional airplanes were too fast and could not hover; balloons went the way of the wind. It was Nicholas Ray who first used a helicopter for aerial shots. On August 21, 1947, cameraman Paul Ivano went aloft to shoot two scenes for RKO's *The Twisted Road*, a car chase and a scene of escaped convicts being pursued through a wheat field. According to Ray, using the helicopter saved $10,000 in production costs.

1947—3-D Feature without Glasses: Most 3-D systems require the viewer to wear anaglyphic spectacles, with one red and one green lens. Soviet scientist S. P. Ivanov developed the first process that successfully dispensed with these. Called Stereokino, the film was projected onto a "radial raster stereoscreen." This was a corrugated metal screen with "raster" grooves designed to reflect the twin images separately to the left and right eye. The process was used for the first time on a Soyuzdetfilm production of *Robinson Crusoe*, the first full-length sound film in color and 3-D. The most difficult scene for director Aleksandr Andreyevsky was one in which a wildcat had to be persuaded to walk toward the camera on a long thin branch. It took the cameraman three nights of filming to secure a single satisfactory shot, but the effect was electrifying in 3-D. Audiences ducked as the animal appeared to prowl over their heads.

1950—Safety Film: As early as 1908 Eastman Kodak had produced a nonflammable safety film on acetate, but it failed to catch on as it tended to shrink and wrinkle. It was only in 1950 that Kodak finally cracked the problem, using a triacetate base immune from shrinkage. Within a year nitrate stock was history, literally so in the case of thousands of films made before 1950 that have now decomposed. In the United Kingdom the organizers of Nitrate Project 2000 are racing against time to transfer 190 million feet of nitrate film—the equivalent of 20,000 full-length features—onto acetate safety film before it is lost to posterity.

1952—Eastman Color: Although the term *Technicolor* is still used metaphorically for anything highly colored, in fact nearly all films produced since 1952 have been on Kodak's Eastman Color stock. The first was the full-length Canadian documentary *Royal Journey*, about the 1952 royal tour of Canada by Queen Elizabeth II. Even films credited "Color by Technicolor" are usually shot in Eastman Color but printed by Technicolor laboratories.

1952—Cinerama Film: Frederick Waller conceived the idea of Cinerama for the oil industry exhibit at the 1939 New York World's Fair, using eleven projectors to display a single film on the wall of the dome-shaped building. After World War II he developed the process to project a film on a vast screen with an aspect ratio of 3:1 using three projectors. The most difficult problem was making the three images that made up the picture appear seamless. When *This Is Cinerama* opened in New York on September 30, 1952, it was impossible to detect where an image joined the next.

1953—Cinemascope: Twentieth Century Fox's *The Robe*, starring Richard Burton and Jean Simmons, was premiered at Grauman's Chinese Theater in Hollywood on September 24, 1953. Cinemascope was an anamorphic system that used a special lens to squeeze a wide image onto standard-gauge film and another special lens on the projector to broaden it out again. The technique had been developed twenty-five years earlier as Hypogonar by French inventor Henri Chrétien and first used by director Claude Autant-Lara for *Contruire en Feu*. Fox acquired the patent rights in 1952 and adapted it as Cinemascope.

1961—French Kiss in a Movie: Kissing in some of the Hollywood classics may have looked passionate enough, but the practice was for both actors and actresses to keep their teeth clenched. Perhaps not surprisingly, it was that prolific lover Warren Beatty who first defied the conventions, when he entered close oracular embrace with Natalie Wood in *Splendor in the Grass.*

1963—Nude Screen Tests: The producers of *Four for Texas* may not have had the dramatic imperatives of the picture uppermost in their minds when they decided that the actresses testing for the lead roles should reveal their hidden attributes. The two who found favor were Anita Ekberg and Ursula Andress. Some actresses had declined the audition, but they need not have worried. All the nude scenes were scissored by the censors.

1967—Black Director of a Mainstream Movie: There had been black directors since the 1920s, but only of black films for black audiences. The first black American to direct a film for multiracial audiences was former San Francisco cable car gripman Melvin Van Peebles, who was unable to break into the closed ranks of Hollywood directors but found the French less color conscious when he wanted to make his own novel *The Pass* into a movie. The story of a black GI on a three-day furlough in Paris who has a brief affair with a shop girl, it was released as *La Permission* in France and *The Story of a Three Day Pass* in the United States. Three years later Van Peebles did make it to Hollywood, directing the hit comedy *The Watermelon Man*, with Godfrey Cambridge as a white insurance salesman who awakes one day to discover he is black.

1967—Unsimulated Sexual Intercourse On-Screen: No prizes for guessing that the Swedes pioneered genuine sex on-screen, honors going to Kenton Gustafsson and Stoffe Svensson for their performance in *They Call Us Misfits*. First Hollywood stars reputed to have gone all the way were Donald Sutherland and Julie Christie in *Don't Look Now* (1973).

1968—Hollywood Ratings System: The Production Code, with its long list of unacceptable practices, especially those relating to nudity, profanity, and obscenity, had come under increasing pressure during the sixties as audiences demanded more mature treatment of human relations in the movies they chose to see. The death knell for the code came in 1968 when two British films containing scenes of oral sex, Michael Winner's *I'll Never Forget Whatshisname* and Albert Finney's *Charlie Bubbles*, succeeded in obtaining United States distribution. The code was replaced with a rating system that enabled films to be released under four classifications: G for general audiences, M for mature audiences, R for restricted, and X for adults only. The latter has tended to signify pornography in the public mind, but in fact the first X-rating was given to Brian de Palma's distinguished *Greetings*, starring Robert de Niro.

1970—Bowel Action On-Screen: Forty years separated the first depiction of urination on screen (see 1930) and the first of evacuation of the bowel. Fittingly, it was Orson Welles, always a pioneer and always of regal bearing, who led the way when he was found on the throne in *Catch-22*. Scatology reached a new low—literally—with a scene in the 1990 British pic *I Bought a Vampire Motorcycle*, shot from inside a lavatory bowl on which someone is going about his business.

1977—Indians Kissing in Indian Film: Kissing was long considered a decadent Occidental custom in Asia and was proscribed in movies. In India it was the producers themselves who imposed the proscription, mainly as a symbolic gesture toward their British rulers. Once independence had been achieved after World War II, there was some relaxation of the rules. A decorous kiss was allowed if one of the partners was a foreigner, or playing the part of a foreigner. There were also "intimate versions" of Indian movies with Indians kissing, but these scenes were cut for home consumption. It was only in 1977 that Shashi Kapoor, India's top box office draw, and former "Miss Asia" Zeenat Aman succeeded in breaking the taboo when their lips met in Raj Kapoor's smash hit *Satyam Shivam Sundaram*, the first Indian "kiss movie" with Indian stars playing Indians to be released in India for nearly half a century.

1985—Colorized Movie: The black-and-white picture *Yankee Doodle Dandy*, with James Cagney as the legendary George M. Cohan, was one of the box office hits of 1942. It took a new lease on life when it was reissued in full and glorious computerized color in 1985, but caused a storm of controversy led by leading Hollywood figures who asserted that such a practice betrayed the integrity of black-and-white screen classics. The company that developed the technique, Color Systems Technology, claims that they go to great efforts to preserve the spirit of the original film, even maintaining a special department whose only function is to research the actual color of the costumes, autos, flora and fauna, buildings, props, and so on, used in the pictures they color. Even the color of the artistes' eyes is true to life.

1987—HDVS Movie: High-definition television (HDTV) is already beginning to attract attention around the world, but a similar process, high-definition video system (HDVS), can be applied to moviemaking. The picture is shot on tape, but with a definition of 1,125 lines—more than twice as much as a conventional TV image. When converted onto film for theatrical exhibition, the clarity is claimed to match that of movies shot on film stock. The benefit of this joint Sony-NHG development to the studios is that it can cut below-the-line production costs by as much as 20 to 30 percent. The first HDVS movie to reach the screen was the Italian-made English-language production *Julia and Julia*, starring Kathleen Turner.

—P.H.R.

MOVIE RECORDS

MOST FEATURE FILMS MADE IN ONE COUNTRY IN ONE YEAR
Nine-hundred and forty-eight in India in 1990. U.S. production peaked at 854 in 1921 and hit a low of 121 in 1963.

MOST FEATURES PRODUCED BY A HOLLYWOOD STUDIO IN A YEAR
One hundred and one by Paramount in 1921. Paramount still makes more in-house productions (as opposed to pick-ups) than any other studio.

MOST FATALITIES ON A MOVIE PRODUCTION
Forty people were killed when fire engulfed the set of the Indian movie *The Sword of Tipu Sultan* (1989). The highest death toll in a Hollywood movie was ten when two planes carrying production crew collided during production of *Such Men Are Dangerous* (1930).

MOST COUNTRIES INVOLVED IN A COPRODUCTION
The record of seven is jointly held by the Soviet/ Bulgarian/Hungarian/German Democratic Republic/Polish/Romanian/Czech production *Sol-daty svobody* (1977) and the Tunisian/Mali/Ivory Coast/Mauritanian/Algerian/Senegalese/French production *West Indies Story* (1979).

LONGEST FILM
The Cure for Insomnia (1987), directed by John Henry Timmis IV and featuring Lee Groban of Chicago reading his 4,080-page poem of the same title, was premiered in its full eighty-five-hour version. The film contained some erotic scenes, and a short, expurgated version was issued that runs only eighty hours. The longest commercially produced movie was the eighteen-part Chinese production *The Burning of the Red Lotus Temple* (1928–31), which ran for twenty-seven hours. The longest to be shown in its entirety was Edgar Reitz's twenty-five-hour-and-thirty-two-minute *Die Zweite Heimat*, which premiered in Munich, the setting of the film, from September 5 to September 9, 1992, with sleep and meal breaks.

LARGEST PRIVATE HOUSE OF A HOLLYWOOD PERSONALITY
Producer Aaron Spelling's 123-room "The Manor" in Holmby Hills, an imitation French

Chateau, was built for $45 million in 1990 on a $10 million site.

LARGEST PUBLICITY BUDGET
The $68 million spent publicizing Universal's *Jurassic Park* exceeded the negative cost of Steven Spielberg's production by $8 million.

MOST REMAKES
Cinderella leads *Hamlet* by ninety-four remakes to seventy-three, with cartoon, modern, operatic, balletic, pornographic, and parody versions among them, following the original 1898 live-action movie starring Laura Bayley.

LONGEST INTERVAL BETWEEN A SEQUEL AND THE ORIGINAL WITH THE SAME STARS
Claude Lelouch's *A Man and a Woman: 20 Years Later* (1986) was released twenty years after *A Man and a Woman* (1966), with Jean-Louis Trintignant and Anouk Aimée. Lelouche has promised *A Man and a Woman: 40 Years Later.*

BIGGEST BOX OFFICE TURKEY
The highest loss was incurred by *1492: Conquest of Paradise* (1992), which had a budget estimated at $50 million and took in $4.4 million at the box office. In terms of budget to box office ratio, however, the critically acclaimed but dire *Orphans* (1987), with Albert Finney, is the all-time turkey with a take of under $100,000 against a negative cost of $15 million.

Albert Finney and Kevin Anderson in the 1987 critically acclaimed failure, Orphans.

MOST-COSTLY FILM
The negative cost of *Waterworld* (1995) came to $172 million. Inflation-adjusted, however, *Cleopatra's* $44 million budget in 1963 would now run more than $200 million.

HIGHEST BUDGET TO BOX OFFICE RATIO
George Miller's Australian production *Mad Max* (1980), starring unknown Sydneysider Mel Gibson, cost $350,000 and took in more than $100 million worldwide, a ratio of 1:285. (For comparison, *Jurassic Park* has a ratio of approximately 1:15.)

HIGHEST FILM RIGHTS FEE
In 1978 Columbia paid $9 million for the rights to Charles Strouse's Broadway musical *Annie.* The highest fee for rights to a novel was $5 million by Warner Brothers for Tom Wolfe's best-seller *Bonfire of the Vanities*, which became a disaster movie mainly because of monumental miscasting.

MOST-FILMED AUTHOR
There have been 307 straight versions of Shakespeare's plays, plus 41 "modern versions" and innumerable parodies. The most-filmed novelist is English thriller-writer Edgar Wallace (1875–1932), whose books and short stories (*The Feathered Serpent*, 1934; *Sanders of the River*, 1935; *The Crimson Circle*, 1936; *The Four Just Men*, 1939) have been made into 179 British, American, and German films.

SHORTEST-DIALOGUE SCRIPT
In Mel Brooks's practically silent *Silent Movie* (United States, 1976), only a single word was spoken. Appropriately, it was delivered by mime artiste Marcel Marceau, who, having been invited by telephone to star in a silent movie, responds "Non!" The person who made the call is asked, in an intertitle, what Marceau replied. "I don't know," says another intertitle, "I don't understand French!"

MOST COWRITERS
In 1994 Universal's *The Flintstones*, with thirty-two scriptwriters, overtook the long-standing 1938 record of MGM's *A Yank at Oxford*, which had thirty-one. The total is even higher if you include Bruce Cohen, Jason Hoffs, and Kate Barker, who brainstormed script ideas with director Brian Levant for an early draft by Gary Ross.

LONGEST INTERVAL BETWEEN SCRIPT AND PRODUCTION
It took nearly forty-four years to bring Dylan Thomas's 1948 screenplay for *Rebecca's Daughters* (1992) to production. About the tollgate

riots in South Wales in the 1840s, the picture starred Peter O'Toole and Joely Richardson.

MOST-OVERUSED LINE

According to a recent survey, 81 percent of Hollywood movies made between 1938 and 1985 contained the line "Let's get outta here" at least once and 17 percent more than once.

LONGEST MONOLOGUE

Apart from solo-performance movies, the longest uninterrupted speech—twenty minutes—was by Edwige Fuillère in the French film L'Aigle a Deux Têtes (1948). Kevin Costner's courtroom summing-up speech as Jim Garrison in JFK (1991) lasted thirty-one minutes and thirty-four seconds, though there were a few brief interventions by the judge and opposing counsel.

FICTIONAL CHARACTER MOST OFTEN PORTRAYED ON-SCREEN

Sir Arthur Conan Doyle's legendary detective Sherlock Holmes has been featured in 211 movies made between 1900 and 1994, with Count Dracula (161 movies) and Frankenstein's monster (117) in second and third place.

HISTORICAL CHARACTER MOST OFTEN PORTRAYED ON-SCREEN

Napoléon Bonaparte has been featured in 194 movies, with Jesus Christ (152 movies) and Abraham Lincoln (137 movies) in second and third place.

MUSICAL WITH MOST SONGS

The 1932 Indian production Indra Sabha had seventy-one songs. The most prolific Hollywood musical was RKO's The Story of Vernon and Irene Castle (1939), with a mere forty-one.

LARGEST CAST

The funeral scene of Sir Richard Attenborough's Gandhi (1982) contained an estimated 300,000 performers, of whom 94,560 were contracted at a rate of one dollar for the day and the remainder were unpaid volunteers summoned by press, radio, and TV announcements and by loudspeaker vans. Eleven camera crews shot 20,000 feet of film—more than the length of the completed 188-minute movie—and this was edited down to 125 seconds for the funeral sequence.

SCREEN ARTISTE TO HAVE PLAYED THE MOST ROLES

Tom London, a locomotive engineer from Louisville, Kentucky, made his screen debut as the locomotive engineer in The Great Train Robbery (1903) and went on to play more than 2,000 other roles until his final appearance in The Lone Texan (1959).

The ubiquitous, but unknown, Tom London.

SCREEN ARTISTE TO HAVE PLAYED THE MOST LEADING ROLES

Indian comedienne Monomara completed her 1,000th film in 1985, often working on as many as thirty pictures at the same time. The Hollywood record pales by comparison, no star having exceeded the 142 roles played by John Wayne.

LARGEST NUMBER OF CREDITED ROLES IN A FILM

There were 381 credited performers in Edgar Reitz's twenty-five-and-a-half-hour-long Die Zweite Heimat (1992), though apart from the premiere this film was generally shown episodically. The largest cast in a film intended for uninterrupted viewing was 260 in the Czech drama Days of Treason (1972), about their betrayal by the Nazis.

ACTOR WITH THE LONGEST SCREEN CAREER

German actor Curt Bois (1900–91) made his screen debut at age eight in Der Fidele Bauer (1908), worked in Hollywood in the late 1930s and 1940s, then returned to Germany and made his last appearance eighty years after the first in Wim Wenders's Wings of Desire (1988).

ACTRESS WITH THE LONGEST SCREEN CAREER

Helen Hayes (1900–93), though chiefly known as a stage performer, had a screen career that lasted seventy-eight years, from her debut at age ten in the title role of Jean and the Calico Doll

John Barrymore planting one of 127 kisses in Don Juan.

(1910) until her final appearance in *Divine Mercy, No Escape* (1988).

MOST ROLES PLAYED BY ONE ACTOR IN A FILM
Rolf Leslie played twenty-seven different roles in Will Barker's biopic of Queen Victoria, *Sixty Years a Queen* (1913).

MOST KISSES IN A MOVIE
The "Great Profile" John Barrymore bestowed 127 kisses on Mary Astor and Estelle Taylor in *Don Juan* (1926).

LONGEST SCREEN KISS
For many years it was claimed that Jane Wyman and Regis Toomey's big clinch in *You're in the Army Now* (1940) lasted for three minutes and five seconds. In fact no screen kiss has lasted longer than the fifty-five sec-onds Steve McQueen and Faye Dunaway spent in passionate embrace in *The Thomas Crown Affair* (1968).

MOST FILMS WITH THE SAME COSTARS
Indian screen heartthrobs Prem Nazir and Sheila had costarred in 130 movies by 1975, somewhat more than the Hollywood record of fifteen costarring roles by husband-and-wife team Charles Bronson and Jill Ireland.

ACTOR WHO HAS PLAYED THE SAME ROLE MOST TIMES
Hong Kong actor Kwan Tak-Hind portrayed the Cantonese martial arts hero Hang Fei-Hong (1847–1924) in seventy-seven films, from *The True Story of Huang Fei-Hong* (1949) to *The Magnificent Butcher* (1980), besides playing the role in a long-running TV series. The Holly-wood record is held by William Boyd, who

played Hopalong Cassidy in sixty-six motion pictures as well as on TV.

OLDEST ACTRESS IN A LEADING ROLE
Lillian Gish (1893–1993) was ninety-three when she costarred with the comparatively youthful Bette Davis, seventy-eight, in Lindsay Anderson's The Whales of August (1987).

OLDEST PERFORMER IN A MOTION PICTURE
Jeanne Louise Calment (b. 1875) of Arles, France, was 114 when she appeared as herself in the Canadian-French production Vincent and Me (1990), a delightful fantasy about a teenage Canadian girl who time-travels back to nineteenth-century Arles to try to persuade Vincent van Gogh to smile. Madame Calment, now the oldest woman who has ever lived, is the last surviving person to have known van Gogh personally, selling him canvas in her father's shop in Arles. Unlike the young heroine of the film, she never saw him crack a smile.

YOUNGEST PERFORMER TO RECEIVE STAR BILLING
Baby LeRoy, real name Leroy Overacker, was six months old when he costarred with Maurice Chevalier in Bedtime Story (1933). His contract had to be signed by his grandfather because not only the star himself but also his sixteen-year-old mother was underage.

MOST HORSES IN A MOVIE
Eleven thousand in Aleksandr Ptushko's Soviet production Sword and the Dragon (1956).

MOST CAMERAS FOR A SINGLE SCENE
Forty-eight cameras were used to film the epic sea battle in Fred Niblo's MGM production Ben Hur (1925).

WIDEST-APERTURE CAMERA LENS
Cameraman John Alcott used an f.7 lens for filming a scene lit only by candlelight in Stanley Kubrick's Barry Lyndon (1975). The lens was developed by NASA for use in space.

SLOWEST SLOW-MOTION SEQUENCE
The climactic explosion scene in Star Trek: The Wrath of Kahn (1982), consisting of 2,500 frames, was filmed by Industrial Light and Magic in a single second. On-screen it lasted 104 seconds.

MOST COSTUMES IN A FILM
Thirty-two thousand were used in MGM's biblical epic Quo Vadis (1951), compared with 26,000 in Cleopatra (1963).

MOST COSTUME CHANGES
Chicago poet, rock musician, folklorist, and ethnologist Lee Groban wore 201 different costumes in the eighty-five-hour-long The Cure for Insomnia (1987), while the record for a mainstream commercial movie is held by Elizabeth Taylor with sixty-five costume changes in Cleopatra (1963). This was exceeded on the small screen, however, by Joan Collins's eighty-seven outfits in the telemovie Sins (1988).

MOST COSTLY COSTUME
Perhaps surprisingly, no costume worn on screen in the last thirty years has exceeded the value of the magnificent $50,000 barzucine sable coat that enfolded a queenly Constance Bennett in Madame X (1965).

LARGEST PRODUCTION CREW
Kon Ichikawa had a crew of 556 on Tokyo Olympiad (1965).

DIRECTOR WITH THE LONGEST CAREER
In 1914 King Vidor (1894–1982) directed his first picture, a two-reeler entitled In Tow, in his home state of Texas at the age of twenty; he filmed his last, a documentary about art called The Metaphor, at age eighty-six in 1980. His sixty-six-year career also included such notable Hollywood classics as The Big Parade (1925), The Crowd (1928), and The Citadel (1938).

DIRECTOR TO HAVE MADE THE MOST FEATURE FILMS
The Hollywood record is held by William Beaudine (1892–1970), with 182 full-length features from Watch Your Step (1922) to Jesse James Meets Frankenstein (1965). He also made 120 short films, starting in 1915.

MOST CODIRECTORS
I Misteri di Roma (1963) had sixteen, each directing his own segment of this subversive portrait of a day in the life of the Eternal City. The most codirectors for nonepisodic films were seven on the James Bond send-up Casino Royale (1967) and on the fantasy flick Dungeonmaster (1985).

LONGEST INTERVAL BETWEEN DIRECTING ASSIGNMENTS
Matilde Landeta, one of Mexico's first woman directors, took time off after Trotacalles (1951) and was not lured back to the set for forty-one years, when she made Nocturno a Rosario (1992).

OLDEST DIRECTOR
Netherlands director Joris Ivens (1898–1989) was eighty-nine when he made the Franco-Italian coproduction Le Vent (1988), sixty years after his debut film.

YOUNGEST DIRECTOR
Also hailing from the Netherlands was the youngest-ever director of a full-length feature film, Sidney Ling. He was thirteen when he

Ramon Novarro and Francis X. Bushman in the chariot scene in the 1925 version of Ben Hur.

directed, produced, scripted, and starred in his professionally made Lex the Wonder Dog (1973).

MOST-EDITED FILM
Howard Hughes shot 2,254,750 feet of film during the four years Hell's Angels (1930) was in production, equivalent to some 370 full-length feature films. This was edited down to 9,045 feet, a ratio of 249:1. The average is 10:1.

MOST-EDITED SCENE
The director Fred Niblo shot more than 200,000 feet of film for the chariot race in Ben Hur (1925), enough for seventeen or eighteen full-length features. It was edited down to 750 feet, a ratio of 267:1.

LEAST-EDITED FILM
D. W. Griffith did no retakes of any scene in his 1919 classic Broken Blossoms, starring the incomparable Lillian Gish, and reduced the 5,500-foot negative by only 200 feet, a ratio of 1.04:1.

MOST-POWERFUL LIGHTING
Lighting cameraman Leon Shamroy used 58,000 amps for some of the interior scenes of Twentieth Century Fox's The King and I (1956), equivalent to 258 "brute" arc lights.

MOST-POWERFUL SINGLE LIGHTING UNIT
Colonel Tim McCoy used a 13,940-amp, 325-million-candlepower arc with a five-foot-diameter lens in California (1927). The beam was strong enough to radiate for ninety miles.

MOST LOCATIONS
Sergei Bondarchuk shot his monumental eight-and-one-half-hour War and Peace (1967) in 168 different Russian and Belarussian locations.

LONGEST MAKEUP JOB
For The Illustrated Man (1969) makeup artist Gorden Bau and a team of eight assistants spent ten hours applying the tattooing to Rod Steiger's torso and another full day tattooing his hands, legs, and lower body.

PRODUCER WITH THE LONGEST CAREER
Parisian Pierre Braunberger (1905–90) was a producer for sixty-five years, starting with Jean

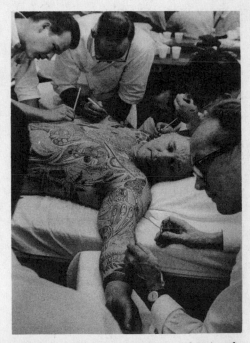

A team of makeup artists prepares Rod Steiger for his role in The Illustrated Man.

Renoir's *La Fille de l'Eau* (1924) and finishing with *Knights of the Round Table* (1989).

MOST-EXPENSIVE PROP
Two thousand Maltese shipwrights were kept in employment for a whole year building a full-scale replica of a Spanish galleon for Roman Polanski's *Pirates* (1986). It cost $12 million. Unfortunately, that is more than the picture took in at the U.S. box office.

PROP MOST OFTEN USED IN MOTION PICTURES
The fabulous Russian Imperial Necklace was hired out by jewelers Joseff of Hollywood for 1,215 different feature films.

LONGEST PRODUCTION SCHEDULE
Brazilian lawyer Alvaro Henriques Goncalves spent eighteen years working on his animated feature *Presente de Natal*, completing it in 1971. This record was broken when Richard Williams, who animated *Who Framed Roger Rabbit*, finally completed his lifework, *The Thief and the Cobbler*. Production began in 1967 and the London-based Canadian animator continued working on it until 1995.

LONGEST PRODUCTION SCHEDULE FOR A DRAMATIC FILM
The record of thirteen years is held by two motion pictures: Leni Riefenstahl's *Tiefland*, which she began before World War II and only completed in 1953 after she had been "unbanned" following de-Nazification, and the Chinese biopic *Dr. Bethune*, completed in 1977 after production had been halted for several years on the orders of Madame Mao during the infamous Cultural Revolution.

SHORTEST PRODUCTION SCHEDULE
Scripting of the British comedy *The Fastest Forward* started on May 14, 1990, and the picture was premiered thirteen days later at London's prestigious Dominion Theater on May 27. The script was completed in five days, the shooting in three, and the editing in another five—well, editors always take time to get their act together. It has to be said that this was a stunt in aid of charity. The swiftest mainstream commercial movie was *Twist Around the Clock* (1961), which was on general release twenty-eight days after Sam Katzman decided to cash in on Chubby Checker's chart-topper.

SHORTEST TIME BETWEEN COMPLETION OF SHOOTING AND PREMIERE
On November 7, 1911, five hours after the final scenes of Alfred Rolfe's Melbourne Cup racing drama *The Cup Winner* had been shot at Flemington Racecourse, the film was on release at five Melbourne theaters. The following day it was showing in Sydney, 640 miles distant.

LARGEST SET
The Roman Forum set, which 1,100 workmen spent seven months building on a site outside Madrid for Samuel Bronston's 1964 epic *The Fall of the Roman Empire*, occupied 55 acres, contained 27 full-size buildings, and had a maximum elevation of 260 feet.

HIGHEST JUMP BY A STUNTMAN WITHOUT A PARACHUTE
Doubling for Burt Reynolds in *Hooper* (1978), stunt artiste A. J. Bakunas fell 232 feet onto an airbag.

MOST MULTILINGUAL FILM-PRODUCING NATION
India has made films in forty-seven different languages since the first talkie (in Hindi) in 1931. One was in German and one in Sanskrit, a classical language no longer spoken.

MOST SCORES FOR HOLLYWOOD MOVIES
Three-time Oscar winner Max Steiner scored 306 feature films for RKO and Warner Brothers over a period of thirty years, starting with the first sound film with a full symphonic score, RKO's *The Bird of Paradise* (1932).

LONGEST MOVIE-SONG TITLE
How Could You Believe Me When I Said I Loved You When You Know I've Been a Liar All My Life (21 words), sung by Fred Astaire and Jane Powell in *Royal Wedding* (1951).

LONGEST MOVIE TITLE
The thirty-seven-word *Night of the Day of the Dawn of the Son of the Bride of the Return of the Revenge of the Terror of the Attack of the Evil, Mutant, Hellbound, Zombified, Flesh-Eating, Sub-humanoid Living Dead—Part 4* (1993). Parts one to three had no existence outside the titler's imagination.

MOST SCREEN CREDITS FOR AN INDIVIDUAL
Art Director Cedric Gibbons, who designed the Oscar statuette, was credited on more than 1,500 films between 1917 and 1955, all MGM productions after 1924.

MOST CREDITS ON ONE FILM
There were 771 names credited on *The Lion King* (1994), most of them for the huge team of animators. *Superman* (1978) had the largest roster of names on a conventional live-action movie with 457.

LONGEST CREDIT SEQUENCE
Credits for Sergio Leone's *Once Upon a Time in the West* (1968) and Richard Donner's *Superman* (1978) each ran for twelve minutes.

It took 343 takes to work out how to get the blind flower girl to mistake Charlie Chaplin for a rich man in City Lights.

LONGEST PRECREDIT SEQUENCE

Two films are known to have had a full thirty minutes of action before the titles and main credits—Dennis Hopper's *The Last Movie* (1971) and Pere Portabella's Spanish production *Pont De Varsoria* (1990).

MOST RETAKES

Charles Chaplin had a hiatus on *City Lights* (1931) because he could not think of a way of making the blind flower girl (Virginia Cherrill) think that the little tramp was a wealthy man. After six months of shooting on and off, he found a solution that worked—the tramp tries to fight his way across a street jammed with traffic, opens the door of a limousine parked by the sidewalk, and climbs out the other side. The flower girl, hearing the door close, assumes that it must be the owner and hands him a flower, taking his last quarter and pocketing the change. Simple—but it was take number 343.

MOST RETAKES OF A SONG SEQUENCE

Josef von Sternberg's classic *The Blue Angel* (1930) was shot in both German- and English-language versions. Unfortunately, when Marlene Dietrich sang *Falling in Love Again* for the latter she could not get her tongue around the word *moths*. It repeatedly came out as *moss*. After 236 takes von Sternberg abandoned the unequal struggle and told the soundman to drown out the offending word by swelling the volume of background chatter from the nightclub revelers.

MOST RETAKES OF A DIALOGUE SEQUENCE

Robert Mitchum said that he ceased to take Hollywood seriously after it had taken costar Greer Garson 125 takes to enunciate the word *No* satisfactorily in *Desire Me* (1947). But even this is exceeded, it is claimed, when the notoriously difficult-to-please Stanley Kubrick made Shelley Duvall repeat a line 127 times in *The Shining* (1980).

MOST CUTS BY CENSOR

John Ford's *The Informer* (1935), set in Ireland during the Troubles, was one of his most admired films—except by the British censors, who made 129 cuts. They scissored every reference to the IRA and the struggle for independence, leaving audiences bewildered as to what the movie was supposed to be about. And this film had no sexual content, unlike Bob Guccione's notorious 1979 skin flick *Caligula*. The Japanese censors imposed 450 "blurs" to shield audiences from the sight of parts of the human anatomy they believed should be revealed only to one's spouse.

LONGEST CARTOON SERIES
Mutt and Jeff, created by Harry "Bud" Fisher, ran for 323 weekly episodes between 1916 and 1936—compared with only 119 Mickey Mouse cartoons.

LONGEST CARTOON FILM
The soft-porn *A Thousand and One Nights* (1969), claimed by Japanese animator Osamu Tezuka as "the first adult cartoon feature," ran for two hours and thirty minutes.

LONGEST SERIAL
Kalem's *The Hazards of Helen* ran for 119 one-reel episodes between 1914 and 1917, with several different actresses in the title role, including Helen Holmes and Helen Gibson. The cumulative running time was more than thirty-one hours.

MOST BIOGRAPHIES OF A STAR
Finnish bibliographer Lennart Eriksson has counted more than 360 full-length works devoted to Charles Chaplin since the first in 1916. Marilyn Monroe has attracted more biographers than any other actress, but has yet to attain these figures.

LARGEST SINGLE-AUDITORIUM MOVIE THEATER
When it opened in March 1927, Samuel Rothapfel's Roxy in Manhattan had 6,214 seats. Since it closed in 1960, the record has been held by the 5,945-seat Radio City Music Hall. Although mainly devoted to live shows, the theater still occasionally hosts movie premieres.

> For 50 cents we took the middle-class man out of his home and gave him an environment that only the Church had given before.
>
> S. Charles Lee, on motion-picture palaces of the 1930s, *Newsweek*, September 10, 1989

LARGEST MULTIPLEX
The Kineopolis in Brussels, Belgium, has twenty-five auditoriums and seats a total of 7,500 patrons.

MOST ADMISSIONS TO FILM PER CAPITA
The first part of the historical trilogy *Khan Asppararoukh* was seen by 6.5 million of Bulgaria's 8.5 million population, or 76 percent, when it was released in 1982.

LONGEST RUN AT ONE THEATER
Emmanuelle, the soft-porn movie that propelled Silvia Kristel to overnight stardom, ran at the Paramount City in Paris for ten years and eight months, from June 26, 1974, to February 26, 1985.

LARGEST AUDIENCE
When the Methodist Centenary celebrations held in Columbus, Ohio, took place on July 4, 1919, one of the events was a special screening of D. W. Griffith's *Boots* on a giant 100-foot-by-75-foot screen at the Oval Amphitheater. A capacity audience of 110,000 saw the picture.

MOST TIMES A PAYING PATRON HAS SEEN THE SAME FILM
Mrs. Myra Franklin of Cardiff, Wales, was so delighted by *The Sound of Music* (1965) that she followed it around Britain from city to city, attending no less than 940 times.

MOST FAN MAIL
According to Walt Disney, Mickey Mouse received 800,000 fan letters during 1933. At an average of 66,000 letters a month, this exceeded the highest number ever achieved by a mere human being—720,000, or an average of 60,000 a month, addressed to seven-year-old Shirley Temple during 1936.

MOST FAN LETTERS IN A SINGLE MONTH
Roy Rogers received 74,852 fan letters in July 1945. Another 200 were addressed to his faithful steed Trigger.

LONGEST CAREER BY A FILM CRITIC
Dilys Powell began reviewing films for the *Sunday Times* of London in 1939 and did so until her death in 1995. She came to the job fairly late, having joined the paper as a columnist in 1924.

LONGEST ACADEMY AWARD ACCEPTANCE SPEECH
Greer Garson did not ramble on for over an hour at the 1943 presentation, as has often been alleged, but her five-and-one-half-minute acceptance speech on receiving the Oscar for best actress in *Mrs. Miniver* was indeed the longest in the history of the Academy Awards.

MOST PEOPLE THANKED IN AN ACCEPTANCE SPEECH
With speeches now restricted to forty-five seconds, it is hard to fit in the names of more than a half dozen or so "wunnerful people." In the pretelevision days, when greater latitude was allowed by the Academy, Olivia de Havilland gushed her gratitude to no fewer than twenty-seven individuals on receiving the best actress award for her role in *To Each His Own* (1946).

—P.H.R.

MOVIE ODDITIES

PLAY IT AGAIN, TITO
Latin lover Tito Lusardo played the romantic lead in *The Day You Leave Me* in 1935. He played the same role again thirty-four years later in the 1969 remake.

MICHAEL'S MOOLAH
Most independent filmmakers borrow the money when they make a film. For unemployed journalist Michael Moore this was not an option when he decided to make a feature-length documentary about the closing of the GM auto plant in his hometown of Flint, Michigan. He raised most of the $250,000 budget for *Roger and Me* (1990), which centered with hilarious and telling effect on his fruitless quest to interview General Motors chief Roger Smith, by running Saturday-night bingo games in Flint. When his source of financing dried up, he scoured the streets for empty soda pop bottles on which he could claim the deposit. Moore's efforts paid off—with a gross of $6.7 million at the U.S. box office as well as TV sales worldwide.

ORSON WELLES'S THRILLER
Orson Welles was desperate for a $50,000 loan. It was 1947 and he was producing a play in Boston but had run out of money. When he called Harry Cohn at Columbia, the mogul resisted his pleas to ante up. Desperate, Welles said he had a thriller in mind that would make a great movie and he was prepared to direct it for Columbia. Cohn asked the title. Welles could not think of an answer, but looking around the room for inspiration his eye fell on the paperback the wardrobe mistress was reading. He signaled to her to hold it up so that he could read the title and told Cohn that the book he wanted to film was Sherwood King's *If I Die Before I Wake*. Cohn lent Welles the $50,000 and Welles brought King's novel to the screen as *The Lady from Shanghai*, also starring in it opposite Rita Hayworth.

THE INVISIBLE PRESIDENT
Every president of the twentieth century has been portrayed on-screen—except one. Warren Gamaliel Harding, who succeeded Woodrow Wilson and preceded Calvin Coolidge, spent two undistinguished years in office between 1921 and his death in 1923. Nothing he did was of sufficient moment to warrant his depiction in a theatrical movie.

WOMAN OF THE WEST
There have been 3,500 westerns made since 1908, apart from the innumerable one-reelers of the early days. Only one has been directed by a woman: Universal's oddly titled '49–'17, made by Ruth Ann Baldwin in 1917.

WARREN THE RED
When Warren Beatty turned his hand to directing on *Reds* (1981), he was determined that even the extras should understand the background to his biopic of Communist sympathizer John Reed. He assembled them on set and lectured them about Reed's belief that wage earners were exploited by their capitalist employers. The extras went away and discussed what had been explained to them. They then returned to Beatty and declared that as they were being exploited, they would strike unless he raised their wages. Realizing he had backed himself into a corner, Beatty conceded with good grace.

GREAT-GRANDPAW WAS A MOVIE STAR
Film actresses Joely and Natasha Richardson and their cousin Jemma Redgrave can claim parents, grandparents, and a great-grandparent who were or are performers in movies. Joely and Natasha are the daughters of Oscar-winner Vanessa Redgrave and her director husband Tony Richardson, while Jemma's father is Corin Redgrave (Giuseppe Conlan in *In the Name of the Father*). Vanessa and Corin, and their sister Lynn Redgrave, are the offspring of Sir Michael Redgrave and Rachel Kempson, and Sir Michael's father, founder of the dynasty, was Roy Redgrave, who made his screen debut in the Australian film *The Christian* in 1911 and was active in Australian cinema until 1920. The only other four-generation dynasty of screen artistes is the Kapoor family in India.

I WAS MY OWN GREAT-GRANDFATHER
A number of actors and actresses have played their own parents on screen and at least two have played their own grandparents, but only one actor has portrayed his own great-grandfather. Michael Palin, formerly of the Monty Python team and remembered for having potato fries stuck up his nostrils by Kevin Kline in *A Fish Called Wanda*, decided to make a movie about how his great-grandfather found romance in the autumn of his years, after coming across his long-lost diary. In a few faded entries the Reverend Edward Palin, a middle-aged classics don at Oxford University forbidden to marry by the statutes of his college, recorded how he had met and fallen in love with a teenage American girl on a walking holiday in Switzerland. The film, titled *American Friends* (1991), recounted how the holiday encounter eventually led to his decision to quit his college fellowship and marry, but for which there would have been no Michael Palin.

ACROSS THE SECTARIAN DIVIDE
The producers of the 1982 picture *The Writing on the Wall*, about the sectarian troubles in

Carmen Nigro (Ken Roady) displays his gorilla suit.

Northern Ireland, found a special way of making their own plea for tolerance. All the Catholic characters were played by Protestant actors and all the Protestants by Catholics.

HOMAGE TO OSCAR WILDE
Alla Nazimova was the lesbian producer and actress briefly married to the sexually ambivalent Rudolph Valentino. In 1923 she decided to make a film from Oscar Wilde's play *Salome*. As an homage to the persecuted playwright, who died shortly after serving a prison sentence for homosexual activity, she employed only gay actors and actresses on the picture.

GORILLA AT LARGE
Many actors have found themselves typecast as cops, military types, or priests, but it was Carmen Nigro's misfortune to be cast as a gorilla in no less than thirty-two movies. Or thirty-three, if his own disputed claim to have played the title role in some of the gorilla scenes in *King Kong* is to be believed.

DON'T TURN OVER
Scope, Color Muda was the only full-length feature film ever to have been made with no cameraman and no camera. The seventy-five-minute animated picture was made in Cinemascope single-handedly by Barcelona artist José Antonio Sistiaga in seventeen months

between 1968 and 1970. He painted each frame separately directly onto the film stock.

SEVEN SHOTS IN ONE
Multiple exposures were often employed to show the same actor playing two or more different roles in a single scene, but latterly they have generally been used for special effects. In *Star Trek* (1979) a septuple exposure was the means of achieving the elaborate sequence in which the starship *Enterprise* first comes into contact with the alien invaders. The different exposures, which included shots of the spacecraft, fog, yellow lights, a star field, and cloud effects, were combined in a scene requiring only thirty seconds of screen time but forty-eight hours of filming.

PEACOCK FINERY
The 1,900 peacock feathers it took to make the fabulous dress with its eighteen-foot train worn by Hedy Lamarr as Delilah in *Samson and Delilah* (1949) were personally gathered by producer-director Cecil B. DeMille. He had spent the previous ten years pursuing molting peacocks on his 1,000-acre ranch until he had enough feathers for this ultimate fashion statement.

WHIPLASH KASHNER
David Kashner learned how to use a long stock whip while herding sheep in Poland and Palestine, cracking the whiplash an inch or so away from the animals without ever striking them. It was an art that stood him in good stead when he drifted to Hollywood in the early thirties. Kashner was hired by the studios as the only professional whipper in town to chastise slaves, malefactors, and winsome young things with sadistic stepfathers for the then-enviable wage of thirty-five dollars a day. During the hungry days of the depression, the five-dollars-a-day extras would eagerly volunteer to portray his victims. Although Kashner could direct the tail of the whip with almost unerring accuracy, just occasionally the lash would strike its subject. It was then that a wailing extra could be confident that the studio would dissuade him from legal redress with compensation sufficient to buy his family food for at least a week.

SOVIET SUPERSTAR MARY PICKFORD
When Mary Pickford made a triumphant visit to the Soviet Union in July 1926, struggling director Sergei Komorov decided that he would star the world's sweetheart in his next movie. As there was no prospect of securing her consent, Sergei decided to make his movie without it. Posing as a newsreel cameraman, he followed her wherever she went, shooting everything he could. He then edited this footage together with scenes shot in the studio to construct a full-length comedy film about a Russian film extra

who is in love with Mary Pickford—and determined to kiss her. Released as *The Kiss of Mary Pickford*, it was a huge success in the USSR. To make a film in which the leading lady was unaware that she was participating was remarkable, but even more amazing was the climactic sequence of the Soviet hero and the Hollywood heroine in close embrace. To this day film technicians argue about how Sergei Komorov achieved this seemingly impossible effect.

BING SINGS . . . SECOND TIME AROUND
Bing Crosby is the only screen star whose debut performance ended up on the cutting-room floor, only to be restored at a later date. As a young unknown in 1930 he performed in a vocal trio accompanying Paul Whiteman's band in *The King of Jazz*, but his scene was edited out before the film was released. By the time the picture was re-released several years later, Crosby had become a major star. Although the studios usually incinerated discarded footage, by rare good fortune the sequence of the trio had been preserved, together with some outtakes that showed Bing in close-up. The reissue with these scenes was released with a poster that gave the popular crooner top billing.

SINDLER'S LIST
Irving Sindler was a hardworking propsman in Hollywood in the late 1930s. Chagrined that members of his humble calling did not receive screen credit, he was determined that his name should be remembered for the films he worked on. So it was that in *Dead End* a delicatessen is called Sindler's, as was a Swedish bakery in *Intermezzo*. His name appeared in Chinese characters emblazoned across a banner in *The Adventures of Marco Polo*, and a gravestone seen in *Wuthering Heights* was inscribed "I. Sindler. A Good Man." In *Raffles* a close-up of a newspaper reveals that "Lord Sindler has just returned from a big-game hunting expedition," while *The Westerner* paid tribute to his mother with a sign over an eatery: "Ma Sindler Home Cooking." The only Sindler production in which he remains in anonymity is John Ford's *The Long Voyage Home*. This was not on account of any newfound modesty. The exterior of a low dive in Limehouse, in whose interior John Wayne and Thomas Mitchell were to have a brawl, announced "Sindler & Son." Unfortunately, Ford decided on a close shot and Sindler's credit to himself was lost to posterity.

TED ALLAN'S LONG MARCH
Many films have taken years to get from development to production, but none has come anywhere near the fifty-one years screenwriter Ted Allan had to wait for the realization of *Bethune, The Making of a Hero*. A biopic of the Canadian doctor who accompanied the Chinese Communists on the celebrated Long March, it was eventually released in 1993, but Allan, who knew Bethune personally, had originally taken the project to Darryl F. Zanuck at Twentieth Century Fox in 1942. The picture was to have starred Canadian actor Walter Pidgeon, but it went into turnaround. During the ensuing years there were numerous attempts to make the film, with Columbia and Warner Brothers interested at various times and Paul Newman and Robert Redford among those named for the role of Bethune. Hollywood never did make the film and it eventually came to fruition as a Canadian/French/Chinese co-production with Canadian actor Donald Sutherland in the leading role. Even after the picture premiered at the Montreal Film Festival in 1990, Ted Allan had to hold himself in patience for another three years to see it go on general release. By that time Allan was seventy-seven years old.

SPECIAL EFFECTS—BY NATURE
The eclipse of the sun in the crucifixion scene of Richard Fleischer's 1962 *Barabbas* was real. The director delayed shooting the scene until the eclipse was due, even though it meant the risk of having to achieve it in a single take. The effect was true to the darkening of the skies recorded in the Gospel, but it is doubtful that audiences were aware that they were watching a phenomenon of nature rather than the artifice of the lighting cameraman.

STUNTS UNLIMITED
Probably the only film in which the stuntmen have outnumbered the actors was Clint Eastwood's 1990 production *The Rookie*. The men who did the derring-do outnumbered the ones who just emoted by more than two to one—eighty-seven stuntmen were credited and thirty-seven actors.

KRISTA REBUILT
Anyone visiting the small town of Krista in Crete will find it well appointed with cafés, shops, and public buildings. It was not so until Jules Dassin decided to film *He Who Must Die* there in 1956. Instead of erecting flimsy, temporary structures for his sets, he insisted they should be solid and permanent. Dassin had widened the road to the town to allow the production vehicles passage, and the twenty-eight truckloads of excavated stone gave him the material for the buildings he needed in the film: a school, a terrace café, a large dwelling, a prison, a post office, and five shops. When Dassin departed he presented the new buildings to the people of Krista for their use in perpetuity.

GOODBYE MR. MASSEY
Visual errors are legion in movies, but mistakes on the sound track are much rarer—usually they can be corrected. One of the few examples occurred in *Abe Lincoln in Illinois* (1940).

One of the seemingly endless series of stunts in the 1990 film The Rookie.

There is a scene at a railroad depot where Lincoln, played by Raymond Massey, is setting out for Washington for his inauguration as president. The crowds wave and cheer and call out "Good-bye Mr. Lincoln!" All except one absent-minded extra who hollers "Good-bye Mr. Massey."

ROLE REVERSAL

Singin' in the Rain (1952) is about a temperamental, self-regarding star of the silent screen, played by Jean Hagen, whose voice is too low class for talkies. Debbie Reynolds plays a well-spoken but struggling newcomer to Hollywood whom the studio hires to dub the older actress's voice. Art mirrored reality. In fact Debbie Reynolds's own voice was not considered classy enough for the supposedly dubbed soundtrack of the film-within-a-film. It was Jean Hagen herself who was heard, speaking in her normal voice.

THE LAST SILENT FILM

Talkies came to Thailand, as to most other countries, in the 1930s. But World War II caused total disruption of the Thai economy and its film industry, with the result that all feature films for the next twenty years were shot silent on 16mm stock. Speech was provided by actors in a booth at the back of the auditorium reading the lines. It was not until 1970 that the practice finally died out, all Thai films after that date being shot on 35mm sound film stock.

LATIN LOVERS

The only English film ever released in England with English subtitles was Derek Jarman's *Sebastiane*, about a sadomasochistic relationship between Saint Sebastian, portrayed as a third-century A.D. soldier in Romano-Britain, and his company commander. The dialogue of the film was entirely in the Latin language, lending it a verisimilitude never achieved by any of Hollywood's Roman epics. The script, written in English, was translated by classicist Jack Welch, who used some ingenious shifts to render Roman barrack-room language into the vernacular. In one instance, though, he was at a loss for a Latin word and had to resort to Greek, converting *motherfucker* into *Oedipus*.

THE PENALTY OF STARDOM

When a relative newcomer to Hollywood named Jon Hall applied for a job as a stand-in on the 1937 Goldwyn production *Hurricane*, he was amazed to be offered the leading role by director John Ford. His enthusiasm might have been tempered had he known that Ford had decided that the sufferings undergone by the South Seas native hero should be for real. Hall found himself diving off the top of the ship's

mast and fighting a shark—and not a dummy
one. When the hero is sentenced to the quarries, it took five members of the production
crew to lift a bag of stones Hall was forced to
carry under a blazing sun. In another scene the
guards fire at him as he attempts to escape and
Ford decreed that it should be with live
ammunition. None of this, though, compared
with the ordeal of the flogging scene, which
the great director said would lack verisimilitude unless Hall was lashed until his back
bled. For two nights afterward he had to sleep
on his stomach, but Ford could have spared
him the pain. The censors cut all the close
shots of his ordeal.

THE ODORATED MOTION
PICTURE MARVEL
It is a base calumny that Switzerland's only
contribution to Western civilization has been
the cuckoo clock. They also gave the world the
first feature-length smellie. Made in Zurich,
Mein Traum (My Dream) starred Paul Hubschmid and Gerta Foster and was premiered at
the Swiss pavilion of the New York World's
Fair on October 10, 1940. Credits included one
for the director of smells, Hans E. Laube, who
claimed that his fragrance process could reproduce more than 4,000 different odors. Audiences were able to savor the scent of flowers,
gasoline, tar, honey, tea, medicaments, smoked
meat, forest pines, and various other aromas.
What the picture did not have was the smell of
success. While neutral Switzerland was making eager efforts to promote the marvel of
odorated motion pictures, the rest of Europe
was too busy making war to notice.

EMPEROR ANTON
Silent-picture director Erich von Stroheim was
one of the first who believed that actors should
not just play their roles, they should live them.
When he cast bit player Anton Wawerka as the
emperor Franz Joseph in his hit movies *The
Merry-Go-Round* and *The Wedding March*, he
ordered that the studio orchestra should strike
up the Austrian national anthem every time
Wawerka came on set. As word spread of this
novel practice, the leading Hollywood restaurants entered the spirit of the thing by playing
the anthem whenever Wawerka was present.
Unfortunately, the previously unknown actor
became so accustomed to being treated as
royalty that he suffered a breakdown after *The
Wedding March* was completed and his imperial privileges were withdrawn.

ALL CHANGE
Foreign distributors often change the English-
language titles of the movies they release, but
not always for the better. *Wayne's World* might
have clicked in Taiwan as it did elsewhere but
for its new title, *The Rambunctious and Clever
Ones*. Australian sleeper *Strictly Ballroom* did
boffo business worldwide except in France,
where the distributors made the bittersweet
comedy sound like a dull documentary by
calling is *Ballroom Dancing*. The French even
succeeded in driving *City Slickers* into box
office oblivion as *Life, Love, and Cars*. There
have been other changes, though, that have
made an unexceptional film a must-see. U.S.
basketball picture *White Men Can't Jump*
brought Italian audiences flocking with the title
amended to *White Men Can't Stick It In*.

MEN ON TOP
Liberal Hollywood may pay lip service to
equal opportunity, but too often it fails to
practice what it preaches. In 1990 no fewer
than 82 percent of all the American films
released gave top billing to the male lead, a
significant increase since 1950, when 72 percent of top-line credits went to men. It was not
always so. Back in 1920, at a time when
women's opportunities in the world at large
were far more limited, Hollywood gave precedence to its female stars. That year top-
lined actresses exceeded actors by 57 percent
to 43 percent.

WHEN BATTLE DID NOT COMMENCE
One of the most unusual contracts ever signed
was between the Mutual Film Corporation and
Mexican bandit Pancho Villa in 1914. This not
only gave Mutual exclusive rights to film
Villa's forces in action but also stipulated that
battles were only to be fought in daylight hours
and at times convenient to Mutual's camera
team. The bandit general may have been a
ruthless fighter, but he proved a good man to
do business with. When Villa was ready to
attack the city of Ojinga, the cameraman was
not available. Battle did not commence until
he reappeared and was able to film a famous
victory.

—P.H.R.

*Mexican guerrilla leader Pancho Villa and his band
of irregulars stage a real revolution for the benefit of
a Hollywood film crew in 1914.*

TOP MALE AND FEMALE MOVIE STARS

Each year Quigley Publications polls motion picture exhibitors to determine the players whose names on the marquee draw the most customers. The number in parentheses indicates overall ranking. For example, the (8) after Jodie Foster's name for 1994 means that seven male stars ranked ahead of her.

	ACTORS	ACTRESSES
1915	William S. Hart	Mary Pickford (2)
1916	William S. Hart	Mary Pickford (2)
1917	Douglas Fairbanks	Anita Stewart (3)
1918	Douglas Fairbanks	Mary Pickford (2)
1919	Wallace Reid	Mary Pickford (3)
1920	Wallace Reid	Marguerite Clark (2)
1921	Douglas Fairbanks (2)	Mary Pickford
1922	Douglas Fairbanks (2)	Mary Pickford
1923	Thomas Meighan	Norma Talmadge (2)
1924	Rudolph Valentino (3)	Norma Talmadge
1925	Rudolph Valentino	Norma Talmadge (2)
1926	Tom Mix (2)	Colleen Moore
1927	Tom Mix	Colleen Moore (2)
1928	Lon Chaney (2)	Clara Bow
1929	Lon Chaney (2)	Clara Bow
1930	William Haines (2)	Joan Crawford
1931	Charles Farrell (2)	Janet Gaynor
1932	Charles Farrell (4)	Marie Dressler
1933	Will Rogers (2)	Marie Dressler
1934	Will Rogers	Janet Gaynor (3)
1935	Will Rogers (2)	Shirley Temple
1936	Clark Gable (2)	Shirley Temple
1937	Clark Gable (2)	Shirley Temple
1938	Clark Gable (2)	Shirley Temple
1939	Mickey Rooney	Shirley Temple (5)
1940	Mickey Rooney	Bette Davis (9)
1941	Mickey Rooney	Bette Davis (8)
1942	Abbott & Costello	Betty Grable (8)
1943	Bob Hope (2)	Betty Grable
1944	Bing Crosby	Betty Grable (4)
1945	Bing Crosby	Greer Garson (3)
1946	Bing Crosby	Ingrid Bergman (2)
1947	Bing Crosby	Betty Grable (2)
1948	Bing Crosby	Betty Grable (2)
1949	Bob Hope	Betty Grable (7)
1950	John Wayne	Betty Grable (4)
1951	John Wayne	Betty Grable (3)
1952	Dean Martin and Jerry Lewis	Doris Day (7)
1953	Gary Cooper	Marilyn Monroe (6)
1954	John Wayne	Marilyn Monroe (5)
1955	James Stewart	Grace Kelly (2)
1956	William Holden	Marilyn Monroe (8)
1957	Rock Hudson	Kim Novak (11)
1958	Glenn Ford	Elizabeth Taylor (2)
1959	Rock Hudson	Doris Day (4)
1960	Rock Hudson (2)	Doris Day
1961	Rock Hudson (2)	Elizabeth Taylor
1962	Rock Hudson (2)	Doris Day
1963	John Wayne (2)	Doris Day
1964	Jack Lemmon (2)	Doris Day
1965	Sean Connery	Doris Day (3)
1966	Sean Connery (2)	Julie Andrews
1967	Lee Marvin (2)	Julie Andrews
1968	Sidney Poitier	Julie Andrews (3)
1969	Paul Newman	Katharine Hepburn (9)
1970	Paul Newman	Barbra Streisand (9)
1971	John Wayne	Ali MacGraw (8)
1972	Clint Eastwood	Barbra Streisand (5)
1973	Clint Eastwood	Barbra Streisand (6)
1974	Robert Redford	Barbra Streisand (4)
1975	Robert Redford	Barbra Streisand (2)
1976	Robert Redford	Tatum O'Neal (8)
1977	Sylvester Stallone	Barbra Streisand (2)
1978	Burt Reynolds	Diane Keaton (7)
1979	Burt Reynolds	Jane Fonda (3)
1980	Burt Reynolds	Jane Fonda (4)
1981	Burt Reynolds	Dolly Parton (4)
1982	Burt Reynolds	Dolly Parton (6)
1983	Clint Eastwood	Meryl Streep (12)
1984	Clint Eastwood	Sally Field (5)
1985	Sylvester Stallone	Meryl Streep (10)
1986	Tom Cruise	Bette Midler (5)
1987	Eddie Murphy	Glenn Close (7)
1988	Tom Cruise	Bette Midler (7)
1989	Jack Nicholson	Kathleen Turner (10)
1990	Arnold Schwarzenegger	Julia Roberts (2)
1991	Kevin Costner	Julia Roberts (4)
1992	Tom Cruise	Whoopi Goldberg (6)
1993	Clint Eastwood	Julia Roberts (6)
1994	Tom Hanks	Jodie Foster (8)
1995	Tom Hanks	Sandra Bullock (6)

Sources: 1915 to 1971, *The Motion Picture Herald and Fame*; 1972– , *The Motion Picture Almanacs*

I never said all actors are cattle. What I said was all actors should be treated like cattle.

Alfred Hitchcock (attributed)

No actor ever had a happy home life. If the affection of those near and dear could have warmed him, he wouldn't have gone out looking to soak up the heat of the multitudes, begging for love from faceless strangers.

Chris Chase, *How to Be a Movie Star, or A Terrible Beauty Is Born*, 1968

The most important thing in acting is honesty. Once you've learned to fake that, you're in.

Sam Goldwyn

ENTERTAINMENT SCANDALS

ROSCOE "FATTY" ARBUCKLE— 1921

In early September 1921, Roscoe "Fatty" Arbuckle was in need of some serious relaxation. The popular silent-film comedian, under contract to Paramount for $1 million per year, had just finished three pictures for the Famous Players—Lasky studio in Hollywood. Arbuckle's brand of slapstick comedy was exhausting, and he had rushed from one stage to another, making the three films at the same time, without a single day off. So he and a couple of his friends, actor Lowell Sherman and director Fred Fischbach, piled into his custom-made, $25,000 Pierce Arrow and headed up the coast to San Francisco, where they checked into a suite of rooms at the St. Francis Hotel.

What happened next is a matter of some dispute, but certain facts are incontrovertible. Arbuckle and friends proceeded to have a party; a considerable amount of bootleg liquor was consumed; various girls, several of dubious reputation, stopped by to join the fun; and one of them, Virginia Rappe, a twenty-six-year-old aspiring actress, became violently ill. She was moved to another room and examined by the

In 1921 Fatty Arbuckle became the first major celebrity to be tried for murder. He was acquitted after three trials.

hotel doctor, who thought she was suffering from too much moonshine. Arbuckle, assured by doctors that she was all right, returned to Los Angeles. Rappe was finally sent to a clinic, but after three days of severe abdominal pain, she died of peritonitis, occasioned by a ruptured bladder.

A woman named Maude Delmont, who had attended the party with Rappe and claimed to be an old friend of hers, soon claimed that Arbuckle had, in effect, killed her. He had herded Virginia into his bedroom, Delmont contended, leered at the other revelers, and said, "I've waited for this for a long time." Arbuckle's suite, Delmont said, soon echoed with bloodcurdling screams; after a while the door opened and Arbuckle appeared; behind him, Rappe's nude, bloody body was sprawled on the floor. "He hurt me, Roscoe hurt me," she allegedly moaned. "I'm dying."

Based on Delmont's testimony, San Francisco district attorney Matthew Brady, a ruthless and ambitious man with an eye on the California statehouse, quickly issued a statement to the press, claiming that the evidence clearly showed that Roscoe "Fatty" Arbuckle had raped or tried to rape Rappe, and that her bladder had been ruptured by the weight of his body. Before the week was out, a voracious press and scandal-hungry public had tried and convicted the biggest star in American comedy.

Brady soon realized, however, that all was not as it seemed. The doctor who had examined Rappe's body just after her death issued a troublesome report stating that the ruptured bladder was "due to natural causes. There were no marks of violence on the body . . . no evidence of criminal assault, no signs that the girl had been attacked in any way." Delmont's story began to fall apart; in addition, she had a long police record and, under the nickname "Bambina," was known as a notorious corespondent, someone who specialized in setting up people in compromising situations for private investigators and divorce cases. Shortly after the death of her "old and dear friend," she sent a telegram to several lawyers in Los Angeles saying, "We have Roscoe Arbuckle in a hole here. Chance to make some money out of him."

For the ambitious district attorney, faced with either ruining the life of an innocent man or dropping the charges, thereby embarrassing himself and destroying his own political future, the choice was clear: Brady decided to proceed to trial. He was aided in his quest for justice by the police judge, who, while noting that he could "find no evidence that Mr. Arbuckle either committed or attempted to commit rape," nonetheless decided to charge Arbuckle with manslaughter. "We are not trying Roscoe Arbuckle alone," the jurist memorably stated. "The issue here is . . . larger than the guilt or innocence of this poor unfortunate man; the issue is universal and grows out of conditions which are a matter of . . . apprehension to every true lover and protector of our American institutions."

Fatty Arbuckle, the judge had as well as admitted, was going to be tried for the crimes of American society. And in this crusade, moral men and women throughout the United States rallied to the cause. Arbuckle's pictures were banned from theaters nationwide. The Anti-Saloon League and the Women's Vigilant Committee of San Francisco fervently proclaimed his guilt. Many called for the death penalty. When such friends as Buster Keaton tried to speak out in Arbuckle's defense, studio heads, eyeing the bottom line, ordered them to distance themselves from the fat man whom the moviegoing public now loved to hate.

At trial, which began in early November, Rappe was revealed to have been not quite the young innocent presented in the press; in fact, she had enjoyed quite a reputation as a party girl who liked getting drunk, taking off her clothes, and falsely accusing men of trying to rape her. Expert medical testimony revealed that Rappe, perhaps as a consequence of her five abortions, had long suffered severe abdominal pain; that the ruptured bladder was the consequence of disease, not violence; and that, when she died, she was pregnant, was seeking another abortion, and was ravaged by gonorrhea. A hotel detective testified that she had unequivocally stated that Arbuckle had not harmed her "in any way." On the stand, Arbuckle's own testimony was clear, cogent, and convincing. He had found Rappe on the bathroom floor, vomiting and screaming in pain, and had helped her to his bed. Returning a short while later, he found that she had fallen again to the floor and had thrown up everywhere. At this point Delmont, feeling the effects of the ten Scotches she had eagerly tossed down, staggered in, followed by a few other, equally inebriated, guests. He had, Arbuckle said, been alone with Rappe for no more than ten minutes.

The jury voted eleven to one for acquittal, the only holdout a woman with links to the Daughters of the American Revolution whose lawyer husband did business with the San Francisco district attorney. At a second trial, the jury deadlocked as well. At the third trial, the jury, after deliberating for just five minutes, brought in a verdict of not guilty. The jury members also issued a statement saying that "acquittal is not enough," that "a great injustice has been done" to Arbuckle, who "is entirely innocent and free of all blame."

The full truth behind the Arbuckle scandal remains cloaked in mystery. In *Frame-Up!* (1991), author Andy Edmonds speculates that Arbuckle may well have been set up by Paramount chief Adolph Zukor, who was infu-riated by the comedian's extremely lucrative contract and who, as he said in a memo, wanted "to bring Arbuckle down a peg or two." The director Fred Fischbach, who had accompanied Arbuckle to San Francisco, would have been part of the scheme. Fischbach would have invited Delmont and Rappe to the party so that they could get compromising photos of Arbuckle that Zukor could then use to force the star to renegotiate his contract. Things went tragically wrong when Rappe became ill and eventually died. Brady may have discovered the intrigue and demanded a payoff; this would explain the rather bizarre fact that the San Francisco district attorney received two checks routed via the Bank of Italy, at the beginning of Arbuckle's first and third trials. Each check was for $10,000, and each was signed by Adolph Zukor.

In any case, Arbuckle would soon discover that his acquittal would not save his reputation. Acting at the behest of Zukor, the Hays Office, established in the wake of the Arbuckle affair to oversee morality in the movies, banned all of Arbuckle's films. Hays later made a formal statement that Arbuckle should be allowed to practice his craft, but the comedian's career was shattered. He spent the next ten years scraping by as a vaudeville performer, directing two-reelers, and telling jokes in a cabaret in Culver City. By 1933 people had either forgiven or forgotten him, and he signed with Warner Brothers to star in a series of comedy shorts. At 2:15 A.M. on June 29, 1933, a few hours after completing the filming of In the Dough, he died in his sleep in a New York hotel, at the age of forty-six. The cause was cardiac arrest. His good friend Buster Keaton, however, said that Fatty Arbuckle had died "of a broken heart."

—E.H.B.

THE CHARLIE CHAPLIN AND JOAN BARRY AFFAIR—1943

Hedda Hopper was working on her popular Hollywood gossip column when an excited red-haired young woman rushed into the office. She said that her name was Joan Barry, that she was pregnant, and that the father of her unborn child was fifty-four-year-old millionaire movie star Charlie Chaplin. Hopper might well have whooped for joy. It was 1943. People were still titillated by the Hollywood marriage, divorce, remarriage cycle. As for documented fornication, that was hot stuff. Hopper understood this culture perfectly. She had made a career of pandering to it, trading in innuendoes just this side of libel—"At the Brown Derby last night, what happily married leading man was snuggling up to . . . ?" So a real live bouncing baby on the way was a scoop.

Moreover, Hedda Hopper hated Chaplin. Already long at the top, he did not need her. And he had never groveled—every gossip columnist's price for good press. He also had a long history of "relationships" with young girls (gossip writing was as priggishly moralistic as it was leering), and he was emotionally sympathetic to a number of left-wing causes. (Like most other successful gossip columnists of the time, Hopper was a Red-baiter.) She printed the story and thus launched a series of trials that were not over until 1946 and led to an extended estrangement between the United States and its greatest film comedian.

Chaplin admitted that he had been intimate with Joan Barry. Indeed, at twenty-two, she was one of the oldest in a long list of his tender-aged Hollywood protégés. Like Errol Flynn, he had a weakness for teenagers. Twice, in 1918 and 1924, he had married a sixteen-year-old just a step ahead of statutory rape charges. During the Barry fracas, he wed Oona O'Neill, then eighteen, daughter of the playwright Eugene O'Neill.

Joan, a pretty but by no means stunning starlet, had come into his life in June 1941. This was in the wake of Chaplin's divorce from Paulette Goddard, and it was no cooing love match. Charlie and Joan were not "seen together." The affair was totally unpublic until Hedda Hopper's ex post facto "exclusive." It sounded like the familiar Hollywood flesh-market story: Joan trading her favors for a teeth-capping job, acting lessons, and the promise of a movie role; Charlie able and happy to pick up the bills.

It is impossible to say whether the two were still having intercourse late enough to conceive the child who was born on October 3, 1943. Chaplin claimed they had gone their separate ways more than a year before. Barry insisted otherwise. She related a tantalizing incident in which she had forced her way into Chaplin's posh house, held a gun on him, and so amused both of them that they had promptly gone to bed together. This was around Christmas 1942, an inauspicious date. Even more damaging: Barry said that in October 1942 she had gone to New York City at Chaplin's expense, had been followed by him, and had had relations with him in his hotel room. This meant that Chaplin could be prosecuted under the Mann Act, a federal law that made it a serious crime (up to twenty-five years in prison and a fine of $25,000) to transport a female across a state line for "immoral" purposes. Originally aimed at organized prostitution (white slavery), the Mann Act was also used as a sort of "interstate intercourse act," a way of prosecuting people the authorities wanted to "get" for some other, not necessarily criminal, reason. Chaplin's leftist sympathies had earned him widespread enmity; Ed Sullivan, at the time a right-wing gossip columnist, charged that the Soviet consulate in Los Angeles had a plane standing by to fly Chaplin and his wife to Moscow should he lose the Mann Act trial—Stalin, Sullivan said, was, after all, a great fan of the "Little Tramp."

With public opinion thus whipped up, Chaplin was prosecuted in federal criminal court as well as sued for child support in a paternity case. In the Mann Act trial, Chaplin was acquitted. His lawyer was Jerry Giesler, already famous for defending Errol Flynn in similar circumstances. Among other convincing arguments, Giesler scored points with his remark that Chaplin had no need to spirit Miss Barry from California to New York City for sex; he could have had it with her in Los Angeles "for as little as twenty-five cents carfare." Further, in a real-life Perry Mason–style defense, Giesler all but put the finger on a more likely sugar daddy, oil tycoon J. Paul Getty. Although the judge prevented Giesler from pursuing the point, it looked very much as if Getty had financed Barry's eastern swing as well as a Mexican trip or two.

The paternity case ended less happily for Chaplin. Assuming it was routine, he dismissed Giesler and relied on his regular, less-expensive attorney. This was a mistake. Giesler may have been more ham than legalist, but he was exactly what was called for. During the paternity trial, Barry fled sobbing from the witness stand after being cross-examined by Chaplin's attorney. In another dramatic scene, a cooing, red-haired baby girl was held up by Barry next to Chaplin, in order for the jury to compare their features. The jury deadlocked seven to five in Chaplin's favor, and a mistrial was declared. A second jury, however, ruled eleven to one in favor of Barry. The anti-Chaplin atmosphere was so intense that Charlie was ordered to pay substantial support despite a blood test showing that his fatherhood was scientifically impossible. Chaplin had in effect been found guilty of behavior offensive to conventional morality. As Joan Barry's lawyer put it in his summing-up: "There has been no one to stop Chaplin in his lecherous conduct all these years—except you. Wives and mothers all over the country are watching to see you stop him dead in his tracks. You'll sleep well the night you give this baby a name—the night you show him [Chaplin] the law means him as well as the bums on Skid Row."

The film career of the cinema's greatest comedian was finished. Monsieur Verdoux (1947) was widely boycotted, and it flopped commercially. Limelight (1952) was well received by the critics but failed to appeal to the mass audience that had made the Little Tramp the best-known and best-loved character in the history of the cinema. In September 1952, Chaplin left on the Queen Elizabeth for a European vacation. Almost as soon as the ship was out of American water, the U.S. attorney general rescinded Chaplin's reentry permit (Chaplin was a British subject), and virtually no one but a few leftists, liberals, and film buffs protested. Chaplin settled in Switzerland, bitter but mostly silent about the country that, if it had given him much, had also taken much of it back. He and his wife would have a long and happy marriage, with eight children.

Only in 1972, when he was more than eighty years old, did Chaplin return to receive Hollywood's homage and the overt acceptance of the American public. He was knighted by Queen Elizabeth in 1975. In failing health, Chaplin was a recluse during his final years, leaving his estate only occasionally. At his last public appearance, a few months before his death in 1977, he attended a performance of a traveling circus troupe. He wore a soft hat pulled down over his forehead and thick glasses that covered much of his face. When the performance ended, he shook hands with one of the clowns.

Chaplin's death at the age of eighty-eight prompted a widespread display of respect and affection.

Oona O'Neill Chaplin died in Switzerland in 1991. Joan Barry had been committed as a schizophrenic to a California state hospital in 1953. Of the innocent cause of it all, the child legally named Carol Ann Chaplin, nothing is known.

—R.S. and E.H.B.

THE BERGMAN-ROSSELLINI AFFAIR—1950

On March 14, 1950, Senator Edwin C. Johnson of Colorado took the floor of the United States Senate and delivered an extraordinary and impassioned harangue. Extraordinary, for in this instance the good senator wasn't rallying against the "Red peril" or his political rivals but against a movie actress. The actress was Ingrid Bergman, and during Johnson's blistering tirade she was labeled a "free-love cultist" and a "powerful influence for evil."

The unusual episode was typical of heated public reaction in 1950 America. For Ingrid Bergman, Hollywood's favorite embodiment of saintliness and virtue, had given birth on February 2 to Renato Roberto Gisuto Giuseppe Rossellini. Little "Robertino" had been conceived not in sunny Hollywood but in far-off Italy, and the child's illustrious father wasn't Ingrid's husband, Dr. Peter Lindstrom, but the noted Italian film director Roberto Rossellini.

Senator Johnson wasn't alone in his righteous wrath. Hell hath no fury like a public scorned, and Bergman and her lover Rossellini had quite literally managed to inflame their public with a passion. The American public could not tolerate a celebrated woman—or, perhaps, any woman—truly assuming her own emotional and sexual freedom. Bergman, after all, had committed the cardinal sin of acting as if her life were her own—not her husband's, not Hollywood's, not America's. Sermons rang from pulpits, women's clubs sniffed through their blue noses, and pickets paraded around theaters showing her films. Producers—already hurt by the infant television industry—cringed, and Hollywood moralists, led by the smut-hungry gossip columnist Louella Parsons, raved in indignation at the adulterous activities of the virginal star of *Joan of Arc* and *The Bells of St. Mary's*.

When idols fall, they land with a crash. The noise was still reverberating a week later when Bergman secured a quick Mexican divorce from Lindstrom and married Rossellini by proxy in Juárez, Mexico.

The whole brouhaha had begun quietly enough with a letter.

Bergman, who had come to the United States from Sweden in 1939 to refilm her Swedish success *Intermezzo* for David O. Selznick, had allowed herself to be talked into a long-term contract. Unhappy with her subsequent film roles, and with no challenging roles in her immediate future, she had let her contract lapse and had begun looking around for opportunities elsewhere. She and her husband had drifted apart. Some of her friends had introduced her to the films of Italian neorealist Roberto Rossellini, and after seeing his masterpiece *Rome, Open City* in 1948, she wrote Rossellini, modestly offering him the use of her talents. Rossellini was delighted and cabled back enthusiastically: "I have just received with great emotion your letter. . . . It is absolutely true that I dreamed of making a film with you and from this very moment I will do everything to see that such a dream becomes a reality as soon as possible."

Rossellini's "dream" may have included more than merely making a film. The forty-three-year-old director had developed a reputation as a playboy and, although technically still married, was keeping several mistresses, including actress Anna Magnani, who was his constant companion.

Elated, Bergman arranged to meet with Rossellini in Paris in 1949 while she was filming Hitchcock's *Under Capricorn* in England. Her husband, acting as her manager, also flew in from the States to offer his advice. The meeting went well, and Rossellini, visiting the United States later that year to accept the New York Film Critics Award for *Paisan* as best foreign film, then went to Los Angeles to schmooze with Hollywood powerbrokers and see Bergman again. He spent some time as the Lindstroms' houseguest, and he and Bergman began discussing plans for a motion picture together.

The Bergman-Rossellini romance apparently began during this period, although it was probably not consummated. Bergman and Rossellini made the rounds of Hollywood together; she soon left to join him in Italy for the filming of *Stromboli*, in which Magnani had originally been slated to star.

Lindstrom did not discourage his wife's trip to Rome. A somewhat stiff and humorless man, he had always encouraged his wife's career and had pursued his own career ambitiously, making an unusual switch from successful dentist to respected neurosurgeon. In any event, the Lindstrom marriage had been shaky for a number of years, and the couple's divergent professions had often kept them apart. She had had other affairs, but this one, Lindstrom knew, would be different.

Stromboli might have been just another Bergman film. The way Rossellini saw it was another matter. Returning to Rome, after his first meeting with Bergman and her husband in Paris, he had told friends, "Swedish women are the easiest in the world to impress, because they have such cold husbands." And the following January, back home after his stay in the United States with the Lindstroms, he had arrogantly announced, "I'm going to put the horns on Mr. Bergman."

When Bergman arrived in Italy, she was given a queen's reception by the public, the press, and Rossellini, who had booked a suite at the elegant Excelsior Hotel. Within a week after filming had begun, Bergman wrote Lindstrom asking for a divorce. "It was not my intention to fall in love and go to Italy forever," she wrote. "But how can I help it or change it? . . . I thought maybe I could conquer the feeling I had for him. . . . But it turned out just the opposite. . . . My Peter, I know how this letter falls like a bomb on our house . . . on our past so filled with sacrifice and help on your part." It would be one and a half years before she saw her daughter again.

The ebullient Rossellini displayed the letter around Rome. While the Italian press howled over the scandal, it often lacked the tone of regally pompous condemnation so widely found in its American counterpart. The magazine *Travaso*, for example, featured a full-page cartoon depicting an armor-clad Bergman as Joan of Arc tied to a stake above a pile of celluloid film, which Anna Magnani, ignoring Rossellini's pleas, was resolutely trying to torch.

And, not surprisingly, much of the Italian public greeted the lovers in a spirit of ardent—if, at times, rather indecorous—celebration. When the couple left Rome to film in Italy's poverty-stricken south, they were treated like visiting royalty. In the town of Catanzaro, for example, the main street was lined with well-wishers. Bergman and Rossellini were given the local hotel's finest room—which, however, did not have its own lavatory. When Bergman went down the hall, she was surprised to find the corridor lined with local dignitaries, who applauded her on her way to—and from—the water closet. The mayor, meanwhile, insisted on lending the couple his silk wedding sheets, which he requested only that they sign before leaving in the morning.

Dr. Lindstrom refused to consent to the divorce, and the heated Bergman-Rossellini romance began making the gossip columns. By the time little Robertino was born, Bergman's career had already slipped. American newspapers, loudly critical of the affair, pontificated on the birth of the child. "St. Joan" had committed adultery. Bergman was enraptured with Rossellini and believed deeply in the purity of his love for her. The willful director, meanwhile, had won his prize, and he would guard it jealously. Both felt, perhaps in different ways, that theirs was a truly great love, a force of nature that could not be denied. In addition to Robertino, they would have two other children—twin girls, one of whom, Isabella, has since become a major star in her own right—yet, over the next six years, their relationship remained tumultuous. They also made more movies, the titles of which could perhaps be said to mirror the arc of a fraught and, finally, fading passion: *The Greatest Love, Journey in Italy, Angst.* These films don't rank with either's best work, and they taught Bergman that, artistically, she and Rossellini were "no good for each other." When Rossellini began an affair with Sonali Das Gupta, the wife of an Indian director, Bergman divorced him in 1957. The ensuing custody battle was bitter and, on Rossellini's part at least, recriminatory.

In the sixties, back in favor with the American public after winning an Academy Award for *Anastasia*—which she had had to film in England—Bergman told the press: "I have had a wonderful life. I have never regretted what I did. I regret the things I didn't do."

What Bergman had done was to shatter a myth she hadn't wanted created in the first place, but it was a blow from which Hollywood never completely recovered.

"Times have changed," she once said to reporters in the 1960s. "No one objects to the Beatles having a holiday with their girls, perhaps because everyone is so pleased they are not taking boys with them." In April 1972 Senator Charles Percy, in an address to the U.S. Senate, apologized for Johnson's vituperative attack of twenty-two years earlier. "Miss Bergman is not only welcome in America," he said. "We are deeply honored by her visits here."

In 1975 Hollywood gave her a "best supporting" Oscar for her work in *Murder on the Orient Express*, in which she portrayed a mousy matron. On June 3, 1977, Rossellini suffered a heart attack and died at his home in Rome. He was seventy-one. In 1978 Ingrid Bergman fulfilled a lifelong dream, acting in Ingmar Bergman's *Autumn Sonata*. She gave what she considered her finest performance, as a middle-aged concert pianist confronting the searing ambiguities of her relationship with her daughter, played by Liv Ullmann. "I don't want to go down and play little parts," Bergman said. "This should be the end." She had developed cancer several years earlier; on August 29, 1982, her birthday, she died at her home in London. Six weeks later, 12,200 people attended a memorial service at London's Saint Martin in the Fields Church. In a tribute, Liv Ullmann said, "Who she was was part of all I understand about life, about being a woman, about being an actress, about sorrow and joy." For his part, Sir John Gielgud simply read a passage from Shakespeare's *The Tempest,* "Our revels now are ended."

—R.S. and E.H.B.

GREAT BALLS OF FIRE!—1958

"Who is the little girl?" the reporters at London's Heathrow Airport called out.

"This is my wife, Myra," Jerry Lee Lewis answered.

"How old is she?"

"Fifteen."

It was a lie. Born July 11, 1944, Myra Gale Brown Lewis was only thirteen as she stepped down from the plane in May 1958, arm in arm with her husband, the rock and roll star nicknamed "the Killer." Yet fifteen was intriguing enough; the reporters pressed for details.

How long had Jerry Lee and Myra been married?

"We were married two months ago, and we're very happy," said Jerry Lee.

Jerry Lee Lewis and his thirteen-year-old wife, Myra, returning to New York, May 28, 1958.

Another lie; they had married the previous December. Had the twenty-two-year-old rock star ever been married before? Yes, twice—the first time when he was fifteen, and the second when he was sixteen. "My second wife was Jane.... It was a long marriage, lasted four years."

Lewis failed to add that his marriage to Jane had been dissolved just the week before he left on this thirty-seven-day tour of England. He had been married to both Jane and Myra for about five months. He also failed to tell the reporters that his new bride happened to be his cousin.

Lewis's manager drew the singer and Myra away to a waiting limousine but not before a reporter shot a question at the petite girl in tight black slacks and black-and-white blouse.

"Don't you think fifteen is too young to be married?"

"Oh no, not at all," she responded. "Age doesn't matter back home. You can marry at ten if you can find a husband."

Within days the London newspapers were calling for British authorities to deport Jerry Lee Lewis as an undesirable alien and—until that was done—for English adolescents to boycott Jerry Lee's thirty-seven concerts to "show that even rock and roll hasn't completely robbed them of their sanity." At the second London concert only about one-quarter of the seats were filled, and the following night's audience greeted the rocker with shouts of "cradle robber," "baby-snatcher," and "Go home, you crumb." He did. Under immense public pressure, the promoters canceled the balance of the tour. Jerry Lee and Myra boarded a plane and went back to Memphis. Phase one—the ascent—of a roller-coaster career had come to an end.

It had been a wild ride so far. Born in Ferriday, Louisiana, on September 29, 1935, Lewis was raised in a fundamentalist Pentecostal family; TV evangelist Jimmy Swaggart (who would have his own career disrupted by scandal) was a cousin and close friend. Jerry Lee would sing hymns with family members gathered around the piano, but then would sneak out to juke joints to hear black rhythm and blues performers. He later admitted that his whole life was dominated by the conflict between Pentecostal righteousness and rock and roll (what he called "the Devil's music") licentiousness. A case in point: he entered Southwestern Bible Institute in Waxahachie, Texas, with the aim of becoming a preacher but was expelled during his first year when he was caught playing a hymn with a rhythm and blues beat.

He started playing clubs, had a modest hit with his first record, "Crazy Arms," in 1956, and then struck solid gold with "Whole Lotta Shakin' Goin' On" and "Great Balls of Fire" (almost rejecting the latter because the lyrics were too sinful). Famous not only for his songs and vocal style but also for his unique approach to playing the piano—pounding it with his fists, feet, head, and other parts of his anatomy—Jerry Lee Lewis emerged as the main contender for Elvis's title of king of rock and roll.

The unexpectedly quick return from England in 1958 marked the beginning of Jerry Lee Lewis's long descent from the realm of rock and roll royalty. Public reaction at home to Lewis's marrying his thirteen-year-old cousin (the bigamy aspect was little noted) led to cancellation of concert bookings and TV appearances. Dick Clark later regretted his role in ostracizing Lewis: "In a very cowardly act I decided to hold off further bookings for Jerry Lee on the show, for which I've been sorry ever since."

Throughout the next decade, Lewis made a modest living by performing in small clubs. But his personal life was wracked with pain. The son Myra had given birth to in 1959 was found dead in the family swimming pool in 1962. Lewis began to drink more heavily, and the more he drank the more he turned on his teenage wife. He beat her, accused her of adultery, and even charged that their son's death had been God's punishment for Myra's carnal wickedness. In 1970 she filed for divorce, charging that she "had been subject to every type of physical and mental abuse imaginable," that Lewis had threatened to hire people to throw her in the river and throw acid in her face, and that he drank constantly.

He married three more times. Jaren Gunn, who became wife number four in October 1971, separated from the singer two weeks later. They later reconciled and had a child together, but by 1982 Jaren was seeking a divorce. On June 8 of that year she was found drowned in a Memphis swimming pool. A year later he married cocktail waitress Shawn Stephens. About two and a half months after the wedding, on August 23, 1983, the fifth Mrs. Lewis was found dead of a methadone overdose in the couple's home in Hernando, Mississippi. Lewis was never formally implicated in either death, but reports in Rolling Stone and on ABC's 20/20 program suggested he had murdered Stephens. Lewis responded to the reports by saying, "These people are trying to make me out to be Jack the Ripper or something. . . . Maybe I should take a lie detector test. Yeah, that's what I should do. I'll take a lie detector test . . . only with my luck, I'll probably fail the damn thing."

Despite all his marital woes, Jerry Lee Lewis managed to get his career back on track by switching from rock and roll to country music. In 1968 he topped the charts for the first time since "Great Balls of Fire" with "To Make Love Sweeter for You." A string of hits followed, and by 1969 he was making more money than ever, charging $10,000 a night by 1970. He added his son Jerry Lee Lewis Jr. (by second wife, Jane) to the band, but Junior turned out to be a drug addict. His father accused drummer Tarp Tarrant of getting the boy hooked, and Tarrant said that Jerry Lee Sr. threatened to kill him. "There were several times on the plane, man," (Lewis bought a DC-3 to fly himself and the band to concerts) "I'd wake up with a knife right here, man—right at the bottom of my throat. . . . See, Jerry was gettin' farther and farther out." In 1973 Jerry Lee Lewis Jr. was killed in an automobile accident.

Though barely surviving a perforated stomach ulcer in 1981 and continuously harassed by the IRS for back taxes, interest, and penalties (totaling $3 million by 1994), Jerry Lee Lewis played on. The scandals and sorrows of his life, however, had taken their toll. In the words of the woman who was at his side during the best and worst of times: "After the death of his kids he turned to drinking and drugs," said Myra in 1984. "He's a man that has been driven totally mad by all the tragedies in his life."

—J.L.K.

CHARLES VAN DOREN AND THE QUIZ SHOW SCANDAL—1959

In June 1955 The $64,000 Question made its debut broadcast on CBS. By July it was the top-rated show on American TV, captivating a weekly audience in excess of 47 million viewers. Revlon, the show's sponsor, enjoyed an enormous surge in sales and profitability; largely as a result of its hit show, Revlon seized a huge lead in the battle for market share among cosmetics makers.

What sort of magic did The $64,000 Question possess? Why did so many Americans so eagerly tune in a quiz show each week? Lou Cowan, the independent television packager who came up with the concept, knew the power of the get-rich-quick opportunity. But he also believed that Americans would be drawn to the spectacle of ordinary people like themselves displaying extraordinary knowledge in a particular field. It was no accident, therefore, that among the show's early winners were a New York City policeman (Shakespeare), a grandmother (the Bible), a shoe repairman (opera), and a Marine captain (cooking). The show also made a winner of Lou Cowan: he became president of CBS.

Yet The $64,000 Question faced a constant peril. What if contestants could not answer questions? The vast audience wanted to see winners, contestants who would capture the $8,000 one-show maximum and return week after week until their winnings reached $32,000. Then the bravest could risk everything on a double-or-nothing attempt at answering the

$64,000 question. This was the drama that made for such compelling TV.

To ensure success, the show's producers began pretesting candidates to find areas of strength and then had questions carefully crafted to assure correct answers. The shoe repairman was asked about Italian opera, not German, about which he knew relatively little. Worse, some contestants found that questions asked during rehearsals reappeared almost verbatim during the live broadcasts. Richard McCutcheon, the Marine captain (and the first to capture the $64,000 prize), believed this practice immoral but remained on the show at the urging of his family.

Not to be outdone, other TV producers rushed in to capitalize on the quiz-show fad. The Big Surprise, Dotto, High Finance, The $64,000 Challenge (a spinoff of the pioneer program), and many others crowded network schedules in 1956 and 1957. In nearly all cases, the producers resorted to manipulation to assure an audience-pleasing outcome. What they discovered early on was that viewers picked contestants they liked and wanted to win and contestants they disliked and wanted to lose. Once the producers determined the popular favorites, it was a simple matter to make sure such contestants received easy questions and advanced past their less-popular rivals.

Without a doubt, the most rigged quiz show was Twenty-One, which made its debut on NBC in September 1956. As developed by producer Dan Enright, Twenty-One paired two contestants who answered questions worth from one to eleven points (depending on difficulty), the winner being the one who stopped with the higher number of points up to and including twenty-one. The formula seemed to lend itself to drama, but Enright had incorporated a fatal flaw. Unlike The $64,000 Question, Twenty-One was not based on narrow expertise; instead, questions were drawn from 108 categories. As a result, it wasn't unusual for contestants on early shows to answer incorrectly, and many shows ended in an embarrassing 0–0 tie. Enright knew he had to take quick action.

He knew just what action to take. In October Enright found a graduate student at City College of New York who desperately wanted to appear on Twenty-One. Herb Stempel claimed that he watched the show frequently and usually knew the answers to questions that contestants flubbed. Although a "little, short, squat guy" (Stempel's self-description), he fit right into the quiz-show success formula of the common man as genius. To make certain the formula would work without a hitch, Enright went to Stempel's home, pulled out a stack of cards, and went over each question and answer in every Twenty-One category.

When Stempel appeared on the show, he defeated his first rival 18–0 in just four min-

utes, winning $9,000 in the process. He stayed on Twenty-One for eight weeks, collecting a grand total of $69,500. Of perhaps even greater importance to the previously unknown graduate student, Stempel became an instant celebrity. People asked for his autograph, and the squat man from Queens reveled in the adulation he received.

But Enright soon decided that Stempel had to go. The public had wearied of the unattractive ex-GI, and Enright had found a tall, handsome professor at Columbia University to become Twenty-One's next champion. Charles Van Doren, son of poet Mark and nephew of Pulitzer Prize-winning biographer Carl, was making $4,000 a year as an English instructor when he decided to apply as a contestant on another Enright quiz show, Tic-Tac-Dough. That show's producer, an Enright lieutenant named Al Freedman, saw in Van Doren the perfect anti-Stempel gladiator.

On November 26, 1956, Freedmen met privately with Van Doren and laid out the entire scenario. There would be a series of tied games at the first Stempel–Van Doren encounter to raise the stakes; then Van Doren would triumph on the following show. Van Doren wondered why he couldn't have the chance to win honestly. Freedman replied that Stempel was "too knowledgeable"; besides, the producer revealed, all quiz shows were fixed. But Freedman's most effective argument was that a Van Doren victory would boost public respect for teachers and intellectuals. Wooed by the lure of wealth and seduced into believing that he was serving a higher purpose, Van Doren gave his assent. The next day Freedman sent a script, including questions to answer and questions to miss.

Stempel was not told of his planned demise until just before the second encounter with Van Doren. Enright then informed Stempel that Twenty-One needed a new champion. Stempel was stunned and resentful, being called on to take a dive so that "a guy that had a fancy name, Ivy League education" could triumph. But he did as he was told, by pretending not to know that Marty had won the 1955 Oscar for best picture. In reality, Marty was one of Herb Stempel's favorite films, dealing, as it did, with an unattractive and unappreciated hero.

Van Doren reigned as Twenty-One champion from November 28, 1956 to March 11, 1957, piling up $129,000 in prize money. He was without question the season's biggest TV star. Time devoted a cover story to the "wizard of quiz." Inundated with book and movie offers, he had to hire a secretary to help deal with the 20,000 letters he received. Each week a massive audience tuned in to watch this superstar of the intellect enter the isolation booth, don a set of headphones, listen intently to the question, furrow his brow, clamp his eyes shut, gnaw at his lower lip, and then deliver the answer he had received from Al Freedman.

When the script finally called for Van Doren to lose, he took a job on NBC's *Today* show at $50,000 a year while maintaining his post as English instructor at Columbia. If only Herb Stempel had kept his mouth shut, the wizard of quiz might have remained all that the public imagined him to be: the engaging though somewhat shy intellectual who could answer some very difficult questions under enormous pressure.

But Stempel could not keep quiet. He told reporters of the fix, but few believed him until contestants on other shows came forward with similar tales of corruption. Finally, in August 1958, as newspapers began to print front-page stories about quiz-show fraud, the New York district attorney announced that a special grand jury would be convened to investigate.

Van Doren denied any culpability, telling the United Press that "at no time was I coached or tutored." He lied to prosecutors, and he lied to the grand jury. It seemed to work. The grand jury took testimony for nine months and wrote a long report detailing how quiz-show producers had rigged the contests, but the presiding judge impounded the report and all the supporting evidence in the apparent belief that the findings would injure innocents like Charles Van Doren.

The end came in 1959. Under growing public pressure, a congressional committee decided to investigate the quiz-show scandals. Subpoenaed to testify, Freedman and Enright confessed. On October 7 the committee invited Van Doren to testify voluntarily the next day. Van Doren responded by disappearing, fleeing in panic to rural New England. For the next ten days the news media seemed to focus on just one subject: where's Charlie?

When he finally resurfaced, Van Doren learned that the committee had issued a subpeona ordering him to testify on November 2. It was time to come clean. He used his ninety-minute testimony to make a full confession. "I would give almost anything I have to reverse the course of my life in the last three years. . . . I was involved, deeply involved, in a deception." Most committee members praised him for his candor, further tormenting Herb Stempel, who had traveled from New York to Washington to see Van Doren excoriated.

But Van Doren found little solace elsewhere. Fired from his jobs at NBC and Columbia University, he was fated to become the symbol of quiz-show crookedness. To escape the glare of publicity in New York, he moved to Chicago and took an editorial position with Encyclopaedia Britannica. Jealously guarding his privacy, he steadfastly refused to comment on the shows or the scandals that had brought him to public prominence. After retiring from Encyclopaedia Britannica in 1982, he authored *The*

Joy of Reading and *A History of Knowledge*. As for Herb Stempel, he worked in the litigation support unit of the New York City Department of Transportation as a professional witness and served as a paid consultant for *Quiz Show*, Robert Redford's 1994 film based on the *Twenty-One* scandal. Dan Enright was forced to find work outside the United States for the next sixteen years. He eventually returned to television and won an Emmy as executive producer of *Caroline*, a CBS Hall-mark Hall of Fame presentation.

—J.L.K.

THE TWILIGHT ZONE MOVIE ACCIDENT—1982

It was to have been a happy ending to a harrowing segment in Warner Brothers' big-screen tribute to the legendary Rod Serling fantasy television series of the 1960s, *The Twilight Zone*. Actor Vic Morrow portrayed a white bigot who finally sees the error of his ways. The scene called for him to carry two Vietnamese children to safety across a river from a menacing U.S. Army helicopter during the Vietnam War. In the episode's final line he tells them, "I'll keep you safe, kids. I promise. Nothing will hurt you, I swear to God."

This line, which Morrow never got to deliver, took on a cruel irony in light of the tragedy that occurred at 2:30 A.M. on Friday, July 23, 1982. During the battle sequence, shot late that night at a motorcycle racing track forty miles north of Los Angeles, a special-effects explosion seriously damaged the huge Bell "Huey" helicopter and sent it spinning out of control. The falling craft crushed six-year-old Renee Chenn, who had been dropped in the water by the running Morrow. The forty-four-foot main rotor blade broke off from the helicopter owing to the extreme heat of the exploding fireball and decapitated both Morrow and seven-year-old Myca Dinh Le before the horrified eyes of more than a hundred actors, crew, and visitors. It was the first time in Hollywood history that children had been killed on a movie set.

Work on the $10 million Steven Spielberg production was suspended while the Federal Aviation Agency and the National Transportation Safety Board investigated the accident. John Landis, director of the segment, and his associates were accused of illegally hiring children, who by state law could not work after 7:00 P.M. The moviemakers readily admitted they were guilty of this charge. They would not, however, admit that the tragic accident was preventable and that Landis deliberately put the three actors in jeopardy by ordering the helicopter to fly lower. Five months later, in his first interview after the tragedy, Landis claimed that his gestures to Morrow to keep moving were misinterpreted by others as signaling the helicopter pilot to descend. "The explosions were much larger than anyone expected," Landis insisted.

But questions surrounding the accident still remained. The following May the Los Angeles County district attorney's office asked the grand jury to conduct hearings on the crash to determine who was responsible. Fines totaling $100,000 were leveled against Landis, Spielberg, and Warner Brothers by state agencies for the violation of safety and child-labor laws. The parents of one of the dead children filed a $200 million wrongful death suit against the filmmakers.

On the same day that Twilight Zone: The Movie was released nationwide—with the Vietnam scenes deleted—the Los Angeles County grand jury indicted Landis, associate producer George Folsey, unit production manager Dan Allingham, special-effects coordinator Paul Stewart, and helicopter pilot Dorcey Wingo on charges of involuntary manslaughter. If convicted, Landis and two of the others could have received a maximum of six-year prison terms. Never before had a film director been held responsible for deaths during the filming of a movie.

Legal maneuvering and further investigation delayed the trial for nearly three years. Jury selection finally began on July 22, 1986. Chief prosecutor Lea Purwin d'Agostino went after the defendants with the righteous wrath of an avenging angel. She put the blame squarely on the shoulders of the filmmakers and their "eagerness for box office success . . . [and] their quest for realism." Landis, known for his manic behavior on the set, was called a "tyrannical director" by d'Agostino.

The defense, led by former Watergate prosecutor James Neal, claimed the accident was unforeseen and resulted from the early detonation of the explosives by the special-effects operator. Indeed, crew member James Comomile admitted in his testimony that he didn't look up from the firing board before setting off the explosives. Landis, for his part, confessed under a fierce barrage of questions in a three-day cross-examination that if he could do the same sequence over, he would "absolutely not" shoot it as he had.

The ten-month trial, with its more than ninety witnesses and hundreds of hours of testimony, finally went to the jury on May 18, 1987. After only one round of balloting, the jury found the defendants not guilty on all counts. "We believe this was all an unforeseeable accident," said jury foreman Lois Rogers, ". . . you don't prosecute people for unforeseeable accidents." The jury claimed that the prosecution never satisfactorily explained how the accident could have been prevented and that their long parade of witnesses was repetitious and unconvincing.

The following February the Directors Guild of America reprimanded Landis, Allingham, and two associates for "unprofessional" conduct in the deaths of the actors. Civil lawsuits filed by the families of the two dead children were later settled for $2 million to each family.

The one positive outcome of the long and expensive trial was a new commitment in Hollywood to safety on the set. An industry safety committee was formed and safety provisions added to the contracts of actors and directors.

Twilight Zone: The Movie was a critical and commercial flop. The remainder of the Landis segment was singled out as one of the weakest episodes. Film critic Richard Corliss wrote that "the story hardly looks worth shooting, let alone dying for." Landis, a high-school dropout who rose to fame on such boisterous, youth-oriented comedies as Animal House and The Blues Brothers, returned to popularity with the hit comedy Trading Places, which marked Eddie Murphy's film debut. But most of his subsequent films failed at the box office. In the early 1990s he became producer of the popular TV series Dream On for HBO. In a rare interview in 1991 Landis confessed, "I live with the 'Twilight Zone' every day of my life."

—S.A.O.

MILLI VANILLI—1989

German record producer Frank Farian, who had produced an international hit with the group Boney M during the disco rage of the 1970s, was creating synthesizer-driven music toward the close of the next decade. Working in a Munich recording studio, Farian produced a pop-dance single called "Girl You Know It's True," whose lyrics he recorded with a trio of studio musicians.

Farian, taking the concept of "prepackaged" song a step beyond merely synthesizing music, decided to substitute the singers who had recorded the lyrics of "Girl" with a flashier though absolutely bogus stage act. He found such flash in the form of a pair of dreadlocked, sequin-wearing young men who could dance to a song though they were quite incapable of singing one. Robert Pilatus, of Germany, and Fabrice Morvan, of Guadeloupe, were living in a neighborhood of musicians in the projects of Munich when they first came to Farian's attention. Neither of the two twenty-somethings had ever sung professionally before. Farian, recognizing their show-biz appeal, signed them up, had them costumed, invented the name Milli Vanilli (which means "positive energy" in Turkish) for them, and sent them on a European tour to promote "Girl You Know It's True." While Milli Vanilli danced and lip-synched their way across the Continent and the song became a hit, Farian put an album together that featured the single.

After their very successful promotional appearances in Europe, Milli Vanilli crossed the Atlantic Ocean and were relaunched by one of the music industry's powerhouses—Arista Records. Music videos were shot featuring Pilatus and Morvan, and the duo joined the Club MTV package tour of the United States. The "Girl You Know It's True" album, which spawned two additional hit singles, wound up selling 7 million copies in America—12 million worldwide.

As sales mounted, egos joined them on the rise. Pilatus was quoted as saying that Milli Vanilli had more talent than Bob Dylan, Paul McCartney, and Mick Jagger. Pilatus and Morvan began getting the idea that they ought to have their voices recorded on the group's next album, an idea that their management either encouraged (according to the duo) or disdained (according to music business insiders).

Milli Vanilli's performance at a benefit concert for AIDS research, at New York City's Radio City Music Hall, foreshadowed their future. While the two performed on stage, the tape that carried the true voices developed glitches, leaving Milli Vanilli looking like a pair of open-mouthed mimes. They fled the stage and the tape resumed its play, blaring out the vocals of singers who were nowhere to be seen. Rumors about the deception of their act spread quickly. In December 1989 the New York newspaper *Newsday* reported that a man named Charles Shaw was crediting himself with singing the rap and chorus vocals on the "Girl You Know It's True" album. Shaw, who soon retracted his claim, actually had laid down the album's vocal tracks, along with Brad Howell and Johnny Davis.

Despite the concert hall embarrassments, the rumors, the clash of wills and egos, and the overall pressures of an industry whose hallmark is overwhelming pressure, Milli Vanilli continued its amazing ascendance. Their take from the sales of the "Girl" album enriched them by an estimated $2 million. Despite *Rolling Stone's* annual Critics' Pick Poll selection of Milli Vanilli as the worst band of 1989 and "Girl" as the year's worst album, others accorded great accolades to the two lip-synching performers. Among the honors bestowed upon them were their being named as best new artist of 1989 at the American Music Awards, and the 1989 Juno Award for best international album, which was presented to them by the Canadian Academy of Recording Arts and Sciences.

Their greatest achievement was, aside from sales, their big win at Los Angeles's Shrine Auditorium on February 22, 1990. There, before a captive audience of those they might have dared think to be their peers, Milli Vanilli received the coveted Grammy Award for best new artist of 1989.

After winning the Grammy, Pilatus and Morvan tried pressuring Frank Farian to produce a follow-up album using their voices. Farian declined to do so and Milli Vanilli fired him. Rather than fade from the controversy, Farian legally restricted the duo from using the Milli Vanilli name and then exposed the sordid secret by admitting to the press that Milli Vanilli had been a sham from its inception.

Newspapers fed on the scandal. Charges and countercharges were made by the parties involved (the duo, producer Farian, new manager Carsten Heyn, and executives at Arista Records and its parent company, Bertelsmann Music Group). Pilatus and Morvan claimed that the record companies were aware of the false credits on the "Girl" album prior to the Grammy Awards. The record companies denied any knowledge of the fraud and were backed up by Farian, who, in turn, was assured that they had no problem with him and would distribute his next effort. The National Academy of Recording Arts and Sciences was outraged by the sordid story behind Milli Vanilli. They stripped Pilatus and Morvan of their Grammy in November of 1990.

The two flash-in-the-pan (non)recording stars tried to redeem themselves by apologizing to their fans and admitting how literally hungry they had been before being hired as Milli Vanilli. Pilatus attempted suicide in 1991 and underwent drug and alcohol rehabilitation after that. In a vain effort to resurrect their careers, the two men formed, in 1993, a duo they dubbed Rob and Fab. They even managed to record an album of their own. The album quickly went bust, however, leaving the two former Milli Vanillians dreaming of another chance at stardom.

—R.N.K.

WOODY ALLEN VERSUS MIA FARROW—1993

Actress Mia Farrow, divorced from Frank Sinatra and André Previn, had been involved in a relationship with filmmaker Woody Allen since 1980. The two were frequently seen together in and around New York, and Farrow had appeared in thirteen of Allen's films over the previous decade. Yet they never lived together, instead maintaining two apartments separated by Central Park; in fact, Allen had never spent a single night in Farrow's home. They nonetheless conceived a son—Satchel—who was born in 1987, and Allen adopted daughter Dylan and son Moses, two of the thirteen children Farrow had begun adopting in the 1970s.

In December 1991, at the same time he was

Woody Allen at a 1994 basketball game with Diane Keaton and Soon-Yi Furrow Previn.

signing the adoption papers, Woody Allen began a sexual relationship with another Farrow adoptee, Soon-Yi Previn. An abused and abandoned Korean girl, Soon-Yi was either nineteen or twenty-one (the Korean birth record is unreliable) when she accepted Allen's invitation to accompany him to a New York Knicks basketball game. That is apparently when their romance began. Until then the fifty-six-year-old director had paid little attention to Soon-Yi—just as he had virtually ignored nearly all of Farrow's large brood except Dylan.

Farrow discovered the romance in January 1992, when she came upon several Polaroid pictures under a box of tissues in Allen's apartment. Each shot showed Soon-Yi in full frontal nudity. Photographer Allen—who claimed to have little skill with a camera—managed to capture both the girl's face and her pudendum in every photo. With her world crashing about her, Farrow dashed from Allen's apartment. Later, recalling her initial viewing of the pictures, she said: "I felt I was looking straight into the face of pure evil."

Although she told Allen by phone to "get away from us," Farrow did not completely sever their relationship. Woody continued to show up

daily at Mia's apartment, where he bestowed so much affection on Dylan that there was an unwritten rule in the household: never leave him alone with the seven-year-old. Ever since Farrow had brought the infant Dylan into her home, Allen had displayed a fondness for the blond little girl that to many observers went well beyond fatherly.

One of those observers was Farrow's mother, actress Maureen O'Sullivan. When Dylan was four, O'Sullivan could hardly believe what she was seeing as Allen applied suntan lotion to the little girl's nude body and began rubbing his finger between her buttocks. Less overtly sexual but nonetheless troubling behavior included Allen's early arrival at Farrow's apartment to sit on Dylan's bed and watch her wake up, his hours of whispering to her and not allowing her to play with anyone else when he was present, his following her from room to room, and his staring at her. Dylan responded to Allen by often locking herself in the bathroom when he arrived at Farrow's apartment or country home in Connecticut.

It was at the country home that the molestation incident supposedly took place. On August 4, 1992, Woody came for a visit. Shortly after his arrival Mia went out shopping with a friend, leaving two babysitters in charge of the children and in charge of enforcing the house rule against Woody's being alone with Dylan. Suddenly, however, the filmmaker and little girl vanished.

The following day one of the babysitters revealed that during the search for Woody and Dylan she had walked into the TV room. There was Dylan on the sofa with Allen kneeling on the floor with his face in her lap. Mia, who had found when she returned from shopping that Dylan was not wearing underpants, began questioning her daughter about what had happened. The little girl said that her father had touched her "private part." Farrow then proceeded to make a videotape of Dylan describing the August 4 encounter.

She took Dylan to her pediatrician, who examined the girl and listened to her story. The doctor told Farrow that he was bound by law to report the incident to the Connecticut state police. Suddenly the tale burst into public view, with Mia and Woody usurping the covers of both *Time* and *Newsweek* from George Bush and Dan Quayle during the Republican national convention. Georgia Republican Newt Gingrich seized on the scandal and accused Bush's opponent, Bill Clinton, of sharing "weird values" with Woody Allen. It was, said Gingrich, "a weird situation [that] fits the Democratic party platform perfectly." Meanwhile, Farrow informed Allen through her lawyers that he could no longer see the children. Allen then counterattacked. Charging that Mia had fabricated the molestation incident in revenge for his involvement with Soon-Yi, Woody asserted that Mia was an unfit mother: she had beaten Soon-Yi after finding the photos; she was constantly strung out on pills; she had threatened and then feigned suicide; she suffered from a compulsive need to adopt troubled and disabled children; she had allowed several of her teenage children to get in trouble with legal authorities; she favored her biological children over her adopted ones; she had even threatened to kill him and poke his eyes out.

Nine days after allegedly molesting his adopted daughter—on August 13, 1992—Woody Allen filed a suit for custody of Dylan, biological son Satchel, and adopted son Moses. At a press conference a week later he denied the molestation charge but confirmed that reports of his romance with Soon-Yi were "happily all true." "The heart wants what it wants," he said.

Allen's custody suit was decided on June 7, 1993, by Acting Justice Elliott Wilk of the State Supreme Court in New York. In nearly every respect, the decision was a total victory for Mia Farrow. Not only did the judge award her custody of all three children, but he denied Allen visiting rights to Dylan and allowed only supervised visits with Satchel. Regarding Moses, Justice Wilk declared that he would honor the boy's wish that he not be forced to see his father.

Woody Allen, the judge observed, "has demonstrated no parenting skills that would qualify him as an adequate custodian for Moses, Dylan, or Satchel." The movie director was "self-absorbed, untrustworthy, and insensitive." Allen's involvement with Soon-Yi, especially his inability to comprehend how the romance impacted on Farrow and her family, only accentuated the filmmaker's lack of fitness as a parent. Regarding Farrow's fitness as a mother—the basis for Allen's custody suit—Justice Wilk merely said: "Ms. Farrow's principal shortcoming with respect to responsible parenting appears to have been her continued relationship with Mr. Allen."

In July 1995 a New York appeals court refused to overturn Justice Wilk's ruling awarding custody of the three children to Farrow.

—J.L.K.

THE MICHAEL JACKSON MOLESTATION CASE—1994

Hailed as "the King of Pop" from Armenia to Zimbabwe, Michael Jackson became not only the world's most popular performer but probably its most controversial as well. While his exceptionally prodigious talents as a singer, song composer, and dancer made him the most famous entertainer in the history of show business, his eccentricities, lifestyle, and legal problems also brought him a measure of infamy.

Jackson was born on August 29, 1958, in Gary, Indiana, the fifth of nine children and the youngest of the five boys born to Joe and Katherine Jackson. Michael soon began showing that he had, as had his siblings, innate musical ability. He had barely become a toddler when he discovered how much he liked creating and practicing dance steps in front of a mirror. His precociousness was even more evident when he sang "Climb Every Mountain" to his kindergarten class.

In 1963, believing in his children's show-business potential, Joe Jackson formed the Jackson 5—an act in which the five-year-old Michael was teamed up with his older brothers, Jackie, Tito, Jermaine, and Marlon. They performed locally and then advanced to club

---

I think I have the type of public image where if I was caught with twelve teen-age girls in bed, or God knows what else, it would not hurt me. I think I'm a publicly avowed pervert and general scrounge."
Woody Allen, as quoted by Eric Lax, 1975

performances in Philadelphia and New York City.

Motown singing star Gladys Knight and pianist Billy Taylor "discovered" the group at the famed Apollo Theater in Harlem. Their recommendation and the support subsequently provided by Diana Ross led to the Jacksons' signing of a record contract proffered by Berry Gordy. The Jackson 5 joined ranks with the Supremes, Smokey Robinson and the Miracles, the Temptations, and the other stellar acts of Gordy's legendary Motown label.

The family moved to Los Angeles in 1969 and the Jackson 5 began their rise to megastardom with four consecutive number one hit songs released over the course of that and the following year. Michael, serving as the lead singer, was well on his way to becoming one of the most identifiable personalities in the world while simultaneously growing up before the public. He was, additionally, the principal (and easily the most dynamic) force driving the group to their staggering accomplishment of selling a total of more than 10 million records on the Motown and Epic labels.

In 1971, at age thirteen, the child prodigy was ready to become an even bigger sensation than the group itself. While continuing to take part in the family act, Michael launched his solo career with what became a number-four hit single, "Got to Be There." His next release, a rendition of the classic "Rockin' Robin," hit number two on the charts and, in October 1972, his recording of the title track from the movie Ben rose all the way to the top.

Cast as the Scarecrow in The Wiz, a 1978 remake of The Wizard Of Oz, Michael demonstrated that he had "star presence" on-screen as well as onstage. The movie work brought him in contact with music industry titan Quincy Jones, who served as the film's musical director. "Get on Down the Road," a duet with Diana Ross from the film's soundtrack, was released as a single and became a monster hit.

Jones produced Michael's next album, "Off the Wall," which sold 7 million copies worldwide and spawned a record-setting four top-ten singles. The biggest-selling hit was the self-composed "Don't Stop till You Get Enough," and it garnered him the Grammy Award for the year's best male rhythm and blues performer.

"Off the Wall" not only made him the biggest star in pop music but gave startling notice, as evidenced by the album cover's portrait photograph, of his physical transformation. Joe Jackson, early on in his youngest son's childhood, had derisively pinned the nickname "Big Nose" on the boy. Now plastic surgery had forever rendered him a squared jaw and thin nose. As time went on, Michael became increasingly androgynous in appearance.

During the 1980s Jackson went from superstardom to a level of international fame and fortune that few had ever reached before. Hit after hit, celebrated music video after music video, world tours generating phenomenal sales, enormous recording contracts, and unrivaled corporate sponsorship deals with Pepsi and LA Gear Sportswear were all generated during the decade. It was a time when Michael dueted with Paul McCartney and bought the rights to 250 Lennon and McCartney songs for $47.5 million. It was the decade during which he starred in a short film, directed by George Lucas, that played in an enormously popular attraction especially built for its exhibition at the Disney entertainment parks.

It was the time when his close relationship with Elizabeth Taylor grew even closer and the time when he left the Jehovah's Witnesses Church and moved out of his family's home and into the Neverland estate he created with its own zoo, Ferris wheel, and other carnival rides. During the 1980s Michael Jackson had his hair catch on fire during the filming of a TV commercial, tried to buy the Elephant Man's bones, and was, as announced by Doubleday Publishers, asked to produce an autobiography to be edited by Jackie Kennedy Onassis.

The decade of the 1980s also marked the remarkable, complex, and emotionally tangled dealings Michael Jackson developed with children. He cowrote "We Are the World," which raised huge sums for charity designated to help famine victims in Africa. He made substantial contributions to children's charities and established his own humanitarian organization, the Heal the World Foundation, to benefit kids of all nations. No one disputed the motives behind his philanthropy—he was honored with the Heritage Award and was feted by Queen Elizabeth as well as by Presidents Ronald Reagan, George Bush, and Bill Clinton.

While fulfilling the role of the world's greatest showman and casting an image so outsized as to be unrivaled by any other public personality, Michael Jackson fiercely protected his private life from scrutiny. He had spokesmen, public relations "spin doctors," lawyers, managers, agents, attendants, and bodyguards—a veritable battalion of people making sure that his inner world was sealed off as much and as often as he commanded it to be.

This shield was penetrated, however, by a series of events that began in Los Angeles, California, in May 1992. One of the most common of occurrences befell this most uncommon of people as Jackson's van broke down on Wilshire Boulevard. A woman, recognizing the stranded superstar, put him in touch with her husband, who worked at Rent-A-Wreck, a nearby car rental agency. The husband of the Good Samaritan went off to pick Jackson up and take him to the rental office. The rental agency's owner, Dave Schwartz, promptly called his wife, June Chandler Schwartz, and told her to come over with his six-year-old stepdaughter and twelve-year-old stepson.

Introductions between the family and the pop idol were made and a twisted relationship between them begun. It was a relationship that was to prove to be the undoing of the magnificently beneficent persona Jackson had spent his life creating.

June Schwartz and her progeny grew close with Jackson over the course of the following months. Michael treated the mother and children to gifts and trips to Disney World, Monaco, Las Vegas, and France, as well as frequently having them as guests at his Neverland Ranch in Santa Barbara County. By the spring of 1993, Michael and the young boy were spending long stretches of time together—hours that included sleep-overs.

Their good times together came to a halt later that summer when the child went to legal authorities with the claim that Jackson had sexually abused him over a four-month time span. The Los Angeles police department began a criminal investigation of these charges on August 17, 1993, and Jackson's private investigator, Anthony Pellicano, responded to them a week later by counterclaiming that the boy's father was trying to extort $20 million from the singer. Jackson began his international "Dangerous" tour in Bangkok, Thailand, one day later.

Events began to snowball as, within less than a week, Jackson postponed his second concert and had Elizabeth Taylor come to his side for moral support. A civil suit accusing Jackson of negligence, fraud, and sexual battery was filed in mid-September. The repercussions of this action not only served to complete the pop idol's fall from grace but also prompted the cancellation of his world tour, a televised admission that he was addicted to painkillers, and the termination of his multimillion-dollar relationship with PepsiCo.

During the months of November and December 1993, Jackson was sued by five of his former bodyguards, who claimed they lost their jobs because they had insider knowledge of Jackson's relationship with young boys. His chauffeur made a sworn deposition that he had been ordered to remove a suitcase and attaché case from the singer's apartment on the same day that the property had been scheduled to be searched for evidence of sexual molestation; Jackson entered a drug clinic for treatment; his sister, LaToya, joined in the accusations about his activities with boys; and his former maid told the press that she had left her job after witnessing Jackson in the nude while in the company of young boys.

Michael Jackson made a televised statement on December 22, 1993, refuting the allegations made against him. Just over a month later, on January 24, 1994, prosecutors announced that they would not be bringing any charges against the boy's father in relation to Jackson's claim that he was a subject of extortion. On the following day, Jackson again declared his innocence and agreed to settle the boy's lawsuit against him out of court. The settlement cost him what is believed to be a sum of $15 million or more. With that done, Jackson was still besieged by grand jury investigations in Los Angeles and Santa Barbara Counties. While the legal process continued its course, Jackson went to the Dominican Republic, where, on March 26, 1994, he secretly married Lisa Marie Presley—daughter of rock and roll king Elvis Presley.

On August 16, 1994, yet another lawsuit was filed against Jackson, this time by the stepfather of the young boy who was at the center of the scandal. He accused Jackson of using fame and fortune to destroy his family. The unprecedented claims and counterclaims, suits and countersuits, and the attending publicity afforded the saga began to dim (though certainly not disappear) as the fall of 1994 approached. On September 21, 1994, prosecutors announced that no charges would be filed against the entertainer because the boy refused to testify against the entertainer in court. That didn't end Jackson's ordeal but it did put it on hold: the case could be reopened anytime within the following six years, which is how long the statute of limitations runs before its expiration.

—R.N.K.

QUOTEBOOK: MOVIES

Hollywood is a place where they'll pay you a thousand dollars for a kiss and fifty cents for your soul.
                                                    Marilyn Monroe

Hollywood—an emotional Detroit.
                                                    Lillian Gish

A celebrity is a person who works hard all his life to become well known, then wears dark glasses to avoid being recognized.
                                   Fred Allen, *Treadmill to Oblivion*, 1954

Chapter 11

TELEVISION

POPULAR TELEVISION SERIES

THE ED SULLIVAN SHOW
(1948–71)

Statistics: *The Ed Sullivan Show* was a sixty-minute Sunday-night variety program that first appeared on CBS on June 20, 1948, and ran weekly until its last telecast on June 6, 1971. Called *Toast of the Town* for its first six years, then officially renamed *The Ed Sullivan Show* on September 18, 1955, it was considered an American institution. It aired twenty-three years, making it the longest-running variety show in television history. Ratings were very steady through the 1950s and 1960s but began to slip in 1968. It was a top-twenty series for thirteen of its seasons. Even the Broadway hit *Bye Bye Birdie* paid tribute to the popularity of the show by including a song called "Ed Sullivan" among its musical numbers. According to Nielsen surveys, the first episode in which the Beatles appeared was still, many years later, one of the five highest-rated episodes of any show of all time.

The Setting: The lavish show was broadcast from CBS's Studio 50 (renamed "Ed Sullivan Theatre" on December 10, 1967) in New York. Sullivan would stand off to the side of the proscenium, employing his peculiar diction and stilted gestures to introduce a wide variety of acts. Some segments and telecasts originated from foreign countries such as Japan, Cuba, Israel, and the Soviet Union. A unique feature of the show was Sullivan honoring celebrity members of the studio audience by having a camera turned on them and introducing them to viewers across the nation.

Cast of Characters: Ed Sullivan, well known as a Broadway columnist for the *New York Daily News*, was an odd choice for television in that he had no particular talent and was, for the most part, wooden, with nervous mannerisms and slurred speech. To his advantage was his newspaper background, which allowed him to sniff out an exciting act and present it with the showmanship it deserved. Besides Sullivan, the only regulars on the show were Ray Bloch, conducting the orchestra; the six original June Taylor Dancers (formerly known as the Toastettes Chorus Line); announcer Ralph Paul; commercial spokeswoman Julia Meade; and, for a time, Jim Henson's Muppets. Guests on the first telecast were Dean Martin, Jerry Lewis, concert pianist Eugene List, Richard Rodgers and Oscar Hammerstein II, comedy team Jim Kirkwood and Lee Goldman, and Ruby Goldstein (a fight referee). Sullivan's son-in-law Bob Precht produced the show for most of its run after the original producer, Marlo Lewis, moved on.

The Creation: The show's concept was to present a vast array of top-rated entertainment acts. One week it could be the Bolshoi Ballet, scenes from a Broadway play, and a rock and roll band; the next week, a stand-up comedian, an opera singer, a magician, and a couple of dancing bears. Virtually every "name" act in music, comedy, film, and theater appeared over the years. Very soon Sullivan became somewhat of an attraction himself. At the top of each broadcast, his familiar utterance "Tonight, we have a really big 'shew' " became a national joke and Sullivan's entire public persona was choice material for a multitude of impersonators—Will Jordan being the most prominent among the bunch.

Highlights and Famous Episodes: Sullivan spotlighted many acts over the years. He presented a ten-year-old violinist, Itzhak Perlman; the seventeen-year-old Liza Minnelli; Bob Hope (his first American TV appearance); Margaret Truman; Humphrey Bogart; Walt Disney; and dozens of black performers at a time when giving blacks network exposure was not a common practice. One of the most frequent guests was a little Italian mouse-puppet, Topo Gigio, for whom Sullivan had a very special affection. Achieving what he considered to be one of his biggest journalistic coups, Sullivan arranged an interview with Cuba's Fidel Castro and aired it before Castro and his revolutionary troops had even reached Havana. It wasn't until after he had aired the segment, between a trained dog act and comedian Alan King, that he realized he'd been duped into believing that Castro was not a Communist. Never did Sullivan come closer to making television history than on February 9, 1964, when he introduced the Beatles to most of America for the first time. The audience was filled with young girls who wept and screamed so loudly, they made it nearly impossible to hear the songs. Two of the Beatles' three appearances on the show garnered Sullivan his highest ratings ever and opened the floodgates for the invasion of countless British rock groups. A common misconception is that Elvis Presley made his television debut on the Sullivan show in September 1956. In fact, the twenty-one-year-old sensation had already made several appearances on the Dorsey Brothers' *Stage Show*, *The Milton Berle Show*, and *The Steve Allen Show*. Sullivan, no fan of rock and roll, noted the huge ratings Presley scored on Allen's show and immediately signed the Tupelo-born crooner to three appearances, for which he was paid the staggering sum (in those days) of $50,000. Presley's first appearance meant instant ratings success for Sullivan's show, which grabbed more than 80 percent of the audience that night. Though the cameras pulled back during a dance sequence, prompting cries of "censorship," it was actually for Presley's third appearance that a decision was made to photograph him in tight close-up, thereby masking his below-the-waist gyrations, which might be considered too risqué.

Behind the Scenes: Ed Sullivan had some well-publicized feuds with Arthur Godfrey, Frank Sinatra, and Jack Paar. His most famous clash was with Steve Allen, who came on NBC opposite Sullivan with his own variety show. In an article for *TV Guide*, Sullivan called Allen a Johnny-come-lately and dismissed his accusations of guest stealing as attempts by Allen at cheap publicity. But probably no on-the-air incident is more infamous than the one involving comedian Jackie Mason. During one of Mason's frequent guest stints, Sullivan, who was running behind, was anxious for Mason to wind up his routine. He began giving the comedian hand signals in plain sight of the audience. This annoyed Mason, who returned a few hand signals of his own—among them, one with his middle finger clearly extended in familiar fashion. This was on camera and it made Sullivan furious. He ultimately accused Mason of offensive conduct and insubordination. Mason's contract, calling for six more appearances, was canceled. The two men didn't

Ed Sullivan with the Beatles, rehearsing for their February 9, 1964, show.

reconcile for more than two years. It is suspected that one of the primary reasons *The Ed Sullivan Show* was canceled was that its appeal was to older viewers and CBS wanted to "modernize" its programming for the 1970s. During the next few years after the show was canceled, Sullivan did a number of specials and a twenty-fifth anniversary show in 1973. He died of cancer on October 13, 1974.

—J.L.

I LOVE LUCY
(1951–57)

Statistics: When thirty-nine-year-old actress Lucille Ball decided to try television, she had little to lose. After a series of forgettable roles in fluff comedies and women's pictures, her career as an actress had stalled. And her marriage to a Cuban bandleader five years her junior was shaky. Yet out of her desperation came "Lucy," arguably the most famous and enduring comedy character in television history.

I Love Lucy premiered on October 15, 1951, and was an immediate hit. The show quickly climbed to third, then first in the ratings, a position it held for four of its remaining five seasons. When the last of the 180 original episodes aired on May 6, 1957, it was still television's top-rated program. *I Love Lucy* earned six Emmy Awards, including two for Lucille Ball and one for supporting actress Vivian Vance. Since then the show has been in nearly continuous syndication around the world.

The Setting: In a New York brownstone at 623 East Sixty-eighth Street, the Ricardo family rented a three-room apartment from their landlords and friends, the Mertzes. During the first years of the series, nearly all the action took place in the Ricardo apartment, the Mertz apartment, or the Tropicana nightclub, where Ricky Ricardo worked. Later the series would go "on the road," incorporating more glamorous locales in California, Florida, and Europe. In the sixth season the Ricardos and Mertzes moved to Connecticut. Nevertheless, the original sets established one of *I Love Lucy*'s basic themes: Lucy's desire to escape from her conventional home life to the glamour of Ricky's show-business world.

Cast of Characters: *I Love Lucy* built its humor on the interplay of four characters. Ricky Ricardo, the Cuban bandleader and conga drum player, was volatile and apt to garble his English or relapse into Spanish. Lucy Ricardo was his flighty, scheming, star-struck wife. Fred Mertz was the skinflint curmudgeon, quick to bicker with his wife, Ethel. As Lucy's patient sidekick,

Ethel's role included calling Lucy's latest scheme "the dumbest thing I've ever heard of."

The Creation: *I Love Lucy* was Lucille Ball's idea. "I *wanted* to be typecast," she said. Reflecting on her film career, she noticed that "there were only three or four scenes that I cared anything about. . . . They were all domestic scenes where I played a housewife."

She also wanted to save her ten-year marriage to Desi Arnaz, which long professional separations had strained to the breaking point. She wanted to work with Desi.

CBS was enthusiastic about a series with Lucy, based on her screwball-wife character from the radio program *My Favorite Husband*. But they didn't want Desi. As CBS officials put it to Lucy, "No one would believe *he* was your husband." Instead, they made Desi host of a radio show, replacing an emerging young emcee named Johnny Carson.

Lucy and Desi fought back, producing a successful vaudeville act and then a pilot episode about Larry and Lucy Lopez, a bandleader and his scheming wife. CBS finally accepted the series idea, although they still hoped Ricky's role and especially his singing could be reduced to virtually nothing; Lucy secretly conspired with the writers to make Ricky's nightclub central to early plots.

To open up more story lines, CBS added the Mertzes. William Frawley was cast as Fred and Vivian Vance as Ethel, Lucy's matronly friend. To Lucy's dismay, Vivian was actually a year younger and, at that time, slimmer than Lucy. "She doesn't look like a landlady," Lucy said at their first meeting. "I photograph dumpy," Vivian reassured her.

Once the cast was set, a bigger problem surfaced. CBS had assumed that *I Love Lucy*, like all television programs at that time, would be broadcast live from New York. The Arnazes refused to leave California—and they insisted on performing before a live studio audience. The impasse ended with a (then) revolutionary idea: videotaping the show on the West Coast. To cover the expense, Desi agreed to reduce their salaries in exchange for complete ownership of the show. He then built a soundstage, complete with bleachers for the audience. Desi had laid the foundation for Desilu Studios. The best production wizards of the day pioneered studio lighting and multicamera filming techniques that are still used for situation comedies filmed today.

Highlights and Famous Episodes: When the real-life Lucy became pregnant at the end of the first season, her writers were delighted by the story-line possibilities. But CBS and the sponsor, Philip Morris, were aghast. At that time even married TV couples slept in twin beds, and the word *pregnant* was taboo. As a result, only delicate references were made to Lucy's "condition," and all scripts had to be screened for decency by a rabbi, a priest, and a Protestant minister. Nevertheless, Lucy and Desi took advantage of the situation by creating six pregnancy stories, building up to the January 19, 1953, airing of "Lucy Goes to the Hospital," which was seen that night on 72 percent of American televisions. In a publicity coup, they arranged to have their real-life son, Desi Arnaz Jr., born by Cesarean that same day.

But I Love Lucy is remembered not for its plots but for certain scenes and comic images. From Buster Keaton, Lucy had learned the secret of comic timing: listen, react, then act. Lucy is most often remembered in some screwball situation, reacting with bulging eyes or scrunched face. Classic examples:

• Challenged to bake bread, Lucy adds too much yeast to the dough. An immense loaf emerges from the oven and pins her to the sink.
• Lucy becomes a TV pitchwoman for Vitameatavegamin, a tonic that is (she discovers) 23 percent alcohol. With each run-through, Lucy downs the prescribed dose and gradually becomes giddily tongue-twisted.
• Lucy and Ethel take jobs on a candy assembly line. All goes well until the line hits full speed, forcing them to stuff candy everywhere, including their mouths, to keep pace.
• Lucy visits an Italian vineyard where wine is made the old-fashioned way. Her spirited attempts to squash the grapes barefoot lead to an all-out grape fight with other workers.
• Lucy encounters Harpo Marx and tries to make him believe she is his reflection in a mirror by pantomiming his every movement.

Behind the Scenes: I Love Lucy was still first in the ratings when Lucy and Desi, sensing an end to story possibilities, ended the show. Their marriage was also ending under the pressure of work and Desi's well-known infidelities.

In 1962 Lucy took over from Desi as head of Desilu Studios. Under her direction, the studio produced two other perennials, Mission: Impossible and Star Trek, before being bought by Gulf and Western in 1967.

Through the years, Lucille Ball held on to "Lucy." "I never found a place of my own, never became truly confident until, in the Lucy character, I began to create something that was truly mine," she said. She returned in 1962 with The Lucy Show, in which she played the widow Lucy Carmichael, with two kids and a sidekick, played by Vivian Vance. But as Lucy Barker in Life with Lucy (1986), she was out of step with the times and quickly canceled. It matters very little. The true Lucy—Lucy Ricardo—may keep mugging forever.

—H.L.R.

THE HONEYMOONERS
(1955–56)

Statistics: The Honeymooners began on the tiny Dumont network in 1950, as just another sketch on Jackie Gleason's first TV show, Cavalcade of Stars.

The Gleason show moved to CBS in 1952, and by 1955 the Honeymooners sketch was sponsored by Buick as a freestanding sitcom. Buick paid more than $6 million for two seasons (seventy-eight episodes) of The Honeymooners. After only thirty-nine episodes in the 1955–56 season, Gleason called the deal off and ended (except for several revival shows) the Honeymooners' original run. A year later Gleason sold the thirty-nine shows to CBS for $1.5 million. The shows soon went into syndication. Today, in many U.S. cities, one can watch The Honeymooners as many as seven nights a week—and that's been the case for nearly thirty years.

Gleason's sitcom finished twentieth in the ratings for the year, a big drop from the second spot that the earlier variety show had held. The Honeymooners was even beaten in its 8:30 P.M. Saturday-night time slot by The Perry Como Show.

For the 1956–57 season, Gleason and CBS returned to the variety format, with The Honeymooners being demoted from a sitcom back to just another recurring sketch.

In 1984 seventy-five "lost" Honeymooners episodes (sketches from Gleason's 1952–55 and 1956–57 CBS variety shows) were grouped into a few hour-long specials and some seventy-five half-hour shows, lightly edited from the originals.

The Setting: The first Honeymooners sketch on Cavalcade (October 5, 1951) was a primitive cousin to later episodes of the show. It was lacking in laughs, devoid of sentiment, and played on a single note of rising rage. Time and experiment would soften the sketch material into its eventual form, half cartoon farce and half subtle psychological study.

The sparse tenement apartment of bus driver Ralph Kramden and his wife, Alice, served as the setting for most episodes. The apartment was usually visited by Ralph's best friend, Ed Norton, a sewer worker. Norton would drop by unexpectedly, causing Ralph to throw him out of the apartment twenty-one times during the thirty-nine episodes. Norton's wife, Trixie, was also a frequent guest, although Ralph only showed her the door twice.

Although Ralph and Alice might fight often, most shows ended with an embrace that showed a healthy physical attraction, which was rare on fifties television. This embrace, followed by Ralph's trademark line "Baby, you're the greatest," ended nine of the thirty-nine episodes.

Ralph Kramden laying down the law to wife, Alice, while Norton and Trixie look on in The Honeymooners.

Cast of Characters: The cast included Jackie Gleason (Ralph Kramden), Audrey Meadows (Alice Kramden), Art Carney (Ed Norton), and Joyce Randolph (Trixie Norton). Pert Kelton played the role of Alice until Gleason switched to CBS in 1952. Carney played a cop in the first sketch but came aboard as Ralph's best friend in subsequent sketches. Elaine Stritch played Trixie once before Randolph took over.

Gleason said that Carney "was responsible for 90 percent of the show's success." Emmy voters agreed and voted Carney as best supporting actor in 1955. *Honeymooners* writer Walter Stone said the dynamic between Ralph's schemes and Norton's happy-go-lucky attitude drove the show.

Ralph's schemes had one common goal—to obtain Alice's respect and justify her continued devotion. Gleason thought Meadows was too pretty to play Alice, until Meadows sent Gleason photos that a photographer took of her at seven in the morning.

Meadows was called "the Rock" because she stuck to the script, yet she never stepped on Gleason's and Carney's ad-libs.

The Creation: Gleason presented the idea to *Cavalcade* writers Joe Bigelow and Harry Crane because they needed an extra sketch to round out the variety show. The ordinary Ralph Kramden was a switch for Gleason because he wasn't bigger than life like the "Poor Soul" and the playboy Reginald Van Gleason III.

Ralph was originally a cop, but he became a bus driver because Gleason wanted to see Ralph constantly, and comically, aggravated. Writers wanted to call the sketch "the Beast," but Gleason voted that title down because he thought the story of the Kramdens was basically an old-fashioned romance—thus, "the Honeymooners."

The show's writers in 1955—head writer Marvin Marx, Walter Stone, Leonard Stern, Syd Zelinka, Andy Russell, and Herb Finn—were among the best in the business. The writers, however, regretted the loss of flexibility they faced in having to make all *Honeymooners* episodes a half hour long instead of being able to vary the running time as content warranted.

Add to that CBS's belief that variety shows, not situation comedies, were the important element in television scheduling, and the outlook was pessimistic for the sitcom success of *The Honeymooners*.

Highlights and Famous Episodes: "TV or Not TV" (October 1, 1955) was the first show and featured Ed and Ralph fighting over custody of a new TV set. "The Golfer" (October 15, 1955) is notable for Ralph's ridiculous golfing outfit that he wears when he pretends he is a great golfer to impress his boss.

"Better Living through TV" (November 12, 1955) features Ralph as the tongue-tied "chef of the future" who, along with Norton, unwittingly destroys a TV studio while filming a late-night commercial on the "superior way to core an apple."

"Opportunity Knocks, But" (May 5, 1956) shows Gleason as a pool shark years before his 1961 film portrayal of Minnesota Fats in *The Hustler*.

"A Man's Pride" (September 22, 1956) was the final episode of the season. In this show, Ralph brags about his success to one of Alice's old boyfriends and gets caught in his lies when the man shows up at the bus garage.

Some of Ralph's best-known expressions were not said as often in the thirty-nine episodes as one would think. Ralph says "One of these days, pow! Right in the kisser" in only one episode, and although he says "bang-zoom" in seven episodes, Ralph never says "Bang-zoom, to the moon."

Behind the Scenes: *The Honeymooners* was filmed twice a week—Tuesday and Friday nights at 8:00 P.M. in the Adelphi Theater on Fifty-fourth Street in Manhattan. More than a thousand people attended each show.

Rehearsal was a dirty word to Gleason. He contended that too much rehearsal destroyed the show's spontaneity. Gleason even had a stand-in for the dress rehearsals. Many of the long speeches Ralph gave to Alice were never written but were Gleason ad-libs.

Off the set, Gleason was the boss and not a close friend of his fellow actors. In the 1955–56 season, both Meadows and Randolph got married and didn't invite Gleason or any other cast members to the weddings. These snubs led to tabloid rumors of a feud.

However, no rumors could dispel the enthusiasm of the Royal Association for the Longevity and Preservation of the Honeymooners (RALPH). The fan club, founded by Peter Crescenti and Bob Columbe in 1982, has grown consistently ever since.

The affection of RALPH members for the show may be as simple as the reason Gleason cited when asked why the *Honeymooners* shows had remained popular for so long: "Because they were funny."

—J.R.O.

60 MINUTES
(1968–   )

Statistics: Since the first episode of *60 Minutes* on September 24, 1968, CBS has made more than $1.3 billion on the highly rated newsmagazine. Ratings were low at first. The show finished the 1975–76 season in fifty-second place, but by the fall of 1976 the show was climbing so fast that it was allowed to "bump the network." This means that East Coast viewers would see the complete show after football, and the rest of the network schedule would be bumped back. *60 Minutes* never looked back and it soon became a perennial top-ten show drawing approximately 30 million viewers a week.

It is one of the only shows, including *The Ed Sullivan Show, Meet the Press, Gunsmoke,* and *The Tonight Show,* to last on television for more than twenty years. This pattern of success has allowed *60 Minutes* to charge more than $400,000 per minute for its national advertising slots.

The Setting: If the opening-credits stopwatch kept running, it would report that the show, minus advertising, is closer to forty-seven minutes. Each of the three segments averages thirteen minutes, Andy Rooney is allocated three minutes, and the remaining five minutes are spent on intros, updates, viewer letters, and the end credits.

Don Hewitt, creator of *60 Minutes,* sought to produce a show different from the single-subject documentaries (*CBS Reports,* NBC's *White Paper*) that drew low ratings and even lower profits. Hewitt believed these shows "seemed to be the voice of the corporation" and he "didn't believe people were any more interested in hearing from a corporation than they were in watching a document."

The philosophy of "looking out for the little guy," tinged with a bit of righteous anger, made *60 Minutes* a favorite because the show wasn't afraid of taking on major corporations. From Ford Motor Company (exploding Pinto gas tanks) to Coors Brewing Company (labor practices) to countless other corporations, *60 Minutes* wrote the book on watchdog journalism.

Hewitt sought to get journalists involved in the stories, departing from the traditional view that reporters should be detached from the stories they are covering. Through this involvement, *60 Minutes* proved to be a unique forum for exposure of suspect politicians, lawyers, doctors, bureaucrats, and the like.

Viewers have responded to *60 Minutes,* sending the show almost 80,000 letters a year—70 percent of the mail CBS News receives. The letters range from insightful to amusing. For instance, a Harry Reasoner segment called "Bloody Ivory," about the slaughter of Kenyan elephants for their tusks, impelled a fifteen-year-old-girl to write that she was as guilty as everyone else and had decided to change soap.

Cast of Characters: Mike Wallace and Harry Reasoner started with the program in 1968. Morley Safer joined in 1970 as a replacement for Reasoner, who would leave for ABC, only to return in 1978. Dan Rather was the third correspondent from 1975 to 1981, until he was chosen to replace Walter Cronkite as *CBS Evening News* anchor. Ed Bradley took over for Rather at that point.

The show's first female correspondent, Diane Sawyer, joined the show from 1984 until 1989, when she left for ABC's *PrimeTime Live.* Sawyer was replaced by Steve Kroft and Meredith Vieira. Vieira was later replaced by Lesley Stahl. The 1994–95 reporting cast was composed of Wallace, Safer, Bradley, Kroft, and Stahl.

Correspondent Andy Rooney keeps his distance from other staff, preferring to produce his small essay segments across the street in the old CBS Broadcast Center.

The show's permanent staff numbers seventy, with only eight of those being staff researchers.

The Creation: The first show, on September 24, 1968, featured presidential candidates Richard Nixon and Hubert Humphrey watching their respective nominations from hotel suites. The show also had a timely (a month after the Democratic National Convention in Chicago) segment about police brutality.

Reasoner's warm, conversational style offset the tough interviewing style of Mike Wallace perfectly and kept a good balance in the program's early years.

Hewitt's philosophy of personal journalism took the lead in such later stories as when Safer (1981) was searched by British guards in Northern Ireland, Rather (1980) was dressed as an anti-Soviet guerrilla in Afghanistan, and Wallace (1979) faced down the Ayatollah Khomeini in the leader's first interview with a U.S. journalist early in the Iran hostage crisis.

Highlights and Famous Episodes: The most famous story that people associate with *60 Minutes* was actually never on the show. Although reported by Mike Wallace, "The Uncounted Enemy: A Vietnam Deception" was actually a CBS News special. This special resulted in General William Westmoreland's suing CBS for $120 million because he believed the network had defamed him in suggesting that he may have falsified troop numbers in the Vietnam War. In 1985 CBS and Westmoreland reached an out-of-court settlement before the case went to the jury.

A 1988 story reported the plight of a homeless woman, Joyce Brown, in her struggle against New York City and its mayor, Ed Koch. Brown had been committed against her will to a psychiatric facility, and this story helped to shape the debate on homeless people and their rights in the eighties.

The program did not stay away from radical positions, such as an interview with Black Panther information minister Eldridge Cleaver in 1970, which drew the attention of the U.S. Secret Service, which was busy investigating groups such as the Panthers and Students for a Democratic Society.

In March 1980 "The Iran File" asked whether Iran was justified in hating the United States because the CIA had restored the Shah to power and allegedly helped to set up Savak, the Shah's secret police.

A 1973 story on Colonel Anthony Herbert questioned the retired officer's claims of a cover-up of Vietnam War atrocities committed by U.S. troops. Herbert sued 60 Minutes, claiming he was falsely and maliciously portrayed as a liar. The suit was dismissed in 1986, but the case led to the requirement that defendants testify to what they knew and were thinking during the entire production process of allegedly defamatory stories.

In 1992 presidential candidate Bill Clinton admitted on the show to "causing pain in his marriage" but declined to be more specific about the rumors of extramarital affairs that were haunting his campaign at the time. An estimated 34 million viewers watched the interview, in part because it followed the Super Bowl.

Behind the Scenes: Hewitt said he has never been stopped from doing a story he wanted to do. He adds that he likes to make the news instead of just processing it.

Making the news has put strain on his reporters' personal lives. Divorce is an occupational problem—Hewitt, Wallace, Reasoner, and Bradley all divorced while on the show.

The show was criticized for using "checkbook journalism" when it paid $15,000 for an interview with Watergate figure G. Gordon Liddy. During the interview, Liddy compared John Dean to Judas. Liddy also admitted that he (Liddy) had threatened to kill Jeb Magruder, his boss at the Committee to Re-Elect the President. The interview did help the show to stay on the trail of the Watergate conspirators. Charles Colson would claim that his unfavorable appearance on 60 Minutes was one of the prime factors that led to his pleading guilty.

Ten thousand dollars bought interviews in 1981 with a pair of American gunrunners in Lebanon, but the $10,000 for a never-aired 1975 story on the whereabouts of missing union leader Jimmy Hoffa's body is one payment the show regrets.

Ex-con Chuck Medlin and former Greensboro Record news reporter Patrick O'Keefe were supposed to take Safer to a rock pile off Key West, Florida, and show him Hoffa's body after the money was delivered to them. But Medlin ran off with the cash and left Safer and O'Keefe in the lurch. Although Medlin was later arrested for being an escaped parolee, 60 Minutes looked very bad for trusting the credibility of a career criminal and a reporter (O'Keefe) who used to write columns describing how the spirit of the Lord came to him while he was having a hamburger at Shoney's.

The major thing that 60 Minutes has done is use journalism to affect the political and judicial processes. A Safer story on how guns from South Carolina were being sold in New York led the South Carolina legislature to pass the state's first restrictive handgun law. A Rather story on the pesticide Kepone resulted in 153 indictments and a $13 million fine against Allied Chemical Corporation for contaminating Virginia's James River.

—J.R.O.

ALL IN THE FAMILY
(1971–79)

Statistics: It began with a warning: "The program you are about to see is All in the Family. It seeks to throw a humorous spotlight on our frailties, prejudices, and concerns. By making them a source of laughter, we hope to show—in a mature fashion—just how absurd they are." Not many people stayed tuned to watch this premier episode, sandwiched between the cornpone comedy Hee Haw and the stately CBS News. Those who did saw the start of one of television's most enduring and controversial situation comedies.

Launched as a midseason replacement on January 12, 1971, All in the Family ran for nine years on CBS. For five seasons it was at the top of the Nielsen ratings; when its 202nd and final episode was broadcast on April 8, 1979, the show was still in the top ten. All in the Family garnered twenty-one Emmy Awards for its writers, directors, and cast and launched two spinoffs: Maude (Edith's politically active, feminist cousin) and The Jeffersons (the Bunkers' socially mobile black neighbors).

The Setting: Each episode began with a shot of 709 Hauser Street in Queens, a working-class borough of New York. The set re-created a drab, lived-in house with cracks in the walls, a worn carpet (it was actually painted on the floor), and living room chairs from a thrift store.

The time was the present. But *All in the Family* wasn't just set in the 1970s; it reflected every trauma, foible, and wart of that decade.

Cast of Characters: Archie Bunker was white, Anglo-Saxon, Protestant, overweight, and blue-collar—he worked on a loading dock and sometimes drove a taxi. With a toehold in the lower middle class, Archie vented rage at everyone and everything that seemed threatening: minorities, liberals, and social change. He was an opinionated bigot and, in the words of one writer, "basically a horse's ass," but not cruel.

Archie's wife, Edith, a.k.a. "Dingbat," was a dimwitted, frumpy housewife who quoted Hallmark cards, told interminable stories, and made obtuse pronouncements, until the frustrated Archie would shout "Stifle yourself." Edith had a kind heart and rosy outlook. Archie sums her up: "You'll stoop to anything to be good."

Daughter Gloria, blond, sexy, and addled, was Archie's princess. But Gloria, to Archie's dismay, had married Mike Stivik, a left-leaning sociology student with a slate of liberal causes. To Archie, "Meathead" was a Commie, pinko, lazy, pervert, atheist Polack. Because Mike was in school "learnin' how to be a subversive," the Stiviks lived under Archie's roof.

The Creation: The Bunkers had British roots. In 1966 a BBC hit, *'Til Death Do Us Part*, about a bigoted dockworker and his family, caught the eye of American producer Norman Lear, who optioned the rights for a U.S. adaptation. But the British characters seemed too sharp, too cruel for Lear. He tempered the Bunkers with memories of his own family. Many of the classic Archie-and-Mike verbal duels were, Lear says, replays of his own fights with his father. And, like Archie, Lear's father held court from a shabby living room chair.

Lear went to ABC, which agreed to shoot a pilot. After Mickey Rooney rejected the role of Archie, Lear turned to Carroll O'Connor, an accomplished character actor. For Edith, he chose stage actress Jean Stapleton. Kelly Jean Peters was cast as Gloria and Tim McIntire as her handsome husband, Richard. ABC saw the pilot and winced. A second pilot was shot, this time with Candy Azzarra and Chip Oliver in the roles of Gloria and Richard. ABC let its option lapse.

Lear then took the series to CBS, which shot another pilot with Sally Struthers as Gloria and Rob Reiner as long-haired Michael Stivic, of Polish descent. The original title, *Those Were the Days*, was changed to *All in the Family*.

Highlights and Famous Episodes: Archie Bunker came out swinging. The show's opening episode was short on plot (a surprise party for the Bunkers' wedding anniversary) but long on fireworks. Viewers heard for the first time such Bunkerisms as "Feinberg, Feinstein—it all comes to the same thing, and I know *that* tribe" and "Let the spades and spics go out and hustle, just like I done." Lear had refused all suggestions to soften its tone, saying "I felt we had to get the network completely wet." Within the first thirteen episodes, Archie dealt with racial stereotypes (Jewish lawyers, black neighbors), homosexuality (his beer-drinking buddy turned out to be gay), women's liberation, fear of job loss, and his daughter's miscarriage—all subjects that were taboo in 1971.

Lear was especially daring when the subject was sex. In addition to Gloria's miscarriage, *All in the Family* addressed impotence ("Mike's Problem," caused by worry over grades), menopause ("Edith's Problem," which Archie called "mental pause"), and Gloria's premenstrual stress ("The Battle of the Month," an episode that brought more outraged mail than any other in the show's history). In "Edith's 50th Birthday," Edith misses her own party when a rapist holds her at gunpoint in her own living room.

The Bunkers also faced most of the decade's social problems. In "The Bunkers and Inflation," Archie's union goes on strike and ends up the loser. Mike's liberal ideals are sorely tested in "Mike's Move," when he loses a teaching job to a comparably qualified black candidate. "Archie's Brief Encounter" shows how infidelity can change a marriage. "The Draft Dodger" pits Mike's war-resisting buddy against the father of a slain Vietnam veteran; the father's unexpected plea for amnesty and healing leaves Archie confused.

Behind the Scenes: When *All in the Family* premiered, CBS prepared for public outrage. It never came. By the end of its first season, the show was getting 100 to 200 letters a week, overwhelmingly favorable.

Problems of another sort arose four years later. O'Connor and Lear disagreed several times about scripts, most seriously in 1974. When O'Connor walked out, the scriptwriters devised a four-part story in which Archie goes to a convention in Buffalo and disappears. Lear threatened to kill off Archie if O'Connor did not return by episode three. But the two reached an accord, and Archie lived.

As a cultural icon, Archie Bunker still lives. Archie's chair, along with Edith's chair and Archie's beer can, are on display at the Smithsonian's National Museum of American History.
—H.L.R.

M*A*S*H
(1972–83)

Statistics: In 1993 *TV Guide* magazine dubbed this powerful sitcom not only the best of the

1970s but the best of all time. Not too bad for a show that finished forty-sixth its first season and had its time slot switched annually for six seasons. M*A*S*H eventually settled into Mondays at 9:00 P.M. Its ratings remained solid after CBS president Fred Silverman surprisingly renewed it for its second year and placed it behind the megahit *All in the Family*. Presently in syndication, M*A*S*H's final episode aired on February 28, 1983. In all, it won thirteen major Emmys during its run. A number of them went to Alan Alda for acting, writing, and directing.

The Setting: Stories centered on the staff of the 4077th Mobile Army Surgical Hospital, which treated the maimed and dying GIs behind the lines during the Korean War. Although the show was about Korea in the 1950s, it could just as well have been about Vietnam in the 1970s. The futility, absurdity, and insanity of the war forced the surgeons to maintain a sense of humor or risk going crazy themselves. The show's regular sets, located at Twentieth Century Fox Studios, included the officers' club, the mess tent, and the operating room. The floor of the compound itself was peppered with an assortment of bushes, rocks, and piles of dirt for authenticity. The original M*A*S*H movie set, which remained standing in Malibu Creek State Park, was often used for the small-screen version's exteriors.

Cast of Characters: The passionate yet world-weary Hawkeye Pierce, who refused to knuckle under to authority, was played by Alan Alda. Although Gary Burghoff (Emmy winner) had played Radar as somewhat sardonic in the feature-film version, he chose to play him much more shy, bumbling, kind-hearted, and naive for TV. Bill Christopher didn't play Father Mulcahy in the pilot episode but took over the role when the series was picked up. Jamie Farr was originally cast as Klinger for one episode only, but his madness added such a unique color to the show that he was kept as a regular. Mike Farrell joined the cast in 1975 as the honest, tolerant, and humorous B. J. Hunnicut, a replacement for the character of Trapper John, who had been played by Wayne Rogers for the first three years. Larry

Hawkeye puts Radar's teddy bear into a time capsule during the last regular episode of M*A*S*H. *Looking on are Major Winchester, Corporal Klinger, and Colonel Potter.*

Linville appeared as the hypocritical and pompous antagonist, Major Frank Burns, from inception until the start of the 1977–78 season. In 1975 veteran actor Harry Morgan joined the cast as career army man Colonel Sherman Potter, the commanding officer you could trust with your life. McLean Stevenson, who left the series in the spring of 1975, was the easygoing Lieutenant Colonel Henry Blake, who would just as soon go fishing and let Radar run his command. David Ogden Stiers portrayed the aristocratic Bostonian, Major Charles Emerson Winchester III, replacing Linville's Frank Burns as the villain the audience loved to hate. Rounding out the cast, Loretta Swit appeared as the fascinating and multifaceted Major Margaret "Hot Lips" Houlihan.

The Creation: William Self, head of Twentieth Century Fox TV, had the idea of a M*A*S*H TV series based on the hugely successful 1970 Robert Altman movie, which was derived from Dr. Richard Hornberger's novel (written under the pseudonym Richard Hooker). In the early 1970s, thanks to Norman Lear, controversial sitcoms were definitely in, so why not an antiwar comedy that was bawdy and bloody? Enthused at the prospect, Fred Silverman assigned the show to producer Gene Reynolds. When CBS promised to give Reynolds a free hand, he recruited Larry Gelbart to write the pilot and, together, the two men set out to achieve their goal: to create a sincerely irreverent comedy series about the horrors of war without the traditional service-gang hijinks and jokes.

Highlights and Famous Episodes: McLean Stevenson's final show, in which his character dies in a plane crash on the way home from Korea, garnered more mail and comment than any episode in the show's history. One of the series' most touching moments was when Radar read the shocking news of Blake's death to the rest of the characters. The series' first two-part episode, "Comrades in Arms," was a turning point for Margaret Houlihan's character. It focused on Margaret and Hawkeye, stranded in a shelled-out house under a barrage of gunfire with little to do but let nature take its course. It was an intimate look at both characters, in which they realized that in spite of their animosities toward each other, there was also a real mutual affection. The most unusual episode of all was the black-and-white interview show, which aired at the end of M*A*S*H's fourth season. Reynolds suggested casting Clete Roberts, a newsman with experience in Korea, as an interviewer who simply interviewed the M*A*S*H characters about their thoughts and experiences of war. It was presented in an extremely effective documentary fashion.

Behind the Scenes: It's interesting to note that the director of Jamie Farr's first episode instructed him to play the part of Klinger with a lisp and a swish, the stereotype of a homosexual. When Gene Reynolds saw the footage, he was appalled, and he agreed with Farr that wearing dresses but playing the character completely straight was what would give it a very funny spin. Reynolds ordered Farr's footage to be reshot. It worked so well that Klinger became a regular. By the tenth season, the cast and writers admitted that a creative dry spell had set in. A vote was taken and the majority of the cast nixed returning for another season. Not thrilled about giving up a hit show, the executives at Twentieth Century Fox and CBS approached Alan Alda with a proposal. If the star could get the entire cast to agree to do an abridged season of sixteen episodes, they would shoot a final episode of feature length that would be the most ambitious ever filmed. Alda went for the idea and talked the others into joining him. Eventually a two-and-one-half-hour episode, "Goodbye, Farewell, and Amen," aired on February 28, 1983. It was intensely promoted and rated higher than any single TV episode up to that time, watched by 125 million viewers.

—J.L.

ROOTS
(1977)

Statistics: This saga of a black American family, which was adapted from Alex Haley's best-selling book, was the first presentation to be called a novel for television. The twelve-hour drama ran eight consecutive nights on ABC beginning January 23, 1977, and won thirty-seven Emmy nominations, going on to win the award in many categories, including acting, writing, direction, and limited series. The show was a staggering ratings success. According to A. C. Nielsen, approximately 100 million viewers saw the final installment, making it the most-watched TV show of all time. In addition, the episodes were the top seven programs of their week, giving ABC the distinction of having the highest-rated week any network has ever had.

The Setting: The serialized story spread over an entire century, beginning in 1750 in Gambia, West Africa, where white slave traders abducted the central character at age seventeen and brought him to Annapolis, where he was sold, then hauled away to a southern plantation in Spotsylvania County, Virginia.

Cast of Characters: Since the story of Roots spanned generations, two actors shared the coveted role of Kunta Kinte. An unknown, Levar Burton, played this most powerfully rendered slave as a teenager, and John Amos portrayed him as an adult. Cicely Tyson appeared as Kunta's mother, Binta, and Thalmus Rasulala played Omoro, Kunta's father. Edward Asner, who won an Emmy, was the conscience-stricken Captain Davies, whose third mate, a somewhat vicious man, was played by Ralph Waite. Other notables were Louis Gossett Jr. (also an Emmy winner) as Fiddler, Leslie Uggams as Kizzy, Olivia Cole (Emmy winner) as Mathilda, and Ben Vereen as Chicken George. Others in the very large cast were Maya Angelou, Lorne Greene, Vic Morrow, Robert Reed, Chuck Connors, MacDonald Carey, George Hamilton, Richard Roundtree, Lloyd Bridges, Burl Ives, and O. J. Simpson.

The Creation: The novel of Alex Haley's own roots was twelve years in the writing. He'd done massive research, including a journey to the village of Juffure in the backcountry of the republic of Gambia and extensive conversation with a griot—a tribal oral historian. ABC's president, Fred Silverman, took a major gamble, transforming Roots into an innovative television format. The actual inception of Roots is credited to Silverman's predecessor at ABC, Martin Starger, and his programming executive, Brandon Stoddard. The idea of serializing a novel on eight consecutive nights was unprecedented in 1977. The irony, insiders claim, was that Silverman and other ABC executives were actually so doubtful of the pulling power of the program that they ordered it "aired and over with" one week prior to the crucial "sweeps week," when viewer ratings determine advertising rates for local stations.

Highlights: The abduction of the Africans, Kunta Kinte among them, was an eye-opening sequence that got the series off to a compelling start. The overall presentation had its share of mature content, including rape and the display of bare breasts in the early African segments. An unforgettable sequence involved the removal of half of Kinte's foot, a punishment for repeated escape attempts. As the series ended, Tom, a free man and great-grandson of Kunta Kinte, ventured to Tennessee to provide a new and better life for his family.

Behind the Scenes: Executive producer David L. Wolper, producer Stan Margulies, and screenwriter William Blinn witnessed the profound effect of Roots on future TV programming. It was hard to imagine nearly half of the entire population of America sitting in front of TV screens just to watch a single dramatic presentation. Countless novels have been brought to the small screen as a result of the unprecedented ratings success of Roots. Though Haley claimed his book was nonfiction, critics had their doubts. They called it a novel and questioned the extent of the cruelty it attributed to racism. They felt that the cruelty of the eighteenth and nineteenth centuries was really to blame—a cruelty that affected whites as much as it did blacks. It was suggested that the slave trade thrived only because African blacks sold their own brothers into slavery as opposed to its rise being due to so-called raids or "white slave parties." Some critics claimed that the historical aspect of the show was distorted and sensationalized. One critic referred to it as the network's "shackles, whips, and lust" view of slavery. A year after the show had aired, Alex Haley was sued for plagiarism by Harold Courlander, the author of a 1967 novel about slavery, The African. During a five-week trial, Haley was subjected to a brutal cross-examination. The judge was certain of Haley's guilt but detested the idea of discrediting a black idol from the bench. Eventually the matter was settled out of court. Haley paid Courlander $650,000 and signed a face-saving two sentence statement: "The suit has been amicably settled out of court. Alex Haley acknowledges and regrets that various materials from The African found their way into his book, Roots." Haley, who had diabetes, died of a heart attack in Seattle, Washington, on February 10, 1992, at the age of seventy.

—J.L.

DALLAS
(1978–91)

Statistics: Dallas premiered on CBS on Sunday, April 2, 1978. After five episodes and three different time slots, the show established itself on Fridays at 10:00 P.M. (some years at 9:00), where it ran for the remainder of its twelve seasons. The show was not an instant success (it ranked near number fifty-five in the Nielsen ratings), but by 1980 it was the most-watched series on network television and was on its way to becoming the most popular nighttime soap opera in the history of the medium. It was in the top-ten Nielsen ratings for half of its years, regularly drawing audiences of 30 to 40 million.

The Setting: The drama about big money, oil, greed, power, betrayal, and sex was played against the backdrop of modern Texas. The stories primarily centered on conflicts within the Ewing family.

A patriarch, his wife, their two sons and their respective wives, and the teenage niece of a third son who had moved to California all lived under one roof, a magnificent ranch called Southfork. Most exteriors were filmed at Duncan Acres (which since has been legally renamed Southfork) in Plano, Texas. The interiors for the series were shot either at the home of Mr. and Mrs. Bruce Calder in Turtle Creek, Texas, or at the

MGM studios in Culver City, California, where the Calder home had been duplicated in detail.

Cast of Characters: The head of the Ewing clan was Jock Ewing, played by veteran actor Jim Davis. The well-known Broadway actress Barbara Bel Geddes played Jock's wife and true love, "Miss Ellie" (portrayed by Donna Reed during the 1984–85 season). The role of J.R., the unscrupulous, unfaithful, and conniving eldest son, went to Larry Hagman, formerly of *I Dream of Jeannie.* The constant thorn in J.R.'s side was his youngest brother, Bobby (played by Patrick Duffy), a young man rife with the morals and values J.R. disdained. Gary Ewing, the somewhat emotionally unstable middle son, played by Ted Shackleford, rarely appeared. Also in the Ewing household was J.R.'s boozy wife, Sue Ellen, played by Linda Gray. Victoria Principal played Bobby's beautiful bride, and rounding out the immediate family was Charlene Tilton in the role of Gary's blond and sexy teenage daughter, Lucy. Other prominent members of the cast were Steve Kanaly as Ray Krebbs, and Ken Kercheval as Cliff Barnes. A multitude of other regulars came and went over the course of the show's long run. Among them were Howard Keel, Alexis Smith, Priscilla Presley, Joan Van Ark, Susan Lucci, Barbara Eden, Leigh Taylor-Young, Mary Crosby, Megan Gallagher, Susan Howard, Tina Louise, Keenan Wynn, David Wayne, and many, many more.

The Creation: During a period in the late 1970s when TV was mainly "jiggle" shows and low-brow sitcoms, the networks were looking for potent drama (cop shows weren't working, mostly because of curbs on TV violence). Five episodes of *Dallas* were filmed to give it a chance to attract some viewers and maybe win a slot on the lineup for fall 1978. It was heavily promoted and got substantial ratings. Larry Hagman's eventual contention was that since there was a recession in the late 1970s and no one had any money, they were interested in staying home and watching TV for entertainment. Also, there was something appealing about watching the rich when you weren't rich yourself, just as audiences during the depression loved to see movies about the wealthy.

Highlights and Famous Episodes: There was no end to J.R.'s shenanigans over the years. He sold worthless Asian oil leases to friends, secretly mortgaged Southfork, attempted to institutionalize his own wife for alcoholism, thwarted other people's plans to marry, and was himself confined to a mental institution and fitted with a straitjacket. However, no other single episode, perhaps in TV history, caused the stir that the final one of the 1979–80 season did. It was a startling cliffhanger in which J.R. was mysteriously shot and rushed to the hospital in critical condition. For that entire summer, neither the fans nor the cast had any idea "who shot J.R." But thanks to publicity mills cranking out endless speculation, the question reached international epidemic proportions. Jimmy the Greek laid odds on his favorite. Betting parlors took in millions on bets. The candidates for the nasty deed were the talk of England and many other countries. Several alternative endings were filmed under tight security. Although Larry Hagman and the producers had seen the final cut and knew the assailant's identity, they kept it a secret. Hagman even nixed an offer by a consortium of European newspapers that offered him $250,000 to name the assassin. On November 21, 1980, the world found out. Jimmy the Greek was right, it was Sue Ellen's sister, Kristin (played by Mary Crosby). The revealing episode was seen by more viewers than any episode of any show in the history of television up to that time. That night, 80 percent of all viewers in front of their sets were tuned in to *Dallas,* 350 million people in fifty-seven different countries.

Behind the Scenes: At the end of the 1983–84 season, Barbara Bel Geddes left the show and was replaced by Donna Reed. When Bel Geddes decided to return a year later, nobody bothered to tell Donna Reed. As she was stepping off a plane in Europe, she was devastated to learn from the awaiting reporters that she'd been fired. It was no secret that Patrick Duffy had also wanted out of the weekly series grind for some time, and at the end of the 1985–86 season, the producers finally accommodated him—Bobby Ewing was killed in a hit-and-run accident and given an elaborate funeral. When his absence caused ratings to sag the following year, Larry Hagman coaxed Duffy into returning to the show. In what was clearly one of the most lame cop-outs in soap opera history, the 1986–87 season opened with a dead and buried Bobby Ewing casually rinsing off in his wife, Pam's, shower. The writers' justification for his remarkable reemergence was that he'd dreamed the entire 1985–86 season. Everything that had happened in all the previous twenty-plus episodes was part of his dream. Bobby was back and nothing more had to be said about it. One way to fathom just how successful *Dallas* was worldwide is to consider that during its heyday, it was reported that in Turkey a parliamentary meeting was cut short once so its members would not miss the show.

—J.L.

THE COSBY SHOW
(1984–92)

Statistics: This 8:00 P.M. half-hour situation comedy premiered on September 20 and became the runaway hit of television's 1984 season. It dominated the Nielsen ratings for most of the 1980s, garnering the number-one spot in its second season and maintaining it five years in a row (1985–90), a record equaled only by *All in the Family*. The show single-handedly revived an endangered species—sitcom. Before Cosby, NBC was anchored in last place in the ratings. Afterward it became the number-one network. Media experts estimate that the show earned NBC a cool billion dollars and made Cosby one of America's wealthiest men. The show won six Emmys, fourteen NAACP Image Awards, a Peabody, and a Humanitas (writing) Award during its run of 208 episodes. Syndicated reruns were sold for an average of $1 million per episode, more than twice the amount ever charged for any previous program.

The Setting: The family-oriented stories took place in Cliff and Clair Huxtable's New York brownstone. Although Cliff was an obstetrician who maintained his office at home and Clair was an attorney, the show focused mainly on their family life with the five children rather than on their professions—almost like a throwback to the domestic comedies of the 1950s. The family problems were often no more complex than bad report cards or overly provocative teenage party dresses. An entire episode might center on reminiscing around a family album. Whenever there were conflicts, they were resolved with love, warmth, and forgiveness, and always tempered with a sense of humor. The Huxtables were strict, caring parents who valued honesty and openness in family communication.

Cast of Characters: The role of Dr. Heathcliff Huxtable, the lovable, warm, and funny husband and father, fit Bill Cosby like a familiar glove. Phylicia Ayers-Allen (later to become Phylicia Rashad after her marriage to NBC

The Huxtable children prepare for the first day of school during a 1985 episode of The Cosby Show.

sportscaster Ahmad Rashad) played Clair Huxtable. The Huxtables' only son, Theo, was played by Malcolm-Jamal Warner, a thirteen-year-old whom Cosby chose on the last day of a nationwide search. Lisa Bonet appeared as sixteen-year-old Denise. When Bonet's character went off to college, Bonet moved on to a spin-off series, *A Different World*, which she remained with for a year, returning to *The Cosby Show* in 1988. Vanessa Huxtable was portrayed by Tempestt Bledsoe, who began the show at age eight. The youngest Huxtable daughter, Rudy, was played by Keshia Knight Pulliam. Although the eldest Huxtable daughter was never seen during the first season because she was in college, Sabrina Le Beauf joined the cast as Sondra for the second season. Over the eight-year run, others joined the Cosby roster: friends of the kids, sons-in-law, grandchildren, Clair's folks, and Cliff's parents. Celebrity guests were usually famous musicians such as Stevie Wonder, B. B. King, Joe Williams, Nancy Wilson, the Count Basie Band, and Sammy Davis Jr.

The Creation: Although the creation of the series is credited to Cosby, Ed Weinberger, and Michael Leeson, it was clearly Cosby's initial vision to bring a successful African-American family into television's mainstream. He didn't want to employ the usual gimmicks and jokes; no jivey jargon or negative stereotypes. He originally pitched the show to ABC as a blue-collar comedy in which the father was a limousine driver and the mother was a plumber. After ABC passed on the idea, Cosby's real-life wife, Camille, suggested he make the parents upscale professionals. Although ABC passed again, NBC bought the show. Cosby insisted on total creative control and wanted the show to be taped at the Kaufman-Astoria Studio in Queens, New York, because he disliked working in Hollywood. (For the first three years it was taped at NBC Studios in Brooklyn.) He was so determined to make the family relations authentic that he even commissioned a highly respected black psychiatrist, Alvin Poussaint of the Harvard Medical School, to review every script for psychological accuracy. The idea was to provide role models and lessons for all races in how to raise a family in a kind and loving manner.

Highlights and Famous Episodes: Among many memorable episodes, one that was especially touching was when little Rudy's goldfish died and was buried at sea (flushed down the toilet). Eight-year-old Vanessa grew up during the course of the series, and never was this more evident than in the eighth season, when she shocked the family by announcing her six-month-old engagement to a maintenance man who was twelve years her senior. One of the finest episodes was the first, when Cosby confronted his son, Theo, for failing in school. Indifferent, the boy declared that his goal in life was to be nothing more than "regular people." Cosby's explanation of what it was really like to be "regular people" was a classic study in reality and a hilarious one. Coming full circle, eight years later, the final episode centered on Theo's graduation from NYU, in which all the major characters who had ever appeared on the show were brought back to reprise their roles.

Behind the Scenes: Although the series was touted and loved by many, it also drew criticism. Some declared the show unrealistic because the Huxtables were educated and affluent. There was even a book written by two University of Massachusetts professors that accused the Huxtables' affluence of desensitizing white Americans to the plight of inner-city blacks. Whatever else *The Cosby Show* did, it

forever changed the way America viewed the black family. The final episode was heavily promoted and scheduled to air on April 30, 1992. That same day, the infamous verdicts for the Rodney King beating trial were announced. Within a short time, there was live coverage on all channels of Los Angeles being burned and looted. NBC was in a delicate position, faced with being deemed insensitive and unsympathetic if they aired the Cosby show or disappointing millions outside Los Angeles who had looked forward to the much-ballyhooed climactic episode. Cosby had even recorded two introductions in the event that the network preempted it. Ultimately, NBC chose to air the episode. When it was completed, a statement by Cosby was read: "Let us all pray that everyone from the top of the government down to the people in the streets . . . would all have good sense. And let us pray for a better tomorrow, which starts today."

—J.L.

HIGHEST-RATED TV SERIES, BY YEAR

The following lists are the ten top-rated evening television series for every year from 1950 through May 1996. The Nielsen TV ratings, compiled by Nielsen Media Research, set the market standards for advertiser-supported TV. Nielsen TV ratings provide an estimate of the audience for just about every program that can be seen on TV. A rating is the percent of a population viewing a TV program during the average minute. For example, a household rating of 67.3 would mean that 67.3 percent of all households equipped with a television set were tuned to that program during the average minute.

OCTOBER 1950–APRIL 1951

Program	Network	Rating
1. Texaco Star Theater	NBC	61.6
2. Fireside Theatre	NBC	52.6
3. Philco TV Playhouse	NBC	45.3
4. Your Show of Shows	NBC	42.6
5. The Colgate Comedy Hour	NBC	42.0
6. Gillette Cavalcade of Sports	NBC	41.3
7. The Lone Ranger	ABC	41.2
8. Arthur Godfrey's Talent Scouts	CBS	40.6
9. Hopalong Cassidy	NBC	39.9
10. Mama	CBS	39.7

OCTOBER 1951–APRIL 1952

Program	Network	Rating
1. Arthur Godfrey's Talent Scouts	CBS	53.8
2. Texaco Star Theater	NBC	52.0
3. I Love Lucy	CBS	50.9
4. The Red Skelton Show	NBC	50.2
5. The Colgate Comedy Hour	NBC	45.3
6. Arthur Godfrey and His Friends	CBS	43.3
7. Fireside Theatre	NBC	43.1
8. Your Show of Shows	NBC	43.0
9. The Jack Benny Show	CBS	42.8
10. You Bet Your Life	NBC	42.1

OCTOBER 1952–APRIL 1953

Program	Network	Rating
1. I Love Lucy	CBS	67.3
2. Arthur Godfrey's Talent Scouts	CBS	54.7
3. Arthur Godfrey and His Friends	CBS	47.1
4. Dragnet	NBC	46.8
5. Texaco Star Theater	NBC	46.7
6. The Buick Circus Hour	NBC	46.0
7. The Colgate Comedy Hour	NBC	44.3
8. Gangbusters	NBC	42.4
9. You Bet Your Life	NBC	41.6
10. Fireside Theatre	NBC	40.6

OCTOBER 1953–APRIL 1954

Program	Network	Rating
1. I Love Lucy	CBS	58.8
2. Dragnet	NBC	53.2
3. Arthur Godfrey's Talent Scouts	CBS	43.6
3. You Bet Your Life	NBC	43.6
5. The Chevy Show (Bob Hope)	NBC	41.4
6. The Milton Berle Show	NBC	40.2
7. Arthur Godfrey and His Friends	CBS	38.9
8. The Ford Show	NBC	38.8
9. The Jackie Gleason Show	CBS	38.1
10. Fireside Theatre	NBC	36.4

OCTOBER 1954–APRIL 1955

Program	Network	Rating
1. I Love Lucy	CBS	49.3
2. The Jackie Gleason Show	CBS	42.4
3. Dragnet	NBC	42.1
4. You Bet Your Life	NBC	41.0
5. The Toast of the Town	CBS	39.6
6. Disneyland	ABC	39.1
7. The Chevy Show (Bob Hope)	NBC	38.5
8. The Jack Benny Show	CBS	38.3
9. The Martha Raye Show	NBC	35.6
10. The George Gobel Show	NBC	35.2

OCTOBER 1955–APRIL 1956

Program	Network	Rating
1. The $64,000 Question	CBS	47.5
2. I Love Lucy	CBS	46.1
3. The Ed Sullivan Show	CBS	39.5
4. Disneyland	ABC	37.4
5. The Jack Benny Show	CBS	37.2
6. December Bride	CBS	37.0
7. You Bet Your Life	NBC	35.4
8. Dragnet	NBC	35.0
9. The Millionaire	CBS	33.8
10. I've Got a Secret	CBS	33.5

OCTOBER 1956–APRIL 1957

Program	Network	Rating
1. I Love Lucy	CBS	43.7
2. The Ed Sullivan Show	CBS	38.4
3. General Electric Theater	CBS	36.9
4. The $64,000 Question	CBS	36.4
5. December Bride	CBS	35.2
6. Alfred Hitchcock Presents	CBS	33.9
7. I've Got a Secret	CBS	32.7
7. Gunsmoke	CBS	32.7
9. The Perry Como Show	NBC	32.6
10. The Jack Benny Show	NBC	32.3

OCTOBER 1957–APRIL 1958

Program	Network	Rating
1. Gunsmoke	CBS	43.1
2. The Danny Thomas Show	CBS	35.3
3. Tales of Wells Fargo	NBC	35.2
4. Have Gun Will Travel	CBS	33.7
5. I've Got a Secret	CBS	33.4
6. The Life and Legend of Wyatt Earp	ABC	32.6
7. General Electric Theater	CBS	31.5
8. The Restless Gun	NBC	31.4
9. December Bride	CBS	30.7
10. You Bet Your Life	NBC	30.6

OCTOBER 1958–APRIL 1959

Program	Network	Rating
1. Gunsmoke	CBS	39.6
2. Wagon Train	NBC	36.1
3. Have Gun Will Travel	CBS	34.3
4. The Rifleman	ABC	33.1
5. The Danny Thomas Show	CBS	32.8
6. Maverick	ABC	30.4
7. Tales of Wells Fargo	NBC	30.2
8. The Real McCoys	ABC	30.1
9. I've Got a Secret	CBS	29.8
10. The Life and Legend of Wyatt Earp	ABC	29.1

OCTOBER 1959–APRIL 1960

Program	Network	Rating
1. Gunsmoke	CBS	40.3
2. Wagon Train	NBC	38.4
3. Have Gun Will Travel	CBS	34.7
4. The Danny Thomas Show	CBS	31.1
5. The Red Skelton Show	CBS	30.8
6. Father Knows Best	CBS	29.7
6. 77 Sunset Strip	ABC	29.7
8. The Price Is Right	NBC	29.2
9. Wanted: Dead or Alive	CBS	28.7
10. Perry Mason	CBS	28.3

OCTOBER 1960–APRIL 1961

Program	Network	Rating
1. Gunsmoke	CBS	37.3
2. Wagon Train	NBC	34.2
3. Have Gun Will Travel	CBS	30.9
4. The Andy Griffith Show	CBS	27.8
5. The Real McCoys	ABC	27.7
6. Rawhide	CBS	27.5
7. Candid Camera	CBS	27.3
8. The Untouchables	ABC	27.0
8. The Price Is Right	NBC	27.0
10. The Jack Benny Show	CBS	26.2

OCTOBER 1961–APRIL 1962

Program	Network	Rating
1. Wagon Train	NBC	32.1
2. Bonanza	NBC	30.0
3. Gunsmoke	CBS	28.3
4. Hazel	NBC	27.7
5. Perry Mason	CBS	27.3
6. The Red Skelton Show	CBS	27.1
7. The Andy Griffith Show	CBS	27.0
8. The Danny Thomas Show	CBS	26.1
9. Dr. Kildare	NBC	25.6
10. Candid Camera	CBS	25.5

OCTOBER 1962–APRIL 1963

Program	Network	Rating
1. The Beverly Hillbillies	CBS	36.0
2. Candid Camera	CBS	31.1
3. The Red Skelton Show	CBS	31.1
4. Bonanza	NBC	29.8
4. The Lucy Show	CBS	29.8
6. The Andy Griffith Show	CBS	29.7
7. Ben Casey	ABC	28.7
7. The Danny Thomas Show	CBS	28.7
9. The Dick Van Dyke Show	CBS	27.1
10. Gunsmoke	CBS	27.0

OCTOBER 1963–APRIL 1964

Program	Network	Rating
1. The Beverly Hillbillies	CBS	39.1
2. Bonanza	NBC	36.9
3. The Dick Van Dyke Show	CBS	33.3
4. Petticoat Junction	CBS	30.3
5. The Andy Griffith Show	CBS	29.4
6. The Lucy Show	CBS	28.1
7. Candid Camera	CBS	27.7
8. The Ed Sullivan Show	CBS	27.5
9. The Danny Thomas Show	CBS	26.7
10. My Favorite Martian	CBS	26.3

OCTOBER 1964–APRIL 1965

Program	Network	Rating
1. Bonanza	NBC	36.3
2. Bewitched	ABC	31.0
3. Gomer Pyle, U.S.M.C.	CBS	30.7
4. The Andy Griffith Show	CBS	28.3
5. The Fugitive	ABC	27.9
6. The Red Skelton Hour	CBS	27.4
7. The Dick Van Dyke Show	CBS	27.1
8. The Lucy Show	CBS	26.6
9. Peyton Place II	ABC	26.4
10. Combat	ABC	26.1

OCTOBER 1965–APRIL 1966

Program	Network	Rating
1. Bonanza	NBC	31.8
2. Gomer Pyle, U.S.M.C.	CBS	27.8
3. The Lucy Show	CBS	27.7
4. The Red Skelton Hour	CBS	27.6
5. Batman (Thursday)	ABC	27.0
6. The Andy Griffith Show	CBS	26.9
7. Bewitched	ABC	25.9
7. The Beverly Hillbillies	CBS	25.9
9. Hogan's Heroes	CBS	24.9
10. Batman (Wednesday)	ABC	24.7

OCTOBER 1966–APRIL 1967

Program	Network	Rating
1. Bonanza	NBC	29.1
2. The Red Skelton Hour	CBS	28.2
3. The Andy Griffith Show	CBS	27.4
4. The Lucy Show	CBS	26.2
5. The Jackie Gleason Show	CBS	25.3
6. Green Acres	CBS	24.6
7. Daktari	CBS	23.4
7. Bewitched	ABC	23.4
7. The Beverly Hillbillies	CBS	23.4
10. Gomer Pyle, U.S.M.C.	CBS	22.8

OCTOBER 1967–APRIL 1968

Program	Network	Rating
1. The Andy Griffith Show	CBS	27.6
2. The Lucy Show	CBS	27.0
3. Gomer Pyle, U.S.M.C.	CBS	25.6
4. Gunsmoke	CBS	25.5
4. Family Affair	CBS	25.5

4. Bonanza	NBC	25.5
7. The Red Skelton Show	CBS	25.3
8. The Dean Martin Show	NBC	24.8
9. The Jackie Gleason Show	CBS	23.9
10. Saturday Night at the Movies	NBC	23.6

OCTOBER 1968–APRIL 1969

Program	Network	Rating
1. Rowan & Martin's Laugh-In	NBC	31.8
2. Gomer Pyle, U.S.M.C.	CBS	27.2
3. Bonanza	NBC	26.6
4. Mayberry R.F.D.	CBS	25.4
5. Family Affair	CBS	25.2
6. Gunsmoke	CBS	24.9
7. Julia	NBC	24.6
8. The Dean Martin Show	NBC	24.1
9. Here's Lucy	CBS	23.8
10. The Beverly Hillbillies	CBS	23.5

OCTOBER 1969–APRIL 1970

Program	Network	Rating
1. Rowan & Martin's Laugh-In	NBC	26.3
2. Gunsmoke	CBS	25.9
3. Bonanza	NBC	24.8
4. Mayberry R.F.D.	CBS	24.4
5. Family Affair	CBS	24.2
6. Here's Lucy	CBS	23.9
7. The Red Skelton Hour	CBS	23.8
8. Marcus Welby, M.D.	ABC	23.7
9. Walt Disney's Wonderful World of Color	NBC	23.6
10. The Doris Day Show	CBS	22.8

OCTOBER 1970–APRIL 1971

Program	Network	Rating
1. Marcus Welby, M.D.	ABC	29.6
2. The Flip Wilson Show	NBC	27.9
3. Here's Lucy	CBS	26.1
4. Ironside	NBC	25.7
5. Gunsmoke	CBS	25.5
6. ABC Movie of the Week	ABC	25.1
7. Hawaii Five-O	CBS	25.0
8. Medical Center	CBS	24.5
9. Bonanza	NBC	23.9
10. The F.B.I.	ABC	23.0

OCTOBER 1971–APRIL 1972

Program	Network	Rating
1. All in the Family	CBS	34.0
2. The Flip Wilson Show	NBC	28.2

3. Marcus Welby, M.D.	ABC	27.8
4. Gunsmoke	CBS	26.0
5. ABC Movie of the Week	ABC	25.6
6. Sanford and Son	NBC	25.2
7. Mannix	CBS	24.8
8. Funny Face	CBS	23.9
8. Adam-12	NBC	23.9
10. The Mary Tyler Moore Show	CBS	23.7

OCTOBER 1972–APRIL 1973

Program	Network	Rating
1. All in the Family	CBS	33.3
2. Sanford and Son	NBC	27.6
3. Hawaii Five-O	CBS	25.2
4. Maude	CBS	24.7
5. Bridget Loves Bernie	CBS	24.2
5. Sunday Mystery Movie	NBC	24.2
7. The Mary Tyler Moore Show	CBS	23.6
7. Gunsmoke	CBS	23.6
9. The Wonderful World of Disney	NBC	23.5
10. Ironside	NBC	23.4

SEPTEMBER 1973–APRIL 1974

Program	Network	Rating
1. All in the Family	CBS	31.2
2. The Waltons	CBS	28.1
3. Sanford and Son	NBC	27.5
4. M*A*S*H	CBS	25.7
5. Hawaii Five-O	CBS	24.0
6. Maude	CBS	23.5
7. Kojak	CBS	23.3
7. The Sonny and Cher Comedy Hour	CBS	23.3
9. The Mary Tyler Moore Show	CBS	23.1
9. Cannon	CBS	23.1

SEPTEMBER 1974–APRIL 1975

Program	Network	Rating
1. All in the Family	CBS	30.2
2. Sanford and Son	NBC	29.6
3. Chico and the Man	NBC	28.5
4. The Jeffersons	CBS	27.6
5. M*A*S*H	CBS	27.4
6. Rhoda	CBS	26.3
7. Good Times	CBS	25.8
8. The Waltons	CBS	25.5
9. Maude	CBS	24.9
10. Hawaii Five-O	CBS	24.8

SEPTEMBER 1975–APRIL 1976

Program	Network	Rating
1. All in the Family	CBS	30.1
2. Rich Man, Poor Man	ABC	28.0

Program	Network	Rating
3. Laverne & Shirley	ABC	27.5
4. Maude	CBS	25.0
5. The Bionic Woman	ABC	24.9
6. Phyllis	CBS	24.5
7. Sanford and Son	NBC	24.4
7. Rhoda	CBS	24.4
9. The Six Million Dollar Man	ABC	24.3
10. ABC Monday Night Movie	ABC	24.2

SEPTEMBER 1976–APRIL 1977

Program	Network	Rating
1. Happy Days	ABC	31.5
2. Laverne & Shirley	ABC	30.9
3. ABC Monday Night Movie	ABC	26.0
4. M*A*S*H	CBS	25.9
5. Charlie's Angels	ABC	25.8
6. The Big Event	NBC	24.4
7. The Six Million Dollar Man	ABC	24.2
8. ABC Sunday Night Movie	ABC	23.4
8. Baretta	ABC	23.4
8. One Day at a Time	CBS	23.4

SEPTEMBER 1977–APRIL 1978

Program	Network	Rating
1. Laverne & Shirley	ABC	31.6
2. Happy Days	ABC	31.4
3. Three's Company	ABC	28.3
4. 60 Minutes	CBS	24.4
4. Charlie's Angels	ABC	24.4
4. All in the Family	CBS	24.4
7. Little House on the Prairie	NBC	24.1
8. Alice	CBS	23.2
8. M*A*S*H	CBS	23.2
10. One Day at a Time	CBS	23.0

SEPTEMBER 1978–APRIL 1979

Program	Network	Rating
1. Laverne & Shirley	ABC	30.5
2. Three's Company	ABC	30.3
3. Mork & Mindy	ABC	28.6
3. Happy Days	ABC	28.6
5. Angie	ABC	26.7
6. 60 Minutes	CBS	25.5
7. M*A*S*H	CBS	25.4
8. The Ropers	ABC	25.2
9. All in the Family	CBS	24.9
9. Taxi	ABC	24.9

SEPTEMBER 1979–APRIL 1980

Program	Network	Rating
1. 60 Minutes	CBS	28.4
2. Three's Company	ABC	26.3
3. That's Incredible	ABC	25.8
4. Alice	CBS	25.3
4. M*A*S*H	CBS	25.3
6. Dallas	CBS	25.0
7. Flo	CBS	24.4
8. The Jeffersons	CBS	24.3
9. The Dukes of Hazzard	CBS	24.1
10. One Day at a Time	CBS	23.0

SEPTEMBER 1980–APRIL 1981

Program	Network	Rating
1. Dallas	CBS	34.5
2. The Dukes of Hazzard	CBS	27.3
3. 60 Minutes	CBS	27.0
4. M*A*S*H	CBS	25.7
5. The Love Boat	ABC	24.3
6. The Jeffersons	CBS	23.5
7. Alice	CBS	22.9
8. House Calls	CBS	22.4
8. Three's Company	ABC	22.4
10. Little House on the Prairie	NBC	22.1

SEPTEMBER 1981–APRIL 1982

Program	Network	Rating
1. Dallas	CBS	28.4
2. 60 Minutes	CBS	27.7
3. The Jeffersons	CBS	23.4
4. Three's Company	ABC	23.3
5. Alice	CBS	22.7
6. The Dukes of Hazzard	CBS	22.6
6. Too Close for Comfort	ABC	22.6
8. ABC Monday Night Movie	ABC	22.5

Mork (Robin Williams) pays a visit to Richie Cunningham (Ron Howard) and the Fonz (Henry Winkler) during an episode of Happy Days.

9. M*A*S*H   CBS   22.3
10. One Day at a Time   CBS   22.0

SEPTEMBER 1982–APRIL 1983

Program	Network	Rating
1. 60 Minutes	CBS	25.5
2. Dallas	CBS	24.6
3. M*A*S*H	CBS	22.6
3. Magnum, P.I.	CBS	22.6
5. Dynasty	ABC	22.4
6. Three's Company	ABC	21.2
7. Simon & Simon	CBS	21.0
8. Falcon Crest	CBS	20.7
9. The Love Boat	ABC	20.3
10. The A-Team	NBC	20.1
10. Monday Night Football	ABC	20.1

SEPTEMBER 1983–APRIL 1984

Program	Network	Rating
1. Dallas	CBS	25.7
2. 60 Minutes	CBS	24.2
3. Dynasty	ABC	24.1
4. The A-Team	NBC	24.0
5. Simon & Simon	CBS	23.8
6. Magnum, P.I.	CBS	22.4
7. Falcon Crest	CBS	22.0
8. Kate & Allie	CBS	21.9
9. Hotel	ABC	21.1
10. Cagney & Lacey	CBS	20.9

SEPTEMBER 1984–APRIL 1985

Program	Network	Rating
1. Dynasty	ABC	25.0
2. Dallas	CBS	24.7
3. The Cosby Show	NBC	24.2
4. 60 Minutes	CBS	22.2
5. Family Ties	NBC	22.1
6. The A-Team	NBC	21.9
7. Simon & Simon	CBS	21.8
8. Murder, She Wrote	CBS	20.1
9. Knots Landing	CBS	20.0
10. Falcon Crest	CBS	19.9
10. Crazy Like a Fox	CBS	19.9

SEPTEMBER 1985–APRIL 1986

Program	Network	Rating
1. The Cosby Show	NBC	33.7
2. Family Ties	NBC	30.0
3. Murder, She Wrote	CBS	25.3
4. 60 Minutes	CBS	23.9
5. Cheers	NBC	23.7
6. Dallas	CBS	21.9
7. Dynasty	ABC	21.8
7. The Golden Girls	NBC	21.8
9. Miami Vice	NBC	21.3
10. Who's the Boss?	ABC	21.1

SEPTEMBER 1986–APRIL 1987

Program	Network	Rating
1. The Cosby Show	NBC	34.9
2. Family Ties	NBC	32.7
3. Cheers	NBC	27.2
4. Murder, She Wrote	CBS	25.4
5. The Golden Girls	NBC	24.5
6. 60 Minutes	CBS	23.3
7. Night Court	NBC	23.2
8. Growing Pains	ABC	22.7
9. Moonlighting	ABC	22.4
10. Who's the Boss?	ABC	22.0

SEPTEMBER 1987–APRIL 1988

Program	Network	Rating
1. The Cosby Show	NBC	27.8
2. A Different World	NBC	25.0
3. Cheers	NBC	23.4
4. The Golden Girls	NBC	21.8
5. Growing Pains	ABC	21.3
6. Who's the Boss?	ABC	21.2
7. Night Court	NBC	20.8
8. 60 Minutes	CBS	20.6
9. Murder, She Wrote	CBS	20.2
10. Alf	NBC	18.8
10. The Wonder Years	ABC	18.8

OCTOBER 1988–APRIL 1989

Program	Network	Rating
1. The Cosby Show	NBC	25.6
2. Roseanne	ABC	23.8
3. A Different World	NBC	23.0
4. Cheers	NBC	22.3
5. 60 Minutes	CBS	21.7
6. The Golden Girls	NBC	21.4
7. Who's the Boss?	ABC	20.8
8. Murder, She Wrote	CBS	19.9
9. Empty Nest	NBC	19.2
10. Anything But Love	ABC	19.0

SEPTEMBER 1989–APRIL 1990

Program	Network	Rating
1. The Cosby Show	NBC	23.1
1. Roseanne	ABC	23.1
3. Cheers	NBC	22.7
4. A Different World	NBC	21.1
5. America's Funniest Home Videos	ABC	20.9
6. The Golden Girls	NBC	20.1
7. 60 Minutes	CBS	19.7
8. The Wonder Years	ABC	19.2
9. Empty Nest	NBC	18.9
10. Monday Night Football	ABC	18.1

SEPTEMBER 1990–APRIL 1991

Program	Network	Rating
1. Cheers	NBC	21.3
2. 60 Minutes	CBS	20.6
3. Roseanne	ABC	18.1
4. A Different World	NBC	17.5
5. The Cosby Show	NBC	17.1
6. Murphy Brown	CBS	16.9
7. Empty Nest	NBC	16.7
7. America's Funniest Home Videos	ABC	16.7
9. Monday Night Football	ABC	16.6
10. The Golden Girls	NBC	16.5
10. Designing Women	CBS	16.5

SEPTEMBER 1991–APRIL 1992

Program	Network	Rating
1. 60 Minutes	CBS	21.9
2. Roseanne	ABC	20.2
3. Murphy Brown	CBS	18.6
4. Cheers	NBC	17.6
5. Home Improvement	ABC	17.5
6. Designing Women	CBS	17.3
7. Coach	ABC	17.2
8. Full House	ABC	17.0
9. Unsolved Mysteries	NBC	16.9
9. Murder, She Wrote	CBS	16.9

SEPTEMBER 1992–APRIL 1993

Program	Network	Rating
1. 60 Minutes	CBS	21.9
2. Roseanne	ABC	20.7
3. Home Improvement	ABC	19.2
4. Murphy Brown	CBS	17.9
5. Murder, She Wrote	CBS	17.7
6. Coach	ABC	17.5
7. NFL Monday Night Football	ABC	16.7
8. Cheers	NBC	16.1
9. Full House	ABC	15.8
10. Northern Exposure	CBS	15.2

SEPTEMBER 1993–APRIL 1994

Program	Network	Rating
1. Home Improvement	ABC	21.8
2. 60 Minutes	CBS	20.9
3. Seinfeld	NBC	19.3
4. Roseanne	ABC	19.2
5. These Friends of Mine	ABC	18.7
6. Grace Under Fire	ABC	18.0
7. Frasier	NBC	17.5
8. Coach	ABC	17.4
9. Murder, She Wrote	CBS	17.0
10. NFL Monday Night Football	ABC	16.3

SEPTEMBER 1994–APRIL 1995

Program	Network	Rating
1. Seinfeld	NBC	20.5
2. E.R.	NBC	20.0
3. Home Improvement	ABC	19.9
4. Grace Under Fire	ABC	18.9
5. NFL Monday Night Football	ABC	17.8
6. 60 Minutes	CBS	17.1
7. NYPD Blue	ABC	16.5
8. Friends	NBC	16.1
9. Murder, She Wrote	CBS	15.6
9. Roseanne	ABC	15.6

SEPTEMBER 1995–MAY 1996

Program	Network	Rating
1. E.R.	NBC	22.0
2. Seinfeld	NBC	21.2
3. Friends	NBC	18.7
4. Caroline in the City	NBC	17.9
5. NFL Monday Night Football	ABC	17.1
6. The Single Guy	NBC	16.7
7. Home Improvement	ABC	16.2
8. Boston Common	NBC	15.6
9. 60 Minutes	CBS	14.2
10. NYPD Blue	ABC	14.1

TELEVISED CONGRESSIONAL HEARINGS

ARMY-McCARTHY HEARINGS

I cannot and will not cut my conscience to fit this year's fashions.

Lillian Hellman, letter to House Committee on Un-American Activities, May 19, 1952

Dates: April 22, 1954, to June 18, 1954

Background: With the closing of the Iron Curtain in 1948 and the Communist victory in China's civil war the following year, American alarm at the spread of Communism had, by the end of the 1940s, reached its most intense level since the Red scare following World War I. When President Harry Truman revealed in September 1949 that Soviet spies had stolen the secret of the atom bomb, American fears reached near-fever pitch. In January 1950 Alger Hiss was convicted of perjury for denying that, while in the State Department, he had spied for the Soviet Union in the 1930s; the next month Joseph McCarthy, a hitherto-unknown Republican junior senator from Wisconsin, made a speech in which he claimed to have a list of 205 State Department employees who were members of the Communist party. When a Senate subcommittee began to investigate, McCarthy was forced to concede that there actually was no list. Only nine individuals were named; and while several careers were ruined, McCarthy's most important targets, Dr. Philip Jessup, ambassador-at-large responsible for U.S. China policy, and Professor Owen Lattimore, of Johns Hopkins University, were both eventually exonerated.

Over the next two years, however, taking advantage of the general hysteria fueled by the Korean War and the trial and execution of accused A-bomb spies Julius and Ethel Rosenberg, McCarthy continued his attacks on the alleged Communist infiltration of the U.S. government. Waging a ruthless campaign of smear and innuendo that imputed darkly subversive sympathies to opponents of all political stripes, the senator began to aim his poisoned arrows ever higher. His targets included such figures as George C. Marshall, former secretary of state, army chief of staff, and architect of the postwar plan to rebuild Western Europe, whose career, McCarthy intoned in a typically hyperbolic 1951 speech, was a product of "a conspiracy . . . so immense as to dwarf any previous such venture in the history of man."

McCarthy was aided in his endeavors by his friend J. Edgar Hoover, who gladly shared nuggets of tactical wisdom gleaned through thirty years of vigorous political blackmail. The FBI chief, for example, regularly made available abstracts of the bureau's security files and advised McCarthy on how to couch his accusations in vague terms that could not easily be rebutted. In January 1953, following a Republican landslide in the 1952 elections, McCarthy became chairman of the Senate Committee on Government Operations and its subcommittee on investigations, thereby gaining vast powers of subpoena and setting a collision course with the new Eisenhower administration, which wished to preserve, against possible congressional encroachment, the prerogatives of the executive branch. White House and Pentagon opposition to McCarthy intensified when, that summer, he expanded his investigations to include rumors of Communist espionage in the U.S. Army.

In the meantime, however, McCarthy himself had become vulnerable, owing, largely, not to the patently unprincipled nature of his own actions but to the bizarre behavior of his subcommittee's chief counsel, Roy M. Cohn. Cohn was an ambitious and utterly amoral young lawyer who also, in a society whose fear of Communism was rivaled only by its terror of sexual nonconformity, happened to be a closet homosexual. As luck would have it, Cohn's friend and aide, G. David Schine, got drafted into the military; drunk with power and terrified at the prospect of losing Schine to some distant posting, Cohn threatened to "wreck the army" unless his friend was given an assignment that, as knowing Washington wags unkindly put it, "would keep him within arm's reach."

Hoover, meanwhile, sensing how the balance of power was now beginning to shift against McCarthy, and realizing his own vulnerability to questions concerning his personal life, ordered the FBI to halt its assistance to the Wisconsin senator. In March 1954, following a secret meeting between top-level White House, Pentagon, and Justice Department staffers, the army warned McCarthy to abandon his investigation or face charges that he and Cohn had violated the law by attempting to influence Schine's posting. When McCarthy refused, the army released its accusations to the press, and the next month the Army-McCarthy hearings began.

Congressional Cast of Characters: The major players were Joseph R. McCarthy, a second-term Republican senator from Wisconsin, friend of Massachusetts power broker Joseph Kennedy, who had given generously to McCarthy's 1946 Senate campaign; Karl E. Mundt, acting committee chairman and Eisenhower Republican from South Dakota; Joseph N. Welch, a masterful, Iowa-born Boston trial lawyer, who had agreed to serve without compensation as special counsel for the army; and two ambitious young attorneys: Roy M. Cohn, chief counsel to the McCarthy subcommittee, and Robert F. Kennedy, counsel to the subcommittee's Democratic senators, whose father had earlier gotten him a position as a McCarthy aide, and who detested Roy Cohn for beating him out of the job as McCarthy's chief counsel the previous year.

Key Witnesses and Testimony: The hearings were the first major congressional event to be televised live, and their long-term effect would be largely influenced by how the various characters in the drama came across on the small screen. In this regard, the army did not emerge unscathed. Testimony revealed that it had attempted to placate McCarthy and Cohn by offering Schine a convenient domestic assignment, and Cohn testified—albeit with questionable veracity—that army counsel John Adams had offered to provide information about other branches of the service, such as an air force base reputedly infested with "sex deviates," if he would call off his army probe.

McCarthy, however, turned out to be the big loser. In contrast to the elegantly calculated manner of Joseph Welch, the senator's dubious methods and shrill, abrasive style were brought home to many Americans for the first time. For example, a key piece of McCarthy's evidence—a photograph showing Secretary of the Army Robert Stevens and Private Schine apparently enjoying a friendly chat—turned out to have been doctored. In a typically acerbic exchange following this revelation, Welch queried a McCarthy assistant about the origin of the cropped photograph. "Did you think it came from a pixie?" he asked. McCarthy broke in. "Will the counsel for my benefit define—I think he might be an expert on that—what a pixie is?" Welch answered, "Yes, I should say, Mr. Senator, that a pixie is a close relative to a fairy. . . . Have I enlightened you?"

The most telling blow in the thirty-six days of hearings came when Welch rebuked McCarthy for alluding to a past, vaguely Communist association of a young lawyer in Welch's firm: "Little did I dream you could be so reckless and so cruel. . . . I fear he shall always bear a scar needlessly inflicted by you. . . . Have you no decency, sir, at long last? Have you no decency?" The army's counsel had accurately understood—as McCarthy had not—that the hearings' most significant repercussions would be played out in the minds of the vast television public; his eloquent emotional outburst crystallized the growing impression held by millions of uneasy viewers that McCarthy was, in fact, nothing but a heartless, brutal bully. Following this exchange, Welch wept tears of moral outrage as he left the Senate Caucus Room—apparently pausing, however, to wink through misty eyes at a friend.

Outcome and Aftermath: The Republican-controlled subcommittee rebuked Cohn and criticized McCarthy for failing to better supervise his staff. Eisenhower's triumph over McCarthy asserted the executive's broad powers over Congress and, ironically, helped pave the way for the kind of imperial presidency that could later wage its own war in Vietnam. Cohn resigned as chief counsel in July; widely reviled, he continued to practice law until he was disbarred for unethical conduct in 1986, the same year he died of AIDS. McCarthy, after being censured by the Senate in December 1954, began to drink even more heavily; he died of liver disease on May 2, 1957. His funeral was attended by J. Edgar Hoover, even though, for the last three years of McCarthy's life, the FBI chief had refused to take his old friend's phone calls.

—E.H.B.

THE WATERGATE AFFAIR

When the President does it, that means that it is not illegal.

Richard M. Nixon, TV interview
with David Frost, May 20, 1977

Dates: June 17, 1972, to August 8, 1974
Background: The Watergate affair was one of the most extraordinary political scandals in American history. For two agonizing years, citizens were drawn to their television sets as the hypnotic, inexorable death throes of the so-called imperial presidency dominated the nightly news.

Richard Nixon, the antihero of this political tragedy, despised and feared the news media. Many commentators cited his poor showing during the televised debates against the handsome and charismatic John F. Kennedy to account for Nixon's breathtakingly narrow defeat during the 1960 presidential election.

In 1962, running against Pat Brown, he had gone on to suffer a humiliating defeat in the California governor's race. Along with his campaign manager, H. R. Haldeman, Nixon had been convicted and fined for unfair campaign practices.

In the aftermath of that election he told a roomful of reporters that he was retiring from politics, adding bitterly, "You won't have Nixon to kick around any more."

But just six years later, the nation watched live broadcasts of Chicago police battling demonstrators outside the hopelessly fragmented 1968 Democratic National Convention, and threw its support to Nixon, the Republican "law and order" candidate, sweeping him into the White House at last.

Entrenched in the Oval Office, Nixon was obsessively determined not to be a one-term president. By the late spring and early summer of 1972, he feared he might once again be facing a Kennedy in the national elections—Senator Edward M. Kennedy of Massachusetts, younger brother of the martyred John and Robert Kennedy.

Compounding Nixon's worries about taking on a strong Democratic challenger was the insurgent third-party campaign of Alabama governor George C. Wallace. Wallace's far-right American Independent Party platform threatened to lure away Nixon's conservative supporters.

Finally, Nixon, the career cold warrior, was bedeviled by his lifelong fear of enemies within. On June 13 the *New York Times* had begun publishing the "Pentagon Papers," a classified history of the war in Vietnam. These secret documents were leaked to the *Times* by a young defense analyst, Daniel Ellsberg.

Nixon was infuriated to learn that the full text of the "Pentagon Papers," including those sections the *Times* had elected *not* to print, had been delivered to the Soviet embassy in Washington. On July 10 the *Times* did it again, publishing the U.S. negotiating position for the Strategic Arms Limitation Talks, then in progress with the Soviets.

Hard-liners within the State or Defense Department may well have been the real culprits behind the SALT talk leaks. But the Nixon White House had already seen "Red" and had, in its own mind, begun fighting back.

Cast of Characters: On June 17, 1972, five "black bag" men on the payroll of CREEP—the Committee to Re-Elect the President—were arrested in the act of bugging and burglarizing the offices of the Democratic National Committee, located in the Washington, D.C., Watergate hotel, apartment, and office complex.

It was not the entry team's first clandestine mission for the White House, nor even their first break-in at the Democratic offices. Several of the same men had previously ransacked the Beverly Hills office of Daniel Ellsberg's psychiatrist, Dr. Lewis Fielding, hunting for evidence they hoped would link Ellsberg to the KGB.

They were unable to find such evidence, but at least they had been lucky enough to avoid arrest. Their confidence was further bolstered by an undetected break-in at the Democratic national office suite on May 28.

The burglars were veterans of the CIA's fitful secret war against Castro's Cuba, experts at what the agency euphemistically called covert entry. But on that predawn Sunday morning in June, one of the experts unaccountably taped a door latch open horizontally instead of vertically, leaving the tape conspicuously visible against the door frame. The taped door was noticed by an alert security guard, Frank Wills, who summoned the police.

Today, most historians believe the burglary was simply intended to gather political intelligence against the Democrats. A popular revisionist theory contends the burglars were really hunting for evidence of suspected financial dealings between National Democratic Chairman Larry O'Brian and reclusive billionaire industrialist Howard Hughes.

Whatever its objective, the "plausible deniability" of the CREEP burglary collapsed later that same day, when a *Washington Post* police reporter got a look at the arrest report. Unbelievably, two of the burglars had been carrying address books listing the name of their controller, E. Howard Hunt, and Hunt's telephone number at the White House. A third carried an expense check signed by Hunt.

It was an astoundingly inept breach of security, and it handed investigators a tantalizing link between the burglars and the highest levels of the Nixon administration.

A retired CIA officer and prolific spy novelist, Hunt had previously worked as an agency

Frank Wills, the security guard who set off the investigation that led to the fall of a United States president.

"destabilization expert" and had a prominent role in the abortive 1961 Bay of Pigs invasion.

Prior to Watergate, Hunt had been best known for creating the 1954 media disinformation campaign that toppled the regime of Guatemala's democratically elected president. Hunt's skullduggery allowed the CIA to install a puppet dictator more sympathetic to the interests of the United Fruit Company, of which agency director Allen Dulles and his brother, Secretary of State John Foster Dulles, were coincidentally stockholders.

Hunt was one of several political mercenaries hired expressly to dig up dirt on Ted Kennedy by the White House hatchet man, Charles Colson. Another "consultant," former New York City detective Anthony Ulasewicz, had been dogging Kennedy's trail on Colson's orders since May 1969, roughly six weeks before the Chappaquiddick incident. (See p. 760.)

Secretly paid from surplus 1968 campaign funds, Ulasewicz had been installed in a Manhattan bachelor pad and commissioned to seduce former friends and coworkers of the late Mary Jo Kopechne, in the hope that one of them might reveal the "real truth" behind the relationship between the senator and the former Robert F. Kennedy campaign worker.

Hunt's immediate superior at the time of the break-in was an ex-FBI agent and prosecuting attorney named G. Gordon Liddy. An unsuccessful candidate for Congress, Liddy had made a splash in Republican circles by prosecuting LSD advocate Timothy Leary. Liddy had later been instrumental in the formation of the Drug Enforcement Administration, and was one of the architects of the administration's much ballyhooed "War on Drugs." His political by-word was "The end justifies the means."

Hunt and Liddy were cofounders and key operatives of CREEP's in-house clandestine-services and dirty-tricks unit. The press would soon refer to this organization as "the plumbers," because its job was ostensibly to plug leaks of classified information.

In fact its mission was entirely political, and thanks to Liddy (a passionate admirer of all things German), the CREEP operatives called themselves ODESSA. The name was borrowed from the underground post–World War II association of former members of the Nazi SS.

Liddy had requested a million dollars to wage clandestine war against the Democrats, but the reckless and sometimes violent excesses of his proposed "Gemstone" plan so alarmed his CREEP superiors that they reined him in. The break-in was actually part of Liddy's watered-down half-million-dollar approach.

Hunt and Liddy had been present at the Watergate on the night of the burglary, monitoring its progress with walkie-talkies from a hotel room facing the Democratic office suite. Liddy went home after the burglars' arrest and told his wife that something had gone wrong and he was probably going to jail.

When a reporter called Hunt at work the next day to ask him why the burglars were carrying his name and phone number, a startled Hunt barked "My God!" into the phone and promptly hung up.

It was now obvious that one or more of the jailed burglars would talk, making the White House dirty-tricks squad a matter of public record. Liddy met with White House counsel John Dean and melodramatically volunteered to present himself as a willing target for administration hit men on the street corner of Dean's choice. Both Dean and Nixon concluded Liddy was mentally disturbed.

The White House publicly dismissed the break-in as "a third-rate burglary attempt" while meanwhile frantically exploring ways to guarantee that the burglars would remain silent. Richard Nixon sought to limit the political fallout by requesting network airtime, solemnly assuring the nation that his administration had had no involvement in the burglary.

But thanks to the well-honed self-preservation instincts of the president's men (and at least in part to the television-fostered perception of the sweating, beetle-browed Nixon as "Tricky Dicky"), almost nobody bought the official protestations of noninvolvement.

> What really hurts in matters of this sort is not the fact that they occur, because overzealous people in campaigns do things that are wrong. What really hurts is if you try to cover it up.
> Richard M. Nixon, August 29, 1972

Key Witnesses and Testimony: In January, under the mounting glare of press scrutiny, the trial of Hunt, Liddy, and the five Watergate burglars got under way in the federal district courtroom of Chief Judge John J. ("Maximum John") Sirica.

Hunt, Liddy, and the burglars were charged with burglary, intercepting wire and oral communications, and conspiracy. A week into the trial, obviously relishing his newfound notoriety, Judge Sirica proclaimed his dissatisfaction with the "kid gloves treatment" the prosecutors were showing the defendants.

All seven CREEP men denied any intent of wrongdoing and, at first, refused to implicate any higher-ups. Sirica threatened to impose lengthy prison terms unless the whole story came out. Eventually, only G. Gordon Liddy stubbornly refused to talk.

In February, with the avuncular seventy-two-year-old Senator Sam J. Ervin of North Carolina as chairman, the Senate set up a seven-member select committee to investigate 1972 presidential campaign activities. A Harvard Law School–trained constitutional expert and a strict constructionist, Ervin cross-examined the frequently slippery committee witnesses with a folksy demeanor that soon made him a somewhat unlikely folk hero.

James W. McCord, a former agent of both the FBI and the CIA, was the first burglary defendant to break. On March 23 Sirica revealed that McCord had written him from jail. Disillusioned when promised support from the White House failed to materialize, McCord, the ODESSA electronic surveillance expert, recounted pressures being exerted on him and his codefendants to keep silent and take the heat.

McCord's letter told how Anthony Ulasewicz had twice offered him executive clemency, and detailed the perjury of high administration officials, as well as the previously undisclosed involvement of John N. Mitchell, the head of Nixon's reelection committee.

It was a chilling and sensational accusation, for Mitchell had until recently been attorney general, the top law-enforcement officer in the United States. McCord claimed that Mitchell, a longtime personal friend of Nixon's, had personally authorized the break-ins and other dirty tricks.

John W. Dean III, counsel to the president, was the next Nixon subordinate to jump ship. Afraid of being made the designated scapegoat for the Watergate affair, on April 2 Dean contacted the U.S. District Attorney's office and bartered an insider's view of the disintegrating Nixon White House in exchange for a limited grant of immunity.

On April 10, Jeb Magruder, who had authorized ODESSA operations in his role of deputy director of CREEP, also struck a deal with prosecutors and started talking.

The White House learned that Dean was casting H.R. Haldeman, Nixon's chief of staff, and John Erlichman, Nixon's assistant for domestic affairs, as principal actors in the cover-up scheme to obstruct justice. In late April, Nixon reluctantly asked for and received the resignations of his two closest aides.

By May the remaining president's men, who had stonewalled the grand jury, the FBI, and the press, were openly sandbagging each other, competing for prosecutorial immunity. They were feverishly currying favor with the media, peddling what press secretary (and former Disneyland tour guide) Ron Ziegler called "an epidemic of press leaks in tidal wave proportions."

Under intense Senate pressure, Nixon appointed Archibald Cox as special prosecutor, with wide-ranging power to investigate all aspects of the Watergate affair. On May 17, 1973, just six months after Nixon's landslide reelection, the Senate Watergate Committee commenced its televised hearings.

John Mitchell blandly denied any knowledge of the break-in, insisting that the president knew nothing of any cover-up. Mitchell instead pointed the finger at Haldeman and Erlichman.

Haldeman and Erlichman did their best to protect their former chief. Both men described Nixon as being above the struggle, too busy during the summer of 1972 with vital national security issues to keep abreast of Watergate. They testified that Nixon had relied on house counsel Dean to keep him informed, and accused Dean of disloyalty to the president. Next it was Dean's turn.

Between June 25 and 29, Dean regaled the senators with famous names from Nixon's enemies list, a roster of "opposition" people targeted for harassment by the IRS and FBI. Dean further revealed that Nixon had ordered him to work on a cover-up plan, not the objective investigation Nixon had claimed to have ordered.

Finally, in the most dramatic testimony of the televised hearings, Dean related that during his March 21 meeting with Nixon, Haldeman, and Erlichman, the president had assured Dean there would be "no problem" in raising a million dollars to buy the silence of the Watergate burglars.

The coup de grâce to Nixon's mortally wounded presidency came on July 16, when Alexander Butterfield, Haldeman's former assistant, revealed that all conversations in the Oval Office had been taped since 1971. Dean had confirmed that criminal activities had taken place in the White House, and now Butterfield had told the senators where the evidence of those crimes could be found.

Nixon desperately fought to keep the tapes to himself. On October 20, 1973, he ordered Special Prosecutor Cox to "cease and desist" his efforts to subpoena the tapes. Cox refused, and Nixon ordered Attorney General Elliot Richardson to fire him.

Richardson refused Nixon's order, and resigned. Nixon next ordered Deputy Attorney General William Ruckelshaus to fire Cox. Ruckelshaus also refused and resigned. Finally Solicitor General Robert Bork was promoted to acting attorney general, and he obediently fired Cox.

When the so-called Saturday Night Massacre hit the airwaves, Nixon's support in Congress and the electorate vanished, and the first calls for his impeachment were heard. It was the first time an American president had faced a serious threat of impeachment proceedings since 1868, when Andrew Johnson had narrowly escaped being thrown out of office.

On November 1, 1973, Nixon named Leon Jaworski the new special prosecutor, and under unrelenting pressure, he released an eight-hour transcript of some of the tapes on April 30, 1974.

The revelations of the tapes, with their unguarded glimpses of a profane, conspiratorial chief executive, appalled the American public. One snippet in which Nixon instructed aides was especially damning: "I want you all to stonewall it, let them plead the Fifth Amendment, cover up, or anything else."

Even more fatal to Nixon's dimming credibility was the eighteen-and-a-half minute gap in the tape of a June 20, 1972, Nixon-Haldeman meeting. Rose Mary Woods, Nixon's longtime personal secretary, loyally insisted she had accidentally erased part of the tape, but experts charged that the gap could only have been the intentional result of five to nine deliberate manual manipulations.

Nixon vainly struggled to restore his tarnished image with a series of speeches before handpicked audiences ("controlled environments" in White House jargon), called Operation Candor. On November 17, while addressing the Associated Press Managing Editors Convention at Disney World, Nixon made one of his more memorable disclaimers: "People have the right to know whether or not their President is a crook. Well, I am not a crook."

Outcome and Aftermath: After eighteen months of denials, the scandal was nearing its climax. On March 1, 1974, Nixon suffered the indignity of being named an unindicted coconspirator in the cover-up indictments of Mitchell, Haldeman, Erlichman, and other aides. The House

Judiciary Committee voted to impeach him on three of five original articles: obstruction of justice, abuse of power, and defiance of congressional subpoenas.

The final act of the drama was played out in July 1974, when Nixon's entire legal staff informed the president they intended to resign en masse unless the president released a key tape—the conversation between Nixon and Haldeman recorded on June 23, 1972.

This was the so-called smoking-gun tape, in which Nixon tried to get the CIA to block the FBI's investigation of the source of the money found on the Watergate burglars. When he listened to it on July 31, 1974, the tape convinced Nixon's personal attorney, James St. Clair, that his client had no choice but to resign.

Nixon's only alternative was to be impeached and thrown out of office. A delegation of Republican leaders called at the White House to persuade the president to relinquish his office.

In a sixteen-minute broadcast on August 8, 1974, Richard Nixon yielded to the weight of the evidence against him and, staring balefully into the cameras, announced his resignation. It was the sixth anniversary of the day he had triumphantly accepted his party's nomination for his first term as president.

On September 8, 1974, President Gerald Ford, Nixon's self-appointed successor, granted the former president a "full, free, and complete" pardon for all offenses against the United States. Ford's decision almost certainly cost him the 1976 presidential election, which he lost to Washington outsider Jimmy Carter.

Although legally Nixon's acceptance of the pardon constituted an admission of guilt for these unspecified crimes, Richard Nixon never really apologized for his part in the Watergate cover-up. During a famous postresignation television interview, he told David Frost, "I fouled up in the area where I'm supposed to be a master—politics." Nixon's critics were quick to respond that he had really fouled up in the area where he had always been suspect: ethics.

Special Prosecutor Leon Jaworski speculated that Nixon could probably have weathered the scandal if he had invoked executive privilege or national security concerns and simply destroyed the tapes. Why the president decided not to is one of the many still-unresolved mysteries of Watergate.

In his 1982 memoirs, Nixon admitted he had considered destroying the tapes, but that the consensus opinion among his advisors was that to do so would have constituted an admission of guilt. Astonishingly, he may even have regarded the tapes as a kind of insurance policy—"I was prepared to believe that others, even people close to me, would turn against me just as Dean had done, and in that case, the tapes would give me at least some protection."

Nixon's political rehabilitation was slow and patient and rooted in his strong point, foreign policy. By the time of his death by stroke on April 22, 1994, he was no longer "that Watergate man," as he ruefully described himself, but a valued advisor and quasi-official emissary of Republican and Democratic presidents alike.

The scandal that destroyed the Nixon administration marked a decisive shift from a secretive, clubbish, and insular political process to a more open yet chaotic and decentralized form of government.

The office of the presidency has permanently lost much of its luster and larger-than-life mystique. For many Americans, the president is no longer the living embodiment of American ideals but merely the latest political gamesman to inhabit the White House.

In 1982 Nixon wrote, "Virtue is not what lifts great leaders above others. The good and bad alike can be equally driven, equally determined, equally persuasive. Leadership itself is morally neutral. It can be used for good or ill."

—M.C.S.

IRAN-CONTRA AFFAIR

We do many things at the federal level that would be considered dishonest and illegal if done in the private sector.

Donald T. Regan, New York Times, August 25, 1986

Dates: May 5, 1987, to August 6, 1987
Background: On October 5, 1986, a U.S. cargo plane was shot down over southern Nicaragua. Two of the crew members died in the crash, but the third, Eugene Hasenfus, parachuted to safety and was captured by the Sandinista army. Led out of the jungle at gunpoint, Hasenfus's very existence set in motion an incredible chain of cover-ups and lies that would mushroom into one of the biggest scandals in American political history. Loosely known as the Iran-Contra affair, a bizarre network of arms sales to Iran designed to win release of U.S. hostages being held in Lebanon *and* raise money to fund the Nicaraguan Contras, the botched enterprise took years to unravel, threatening both the Reagan and Bush presidencies in the process.

The highlight of the Iran-Contra affair came on May 5, 1987, when Congress began televised hearings into the matter that kept Americans riveted to their TV sets for the next twelve weeks. The hearings made household names of mid- to upper-level bureaucrats such as Oliver North, Richard Secord, John Poindexter, Robert McFarlane, and Elliott Abrams, and flushed out colorful bit players such as Washington secretary Fawn Hall, Iranian businessman Albert Hakim, and Saudi billionaire Adnan Khashoggi. But if the truth proved hard to ascertain—thanks, in large part, to the illegal shredding of key documents by North and his staff—the hearings did expose huge tracts of the U.S. government as weak and unprincipled, contributing to the nation's growing distrust in the political process by the early 1990s.

Convictions were rare in the Iran-Contra affair (North's and Poindexter's were overturned on appeal), and the few verdicts that were handed down in court amounted to little more than slaps on the wrist. On December 24, 1992, outgoing president George Bush pardoned former secretary of defense Caspar Weinberger and five other defendants, asserting that it was "time for the country to move on." But independent counsel Lawrence Walsh, who spent more than seven years and $40 million untangling the scandal and issued his own report on it in January 1994, saw it differently. "The Iran-Contra cover-up," he said, ". . . has now been completed."

The Iran-Contra affair was the direct result of two major dilemmas facing the Reagan administration in the early 1980s: (1) how to fund, train, and arm an army of Nicaraguan exiles (known as Contras) to overthrow the socialist Sandinista government, especially after the U.S. Congress made it illegal to do so in 1982, and (2) how to win release of American hostages being held by Islamic radicals in Beirut.

Although the CIA was originally authorized to oversee the Contras' efforts in 1981, and CIA director William Casey embraced the mission wholeheartedly, Congress passed legislation two years later ordering the CIA to pull out. The so-called Boland Amendment made it illegal for the CIA either to aid the Contras or to provoke a war between Nicaragua and Honduras, and was toughened to include all sectors of the U.S. government with the passage of the Boland Amendment II in 1984. But by that time, responsibility for supporting the Contras' campaign had been shifted from the CIA to the National Security Council (NSC), where it wound up on the desk of Oliver North, the deputy-director for political-military affairs. A decorated Vietnam veteran with little or no regard for the law, North quickly established a vast and secret military supply system that employed retired CIA and Defense Department personnel, mercenaries, terrorists, and foreign saboteurs. Yet North never acted alone. In addition to revealing the mentorlike guidance of William Casey, declassified documents make it clear that knowledge, and in some cases, direct approval, of the Contra-support effort existed in virtually every wing of the Reagan White House, including the Oval Office itself.

As the Nicaraguan civil war raged on, the Reagan administration became increasingly preoccupied with the growing number of Americans kidnapped in Lebanon. When Iran—a nation that held fifty-two Americans hostage from 1979 to 1981—offered to use its influence to negotiate the release of the hostages in Beirut in exchange for the opportunity to buy U.S. weapons, Reagan's men agreed. The fact that Israel, a country reviled by most militant Muslims, agreed to serve as the go-between in the arms sales only adds to the strange nature of the deal.

Unfortunately, North, who assumed command of the arms sales in late August or early September 1985, and McFarlance, who helped him, turned out to be naive bumblers who were no match for the wily Iranian negotiators. Every time a U.S. hostage was released, another was taken. Meanwhile, North cross-pollinated the Contra and Iran initiatives. By artificially inflating the prices of the arms, North was able to reap profits that could be diverted to funding the Contras. The arms shipments lasted from August 20, 1985, to October 28, 1988, and a total of more than 2,000 missiles and spare parts were shipped to Iran. But of the $16.1 million in profits raised, only $3.8 million ever went to the Contras. The rest was used to purchase equipment, such as a cargo freighter, that could be used in future unspecified operations.

But when the plane carrying Hasenfus was shot down—and Hasenfus told his captors he believed he was working on a CIA-sanctioned operation, identifying two other operatives by their code names in the process—the entire Iran-Contra scheme quickly collapsed. Vice President George Bush's office was informed that a plane was missing just hours after Hasenfus was taken prisoner, and a CIA station chief in Costa Rica quickly followed with a coded message that warned the "situation requires we do necessary damage control."

In the case of North and other officials at the NSC, that meant shredding incriminating notes and documents and falsifying others to provide cover. But not before President Ronald Reagan and Attorney General Edwin Meese went on national television at noon on November 25, 1986, to report the "discovery" of these interrelated Iran and Contra operations and attempt to pin as much of the blame on North as possible. One hour later North was fired and his boss, NSC adviser John Poindexter, was allowed to resign.

A "blue-ribbon" panel headed by former U.S. senator John Tower was appointed to investigate the Iran-Contra affair; it issued its final report on February 26, 1987. But while generally scolding President Reagan for his "hands-off management style," the report proved cursory and unwilling to tackle the scandal head-on. The televised congressional hearings that followed the Tower Commission made a temporary national hero of North and revealed the entire investigation as flawed; in order to obtain the testimony of key players such as North and Poindexter, Congress granted them immunity, undermining the ability of Lawrence Walsh, the independent counsel, to successfully prosecute them afterward.

Congressional Cast of Characters: As chairman of the joint congressional panel, Senator Daniel Inouye (D-Hawaii) was expected to display the same vigorous accountability and determination he had shown as a member of the Senate Watergate committee in the 1970s. But Inouye never came to life during the Iran-Contra hearings, even though he had been a staunch foe of the Reagan policy toward Central America since 1983. Looking sad and disinterested, Inouye's half-hearted leadership set the tone for the Democrats on the panel.

Representative Lee Hamilton (D-Indiana) chaired both the House Intelligence Committee and the special committee investigating the Iran-Contra scandal, but was lied to again and again by witnesses such as Oliver North and Elliott Abrams. During one round of hearings in 1986, Hamilton even thanked Poindexter for his participation and later told a colleague that "published press allegations cannot be proven."

Senator George Mitchell (D-Maine), a member of the Senate Iran-Contra committee, did more to clear up the mess than anybody else (albeit afterward) by coauthoring a book entitled *Men of Zeal: A Candid Inside Story of the Iran-Contra Hearings.*

Senator Thomas Eagleton (D-Missouri), a member of the Senate Intelligence Committee, was responsible for one of the few outbursts of anger at Abrams's casual lies during testimony. Mocking Abrams's assertion that the U.S. government was "not in the fund-raising business," Eagleton concluded by saying, "I've heard [Abrams's testimony] and I want to puke."

Senator Warren Rudman (R-New Hampshire), vice chairman of the congressional panel, was better known as the latter half of the Gramm-Rudman deficit reduction measure. A close friend of the Reagan White House and of eventual chief of staff Howard Baker, Rudman proved almost invisible during the Iran-Contra hearings.

Taking advantage of the general weakness of the Democrats, most of the other Republican members of the panel ignored their investigatory mandate and used the hearings as a propaganda forum in support of the Contras.

Key Witnesses and Testimony: Although most Americans struggled to comprehend the complex network of arms sales and Contra resupply that North and his associates had created, the joint House and Senate Iran-Contra hearings were nonetheless entertaining. Beginning May 5, 1987, and lasting until August 6, 1987, they featured more than 250 hours of testimony from thirty-two witnesses. And if no bombshells were dropped by either the witnesses or the lawmakers—and no "smoking gun" was ever uncovered linking President Reagan directly to the whole affair—America still found itself with a whole new set of heroes and villains.

There was Fawn Hall, North's striking secretary, who testified that she shredded some classified documents and smuggled others out of the NSC building by stuffing them down her boots and in the back of her blouse. There were Reagan staffers and Cabinet secretaries such as Donald Regan, Edwin Meese, Robert McFarlane, Elliott Abrams, and George Shultz, who provided details of a White House overrun with private-sector intermediaries. And there was a seemingly endless parade of low-level bureaucrats and shady arms dealers caught up in the web.

Coincidentally, the one witness who surely had the most to tell, CIA director Casey, was discovered to have a brain tumor and died the day after the hearings got under way. Casey reportedly admitted his involvement, in a deathbed interview with *Washington Post* reporter Bob Woodward, although Casey's widow denies Woodward ever got near her husband's room.

North's testimony from July 7 to 14 proved to be the most colorful, and he was so electric that the networks preempted their daytime soap operas to stay on the air. Wearing his green U.S. Marines uniform for the first time in years—North normally wore a coat and tie at the NSC—he bullied the congressional panel with equal parts pathos and patriotism, getting teary-eyed at will and wrapping himself in the American flag. Although North brazenly admitted to lying before Congress, destroying evidence, operating U.S. initiatives in violation of U.S. law, and participating in a cover-up, he said he did so in defense of America and added that President Reagan had called him a national hero.

When it was disclosed that North had accepted a $13,800 fence and security system as a gift from businessmen who were profiting on the arms sales, North testified that the fence was necessary to protect his family from terrorists. In order to distract public attention from this obvious and extremely unpatriotic case of bribery, North's lawyers displayed a huge photograph of noted terrorist Abu Nidal. "I want you to know," said North, "that I'd be more than willing—and if anybody else is watching overseas, and I'm glad they are—I'll be glad to meet Abu Nidal on equal terms anywhere in the world, O.K.?"

With that, "Ollie mania" was born, thrilling much of America to its heartland and completely cowing congressional investigators, who either lacked the stomach to confront a vainglorious egomaniac like North or faced difficult reelection prospects in the upcoming year. Others simply could not bear the prospect of impeachment hearings, especially with the Reagan administration poised to reopen nuclear disarmament talks with the Soviet Union. Tired of the whole Iran-Contra affair, the joint congressional panel promptly closed up shop following Poindexter's testimony in August, and issued

Oliver North, seated with his lawyer, Brendan "Potted Plant" Sullivan, displays an enormous blowup of terrorist Abu Nidal in an attempt to distract the American public from the fact that he committed the unpatriotic act of taking a bribe.

its final report on November 17, 1987. Not surprisingly, that report conferred "ultimate responsibility" on the Reagan White House but allowed as how a "cabal of zealots" therein had "undermined the powers of Congress as a co-equal branch and subverted the Constitution." A minority report, however, signed by eight of the Republicans on the twenty-six-member committee, found only errors of judgment, "no constitutional crisis, no systematic disrespect for the 'rule of law,' no grand conspiracy and no administration-wide dishonesty or cover-up."

Outcome and Aftermath: Although Walsh, a staunch Republican, doggedly compiled cases against the Iran-Contra conspirators, even as he turned eighty years of age in 1992, it was all for naught. Eleven defendants were convicted of crimes. The original charges ranged from perjury to defrauding the U.S. Treasury, but these were plea-bargained down to minor felony and misdemeanor charges. McFarlane, who pleaded guilty to four counts of "withholding information," received the harshest penalty (two years' probation, a $20,000 fine, and 200 hours of community service), but he was one of those pardoned by George Bush. The convictions of North (three counts of obstruction of justice, misleading Congress, and accepting an illegal gratuity) and Poindexter (five counts of conspir-

acy, obstruction of Congress, and false statements) were overturned on appeal because they had been granted immunity. Former CIA operative Thomas Clines was the only defendant to receive a prison sentence—for falsifying tax records.

In his final report on the Iran-Contra affair, which was published January 18, 1994, Walsh concluded that both Reagan and Bush knew of the burgeoning scandal and participated "or at least acquiesced" in the cover-up, but could find no evidence that either broke the law. Aftershocks from the Iran-Contra affair had dogged Reagan throughout his second term and may have contributed to Bush's failed reelection bid in 1992. But it's hard to know for sure. Distracted by events such as the 1991 Gulf War, the nation gradually lost interest in Iran-Contra, and it is doubtful that many Americans ever fully understood the scandal and its implications. In the end, all anybody knew was that a lot of politicians were breaking the laws and lying to the country again, and this manifested itself in the deep cynicism many Americans began to harbor toward the political process.

While most of the players retired to lives of consulting or private business, only North stayed in the spotlight. Portraying himself as an antiestablishment politician and drawing support from conservative groups, North won the Republican nomination for the U.S. Senate in Virginia in 1994. He spent $17.6 million on his campaign—often battling denunciations from prominent Republicans such as Reagan and Senator John Warner—but narrowly lost to the incumbent, Charles Robb.

—D.W.C.

CLARENCE THOMAS HEARINGS

Dates: October 11 to October 14, 1991
Background: Late on the afternoon of September 12, 1991, as he presided over the dreary confirmation hearings of Supreme Court nominee Clarence Thomas, Senator Joe Biden received a tap on the shoulder from an aide and was beckoned into a private room. There Biden first heard the news: a young law professor who had worked under Thomas at the Equal Employment Opportunity Commission (EEOC) was saying that Thomas had sexually harassed her. She seemed to be telling the truth, he was told, and might even agree to testify. Clearly shaken, Biden returned to his seat without saying a word to his fellow senators, and that day's hearing proceeded without incident. But it would not be long before the entire United States was arguing the case.

Anita Hill's charges of sexual harassment against Thomas—televised live for twenty-one engrossing hours from October 11 to October

14, 1991—did more than reveal the Supreme Court nomination process in all its partisan squalor. They touched off a firestorm of debate in the United States, polarizing the country along battle lines of gender, race, and age, and literally introduced millions of Americans to the notion of sexual harassment. In addition, important constitutional rights such as privacy and due process were trampled, while wild media speculation often appeared to drive the case. Through it all, voters were treated to the sight of their senators—all white, all male, all struggling to be fair—mishandling the hearings at every turn.

The Thomas-Hill case was no easy call. Both appeared sincere, yet one of them was lying. Biden, who chaired the Judiciary Committee, which was charged with either confirming or denying Thomas, understood the implications of the case from the start. "This ain't about Anita Hill and this ain't about Clarence Thomas," he said repeatedly. "This is about a power struggle going on in this country between men and women. This is the biggest thing you can imagine."

Born on June 23, 1948, in Pin Point, Georgia, Clarence Thomas rose quickly from rural poverty to national prominence. Reared predominantly by his grandparents, Thomas recalled that his upbringing was "strong, stable and conservative." In a 1987 speech, he said that "God was central. . . . Crime, welfare, slothfulness and alcohol were enemies." Although he studied to be a priest, Thomas changed his mind after hearing a classmate utter a racist remark. He graduated from Holy Cross in 1971. Thomas received his law degree from Yale University in 1974.

As he began a career in government, Thomas transformed from a liberal Democrat who voted for George McGovern in 1972 into a conservative Republican with harsh views toward race-conscious programs such as Affirmative Action. "The Democratic Party just did not level with me," he once said. "They continued to promise some kind of salvation for minorities, talked down about poverty programs, always enshrined everything in civil rights." Once the Reagan administration took power, Thomas hit the fast lane, serving in the Department of Education from 1981 to 1982 before heading up to EEOC from 1982 to 1990. Later that year, Thomas was appointed to the U.S. Court of Appeals for the District of Columbia.

Yet many legal experts considered Thomas a poor choice for the Supreme Court. Nominated by President George Bush to fill the position vacated by Thurgood Marshall, the first and only African American to sit on the court up to that time, Thomas bore the stamp of tokenism from the start. He had no significant legal experience as a prosecutor, defense attorney, trial lawyer, law professor, or judge, and when

pressed during his confirmation hearings to cite some landmark cases, he drew a blank. In fact, the American Bar Association gave Thomas's nomination a lackluster "qualified" rating, the lowest it had given a Supreme Court nominee in modern times. Still, Bush thought him "the best man for the job."

Troubling, too, was Thomas's private life, especially to those who knew him well. Divorced in 1984 after a three-year separation from his first wife—and not remarried until 1987—Thomas delved heavily into pornography at the time, plastering the walls of his Washington, D.C., apartment with nude centerfolds and renting hundreds of X-rated videotapes. Although friends and associates thought it odd, Thomas's behavior would not come into consideration until Hill's charges.

Anita Hill, meanwhile, had a similarly rural upbringing. Born July 30, 1956, in Morris, Oklahoma, she was the youngest of thirteen children in a close-knit, religious family. Hill attended integrated high schools, earned a degree in psychology from Oklahoma State University in 1977, and, like Thomas, graduated from Yale Law School (1980). Friends described Hill as sweet, proud, intensely private; she wasn't even a registered voter. "She was a real straight arrow," said Michael Middleton, who worked with both her and Thomas in Washington. ". . . She certainly was no bimbo."

Hill worked for a Washington law firm for a year before joining Thomas as his assistant from 1981 to 1983, first at the Department of Education and then at EEOC. It was at the latter post that Thomas's alleged sexual harassment of Hill occurred. She then left Washington to join the law school faculty at Oral Roberts University and later the University of Oklahoma.

Word of Hill's alleged sexual harassment first reached Washington in the summer of 1991, when she casually mentioned it to a friend in government who, in turn, mentioned it to an employee of a liberal group opposing Thomas's nomination. On September 10 a member of Senator Howard Metzenbaum's staff who attended Yale Law School with Hill heard her story and told his boss. Metzenbaum ordered that Biden's staff be informed.

But Hill was a reluctant witness. She agreed to testify to the committee only if her name was kept secret, even from Thomas, apparently believing that, once accused, he would just quietly withdraw. Only pressure from the press (the Judiciary Committee was riddled with news leaks) forced her into the spotlight.

Yet there was no denying the dramatic impact Hill's allegations had already had on the proceedings, whether her identity was known or not. Although rumors of her charges were making committee members squirm, it wasn't until Hill's nationally televised press conference, on October 7 in Oklahoma, that Biden gathered the momentum he needed to delay a scheduled vote on Thomas. The result, predictably, was chaos.

Congressional Cast of Characters: As chairman of the Judiciary Committee, Biden (D-Delaware) tried to conduct a fair hearing, struggling with "how to get the truth—but without conducting a Star Chamber." Yet he was handcuffed from the start. Savage press attacks on Biden in 1987, when he was accused of plagiarizing parts of a speech from a British politician, made him wary of probing anyone's personal life unfairly. He tried to keep the hearing focused narrowly on whether sexual harassment had occurred in this particular instance, but wound up losing control of the larger issues at stake. In retrospect, Biden believed the process was unfair to both Thomas and Hill.

Edward Kennedy (D-Massachusetts) might normally have flexed his liberal might and championed Hill's cause. But with rape charges pending against his nephew, William Kennedy Smith, and testimony in that case featuring tales of Edward Kennedy's bar-hopping antics, he was in no position to do anything but sit through the Thomas hearings in embarrassed silence. A year later, to shore up his reputation, Kennedy apologized to his constituents for his personal behavior and also remarried.

Arlen Spector (R-Pennsylvania) approached the hearings like a trial and sparred with Hill over discrepancies in her testimony, earning the ire of feminists. He faced a strong female challenger, Lynn Yeakle, in 1992 but narrowly defeated her to win reelection.

Orrin Hatch (R-Utah), though by then a millionaire, also grew up poor and identified with Thomas. In addition to coaching the Supreme Court nominee on his testimony, Hatch made the strongest bid to undermine Hill's testimony.

Key Witnesses and Testimony: The setting was the Old Senate Caucus Room, the same chambers that had witnessed the Army-McCarthy, Watergate, and Iran-Contra hearings. This time the public saw two poised, professional African Americans—one male and one female—facing a panel of fourteen powerful white males.

Thomas was the first to appear. The cautious, controlled judge of the preceding weeks was gone. Saying he was "shocked, surprised, hurt and emotionally saddened" to learn of Hill's charges, Thomas swore, "I have not said or done the things that Anita Hill has alleged. God . . . is my judge." Angrily, he continued: "No job is worth what I've been through—no job. No horror in my life has been so debilitating. Confirm me if you want. Don't confirm me if you are so led. I'll not provide the rope for my own lynching." He then blasted the confirma-

tion process itself, calling it "Kafkaesque. It has got to stop," he continued.

Hill followed. Cool and unflappable, she looked the senators in the eye and answered without hesitation. From this demure, polite woman came shockingly graphic testimony: "He talked about pornographic materials depicting individuals with large penises or large breasts involved in various sexual acts. . . . On several occasions, Thomas told me graphically of his own sexual prowess. . . . He referred to the size of his own penis as being larger than normal and he also spoke on some occasions of the pleasures he had given women with oral sex." Hill also testified that Thomas made references to a porn actor called Long Dong Silver and once asked loudly who'd placed a pubic hair on his can of Coke.

Although Biden had originally wanted to cut the testimony off at this point, White House lawyers bullied him into letting Thomas speak first *and* last, in order to rebut the charges. So while Hill's R-rated allegations played to a daytime audience, Thomas closed the show in prime time, when a much larger audience was watching. The nominee, fighting back tears as his wife wept beside him, was even angrier than before. "I . . . unequivocally, uncategorically . . . deny each and every single allegation against me today," he began. "I am incapable of proving the negative. It did not occur." Thomas again raged at the process, calling it a "high-tech lynching for uppity blacks who in any way deign to think for themselves. . . . You have spent the entire day destroying what it has taken me forty-three years to build . . . and you can't give it back to me."

Each side then introduced witnesses. Hill's insisted she had no motive for lying and recalled her mentioning the harassment at the time it occurred. Thomas's portrayed him as a dignified, respectful manager, and pointed out that Hill had willingly transferred with him to the EEOC. In addition, Thomas's telephone logs indicated he received at least eleven calls from Hill over the years, all of which seemed odd if their relationship was so strained.

Some of the most potentially damaging witness testimony was never heard. Angela Wright, another former EEOC staffer who claimed to have been harassed by Thomas, was kept waiting in an anteroom all weekend but never introduced. It seems the Republicans unearthed personnel records that were unflattering, and the Democrats feared it would undermine her credibility. Other potential witnesses who could either have shed light on Thomas's character or corroborated Hill's testimony were never called.

The committee, meanwhile, was no help at all. While most members were reluctant to say words like *penis* and *breast* in public, none wanted to attack a black man seeking higher office, especially once he referred to the hearings as a lynching. After some sparring with Thomas and Hill, Biden gaveled the hearings to a close in the early-morning hours of October 14, 1991.

Outcome and Aftermath: A slim majority of Senators—fifty-two to forty-eight—decided that charges of sexual harassment that occurred ten years ago and could not be proved should not destroy Thomas's career. At the time, the public agreed. Opinion polls showed that 60 percent of the U.S. public believed Thomas and only 20 percent sided with Hill immediately after the hearings, but those numbers changed with time. Just one year later, polls showed a 38–38 percent split, with support for Hill's version continuing to rise.

Anita Hill returned to her faculty position in Oklahoma. She also took on a national role, speaking on the subject of sexual harassment. Although she testified that she would not write about her experiences, Hill signed a $2 million contract to write two books in 1993.

Clarence Thomas was sworn in as a Supreme Court justice on October 18, 1991, in a hurried ceremony designed to thwart rumors that even more scandalous stories about him were in the works. He now leads a quiet life, and is outwardly bitter toward the press. On the Court, Thomas frequently aligns himself with the most conservative members, which may be the most enduring outcome. As Thomas himself said: "I'm going to be [on the Court] for forty years. For those who don't like it, get over it."

—D.W.C.

QUOTEBOOK: TELEVISION

Television is a triumph of equipment over people, and the minds that control it are so small that you could put them in a gnat's navel with room left over for two caraway seeds and an agent's heart.

Fred Allen

Television has done much for psychiatry by spreading information about it, as well as contributing to the need for it.
Alfred Hitchcock, *Alfred Hitchcock Presents*, c. 1960

Television is a vast wasteland.

Newton Minow, 1961

Television has brought back murder into the home—where it belongs.
Alfred Hitchcock, the *Observer*, December 19, 1965

Television is an invention that permits you to be entertained in your living room by people you wouldn't have in your home.

David Frost

Children who have been taught, or conditioned, to listen passively most of the day to the warm verbal communication coming from the TV screen, to the deep emotional appeal of the so-called TV personality, are often unable to respond to real persons because they arouse so much less feeling than the skilled actor. Worse, they lose the ability to learn from reality because life experiences are more complicated than the ones they see on the screen, and there is no one who comes in at the end to explain it all. The "TV child" . . . gets discouraged when he cannot grasp the meaning of what happens to him. . . . If, later in life, this block of solid inertia is not removed, the emotional isolation from mothers that starts in front of TV may continue. . . . This being seduced into passivity and discouraged about facing life actively on one's own is the real danger of TV.
Bruno Bettelheim, in Martin Mayer's
About Television, 1972

Television is the first truly democratic culture—the first culture available to everybody and entirely governed by what the people want. The most terrifying thing is what the people do want.
Clive Barnes, in the *New York Times*, 1969

Chapter 12

ARTS AND PERFORMERS

PEOPLE WHO NEVER WERE—
YET LIVE TODAY

BATMAN (a.k.a. BRUCE N. WAYNE) (b. 1914)
Batman, also known as Bruce Wayne, has earned the reputation of being America's premier detective by fighting crime successfully for more than fifty-five years. His prowess in subduing the criminal element—with the help of Robin the Boy Wonder—has prompted gangland figure "Knuckles" Conger to state, "It's amazing how one man and a boy can terrorize the whole underworld!"

Born in 1914 to Thomas and Martha Wayne of Gotham City, Bruce Wayne was orphaned at the age of ten when a small-time mugger named Joey Chill murdered his parents during a robbery attempt. The indomitable lad, bearing the psychological scar caused by his parents' senseless death, swore "by the spirits of my parents to avenge their deaths by spending the rest of my life warring on all criminals."

Since the Wayne estate made him fabulously wealthy, Bruce Wayne was able to devote his adolescence to the study of science, the training of his body, and a scrutiny of the criminal mind. As an adult, he was well equipped for his life's work. He was a master scientist and inventor. He was a highly trained gymnast. And most important, perhaps, he was an expert in the labyrinthine twistings of the criminal mind.

But before embarking on his crusade against crime, he needed a disguise. He decided that a creature of the night would strike terror into criminals, who were generally a superstitious and cowardly lot. As he mused about this one night, a bat flew in through the window of his study. Instantly, he chose the bat as his symbol. Thus did Bruce Wayne, the flamboyant millionaire and playboy, become Batman, one of the world's greatest detectives.

Batman's initial onslaughts against the underworld, which began in 1939, drew the ire of police officials, who refused to condone his extralegal vigilante activities. However, after 1941, when he was made an honorary member of the Gotham Police Force, Batman was able to escalate his crime-fighting endeavors. From tilting with small-time hoodlums, he moved on to tackling mightier foes in higher places. Realizing that he could use an assistant, he chose Dick Grayson, a young aerialist with a traveling circus, whose parents had been killed by extortionist racketeers. Bruce Wayne adopted the boy and trained him to be a junior edition of Batman himself.

Together Batman and Robin the Boy Wonder have engaged in a never-ending battle against the forces of chaos in society. This battle has taken them not only to the four corners of the earth but also to distant planets and different time dimensions. But the scene of their greatest victories has been Gotham City.

Perhaps the fiercest of Batman's archenemies has been the Joker, a green-haired harlequin figure who announces his crimes in advance and leaves a joker as his calling card. They first met in 1940, when the Joker instigated a series of daring jewel thefts that left the authorities baffled. Despite his broadcasting a warning of his intended crimes over the radio, he was able to steal the jewels and murder his victims, leaving them with their faces contorted in gruesome smiles.

Even in these early encounters, Batman displayed the qualities that were to ensure his unparalleled success in the following years. These qualities include his matchless capacity for dealing with disaster and his penchant for glib repartee while engaged in mortal combat. "You may be the Joker," said Batman as he dealt his opponent a knockout blow during one fray, "but I'm the King of Clubs." In spite of Batman's success in more than thirty-five encounters with the Joker, his miraculous escapes have allowed him to remain Batman's primary foil even today. As Batman himself explained to Robin, "He's cheated death so often you just can't trust that guy."

World War II saw Batman and Robin defending the home front against enemy spies and subversive elements in addition to their usual racket-busting crusades. In January of 1942, for instance, they were instrumental in smashing the Nazi spy ring headed by the sinister Count Felix. (It was during this period, also, that Batman ordered Robin to abstain from crime fighting until his report card showed improvement.)

During the 1950s, Batman and Robin began a series of adventures that took them into the past and matched them with such notable characters as the Three Musketeers, Aladdin, Franken-stein, and Bat Masterson.

Second only to the Joker as Batman's arch foe is Oswald Cobblepot, the Penguin, whose nick-name derives from his rotund appearance and waddling gait. Noted for his vanity and his flowery language, he is even more renowned for his passion for birds and his ingenious use of umbrellas. "The perfect crime is a work of art!" the Penguin has stated. It has proved an elusive goal for him, though, as Batman has met and defeated him on some thirty different occa-sions. In 1965, the Penguin began a series of bizarre episodes based on trick umbrellas. The Penguin was eventually captured and sent to prison while attempting to escape on his "jetumbrella." Once out of prison, he ran, unsuccessfully, for mayor of Gotham City.

Other foes have included Harvey Dent, known as Two-Face, and Edward Nigma, the Riddler. Two-Face, a schizophrenic, trusted his fate to a half-defaced silver dollar. If the dam-aged face of the coin landed up when tossed, he would commit a crime; if the unmarked side landed up, he would not. The Riddler, the man of many questions, tested Batman's skill by leaving clues to his crimes in the form of riddles. Another frequent enemy has been Selina Kyle, the Catwoman. In more recent years, Batman has taken on extraterrestrial aliens as well as criminals from the future.

Robin eventually left Batman to become Night-wing and Bruce Wayne took on other protégés. Batman's daylight hours are spent directing the Wayne Foundation, a large philanthropic orga-nization, and he resides in the penthouse atop the Wayne Foundation Building. Although he spends little time at Wayne Manor, the family estate with its accompanying subterranean Bat-cave complex, he maintains this mansion, as well as a plush Gulf Coast beach house in Florida. He continues to live with his faithful English butler, Alfred Pennyworth.

During the night hours, when evil threatens, Bruce Wayne becomes the caped crusader, Batman—defending the just and punishing the lawless, as he continues to strike terror into the hearts of the underworld. Originally Batman vowed not to kill, but as he aged and Gotham City grew more violent, the caped crusader renounced his vow.

—J.B.M.

JAMES BOND (b. 1920)

Dashing good looks, coolness under fire, and a penchant for high living have elevated James Bond to legendary status as the British agent licensed to kill and have rightfully earned him the reputation of secret agent extraordinaire.

James Bond was born in 1920 to Andrew Bond of Scotland and Monique Delacroix of Switzer-land. Andrew Bond's position as foreign repre-sentative for the Vickers armament firm took the family to numerous European cities, and conse-quently James was fluent in French and German as well as English by age nine. When he was eleven, his parents died in a climbing accident in the Aiguilles Rouges above Chamonix. Bond's rearing, such as it was, was left to his maiden aunt, Charmian Bond of Kent, England.

At thirteen he entered Eton College, but after what has been described as a "brief and undis-tinguished career," he was expelled because of some alleged trouble with one of the boys' maids. He then transferred to Fettes, where he distinguished himself as the school's light-weight boxing champion and the founder of the first serious judo class in a British public school.

On his graduation from Fettes at seventeen, he entered the University of Geneva. It was during this time that his reputation for fast living and rugged physical endurance attracted the atten-tion of the local British Secret Service operative. He was subsequently recruited into the service as a low-level agent and soon became addicted to the fast-paced and dangerous lifestyle.

In 1941 he entered the Ministry of Defense and attained the rank of lieutenant. The under-cover activity continued, and after several spec-tacular successes, he ended the war with the rank of commander. Two assignments during this time were to shape his future. In the first, he killed a Norwegian double agent with his bare hands in a Stockholm hotel room. In the second, he killed a Japanese code breaker on the thirty-sixth floor of the RCA Building in Rocke-feller Center. These two daring feats made him eligible for the Double-0 section of the Secret Service. He accepted the commission in 1952 and was issued the number 007—his license to kill in the line of duty.

The years 1953 to 1959 saw Bond primarily occupied with the destruction of SMERSH, the Soviet counterespionage organization, whose name means "death to spies." Among his assignments were the now famous Casino Royale affair, where he defeated Le Chiffre in a high-stakes baccarat game, preventing him from regaining misappropriated SMERSH funds. Then he stopped Mr. Big, leader of the international Black Widow voodoo cult, from turning over a vast pirate treasure to SMERSH. In the Moonraker affair, 007 prevented Soviet-controlled Hugo Drax from destroying London by atom bomb.

In his one adventure away from SMERSH during this period, Bond entered an American diamond-smuggling pipeline that began in South Africa and ended in Las Vegas, and sealed both ends (1956).

In 1957 he successfully thwarted an elaborate SMERSH plot for his own assassination and followed this coup with the destruction of Dr. No, a German-Chinese scientist who was running an American missile-sabotaging operation under the cover of a Caribbean bird guano business. The following year saw one of Bond's most incredible adventures and the virtual destruction of SMERSH. In that assignment he pitted himself against master criminal Auric Goldfinger, who had devised a plot, backed by SMERSH, to steal all of the gold in Fort Knox.

Having undermined the effectiveness of SMERSH, Bond turned his attention to a new threat, SPECTRE—the Special Executive for Counterintelligence, Terrorism, Revenge, and Extortion—and its diabolical leader, Ernst Stavro Blofeld.

In 1961 Bond sabotaged SPECTRE's attempted blackmail of Western nations with hijacked nuclear devices, in what was then termed Operation Thunderball. Although SPECTRE was stopped, Blofeld escaped, but Bond found and defeated him one year later. This time Blofeld was trying to ruin England's economic base by means of biological infestation of crops and livestock. Bond was successful with the help of Marc-Ange Draco, leader of France's counterpart of the Mafia, the Union Corse. Blofeld escaped again, however, and was able to kill Bond's wife of one day, Tracy di Vicenzo, the daughter of Draco, only minutes after the wedding.

Bond was completely demoralized after this episode. He lost his Double-0 number and was sent on a diplomatic mission to Japan. Here he uncovered the maniacal Blofeld for the last time. He was keeping a Japanese "suicide garden" on a remote island fortress. Bond destroyed the island and killed Blofeld, but the assignment nearly cost him his life. As it was, he suffered a complete loss of memory and eventually fell into the hands of the Soviets, who brainwashed him and sent him back to assassinate the head of the British Secret Service. The plot was foiled, and in 1964 Bond was deprogrammed and sent on his last notable assignment, against freelance assassin Paco "Pistols" Scaramanga—the man with the golden gun.

Over the years, Bond faced great physical pain: one time his testicles were smashed with a carpet beater, another time the side of his face was burned with a blowtorch.

Although Bond's spectacular adventures contributed much to his reputation, they were not the only factor. He was a high liver and prolific lover of the first order. From his modified 1939 Bentley to his custom-made Morland Special cigarettes with the triple gold rings, he was a man with a discriminating palate and particular tastes. And the women in his life, invariably tall, athletic, and independent, had names as exotic as their lifestyles—Pussy Galore, Kissy Suzuki, and Honeychile Rider, to name just a few. But no woman was able to hold him, because he was in essence married to M, the irascible Admiral Sir Miles Messervy, head of the British Secret Service, the man whom Bond claimed "holds a great deal of my affection and all of my loyalty and obedience."

Bond has been retired from the Ministry of Defense since 1965 and continues to reside in his flat off Kings Road in London. But if a threat of sufficient proportions should arise, it is certain that Bond would be reissued his license and would take the field once again as Secret Agent 007.

—J.B.M.

SHERLOCK HOLMES (b.1854?)

Not much is known of the early life of Sherlock Holmes, genius of detection, who, in his deerstalker cap and inverness coat, solved criminal cases that even Scotland Yard could not crack.

Basil Rathbone in The Adventures of Sherlock Holmes.

Through clues in books published by his chronicler, Dr. John H. Watson, most biographers have come to the conclusion that he was probably born on January 6, 1854, in Yorkshire. Though Holmes was related to the Vernets, Parisian artists, his ancestors were mostly country squires. He had a brother Mycroft, seven years older than he, who, behind the scenes, ran the British government.

Probably in 1871 Holmes went to a university (whether Cambridge or Oxford is not known). He was a loner, choosing to spend his time in solitary analytical thought, forming the theoretical bases of his extraordinary methods of detection. During this time an incident, in which a bull terrier bit him on the ankle, brought about a friendship with a certain Victor Trevor, which in turn hurled Holmes into his first case, "the Gloria Scott," involving the decoding of a mysterious message about flypapers and hen pheasants. His success in this case suggested to him that he might devote his life to the detection and prevention of crime.

It was in 1881 that Holmes met Watson, then recuperating from a war wound. Holmes's description of Watson reveals his tremendous powers of observation: "Here is a gentleman of a medical type but with the air of a military man. Clearly an army doctor, then. He has just come from the tropics, and his face is dark, and that is not the natural tint of his skin, for his wrists are fair. He has undergone hardship and sickness, as his haggard face says clearly. His left arm has been injured. He holds it in a stiff and unnatural manner. Where in the tropics could an English army doctor have seen such hardship and got his arm wounded? Clearly in Afghanistan."

By the time he met Watson, Holmes was already in the detective business. The two almost immediately saw the possibilities in a relationship between them and soon set up housekeeping at 221B Baker Street.

They made a truly odd couple. Watson objected to Holmes's strange habits: keeping his cigars in a coal scuttle and his tobacco in a Persian slipper, impaling his correspondence to the mantelpiece with a jackknife, and, most serious, sniffing cocaine (three doses a day by 1887), a habit that Watson probably weaned him from eventually.

Though Watson did set up a medical practice from time to time, he found his true vocation as general factotum and chronicler of Holmes's career in detection.

A Study in Scarlet was the first book Watson published. Holmes didn't think much of it, telling his friend, "Honestly, I cannot congratulate you on it. Detection is, or ought to be, an exact science, and should be treated in the same cold and unemotional manner. You have attempted to tinge it with romanticism, which produces much the same effect as if you worked a love story or elopement into the fifth proposition of

Euclid." In spite of this bucket of cold water, Watson continued to write stories, some sixty of them, about Holmes's cases, each as "romantic" as the first. The cases involved a number of strange items and happenings: the worm unknown to science, the giant Sumatran rat that haunted the good ship Matilda, the Sussex vampire, the opal tiara, the singular affair of the aluminum crutch, the blue carbuncle, the speckled band, the redheaded league.

> It is an old maxim of mine that when you have excluded the impossible, whatever remains, however improbable, must be the truth.
>
> Sherlock Holmes, in Sir Arthur Conan Doyle's The Berly Coronet

The most famous master criminal with whom Holmes dealt was the dastardly Professor Moriarty, who was, in Holmes's words, "a genius, a philosopher, an abstract thinker" with a "brain of the first order." Moriarty's operation was huge, a criminal network that covered Europe. After Moriarty tried to murder Holmes and burn the rooms at Baker Street, Holmes went in pursuit of him. They met in a death struggle above Reichenbach Falls in Meiringen, Switzerland, where, it is said, the redoubtable Holmes wrestled the master criminal over the edge of the cliff to fall to his death below. There is some controversy about what happened next to Holmes, for he disappeared for two years. He himself claimed that he went on a long journey under the name of Sigerson: to Tibet, where he met the head lama, to Persia, to Khartoum, ending up in Paris, where he conducted some research into coal-tar derivatives. There are those who believe that Holmes in actuality had amnesia during this period.

After that he resumed his career, and Watson resumed writing books about it. The good doctor delighted in telling of Holmes's disguises: a plumber, a loafer, an old salt, a drunken groom, an old woman, an Italian priest, a crippled bookseller. He delighted also in telling about the great detective's uncanny ability to extract from the smallest piece of evidence a whole story of crime. It is no accident that Holmes was the author of a little-known classic monograph on more than a hundred varieties of tobacco ash. Among Holmes's other published works are Upon the Tracing of Footsteps and Upon the Influence of a Trade Upon the Form of a Hand. For some reason, Holmes and Watson quarreled in 1896, and Holmes was left without his Boswell for a period of time. It had happened before that Watson had left the scene (usually to get married), but this was the first time the two had had a falling out.

They made up, and the two stayed together

until Holmes's retirement, in 1912, to a small farm on the South Downs, overlooking the Channel, where he took up beekeeping. So engrossed was he in this retirement hobby that he wrote a book about it: *A Practical Handbook of Bee Culture, with Some Observation upon the Segregation of the Queen.*

Holmes came out of retirement once to break a World War I master-spy ring that was threatening the security of the British Empire.

The circumstances of his death are uncertain. The late W. S. Baring-Gould claims that Holmes died at the age of 103, just after sunset, with the word *Irene* on his lips. Irene Adler, glamorous American-born opera singer, may have been The Woman in Holmes's life.

E. V. Knox said that Holmes died at the age of ninety-eight from a sting by one of his bees, possibly an Italian queen.

There are equally conflicting versions of the death of Watson.

—A.E.

PHILIP MARLOWE (b. 1900?)

Philip Marlowe was born in Santa Rosa, California, in that time-out-of-time that allowed him to be thirty-three years old in 1933, forty-two in 1953, and forty-three and one-half in 1958. He attended university in Oregon but never graduated. He worked as an investigator for an insurance company and was once employed as an investigator by Taggart Wilde, district attorney of Los Angeles, but was fired for insubordination. In many ways Marlowe was the very model of a perfect private investigator: slightly over six feet tall and 190 pounds, with brown eyes and brown hair. He liked liquor, women, and working alone. His independent detective agency was a shoestring operation that he ran from a pair of musty, scantily furnished rooms on the sixth floor of the Cahuenga Building on Hollywood Boulevard.

Although Marlowe would have said that his principal hobby was replaying championship chess games taken from books, his greatest pleasure was solving murders and related crimes, as evidenced by the fact that he worked for free as often as he did for money. As he told his old pal Lieutenant Bernie Ohls, assistant chief of homicide for the Los Angeles sheriff's office, "I'm a romantic, Bernie. I hear voices crying in the night and I go to see what's the matter. You don't make a dime that way. . . . No percentage in it at all. No nothing, except sometimes I get my face pushed in, or get tossed in the can, or get threatened by some fast-money boy."

Marlowe's romanticism stemmed in part from his desire to instill some humanity into the hard, fast, superficial world of Hollywood and Los Angeles, where he lived and worked. Often he was tempted to go far beyond the extent of his responsibility to his clients, but almost

invariably he held fast to his principles, and he was loyal to a fault.

In 1939 Marlowe did not reveal his knowledge of a murderer's identity because she was insane and subject to epileptic seizures, and her discovery would have benefited no one. Despite the fact that she had also tried to shoot him for refusing to sleep with her, Marlowe gave her sister a three-day grace period to get the girl to a hospital where she would be kept under constant observation, and where she might be cured. In 1944, pursuing a lead in a complicated set of murders arranged to look like a series of unrelated suicides, he was viciously beaten by corrupt policemen and sent to jail. When the police captain found out that his officers had punched and kicked Marlowe, had hit him with a blackjack, and had made him drink whiskey so they could arrest him for drunken driving, he asked if Marlowe wanted to file charges against them. Marlowe replied, "Life's too short for me to be filing charges of assault against police officers." Later Marlowe discovered that the murderer he was looking for was Al Degarmo, the most corrupt of all the dirty cops. He told Degarmo shortly before the pinch, "I'm all done with hating you. It's all washed out of me. I hate people with hate, but I don't hate them very long." In 1949 he was arrested twice and slapped around by the police because he was shielding a movie star who was prepared to confess to a murder she hadn't committed. In 1953, protecting the memory of a friend he thought had died, Marlowe was again beaten by the police, sent to jail, and later set up as bait to trap a big-time racketeer who wanted Marlowe dead. In that same year, while earning only $25 a day, he received $5,000 from a would-be client but refused to spend it because "there was something wrong with the way I got it."

Marlowe was threatened with jail, bodily harm, loss of his detective's license, and/or death in every major case he undertook. Yet, whether confronting crooked cops, petty thieves, junkies, syndicate hit men, or clients who refused to save themselves, Marlowe endured, fending off guns and knives with sarcastic witticisms, keeping his head clear enough to have no illusions about himself or the people he dealt with, bearing no grudges, and demonstrating, when the occasion demanded, that he was a dead shot and a tough fighter. During his entire career, he killed only one man.

Marlowe was more than simply a detective. He discussed T. S. Eliot with a mistress's chauffeur, cited Flaubert's work habits to a popular hack writer, and quoted Browning to another mistress. When a woman with whom he had spent the night asked him, "How can such a hard man be so gentle?" he replied, "If I wasn't hard, I wouldn't be alive. If I wasn't gentle, I wouldn't deserve to be alive."

Although in 1939 Marlowe told General Guy

de Brisay Sternwood, "I'm unmarried because I don't like policemen's wives," he had numerous erotic encounters with women over the years. In 1939 he spent one night necking in his car parked high above the Pacific Ocean with Vivian Sternwood Regan, who wanted very much to sleep with him. When she found out he was playing along in order to pump her for information about a murder, she flew into a rage and had him drive her home. When he walked into his own apartment later that night, Vivian's sister Carmen was lying naked on his bed, giggling.

In 1949 sweet young Orfamay Quest came all the way from Manhattan, Kansas, to hire Marlowe to find her lost brother, Orrin. In the process of discovering that Orfamay had fingered Orrin so that a gangster could gun him down, Marlowe also learned that she was exceedingly easy to kiss. He later discovered that her sister Leila, a film star better known as Mavis Weld, was being blackmailed by Orrin, and that Mavis was even easier to kiss. And he found out that Mavis's roommate, a B-film actress named Dolores Gonzales, was as much fun to kiss as either of the Kansas girls and even more accessible.

In 1953, working on a double-barreled case that involved uncovering the truth about one disappearance and two apparently unrelated murders, Marlowe met Mrs. Linda Loring. Her sister was one of the two murder victims in this case. Linda was the daughter of a powerful multimillionaire and the wife of a physician whose specialty was prescribing uppers and downers for his high-society patients. Linda and Marlowe met over drinks a few times, and when she determined to divorce her husband, she spent a night in Marlowe's bed. When she left in the morning, Marlowe never expected to see her again. But his night with Linda was clearly more than just another trick to him, and he realized that to "say good-bye is to die a little."

In 1958, after a simple tailing job led Marlowe to discover both a murder and a murderer near Del Mar, California, he broke one of his unspoken rules. "When I want your beautiful white body," he said to Betty Mayfield, "it won't be while you're my client." Minutes later she was saying, "Take me, I'm yours—all of me is yours. Take me." And he did.

But when he returned home from Del Mar, he had a phone call from Paris, where Linda Loring had been living since their brief encounter. She told him she loved him and wanted to marry him, and—tacitly—he agreed. She invited him to come to Paris on her money, but Marlowe refused: "Sure, you have the money for 500 plane tickets. But this one will be my plane ticket. Take it or don't come." She accepted, and for Marlowe "the air was full of music."

—B.H.

JANE MARPLE (b. c. 1850s)

Among female detectives there are few that are as unlikely and as endearing as Miss Jane Marple. This intrepid senior has used her wide understanding of the human condition to solve many a bloody murder.

She was born in the quiet village of Saint Mary Mead in Radfordshire, England, in the 1850s, but little more is known about Jane Marple's early life. Two of her uncles were canons in the Church of England, and it is believed her father was a clergyman. This strong religious background may account for Miss Marple's solid sense of morality and firm belief in the power of both good and evil. Her father, whatever his profession, was a strict Victorian, ending his daughter's only known romantic attachment to a young man who later turned out to be a cad. After that, Jane never married.

Thin and tall, with a pink-and-white complexion, Miss Marple has fluffy white hair and large china-blue eyes that miss nothing, especially when following the twisting trail of murder and mayhem. Conservative by nature, she favors lace and home-knitted shawls. She has lived in Saint Mary Mead all her life and resides in a quaint cottage, next to the vicarage, scene of her first important murder case. Her hobbies are knitting and gardening, the latter of which she has had to forego in recent years at the order of Dr. Haydock, her personal physician and neighbor, to counteract her worsening rheumatism. She also is an avid bird-watcher, although she has often used this as an excuse to observe the activities of murder suspects through her binoculars.

Miss Marple first became involved in crime-solving at the advanced age of seventy-four, when her nephew and closest relative, the successful novelist and sometime poet Raymond West invited her to join a rather unusual club. The "Tuesday Night Club" meets weekly to discuss and solve unsolved mysteries, most of them dealing with murder. The other members are Dr. Haydock; Joyce Campriere, a painter; Mr. Pitherick, a local solicitor; Dr. Pender, a clergyman; and Sir Henry Clithering, an ex-commissioner of Scotland Yard. Although they all have keen analytical minds, it is inevitably Miss Marple who manages to solve the armchair crimes with her uncanny use of analogies and deep understanding of the dark side of human nature. In the village of Saint Mary Mead, she has found a microcosm of the larger world, seething with passion and wickedness under life's placid surface that all too often erupts in murder. This has led this genteel lady to a surprisingly cynical view of life. "I always believe the worst," she said during one of her more bizarre cases. "What is so sad is that one is usually justified in doing so."

Her success at the Tuesday Night Club, and the admiration and respect of her fellow club members, led to her first real murder case at the vicarage in 1932. Although seen by some as a gossipy village busybody, Miss Marple exposed the killer and caused the vicar himself to declare, "There is no detective in England equal to a spinster lady of uncertain age with plenty of time on her hands."

Most of Miss Marple's subsequent cases, for which her help is usually unsolicited by the authorities, have taken place in Saint Mary Mead and surrounding villages. Occasionally she has been at the scene of the murder, but usually a friend or acquaintance draws her into the case. In one of her most intriguing cases, in 1957, her friend Mrs. McGillicuddy witnessed a woman being strangled on a passing train. Suffering the afflictions of old age, Miss Marple had to use her assistant Lucy Eyles-barrow to collect the evidence that led her to the killer.

In later years, thanks to the generosity of her affluent and doting nephew, Miss Marple has been able to extend the range of her sleuthing. She solved one murder while on a vacation in the Caribbean in 1964 following a bout with pneumonia, another at London's posh Bertram Hotel a year later, and a third on a bus tour of famous homes and gardens of Great Britain in 1971. Other unusual settings for her cases have included a school for young delinquents and a country home where a parlor game of mock murder ended in a very real one.

Although her keen mind has brought her to the solution in every investigation she has undertaken, Miss Marple has never taken credit for her successes, preferring the publicity to go to the police. As a lady and an amateur, she has avoided the spotlight. "Nothing was said of Miss Marple's share in the business," reported the vicar in her first case. "She herself would have been horrified at the thought of such a thing."

Since 1979 Miss Marple has been largely inactive, busying herself with her knitting and good works for the children of Saint Faith's Orphanage, her favorite charity. Yet the day may come when she returns to the game should murder rear its ugly head again in her peaceful environs. For as she has said once, "There is a great deal of wickedness in village life."

—S.A.O.

"UNCLE" SCROOGE McDUCK (b. c. 1860s)

Scrooge McDuck was born in Scotland, son of a Glasgow miner. As a youth he earned money shining shoes and gathering and selling firewood. In 1879 or 1880, he left Scotland and moved to the United States, where his uncle was a riverboat captain on the Mississippi. He traveled across the country until he ran out of money in Montana, failed as a prospector, then hired on as a cowboy in 1882. He staked a land claim, built a shack, and mined for copper. The

mine boomed and Scrooge was able to return to Scotland as a wealthy duck in 1884.

He traveled widely and his lust for money led him to Africa, where he found and developed the Star of the World diamond mine and became a millionaire. He left the mine to be run by employees and continued his travels. Scrooge traded pearls in Indochina, bought and sold yaks in Tibet, and financed a network of salesmen in the Gobi Desert. In 1898 he heard about the Alaska gold rush and crossed the Bering Strait. He worked hard, saved his money, and met the woman of his life—Glittering Goldie, the "Star of the North." Eventually Scrooge tired of mosquitoes, mud, and ice, so he moved to town and opened a bank and general store. By 1902 he had made his first billion.

After more travels Scrooge found his home for life. On the site of Old Fort Duckburg on the Tulebug River, he staked a claim to ten acres and built a wooden money bin. It was in this period that Scrooge remarked:

No man is poor who can do what he likes to do once in a while
And I like to dive around in my money like a porpoise
And burrow through it like a gopher . . .
And toss it up, and let it hit me on the head.

He financed a chemical gas factory, a smelter, and other industries. By 1910 his business was a colossus and the city of Duckburg was growing. The challenge was gone so Scrooge hit the road again.

He sold rain hats in Arabia and lawn mowers in the Sahara, and started a salt business in Egypt before being forced out by the political situation. He discovered a diamond mine in the Congo and in 1916 he prospected for emeralds in South America. Scrooge returned to New York in 1921 and hit the stock market—he bought RCA for 5¢ a share and sold it for $538 a share in 1929. Staunchly conservative during the Roosevelt years, his industrial business was tripled by World War II. By the late 1940s he possessed three cubic acres of money. His health declined because his pores became clogged with gold dust and minerals from his habit of swimming in his money. He also became addicted to Amazonian Nutmeg Tea. In his later years, he became nasty and greedy and obsessed with protecting his fortune, particularly from the Beagle Boys, a family of thieves who made ten attempts to get Scrooge's money. Because of his lower-class origins, Scrooge had an intense need for social acceptance by the traditionally wealthy of the duck world.

In his old age, he was driven by the need to prove himself as good as ever through making such deals as selling the people of tropical Indochina an enormous stove used for heating aircraft hangars. Uncle Scrooge McDuck is believed to be alive today, although his where-abouts are unknown. His fortune, said to exceed that of Bill Gates, is estimated at $91 multiplijillion, 9 obsquatumatillian, 623.62.

Scrooge's adventures have been admirably chronicled by Carl Barks, a former dishwasher, miner, sailor, and lumberman who went to work in the Disney studios during the 1940s. Barks first undertook the illumination of the crusty capitalist's life with the book *Only a Poor Old Man* in *Uncle Scrooge #1* (1951). This is gener-ally believed to be the first authorized chapter in the great duck's biography. Barks's various oils depicting Scrooge amid his wealth are consid-ered to be the finest visual presentations of the reclusive tycoon, since no photographs exist.

—D.W.

JOHN RAMBO (b. 1947)

In the 1980s, John Rambo became the exemplar of the American fighting man: a veritable one-man army whose can-do spirit was a shining symbol of the country's willingness to over-come "the Vietnam syndrome" of the seventies. But for Rambo himself, life was always a struggle.

John J. Rambo was born in 1947 in Bowie, Arizona, of mixed German and Native Ameri-can heritage. His family was poor—often un-able to buy food—and his mother died when he was young. His father was an abusive alcoholic who once tried to kill his son with a knife. Rambo ran away from home that night, but not before shooting his father with a bow and arrow, nearly killing him.

At seventeen Rambo enlisted in the U.S. Army, figuring he'd be drafted soon anyway. In the service he received extensive psychological testing and—despite much evidence to the contrary—was found to be normal. Rambo was recruited for the Green Berets by his friend and mentor, Colonel Samuel Trautman, who often called Rambo the best student he'd ever had: "He's a man who's been trained to ignore pain, ignore weather, to live off the land, to eat things that would make a billy goat puke." Besides learning to kill with guns, knives, and his bare hands, Rambo was cross-trained as a medic and learned to speak Vietnamese, fly helicopters, and survive in the wilderness with only a knife.

During his three-year tour, Rambo was cred-ited with fifty-nine confirmed kills and was decorated with two Silver Stars, four Bronze Stars, four Purple Hearts, the Distinguished Service Cross, and the Congressional Medal of Honor.

The seminal event in Rambo's military career was a guerrilla mission behind enemy lines, where his unit was ambushed and Rambo was shot in the leg and captured. At the jungle prison camp, Rambo was tortured with a knife and kept in a ten-foot hole, but he never revealed any information to his captors. As a prisoner, Rambo was required to do heavy labor and was deprived of sleep and food. But, as Rambo himself later recalled it, there was not much they could do to him that his instructors had not already put him through. He eventually escaped by giving himself dysentery: his guard left him alone to go get help and Rambo had his chance to run.

Despite his many honors, Rambo ended his service with a nervous breakdown and "a job greasing cars," according to Trautman.

Rambo had trouble adjusting to civilian life. He couldn't find steady employment and spent several years as a drifter. In 1982 he was arrested for vagrancy in a small town in the Pacific Northwest, where he was beaten by local sher-iff's deputies. In a flashback-induced rage, he broke free and escaped into the mountains. After one of the deputies was accidentally killed, Rambo tried to surrender, but the undisciplined lawmen shot at him anyway. Rambo used his jungle-warfare know-how to repulse his pursu-ers. When some 200 state police and National Guardsmen joined the manhunt, Rambo became a celebrity outlaw.

Trautman arrived to ask Rambo to surrender: "We can't have you out there wasting friendly civilians." Rambo replied: "There are no friendly civilians."

Though he was presumed dead after the abandoned mine entrance he was hiding in was blown up, Rambo escaped and proceeded to vent his famous rage on the town with an M-60 machine gun. He did, however, finally surren-der at Trautman's behest.

Rambo's story might have ended there—with Rambo doing hard time in prison—but in 1985 Trautman offered him the possibility of a presi-dential pardon if he would parachute into Viet-nam to search for POW/MIAs. Rambo agreed, but asked: "Sir, do we get to win this time?"

Rambo disdained high-tech gadgetry ("I've always believed that the mind is the best weapon"), although he did seem to get a lot of use from M-60s and his special explosive-tipped arrows, which could down a helicopter with a single shot.

With Co Bao, his beautiful Vietnamese con-tact, Rambo quickly found the camp and freed one of the prisoners. But his U.S. government handlers—Trautman excepted—didn't really want Rambo to find any POWs (they had hoped that he would find an empty camp so that the whole messy POW/MIA issue could finally be put to rest); they aborted the mission and allowed Rambo to be captured. Co rescued Rambo from interrogation by a sadistic Russian commander. Rambo then slaughtered scores of enemy soldiers before escaping to Thailand with the freed POWs in a Soviet helicopter. On landing, he let out his patented warrior's howl as he shot up the mission's headquarters with his M-60.

Trautman asked Rambo not to hate his country. Rambo replied: "Hate it? I'd die for it. I want what every other guy who came over here and spilled his guts wants—for our country to love us as much as we love it." With that, Rambo headed into the jungle.

Three years later, Rambo was living in a Thai Buddhist monastery, where Trautman found him and asked him to join him on a mission to aid the rebels in Afghanistan. Rambo refused to go . . . until he heard of Trautman's capture by the Soviets. (Coincidentally, the Soviets began pulling out of Afghanistan the same month Rambo went in.)

Joined by mujahedin rebels, he pulled off a daring rescue, but as Rambo and Trautman made their way on foot toward the border, they were blocked by what seemed to be the entire Soviet Red Army in Afghanistan. Just when things seemed bleakest, a mounted horde of mujahedin came to their rescue. As the Soviets retreated, the mujahedin asked Rambo to stay and help their struggle. Rambo's last words were only, "I have to go."

—A.B.C.

SPOCK (b. 2230)

The dignified, imperturbable first officer of the starship Enterprise was born in 2230 on the planet Vulcan to a Vulcan father and a human mother. Like all Vulcans, he has pointed ears and green blood as well as superhuman strength and intellect. From early childhood he was taught to suppress all emotion, abhorred by Vulcans as the prime cause of violence, and to exalt logic.

Spock's father, Sarek, was a distinguished scientist and ambassador; his mother, Amanda Grayson, was a teacher. Sarek never explained his odd choice of a human (that is, emotional) mate, except to say, "It seemed the logical thing to do." Although Spock loved his mother, he never told her so; he was ashamed of his feelings and his human ancestry. A lonely child, without brothers or sisters, Spock was teased by his Vulcan playmates for being different.

Around the age of seven he was married, Vulcan-fashion, to a child bride named T'Pring, in a telepathic bonding ceremony arranged by the young couple's parents. Theoretically, Spock and T'Pring would come together in adulthood at the "time of mating." Mature Vulcan males feel an overwhelming physical mating urge about every seven years, and their females submit passively at this time.

Spock's father taught him science and computer technology and wanted him to enter the Vulcan Science Academy and devote his life to pure research. However, Spock's restlessness and insatiable curiosity, the human elements in his personality, led him to choose the Space Service instead. As a consequence, his tradition-bound father stopped speaking to him.

After eight years at the Space Academy, Spock joined the crew of the U.S.S. Enterprise, first under the command of Captain Christopher Pike and then under the command of Captain James T. Kirk. The Vulcan rose to the rank of commander and became known as "the best first officer in the fleet." The feud with his father lasted eighteen years, and during this time Spock seldom visited Vulcan. Then Sarek, on an ambassadorial mission, ran into his son aboard the Enterprise. Because of a sudden illness, the stiff-necked ambassador needed a blood transfusion, and only Spock could provide the rare T-negative blood needed to save his life. This incident resulted in a reconciliation between father and son.

The Enterprise, with a crew of more than 400, is the largest starship in the fleet of the United Federation of Planets. Its mission is peaceful exploration of the galaxy. Its captain must observe the Prime Directive: noninterference with other life-forms. Unless alien life-forms constitute a threat, this directive must never be violated. The Klingons, a warlike and unscrupulous but technologically advanced people, continually harass the mission.

Spock is second in command and the ship's science officer, working at the library computer station on the bridge. The only Vulcan aboard, he is uniquely qualified to assist Captain Kirk. In addition to having unflinching courage, Spock is gifted with supersensitive sight and hearing, telepathic powers, total recall, and the ability to calculate with fine precision and lightning speed. He can deliver a deft pinch on the neck that renders an enemy helpless but does not kill. As a Vulcan he abhors killing but can kill efficiently for a logical reason (Spock is, incidentally, a strict vegetarian). He is no narrow specialist, but well versed in art, history, and music. He won second prize in the All-Vulcan Music Competition. His instrument is the Vulcan harp.

Three-dimensional chess is Spock's favorite form of recreation. The fact that Kirk can beat his first officer at chess is symbolic of the relationship between them. The captain's fully developed human imagination and intuition often prevail over Vulcan logic. Spock understands this and gladly serves under Kirk—whom he admires above all other men—without jealousy or rivalry. The Vulcan's relationship with the rest of the crew is distant. His pride, computerlike intellect, and inability to make small talk preclude intimacy.

The ship's chief medical officer, Dr. Leonard McCoy, often attempts to probe beneath Spock's impassive surface by making sarcastic and, at times, cruel remarks that are designed to provoke a "human" emotional response. Although the two are mutually supportive in large matters, they bicker constantly over small ones, seldom verbalizing their genuine respect and concern for each other. Spock can never forget that he is a half-breed, effectively alienated from humans as well as Vulcans.

After he had not seen T'Pring, his child bride, for many years, Spock was suddenly seized by the mating urge. He became highly irrational as instinct took over. Shocked by the change in their friend, Captain Kirk and Dr. McCoy accompanied Spock to Vulcan to claim his wife. She, however, rejected Spock in favor of another Vulcan male. Vulcan law allowed her to select a champion to fight Spock to the death. She chose Kirk. Spock, in a trancelike state, nearly killed his friend during the ensuing duel. Kirk was saved only by the quick thinking of McCoy, who administered a death-simulating injection to the captain. Later, his mating urge sublimated in battle, the brokenhearted Spock uncharacteristically displayed the human emotions of grief and subsequent joy as Captain Kirk returned seemingly from the dead.

Between mating times, Vulcans have no interest in sex, let alone in love. Spock does not respond to the devotion shown by *Enterprise* nurse Christine Chapel. There have been rare occasions when, under the influence of mind-altering drugs or time warps, his repressed emotions have surfaced and he has evidenced a love for human females. On Omicron Ceti III, for example, after being exposed to the spores of a plant that worked on the central nervous system, he fell in love with Leila, an Earth woman. But in each case, once the mind-altering condition ended, he has reverted to his normal celibate habits.

At the end of Kirk's five-year mission, Spock retired from Starfleet. He returned to Vulcan to pursue the discipline of Kolinahr, the complete purging of all emotions, but he was called back to the *Enterprise.*

In 2271 he mind-melded with the alien menage V'GER, only to discover that it was a machine with consciousness, suffering from an existential dilemma. He nearly died during this encounter, but while recovering in sick bay he shed a tear for V'GER's plight and told Kirk, "Logic and knowledge are not enough." Spock remained with Starfleet and was promoted to *Enterprise* captain when the ship was assigned as a training vessel.

In 2285 Spock heroically sacrificed his life to save the crew of the *Enterprise.* Entering the ship's reactor room, he manually repaired the space drive, preventing the detonation of the deadly Genesis device set by the evil Khan Noonien Singh. The Vulcan's body was torpedoed through space to the surface of the newly formed Genesis planet. Unknown to anyone, before his death Spock imprinted his *katra,* or soul, into the body of the ship's doctor, McCoy.

In an attempt to restore Spock's soul, Captain Kirk later hijacked the *Enterprise* and headed to planet Genesis. Crew members from another

Leonard Nimoy as Spock in Star Trek: The Wrath of Khan.

Starfleet ship had found a youthful but quickly aging Spock, his body regenerated by the fruitful planet but his mind blank. The mind transfer was finally completed by a Vulcan high priestess, and Spock was reborn. He received several months of reeducation in the Vulcan way, but his mother grew concerned that his human side was being neglected. Spock decided to return to Earth with his shipmates.

In later years Spock became a diplomat. He served as Federation envoy to the Klingons, and in 2368 he secretly traveled to Romulus on a personal mission to further Romulan/Vulcan reunification. Here he worked in the Romulan underground, aiding dissidents. After the death of his father, Sarek, Spock learned that Sarek had mind-melded with Jean-Luc Picard, who allowed Spock to enter his thoughts and discover, at long last, his father's love for him. Today Spock continues his activities on Romulus.

Although Spock's is a dangerous life, it is challenging and fulfilling for one with his capabilities. True to his Vulcan heritage, he does not seek to be happy but only to serve, governed by the highest principles of loyalty, devotion to duty, and belief in personal honor.
—M.B.T. and A.W.

SUPERMAN (a.k.a. CLARK KENT AND KAL-EL) (1938–92; 1993–   )

Superman was born Kal-El, son of the scientist Jor-El and his wife, Lara, of the doomed planet

Krypton. Jor-El predicted the planet-devouring Kryptonian explosion for years in the Kryptonian senate, but no one would listen. Finally, in desperation, he constructed a one-man rocket ship to save his infant son Kal-El. The rocket escaped fiery destruction by scant seconds as Krypton was consumed by an atomic fire.

The rocket landed near Smallville, Illinois, where the infant Kal-El was found and adopted by Jonathan and Martha Kent. His foster parents soon discovered that their new son had amazing powers, including the power of flight, super strength, heightened sensory perception, great speed, and invulnerability. Fortunately for young Clark and the world at large, the Kents recognized that there was both a potential for good and a potential for evil in their son's abilities. Wisely, they instilled in him a strong moral obligation to aid people all over the world. Their contribution cannot be overstated. It was due to the Kents' encouragement that Clark first became Superboy, using a costume constructed from materials found in the crashed Kryptonian spaceship.

Several explanations have been offered for Superman's amazing abilities, but it is generally considered that he owes his powers to the difference between Krypton's original red sun and the earth's yellow sun. All survivors of the planet Krypton, including Clark's cousin Linda (Supergirl) Lee and the citizens of the miniature city Kandor (shrunk and placed in a bottle by the evil genius Braniac), have super powers when exposed to the earth's sun.

After Clark graduated from Smallville High he went to work as a reporter for the *Metropolis Daily Planet*, under the direction of editor Perry White. Superman discovered that he could use his "mild-mannered" reporter's guise to further his personal cause of achieving world justice. He also found that his prowess at supertyping was an advantage in meeting a journalist's deadlines.

Eventually the *Daily Planet* was taken over by a giant conglomerate, Galaxy Communications, headed by the mysterious Morgan Edge. Edge switched Kent from his job on the newspaper to Galaxy Broadcasting, where Kent established himself as a perceptive and resourceful reporter on the network's evening news program. Kent also tried his hand at writing spy thrillers before he returned to his old job as a reporter for the newspaper. The *Daily Planet* was sold again, this time to David Warfield, a media magnate intent on turning the paper into a sensational tabloid. Kent, however, retained his idealism and journalistic ethics.

Superman, as Clark Kent, has dated many girls over the years, including Lana Lang, a high-school chum; fellow reporter Lois Lane; the mermaid Lori, inhabitant of an undersea city on Atlantis; and Lacy Warfield, daughter of the *Daily Planet* owner. Superman recently became engaged to Lois Lane, and she is the only person to know him in both his Superman and Clark Kent identities. Superman has saved Lois from numerous serious scrapes since they first met, including rescuing her from terrorists who held her captive in the Eiffel Tower. He also once brought her back to life when she had been killed by a nuclear bomb explosion. He accomplished this amazing feat by reversing the rotational force of Earth.

Although Clark Kent has taken part in U.S. wars, he maintains a strictly nonpartisan stance in his Superman activities, preferring to deal with criminals of both human and alien descent. Great heroes attract great villains. Superman has been plagued by his archenemy Lex Luthor, a boyhood genius who might have devoted his prodigious scientific talents to the good of humankind had not the enthusiastic Superboy caused an accident that left Luthor bald. Luthor traditionally pursues two goals: world domination and the destruction of Superman.

Superman has also dealt with the fiendish Braniac, a computer that successfully masqueraded for many years as a green human being. Superman has also confronted Mr. Mxyztplk, the Imp from the Fifth Dimension, who can be returned to his home only by being tricked into pronouncing his own name backward. Another challenging nemesis Superman faced more recently was Nuclear Man, a solar-energized Titan who was cloned from a hair off Superman's head.

For many years Superman was plagued by chunks of kryptonite, radioactive remnants of his home planet, which had the power to weaken and possibly kill him. Of kryptonite's various forms, green was the most deadly and the most common. It was thought that a freak accident in 1970 at a secret government testing laboratory in New Mexico rendered all kryptonite harmless, but Lex Luthor later found a potent supply of the rocklike substance. Another of Superman's enemies, businessman Ross Webster, head of an international cartel, employed a computer genius by the name of Gus Gorman to create a synthetic kryptonite. Although it didn't strip Superman of his powers, the experimental kryptonite did create temporary personality problems in the man of steel. In an altered state, he blew out the Olympic flame, straightened the Leaning Tower of Pisa, and pulled other adolescent pranks that he remedied later when he returned to himself.

Superman's adventures took a tragic turn in 1992 when he faced off against a warrior named Doomsday. Battling the gray exoskeletal monster in the streets of Metropolis, Superman was mortally wounded in hand-to-hand combat. He had enough strength to defeat Doomsday, but he died in the arms of Lois Lane. Superman's death made headlines around the world. A two-hour memorial service was held in Metropolis; Clark Kent was missing and did not attend.

Since no one could believe that the invincible hero had truly died, it left an open field for pretenders. Among those claiming to be Superman in the days ahead were the Eradicator, an Elvis look-alike on a vigilante mission, and John Henry Irons, an African-American steelworker cloned from Superboy.

As it turned out, the Eradicator rescued Superman from the grave and placed him in a regeneration matrix, a flotation chamber with a life-support system on the ocean floor. Later the Eradicator transported him to the Arctic Fortress of Solitude. After Superman regained his strength, he returned to Metropolis, where he kissed a joyous Lois Lane. Clark Kent reappeared about the same time—he had been trapped under rubble from buildings felled during the Doomsday battle. Superman himself was perplexed by his amazing comeback and said simply, "Perhaps some outside agency intervened."

Superman's last known address was 344 Clinton Avenue in Metropolis. He also maintains his retreat home in the Arctic. Those interested in contacting him are urged to write to him in care of the *Daily Planet*.

—M.B. and L.A.C.

TARZAN (JOHN CLAYTON) (b. 1888)

Tarzan of the Apes, also called Tarzan the Terrible and Son of God, was born in a cottage made of packing crates and mud on the shores of Africa on November 22, 1888. His real name was John Clayton, and he was the son of Lord Greystoke and his delicate wife, Alice, who, not long before John's birth, were marooned on those wild shores by savage mutineers. Had it not been for this disaster, the young lord might have been born in an English castle.

His mother, shocked into vague madness by an encounter with a 350-pound ape (which she bravely shot and killed), died a year after his birth. Clayton, heartbroken, then wrote in his diary, "My little son is crying for nourishment—Alice, Alice, what shall I do!" Though Clayton was not to know it, help for the baby did come, and from unexpected quarters. It wasn't long after that that Kerchak, king of the apes, and his troop went on a rampage, entered the cabin (Clayton had carelessly left the door open), and killed the grief-stricken husband and father. Had it not been for Kala, mate of Tublat, who was mourning the loss of a baby, little John Clayton might have been killed too. However, Kala grabbed him to her bosom and adopted him as her own.

Thus began the strange, fantastic story of Tarzan, boy of the jungle, who grew up as an ape child. (The name Tarzan is ape language for "white-skinned ape.") For the next nineteen years, Tarzan led an almost idyllic life, swinging through the trees (but not on vines, as Hollywood would have it), playing tricks on his foster father, and growing up to be an athletic miracle. At the age of ten, he was as strong as a man of thirty. At nineteen he had, according to his biographer, Edgar Rice Burroughs, "the grace of a Greek god" and "the thews of a bull."

However healthy the life, it had done little for his intellectual development. That he did for himself. Visiting the cabin where he was born, he found books in which were what he called "little bugs." With his natural mental endowments, it wasn't long before he was able to decipher those little bugs and read English, using a children's illustrated alphabet and a dictionary. It was inevitable, however, that the child of the jungle, self-taught, would have holes in his education.

Tarzan was somewhat lonely, for as he grew he surpassed the apes in intellectual achievement. He made friends with Tantor, the elephant, and later with Sheeta, the leopard, but this did not end his yearning to be with his own kind: the men he had seen in his father's books.

In his teenage years, a tribe of Pygmies did settle nearby. However, they earned Tarzan's eternal enmity, for it was a Pygmy cannibal who killed Tarzan's mother Kala with a poisoned arrow. He, in turn, killed the assassin and, hungry, almost ate a piece of the dead warrior. Something stopped him. (Burroughs says it was a hereditary repulsion toward cannibalism.)

In 1908 Tarzan met Jane Porter, who by sheer coincidence was marooned on that same shore. She was nineteen, with long yellow hair and blue-gray eyes, a fit match for the bronzed, gray-eyed young god. Jane was accompanied by her addlepated old father, his companion, equally eccentric, her maid, and, believe it or not, Tarzan's second cousin, Lord Greystoke, who unwittingly was holding the title that rightfully belonged to Tarzan.

Tarzan and Jane fell in love, of course, pledging that love in a woodland bower where Tarzan did "what no red-blooded man needs lessons in doing. He took his woman in his arms and smothered her upturned panting lips with kisses." He did no more. In spite of the fact that he had been brought up by animals, he had somehow, through a kind of hereditary understanding, developed a full-blown sense of Victorian sexual morality.

Through a series of misadventures involving the cannibals, some pirates, buried gold, and abductions, Tarzan and Jane were separated. She sailed back to her native United States. He, with a new-found friend, a Frenchman, followed her there.

It was several months later that Jane, living on a farm in Wisconsin and facing marriage for financial reasons to a cold-hearted villain, saw a four-cylinder French touring car drive up.

Who should step out of it but Tarzan. In short order he saved her from the villain and a forest fire, only to have to renounce his true love because she, in a weak moment, had agreed to marry Tarzan's second cousin. Two years later, Tarzan had his heart's desire and married Jane. In the interim, however, he had some spine-tingling adventures: a duel, a fight with Arab bandits, a brief fling with a countess. Though his heart always belonged to Jane, Tarzan was wildly attractive to women, including the beautiful Russian countess and the queen of La, a lost Atlantis in the heart of Africa. He wasn't always able to fight them off, though what did take place would hardly shock anyone today. He also learned to drink absinthe and smoke cigarettes.

During the rest of his life, Tarzan lived either at his English country estate (he got his title at last) or his African estate, and when he grew bored with both, he traveled the world. Though outwardly urbane, he never did shake off his jungle childhood. Once, on the green lawn of Westerfalcon Hall, he found and ate an earthworm, a treat for an ape, much to Jane's horror.

During his lifetime Tarzan had two sons, one adopted, whom, along with his wife, he was always rescuing from horrible fates. He conducted a running battle with the dastardly Rokoff and sundry other villains: the River Devil, the Lion Man, a Minunian scientist who shrank him to the height of eighteen inches, and the monster Numa, a celestial lion that threatened to eat up the moon. (Biographers other than Burroughs doubt the truth of this story.) In World War I he lassoed a bomber. In World War II he joined the RAF and flew planes over Burma, China, and Japan. He also served in the Foreign Legion. Though most of his adventures were in Africa, where he visited such little-known places as the Great Thorn Forest, he also traveled throughout the world, including Hollywood, where moviemakers made fortunes chronicling his life and those of his sons.

There is no record of what happened to Tarzan after 1946.

—A.E.

POPULAR SONGS AND THEIR STORIES

"VISSI D'ARTE," Giacomo Puccini (1900)

"Vissi d'arte" is one of two well-admired arias from Giacomo Puccini's opera *Tosca*, which premiered at the Teatro Costanzi in Rome on January 14, 1900. The play *La Tosca*, by playwright Victorien Sardou, had opened in Paris in November 1887, featuring the renowned Sarah Bernhardt. Two years later Puccini saw Bernhardt in a production of the play, and although he did not understand French, he sensed the highly dramatic subject and knew that he could turn it into an effective opera.

He expressed his interest to his publisher, Giulio Ricordi, who commissioned Luigi Illica to write the libretto. When Puccini's interest in the project later waned, Ricordi gave the libretto to Alberto Franchetti, another composer whose works he published. Then Puccini's interest in *Tosca* was rekindled, perhaps because the composer Verdi had judged the play a worthy subject for an opera but felt himself too old to undertake the task. It fell to Ricordi and Illica to trick Franchetti into relinquishing his rights to the piece. This they managed to do by convincing him that *Tosca* was too violent and too political to be the subject of an opera. The day after Franchetti gave up his rights to the libretto, Puccini acquired them.

Another librettist, Giuseppe Giacosa, was brought into the project to help with the versification. Puccini was a difficult taskmaster for his librettists and the writing phase was characterized by many cuts, revisions, and disagreements.

An atmosphere of violence pervades the whole of *Tosca*. Underlying Puccini's music is a strong melancholy and sadness. This is particularly prominent when Floria Tosca sings her "Vissi d'arte": "I lived for art, I lived for love. I have never harmed a living soul!" She bemoans her apparent fate at the hands of the evil Scarpia, "In my hour of misery why, why O Lord, ah . . . why do you repay me thus?" Though filled with misery, her lyrical, flowing aria is especially touching, as it comes after the whole of act 2, which is nonlyrical in song and violent in plot.

—B.S.

"SWEET ADELINE," Richard H. Gerard and Henry Armstrong (1903)

"Sweet Adeline" is a song loved and sung by generations of Americans, especially when in a mellow mood.

Although the song as it is now known dates from 1903, the melody was written by Henry Armstrong in 1896, when he was eighteen years old. It did not for a time have any words, but when young Henry traveled from Boston to New York and went to work for Witmark, the music publishing house, he met another young man, Richard H. Gerard. He asked Gerard to write some lyrics for the tune, and the song became "You're the Flower of My Heart, Sweet

Rosalie." This song went from publisher to publisher without finding a taker. Then Gerard suggested that maybe a change of title would help.

According to the story, about this time Gerard and Armstrong happened to see a poster announcing the farewell concert tour of the famed prima donna Adelina Patti. That was it. The girl in the song would be Adeline and the title shortened to, simply, "Sweet Adeline."

In 1903 Witmark accepted and published the song. However, it still did not sell well. About a year later, the Quaker City Four, a vaudeville quartet, came to Witmark's looking for new material. They turned down song after song until they were shown "Sweet Adeline." "That's what we've been looking for," one of them said. They sang the song shortly afterward in a program given at the Victoria Theatre in New York City. It was a hit right away and soon it was being sung everywhere.

Barbershop quartets especially found "Sweet Adeline" a great song for the "rough and ready choral harmonization" that has always been their trademark. Today it is not only a favorite with members of the Society for the Preservation and Encouragement of Barber Shop Singing, founded in Tulsa, Oklahoma, in 1938, but has also furnished the name for the female equivalent of the male barbershop singers, the Sweet Adelines.

"Sweet Adeline" was also used as the title of a musical comedy, written by Jerome Kern and Oscar Hammerstein II, which was made into a movie in 1929. This was not a success. However, John J. Fitzgerald—President John Kennedy's grandfather—used "Sweet Adeline" as the theme song for a successful campaign that resulted in his being elected mayor of Boston.
—E.S.L.

"DOWN BY THE OLD MILL STREAM," Tell Taylor (1908)

With both words and music by Tell Taylor, this classic of the barbershop quartet genre was one of the leading hit songs of its decade, selling more than 2 million copies of sheet music.

Tell Taylor composed about 200 songs, most of them sentimental ballads, with nearly a hundred big sellers to his credit, including "Rock Me Asleep in an Old Rocking Chair" and "He Sleeps Beneath the Soil of France."

After leaving his hometown of Findlay, Ohio, Taylor established himself as a popular songwriter; he wrote two hit Broadway shows and starred in musical productions as well. In the summer of 1908 the thirty-two-year-old Taylor went home to Findlay for a rest. While he was fishing on the banks of the Blanchard River, his thoughts went back to cherished scenes of his boyhood, such as playing around the old Misamore grist mill a few miles upstream. His daydreams also turned to a girl he had had a crush on so long ago, and this provided the inspiration for the words and melody that he jotted down that day while fishing.

Taylor did nothing with his composition for two years, until the Orpheus Comedy Four, a vaudeville act, asked him for a song for their opening in Saginaw, Michigan; "Down by the Old Mill Stream" was an overnight sensation. When the sheet music was published, it also was an instant hit. In Chicago 2,500 copies sold in one hour, and in Saint Louis, 200,000 copies in one week.

Becoming his own song plugger, Taylor took "Down by the Old Mill Stream" on the road to introduce the song to the public, sometimes playing and singing it himself in music stores and selling copies of its sheet music. Tell Taylor became a millionaire with this one hit.

Eventually Hollywood decided to make a feature film based on "Down by the Old Mill Stream," but Tell Taylor died in 1937 while on his way to California to help in the movie production; the film never materialized.

Although it was a familiar barbershop quartet selection and was sung extensively by amateurs, the song has also been recorded by Bing Crosby, Gene Krupa, and Arthur Godfrey and His Chordettes.

Because it embodies a little of the quiet of the countryside, a looking back at the past, and daydreaming about an old sweetheart, "Down by the Old Mill Stream" had a long-standing appeal for Americans. It was the kind of song that passed into oral tradition, a harmonizing favorite that could easily be remembered and sung by anyone.
—B.S.

> *What's the use of worrying?*
> *It never was worth while,*
> *So, pack up your troubles in your old kit-bag,*
> *And smile, smile, smile.*
> George Asaf (George H. Powell),
> "Pack Up Your Troubles in Your Old Kit-Bag,"
> 1915

> *Over there, over there,*
> *Send the word, send the word over there*
> *That the Yanks are coming, the Yanks are coming,*
> *The drums rum-tumming everywhere.*
> *So prepare, say a prayer,*
> *Send the word, send the word to beware.*
> *We'll be over, we're coming over*
> *And we won't come back till it's over, over there.*
> George M. Cohan, "Over There," 1917

"RHAPSODY IN BLUE," George Gershwin (1924)

Premiered to a large and enthusiastic crowd in 1924, "Rhapsody in Blue" was praised by Henry

O. Osgood, the editor of *Musical America*, as greater than Stravinsky's *Rite of Spring*. Whether or not it is that, certainly it is one of the most popular pieces ever written. It was the link between popular music of its day and classical music.

George Gershwin was just twenty-five years old, a composer of a half dozen musical-comedy scores and other songs, when Paul Whiteman, the self-proclaimed "king of jazz," asked him to produce a new piece of music for Whiteman's "Experiment in Modern Music," a concert to be presented February 12, 1924. Years later, Gershwin recalled that the evolution of the music began on a train ride from New York to Boston. The rhythms of the rattling train stimulated Gershwin's musical imagination and he envisioned the whole construction of the rhapsody. "I heard it as a musical kaleidoscope of America, of our vast melting pot, of our national pep, of our blues, our metropolitan madness."

Gershwin began writing on January 7, 1924, at his parents' apartment on 110th Street and Amsterdam Avenue in New York, where he lived along with his brothers and sister. Whiteman's talented arranger Ferde Grofé was there to snap up Gershwin's manuscript almost page by page; Grofé finished the orchestration on February 4.

The never-before-heard opening whoop of the clarinet was the contribution of the brilliant clarinetist Ross Gorman. Instead of playing the seventeen-note scale ascent with each note tongued separately as Gershwin had written it, Gorman during a rehearsal smeared the notes to the top register so that it sounded almost like a siren wailing. Gorman did this with such precision that it established the mood for the whole rhapsody. It was an extraordinary opening and a signature piece.

Pressed for time, Gershwin left several pages blank in Whiteman's score as piano solos for himself that he would improvise on stage. Partly because of this, the audience at the premiere in Aeolian Hall heard a performance that was quite different from what is now familiar to audiences. Whiteman's band had eighteen musicians who played twenty-three instruments that day. Two years later Grofé reorchestrated "Rhapsody in Blue" for symphony orchestra, and it is this version that is usually played today.

In 1924 alone, the Whiteman band played the piece eighty-four times, and also that year Whiteman and Gershwin recorded "Rhapsody in Blue" for the Victor Blue label. The composition has become part of the repertory of major American symphony orchestras and has been performed throughout Europe as well. "Rhapsody in Blue" has been scored in many variations, including ones for an orchestra of harmonicas, a mandolin orchestra, even an a cappella chorus.

While still not embraced by many highbrow critics and composers, "Rhapsody in Blue" was the centerpiece of that February 1924 concert, which became a legend as a milestone in American musical history.

—B.S.

> George [Gershwin] died on July 11, 1937, but I don't have to believe that if I don't want to.
> John O'Hara, *Newsweek*, July 15, 1940

"BOLÉRO," Maurice Ravel (1928)

Maurice Ravel's most widely known and popular composition, "Boléro," was the result of a commission from his friend, the Russian ballerina Ida Rubinstein.

After a successful four-month tour of the United States and Canada, Maurice Ravel returned to France in April 1928 and took a short vacation in Saint-Jean-de-Luz on the Basque coast. One morning before going for a swim with his friend Gustave Samazeuilh, Ravel went to the piano and with one finger played a tune that he felt had an insistent quality about it. He told Samazeuilh that he was "going to try and repeat it a number of times without any development, gradually increasing the orchestra as best I can."

With that beginning Ravel went on to compose a piece that emphatically departs from a thousand-year tradition of Western musical thinking. There is no variation in theme, the whole of "Boléro" being an insistent repetition of the same two sections of one theme. Ravel himself described it as "a rather slow dance, uniform throughout in its melody, harmony, and rhythm, the latter being tapped out continuously on the drum. The only element of variety is supplied by the orchestral crescendo." But the crescendo is long and meticulously controlled, with a building of tension that appeals primarily to the senses rather than the analytical mind.

Maurice Ravel (right) playing the score from Daphnis et Chloé *with Vaslav Nijinsky, 1912.*

Although Ravel's knowledge of things Spanish was quite extensive, his composition in its form, tempo, and rhythm has only a slight similarity to the authentic Spanish dance, prevalent in Andalusia and Castile, known as the bolero.

Much to Ravel's surprise, "Boléro" became incredibly popular soon after its premiere on November 22, 1928, at the Paris Opéra. Hélène Jourdan-Morhange, a close friend, wrote that Ravel attributed this popularity to "the obsessive, musico-sexual element in the piece."

An incident that helped bring "Boléro" to the forefront of the musical world occurred in early 1930 when the great Arturo Toscanini conducted the music at the Paris Opéra. Ravel was infuriated because Toscanini increased the tempo to what Ravel called "a ridiculous speed." After the performance, a livid Ravel refused to stand up when Toscanini tried to get him to take a bow.

First conceived as a ballet and subsequently performed as an independent symphonic work, "Boléro" eventually found its way onto the silver screen. In 1934 Paramount released the film *Bolero*, with Carole Lombard and George Raft, in which the music played a significant part. In 1979 Blake Edwards directed the film *10*, with Henry Mancini conducting "Boléro." After Bo Derek tells costar Dudley Moore that "Boléro" is the only music to make love by, the public responded with renewed interest in the music, buying 25,000 copies of it in a ten-day period. Maurice Ravel's suspicion about "Boléro's" carnal appeal seems to have been justified.
—B.S.

"STARDUST," Hoagy Carmichael and Mitchell Parish (1929)

Hoagy Carmichael's haunting torch song "Stardust" is one of the world's three most-played popular songs. It has been recorded almost 500 times in forty-six different arrangements for every possible instrument, including the xylophone and the Hawaiian guitar. The lyrics have been translated into forty languages.

Returning in 1927 to his alma mater, Indiana University, to visit old friends and old haunts, Hoagy Carmichael, then twenty-seven years old, eventually found himself one night sitting alone on the campus "spooning wall" engrossed in his memories. He described the evening as "sweet with the death of summer and the hint and promise of fall." His thoughts turned to his college sweetheart, Dorothy Kelly, who recently had sent him a telegram saying she was going to marry someone else. Sitting on the wall he whistled the melody that became the immortal "Stardust." He ran to his old hangout, the Book Nook (so named because it was conspicuously unliterary), where he pounded out the tune on the old backroom player piano.

His college roommate, Stu Gorrell, christened the composition "Stardust" because he said it "sounded like dust from the stars drifting down through the summer sky."

The way Carmichael wrote it that night was as a snappy, upbeat fox-trot, a solo instrumental for the piano, but with an unusual melodic structure and key changes, one that was very unconventional for the late 1920s. In the motif of "Stardust," some have seen the influence of Bix Beiderbecke, the legendary jazz cornetist, who was Carmichael's personal idol as well as friend.

As the jazzy piano instrumental first played by Don Redman and his orchestra, the tune made little impression. Soon, however, Victor Young of the Isham Jones orchestra arranged "Stardust" in a slower tempo, as an ethereal ballad, and the orchestra recorded it that way. In 1929 the Mills Music Company, Carmichael's publisher, commissioned Mitchell Parish to write lyrics for the song—starting with the well-known verse "And now the purple dusk of twilight time . . . steals across the meadows of my heart."

In that incarnation it made its debut at the Cotton Club in Harlem; then more and more singers and bandleaders added "Stardust" to their repertoire, until it became a standard popular song. In the 1930s gossip columnist Walter Winchell fell in love with the song and, as Carmichael recounts it, forced fellow newsmen to put down their drinks while he held them by the lapels and whistled the tune. For years Winchell repeatedly quoted the song lyrics in his column, contributing to the number's growing popularity.

Artie Shaw and his orchestra recorded "Stardust" in 1940 and that recording sold more than 2 million copies within a five-year period. It has been estimated that Shaw's record had worldwide sales of 15 million copies.

In 1936 "Stardust" became the first song ever recorded on both sides of the same record—one side by Tommy Dorsey and his orchestra and the other by Benny Goodman and his band. Other well-known artists who have recorded the immortal tune have included Bing Crosby, Louis Armstrong, Dinah Shore, Guy Lombardo, Dick Haymes, Glenn Miller, André Kostelanetz, and Frank Sinatra.

In 1957, thirty years after the melody first came into being, "Stardust" was again on the best-seller lists in a recording by Billy Ward.
—B.S.

"PETER AND THE WOLF," Sergei Prokofiev (1936)

Perhaps Sergei Prokofiev's most famous and most often-recorded work, "Peter and the Wolf" was composed specifically for the Moscow Children's Musical Theatre in 1936. Natalie Satz, its thirty-three-year-old director, asked internationally known Prokofiev to compose a

They used to tell me I was building a dream,
And so I followed the mob
When there was earth to plough or guns to bear
I was always there right on the job

They used to tell me I was building a dream
With peace and glory ahead
Why should I be standing in line
Just waiting for bread?

Once I built a railroad, made it run,
Made it race against time.
Once I built a railroad,
Now it's done
Brother, can you spare a dime?

Once I built a tower, to the sun.
Brick and rivet and lime,
Once I built a tower,
Now it's done,
Brother, can you spare a dime?

Once in khaki suits
Gee, we looked swell
Full of that Yankee Doodle-de-dum.
Half a million boots went sloggin' thru Hell
I was the kid with the drum.
Say, don't you remember, they called me Al
It was Al all the time
Say, don't you remember I'm your Pal!
Buddy, can you spare a dime?

Jay Gorney and E. Y. (Yip) Harburg,
"Brother, Can You Spare a Dime?"
1928, first performed October 5, 1932

piece that would help children become acquainted with the various instruments of the symphony orchestra. Prokofiev was so enthusiastic about composing for children that he offered to do the task for whatever fee Satz could afford.

Agreeing that the most important thing was to be as concrete as possible in their sounds and images, Prokofiev and Satz decided to create a story involving animals and at least one human and that each character would be identified by its own musical instrument.

Satz engaged the poet Nina Saksonskaya to write the story but Prokofiev was dissatisfied with the result, complaining that there were far too many rhymes and too much clichéd language. He undertook the text himself. The story, the musical score, and the orchestration were completed by April 24, 1936, the day after Prokofiev's forty-fifth birthday.

When Prokofiev tried it out the first time for Natalie Satz at the theater, a group of children listened attentively and became so excited that they asked the composer three times to repeat the final march of the hunters.

This symphonic fairy tale was premiered in May 1936, and although Prokofiev's close collaborator, Natalie Satz, was scheduled to read the narration, she was unable to do so. Several months later she was arrested and sent to a concentration camp because her husband was on trial for treason. Although he was eventually executed, Natalie Satz was released. She was still reading the narration of "Peter and the Wolf" for the Moscow Children's Theatre when she was well into her eighties.

"Peter and the Wolf" has been enormously popular and endlessly recorded in different languages with a variety of narrators, including Sir Ralph Richardson, Mia Farrow, Sean Connery, David Bowie, Hermione Gingold, William F. Buckley Jr., Leonard Bernstein, and former New York Mets pitcher Tom Seaver.

Musically, the tale is another example of the composer's special talent for presenting characters in rhythm, melody, and timbre. For example, the wolf has a masculine brass fanfare, the hunters a full orchestral march, and Peter the confident rhythm of a string quartet. Each portrait is distinct and appropriate for the mood.

—B.S.

"IN THE MOOD," Joe Garland (1938)

"In the Mood" is one of those renowned songs that for millions of people today represent the swing era in American music. It had just the right tempo for dancing; young crowds found it perfect for jitterbugging.

"In the Mood" was first released by the Glenn Miller Band in 1939 on the Bluebird label by RCA Victor. The song, however, had many incarnations before that. The underlying riff goes back to the late 1920s. New Orleans trumpeter Wingy Manone used the basic theme in a Chicago-style recording in August 1930 called "Tar Paper Stomp." Seven months later, Horace Henderson incorporated the same motif in a tune entitled "Hot and Anxious," recorded both by his brother Fletcher Henderson's band and by the Don Redman band. In 1935 Joe Garland arranged the theme into a song called "There's Rhythm in Harlem" for the Mills Blue Rhythm Band.

Renaming the composition "In the Mood," Joe Garland and Edgar Hayes recorded it in February 1938 as a big band number. Garland copyrighted the song in June and offered it to Artie Shaw, who played it but did not record it. Subsequently, Garland submitted it to Glenn Miller. By trimming Garland's arrangement down to essentials and adding in two solo sections, Miller magically transformed the piece into one of the most successful big band era recordings. The beautifully constructed piece is famous for its fadeaway ending, as Miller baits his listeners with the riff repeated three times at ever-softer levels before the band roars into the rousing, explosive, full-ensemble finale.

Andy Razaf, a well-known lyricist who worked with Fats Waller and Eubie Blake, was hired for $200 cash on the spot in the recording studio to provide lyrics for Miller's "In the Mood." Based

on one of his and Waller's unpublished songs, "Whatcha Got on for Tonight?," Razaf's lyrics were reintroduced to a new generation of listeners in 1973 when Bette Midler recorded the song with some modifications to suit her own persona.

—B.S.

"OVER THE RAINBOW," Harold Arlen and E. Y. (Yip) Harburg (1938)

Following the premiere of The Wizard of Oz in 1939, "Over the Rainbow" became Judy Garland's personal theme song, and as she once said, "It has become a part of my life. . . . It's still the song that's closest to my heart." It was the one that always had the most dramatic effect on her audiences over the years.

Film producers Mervyn LeRoy and Arthur Freed hired composer Harold Arlen and lyricist E. Y. Harburg in May 1938 for $25,000 to write the complete musical score for Wizard. This was the first time in motion-picture history, except for animated cartoons, that the music would be prescored throughout. This integrated musical score meant that every song commented on a movie character or advanced the plot in some way. Freed wanted Arlen and Harburg to create a ballad to serve as a transition from Kansas to the Land of Oz. They decided that it would be "a song of yearning . . . to delineate Dorothy and to give an emotional touch to the scene where she is frustrated and in trouble."

While Harold and his wife, Anya, were driving to Grauman's Chinese Theater in Hollywood to see a movie, the broad, windswept melody came to Arlen and he hurriedly jotted it down while sitting in the car in front of Schwab's Drug Store. When he first played it for Yip Harburg, with its slow tempo and a rich harmonization, Yip was clearly disappointed. "It's full of crescendos! It's too lush! That's for Nelson Eddy, not for a little girl from Kansas." It was too majestic and serious, too solemn, and too old-sounding for the thirteen-year-old character.

They asked their friend Ira Gershwin to listen to the composition and he suggested a quicker tempo and a thinner harmonic texture, which was precisely what it needed.

Harburg then set about the lyrics and the development of the rainbow image (something that was not in the book by L. Frank Baum) as the bridge from the black-and-white landscape of Kansas to the saturated colors of the Land of Oz. And so the famous opening "Somewhere over the rainbow" was created.

In spite of its dramatic importance, MGM executives tried three times to take the song out of the film. It was ultimately saved by the outrage of producer Arthur Freed, who declared, "The song stays—or I go! It's as simple as that."

In February 1940, "Over the Rainbow" won an Oscar for best song. Judy Garland, after receiving a special juvenile award, entertained the audience by singing the ballad. Later in her career, after personal setbacks and professional disasters, Garland made a dramatic comeback in 1967. Sitting on the stage with her feet dangling over the orchestra pit, she sang an emotional rendition of the song that, once again, completely captivated her audience.

Part of the continuing enchantment with the song has been due to its association with Judy Garland. Both the song and the performer have an underlying melancholy and sadness that elicits empathy from the listener.

—B.S.

"THIS LAND IS YOUR LAND," Woody Guthrie (1940)

Written and composed by Woody Guthrie, "This Land Is Your Land" is an American classic folk ballad that was inducted into the National Academy of Recording Arts and Sciences (NARAS) Hall of Fame in 1989. Some have even suggested that it replace the "Star-Spangled Banner" as America's national anthem.

Guthrie, born July 14, 1912, in Indian territory in Oklahoma, was a refugee from the poverty of the Oklahoma dust bowl. During the 1920s and 1930s he roamed the country, living as a hobo, working at menial jobs, and performing wherever he could—saloons, union halls, picket lines. He crafted his modest songs out of his firsthand experiences of the hardships of the depression, the dust bowl drought, and the lives of the impoverished. Being a deep-rooted left-winger, he felt himself a spokesperson for the working class. He once told his audience, "I am out to sing the songs that will make you take pride in yourself and your work."

Using a tune from the Carter Family's song "Little Darlin', Pal of Mine," which itself had come from an old Baptist hymn, "Oh My Lovin' Brother," Guthrie wrote on February 23, 1940, six verses of a song he named "God Blessed America." With two of its verses, Guthrie's song seemed to parody Irving Berlin's "God Bless America":

Was a big high wall there that tried to stop me
A sign was painted said: Private Property,
But on the back side it didn't say nothing—
God blessed America for me.

One bright sunny morning in the shadow of the steeple
By the Relief office I saw my people—
As they stood hungry, I stood there wondering if
God blessed America for me.

Near the end of his life Woody Guthrie had his son Arlo memorize these meaningful verses because he was afraid they would be forgotten in time, as popular sentiment already was diluting his original intensity of feeling.

Four years after writing the song, Guthrie changed the tag line of each verse from "God blessed America for me" to "This land was made for you and me." He recorded the song as "This Land Is Your Land" in April 1944 in the studio of Moe Asch who was recording the music of such people as Leadbelly, Cisco Houston, Bess Lomax, and Sonny Terry.

Having written more than a thousand songs of social and political significance, Woody Guthrie provided inspiration for a later generation of popular folksingers such as Bob Dylan, Joan Baez, Jack Elliott, Tom Paxton, and Phil Ochs. "This Land Is Your Land" was the theme song in George McGovern's 1972 presidential campaign and has been used as an advertising jingle by United Airlines and the Ford Motor Company. Guthrie's song has been recorded by the Wayfarers; Glen Yarborough; the Kingston Trio; the Brothers Four; the Limeliters; the New Christy Minstrels; Peter, Paul and Mary; Trini Lopez; Harry Belafonte; Jay and the Americans; Glen Campbell; Bing Crosby; the Staple Singers; Tex Ritter; Connie Francis; Country Joe McDonald; Paul Anka; Jim Croce; the Mike Curb Congregation; and the Mormon Tabernacle Choir. It is not known how many of these recording artists, not to mention the corporate giants, were aware of the song's original leftist commentary on Berlin's "God Bless America."

—B.S.

> *I hate a song that makes you think that you're not any good. I hate a song that makes you think that you are just born to lose. Bound to lose. No good to nobody. No good for nothing. Because you are either too old or too young or too fat or too slim or too ugly or too this or too that. Songs that run you down or songs that poke fun at you on account of your bad luck or your bad traveling.*
>
> *I am out to fight those kinds of songs to my very last breath of air and my last drop of blood.*
>
> *I am out to sing songs that will prove to you that this is your world and that if it has hit you pretty hard and knocked you for a dozen loops, no matter how hard it's run you down and rolled over you, no matter what color, what size you are, how you are built, I am out to sing the songs that make you take pride in yourself and in your work. And the songs I sing are made up for the most part by all sorts of folks just about like you.*
>
> Woody Guthrie

"WHITE CHRISTMAS," Irving Berlin (1942)

"White Christmas" is one of the three or four most widely known and best loved of the 900 melodic and lyrical creations by that dean of American popular song, Irving Berlin. "White Christmas" began as part of the movie score written in Hollywood in 1942 for *Holiday Inn*. The film, produced by Paramount, starred Bing Crosby and Fred Astaire. When it came time to record the song, musical director Walter Scharf asked Berlin to leave the set. He was later discovered hiding behind a screen so that he could monitor Crosby's performance.

After being sung by Crosby, the song stepped right out of the movie and became an immediate hit. It earned an Academy Award as best song of 1942 for its composer; it also earned him the gratitude of thousands of World War II Yanks fighting in the jungles and swamps of the Pacific, since it brought them a nostalgic recollection of home—with its white Christmases and Yuletide cheer and peace.

Sales figures show that since then the song has had a sheet-music sale of about 5 million. Its record sales are some 180 million copies. In addition to the Oscar given by the Academy of Motion Picture Arts and Sciences, its widespread popularity—a continuing popularity—was proved by its appearance on *The Hit Parade* radio (and later TV) program a record-breaking thirty-two times during the program's quarter-of-a-century airing. The song also provided the title for the movie *White Christmas*, made in 1954.

—E.S.L.

"WE SHALL OVERCOME," Zilphia Horton, Frank Hamilton, Guy Carawan, and Pete Seeger (1945)

"We Shall Overcome" began as a gospel hymn and union song, but it was transformed by its four authors into the rallying cry of the black freedom movement for civil rights.

The music may derive from a 1794 hymn called "O Sanctissima," or "Prayer of the Sicilian Mariners," though some parts of the song are more recent. The words "I'll overcome some day" first appeared in a hymn by C. Albert Tindley and Reverend A. R. Shockly in *New Songs of the Gospel* (1900); however, the tune of that hymn was not the one we associate with the present-day song.

In 1945 the words and tune came together in a song called "I'll Overcome Some Day," with additional words by Atron Twigg and a revised musical arrangement by Kenneth Morris, a Chicago gospel singer. Roberta Martin wrote another version, the last twelve bars of which are part of the current version of "We Shall Overcome."

Zilphia Horton, wife of the founder of Highlander Folk School in Monteagle, Tennessee, first heard the song in October 1945. One story says she joined a picket line of the Congress of Industrial Organizations (CIO) Food and Tobacco Workers' strike in Charleston, South Carolina, on a cold winter's day and heard it then. Another story says that two of the picketers came to a labor workshop at the school and sang it for her. Whichever story is true, we do know that she did hear the song and turned it into a union song. Later she taught it to Pete Seeger, the folksinger. She also sang it up North and added more verses ("We'll walk hand in hand" is one of these). Folksinger Frank Hamil-

The Woolworth lunch counter sit-in, Greensboro, North Carolina, February 2, 1960. From left to right: Joseph McNeil, Franklin McCain, Billy Smith, and Clarence Henderson.

ton popularized the song, as did Guy Carawan, another white folksinger, who sang it to the black students who protested "white only" restaurants with sit-ins.

The song was recorded in 1950 by Joe Glazer and the Elm City Four and released by the CIO Department of Education and Research. When the song was published in 1960, the four authors dedicated it to the freedom movement and designated that all royalties resulting from its sale were to go to the movement. The popular version of the song is copyrighted under the names of Horton, Hamilton, Carawan, and Seeger.

"We Shall Overcome" was the song of the freedom movement. People sang its powerful, almost hypnotic lyrics—often repeating verses after a song leader—with their arms linked, as they swayed back and forth.

Martin Luther King Jr. said that the song lent unity to the freedom movement. Mrs. Viola Liuzzo, a white civil rights worker murdered in Alabama in 1965, sang "We Shall Overcome" as she lay dying. So did John Harris as he stood on the gallows of the prison in Johannesburg, South Africa, on April 1, 1965, waiting to be hung. It was suppressed in South Africa for decades after.

In the late 1960s, when the civil rights movement in the United States split between nonviolent moderates and violent militants, the militants criticized "We Shall Overcome" as being too passive, suggesting the lyrics be changed to "We shall overrun." Malcolm X and others also criticized the concept "We shall overcome *someday*," noting that black Americans wanted freedom not "someday" but now.
—A.E.

"ROCK AROUND THE CLOCK," Max Freedman and Jimmy DeKnight (1953)

Don't just play—do something.

Bill Haley, 1957

Bill Haley and the Comets' "Rock Around the Clock" wasn't the first rock song ever recorded. It was, however, the first to be recorded by a major label (Decca), the first to reach a national audience, and the first to frighten adults with their collective nightmare come to life: teen rebellion. After Haley, major record companies could no longer ignore the profits generated by the youth market that the independent labels catered to. For these accomplishments alone Bill Haley has to be considered one of the founders of rock and roll. The record appeared on the charts in May 1955 and stayed there for twenty-nine weeks, eventually selling more than 25 million copies. It remains one of rock's biggest hits.

"Rock Around the Clock" almost didn't make it. Bill Haley, from Chester, Pennsylvania, started out as a small-time country western singer recording covers of country hits on little-known labels. In 1951 he decided to concentrate on rhythm and blues, transforming himself into a "hep cat" replete with spit curl and outlandish dinner jackets. On the basis of "Crazy, Man, Crazy," which went to number

Bill Haley (center) and the Comets, London, February 6, 1957.

fifteen on the charts, Haley and his Comets signed with Decca in 1954. He recorded "Rock Around the Clock" as the "B" side of "Thirteen Women." Although Decca promoted the record heavily, it sold a respectable but far from spectacular 75,000 copies. Since the term *rock and roll* had not been coined as a musical category, "Rock Around the Clock" was designated a "novelty fox-trot" by the label.

Haley next released a highly sanitized version of Joe Turner's lowdown rhythm and blues number, "Shake, Rattle, and Roll," which broke the top ten in the charts. Then the movie *Blackboard Jungle* used "Rock Around the Clock" for its soundtrack, and Haley really took off. The movie, released in May 1955, was controversial, with its theme of rebellious youth. Even though it garnered decent reviews and received four Oscar nominations, adults found the movie and its loud music threatening. Clare Booth Luce, then ambassador to France, used her influence to have the film withdrawn from the Venice Film Festival. A number of cities in the United States banned the film outright, including Memphis, home of Sun Records and Elvis Presley. Public outrage made the movie and the song even more popular with postwar youth. Decca rushed the record into rerelease and Haley became rock's first king.

Haley's reign at the top didn't last long. He starred in a quickie movie called *Rock Around the Clock* that reprised the song in 1956. The film was highly profitable, but teenagers could not identify with Haley, who was cast as a family man and was overweight and balding to boot. At the time Haley started to slide, Elvis Presley was beginning his meteoric rise. Teens found a new hero in Elvis, whose sultry looks and hip-shaking moves made Haley appear old by comparison. Haley had a few minor hits following "Rock Around the Clock," but by 1960 his career was over. He tried to make a comeback as a revival act in the seventies and then dropped out of sight. In a rare public statement in the late seventies, he said, "The story has got pretty crowded as to who was the Father of Rock and Roll. I haven't done much in life except that. And I'd like to get credit for it." He gradually lapsed into alcoholism and dementia. Haley died of a heart attack on February 9, 1981.

—D.W.C.

"DON'T BE CRUEL," Otis Blackwell and Elvis Presley (1956)
"HOUND DOG," Jerry Lieber and Mike Stoller (1952)

"Don't Be Cruel" and "Hound Dog" are synonymous with Elvis Presley and rocketed his career into the stratosphere in the fifties, yet few people know of the songs' histories or composers.

Otis Blackwell, a struggling New York songwriter, wrote "Don't Be Cruel" and sold it along with five other tunes for twenty-five dollars apiece to Shalimar, a music publisher. "Don't Be Cruel" entered rock history and the other five vanished into obscurity. When Elvis showed interest in the song, his new manager, Colonel Tom Parker, would allow him to record it only if Blackwell agreed to share writing and publishing royalties. At the time Blackwell had no idea who Elvis Presley was. Moe Gayle, Shalimar's co-owner, convinced Blackwell that the possibility of half the royalties of a hit with Elvis was better than not recording it at all.

Blackwell may also have been an unwitting but important influence on Elvis's style. Those who have heard his demonstration disks of "Don't Be Cruel" claim that there is a remarkable similarity to Elvis's recording, right down to the quivering passion and vocal inflections. The theory is plausible, since Elvis's musicians could not read music and had to follow the demo disk note for note when they recorded the song.

In his lifetime, Blackwell wrote more than 900 songs, including "All Shook Up" and "Return to Sender" for Elvis, and "Breathless" and "Great Balls of Fire" for Jerry Lee Lewis.

"Hound Dog" was written by Jerry Lieber and Mike Stoller, a Los Angeles songwriting team, specifically for Willie Mae "Big Mama" Thornton, a popular blues artist. Her recording of the song went to number one on the rhythm and blues charts in 1953. A group called Freddie Bell and the Bellboys later did a humorous take on the number, which Elvis happened to hear during his first appearance in Las Vegas after he released "Heartbreak Hotel." Elvis thought their version was hilarious and began to include it in his act. Afterward, no one remembered that the original song was about a gigolo.

Elvis introduced "Hound Dog" to the United States on Milton Berle's TV show in June 1956 and caused a nationwide scandal with his pelvic gyrations. Ed Sullivan, whose Sunday-night variety show was the undisputed champion, declared that Presley would never be allowed on, and Elvis performed on other TV shows including Steve Allen's instead. In order to avoid controversy, Allen tried to tame Elvis's wild image by having him appear dressed in white tie and tails. Elvis took it in stride, even though he was reduced to singing "Hound Dog" to a live basset hound while standing perfectly still. Elvis's fans hated Allen's attempt to change Elvis, but the show beat Sullivan in the ratings. Sullivan relented and paid Elvis $50,000 for three appearances—an unheard of amount at the time. When Elvis performed "Hound Dog" and "Don't Be Cruel" on September 9, 1956, an estimated 54 million viewers (a third of the U.S. population) tuned in. Elvis sang "Hound Dog" and "Don't Be Cruel," among other numbers, on all three of his Sullivan appearances.

After "Hound Dog," Lieber and Stoller continued to write hits, including "Kansas City" and "Jailhouse Rock." It could have been otherwise. Mike Stoller and his wife were returning from Europe aboard the liner *Andrea Doria* when it was rammed and sunk by the Swedish ship *Stockholm*. They escaped in a lifeboat and were rescued at sea. Jerry Lieber, frantic with worry, rushed to the docks to meet the freighter that brought the survivors home. Upon finding the Stollers, a relieved Lieber exclaimed, "Elvis Presley recorded 'Hound Dog!' "

"Don't Be Cruel" was originally released as the "B" side of "Hound Dog" but proved more popular and was number one for eleven weeks on the charts, while "Hound Dog" followed at number two. The double-sided hit went on to become the number one record of 1956 and sold more than 5 million copies in the United States alone.

—D.W.C.

"THE SOUND OF MUSIC," Richard Rodgers and Oscar Hammerstein II (1959)

Title song of the musical play and film, "The Sound of Music" was composed by Richard Rodgers with lyrics by Oscar Hammerstein II. The stage production, which opened on November 16, 1959, was a remarkably successful audience pleaser. On Broadway it ran for more than three years—1,443 performances to be exact—and was still playing on the London stage when the film version premiered in 1965.

Taken from Maria Augusta Trapp's autobiography, the play and the movie were romanticized and inaccurate versions of the life of the Trapp family of Austria. Maria, a novice at the Nonnberg Abbey, was sent to be the governess for the seven children of the widower Baron Georg von Trapp. She and the much-decorated naval captain fell in love, married, and with the help of their priest and friend, Father Franz Wasner, formed a choral ensemble. Known as the Trapp Family Choir, they performed throughout Europe. After the takeover of their country by Hitler's Third Reich in 1938, the Trapp family was forced to flee from their Austrian estate.

The fade-in of the play presents a forested mountainside with Maria in her nun's habit sitting under a tree, looking out dreamily and regretting that her day has come to an end. She sings the title song, describing her surroundings as being filled with "the sound of music" and portraying her heart as wanting to sing all the songs it hears.

Hammerstein's lyrics flow easily; he uses a simple vocabulary, colloquialisms, and everyday catchphrases. As he once wrote, "A rhyme should be unassertive, never stand out too noticeably."

The Sound of Music was a cross between an operetta and a musical play. It had an abundance of tenderness, sweetness, and innocence, and because of its sentimentality, it has been labeled old-fashioned. Most critics praised the musical score. But Walter Kerr wrote in the *Herald Tribune:* "The show is handsome ... and it is going to be popular ... but before [it] is halfway through its promising chores, it becomes not only too sweet for words but almost too sweet for music." Despite such criticism, *The Sound of Music* was what the public wanted to see and hear. It proved what Richard Rodgers had often said about the only smart people in show business being the audiences.

It was a triumph that the lyricist shared for only a brief time: Oscar Hammerstein II died on August 23, 1960. That night all the theaters on Broadway and in London's West End dimmed their lights for three minutes. The stage production with Mary Martin won six Tony Awards, including the one for best musical score. When the film version starring Julie Andrews came out in 1965, it set a gross receipts record of $66 million and the soundtrack album went gold that same year.

—B.S.

> Come mothers and fathers,
> Throughout the land
> And don't criticize
> What you can't understand.
> Your sons and your daughters
> Are beyond your command
> Your old road is
> Rapidly agin'
> Please get out of the new one
> If you can't lend your hand
> For the times they are a-changin'!
>   Bob Dylan, "The Times They Are A-Changing,"
>   1964

"YESTERDAY," John Lennon and Paul McCartney (1965)

"Yesterday," one of the most-recorded songs in music history, with more than 2,500 cover versions, was originally known as "Scrambled Eggs." According to composer Paul McCartney, the music came to him shortly after waking one morning. He simply ambled over to his bedside piano and played the chords. For a long time, however, the only lyrics he had were, "Scrambled eggs / Oh, how I loved your legs."

The song was the first solo single by one of the Beatles and the first to be backed by strings. McCartney recorded it alone with a guitar in the Abbey Road studios in 1965. Producer George Martin suggested the addition of a string quartet. Although McCartney thought the idea was ludicrous, he allowed Martin to work out the arrangement and was pleased with the result. It was the first step toward more complex and sophisticated musical arrangements that became Beatles hallmarks with the albums *Rubber*

Soul, Revolver, and *Sgt. Pepper's Lonely Hearts Club Band.*

Although "Yesterday" was written in its entirety by McCartney, Lennon shared songwriting credits through a prior agreement. "Yesterday" signaled the beginning of the end of Lennon and McCartney's collaborative songwriting efforts. Although the pair continued to write together, each became more interested in following his own musical direction. In April 1970 McCartney released his first solo album, one month before the release of the Beatles' *Let It Be.* Later that same year Lennon and McCartney formally dissolved the most successful band in rock history.

In 1984 McCartney wanted to use "Yesterday" in his film *Give My Regards to Broad Street,* but he had to apply to the publishers, since he no longer held the copyright to the song. "Yesterday," along with much of the rest of the Beatles' catalog, is owned by pop star Michael Jackson.

—D.W.C.

DR. DEMENTO'S STRANGEST SONGS OF THE TWENTIETH CENTURY

The private collection of more than 200,000 records of radio personality Dr. Demento is said to be one of the world's largest. He puts his library of disks to use on *The Dr. Demento Show,* which is heard on 200 radio stations in the United States and on the Armed Forces Radio Network. From his collection, he has chosen the century's strangest songs.

"Destruction of San Francisco" (1900s): The century's first decade was also the phonograph's first decade as a true mass medium. Along with operatic excerpts, concert band selections, and the pop hits of the day, record makers turned out numerous so-called descriptive records. These used dialogue, music, and sound effects to paint humorous audio pictures of such colorful scenes as a hair-raising ride on an early-day automobile, or those described in "Passing of a Circus Parade" and "The Dog Fight" (this was twenty years before radio or sound movies became part of American life). The great San Francisco earthquake of 1906 inspired Columbia Records to alter the formula and produce one of the very few serious "descriptive" disks. Like the others, it uses music (serene at the start, a little mock Wagner for the quake and fire, a funeral dirge at the end), sound effects, and dialogue ("It's an earthquake, run for your lives! The city is in flames. . . . Shoot every man caught plundering!"). It's unreal, in every sense of the word.

World War I songs (1910s): "I Didn't Raise My Boy to Be a Soldier," the pacifist anthem that hit number one in 1915, was rudely swept off to oblivion as Tin Pan Alley celebrated America's 1916 entry into the war with the greatest barrage of military pop songs ever known. There were literally hundreds—"We're All Going Calling On the Kaiser," "Just Like Washington Crossed the Delaware (General Pershing Will Cross the Rhine)," "When I Send You a Picture of Berlin," "When Alexander Takes His Ragtime Band to France," "We Don't Want the Bacon (What We Want Is a Piece of the Rhine)," and the only one anybody remembers today, "Over There." There was one more good one just after the Armistice— "How Ya Gonna Keep 'Em down on the Farm (After They've Seen Paree)." How prophetic that would turn out to be.

"Yes, We Have No Bananas" (1920s): The year 1923 produced a vintage crop of humorous hits—"Barney Google," "I Love Me," "Old King Tut"—but the biggest and most peculiar of all was "Yes, We Have No Bananas." This song, which gleefully mocked the broken English of a Greek-American fruit-stand owner, sold millions of records and music sheets alike without a whisper of protest about political incorrectness. (Admittedly it wasn't quite up there, or down there, with the "coon" songs that ran rampant around the turn of the century, with their outrageous stereotypes of African Americans. One of those, "The Preacher and the Bear" [1905], was the first phonograph record ever to sell a million copies.)

"Gloomy Sunday" (1930s): Many of the pop songs that came our way during the Great Depression were cheerful, optimistic, escapist— "We're in the Money" was far more typical, if less truthful, than "Brother, Can You Spare a Dime." Just as we were well on the way to recovery, though, "Gloomy Sunday," the Famous Hungarian Suicide Song (as it was advertised on some record labels) arrived in America, with a reputation for having actually increased the suicide rate in its native land. Billie Holiday's is the best-known rendition today, but it's basso profundo Paul Robeson's performance that truly plumbs the depths. The alternative-rock angstmeisters so popular in the 1990s sound positively joyful by comparison.

"Huggin' and Chalkin' " (1940s): In a close race, our prize for delightful strangeness (not to mention political incorrectness) in this decade goes to "Huggin' and Chalkin' "—the 1947 number one hit about a woman so large she could be hugged only in sections, as the hugger kept track of his progress by making chalk marks on her person. Runners-up include that genealogical puzzle in song "I'm My Own Grandpaw," Slim Gaillard's eloquent nonsense "Cement Mixer" (later hilariously rendered by Liberace), and "Jesus Hits Like the Atom Bomb."

"George" (1950s): Two lovers stroll through the park, accompanied by George, a person of unspecified age who promptly falls into a brook and drowns, leaving the pair to do what lovers do. One hates to give away the ending, because this pop ballad is sung so sweetly and nonchalantly by Dolores Hawkins on her 1955 recording that you might not even notice its *Twilight Zone* creepiness the first time through.

"They're Coming to Take Me Away, Ha-Haaa!" (1960s): Jerry Samuels was a moderately successful songwriter and journeyman piano-bar entertainer until the Great Muse of Strangeness snuck up behind him and whacked him upside the head. In a one-and-a-half-hour 1966 recording session, Jerry created the greatest, most succinct song about mental illness ever invented by man, which Warner Brothers Records promptly bought and released under the name "Napoleon XIV." His follow-up album was a low-budget hoot, but Warner Brothers wouldn't touch his next LP, a serious (and brilliant) concept album about insanity. Soon it was back to the piano bars for Jerry—but there's a happy ending. Positioning himself splendidly for the graying of America, Jerry is now a booking agent specializing in entertainers for convalescent homes.

"Boogie Woogie Amputee" (1970s): "I love to dance with Peg Leg Sue / She's got one and I got

two!" Handicapped parking spaces were just becoming familiar when Barnes and Barnes released this lively dance-rocker on a 1979 single. Barnes and Barnes are quite a story in themselves: the duo consists of former child actor Bill(y) Mumy (he was little red-headed Will Robinson in *Lost In Space*) and keyboardist-singer Robert Haimer. Their 1978 "Fish Heads" is the all-time most-requested song on the Dr. Demento Show.

"A Blind Man's Penis" (1980s): You've seen the little ads in pulp magazines . . . "WE WILL SET YOUR SONG POEMS TO MUSIC, HAVE THEM RECORDED BY TOP HOLLYWOOD ARTISTS AND DISTRIBUTED TO RADIO STATIONS." In the process of separating Middle America's more gullible amateur songwriters from their hard-earned cash, these operators have created more than their share of strangeness. As an experiment, radical singer-songwriter-provocateur John Trubee wrote a lovely song poem one day, with the refrain "A blind man's penis is erect because he's blind," and sent it off to one of those advertisers with a check. The cassette he got in return became the strangest indie-label 45 rpm of 1983 and, probably, the decade.

"Rudy Rudy" (1990s): Strangeness doesn't have the novelty value it used to have, now that singers and bands whose only discernible talent *is* strangeness routinely get CDs and tapes released. Sublime strangeness still comes from unexpected places, though. "Rudy Rudy" by Harry Jeremy (1992) starts out as a cheerful, affectionate ode to "the dog of my childhood." As the singer goes on to describe Rudy's fatal encounter with a truck, the dog's gruesome, lingering death, and its ghoulish aftermath in excruciating detail, his cheerful demeanor never changes, nor does the song's jaunty melody and bouncy beat.

BEST-SELLING BOOKS OF THE TWENTIETH CENTURY

HARDCOVER, FICTION

1900 *To Have and to Hold*, Mary Johnston
1901 *The Crisis*, Winston Churchill
1902 *The Virginian*, Owen Wister
1903 *Lady Rose's Daughter*, Mary Augusta Ward
1904 *The Crossing*, Winston Churchill
1905 *The Marriage of William Ashe*, Mary Augusta Ward
1906 *Coniston*, Winston Churchill
1907 *The Lady of the Decoration*, Frances Little
1908 *Mr. Crewe's Career*, Winston Churchill
1909 *The Inner Shrine*, anonymous (Basil King)

1910 *The Rosary*, Florence Charlesworth Barclay
1911 *The Broad Highway*, John Jeffery Farnol
1912 *The Harvester*, Gene Stratton Porter
1913 *The Inside of the Cup*, Winston Churchill
1914 *The Eyes of the World*, Harold Bell Wright
1915 *The Turmoil*, Booth Tarkington
1916 *Seventeen*, Booth Tarkington
1917 *Mr. Britling Sees It Through*, H. G. Wells
1918 *The U.P. Trail*, Zane Grey
1919 *The Four Horsemen of the Apocalypse*, Vicente Blasco-Ibáñez
1920 *The Man of the Forest*, Zane Grey

Sinclair Lewis, author of Main Street, Babbitt, Arrowsmith, *and* Elmer Gantry.

1921 *Main Street*, Sinclair Lewis
1922 *If Winter Comes*, A. S. M. Hutchinson
1923 *Black Oxen*, Gertrude Horn Atherton
1924 *So Big*, Edna Ferber
1925 *Soundings*, Arthur Hamilton Gibbs
1926 *The Private Life of Helen of Troy*, John Erskine
1927 *Elmer Gantry*, Sinclair Lewis
1928 *The Bridge of San Luis Rey*, Thornton Wilder
1929 *All Quiet on the Western Front*, Erich Maria Remarque
1930 *Cimarron*, Edna Ferber
1931 *The Good Earth*, Pearl S. Buck
1932 *The Good Earth*, Pearl S. Buck
1933 *Anthony Adverse*, Hervey Allen
1934 *Anthony Adverse*, Hervey Allen
1935 *Green Light*, Lloyd C. Douglas
1936 *Gone with the Wind*, Margaret Mitchell

I'm tired of everlasting being unnatural and never doing anything I want to do. I'm tired of acting like I don't eat more than a bird, and walking when I want to run and saying I feel faint after a waltz, when I could dance for two days and never get tired. I'm tired of saying, "How wonderful you are!" to fool men who haven't got one-half the sense I've got and I'm tired of pretending I don't know anything, so men can tell me things and feel important while they're doing it.

Scarlett O'Hara in Margaret Mitchell's
Gone with the Wind, 1936

1937 *Gone with the Wind*, Margaret Mitchell
1938 *The Yearling*, Marjorie Kinnan Rawlings
1939 *The Grapes of Wrath*, John Steinbeck
1940 *How Green Was My Valley*, Richard Llewellyn
1941 *The Keys of the Kingdom*, A. J. Cronin
1942 *The Song of Bernadette*, Franz Werfel
1943 *The Robe*, Lloyd C. Douglas
1944 *Strange Fruit*, Lillian Smith
1945 *Forever Amber*, Kathleen Winsor
1946 *The King's General*, Daphne du Maurier
1947 *The Miracle of the Bells*, Russell Janney
1948 *The Big Fisherman*, Lloyd C. Douglas
1949 *The Egyptian*, Mika Waltari
1950 *The Cardinal*, Henry Morton Robinson
1951 *From Here to Eternity*, James Jones
1952 *The Silver Chalice*, Thomas B. Costain
1953 *The Robe*, Lloyd C. Douglas
1954 *Not as a Stranger*, Morton Thompson
1955 *Marjorie Morningstar*, Herman Wouk
1956 *Don't Go Near the Water*, William Brinkley
1957 *By Love Possessed*, James Gould Cozzens
1958 *Doctor Zhivago*, Boris Pasternak
1959 *Exodus*, Leon Uris
1960 *Advise and Consent*, Allen Drury
1961 *The Agony and the Ecstasy*, Irving Stone
1962 *Ship of Fools*, Katherine Anne Porter
1963 *The Shoes of the Fisherman*, Morris L. West
1964 *The Spy Who Came in from the Cold*, John Le Carré
1965 *The Source*, James A. Michener
1966 *Valley of the Dolls*, Jacqueline Susann
1967 *The Arrangement*, Elia Kazan
1968 *Airport*, Arthur Hailey
1969 *Portnoy's Complaint*, Philip Roth
1970 *Love Story*, Erich Segal
1971 *Wheels*, Arthur Hailey
1972 *Jonathon Livingston Seagull*, Richard Bach
1973 *Jonathon Livingston Seagull*, Richard Bach
1974 *Centennial*, James A. Michener
1975 *Ragtime*, E. L. Doctorow
1976 *Trinity*, Leon Uris
1977 *The Silmarillion*, J. R. R. Tolkien
1978 *Chesapeake*, James A. Michener
1979 *The Matarese Circle*, Robert Ludlum
1980 *The Covenant*, James A. Michener
1981 *Noble House*, James Clavell
1982 *E.T. The Extra-Terrestrial Storybook*, William Kotzwinkle
1983 *Return of the Jedi Storybook*, adapted by Joan D. Vinge
1984 *The Talisman*, Stephen King and Peter Straub
1985 *The Mammoth Hunters*, Jean M. Auel
1986 *It*, Stephen King
1987 *The Tommyknockers*, Stephen King
1988 *The Cardinal of the Kremlin*, Tom Clancy
1989 *Clear and Present Danger*, Tom Clancy
1990 *The Plains of Passage*, Jean M. Auel

1991 *Scarlett: The Sequel to Margaret Mitchell's "Gone with the Wind,"* Alexandra Ripley
1992 *Dolores Claiborne,* Stephen King
1993 *The Bridges of Madison County,* Robert James Waller
1994 *The Chamber,* John Grisham
1995 *The Rainmaker,* John Grisham

HARDCOVER, NONFICTION

1912 *The Promised Land,* Mary Antin
1913 *Crowds,* Gerald Stanley Lee
1914–16 Records not kept
1917 *Rhymes of a Red Cross Man,* Robert W. Service
1918 *Rhymes of a Red Cross Man,* Robert W. Service
1919 *The Education of Henry Adams,* Henry Adams
1920 *Now It Can Be Told,* Philip Gibbs
1921 *The Outline of History,* H. G. Wells
1922 *The Outline of History,* H. G. Wells
1923 *Etiquette,* Emily Post
1924 *Diet and Health,* Lulu Hunt Peters
1925 *Diet and Health,* Lulu Hunt Peters
1926 *The Man Nobody Knows,* Bruce Barton
1927 *The Story of Philosophy,* Will Durant
1928 *Disraeli,* André Maurois
1929 *The Art of Thinking,* Ernest Dimnet
1930 *The Story of San Michele,* Axel Munthe
1931 *Education of a Princess,* Marie, Grand Duchess of Russia
1932 *The Epic of America,* James Truslow Adams
1933 *Life Begins at Forty,* Walter B. Pitkin
1934 *While Rome Burns,* Alexander Woollcott
1935 *North to the Orient,* Anne Morrow Lindbergh
1936 *Man the Unknown,* Alexis Carrel
1937 *How to Win Friends and Influence People,* Dale Carnegie
1938 *The Importance of Living,* Lin Yutang
1939 *Days of Our Years,* Pierre van Paassen
1940 *I Married Adventure,* Osa Johnson
1941 *Berlin Diary,* William L. Shirer
1942 *See Here, Private Hargrove,* Marion Hargrove
1943 *Under Cover,* John Roy Carlson
1944 *I Never Left Home,* Bob Hope
1945 *Brave Men,* Ernie Pyle
1946 *The Egg and I,* Betty MacDonald
1947 *Peace of Mind,* Joshua Loth Liebman
1948 *Crusade in Europe,* Dwight D. Eisenhower
1949 *White Collar Zoo,* Clare Barnes Jr.
1950 *Betty Crocker's Picture Cook Book*
1951 *Look Younger, Live Longer,* Gayelord Hauser
1952 *The Holy Bible: Revised Standard Version*
1953 *The Holy Bible: Revised Standard Version*
1954 *The Holy Bible: Revised Standard Version*
1955 *Gift from the Sea,* Anne Morrow Lindbergh
1956 *Arthritis and Common Sense,* Dan Dale Alexander

1957 *Kids Say the Darndest Things!* Art Linkletter
1958 *Kids Say the Darndest Things!* Art Linkletter
1959 *'Twixt Twelve and Twenty,* Pat Boone
1960 *Folk Medicine,* D. C. Jarvis
1961 *The New English Bible: The New Testament*
1962 *Calories Don't Count,* Dr. Herman Taller
1963 *Happiness Is a Warm Puppy,* Charles M. Schulz
1964 *Four Days,* American Heritage and United Press International
1965 *How to Be a Jewish Mother,* Dan Greenburg
1966 *How to Avoid Probate,* Norman F. Dacey
1967 *The Death of a President,* William Manchester
1968 *Better Homes and Gardens New Cook Book*
1969 *American Heritage Dictionary of the English Language,* William Morris, editor
1970 *Everything You Wanted to Know about Sex but Were Afraid to Ask,* David Reuben, M.D.
1971 *The Sensuous Man,* "M"
1972 *The Living Bible,* Kenneth Taylor
1973 *The Living Bible,* Kenneth Taylor
1974 *The Total Woman,* Marabel Morgan
1975 *Angels: God's Secret Agents,* Billy Graham
1976 *The Final Days,* Bob Woodward and Carl Bernstein
1977 *Roots,* Alex Haley
1978 *If Life Is a Bowl of Cherries—What Am I Doing in the Pits?* Erma Bombeck
1979 *Aunt Erma's Cope Book,* Erma Bombeck
1980 *Crisis Investing: Opportunities and Profits in the Coming Great Depression,* Douglas R. Casey
1981 *The Beverly Hills Diet,* Judy Mazel
1982 *Jane Fonda's Workout Book,* Jane Fonda
1983 *In Search of Excellence: Lessons from America's Best-Run Companies,* Thomas J. Peters and Robert H. Waterman Jr.
1984 *Iacocca: An Autobiography,* Lee Iacocca with William Novak
1985 *Iacocca: An Autobiography,* Lee Iacocca with William Novak
1986 *Fatherhood,* Bill Cosby
1987 *Time Flies,* Bill Cosby
1988 *The 8-Week Cholesterol Cure,* Robert E. Kowalski
1989 *All I Really Need to Know I Learned in Kindergarten,* Robert Fulghum
1990 *A Life on the Road,* Charles Kuralt
1991 *Me: Stories of My Life,* Katharine Hepburn
1992 *The Way Things Ought to Be,* Rush Limbaugh
1993 *See I Told You So,* Rush Limbaugh
1994 *In the Kitchen with Rosie,* Rosie Daley
1995 *Men Are from Mars, Women Are from Venus,* John Gray

15 UNUSUAL BOOK TITLES FROM THE LIBRARY OF *THE PEOPLE'S ALMANAC*

1. *Old Age: Its Cause and Prevention,* by Sanford Bennett. New York: Physical Culture Publishing Co., 1912.
   Mr. Bennett, "the man who grew young at 70," also authored the book *Exercising in Bed.*

2. *Carnivorous Butterflies,* by Austin H. Clark. Washington, D.C.: U.S. Government Printing Office, 1926.

3. *I Knew 3,000 Lunatics,* by Victor R. Small. New York: Farrar and Rinehart, 1935.

4. *The Dynamics of Psychosomatic Dentistry,* by Joseph S. Landa. Brooklyn, N.Y.: Dental Items of Interest Publishing Co., 1953.

5. *My Duodenal Ulcer and I,* by "Dr. Stuart Morton." London: Christopher Johnson, 1955.
   Fans of this book might also enjoy the more grammatically satisfying *My Prostate and Me,* by William Martin (New York: Cadell and Davies, 1994).

6. *The Magic of Telephone Evangelism,* by Harold E. Metcalf. Atlanta, Ga.: Southern Union Conference, 1967.

7. *Practical Candle Burning,* by Raymond Buckland. St. Paul, Minn.: Llewellyn Publications, 1970.

8. *Your Destiny in Thumb: Indian Science of Thumb Reading,* by R. G. Rao. Bangalore, India: The Astrological Office, 1971.

9. *How to Rob Banks Without Violence,* by Roderic Knowles. London: Michael Joseph, 1972.

10. *Careers in Dope,* by Dan Waldorf. Englewood Cliffs, N.J.: Prentice-Hall, 1973.

11. *Learning from Salmon,* by Herman Aihara. Oroville, Calif.: George Ohsawa Macrobiotic Foundation, 1980.

12. *Sodomy and the Pirate Tradition,* by B. R. Burg. New York: New York University Press, 1984.

13. *Engineering for Potatoes,* by B. F. Cargill. St. Joseph, Mich.: American Society of Agricultural Engineers, 1986.

14. *How to Shit in the Woods,* by Kathleen Meyer. Berkeley, Calif.: Ten Speed Press, 1989.

15. *How to Become a Schizophrenic,* by John Modrow. Everett, Wash.: Apollyon Press, 1992.

—D.W.

19 CURIOUS HISTORIES AND ESOTERIC STUDIES FROM THE LIBRARY OF *THE PEOPLE'S ALMANAC*

1. *The Direction of Hair in Animals and Man,* by Walter Kidd. London: Adam and Charles Black, 1903.
   In his preface, Dr. Kidd states, "No doubt many of the phenomena here described are intrinsically uninteresting and unimportant." However, if you have ever yearned for a book that analyzes the direction in which hair grows on lions, oxen, dogs, apes, tapirs, humans, asses, anteaters, sloths, and other animals, you won't be disappointed.

2. *A Study of Splashes,* by A. M. Worthington. London: Longmans, Green, and Co., 1908.
   This pioneering classic makes use of 200 photographs to help answer the question "What actually happens when a drop falls and splashes?" Worthington's book was considered so valuable to students of physics that it was reissued as recently as 1963.

3. *Little-Known Sisters of Well-Known Men,* by Sarah G. Pomeroy. Boston: Dana Estes, 1912.
   A review of the lives of eight little-known sisters, including Sarianna Browning, Sarah Disraeli, and Sophia Thoreau, as well as two known sisters of English writers, Dorothy Wordsworth and Mary Lamb.

4. *The Quick Brown Fox,* by Richard G. Templeton Jr. Chicago: At the Sign of the Gargoyle, 1945.
   Thirty-three examples of sentences that include all twenty-six letters of the English alphabet. Included are classics such as "The quick brown fox jumps over the lazy dog" and "Pack my bags with five dozen liquor jugs," as well as the less well known "The July sun caused a fragment of black pine wax to ooze on the velvet quilt" and

"Very careful and exact knowledge should be emphasized in adjudging a quadrant."

5. *Paintings and Drawings on the Backs of National Gallery Pictures*, by Martin Davies. London: National Gallery Publications, 1946.
   A rare opportunity to view the flip side of forty-two famous works of art.

6. *The History and Romance of Elastic Webbing*, by Clifford A. Richmond. Easthampton, Mass.: Easthampton News Company, 1946.
   A lively account of the birth and growth of the elastic webbing industry in the nineteenth century. In the words of the author, once a man has "got the smell of rubber in his nostrils ... he either stays with rubber or is thereafter ever homesick to get back into the rubber industry."

7. *The One-Leg Resting Position (Nilotenstellung) in Africa and Elsewhere*, by Gerhard Lindblom. Stockholm: Statens Ethnografiska Museum, 1949.
   A survey of cultures in which people commonly rest while standing by placing one foot on or near the knee of the other leg. Contains fifteen photographs from Africa, Sri Lanka, Romania, Australia, and Bolivia, as well as a foldout locator map of Africa.

8. *The Ants of Colorado*, by Robert E. Gregg. Boulder, Colo.: University of Colorado Press, 1963.
   The author traveled 15,500 miles over a sixteen-year period in his search for the 165 kinds of ants that can be found within the borders of the state of Colorado. The book is 792 pages long and contains a locator map for each species and subspecies.

9. *Early United States Barbed Wire Patents*, by Jesse S. James. Maywood, Calif.: self-published, 1966.
   A definitive listing of 401 barbed wire patents filed between the years 1867 and 1897.

10. *Dirt: A Social History As Seen Through the Uses and Abuses of Dirt*, by Terence McLaughlin. New York: Stein and Day, 1971.
    Readers who are drawn to dirty books might also enjoy *Smut: An Anatomy of Dirt*, by Christian Engensberger (New York: Seabury, 1972); *The Kingdom of Dust*, by J. Gordon Ogden (Chicago: Popular Mechanics, 1912); and *All about Mud*, by Oliver R. Selfridge (Reading, Mass.: Addison-Wesley, 1978).

11. *Manhole Covers of Los Angeles*, by Robert and Mimi Melnick. Los Angeles: Dawson's Book Shop, 1974.
    Despite its title, this book's scope is not limited to manhole covers—it also deals with handhole covers, which provide access to valves and meter boxes. There are 144 photographs. The authors lament the standardization of manhole cover making, which has put an end to the creative designs of the early part of the century.

12. *Movie Stars in Bathtubs*, by Jack Scagnetti. Middle Village, N.Y.: Jonathan David Publishers, 1975.
    One hundred and fifty-six photographs of movie stars in bathtubs. There are also numerous shots of actors, actresses, and animals in showers and steambaths.

13. *America in Wax*, by Gene Gurney. New York: Crown Publishers, 1977.
    A complete guidebook to wax museums in the United States, with 678 illustrations, including Brigitte Bardot, Nikita Khrushchev, and the Battle of Yorktown.

14. *The Gender Trap*, by Chris Johnson and Cathy Brown with Wendy Nelson. London: Proteus, 1982.

Cathy (right), who once was a man named Eugene, and Chris (left), who once was a woman named Anne, with their daughter, Emma. After Emma's birth both parents changed sexes.

The autobiography of the world's first transsexual parents. Chris and Cathy began life as Anne and Eugene. Anne was a social worker who wished she was a man; Eugene was a Kung Fu instructor who wished he was a woman. They fell in love, Anne gave birth to a baby girl, Emma, and then Anne and Eugene switched sexes. Anne, now Chris, became Emma's father and Eugene, now Cathy, took over the role of mother.

15. *I Dream of Woody*, by Dee Burton. New York: William Morrow, 1984.

Burton presents the cases of seventy people from New York and Los Angeles who have dreamed about Woody Allen. Fans of books about people who dreamed about a famous person will also want to track down *Dreams About H. M. the Queen*, by Brian Masters (Frogmore, Saint Albans, Herts: Mayflower, 1973), a collection of dreams about Queen Elizabeth II and other members of the British royal family; and *I Dream of Madonna*, by Kay Turner (San Francisco: Collins, 1993).

16. *Out of Our Kitchen Closets: San Francisco Gay Jewish Cooking*. San Francisco: Congregation Sha'ar Zahav, 1987.

One hundred fifty recipes submitted by the members, families, and friends of a gay and lesbian synagogue. Seventeen of the recipes are for kugel.

17. *Misfits! The Cleveland Spiders in 1899*, by J. Thomas Hetrick. Jefferson, N.C.: McFarland and Co., 1991.

The 1899 Cleveland Spiders were the worst team in the history of major-league baseball. The Spiders got off to a bad start, winning only three of their first twenty-three games. Then they settled down to a terrible midseason streak before collapsing completely and losing forty of their last forty-one games. In a twelve-team league, the Spiders' final record of 20 wins and 134 losses left them thirty-five games behind the eleventh-place team. Their average home attendance was 150. In fact, fan support was so anemic that the Spiders gave up playing in Cleveland and played 113 of their games on the road.

18. *Sell Yourself to Science*, by Jim Hogshire. Port Townsend, Wash.: Loompanics Unlimited, 1992.

The subtitle says it all: *The Complete Guide to Selling Your Organs, Body Fluids, Bodily Functions, and Being a Human Guinea Pig*. If you are reasonably healthy, but have no job skills, this is the book for you. Hogshire explains how to earn $100 a day as a subject for drug studies and other scientific experiments, and how to sell your blood, sperm, hair, breast milk, and bone marrow.

19. *The Life and Cuisine of Elvis Presley*, by David Adler. New York: Crown, 1993.

In exquisite detail, Adler traces the evolution of what Elvis ate from the time he was a baby (corn bread soaked in buttermilk) through his years in the army, Las Vegas, Hollywood, and Graceland, and finally the bingeing that weakened his health. Elvis gobbled a dozen honey doughnuts in a cab before a visit to the White House and once ate five chocolate sundaes for breakfast before passing out. Included are recipes for fried squirrel, peanut butter and American cheese sandwich, and Elvis's last supper, which was actually ice cream and cookies.

—D.W.

POPULAR BROADWAY SHOWS
(PLUS ONE OFF-BROADWAY SHOW)

ABIE'S IRISH ROSE

by Anne Nichols
Opened May 23, 1922
2,327 performances
The Fulton Theatre
Directed by Laurence Marston
Produced by Anne Nichols
Cast: Robert B. Williams (Abraham Levy); Marie Carroll (Rosemary Murphy); Alfred Wiseman (Solomon Levy); John Cope (Patrick Murphy); Mathilde Cottrelly (Mrs. Isaac Cohen); Bernard Gorcey (Isaac Cohen); Howard Lang (Dr. Jacob Samuels); Harry Bradley (Father Whalen); Dorothy Grau (Flower Girl)

H. L. Mencken regarded this show as a potboiler, calling it "America's third-largest industry." The *New York Globe* labeled it "a dramatization of the Sunday comic strip." The *New York World* sneered that it had "not so much as a single line of honest writing." But *Abie's Irish*

Rose survived these critical putdowns to become the all-time record holder for long runs until *Tobacco Road* eclipsed it more than a decade later.

The comedy, which reviewers castigated for its simplistic characterizations and religious stereotyping, poked fun at interfaith intolerance with its story of a Jewish boy falling in love with a Catholic girl. They are initially married by a Protestant minister. To please their respective quarreling families, the couple is later entwined by both a Jewish rabbi and a Catholic priest. Between weddings, there are jokes about the eating habits and broken English of both clans. The play ends with the rabbi and the priest preaching harmony and the arrival of the couple's offspring—twins named Rebecca and Patrick Joseph.

Anne Nichols, a former actress, stated that she wrote the play to promote understanding between followers of different faiths. "My own people hated both the Jews and the Catholics," she told the *New York Times*. "When I was eleven years old I was spanked for giving a Catholic girl a prayer book of her Church for a birthday present. That explains why I knew something of religious intolerance."

She was determined to get her play on Broadway at any cost. *Abie* was first optioned by Oliver Morosco for a run in Los Angeles. When Morosco showed no signs of moving the California company to New York, Nichols mounted a Broadway production with her own funds. When Morosco sued to stop the rival East Coast *Abie*, Nichols countersued for nonpayment of royalties and control of the rights on the West Coast production. She eventually won, only to have her production greeted with hostility by the press.

To keep the show on, Nichols mortgaged her home, and the actors took a pay cut. An audience was gradually built up through word of mouth, giving Nichols the last laugh on the critics. She invited each of the reviewers who panned the opening to the closing 2,327th performance. An estimated 11 million people saw the comedy either on Broadway or in the dozens of cities around the world (including Shanghai) where it played.

But all was not rosy for *Abie*. In 1930 Nichols sued Universal Pictures for $3 million over what she saw were similarities between her play and the studio's *The Kellys and the Cohens*. In order to get the "official" version on celluloid, the author signed a contract with Adolph Zukor's Famous Players–Lasky Corporation for $300,000 in exchange for gaining the movie rights on the day the play reached a performance total of 2,000. It was filmed twice (1928 and 1946) with middling results. Again the critics blasted it, and this time audiences stayed away. A radio series based on the play aired in 1942.

Revivals in 1937 and 1954, both directed by Nichols, were unsuccessful because of the outmoded ethnic humor.

Nichols wanted to be remembered as more than the author of just one play. At one point she announced that a sequel to *Abie* was forthcoming, but she never finished it. Her subsequent output consists of a few forgotten comedies.

TOBACCO ROAD

by Jack Kirkland, based on the novel by Erskine Caldwell
Opened December 4, 1933
3,182 performances
The Masque Theatre
Directed and produced by Anthony Brown
Cast: Henry Hull (Jeeter Lester); Margaret Wycherly (Ada Lester); Maude Odell (Sister Bessie Rice); Sam Byrd (Dude Lester); Ruth Hunter (Ellie Mae); Patricia Quinn (Grandma Lester); Dean Jagger (Lov Bensey); Ashley Cooper (Henry Peabody); Reneice Rehan (Pearl); Lamar King (Captain Tim); Edwin Walter (George Payne)

A 1941 *New Yorker* cartoon shows an old couple sitting at home as a younger husband and wife get ready for a night on the town. The caption of the older man speaking to his spouse reads: "Mother, do you remember when we went to see *Tobacco Road*?" The longevity of Jack Kirkland's dramatization of Erskine Caldwell's steamy best-seller about dirt-poor Georgia sharecroppers was the subject of many such quips. Lorenz Hart even mentioned it in his lyrics for "Give It Back to the Indians," an ode to Manhattan Island.

Despite its later success, Kirkland had a difficult time getting the show produced. Although the language and actions of Jeeter Lester and his family of turnip eaters would be considered mild by audiences used to David Mamet and Sam Shepard, the producers of 1933 found the material too racy to risk their funds on. Kirkland finally had to do it himself. With his director, Anthony Brown, as producer, he spent his last $6,000 to make *Tobacco Road* a part of the Great White Way. (It eventually earned back almost a hundred times the original investment.) On the last night of Prohibition, *Tobacco Road* opened.

Like its record-breaking predecessor, *Abie's Irish Rose*, *Tobacco Road* received deprecating reviews. Brooks Atkinson of the *New York Times* called it "one of the grossest episodes ever put on the stage. The theatre has never sheltered a fouler or more degenerate parcel of folks." But he admitted it did leave a "vivid impression." Percy Hammond of the *New York Herald-Tribune* genteelly described it as a play "for those who get a naughty thrill from dark disclosures of the primitive human animal while writhing in the throes of gender." But all the critics praised Henry Hull's performance as Jeeter.

Initial receipts were so low at the box office that the landlord at the Masque Theatre forced the production to move. Business picked up at the show's new home, the 48th Street Theatre, when an editorial in the *Daily News* came out comparing the play to the works of Émile Zola and Theodore Dreiser for truthfully depicting the deplorable conditions of its characters.

Tobacco Road was now a succès de scandale, with the public flocking to see it, expecting obscenity. Another controversy helped the box office: During the first of many national tours, the mayor of Chicago attended a performance and immediately banned it from further showings there. People had to see what was so dirty that it couldn't be seen on the stage in a big city like Chicago. There were further censorship problems in Boston, New Orleans, and Atlanta. In Indiana City, Michigan, where the local fathers had forbidden the Jeeters from setting a bare foot in their town, the play was performed on a showboat moored just outside the jurisdiction of the local government. Despite, or maybe because of, these censorship problems, the various road tours played 327 cities, some returning as many as eight times.

The show even inspired congressional action, both praising and damning the production. Representative Charles Kramer of California asked for a congressional investigation of the economic conditions of citizens living in real-life tobacco roads, while Braswell Deen of Georgia attacked the play from the floor of the House while it was playing in Washington, D.C. He called the treatment of his home state "untruthful, undignified, undiplomatic, and unfair."

Meanwhile, back on Broadway, the New York company was doing so well that Kirkland was able to move it to the Forrest Theatre and take over the lease. It was an eventful eight-year run: an actress died in her dressing room during a performance, the playwright married a member of the company, and the box office was robbed at gunpoint.

The biggest backstage brouhaha involved James Barton, Henry Hull's successor in the lead role. Ironically, he was called before the board of Equity Actors Association for cursing at fellow cast members offstage and received an official reprimand from that union. Barton left the company soon after. The role was played on Broadway by five different actors, the last of whom was Will Geer, now best remembered as the grandfather on *The Waltons* television series.

Twentieth Century Fox released John Ford's film version in 1941. Charley Grapewin (who played Uncle Henry in *The Wizard of Oz*) was Jeeter. *Tobacco Road* reappeared on Broadway a total of four times.

LIFE WITH FATHER

by Howard Lindsay and Russel Crouse, based on the book by Clarence Day
Opened November 8, 1939
3,224 performances
The Empire Theatre
Directed by Bretaigne Windust
Produced by Oscar Serlin
Cast: Howard Lindsay (Father); Dorothy Stickney (Vinnie); John Drew Devereaux (Clarence); Teresa Wright (Mary); Richard Simon (John); Raymond Roe (Whitney); Larry Robinson (Harlan); Ruth Hammond (Cora); Richard Sterling (The Reverend Dr. Lloyd); Katherine Bard (Annie); Dorothy Bernard (Margaret); Portia Morrow (Delia); Nellie Burt (Nora); A. H. Van Buren (Dr. Humphreys); John C. King (Dr. Somers); Timothy Kearse (Maggie)

Among all the nonmusical long-run shows, *Life with Father* ranks as the record holder; its eight-year record still holds after nearly five decades. When you count the musicals, its record is still impressive. Only *A Chorus Line*, *Oh! Calcutta!*, *42nd Street*, *Grease*, *Fiddler on the Roof*, and *Cats* have run longer.

Like several later comedies (*My Sister Eileen*, *Junior Miss*), *Life with Father* first appeared on the pages of the *New Yorker* as a series of articles—Clarence Day's reminiscences of his growing up in Victorian-era New York centered on his crusty father ruling over his loving, cleverer wife and his four sons. Producer Oscar Serlin recognized the potential for a film or stage play in Day's pieces and obtained an option from the author's widow on the material.

Serlin first conceived of a Paramount film with W. C. Fields as Father. He commissioned a screenplay tailored to Fields's talents, but Mrs. Day, sensing that the bulbous-nosed comedian did not present the right image, nixed the project. Undaunted, Serlin brought the property to Howard Lindsay, who had read the Day articles to his wife, actress Dorothy Stickney, while her eyes were bad. Lindsay enthusiastically assented to tackling the assignment of adapting the material to the stage. He brought in Russel Crouse, his collaborator on the books of three previous musicals, including *Anything Goes*. Crouse had also written three books on the American Victorian era, so he was an expert on the period.

Without an advance from the producer or the Day family, Lindsay and Crouse spent two years on their stage adaptation, most of the time talking and working out the scenes. Nothing was committed to paper until it had been meticulously plotted beforehand. Unlike the Fields movie script, the new version proved to be satisfactory to the Day family, and production was allowed to proceed.

The first choice for the roles of Father and

Mother Day were Alfred Lunt and Lynn Fontanne, Broadway's most celebrated acting couple. While Lunt was enchanted with the idea of playing the blustering patriarch, the elegant Fontanne could not see herself as the mother, who hides her ability to manage Father behind an ingenuous persona. Walter Connolly, Roland Young, John Halliday, and Walter Huston also rejected the leading role. It finally fell to Lindsay himself to enact Father opposite his wife as Mother. This was not so undesirable, for the coauthor had wanted to play the role all along.

Investors were hard to come by. They couldn't imagine much mileage in the pleasant snapshot of family life in the 1880s. An offer came to mount the play at a summer theater in Skowhegan, Maine, but there was still no money. Lindsay was so determined to get *Life with Father* on and to act in it that he and Stickney mortgaged their home and anything of value they owned. After the summer-stock run, on a shoestring budget, enough backers were attracted to attempt a New York mounting.

Bretaigne Windust, who had made a hit with his staging of Robert E. Sherwood's drama *Idiot's Delight*, signed on as director. There were few cast changes from Skowhegan. A young Montgomery Clift almost played Clarence, but he was judged too sophisticated for the virginal eldest son, so John Drew Devereaux from the summer cast repeated the role. Mrs. Day was at all the rehearsals to ensure that the sacred memory of her husband's work was never compromised. As owner of 50 percent of the rights, she was also protecting her financial interests.

After a week's tryout in Baltimore, the show opened at the Empire Theatre on Broadway. Before the premiere, Lindsay remarked to Crouse, "We've got a nice little comedy here. We might even get six months out of it." What they got was one of the longest Broadway runs in history. At the closing performance, Lindsay and Stickney sent a telegram to the company reading "Better luck next time." In fact, in 1948 the authors penned a sequel entitled *Life with Mother*. The second play on the Days had a modest success and ran 265 performances.

William Powell starred with Irene Dunne in the 1947 film of the play with a young Elizabeth Taylor. A television series based on the play ran from 1953 to 1955, with Leon Ames and Lurene Tuttle as Father and Mother.

MY FAIR LADY

Book and lyrics by Alan Jay Lerner, based on the play *Pygmalion*, by George Bernard Shaw
Music by Frederick Loewe
Opened March 15, 1956
2,717 performances
Mark Hellinger Theatre

Julie Andrews and Rex Harrison in My Fair Lady.

Directed by Moss Hart
Choreographed by Hanya Holm
Produced by Herman Levin
Cast: Rex Harrison (Professor Henry Higgins); Julie Andrews (Eliza Doolittle); Stanley Holloway (Alfred P. Doolittle); Robert Coote (Colonel Pickering); Cathleen Nesbitt (Mrs. Higgins); John Michael King (Freddy Eynsford-Hill); Philippa Bevans (Mrs. Pearce); Viola Roache (Mrs. Eynsford-Hill); Cordon Dilworth (Harry/Lord Boxington); Ron McLennon (Jamie/Ambassador); Olive Reeves-Smith (Mrs. Hopkins/Lady Boxington); Christopher Hewett (Bystander/Zoltan Karpathy); David Thomas (Bartender); Reid Shelton (1st Cockney/Butler); Glenn Kezer (2nd Cockney); James Morris (3rd Cockney); Herb Surface (4th Cockney); Barton Mumaw (Chauffeur/Constable); Cathy Conklin (Flower Girl); Paul Brown (Flunkey); Maribel Hammer (Queen of Transylvania); Judith Williams (Mrs. Higgins's Maid)

Like so many other smash hits, *My Fair Lady* was not given a ghost of a chance by most Broadway professionals when it was first conceived. Many talents, such as Rodgers and Hammerstein and Noël Coward, had essayed musicalizing G. B. Shaw's *Pygmalion*. But it was Alan Jay Lerner and Frederick Loewe who, with a little bit of luck and lots of hard work, finally made Professor Henry Higgins and Eliza Doolittle dance all night—for six and a half years on Broadway and for almost forty around the world. Film producer Gabriel Pascal owned the rights to Shaw's plays and had made successful movies of many of them. He felt a musical version of *Pygmalion*—Shaw's story of an arrogant phonetics expert transforming a Cockney flower seller into a lady by changing her speech—would be a natural. The producer encountered Lerner while the lyricist was in Hollywood and hired him and Loewe to do the transformation. The team were later to find out why Rodgers and Hammerstein and Coward had given up on the project. The play is a non-love story.

Eliza leaves Higgins at the final curtain, and in an epilogue, Shaw made it clear that the former flower girl marries the foppish Freddy Eynsford-Hill. They also found it difficult to cut any of Shaw's brilliant dialogue and to move the action out of Higgins's study.

Lerner and Loewe dropped the project in 1952, and their partnership was temporarily severed. The death of Pascal brought the two together again. As a result of the producer's passing, the rights to *Pygmalion* were in question, and the pair were eventually able to acquire them. They met to recommence work on the musical version, solved the problems encountered during their first attempt by following the screenplay rather than the play, and altered the ending to have Eliza come back to Higgins.

For the role of the misogynist linguist, Lerner wanted Rex Harrison, an experienced Shavian actor. Mary Martin had initially expressed interest in playing Eliza, but when she heard what the team had written so far, she immediately concluded that they had lost their talent. Harrison was more pleased about the production, but he still had to be persuaded. The actor had little confidence in his singing voice. After promising to tailor the material to his talent, Lerner and Loewe finally got the actor to accept the role. For Eliza, they chose a new young star, eighteen-year-old Julie Andrews, who had made a hit in *The Boy Friend*, a parody of 1920s musicals, in London and New York.

Moss Hart, coauthor of many hits with George S. Kaufman and director of several smashes by others, as well as his own musical *Lady in the Dark*, was hired to stage the work, which was still titleless as the company was leaving for New Haven for tryouts. After rejecting *Liza* and *The Lady Liza*, the authors settled on the title that they hated least: *My Fair Lady*.

In New Haven Harrison's fear of singing resulted in his near refusal to go on for the opening night, but the star reluctantly did. *My Fair Lady* became an immediate success and went on to break *Oklahoma*'s record as the longest-running musical on Broadway (a distinction that it held for more than nine years). Like the New York edition, the touring company, originally with Brian Aherne and Anne Rogers, played for more than six years.

The show owes its longevity to the perfect marriage between the brilliant libretto and the sparkling score. Loewe's music was lush and romantic. Lerner's clever lyrics seemed to be an extension of Shaw's dialogue, and Harrison's caustic speak-singing of them established a new style of performing. Eliza was transformed from a dirt-smudged guttersnipe to an independent young woman and Andrews from an unknown to a Broadway star.

For the 1964 film version, producer Jack L. Warner insisted on internationally known performers, since movie musicals were becoming harder to sell. Cary Grant was his choice for Higgins and Audrey Hepburn for Eliza. Grant refused the role, stating he could never follow Rex Harrison, who then did play the role on screen. Andrews was not considered a large enough draw, so Hepburn was the movie Eliza (with vocals supplied by Marni Nixon). (As if to compensate for the loss, Andrews was immediately cast in the title role of Walt Disney's film musical *Mary Poppins*. While the Academy Awards that year graced *Lady* with eight Oscars, including best picture, and best actor for Harrison, Andrews got her revenge by winning best actress for *Poppins*.)

In addition to thousands of productions all over the world, *My Fair Lady* has had three Broadway revivals. Ian Richardson and Christine Andreas starred in the 1976 production, for which George Rose won a Tony as Eliza's father, Alfred P. Doolittle. Harrison returned to play Henry Higgins in 1981, with Nancy Ringham as Eliza and Milo O'Shea as Doolittle. Richard Chamberlain headlined a touring version that played Broadway in 1993–94.

THE FANTASTICKS

Book and lyrics by Tom Jones
Music by Harvey Schmidt
Opened off Broadway May 3, 1960
Still running (14,927 performances as of May 21, 1996)
Sullivan Street Playhouse
Directed by Word Baker
Produced by Lore Noto
Cast: Jerry Orbach (El Gallo); Rita Gardner (The Girl); Kenneth Nelson (The Boy); William Larsen (The Boy's Father); Hugh Thomas (The Girl's Father); Thomas Bruce (The Old Actor); George Curley (The Man Who Dies); Richard Stauffer (The Mute); Jay Hampton (The Handyman)

The longest-running musical either on or off Broadway—or anywhere in the world—is *The Fantasticks*, the charming show of romance and magic that opened at the Sullivan Street Playhouse in 1960 and is still going strong. The deceptively simple plot involves a pair of young lovers whose fathers pretend to quarrel in order to spur their offspring's union.

The story is derived from *Les Romanesques*, an 1894 play by Edmond Rostand, author of *Cyrano de Bergerac*. Harvey Schmidt and Tom Jones began adapting the piece into a one-act musical while they were both students at the University of Texas. Originally their adaptation was an elaborate extravaganza set on a Texas ranch, with the boy and the girl living on opposite sides of the Mexican border. It sported the ungainly title of *Joy Comes to Dead Horse*.

The collaborators were forced to rework the piece when *West Side Story* opened with its similar theme of a star-crossed romance. Fellow classmate Word Baker offered Jones and Schmidt the opportunity to mount their new version, called *The Fantasticks*, at Barnard College's Minor Latham Theatre. The new take on the material was presentational, as Baker conjured up the story with deliberate theatricality on a bare stage. Producer Lore Noto saw the show at Barnard and agreed to mount the production off-Broadway if it were expanded to two acts.

Critical reaction was lukewarm, and the production almost closed within a week, but good word of mouth kept the show open.

There have been at least 11,000 productions of *The Fantasticks* in the United States alone, as well as 700 foreign mountings in sixty-eight different countries. Some of the better-known names to have appeared in it are F. Murray Abraham, Anna Maria Alberghetti, Richard Chamberlain, Glenn Close, Bert Convy, Elliott Gould, Robert Goulet, Edward Everett Horton, Liza Minnelli, John Wood, and producer Noto, as well as author Jones (who played the role of the Old Actor under the name of Thomas Bruce).

A 1964 telecast on NBC's *Hallmark Hall of Fame* featured Ricardo Montalban, Bert Lahr, Stanley Holloway, Susan Watson (the original Luisa at Barnard), and John Davidson.

FIDDLER ON THE ROOF

Book by Joseph Stein, based on the stories by Sholom Aleichem
Music by Jerry Bock
Lyrics by Sheldon Harnick
Opened September 22, 1964
3,242 performances
Imperial Theatre
Directed and choreographed by Jerome Robbins
Produced by Harold Prince
Cast: Zero Mostel (Tevye); Maria Karnilova (Golde); Beatrice Arthur (Yente); Austin Pendelton (Motel Kamzoil); Joanna Merlin (Tzeitel); Julia Mignes (Hodel); Tanya Everett (Chava); Marilyn Rogers (Shprintze); Linda Ross (Bielke); Bert Convy (Perchik); Michael Granger (Lazar Wolf); Joe Ponazecki (Fyedka); Helen Verbit (Shandel); Zvee Scooler (Mord-

cha); Gluck Sandor (Rabbi); Leonard Frey (Mendel); Paul Lipson (Avram); Maurice Edwards (Nahum); Sue Babel (Grandma Tzeitel); Carol Sawyer (Fruma-Sarah); Mitch Thomas (Yussel); Joseph Sullivan (Constable); Robert Berdeen (Sasha); Gino Conforti (The Fiddler)

Zero Mostel followed his side-splitting Pseudolus in *A Funny Thing Happened on the Way to the Forum* with the long-suffering Tevye in *Fiddler on the Roof*. The musical retelling of Yiddish writer Sholom Aleichem's stories about the trials of Tevye the milkman in Czarist Russia ran for almost eight years. It was Broadway's longest-running show until 1979, when *Grease* slid by *Fiddler*'s record. Mostel explained *Fiddler*'s longevity in a *New York Times* interview: "Tevye is universal. He has no nationality really, because he symbolizes the underprivileged in every country—no matter what adversity he meets, he just puffs up his chest and goes on."

The show opens with the cast extolling the importance of "tradition" in their little Jewish Orthodox community of Anatevka. But as the tale unfolds, Tevye, his family, and the entire village are bereft of their way of life. Three of Tevye's five daughters marry against Orthodox customs. At one of the weddings, tradition is broken as men dance with women. Near the final curtain, a government official announces that the town will be destroyed in a pogrom and that every Jew must leave the country. As the townspeople are scattered, Tevye and his family hope for a new life in America.

Mostel lightened the dark mood with comic conversations with God ("With your help, I'm starving to death," he complains to the deity). The songs "If I Were a Rich Man," "Matchmaker, Matchmaker," "Sunrise, Sunset," and "Do You Love Me!" proved hits. Jerome Robbins's staging of a hilarious dream sequence and a bottle dance were highlights.

The idea for the show was born with composer Jerry Bock, lyricist Sheldon Harnick, and librettist Joseph Stein, who had collaborated on *The Body Beautiful* (1958), a boxing musical. The songwriters wanted to work with Stein again and suggested that they adapt *Wandering Star*, a novel by Aleichem.

Stein told the *New York World-Telegram*, "I didn't like it for a musical. But it joggled my memory. When I was a child in the Bronx, my father used to read to me Sholom Aleichem's short stories about Tevye and his daughters. I suggested the stories, and Jerry and Sheldon were intrigued. We decided not to approach a producer until we were finished. We were in love with it, but weren't sure it would work. It was pure speculation and pure affection." This would not be the first time Tevye had appeared in theatrical form. A Yiddish theater production entitled *Tevye the Dairyman* had opened in

1935 and was filmed in 1939. *Tevye and His Daughters* had appeared in 1957.

Once a script was finished, producer Fred Coe optioned the show but had trouble raising the necessary capital. Then Harold Prince, director and producer of Bock and Harnick's *She Loves Me*, stepped in as coproducer. When the partnership didn't work out, Prince bought out Coe's interest and became sole producer.

Before rehearsals began, the title was changed from *Tevye and His Daughters* to *Fiddler on the Roof*, inspired by Marc Chagall's surrealist painting in which a fiddler soars over a small eastern European town. Boris Aronson's stylized set also reflected Chagall's influence.

For the vital role of Tevye, stars such as Danny Kaye, Danny Thomas, Tom Bosley, and Howard Da Silva were considered. Prince wanted Mostel. Despite the actor's hijinks during the run of *Forum*, the producer was sure Mostel was the right candidate. Mostel drew critical raves and won another Tony Award, but he continued to mug and ad-lib during his nine-month tenure. When his contract was up, he was followed by six Tevyes: Luther Adler, Herschel Bernardi, Harry Goz, Jerry Jarrett, Jan Peerce, and Paul Lipson, with no slackening at the box office. Bette Midler and Pia Zadora appeared as two of Tevye's daughters during the Broadway run. The national tour was headlined by Luther Adler.

Mostel returned to the role in a national tour that stopped in New York in 1976. Topol, who played Tevye in the London production and the 1971 film, starred in a 1990 revival.

OH! CALCUTTA!

Devised by Kenneth Tynan
Sketches by Samuel Beckett, Jules Feiffer, Dan Greenberg, John Lennon, Jacques Levy, Leonard Melfi, David Newman and Robert Benton, Sam Shepard, Clovis Trouille, Kenneth Tynan, and Sherman Yellen
Music and lyrics by The Open Window (Robert Dennis, Peter Schickele, and Stanley Walden)
Opened February 26, 1971
610 performances, after a run of 704 performances off Broadway
Belasco Theatre
Directed by Jacques Levy
Choreographed by Margo Sappington
Produced by Hillard Elkins
Cast: Mel Auston, Raina Barrett, Ray Edelstein, Samantha Harper, Patricia Hawkins, William Knight, Mitchell McGuire, Pamela Pilkenton, Gary Rethmeier, Nancy Tribush

"Some time ago," wrote the British theater critic Kenneth Tynan in the *Village Voice*, "it occurred to me that there was no place for a civilized man to take a civilized woman to spend an evening of civilized erotic stimulation. At one end there's burlesque, at the other an expensive nightclub, but no place in between. We're trying to fill the gap with this show." The show Tynan was referring to is *Oh! Calcutta!*, the world's longest-running erotic musical. For the sexually explicit revue, Tynan solicited contributors from such diverse writers as the Nobel Prize–winning Samuel Beckett, former Beatle John Lennon, cartoonist Jules Feiffer, and playwright Sam Shepard.

"He said that we could write about anything in the world within the realm of sexuality," David Newman, one of the contributors, told *Time* magazine. "The only other caveat was that our piece should have absolutely no redeeming social value." The songs were by a group called The Open Window (Robert Dennis, Peter Schickele, and Stanley Walden); Schickele had achieved fame by spoofing classical music in his P.D.Q. Bach concerts.

Not only did the skits deal frankly with such sexual matters as masturbation, wife swapping, and fetishes, but the production also featured frontal nudity. The cast of *Hair* had briefly flashed their birthday suits for a few dimly lit moments at the end of their first act. *Calcutta* opened with the eight-member cast standing downstage in full lighting and in bathrobes, then stripping down so that their only costumes were dimples and freckles.

The show opened off-Broadway on June 17, 1969, at the Eden Theatre, with a cast that included Bill Macy, Alan Rachins, and the choreographer Margo Sappington.

The critics found the revue tasteless and gratuitous. Clive Barnes of the *Times* sneered, "Voyeurs of the city unite. You have nothing to lose but your brains." But audiences were attracted by the enormous publicity surrounding this first-ever legitimate production featuring extensive nudity. After a run of 704 performances, *Oh! Calcutta!* moved to Broadway's Belasco Theatre, where it continued for another 610 performances.

Then, in September of 1976, Norman Kean, general manager for the original production, revived the show. Kean's strategy was to attract tourists visiting New York for the nation's bicentennial celebrations. The new *Calcutta!* opened at the Edison Theatre, a converted ballroom in the Edison Hotel, playing in repertory with *Me and Bessie*, a revue starring Linda Hopkins as blues singer Bessie Smith. *Me and Bessie* closed that December, but *Calcutta!* continued 5,959 times, for the second-longest run in Broadway history. Because it was sometimes performed ten or eleven times a week, as opposed to the traditional eight common to most shows, for a while *Calcutta!* had more performances racked up than any other show on the main stem, including *A Chorus Line*. (*Chorus Line* closed after the nudie revue to claim the title of longest run.)

Tourists, mainly those from Japan, where onstage nudity was forbidden, became the main audience for *Calcutta!* during its phenomenally long life. Kean played to this market by advertising in Japanese publications and offering a simultaneous Japanese translation, and by providing translations of the sketches in nine languages.

Business began to fall off in the late 1980s. For one thing, the specter of AIDS dampened the fun of the show's licentious humor. There were also waves of negative publicity, understandably, when producer Kean murdered his wife, actress Gwyda DonHowe, and then leaped to his death from their apartment. The final blow came when the Japanese tourist trade slowed. The cast threw in the towel for the last time on August 6, 1989. It was estimated that *Oh! Calcutta!* had grossed more than $350 million and had been seen by 85 million people around the world.

A CHORUS LINE

Conceived by Michael Bennett
Book by James Kirkwood and Nicholas Dante
Music by Marvin Hamlisch
Lyrics by Ed Kleban
Opened October 19, 1975
6,137 performances, after an off-Broadway run at the Public Theatre
Shubert Theatre
Directed by Michael Bennett
Choreographed by Michael Bennett and Bob Avian
Produced by Joseph Papp, New York Shakespeare Festival
Cast: Donna McKechnie (Cassie); Robert Lu-Pone (Zach); Sammy Williams (Paul); Carole Bishop (Sheila); Priscilla Lopez (Diana); Pamela Blair (Val); Wayne Cilento (Mike); Scott Allen (Roy); Renee Baughman (Kristine); Chuck Cissel (Butch); Clive Clerk (Larry); Kay Cole (Maggie); Ronald Dennis (Richie); Donna Drake (Tricia); Brandt Edwards (Tom); Patricia Garland (Judy); Carolyn Kirsch (Lois); Ron Kuhlman (Don); Nancy Lane (Bebe); Baayork Lee (Connie); Cameron Mason (Mark); Don Percassi (Al); Michael Serrecchia (Frank); Michel Stuart (Greg); Thomas J. Walsh (Bobby); Crissy Wilzak (Vicki)

Along with *Show Boat, Oklahoma!,* and *West Side Story, A Chorus Line* is acknowledged as a milestone in American musical theater history and holds the record for longest-running show of any kind—play or musical—on Broadway. Using the framework of an audition for an unnamed musical, the show exposes the souls, dreams, and desires of a group of dancers. Eschewing the traditional plot-oriented book, *Chorus Line* offers brief glimpses into the lives of the auditioners so that they are seen as individuals. In the dazzling finale, "One," they don identical golden top hats and tails and their uniqueness vanishes as they form a perfect, uniform line. More than an inside "show-biz" story, the musical is about anyone who's ever had to prove himself or herself in order to get a job.

Director Michael Bennett, who was credited with conceiving the show, stated to *Playbill* magazine that he wanted to do a show "for my people—Broadway's beautiful, brilliant chorus dancers. . . . Every single one of them is very special, and I wanted them and audiences to know it."

No less than four books detail the creation of this production (two biographies of Bennett and two histories of *Chorus Line*). The seed for the show was sown in 1974, when dancers Michon Peacock and Tony Stevens were depressed after appearing in a flop musical (*Rachel Lily Rosenbloom*) and determined to do something to improve the lot of the Broadway chorus performer. They contacted Bennett with the desire to create a show or repertory company of their own. As a result, twenty-four veteran chorus dancers gathered in a rehearsal studio and stayed up all night talking about their experiences on the chorus line; Bennett conducted the session and taped the talks. Using the tapes as raw material, Bennett and Nicholas Dante, one of the dancers who was also a writer, began to fashion a script.

A nonprofit off-Broadway theater provided the birthplace for Broadway's biggest hit. Joseph Papp of the New York Shakespeare Festival had wanted Bennett to direct a revival of *The Threepenny Opera.* Bennett was not interested in revivals but asked Papp to sponsor a workshop to develop his musical about dancers. Papp agreed to foot the bill. This led to a whole new way of writing musicals. Material could be written, tried out, and staged without the pressure of performing it for paying audiences. As out-of-town tryouts in Boston, New Haven, and Philadelphia became too costly, workshops became the new wave of creating musicals.

During the resultant two *Chorus Line* workshops, Bennett and Dante were joined by composer Marvin Hamlisch; lyricist Ed Kleban; playwright James Kirkwood, who would collaborate with Dante; and Bennett's fellow choreographer, Bob Avian. The final product was four hours and twenty minutes long. As Kirkwood wrote in *Playbill* magazine, "Had we been going the usual route (Boston, Philly, etc.) we could have achieved nothing more from night to night, what with paying customers to please, than cosmetic surgery, applying a Band-Aid here, taking a snip or tuck there. Knowing we were only returning to West 19th Street with no audience to please but ourselves, we could perform major surgery without benefit of press or public scrutiny."

When the revised, two-hour-long production began previews at the Newman Theatre, one of the stages at the Shakespeare Festival's Public Theatre, in April of 1975, it took off. The Broadway transfer took place in July, where the show previewed until October. A Chorus Line won every award imaginable, including the Tony, New York Drama Critics Circle, Drama Desk, Outer Critics Circle, Pulitzer Prize, and even an Obie for its off-Broadway run.

Many of the characters' lives that the original cast were enacting paralleled their own. Donna McKechnie's unhappy sojourn in Hollywood was repeated in her character Cassie, and her personal relationship with future husband Bennett was mirrored by Cassie's ties to the character of Zach, a director who is auditioning the dancers. Several original cast members returned to the Broadway company and to two national touring companies.

On the night of September 29, 1983, A Chorus Line broke the record held by Grease to become the longest-running show in Broadway history. In a gala performance, 332 cast members from the Broadway, touring, and international companies joined for a once-in-a-lifetime celebration. The final showing on April 28, 1990, was anticlimactic after the spectacular 1983 performance. Many of the show's creators, including Michael Bennett, James Kirkwood, and Ed Kleban, had died.

Richard Attenborough directed the 1985 movie version, which was unable to recreate the dynamism of the stage show.

CATS

Music by Andrew Lloyd Webber
Lyrics taken from Old Possum's Book of Practical Cats, by T. S. Eliot
Opened October 7, 1982
Still running (5,685 performances as of May 21, 1996)
Winter Garden Theatre
Directed by Trevor Nunn
Choreographed by Gillian Lynn
Produced by Cameron Mackintosh, the Really Useful Company, David Geffen, and the Shubert Organization
Cast: Betty Buckley (Grizabella); Ken Page (Old Deuteronomy); Hector Jaime Mercado (Alonzo); Stephen Hanan (Bustopher Jones/Asparagus/Growltiger); Donna King (Bombalurina); Steven Gelfer (Carbucketty); René Ceballos (Cassandra); René Clemente (Coricopat/Mungojerrie); Wendy Edmead (Demeter); Christine Langner (Etcetra/Rumpleteazer); Bonnie Simmons (Jellyloru/Griddlebone); Anna McNeely (Jennyanydots); Timothy Scott (Mistoffolees); Harry Groener (Munkustrap); Kenneth Ard (Plato/Macavity/Rumpus Cat);

Herman W. Sebek (Pouncival); Terrence V. Mann (Rum Tum Tigger); Whitney Kershaw (Sillabub); Reed Jones (Skimbleshanks); Janet L. Hubert (Tantomile); Robert Hoshour (Tumblebrutus); Cynthia Onrubia (Victoria)

Cats was British wunderkind Andrew Lloyd Webber's first hit without his former partner, Tim Rice, and it established him as the dominant musical force both on Broadway and in London's West End. By 1983 Lloyd Webber had six productions running simultaneously in New York and London: Joseph and the Amazing Technicolor Dreamcoat, Evita, and Cats in America; and Evita, Cats, and Song and Dance in his native land.

Cats marked the beginning of a wave of British megahits with lots of flashy spectacle and little story. Instead of a narrative, the show is a series of songs and dances, as an ensemble of actors in John Napier's elaborate cat costumes cavort around a junkyard. Each feline is given his or her own moment to meow in the spotlight. There's Macavity, the mystery cat; Skimbleshanks, the railway cat; and Grizabella, the glamour puss who provides the evening's only bit of plot: she is chosen to ascend to "the heavy-side layer," the cats' version of heaven. Singing the show's haunting pop hit "Memory," the formerly elegant but now frazzled feline (a sort of furry Evita) is led to her reward by the sagacious Old Deuteronomy. This scene provided the show with its most stunning visual effect, as the two are lifted on a giant tire to the upper reaches of the theater. Later British pop musicals mimicked this device in the crashing chandelier in Phantom of the Opera and the helicopter in Miss Saigon.

The remarkable source for this fantasy was the Nobel Prize–winning poet T. S. Eliot, whose The Love Song of J. Alfred Prufrock and The Waste Land are masterpieces of modern poetry. But Eliot, a true cat lover, showed his lighter side when he wrote Old Possum's Book of Practical Cats, a collection of verse for children that he first circulated only among friends, then eventually published in 1939. Lloyd Webber originally set these poems to music for the amusement of his friends, much as Eliot had written them. The composer explained his interest in the poems to Playbill: "I suddenly realized there were very musical rhythms in them, an extraordinary rhythm that really is the rhythm of lyrics. The words themselves dictate that certain musical phrases have to be there. . . . I couldn't say why I was drawn to setting the poems; I suppose it was because it was a book I knew very well and I was very much intrigued to see if I could write music to existing words, which I hadn't done before."

The few songs written for weekend afternoons soon grew into a full production. The composer originally intended to present them as a one-act musical. It was to be coupled with

Tell Me on a Sunday, a one-woman song recital that later became the "song" half of *Song and Dance* (1985). *Cats* expanded into a full evening. When the material in the original Eliot work was exhausted, other Eliot works were used. Then director Trevor Nunn and lyricist Richard Stilgoe supplied additional lyrics. The poet's widow, Valerie Eliot, gave Lloyd Webber a previously unpublished fragment of her husband's work, which was transformed into "Memory." This song gave the show a pop hit when Barbra Streisand and Judy Collins each recorded it.

Few thought a musical about dancing cats would be a success, but producer Cameron Mackintosh had instincts that told him otherwise. Along with Lloyd Webber's new production entity, the Really Useful Company, Mackintosh mounted the show in New York and London to a tumultuous public response, despite a somewhat lukewarm press.

The advertising slogan for *Cats* states: "Now and forever." As of this writing it is the longest-running Broadway show still playing, and is outdistanced only by *A Chorus Line* and *Oh! Calcutta!* in total number of performances. It has played all over the world, earning in excess of $100 million. The slogan's boast may be an understatement.

Source: *It's a Hit: The Back Stage Book of Longest-Running Broadway Shows, 1884 to Present*, by David Sheward. New York: Back Stage Books, 1994. Reprinted with permission.

THE 10 GREATEST MAGICAL EFFECTS OF THE TWENTIETH CENTURY

1. LEVITATION OF PRINCESS KARNAC (c. 1904)

Invented and performed by John Nevil Maskelyne: a woman floated upward from a couch on a brightly lit stage, a hoop being passed around her body to prove that wires were not used. The principle employed inspired many later versions of the effect, most recently David Copperfield's "Flying" illusion.

There is a popular story that American magician Harry Kellar strode onstage during Maskelyne's performance of this illusion to learn how it was done. It is, however, more likely that Kellar gained his knowledge by a time-honored means—hiring away a Maskelyne coworker. Only months after Paul Valadon moved from Maskelyne's show to Kellar's, the latter began to feature the illusion; it stayed in his show for many years.

2. MASCOT MOTH (1905)

Invented and performed by David Devant: a woman (dressed in mothlike costume) standing on a bare stage visibly vanished. In the late twentieth century, featured by Doug Henning (in his Broadway show *Merlin*) and by Siegfried and Roy.

Stunningly simple in effect, the illusion is so complex—requiring complex mechanics and faultless teamwork by the magician and his assistants—that with the exception of the performers mentioned, it has rarely been seen since Devant's time.

3. WALKING THROUGH A BRICK WALL (1914)

Invented and performed by P. T. Selbit and featured by Houdini: a brick wall was built onstage and the performer (briefly concealed by screens at each side) passed through the solid obstacle. Doug Henning performed his version in a 1977 television special; in 1986, also for television, David Copperfield "walked" through the Great Wall of China.

Like many illusions, this has a cloudy history; other claimants to its invention include Sidney Josolyne, whose version was used by Houdini, and C. A. Alexander, a very successful American performer of the first decades of this century. Alexander's version involved walking through a barrier made of blocks of ice. Curiously, these two creators of a spectacular magical effect were professional mentalists (mind readers) rather than magicians.

4. VANISHING ELEPHANT (1918)

Invented by Charles Morritt and featured by Houdini (more for the publicity angle than the mystery): a five-ton elephant, placed in a large box, was made to disappear. Mystery writer Walter B. Gibson joked: "Four men push a cabinet on stage, an elephant is put inside and vanished; sixteen men push the cabinet off stage; where did the elephant go?" In actuality the illusion was said to be quite baffling.

Later versions have been performed by Doug Henning (for a 1976 television special) and Siegfried and Roy.

5. SAWING A WOMAN IN HALF (1921)

Invented and performed by Horace Goldin (based on an earlier P. T. Selbit illusion): a woman, placed in a box with head and feet showing, was cut into two pieces and then restored. Later versions have used swords, cleavers, and buzz saws.

Perhaps the strangest of all versions of this effect was that performed by Rajah Raboid; this magician/mentalist brought up a man from the audience, placed him in a box, and then apparently cut him in half and restored him. When the man stood up, however, the top half of his body leaped off the bottom half, and the two halves ran off the stage in opposite directions. This unique presentation was possible only because the stooge from the audience, a man of normal stature, was the identical twin brother of "half-man" Johnny Eck (featured in the Tod Browning film *Freaks*), whose body ended at the waist. A midget wearing a pair of pants completed the illusion, the two being switched for the normal twin inside the box.

After a week Eck demanded a better salary, which Raboid refused, closing this odd chapter in the history of the illusion.

6. MILLION-DOLLAR MYSTERY (c. 1928)

Invented by Walter Jeans and featured by Howard Thurston: from an eighteen-inch-square box, isolated from scenery and stage traps, items appeared and vanished—including a girl and a solid five-foot railroad tie. The basic principle has since been used to produce baby chicks— and vanish elephants.

It is a curious paradox that magicians often use "invisibility" as a dramatic premise in a magical presentation; here such a premise is not used—yet this illusion depends on the spectator's looking directly at a large solid object and being unable to see it.

7. HOOKER RISING CARDS (c. 1935)

Invented by Dr. Samuel Hooker: an elaborate version of a classic effect in which chosen cards rise mysteriously from the deck. Hooker's presentation, where any card called for would rise, where cards would float within a glass dome, and much more, was so baffling that many magicians thought the effect was a myth until the early 1990s, when illusion designer/builder John Gaughan recreated the routine.

As with the "Mascot Moth" mentioned above, this apparently simple routine is so complex in method and performance that it is unlikely that it will ever again be performed on a regular basis.

8. OUT OF THIS WORLD (1942)

Invented by Paul Curry: dealing cards facedown into two random piles, a spectator is mysteriously able to separate them into red and black

suits. Often voted by magicians as the greatest card trick of all time.

The effect is so appealing that Winston Churchill once delayed a World War II meeting of Parliament to watch repeated performances of it by actor/magician Harry Green. More recently, noted writer and expert on the paranormal Colin Wilson was shown this feat by psychic-debunker James Randi. Wilson's reaction: "If Randi had told me he did *that* trick by supernatural means, I might have believed him!"

9. LINKING FINGER RINGS (c. 1960)

Invented by Harvard math professor Dr. Persi Diaconis: three borrowed finger rings are linked together in a chain, examined by spectators, and unlinked. Featured by Harry Anderson, illusionist Jonathan Pendragon, and magician Kreskin.

An earlier version of this effect, in which a dozen or so rings, borrowed from audience members, were linked into a long chain, was invented and featured in his *Mercury Wonder Show* by actor/magician Orson Welles.

10. ZIG-ZAG (1970)

Invented and performed by Robert Harbin: a woman is placed in a cabinet, the center section of which is then slid out to the side, apparently trisecting her. The effect can be performed with an audience on all sides, under almost any conditions; this, and its strong visual appeal, make it the most popular illusion of the late twentieth century.

This popularity has led to a less desirable distinction: the "Zig-Zag" is also the most pirated illusion of the last thirty years, with unauthorized copies of the apparatus numbering in the hundreds. Few of the copyists have been able to perform the illusion with the mystery and charm of its inventor.

Note: The above list does not include several "once-only" effects done for publicity or television specials, as for example, Ricky Jay's "Creation of Life" (in which a cigarette paper becomes a living butterfly) or David Copperfield's "Vanishing Statue of Liberty." Except where noted, these effects were (and are) performed as part of a regular performance.

List compiled by T. A. Waters, author of the *Encyclopedia of Magic and Magicians.*

FOOTNOTE PERFORMERS AND ARTISTS

HADJI ALI (1892–1937), Regurgitator

Would you pay good money to watch someone throw up?

Thousands once did, gladly, on both sides of the Atlantic. Born in Egypt in 1892, Hadji Ali traveled to the United States in the early 1930s,

appearing in fairs, carnivals, and vaudeville. Billed variously as "the Amazing Regurgitator" and "the Egyptian Enigma," Ali would swallow a variety of household objects—coins, buttons, stones, watermelon seeds, hickory nuts, costume jewelry, even live goldfish—and wash them down with copious amounts of water. Then, as audience members called out specific items, he would spit them up, one at a time. Ali acquired a small but enthusiastic following; his grand finale brought down the house every night.

His assistant would set up a toy castle in a corner of the stage while Ali gulped down a gallon of water chased with a pint of kerosene. To the accompaniment of a dramatic drumroll, he would spit out the kerosene in a six-foot arc across the stage, setting the castle on fire. Then, with the flames shooting high into the air, Ali would upchuck the water and extinguish all traces of the fire.

Ali remained more a sideshow curiosity than a true vaudeville headliner; according to Joe Laurie Jr. in his book *Vaudeville: From the Honky Tonks to the Palace*, Ali "lasted four weeks" in one theater "before they got wise that he was killing their supper shows."

Even so, Ali's remarkable talent was recorded in at least three films: *Strange As It Seems*, a 1930 short subject, *Politiquerias*, a Spanish-language comedy made in 1931, and *Gizmo*, a documentary filmed in the 1930s that is occasionally shown on cable television. He was also featured at Grauman's Chinese Theater in Hollywood from 1930 to 1931. He died during a theatrical tour of Great Britain in 1937.

To be sure, Ali's genius for selective regurgitation was not unique or unprecedented. A performer named Mac Norton, headlined as "the Human Aquarium," made a living in Europe ingesting and disgorging live fish and frogs on stage. He tried to bring his act to the United States but was prevented from doing so by the American Society for the Prevention of Cruelty to Animals in the 1920s. Around the same time, German-born Hans Rohrl gained fame as "the Living Hydrant." He wowed audiences by propelling a mouthful of water fifteen feet across a stage in a spray nearly seven feet wide.

In fact, voluntary upchucking, through controlled expansion and contraction of the throat and stomach muscles, has been a popular form of entertainment since the 1600s. A French medical text published in 1812 noted that a highly distinguished member of the Faculty of Paris was capable of vomiting the contents of his stomach at will, without nausea or excessive effort. Unlike Hadji Ali, however, there is no indication that anyone paid to see him perform.
—B.F.

CHRISTO (b. 1935), Wrap Artist

October 1991, the Tejon Pass, about sixty miles north of Los Angeles.

It looked like the setting from a movie billed to have "a cast of thousands." But the thousands, actually about 900 workers, had not gathered to remake the battle scene from *Spartacus*. Instead they came to raise umbrel-

las. Gradually the umbrellas—a total of 1,760 of them—budded up like giant yellow dandelions. They weren't the kind one finds on the beach. These were more like satellite-dish antennae, large ones. Made of aluminum, nylon, and steel, they weighed 488 pounds apiece. And California was not the only site of the raising of an umbrella forest. Seven time zones away, in Ibaraki Prefecture, north of Tokyo, Japan, stood 1,340 blue parasols. The joint California and Japan project employed 2,000 workers, used 50 acres of fabric, and cost $26 million. This incredible effort was inspired by environmental artist Christo. "With 'The Umbrellas' temporariness is more important than in my other works of art," Christo said. "What especially appeals to me is the ability of the umbrellas to open and close rapidly. That dynamic is very much in keeping with my philosophy—that the work will appear like flower blossoms, and disappear after three weeks."

Christo Javacheff (he deliberately dropped his last name) was born June 13, 1935, in Gabrovo, Bulgaria. He never doubted his destiny. "From childhood on, I had only one thought: to become an artist." As a teenager he attended the Fine Arts Academy in Sofia. It was a Stalinist-era state-run school where students were encouraged to paint scenes of smiling factory workers toiling over drill presses. One school assignment, however, intrigued Christo. He and teams of young artists were sent to agricultural co-ops, where they instructed farmers to cover their haystacks with tarps to improve the looks of the rural landscape. Covering or wrapping large familiar objects fascinated the youthful Christo. It was a way of transforming everyday sights into works of art.

In 1958 Christo moved to Paris and joined a *nouveau realistes* group of artists who were devoted to grandiose projects. His first memorable piece was erected in 1962, when he blocked a Paris street, the Rue Visconti, with a wall of 204 oil drums. The work was a political snub against the Berlin Wall, built a year earlier. The *Wall of Oil Drums* attracted little attention in the world press, but it caused a massive traffic jam in the City of Light. Christo later asked Parisian officials for permission to wrap the Eiffel Tower, but he was turned down.

Christo left Paris and moved to New York in 1964. In America he turned to wrapping objects on a huge scale. He wrapped the Museum of Contemporary Art in Chicago with sixty-two pieces of brown tarpaulin, all strung together with two miles of brown rope. Then, always stretching his limits, he wrapped one mile of jagged Australian coastline near Sydney with 1 million square feet of polythene sheets entwined by 36 miles of rope.

Wrapping objects was only one of his enterprises. Journeying to Rifle, Colorado, in 1972, he completed *Valley Curtain*, a great net that he hung like a spiderweb between a pair of mountains more than 1,000 feet apart. Two years later he erected *Running Fence*, an eighteen-foot-high nylon fence that serpentined along twenty-four miles of California countryside north of San Francisco. For *Running Fence*, he needed to get written permission from fifty-nine homeowners and farmers and fifteen government agencies. No problem. The artist claimed that working with property owners was a part of the creative process he always enjoyed. Strangely, the toughest opposition against *Running Fence* came from an association of California artists who said the work made a mockery of art. One of Christo's most sublime creations was completed in 1983, when he ringed eleven small islands in Florida's Biscayne Bay with bright pink fabric. He said *Surrounded Islands* stood as "my water lilies."

Christo finances all of his projects through the sale of sketches, models, and details of his work. A Christo sketch can fetch as much as $100,000. He accepts no money from governments or institutions. His decorations stand for two to three weeks. All the material he uses is recyclable. For these reasons he has made few enemies, despite the bizarre nature of his art. When one of the mammoth parasols in *The Umbrellas* tore loose in a gust of wind and killed a viewer, a deeply shaken Christo ordered the exhibit closed immediately.

In 1995, after twenty-four years of lobbying the German parliament, Christo wrapped the Reichstag in Berlin with a million square feet of silver fabric and nine miles of blue rope. This is the same building that historians believe the Nazis once burned in order to stir up the German masses and sweep their leader, Adolf Hitler, into power.

—R.C.S.

PERLA SIEDLE GIBSON (1888–1971), Singer

During the Second World War, the South African port of Durban was a major maritime crossroads on the route to several theaters of war. Three million soldiers, sailors, and airmen passed through, and few would ever forget the Lady in White.

As their ships passed through the harbor's narrow entrance, men would crowd the decks for their first sight of land in perhaps forty days. There, standing alone on the North Quay, would be a stout little woman in her fifties dressed in white, serenading them in a rich soprano voice, beating time with a silk scarf. They would listen in silent astonishment, or cheer, shouting requests and singing along with her.

To Americans she was Katie Smith, or the Dockside Diva; to Britons, the Lady in White. Her name was Perla Siedle Gibson.

Born on April 30, 1888, Perla Siedle studied music and painting in Europe. After some years as a professional singer in London, she returned to her native South Africa in 1923 with her husband, Jack Gibson, and settled into the comfortable life of a wealthy white housewife, dividing her time between family life, painting, and music. As a member of the South African Society of Artists and the first president of the Natal Society of Artists, she exhibited her work regularly, including shows in Paris and London. Her pictures were bold and optimistic studies of Durban and its people, full of light and color. She was especially fond of painting Zulus.

On the outbreak of war, her husband and both sons joined the forces and she volunteered to help run a refreshment stall for the Seaman's Institute. This was where she began her second singing career. She described the moment in her autobiography, *The Lady in White* (1964):

"It was April 1940. I was standing at a Durban dockside canteen, being called 'Ma' by thousands of young khaki-clad soldiers lining the rails of a giant troopship slowly gliding by.

" 'Sing us a song, Ma!' 'Come on, be a sport, Ma!' 'Give us "Land of Hope and Glory," Ma!'

"I cupped my hands wide over my mouth. At the first notes of that most moving of patriotic songs a hush fell. Then a full-throated chorus of thousands took up the refrain."

After years of appearing in opera or giving recitals, she realized she now had a mission to sing to passing ships. "I vowed inwardly," she wrote, "that I would never fail those men and the countless more who were to follow them, for they, separated from their own loved ones, saw in me, standing alone, the yearning personification of all that home, love and gentleness meant." The war was a deadly struggle for civilization in which all she could offer was "a God-given voice and a burning determination to fulfill destiny that had opened up before me, almost like a revelation."

While hostilities lasted, she serenaded every merchantman, troopship, warship, and hospital ship that entered or left the harbor. She arrived in her chauffeur-driven car regardless of time of day or weather conditions to sing in fierce heat or driving rain. She never missed a single appointment—not even on the day on which she learned of her son's death in action in Italy.

As the war progressed, her repertoire widened. To the unglamorous and underappreciated merchant marine she sang a song especially composed by her father. When the first Americans arrived, she hurriedly got a group of Marines to teach her "The Shores of Tripoli," and was soon singing "God Bless America" to any ship flying the Stars and Stripes.

She was even credited with preventing mutiny. On one occasion, soldiers on a British troopship, wearied by a long, uncomfortable, and dangerous journey, had resolved, despite their officers' threats and pleas, to walk ashore as soon as they docked. Gibson was later told that as the ship reached the harbor and she sang "There'll Always be an England" and "Land of

Hope and Glory," the rebellion crumbled. "The effect was miraculous," a military policeman later told her. ". . . The mood changed from sullen resentment to cheerfulness in minutes and soon the men were lustily singing with you. We, braced for what we fully expected was to be one of the toughest spells ever spent ashore, found ourselves dealing with men who behaved like lambs." On another occasion she had a similar effect on a shipload of mutinous Australians by singing "Waltzing Matilda."

After the war, she confined her serenades to British and American warships visiting Durban. She continued to paint, wrote her memoirs, and corresponded with the huge number of acquaintances worldwide that her wartime exploits had won her. One man, repatriated after losing his eyesight, had vowed he would visit her to thank her for singing him a few songs while he was being taken from a hospital ship. This, in the days before routine international air travel, was a major undertaking, but after an operation restored his sight, he signed up as a musician on a liner solely for the purpose of calling on Perla Gibson in Durban to thank her personally for her few minutes' kindness.

She made several trips to Britain for old comrades' reunions and a hugely successful TV appearance. In a newspaper interview she tried to summarize why she was held in such affection: "I was once called 'the mother of them all' and I suppose that sums me up. I've given all those men that touch of home. I've epitomized their mums—no glamorous blondes or Marlene Dietrich, just an old mother."

—E.B.

FLORENCE FOSTER JENKINS (1868?-1944), "Singer"

Of her singing, *Newsweek* wrote, "There was no awareness of pitch, and her vocal gait rocked like a drunken sailor in a gale." Florence Stevenson of *Opera News* reminisced that she was "a prima donna in everything but her voice."

Despite what many called a breathtaking lack of talent, Florence Foster Jenkins, a putative coloratura soprano, was unquestionably a legend of the American musical stage—even if to many it was as a figure of fun.

To critics the dubious diva was more notable for the exuberance and ambition of her performances than for their quality or excellence. An entry in *The New Grove Dictionary of American Music* describes her thus: "She seems to have taken her singing seriously and to have been unaware of the gulf that lay between her technique and the repertory she undertook. . . . But whether or not she understood the reasons for her popularity, it continued to grow."

Despite her vocal shortcomings, she never lacked for fans. Her concert tickets commanded top dollar. Her admirers included Enrico

The stunningly untalented Florence Foster Jenkins.

Caruso, Katharine Cornell, and Lily Pons. Cole Porter wrote a song for her. RCA Victor released her records. She even sang at the White House for President Calvin Coolidge (he was never known for his artistic discernment).

Though some who attended her concerts came to jape and jeer (Jenkins would claim they were in the employ of jealous rivals), many others were entirely earnest in their appreciation. Even one of her detractors had to concede that "the applause was real."

Florence Foster was born into a well-to-do Wilkes-Barre, Pennsylvania, family. She asked her father to send her to Europe to study singing, but he refused, and she eloped with a young physician, Frank Jenkins, who was equally unsupportive of her art. They divorced in 1902.

Without family money, Jenkins supported herself as a pianist and music teacher until 1909, when she inherited her father's fortune and launched—she was then in her early forties—what became a remarkable, if improbable, singing career.

Before she began singing in public, her artistic reputation stemmed from her generous philanthropic support for young musicians through the Verdi Club, which she founded in New York. Charter members included the great Caruso. The club held annual fund-raising recitals at the Plaza and the Ritz. Jenkins later used the same format for her own annual performances, which she began giving in 1912 before society-lady audiences in New York, Washington, Boston, Newport, and Saratoga Springs. In 1943 she was involved in a taxi collision that, she said, left her able to warble a higher F than ever before.

Jenkins's recitals were soon renowned as lavishly staged events featuring elaborate floral sets and numerous costume changes. Among her outfits: a Russian peasant, a Mexican with sombrero, and, most famously, an angel with wings. As a Spanish señorita, with shawl and large fan, she wowed the crowd by tossing handfuls of rosebuds at the audience from a wicker basket—then throwing the basket itself. Then she would send her accompanist into audiences to retrieve the buds so she could do it all over again.

Her self-regard was a marvel. Jenkins wrote in a program note: "Tetrazzini took three breaths to sing this phrase, I do it in one." (A witness said it actually took twenty-four.) She always chose the most difficult pieces, such as the "Queen of Night" aria from The Magic Flute and "Adele's Laughing Song" from Die Fledermaus. "People expect virtuoso performances from a virtuoso," she said.

Some critics agreed. "In our time," wrote Robert Lawrence in the Saturday Review, "only two prime donne assolute [have been] intrepid enough to attempt every phase of high soprano literature: Florence Foster Jenkins and Maria Callas. Each has her adherents; and while it cannot be denied that Mme. Callas is interpretively the more accomplished . . . Mme. Jenkins is acoustically the more picturesque." He went on to say that "her singing at its finest suggests the untrammeled swoop of some great bird." Newsweek said that "in high notes, Mrs. Jenkins sounds as if she was afflicted with low, nagging backache."

Robert Bager of the New York World-Telegram wrote: "She was exceedingly happy in her work. It is a pity so few artists are. And her happiness was communicated as if by magic to her listeners who were stimulated to the point of audible cheering, even joyous laughter and ecstasy by the inimitable singing."

Throughout her career and since, there has been a debate whether the whole act was an elaborate put-on—or just an egregious case of self-deception. Some suspected Jenkins's favorable notices came from reviewers eager to prove they were in on the joke.

Jenkins capped her career with a sold-out farewell performance at Carnegie Hall (her first and only appearance there) on October 25, 1944. Two thousand patrons were turned away—all with an "acute sense of humor" said the New York Post—and scalpers got as much as twenty dollars per ticket. Jenkins died one month later. In a quote that might sum up her career, she once said: "Some may say I couldn't sing, but no one can say that I didn't sing."

—A.B.C.

MICKEY MOUSE (b. 1928), Actor

Mickey Mouse was born on a train en route to Los Angeles from New York. His early life is somewhat of a secret, and it was not until he applied for work at the Disney studios that Mickey's film career was launched and carefully recorded. In his first silent film, Plane Crazy, he met and fell in love with his leading lady, Minnie Mouse, who also appeared in Mickey's second film, Gallopin' Gaucho. Although he could not find financial backing for his silent movies, Mickey, confident of his talent, made a talkie, Steamboat Willie. The addition of a synchronized sound track made Mickey's character come fully alive, even though his voice was rather squeaky. Steamboat Willie premiered in New York City, where it was a box-office sensation.

Mickey's early pictures revolved around his talent as an entertainer, particularly as a violinist and pianist. Not satisfied to be known only as a musician, Mickey insisted on "juicier" roles. In 1930 and 1931, he starred in twenty-one films in which he played such characters as a fire chief, soldier, hunter, cowboy, prisoner, and great lover. The studio began making color films in 1932, but Mickey, always modest and concerned with the welfare of others, continued to appear in black and white, allowing the studio to use more of its available funds to add color to their other film endeavors.

By 1935 Mickey Mouse was an internationally renowned star. Germany had chosen one of his films as one of the ten best pictures of the year (1930). Awards came in from Argentina and Cuba. Russia sent him an antique cut-glass bowl from the first Soviet Cinema Festival. When Mickey made his initial color film, The Band Concert, he received awards from the third International Cinematographic Arts Exhibition in Venice and from the Brussels International Festival. Not to be outdone by foreign praise, Worcester, Massachusetts, officially proclaimed May 12 as Mickey Mouse Day.

Although Mickey starred in sixteen pictures in 1936 and 1937, he was losing ground to other Disney studio stars—particularly a sailor-suited duck named Donald and a canine actor called Pluto. During the four years preceding World War II, Mickey appeared in fewer films, and he sometimes took second billing to Pluto. However, his popularity was reinstated with Fantasia (1940) and his role as the Sorcerer's Apprentice.

When war broke out, he retired to concentrate on aiding the war effort. His dedication and service were duly acknowledged—the password of the Allies on D-Day in 1944 was "Mickey Mouse." Unfortunately, Mickey's films, like all American films, were banned in France during the German occupation. An entire editorial column, "Au Revoir, Mickey," appeared in a noted French newspaper in 1942. When France was liberated, another editorial, "Bonjour, Mickey," welcomed back the skinny-legged mouse who "got the best of the invincible Fuehrer."

With the war ended, Mickey returned to Hollywood, but he was finding it increasingly difficult to add scope and depth to the characters he portrayed. Always the "good guy," he was not supposed to lose his temper or do anything sneaky. When he erred, critical fan mail poured into his office.

In 1955 Mickey made a smash comeback with *The Mickey Mouse Club*, a show that played five days a week on national television. A cast of twenty-four Mouseketeers aided him. They sang, danced, and, in general, helped him make each day a glorious one—Monday was "Fun with Music Day"; Tuesday, "Guest Star Day"; Wednesday, "Anything Can Happen Day"; Thursday, "Circus Day"; and Friday was "Talent Round-Up Day."

In 1959 Mickey realized that he enjoyed public relations more than filmmaking and agreed to become the official host for Disneyland in California and later for Walt Disney World in Florida, as well as Disney ventures in Japan and France. Currently, he is busy shaking hands, leading parades, and having his picture taken with visitors to the Magic Kingdoms.
—C.O.M.

ALESSANDRO MORESCHI (1858–1922), Castrato

Extinctions are normally a cause for regret, but when Alessandro Moreschi died in Rome on April 21, 1922, one can only hope that his kind went the way of the dodo and the passenger

Alessandro Moreschi, the last castrato.

pigeon. As a child, Moreschi, like thousands of boys before him, had been deliberately castrated. It was a career move.

Saint Paul the Apostle had said, "Let women be silent in churches," so the Catholic Church forbade women in its choirs. But as sacred music became more elaborate after the Middle Ages, composers and choirmasters demanded more vocal flexibility. Boys were usually used for the higher ranges, but boys' voices broke before they could be trained to true excellence.

Somehow, eunuchs were hit on as a solution. By 1565 there were castrati singing at the Pope's private place of worship, the Sistine Chapel. By the mid-seventeenth century castrati were in church choirs throughout Italy and in many cities north of the Alps.

The operation was usually carried out between the ages of six and eight. Between primitive surgical techniques and an incomplete appreciation of antisepsis, many boys must have failed to survive. Since the church's official line was that mutilation was unlawful, it was rarely openly admitted that the boys had been deliberately mutilated; their condition was usually ascribed to illness, mishap, or deformity.

After the operation the boys were enlisted in—or sold to—church or orphanage musical schools, where they endured a very tough training regime. They grew to adulthood, training uninterrupted by puberty, achieving a wider vocal range than other singers. In many, castration led to overdevelopment of the chest cavity, giving the voice formidable power and stamina.

"What singing!" said one writer on hearing a castrato for the first time. "Imagine a voice that combines the sweetness of the flute and the animated suavity of the human larynx—a voice which leaps and leaps, lightly and spontaneously, like a lark that flies through the air and is intoxicated with its own flight."

If they had stayed in church choirs, castrati would have remained an ecclesiastical freak show. By the seventeenth century, however, they had moved into Italy's burgeoning new art form; in opera, a castrato—known as an *evirato* (unmanned) or *musico*—could take male or female roles.

"Eviva il coltello!" audiences cried as the curtain came down—"Long live the knife!" *Evirati* became a byword for tantrums, vanity, and bad acting, but by the 1700s the castrati could earn huge salaries. Names such as Senesino, Crescentini, Velluti, Pacchierotti, and the great Farinelli (reckoned by some to be the best singer who ever lived) were Europe's first musical superstars, which is why at that time an estimated 4,000 Italian boys a year were mutilated at their parents' behest.

Stories of their amorous adventures—mostly heterosexual—abound. Some even attempted marriage. Though the castrato's testicles were removed, the scrotum remained in place, and it was by all accounts possible for a castrato to lead an active sex life. One medical authority suggests that the operation did not inhibit the body's production of testosterone. It was said by some that a eunuch was a better lover than a regular guy—and he posed no risk of pregnancy.

Castrati featured in opera until the early nineteenth century; Monteverdi, Gluck, Handel, Mozart, and even Rossini wrote roles for castrati. They continued to sing in the Sistine Chapel until the early 1900s.

Alessandro Moreschi, the last known castrato, was born on November 11, 1858, in Montecompatri, Italy, and studied at the schola cantorum of San Salvatore in Lauro and later under composer Gaetano Capocci, musical director of the Cappella Lateranese. He joined the Sistine choir as a soloist in 1883, but sang at other churches and at private and public concerts. Known as "the Angel of Rome," Moreschi was in great demand in Roman society for many years.

Described as a short, plump man, he appears to have led a blameless life, uncluttered by the vices of his predecessors—apart possibly from vanity. Witnesses write of his strolling around the Vatican with a white scarf around his neck, graciously accepting the compliments of his admirers. In conversation, his voice was described as "high-speaking tenor."

Moreschi was secure enough in his position to cancel church appointments when he felt like it, causing one enraged Vatican official to disparagingly refer to him as "a hermaphrodite." He nonetheless became musical director of the Sistine choir at the turn of the century. Here, recordings were made of his singing, both as soloist and as choir member, in 1902 and 1904.

The recordings, including Rossini's "Crucifixus," Laibach's "Pie Jesu," and the Bach-Gounod "Ave Maria," are the only clues we have of what the castrato voice sounded like. When they were reissued on CD in the 1980s, one critic described Moreschi's singing as "afflicted with a constant sobbing quality that he thought was expressive." Another said of Moreschi's rendition of Tosti's "Ideale" that "the voice is direly afflicted, the style gusty and the total effect sadly comical." Moreschi's pitch was sometimes unreliable, although his voice would by then have been past its peak, since he was in his forties and had been a soloist for more than twenty years.

Castrati were finally banned from the papal chapel by Pope Pius X in 1903. Professor Moreschi was permitted, however, to stay on as conductor and probably soloist, too, until his retirement in 1913.

—E.B.

PERVYI SIMFONICHESKII ANSAMBL (1922–32), Conductorless Orchestra

Conductor Otto Klemperer was once invited to lead the Pervyi Simfonicheskii Ansambl in a concert in Moscow. Midway through the program, however, Klemperer laid down his baton and took a seat in the audience, and the ensemble finished without him.

A remarkable feat on the face of it, and yet no one present was surprised in the least, for the group, known more familiarly by the abbreviation Persimfans, had been making its mark, since its premiere performance in February 1922, as the world's first and greatest conductorless orchestra. (Pervyi Simfonicheskii Ansambl means "first symphonic ensemble.")

"It isn't that we're opposed to conductors," the group's founder, violinist Lev Zeitlin, once remarked, "just bad conductors." But Zeitlin and company, in keeping with the egalitarian philosophy of Karl Marx, eschewed all men with batons, with the occasional exception of invited guests like Klemperer. As musicologist Nicolas Slonimsky put it, the Persimfans "was intent on demonstrating that in a proletarian state orchestra, men do not need a musical dictator."

Indeed, the Persimfans fared admirably without a leader, although its successes came only after endless racking rehearsals and conferences during which every performer had to become familiar with the entire score. Works by Haydn, Mozart, and their contemporaries were simple enough to present few problems. But the group was challenged severely by the orchestral excesses of the Romantics and the complexities of twentieth-century compositions.

Within the ensemble, a smaller committee of musicians was elected to meet regularly to decide on such intangibles as the volume, dynamics, tempo, and style of specific concert pieces. Then, at rehearsals, one of the committee members would sit in the balcony to monitor and report back on the effect.

Onstage, the group played in a circle so that each musician was plainly visible to all of his colleagues. "The utmost concentration and attention is demanded of each player, all of whom are fully conscious of their responsibility in that magic circle," the French pianist Henri Gil-Marchex, who once performed with the Persimfans, once wrote. "Each member of the orchestra has his own important part to play, and glances, raising of the brow, and slight motions of the shoulders are done by each instrumentalist, but so discreetly that the listener . . . seldom notices it." In January 1927, Sergei Prokofiev appeared with the Persimfans in a program that included his Piano Concerto no. 3, as well as his orchestral suites from Chout and The Love for Three Oranges. "The conductorless orchestra coped splendidly with difficult programs and accompanied soloists as competently as any conducted orchestra," Prokofiev, who was rarely quick to praise, later said. "Their main difficulty lay in changing tempo, for here the whole ensemble had to feel the music in exactly the same way. On the other hand, the difficult passages were easily overcome, for each individual musician felt himself a soloist and played with perfect precision."

The Persimfans won worldwide acclaim throughout the 1920s and inspired imitators in Paris, Berlin, and New York. In 1927 they were named an Honored Collective by the Soviet government. Ultimately, however, dissension within the ensemble—coupled with a relaxation of the state-held view that guidance and leadership by a trained individual are always ideologically offensive—proved the group's undoing. In 1932 the Persimfans was disbanded.

—B.F.

WARNER SALLMAN (1897–1968), Painter
What, exactly, did Jesus look like?

In the absence of photographs and home movies, we'll never know for certain. Nonetheless, for more than a half century, Christians around the world have carried as vivid a mental image of Jesus as if they knew him intimately. Their Jesus had flowing hair, blue eyes, a neatly barbered beard and mustache, and a warm, beatific look.

They didn't make it up: the image comes directly from *Head of Christ,* a head-and-shoulders portrait that may well be the best-known icon of popular culture in the twentieth century.

The artist was Warner E. Sallman, whose own fame pales next to that of his work. While few

"Head of Christ," created in 1940 by Warner Sallman, has been reproduced more than a billion times.

people know his name, more than 500 million copies of *Head of Christ* have been printed since 1940; Sallman also painted scores of scenes depicting Jesus in modern-day settings, offering kindness and paternal protection to typical Americans. Among the best-known are *Christ at Heart's Door,* showing the subject knocking on the door of a house, and a Sputnik Christ, which portrays a gargantuan Jesus standing astride the earth, his head in outer space.

All told, more than a billion reproductions of Sallman's Jesus have adorned magazines, religious tracts, calendars, clocks, lamps, pins, posters, and tacky souvenir items. To this day they're found everywhere, in homes, offices, barber shops, and church vestries. During World War II, U.S. fighting men carried snapshot-sized Sallmans into battle along with their mess kits and M16s. "Ex-G.I.s would weep as they told me stories about carrying 'Head of Christ' in their wallets, and how it kept them alive," says Jason Knapp, director of the Jesse C. Wilson Galleries at Indiana's Anderson University, where many of Sallman's paintings are on display.

Sallman was born in Chicago in 1897 and brought up in the Evangelical Covenant Church by his European-born parents. After studying commercial art at the Art Institute of Chicago, he began a career as an illustrator for advertising agencies and religious publishers. One night in 1924, he was struggling to come up with a suitable illustration for the magazine *Covenant Companion,* of which he was art editor. Though his deadline was the next day, he drew only blanks. Finally he gave up and went to bed.

He awoke around 2:30 A.M., he later recalled, and "suddenly there appeared to my mind's eye a picture of the Christ just as if it were on my drawing board." Sallman roughed out the concept in charcoal in the morning and got it in to the magazine the next afternoon moments before the 4:30 deadline. He called his work *Son of Man.*

In the early 1930s, an Indianapolis religious publisher, Kriebel and Bates, bought the rights to *Son of Man* and, in 1940, commissioned Sallman to execute a color rendering. The resulting effort reflected a merging of two styles—that of nineteenth-century American and English religious painters and mid-twentieth-century advertising. Some called it genius, others called it kitsch. But one thing was unarguable: *Head of Christ* became an overnight blockbuster.

At a 1994 symposium on Sallman's art at Yale University, as reported in the *Los Angeles Times,* one academic explained its popularity in terms of its easy accessibility to ordinary people. "He was not depicted in a specific time and place," she noted, "but interacting with people like you and me." But not everyone who took part in the symposium was sold on Sallman's Jesus. One participant said he looked like "a well-built farm kid who grew a beard." Another likened him to the Breck Girl, star of the famous shampoo ad campaign, with flowing, squeaky-clean hair and immaculate complexion.

Indeed, Sallman's critics have long derided his Jesus for appearing insufficiently masculine. As one professor at a Lutheran seminary put it, "We have a pretty picture of a woman with a curling beard who has just come from the beauty parlor with a Halo shampoo, but we do not have the Lord who died and rose again." In the early 1960s, Sallman gave his Jesus a makeover, painting him in *Lord and Master* with shorter hair and a tougher, even macho expression. It satisfied the critics but failed to catch on.

Sallman, who died in 1968, always insisted that the vision of Jesus that appeared to him that winter night in 1924 sprang wholly from his own mind. But it clearly owed something to *The Friend of the Humble*, a painting by Frenchman Léon Lhermitte that had appeared in the December 1922 *Ladies Home Journal*. Asked by an interviewer to comment on the similarity, Sallman was less than forthcoming. "Isn't everything we create a composite of what we have stored subconsciously through the years?" he replied.

To the millions of Christians who have cherished Sallman's vision for generations, his debt to Lhermitte is unimportant. As one woman explained, what makes *Head of Christ* so uniquely wonderful is that it shows "just exactly what Jesus looked like."

—B.F.

QUOTEBOOK: ARTS AND PERFORMERS

THE RESPONSIBILITY OF ARTISTS

In any society, the artist has a responsibility. His effectiveness is certainly limited and a painter or writer cannot change the world. But they can keep an essential margin of non-conformity alive. Thanks to them the powerful can never affirm that everyone agrees with their acts. That small difference is very important.
Luis Buñuel

Art must hurt. First, it must hurt the artist himself; the artist must experience pain before he creates. Otherwise, he won't be able to produce tears. A true artist must describe the things he is most afraid of, all that which he wished to avoid.
Itamar Yaoz-Kest

LITERATURE

In America only the successful writer is important, in France all writers are important, in England no writer is important, in Australia you have to explain what a writer is.
Geoffrey Cotterell

Literature is mostly about sex and not much about having children and life is the other way round.
David Lodge, The British Museum Is Falling Down, 1965

Writing is turning one's worst moments into money.
J. P. Donleavy, quoted in 1968

POETRY

We make out of the quarrel with others, rhetoric, but of the quarrel with ourselves, poetry.
W. B. Yeats, "Anima Hominis," Essays, 1924

If there is no money in poetry, neither is there poetry in money.
Robert Graves, speech at London School of Economics, December 6, 1963

"How are you?"
"Not very well. I can only write prose today."
W. B. Yeats in conversation

The poet speaks to all men of that other life of theirs that they have smothered and forgotten.
Edith Sitwell, Rhyme and Reason, 1930

SHOW BUSINESS

There's no business like show business.
Irving Berlin, Annie Get Your Gun (film), 1946

Night clubs are places where the tables are reserved and the guests aren't.
Frank Caspar, 1942

COMEDY

It is the truth: comedians and jazz musicians have been more comforting and enlightening to me than preachers and politicians or philosophers or poets or painters or novelists of my time. Historians in the future, in my opinion, will congratulate us on very little other than our clowning and our jazz.
Kurt Vonnegut, foreword, The Best of Bob and Ray, 1974

This was some great act this guy had; Jack Benny carried a violin that he didn't play, a cigar he didn't smoke, and he was funniest when he said nothing.
George Burns, All My Best Friends, 1989

There is not one female comic who was beautiful as a little girl.

Joan Rivers, *Los Angeles Times*, May 10, 1974

ART

Art is the unceasing effort to compete with the beauty of flowers—and never succeeding.

Marc Chagall, 1977

Drawing is the art of taking a line for a walk.

Paul Klee

I unconsciously decided that, even if it wasn't an ideal world, it should be and so painted only the ideal aspects of it—pictures in which there are no drunken slatterns or self-centered mothers . . . only foxy grandpas who played baseball with the kids and boys who fished from logs and got up circuses in the backyard.

Norman Rockwell, *Washington Post*, May 1972

Explaining how he achieved such lifelike flesh tones in his paintings of nudes:

I just keep painting till I feel like pinching. Then I know it's right.

Pierre Auguste Renoir, attributed, 1919

MUSIC

I'd like to think that when I sing a song, I can let you know all about the heartbreak, struggle, lies and kicks in the ass I've gotten over the years for being black and everything else, without actually saying a word about it.

Ray Charles, interview, *Playboy*, 1970

OPERA

No opera plot can be sensible, for in sensible situations people do not sing.

W. H. Auden, *Times Literary Supplement*, November 2, 1967

Opera is when a guy gets stabbed in the back and, instead of bleeding, he sings.

Ed Gardner, in *Duffy's Tavern*, 1940s American radio program

COMPOSERS

Never compose anything unless the not composing of it becomes a positive nuisance to you.

Gustav Holst, letter to W. G. Whittaker, 1921

Every composer's music reflects in its subject matter and in its style the source of the money the composer is living on while writing the music.

Virgil Thomson, *The State of Music*, 1939

Composers shouldn't think too much—it interferes with their plagiarism.

Howard Dietz, letter to Goddard Lieberson, November 1974

On being asked on TV why his compositions contained so many sharps and flats:

Down South where I come from you don't go around hitting too many white keys.

Eubie Blake, 1983

The basic difference between classical music and jazz is that in the former the music is always greater than its performance—whereas the way jazz is performed is always more important than what is being played.

André Previn, 1967

CRITICS

I am sitting in the smallest room of my house. I have your review before me. In a moment it will be behind me.

Max Reger, letter to Munich critic Rudolph Louis in response to his review in *Münchener Neuste Nachrichten*, February 7, 1906

Asking a working writer what he thinks about critics is like asking a lamp-post what it thinks about dogs.

Christopher Hampton, 1977

There is probably no hell for authors in the next world—they suffer too much from critics and publishers in this.

Christian Nastell Boyce, *Summaries of Thought*

I can take any amount of criticism, so long as it is unqualified praise.

Noël Coward

Critics are like eunuchs in a harem: they know how it's done, they've seen it done every day, but they're unable to do it themselves.

Brendan Behan, attributed

If upon reading the notices in the newspapers after the first night it is found that different critics take exception to different scenes, you can safely predict a successful run.

If the critics unanimously take exception to one particular scene it is advisable to move that scene to a more conspicuous place in the programme.

If, on the other hand, no particular critic dislikes any particular scene and they all write praising the production, it either means that you have such a good show that they haven't the face to attack it, or such a bad show that they like it. In either case it will probably be a failure.

Noël Coward

What you said hurt me very much. I cried all the way to the bank.

Liberace, replying to critics, 1954

Chapter 13

NEWS

News is the first rough draft of history.
Benjamin Bradlee

9-DAY WONDERS—ON THE 10TH DAY

A nine-day wonder is a person who dominated the news briefly and then disappeared from the headlines.

HEADLINE—1926: GERTRUDE EDERLE
At the Peak: At 7:09 on the morning of August 6, 1926, Gertrude Ederle—"Trudy" to her friends—dived into the choppy waters at Cap Gris-Nez, in France, to attempt what no woman had ever done before: the crossing of the English Channel. Nineteen and confident, she was determined not only to cross the thirty-five-mile-wide channel but to do it in record time. The *New York Daily News* and the *Chicago Tribune*, evidently sharing her confidence, were backing her attempt, and noted reporter Westbrook Pegler, assigned to ghost-write Trudy's account of the crossing for the *Tribune*, followed alongside her in a small boat, accompanied by his wife and by Ederle's trainer, Thomas Burgess. Optimism was the prevailing mood.

Not that it would be a breeze. She had attempted the channel once before, in 1925, and had failed, as had countless other swimmers, both male and female. On this trip, waves and winds buffeted her so mercilessly that after she'd been in the water twelve hours, Burgess was moved to beg her to come out. Ederle looked up and without missing a stroke asked, "What for?" At 9:40 that evening, she clambered out of the water onto the beach at Kingsdown, England, where a British immigration officer wryly asked for her passport. It had taken her fourteen hours and thirty-one minutes to swim the channel, the best time ever recorded by man or woman.

Ederle had been swimming competitively since she was a young girl. She won three medals in the 1924 Olympics—a gold medal as a member of the 4x100-meter relay and two

In 1926 Gertrude Ederle became the first woman to swim the English Channel, breaking the men's record in the process. As she emerged from the water at Kingsdown, England, a British immigration official asked her for her passport.

bronzes in the 100-meter and the 400-meter freestyle. But it is for conquering the Channel that she will be remembered.

On the morning of the famous swim, the *London Daily News* ran an editorial that pronounced, "Even the most uncompromising champion of the rights and capacities of women must admit that in contests of physical skill, speed and endurance, they must remain forever the weaker sex." Ederle's time beat the best men's record by two hours. "People said women couldn't swim the Channel," Ederle has said, "but I proved they could."

Back in the States, Ederle, the daughter of a Manhattan delicatessen owner, was hailed as a heroine and feted with a ticker-tape parade in New York City. She went on tour for two years and her endorsements, public appearances, and a 1927 movie called *Swim, Girl, Swim* earned her $2,000 a week, most of which she donated to the Woman's Swimming Association, which had sponsored her first try at crossing the channel.

While on tour, Ederle realized that her hearing had been impaired by her fourteen-and-a-half-hour odyssey, and she was forced to curtail her engagements. At the age of twenty-one she suffered a nervous breakdown, and in 1933, while visiting friends in Hempstead, Long Island, she fell, suffering a fractured pelvis and an injured spine. She was in a cast for four years. With determination, Ederle recovered and made a comeback at Billy Rose's Aquacade at the 1939 New York World's Fair.

And After: Gertrude Ederle, now an octogenarian, lives with a care-giving companion in Manhattan. She has compensated for her hearing loss by wearing a hearing aid and learning to read lips. In her late sixties, she taught swimming to youngsters at the Lexington School for the Deaf in New York City.

One of her last public appearances was in 1975 at a ceremony to dedicate a park in her honor; the park, in Highlands, New Jersey, overlooks the Shrewsbury River. It was on this stretch of beach that the young Trudy, age nine, taught herself the crawl by observing two boys swimming the stroke. After childhood, Ederle spent her summers in Highlands and it was in these same waters that she trained for her world-famous swim.

In her speech at the park dedication, Ederle claimed that she is responsible for another first: "I also invented the two-piece bathing suit, although I didn't have the sense to patent it." For her channel swim, she said, "I cut up my favorite training suit so that it wouldn't weigh me down or chafe, and I would be decent in case I failed and they had to drag me out." The suit and the swim on that day in 1926 were both a success.

—**B.F. and L.A.C.**

HEADLINE—1929: ROY RIEGELS
At the Peak: Roy Riegels was a better-than-competent defensive lineman for the University of California's championship football team and had been elected captain by his teammates toward the end of the 1928 season. But history remembers him only as the man who blew the

1929 Rose Bowl for his team on New Year's Day by carrying the ball sixty-nine yards in the wrong direction. It was a blunder of epic proportions, for it provided opposing Georgia Tech with the winning edge in a game that gridiron pundits had said would determine which team was the best in college football.

Seventy-two thousand people were on hand at Pasadena, cheering wildly as the Tech quarterback, Stumpy Thomason, fumbled on his own thirty-six-yard line midway through the second quarter. A mad scramble ensued, and Riegels, a lineman who rarely had the opportunity of getting his hands on the ball, grabbed the pigskin and started running.

At this point a confused Riegels apparently lost his bearings in the blur of uniforms, spun around, and reversed field. A few startled Tech players made a stab at tackling him, but then thought better of it and let Riegels dig his own grave. Galloping off into the sunlight toward his own goal line, he evidently had no idea that he was in error. A lone California teammate, Benny Lom, renowned for his speed, chased after Riegels, screaming, "No, Roy, no—not that way!" but his pleas were drowned out in the roar of the crowd.

Lom caught up with Riegels on the California ten-yard line and dragged him to a halt on the three; he got the bewildered ball carrier to turn around momentarily, in the hope of blocking for him and gaining back some of the lost yardage. But Tech was already there and they hit Riegels with all they had, stopping him cold on the one-yard line. Dejected beyond words, Riegels sat on the ground. His teammates tried their best to console him.

On the next play, kicker Lom dropped back into the end zone to punt, but the kick was blocked and Tech scored a two-point safety. Tech went on to win eight to seven.

Riegels took a sound drubbing in the nation's press for many days to come ("BLUNDER DEFEATS CALIFORNIA: CAPTAIN ELECT RUNS 69½ YARDS TO WRONG GOAL," was the headline on the story the *Chicago Daily Tribune* ran the next day), and his name became a household word. He had asked to leave the game after the mishap, but at the urging of his teammates, he returned in the second half. In the wake of the disaster, California coach Nibs Price said that Riegels was his smartest player, and "it was an accident that might have happened to anyone."

Riegels got plenty of ribbing for running the wrong way. Companies tried to recruit him as a sponsor for upside-down cakes, ties with stripes out of kilter, and backward walkathons. Reigels, however, kept his sense of humor. In 1964 he generously sent a letter to console Minnesota Viking Jim Marshall, who had run sixty yards into his own end zone. Riegels advised him, "Learn to take it and laugh with the crowd."

And After: After he graduated, Riegels became a teacher and coached high-school football in California. He served in the United States Army Air Corps as a major during World War II. From 1955 until his retirement in 1976, he owned the Roy Riegels Chemical Company in Woodland, California, an agricultural chemical business. Riegels died from complications of Parkinson's disease at his home in Oakland, California, on March 25, 1993. He was eighty-four years old.

In an interview some years before his death, he said, "All the times I've run across or heard people saying 'wrong way,' even though they weren't referring to me, I immediately turned around to see if they were speaking about me. I still don't understand how I did it."

Reporters are no longer able to call Riegels every year at Rose Bowl time, but he won't be forgotten. Two years before he died, he was inducted into the Rose Bowl Hall of Fame.
—B.F. and L.A.C.

In the future, everyone will be famous for 15 minutes.

Andy Warhol

HEADLINE—1934: THE DIONNE QUINTUPLETS

At the Peak: The birth of five identical daughters to Elzire Dionne on a small farm in the backwoods of northern Ontario on the bleak morning of May 28, 1934, made instant headlines throughout the world and was universally hailed as a miracle of human fertility.

Nonetheless, Elzire and her husband, Oliva, were more depressed than exhilarated. They were already supporting six children on a monthly income of barely $100 and were not sure how they would manage to pay the delivery fees for the quints, much less feed them.

Trading on the fame of their new offspring was one solution. Within forty-eight hours of the birth, representatives of the Chicago World's Fair had telephoned Oliva Dionne, inviting him to place the infants on exhibit at the fair in return for 23 percent of the gate receipts. Confused, depressed, and in desperate need of cash, Dionne agreed at once.

But the contract was quickly questioned when Dr. Allan Dafoe, the quints' physician, stepped in, insisting that the girls were still much too small and frail to be moved. The Canadian prime minister, ostensibly outraged by the prospect of vaudeville tours and film contracts for infants barely old enough to open their eyes, interceded and made the quintuplets wards of the state, establishing a board of four guardians, which included Dafoe, and a trust fund of $1 million to care for the infants. Dafoe was to have authority to raise them, assisted by

a round-the-clock staff of nurses and nuns in a specially built, nine-room nursery on the Dionne farm. The parents and their older children were to remain segregated in the old farmhouse. The parents were allowed daily visits to the compound, but the older siblings were initially forbidden to play with the quints.

For nine years the girls lived a goldfish-bowl existence. Three million tourists (as many as 6,000 a day) came to gawk at them through one-way windows, and a miniature empire of souvenir shops, motels, gas stations, quick-food stands, and bus lines sprouted up in the fertile soil surrounding the Dionne farm. An official photographer, Fred Davis, was allowed one hour every morning to photograph the sisters. They were in great demand in the media and in advertisements for a multitude of products—everything from cod liver oil to General Motors cars. Dr. Dafoe, a country doctor and a widower with one child of his own, grew rich on product endorsements and royalties from books, films, and newsreels. The Ontario government profited enormously from tourism revenue, including some $4 million in gasoline taxes.

In 1941, after years of legal struggles, Elzire and Oliva Dionne regained from Dafoe the custody of their daughters, and North America's "number one peep show" drew to a close. But the quints remained in enforced isolation behind a barbed-wire fence surrounding a new, heavily guarded seven-bedroom family home that had been built on the Dionne farm. Their privacy abused and their freedom denied them, the girls were treated harshly by their parents and deprived of the $30,000 a year due them from movie appearances and endorsements. Later, the girls were to write retrospectively that they had had "a painfully unhappy childhood."

And After: The years since they faded from the public eye have not been kind to the Dionne quintuplets. Emilie, who was studying to be a nun at a convent in the Laurentians, suffocated in 1954 during an epileptic seizure. Marie died sixteen years later in squalid obscurity, in a Montreal apartment. The most troubled of the quintuplets, she had also sought happiness as a nun but had failed to find it. She suffered a nervous breakdown in the spring of 1957. On the road to emotional security, the next year she had married a civil servant, Florian Houle, fourteen years her senior. But Marie, who bore two children, was haunted by several miscarriages, and the frequent work-related absences of her husband strained their marriage. She had been separated from Houle and living alone for several years drinking heavily and suffering from depression, when she died of a blood clot to the brain on February 27, 1970.

The three surviving sisters—Yvonne, Cécile, and Annette—live today in Saint Bruno, a suburb of Montreal. Yvonne, who has never

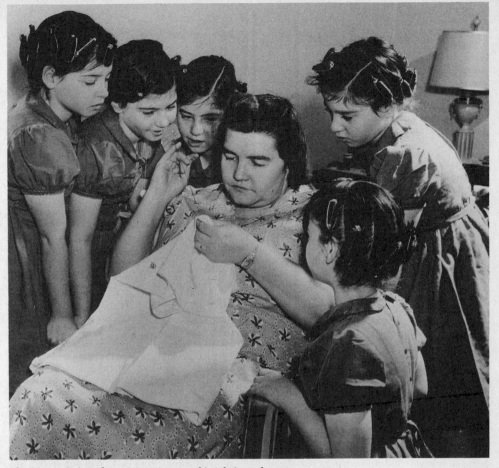

The Dionne Quintuplets, at age nine, watching their mother sew.

married, came with Cécile to Montreal in the mid-1950s to attend nursing school. Annette also moved to Montreal to enroll in college. It was during that time that Cécile met Philippe Langlois and Annette began to date Germain Allard. These were the girls' first boyfriends and they were both married within two years.

Cécile and Langlois moved to Quebec City. They were beset by tragedy when one of their twin boys died in infancy. Some years later, Cécile sued for divorce and custody of their surviving children and returned to the Montreal area to be near her sisters. Their closeness put such a strain on Annette's marriage that her husband, Germain, finally gave her an ultimatum, "The only way to save our marriage is to sell the house and move out of this circle of you and your sisters and try to start all over again." Annette chose her sisters, Cécile and Yvonne.

While Yvonne managed to live comfortably on her income from the quintuplets' trust fund, the two divorced women struggled to support their families. Cécile's share of the trust fund had dwindled to $50,000 and, partly because of her ex-husband's lavish spending, she was forced to work as a checker in a local supermarket.

The three surviving quintuplets did not see their parents for nearly a dozen years. Their father, Oliva, had been deeply hurt by the 1965 book *We Were Five* (by Marie, Annette, and Cécile; Yvonne did not participate), in which the women described their unhappiness in the strict Catholic family home. Oliva died in 1979 and his wife, Elzire, died in 1986. The couple had remained in the large family home built for them and their thirteen children by the Ontario government in 1941.

Today, Yvonne, Cécile, and Annette guard their privacy and live inconspicuously on their modest incomes in Saint Bruno. They detest the term quintuplets. In 1993 they hired an attorney to sue the city of North Bay, Ontario, for operating The Dionne Quints Museum and using their name without permission. The city had purchased the original Dionne homestead in 1985 and runs it today as a museum and gift shop open during the summer months. Settling out of court, the city agreed to pay them 15 percent of the museum's entry fees. The sisters stand to gain only a few thousand dollars a year—and perhaps the satisfaction that at last they themselves have something to say about the public merchandising of the Dionne quintuplets.

—B.F. and L.A.C.

HEADLINE—1952: CHRISTINE JORGENSEN

At the Peak: Before the fuss began, Christine was just plain George Jorgensen, a kid from the Bronx who was never very happy, back in the 1930s, when his father encouraged him to play baseball and football like the rest of the boys. It seemed George was always happier dressing up dolls or playing hopscotch with the girls. And all through school and a series of photographer's jobs, and even in the U.S. Army, it was the same story: George wanted to be a girl. So in 1950 he went to see some doctors in Denmark he'd heard about and asked them to make him one.

Two years later, after a series of operations and almost 2,000 hormone injections, Jorgensen returned to New York amid a flurry of unwanted publicity as Christine, the first sex-change woman known to the American public. The fashion editor of the *Los Angeles Times* enthused, "Christine Jorgensen is pretty, personable and pleasant—by any standard. She's courteous and intelligent, too. Over lunch at the Statler yesterday, this reporter forgot to remember her past maleness and saw only her present femininity and charm." Of course, not everyone was convinced that the switch had been a success. Here's how the *New York Daily News* reported the homecoming: "Christine Jorgensen, the lad who became a lady, arrived home from Denmark yesterday, lit a cigarette like a girl, husked 'Hello,' and tossed off a Bloody Mary like a guy, then opened her fur coat. Jane Russell has nothing to worry about."

When the first flurry of jokes and news stories had faded away, Christine went on to play some minor stage roles, star in her own nightclub act, write her autobiography, and become involved in two well-publicized romances that led to engagement but not marriage. She also appeared occasionally on talk shows and made the circuit as a campus lecturer, giving talks on "how to deal with being different."

Interviewed in 1978, when sex-change surgery was almost commonplace, the fifty-one-year-old Jorgensen commented, "Twenty years ago I met with almost complete hostility. Today there's almost complete comprehension. I am the woman I always wanted to be. I'm happy and I love life. And it is a fairly normal life, too. I date quite a bit."

And After: Christine Jorgensen died May 3, 1989, in San Clemente, California, after a two-and-a-half-year struggle with cancer that started in her bladder and spread to her lungs. She attributed her disease to a family history of cancer and a two-pack-a-day cigarette habit—not to her heavy hormone usage.

Although Jorgensen played a large role in changing people's attitudes toward transsexuals, she did not like to be labeled by that term. She referred to herself simply as having undergone a "sex change." In the year before her death, she told a reporter, "What people still don't understand is that the important thing is identity. You don't do it primarily for sexual reasons, you do it because of who you are. Most people can't accept that no animal is 100 percent male or 100 percent female. We are dealing with a series of degrees."

At the time of her death, Jorgensen was working on a sequel to her 1967 autobiography. She bequeathed her personal papers and other documents to the Royal Library in Copenhagen, the city where her life as a woman began.

—G.G. and L.A.C.

HEADLINE—1955: ROSA PARKS

At the Peak: It was only a two-letter word and it was uttered quietly. But it was heard throughout the city of Montgomery, the state of Alabama, the United States of America, and the world. No. Rosa Parks said no. She would not give up her seat to a white man. No. She would not go stand at the back of the bus.

It was not a premeditated ploy for attention. She didn't plan to create an explosive situation. Although she was active in the NAACP (National Association for the Advancement of Colored People), Rosa Parks was not a rebel. She simply was tired and her feet hurt. It had been a long day at the Montgomery Fair, the department store where she worked in alterations. Perhaps because she was weary, her tolerance for injustice was low. Anyway, slim as the proverbial straw, the neatly dressed seamstress managed by her action to break the patience of the people of her color and motivate them to unite and start overcoming.

It was after six o'clock on the cold, dark evening of Thursday, December 1, 1955, that forty-two-year-old Rosa Parks, by remaining seated, stood up against discrimination. This caused her to be referred to often as the mother of the civil-rights movement.

In Montgomery, blacks formed 70 percent of the bus riders, but they were forced to pay fares at the front of the bus, disembark, then reboard through the back door to sit in the black section. They were never allowed in the white-only section, even if the bus was empty. On this December evening, Rosa Parks's bus quickly filled with passengers. The bus driver, J. F. Blake, noticed a white man standing and ordered all those sitting in Rosa Parks's row to vacate their seats in the black section to make room for the white passenger. Three of the blacks reluctantly moved to stand in the back of the bus, but Rosa Parks, on her way home with a full bag of groceries, did not.

In recalling what happened on the bus, Mrs. Parks said, "The bus driver turned around and looked at me. 'If you don't move,' he said, 'I'll call the police and have you arrested.' " She remembers saying, "Have me arrested. I'm not going to move."

Within minutes two officers boarded the bus to escort Parks to jail, where she was finger-printed and booked for violating the bus segregation laws. Word of the arrest quickly spread in the black community to Edgar Daniel Nixon, head of the local NAACP. Rosa Parks was a volunteer worker and elected secretary for the association. Nixon made an unsuccessful call to the police to determine the charges and then headed down to the station, accompanied by Clifford Durr, a white civil-rights lawyer, and his wife, Virginia, also an activist, where he signed a $100 bond for Parks's release.

Mrs. Parks said she was glad she didn't have to remain in jail until her trial, which was set for Monday, four days away. She felt that already her husband and mother must be terribly worried about why she was so late getting home from work.

That weekend, indignant members of the civil-rights community went into action. Blacks had been arrested and fined many times before for violation of the bus segregation laws. The NAACP and the Women's Political Council, a group of black teachers and professional women, had been keeping an eye out for a test case to challenge these unjust race laws in court and to create a focus for public protest. The arrest of hard-working, dignified Rosa Parks presented a solid symbol for challenge.

By fighting the charges against her, Mrs. Parks knew she was entering a dangerous battle. Although her husband, Raymond, a barber, was against it, telling her, "The white folks will kill you, Rosa," she made her own decision and announced to Nixon and the Durrs, "If you think it will mean something to Montgomery and do some good, I'll be happy to go along with it."

Nixon immediately began calling community and religious leaders, who met to plan a protest. There is some dispute as to whether the idea for the bus boycott came from Nixon or the Women's Political Council. In any event, a boycott of public transportation was quickly planned for that Monday. The Women's Political Council blanketed Montgomery with 52,000 leaflets announcing the boycott. The group assembled by Nixon called themselves the Montgomery Improvement Association and asked the new pastor of the Dexter Avenue Baptist Church, an unknown twenty-six-year-old who had a way with words, to be the spokesman for the protest. The young man's name was Martin Luther King Jr.

On Monday some 500 blacks crowded the hallways and entrance of the courthouse.

Rosa Parks was tried, found guilty, and fined fourteen dollars, which she refused to pay. Her case was appealed. On that same day, the bus boycott by blacks started. It was an unqualified success. Taxicabs were used and private cars were recruited to form a carpool system that eventually transported 30,000 people a day. Planned originally for one day, the boycott ended 381 days after Rosa Parks's resistance triggered it. And the blacks discovered, perhaps to their amazement, that they did have an effective source of power—pocketbook power. The nearly empty buses meant losses in revenue, and in time the company went broke.

The leaders of the Montgomery Improvement Association filed suit in federal court to have segregated bus seating declared unconstitutional. The court ruled in their favor and, on appeal, the Supreme Court upheld the ruling. On December 20, 1956, the highest court in the land served its order on Montgomery officials that the city's buses must be integrated.

Blacks as well as white sympathizers rejoiced, and persuasive preacher Martin Luther King, with a Ph.D. from Boston University, was catapulted into the lead position of the struggle for civil rights. The still-pending Rosa Parks case was dropped.

And After: Rosa Parks and her husband, Raymond, who died in 1977, settled in Detroit, Michigan, in 1957. Moving north apparently had nothing directly to do with what happened

Rosa Parks being fingerprinted by Deputy Sheriff D. H. Lackey in Montgomery, Alabama.

to her in the South, although she did lose her job because of her role in the boycott.

"We moved to Detroit because my only brother lived there and I wanted to be near him," Rosa Parks is quoted as saying. She explained that they stayed in Montgomery until things were quiet, which was before the students became active.

In Detroit, in order to supplement the income of her husband, she worked as a seamstress until the spring of 1965. After that she was hired as a secretary in the office of Congressman John Conyers Jr. (D-Michigan), where she worked until her retirement in 1988.

There are those of her admirers who feel she never has been given enough recognition. It is doubtful whether Mrs. Parks shares this feeling. Throughout the years she has been the recipient of many honors, including ten honorary college degrees, and frequently she was photographed with Martin Luther King Jr. She celebrated her seventy-seventh birthday in 1990 at Lincoln Center, honored by a crowd of 3,000 black leaders, politicians, and entertainers.

A major street and a $3 million junior high school in Detroit bear her name.

In August 1994, Rosa Parks made headlines as the victim of urban crime. She was attacked in her Detroit home and robbed of fifty-three dollars by a twenty-eight-year-old black man. She was briefly hospitalized and treated for lacerations on her face. Letters from across the country and as far away as Japan poured in, expressing sympathy for Parks and outrage at the crime. Her attacker, Joseph Skipper, a drug addict, was arrested and held separately from other prisoners in the county jail for fear of reprisals. Only ten days after the assault, Parks underwent surgery to replace her pacemaker; her doctors were not sure if the problem was related to injuries sustained in the attack.

Rosa Parks doesn't have children of her own to perpetuate her existence. However, it seems unlikely her name will be forgotten by future generations. It is firmly inscribed in her country's history.

—L.A.C.

HEADLINE—1963: CHRISTINE KEELER

At the Peak: London's tabloid News of the World paid her £20,000 for the serialization of her life story, and several books and two movies have been produced about her sub rosa exploits among the British upper crust. Christine Keeler, whatever her ultimate intent may have been, helped to topple the Tory government of 1963 and possibly endangered the national security of her country. Here is a hindsight look at what has come to be known as the Profumo Affair.

Born in Middlesex in 1942, Christine grew up in a converted railway car with her mother and stepfather, Ted Huish. She left school at age fifteen and a year later stole a car to get to

London, where she hoped to have a glamorous life as one of the "models" written about in the gossip columns. For perhaps a year she worked as a waitress in London, then was hired as a showgirl at Murray's Cabaret Club. After the chorus show, the girls would sit with customers to encourage their drinking, for which they earned a share of the house profits. If they chose to take a man home, which Christine may have done from time to time, they might make twenty-five pounds of their own for the enterprise. At the club Christine met and frequently entertained a wealthy Arab who in turn introduced her to the man who was to change her life—Dr. Stephen Ward, an osteopath.

Ward fingered the spines of only the wealthy and titled. His patients included such politicians as Winston Churchill and such celebrities as Elizabeth Taylor and Ava Gardner. His sidelines were sketching portraits of his famous patients and ingratiating himself with lords and tycoons by providing introductions to attractive, willing young women. London in the early sixties was heady with the "new morality," and Ward, who had a voyeuristic streak, enjoyed initiating sexual games. Ward himself shared his London flat with a series of young women, including Christine Keeler and her blond, pixie-faced coworker at the cabaret, Marilyn ("Mandy") Rice-Davies, then sixteen years old. During and after the scandal that later unfolded, both women denied any sexual relationship with Ward.

Ward was a good friend of the playboy Viscount Astor and had penetrated Astor's "Cliveden set" of wealthy right-wing politicos. Lord Astor rented a cottage on his estate to Ward for one pound a year. In exchange, Ward hosted weekend parties for the elite with bacchanalian entertainment. At a party at the Cliveden estate in July 1961, Ward introduced Christine, naked in a swimming pool, to Lord John Dennis Profumo, war minister of the government. Profumo was married to actress Valerie Hobson, who had appeared in such films as Great Expectations and The Bride of Frankenstein, but he wasted no time in seeing Christine again.

What followed was an affair of brief duration between Christine and Profumo, conducted at Ward's flat in Wimpole Mews. Whether the lord knew or not, Christine had frolicked on the same premises with Eugene "Huggy Bear" Ivanov, assistant naval attaché to the Russian embassy and known by MI-5 to be a Soviet spy. After receiving security warnings, Profumo ended the meetings with Christine in an affectionate farewell note to her. Not long afterward, Christine took up with some West Indian blues musicians and drug users. She lived with one of the crew, a Jamaican named Johnnie Edgecombe, who grew jealous of her other boyfriends, even attacking a rival, Aloysius "Lucky" Gordon, with a knife. One night in December 1962 when Christine was visiting Mandy Rice-Davies, then a roommate at Ward's flat, Edgecombe showed up and started shooting wildly through the door. When he was brought to trial, Christine was a key witness, but she fled to Spain to avoid testifying. Before her departure, she had discussed with friends, including a former Labour M.P., facts about her past that might be revealed on the witness stand—namely, her liaisons with Ivanov and Profumo. She had also decided to sell her story to London's *Sunday Pictorial*.

While Keeler was in Spain, all hell broke loose. On March 22, 1963, in a speech before the House of Commons, Profumo denied that he had ever been to bed with Christine Keeler. But the London paper was in possession of the farewell letter he had written to Christine. It was addressed to "Darling" and seemed to contradict his testimony. Stephen Ward had sent a letter to Prime Minister Harold Macmillan's private secretary, and the contents became known to the House of Commons. A full investigation by British MI-5 intelligence showed that Huggy Bear Ivanov had asked Ward to find out from Profumo when the United States would deliver nuclear warheads to West Germany. The purpose was to forestall a U.S.-Soviet showdown over the Cuban Missile Crisis. The assumption was made that Ward had put Christine up to the task during her intimate moments with Profumo. By the time of the Edgecombe trial, Ivanov had been recalled to Moscow, where he was treated to an early retirement.

By the summer of 1963, the Profumo affair was café and bar talk the world over. Profumo confessed publicly to an "impropriety" with Keeler, although he adamantly denied that any breach of national security had taken place. His real crime was lying to the House of Commons in his previous denial, and political pressure forced him to resign in early June. Within days, Ward was stopped in his white Jaguar and arrested by Scotland Yard, who had received anonymous letters about him. Released on a bail equivalent to $8,400, Ward was ordered to stand trial on eight counts, the charges ranging from running a brothel to arranging for abortions.

The police had conducted a massive investigation, interviewing some 140 people to find evidence against Ward. The trial itself, in July and August, was a kind of Rabelaisian Miss Universe pageant, with a parade of vivacious showgirls and prostitutes taking the stand and swapping stories of two-way mirrors, sadomasochistic play with whips and marijuana, and even mention of a naked, masked, male "host" whose real identity was too sensitive for the world to know. The stars of the extravaganza were Mandy Rice-Davies and Christine Keeler. Christine testified she had not repaid loans Ward had made to her, but stated clearly, "I am not a prostitute and never have been." Mandy admitted to sleeping with Lord Astor and the

actor Douglas Fairbanks and said Ward had encouraged her to have sex with other men—an admission she later retracted in her memoirs. In her book *The Mandy Report*, published in 1964, she wrote, "No one would deny that Stephen was a depraved and immoral man. . . . He most certainly never influenced me to sleep with anyone, nor ever asked me to do so."

Ward claimed in his testimony that he was an agent of MI-5, hired to keep tabs on and entrap Ivanov. By introducing Ivanov to Keeler and reporting the Profumo-Keeler affair to the government, he said, he was just doing his job for British intelligence. At the time of the trial, MI-5 denied any such doings.

On the last day of the trial, Ward overdosed on barbiturates and lay in a coma as the jury returned their verdict—he was found guilty of living on immoral earnings. He died on August 3, 1963, before the judge could pronounce his sentence. Three months later, Prime Minister Macmillan was forced out by the scandal, resigning on the grounds of ill health. His ignominious exit made room for the Labour Party's victory in the next year's elections and ended thirteen years of Conservative rule.

Keeler's personal life was further exposed in another trial in the Old Bailey by conflicting accounts of her affair with the Jamaican jazz singer Lucky Gordon. In a sober state, Keeler testified that Gordon had beaten her up in April, after her return from Spain. Gordon retorted that all he got from her in return for marijuana was VD. In a drunken tape-recorded confession, Keeler finally admitted that Gordon was not guilty of the assault charge, and he was released. In December 1963, Christine Keeler was sentenced to nine months for perjury and conspiracy to obstruct justice. "All I want," she said tearfully after the court adjourned, "is for everyone to let me be a normal girl again."

And After: Some of the cast of characters in the Profumo affair still live in London, and some have died. Lord Astor saw his last days at Cliveden in 1966, during which his wife had the estate exorcised by a priest. She then leased the mansion to Stanford University. Today Cliveden is a luxury hotel.

Profumo's political career was ended forever by his "indiscretion," but his family's wealth has been enough to sustain him in a lordly fashion. He has worked as a volunteer with drug addicts, alcoholics, and the homeless in London's East End, and was redeemed in the eyes of Queen Elizabeth, who named him a Commander of the Order of the British Empire in 1975. Profumo is still married to Valerie Hobson. The two maintained an unbroken silence about the affair for thirty years, until they won a successful libel suit against Ivanov in 1992. In his book *The Naked Spy*, Ivanov had alleged that he stole documents from the Profumo home while Valerie Hobson made tea for him. Apparently that charge was too much for the stoic wife of Profumo.

Ivanov himself died in Moscow in 1994, ravaged by the effects of a heavy vodka habit. In the years before his death, Christine Keeler visited him in Moscow and he offered an apology for having slept with her in hopes of learning military secrets from Profumo.

While Keeler reconciled with Ivanov, she and Mandy Rice-Davies have not spoken for years. Mandy moved on from the days of scandal to work as a cabaret singer in Europe and Israel. She married an Israeli flight attendant and the couple owned several successful restaurants in Tel Aviv. Today she and her second husband, a businessman, have homes in Miami and London and Rice-Davies is a published novelist.

The postscript for Christine Keeler is not so upbeat. After serving six months of her jail sentence, she was married briefly to a laborer, a union that produced a son. During the late sixties, she sold her life story to Rupert Murdoch's News of the World and was sighted about London with such bohemians as Penelope Tree and Marianne Faithfull. In the next two decades, however, she fell on very hard times, living on social security in government-owned housing and occasionally taking jobs in telemarketing and at a dry cleaner's. A second brief marriage, to a business executive, ended in his bankruptcy, divorce, and a bitter custody battle over their son, Seymour.

In 1989, at age forty-seven, Keeler attended the world premier of the movie Scandal! about her youthful exploits, on the arm of her seventeen-year-old son. Her celebrity status has netted her neither riches nor success with men; she now lives with two cats as company.

Today Keeler claims that Ward was engaged in espionage, possibly as a double agent, but she denies that any government secrets were revealed during the one time she slept with Ivanov or the four or five times she bedded Profumo.

Recently the London Times confirmed anonymous sources within MI-5 that Ward had, in fact, been in its employ. The full story will have to wait, however, until more documents are revealed—documents being held by the government until "an unspecified time." In the meantime, followers of the story can visit London's National Gallery to view a portrait of Christine Keeler drawn by Stephen Ward.

—W.F.R. and L.A.C.

HEADLINE—1975: OLIVER SIPPLE

At the Peak: At 3:29 P.M. on the twenty-second of September 1975, an act of sublime intervention by Oliver W. Sipple thwarted an assassination attempt on President Gerald Ford. Sipple was part of a crowd of about 3,000 people who had gathered outside San Francisco's Saint Francis Hotel to see the president. Ford, just emerging from the building, was vulnerable despite heavy security protection. Sipple noticed that the woman next to him had pulled and leveled a .38-caliber pistol as Ford headed to his limousine. Reacting instinctually, Sipple lunged at the woman, Sara Jane Moore, just as her finger squeezed the trigger. He managed to jar her arm slightly. It was enough of a jar, however, to deflect her aim and cause the bullet to veer five feet wide of its mark. Had it not been for Sipple's action, the bullet would have struck the president in the head.

Sipple was no stranger to gunfire. He had served in the marines and saw action in Vietnam. Shrapnel wounds suffered in December 1968 caused him to finish out his tour of duty in a Philadelphia veterans hospital, from which he was released in March of 1970. He later spent six months in San Francisco's VA hospital and, at the time of the assassination attempt, was frequently being readmitted into the hospital. Listed as being 100 percent disabled on psychological grounds, he was unable to hold a job and was receiving disability pay. He lived, with a merchant seaman roommate, in a fourth-floor walk-up apartment located in San Francisco's Mission District.

And After: The police and Secret Service immediately commended Sipple for his action at the scene, while Ford thanked him in a letter. Unfortunately, Sipple became not only an instant hero but an instant victim as well. The media not only hailed and celebrated his deed, they also disclosed his private life. Though he was known to be a homosexual by various fellow members of San Francisco's gay community, Oliver W. Sipple had not publicly "come out of the closet." His sexual identity was something he had always kept secret from his family. He asked the press reporters to leave him alone, making it clear that neither his mother nor his employer had knowledge of his sexual orientation.

Despite his wishes, gay activist and politician Harvey Milk (who was later assassinated by Dan White), publicly proclaimed Sipple and said his act "will help break the stereotype of homosexuals." Gay liberation groups petitioned local media to give Sipple his due as a gay hero. Then columnist Herb Caen published the private side of the ex-marine's story in the San Francisco Chronicle. Six other papers ran the column as well. After discovering her son's secret, Sipple's mother reacted to the public harassment she began to endure by cutting off contact with him.

Sipple, the reluctant hero, filed a $15 million invasion-of-privacy suit against Caen, the seven newspapers that published his disclosures, and fifty "John Doe" publishers for invading his privacy. A San Francisco superior court judge dismissed the suit by Sipple, who continued his legal battle until May 1984, when a state court of appeals upheld the original dismissal.

Sipple's mental and physical health sharply declined over the years. He drank heavily, was fitted with a pacemaker, became paranoid and suicidal. His weight went up to 298 pounds. On February 2, 1989, he was found dead in his bed, with a half-gallon bottle of bourbon at his side. The forty-seven-year-old Sipple had been dead for two weeks.

Sara Jane Moore, convicted of attempted assassination and given a life sentence, is currently imprisoned at the Federal Correctional Institution in Dublin, California.

—R.N.K.

HEADLINE—1982: MICHAEL FAGAN

At the Peak: At 6:45 on the morning of July 9, 1982, Michael Fagan, a thirty-one-year-old unemployed painter and decorator under the occasional delusion that he was the son of Rudolf Hess, climbed a fence into the grounds of Buckingham Palace.

He entered the palace through a ground-floor window, set off an alarm (which was ignored), retreated, then shinnied up a drainpipe to climb through an open window on the floor above. He wandered the palace unchallenged for fifteen minutes before entering the queen's bedroom carrying a piece of broken glass from an ashtray. He half intended, he later said, to use it to cut his wrists in front of the queen.

The queen pressed an alarm bell, which failed to get any response. Twice she used her bedside telephone to call officers from the palace police lodge to her room. None came.

Meantime, Fagan sat on her bed and told her of his family problems. The queen responded with gracious small talk (she'd had years of practice), observing that he'd be about the same age as her son Charles. When Fagan asked for a cigarette, she managed to leave the room, promising to find one. Outside she found a chambermaid, to whom she explained the problem. "Bloody hell ma'am!" said the maid. "He shouldn't be in there!"

In retelling the story, the queen reportedly said she was less scared of Fagan than the prospect that Prince Philip might enter the bedroom while he was there. "I knew that all hell would break loose if that happened. That's all I was really thinking about."

The chambermaid and the queen led Fagan into a pantry as a footman arrived from walking the queen's corgis. He plied Fagan with cigarettes while the queen kept the dogs at bay. Finally, one policeman, then another, arrived to take Fagan away.

The episode provoked a huge security scare, especially when it emerged that Fagan had penetrated the palace five weeks previously, during a state visit by President and Mrs. Reagan, when security was supposed to be watertight. The British press fell gleefully on the story, reporting that the queen was wearing a short nightdress and had her hair in pins. They were intrigued that the queen and her husband slept separately and many column inches were expended on impertinent speculation about the royal love life.

An indirect victim of the scandal was Commander Michael Trestrail, who resigned as head of the queen's security after confessing to being gay. This had emerged when a male prostitute tried to cash in on the Fagan story by selling details of his relationship with Trestrail to the press. Trestrail was not guilty of any dereliction of duty, but by the idiomatic reasoning of the British establishment, "homosexual" usually equals "security risk."

Under English law, Fagan could not be prosecuted for trespass, a civil offense, but was charged with the theft of a half bottle of wine on his first visit. He was acquitted by a jury, which felt he had had no criminal intent, and on the basis of medical opinion sent to a mental hospital. Later in 1982 he was charged with stealing a motor vehicle in an unrelated incident and was committed indefinitely.

And After: In January 1983 Fagan was discharged from a maximum security hospital in Liverpool on the recommendation of a mental health tribunal, which ruled that while he was still mentally ill there was no need for him to be detained.

The security of Buckingham Palace had been breached several times before. In December 1838, early in Queen Victoria's reign, a twelve-year-old boy was caught who had been living in the palace for a year. In 1840 and 1841, seventeen-year-old Edmund Jones made three break-ins. He sat on the throne and fell asleep in the queen's sitting room. He was twice sentenced to the treadmill before being enlisted in the Royal Navy. "Supposing he had come into the bedroom! How frightened I should have been!" wrote Victoria.

Several people have been caught in the palace grounds in recent years, most notably three German backpackers who camped there for a night on June 14, 1981, thinking they were in Hyde Park. In June 1994, thirty-year-old American James Miller paraglided onto the palace roof, then stripped off his pants to reveal that he was painted green from the waist down. Her Majesty was not in residence at the time.

—E.B.

HEADLINE—1984: BERNHARD GOETZ

At the Peak: Bernhard Goetz was a thirty-seven-year-old, self-employed engineer who lived on West Fourteenth Street on the outskirts of Greenwich Village when fear and fate worked in tandem to cause this soft-spoken man to become known as the notorious Subway Vigilante. Goetz, who had been active in community-improvement campaigns, had been a victim of urban crime in January of 1981. Three black teenagers beat and mugged him in a subway station. Two of his assailants escaped capture, the third was caught by police and let go after less than three hours. Goetz was questioned for six hours. Seeking to protect himself from any such brutalization in the future, he attempted to obtain a permit to carry a handgun. His permit request was denied and so Bernhard Goetz circumvented the law by buying a revolver in Florida.

Goetz was carrying this pistol on December 22, 1984, when he boarded a subway car at New York City's Fourteenth Street subway station. He took a seat in an uncrowded car. Sharing the car were four black teenagers—Barry Allen, Darrell Cabey, Troy Canty, and James Ramseur. Canty asked Goetz how he was doing. Goetz responded that he was doing fine. According to testimony that Goetz later gave in court, the teens stood up and moved toward him— forming a wall between him and the subway doors. Canty now demanded that Goetz give him five dollars. Goetz stood up and unzipped his jacket and asked that the demand be repeated. When it was, Goetz responded by pulling out his gun and firing a bullet into each of the four teenagers. After surveying their injuries Goetz discovered that one of the wounded, Darrell Cabey, did not seem to be bleeding. "You seem to be all right," said Goetz, "here's another." Then he shot a fifth bullet, which blasted into the boy's spine—paralyzing him from the waist down and leaving him with permanent brain damage.

When the train pulled into its next stop, Goetz was accosted by a conductor, who asked him if he was a cop. Goetz told him that he wasn't, that "they tried to rip me off." He then jumped out onto the subway tracks and headed into the darkness of a subway tunnel.

Goetz rented a car that same afternoon and drove it north to Vermont and into New Hampshire. Nine days later, in the middle of the last day of the year, he entered a police station in Concord, New Hampshire, and gave a two-hour confession recorded on audio tape and a two-hour confession recorded on video. Turned over to authorities in New York State on January 3, 1985, Goetz was subsequently placed in Rikers Island Prison. He posted $50,000 bail on January 7 and was released.

His criminal trial began in December of 1986. On June 16, 1987, he was acquitted of twelve charges but found guilty of a thirteenth—illegal gun possession.

And After: Goetz, who received a one-year sentence, served 250 days in jail owing to a reduction for good behavior. He was released from the Brooklyn House of Detention on September 21, 1989. His troubles, however, did not end. He faced a $50 million civil lawsuit filed by Darrell Cabey, the man whom Goetz

paralyzed with the fifth bullet he fired. In April 1996, a New York civil court jury found Goetz guilty of reckless behavior and ordered him to pay $43 million in damages to Cabey.

—R.N.K.

HEADLINE—1987: MATHIAS RUST

At the Peak: On the day that *Pravda* marked Soviet Border Guards Day with an editorial saying that "every meter" of the USSR's frontier was "under reliable surveillance," a nineteen-year-old German flew across 750 kilometers of supposedly well-defended Soviet airspace and landed in one of Russia's most sacred places.

A neat and introverted character who lived with his parents near Hamburg, Mathias Rust was obsessed with flying. Virtually all his earnings as a computer operator for a mail-order trinket company went on flying. On May 28, 1987, while on a flying tour of Scandinavia in a single-engine Cessna 172 that he had chartered, he left his stated course from Helsinki to Stockholm and flew to Moscow. He landed near Red Square at around 7 P.M. and, after signing autographs, was arrested.

Soviet officials defensively claimed that Rust had not actually evaded the USSR's air defenses, but that they had chosen not to shoot him down because nobody could decide what to do about his apparently harmless civil aircraft.

Mathias Rust's Cessna parked in Moscow's Red Square, May 29, 1987.

The West German government condemned his "foolhardy act," but the Soviet Communist daily *Pravda* alleged that Rust had been on a politically motivated suicide mission. Others suggested that his motive could be found in a World War II German aviators' drinking song, "On Ascension Day We Land in Red Square" (May 28, 1987, was Ascension Day).

A month later, in the Moscow Supreme Court, he stated he had been on a peace mission. The court didn't buy it, said his journey was an ego trip, and gave him four years for malicious hooliganism, three years for violating international flight rules, and two years for illegal entry to the USSR, all sentences to run concurrently. In Moscow's Lefortovo Prison, he repaired books for the prison library and practiced his Russian and English with other inmates. He was released eleven months later, following a visit to Moscow by West Germany's foreign minister. His family sold their story exclusively to Germany's mass-circulation *Stern* magazine for an undisclosed fee, some of which Rust spent on a Mercedes-Benz and a horse.

Rust's flight was not entirely without precedent. On November 13, 1938, a Briton named Brian Grover landed a light plane in the village of Noginsk, 125 miles north of Moscow. He had hoped to be reunited with his sweetheart Yelena Golius, a pharmacist's assistant in Grozny. After spending a month in jail, he was allowed to marry Golius, after which the couple moved to England.

And After: As a conscientious objector, Mathias Rust avoided military service by working as an orderly in a Hamburg hospital. There, on November 23, 1989, he stabbed a student nurse three times with a switchblade. Had she not already been in a hospital she would have died.

Newspapers that had once compared Rust to the Red Baron now dubbed him "Mac the Knife." He insisted on opening and reading every letter in the sackload of hate mail he received. "It makes him happy," said his attorney, Yitzhak Goldfine. "They become his imaginary friends."

At his trial for attempted manslaughter in April 1991, the court heard how Rust had had a crush on nursing student Stefanie Walura. On November 23, 1989, he followed her into a locker room; as he approached her, she feared he was about to kiss her and screamed. Rust backed off and Walura started to leave, when he knifed her. He claimed she had taunted him.

Goldfine portrayed Rust as friendless and confused. A psychiatrist testified that he suffered from "narcissistic neuroses." Goldfine hinted that KGB officers had drugged him in Moscow and that such drugs might cause aggression years later. The court accepted that the attack was not premeditated and Rust got two and a half years' imprisonment. Spectators in the courtroom jeered the leniency of the sentence.

Mathias Rust was freed in October 1993. Before his trial he became engaged to a Polish woman and said he planned to train as a veterinary surgeon and leave Germany forever.

—E.B.

HEADLINE—1992: REGINALD DENNY

At the Peak: In the late afternoon of April 29, 1992, in south central Los Angeles, Reginald Denny was listening to "soothing music" while driving his 80,000-pound, 18-wheeler truck loaded with gravel through the intersection of Florence and Normandie Avenues after taking a shortcut off the freeway.

A few hours earlier, about thirty miles away, in the white surburban community of Simi Valley, California, a nearly all-white jury acquitted four white Los Angeles police officers of beating a black motorist named Rodney King.

Those two events were forever linked when some black citizens, angry at the verdicts, stopped Denny's semi, pulled him from the driver's seat to the ground, and then proceeded to beat him relentlessly. It was the start of the 1992 Los Angeles riots.

The beating was almost celebratory in nature. But it was also violent and ugly as Denny was pounded by the angry crowd. The culmination of the incident came as a dazed and bloody Denny seemed to be rising up. He got on his knees. But then from behind, one of the angry blacks, from almost point-blank range, threw some hard gravel at Denny's head. He collapsed to the ground as his assaulter raised his arms in triumph and seemed to be dancing.

The incident became a defining moment for Los Angeles's 1992 riots, which continued for several days following the King verdict and resulted in the deaths of more than fifty people. As the beating was taking place, one of the many television news helicopters photographing the riots was overhead. The beating of Reginald Denny was shown live on Los Angeles television and replayed on stations worldwide in the days after.

Denny himself would probably have died if it had not been for the courageous efforts of Lei Yuille, Bobby Green, Terri Barnett, and Titus Murphy, who saw the attack on television. With the riots growing in intensity and violence, these citizens, who lived nearby, came to the intersection of Florence and Normandie. Amazingly, the battered Denny had been able to lift himself off the ground and climb back into the driver's cab. Bobby Green persuaded Denny to move over and they sped, with horns blaring, to a nearby hospital.

As Denny was being driven to the hospital, he was falling in and out of consciousness. While paramedics were taking him inside the emergency room, Denny began to go into convulsions. Doctors discovered Denny had a large

Reginald Denny being beaten by Damian Williams, Henry Watson, and two others, on April 29, 1992.

depressed skull fracture of the right side of his head and between 90 and 100 hundred fractures in his face. His left eye dropped three-quarters of an inch behind his cheekbone and an emergency operation had to be performed to place a breathing tube in Denny's throat because Denny was beginning to strangle on his tongue. He remained in a coma for six days.

Doctors said afterward that Denny came within minutes of dying. They were able to save Denny's life, but it required a heroic effort and Denny required massive reconstructive surgery to make his face look normal again.

The man whose life "was a bore . . . and I liked it," became a celebrity. More than 25,000 letters were sent to the hospital, where he remained for thirty-three days. He once sneaked out of the hospital to go watch some boats drag racing at a lake. The event overcame Denny, who began to cry while the boat racers all hugged him.

Denny remembers the events leading up to his beating but doesn't remember the beating itself. "It was just one big wallop," he recalled.

After the Denny incident, four blacks were arrested in connection with the assault and put on trial. It was yet another one of a series of cases that gripped Los Angeles after the Rodney King beating. Jurors acquitted the two main defendants, Damian Williams and Henry Watson, of attempted murder, but both were found guilty of lesser charges relating to the riots.

And After: Denny still takes medication and lives in the Los Angeles area. His head injuries prevent him from ever going back to work. Denny has always displayed a remarkably nonbitter attitude, refusing to blame anyone for his plight. At the trial of the two men accused of beating him, Denny went up to the mothers of the two defendants and hugged them.

—S.F.

8 NEWS STORIES THAT NEVER HAPPENED

1. THE ANNIVERSARY OF THE BATHTUB
(*New York Evening Mail*, 1917)
H. L. Mencken was an iconoclastic newspaper writer and editor who flourished in the first half

of the twentieth century. He hurled barbs and bitter quips at groups and individuals who attracted his jaundiced eye, and achieved great notoriety in his heyday. Mencken did not have much hope for the mentality of the mass of men; he even coined the term *booboisie* to express his contempt for the majority of his fellows on earth. It is surprising, then, that he affected to be startled by the unquestioning acceptance given to an article he wrote for the *New York Evening Mail* on December 28, 1917.

Mencken called his piece "A Neglected Anniversary." In it he purported to give the natural history of the plumbed bathtub in America. Mencken advised his readers that December 10 of that year had been the seventy-fifth anniversary of the introduction of this indoor facility to America. He said the convenience had been seen first in Cincinnati in 1842.

Mencken said a man named Adam Thompson had become acquainted with the device while on a European jaunt. In England Thompson had met Lord John Russell, who supposedly had introduced tubbing to that country. Thompson decided to be the innovator in America.

Upon returning to the United States, Thompson ordered the construction of a splendid mahogany unit lined with lead to prevent rot. The tub was introduced at a Cincinnati stag party, at which the chief source of merriment was stripping to the buff and settling down into the contrivance, each man in his turn.

Mencken said that Thompson was a wealthy man, a dealer in cotton and grain, and that he hoped mainly for prestige from his introduction of the bathtub. He did not expect to make money; rather, he wished merely to be recognized as a public benefactor for having brought the tub to the attention of his countrymen.

Alas, reported Mencken, it did not turn out that way. Physicians decried the tub, saying it was dangerous to a person's health to use it. Three cities charged extra for any water used in the newfangled devices. The Boston city fathers prohibited its use, except under stringent medical supervision. Philadelphia, Mencken wrote, almost passed a law forbidding bathtub use in winter months.

But the bathtub had somehow caught the public's fancy despite initial opposition. Finally President Millard Fillmore, ignoring negative grumblings, bravely ordered the installation of a tub in the White House and took the first presidential bath.

The column eventually came to an end, but not the legend it had started. The information in the piece was picked up by various sources as a "straight" news story, and before long Mencken began to see the "facts" he had created used in earnest writings by other men, obviously sincere, who took it all at face value. What particularly galled Mencken was that chiropractors (a group heading the list of his pet hates) used the "information" to prove the stupidity of physicians in their reluctance to try new and supposedly beneficial treatments for mankind's ills. Or so he wrote in a retraction of sorts,

"Melancholy Reflections," which was syndicated May 23, 1926, in a number of newspapers.

Mencken noted in the same article that physicians now cited the "facts" he'd invented as proof of the advance of public health measures throughout the years, and that these "facts" were beginning to appear in standard reference books, were discussed in Congress, and were referred to in scholarly journals.

Mencken may have thought his revelation would settle matters. After all, he had only written the original piece in an effort to lighten the darker days of World War I; it had never occurred to him, or so he said, that anyone would take the piece seriously. But the joke had got out of hand, and now it was time for a correction.

It didn't work out that way. The *Boston Herald* published Mencken's retraction along with an editorial cartoon satirizing the willingness of the public to believe what it was told. However, three weeks later the same paper reprinted the virginal ten-year-old hoax article as a piece of uncontested, "real" news, thereby proving that editors can be just as gullible as their readers.

A few weeks later, Mencken wrote another column, also widely syndicated, in which he pointed out the *Herald*'s error and once again disclaimed any valid source for the "facts" people were so willing to believe about the bathtub and its history in America. Again, it didn't do any good.

Mencken's original tale was alluded to in articles and books for years afterward. The ridiculous information appeared in newspapers ranging from Hearst's *American Weekly* to the staid, proper, punctilious *New York Times*. Twice Mencken's own paper, the *Baltimore Sun*, was "stung" by the resurfacing of "facts" from the original article. And President Harry Truman, while showing friends and guests about the White House, used to repeat the "fact" that a predecessor, Millard Fillmore, had introduced the first bathtub there. Truman supposedly even included a sketch of the whole story in a speech he gave in Philadelphia, by way of illustration of progress in public health. That was in 1952, some thirty-five years after the original piece was published and twenty-six years after Mencken published his second retraction.

Is the Bathtub Hoax still around? It's difficult to say. But if you ever come across a reference to Cincinnati as the home of the bathtub, or to Millard Fillmore as our first tubbing president, you'll know it hasn't died out altogether.

2. THE NEW YORK SIN SHIP (*New York Herald Tribune*, 1924)

Stories of mythical ships have been a staple throughout history, from the magical boats of Sinbad to the *Flying Dutchman*. Such a story was that of the "sin ship" anchored outside the twelve-mile limit of New York harbor; it was, however, presented as a factual news story.

An article by *New York Herald Tribune* writer Sanford Jarrell appeared in the paper's August 16, 1924, edition; it described a floating saloon catering to the wealthy and gave a vivid account of the free-flowing liquor and free-living chorus girls on board. To a readership enduring Prohibition, here was a fantasy they wanted to believe. Many boats set out in search of the ship but were unable to locate it. Jarrell, however, continued for a week to publish articles giving more details and speculations about the mystery vessel. In one he told of extensive searches by the Coast Guard; in another, of how the ship might be the *Kaiser Friedrich*, a ship with a long and checkered history.

Finally—eight days after publishing the original story—the *Tribune*'s editors told the public that it was a hoax, and that Jarrell had admitted fabricating the tale. Jarrell resigned in disgrace—and was immediately offered employment by more than half a dozen competing newspapers.

3. HUNGER MARCHERS STORM BUCKINGHAM PALACE (*New York Mirror*, 1932)

In the early 1930s, William Randolph Hearst, the colorful newspaper magnate, was pro-labor, and his papers were in the habit of concocting stories that enhanced his stand. An example: In a 1932 issue of the *New York Daily Mirror*, an article described hunger marchers storming Buckingham Palace in London. To back up the story, the paper ran a photograph reputedly showing such a scene. In actuality, the photograph had been taken in 1929 and the crowd of people in it was anxiously waiting for news about the health of ailing King George V.

4. SEVERE CROP FAILURE IN SOVIET UNION (Hearst Newspapers, 1935)

Virulently anti-Soviet, Hearst used his papers to spread propaganda, often based on untruths, against the Russians. For example, in 1935 Hearst papers ran a series of articles about severe crop failures in the USSR; these were written by a self-styled reporter using the alias Thomas Walker, who turned out to be an ex-jailbird named Robert Green who had escaped from a Colorado state prison in 1921. Ironically, the same papers carried another series of articles, written by foreign correspondent Lindsay Parrott, which spoke glowingly of the fruitful Russian harvest of 1935. Hearst's other "hoaxes" included atrocity stories that helped foment American intervention in Cuba and the Spanish-American War; faked stories and pictures that helped to create resentment against Mexico in 1927; and photographs of rebel atrocities mislabeled as Loyalist atrocities during the civil war in Spain.

5. THE GREAT MARTIAN INVASION (*Mercury Theatre on the Air*, 1938)

"Everybody was terribly frightened. Some of the women almost went crazy. The men were a little calmer. Some of the women tried to call their families. Some got down on their knees and prayed. Others were actually trembling. My daughter was terribly frightened and really suffered from shock. A ten-year-old child that was here was petrified. He looked like marble." For the New Jersey nurse who spoke these words—and thousands of other Americans—what had started out as a relaxed Sunday night in front of the radio turned into a night of fear, confusion, and panic. For it was October 30, 1938, the night before Halloween and the night the Martians invaded the Earth. It was the night Orson Welles's *Mercury Theatre on the Air* terrorized America with a radio dramatization of H. G. Wells's *War of the Worlds*.

The play, loosely adapted from the classic science-fiction story, was only an hour long. What was there about it, then, that could make people dash hysterically through the street or abandon their homes or fatalistically face death at the hands of the invaders as one woman in Pittsburgh did, who was found in her bathroom clutching a bottle of poison and shrieking, "I'd rather die this way than like that"?

Making a radio play from Wells's novel was Orson Welles's idea. He and the Mercury Theatre Company were then broadcasting an hour-long play from CBS every Sunday at 8:00 P.M., competing against the ultrapopular *Chase and Sanborn Hour*, which featured ventriloquist Edgar Bergen and his red-headed, smart-mouthed dummy, Charlie McCarthy. There were those in radio circles who said no one listened to the *Mercury Theatre*. Obviously, they were wrong.

Writer Howard Koch, given the task of creating the script, said it was impossible. But somehow he got it done, and somewhere along the line, his employer decided to turn the novel into a broadcast of simulated news bulletins and to change the setting to the United States. Koch set to work with a map of New Jersey he had picked up at a gas station, choosing place names to put in the script—the Pulaski Skyway, Bayonne, Route 23. He chose the landing spot of the Martians—Grovers Mill, twenty-two miles from Princeton—by covering his eyes and stabbing at random with his pencil point.

To increase the air of reality, an actor cast as a radio announcer listened over and over to a recording of the hysterical voice of Herb Morrison, who had reported the explosion of the *Hindenburg*, and then copied his intonations.

Welles, who played Princeton scientist Professor Pierson, seemed to have a presentiment of what was about to happen, for he spotted announcements throughout the broadcast explaining that it was only a play.

Reaching an audience that numbered about

12 million, the show began as usual with a few bars of Tchaikovsky's Piano Concerto no. 1 in B-flat Minor and an announcement of the show. After a weather report, an announcer said, "We now take you to the Meridian Room in the Hotel Park Plaza in downtown New York, where you will be entertained by the music of Ramón Raquello and his orchestra." The music began, and then was interrupted by a series of news bulletins—a report of mysterious gas eruptions on Mars as seen by astronomers and an interview between announcer Carl Phillips and Professor Pierson, ostensibly on their way to Grovers Mill to investigate an object that had fallen from the skies, perhaps a meteor. In the background were the sounds of crowds and emergency sirens. Then more music and another bulletin, which advised that the "meteor" was actually a humming metal cylinder.

Meanwhile, at 8:12 Edgar and Charlie completed a skit; they were followed by a commercial for Chase and Sanborn coffee and Nelson Eddy crooning a love song. Millions of people switched to CBS and heard:

ANNOUNCER: I'll move the microphone nearer. Here. [Pause.] Now we're not more than twenty-five feet away. Can you hear it now? Oh, Professor Pierson!
PIERSON: Yes, Mr. Phillips?
ANNOUNCER: Can you tell us the meaning of that scraping noise inside the thing?
PIERSON: Possibly the unequal cooling of its surface.
ANNOUNCER: Do you still think it's a meteor, Professor?
PIERSON: I don't know what to think. The metal casing is definitely extraterrestrial . . . not found on this earth . . .
PHILLIPS: Just a minute! Something's happening! Ladies and gentlemen, this is terrific. The end of the thing is beginning to flake off! The top is beginning to rotate like a screw! The thing must be metal!

The crowd noises increased as the top came off, and the announcer went on:

ANNOUNCER: Ladies and gentlemen, this is the most terrifying thing I have ever witnessed! . . . Wait a minute! Someone's *crawling out of the hollow top.* Someone or . . . something. I can see peering out of that black hole two luminous discs . . . are they eyes? It might be a face. It might be . . .

And he proceeded to describe the tentacles of the creature, its size (large "as a bear"), its black eyes (which gleamed "like a serpent"), and its mouth ("V-shaped with saliva dripping from its rimless lips that seem to quiver and pulsate").

Between musical interludes, the horrors mounted. The police approached the cylinder, only to be turned into flaming torches by the Martians' flamethrower, a kind of "heat ray" emanating from a mirror.

Meanwhile, back in the real world, the panic began. Those who tuned in late accepted what they heard. Switchboards at police stations were jammed with calls, and some people fled their homes to mill about in the streets.

As the broadcast continued, the governor had the commander of the state militia put part of New Jersey under martial law; more spaceships arrived (one was found by coon hunters); thousands of National Guardsmen and the entire Army Air Corps were wiped out; communication lines were down and railroads were torn up; highways were "clogged with frantic human traffic"; the president declared a national emergency; and the secretary of the interior (played by Kenneth Delmar, who later portrayed Senator Claghorn on the *Fred Allen Show*), gave an inspirational speech in an authoritative voice that sounded a lot like President Franklin D. Roosevelt's. Those Martians were indeed, as the script said, able to "move at express-train speed." In less than a half hour of real time, they had annihilated most of New Jersey. In Newark "poisonous black smoke," according to "a telephone operator," was pouring in from the marshes. Hearing that report come over their radios, many Newark residents abandoned their homes. In one block, twenty families rushed out with wet handkerchiefs over their heads and faces, trying to escape the gas.

The drama switched to New York, where a lone announcer stood on a rooftop watching the Martians—tall as skyscrapers—preparing to wade the Hudson River and said: "Now they're lifting their metal hands. This is the end now. . . . People in the streets see it now. . . . They're running toward the East River . . . thousands of them, dropping like rats. . . . Now the smoke's crossing Sixth Avenue . . . Fifth Avenue . . . 100 yards away . . . it's fifty feet. . . ." Then the mike went dead. And in New York, listeners rushed out of their doors to hallucinate in the streets, seeing those Martians and their machines over on the Jersey Palisades.

In the radio studio, police mobbed the control room, having already surrounded the building, after officials became aware of the magnitude of the panic. Calls continued to come in, one from the mayor of Flint, Michigan, who reported mobs, violence, and looting. "Women and children are huddled in the churches," he said, and if he were to find out that the whole thing was "nothing but a crummy joke," then he planned to come to New York to "punch the author of it in the nose."

Although hundreds of thousands of Americans were in the streets, governors announced that there was no martial law. People prayed in churches or slugged down booze, depending on their individual persuasions. Calls to local radio stations increased 500 percent. Most listeners missed the station break, which clearly said that the "Martian landing" was part of a radio drama, and they did not hear the second half of the show, which was set in a time weeks later and told of the Martians' final defeat by bacteria, the "humblest thing that God in his wisdom put on earth." And few heard Welles's jocular sign-off.

The police in the studio began to question the cast, citing suicides, traffic deaths, and a "fatal stampede in a Jersey hall." These reports were either exaggerated or completely untrue. But the panic was real, and it went on in spite of CBS announcements during the evening that said that "the entire story and all its incidents were fictitious."

The following morning, newspapers headlined the broadcast. A Nazi Party paper blamed the panic on the Jews, and an Italian paper said that the program had plunged a "third-grade democracy into confusion." While the *New York Times* pompously hinted of censorship and chided radio, talking of its "adult responsibilities" and its lack of mastery over "itself or the material it uses," the *New York World Telegram*, agreeing that such an event should never happen again, said, "If so many people could be misled unintentionally when the purpose was merely to entertain, what could designing politicians not do through control of broadcasting stations?"

Dorothy Thompson, in a much-quoted column, wrote, "Nothing about the broadcast was in the least credible, no matter at what point the listener might have tuned in," and went on to say that Welles had done the country a service by demonstrating how easy it would be to start a panic in time of war.

Fearing investigation by the Federal Communications Commission, the chairman of CBS called the show "regrettable" and made a public statement of apology, as did Welles.

A study of the effects of the show was undertaken by a group at Princeton University. Aside from its statistics, the group made an invaluable contribution by recording actual reactions people had had during the panic. Some examples:

A New Jersey housewife named Ferguson: "I knew it was something terrible and I was frightened. But I didn't know just what it was. I couldn't make myself believe it was the end of the world. I've always heard that when the world would come to an end, it would come so fast nobody would know—so why should God get in touch with this announcer? When they told us what road to take and get up over the hills and the children began to cry, the family decided to get out. We took blankets and my granddaughter wanted to take the cat and canary. We were outside the garage when the neighbor's boy came back and told us it was only a play."

Helen Anthony, a high-school girl from Pennsylvania: "I was really hysterical. My two girl friends and I were crying and holding each other, and everything seemed so unimportant in the face of death. We felt it was terrible we should die so young."

A man who had spent all his money trying to escape wrote: "I thought the best thing to do was to go away, so I took three dollars and twenty-five cents out of my savings and bought a ticket. After I had gone sixty miles, I heard it was a play. Now I don't have any money left for the shoes I was saving up for. Would you please have someone send me a pair of black shoes, size 9-B."

Midwesterner Joseph Hendley: "That Halloween boo had our family on its knees before the program was half over. . . . My mother went out and looked for Mars. Dad was hard to convince, and skeptical, but even he got to believing it. Brother Joe, as usual, got more excited than anyone. . . . Lillie got sick to her stomach. I don't know what I did exactly, but I know I prayed harder and more earnest than ever before."

An eastern college student: "One of the first things I did was try to phone my girl in Poughkeepsie, but the lines were all busy, so that just confirmed my impression that the thing was true. We started driving back to Poughkeepsie. We had heard that Princeton was wiped out and gas was spreading over New Jersey and fire, so I figured there wasn't anything to do—we figured our friends and families were all dead. I made the forty-five miles in thirty-five minutes and didn't even realize it. . . . I thought the whole human race was going to be wiped out—that seemed more important than the fact we were going to die. It seemed awful that everything that had been worked on for years was going to be lost forever."

Of course, not everyone who tuned in to the broadcast believed it. Some who had read the original Wells novel recognized the story line. Others caught on as the incidents in the play began occurring much too fast to be taking place in real time. And yet others, who feared an invasion from across the sea, concluded that the Nazis were storming the Atlantic beaches.

So was it just the play that caused the panic on that October night? Or was it something else for which the *Mercury Theatre* broadcast served merely as a catalyst: a combination of the anxiety and tension permeating a world on the brink of war, the low mental defenses of a people exhausted by the Great Depression, and the firmly held belief that what was said by authoritative voices over the medium of the radio had to be the truth?

6. THE GULF OF TONKIN INCIDENT (1964)

Throughout the ages great and bloody conflicts have begun with seemingly small events:

Helen's abduction and the subsequent siege of Troy; the assassination of Archduke Ferdinand at Sarajevo, which signaled the beginning of the First World War; and the attack on patrol boats in the Gulf of Tonkin, the incident that led to American involvement in the Vietnam conflict. The tale of Helen is likely a myth; the murder of Archduke Ferdinand, actual history—and what really happened in the Gulf of Tonkin will probably forever lie somewhere between history and myth. More than thirty years after the event, it remains what can only be called a muddle.

That something happened between U.S. and North Vietnamese patrol boats in the Tonkin gulf is not disputed, but even the commanders and their crews on the scene were uncertain as to just what it was. This uncertainty was clear in the initial cables sent by Captain John Herrick (aboard the destroyer *Maddox*) at the time of the event. What apparently did happen was this:

In the early afternoon of August 2, 1964, the U.S. Navy's Seventh Fleet destroyer *Maddox* was patrolling the South China Sea off Vietnam. Three North Vietnamese PT boats appeared and began what appeared to be attack maneuvers. The *Maddox* and the PT boats were probably hit by each other's gunfire, sustaining minor damage. If torpedoes were fired by the North Vietnamese, they failed to find their mark. Crusader jets from the nearby carrier *Ticonderoga* came to the *Maddox*'s aid, sinking one North Vietnamese boat and crippling another.

It was, however, a supposed second attack on the *Maddox* two nights later that was the spur for U.S. reprisals. The sonar, which had been behaving in erratic fashion, indicated the presence of several enemy boats to its inexperienced operator—who, it was later said, might have been picking up "anything from rain and waves to the whir of their own propellers."

Another destroyer in the area, the *Turner Joy*, had also picked up sonar indications of enemy ships; both U.S. ships fired for several hours into the darkness at targets they couldn't see. At first Captain Herrick (commanding the *Maddox*) thought his ship had destroyed two or three enemy craft, and so reported to higher command. Later he was less certain, and his subsequent cables were cautionary and circumspect. A *Ticonderoga* pilot, Commander James B. Stockdale, was more certain; he had flown over the area for more than ninety minutes and seen no evidence of the presence of any but U.S. ships.

President Lyndon Johnson did not indicate any doubt as to the reality of the attack in a speech on the subject; he pushed hard for the Gulf of Tonkin Resolution, which allowed for punitive air strikes against North Vietnam. Though such reprisals would be technically illegal under international law even if the supposed attack had actually occurred, the Senate passed the resolution after a few hours of discussion, the House after only forty minutes. The first steps on the march that would cost over one million lives—including more than 58,000 Americans—had begun.

Three years later the Tonkin incident was the subject of extensive hearings in which Secretary of Defense Robert H. McNamara was questioned at length by Senator J. William Fulbright and others. The investigating committee was, however, limited to information provided by the administration and the Defense Department, and in the final analysis learned nothing of substance. For several more years the United States fought a war that was at least in part brought about by an incident that probably never happened.

7. THE EIGHT-YEAR-OLD HEROIN ADDICT (The *Washington Post*, 1980)

The *Washington Post* has long been considered one of the finest newspapers in the United States; it is perhaps best known for the epochal coverage of the Watergate break-in by reporters Bob Woodward and Carl Bernstein. Accordingly, a story that appeared in its pages on September 28, 1980, in which the tragic ghetto life of Jimmy, an eight-year-old heroin addict, was described by reporter Janet Cooke, drew immediate attention. Police and social workers searched for the boy; unable to find him, they contacted Cooke, who told them that revealing information would put both Jimmy and herself in danger. She stood on her First Amendment rights, and the *Post*—not without misgivings, since its own investigations had begun to cast doubt on the story—stood behind her. Interest in the precise details of the story slowly dwindled away.

It might well have ended there but for the *Post*'s submitting the story for consideration by the Pulitzer Prize committee; Woodward later explained that not to submit such a prominent story would have indicated the newspaper lacked faith in its veracity. When the story won, Cooke was asked to supply biographical information to the committee; the résumé she provided was so filled with errors and inconsistencies that it brought the Jimmy story into doubt. Questioned by Woodward and Executive Editor Ben Bradlee, Cooke finally confessed to making up the story. The next day she publicly apologized and resigned; the *Post* returned the Pulitzer and ran a story describing the hoax. Not content with that, a few days later the *Post* carried a 12,000 word article on the hoax by reporter Bill Green.

The *Post* survived with its credibility almost intact; not so Janet Cooke. The twenty-five-year-old black reporter, who had seemed destined for a major career with the *Post*, faded from public view.

8. THE PATRIOT MISSILE SUCCESSES (1991)

One of the technological heroes of the Gulf War seemed to be the Patriot missile. The U.S. Army claimed that the Patriot "intercepted" forty-five of forty-seven Iraqi Scud missiles; President George Bush claimed forty-one of forty-two—a far better success rate than its own builders had predicted. Many Americans who get their news primarily from broadcast television still believe the Patriot to have been a major success story. Informed analysts are not so sure.

> The first casualty when war comes is truth.
> Hiram Johnson, speech, 1917

For one thing, the Patriot was designed to protect military targets, not dense civilian populations; when a Patriot hit its target, the Scud would often break up into several pieces. The falling fragments could do damage over a far wider area than an intact Scud.

Later analysis of videotapes indicated that target hits were rare indeed; of thirty-three Patriots fired, twenty-five were complete misses, while the other eight might have done some damage—but even this latter speculation could not be proved. A Massachusetts Institute of Technology study indicated that "there is literally no evidence of destruction of a Scud warhead." An Israeli Air Force study agreed with the MIT study; the Pentagon, predictably, did not.

It was argued by the military that the Scud missile would often break up when reentering the atmosphere, and the Patriot was not really designed to hit multiple targets; the Patriot had originally been designed as an antiaircraft weapon, and only later modified to meet the threat of Scud attacks. Raytheon Corporation (a prime contractor for the Patriot) also disputed the conclusions reached by the study's author.

Nonetheless, the Patriot—scheduled to be phased out of production after Desert Storm—was given another chance: an appropriation to purchase 158 Patriots was approved. The cost for these improved models of the Patriot: $214 million. And what about all those "intercepts" that the army had claimed? Brigadier General Robert Drolet explained that President Bush had not lied to the press and public, he had simply used a different definition of the word "intercept." According to the U.S. Army, "intercepted" did not mean "destroyed," it meant "a Patriot and Scud passed in the sky."

—A.E., M.G., and T.A.W.

General H. Norman Schwarzkopf misled the public about the effectiveness of the Patriot missile.

PHOTOGRAPHS OF HISTORY IN THE MAKING

Thomas Howard of the Chicago Tribune snapped this forbidden photo of Ruth Snyder being executed for the murder of her husband by strapping a miniature camera to his leg and running a cable release inside his trousers and into his pocket. The execution took place at Sing Sing Prison in Ossining, New York, on January 12, 1928.

This photo of German soldiers rounding up Polish Jews in Warsaw was taken from an SS commander's report to his superior officer. The fear and disbelief in the child's face brought home to the world the terrorism of the Nazis when it was introduced as evidence at the Nuremberg War Crimes Trial.

Joe Rosenthal took this picture of United States Marines raising the American flag on top of Mount Suribachi on the island of Iwo Jima on February 23, 1945. It was actually the second U.S. flag raised on the island, so some critics contended the shot was staged.

The smile on Harry Truman's face tells it all in this Frank Cancellare photo: the Chicago Tribune was premature in announcing that Thomas Dewey had won the 1948 U.S. presidential election.

Vietnamese Buddhist monk Thich Quang Duc commits suicide on the streets of Saigon on June 11, 1963, to protest government persecution of Buddhists. Malcolm Browne captured this moving image.

In this photo by Eddie Adams, South Vietnamese police chief Nguyen Ngoc Loan executes a Viet Cong suspect in Saigon, 1968. This shot, and its newsreel equivalent, came to symbolize the brutal, undemocratic nature of the U.S.-supported South Vietnamese regime. The victim had just killed a policeman.

During the 1989 pro-democracy demonstrations in Beijing, an unknown man stands down a convoy of government tanks.

QUOTEBOOK: NEWS

Freedom of the press is guaranteed only to those who own one.

A.J. Liebling, attributed

Freedom of the press in Britain is freedom to print such of the proprietor's prejudices as the advertisers don't object to.

Hannen Swaffer, attributed, c. 1928

Newspapers have two great advantages over television. They can be used by men as barriers against their wives. It is still the only effective screen against the morning features of the loved one, and, as such, performs a unique human service. The second advantage is that you can't line a garbage pail with a television set—it's usually the other way around.

Marya Mannes, speech, Women's National Press Club, 1960

Editor: a person employed by a newspaper, whose business is to separate the wheat from the chaff, and to see that the chaff is printed.

Elbert Hubbard, Roycroft Dictionary, 1914

You cannot hope
to bribe or twist,
thank God! the
British journalist.
But, seeing what
the man will do
unbribed, there's
no occasion to.

Humbert Wolfe, "Over the Fire," The Uncelestial City, 1930

Advice to aspiring war correspondents:

Never sound excited. Imagine yourself at a dinner table back in the United States with the local editor, a banker and a professor talking over coffee. You try and tell what it was like, while the maid's boyfriend, a truck driver, listens from the kitchen. Try to be understood by the truck driver while not insulting the professor's intelligence.

Edward R. Murrow, 1944

The world really isn't any worse. It's just that the news coverage is so much better.

Anonymous, English Digest, March 1965

Chapter 14

SCIENCE AND TECHNOLOGY

SCIENCE

It is good morning exercise for a research scientist to discard a pet hypothesis every day before breakfast. It keeps him young.

Konrad Lorenz, On Aggression, 1963

That is the essence of science: ask an impertinent question and you are on the way to a pertinent answer.

Jacob Bronowski

Every answer given arouses new questions. The progress of science is matched by an increase in the hidden and mysterious.

Leo Baeck, Judaism and Science, 1949

Science is wonderfully equipped to answer the question "How?" but it gets terribly confused when you ask the question "Why?"

Erwin Chargaff, Columbia Forum, Summer 1969

In science the credit goes to the man who convinces the world, not to the man to whom the idea first occurred.

Sir Francis Darwin, Galton Lecture to the Eugenics Society, published in Eugenics Review, April 1914

GREAT SCIENTISTS AND THEIR DISCOVERIES

MAX PLANCK CREATES QUANTUM PHYSICS (1900)

Max Carl Ernst Planck was that rare scientist, one whose discoveries were truly revolutionary, marking a watershed moment in the history of humanity's understanding of the nature of the world.

Planck was born in Kiel, Germany, on April 23, 1858, into a family of scholars, lawyers, and public servants. At the age of twenty-one he earned a doctorate in physics from the University of Berlin. After teaching at Munich and later at Kiel University in his hometown, Planck joined the faculty at Berlin as professor of theoretical physics.

Although fascinated by optics, electricity, and mechanics, it was in the area of heat and energy that his most important discoveries occurred. His interest focused on objects called black bodies, that is, objects that absorb all frequencies of electromagnetic radiation. Classical physics posited the notion that such objects should radiate heat at certain frequencies but Planck and others noted that the *should* was not backed up by what actually happened.

There was something fundamentally wrong with the way in which scientists thought of energy. It did not exist as a continuous variable that could take on any value at all, but as a flow of discrete "packages" to which Planck gave the name "quanta." Most physicists considered the notion—which he first announced as a formula in October 1900, then backed up with a theoretical basis in December 1900—too revolutionary, but Planck soon earned the agreement and respect of Einstein and Bohr. Quantum physics was to become a powerful tool in learning the true inner workings of the atom. Planck was awarded the Nobel Prize in physics in 1918.

> *We have no right to assume that any physical laws exist, or if they have existed up to now, that they will continue to exist in a similar manner in the future.*
> Max Planck, The Universe in Light of Modern Physics, 1931

He stayed in Germany after the rise of Adolf Hitler and sought to protect Jewish scientists. His son was executed in 1944 for plotting to overthrow Hitler. His home and library were destroyed in the war, but he was rescued by American troops and lived out the last years of his long life in Göttingen, where he died on October 3, 1947.

KARL LANDSTEINER RECOGNIZES BLOOD GROUPS (1901)

Without the creative contribution of Karl Landsteiner, born in Austria on June 14, 1868, countless thousands of people would have risked unnecessary death because of the severe danger caused by blood transfusions before his research.

The theoretical underpinnings of blood transfusions date back to William Harvey's discovery, published in 1618, that blood circulates through the body. The first successful transfusion performed on a human was by French physician Jean-Baptiste Denis, doctor to King Louis IV—he used lambs as donors. When one of his patients died after a transfusion, he was arrested and the practice outlawed even though the dead man was later found to have been poisoned by his wife.

The practice of transfusion was revived in the early nineteenth century, but it was still very risky, even with humans as donors, mainly because the transfused blood often clotted, and severe kidney failure could occur.

Working on the assumption that there were intrinsic similarities and dissimilarities in the blood of humans, Landsteiner began the analyses that resulted in 1901 in a relatively simple way of knowing who could give and receive safe transfusions. Group A subjects could receive blood from A and O donors, group B subjects from B and O donors, O only from O donors, and AB, discovered the next year, from all donors.

Not only could transfusions now be safely performed, but blood banks could be established, which allowed operations to be performed that were previously impossible. Blood typing could also be used in helping to determine disputed paternity, and also in the investigation of crimes where the identification of blood at a crime scene was important.

Landsteiner isolated the poliomyelitis virus and was the first to use monkeys in experiments on polio. He also, with Alexander Weiner and Phillip Levine, discovered the Rhesus (Rh) blood factor in studies with Rhesus monkeys.

A timid man who shunned publicity and loved nothing better than to hole up in his laboratory, he died at his lab bench on June 26, 1943, of a heart attack.

WALTER SUTTON AND THEODOR BOVERI CREATE CHROMOSOMAL THEORY OF HEREDITY (1902)

Walter Sutton spent his early years on a farm in Kansas. Born on April 5, 1877, he entered the University of Kansas in Lawrence in 1896 to study engineering, but the following year his youngest brother died of typhoid fever and Sutton turned to the study of medicine.

He studied biology at the university under the inspiring influence of Clarence E. McClung and soon was attempting to understand the function and structure of chromosomes by experimenting with a plentiful Kansas creature, the grasshopper.

Cytologists already suspected that chromosomes played a role in heredity, but it was Sutton who showed the relationship between the behavior of chromosomes and the theories of Gregor Mendel. In two papers, one released in 1902 and the other in 1903, Sutton hypothesized that chromosomes carry the units of inheritance. He created detailed charts of grasshopper chromosomes showing the various phases of development and determined that all chromosomes exist in pairs, one from each parent.

Sutton died of a ruptured appendix on November 10, 1916.

Another scientist, Theodor Boveri, a world away in Munich, came to almost exactly the same conclusions as Sutton. Working with the eggs of a species of roundworm, he also determined that certain chromosomes were responsible for certain characteristics in the organism.

Born in Bamberg, Germany, on October 12, 1862, Boveri studied at Munich University and later became professor of zoology at the University of Würzburg, where he taught for the rest of his life.

Although brilliant, he led a troubled life, subjected to fits of severe depression. "My brain is frozen," he wrote in a letter to his brother, "and every bit of intellectual activity . . . is forbidden me." He spent some time in a sanitarium, which seemed to help, but he remained prone to periods of deep melancholy.

His health got much worse following the beginning of World War I, and he died at age fifty-three on October 15, 1915.

ALBERT EINSTEIN PUBLISHES THEORIES OF RELATIVITY (1905, 1915)

Widely accepted in his own lifetime as one of the most powerful and original intellects in the history of mankind, Albert Einstein is today best known for his theories of relativity. In creating his theories, Einstein looked at such concepts as time and space and came up with stunningly original new ways to view them.

Not only were scientists given challengingly new theoretical visions of the universe, but literally earth-shattering results grew out of Einstein's theorizing in the form of the atom bomb. In the realm of ideas, and in the new and terrifying nature of war, the planet and its inhabitants would never be the same again.

Born on March 14, 1879, in Ulm, Germany, Einstein was a mediocre student at best, in spite of his early interest in mathematics. He rebelled

Marie and Pierre Curie with their seven-year-old daughter Irène. Eventually all three of them won Nobel prizes. Marie and Pierre won the 1903 physics prize for their research into the phenomenon of radiation. After Pierre died in a traffic accident, Marie won the chemistry prize in 1911 for the discovery of radium and polonium. Irène earned the Nobel Prize in chemistry in 1935, along with her husband, Frédéric Joliot, for research into the synthesis of radioactive elements. Irène and her mother both died from leukemia caused by overexposure to the radioactive materials used in their experiments.

against the rigid regimentation of the German school system of his time, and with his poor grades could only gain a post as a junior patents clerk in Berne, Switzerland, to where his family immigrated.

With a simple job and plenty of time on his hands the young man sat down with three things: paper, a pencil, and a brain that scientists would carefully scrutinize after his death.

He took the first steps toward his revolutionary theories. In 1905 he published his *Special Theory of Relativity*, which challenged concepts of time and space that had been accepted since Newton's time, presenting a remarkable new picture of the universe. Mass, length, and time were not unvarying as had been assumed, Einstein said, but depended on the relative motion between the observer and the thing observed.

In 1915 his general theory of relativity described a continuum of space and time in the form of a complicated four-dimensional curve. A violent controversy raged—many scientists found his ideas incomprehensible, and the ones who could understand the math rejected his conclusions because they were so contrary to common sense.

Einstein won the 1921 Nobel Prize in physics, and his ideas were accepted by most of the world as the work of a genius. He was attacked by Adolf Hitler. His property was confiscated and he was welcomed to the United States. Hitler himself said that no Jew could have formulated Einstein's theories, that they must have been stolen from a German army officer who had been killed in World War I.

As World War II heated up, scientists in the free world came to fear that the Germans could apply Einstein's ideas and convert mass directly to energy, that a minute piece of mass could unleash a vast amount of energy—nuclear energy. Torn between his pacifist beliefs and the fear that the Nazis would win the war, Einstein urged President Franklin D. Roosevelt to win the race for the A-bomb.

He spent his last years in semiretirement in Princeton, where he continued to work and teach. He died on April 18, 1955.

WALTHER NERNST PROPOUNDS THIRD LAW OF THERMODYNAMICS (1905)

When the young man abandoned the writing of poetry for scientific pursuits, the first step was taken in his accomplishments in the relatively new area of thermodynamics. He referred to the new discipline as "the meeting of two sciences hitherto somewhat independent of each other."

The new subject sought to understand heat as energy, and the young man who devoted his life to it was Hermann Walther Nernst, born in what is now Wabrzezno, Poland, on June 25, 1864. From the beginning he was an excellent student, forsaking his interest in poetry because of the inspiration of an early chemistry teacher. He went on to study at the Universities of Zurich, Berlin, Graz, and Wurzburg.

Still in his midtwenties, he earned international acclaim for his work—called the Nernst equation—on the behavior of electrolytes in the presence of electric currents. The Nernst equation is important in the fields of medicine and biology, since it made possible an analysis of the distribution of substances in different parts of a living organism.

In 1894 he established the Kaiser Wilhelm Institute for Physical Chemistry and Electrochemistry at Göttingen and invited an international group of scholars to help him investigate such topics as polarization, dielectric constants, and chemical equilibria. He moved on to a chemistry professorship at the University of Berlin, where, in 1905, he proposed his "heat theorem"—what is now known as the third law of thermodynamics—by which predictions can be made about how far a chemical reaction can go before it reaches equilibrium. In 1912 he expressed this theorem as the basic unattainability of absolute zero.

Nernst was known as a man with a strong

ego, a good sense of humor, and a lively interest in life. He loved to drive automobiles, and volunteered as an ambulance driver in World War I. Toward the end of his career he became fascinated with cosmological questions and opposed the notion of the heat death of the universe. He also opposed Adolf Hitler's attempts to discredit the accomplishments of Albert Einstein and other Jewish scientists. He died suddenly of heart failure on November 18, 1941.

HEIKE KAMERLINGH ONNES DISCOVERS SUPERCONDUCTIVITY (1911)

Born in Groningen, the Netherlands, on September 21, 1853, Kamerlingh Onnes went on to study at the Universities of Groningen and Heidelberg, and was later appointed to a professorship of physics at the University of Leiden.

Early in his career he came into contact with the great scientist Johannes van der Walls, who sparked his interest in problems related to the molecular theory of matter. Van der Walls was to remain an important influence on Kamerlingh Onnes.

Kamerlingh Onnes was a man of great focus, almost to the point of obsession, and the subject that fascinated him was the characteristics and behavior of matter at extremely low temperatures. He made the Cryogenic Laboratory at Leiden the worldwide center for low-temperature research. For years he had a virtual monopoly on low-temperature studies because the liquid-helium facilities he created were unique.

Kamerlingh Onnes tackled first the very practical problem of the lack of techniques and devices to create temperatures as near to absolute zero as possible. A subject of great interest to him was the electrical resistance of metals at very low temperatures. He started with the assumption that resistance would increase as the metal's temperature lowered, reaching the maximum near absolute zero.

He was, however, astonished to note that the resistance of certain metals actually decreases, reaching zero resistance at a temperature close to absolute zero. He discovered this phenomenon in 1911, calling it supraconductivity, a term later changed to superconductivity.

A man whose interest went beyond mere lab work and theorizing, he studied practical ways to use refrigeration, such as for transporting and storing foods.

Kamerlingh Onnes was a taskmaster in the laboratory and drove his assistants hard. The story is told that, at his funeral, his lab assistants, walking behind the hearse, had to break into a run as the vehicle picked up speed to make up for a delay. One said to another: "The old devil—even after he has gone he makes us run."

He received the Nobel Prize in physics in 1913, and died in Leiden on February 21, 1926.

NIELS BOHR PROPOSES ATOMIC MODEL (1913)

Enormous progress has been made since the early 1900s in the understanding and use of atomic energy, but the work of Niels Bohr remains important and at the very heart of the research.

The son of a professor of physiology, Bohr grew up in Copenhagen in a family where intellectual and cultural pursuits were a matter of course. He was determined to follow his father in an academic career, but the young man was also enthusiastic about sports—soccer, skiing, and sailing—an interest he enjoyed all his life.

At Cambridge University, Bohr met Ernest Rutherford and under this great man's influence he became fascinated with the structure of the atom. By 1913 he had developed a revolutionary new theory that was to make him famous.

Although Bohr was impressed by Rutherford's image of the atom as a kind of miniature solar system, there was a flaw. He noted that by the known laws of physics, electrically charged particles moving in circles should emit electromagnetic radiation, lose energy, and spiral to the center.

Bohr posited the idea that electrons could revolve at what he called a ground state—the electron would not emit energy and could therefore continue revolving around the nucleus forever. But if energy were fed into the atom, the electron could "jump up" to an orbit of higher energy, and then "jump down" to its ground state. As it did all this it would shed energy in "quanta," as Max Planck had predicted in his quantum theory.

Bohr's theory of specific energy levels within the atom remains basic to science's knowledge of the atom. In 1922 he was awarded the Nobel Prize in physics.

When the Nazis invaded Denmark, they came after Bohr to join their team to create an atom bomb. He risked arrest by defying them and, in 1943, he knew he had to flee. He dissolved in acid the gold from his Nobel medal and hid the bottle. When he returned to his homeland later, he had the medal recast. He died in 1962.

HENRY MOSELEY CREATES IDEA OF ATOMIC NUMBERS (1914)

Henry Moseley's life, even though cut tragically short, was nevertheless rich in scientific accomplishment. He was born in England on November 23, 1887, into a family with a long and rich scientific tradition: his father had been a professor of anatomy and his grandfather a well-known mathematician.

In 1914, only twenty-seven years old, Moseley studied X rays emitted by metals under certain conditions and evolved the idea of atomic numbers. His creation, for the first time, made clear sense out of the periodic table and was a big step toward understanding the actual structure of the atomic nucleus. According to Moseley's theory, elements can have only integral numbers (nuclear charges). This idea showed experimenters where to look for as-yet-undiscovered elements, a search that turned out to be very fruitful in a relatively short time.

The very next year after Moseley's discovery, however, Moseley felt the patriotic stirrings of other young men his age and enlisted to fight in World War I. Military leaders, in a spectacular show of moronic simplemindedness, sent him to the front, and in the badly mismanaged Gallipoli campaign, a sniper's bullet cut short the scientific career of a bona fide genius. He died on August 10, 1915.

"To use such a man as a subaltern," wrote Ernest Rutherford in *Nature* magazine, "is economically equivalent to using the *Lusitania* to carry a pound of butter from Ramsgate to Margate." The daily press ran headlines such as "Sacrifice of a Genius," and "Too Valuable to Die."

The French referred to his loss as a *mort*

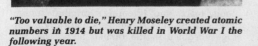

"Too valuable to die," Henry Moseley created atomic numbers in 1914 but was killed in World War I the following year.

glorieuse, and even the Germans called the event "a matter of great regret." In all probability, Moseley would have won, perhaps jointly with Charles G. Barkla, the 1917 Nobel Prize in physics.

—R.W.S.

EDWIN HUBBLE FINDS NEW GALAXIES (1923)

When the United States launched the Hubble Space Telescope (a space observatory) in 1990, it was so problem plagued that "Hubble" became something of a joke, a synonym for failure. But there was little failure in the career of its namesake. Edwin Hubble's observations altered our understanding of the universe, especially its size.

The son of a Missouri lawyer, Hubble seemed destined to follow in his father's footsteps. Although he showed an early interest in astronomy and majored in it at the University of Chicago, he went on to study law at Oxford and opened a practice in Louisville, Kentucky. One year was enough. He went back to the University of Chicago, earning a Ph.D. in astronomy in 1917.

Offered a position at the Mount Wilson Observatory in California, Hubble turned it down. "Regret cannot accept your invitation to join the Mount Wilson staff," he telegraphed. "Joined the army instead. Am off to war." The United States had just entered the First World War, and Hubble put service to country before career advancement. Not until 1919 did he begin peering at the heavens through Mount Wilson's giant telescope.

Hubble's special interest was nebulae—fuzzy patches of light that no one understood in terms of character or location. Were these objects part of our galaxy or did they lay beyond our galaxy's outermost stars? In the early 1920s, many astronomers believed that nothing existed beyond the Milky Way. But Hubble figured out that the giant Andromeda nebula was 900,000 light-years from Earth—well beyond the Milky Way. Not only was the universe much larger than the Milky Way, but the universe was filled with an uncounted multitude of galaxies. In determining that our galaxy was nothing special, Hubble revolutionized understanding of the universe and Earth's place in it.

By 1929 Hubble had determined the distances from Earth to twenty-two galaxies. It was then that he announced "Hubble's law." By studying the light that reached Earth from distant galaxies, he was able to conclude that the farther a galaxy was from Earth the more rapidly it was moving away from Earth. The universe, therefore, is not only much larger than previously thought, but it is also constantly growing. Hubble's discovery of an expanding universe supported the subsequent big bang theory of creation.

ROBERT MILLIKAN DISCOVERS COSMIC RAYS (1926)

Robert A. Millikan received the 1923 Nobel Prize in physics for his research into electrons and the photoelectric effect, but not until 1927 was he accorded the ultimate honor: he appeared on the cover of Time magazine. In the accompanying article Time gushed that Millikan had "detected the pulse of the universe."

That pulse consisted of what Millikan had dubbed "cosmic rays." Scientists before Millikan had noted the existence of radiation in the atmosphere and had assumed that it resulted from radioactive elements on Earth. Through several elegantly designed experiments, Millikan demonstrated conclusively that the origin of what was termed "penetrating radiation" was outer space. Thus, penetrating radiation became cosmic rays.

Initially, Millikan was convinced that cosmic rays were evidence of the "birth cries" of infant atoms. Whether by fusion or by electron capture, new atoms were constantly being formed in outer space. He claimed that space, in fact, was home to "obstetrical wards" where the elements that constitute the bulk of the earth—helium, oxygen, and silicon—were created and sent on their way. He later retreated from this position, however, when challenged by scientists who doubted his atom-building hypothesis.

He also faced opposition regarding his unshakable insistence that science and religion were compatible. The son of a Congregational minister, Millikan was imbued with the Protestant ethic—that is, fear God and respect hard work. To him, the existence of cosmic rays proved that the Creator was "continually on His job." This blending of old-time religion with his stunning success as a researcher made Robert Millikan the most famous American scientist of his era. He used his fame to build the California Institute of Technology (Caltech) into one of the nation's leading scientific institutions, and he did much to create the modern linkage of academic, industrial, and governmental bodies in scientific research.

WERNER HEISENBERG FORMULATES THE UNCERTAINTY PRINCIPLE (1927)

The question was, "Does God throw dice?" At least, that's the way Albert Einstein saw it. Einstein, to the end of his days, believed in classical physics, which held that the universe is governed by the knowable, predictable relationship between matter and energy. He could not accept the notion that, at the level of the atom, such determinism did not hold. If it did not hold, then the universe was ultimately unknowable—and an unknowable universe was one in which God could be throwing dice.

Einstein's ruminations on God and dice were prompted by the uncertainty principle, an idea conceived by a young (twenty-six-year-old) German physicist named Werner Heisenberg. The son of a classics professor, Heisenberg studied physics in Germany before going to Denmark in the 1920s to work with Niels Bohr. Bohr was the leading figure in atomic theory, winning the 1922 Nobel Prize in physics for his work on atomic structure. But Bohr's model for the atom failed to explain certain observed phenomena. Heisenberg tried to reconcile the model with the observations, failed, and then reflected on the reason for the failure.

Working late one night in 1927 at Bohr's Institute for Theoretical Physics, Heisenberg decided to go for a walk. During his walk in the cold March air Heisenberg had a revelation. On the subatomic level, the very act of observation changed what was being observed. To identify the position of a subatomic particle, for example, one necessarily altered its velocity. To measure a particle's velocity, one had to change the particle's position. One measurement always made the other measurement uncertain. So much for the knowable, predictable relationship between matter and energy.

Heisenberg's revelation that night came to be known as the uncertainty principle. While it was meaningful only at the atomic level, not affecting our understanding of the behavior of everyday objects, the uncertainty principle simply crushed the concept of determinism in physics, evoking Einstein's anguished query about God throwing dice.

Largely owing to his formulation of the uncertainty principle, Werner Heisenberg was awarded the 1932 Nobel Prize in physics. He remained in Germany throughout the Nazi era, though he apparently was no Hitlerite. Looked to for leadership in the development of a German atomic bomb, he may well have scuttled the project by exaggerating the dangers and difficulties inherent in such a project.

SIR ALEXANDER FLEMING DISCOVERS PENICILLIN (1928)

It made a great story: Scientist accidentally contaminates bacteria sample with mold, then discovers that the mold is actually a powerful antibacterial agent. His accidental discovery, penicillin, later saves countless lives and the lucky scientist is rewarded with the Nobel Prize for medicine.

Most of the story was true. Like a good many bacteriologists of his day, Alexander Fleming (later "Sir" when he was knighted in 1944) was searching for the "magic bullet"—a substance that would kill disease-producing bacteria without damaging, or even interacting with, a patient's tissues. In 1922 he discovered lysozyme, an antibacterial substance found in saliva, blood, tears, and (Fleming's original source) nasal mucous. Lysozyme, as a naturally occurring substance in the human body, was safe enough, but it had one serious flaw—the only bacteria it killed were those that did not cause illness. Lysozyme clearly was not the magic bullet.

The breakthrough occurred in 1928. The Scottish-born bacteriologist had grown cultures of the staphylococci bacteria in petri dishes, then allowed the cultures to remain on his bench while he went on a brief vacation. When he returned he found that mold had contaminated some of the dishes and that where the mold had grown the bacteria were destroyed.

The contaminating mold was *Penicillium*, a rare organism that the laboratory on the floor below Fleming's lab just happened to be growing at the time. Fleming figured out that penicillium mold produced an antibacterial substance, and he named the substance "penicillin." Remarkably, however, he did little to pursue the possibilities that penicillin presented. Not a chemist, he failed to isolate the bactericidal substance from the mold "broth." And although he applied the mold broth to laboratory animals, learning in the process that it was nontoxic even in large concentrations, Fleming apparently had no clue that he had stumbled on the magic bullet that could cure terrible diseases.

Fleming turned his attention elsewhere, and research into penicillin languished for twelve years. It was not until 1940—following the outbreak of World War II—that interest in Fleming's serendipitous discovery revived. Howard Florey and Ernst Chain, two bacteriologists in search of the magic bullet, read a paper Fleming had written and began to work with penicillin. They succeeded in isolating the drug, then tested it on humans and garnered the necessary financial resources to put it into mass production. It was largely due to Florey and Chain that penicillin became immediately available to thousands of wounded soldiers who may well have died had they not received injections of the first antibiotic.

Florey and Chain shared the Nobel Prize with Fleming in 1945, but they never shared in the public acclaim accorded the lucky Scot. Their solid science was far more responsible for bringing penicillin to fruition, but Fleming's contaminated petri dish made a far better story.

—J.L.K.

KURT GÖDEL FORMULATES GÖDEL'S THEOREM (1931)

As a child, in spite of the fact that he was shy and introverted, this Austrian-born mathematician acquired the nickname "Herr Warum" (Mr. Why); as an adult he became a reclusive figure whose thoughts and theories caused observers to compare him, in the same breath, to Albert Einstein and Franz Kafka.

Born on April 28, 1906, in what is now Brno, in the Czech Republic, he died on January 14, 1978, in a New Jersey hospital of a bizarre cause—self-imposed starvation. As a climax to a long-time tendency to hypochondria and deteriorating mental health, he came to believe that someone was poisoning his food.

He studied at the University of Vienna, and later became associated with the Institute for Advanced Studies at Princeton.

In his lifetime, Gödel became famous as one of the planet's most creative logicians and mathematical theorists. His celebrated theorem, expressed in 1931, was so novel and complex that even other mathematicians had difficulty understanding it.

Simply put, if that is possible, it suggests that logical reasoning can never comprehend ultimate truth, that certain mathematical theories can never be proved or disproved, that mathematics is necessarily incomplete. As was Kafka's K in *The Castle*, mathematicians are doomed to scurry up and down endless corridors of thought, banging on doors, conducting investigations that can yield no final answers.

He also thought a lot about time, considering man's ordinary view of the subject to be an illusion. He constructed a mathematical explanation of a possible universe in which time travel would be possible.

If Gödel's ideas struck many as strange, his personality was a perfect match. Often plagued with severe depression, he found some relief by taking strolls with his friend Einstein and chatting about relativity. With a high singsong voice and laughter that struck observers as curious, his sentences often trailed off into an amused hum. As he grew older he lived in more and more complete isolation, and ever-deepening silence, almost completely limiting his contact to his wife, Adele.

—R.W.S.

OTTO HAHN AND LISE MEITNER UNLOCK THE SECRET OF NUCLEAR FISSION (1938)

Workmates for more than thirty years, Otto Hahn and Lise Meitner made their greatest discovery while separated, he in Germany, she in forced exile in Sweden. They had started working together in 1907, when Meitner—a young physicist from Austria—came to study in Berlin. Barred from working in laboratories with male students, she found a place in Hahn's lab at the Chemical Institute. Hahn, who had disappointed his German parents by opting to study chemistry rather than architecture, was already highly regarded for his investigations of radioactive elements.

The Hahn-Meitner collaboration focused on these elements and their isotopes. The duo was separated during World War I—Hahn fighting on the western front while Meitner served as a nurse—but by 1917 they were back in Berlin, working at the Kaiser Wilhelm Institute for Chemistry on the chemical and physical properties of radioactive elements.

In 1928 Hahn became director of the institute, a position he maintained despite his opposition to the Nazis' ridding the place of its Jewish scientists. Meitner, a Jew, was at first unaffected by the anti-Semitic regulations because she wasn't German. By late 1938, however, she was forced to flee. She went first to Holland and later to Sweden, where, for the most part, she remained for the rest of her life.

From 1934 until her departure, Meitner worked with Hahn on the effects of bombarding uranium with neutrons. Other scientists—such as Enrico Fermi—had performed similar experiments, but no one had yet been able to figure out just what happened when the heavy uranium nucleus was subjected to the neutron bombardment. Fermi suspected that the result was creation of an element heavier than uranium (the heaviest element existing in nature).

At Christmas 1938, Hahn wrote to the exiled Meitner in Sweden. He and his new partner, Fritz Strassmann, seemed to have found barium resulting from the neutron bombardment of uranium. But that was impossible. Uranium had an atomic number of 92. Fermi had theorized that neutron bombardment might yield a heavier element with the atomic number 93. Barium had an atomic number of 56. Hahn concluded his letter by surmising that he and Strassmann must have made a mistake.

But Meitner knew better. With her nephew, Otto Frisch (who was visiting his aunt in Sweden for the holidays), she figured it out. Hahn was too good a scientist to make a mistake. The uranium bombardment experiment had indeed yielded barium and, she predicted, an isotope of the gaseous element krypton—atomic number 36 (barium's 56 plus krypton's 36 equals uranium's 92). When the uranium atom was hit by a neutron, its nucleus split, or—in Meitner's term—it fissioned. In January 1939, Meitner and Frisch published their theory of nuclear fission in the British scientific journal *Nature*. The following month, Hahn and Strassmann published results of a confirming study in which they found the Meitner-predicted traces of krypton.

It was nuclear fission that—in a sustained chain reaction of splitting uranium atoms—would be the basis for nuclear weapons. Although Meitner realized that fission must release an enormous amount of energy, neither she nor Hahn saw the possibilities, for good and ill, of the chain reaction. She stayed in Sweden during World War II, became a Swedish citizen in 1949, and continued to do research in nuclear physics. In 1960 she retired to Cambridge, England, and in 1966 she received the Enrico Fermi Prize for her insight into the fission of uranium.

Hahn remained in Germany. Although he could not help but become involved in the German War Department's nuclear research office, Germany never launched an atomic bomb program. He was briefly interned by Allied forces at the end of the war, during which time he learned of the atomic bombings of Hiroshima and Nagasaki. Consumed by guilt for his role in the creation of such horrific weapons, he considered suicide. He ultimately rejected the thought, but Hahn was an ardent opponent of nuclear weaponry to the end of his life.

WILLARD LIBBY DEVISES CARBON 14 DATING (1949)

Willard Libby loved isotopes—those forms of a chemical element that are identical in atomic number (same number of protons) but differ in atomic weight because of different numbers of neutrons. It was Libby who researched techniques for separating uranium isotopes for the Manhattan Project, thereby playing a crucial role in the production of the atomic bomb.

It was carbon isotopes, however, that most interested Libby. He knew that when cosmic rays strike atoms in the earth's atmosphere, neutrons are released. These neutrons are then absorbed by nitrogen, creating the isotope nitrogen 14. The nitrogen 14 decays into carbon 14, a radioactive isotope of carbon. These radioactive isotopes eventually form carbon dioxide, which is absorbed by plants during photosynthesis and eventually ingested into animal tissues as well. All living matter contains carbon 14.

That was the key for Willard Libby. Since carbon 14 decays at a steady rate, Libby thought that he should be able to determine any organic substance's date of death by measuring how much carbon 14 he could find in it. The yardstick of measurement was carbon 14's half-life—half of any given concentration would decay in 5,730 years.

Libby needed an extraordinarily sensitive Geiger counter to measure the radioactivity of a dating sample, and he needed to shield that Geiger counter from interference by cosmic rays or other sources of radiation. He surrounded his main Geiger counter with iron walls eight inches thick to absorb terrestrial radiation, and he set up eleven smaller Geiger counters around the main unit to detect cosmic rays. When such rays were detected, the main Geiger counter was shut down for a fraction of a second.

Libby's method of radiocarbon dating worked. It worked so well, in fact, that archaeologists and historians and other scholars had to revise their time lines. For example, Libby discovered that the last ice age in North America ended 10,000 years ago, not the 25,000 years that geologists had asserted.

FRANCIS CRICK AND JAMES WATSON DECODE THE STRUCTURE OF DNA (1953)

In determining the structure of deoxyribonucleic acid, Francis Crick and James Watson revealed how the master molecule that contains the genetic code could divide and replicate itself. It was an astounding achievement, earning both men the 1962 Nobel Prize for physiology and medicine.

Theirs was something of an odd pairing—the older Crick, who had not yet completed his doctorate and was looking for a job, teaming with the prodigy Watson, who was looking for a Nobel Prize. They met at Cambridge University's Cavendish Laboratory in 1951. There Watson convinced Crick to help develop a DNA model. Eighteen months later—in April 1953—they announced their breakthrough in the British magazine *Nature*: "We wish to suggest a structure," they began, "for the salt of deoxyribonucleic acid (DNA). This structure has novel features which are of considerable biological interest."

It was an uncharacteristically modest presentation for two men with substantial egos. Watson's book *The Double Helix*, which describes the search for DNA structure, begins with the sentence: "I have never seen Francis Crick in a modest mood." James Watson was no shrinking violet either. Born in Chicago in 1928, he quickly showed evidence of genius. Possessing a photographic memory, he appeared on the radio contest *The Quiz Kids*, entered the University of Chicago at the age of fifteen, graduated with a degree in zoology, and went on to graduate school at Indiana University; he was just twenty-two when Indiana awarded him a Ph.D.

Watson, who had attended Chicago and Indiana on scholarships, then went to the University of Copenhagen on a National Research Council grant. It was there that he began to examine the biochemistry of DNA. A grant from the National Foundation for Infantile Paralysis took him to the Cavendish Laboratory, where he met physicist-recently-turned-biologist Francis Crick.

Crick, born in Northampton, England, in 1916, had begun his study of physics at University College in London in 1934, when Watson was just six years old. Crick remained at University College for graduate work, but progress toward his doctorate was interrupted by the outbreak of World War II. He spent the war years working on the development of mines for the British Admiralty, then decided he'd rather be a biologist. In 1949 he began research into the chemical basis of genetics at the Cavendish Laboratory.

By the time Watson and Crick formed their partnership, much was known about the composition of DNA. Scientists knew that DNA is constructed of five-carbon sugar molecules, phosphate, and four nitrogen-containing bases.

Two University of London researchers—Maurice H. F. Wilkins and Rosalind Franklin—had made X-ray pictures of DNA crystals, revealing the basic shape of the molecule. What was not known was how the various components were linked, enabling DNA to divide and replicate itself.

Watson and Crick figured it out. Doing very little laboratory work, they instead used beads, pieces of wire, and cardboard to create a model that would match what was known about DNA's chemistry and shape. The model revealed the shape to be a double helix—a ladder twisted to form a spiral. Two strands of sugar and phosphate are joined by pairs of bases inside the helix. Hydrogen bonds attach the bases to one another: adenine paired with thymine, guanine paired with cytosine. DNA separates at the hydrogen bonds, a new molecule forms opposite each half of the old one, with the bases of the old acting as a template for the new molecule. Within hours of determining the double-helix structure, the two scientists were proclaiming "that we had found the secret of life." Watson was just twenty-five years old.

It was all very elegant science, and Crick and Watson reaped the rewards of revealing how life's genetic matter replicates. Crick finally got his Ph.D., and Watson accepted a professorship at Harvard. Except for a brief time in 1955–56, the two never worked together again. Most recently, Watson has been involved in cancer research and directing the human genome project—an attempt to identify all human genes. Crick has been doing brain research and investigating the notion that life originated on Earth as a consequence of seeds sent here from a distant planet—"directed panspermia," he calls it.

—J.L.K.

DAN McKENZIE AND R. L. PARKER INTRODUCE THEORY OF PLATE TECTONICS (1967)

The geologic theory of plate tectonics maintains that the surface of the planet is made up of about seven distinct major plates and many smaller plates that move at extremely slow speeds. The movement of these huge chunks of the earth causes—along with the continental drift described by Alfred Wegener—earthquakes, volcanoes, mountains, troughs, rifts, ridges, and ocean basins.

Observers have noted, almost since the time when relatively complete and accurate maps were available, that the continents seem to be huge pieces of some jigsaw puzzle. Until Wegener introduced the idea of continental drift, and McKenzie and Parker introduced the idea of plate tectonics in 1967 and later backed it up with seafloor surveys, the idea that such huge and solid masses could be drifting across the face of the planet was simply beyond belief.

The notion of plate tectonics presents some odd facts: geologically speaking, San Francisco, Los Angeles, and most of the coast of California are not part of North America—they actually are on the eastern edge of the Pacific plate. The Atlantic Ocean is getting wider, and the Pacific Ocean is shrinking. Along the western edge of the Pacific plate there exists tremendous pressure as it pushes against the Asian plate, hence the numerous volcanoes that ring the northern and western edges of the Pacific Ocean.

We can see, as Parker and McKenzie did, and as Wegener did, the results of continental drift and plate tectonics, but without the patience of the gods, we can never actually see it happening—until perhaps beachfront property in Southern California butts up against the suburbs of Tokyo.

—R.W.S.

GREAT INVENTORS AND THEIR INVENTIONS

MARCONI'S "STILL, SMALL VOICES": RADIO IS BORN (1901)

A family legend surrounds Guglielmo Marconi's birth on April 25, 1874. A gardener supposedly said of the newborn: "What big ears he has!" Marconi's mother was Annie Jameson, of Ireland's Jameson whiskey distillers. While studying music in Italy, she eloped with the widower Giuseppe Marconi. Perhaps thinking of the leprechauns in her native Belfast, Annie told the gardener: "With these ears he'll be able to hear the still, small voices of the air."

As his domineering father often told him, Marconi was a mama's boy, a loner, and a good-for-nothing. He flunked out of high school and failed entrance exams to the University of Bologna and the Italian Naval Academy. He finally got into technical school, where two people changed his life: a physics professor introduced him to electromagnetic theory, and a blind telegrapher taught him Morse code.

Morse code was then dependent on a network of wires. In the 1860s, British physicist James Clerk Maxwell had theorized about invisible electromagnetic waves. Heinrich Hertz in Germany generated such signals, which he called "Hertzian waves." (His name is preserved today as the unit of measurement for radio frequencies—a Hertz is one cycle per second.)

In 1894, the year Hertz died, Marconi read a magazine article about the invisible waves. He had a brainstorm—using Hertzian waves to send Morse code. Marconi was amazed that no one else had done it and resolved that he would be the first to transmit signals without wires.

Back home he set up an attic laboratory and labored for months. One night he called his mother in. Marconi tapped a telegraph key. On the other side of the attic, a bell rang. Between key and bell were no wires—only air.

Marconi knew this was simply a parlor trick. Wireless transmission would succeed only if it conquered distance. By 1895 Marconi had sent Morse code more than one and a half miles. His father told him he was wasting his life.

The Italian military agreed, when Marconi demonstrated his invention. After his own government ignored him, Annie took her son to London in 1896. Sir William Preece, chief engineer of the British postal service, immediately saw a need for "wireless."

By 1899 Marconi was transmitting thirty-one miles across the English Channel. Many scientists believed radio waves traveled like light, in a straight line. If true, this meant the waves could travel only as far as the visible horizon—about 200 miles.

The experts were proved wrong on December 12, 1901. At a transmitter in England, Marconi tapped out three dots, the Morse letter S. His signal was received in Newfoundland, Canada, 2,137 miles across the Atlantic. Wireless transatlantic communication was a reality.

Marconi never lacked critics. He was called a mere synthesizer of ideas, not a "true" scientist. But even his harshest critics concede that Marconi was the first to successfully transmit wireless radio waves over long distances.

Marconi died on July 20, 1937. The next day, radio operators all over the world shut down their transmitters for two minutes in his memory.

Guglielmo Marconi at his receiving set at St. John's, Newfoundland, December 12, 1901.

BAEKELAND AND (A DAY LATE) SWINBURNE: PLASTIC (1907)

Plastic, a remarkable material, was invented almost simultaneously by two remarkable men.

Leo Hendrik Baekeland (1863–1944) was born in Belgium, the son of an illiterate cobbler and a maid. He won a university scholarship and, at twenty, was graduated *maxima cum laude* with a doctorate. Inspired by Benjamin Franklin's autobiography, Baekeland emigrated to America. He was determined to get rich.

In 1891 his improvement to Velox photographic paper allowed photos to be developed cheaply under artificial light. En route to meet Kodak president George Eastman, Baekeland decided he would try to sell his patent for $50,000 but would settle for $25,000. Eastman offered him $750,000.

The newly rich Baekeland soon hit on another money making idea: artificial shellac. At the time, shellac was an expensive natural substance made from the wings of Southeast Asian insects. A cheap synthetic shellac would be a big seller.

In 1872 the German chemist Adolf von Baeyer had created a synthetic resin by combining phenol (carbolic acid) and formaldehyde. The chemicals formed a sticky black gunk that dried rock hard. In liquid form this would be a perfect shellac: tough and weatherproof. But Baekeland had to find a way to dissolve the stuff into a liquid.

He failed. But at some point, Baekeland reversed his thinking: a hard synthetic resin might also have practical uses.

In contrast to Baekeland, James Swinburne (1858–1958) was born into an old, eccentric Scottish family. Not a clock in the house worked until twelve-year-old James showed his budding technical ability by repairing them all.

Swinburne became an electrical engineer. He created the words rotor and stator to describe the parts of an electric motor. In 1904 he was studying long-distance transmission of high-voltage electricity. One problem had to be solved: high-voltage insulation constantly broke down, limiting transmission distances.

Searching for a better insulator, Swinburne experimented with the same chemicals that interested Baekeland. A careful man, Swinburne did not want to publicize his work until he was successful. In 1907 he was ready to patent his new material. He discovered that one day before his application, an identical patent had been awarded to Baekeland.

Baekeland had created a hard, clear resin that could be easily molded and colored. It was impervious to solvents, electricity, and heat. He called it Bakelite.

Bakelite was the first thermosetting plastic, that is, one that held its shape after heating. An ancestor, celluloid, was a thermoplastic, which softened when heated. In just a few years,

Bakelite was everywhere, in ashtrays, radios, fountain pens, and thousands of industrial products—including high-voltage electrical insulators. Baekeland kept control of the patent, and Bakelite made him a multimillionaire.

Swinburne eventually came up with a tough lacquer for protecting polished metal. He named it Damard (short for "damn hard"). In 1916 Baekeland visited England to establish a subsidiary. He met Swinburne, acquired his Damard Lacquer Company, and made Swinburne chairman of the new Bakelite Limited.

Baekeland retired to his Florida mansion in 1939. He became a miserly recluse, shunning his family and eating his meals from tin cans. He died on February 23, 1944.

Swinburne served as chairman of Bakelite until 1948, when he retired at ninety. He was granted more than a hundred patents and died in 1958, one month after his 100th birthday.

ARMSTRONG'S GREATEST HITS: RADIO GROWS UP (1912–33)

The inventions of Edwin Howard Armstrong live in every radio and TV today. Yet his own life reads like a Greek tragedy, with lawyers replacing the more classical antagonists.

Armstrong was born in New York on December 18, 1890. As a child he built his own radio receivers from scratch and broadcast over a homemade transmitting station.

While a student at Columbia, Armstrong developed his first great invention. On the night of September 22, 1912, Armstrong's sister Ethel awoke to his cries of "I've done it!" Then she heard another sound—loud dots and dashes of Morse code.

Armstrong had improved the Audion, Lee De Forest's triode vacuum tube. Though better than earlier receivers, the curse of the Audion was weak reception; radio listeners had to wear uncomfortable headphones. By feeding part of the Audion output current back to its input, Armstrong made the tube a powerful amplifier. He called his invention the "feedback" or "regenerative" circuit, and it became a basic principle of radio electronics.

Armstrong did not file a patent until he finished college in 1913. He was immediately snarled in lawsuits. De Forest kept the case in court for more than ten years, refusing to concede when Armstrong's patent was upheld. With the unlimited legal backing of his patent owner, AT&T, De Forest finally appealed to the Supreme Court and won on a technicality.

Armstrong made his next great discovery while serving in France during World War I. His superheterodyne circuit eliminated several problems with existing receivers and greatly improved the reception of weak signals.

Though the De Forest suits dragged on, Armstrong prospered in the 1920s. He sold his "superhet" patent to Westinghouse and married

Marion MacInnis. She was the secretary to one of the most powerful men in radio and Armstrong's longtime friend: David Sarnoff, manager of RCA, which owned the NBC radio networks.

Next Armstrong went to work on the problem of noise, which was inherent in the standard broadcast method of amplitude modulation (AM). In 1933 Armstrong patented a whole new system: frequency modulation (FM), which produced a noise-free signal.

Armstrong expected FM to catch on immediately, but the radio industry saw it as a threat. Under industry pressure, the Federal Communications Commission (FCC) waited seven years before issuing Armstrong an FM broadcast permit. World War II further delayed the new medium. By the late 1940s fifty FM stations were broadcasting to more than 500,000 receivers. Then, again influenced by the broadcast industry, the FCC forced FM to a higher frequency band and drastically limited its power. Overnight, existing FM stations and receivers were obsolete. Armstrong was stunned.

Then the industry began using FM to provide sound in its newest product—television. Armstrong believed that, more than patent infringement, this was outright theft. He saw the mighty RCA as the worst offender. A friendship of three decades ended with Sarnoff and Armstrong talking only through lawyers.

By the early fifties legal battles had left Armstrong nearly broke, and his health was visibly failing. On Thanksgiving 1953, Armstrong and Marion began arguing about the lawsuits. Normally a mild man, Armstrong swung a fire poker. The blow bruised Marion's arm and shattered their marriage. Armstrong spent Christmas alone in his Manhattan apartment. His lawyers told him that the FM lawsuits would probably continue for another decade.

On Sunday, January 31, 1954, the meticulous inventor dressed in a fresh suit with overcoat, scarf, and gloves. He wrote a note to Marion: "I would give my life to turn back to the time when we were so happy and free." His apartment was on the thirteenth floor; he wasn't superstitious, and he had loved heights since climbing his first antenna mast as a boy. Howard Armstrong stepped out of a window, into eternity.

Armstrong's contribution to electronics is incalculable. He would no doubt have accomplished even more without the constant stress of his legal problems. After Armstrong's death, Marion filed twenty-one lawsuits in his name. She won them all.

A LOOK INSIDE: RABI AND MAGNETIC RESONANCE IMAGING (1931)

Magnetic resonance imaging (MRI) allows doctors to look inside the human body without harmful X rays or painful dye injection. MRI became a medical procedure by a long and serendipitous route; it was originally developed to study the behavior of atomic particles.

Isidor I. Rabi (1898–1988) was a Polish-born American physicist who observed that the nucleus of an atom "spun" at precise frequencies. In 1931 Rabi set up a magnetic field that could be tuned to these frequencies, somewhat like a radio transmitter. When hit with the correct frequency, the "spin" of the nucleus reversed. Turning off the magnetic field returned the nucleus to its original state, causing pulses of energy to be emitted. These pulses could be measured, revealing nuclear secrets. Rabi's discovery won the 1944 Nobel Prize in physics.

His work led directly to another pair of Nobels in 1952. Felix Bloch (1905–83) and Edward Purcell (b. 1912) won the prize by making the Rabi method more precise. More important, they eliminated the need to vaporize a sample, thus destroying it. This paved the way for medical MRI.

The first person to use MRI on living tissue was Raymond V. Damadian (b. 1916). Experimenting on animals, then humans, Damadian discovered that MRI could locate diseases in the body. Cancer cells had a distinctive resonant frequency, allowing that killer disease to be quickly pinpointed. In 1978 a group of British researchers used MRI to take the first look inside a living human brain.

However, the process that Rabi began in 1931 is still in its medical infancy. In October 1991, Dr. Richard R. Ernst (b. 1933) was flying from his native Switzerland to New York; the pilot informed Ernst that he had won the Nobel Prize in chemistry. Ernst's Nobel Prize represented twenty-five years of MRI improvements. The innovations of Ernst and his American colleague, Dr. Weston Anderson, extracted more information from nuclear signals with greater accuracy. The Nobel citation noted that the difference before and after Ernst's work was "like looking at the skyline of a mountain range, and then looking at the whole range from an aircraft above."

ATOMIC HAMMER: COCKCROFT AND THE PARTICLE ACCELERATOR (1932)

John Douglas Cockcroft was the stereotypical absent-minded professor. He once left his wife in the car while visiting a friend, then took the train home, forgetting both car and wife. Yet this gentle mathematician unleashed the violent elemental forces that led to the creation of the atomic bomb.

Cockcroft was born May 27, 1897, to a family of textile manufacturers in Todmorden, England. He showed mathematical brilliance as a boy and entered Manchester University in 1914. When World War I began, Cockcroft left school for the army. He survived some of the war's fiercest fighting.

Home again, he worked at a power plant while taking a college apprenticeship in electrical engineering. His supervisors recognized Cockcroft's abilities and urged him to pursue higher-level university work. Cockcroft entered Cambridge and studied physics under Ernest Rutherford, one of the first atomic physicists.

When Cockcroft received his B.S. in 1924, he was recruited for Rutherford's atomic research team at Cavendish Laboratory. The Cavendish geniuses knew that the nucleus of an atom contained densely compacted energy. If the nucleus could be cracked open, the energy would be released.

Along with formidable intelligence, Cockcroft brought to this problem his practical experience in high-voltage electricity. With a brilliant assistant, Ernest Walton (1903–1995), Cockcroft began building a particle accelerator. The device was a gigantic spiral capable of generating 300,000 volts. According to Cockcroft's calculations, a proton would travel around the accelerator spirals, gaining speed and energy until it struck a lithium nucleus at the other end. If the target nucleus were split, it would no longer be lithium.

On April 30, 1932, Cockcroft and Walton introduced hydrogen particles, made unstable by an additional proton, into one end of the accelerator. When the experiment ended, the single lithium target nucleus had become two nuclei of helium. It was the first artificial nuclear transformation; the atom had been split.

Cockcroft and Walton shared a 1951 Nobel Prize for their particle accelerator. Cockcroft also played a major part in developing radar and later directed Britain's Atomic Energy Research Establishment. He died on September 18, 1967.

LISTENING TO OTHER WORLDS: REBER'S RADIO TELESCOPE (1937)

Grote Reber (b. 1911) was not just the first radio astronomer; he was the world's only radio astronomer until the late 1940s. Even more remarkably, Reber was an amateur with no funding from colleges, governments, or science. Reber figured out how to design radio telescopes, paid for their construction out of his own pocket, and built them in his backyard in Wheaton, Illinois.

Reber always credited the invention of radio astronomy to Karl Jansky (1905–50). In 1928 Jansky was an engineer for Bell Laboratories. He was assigned to study all the sources of noise that interfered with long-distance radio signals. Jansky cobbled up a weird array of rectangular antennas. Needing to track noise by rotating the antennas, he mounted the array on wheels from a junked Model T. Jansky had accidentally invented the first radio telescope, though he didn't know it yet.

By 1932 Jansky had identified all the sources of radio interference except one persistent hiss. At first he suspected solar noise, but in tracking the hiss over several months, Jansky noted that it moved away from the Sun. He then deduced that the noise was coming from the Milky Way: static from the stars. Jansky published his findings and urged his employer to investigate further. But Bell was only interested in Jansky's primary task, eliminating radio noise, which had solid commercial applications.

In Wheaton, Illinois, Grote Reber was fascinated when he read of Jansky's cosmic static. A radio fanatic since his youth, Reber made his living designing radio receivers. In 1937 he began designing the world's first purpose-built radio telescope.

The device slowly took shape in Reber's backyard. He built it from lumberyard rafters and old car parts. Its thirty-one-foot parabolic antenna was common galvanized sheet metal. Looking like something from an H. G. Wells novel, the antenna attracted a lot of attention, not all of it favorable. When a small airplane was forced down in Wheaton with engine failure, rumors spread that Reber had grounded the aircraft with a death ray from his strange invention.

Reber's first attempts to eavesdrop on the universe were unsuccessful. Finally, in 1939 a chart graph connected to the telescope recorded radio emissions at a wavelength of 1.87 meters (160 megahertz).

He began carefully mapping "radio stars." One of the weakest turned out to be the Sun. One of the strongest was the Crab Nebula, a supernova whose death throes had first been observed in the year 1054. Another source was not a star at all, but a pair of galaxies beyond the Milky Way colliding with each other.

Reber's backyard creation was the first step in the new science of radio astronomy. Within his lifetime that science would lead to astonishing revelations about the nature and history of the universe.

THE INVISIBLE BASTION: WATSON-WATT AND RADAR (1940)

In the early days of radio, broadcasters noticed an irritating phenomenon. When an object passed in front of a radio beam, the waves bounced off, creating reflected echoes. A few scientists thought the bouncing beams could serve as an early-warning system, but the military was not interested.

Things had changed by the 1930s, when the world was clearly headed for war. Britain, America, France, and Germany began crash programs to develop radio-based warning sytems. These systems were called radio detecting and ranging, or radar.

One of radar's earliest advocates was a Scottish physicist, Robert Alexander Watson-Watt.

Born in Aberdeenshire on April 13, 1892, Watson-Watt was a scientific prodigy who fell in love with "wireless." By 1915 he was using radio waves to locate thunderstorms. In 1919 he patented echo-location, or bouncing radio waves off objects to find them.

He also hit on the idea of visual tracking. He believed this was possible with the cathode-ray tube (CRT), the new "picture tube" used in oscilloscopes. Watson-Watt proposed the idea in 1916 but didn't get a CRT until one arrived from America in 1923. His idea proved correct.

Watson-Watt spent the next decade developing his theories while working for the British government. In 1934 he was sent to the Air Ministry as scientific adviser. His top-secret mission: build a radar network to protect Britain from air attack.

More than anyone else, Watson-Watt knew how much work lay ahead. Early radar used continuous wave beams, which could only detect the presence of an approaching object. Two separate antennas were required, for transmitting the powerful search beam and receiving its weak "echo." The echo was susceptible to weather interference. Radar transmitters were physically huge and consumed prodigious amounts of energy.

Watson-Watt helped solve each problem. In 1936 the continuous-wave beam was replaced by a pulsed signal, which could detect an incoming aircraft and also pinpoint its location. Transmit and receive functions were combined in a single antenna, the duplexer. In 1939 a microwave transmitter allowed radar to "see" through clouds and fog. One of the most critical developments was a smaller and more efficient transmitter, the cavity magnetron.

By the time Luftwaffe bombers appeared over England, in August 1940, Watson-Watt had built an extensive radar network. The British called it "an invisible bastion." Radar operators saw the Luftwaffe coming 150 miles away, at altitudes up to 30,000 feet.

Watson-Watt visited the United States in 1941 to share his research. Radar was mistrusted at first. When a GI once reported "the biggest blip I've ever seen," headquarters told him not to worry. He shut down his transmitter and went to breakfast . . . on the morning of December 7, 1941, at Pearl Harbor, Hawaii.

For his contributions to radar, Watson-Watt was knighted in 1942. Radar development continued after the war, finding many civilian uses. Watson-Watt died on December 5, 1973. He is still remembered as the father of radar.

SMALL WONDERS, PART 1: THE TRANSISTOR (1948)

For four decades the main component in electronic equipment was the vacuum tube. Its limits were highlighted in 1946, when the first general-purpose computer appeared. The thirty-ton ENIAC (Electronic Numerical Integrator and Calculator) used 500 miles of wire to connect 17,468 vacuum tubes. The hot, glowing tubes required room-sized air conditioners and drew swarms of moths. Those moths were often zapped by high voltage, creating short circuits—and a computer term still used today; ENIAC had to be literally "debugged."

As ENIAC went on-line, the replacement for the vacuum tube was being developed. Since 1931 Walter H. Brattain (1902–87) had researched solid-state physics at Bell Laboratories. He had found some odd electrical properties in crystals such as silicon and germanium. Most materials were either electrical conductors (such as metal) or insulators (such as rubber). Pure silicon was an insulator, but when chemically treated, its atomic structure was altered and the crystal conducted electricity.

Because the treated silicon was neither insulator nor conductor, it was called a semiconductor. On December 29, 1939, a Bell employee named William Shockley (1910–89) wrote in his lab notebook: "It has today occurred to me that an amplifier using semiconductors rather than vacuum [tubes] is possible." If Shockley was right, tiny crystals might replace the bulky, inefficient vacuum tube, but World War II interrupted his research.

During the war, Brattain developed silicon rectifiers for radar sets. In 1945 Shockley, Brattain, and John Bardeen (1908–87) began trying to develop semiconductor amplifiers. Brattain was a hands-on experimenter, Bardeen was a brilliant theorist, and Shockley was a little of both.

After two years of failure, late in 1947 the team produced an amplified signal in germanium. Because current had been transferred from a low-resistance input to a high-resistance output, the invention was soon called the transfer resistor. This was soon shortened to transistor.

On July 1, 1948, Bell Labs introduced the transistor to the world. Its first consumer use came in 1953—the transistorized hearing aid. The founder of AT&T and Bell Labs, Alexander Graham Bell, had spent much of his life trying to help the deaf. In Bell's memory, AT&T allowed the transistor to be used royalty free in hearing devices.

In 1956 Shockley, Brattain, and Bardeen shared a Nobel Prize in physics. One member of the trio was not overjoyed by some of the changes his invention wrought. "The thing I deplore most," Brattain said in 1973, "is the use of solid-state electronics by rock-and-roll musicians to raise the level of sound to where it is both painful and injurious." Brattain spent his entire career at Bell Labs, retiring in 1967.

John Bardeen was the first person to win the Nobel Prize twice in the same field. In 1972 he shared a second Nobel in physics for his contributions to superconductor theory.

William Shockley improved the first crude transistors, and later taught engineering at Stanford University. Then he took up genetics, a field in which he had no training. He advocated sperm banks to create an intellectual master race and authored the "dysgenics" theory, which said, in essence, that nonwhite people are dumber than whites and have too many kids. During the 1960s protesters often gathered outside Shockley's office at Stanford. Their death threats were delivered at a loud volume thanks to a portable amplifier that used Shockley's transistors.

FREE ENERGY: THE PHOTOVOLTAIC CELL AND SOLAR POWER (1954)

Every forty days, sunlight produces as much energy as the earth's total known reserves of oil, coal, and natural gas. Harnessing all that free energy has long occupied scientists. Charles Fritts invented a working photovoltaic cell (or solar cell) in 1886. He used the element selenium, which conducted more electricity in sunlight than in the dark.

Scientists considered Fritts a fraud; his "free energy" sounded suspiciously like a perpetual-motion machine. Not for the last time, solar power was relegated to the scientific basement.

Years later, after quantum mechanics had explained how selenium worked, Fritts's idea was rediscovered. In 1954 Bell Laboratories of AT&T assigned Daryl Chapin to develop an efficient selenium solar cell. In another department, Gerald Pearson led a team investigating semiconductors. A member of Pearson's team, Calvin Fuller, had years of semiconductor experience. By using a new chemical process to treat silicon, Fuller developed a semiconductor solar cell.

The device initially converted 4 percent of incoming sunlight into electricity, making it five times more efficient than selenium. Steadily improved by Fuller, Pearson, and Chapin, this increased to 6 percent, then 10 percent.

In 1954 the three men announced their discovery. "We tried to avoid making too much claim for it," Chapin said. The media were under no such restraints. Magazines predicted sun-powered convertibles and unlimited free electricity.

In Americus, Georgia, during 1956, the new solar cells were used to power a telephone amplifier. Mounted on phone poles, 432 solar cells provided nine volts of power to charge a nickel-cadmium battery. The six-month test was a success.

But this was a long way from a sun-powered car, and the public lost interest. Bell's 1956 solar cells could not financially compete with conventional electricity. Though silicon is literally common as dirt—it appears in one form as sand—solar cells required especially "grown" and uncommonly pure silicon, which then had to undergo several costly chemical processes.

As had happened in the nineteenth century, the whole technology was almost scrapped. It was saved by the space race. Satellites needed a simple, renewable power source, and solar cells were perfect (there are no clouds in space to obscure the Sun). In 1958 the first American orbiting satellite, Vanguard I, used silicon solar cells. They have powered all American satellites since. In 1980 Dr. Paul MacReady built the world's first solar-powered airplane, the Solar Challenger (see page 339).

The last quarter of the twentieth century has suffered several energy crises and nuclear-power accidents, with renewed interest in solar power after each. This interest tends to die out quickly. One reason is the old curse of solar power: inflated expectations. Another reason is that the nuclear energy and fossil-fuel industries have powerful, well-financed lobbies, which are not countered by an equivalent solar lobby.

TO SEE AN ATOM: MÜLLER'S MICROSCOPES (1955)

The German physicist Erwin Wilhelm Müller (1911–77) had one lifelong obsession: to look through a microscope and study a single atom. The microscope of Müller's youth had changed little since the seventeenth century, when Antoni van Leeuwenhoek's lenses improved the compound microscope purportedly invented by Zacharias Janssen about 1590.

By the time Müller was a student at Berlin's Technical University, the electron microscope had been invented. This device showed hitherto unseen particles, such as bacteria and molecules, but not atoms. Like many young scientists, Müller believed the ability to see individual atoms was critical to the revolutionary new science of subatomic theory.

Müller began working on an improved microscope in college, basing his work on theories of quantum mechanics proposed by Robert Oppenheimer. Just a year after he graduated, in 1936, Müller unveiled his field emission microscope. A metal needle was subjected to a powerful electric field, causing the emission of negative electrons onto a positively charged fluorescent screen. The screen displayed an enlarged view of the needle's atomic structure.

Müller's device could photograph molecules only a quarter-millionth of an inch in diameter. But he still could not see the structure of one atom. Müller went on working, though during World War II Germany could spare no funding for his nonlethal science.

He emigrated to the United States in 1952 with an improved design, the field ion microscope. The basic principles were the same, but Müller reversed the polarity, sending positively charged ions toward a negative screen.

On a hot day in August 1955, Müller recalled, "I became the first person to see an atom. On that day, the regular array of atoms and a crystal lattice became clearly visible."

Müller's dream had come true. His field ion microscope is still the most powerful optical instrument in the world, and the only microscope capable of revealing flaws in metal at the atomic level.

SMALL WONDERS, PART 2: THE INTEGRATED CIRCUIT (1958)

The transistor revolutionized electronics but created its own problems. Freed from the limitations of the vacuum tube, engineers designed complex transistor circuits with thousands of connections. The connections had to be hand-wired, a slow, expensive, and sometimes impossible process. During the 1950s the answer became obvious: components and connections had to be integrated, or combined, in one circuit.

Robert Noyce, seen here in 1989 holding a semiconductor wafer, coinvented the integrated circuit in 1958.

The transistor was the opening shot of the modern technology revolution, but the heavy artillery was the tiny integrated circuit, or microchip. As is true of many inventions, the first working integrated circuit was developed simultaneously by two independent inventors.

Robert Norton Noyce (1927–90) described his career as "the result of a series of dissatisfactions." Those dissatisfactions, which led Noyce to start two of the world's most famous technology companies, began during 1956 in an old apricot barn near Santa Clara, California.

The converted barn was the lab of William Shockley, coinventor of the transistor and aspiring entrepreneur. Shockley had lured Noyce and seven other young physicists to California. They were known as the Shockley Eight. Before long Shockley called them the traitorous eight. In 1957 the eight left to form their own company, Fairchild Semiconductor. Shockley was a brilliant inventor but a lousy businessman. Noyce would turn out to be extremely talented in both areas.

Like any new company, Fairchild had to scramble for work. In the late 1950s, that meant cranking out lots of transistors. But Noyce began thinking more and more of integrated circuits.

A thousand miles away, the same thoughts occurred to an engineer at Texas Instruments. During the summer of 1958, while his coworkers were on vacation, Jack Kilby (b. 1923) stayed in the lab. Kilby hand-crafted in miniature the three basic electronic components: the transistor, resistor, and capacitor. He glued his parts onto a one-inch chip of silicon and connected them with tiny gold wires. The tiny circuit worked, and in February 1959, Texas Instruments applied for a patent.

Noyce tried another approach, the "planar process," which sandwiched layers of semicon-ductors between insulators and eliminated wires completely. Fairchild filed for a patent in July 1959.

The two companies battled over the patent for a decade. It went to Noyce in 1969, but the point was largely moot by then. Fairchild and Texas Instruments had already cross-licensed each other, allowing both to collect royalties from other integrated circuit makers. Kilby and Noyce considered themselves coinventors, as did the scientific community.

In 1965 Kilby supervised the design of a pocket calculator. It was a huge success, and Kilby was promoted—to a point where management duties interfered with the inventing he loved. In 1970 he left Texas Instruments to be a freelance inventor.

Noyce left Fairchild in 1968 to start a new company, Intel. The first integrated circuit that combined all the logic functions of a computer on one chip—the first microprocessor—was the Intel 4004. By the 1980s, Intel's chip designations were becoming household numbers: the (80)286, 386, and 486 were the heart of the personal computer. The microprocessor also found its way into cars, telephones, coffeemakers, and thousands of other devices.

Back in 1971, Intel built the 4004 for a Japanese company, Busicom. In 1988 Noyce helped start Sematech—a consortium formed to help American companies catch up to the Japanese in the design and manufacture of integrated circuits.

LIGHT FANTASTIC: GOULD, MAIMAN, AND THE LASER (1960)

The first lasers seemed useless. Scientists called the laser "a solution looking for a problem." An inside joke resulted from a favorite lab experiment: using the laser beam to burn holes in a razor blade. For a while the unofficial unit of measurement for laser power was the "gillette."

Today lasers have thousands of profitable uses, from compact disc players to microsurgery. Laser is an acronym for "light amplification by stimulated emission of radiation." The word was coined in 1957 by Gordon Gould (b. 1920), who is generally credited with the designs that led to working lasers.

The concept of "stimulated emission" originated with Albert Einstein. Normal, visible light is caused by spontaneous emission when atoms throw off excess energy. This light is a mix of different colors and wavelengths, which diffuses and grows weaker as it travels. Einstein theorized that atoms could be stimulated to produce light of a uniform wavelength (coherent light) and color (monochromatic light). Instead of diffusing, these lightwaves would amplify each other.

In 1953 Charles Townes used these theories to amplify invisible microwave energy, creating the maser (microwave amplification by stimulated emission of radiation). The next step would be a device to amplify visible light, which Townes called the optical maser.

Gordon Gould called it a laser. During World War II he had worked on the Manhattan Project, which developed the first atomic bomb. Unfortunately for his future, in 1943 Gould briefly attended a Marxist study group led by an undercover FBI agent.

Gould said that his 1957 inspiration for the laser came in a "flash of insight." He sketched some designs in his notebook, and had the notebook notarized in a Bronx candy store. Gould believed, incorrectly, that he had to build a working laser before he could get a patent.

Gould took his ideas to a small New York company, TRG. The Pentagon gave TRG a million-dollar development contract for the laser. Then Gould's brief fling with Marxism was uncovered, and he was denied a security clearance. The Pentagon classified his notebooks and refused Gould permission to read his own writings.

In 1958 Charles Townes and Arthur Schawlow patented a laser remarkably similar to a design in Gould's 1957 notes. Gould began contesting this patent in court.

Neither Townes nor Gould built the first working laser, an honor that belongs to Theodore H. Maiman (b. 1927). Maiman's laser was a ruby cylinder with silver-coated ends that acted as mirrors. An intense flash of light triggered a chain reaction in the ruby. The mirrored ends bounced the light energy back and forth (amplified it) until it was strong enough to escape from one end of the ruby as an intense beam.

Maiman built his laser in 1960. By the 1970s Gould's original designs were used in 90 percent of working lasers, including the ubiquitous bar-code price reader.

After twenty years of legal struggle, Gould was issued a patent for his 1957 designs on October 11, 1977. The hard-won patent didn't bring him any royalties until 1986. Several lawsuits for infringement were successful, though they cost several million dollars and lasted into the late 1980s.

LINKING THE WORLD: PIERCE AND HIS SATELLITES (1962)

In a 1945 magazine article, Arthur C. Clarke described the communications satellite network of the 1980s. He correctly predicted that satellites would sit 22,300 miles above the Equator in geosynchronous orbit (that is, always at the same point above Earth's surface).

The writings of Clarke and others inspired John Robinson Pierce (b. 1910); according to Clarke, Pierce "has done more than any other individual to bring about the age of space communications." A boyhood love of science fiction led Pierce to a scientific career. Armed with his new Ph.D. in 1936, Pierce went to work for Bell Laboratories, the research arm of AT&T.

In the early 1950s, Pierce wrote several theoretical articles about communications satellites. At the time, the National Aeronautics and Space Administration (NASA) was launching balloons 1,000 miles into the sky for atmospheric research. Pierce suggested that one of these balloons might also work as a passive satellite (which only relays signals; an active satellite can both receive and transmit).

On August 12, 1960, a missile launched a canister from Cape Canaveral. The canister contained a metallic balloon that inflated to a diameter of 100 feet. During its second orbit of the earth, the crude satellite, called Echo 1, bounced the voice of President Dwight Eisenhower from California to New Jersey.

Echo 1 caught the world's attention. Early in 1961, Britain and France agreed to build receiving stations for future communications satellites. Pierce urged AT&T to build those satellites.

The biggest stumbling block was a launch vehicle; NASA had a monopoly on American missiles. AT&T negotiated for launch services. The terms were stiff: NASA demanded $3.5 million per launch and a worldwide license to any inventions flowing from satellite research. AT&T was famous for zealously guarding patents, and it was a measure of confidence in Pierce that AT&T agreed to the NASA demands.

The new satellite was Telstar 1, a 175-pound solar-powered ball. Basically a two-way radio in space, its microwave circuits could handle 600 simultaneous phone calls or one TV channel.

Telstar 1 left Cape Canaveral atop a Thor-Delta missile at 3:35 A.M. on July 10, 1962. At 6:47 P.M., a French station picked up the first TV picture ever broadcast across the Atlantic. Though Telstar was only a low-altitude satellite, it immediately revolutionized communications by providing live television coverage around the world.

Clarke's 1945 dream had to wait for more powerful missiles, which could boost satellites into geosynchronous equatorial orbit. This allowed simpler antennas, that is, the "dishes" that citizens all over the world erected in their backyards.

Aside from their technical benefits, communications satellites prodded nations into cooperating on the peaceful use of outer space. They may have succeeded too well; today the geosynchronous orbit is so crowded that interference is a problem. John Pierce summarized his work perfectly in a 1988 article: "The future is more complicated than the past."

CRACKING THE HUMAN CODE: RECOMBINANT DNA (1973)

What makes you "you?" A major factor is about 100,000 genes in your body, occurring as deoxyribonucleic acid (DNA). DNA is a set of chemical sequences that act as a virtual instruction manual of heredity. If nature alters a single DNA sequence at birth, the result can be a genetic disorder such as cystic fibrosis or sickle-cell anemia.

The new science of genetic engineering, also known as biotechnology, gene splicing, or cloning, deliberately alters DNA. By doing so, it may one day eliminate genetic disorders.

The invention of genetic engineering was a long, collaborative process. It began with the study of the simplest life-forms, single-celled bacteria. In 1952 Joshua Lederberg discovered that a virus-attacking bacteria could carry genetic material. A human intestinal bacteria, E. coli, was an excellent case study because it contains a single DNA molecule with 2,000 to 3,000 genes. E. coli was accompanied by "genetic loose change": tiny, semi-independent molecules called plasmids, with only five to ten genes.

Researchers suspected that the plasmid could carry recoded genetic material. Swiss molecular biologist Werner Arber discovered a special type of plasmid called a restriction enzyme, which can recognize specific DNA sequences. It can also cut a DNA chain, allowing foreign material to be spliced in. Arber and two other researchers, Daniel Nathans and Hamilton Smith, shared a 1978 Nobel Prize in physiology and medicine for their work with restriction enzymes.

Their accomplishments laid the foundation for the work of Paul Berg (b. 1926), who is often called the father of genetic engineering. In 1973 Berg joined DNA from two different organisms. His process won a Nobel Prize in chemistry, but it was slow and laborious.

The real breakthrough came later in 1973, with the work of Stanley Cohen (b. 1935) and Herbert Boyer (b. 1936). After Cohen and Boyer simplified Berg's process, they mixed DNA from two separate plasmids for the first time. Because genes from two different sources were combined, the end result was called "recombinant" DNA.

This new science has already provided tremendous benefits. In December 1980 a diabetic was injected for the first time with genetically engineered human insulin. Other medicines once extracted with great difficulty from humans or animals, such as growth hormones and cancer-fighting interferons, are also manufactured in the lab today. In agriculture, genetically altered plants may alleviate world famine.

However, genetic engineering poses immense ethical and social questions. As soon as Cohen and Boyer completed the first recombinant DNA experiment, scientists began to worry that a lab accident could unleash deadly altered genes. Boyer helped establish guidelines for genetic research in 1975, and some types of experiments were banned outright.

The science-fiction threat, cloned people, is a long way off; humans are just too genetically complex. By the mid-1990s, biologists armed with the world's most powerful computers were only beginning to "map" our complete genetic makeup.

WIRED LIGHT: MILLER, KAO, AND FIBER OPTICS (1977)

Four years after he invented the telephone, in 1880, Alexander Graham Bell created the "photophone." This device transmitted speech on a beam of light. Bell wrote: "I have heard a ray of sun laugh and cough and sing." But a ray of sun couldn't transmit sound very far with any reliability. Bell's dream had to wait for a stable, artificial light source: the laser.

The company Bell founded, AT&T, was by the mid-1960s building small, low-temperature lasers. Such lasers were required for a twentieth-century version of the photophone: "optical communications." A pioneer in the field, Stewart Miller of Bell Labs, saw that the laser could transmit "tremendous amounts of information."

But how to transmit it? The light would carry signals, such as voice or video, which had to be precisely transmitted and received. Firing lasers through the atmosphere was a dismal failure because of clouds, fog, and ground obstacles. The light would have to travel through a controlled environment, or conduit—just as electrical signals traveled through wires.

After three years of research, an answer came from Charles Kao and G. A. Hockham, of Britain's Standard Telecommunications Laboratories. Kao and Hockham suggested that the ideal light conduit was optical fibers, in the form of tiny glass tubes. Soon the field of optical communications had adopted the name of its transmission medium—fiber optics.

Developing that medium was a trip into the unknown. Kao had shown that the glass must be extremely pure to avoid signal losses. Transparency equalled purity, but no test equipment could measure signal loss as a function of glass purity. No standards existed. The problem was attacked by both AT&T and the Corning Glass Works. A member of the Corning team, Peter Schultz, expressed the dilemma: "How transparent could glass be?"

AT&T tried one method, Corning another, though their processes were similar. The components of fiber optics begin as a glass tube, coated inside with more than a hundred thin glass layers. The tube is heated until it collapses, then the layers are pulled into individual fiber optic strands.

In 1970 Corning developed fibers with losses of less than 20 decibels per kilometer—the magic number. By early 1976, 2,100 feet of fiber optics snaked through the Bell Labs Product Engineering Center in Atlanta. It was the prototype system, capable of carrying 50,000 telephone calls.

Today, telephone service is cheaper and better because of fiber optics. A half-inch fiber optic cable carries more signals than a ten-inch bundle of copper. At 1 percent the weight of copper cable, fiber optics cable is impervious to interference and much safer, since it carries light and not electricity.

Fiber optics also has other uses; the medical fiberscope can look inside the human body without surgery or X rays. New jobs for fiber optics seem to be discovered daily, especially in communications and data transmission, and the future of this young technology is unlimited.

CHEATING DEATH: JARVIK AND THE ARTIFICIAL HEART (1982)

For centuries humanity dreamed of replacing worn-out body parts. One of the most likely candidates was also one of the most criticial: the heart, which is basically a pump for blood. It seemed logical that this organ could be replaced by a mechanical pump.

The dream had to wait for twentieth-century technology. The first total artificial heart (TAH) was developed by Dr. Willem Kolff in 1957 and implanted in a dog. Animal experiments continued for more than a decade. In 1969 Dr. Denton Cooley implanted the first artificial heart in a human. The plastic and Dacron device was only a temporary measure until the patient could receive a transplanted human heart.

Doctors learned early about a problem with the TAH: the fierce resistance of the body, which rejects any foreign matter. In the case of the TAH, one form of this resistance was blood clotting, which could lead to strokes and other complications.

Dr. Robert Jarvik (b. 1946) was a doctor's son who grew up watching his father perform surgery. Even as a child, Jarvik showed an interest in the design of medical tools. After his father died of heart disease, Jarvik set his mind on becoming a doctor and helping future cardiac patients.

He moved to Utah and worked with the artificial heart pioneer, Dr. Willem Kolff. Jarvik began designing a TAH in 1972, while also inventing a number of surgical tools. In 1979 he patented the Jarvik-7. This small TAH fit comfortably in the chest, though it was powered by a big roll-around air compressor. Hoses from the compressor would pass through two permanent incisions in the patient's abdomen.

In December 1982, retired dentist Barney Clark, with terminal heart disease, was given only hours to live. Clark's doctor, William C. DeVries, suggested the Jarvik-7. Clark awoke hours later with an artificial heart beating in his chest.

The successful operation was cheered by many, though it touched off arguments over several moral issues. These included debates on mere survival versus quality of life, and the ethics of an operation that few could afford (the procedure cost about $200,000).

The bright future of the TAH tarnished quickly. By 1985 seven patients had received Jarvik hearts. Three were dead, including Clark, who lived 112 days after his operation. Four had suffered debilitating strokes. Besides the problems with blood clotting, doctors noted severe infections that resisted antibiotics. The incisions required for the air compressor were an open door to infection, and the metal and plastic of the TAH itself attracted germs. The longer a patient used a TAH, the more likely was the result of stroke or fatal infection.

Human heart transplants, meanwhile, became easier, though the demand for hearts always exceeded supply. By 1988 the TAH had temporarily regressed back to 1969: doctors recommended that the Jarvik heart be used for a maximum of 30 days, while a patient awaited a human heart.

Robert Jarvik continues to improve the TAH, aware of his invention's shortcomings. The ultimate artificial heart, Jarvik has written, must be "more than functional, reliable and dependable. It must be forgettable."

—M.S.S.

THE CURRENT WARRIORS

THOMAS EDISON (1847–1931)

The immense reservoir of creative energy and dazzling array of important technological innovations of inventor Thomas Edison, dubbed "the Wizard of Menlo Park" by his contemporaries, has long been the stuff of modern legend.

Although he is typically associated with the development of such devices as the incandescent light bulb, the phonograph, and the motion picture camera, perhaps his most crucial accomplishment was in the transformation of the invention process itself.

Edison's life easily rivals a Horatio Alger story. Born in Milan, Ohio, he was the seventh—and last—child of his family. When he was a young boy, Edison had a manner that set him apart from the other children and often puzzled adults. Shortly after starting school, his teacher concluded he was "addled," so after only three months of formal education, Edison's mother, a former teacher herself, decided to instruct the young boy at home. Edison became a voracious reader and although he was not particularly fond of mathematics, he became intensely interested in chemistry and electricity. Insatiably curious, he constructed a makeshift laboratory in the basement of his house to pursue various experiments.

In order to buy more chemicals and apparatus for his lab, the twelve-year-old Edison got a job selling newspapers and snacks aboard the Grand Trunk Railway. On his off hours, he'd spend time plowing through the shelves at the Detroit Library. Edison took the earnings from his work and purchased some used printing equipment. He set up the machinery in a baggage car and began publishing his own newspaper, the *Weekly Herald*. The young entrepreneur began to employ other children to help in his operation.

In order to have more time for experimentation, Edison also received permission to relocate his basement lab to the baggage car. However, after a jar of phosphorous fell off a shelf and ignited a fire in the car, the mobile lab was shut down by an angry train conductor.

In 1862 Edison rescued a boy who was about to be killed by an oncoming train. The child's father was grateful but poor and offered to reward Edison by teaching him telegraphy. At the time, telegraphy was an essential channel of communication and operators were in high demand. Edison quickly established a reputation as one of the premier operators in the United States.

During roughly the same period, Edison began to grow increasingly deaf. He attributed the hearing loss to an incident in which he attempted to get aboard a moving freight train and the conductor pulled him up by his ears. Some have speculated that the disorder was actually brought on by genetic factors or by scarlet fever. Whatever the cause, the partial deafness is thought to have played a significant role in some of his later work refining the phonograph system.

In 1868 Edison simultaneously patented his first invention and learned a painful lesson in real-world practicality. He took his new electric vote-recording machine to Washington, D.C., for a demonstration before a congressional committee. He was later told that the device was too efficient and would not give the politicians enough time for negotiations and assorted legislative maneuvers. After this experience, the chastened inventor vowed that he would never invent a device without first being sure it was needed.

Another twist of fate, in 1871, gave Edison an important career break. While he was waiting for a job interview, a telegraph broke down in the office. Edison promptly fixed the machine and got a better job than the one he was originally seeking. Shortly afterward he devised an improved version of the stock ticker. He offered the machine for sale but was afraid to ask the $5,000 that he wanted for it. Edison allowed the prospective buyers to name the price. They gave him $40,000.

At the age of twenty-three, he took his earnings and set up an engineering firm in Newark, New Jersey, where, during the next six years, he developed the mimeograph and made improvements on the telegraph and typewriter. The kinds of inventions varied widely. With the help of Mary Stilwell, a woman he later married, he created waxed paper.

By 1876 Edison wanted to expand. He envisioned an "invention factory" where he could turn out a constant stream of assorted, and potentially lucrative, gadgets. The facility he created in Menlo Park, New Jersey, became the predecessor of the modern commercial research laboratory. Edison said he wanted to turn out a new invention every ten days. As bold as this challenge was, he often exceeded his goals and obtained a new patent every five days. Although the hours were often long and the money sometimes short, he had many loyal employees. (A group of assistants was referred to as the insomnia squad.) Although not all of the inventions they churned out were significant in the long term, many had a major impact on modern society.

The first significant device to come out of Menlo Park was the carbon telephone transmitter, a device that greatly improved the sound clarity of the telephone. The second major product to come from Menlo Park was one of Edison's most original and personal favorites— the "talking machine." While many of Edison's patents were for improvements to other people's inventions, the phonograph was, in many ways, his brainchild. He put tin foil on a cylinder that could be etched by a needle that moved in response to sound waves. He realized that the etched foil represented a physical record of the vibrations and could be used to reproduce the original sounds. He recited the nursery rhyme "Mary Had a Little Lamb" while cranking his new device and then played back the recorded voice to stunned listeners. The phono-

In 1929, Thomas Edison (right) compares one of his original lightbulbs and a new one held by Henry Ford.

graph was an instant sensation and cemented his reputation as a magician.

Although the idea for an electric light had been around for some time, no one had been able to make it work for long periods. Edison undertook an exhaustive search for a filament that would generate light without quickly burning out. Using scorched cotton thread, he constructed a light that stayed lit for forty hours straight. Perhaps even more important than the light itself, he helped to create an electricity system that could supply homes and businesses.

> We owe a lot to Thomas Edison—if it wasn't for him, we'd be watching television by candlelight.
> Milton Berle

Edison's first wife died of typhoid fever in 1884 and he married Mina Miller two years later. Shortly after his second marriage, Edison moved to West Orange, New Jersey, and continued to churn out inventions. With the help of William Dickson, he developed the kinetoscope—an early motion picture camera. Like so many other devices, the idea was not originally Edison's.

However, his innovative refinements were crucial in its development.

In 1915 Edison was rumored to be a strong contender for the Nobel Prize in physics, along with inventor and former employee Nikola Tesla. However, the two men had long been embroiled in an acrimonious dispute over the merits of direct versus alternating current. The gossip was that Tesla and Edison refused to share the prize. The committee gave it to a British father-and-son team, W. H. and W. L. Bragg, for their study of the structure of crystals.

As he grew older, Edison tended to be increasingly autocratic and rigid. These traits often hindered his bid to promote his phonograph and other inventions. He also lost millions of dollars on projects that were technologically impressive but financial white elephants. After a life of spectacular successes and failures, Edison died peacefully in West Orange.
—H.X.W.

NIKOLA TESLA (1856–1943)

Nikola Tesla's reputation as a mad visionary and mesmerizing showman has often obscured the fact that he was instrumental in the development of the basic system of electrical distribution used worldwide. The man who, later in his life, claimed to have invented a powerful "death beam" and had attempted to communicate with life on other planets also developed essential components for generating and distributing alternating current (AC).

Tesla, a native of Smiljan, Croatia, was the son of a clergyman and an illiterate mother who had a knack for inventing useful implements for the family farm. Early on, "Nikki" displayed a profound and, occasionally, reckless interest in mathematics, mechanics, and physics. In an abortive attempt to fly, he landed himself in the hospital for six weeks with three broken ribs.

At the age of nineteen, Tesla received technical training at the University of Graz and went on to the University of Prague to study philosophy. While he was a student at Graz, Tesla remarked during a lab demonstration that it might be possible to make an electric motor that was much more efficient than the direct current (DC) models then available. Despite being ridiculed by the head of the physics department, Tesla became obsessed with creating such a device.

The breakthrough came late one afternoon as he strolled through a Budapest city park with a close friend. Tesla had been reciting lines from Goethe's *Faust* when the idea for the induction motor flashed, fully formed, into his mind. He grabbed a stick and scratched out the basic diagrams in the sand. His idea was to use alternating current to create a rotating magnetic field that could drive a motor. Not only was Tesla's machine a clear improvement over the currently available motors, but it also repre-

Nikola Tesla generating artificial lightning in his laboratory.

sented an important breakthrough for combating a problem faced by the budding electricity industry. In order to distribute electrical power efficiently over long distances, power companies needed the ability to raise and lower voltage as needed. However, this was not possible with the direct current system strongly favored by Thomas Edison. On the other hand, with the help of transformers, AC could be effectively manipulated and transported far from the power source. Tesla's induction motor helped to make AC feasible.

Tesla decided that his best chances of developing his machine lay overseas, so he sailed to the United States in 1884. Although Tesla had virtually no money, he did possess a glowing letter of introduction to present to Thomas Edison, and he soon began to work for the American inventor. Tesla showed himself to be a capable and tireless worker—no small feat in Edison's labs. Nevertheless, the two strong-willed men were completely unsuited to work together. While Tesla was a fervent believer in the benefits of AC, Edison had firmly dug his heels into the DC camp. The seeds of the acrimonious "current wars" were sown.

Tesla left Edison and began working for a company that focused on making industrial arc lights. The restless genius found the work unsatisfying, and resigned. Never a good manager of his own money, Tesla barely supported himself digging ditches and doing other odd jobs. However, his fortunes were soon to change. By 1887 people with the Western Union Telegraph Company helped him to form a new business. For the next two years, Tesla experienced a creative surge that yielded many important devices. Designs for split-phase, induction, and synchronous motors; generators; transformers; and a variety of other devices flowed from the lab.

> It is providential that the youth or man of inventive mind is not "blessed" with a million dollars. The mind is sharper and keener in seclusion and uninterrupted solitude. Originality thrives in seclusion free of outside influences beating upon us to cripple the creative mind. Be alone—that is the secret of invention: be alone, that is when ideas are born.
>
> Nikola Tesla

A prominent businessman by the name of George Westinghouse became interested in Tesla's work. The magnate gave Tesla financial backing to pursue the development of an AC system. Meanwhile, DC proponent Edison mounted an often ruthless public relations assault on his competitors. He arranged graphic demonstrations of animals being electrocuted with high-voltage AC to portray its dangers. Edison also lobbied for the use of AC in New York State's electric chair, citing its lethality, and suggested that electrocutions should be described as being "westinghoused."

Despite concerted attacks, AC won out over DC. The mid-1890s marked one of Tesla's crowning achievements—the world's first hydroelectric generating plant with a long-range distribution system came on line in Niagara Falls. The facility represented a vindication of Tesla's vision.

Tesla continued to work on a variety of innovations and often showed an amazing ability to predict future trends in technology. He felt that it would eventually be possible to communicate and transmit energy without wires and foresaw the use of radar. He built a model radio-controlled ship and devices that could create bolts of artificial lightning. Tesla was also an early advocate of harnessing solar and geothermal power. In 1915 a story was spread that Tesla would be a cowinner of the Nobel Prize in physics with Thomas Edison. Because of their bitter rivalry, it was rumored that one or the other had turned down the award when the physics prize went to a British father-and-son research team rather than to either of the two old enemies.

As he grew older, Tesla became increasingly more eccentric and developed a severe germ phobia. He never married and eventually withdrew from society and lived in a run-down New York hotel room and spent much of his time tending to pigeons. He died peacefully in his room.

—H.X.W.

> I just invent, then wait until man comes around to needing what I've invented.
> R. Buckminster Fuller, Time, June 10, 1964

INVENTION OF EVERYDAY OBJECTS

1900—Kodak Brownie Camera: George Eastman had ushered in the era of snapshot photography when he introduced his box camera in 1888. Now, as a new century dawned, he wanted to bring the joys of photography to children—with a camera that would retail for just a dollar. It was named the Brownie, after the industrious little elves created by the Canadian writer Palmer Cox—Brownies were known for working well, which was what Eastman wanted his cameras to be known for. There was hardly any profit from the sale of a one-dollar camera, but at fifteen cents for a film with six exposures, there was plenty to be made out of the photographs it took. So successful was the Brownie that it remained on the market, in various sizes and styles, until replaced by the Instamatic in the 1960s.

1900—Paper Clip: Many, perhaps most, inventions were earlier than you would suppose. Just a few were later. Why did it take until the twentieth century to produce an idea as simple as the paper clip? It was a Norwegian, Johann Vaaler, who first bent a piece of wire into a double oblong shape and so solved the problem of holding loose papers together. Patented in Germany, the paper clip is a rare example of an invention that has seen scarcely any improvements in design. The only significant development, made in Britain in the 1950s, was to bend the tip of the inner oblong upward to make it easier to guide onto the papers to be clipped.

1900—Escalator: The first public escalator with steps was designed by Charles D. Seeberger and built by the Otis Elevator Company for use at the Paris Exposition. Earlier escalators had consisted of an inclined endless-belt conveyor, which required a much shallower incline—and therefore a lot more space—than a moving staircase. Some people found the idea of stepping on and off stairs that moved an alarming one. When the first Seeberger escalators were installed in the London underground in 1911, a man with a wooden leg, called "Bumper" Harris, was engaged to ride up and down them all day to provide reassurance for the fainthearted.

1902—Air Conditioning: The first effective air-conditioning unit, one that would dehumidify as well as cool the air, was invented not for human comfort but as a means of improving the quality of color printing. Willis H. Carrier, "the father of air conditioning," was working for the Buffalo Forge Company when he was assigned to the Sackett-Wilhelms Lithographing and Publishing Company of Brooklyn, New York. His task was to find a solution to the contraction and expansion of the coated papers used for color printing that occurred during hot and humid weather. Using ammonia as a refrigerant, Carrier built a thirty-ton, cold-water-spray apparatus that absorbed humidity from warm air. In 1917 Sam Katz and the Balaban brothers, proprietors of the Central Park Theater in Chicago, decided they could attract moviegoers during the traditionally dead summer months by installing air-conditioning—the first use of Carrier's invention for human comfort.

1902—Vacuum Cleaner: Anyone who had been in a restaurant in London's Victoria Street the day that Cecil Booth placed a handkerchief over the back of the plush seat on which he was sitting, sucked hard, and nearly choked from the dust in his mouth, might have concluded the man was mad. In fact he had just proved to his own satisfaction that dirt could be removed by suction, a ring of black spots on his handkerchief providing visible evidence. Devising a machine to do the same thing on a scale sufficient to clean carpets and drapes was far from simple. Booth's first commercially produced vacuum cleaner was so large that it was mounted on wagon wheels and parked in the street outside the households to be cleaned. Hoses as long as 800 feet were passed through the windows and the cleaning done by Booth's own operators. Fashionable ladies in London would hold vacuum-cleaning parties at which guests could actually watch the transmission of the dirt, since Booth had thoughtfully inserted glass-covered apertures at intervals in the sides of the hose. Portable vacuum cleaners that could be purchased for home use appeared in America in 1905, but even these machines weighed a formidable ninety-two pounds.

1902—Teddy Bears: When President Theodore "Teddy" Roosevelt visited Mississippi to settle a border dispute with Louisiana, the organizers of a hunting expedition staked a bear cub to the ground to ensure that the President could not miss. Roosevelt, a true sportsman, refused to fire. A political cartoon by Clifford Berryman based on this incident was syndicated in the newspapers and seen by Morris Mitchom, a Russian immigrant who sold sweets and toys in a small shop in Brooklyn. He was greatly taken by the drawing of the reprieved bear cub and made up a toy version in soft plush, which he placed in the window with a copy of the cartoon and a placard declaring "Teddy's Bear." Coming from a country in which the ruler's name was not to be taken lightly, Mitchom decided it would be prudent to seek permission before making bears for sale. The president gave his assent in a note written in his own hand, but added, "I don't think my name is worth much to the toy bear cub business." Fortunately for Morris Mitchom, Teddy Roosevelt had misjudged either the appeal of cuddly bears or the pulling power of his own name. Either way, the bear mania that seized America was so complete that a pastor in Michigan denounced the placid Teddy for "destroying all instincts of motherhood and leading the nation to race suicide."

1903—Safety Razor: Without the invention of the crown cork bottle cap, there might not have been razor blades. For it was the inventor of the former, William Painter, who told his employee King Camp Gillette that the way to a fortune was to devise something to be used, discarded, and replaced. The idea for the safety razor came to Gillette one day in 1895 while he was shaving with his cut-throat razor. Only the edge of the blade was used for the cutting action, he reasoned, so why not dispose of the expensive

steel backing? In fact it took another six years to produce wafers of steel sufficiently thin, tough, and sharp to serve his purpose and a further two years to start production. Even then there was little indication that America was willing to abandon the razor strop, with sales of only 51 safety razors and 168 blades. Suddenly, however, the idea caught on, and by the end of 1904 Gillette had sold 90,000 razors and no fewer than 12.5 million blades. The "disposable" era was under way.

1903—Telephone Booth: The world's first outdoor phone booth was a hexagonal kiosk erected by the Great Central Railway in High Holborn in London, England. Each of the six sides carried posters for the railway company, illuminated at night. Most early telephone booths in Britain were made of wood, but in port areas they were made of galvanized iron because it was feared that a wharf worker who had failed to get through and lost his money would try to kick the door down. In 1912 the booths were equipped with doodle pads to discourage frustrated callers from decorating the walls with graffiti.

1904—Thermos Flask: Most people use a thermos to keep liquids hot, but the inventor was only interested in keeping them cool. Scottish scientist James Dewar, discoverer of the means of making liquid hydrogen, invented the double-walled glass vessel in 1892 to keep gases and chemicals at a constant low temperature. His wife had doubts about the scientific principle of extracting the air between the walls to create a vacuum and knitted an elongated "tea cosy" for the prototype thermos. Dewar himself saw no commercial application for his invention and neglected to patent it. One of his ex-pupils, Reinhold Burger, was more farsighted, and after returning to his native Germany, he started to manufacture vacuum flasks for domestic use in 1904. To find a name he held a public competition, won by a citizen of Munich with the suggestion "Thermos" from the Greek word for heat, therme. Easily broken, none of the early flasks manufactured by the firm of Burger and Aschenbrenner survives, but Dewar's 1892 prototype may be seen at London's Science Museum—still in its knitted cosy.

1906—Radio Broadcasting: The audience for the world's first broadcast consisted of no more than the surprised radio operators of a few ships passing by Brant Rock on the coast of Massachusetts at midnight on Christmas Eve 1906. The voice they heard reciting verses from the Gospel of Saint Luke and wishing them seasonal good cheer was that of Professor Reginald Aubrey Fessenden, the Canadian-born pioneer of radio telephony. The program, broadcast over a five-mile radius from the

National Electric Signaling Company's 420-foot-high radio mast at Brant Rock, also consisted of Fessenden rendering Gounod's "O, Holy Night" on his violin and a phonograph record of Handel's "Largo." Fessenden simply wanted to prove that his discovery of amplitude modulation of radio waves would enable speech and music to be carried through the ether. Neither the sleepy ship's radio operators, suddenly aroused by a disembodied voice calling to them out of the night, nor Professor Fessenden himself was aware that the experiment signaled the birth of the first powerful leisure and communications medium of the twentieth century.

1906—Soap Flakes: Soap flakes have probably existed as long as soap, but it was the housewife or laundry worker who had to scrape them from a bar of soap with a knife. Only in 1906 were washday chores lightened by the introduction of prepackaged soap flakes ready for use, a commercial triumph for the giant Lever Brothers soap works at Port Sunlight in the north of England. Lux flakes were one of the most heavily promoted household products of the early twentieth century, leading Lever Brothers' chairman, Lord Leverhulme, to make the classic observation that has become part of merchandising lore: "Half my advertising budget is wasted. I wish I knew which half."

1908—Geiger Counter: The earliest form of the Geiger counter, a device for measuring radiation, was built by German-born Hans Geiger while he was working as a research assistant for Professor Ernest Rutherford at the Manchester University physical laboratories in England. The prototype counter consisted of little more than a wire contained in a sealed metal tube with a mica window at one end, but connected to a power source, it enabled Geiger and Rutherford to locate and count alpha particles, a constituent of the rays emitted by radioactive decay.

1908—Gun Silencer: The report of a gun being fired comes mainly from the escaping gases exploding from its muzzle. Hiram Percy Maxim, son of the inventor of the Maxim machine gun, thought he had solved the problem with a cylinder containing several small chambers that screwed on to the barrel of a gun. These chambers were divided by metal rings, and as the bullet passed through their center, the gases were dispersed through the chambers sufficiently to prevent explosion. This worked to an extent, but the crack of a bullet passing through the sound barrier still produced a loud noise in itself. The answer was for snipers to use the silencer together with low-velocity ammunition, which traveled at slightly less than the speed of sound.

1909—Outboard Motor: The story of the outboard motor begins on a small island in Lake Michigan where Norwegian immigrant Ole Evinrude had taken his sweetheart, Bessie Cary, for a picnic. The day was a hot one and Bessie expressed a wish for ice cream. Ole rowed back to shore and bought the ice cream, but by the time he had rowed two and a half miles back to Bessie, it had melted. Disappointment was tempered by the germ of an idea, and after Ole and Bessie had married they set up a company to build motors that could be clipped on to rowboats. Despite its low power, the single-cylinder, 1.5-horsepower outboard motor rapidly caught on with tired oarsman, and as swifter, more powerful engines followed, the fortune of the Evinrudes was assured.

1910—Neon Light: The first neon lamps were two forty-foot-long tubes used to illuminate the peristyle of the Grand Palais in Paris where the annual French motor show was being held. They were the invention of physicist Georges Claude, who intended them for ordinary lighting purposes rather than decorative use. But because early neon glowed red, he was persuaded by a friend in the advertising business that it would be better used for signs. In 1912 the world's first neon advertising sign, consisting of the single word CINZANO, was erected in the boulevard Haussmann in Paris.

1912—Cellophane: At the local café in Paris where Jacques Brandenberger took his coffee, the tablecloths were usually stained by spilled wine or food. A lesser man might have changed cafés, but Brandenberger was determined to produce a see-through covering that would protect tablecloths. Considering that it took him eight years of research before he perfected a technique for producing viscose in the form of a thin film, it is ironic that cellophane was never used for the purpose Brandenberger intended. But it did create a packaging revolution, particularly after DuPont, who held the United States rights, developed a moisture-proof version in 1924. The only problem was getting it off the carton, and that was solved in 1931 when Wrigley's introduced the tear strip on their cellophane-wrapped chewing gum packages. As for the tablecloths, the world still awaits deliverance from spilled coffee.

1915—Pyrex: The first ovenproof glass vessel was not intended as such by the Corning Glass Works of Corning, New York. It was the base of an electric storage battery, but Mrs. Becky Littleton, wife of Corning's chief physicist, decided to use it for baking. Jesse Littleton was so impressed by the fact that the sturdy vessel baked uniformly and did not break that Eugene G. Sullivan and William C. Taylor were assigned to develop a much thinner, lead-free glass that would be equally heat resistant. They came up with a formula of soda, sodium, borax, and alumina, which was fired at more than 2,500 degrees Fahrenheit. This was called Nonex (a contraction of nonexpanding), but it was soon replaced by an improved version named Pyrex. Within five years it had created a revolution in the kitchen, with some 5 million items of ovenproof glassware in use in North America and production already under way in Britain.

1916—Loudspeaker: On July 3, 1916, the annual convention of the National Educational Association opened at Madison Square Garden in New York City. The number of delegates was so great that those at the back of the huge concourse were beyond normal voice range. But in fact they heard perfectly, thanks to a new technical miracle called the loudspeaker. The instrument had been perfected by AT&T using the Audion triode developed by the radio pioneer Lee De Forest to provide clear and undistorted amplification. This was the first time it was used to reach an audience of a size too large for the unamplified human voice.

1922—Snowmobile: Joseph-Armand Bombardier of Valcourt, Quebec, was just fifteen years old when he built his prototype snowmobile. He adapted the family sleigh by mounting a Model T Ford engine on the chassis, which drove a hand-carded wooden propeller. His father was so fearful of the danger to life and limb that he made young Joseph-Armand dismantle it again. Far from being discouraged, the boy continued his experiments and eventually, in 1937, established L'Auto-neige Bombardier to manufacture snowmobiles on a regular basis. In 1940 he made his breakthrough to commercial success with a tracked vehicle powered by a Ford VS engine that could carry a dozen passengers—the snowmobile bus.

1923—16mm Home Movie Camera: Home movies are almost as old as cinema, with the first complete camera-projector outfit for the amateur on sale in Britain as early as 1896. The big breakthrough, though, came with the introduction of the 16mm Kodak Model A camera and projector on July 5, 1923. This achieved for home movies what the Kodak No. 1 box camera had done for snapshot photography fifty-five years earlier.

1924—Masonite: This synthetic hardboard was one of those inventions that came about by a fortunate accident. William Mason wanted to find a use for the wood chips carpeting the floor of every sawmill and thought that they could be pressed into a composition insulating material. He obtained an old steam press dating from the previous century with funds provided by a lumber company in Wausau, Wisconsin, and set to work. One day Mason went to lunch and left the steam running by mistake. On his return he was amazed to find that the wood chips had bonded into hardboard. Moreover, it proved resistant to weathering. Abandoning his plans to produce insulation, he established what was to become the Masonite Corporation and began manufacturing the new versatile and durable building material.

1926—Electric Blanket: The principle on which the electric blanket works was developed by American physician Sidney Russell in 1912, when he made up heating pads for patients that contained insulated metal tape. No one in America, however, saw the commercial possibilities of Russell's invention and it was only in 1924 that the Ex-Services Mental Welfare Society in Britain, looking for a new product that could be manufactured by shell-shocked World War I veterans, began production of the Thermega underblanket.

1926—Pop-Up Toaster: The first domestic-model pop-up toaster came on the market in June at $13.50. It was manufactured by the McGraw Electric Company of Minneapolis.

1927—Transatlantic Telephone Calls: The Bell Telephone Company in the United States and the General Post Office in the United Kingdom inaugurated the first transatlantic telephone service. Communication tended to be confined to urgent business of major import rather than social chit-chat. At $75.00 for three minutes' conversation—about half the cost of a Model T Ford—nobody was going to call London to say "Hi."

1928—Scotch Tape: The first cellulose self-adhesive tape went on sale on January 31. It had been developed by the 3M Company of Saint Paul, Minnesota, as a masking tape for the spray-paint workshops of auto-manufacturing plants. In order to reduce cost, the adhesive was in two thin strips at the margins of the tape. Unfortunately, this meant that it tended to peel off car bodies as the paint was being applied, much to the distress of the sprayers. According to different versions of the legend, they either told the 3M salesmen to take the "Scotch" tape back to their bosses or they told them to take the tape back to their "Scotch" bosses. Whichever, the bosses recognized a good brand name when they heard it, and at the same time they made the decision to stop being Scotch and spread the adhesive over the entire press-down surface of the tape.

1928—Pap Test: Also known as the smear test, this technique for detecting the two most fatal forms of cancer in women, cervical and uterine, was developed by Greek-born Dr. George Papanicolaou of Cornell Medical School in New York. The importance of the test is that it enables the diagnosis of these cancers before the symptoms are apparent, giving patients a very high chance of recovery. Following the widespread adoption of the Pap test in 1943, cervical cancer dropped from being the most common cause of death for American women to third place among fatal diseases. When diagnosed in its earliest stages, it is almost 100 percent curable.

1931—Electronic Flash Photography: Harold Edgerton of Boston's MIT devised a reusable stroboscopic flashbulb in order to photograph objects moving at high speed without blurring. Some of his classic photographic studies showed multiple images of such phenomena as a crown of droplets rising in the air as an object was dropped into a glass of milk and the passage of a bullet as it cut through a playing card from one edge to the other. The technique was probably most effective for sports reportage, enabling a baseball to be seen in flight or at the point of impact. Edgerton's work on high-speed photography led to the production of the first commercially available electronic flashbulb, the Kodatron Strobe, which was introduced by Kodak in 1940. During World War II the United States Army Air Force used Edgerton's electronic strobes to take the world's first night reconnaissance photographs over the enemy-held fortress of Monte Cassino in Italy.

1931—Long-Playing Record: The long-playing record was one of those inventions launched before its time had come. The first microgroove 33⅓ rpm LPs were marketed by RCA Victor in November 1931, led by a recording of Beethoven's Fifth by the Philadelphia Orchestra under Leopold Stokowski—the first time a complete orchestral piece had been issued on a single record. But at the height of the depression few could afford the expensive long-playing record players, which ranged from $247.50 to $995. The microgroove 33⅓ rpm LP was revived in 1948 by Columbia, using an improved recording technique developed by Dr. Peter Goldmark. This time the economy was in better shape, the equipment was much cheaper (as little as $29.25 for an adapter for a standard record player), and the vinylite records, unlike RCA Victor's LPs, were unbreakable. Columbia's revolution in sound recording was to oust the 78 rpm disk in about the same time that it would take for CDs to kill off the 33⅓ rpm LP a generation later. Goldmark himself never received a penny in royalties. Instead he was given a copy of every LP produced by Columbia.

1932—Stereo Recording: Arthur Keller of Bell Telephone Laboratories made the first ex-

perimental stereophonic disks, a number of recordings of the Philadelphia Orchestra under Leopold Stokowski. These were demonstrated publicly at the Chicago World's Fair the following year. While reproduction was of a high standard, the technique was too complex and expensive to be readily adapted to commercial use. It would be more than twenty years before stereo recordings were available to the public, and the first ones, issued by Livingston Electronic of New York in May 1954, were on tape. Stereo disks followed three years later.

1934—Laundromat: The first self-service laundry was called a washateria. Opened at Fort Worth, Texas, by J. F. Cantrell, it had four electric washing machines, which were rented by the hour. Customers were told to bring their own soap powder.

1935—Fluorescent Lamp: Today fluorescent lamps supply about two-thirds of all lighting worldwide. The very first one exhibited in public was displayed by GEC at the Illuminating Engineering Society's convention in Cincinnati in September. The light emitted from the two-foot-long tube glowed a brilliant green. A label stated simply: "The fluorescent lumiline lamp—a laboratory experiment of great promise." The following year the promise was fulfilled when fluorescent lamps had their first practical application. On the occasion of the U.S. Patent Office's centenary, a grand reception was held for more than a thousand people. As the names of America's twelve greatest inventors were read out, the house lights dimmed and suddenly the vast hall was ablaze with the hard white light of this latest miracle of American technology.

1935—Color Roll Film: The first successful three-color roll film for amateurs was Kodachrome, developed by Leopold Mannes and Leopold Godowsky. Earlier color roll films had been introduced in Germany in 1924 and Britain in 1929, but these were two-color processes. Kodachrome was suitable only for making transparencies. Kodacolor followed in 1942 as the first color roll film designed for making color prints.

1938—Xerox Photocopy: The first Xerox photocopy was made by Chester Floyd Carlson, and it read "ASTORIA 10–22–38"—the place and date of this technological breakthrough. Exactly ten years later to the day the world's first dry copier, the Xerox Model A, was unveiled by the Haloid Company. The 600-pound machine was so large and graceless it soon acquired the nickname "the Ox Box," but it was the beginning of the end for the messy and complicated wet copiers that had preceded it.

1938—Nylon: The first nylon product to come on sale was not stockings, as popularly supposed, but Dr. West's Miracle Tuft Toothbrush in September 1938. Nylon had been developed by Dr. Wallace Corothers of DuPont, though tragically he had committed suicide before seeing the commercial realization of his invention. Manufacture of nylon yarn began the following year, and the first stockings in the artificial fabric went on sale in Wilmington, Delaware. By 1941 American women had bought no fewer than 60 million pairs and soon afterward American GIs were buying them too. Those bound for Britain knew that English girls, so short of stockings that they painted their bare legs with dye and drew a "seam" up the back, would do almost anything in return for nylons. It was said that many a war baby was a testimony to the bargaining power of the luxurious new hosiery.

1938—Teflon: Whenever there is a need to justify the expenditure on space exploration, Teflon is cited as one of the benefits it has conferred on mankind. While it is true that Teflon has been used extensively on nose cones, fuel tanks, and heat shields for spacecraft, its discovery long precedes the space race. It was on April 6, 1938, that Roy J. Plunkett of DuPont discovered Teflon accidentally. He was conducting research on refrigerants when he found that a cylinder of tetrafluorethylene that he had stored in a cold box no longer contained the gas. On cutting it open he was surprised to see that it was full of a waxy substance that slid and slithered around without ever adhering to the walls of the cylinder. Thus Teflon was born. At first its uses were strictly military and it was not until 1954 that anyone found a domestic use for it. Then in France research engineer Mare Gregoire tried using it to improve the efficiency of fishing rods and in the process discovered how to coat metal with Teflon. He founded the Tefal company, which launched the world's first nonstick pans on the market in Nice in May 1956. So it was not NASA that gave us nonstick kitchenware but a French kitchenware company that gave NASA the means to use Teflon in space.

1943—Scuba Gear: The aqualung has been known since 1867 but was only perfected during World War II when Jacques Cousteau and Emile Gagnan added the demand regulator—a device that delivered oxygen to the diver at the same pressure as the water around him. It had been developed by Gagnan, an engineer, as a pressure-reducing valve to enable cars to run on propane during the wartime gasoline shortage. Scuba is an acronym for self-contained underwater breathing apparatus.

1944—Ballpoint Pen: The first ballpoint pens were manufactured in Reading, England, by a workforce of seventeen women occupying a disused aircraft hangar. The entire first year's output of 30,000 pens was destined for the Royal Air Force, enabling navigators to write their calculations in ink—ordinary fountain pens would not operate in unpressurized cabins at high altitudes. The development of the ballpoint had started shortly before World War II in Hungary, where its inventor, László Biró, was a journalist, and completed in Argentina, to which he had gone as a refugee. He patented it in 1943, the year he met Henry Martin, who was in Buenos Aires on a mission for the British government. Martin acquired the British rights and later set up the manufacturing plant in Reading. The first ballpoints available to the public were launched by the Eterpen Company of Buenos Aires early in 1945. These were seen by a visiting American businessman, who discovered that Biró had failed to patent the pen in the United States and began manufacture on his own account. Quaintly advertised as "the first pen that writes under water," it went on sale at Gimbel's in New York on October 29, 1945, and 10,000 had been sold at $12.50 each by closing time.

1945—Microwave Oven: Percy LeBaron Spencer of the Raytheon Company in Waltham, Massachusetts, conceived the idea of the microwave one day when he happened to stand in front of a radar power tube in the factory and found, when he reached into his pocket, a gooey brown mess where formerly there had been a candy bar. The next day he put an egg in a kettle with a hole cut in the side and placed it in front of the power tube. One of Spencer's colleagues passed by, lifted the lid of the kettle to see what lay inside, and received a faceful of half-cooked egg as the shell exploded under pressure. The first microwave oven to go on sale was marketed by Raytheon at $3,000 in 1947 as the Radar Range—it was, after all, simply a radar set you could use for cooking.

1946—Slinky: The coiled spring that walks down steps of its own volition was not so much an invention as a simple technical phenomenon. Marine engineer Richard James was sitting in his office at the Cramp Shipyard in Philadelphia in 1945 when a torsion spring fell off a shelf and ambled over a pile of books. He and his wife, Betty, borrowed $500 and used it to produce 400 springs, dreamed up the name Slinky, and launched the product in 1946 at Gimbel's of New York. When all 400 sold out in ninety minutes, the Jameses knew they had found something that captivated the small boy or small girl in every American.

1947—Instant Camera: The idea of the instant camera came to Edwin Land on a family picnic in 1943. When he took a snapshot, his three-year-old daughter hopped up and down in impatience to see the result. As he explained to her that it would take several days, the thought came to him that it should be possible to see the picture immediately. Four years later he produced the Polaroid Land Camera, which developed the photograph with chemicals secreted in a pod at the side of the film. As the film passed between twin rollers, the pod was crushed and the developing fluid was released onto the surface of what was about to become an image.

1949—Telephone Answering Machine: It was called the Ipsophone, was more than three feet high, and weighed more than 300 pounds. This monster machine was manufactured by Buhrle and Company of Oerlikon, Switzerland, and despite its complexity it was remarkably efficient. One advanced feature was a device that enabled owners to call in when absent to hear their messages, but they were able to do so only after proving their identity by recognizing a preselected pair of digits spoken by the machine. Among early users were Orthodox Jews. The Ipsophone enabled them to receive messages on the Sabbath without activating electricity themselves.

1949—Silly Putty: It was one of those inventions no one could find a use for. During World War II, General Electric engineer James Wright created a bouncing compound by combining boric acid with silicone oil while experimenting on substitutes for rubber. Not until 1949 did anyone show an interest in it as a commercial proposition. Peter Hodgson of New Haven, Connecticut, was an advertising copywriter who had been made redundant. He borrowed $147, bought a vast consignment of the substance from General Electric, and hired a Yale student to cut it into one-ounce lumps. These he put into plastic eggs and retailed as Silly Putty for one dollar each through Doubleday bookshops. The venture was so successful that when Peter Hodgson died many years later, he left $140 million—almost $1 million for every dollar he had originally invested in General Electric's throwout.

1949—Disposable Diapers: Britain led the diaper revolution, though it was not called that because in England they are known as nappies. The pioneer was Robinson's of Chesterfield, who launched an absorbent pulp-paper diaper in November 1949. It was followed by Drypers and KDs in the United States, but all these paper versions had a distressing tendency to leak. Cost was also a problem. It was not until Procter and Gamble launched their tape-on Pampers in 1961 that the disposable began to make inroads into the toweling diaper market. Even then the leak problem remained, eventually overcome in the early 1980s when leg

elastics were successfully introduced. Nowadays disposables have about 90 percent of the diaper market, compared with less than 1 percent in 1956. Highest penetration is in France at 98 percent.

1951—Direct Dial Telephone Calls: It was a world first when Mayor M. Leslie Dennying of Englewood, New Jersey, dialed Mayor Frank P. Osborne of Alameda, California, on November 10, inaugurating Bell Telephone's coast-to-coast "no operator" service.

1951—Geodesic Dome: Ever associated with the name of visionary architect Buckminster Fuller, the geodesic dome was patented in 1951 as a lightweight structure offering no resistance to wind. The first permanent installation was at the rotunda at the Ford Motor Company headquarters in Detroit. A conventional dome would have weighed about 160 tons; Fuller's creation for Ford was a mere 8½ tons. The U.S. Defense Department became Fuller's biggest client for geodesic domes, especially for housing sensitive radar equipment in remote areas.

1951—Cable TV: On January 1 a new entertainment medium was born, but apart from the employees of Chicago's Zenith Radio Corporation, only the 300 subscribers to Zenith's Phonevision Service knew about it. On the opening day of cable television there was a choice of three movies: *April Showers* with Jack Carson, *Welcome Stranger* with Bing Crosby, and *Homecoming* with Clark Gable. Scrambled signals were unscrambled via the telephone circuit—provided you were willing to pay the dollar-a-movie fee for being a pioneer cable TV viewer.

1952—Tranquilizer: The first tranquilizing drug was Reserpine, developed by the British biochemist Robert Robinson and the Swiss pharmacologist Emil Schittler. The two scientists had observed that the powdered root of the Indian shrub *Rauwolfia serpentina* had a quieting effect on troubled persons. The drug was first produced for clinical use by the Swiss chemical giant Ciba Laboratories.

1955—Artificial Diamonds: The General Electric Company was the first to make synthetic diamonds, heating carbon to a temperature of 4,700 degrees Fahrenheit at a pressure of more than 100,000 atmospheres. These stones, created for industrial use, are scarcely a millimeter in length and usually black. By increasing the temperature at which the carbon is baked, it is technically feasible to create clear gemstones, but they lack the quality of the real thing and in any case would cost more than nature's version.

1955—Transistor Radio: Although Bell Telephone made the first commercial application of the transistor in 1951, it was the Japanese who saw its potential for miniaturized electronic consumer goods. Sony was the pioneer, launching the first transistor radio, the TR-55, in August 1955, though America was quick to respond when Regency Electronics of Indianapolis brought out its TR-1 in October. Early transistor radios were expensive, but within five years it was possible to buy a reliable pocket set for as little as five dollars.

1956—Typing Correction Fluid: Bette Nesmith Graham's success story would not have happened had she been a better typist. Prone to making errors in her typing as a secretary at Texas Bank and Trust in Dallas, she needed a surefire way of correcting them without leaving smudges. Her solution was inspired, even though it did not require any inventive skills. She simply poured white tempera waterbase paint into a small bottle and took it to work with an eyebrow brush. When other typists began asking for her "correcting fluid," she began bottling it in the garage with the help of her son Michael. He was later to achieve fame and fortune as Michael Nesmith of the pop group The Monkees. Bette achieved her fame and fortune with what was to become Liquid Paper, a hugely successful venture that was worth $47 million when she sold out to Gillette in 1979. And on top of that, the deal gave her and Michael royalties on every bottle sold until the end of the century.

1957—Velcro: When George de Mistral established the Velcotrex factory at Aubonne in Switzerland to manufacture the first Velcro fasteners, it was the culmination of fifteen years of intensive research and development. The idea was simple, even if its realization was not. It began with an unlucky accident that had spoiled an evening out in 1941. The zipper on Madame de Mistral's dress jammed and would not unjam. De Mistral decided there had to be a better method of fastening fabrics, but it was not until a few months later, when he was out hunting with his dog, that the solution presented itself. The dog's ear became covered in burrs from brushing against burdock weed. On examining the burrs under a microscope, de Mistral saw that they bristled with tiny hooks. The principle of Velcro had been revealed—all that remained was to apply it. When at last he succeeded, his invention spread rapidly around the Earth—and beyond it. Among its beneficiaries were the first astronauts to fly to the Moon. They used Velcro not only on their spacesuits but also to fix objects to the cabin walls that would otherwise have floated in weightless space.

1958—Skateboard: Some Californians called it sidewalk surfing and some terra-surfing when Bill Richards and his son Mark of the Val Surf Shop in Dana Point introduced a brand new sport designed to appeal to surf bums on dry land. Their first skateboards were rudimentary by today's standards. They gave the Chicago Roller Skate Company an order for the wheel assemblies from roller skates. These they mounted beneath square wooden boards, and for just eight dollars anyone could play. In the early years the wheels of the boards had insufficient grip for the kind of maneuverability that would turn a cult into a craze, but that changed when polyurethane wheels were introduced in 1973 by Frank Nasworthy. Curiously, they had proved useless for roller skates but were the missing link for skateboards.

1958—Heart Pacemaker: The first implantable pacemaker, which had an external coil and an internal receiver, was inserted into the chest of Swedish cardiac patient Arne Larson by Dr. Ake Senning in Stockholm on October 29, 1958. Even with a pacemaker, people who suffered from heart defects had to regulate their activity. In 1986 the German company Biotronik introduced a programmed pacemaker that gave wearers much more freedom to lead a normal life. By measuring blood temperature, the device increases the heartbeat rate as the patient exerts more energy, as for instance when climbing stairs.

1958—Audiocassette: The tape recorder had been around since 1929, but it could not compete with the disk record player as an entertainment medium until RCA Victor introduced the cassette player in June 1958. Even then the audiocassettes, which used half-inch tape, were too big and had too short a playing time to make serious inroads into the market for vinyl LPs. The breakthrough came with the "compact cassette," developed by the Dutch electronics firm Philips in 1963. This used 3.8mm tape and established the present worldwide audio cassette standard.

1964—Fax Machine: Although facsimile transmission was pioneered by AT&T in 1925, the office fax was born on May 5, 1964, when Xerox unveiled the LDX at its Fifty-second Street showroom in New York. It was not the slimline desktop device of today. There were separate units for scanning, transmitting, and receiving, and it could not operate over ordinary telephone lines—you needed a dedicated line or a wideband microwave link. And at $850 a month rental, plus line charges, it was not for the small-business man. But ten years later two events happened that were ultimately to bring the fax into almost every office and millions of households. The United Nations set international standards, which meant that the new generation of faxes could all communicate with each other, regardless of make or country of origin. Also in 1974 the Japanese, who would soon dominate the fax market, introduced the first fax machine able to send an A4 sheet over conventional telephone lines in under a minute. The fax had come of age and the globe had taken one step further toward becoming that proverbial village.

1964—Aseptic Packaging: The Tetra-Pak was the first aseptic packaging, a means of keeping food from spoiling by first sterilizing it and then sealing it in a sterilized container. Although developed in Sweden, the earliest commercial application was made in Switzerland when the Verbands Molkerai of Thun used Tetra-Paks for the introduction of the world's first long-life milk.

1966—Antishoplifting Tag: When Arthur J. Minasy was growing up in Astoria, Queens, he shoplifted marbles and tennis balls from the local Woolworth's five-and-ten. By the early 1960s he was working as a consultant for the New York City Police Department, trying to solve the growing problem of shoplifting. In 1964 he beat out other inventors by creating in his garage an electronic tag that deterred shoplifting. The tags, attached to items in a store, would set off an alarm when they passed through a security system near the door. A prototype of Minasy's invention, which he called the Knogo (as in no-go) and upon which his international Knogo Corporation was founded, was accepted into the permanent collection of the Smithsonian's National Museum of American History in 1991.

1970—Liquid Crystal Display: The LCD not only gives high visibility even in direct sunlight but also uses a thousand times less electricity than the LED (light-emitting diode). The first system capable of commercial application, the Twisted Nematic LCD, was patented in 1971 by Hoffmann–La Roche and Company of Switzerland.

1970—Pocket Calculator: In Tokyo on April 15, 1970, Canon Business Machines announced the introduction of the Pocketronic Printing Calculator. It was another successful Japanese launch of an American invention. This "miniature electronic calculator" had been patented by Jack Hilly, Jerry Merryman, and James Van Tassel of Texas Instruments following a challenge by TI president Patrick Haggerty to put the newly invented microchip to use on every office desk. The Pocketronic cost $150, it gave you your answer on paper tape rather than a liquid crystal display, and for a machine designed for the pocket it weighed in at a not inconsiderable two and a half pounds. But for the first time the mathematically illiterate could multiply and divide without exercising their brains.

1970—International Direct Dial Telephone Calls: AT&T and Britain's General Post Office got into bed together and the world shrank again. On March 1, for the first time, you could dial direct from New York to London.

1972—CAT Scanner: CAT stands for computerized axial tomography, a way of taking photographs of cross sections of diseased tissue 100 times more detailed than by the traditional X-ray method. The inventor was Godfrey Hounsfield of Britain's Electrical and Musical Industries, the company that first brought television into the home. The first CAT scanner in clinical use entered medical history in 1972 when it was used to diagnose a brain tumor in a woman patient at Wimbledon, England's, Atkinson Morley's Hospital. Hounsfield shared the 1979 Nobel Prize for physiology and medicine with American inventor Allan Cormack, who had independently worked on the principles of CAT scanning.

1972—Video Games: It was a pale November day and there was a new attraction at Andy Capp's Tavern in Sunnyvale, California. Patrons were so eager to play the electronic game called Pong—a video version of table tennis—that the machine seized up because it was jammed with coins. The brain behind what was to become a world revolution in leisure-time activity belonged to Nolan Bushnell, a bright young engineer with the Ampex corporation. Others had experimented with video games but failed because the equipment was always too large and too expensive to be a commercial proposition. Bushnell harnessed the might of the microprocessor to the kind of game that had been played in amusement arcades for generations. He founded Atari to market the concept, and when he sold out to Warner Brothers ten years later his personal profit from the deal was $15 million.

1973—Plastic Soda Pop Bottles: Plastic bottles had first been made with blow-molding machinery in the 1940s, but these could not withstand the pressure of carbonated soft drinks without bursting. It was only in 1973 that Nat Wyeth, an engineer with the DuPont Chemical Company, found a technique for making bottles tough enough to be 100 percent safe even if they were shaken hard.

> The marvels of modern technology include the development of a soda can which, when discarded, will last forever—and a $7,000 car, which, when properly cared for, will rust out in two or three years.
>
> Paul Harwitz, *Wall Street Journal*

1974—VCR: "The start of a revolution in home entertainment" is how the Dutch firm Philips hailed the introduction of their N1500 videocassette recorder, the first to be designed for domestic use. In fact the revolution failed to start. The half-inch tapes played only for an hour, which meant a changeover if you wanted to record a movie. And they were too expensive at fifty dollars each. But it did start two years later when the JVS and Matsushita companies of Japan launched the VHS format, which, after a battle with Sony's rival Betamax format, eventually became the industry standard.

1974—Bar Codes: At one minute past eight o'clock on June 26, a retailing revolution began. For the first time a product pack was scanned at the checkout of a supermarket. The place was Troy, Ohio. The store was Marsh Supermarket. And the pack? Those who saw a small slice of history being made cannot agree whether it was a ten-pack of Wrigley's chewing gum or just a single packet.

1977—Rubik's Cube: Professor Erno Rubik was a lecturer in architectural design in his native Budapest when he patented the exasperating cube that bears his name. Each of the six faces of the cube had nine moveable squares of different colors and the idea was to make each face all one color. In 1979 the Ideal toy company of New York (now Hasbro) acquired the manufacturing rights and sold more than 100 million cubes worldwide, making Rubik one of the only millionaires in what was then the Communist bloc.

1978—Test-Tube Baby: In-vitro fertilization (IVF) is a technique for fertilization of sperm and egg outside the human body. In fact it takes place not in a test tube but in a glass petri dish, from which *in vitro* (in glass) is derived. This method of enabling infertile women to have babies was first employed successfully by gynecologist Dr. Patrick Steptoe and Cambridge University physiologist Dr. Robert Edwards at Oldham, in Lancashire, England, where the first "test-tube baby," Louise Brown, was born on July 25, 1978.

1979—Post-It Notes: The special gum that enables the ubiquitous little paper rectangles to "stick without sticking" was developed by chance in 1973 by Dr. Spencer Silver of the Minnesota Mining & Manufacturing (3M) Company. Nobody could think of a use for it until his colleague Arthur Fry, a member of a local choir, used the unwanted gum to make markers for his music book that would not fall out. The market for bookmarkers, however efficient they may be, is limited. But one day Fry had occasion to make a brief comment on a report. He used one of his markers to write a note, stuck it on the report, and sent it to his boss. The boss's reply came back written on the same note. This was the moment of revelation—the stickers could be marketed as notelets for short comments, instructions, or reminders. But when they were

sales-tested as Press'n'Peel pads, there was no demand. Only when 3M bombarded Boise, Idaho, with a campaign they called the "Boise Blitz" and changed the name of the product to the catchier Post-it, did it take off.

1979—Walkman: It is not a true invention, because it involved no innovative technology, but it was a brilliant marketing concept. According to Sony legend, chairman Akio Morita was fed up with having to listen to rock music blaring from his children's hi-fi. He determined to give teenagers a miniature tape player with headphones, which would release their long-suffering parents from the miseries of modern music. It was launched in Japan as the Walkman, but Sony's American agents told them the name did not make sense and it was introduced in the United States, in December 1979, as the Soundabout. The British agreed that it was a meaningless name, but they decided to call it the Stowaway. When tourists started bringing home-grown Walkmans back from Japan, a serious confusion developed over brand identity. Within a few months Sony had decided that a Walkman would be a Walkman worldwide, and nobody seems to have found the name senseless ever since.

1980—Compact Disc: It took the Dutch electronics company Philips fifteen years to develop the CD. When they demonstrated the grooveless, laser-read miniature disks at the Salzburg Festival in April 1980, the great conductor Herbert von Karajan declared that "all else is gaslight." In a joint venture two years later, Philips and Sony launched the first compact disc players in Japan, and they reached Europe and the United States in 1983. Before the end of the decade, CDs were outselling vinyl LPs, and they would kill them off altogether in the 1990s.

1980—Rollerblade Skates: In-line roller skates were a reinvention. They had first been demonstrated in London in the 1820s but afterward forgotten for 150 years. Then a young Minnesotan, twenty-year-old Scott Olson, decided he wanted a means of continuing his hockey training out of season (he was a semipro hockey player for the Winnipeg Jets). In 1978 Olson saw someone distributing ice skates with wheels on them—the perfect, if somewhat clunky, answer. He purchased the patent, and he and his brother Brennan began to improve the design in 1980. They set up manufacturing in their parents' home in Bloomington, Minnesota. The in-line skate with its "blade" of polyurethane wheels was capable of the same kind of speed on land as conventional skates on ice.

1987—Genetic Fingerprinting: In January 1988 Colin Pitchfork was found guilty at Leicester Crown Court in England of the rape and murder of two schoolgirls. He was the first murderer in the world convicted on the evidence of genetic fingerprinting. This technique of criminal detection was based on the discovery by Dr. Alec J. Jeffreys of Leicester University that the unique genetic identity of any individual could be determined by analyzing sections of DNA from samples of blood, semen, or saliva. The method had been introduced in January 1987 when Leicestershire's police department began collecting samples of blood or saliva from 2000 men aged sixteen to thirty-four in the area where the teenagers had been strangled. Only two men refused, one of whom was Pitchfork. Later he was pressured to comply but hired a substitute to supply the sample in his stead. When this man confessed to the deception, Pitchfork was DNA tested and arrested. In the resulting murder trial his "genetic fingerprint" was proved to be identical to that identified from the semen found in the bodies of his victims.

—P.II.R.

DONALD DUCK CREDITED WITH INVENTION

In 1964, when the freighter *Al Kuwait* capsized in the harbor of Kuwait with a cargo of 6,000 sheep, local citizens feared that the rotting carcasses would poison their supply of drinking water.

Fortunately, Danish manufacturer Karl Kroyer remembered a 1949 Walt Disney comic book in which Donald Duck and his nephews, Huey, Dewey, and Louie, raised a sunken yacht by stuffing it full of Ping-Pong balls.

Putting this duck wisdom to good use, Kroyer ordered 27 billion polystyrene balls to be injected into the hull of the *Al Kuwait*. The freighter was successfully raised to an even keel, and the Kuwaiti water supply was saved. Few people who admired this great engineering feat were aware that credit for the idea belonged to four fictional ducks—and the man who drew them, cartoonist Carl Barks.

MILESTONES IN COMPUTER HISTORY

THE GREAT BRASS BRAIN, 1910
In the 1880s the affable William Thompson, Lord Kelvin, a witty man who looked like Santa Claus, tried to invent a calculating machine for solving differential equations. He believed that by substituting "brass for brain," computing could be done faster. He failed in his enterprise, at least partly because Victorian technology just wasn't up to the demands of his machine. However, he did invent one successful operating device, one that predicted the times when tides rose and fell at seaports in Britain.

In 1905 two other men—Rollins Harris and E. G. Fisher of the U.S. Coast and Geodetic Survey—began working on a similar machine. Completed in 1910, their Great Brass Brain, a 2,500-pound mechanical device eleven feet long and seven feet high, predicted tides with great accuracy. Its rotating shafts, cams, and gears groaned through calculations for tidal charts after an operator set thirty-seven separate dials, each representing a variable, and turned a crank. The Brass Brain was so good at its job that it was not retired until 1966.

THE DIFFERENTIAL ANALYZER, 1935
In the 1920s a young American engineer, Vannevar Bush, thought he saw a way that Lord Kelvin's "brass brain" for differential equations

could be built. The need was there—as science and engineering had grown, so had the requirement for fast calculation. Engineers were stockpiling differential equations, unable to solve them quickly enough on the calculating machines of the day. To build his machine, Bush had a tool Kelvin had not: a servomotor (small electric motor that was reliable). The Bush Differential Analyzer took five years to make. Looking something like a printing press, with its wheels and gears and axles and rotating rods, it took up several hundred square feet of space and weighed 100 tons. To program it, an operator needed screwdrivers and hammers. Yet it was a sophisticated number cruncher for the time.

The Moore School at the University of Pennsylvania, Massachusetts Institute of Technology, and the U.S. Army collaborated in building two Bush Differential Analyzers; they were completed by 1935. The machines were important to ballistics research because they were able to quickly produce artillery firing tables for making corrections for winds, temperature, and other variables.

COLOSSUS, 1948
In 1939, when Konrad Zuse and Helmut Shreyer went to a German government official

with the idea of building a computer to decipher enemy codes, the official turned them down flat. The basis for his refusal: Zuse and Shreyer estimated that it would take a year to build the computer, and Hitler thought the war would be over in six months.

Meanwhile, in England a much less confident government was all too happy to spend money on an electronic decoding machine. To this end it assembled a motley and eccentric crew of mathematicians, chess experts, and other creative folk (Ian Fleming, creator of the James Bond thrillers, among them) at Bletchley Park (a manor). Their job was to design a machine to break the Enigma system used by the Germans to encode messages. Their first effort, the Bombe, which made a noise like clicking knitting needles, worked well until the Germans improved on Enigma, multiplying possible keys for encoding by a factor of twenty-six, so that it was capable of a sextillion—1,000,000,000,000,000,000,000—settings. It now took a month to decode messages, giving the German U-boats almost free rein in the Atlantic to send messages. Something better than the bombe was needed. The final product, Colossus, was digital and programmable. It had 1,500 beer-can-sized vacuum tubes, which made it so hot that operators were advised to take off their shirts while working on it. It was about three feet deep and as wide and high as a highway billboard. Like humans, it had its eccentricities—for instance, it suffered from a kind of machine epilepsy, causing it to become temperamental from time to time.

Everything about Colossus was top secret. In fact, it was not until thirty years after the war that any information of value was released about it, even though more than a thousand people worked on the project.

EDVAC (Electronic Discrete Variable Automatic Computer), 1950

An elegant fat man, mathematical genius John von Neumann (born 1903 in Hungary) was a "species greater than man," according to one who knew him, and "Saint Johnny" to another because he had so many admiring disciples. In fact the admiration was deserved, though he did sometimes make mistakes. Among his many accomplishments were the invention of game theory and pivotal work on the nuclear bomb.

In a 101-page document, *First Draft of a Report on the EDVAC*, von Neumann laid out the principles for a hypothetical digital electronic computer that would have a central arithmetical unit, a central control unit to tell the computer what to do and in what order, a memory unit, an input device, an output device, and a recording device.

The idea came to reality at the Moore School

of Engineering, University of Pennsylvania. Designed by John Brainerd, J. Presper Eckert Jr., John Mauchly, and others, EDVAC used mercury delay storage lines (waves in fluid metal) to beef up memory, in place of vacuum tubes. This allowed the inclusion of a stored program (a set of commands to go along with data).

COBOL, 1950

"Amazing Grace" Hopper (1906–92), née Grace Brewster Murray, was considered the mother of COBOL, a business programming language, even though she herself did not actually write it. Having spent her earlier years as a mathematics professor at Vassar, she began programming for the armed services during World War II. She eventually achieved the rank of rear admiral. In 1952 she became systems engineer and director of automatic programming for UNIVAC Division of Sperry. There she developed the language compiler (assembly language or assembler) software that first translates high-level symbolic language instructions into an organized program in a computer's binary language, then carries it out. Her team produced Flow-matic (a.k.a. B-0) in 1957. It was the first language that used English words and syntax as commands—"stop," "add," "execute." This notion was later incorporated into COBOL. COBOL also separated processing from data so that the programmer could change part of the code, and it was good at handling files and managing large amounts of data. However, it was so slow-starting in sales that early on Howard Brumberg of RCA sent a tombstone labeled COBOL to the Pentagon to point out the fact that it was dead. His pessimism was misplaced.

UNIVAC, 1951

UNIVAC (Universal Variable Computer) achieved early fame when, a year after it was completed, it predicted that Dwight D. Eisenhower would win the presidential election with 438 electoral votes—a remarkably precise prediction. (In actuality, Eisenhower won 432 electoral votes.) About fifty UNIVACs, at prices of about $1 million each, were sold over its lifetime. For its time it was capable of long and ponderous calculations, partly because of its magnetic tape permanent storage (programs that can be read into memory to tell the computer how to process data). This made it valuable for such tasks as analyzing census data.

The main players in the creation of UNIVAC, John Mauchly and J. Presper Eckert, started their own company—Mauchly Eckert Computer Company—in 1946, when they started building UNIVAC. Mauchly, professorial but flamboyant, was an engineering genius. At eight he wired light switches so that his relatives could turn on a light from either of two points. This "lazy man's switch," as he called it, was

The UNIVAC computer gained attention when it was used to predict trends in the 1952 United States elections.

similar to binary switching circuits in computers. Electrical engineer J. Presper Eckert was famous for making a sound system to play chimes in graveyards to drown out the noise of the crematorium—as well as for less interesting but more weighty innovations.

Unfortunately, the company lost $2 million in government contracts when, in that Red-baiting era, it was discovered that a Mauchly-Eckert secretary had gone out with a man who had attended a few Communist Party meetings. American Totalizator Corporation, which made pari-mutuel machines for racetracks, invested $500,000 in the company and later took control. In 1950 the company was acquired by Remington Rand.

WHIRLWIND, 1951

Without the Cold War, Whirlwind, a marvel of early computing but very costly in time and money, might never have been made. Seeing a threat in Soviet atomic weapon explosions and the invasion of South Korea, the government sought to develop a sophisticated computer to strengthen national defense by quickly modernizing the air force. Such a computer should be able to do lightning-fast and accurate flight simulations, among other things. To that end, the government threw money at the Whirlwind project. A team effort of 175 people over three years, it required a $1 million annual budget. When finished, Whirlwind, a high-speed electronic computer, featured a digital stored program—instructions could be fed into the machine through tapes and other external devices. It could multiply in twenty microseconds. It also took up 2,500 square feet and contained 4,000 vacuum tubes and a walkthrough corridor.

Perhaps the most important individual behind Whirlwind was Jay W. Forrester, who early became an engineering whiz—as a teenager, he built a wind-driven electrical system to supply his parents' cattle ranch. It was Forrester who solved several of Whirlwind's problems. For example, in the beginning Whirlwind cost $32,000 a month for memory because its storage tubes failed so often. So Forrester developed magnetic-core memory—several doughnut-shaped ferrite-magnetic cores, strung on a wire grid, each representing a computer address. Put into Whirlwind in 1953, this system made the computer twice as fast and far cheaper and more reliable.

THE INTERNET, 1973

A worldwide public mega-network for connecting all the world's computers together, the Internet is designed to operate over almost any kind of telecommunications transport medium, from telephone lines and optical fiber to satellites, and to connect to just about anything with a computer chip in it. More than just a network, it is an enormous cross section of people and organizations constantly sharing information, collaborating, and developing new ideas and products.

> The new electronic interdependence recreates the world in the image of a global village.
> Marshall McLuhan, Gutenberg Galaxy, 1962

Originally created in 1973 by the U.S. Department of Defense as a way to integrate its research facilities and people, it began to be heavily used worldwide in the 1980s for scientific research and education. With the widespread use of personal computers in the 1990s, the Internet quickly became a way for business and the general public to reach just about everyone else.

By mid-1995, the Internet encompassed more than 7 million computers and tens of millions of users all over the world. During the 1990s, one Internet use in particular—the World Wide Web (WWW)—grew so popular that it became the basis for much of the Internet's expansion. The WWW allows multimedia presentations and navigation through cyberspace, filling out forms, or even making purchases by just pointing and clicking on a computer screen. It also enables people to participate in discussion groups, send and receive electronic mail, distribute software, and play interactive games.

BASIC, 1975

In 1975 Paul Allen saw an ad for a knocked-down, do-it-yourself computer, the Altair 8800, made by MITS of Albuquerque, New Mexico. He raced to show it to his long-time friend William Gates (they met in prep school), then a student at Harvard. They bought an Altair and called the president of MITS, claiming that they had written a version of BASIC, a high-level programming language, for his computer. In actuality, Gates and Allen had just started working on their version of BASIC—it took them six weeks of nearly sleepless days and nights to finish it. They called their version GW-BASIC—the GW stood for Gee Whiz. The original BASIC, Beginner's All-purpose Symbolic Instruction Code, had been created in 1964 by two Dartmouth mathematics professors—John Kemeny and Thomas Kurtz. They had allowed their version of BASIC to fall into the public domain.

GW-BASIC was a success. In 1975, partly based on that success, Gates, then only nineteen years old, and Allen founded Microsoft, the giant dominating the software industry in the 1990s. (It was not the first time they had collaborated in business. Still in high school, they started a company called Traf-o-Data, which, using a computer, was to figure out and help control traffic patterns in Seattle.) They sold BASIC to individuals for $500 alone or for $75 if they bought an Altair and its peripherals too. They also sold to hardware computer companies, including Apple, Commodore, and Radio Shack. When they secured one fat contract for more than $1 million, Gates celebrated by drinking and jumping up on the hoods of taxicabs. It was not unusual behavior for this enigma of a man, reputed to like fast cars and work, champagne, and hamburgers. Savvy as well as colorful, he refused a buyout from Ross Perot when he was only twenty-three years old.

CRAY 1 SUPERCOMPUTER, 1976

The Cray 1, the benchmark supercomputer, could operate at 150 megaflops—that is, it could, in one second, perform 150 million floating point mathematical calculations. A floating point calculation is addition, subtraction, multiplication, or division of two numbers so small or large that they are described in scientific notation—for example, 3.45692×20^{31}. The Cray 1 was 300,000 times faster than the 1981 IBM personal computer and at least forty-five times as fast as IBM's biggest mainframe. A cylinder only six feet high and eight feet around, called by some "the world's most expensive love seat," the Cray 1 contained sixty miles of wiring, 34,000 integrated circuit boards, and 200,000 semiconductor chips. It was considered the first supercomputer—though others, such as the CDC 6600, also created by Cray, might claim the same honor. Each individual machine also cost in the millions of dollars. For certain purposes, though, it was worth it. Supercomputers use differential equations to model complex physical phenomena such as nuclear explosions, how a hurricane will act, how air flows over an airplane wing, atomic activity, or the birth of the universe. It can test hypotheses that cannot be tested any other way (those involving the universe) or are too dangerous or expensive to test any other way (nuclear explosions). It was no accident that the first Cray 1 to be built was installed at Los Alamos National Laboratory in 1976.

The mastermind behind the Cray is a reclusive genius, Seymour Cray, born in 1925. Cray sees himself as an artist, trying, as he says, "to hear what is going on inside his ideas."

WORDSTAR, 1979

In 1979 Seymour Rubenstein, hardware entrepreneur and head of MicroPro, saw a demand for a word processing program. People were sending him letters asking for something like, but better than, Michael Shrayer's Electric Pencil, the first commercial word processing program for microcomputers.

Rubenstein brought in a hot programmer, Rob Barnaby, to create WordStar, released in the middle of 1979. It was immediately successful—perhaps the best software moneymaker of all time—and retained its success at least until 1985.

It is difficult to overstate the importance of computer word processing. It revolutionized the office, eliminating the typing pool. It changed forever the way people write. And it turned the typewriter and attendant eraser into artifacts.

dBASE, 1980

In 1974, in the Jet Propulsion Laboratory (JPL) near Pasadena, California, engineers and scientists started using Jeb Long's JPLDIS (JPL Data-Management and Information Retrieval System) to analyze information from unmanned space probes. A systems designer at JPL, Wayne Ratliff, took JPLDIS as a model to write new software, eventually called VULCAN, which he advertised in BYTE magazine in 1980. In August of that year, he came out with an advanced version of VULCAN, but only fifty copies were ever sold. Along came George Tate, that summer of 1980, and a deal was struck through which Tate would distribute the product, a sophisticated program for manipulating data files, and give Ratliff generous royalties. The name of the program was changed to dBASE II—dBASE I had never existed. Tate devised strange ads comparing dBASE II to a bilge pump, which sucks stuff from the underwater part of a ship. Bilge pump manufacturers and other database manufacturers alike disliked the ad, but it sold the product. The company Ashton-Tate was formed as marketer.

MS-DOS, 1980

In 1980 Tim Paterson of Seattle Computer cloned—more or less—a still-in-the-works operating system called CP/M-86 (Digital Research) and called it QDOS (Quick and Dirty Operating System). Bill Gates's company Microsoft bought QDOS outright from Paterson for $50,000. It was a very important purchase—a good operating system is the translator between user and computer—and more.

Bill Gates got the contract to license MS-DOS (Microsoft Disk Operating System) to IBM in 1980. Part of the reason he was able to beat out the competition had to do with his family—IBM president John Opel knew Mary Gates, Bill's mother, from serving on the national board of the United Way.

Before MS-DOS could be installed in the IBM personal computer, known as HAL (from the film 2001), it had to be adapted by Microsoft. So important was the exclusivity of MS-DOS to IBM that IBM required Microsoft personnel to work on the program revision in secrecy in a windowless storage closet. By 1995, 90 percent of the world's IBM PCs and compatibles used MS-DOS.

LOTUS 1-2-3, 1982

In a matter of days from the time Lotus 1-2-3 was introduced at COMDEX, a computer trade show, in the fall of 1982, the company received millions of dollars in advance orders. Lotus was a phenomenal best-seller, even before it was released early in 1983. The first integrated package of office functions in one program, it combined spreadsheet, graphics program, and database manager.

The program was the work of Mitch Kapor, who started Lotus, and Jonathan Sachs, an assembly language genius. Kapor, who had been involved in teaching Transcendental Meditation, among other counterculture endeavors, began his love affair with computers with the TRS-80 Model 1, then went on to own an Apple computer. Overnight he turned into an Apple programmer. In 1977 he started a users' group of seven people in his living room. There he met MIT grad student Eric Rosenfeld, who was working on computer research analysis of his data on the university computer. Kapor wrote Rosenfeld a program in BASIC that would work on an Apple. He called it Tiny Troll. With Rosenfeld he created for the publisher Personal Software two new programs based on Tiny Troll—VisiTrend and VisiPlot. In 1982 VisiCorp (Personal Software under a new name) bought out the contract for the two programs for $1.2 million, providing startup money for Kapor's new company—Lotus—and the development of Lotus 1-2-3.

DESKTOP LASER PRINTER, 1984

In 1969 Xerox Corporation put Gary Starkweather to work adapting copier technology to printing. This was more complicated than it sounds. It involved using a laser beam to put a pattern of charged dots on a light-sensitive drum, exposing the resulting electrostatic image to toner particles oppositely charged, then transferring the result to paper. The effort was worth it because a laser printer promised to be quieter and faster than a daisy wheel or dot-matrix printer, which sounded like clacking typewriters and printed words one letter, or set of dots, at a time. And it would provide higher resolution output than the dot-matrix printer with its often smudgy dot pattern. Unlike the daisy wheel, it had the potential to print landscape (sideways), with characters of any size that could fit the page.

But there was a big problem: cost of components. For instance, in 1977 Xerox introduced a laser printer that could produce 7,000 lines a minute at 300-dot-per-inch density—however, it cost a hefty $350,000. By 1983 Canon had developed a printer engine that sold for $1,000 or less, which meant that printers could sell for under $7,000. Hewlett-Packard used the engine to produce the HP LaserJet, the first desktop laser printer, the following year.

WINDOWS, 1985

When it first came on the market, Windows, a product of Bill Gates's Microsoft, was a sensation. It was an operating environment with GUI (pronounced "gooey"), or graphical user interface, that could be used to connect one program to another. It had icons, it had WYSIWYG ("What you see is what you get," a phrase lifted from comic Flip Wilson's character Geraldine). It had windows, a mouse, and hot-link programs. The user could move files and cut material from one program to the other and paste it in. It made the PC look a lot like a Macintosh.

Windows had had a rocky development. When it looked as if the project was in trouble, Gates brought in Neil Konzen, a young Macintosh genius barely out of his teens, to look at it. Konzen said Windows was "actually in hell." And in six weeks he rewrote it. Someone else said that it had become the "death project"— IBM, which had licensed other Microsoft products, was not interested in it. In fact, IBM personnel called Gates the Prince of Darkness and his employees Hitler Youth. Apple wasn't happy either, for obvious reasons. Moreover, Windows was slow, and it didn't always work. But it cornered the PC multitasking market, and Windows 3.0 alone sold millions of copies.

VIRTUAL REALITY, c. 1985

Student pilots go down in flames but emerge unscathed from an unwrecked cockpit. An amateur musician performs Jimi Hendrix music on an "air guitar." Prospective buyers "walk" through a building that is as yet unbuilt. Doctors practice threading sophisticated surgical instruments through a simulated body—and no one gets hurt. All this is courtesy of "virtual reality"—interaction with computer-generated artificial worlds.

Jaron Lanier, king of the virtual reality fantasy realm, calls virtual reality electronic LSD. Six feet tall, with blond dreadlocks, Lanier is a character—it is said that he rarely bathes and wore his shirts sideways as a child. The electronic DataGlove his company, VPL, created provides the open sesame to interaction in a computer-generated world that seems real. By raising the glove, participants experience the sensation of flying, and they can use it to grab at an artificial object in the world and move it around. Other equipment includes goggles with a magnetic tracking device that, by reacting to head movements of the wearer, shifts the field of vision in the artificial world. A data suit contains sensors that give the viewer the illusion of moving through an artificial scene.

But virtual reality is not all fun and games. It can also be a serious training tool. For instance, at Wright-Patterson Air Force Base, a "super cockpit" simulates flying high-speed aircraft so students can experience piloting a plane without danger. With telepresence, another form of virtual reality, computerized entities, like robots, are placed in distant or dangerous environments, such as the depths of the ocean, space, or a furnace, but manipulated by human beings in safer places.

—A.E.

ENVIRONMENTALISTS

ALDO LEOPOLD (1886–1948)

Aldo Leopold was an author, naturalist, and philosopher who was one of the forerunners of the American conservation movement.

Rand Aldo Leopold (his first name, Rand, was never used) was born in Burlington, Iowa, on January 11, 1886. When Leopold was born, there was no forestry profession to speak of in America. Most of his youthful instruction came from his father, Carl, who had a well-developed code of personal sportsmanship.

Leopold received his preparatory education at the Lawrenceville School in New Jersey and then entered the newly created School of Forestry at Yale. Following graduation with a master's degree in 1909, Leopold joined the U.S. Forest Service and was sent to the Southwest

(Arizona and New Mexico), where he met his wife, Estella, and where he remained for fifteen years.

Aldo Leopold's intellectual development mirrors the history of ecological and evolutionary thought. Ecology as a scientific discipline is a product of the twentieth century.

Leopold's involvement in intellectual wildlife conservation instead of the more overtly physical labors of the Forest Service came about almost by accident. While settling a range dispute in a remote part of the Carson National Forest in New Mexico, Leopold was caught in a blizzard and began to suffer from a severe inflammation in his knees. A country physician wrongly diagnosed Leopold's ailment as rheumatism and prescribed the worst possible treatment, and Leopold almost died from a case of acute nephritis.

A recurrence of the disease, which could occur from overexertion, was considered in all cases fatal. This was when Leopold shifted his focus to wildlife conservation work.

Leopold actually left the Forest Service in 1918 to serve as the secretary of the Albuquerque Chamber of Commerce, where he hoped to more effectively promote the cause of game preservation. He also promoted victory gardens, agricultural drainage of the Rio Grande Valley, public parks, and a civic center for Albuquerque. Leopold would return to the Forest Service in 1919.

Leopold came to be known as the father of the profession of wildlife management in America. He was given the first professorship in game management in the United States at the University of Wisconsin in 1933. In the same year, Leopold published the textbook *Game Management*, which is still regarded as a basic statement of the profession of wildlife management.

In Leopold's theory of game management, the objective was to preserve the healthy functioning of the ecological system, rather than primarily trying to protect individual animals. Leopold's most important essay, *The Land Ethic*, concluded that "a thing is right when it tends to preserve the integrity, stability and beauty of the biotic community."

Leopold also wrote with a wit and style that was unusual for his field.

When Karl Frederick, then president of the National Rifle Association, said that the killing of eagles was "the purest of all rifle sports," Leopold told Frederick that he "would infinitely rather that Frederick would shoot the vases off my mantelpiece than the eagles out of my Alaska."

Despite the numerous wildlife subjects Leopold investigated, he said that there were really only two things that interested him—"the relation of people to each other, and the relation of people to land."

Even though he was a strong advocate of conservation, Leopold was not an enemy of the hunter. It must be remembered that Leopold was a hunter first, who later became a conservationist through his many wildlife experiences. The shift in Leopold's career, away from forestry proper and toward the protection of wildlife, paralleled a shift in the direction of the conservation movement as a whole. Leopold saw hunting not as an abomination, nor as an inconsistency, but as active participation in the drama of life, to be conducted in a civil manner.

The second of Leopold's major works was *A Sand County Almanac and Sketches Here and There*, published in 1949, a year after Leopold's death. The book reflected literary brilliance alongside a subtle appreciation for the natural

world. Most important, the book detailed Leopold's philosophy of a "land ethic." This concept stated that it was each citizen's responsibility to become a steward of the landscape—a concept that would lead the way to a modern ecological ideology.

Sand County won critical praise for its innovative nature writing. The comprehensive writing was highly personal, rich in humor and irony, and imbued with a sense of respect and wonder. Because of *Sand County*, Leopold became firmly established as a major figure in conservation history, alongside such luminaries as Henry Thoreau and John Muir.

Leopold died of a heart attack on April 21, 1948, while fighting a grass fire that was threatening his farm in Sauk County, Wisconsin. His land ethic, coupled with his assertion of individual obligation, remains Leopold's most enduring contribution to the field of wildlife management.

—J.R.O.

> We face the question whether a still higher "standard of living" is worth its cost in things natural, wild, and free. For us of the minority, the opportunity to see geese is more important than television.
> Aldo Leopold, *A Sand County Almanac*, 1949

RACHEL CARSON (1907–64)

Rachel Carson, with the publication of *Silent Spring* in 1962, transformed and energized the ecology movement before it knew it was a movement.

DDT was considered a wonder pesticide. Its creator, Paul Müller, won a Nobel Prize in 1948. However, when Olga Owens Huckins, a friend of Rachel Carson's, suggested that DDT might be dangerous, Carson began to research and collect data that led her to the conclusion that organopesticides build up in crops on which they are sprayed and are then transferred to birds and other animals. DDT had, until the publication of *Silent Spring*, been hailed as one of the greatest scientific leaps forward in history. DDT was actually a result of research conducted by the military on biological warfare. Researchers noticed that agents such as DDT, while not immediately poisonous to humans, killed almost all insects. In the 1940s and 1950s it achieved extensive use as a pesticide on a wide variety of crops. Crop yields were dramatically increased. The battle against pests that preyed on grains, fruits, and vegetables seemed about to be won in a great burst of mid-twentieth-century optimism.

Silent Spring shattered that optimism forever. What was the triumph of science in the form of greater crop yields balanced against the poisoning of millions of birds? *Silent Spring* posed questions that are still relevant. How do we balance our industrial and agricultural needs with the dangers they pose to the environment? What is progress when synthetic chemicals that increase agricultural production also destroy the quality of life?

> Over increasingly large areas of the United States, spring now comes unheralded by the return of the birds, and the early mornings are strangely silent where once they were filled with the beauty of bird song.
>
> Rachel Carson, The Silent Spring, 1962

It was the poetry of Rachel Carson's writing that awakened the conscience of Americans as much as the rigor of her data. Ultimately she was using scientific inquiry as a way of educating her readers about the interrelatedness of all life. While she did not, as her detractors suggested, demand the end of pesticide use, she argued that scientists and politicians must be involved in studying the long-term effects of pesticides on nature, not just the short-term economic benefits. But her arguments were phrased in such a way as to arouse universal concern for nature. As she states in the concluding chapter of Silent Spring, "The 'control of nature' is a phrase conceived in arrogance, born of the Neanderthal age of biology and philosophy, when it was supposed that nature exists for the convenience of man. . . . It is our alarming misfortune that so primitive a science had armed itself with the most modern and terrible weapons, and that in turning them against the insects it has also turned them against the earth."

Rachel Carson.

Silent Spring set in motion events that led to the creation of the Environmental Defense Fund, which later became the Environmental Protection Agency. And while the process of bureaucracy moved with its customary slowness, DDT was finally banned in the United States in 1972. Its derivatives, aldrin and dieldrin, heptachlor and chlordane, were banned in 1975.

Pesticide companies, such as Monsanto, responded by claiming that without pesticide spraying, the world faced pestilence and famine. Time magazine called Silent Spring "unfair, one-sided, and hysterically over-emphatic." And of course, while over and over Carson's thesis has been found to be true, pesticide companies have continued to create new products that have continued the process of destruction. When the most dangerous pesticides are banned in the United States, they are sold in foreign markets, such as Mexico, where there is less regulation, and the resulting crops are exported back to supermarkets in the United States.

While she was attacked as an alarmist at the time Silent Spring was published, most scientists and environmentalists now believe her most dire predictions were understatements. The dangers posed by Peb, dioxin, and resistant strains of bacteria were unknown in 1962. Unknown also were the effects of fluorocarbons and carbon dioxides, which had led to ozone depletion and global warming. Forty years after the publication of Carson's The Sea around Us, estimates agree that most of the fish population has been depleted worldwide.

Rachel Carson lived modestly in Maryland and never married. When her niece died, she adopted and raised her niece's son. Her early career was spent working for the Bureau of Fisheries. The success of her first books, Under the Sea-Wind and The Sea around Us, the latter of which became a best-seller, allowed her the freedom to research and write full-time. She was, however, uncomfortable with celebrity and public advocacy. She died of breast cancer on April 14, 1964.

—D.C.

> It strains belief to know that Neil Armstrong can walk on the moon, 250,000 miles away, but that he cannot swim in Lake Erie, a few miles from his home.
>
> Edward M. Kennedy, January 26, 1970

Chapter 15

HEALTH

FOOD FIRSTS

1900—Hamburger: Birth of the twentieth century, birth of a twentieth-century icon at Louis Lunch, a three-seat lunch counter in New Haven, Connecticut. Louis Lassen ground up prime lean beef costing all of seven cents a pound, broiled it, and served it between slices of toast. Buns came later when hamburgers first met a wider public at the Saint Louis Exposition of 1904, but at Louis Lunch, which continues to flourish, the original burger-on-toast is still the order of the day.

1901—Peanut Vending Machines: These were first installed at the Pan-American Exposition at Buffalo by the Mills Novelty Company, those wonderful folk who also gave the world the one-arm bandit.

1901—Instant Coffee: A crude type of instant coffee in powdered form was sold from a stall at the Pan America Exhibition in Buffalo, New York, by Japanese-American Sartori Kato. This failed to convert housewives from the laborious traditional ways of making coffee, and it took a glut of coffee beans in Brazil in the early 1930s to effect the change. Unable to export the beans during the worldwide Great Depression, the Brazilians used them by the ton as fuel for steam locomotives. Then Brazil's Institute of Coffee decided a soluble coffee powder would help to revive the trade and asked the Swiss company Nestlé to help. The result, after several years of research, was Nescafé, an immediate success when it was launched in 1938.

1903—Decaffeinated Coffee: When German coffee wholesaler Ludwig Roselius received a shipload of coffee beans that had been soaked in seawater he thought it was a disaster. In fact it was the making of his fortune. The process he developed to restore the beans had the effect of removing the caffeine from them; so, making a virtue of necessity, he coined a special brand name for them—Sanka, a contraction of "sans

caffeine." In 1923 it was launched in the United States and "decaf" became part of the American way of life.

1903—Ice-Cream Cone: The first mold for producing cornets or cones for ice cream was patented by Italian ice-cream salesman Italo Marcioni of New Jersey on December 13, 1903. There are numerous claimants to the invention of the ice-cream cone, and various picturesque tales about its inception, but only Marcioni had a patent to prove his precedence.

1904—Milk Shake Maker: The electric shake mixer was introduced by George Schmidt and Fred Osius of Racine, Wisconsin.

1905—Pizzeria: Gennaro Lombardi established America's first pizza joint at 53½ Spring Street in New York City's Little Italy.

1906—Hot Dogs: English immigrant Harry Mosley Stevens held the ice-cream and soda pop concession at the Polo Grounds in New York, home of the New York Giants. One spring afternoon the fans were shivering with cold and the last thing anyone wanted was ice cream. Stevens reckoned they needed something hot, but it had to stay hot while his vendors went around the stands. The thought occurred to him that a German "dachshund" sausage would stay warm in its skin and warmer still encased in a roll. He summoned the vendors and told them to sweep the neighborhood for all the dachshund sausages they could find. "You've got to have a slogan to go with the sausage," Harry told his men. "Here's what I want you to yell. They're red hot. Get your dachshund sausages while they're red hot."

Attending the ball game that afternoon was New York's leading cartoonist, Tad Dorgan. Seeing the popularity of Harry Stevens's new fast-food idea, Dorgan decided it would make a cartoon. As he did not know how to spell dachshund, he called the sausage in a roll a "hot dog" and his cartoon showed two of them barking at each other. The name caught on and ultimately helped to make the product a success—but only after Stevens had quashed persistent rumors that the sausages were made of dog meat.

1906—Milk Cartons: Originally milk was dispensed straight from a pail into the customer's own jug. Later it came in bottles. Then in San Francisco in 1906 G. W. Maxwell introduced the waxed carton, a handier and more hygienic method of retailing milk.

1907—Canned Tuna: Imagine a world without tuna fish sandwiches or tuna fish salads. But they did not exist before A. P. Halfhill of San Pedro, California, began packing tuna in cans.

1908—Coffee Filters: The Melitta filter is one of the few eponymous inventions to bear the forename of its inventor rather than the surname. Melitta Bentz was a German housewife who wanted to make better-tasting coffee for her family and do it more quickly than a percolator. She pierced holes in the bottom of a tin can, cut out a disc of absorbent paper to line it with, piled ground coffee on top, poured on the boiling water—and had a perfect cup of coffee. The whole technique was developed in a matter of minutes and it was to reap her a fortune.

1910—Vichyssoise: This was another innovation that did not take long to develop. Soupe bon femme was popular at the Ritz-Carlton Hotel in New York. The chef, Louis Diat, figured it would taste just as good served cold on a summer's day. But would anyone be prepared to order cold soupe bon femme? They would if it was called something different, so vichyssoise it became.

1910—Electric Food Mixer: Although food mixers made little impact before the 1930s, they were produced as early as 1910 by the Hamilton Beach Manufacturing Company of Washington, North Carolina.

1910—Cona Coffee Maker: Melitta filters use a cone and Cona doesn't. In fact the name is derived from that of its inventor, Alfred Cohn of London, England. Cona was the first all-glass coffee maker.

1912—Combination Candy Bar: There had been chocolate bars with creme filling before and chocolate bars with nuts, but no chocolate-coated candy bars with a combination of fillings until the Standard Candy Company of Nashville, Tennessee, brewed up a mixture of marshmallow, caramel, and fresh-roasted peanuts in a copper kettle and enrobed the result in sweet milk chocolate. They called it the Goo Goo

Cluster and nobody can precisely remember why except that it had something to do with babies going goo-goo when they are happy. Goo Goo Clusters are still sold in Tennessee and neighboring states and fans who live elsewhere send in mail orders from as far away as Canada. The South's own candy bar found new fame when it was featured in Robert Altman's 1975 hit movie Nashville.

1912—Ready-Made Mayonnaise: If you wanted mayo before 1912, you made it yourself. Then Richard Hellman, proprietor of a Manhattan deli, began selling mayonnaise made to his own recipe in one-pound wooden "boats." He started packing Hellman's in glass jars the following year.

1914—Meal Served in an Airplane: Igor Sikorski is celebrated as the father of the helicopter. He also designed the world's first airliners. It was aboard one of these, the Ilya Mourometz, that a full meal with wines was served during a proving flight from Petrograd (now Saint Petersburg) in Russia to Kiev in Ukraine on June 29, 1914.

1915—Processed Cheese: James Lewis Kraft was a Canadian who went to Chicago at the age of sixteen and decided to dedicate his life to cheese. He determined to produce a cheese that would be long lasting, would be uniform in quality, would appeal to the American palate (that is, bland), and could be packaged without waste. After years of experimenting, he was ready to launch his American-Cheddar Process Cheese in Canada in 1915. Two years later, with America's entry into World War I, Uncle Sam became his biggest customer and processed cheese became a staple of life on the western front.

1916—Fortune Cookies: In China there was a parlor game played with miniature cakes containing messages. George Jung of the Hong Kong Noodle Company of Los Angeles adapted the idea to produce the first fortune cookies.

1919—Canned Grapefruit: Yankee Products Limited of Puerto Rico introduced canned grapefruit.

1919—Airline Meals: Passengers flying between London and Paris with Handley Page Transport were able to buy prepacked lunch boxes on the airplane for three shillings (seventy-five cents). Hot meals in the air were introduced by the French, when Air Union offered a five-course gourmet meal with wines in 1925.

1919—All-Bran: The high-fiber cereal All-Bran was launched by Kellogg's of Battle Creek, Michigan.

1920—Ice Cream On a Stick: Harry Burt pioneered ice cream on a stick when he launched his Good Humor Bar in January 1920.

1920—Bloody Mary: It was Fernand L. Petiot, bartender at Harry's New York Bar in Paris, who had the idea of mixing vodka and tomato juice and adding a dash of Worcestershire sauce. He changed the name to Bloody Mary when it did not move too fast under its original moniker—Bucket of Blood.

1921—Drive-In Restaurant: Dallas candy wholesaler J. G. Kirby figured "people with cars are so lazy they don't want to get out of them to eat." That Kirby had figured right was proved when he opened a pork barbecue eatery with attendant carhops on the Dallas–Fort Worth Highway. He called it the Pig Stand and within ten years he had a chain of the same name throughout the Midwest and on both the Pacific and Atlantic coasts.

1921—Chocolate-Covered Ice-Cream Bar: Christian K. Nelson was a teacher in Onawa, Iowa, who ran a candy store in his spare time. One day an eight-year-old boy, undecided between a chocolate bar and an ice cream, decided to have both. It was this which gave Nelson the idea of combining the two. He launched his ice-cream bar in 1921 as the I-Scream bar and coined the slogan "I scream, you scream, we all scream for ice cream." This became a hit song when it was set to music, but Nelson was worried that once the song was forgotten, so would the I-Scream bar. The new name he came up with endures to this day—Eskimo Pie.

1921—Burger Chain: Long before McDonald's, the White Castle chain stretched across America. It began with a weird-looking miniature castle opened by fry cook Walt Anderson and insurance agent Bill Ingram in Wichita, Kansas. And because their five-cent steamed hamburgers were on the small side, they dreamed up the slogan "Buy 'em by the sack." The secret of their success was absolute uniformity of product quality and service standards, so that visiting a White Castle was as reassuringly the same in Los Angeles or New York City as it was in Wichita.

1922—Canned Baby Food: Harold and Anna Clapp were the first to produce strained baby food in cans when they started preparing Clapp's Vegetable Soup in the kitchen of their restaurant in Rochester, New York. Large-scale production of canned baby foods was begun in 1929 by Gerber's, but sales dropped off when mothers sampled the salt-free preparations and declared them tasteless. Infants have insufficient sense of taste to know the difference, but Gerber's succumbed to matriarchal decree and added the unnecessary salt.

1923—Popsicle: Lemonade-mix salesman Frank Epperson had been demonstrating his product in New Jersey when he left a glass of it in front of an open window on a cold winter's night. In the morning the lemonade was frozen and when Epperson tugged on the spoon he had left in the glass he found he was holding the prototype Popsicle. The product was launched by the Joe Lowe food processing company, who bought the rights from Epperson.

1923—Canned Tomato Juice: Tomatoes had been packed in cans since the 1860s, but no one thought there was a market for tomato juice in cans until Libby's of Chicago proved that America was waiting for it.

1924—Caesar Salad: Caesar Gardini concocted this salad of romaine lettuce, coddled egg, Parmesan cheese, Worcestershire sauce, and garlic-flavored croutons for a party of Hollywood movie stars celebrating July 4 at his Caesar's Place restaurant in Tijuana, Mexico. (Anchovies and bleu cheese were a later variation.)

1926—Prepacked Yogurt: Known for its health-giving properties and believed to promote longevity, yogurt has been eaten since biblical times. When Barcelona yogurt maker Isaac Carasso settled in Paris, he decided he could only reach a wide market by packing it in cartons. Adding fruit for flavor, he launched the product as Dannone, derived from the name of his son Daniel. Stateside it became Dannon and helped to turn America health conscious in the 1960s.

1928—Sliced Bread: The father of the precut loaf was former jewelry store owner Otto Frederick Rohwedder, who had started work on a slicing machine back in 1912. When bakers told him that sliced bread would go stale too quickly, he devised an apparatus for holding the slices together with hat pins. Unfortunately, the pins kept falling out. The obvious solution of an overall wrapper was not so obvious, because wrapped bread did not exist. It was this, though, that proved the key to success, and in May 1928 a bakery in Battle Creek, Michigan, began turning out the first sliced bread, using Rohwedder's latest slicer, which also wrapped and sealed the loaf.

1929—Rice Krispies: The sound of snap, crackle, and pop was introduced to breakfast time by Kellogg's.

1929—Frozen Food: Clarence Birdseye is usually credited with inventing the frozen food process, but Dr. Archibald Huntsman of the Fisheries Experimental Station at Halifax, Nova Scotia, saw his deep-freezing process in commercial use a full year earlier than Birdseye. The world's first prepackaged frozen food product went on sale in one-pound packs labeled Fresh Ice Fillets in Toronto, Canada, in January 1929. This was haddock, but cod, halibut, flounder, swordfish, and cusk were soon added to the range. Meanwhile, on the other side of the border, Birdseye was completing negotiations with the Postum Company, who acquired the rights to his process for $22 million (Dr. Huntsman did not make a cent out of his because he was a government employee). The first Birds Eye frozen products, including meat, fish, vegetables, and fruit, went on sale at ten stores in Springfield, Massachusetts, on March 6, 1930. Although this was in the depths of the depression, within three years there were more than 500 frozen food outlets in the United States.

1929—7-Up: C. L. Grigg had been manufacturing an artificially flavored orange soda called Howdy since 1920 when new legislation, introduced at the behest of the citrus growers, required that real orange pulp be used. Grigg replaced Howdy with a new lemon-lime drink, which he called by what must surely be one of the most inept brand names of all time: Bib-Label Lithiated Lemon-Lime Soda. Wiser counsels prevailed and he was persuaded to change it to 7-Up. Many people have speculated about the significance of the seven. It is nothing more mysterious than the fact that Grigg's best-selling soda pop came in a seven-ounce bottle.

1930—Cereal Baby Food: Pablum was launched commercially by Mead Johnson. The precooked vitamin-enriched cereal had been devised as a strengthener for weakly infants by Canadian physician Dr. Alan Brown of the Toronto Hospital for Sick Children. He named it Pablum from the Latin word *pabulum*, meaning food. Royalties from the sale of Pablum went to the hospital's Pediatric Research Foundation.

1933—Chocolate Chip Cookies: Ruth Wakefield, owner of the Toll House Inn, in Whitman, Massachusetts, was in a hurry to make some butter drop-do's and rather than melt the chocolate in advance, she added chips of chocolate from a Nestlé semisweet bar to the dough, assuming they would melt while baking. To her surprise the chips stayed intact. Toll House cookies became so popular after the recipe had been published in a Boston newspaper that Nestlé was surprised to learn that sales of their semisweet chocolate had skyrocketed in the area. They responded by selling ready-made chocolate chips in packets and later bought the rights to the Toll House cookies recipe from Ruth Wakefield.

1934—Soft Ice Cream: Greek immigrant Thomas Carvelas of Yonkers, New York, borrowed fifteen dollars from his fiancée to buy an old truck from which he could peddle his "frozen custard." The investment paid off handsomely, with Carvel soft-ice-cream stands spreading throughout the northeastern United States.

1934—Pavlova: Unkindly described as Australia's only contribution to international cuisine, pavlova was created by Bert Sachse of the Esplanade Hotel in Perth, Western Australia. He added corn flour, vinegar, and vanilla to a meringue mixture and the result was, according to the Esplanade's manager, Harry Nairn, "as light as Pavlova."

1934—Cheeseburger: The marriage of a cheese slice and burger patty was consummated at Kaelen's burger bar in Louisville, Kentucky.

1935—Canned Beer: First to put beer in cans was the Krueger Brewing Company of Newark, New Jersey, who began test-marketing their Cream Ale this way in Richmond, Virginia, on January 24, 1935.

1937—Spam: It was to have been called Brunch, but the brother-in-law of Hormel's chairman came up with the idea of an acronym of shoulder pork and ham. It came into its own in World War II, feeding million of GIs, helped to keep Britain going through the rigors of rationing, and even sustained the Russian front. "Without Spam," wrote Nikita Khrushchev in his memoirs, "we shouldn't have been able to feed our army." And Ike sent a testimonial to the Hormel company when it was all over that just about summed up the feelings of everyone who had fought through to victory: "I ate my share of Spam along with millions of other soldiers. I'll even confess to a few unkind words about it— uttered during the strain of battle, you understand. But as the former Commander-in-Chief of the Allied Forces, I believe I can still forgive you for your only sin: sending us so much of it."

1938—Baked Potatoes with Toppings: It seems like an obvious idea, but nobody thought of it until Lawrence L. Frank offered the rich and famous of Beverly Hills the simple pleasure of baked potatoes with toppings of bacon, chives, cheese, and the like, at his Lawry's The Prime Rib Restaurant.

1939—Precooked Frozen Meals: Most people think that TV dinners were the first, when they were introduced in 1954, but fifteen years earlier Birds Eye had offered frozen chicken fricassee and frozen criss-cross steak. Before the end of 1939 other frozen-food manufacturers had added creamed chicken, beef stew, and roast turkey with dressing. Were they inspired by the fact that regular TV programming began that year?

1939—Home Freezer: Or maybe it was because General Electric had just introduced the first refrigerator with a freezer compartment.

1942—Sell-By Date: History does not record the first product pack with a sell-by date on it. But the earliest known is a carton of Lyons coffee, now preserved at the Museum of Advertising and Packaging in Gloucester, England, which is well past its sell-by date of October 17, 1942.

1943—Irish Coffee: The transatlantic flying boat service that had been inaugurated in 1939 by Pan American Airways continued during World War II for VIP passengers on urgent official business. Those arriving at the terminal in Foynes, on Ireland's Atlantic coast, had to brave a short, but nevertheless windswept and choppy, crossing by launch from the airplane to the shore. Joe Sheridan, chef of the Airport Building restaurant, watched them arriving shivering with cold. What they needed, he reasoned, was warming up. And what would warm them up better than hot coffee with a slug of Irish whiskey, topped with a head of whipped cream for that extra touch of Irish welcome? After the war, patrons of Joe Sheridan's concoction at Shannon Airport, as it had become, included George Bush and Fidel Castro. Irish coffee reached America in the 1950s via the Buena Vista bar on San Francisco's Fisherman's Wharf, where Joe Sheridan himself was later to work after his retirement from Shannon. It became so popular in the Bay Area that at one time consumption of Irish whiskey in San Francisco was actually higher than in the whole of Ireland.

1947—Food Product in Aerosol Can: The aerosol can had been invented in 1926 by a Norwegian named Eric Rotheim, but it took the American know-how of Reddi-Whip Incorporated to shovel aerated whipped cream into it.

1947—Frozen Orange Juice Concentrate: A citrus cooperative in Lake Wales, Florida, produced the first orange juice that you could keep until you needed it.

1948—McDonald's: Richard and Maurice McDonald decided to convert their drive-in restaurant on E Street in San Bernardino, California, to self-service in December 1948. They offered fast food—with burgers at fifteen cents, fries at ten cents, and shakes at twenty cents—fast service, and no frills (crockery out, cutlery out). The rest was history.

1952—Coffee Creamer: Coffee has not tasted the same since the introduction of Pream by M and R Dietetic Laboratories of Columbus, Ohio.

1952—Diet Soda Pop: No-Cal Ginger Ale was the first soft drink sweetened with cyclamates, which were banned in the United States after tests on rats fed with the sugar substitute showed a high incidence of bladder cancer. It was introduced by Kirsch Beverages of Brooklyn, New York.

1962—Tab-Opening Drink Can: Ermal Clayton Fraze of Dayton, Ohio, was on a family picnic in 1959 when, like so many other fathers, he found he had left the can opener behind. To open a can of beer he had to bash it against the fender of his car, losing half the contents as the top caved in. There had to be a better way and Ermal found it. His tab-opening all-aluminum can was introduced in 1962, when it was adopted for Pittsburgh's Iron City Beer.

1975—Cereal Bar: General Mills introduced high-fiber Nature Valley Granola Bars. They came in coconut, cinnamon, and oats 'n' honey flavors.

1982—Diet Coke: Thirty years after the advent of the first diet soda the mighty Coca-Cola Company allowed the word *Coke* to be linked to the word *diet* for the first time.

1986—Nicotine Chewing Gum: If willpower failed, smokers could get a nicotine fix from Nicoret. It was developed by Pharmacia Les Therapeutics AB in Sweden.

1991—Edible Tableware: From Taipei in Taiwan has come the answer to the dishwashing menace. You eat your meal from plates made of compressed oatmeal. Then you eat the plates.

—**P.H.R.**

QUOTEBOOK

ALCOHOLISM

Alcoholism isn't a spectator sport. Eventually the whole family gets to play.
Joyce Rebeta-Burditt, The Cracker Factory, 1977

Alcohol is like love: the first kiss is magic, the second is intimate, the third is routine. After that you just take the girl's clothes off.
Raymond Chandler, The Long Goodbye, 1953

My dad was the town drunk. A lot of times that's not so bad—but New York City?
Henny Youngman, Henny Youngman's Greatest One Liners, 1970

Work is the curse of the drinking classes.
Oscar Wilde, attributed, 1900

Abstainer, n.: a weak person who yields to the temptation of denying himself a pleasure.
Ambrose Bierce, The Devil's Dictionary, 1911

If you resolve to give up smoking, drinking and loving, you don't actually live longer, it just seems longer.
                Clement Freud, quoted in the *Observer*, 1964

The beneficial effects of the regular quarter of an hour's exercise before breakfast is more than offset by the mental wear and tear in getting out of bed fifteen minutes earlier than one otherwise would.
                Simeon Strunsky, *The Patient Observer and His Friends*, 1911

EXERCISE

I believe every human has a finite number of heartbeats. I don't intend to waste any of mine running around doing exercises.
                Neil Armstrong

The only reason I would take up jogging is so that I could hear heavy breathing again.
                Erma Bombeck

DEADLY DISEASES

AIDS

As enigmatic as it is deadly, acquired immune deficiency syndrome (AIDS) is a progressive, degenerative disease that afflicts the immune system as well as other major organ systems. AIDS appears to have begun its worldwide onslaught in the late 1970s and early 1980s.

The human immunodeficiency virus (HIV) is generally believed to be the cause of AIDS. The virus infects T-lymphocytes (T-cells), which are a variety of white blood cells that perform essential roles in mounting an effective immune defense. In what amounts to a molecular hijacking, HIV inserts its own set of genetic instructions into the T-cells' chromosomes. Once the infected lymphocytes have been reprogrammed, they can be living factories that help churn out hundreds of new copies of the virus. Some of the host cells are killed in the process, while others can survive and serve as HIV storehouses. There is no way to delete the embedded viral programming without destroying the host. HIV can also infect other cell types, including some located in the brain. Although AIDS patients can die from the damage inflicted directly by HIV, many succumb to secondary infections that overwhelm the weakened immune system. Standard treatments include the drugs azidothymidine (AZT) and dideoxyinosine (DDI), which are highly toxic and of limited efficacy.

HIV can be transmitted through exposure to infected blood or other bodily fluids. The most common modes of transmission include unprotected sexual contact with infected individuals and the sharing of needles among intravenous drug users. The virus can also be passed along during transfusions of infected blood products and from mother to child before or during birth or during breastfeeding. In the United States, the Caribbean, and Europe, the disease originally spread rapidly through homosexual men and intravenous drug users. However, it has become increasingly prevalent in the heterosexual populations. In Africa and Asia, AIDS spreads primarily in heterosexuals. In 1995 it was estimated that about one-half million people in the United States had full-blown AIDS and that globally the disease had stricken 4.5 million and had killed 1 million. Approximately 20 million people worldwide were infected with HIV by 1995, and it was predicted that number would climb to between 40 and 110 million by the year 2000.

You're not just sleeping with one person, you're sleeping with everyone they ever slept with.
        Theresa Crenshaw, *Men, Women, Sex and AIDS*, NBC-TV, January 13, 1987

ORIGINS AND EARLY SPREAD
The origins of AIDS remain unclear and largely a matter of conjecture. Some scientists think HIV may have developed from a virus harbored in African monkeys that eventually made its way into the human population. Others believe that HIV has been present for centuries in small undetected pockets scattered around the world. There are two major types of HIV (HIV-1 and HIV-2). The former is predominant in North America and Europe, whereas the latter is considered rare outside of West Africa.

In the late 1970s and early 1980s, a few American physicians began noticing that some of their previously healthy homosexual patients had developed Pneumocystis carinii pneumonia (PCP) and Kaposi's sarcoma—two diseases that can signal a malfunctioning immune system.

Epidemiologists with the U.S. Centers for Disease Control in Atlanta, Georgia, as well as other investigators began searching for the causes and sources of the disease. Gaetan

Gaetan Dugas, an Air Canada flight attendant, became known as "Patient Zero" because he was the first person to be recognized as a major transmitter of AIDS. He died of the disease on March 30, 1984.

Dugas, a gay Air Canada flight attendant, became a notorious figure in the early efforts to track the disease's spread across the United States. Nicknamed "Patient Zero," Dugas, who was diagnosed with the disease, reportedly had about 250 sexual partners a year as he traveled across the country. Despite being warned that he presented a serious risk to others, he continued to have unprotected sex until his death in 1984 at the age of thirty-two.

RESEARCH AND CONTROVERSY
The intense search for the cause of AIDS in the early eighties ignited a bitter dispute between French and American virologists and cast a shadow over the scientific conduct of Robert Gallo (b. 1937), a National Institutes of Health researcher. In 1983 a team of researchers working at the Pasteur Institute in France under Luc Montagnier (b. 1932) announced that they had isolated the virus responsible for AIDS. However, Gallo expressed skepticism about the report and said that AIDS was caused by a kind of leukemia virus or HTLV (human T-lymphotropic virus). The following year, Gallo stated that he had discovered the virus responsible for AIDS. However, it turned out not to be a member of the HTLV family. Instead, it was the same virus the French had identified earlier. During the protracted battle, Gallo denied deliberately appropriating the French samples. An agreement was finally reached that lists Montagnier and Gallo as "codiscoverers" of the virus.

Although most scientists believe HIV is the cause of AIDS, a vocal minority, including controversial University of California, Berkeley, biologist Peter Duesberg, argues there are other factors involved. They believe this is part of the

reason the search for a vaccine and effective drugs to combat AIDS has been disappointing. Nevertheless, in October 1994 the World Health Organization announced plans for a large-scale trial of an HIV vaccine. And in 1995 a U.S. Food and Drug Administration advisory panel recommended trials on 5,000 volunteers of a vaccine developed by Dr. Jonas Salk. If Salk's treatment is proved to be effective, he will have helped stop two deadly diseases in the twentieth century (see "Polio," page 604).

—H.X.W.

CANCER

Cancer comprises more than 150 related diseases, all caused by uncontrolled growth of abnormal cells within the body. These cellular renegades can arise from tissues ranging from skin to bone and are able to invade and destroy surrounding normal cells. In a process called metastasis, they enter the bloodstream or lymphatic system and migrate to various areas of the body. Once implanted in these other regions, they can form new colonies. As the disease progresses, the aberrant cells bear less resemblance to the tissues from which they originated.

Not all tumors are considered cancerous. Localized swellings that do not penetrate other tissues or metastasize are known as benign tumors. These noncancerous overgrowths, as the name implies, are relatively harmless and often readily removed by surgery. Malignant tumors, on the other hand, are more aggressive, invasive, and mobile.

Malignancies are classified into two major types: carcinomas and sarcomas. The former come from epithelial tissue such as the skin, as well as the linings of the mouth, stomach, and lungs. The latter develop from fibrous connective tissue as well as from muscle, fat, and cartilage. Although leukemias and lymphomas can be viewed as subsets of cancers of the connective tissues, they are typically classified separately.

Cancer mortality varies in different regions of the world. A 1990 comparison of fifteen developed nations revealed that the Scandinavian countries and Japan had some of the lowest mortality rates, while France and Scotland had some of the highest. In these age-adjusted mortality figures for men and women aged thirty-five to seventy-five, the United States had a tenth-place rank. U.S. males had a death rate of 315.3 per 100,000, compared with 228.0 for females.

PRE-1900 KNOWLEDGE AND TREATMENT
The emergence of cancer may predate recorded history. There is evidence in fossilized bones

suggesting that some dinosaurs may have been afflicted with the disease. Malignant tumors have been found in 5,000-year-old Egyptian mummies, and descriptions of cancer cases appear in medical writings found on 3,500-year-old papyrus records. The ancient Greeks thought these tumors had a crablike appearance, a fact reflected in the name "cancer," which comes from *karkínos*, the Greek word for crab.

In 1775 Percival Potts, an English surgeon, was the first to recognize that cancer could be caused by an external substance. He believed that the high incidence of scrotal cancer among young chimney sweeps was due to their constant exposure to the soot in the flues.

During the same period, many physicians thought tumors were formed by substances in the blood. Another English surgeon, John Hunter, called the substance coagulating lymph. Cancer treatments often included such techniques as bloodletting and cauterizations.

POST-1900 DISCOVERIES

Because cancer is not a single disease and does not stem from a single cause, research in the field has been complicated and occasionally contentious. Scientists have found a myriad of different environmental and genetic factors that can, to varying degrees, influence the development of malignant tumors. The external agents include ionizing radiation, assorted chemicals, and certain viruses. Inside the body, several genes have been identified that can transform normal cells into potential killers.

In the early 1900s there was a pervasive view that cancer was essentially a hereditary disease. Many researchers dismissed the notion that infectious agents could play a role in the development of the illness. However, in 1911 an American physician, Francis Peyton Rous (1879–1970), demonstrated that a virus (the Rous avian sarcoma virus, or RSV) was able to induce muscle tumors in chickens. Some pathologists and geneticists felt Rous's work undermined their own theories about the hereditary basis of cancer. In addition, some researchers had difficulty replicating Rous's results. Consequently, he was condemned by some scientists and his work was ignored for decades. However, his efforts were finally rewarded in 1966 with a Nobel Prize.

Although Percival Potts made his groundbreaking observations about the influence of chimney soot on cancer in 1775, many important carcinogenic substances were not identified until the second half of the twentieth century. In 1957, for example, Surgeon General Leroy E. Burney reported that scientific studies on cigarettes showed a "direct relationship between the incidence of lung cancer and the amount smoked." Hundreds of chemicals, both manmade and naturally occurring, have been

shown to produce tumors in laboratory animals, and many of these are carcinogenic to humans as well. Substances implicated in human cancer range from PCBs (a group of chemicals used in paints, adhesives, and batteries) to aflatoxin (a substance produced by fungi that grow on peanuts and other plants).

Evidence of the cancer-causing properties of radiation first began to emerge at the beginning of the 1900s, when physicians who used X rays and radium in their practices began developing cancer. Other forms of radiation have been identified as potential threats. Chronic, unprotected exposure to ultraviolet light from the sun is considered a risk factor in the development of skin cancer, particularly for light-skinned individuals.

Damage to the body's cells, whether it's from viruses, chemicals, or radiation, can trigger a cascade of events that lead to cancer. Mutations to the cells' genetic blueprint, or DNA, are believed to be central to this process. Scientists have begun to focus on a specific set of genes, called oncogenes, that regulate various aspects of cell division. When oncogenes are altered, normal functions can go awry and lead to the uncontrolled growth associated with cancer. Some individuals may inherit copies of these genes, making them especially vulnerable to developing certain forms of the disease.

People who have cancer typically undergo a variety of treatments aimed at eradicating the abnormal cells. Therapies include surgically removing tumors, bombarding cancer cells with radiation, or destroying them with potent drugs. However, scientists are searching for other kinds of approaches that are more targeted and less debilitating to the patients.

Beginning in the 1970s, researchers began to find ways to help stimulate the patient's immune system to quash the cellular rebellion. Diseases such as pancreatic cancer and melanoma have been experimentally treated by inoculating patients with vaccines made from their own inactivated tumor cells. These vaccines are believed to give the immune system an edge in combating the often well protected cancer cells.

Cancer researchers have also turned to oncogenes in the hope they may offer insights into new ways to treat the disease. Among the genes that have received the most attention are p16, p53, and MTSI. Molecular biologists believe that by studying the kinds of proteins they help produce, it may be possible to develop new generations of drugs that could halt the growth of malignant cells. This trend in research is not so much to find ways to destroy the aberrant cells with highly toxic compounds as to devise drugs that can alter the cells' life cycle and induce them to shut down on their own.

As the tools of molecular biologists continue to improve, they will have more ways to keep the rebellious cells in check.

—H.X.W.

DIABETES MELLITUS

Diabetes is the fourth most deadly disease in the United States, killing more than 160,000 people each year. Worldwide data are sketchy, but this disease is definitely global, though unevenly distributed. It is prevalent in northern Europe and rare in Asia—yet recent outbreaks have occurred in New Zealand and Japan. It is more common among certain ethnic groups, including African Americans, Hispanics, American Indians, Australian Aborigines, Polynesians, and Middle Eastern populations.

Diabetes is a failure to metabolize carbohydrates. Normally, digestion converts carbohydrates in food into sugar (glucose), and the pancreas releases a hormone called insulin that allows the body's cells to use the glucose for food. Without insulin, glucose builds up in the blood. Meanwhile, the starved cells turn to fat for fuel, which results in abnormally high acid levels in blood and tissues. If untreated, a diabetic will fall into a coma or waste away. Even with modern treatment to control blood sugar, diabetes affects the blood vessels and eventually can cause strokes, heart attacks, kidney failure, and blindness. It also degenerates nerves, causing numbness in hands and feet. Diabetes takes two forms. Juvenile (type I) diabetes, which strikes children, is less common but more serious because the pancreas produces no insulin. Most diabetics have maturity onset (type II) diabetes, often associated with obesity and sedentary lifestyles. They either do not produce enough insulin or cannot use what they produce. Though easier to treat, type II diabetes can result in the same severe complications as type I diabetes.

PRE-1900 KNOWLEDGE AND TREATMENT
Physicians in ancient Egypt, India, China, Japan, and Rome all recognized the symptoms of diabetes: excessive thirst and copious urine (as the body tries to wash out glucose) and weight loss (as the body burns fat and protein to stay alive). But they didn't know its cause and had no treatment. Diabetes meant death.

English physician Thomas Willis (1621–75) found a significant clue when he noticed that the urine of diabetics tasted sweet. In 1889 German physicians Joseph von Mering (1849–1908) and Oskar Minkowski (1858–1931) experimented with dogs to confirm the suspected link between diabetes and the pancreas. English scientist Sir Edward Sharpey-Schäfer (1850–1935) identified insulin as the relevant hormone.

POST-1900 DISCOVERIES
Until the 1920s, diabetes treatment was as grim as the disease. Dr. Frederick M. Allen (1879–1964), of the Rockefeller Institute in New York, noted that diabetics had trouble metabolizing all food, so he prescribed—dieting. For his skeletal patients, Allen prescribed liquid fasts followed by strict low-calorie regimes, plus strenuous daily exercise.

The breakthrough came in 1921 when Canadian doctors Frederick Grant Banting (1891–1941) and John J. R. Macleod (1876–1935) discovered insulin. For this work they shared the 1923 Nobel Prize for physiology and medicine—though by then the two were barely speaking. Macleod had sponsored Banting and his assistant, Charles Best, as they developed and tested insulin using dogs. But Macleod asked Dr. J. B. Collip (1892–1965) to develop a purified extract for human testing. Banting believed those two were stealing his research; Macleod and Collip thought Banting was paranoid.

Caught in the middle was Leonard Thompson, a fourteen-year-old charity patient whom Allen's treatment had already reduced to sixty-five pounds. First Banting and Best injected Thompson with their insulin extract, a "thick brown muck" derived from ground beef pancreas. It had little effect. Meanwhile, Collip, who practiced what he himself called "bathtub chemistry," developed a better extract. With this, Thompson improved. But Collip refused to share his process with Banting, and the two quarreled, apparently coming to blows. A frigid truce came only after all four men signed a pact forbidding them from patenting one another's work.

Banting carried out medical research until his death in a wartime air crash. Frederick Allen developed another diabetes treatment, Myrtillin, an extract of mulberry leaves based on an Austrian folk remedy, which also failed. Leonard Thompson grew to adulthood, became a factory assistant, and died at twenty-seven from pneumonia complications.

Today research is leading to better treatment for diabetes. Extensive clinical tests completed in 1993 show that diabetics who monitor their glucose levels and take insulin several times a day can reduce diabetic complications by 50 to 75 percent. New drugs, plus treatment such as pancreatic cell injections, are also being tried. Most important, scientists are beginning to understand the causes of diabetes. In 1994 Oxford University researchers identified at least eighteen genes that together lead to the onset of type 1 diabetes; people with a genetic predisposition then become diabetic after something, such as a virus, triggers the immune system to attack the pancreas. Armed with this knowledge, researchers hope they can eventually prevent the attack from ever happening.

—H.L.R.

HEART DISEASE

Heart disease is the world's number one killer. The term *heart disease* encompasses a variety of diseases, including heart attacks (heart failure), diseases of heart rate (such as arrhythmia), problems with blood pressure, and various stenoses (narrowing of the arteries). Our knowledge of the heart and its functions, and how to treat its various ailments, was poorly understood through most of human history. The greatest advances have come in only the last 150 years.

The causes of heart disease have changed little through history. Stress, diet, smoking, and level of activity all play a role in coronary health. To understand heart disease is to understand the history of man's attempts at learning about the heart and the ways to diagnose and treat heart disease. This progress is interwoven with the development of technologies that made possible increasingly detailed observation of the heart. Without these technologies, much of what today is common knowledge would remain hidden from observation, greatly limiting diagnosis and treatments.

PRE-1900 KNOWLEDGE AND TREATMENT

In 1628 Englishman William Harvey published an accurate description of the heart as a pump that circulates blood, but most physicians still believed that blood ebbed and flowed like the tides. Harvey's work was reinforced by Marcelo Malpighi in 1661, when he proved the existence of the microscopic vessels that circulate the blood.

In 1816, to better hear the "clacking" that Harvey had described when he put his ear to a patient's chest, René Laënnec invented the stethoscope, one of the most important tools used in diagnosing heart disease. His first form of the instrument was a rolled up paper tube, and it remained a rigid device until the advent of vulcanized rubber. In 1852 George Cammann refined the stethoscope to its modern form.

One of the first drugs used to treat heart disease was digitalis. An eighteenth-century physician, William Withering, studied a remedy for dropsy that had been devised by an old woman in Shropshire, England. The active ingredient in her concoction was foxglove (digitalis), and Withering correctly surmised that it slowed the pulse rate. Unfortunately, in the wrong dose, it also killed patients.

Early research into the electrical functions and dysfunctions of the heart centered on developing more sensitive instruments to measure heart activity without surgery. In the late 1700s, Alessandro Volta and Luigi Galvani contributed to the discovery that the heart produces its own electricity and beats involuntarily. (Surprisingly, it was not until 1952 that electric shock was first used to restart a pa-

tient's heart.) In the 1870s, French physicist Gabriel Lippmann developed the "capillary electrometer," which measured small electrical voltages; Augustus Waller, another French scientist, used Lippmann's device to measure electrical changes within the heart.

POST-1900 DISCOVERIES

By 1903 the capillary electrometer was refined into a "galvanometer," a more sensitive device capable of recording the heart's electrical impulses. In 1924 Willem Einthoven received the Nobel Prize for this device, which is now known as the electrocardiograph.

The 1960s and 1970s saw technological advances and refinements in surgical techniques, the use of drug therapy, and scientifically informed preventative care.

Drug therapy involved the use of diuretics, anticlotting agents (such as aspirin), and others such as adrenaline (first used in 1905 to restart the heart). Though many of these compounds were developed much earlier, it has only been in the twentieth century that they have seen direct use as cardiac care agents. Many, such as digitalis (now safely used to control heart rate), reserpine (for hypertension), and quinidine (an antiarrhythmic), were botanically derived. However, the greatest gains came with the advent of the "synthetic chemist." This new breed of chemist could produce exotic agents that could target the area needing treatment.

The first successful open-heart surgery was performed on an animal in 1914 by Dr. Alexis Carrel. However, successful operations on humans eluded medicine for some fifty years more. The 1950s saw the advent of heart massage (1950), the mechanical heart (1952), and the heart-lung machine (1953). By 1960 the pacemaker was finally developed.

In 1967 South African surgeon Christiaan Barnard performed the first heart transplant on Louis Washkansky, who lived for eighteen days. A year later Dr. Denton Cooley performed seventeen successful heart transplants. On July 11, 1994, Dirk van Zyl, the longest-lived heart-transplant survivor and a patient of Barnard's, died at the age of sixty-eight. Zyl, who received his new heart in 1971, lived a record twenty-three years after the surgery. Worldwide, about 3,500 heart transplants are now performed each year—most in the United States.

The first totally artificial heart was made of Dacron and was successfully implanted by Cooley in 1969. The longest-lived recipient of an artificial heart was William J. Schroeder, who survived for nearly two years before dying in 1986.

The first nonhuman heart implant took place in 1984 with great controversy. Baby Fae, a fifteen-month-old baby girl, received a baboon's heart and lived for nearly a month.

A whole new branch of treatment known as interventional also arose. *Interventional* refers to any treatment that uses cardiac catheterization. These treatments include the now widely used angioplasty. A probe is inserted through the arteries via a catheter and is then ballooned in order to reexpand a narrowed artery.

The modern cardiologist must be able to attack heart disease on many levels. In 1961 the American Medical Association linked smoking, diet (especially the consumption of excess sugars and animal fats), and stress to heart disease, which led to better preventive care. The common aspirin is also proving to be a powerful ally. Results of surveys in the early 1990s bolster evidence that there is a lowered occurrence of heart disease for individuals who maintain a controlled daily dosage of aspirin. As with progress in the past, time, experience, and perseverance will be our greatest weapons against this age-old widespread disease.

—M.E.R.

MALARIA

While malaria lacks the public relations of cancer and AIDS, it is the world's major infectious disease. More than 2 billion people are presently at risk. There are 100 million cases of malaria each year, and more than 2 million die of the disease. It was once thought that the disease could be controlled by spraying DDT to kill the mosquitoes and using quinine or chloroquinine to prevent and cure it. The mosquito that causes malaria, however, has developed resistance to DDT, and the parasite is now resistant to all known drugs. Symptoms of the disease include repeated attacks of shaking, high fevers, headache, and profuse sweating.

The parasite, *Plasmodium*, which causes malaria in humans, is carried by the female anopheles mosquito. When an infected mosquito bites a person, it injects a form of the parasite known as a sporozoite. The sporozoite enters the bloodstream and quickly invades the liver. There it begins to divide, eventually invading the red blood cells where it multiplies and begins to cause symptoms. When the red blood cells rupture, male and female forms of the parasite, called gametocytes at this stage, are released. These gametocytes do not mate in humans, but when another mosquito comes along and takes a meal of blood, they hitch a ride and, inside the insect's stomach, they fuse to form a fertilized egg cell. The cycle continues when the egg develops into a sporozoite, which migrates to the mosquito's salivary glands, from where it can be injected into the next human the mosquito bites.

PRE-1900 KNOWLEDGE AND TREATMENT
Malaria is one of the oldest diseases known to man. It existed in ancient China and Mesopota-

mia. In the fifth century B.C., Hippocrates described the different forms of fever. It is mentioned in Greek, Roman, Indian, and Chinese medical records. The name malaria comes from the Italian for "bad air," for it was associated with humid, swampy regions of Italy. Early Roman public works involved the draining of swamps and the securing of sources of pure water.

It is also both a result and a cause of poverty and economic and social decline. It follows behind war, famine, and social disintegration, creating a devastating downward spiral. When the use and care of the land declines, it favors the emergence and transmission of the disease, which creates further neglect of the land.

The first relief came in the 1500s when a Peruvian chief offered the bark of the "fever tree" to a Jesuit missionary, Juan Lopez. The bark of the cinchona tree is the source of quinine, which gave Europeans their first hope. Even with quinine and improved living conditions, malaria provoked major disasters during the nineteenth and early twentieth centuries. It was a major factor in the monumental difficulties encountered during the building of the Panama Canal and the Mamore-Madeira Railway in Brazil, of which it is said that one worker died for each tie laid. A further irony is that, while the Peruvian chief offered the first cure, it was the European explorers who imported the disease to the Americas.

It was only in 1880 that a French physician, Charles Laveran, while stationed in Algeria, noted unusual shapes in the red blood cells of malaria patients. In 1897 a British army physician, Ronald Ross, while stationed in India, confirmed the relationship of mosquito and parasite.

POST-1900 DISCOVERIES
From the late seventeenth century until 1920, quinine was the only specific drug available to combat the symptoms of malaria. After 1920 synthetic drugs chloroquinine and mafloquinine came into use. These drugs, however, gave relief only from the symptoms of the disease, not the cause. Only eradication of the anopheles mosquito could offer a way to control the disease, and in the 1950s and 1960s the World Health Organization launched a worldwide campaign using the insecticide DDT to kill anopheles. The disease disappeared in several countries but returned when the mosquito became DDT resistant. DDT was banned in 1972 after it was shown to be poisonous to humans and animals. Since the 1970s, owing to reduced insecticide use, mosquito resistance, and the downward economic spiral in tropical African nations, malaria has continued to affect mass populations.

Only in the last few years has there been any success in the discovery of a vaccine. A Colombian biochemist, Manuel Patarroyo, claims that preliminary indications show that his vaccine has been from 30 to 60 percent effective in tests conducted in Gambia. In the meantime, the most successful program has been the decidedly low-tech approach of soaking mosquito nets in insecticide.

The final irony is that just as a successful vaccine seems within grasp, the U.S. government is drastically cutting malarial research funding for the Agency for International Development as part of its budget-reduction package.

Medical researchers and health officials agree that resistant strains of viral, bacterial, and parasitic infections now pose the greatest threat to human populations. They caution that by the year 2000, humankind will have returned to a preantibiotic condition, a condition where diseases will mutate faster than scientists can design drugs to treat them. Malaria will be, for the foreseeable future, in the vanguard of those diseases.

—D.C.

POLIO

Poliomyelitis is an infectious disease caused by a virus, the kind of microorganism that produces chicken pox, measles, influenza, warts, and acquired immune deficiency syndrome. Actually, there are three different forms of polio, each traceable to a particular form of the virus, but only one of them penetrates the central nervous system's brain and spinal cord, destroying motor nerve cells and causing lasting paralysis and even asphyxiation. This is the type that swept through the United States during the 1940s and 1950s, infecting millions and leaving some 640,000 "polios" or paralyzed children.

The virus almost always enters the body through the mouth and lodges in the warm, moist environment of the throat and intestinal tract, where it continues to reproduce itself. In the best-case scenario, the virus is stopped in its tracks by the body's immune response, causing no effects whatsoever or, at most, a short bout of fever. At worst, it paralyzes. In either case, some of the virus is excreted in the stool and passed hand-to-hand or hand-to-mouth by people who do not wash their hands often or well enough.

Advances in hygiene at the turn of the nineteenth century inadvertently led to polio. Before that time, open sewers were everywhere, exposing infants, who rarely suffered from paralysis but did, on the other hand, develop antibodies that gave lasting immunity. Before the introduction of polio vaccines, virtually 100 percent of the population in densely populated European and American cities with poor sanitation acquired immunity to all three polio viruses by six years of age. As public health

officials cleaned and closed the sewers, the threat of polio grew. The first U.S. epidemic was in New York City in 1916 and after that not a year passed without an epidemic somewhere. The tolls were terrible: 27,000 people were paralyzed in the epidemic of 1916, and 6,000 of them died. Twenty-five thousand cases of polio were reported in 1946, 58,000 in 1952, 35,000 in 1953. Then, suddenly, the epidemic ended, vanquished by a vaccine that, by 1957, had reduced the number of reported cases to 5,000, and to 3,000 in 1960.

In 1985 the World Health Organization (WHO) launched a campaign to eradicate polio in the Americas by the year 2000. Since 1994 no case of poliomyelitis due to wild polio virus has been reported in the Western Hemisphere, and transmission of these viruses is disappearing from Europe, North Africa, southern Africa, the Middle East, China, and the Pacific. In 1992, 15,587 cases of poliomyelitis were reported throughout the world, although WHO estimates that the actual number of cases may be as high as 140,000.

PRE-1900 KNOWLEDGE AND TREATMENT
Before the discovery of the polio virus in 1908, treatment was based on conjecture and recovery was strictly by chance. Not knowing what the disease was made it difficult to name it. The name that stuck—from its first use in the late 1700s as a kind of observation—was infantile paralysis. It wasn't necessary to explain the disease, the terrifying image was enough.

Physicians of the day considered diagnosis inconsequential; it was their job to do something "useful" for patients. Consequently, they simply accepted and perpetuated the notion that the paralysis had something to do with teething in infants. The great English author Sir Walter Scott (1771–1832), who was afflicted with the "lameness" in 1773, later wrote of the "fever which often accompanies the cutting of large teeth," which held him for three days and left him with a shrunken and contracted leg. The teething theory lasted well into the 1800s. During that time plenty of children cut their teeth and never suffered from paralysis at all.

The few who did try to determine a reason for the paralysis had definite opinions—most of them differing. One London surgeon, John Shaw (1792–1827), got it backward with his theory that paralysis and wasting of the limbs during infancy "frequently produce distortion of the spine." Finally, the German orthopedist Jacob von Heine (1800–79) set the record straight with a seventy-eight page volume with seven lithographed full-page plates, mostly illustrating the condition of affected limbs before and after correction, in addition to the apparatus with which the treatment was done. He concluded that, all in all, these symptoms "point to an affection of the central nervous system, namely the spinal cord." So impressive was his work that subsequent writers named the paralysis Heine-Medin disease, a name that held for more than a dozen years. By the late 1800s, though, the accepted medical term was poliomyelitis from the Greek for "inflammation of the gray marrow."

Meanwhile children were bled, either by leeches or cut cups, and blistered and burned with a red-hot iron to produce a scab and then an ulcerous sore. Finally, in 1880 in his *Principles and Practice of Medicine,* Dr. William Osler (1849–1919) castigated the medical treatments as "medieval."

POST-1900 DISCOVERIES
At the turn of the century, virology was in its infancy. Experiments in Vienna in 1908 and in New York in 1909 suggested that polio was an infectious disease. But nobody knew what caused the infection or why it struck children. And for four decades nobody bothered to find out.

In 1948 Dr. Jonas Edward Salk (1914–1995), an American virologist, was put in charge of the virus-typing project at the University of Pittsburgh, which would ultimately confirm that there were no more than three types of polio virus.

Salk saw the potential for a vaccine that not only would save children but might also make him a hero and allow him to leave his $4,700-a-year job. His objective was a killed-virus vaccine, which inactivates the virus by heat, radiation, or a formaldehyde bath so that it is no longer capable of reproducing within the living cell. The foreign virus—dead or alive—should stimulate an antibody response; the trick is to be sure that every single virus particle in the vaccine is really dead. By contrast, live-virus vaccines are made from viruses that are bred in a laboratory or in an animal to be weaker and weaker, until they will produce antibodies but not the disease itself. The live-virus vaccine offers stronger, longer-lasting immunity than the killed version. Moreover, it offers "herd immunity" on the unvaccinated population as well. For several weeks after immunization the live vaccine replicates in the gut and can be passed on to other people the child comes in contact with, providing indirect immunization.

From the start, the scientific community was polarized. But Salk, undaunted, pushed forward. In 1953 the vaccine was ready for its debut. Officially the Salk polio vaccine was introduced on April 26, 1954, in a field trial that eventually involved more than 650,000 children in 211 health districts of forty-four states. Unofficially, as he later admitted, Salk tested the vaccine on himself. The field trial—conducted on the basis of three successful smaller trials—was designed to confirm the safety and efficacy of the vaccine for the medical community. For the public, however, the answer was already in.

Dr. Jonas Salk, seen here in his laboratory, gained international celebrity as the discoverer of the polio vaccine.

In September 1954 Salk and almost every other virologist and polio epidemiologist in the world met in Rome for the Third International Poliomyelitis Conference. From the start, the austere scientific conference took on the aura of a back-room political caucus as live-virus and killed-virus proponents tried to manipulate the neutral members of the meeting to join their camps. Salk was devastated and refused to attend subsequent meetings.

Critics continued to hammer away at the safety issue. Even before the field trials were launched, concerns were planted in the public mind by news broadcaster Walter Winchell, who announced that the new vaccine contained deadly live virus and that the National Foundation for Infantile Paralysis was stockpiling little white coffins in depots around the country to be ready for the children who would be killed during the field trial.

Then in 1955 came the "Cutter incident," named after one of the manufacturers of the vaccine, in which some of the virus wasn't killed and more than 250 people got polio. Nothing like this ever happened again, but suddenly the image was tarnished.

The climate was right for a new vaccine, and Dr. Albert Sabin (1906–93) was already at work on a live vaccine that had the added advantage of eliminating the use of needles, which terrified children because they hurt and doctors because they carried a risk of contamination. The new vaccine would be taken on a cube of sugar. The Sabin live vaccine was licensed in 1961 and by the late 1960s it was almost impossible to get any other vaccine.

That might have been the end of the story, except for one thing: the live vaccine carries a small but real danger of causing the very disease it is designed to prevent. In the late 1980s, the annual rate of polio paralysis in the United States was four per million, all associated with the Sabin vaccine.

As long as there are unvaccinated children—such as those in developing countries, and even in the United States before they are required to be immunized in order to go to school—polio will continue to be a threat. Certainly a drug to combat the virus would be welcomed; indeed, in 1989 scientists discovered the attachment site at which polio viruses begin their invasions of human cells, which means that a drug to cure polio is a possibility—perhaps in the twenty-first century.

—S.B.

SMALLPOX

Sometimes known as the great fire or the spotted death, smallpox was once a common, highly contagious, and often fatal disease caused by the variola virus. Over thousands of years, recurring plagues have scarred, blinded, and killed an estimated hundreds of millions of people worldwide. Typically, one in four of its victims died. However, a massive vaccination and quarantine campaign launched by the World Health Organization (WHO) in 1967 led to eradication of the illness in the late 1970s. The last specimens of variola remain in two closely guarded refrigerators—one in the United States (Atlanta, Georgia) and the other in Russia (Moscow). Amid considerable controversy, some health officials have recommended destroying the remaining stocks of the virus.

The brick-shaped variola belongs to the orthopoxviruses that represent the largest and most complex group of animal viruses. Other members include monkeypox, buffalopox, camelpox, cowpox, and vaccinia. Although people can be affected by some of the other poxviruses, humans are variola's only natural host. The disease was transmitted by inhalation or through close physical contact with infected individuals or contaminated objects. Smallpox victims experienced severe, flulike symptoms followed by rashes that turned into pus-filled blisters. If the victim lived, the pustules gradually dried up and formed crusts or scabs that fell off, revealing deep, permanent pockmarks on the affected skin. Smallpox survivors were then immune from the disease for the rest of their lives.

The prognosis for the disease depended on many factors, including age and general health of the victim. The illness could be relatively mild or turn into a highly fatal, hemorrhagic form called black smallpox.

PRE-1900 KNOWLEDGE AND TREATMENT
In the eleventh century A.D., a Buddhist nun in China popularized the idea that smallpox deaths could be reduced by preemptive infections with milder forms of the disease. The procedure involved collecting "heavenly flowers," a remarkably poetic term for smallpox pustules. These "flowers" typically came from people who had not exhibited severe cases of the disease. Patients inhaled the powdered scabs as snuff and then developed what they hoped would be a mild case of the illness. Although this approach was successful at protecting some individuals, it was an extremely dangerous and uncertain treatment.

In the late 1700s, a brilliant English physician named Edward Jenner (1749–1825) demonstrated a safe and effective method to prevent smallpox and paved the way for its total eradication. Until that time, children were often deliberately exposed to smallpox in the hope that they would develop a mild case and recover, immune. It was a dangerous practice.

Orphaned at the age of five, Jenner was raised by an older brother and went on to study medicine and natural history. During his medical training, he heard a milkmaid mention that she could not be infected by smallpox because she had already had cowpox. On May 14, 1796, Jenner inoculated eight-year-old James Phipps with cowpox lymph collected from an infected milkmaid. The child experienced only a mild reaction to the procedure. On July 1 Jenner exposed the boy to material from a smallpox victim, but Phipps showed no significant signs of illness.

Jenner submitted his findings to the Royal Society for Improving Natural Knowledge, a prestigious scientific organization. However, they rejected his work and warned that his experiment could jeopardize the good reputation he had earned from his earlier paper on the nesting habits of the cuckoo bird. Undaunted, Jenner inoculated more children with cowpox and obtained the same results. He coined the term *variolae vaccinae* (from *vacca*, the Latin word for cow), which then grew into the word *vaccine*. Jenner's pioneering vaccination experiments inspired later generations of scientists to control a wide variety of other viral illnesses.

POST-1900 KNOWLEDGE AND TREATMENT

Beginning in 1967, WHO initiated a massive smallpox vaccination campaign. The treatment efforts were so successful that by 1977 a hospital cook named Ali Maow Maalin in Somalia became the last person to contract smallpox through natural transmission. However, he was not variola's last victim. In 1978 Janet Parker, an English medical photographer who worked on the floor above a smallpox laboratory, became infected, possibly through the duct system, and died. Professor Henry Bedson, an authority on smallpox and the person responsible for lab safety, was so despondent over the incident that he committed suicide.

Some members of WHO recommended that the remaining samples be genetically mapped and then destroyed on December 1, 1993. However, many scientists asked for a stay of execution. They contended that variola has unique characteristics that could help researchers discover new ways to combat a variety of diseases. Others argued that the risks of keeping the virus outweighed the potential benefits. In May 1996 WHO approved a plan to destroy the last stocks on June 30, 1999.

—H.X.W.

STROKE

The medical term for a stroke is CVA (cerebrovascular accident) or, historically, apoplexy. A stroke occurs when the supply of oxygen and nutrients to the brain is interrupted, resulting in injury to the nervous system. Typical symptoms include paralysis, impaired sensation, and difficulties seeing or communicating and can result in death if breathing stops.

PRE-1900 KNOWLEDGE AND TREATMENT

Strokes have been known to exist since the time of the Greeks. About 440 B.C., Hippocrates described them as attacks of numbness and "anesthesia" that were signs of impending "apoplexy." In third-century B.C. Egypt, the first dissections were performed and the structures of the heart and brain began to be better understood.

Perhaps the single biggest leap in our understanding of the anatomy of the brain occurred with the publication of *Fabrica* by Andreas Vesalius (1514–64). These volumes contained some of the most outstanding neuroanatomical drawings and were rooted in Vesalius's strong foundation of understanding anatomy through solid observation.

The first study linking brain function with apoplexy was published in 1619 by Gregor Nymman (1594–1638). The most significant leap in understanding the link of cerebral hemorrhaging (bleeding) to apoplexy was made by Johan Jakob Wepfer (1620–95). Through meticulous observations, Wepfer correctly deduced the causes of apoplexy and also understood that obstructing the flow of blood to the brain could cause apoplexy. He was first to recognize the risk factors of obesity, hypertension, and heart disease as increasing the likelihood of an apoplectic attack. He also realized that there were varying degrees of apoplexy, depending on which part of the brain was affected and to what extent arteries were blocked.

Wepfer, however, did not realize that in an apoplectic attack, the part of the brain affected is always opposite the side that suffers paralysis. Though this observation dated back to the time of the Romans, it was Giovanni Battista Morgagni (1682–1771) who backed it with evidence in 1761. Though aphasia (speech impairment) was long known to be attributed to apoplexy, it was the Swedish botanist Carolus Linneaus (1707–78) who first accurately described the ability of the stroke victim to fully comprehend speech and writing while not being able to speak himself.

Sir George Burrows, through clinical experiments and accumulated data, showed in 1846 that there was a relationship between cerebral anemia (loss of blood to the brain), a fall in blood pressure, and apoplexy. By the end of the 1800s it was generally recognized that apoplexy could result from cerebral hemorrhaging of diseased cerebral arteries. It was also known that aneurysms (dilation of a blood vessel from disease of the vessel wall) and embolisms (an abnormal particle, such as an air bubble or blood clot, suddenly blocking a blood vessel) could result in apoplexy.

POST-1900 DISCOVERIES

In 1905 H. Chiari was the first to link atherosclerosis to stroke. In 1914 J. Ramsay Hunt added to this knowledge with his recognition that strokes could arise from blockage of arteries outside the brain. Unfortunately, the findings of Chiari and Hunt were ignored for about forty years. This changed with the advent of the noninvasive procedure called carotid arteriography, which could be performed on living patients.

By the 1960s considerable progress had been made in understanding the relationship of atherosclerosis to strokes. It was shown by researchers, such as B. C. Eikelboom (1981), that as plaque accumulated on the walls of arteries and narrowed them severely, a stroke would result.

In the 1920s and 1930s, researchers such as Heinrich Hering, Corneille Heymans, S. Weiss, and J. P. Baker all added to the understanding of the relationship of changes in blood flow through the carotid arteries of the neck to brain response. The discovery of X rays by Wilhelm Roentgen in 1895 forever changed the scientific and medical world. In 1923 J. A. Sicard and G. Forestier were able to inject iodized poppyseed oil into a living patient and flouroscopically follow its progress through the circulatory system. Injections of fluids, known as contrast mediums, immediately met with improvements, including the use of less toxic substances. In 1924 Barney Brooks became the first to use this new science, angiography, to decide how to treat a patient. By 1927 António Egas Moniz was able to successfully use the procedure to reveal cerebral circulation in a living human being.

These developments led to more complex methods of imaging arteries and blood flow. Many of these technologies could provide a view of an artery at any level, or view plane, and allow observation in real time. The evolution of powerful computers permitted a major breakthrough, with the development of computed tomography in 1973. CT allowed for detailed studies of soft tissues not visible using other techniques.

These techniques allowed varying levels of two-dimensional viewing. In 1946 nuclear magnetic resonance imaging, or MRI, was created at the Massachusetts Institute of Technology and Stanford University for the purpose of determining precise chemical structure. Later, its ability to create high-resolution, three-dimensional images was used for medical imaging. By the 1980s MRIs were in common use.

All these new technologies, coupled with drug therapy (which relied on the anticlotting medicines developed for heart disease) and preventive care, have proven to be powerful tools against strokes. Data on stroke patients prior to the 1960s are sparse, as few detailed records were available. Now, with the help of computers and these new technologies, extensive data are available for analysis.

These data indicate that, although the population is aging, the death rate from strokes has been falling. The exact reasons for this decline are not yet fully understood. It is suspected that, because of the historical gains that have been made in understanding the disease, the advent of technologies that enable preemptive screening allow preventive medicine to be applied. Understanding the roles of obesity, hypertension, cholesterol levels, social awareness, and treatment accessibility is vital in fighting strokes. These factors have especially proven important among blacks, who are at greater risk of getting strokes because of higher-than-average incidence of high blood pressure, obesity, and diabetes. Advanced surgical techniques and drug therapies, on the other hand, have played a critical role in maintaining a high survival rate among stroke victims.

—M.E.R.

SYPHILIS

A chronic and potentially fatal venereal disease, syphilis is caused by a slender, corkscrew-shaped spirochete bacterium called *Treponema pallidum*. Humans are the microorganism's only natural host. Although it is typically transmitted during sexual contact through tiny breaks in the skin or mucous membranes, *T. pallidum* can also be passed along congenitally. If left untreated, the spirochete can inflict severe internal damage and incapacitate the heart, spinal cord, and brain.

Because its wide array of symptoms—ranging from fever and rashes to heart disease and mental deterioration—resemble other illnesses, syphilis has been described as the great mimic. A characteristic chancre (a small, painless ulcer) commonly emerges at the sight of infection and signals the onset of the illness. The chancres frequently develop in concealed areas and disappear within days or weeks, so infected individuals may never become aware of their presence. However, several tests can detect the disease. After a diagnosis, the infection can be effectively treated, particularly in the early stages, with penicillin or other antibiotics.

Although there are effective tests and treatments, they are not always readily available in some regions. As a result, syphilis remains a global problem. Although there are no precise data on worldwide incidence rates, by some estimates there are upward of 20 million cases a year. After a period of decline in the United

States around the middle of the twentieth century, the number of people who have become infected is rapidly going up. In 1987 there were 35,241 reported cases of primary and secondary syphilis—a 30 percent rise over the previous year. In 1990 the U.S. Centers for Disease Control (CDC) in Atlanta, Georgia, reported 50,223 cases. These increases are believed to stem from changes in sexual behavior over the last few decades.

PRE-1900 KNOWLEDGE AND TREATMENT

The precise origins of the disease are murky, and historians debate where and when it first arose. Evidence in the skeletons of pre-Columbian South American Indians suggests that the disease was present in the New World prior to Columbus's arrival. Some historians believe Spanish sailors who had contracted syphilis in the West Indies during their voyages with Columbus were responsible for its spread across Europe.

As it spread across the European continent, the French called it the Neapolitan disease or the Spanish sickness. The Spanish and Italians, in turn, called it the French disease. Germans described it as the Polish pox, while the Poles predictably labeled it the German pox. In 1530 an Italian physician and poet named Girolamo Fracastoro (1478–1553) wrote an epic poem about a shepherd lad named Syphilis who angered the sun god and was punished by becoming the first victim of the disease. The fictional shepherd's name eventually became synonymous with the illness itself, thereby putting an end to the nationalistic name-calling.

For many years, some physicians believed that the symptoms of syphilis and gonorrhea were different manifestations of a single illness. Others were not convinced. In an unfortunate attempt to answer the question, a Scottish surgeon named John Hunter deliberately infected himself with the fluid from an individual known to have gonorrhea. Unfortunately, unbeknownst to Hunter, the person also had syphilis.

For the rest of his life, Hunter argued vigorously that the two diseases were one and the same. Another, less personally daring Scottish physician, Benjamin Bell, performed inoculation experiments on his students and demonstrated that the two diseases were clinically different.

POST-1900 DISCOVERIES

Some of the most important developments in identifying and treating syphilis came in the early 1900s. In 1905 German zoologists Fritz Schaudinn (1871–1906) and Erich Hoffmann were the first to observe the shadowy spiral of *T. pallidum* in their microscopes. A German physician, August von Wassermann (1866–1925), developed a diagnostic blood test for the disease in 1906.

Prior to the twentieth century, mercury-based ointments, pills, and vapor baths were the treatments of choice for syphilis. Patients who underwent such therapies faced the possibility of abdominal pains, tooth loss, and rotted bones, among other side effects. In 1908 a German research physician named Paul Ehrlich (1854–1915) and his Japanese colleague, Sahachiro Hata, began working with arsenic-based preparations that were hoped could kill various parasites. They found that a substance designated as 606 was effective in combating *T. pallidum*. Despite its arsenic content, 606, later named Salvarsan (I save), was hailed as a relatively safe and effective cure for the disease. Ehrlich won a Nobel Prize for his work in 1908. Ehrlich also suffered personal and professional attacks for his work on an antisyphilis medication. A few detractors felt that the disease was a just punishment for sinful behavior and Ehrlich was interfering in the process. Others argued that the treatment regimen was too complicated.

Salvarsan was eventually replaced by penicillin and other antibiotics following work in the mid-1940s by U.S. physician John F. Mahoney (1889–1957). Syphilis can be effectively treated with these drugs.

—H.X.W.

FOOTNOTE PEOPLE

CHARLES ATLAS (ANGELO SICILIANO) (1893–1972)

Angelo Siciliano was a fairly husky boy in southern Italy. When he went with his mother to Brooklyn at the age of eleven, however, he began to sicken and grow spindly. He lost interest in school and could not climb the steps to the family flat. "I was a ninety-seven-pound runt," he later recalled. "I was skinny, pale, nervous, and weak." One Halloween he was beaten by a boy wielding a sock full of ashes.

Then, at the age of sixteen, he looked at a statue of Hercules in the Brooklyn Museum and marveled at his muscles.

A week later he joined the YMCA and began to lift dumbbells, pull elastic stretchers, and toss medicine balls. For home use he built a barbell out of a broomstick and two rocks. He wrote away for the Swoboda Course and investigated Strongfortism. He became obsessed with strength.

One day he watched a tiger stretching in the zoo and asked himself, "How does Mr. Tiger keep in physical condition? Did you ever see a tiger with a barbell?" He concluded that lions and tigers became strong by pitting muscle against muscle. Angelo abandoned his barbells and fell to staging tugs-of-war between hands, legs, fingers, and thighs. By means of such exercises, he doubled his weight and returned the beating of his Halloween tormentor.

He acquired a mighty form: a chest that expanded to 54¾ inches and biceps of 17 inches. His friends at the gymnasium took notice and declared that he looked just like the statue of Atlas on the corner bank building. The name stuck and eventually Angelo legally changed his name to Charles Atlas.

As a young man he took a job as strongman in the Coney Island Circus sideshow. He tore telephone books in two, smashed nails through blocks of wood with his bare hands, lifted two men off the floor, and lay on a bed of 7,000 nails eating a banana while three spectators stood on his chest. "Women used to faint when I did that," he said. "They couldn't stand watching a beautiful body like mine being abused." But the feat of strength that really brought Atlas renown was an unplanned one. One day some rowers at Brooklyn's Dike Beach lost their oars. Atlas swam out and saved them by tying the boat's

bow rope around his waist and towing it a mile to the shore.

At the sideshow he was noticed by an artist who asked him to pose. Soon he became a popular sculptors' model, and parts or all of his image appeared on public buildings around the country. His upper body became a torso on a centaur in the lobby of the Capitol Theater on Broadway. He became George Washington in New York's Washington Square, Alexander Hamilton in front of the U.S. Treasury Building in Washington, the Dawn of Glory in Brooklyn's Prospect Park, Patriotism in the Elks National Headquarters in Chicago, and Energy in Repose in the Federal Reserve Bank of Cleveland. He made enough money to quit Coney Island.

In 1922 Bernarr Macfadden, publisher of *Physical Culture* magazine, selected Atlas as the world's most perfectly developed man. The title and prize money enabled Atlas to set up his own mail-order muscle-building business. Advertisements in comics, pulps, and sports and movie magazines showed Atlas clad in a tight-fitting leopard skin, muscles bulging. A 1925 appeal asked, "Do you want to be a tiger?" and opined, "It's the Tiger Men who grab everything they want these days. The new race of Tiger Men win the battles of pelf and power in the mad, dizzy, jazzy marathon for personal success. They whiz by you in stunning big limousines and have fine homes and bulging bank accounts."

In 1928 Charles Roman took over the marketing of the Atlas course and rewrote the ads. He coined the term *dynamic tension* to describe Atlas's isometric exercises and concentrated on selling just plain muscles. "Just tell me where you want handsome steellike muscles," the ads proclaimed. "I'll add five inches to your chest." Later Roman created a comic-strip panel that showed the newly muscled he-man returning to punch the bully who had kicked sand in his face and stolen his girl.

Atlas supplemented Roman's ads with personal appearances. He bent railroad spikes and gave them away as souvenirs. He ordered the spikes in kegs from ironworks and bent 1,500 a year. He pulled six automobiles down a mile of road. He pulled a 145,000-pound railroad observation car 112 feet down a track and a boatload of friends around New York Harbor. Once he broke iron bars in front of 2,000 prisoners at Sing Sing prison.

Subscribers paid thirty dollars for twelve lessons in such arts as deep breathing, arm wrestling with oneself, doing push-ups on chairs, relaxation, and diet. He-men were told to avoid alcohol, tea, white bread, and doughnuts. Character building was an essential part of the training. Atlas told kids who came into his office: "Live clean, think clean, and don't go to burlesque shows." He refused to visit nightclubs, which he claimed were "filled with

Charles Atlas, former ninety-seven-pound weakling, poses on the beach at the age of seventy-eight.

germs." He told a businessman: "Burn your bonds. Tear up your stocks. Give away your property. Get on a healthy basis. My God, man, it's the body that counts!" Atlas believed that he was building character. "With good health goes honesty and integrity. If you've got good health, you think twice before you do anything wrong."

By World War II Atlas had branch offices in London and Buenos Aires and students all over the world. Among his alumni were champion boxers Max Baer and Rocky Marciano, comic Fred Allen, baseball hero Joe DiMaggio, and piano manufacturer Theodore Steinway.

Ultimately, 6 million aspiring he-men bought the course, making Atlas a millionaire several times over. He bought a seaside home at Point Lookout, Long Island, and lived in semiretirement, there and in Palm Beach, Florida, building furniture out of driftwood, working out at the New York City Athletic Club, and posing for publicity photos as a remarkably vigorous septuagenarian, while Roman directed the mail-order business. He died of a heart attack at the age of seventy-nine. The isometric exercises he had pioneered had long since become part of the training used by the armed forces and professional athletes.

—P.S.

TIMOTHY LEARY (1920–1996)

No individual more fully embodied the psychedelic drug culture of the 1960s than Timothy Leary. Leary's invitation to "turn on, tune in, drop out" was taken up by a generation of young Americans to whom he advocated the use of mind-expanding drugs with the zeal of a missionary.

Timothy Francis Leary was born in Springfield, Massachusetts, on October 22, 1920, to a distinguished New England family. One of his forefathers and his namesake was the medical examiner of Boston and a leading expert on blood circulation. His paternal grandfather was, according to Leary, "the richest Irish Catholic in western Massachusetts," and one of his uncles was a Roman Catholic priest.

Leary studied briefly at Holy Cross in Worcester but reacted against "the scholastic approach to religion" taught by the Jesuits. He went on to West Point, which pleased his father, a former West Point captain and army dentist. He lasted there only eighteen months before settling down at the University of Alabama, where he earned a B.A. in psychology.

During World War II Leary worked as a psychologist at a U.S. Army hospital in Pennsylvania. After earning his doctorate at the University of California at Berkeley, he was hired on there as an assistant professor of psychology.

By the late fifties, Leary had become a respectable figure in academia. He had written several works in his field and in 1955 became director of psychological research at a hospital in Oakland, California. But Leary was not a happy man. He later referred to himself as "an anonymous institutional employee who drove to work each morning in a long line of commuter cars and drove home each night and drank martinis . . . like several million, middle-class, liberal intellectual robots."

On his thirty-fifth birthday he left home after a drunken fight with his wife, Marienne, and returned the next morning to find her dead in their exhaust-filled garage, a suicide. To escape his grief he began to travel, eventually settling in Spain with his two children. He returned to the United States in 1959 and joined the faculty of the Harvard University Center for Personality Research.

In August 1960 he first tried psychedelic drugs in their natural state, in Cuernavaca, Mexico. "I ate seven of the sacred mushrooms of Mexico," he later wrote, "and discovered that beauty, revelation, sensuality, the cellular history of the past, God, the Devil—all lie inside my body, outside my mind."

Back at Harvard, Leary made taking LSD, or "dropping acid," a regular part of his curriculum at the Research Center. His fellow trippers included not only his colleagues and students but such celebrated writers as Allen Ginsberg, Jack Kerouac, Arthur Koestler, and Aldous Huxley. Leary's growing notoriety as a drug guru did not please Harvard, despite the fact that his experiments using psychedelic drugs for the treatment of alcoholics, schizophrenics, and imprisoned criminals had proven valid therapy. In 1963 Harvard dismissed him from his post.

A millionaire friend gave Leary free use of a sixty-four-room mansion in Millbrook, New York, which he converted into a center for sixty of his disciples. In 1966 Leary founded the League for Spiritual Discovery, which he called "a legally incorporated religion." His mission, as he saw it, was to overthrow "original sin, the Book of Genesis and the whole Judeo-Christian bad trip." His daughter Susan described life at Millbrook as "like living in a church with jolly people."

Law enforcement agencies, however, did not look so benignly on Leary's liturgical activities and he complained of increasing police harassment. In December 1965 Leary and Susan were arrested at an immigration station in Laredo, Texas, when a snuffbox full of marijuana was found in Susan's panties. He was sentenced to thirty years in prison, a conviction that was later overturned by the Supreme Court. But Leary's troubles with the law were far from over. He was arrested again on marijuana charges in California, where he now lived, and was sentenced to ten years at the minimum-security section of the California State Prison near San Luis Obispo. Along with another ten-year sentence in Laredo, Leary faced a possible twenty years behind bars.

> If you take the game of life seriously, if you take your nervous system seriously, if you take your sense organs seriously, if you take the energy process seriously, you must turn on, tune in and drop out.
>
> Timothy Leary, lecture, June 1966

On September 13, 1970, Leary, considered a "model" prisoner by authorities, scaled the prison's twelve-foot fence and escaped. He fled to Algiers on a false passport with his wife, Rosemary Woodruff, a former airline stewardess and model. There he joined exiled Black Panther leader Eldridge Cleaver. In exile Leary's political consciousness was raised significantly. He wrote a letter to the media in which he proclaimed his commitment to "stay high and wage the revolutionary war." It was pronouncements such as this that led Richard Nixon to call him the most dangerous man alive.

But the revolution came to an end for Leary in January 1973 when he was recaptured, according to him, by CIA agents. He was paroled after two more years in prison and dropped into obscurity.

Sometime in the seventies, Leary discovered a new mind-expanding experience that was legal and highly profitable—computers. "People need some way to activate, boot up and change the discs in their minds," he said in 1986. "LSD may not be as necessary now." He wrote six computer programs and became a consultant to several software companies. Mind Mirror, his self-analysis software program, sold more than 30,000 copies. By the 1990s Leary had taken up the cause of "virtual reality," the computerized re-creation of a 3-D environment, a technological development that the *Wall Street Journal* referred to as electronic LSD.

As a gray-haired grandfather who lived in Los Angeles's Benedict Canyon, Timothy Leary led the good life in his second reincarnation as a media star. He appeared in ads for jeans, traveled the lecture circuit with Watergate burglar G. Gordon Liddy, appeared in musical videos for the MTV generation, and had a film company option his fifth autobiography, *Flashbacks*.

But Leary's outlaw days were not entirely over. On May 10, 1994, he was arrested and released for smoking a cigarette (tobacco) in the smoke-free Robert Mueller Municipal Airport in Austin, Texas. He died of prostate cancer on May 31, 1996. His last words were, "Why not?" and "Yeah."

—S.A.O.

> Drugs have taught an entire generation of American kids the metric system.
>
> P. J. O'Rourke, Modern Manners, 1983
>
> Cocaine is God's way of saying you're making too much money.
>
> Robin Williams

HERMANN RORSCHACH
(1884–1922)

When he was in high school, the inventor of the world-famous Rorschach inkblot test was called Kleck, or "inkblot," by his chums. Like many other youngsters in his native Switzerland, Rorschach enjoyed Klecksography, the making of fanciful inkblot "pictures." Unlike the other youngsters, Rorschach would make inkblots his life's work.

An art teacher like his father, Rorschach showed great talent at painting and drawing conventional pictures. When it was time for him to graduate from high school, he could not decide between a career in art and one in science. He wrote a letter to the famous German biologist Ernst Häckel to ask his advice. Predictably, the scientist suggested science, and Rorschach enrolled in medical school at the University of Zurich.

It was an exhilarating time to be studying science, particularly in Europe and particularly in the field of medicine. A Viennese physician, Sigmund Freud, had delved into the subconscious mind, and his findings about the human personality caused much traditional science and morality to be questioned. Rorschach was also fortunate in having the eminent psychiatrist Eugen Bleuler for a teacher. Bleuler had taught another doctor who was making a name for himself in Zurich, Carl Jung.

The excitement in intellectual circles over psychoanalysis constantly reminded Rorschach of his childhood inkblots. Why, he wondered, might two people see entirely different things in the same inkblot? While still a medical student, he began showing inkblots to schoolchildren and analyzing their reactions. He was aided in these first tests by a friend he had played Klecksography with in high school, who had become an art teacher. The two men wanted to know if gifted students fantasized more in their interpretations of inkblots than average students. Unfortunately, the results of these early tests and the inkblots used have been lost.

Rorschach was intrigued by Freud's work in interpreting dreams, but a dream he himself had had left him puzzled. The night after he witnessed his first autopsy, Rorschach dreamed that he had died and his body was being autopsied. Although he was dead in his dream, he could see and feel what was happening as the presiding physician sliced through his brain. The dream helped convince Rorschach that there was a strong tie between perception and the unconscious. He chose the symbolism of hallucinations as the topic for his doctoral dissertation.

After he received his M.D. in 1912, Rorschach worked briefly in Russia and then returned to work in mental hospitals in Zurich. He stepped up his inkblot research, testing 300 mental patients and 100 "normal" persons. In 1921 his now famous work *Psychodiagnostics*, which set forth his methods of using inkblots to probe the unconscious, was published.

The Rorschach test consists of ten cards, each containing one ornate inkblot. Five are in black and white and five are in color. The examiner shows the subject the cards one at a time and records the subject's responses. Subjects are asked to describe what they see in the blots or what the blots remind them of. They are then shown the cards a second time and asked to explain ambiguous responses and to point out the parts of the inkblots that prompted various reactions. The examiner also notes each subject's social behavior, for example, whether the subject feels challenged or intimidated by the test.

The test results are evaluated by four main criteria: (1) Location: does the subject respond to the entire blot or specific details of the blot? (2) Quality: does the subject react to the color, shade, or what he or she sees as movement in the blot? (3) Content: does the subject perceive humans or animals, animate or inanimate objects? (4) Degree of conventionality: how do the responses compare statistically with the responses given by most people?

In the most general terms, subjects who see whole figures in Rorschach's blots are usually highly intelligent and ingenious. Noting small, individual details indicates an introverted personality and possible emotional conflicts. Numerous responses to color signify impulsiveness and possibly emotional instability. Noticing third-dimensional shading indicates anxiety. Seeing forms in motion means a vivid imagination, but seeing mostly animals is evidence of low intelligence. If most responses are determined by shape or form, it is a sign of normalcy and healthy emotional control.

Psychologists and psychiatrists in Europe and elsewhere quickly recognized the test as a valuable tool. With Rorschach's inkblots they could explore the private fantasy world of a patient without direct questioning and greatly reduce the time required for psychoanalysis. Jung claimed to have discovered a murder as a result of a Rorschach test. The test could also quantify the theretofore purely qualitative approach to personality study. Repeated testing of a patient could check a patient's progress or determine the developmental growth of children. More recently, social workers have used the inkblots to assess the severity of clients' emotional problems, and anthropologists have been able to learn how emotional makeup varies among cultures.

Apparently Rorschach never took his own test. If he had, the test might have revealed an aberration within the personality of its inventor. Less than a year after completing his brilliant treatise, Rorschach began to suffer severe abdominal pains. As a physician he must have known he had an infected appendix. Yet he did nothing. When he finally went to the hospital, the attending surgeon was astounded that Rorschach had let the ailment progress so far. Rorschach was operated on immediately, but he died the next morning of peritonitis. He was only thirty-seven years old.

Today the accuracy of the Rorschach test is questioned by some psychologists, but it remains the most widely used projective test throughout the world. It would be hard to overestimate its importance in clinical psychology and psychiatry. Freud discovered the hidden world of the unconscious; Rorschach provided a compass for quickly surveying that difficult terrain.

—A.L.

Inkblot number one of the Rorschach test.

HUMAN BEHAVIOR EXPERIMENTS

CROSSING ON THE RED LIGHT
Title of Experiment: Status Factors in Pedestrian Violation of Traffic Signals

Conducted by: Monroe Lefkowitz, Robert R. Blake, and Jane Srygley Mouton in Austin, Texas

Reported in: *Journal of Abnormal and Social Psychology* 51, no. 3 (1955): 704–6

Object: To determine whether people are more likely to disobey a prohibition (in this case, a street signal) if they see a high-status person disobey it than if they see a low-status person disobey it. The experimenters also wanted to know if obedience by a high-status person increased other people's obedience.

The Experiment: The experiment was conducted at three street corners in downtown Austin on three successive afternoons. The 2,103 pedestrians who passed the corners during the tests served as subjects. The experiment included several different situations. In one an experimenter's model, dressed as a "high-status" pedestrian (suit, white shirt, tie, shined shoes), obeyed the "wait" signal at the crosswalk for five trials. Then pedestrians were observed for five more trials with the model absent. Next the model returned as a "low-status" pedestrian, in scuffed shoes, soiled trousers, and an unpressed denim shirt. This time he crossed the street even though the signal said "wait." The next day the order was inverted, so that the model would be violating the signal as a high-status pedestrian and conforming to it as a low-status pedestrian. The Traffic Department of the Austin Police Department had been informed of the experiment, and no police officers were around to inhibit the testing.

Conclusions: Only 1 percent of the pedestrians disobeyed the signal when the model was not present. Obedience was so high without the model that the experimenters could not tell whether the presence of an obedient model made any difference. A disobedient model, however, did change pedestrians' behavior. When the low-status model disobeyed the signal, 4 percent of the pedestrians followed his lead. But even more—14 percent—disobeyed the signal when the model in high-status dress did. In other words, class counts.

—C.P.

ONLY FOLLOWING ORDERS
Title of Experiment: Behavioral Study of Obedience

Conducted by: Stanley Milgram, Yale University

Reported in: First experiment described in *Journal of Abnormal and Social Psychology* 67 (1963): 371–78; all eighteen experiments described in *Obedience to Authority: An Experimental View* (New York: Harper and Row, 1974)

Object: To study destructive obedience by ordering a naive subject to administer increasingly severe punishment to another subject in the name of a learning experiment, and to determine the conditions under which the first subject will submit to authority (and continue the punishment) or defy authority (and stop the punishment).

The Experiment: This series of eighteen experiments dealt with the specific situation of conflict between an experimenter's instructions and a subject's conscience. They also considered the degree to which an individual is willing or is forced by some part of his or her internal makeup to submit to an arbitrary outside definition of who he or she is.

The experiments, which involved 1,000 subjects over the years from 1960 to 1963, were set up as a learning trial. Two subjects entered the laboratory together. One was actually an actor. They were told that they were to participate in a test of memory in which one of them would be the "teacher" and the other the "pupil." The situation was rigged so that the actor always got the role of pupil and the real subject became the teacher. The experimenter then explained the procedure. The teacher was to read off word pairs that the pupil was to memorize. Then the teacher was to repeat the first part of each pair and several alternatives for the second part. If the pupil answered incorrectly, the teacher was to administer an electric shock to the pupil via a realistic-looking machine complete with dials and voltage indicator lights, the highest level being 450 volts. With each wrong answer, the teacher was to increase the voltage of the shock. Though the upper levels of shock could be painful, the experimenter carefully explained, they could not cause permanent tissue damage. The ostensible purpose of the experiment was to determine the effect of punishment on memory and learning ability.

The experiment then proceeded. At lower to middle shock levels, the actor expressed pain and asked to be released from the rest of the experiment. In many trials, the actor spoke of being afraid to participate because he had a bad heart, and at middle levels of shock complained that his heart was bothering him. At upper levels of shock the actor screamed in agony and pleaded with the "teacher" to stop, and finally, at the highest levels, he was silent, after saying he would no longer cooperate. Since the actor was out of sight in the next room, many subjects feared that he had been killed.

Conclusions: Most "teachers" protested and argued with the experimenter about inflicting pain, but most went on with the shocks when the experimenter refused to budge from the position that "the experiment must go on," and "the experiment requires that you continue." Fully 65 percent of the teachers went on to administer the highest level of shock despite the agonized protests of the actor-victim. Even when the teachers believed the victim to have heart disease, it made no difference in their obedience, though they displayed great emotional conflict in having to go on.

The series of experiments included variations such as changing the institutional context (moving the site from Yale to an office building in downtown Bridgeport, Connecticut), using women as subjects, and changing personnel in the middle of a test. Milgram found that the closer the victim was to the teacher in physical proximity, the greater was the number of disobedient teachers. When administration of the shock involved actually pushing the pupil's hand down on the shock plate, only 30 percent of the teachers obeyed (still an astounding figure). Also, most teachers would "cheat" when given a chance, such as when the experimenter left the room, by giving the minimum shock to the actor. This fact seemed to indicate that teachers in the tests were not inherently vicious, merely obedient. Further, in a variation in which the experimenter received the shocks, not a single subject proceeded after the experimenter's initial protests and requests that the experiment be terminated, despite the fact that he had agreed to see it through to the end. Clearly it was the authority figure rather than any sense of scientific requirement that was being obeyed.

The implications of Milgram's work are frightening. Few people are able to stand up for what they know is right even when challenged by a self-appointed authority with no ability to enforce his instructions. Few people weigh the words of another person just like themselves as heavily as those of a person they believe to be somehow "above" them. Most individuals ignore the dictates of their own conscience when pressured by a "superior's" expectation of a given behavior or response.

Milgram noted that most of the obedient subjects displayed a high degree of tension characterized by flushing, sweating, increased heartbeat, and other signs of physiological arousal. Those who were quickest to refuse to continue administering shocks remained the most placid. These individuals were "centered." They experienced little tension and their bodies reflected their emotional calm. Why were these individuals so centered when many others experienced such painful conflict? Milgram attributes obedience to the hierarchical structure in the blood of the human race, to the tendency to shift responsibility for an action from the person who performs it to the highest member of a hierarchy who is involved in it, and to social influences that encourage one to conform. He doesn't explain why 35 percent of the subjects were able to overcome all these factors and say no.

Few people would correctly predict the results of this experiment (some Yale psychology majors estimated that only 1.2 percent of the teachers would administer the full shock). Even fewer would predict that they would find themselves in the obedient majority. Each person must ponder these results and must watch out for situations in which one evades personal responsibility for one's actions. Many of Milgram's obedient subjects, like many Nazi war criminals at the Nuremberg war crimes trials or the participants in the My Lai massacre, claimed to be innocent, saying "I was only following my orders." The answer to the question of where each person would stand in a conflict between authority and conscience is present, unnoticed and tragic, in our normal behavior, in everyday life.

—D.R.

SELF-FULFILLING PROPHECY

Title of Experiment: Pygmalion in the Classroom: Teacher Expectation and Pupils' Intellectual Development

Conducted by: Robert Rosenthal, Harvard University, and Lenore Jacobson, South San Francisco Unified School District

Reported in: Symposium of the American Psychological Association, 1966, and in *Pygmalion in the Classroom: Teacher Expectation and Pupils' Intellectual Development* (New York: Holt, Rinehart, and Winston, 1968)

Object: To learn whether innocent subjects are affected by another person's expectations of them and how expectations change the interaction between any two people.

The Experiment: The research was conducted in 1964 in an elementary school referred to as the Oak School, in the San Francisco area. The entire student body was given an intelligence test. Teachers were told the test revealed which children were about to "bloom," that is, go through a learning spurt. The names of those students, which included some minority children, were given to the teachers. Children designated "bloomers" were actually picked at random from all levels of intelligence—but the teachers were unaware of that fact.

Conclusions: Teachers did not change their methods or materials for teaching these exceptional pupils, yet when the test was administered again in 1965 and 1966, first and second graders who had been designated as potential bloomers at the time of the first test had gained twice the number of IQ points as other children. Some of the minority children, who had been below-average learners but were in the group expected to bloom, were suddenly found to be above average or even gifted.

In grades three to six the difference in IQ gain was much less dramatic. The experimenters theorize that the younger children were more malleable and had less established reputations so that teachers were open to new ideas about their abilities. But how can one explain the great difference in IQ gain between the special group and their peers? The experimenters cite another experiment in which three identical groups of rats were designated as fast and slow learners and then given to laboratory assistants to be taught a maze. The rats that the assistants expected to be smarter did in fact perform better. These results at first seem incredible, since the rats were truly identical in intelligence. But when the lab workers were questioned, it turned out that they had been more patient with the "fast" learners, had led them through more trials, and had treated them more kindly. The same phenomenon, said Rosenthal and Jacobson, happened with the specially designated students. They performed better because they were given more attention. Teachers challenged them more because they expected more from them, and gave more positive reinforcement for each success. The experimenters concluded that behavior and achievement really can be affected by another's expectations.

The Rosenthal-Jacobson study became one of the best-known behavioral science studies of the 1960s thanks to the media attention it received. But it was also attacked by many researchers. It prompted Janet Elashoff and Richard Snow, both of Stanford, to write *Pygmalion Reconsidered* (1971). Their opinion was that Rosenthal and Jacobson had overdramatized their results and that teacher expectancy probably does not affect IQ, but it may affect a student's achievements and behavior. *Pygmalion in the Classroom* was rereleased in 1992; the new edition included both negative and positive reviews of the original study.

—D.R.

TO THE RESCUE

Title of Experiment: A Lady in Distress: Inhibiting Effects of Friends and Strangers on Bystander Intervention

Conducted by: Bibb Latané and Judith Rodin at Columbia University, New York City

Reported in: *Journal of Experimental Social Psychology* 5, no. 2 (1969): 189–202

Object: Earlier studies had shown that a single bystander was more likely to intervene in an emergency than groups of bystanders. In other words, there is not necessarily safety in numbers: on March 13, 1964, in Queens, New York, thirty-eight people witnessed Kitty Genovese's murder. Researchers suggest that such nonintervention stems not from urban "apathy" but from

"social inhibition effects"—factors in the relationship of the bystanders to each other. Latané and Rodin set out to explore these factors further. Would two bystanders who knew each other be more likely to intervene than two bystanders who did not know each other? Would friends move in where strangers feared to tread?

The Experiment: A randomly selected group of 120 Columbia male undergraduates accepted an offer to participate (for a small fee) in a survey of game and puzzle preferences. The students were asked to recommend friends who would also be willing to participate. When a student showed up for testing, a market research representative gave him a questionnaire to fill out. Then the representative retired to her office, divided from the testing room by a collapsible curtain that was easily opened. Each student found himself in one of four situations: he was alone in the testing room; he was with a stranger who was a confederate of the experimenter and who was generally unresponsive; he was with a stranger who was, like himself, a student subject in the experiment; or he was with a friend.

As the student or students filled out their questionnaires, a loud crash and a scream came from the representative's office. "Oh, my god, my foot . . . I . . . I . . . can't move it," she moaned (on tape). Further moaning and, finally, recovery continued for a total of 130 seconds. In a subsequent interview, students were asked about what they had heard, their reactions, and why they had acted or not acted to help the representative. Then they were told the experiment's real purpose.

Conclusions: Although all students said they believed the market research representative had really fallen and hurt her foot, not all did something about it. As in previous experiments of this kind, the most helpful bystanders were those bystanding alone; 70 percent of them offered the victim help. The least helpful were students in the company of the unresponsive confederate; only 7 percent of those students intervened. If the pair of bystanders were both student subjects and strangers to each other, at least one of them offered help in 40 percent of the trials. The odds for two friends helping appeared to be about as good as the odds for a single bystander; at least one of the friends helped out in 70 percent of such cases. However, Latané and Rodin pointed out that since there were two people free to act, the rate should have been higher. Consequently, friends, like strangers, do inhibit each other from acting, although not as much so.

Latané and Rodin offered two explanations for a bystander's hesitancy to intervene when he is with someone else: "social influence" (each bystander may hide his uncertainty about what to do by trying to appear poised; the other bystander is thus encouraged to believe the situation is not serious) and "diffusion of responsibility" (if a bystander turns out to be wrong in not acting, at least he shares the responsibility). Friends may be less likely to hide their feelings or put their responsibility off on each other. The results of the experiment may explain why large cities seem less safe than small towns. There are too many strangers in cities. "If you are involved in an emergency," concluded Latané and Rodin, "the best number of bystanders is one."

—C.P.

SNEAKING INTO THE CUCKOO'S NEST
Title of Experiment: On Being Sane in Insane Places

Conducted by: D. L. Rosenhan, Stanford University

Reported in: Colloquiums of the psychology departments at the University of California at Berkeley and at Santa Barbara, the University of Arizona at Tucson, and Harvard University at Cambridge, Massachusetts; later published in *Science* 179 (January 19, 1973): 250–57

Object: How do we recognize the difference between the sane and the insane, and how does expectation affect that recognition?

The Experiment: Rosenhan and eight volunteers (three women, five men) gained admittance to twelve mental institutions. They complained to staff psychiatrists of hearing voices that said "hollow," "empty," or "thud." They reported no other symptoms. The "patients" were chosen for the experiment on the basis of being normal everyday people and they represented a wide range of occupations, from housewife to painter to pediatrician. After being admitted to the hospitals, all pseudopatients told the staff that their symptoms had disappeared, and all acted normally.

Conclusions: In the twelve different hospitals, it took the pseudopatients between seven and fifty-two days to be released. In almost all cases, they were discharged with a diagnosis of "schizophrenia in remission"; not once were they discharged as being sane.

On reading these astounding facts, one might assume that the experiments were conducted in hospitals chosen for inadequate or incompetent staff or overcrowding. This was not the case. Most of the hospitals tested, which were located on both the East and the West Coast of the United States, were funded by local, state, or federal governments, and several were considered excellent. They varied as to newness and number of staff, though one well-staffed, expen-

sive, and modern hospital was included in the test. Results were no different there.

Once the pseudopatients were in the mental hospitals, they observed many enlightening facts about what happens to a person when people think he is crazy. They found that patients were considered less than human and were treated as though they were invisible. Often they would address staff with simple questions such as asking when a given doctor would be in, and they would be totally ignored, with the staff member walking straight past them, or would receive a curt nonreply such as "Hello, how do you feel today?" There was little privacy or activity allowed the patients, but when disorders arose from these stultifying conditions, they were attributed to the patient's "disease." Many pseudopatients took notes of their observations, first secretly and then openly when they found that nobody cared. One nurse, commenting on her patient's "psychosis," mentioned his "compulsive note-taking behavior." Another pseudopatient overheard a staff psychiatrist complaining about patients' "oral acquisitiveness" in lining up in the cafeteria lounge a half hour before lunch. The good doctor overlooked the fact that in the hospital there was little else to do but eat. Treatment was minimal. Drugs replaced a doctor's time. All the pseudopatients were given a surprising variety of medicines—numbering a total of 2,100 pills, including Elavil (an antidepressant) and Thorazine (a tranquilizer)—which they, like many real patients, discarded.

An interesting sidelight to the experiment was the fact that during the first few hospitalizations, although not one psychiatrist, nurse, or attendant suspected the hoax, 35 patients of the 118 residing in admittance wards with the experimenters suspected they were faking. "You're not crazy, you're some journalist (or professor) checking up on conditions here," was heard over and over again.

To verify these disturbing findings, the researchers notified a leading teaching hospital that in a given three-month period, one or more pseudopatients would attempt to gain admission to their hospital. The hospital staff was well acquainted with the experiment. Of 193 patients admitted during the three-month period, 41 were alleged to be pseudopatients by staff members, including 23 by psychiatrists with the greatest amount of training. Actually, not one pseudopatient presented himself during that period.

Dr. Rosenhan was forced to conclude that insanity is very poorly defined and that the label of insanity, once applied, is far less a product of a person's behavior or characteristics than of the context in which a person is encountered.

—D.R.

JUDGING A BOOK BY ITS COVER

Title of Experiment: Beauty Is Talent: Task Evaluation as a Function of the Performer's Physical Attractiveness

Conducted by: David Landy and Harold Sigall, University of Rochester, Rochester, New York

Reported in: *Journal of Personality and Social Psychology* 20, no. 3 (1974): 224–304

Object: To test the hypothesis that individuals attribute more positive qualities and expect better performance from physically attractive people than from physically unattractive ones. It had been shown in several previous experiments and studies that teachers expected their physically attractive pupils to have better relationships with their peers and greater scholastic potential than unattractive students, and that students expected attractive peers to have more fulfilling careers and marriages than unattractive ones.

The Experiment: The experimenters prepared two essays, using as a topic the role of television in society. The essays discussed similar issues and were of equal length. However, one essay was well written, well organized, clear, and grammatically correct, while the other was simplistic, disorganized, full of clichés and errors in usage, and in general poorly written.

Two photographs of female students were selected from the college yearbook for use in the experiment. One was of an attractive coed, the other of a physically unattractive woman. Thirty copies were made of each of the essays, and pictures, supposedly of the author, were attached to twenty of them—the attractive coed in ten cases and the unattractive one in ten. To the remaining ten essays, no picture was attached.

The subjects, sixty male undergraduate psychology students, were asked to judge one of a number of essays that had ostensibly been submitted in a freshman English class. The men were told that the English instructor had assigned the essay to his students for submission to a contest being conducted by a local television channel.

When each subject had finished reading the essay, he was asked to evaluate it on a scale of one to nine on each of four dimensions: creativity, ideas, style, and general quality. In addition, he was asked to rate his impressions of the writer of the essay in four areas: intelligence, sensitivity, talent, and overall ability.

Conclusions: The attractive woman made a clean sweep in every category, with the greatest difference occurring when the poor essay was being rated. The experimenters suggested that "if you are ugly, you are not discriminated against a great deal so long as your performance is impressive. However, should performance be below par, attractiveness matters." They concluded that a beautiful person may be able to get by with inferior work because others expect that attractive people will perform well and therefore give them the benefit of the doubt when work is substandard or of dubious quality.

—G.P.W.

DETECTING LIES

Title of Experiment: The MEGALAB Truth Test

Conducted by: Dr. Richard Wiseman, University of Hertfordshire, England, in conjunction with the BBC, Radio 1, and the *Daily Telegraph*, on March 25, 1994, marking the end of National Science Week.

Object: To determine how various mass media affect the public's ability to discern whether someone is telling the truth or lying.

The Experiment: Dr. Wiseman taped two interviews with Sir Robin Day, an English political commentator, in which Sir Robin discussed his favorite films. In one interview Sir Robin told the truth, stating that his favorite film was *Some Like It Hot*. In the other he lied throughout, claiming his preference for *Gone With the Wind*, a movie he actually found "crashingly boring." Both interviews were then broadcast on Radio 1, shown on the television program *Tomorrow's World*, and printed in the *Daily Telegraph*. Listeners, viewers, and readers were asked to provide their opinions regarding which interview was truthful and which was not. The BBC set up a special telephone network, able to handle as many as 26,500 calls per minute; 37,000 viewers responded in five minutes; the *Daily Telegraph* generated 3,400 responses; Radio 1, about 1,000.

Conclusions: The lying interview was accurately detected by some 73 percent of radio listeners and 64 percent of newspaper readers, but only by 52 percent of television viewers. This data provided ample material for reflection. According to Dr. Wiseman, "When people try to spot liars, they tend to concentrate on body language and other visual clues. For example, most people think that liars do not look you straight in the eye. . . . This is a fallacy. Deceivers understand the way in which their prey thinks. They are aware, for example, that . . . they must maintain eye contact. . . . Good liars fake honesty by skillfully controlling their visual giveaways."

The experiment suggests, then, that when seeking the truth, it is better to avoid such decorations as eye contact and body language (an actor/politician, one realizes, could easily mislead millions), and focus on the most reliable and unadorned part of the message—the words themselves. Sir Robin, for example, used eighty-three words to convey his honest passion for *Some Like It Hot* but was able to muster only forty-three words regarding the Civil War epic.

Dr. Wise also notes that scientists "are beginning to explore the art of deception . . . the psychology of political skulduggery, military deception . . . and business fraud." Not surprisingly, this experiment demonstrates clearly that people are least able to discern between truth and falsehood when lies are broadcast on TV. Since the percentage of the public who reads is fast diminishing, and since, for many, television is quickly becoming the only means of obtaining information, the future would seem to bode ill for the truth, yet another increasingly endangered species. Of course, another possible—indeed, many would say obvious—conclusion to be drawn from this experiment is simply that, generally speaking, compared with the audiences of radio and print media, the public that watches television contains a particularly high percentage of suckers.

—E.H.B.

12 TRAVESTIES OF MODERN MEDICAL SCIENCE

1. THE INFAMOUS TUSKEGEE SYPHILIS STUDY

In 1932, 412 African-American males of Macon County, Alabama, suffering from syphilis, and 200 uninfected men, were entered in a study directed by the U.S. Public Health Service to determine how the syphilitic men would fare over a long period of time if left untreated. Although the men assumed they were receiving medical care (medical personnel visited them often), they did not receive any treatment during the forty years of the study. Despite acknowledgment that the study was of no medical value after penicillin became available for the treatment of syphilis, the program was not ended until 1972—and only after an estimated 20 to 100 of the infected men had died prematurely. Once the deception was revealed, the U.S. medical community established rules on "informed consent," requiring that a patient or test subject be told of an experiment's risks or benefits. In 1974 a $9 million settlement was negotiated for the survivors and families of the dead.

2. THE CHLOROMYCETIN CONFRONTATIONS

The antibiotic chloramphenicol was discovered in 1947 and soon hailed as a new wonder drug because of its ability to act against a variety of infectious diseases. Eventually it was administered to 40 million Americans. In 1952, after three years of record sales around the world, the drug was found to produce aplastic anemia, a fatal blood disorder, in a small but significant group of people. The Parke Davis Company, which controlled the production and distribution of chloramphenicol (trade name Chloromycetin), minimized the dangers of the drug and made a special effort to convince doctors of its safety. Thousands of deaths in the United States alone have occurred as a result of this misrepresentation, and yet the drug sales of Chloromycetin continued to be high until 1967, when publicity generated by a congressional hearing slowed down its sales in the United States. The drug is still sold in large quantities in other countries and continues to be used to treat Lyme disease and other disorders in the United States.

3. THE THALIDOMIDE TRAVESTY

Thalidomide, sold as a sedative, a cure for the flu, and a treatment for morning sickness, was produced and irresponsibly promoted for human use by a small German pharmaceutical firm (Chemie Grünenthal) without adequate pretesting in animals and with only cursory testing on humans. Distributed from 1957 in many countries as an over-the-counter drug, it was discovered in 1961 to be the cause of severe deformities, including missing arms, legs, and

Butch Lumpkin's mother took Thalidomide while she was pregnant, leaving Lumpkin with short arms and deformed fingers. Undeterred, Lumpkin grew up to be a tennis instructor at the Horseshoe Bend Tennis Club in Roswell, Georgia.

even anal openings in infants. The Thalidomide babies were born to mothers who, in early stages of pregnancy, had taken the drug on the advice of their physicians. Twelve thousand afflicted infants were born worldwide, mostly in West Germany, but also in the United Kingdom, the Scandinavian countries, the United States, and Canada. The drug was finally removed from the market in 1961 through the efforts of Dr. Frances Kelsey, the head of the Food and Drug Administration (FDA), who fought hard to keep it off shelves in the United States, and Dr. William McBride in Australia, who first raised the alarm.

In the 1990s, Thalidomide was making a comeback. It was being used in the treatment of Hansen's disease (leprosy) and it was being studied for possible use in the control of AIDS, leukemia, and some forms of arthritis. Doctors expressed hope, though, that they could synthesize a less dangerous form of it—it still had the potential for causing birth defects.

4. THE PAINFUL UGDP LESSON

In a report released in 1970, the University Group Diabetes Program, a research group involving twelve university medical centers and more than a thousand patients, indicated that tolbutamide, one of the drugs used to treat diabetes, was not only ineffective but also dangerous. Patients on the drug ran an increasing risk of cardiovascular disease, including heart attacks. Drug industry spokesmen immediately began discrediting the UGDP with such allegations as faulty trials design, poor management, and unethical procedures in recruiting patients. Despite this attack, the UGDP warnings were confirmed in 1978 and led to the imposition of restrictions on the drug's use. The delaying tactics of the drug industry paid off quite handsomely in their profits, although the FDA estimated that hundreds of deaths annually were included in the price.

5. THE 1976 SWINE FLU FIASCO

When a virus with swine flu characteristics appeared among soldiers at Fort Dix in New Jersey in February 1976, great apprehension was expressed by government health officials that an overdue flu epidemic was brewing. In March, President Gerald Ford called for a federal campaign to vaccinate virtually the entire U.S. population, and Congress passed an appropriation bill for $135 million for the project. Vaccinations began the following fall, and although no additional cases of swine flu were discovered, there were a disturbing number of cases of adverse reactions to the vaccine, including heart attacks and paralysis. By the time the program was suspended, twenty-three persons were reported dead. Because of these cases and the government's legal liability for

them, the program was ended in December 1976. Hundreds of claims running into the millions of dollars were filed against the U.S. government for damages involving the vaccine.

6. THE UNSCRUPULOUS DR. STOUGH

Through close working relations with a number of drug companies in the 1950s and 1960s, Dr. Austin Stough developed a lucrative commercial business supplying blood plasma and conducting large-scale testing of drugs in prisons in Alabama, Arkansas, and Oklahoma. His unsanitary procedures for obtaining blood plasma resulted in more than 500 cases of hepatitis among prisoners and at least three deaths. Despite knowledge of Stough's dangerous operating conditions, neither the drug companies nor the FDA made any move to regulate testing or disqualify Stough. It was only after public disclosure of his operation that Stough was relieved of some of his duties, but Alabama authorities permitted him to continue his drug testing, and Arkansas permitted him to continue his blood plasma program. No criminal charges against Stough were filed.

7. THE SOUTHAM-MANDEL CANCER CELL INOCULATIONS

On July 16, 1963, Dr. Chester Southam, an established cancer researcher, with the approval of Dr. Emanuel Mandel, the hospital medical director, inoculated twenty-two elderly patients at the Jewish Chronic Disease Hospital in Brooklyn, New York, with live cancer cells. The patients were merely asked to consent to a test that would determine their resistance to disease; they were not told they would receive an injection of live human cancer cells for purposes unrelated to their illnesses. Although none of the patients appeared to develop cancer as a result of the inoculations, the Board of Regents of New York censured Dr. Southam and Dr. Mandel for fraud and deceit and prohibited them from practicing medicine for one year.

8. THE ILLUSORY PRACTICE OF PREFRONTAL LOBOTOMY

From 1936 to 1960, prefrontal lobotomies were performed on some 50,000 mentally ill patients in the United States in an attempt to relieve intractable emotional and psychological symptoms. The conventional method was to drill holes in the skull and insert and rotate a knife to cut connections in the brain. Although apparently alleviating symptoms in some patients, the lobotomies reduced other patients to a near vegetative condition, or else had little visible effect on them. The operations were curtailed in the late 1950s because of professional and public criticism. However, in 1973 it was revealed that an estimated 100 to 1,000 lobotomies were still being performed annually in the United States, often in programs receiving federal funding.

9. THE NAZI EXPERIMENTS IN DEATH

The Nuremberg Tribunal in 1946 confirmed that prisoners of the Nazi state had been used as human guinea pigs by German physicians. Healthy prisoners were injected with doses of typhoid, smallpox, diphtheria, and malaria to test even the most unlikely antidotes. Young men were subjected to prolonged exposure to X rays, and after a period of two to four weeks they were castrated so that their organs could be dissected and studied. In experiments dealing with muscle regeneration and bone transplants, healthy legs, arms, shoulder blades, and muscles were removed in operations without any anesthesia. Thousands of people died in agony from these and many other experiments. Of the twenty-one Nazis actually tried at Nuremberg, eleven were sentenced to hang, seven were given prison sentences, and three were acquitted.

10. CHARITY HOSPITAL

Charity Hospital in New Orleans, Louisiana, treated the poorest of poor blacks in the segregated South of the 1940s. To bring funding into the hospital, the U.S. War Department and researchers from Tulane University were allowed to conduct radiation experiments on about 300 of the hospital's patients. Most tests involved only small amounts of radiation, equivalent to natural exposure to radioactive sources such as the Sun. But some included exposing patients to radioactive concoctions up to 100 times stronger than chest X rays. Some of the patients—one as young as fourteen years old—suffered cramps and diarrhea from oral radioactive mercury. On some, topical radioactive mercury was applied to open wounds to test how quickly the mercury was absorbed by the body. The tests went on into the 1950s, long after the Nuremberg trials had ended.

11. THE VANDERBILT AND OTHER RADIATION TESTS

In 1948, 751 pregnant women were fed radioactive iron at Vanderbilt University in Nashville, Tennessee, as part of a nutrition study. The women had come to the university's clinic for free prenatal care but became test subjects instead. A follow-up study done in the mid-1960s showed that three of the babies born to these women died of rare forms of childhood cancer.

In other radiation studies, more than 130 inmates in Oregon and Washington prisons were paid $5 a month to have their testicles dosed with radiation so that researchers could determine what effect radiation had on sex organs. The inmates got a $10 bonus to let the doctors biopsy their testes and $100 for going through the whole program.

Some 600 people in 800 experiments run by the Atomic Energy Commission were exposed to plutonium in the 1940s and 1950s. Eighteen U.S. government workers were injected with plutonium as part of the Manhattan Project in the 1940s—all eighteen had died by the 1990s. In 1993 the release of classified documents showed that the actual numbers of people—pregnant women, children, inmates, the poor—used in radiation tests were higher than suspected. In 1995, through the Human Experiments Litigation Project and other inquiries, it was revealed that at least 16,000 Americans had been guinea pigs for radiation testing, and Pentagon records declassified in 1995 showed that 40,000 military men were exposed to radiation during troop exercises.

12. LSD EXPERIMENTS

From 1949 to 1973, the U.S. Central Intelligence Agency (CIA) secretly funded a $25 million program of mind-control experiments at universities, prisons, and hospitals. Within the CIA the program was variously known as Project Bluebird, Project Artichoke, and MK-ULTRA. At least 39 of the more than 150 separate projects involved human subjects, many of whom did not know they were acting as guinea pigs, even though the Nuremberg Code of 1947, adopted by the United States in 1953, clearly states that medical research should be conducted only with the full consent and knowledge of the subjects.

Dr. Frank Olson was a biochemist working on top-secret germ warfare at Fort Detrick, Maryland, when he was given LSD as part of a 1953 experiment. During the following two weeks, his personality changed. His wife later reported that "he was very melancholy and talked about a mistake he had made." She did not know of her husband's LSD trip; it is questionable whether he himself knew what had happened to him. Olson went for psychiatric treatment to Dr. Harold Abramson (who later conducted CIA drug experiments at New York's Mount Sinai Hospital), but he remained disturbed. On November 28, 1953, two weeks after he took the LSD, Olson—probably unwittingly—ran across his room on the tenth floor of the Statler Hotel in Manhattan and jumped to his death through pulled drapes and a closed window. It was not until June 1975 that his family found out about the drug experiments by reading the Rockefeller Commission report on CIA activities. His widow and three children sued the government. President Gerald Ford apologized, and the family withdrew the suit. However, a private bill to compensate the family for suffering was introduced into Congress, and in 1976 Olson's widow was awarded $750,000. Olson's body was exhumed in 1994 and tests were conducted to determine whether he had been thrown out of the window in 1953. The results were inconclusive.

—The Eds.

QUOTEBOOK

DOCTORS

One of the first duties of the physician is to educate the masses not to take medicine.

Sir William Osler, ca. 1905

Doctors think a lot of patients are cured who have simply quit in disgust.

Don Herold

A hospital bed is a parked taxi with the meter running.

Groucho Marx, Reader's Digest, March 1973

Chapter 16

FAMILY AND LEISURE

LEISURE ACTIVITIES AND FADS

PING-PONG

Ping-Pong or table tennis? The controversy over what to call this popular indoor sport has raged almost since the game's inception in England in the 1880s. Ping-Pong, named after the sound made by a celluloid ball when it strikes the paddle's surface, is a casual game for basement dens. Table tennis, as it is called by connoisseurs, is a fast and demanding sport worthy of the Olympics, where it was first played competitively at Seoul in 1988.

In the beginning the game was strictly a drawing room amusement. The ball, a champagne cork, was hit by a cigar-box lid, the first paddle or bat, across a makeshift net fashioned from a row of books. James Gibbs, a founding member of the Amateur Athletics Association, introduced celluloid toy balls from America about 1891. A London sports goods company quickly put the balls, vellum "battledores," and a real net into production.

By 1900 Ping-Pong was growing in popularity in Great Britain and on the Continent. The initial fad soon faded, however, and the game's popularity didn't return until the 1920s, when the Ping-Pong Association changed its name to the more respectable Table Tennis Association. A few years later the game finally caught on in the United States. Parker Brothers, a game manufacturer in Salem, Massachusetts, copyrighted the name "Ping-Pong" and helped found the American Ping-Pong Association, which held national tournaments annually.

But the nation that dominated the sport for well over a decade was, curiously, Hungary, where it was the number one sport. The Hungarians won the first world championship, held in 1927, and Victor Barna, a young Hungarian champion, dazzled American audiences as he toured the country, smashing the ball from sometimes ten feet away from the table. His power game made table tennis a popular sport and helped sell 5 million Ping-Pong tables to American families during the 1930s.

Only with the outbreak of World War II did table tennis's popularity again flag, to be revived in the 1950s by new technology. The Japanese, who had been avid players since a visiting Japanese professor first brought the game home from England in 1902, introduced a new "sponge"-coated paddle that gave players much more control over the ball.

The game's greatest moment came in April 1971, when the American Table Tennis team received an invitation to play in the People's Republic of China, where Ping-Pong is as popular as baseball is in the United States. It was the first major thaw in U.S.-Chinese relations in more than two decades. The invitation was accepted, and although the Americans lost to the superior playing of the Chinese (men's, 5–3; women's, 5–4), they brought home an incredible diplomatic victory.

When Chinese premier Chou En-lai received the Americans the day after the match in Beijing's Great Hall of the People, he announced, "We have opened a new page in the relations of the Chinese and American people." The so-called Ping-Pong diplomacy smoothed the way for President Richard Nixon's historic trip to China in February 1972. "Probably never before in history has a sport been used so effectively as a tool of international diplomacy," said Time magazine.

A consummate politician, Nixon was quick to declare, during the American athletes' visit to China, "I was quite a Ping-Pong player in my days at law school. I might say I was fairly good at it."

The sport again took center stage in international relations twenty years later, when the South Koreans and the North Koreans joined together to defeat the Chinese team at the table tennis world championships in Japan in May 1991. It was the first time people from this divided land had worked together peacefully since their country was first split in half in 1945.

Today 66 nations belong to the International Table Tennis Federation (ITTF), which holds world championships every two years.

—S.A.O.

CROSSWORD PUZZLES

Newspaperman Arthur Wynne created the first modern crossword puzzle that appeared in a publication in the United States. An English-man born in Liverpool, editor Wynne placed the puzzle in the December 21, 1913, "Fun" page of the Sunday supplement to the *New York World*.

Did the idea of the crossword puzzle spring full-blown into Wynne's mind? Well, no—editor Wynne wanted something bright and new as a steady space filler. He had a vague recollection of a word puzzle he'd once seen in the London *Graphic*. So the first American crossword puzzle was born.

This puzzle was an instant if modest success with the readers of the *World*. It was diamond-shaped, with some of the following clues: a written acknowledgment (seven letters) (an-swer: receipt); the fiber of the gomuti palm (three letters) (answer: doh); to sink in mud (five letters) (answer: mired).

Wynne made other puzzles and is also given credit for the first insertion of black squares in the spaces between the letters. Although he deserves credit for this innovation, crosswords of many shapes and kinds had appeared before 1913 in nineteenth-century English periodicals for children. The mid-Victorian puzzles were derived from the "word square," a group of words arranged so the letters read alike verti-cally and horizontally. According to Margaret Petherbridge Farrar and Prosper Buranelli, the *World*'s puzzle experts in the 1920s, "A magical relation was thought to exist between the words in a word square." Such squares had a cabalistic force in the minds of the readers.

In 1913 English adults paid little attention to the American revival of the crossword puzzle; but when this interest became a positive craze in the 1920s, English enthusiasm grew. Soon almost all daily papers in the United States and Great Britain had crossword features. Not only that, but *les mots croisés* appeared in France, and puzzles sprang up in most other languages except those which do not lend themselves to vertical and horizontal word arrangement by letter, such as Chinese.

There are national differences in the style of crosswords. According to Margaret Pether-bridge Farrar, later the puzzle editor of the *New York Times*, the British style uses many un-keyed letters with no cross clues, eliminates most short words, and features difficult defini-tions. In the United States, conservative rules usually call for symmetrical patterns, no more than one-sixth of the squares black, allover interlock of words, no cutoff segments or un-keyed letters. The quality of the puzzle is judged by the ingenuity of word combinations and the skill in selection of definitions or clues.

The golden age of the crossword puzzle in the United States was during the 1920s, when many fads swept the country—from goldfish swallow-ing to making bathtub gin. As *Publishers Weekly* reported, "The crossword puzzle was America's favorite licit indoor activity in the days before television." F. Scott Fitzgerald considered the popularity of crossword puzzles a sign of "widespread neurosis."

Interest in working crossword puzzles was intense. The Baltimore and Ohio Railroad pro-vided dictionaries in each car on its main commuter line. In Budapest a waiter left a suicide note in the form of a crossword puzzle. In 1924 the first book of crossword puzzles, the *Crossword Puzzle Book*, appeared under the imprint of the Plaza Publishing Company. It became a best-seller and turned Simon and Schuster into a top publishing firm. Amazingly, the publishers did not want their names on the book because they were not sure it would be a success.

Popular interest in the 1920s is shown by aids that were marketed to help puzzle solvers. One was a crossword "tinder," an indicator with a series of movable alphabets on paper strips that were supposed to aid in forming proper letter arrangements before they were written in the square. The device allowed the trial of test words, "saving erasures and changes on the puzzle chart. The indicator, which can be carried in the pocket, does not require a pencil for marking and its construction permits as ready operation as a small adding machine" (*Popular Mechanics*, March 1925).

The main interest among fans in the 1920s was in the puzzle as an aid to language development. The literary intelligentsia, includ-ing Franklin P. Adams, Heywood Broun, Robert Benchley, and Emily Post, took up the puzzle and fed this interest. In the *Literary Digest* of June 6, 1925, Arthur Maurice, former editor of the *Bookman*, claimed to have found forty words that had grown unfamiliar through gen-eral mental laziness but were now resurrected due to the crossword puzzle craze.

Maurice said, "It is the subtle restoration of these words, a direct result of the crossword puzzle, that is galvanizing casual talk into a new and healthy flexibility. A cathedral, for example, is no longer a blur of vague images. The picture has cleared with the rescued under-standing of 'apse' and 'nave.' "

Another reason for the extraordinary success of crossword puzzles, according to Columbia University professors of psychology H. E. Jones and Prescott Leeky, was the low cost of working them, and, the professors added, "The puzzles appeal to the sex instinct in that they supply a new reason for social gatherings, of young particularly."

In the 1920s, as now, there were two schools of puzzle-solution fans: those who grimly armed themselves with dictionaries, gazeteers, and classical Latin phrase books, and free souls "who'd sooner die in the flames than consult a reference book" (*Publishers Weekly*).

Among feats recorded: The fastest time for completing the *London Times* crossword is three minutes, forty-five seconds. This record was set by Roy Dean, age forty-three, of Bromley, Kent, in the British Broadcasting Corporation's "Today" radio studio on December 19, 1970. On the other hand, in May 1966 the *Times* received an announcement from Mr. and Mrs. D. T. Lloyd, a British couple stationed in Fiji, that Mrs. Lloyd had just succeeded in completing their crossword No. 673 from the April 4, 1932, issue—it had gone unfinished for thirty-four years, having been used to wrap a package. The daily *New York Times* record of two minutes, ten seconds, set on May 4, 1989, is held by Stanley Newman.

The world's largest published crossword puzzle, with 12,489 clues across and 13,125 down, was constructed by Robert Turcot of Quebec, Canada.

—M.J.M.

BRIDGE

A card game played by two opposing teams of two partners, bridge evolved out of the English game of whist, although leading bridge expert Charles Goren was quick to point out that whist is "as much like twentieth century contract bridge as the Wrights' airplane is like the X-15."

The game was introduced in England by Lord Brougham in 1894, after he learned it in the south of France. When bridge replaced whist at the venerable Portland Club, one member declared, "It is disgusting to find the temple of whist thus desecrated." He later changed his mind, and announced that there was "no game of cards in the world wherein skill, sound judgment, and insight into the adversary's methods will meet with more certain reward than they will in bridge."

While bridge originally continued the polite and antique trappings of its predecessor, it quickly evolved into a more aggressive and exciting game. Whist-bridge was soon supplanted by "auction" bridge, where the fourth hand was auctioned among three players. By the beginning of the 1900s, auction bridge was replaced by "contract" bridge, in which the bidder can only get the points he contracts to make in a game. This novel idea was dreamed up by American yachtsman and avid card player Harold Vanderbilt during a long cruise from San Francisco to Havana in 1926. Vanderbilt's three companion players were delighted with his "jazzed up" version of the game, which also offered a simpler system for scoring.

The 1930s saw bridge transform itself from a game of the leisure class to the favorite pastime of millions of middle-class Americans. The same Great Depression that made Monopoly a household word made bridge the most popular card game in America. More than a thousand newspapers ran syndicated columns on how to play and win the game. It was the subject of poems and referred to in plays, movies, and novels. Bridge experts such as Ely Culbertson became national celebrities.

Culbertson was contract bridge's greatest exponent and one of its most colorful characters. He claimed to have been born in Romania to an American engineer and the daughter of a Cossack chieftain. A rival once called him "the racketeer of the bridge world," but his talent for self-promotion left even his enemies in awe. To further his career and promote his forthcoming books on bridge, Culbertson challenged the British to a showdown game. He and his American partner beat three British teams. When his egotistical behavior started to annoy even his American colleagues, they joined together to formulate their own system of bridge and pitted it against his. In 1931 Culbertson challenged Sidney Lenz, representative of "the Official System," to what came to be called the bridge battle of the century.

A small legion of journalists set up house in Culbertson's apartment, where he provided entertaining copy for their newspapers with his antics. Once he horrified the fastidious Lenz by eating a steak as they played. When Lenz asked, "Why don't you eat at the proper time, like the rest of us?" Culbertson coolly replied, "My vast public won't let me."

After four weeks of such psychological warfare, Culbertson and his partner won by 8,980 points. The publicity succeeded—*Culbertson's Own Summary of Bids and Responses* was on the list of the ten best-selling nonfiction books in America in 1931 and 1932, and his *Contract Bridge Blue Book* made the list in 1931 and 1933.

When bridge sagged in popularity after World War II, Culbertson's successor, Charles Goren, brought it back to life with a simplified system of evaluating hands before bidding. The possible bridge hands that can be dealt have been calculated by computer at 635,013,559,599.

The game has even been used by the defense in a court of law. Pauline Harrison, heir to the DuPont fortune, suffered a stroke in May 1990 and her children claimed she was incompetent to handle her affairs. Her lawyers argued convincingly for Mrs. Harrison's competence, telling the court she had played bridge, and won, three weeks after her stroke.

—S.A.O.

MONOPOLY

The all-time king of board games was almost rejected by the company it subsequently made rich. Parker Brothers of Salem, Massachusetts, found the game had "fifty-two fundamental errors," not the least of which were that it was too complicated, took too long to play, and had no final objective or goal, other than to drive the other players into bankruptcy.

Monopoly was created in 1933 by Charles B. Darrow, an out-of-work salesman for an engineering firm from Germantown, Pennsylvania. Darrow thought up board games at home to stave off boredom and grim thoughts about his future. He hand-drew the first Monopoly game on a round piece of linoleum and fashioned the houses and hotels from bits of wood he found in a lumberyard. He named the properties after the streets of Atlantic City, where he and his wife had spent their last vacation before the stock market crashed. Since he could find only three railroads that passed through Atlantic City, Darrow cheated and made Short Line, a bus company that carried freight, into the game's fourth railroad.

When friends who played the game at his house asked for their own copy, Darrow obliged. He charged $4.00 a copy, making a profit of $1.75 on each set. As word of Monopoly got around, Darrow found himself unable to keep up with the demand, and he made a deal with a printing company to manufacture the game for him. After he sold 17,000 copies, Darrow decided his cottage industry was ready to become big business and began looking for a commercial manufacturer.

Parker Brothers' initial reluctance to buy the game was overcome when a friend of George Parker's daughter Sally told her she had bought a copy of the game at the famous New York toy store F. A. O. Schwarz and fallen in love with it. Sally's husband, the company's president, bought a copy and stayed up until one in the morning playing it. The very next day he offered to buy the game outright from Darrow, who agreed. "Taking the precepts of Monopoly to heart, I did not care to speculate," the game's inventor later explained.

Orders for the game flooded in so quickly that Parker Brothers had to store them in laundry baskets in the hallways. By 1935 the company was turning out 20,000 sets of Monopoly a week. Within the year, sales reached the $1 million mark. As for Darrow, his modest royalty made him a millionaire by age forty-six.

Even after its initial success, however, Parker Brothers expected the "fad" for Monopoly to fade quickly. On December 19, 1936, company president Parker sent a memo to the manufacturing plant ordering them to "cease absolutely to make any more boards or utensil boxes. We will stop making Monopoly against the possibility of a very early slump."

But Monopoly's popularity has never ended. Today it is an international success, published in twenty-seven nations and fifteen languages, including Greek, German, Hebrew, and Chinese. The only place where Monopoly was not played for many years was the former Soviet Union, which, predictably, found the game "too capitalistic."

How to explain Monopoly's incredible run as the number one copyrighted board game in the world? (It was unseated from that position only briefly by Scrabble and Trivial Pursuit.) Many experts tie its initial popularity to the depression. People could turn from grim economic realities to the fantasy world of high finance, where players bought up properties and grew as rich as Rockefeller. To support this theory, the game's popularity has risen proportionally every time since then that the economy has taken a dip.

To illustrate the game's preeminence, when the city fathers of Atlantic City proposed to rename Baltic and Mediterranean Avenues in early 1973, Monopoly players everywhere were outraged. The bill was unanimously killed by city commissioners in response to the protest, which led Commissioner Joseph Lazarow to compose this ditty:

To this ordinance vote no.
To our residents it presents a great woe.
Baltic and Mediterranean are the streets we know.
Without them we could never pass GO.

Monopoly is a required part of a course on financial accounting on the Bloomington campus of Indiana University. Students grade each other on their ability to record Monopoly transactions on double-entry accounting ledgers. In November 1994 three prisoners in Conway, Arkansas, broke out of the Faulkner County Jail by using the wheelbarrow from a Monopoly set to remove tamper-resistant screws on the air duct coverings in their cell.

For the record, the most frequently landed-on square, according to computer calculations, is Illinois Avenue. The longest recorded single game lasted 820 hours in the summer of 1971 and involved twenty players in Danville, California.

—S.A.O.

SCRABBLE

For many Americans, 1931 was the cruelest year of the Great Depression. Almost one in four workers was unemployed, including an architect from Rhinebeck, New York, named Alfred Mosher Butts. "There I was, out of a job, needing something to do," Butts remembered. Then an idea came to him—not a flash, just a gentle nudge that sent him into motion. Said Butts, "I happened to be a games buff, and I got the notion that I could invent a successful game."

Butts created a word game played with tiny wooden letter tiles that were distributed to players randomly, like surprises from a grab bag. Using the tiles, one player spelled out a word, leaving the opposing player the task of creating a separate word attached to at least one letter of the first word. Piecing out words containing infrequently used letters increased one's chances of winning. For example, using the letter z earned a person ten points, while the five vowels were worth only one point each.

In 1938, seven years after the game's creation, Butts designed a special board consisting of 225 squares. Players now laid their tiles on the board and scored bonus points when they covered a premium square. The board gave the game a chess-playing element, the need to stretch one's mind and anticipate the opponent's moves. When the board became crowded, each new word or letter changed the pattern of play and profoundly altered strategy.

Throughout the 1930s Butts tried to sell his game for the modest price of $1.50 a set. Sales were dismal. Also, none of the board-game companies were interested in marketing it because, as Butts complained, "[they all] wanted childish games and rejected it without ever playing it." Meanwhile, board games such as Monopoly and mahjong enjoyed wild success during the depression era, when a night out for dinner or the movies put a strain on the budget of most families.

No doubt the lack of a catchy name also dampened sales. As imaginative as Butts was when dreaming up his brainchild, he drew a blank when it came to naming the new baby. At one point he called it Lexico, and at another simply It. When he introduced the board he renamed the game Criss-Cross Words. None of these names stuck, none inspired people to play.

In 1948 James Brunot, a friend who often played with Butts and his wife, agreed to manufacture and sell the game. Brunot was a prominent government official who had recently retired and hoped marketing this "intellectual word game" would earn him a little extra money. It was Brunot who gave it a new name: Scrabble. According to the dictionary, the word meant "to scratch, scrape, or paw with the hands or feet." Brunot decided this was an apt description of a player "scrabbling" to fit a word onto the board.

During its first year of operation, Brunot's company sold only 2,500 sets. But the Scrabble skyrocket was beginning a countdown for a spectacular lift-off. The women of Smith College were the first to be bitten by the Scrabble bug after one young lady brought the game on campus and word buzzed from dorm to dorm. The success at Smith established Scrabble as a favorite board game among intelligent, college-bred people. Next an executive from Macy's department store tried the game, was smitten by it, and placed a large order. At the time, the

Macy's Manhattan establishment was billed as "the world's largest department store." In 1952 Brunot's tiny distributing company, which was based in his living room, was suddenly swamped by orders for 60,000 sets. Brunot said, "It was like pumping them into a bottomless pit."

Sales soon topped 1 million sets, and in 1954 Selchow and Righter, a Long Island–based company, bought the manufacturing and marketing rights to Scrabble from Brunot and Butts. Selchow and Righter was one of the many companies that had rejected the game when Butts offered it to them in the 1930s.

Today, some 100 million sets later, Scrabble is played in German, Italian, French, Russian, Hebrew, and English braille. Hollywood has marketed a dirty-word version, and someone else came up with Strip Scrabble. The tiles are made, as they have been since the early 1950s, of Bavarian Black Forest maple, because the consistent grain prevents experts from recognizing the highest-scoring pieces by the grain patterns on the back of the tiles.

Scrabble clubs sponsor some seventy-five tournaments of traditional Scrabble each year. The first world championship was held in London in 1991. Tournament players, armed with the game's ultimate rulebook, *The Official Scrabble Players Dictionary*, delight in fashioning words such as *quaids* (meaning Far Eastern rulers) and *xu* (a monetary unit). Other Scrabble-spoken concoctions include: *beigy, duvetyn,* and *tirrivee*. The highest word score ever achieved was 302 points, by American Jeff Clark for *methodize* and by Canadian Ron Manson for *reequips*. For the record, the number of q words without a u is nine.

Alfred Butts, Scrabble's inventor, died on April 4, 1993. He was ninety-three years old. Throughout his life he remained mystified as to how his creation, his humble attempt to make some money during the bleak depression years, blossomed into a game played with passion by millions of very bright people. He once said, "I invented the dern game, and what happened is still crazy to me."

—R.C.S.

HULA HOOPS

How a circle of polyethylene plastic held together by staples and a wooden plug began one of the greatest fads in modern times remains something of a puzzle.

This most American of fads actually started in Australia, where a toy manufacturer created a bamboo ring that became a popular form of exercise in school gym classes in the early 1950s. The ring fitted around a student's midsection and swung from side to side as the body gyrated. Richard Knerr and Arthur "Spud" Melin, two enterprising Americans, saw the potential of the toy and bought the rights for their company, Wham-O (named for the sound made by their first novelty, a slingshot).

Wham-O transformed the wooden hoop into a light but stiff plastic one, called it the Hula Hoop, and retailed it for three dollars in the spring of 1958. Promotion of the Hula Hoop consisted mainly of public demonstrations by Melin at southern California parks, beaches, and schools. Within days word of mouth had made the Hula Hoop a hot item on the West Coast. The hip-gyrating sport became an obsession for young people and their parents, who saw it as a combination of good, clean fun and exercise. Psychologists who studied the phenomenon saw a more sexual attraction, based on the hip-grinding movement required to keep the hoop in motion. They also claimed the hoop was a symbolic vagina. Stepping into it was akin to reentering the womb. Other experts saw it as a mild form of youth rebellion. According to Dr. Joyce Brothers, kids "delight in the fact that they can keep the hoops spinning in orbit, while many adults can't." Economists saw it more simply as a way for Americans to forget temporarily the current national recession.

Whatever the reason for the attraction, the Hula Hoop craze quickly spread across the nation. Before, most fads had moved from east to west. From now on the process would be irrevocably reversed.

Wham-O ceased production of its other products, including the fledgling Frisbee, and began cranking out 20,000 Hula Hoops a day. But they still couldn't keep up with the demand. Other manufacturers quickly jumped in. Although Wham-O had made the Hula Hoop their exclusive trademark, their loose patent on the product couldn't stop a plethora of imitators, including Spin-a-Hoop, Wiggle-A-Hoop, Hoop-Zing, Hooper Dooper, and the Whoop-De-Do.

Part of the attraction of the hoop was its utter simplicity, although keeping it airborne took considerable skill. Instructions for the Spin-a-Hoop evoked another fad that would have more staying power—rock and roll: "Hug the hoop to the backside. . . . Push hard with the right hand. . . . Now rock, man, rock! . . . Don't twist. . . . Swing it. . . . Sway it. . . . You got it!"

By midsummer, Americans had bought 70 million hoops and the craze had spread to Great Britain, continental Europe, and even Japan. The "hura hoopu," however, suffered a setback when a girl was killed chasing her hoop into Tokyo traffic, causing the toy to be banned in that city in November.

By then the hoop had lost its allure for Americans as well. Saturation and the approach of colder weather ended the hoop craze as quickly as it had begun. Wham-O, ironically, had just been granted a protective patent for its product when the bubble burst. The company was stuck with thousands of hoops and it nearly folded. Frantic dealers tried new gimmicks to unload their inventory. They added bells and rainbow colors and attached rope lariats so the hoop could double as a pet leash. Some even punched holes in their hoops and tried to sell them as lawn showers. All to no avail.

But Wham-O, revived by the more steady sales of the Frisbee, believed lightning could strike twice. In the mid-sixties they came out with a Hula Hoop with a ball bearing inside that made a noise when it was gyrated. The Shoop Shoop Hoop did not come close to the popularity of the original, but it continued to sell steadily.

In 1982 Wham-O tried still again with a striped, candy-scented Peppermint Hula Hoop. This time the company went all out with an expensive ad campaign that included Miss U.S.A. gyrating a hoop at the New York Toy Fair. But the public didn't buy it and the new version was a resounding flop. Maybe they should have sent Spud Melin out to a few beaches instead.
—S.A.O.

FRISBEE

Few toys have had as complicated a history as the Frisbee. The very origin of its odd name is a matter of debate. Some say it came from the Mother Frisbie Pie Company in Bridgeport, Connecticut, whose tins were more popular with Yale students than the pies they contained. As far back as the 1870s, students would hurl the tins through the air, yelling "Frisbee!" as a golfer might holler "Fore!" Others claim the term originated even further back, in 1827, when a Yalie named Frisbee threw a collection plate 200 feet in protest against the school's required chapel services. Frisbee manufacturer Richard Knerr claimed he named the disc after a character in a newspaper comic strip—Mr. Frisbee.

Knerr, however, didn't dream up the disc itself. It was the brainchild of two men, on only one of whom fortune smiled. New Hampshire furniture maker Bill Robes created what he called his "Space Saucer" in the shape of a tin-can lid. He sold them to students for fifty cents apiece. Seeing potential in his product, he took it to Parker Brothers, makers of Monopoly and other board games. They wanted to manufacture Robes's saucer, but he didn't like the deal they offered him and turned them down.

Meanwhile, across the country in Los Angeles, twenty-eight-year-old building inspector Frederick Morrison had created his own flying disc, the Flyin' Saucer, which he later renamed the Pluto Platter. Morrison had a touch of the con man in his soul and would pitch his platters at country fairs and public beaches. At the Pomona Fair he claimed the saucer was controlled by an "invisible wire," which he sold to patrons for one dollar. The Platter came free.

Knerr and Arthur Melin, co-owners of the Wham-O novelty company, bought the rights to

Morrison's invention in 1956, changed the metal to plastic to make it less dangerous, and added ridges along the disc's surface to break up the airflow and keep it stable when airborne. The following year Wham-O came out with the first Frisbee. Unlike the firm's next big product, the Hula Hoop, the Frisbee's sales took off slowly but steadily, like the airborne disc itself.

Robes, who had developed his saucer several years before Morrison, thought the other man had stolen his idea, but he later realized they had been working independently.

In the late 1960s, a new generation of athletes discovered the Frisbee and were not content with merely tossing it back and forth across a lawn. They came up with complicated team sports for the versatile disc, most notably Ultimate Frisbee, a challenging game that combines football, soccer, and basketball. Invented in the parking lot of Columbia High School in Maplewood, New Jersey, in 1969, Ultimate Frisbee grew in popularity and was being played by 6,000 Americans by 1988.

Each year a sixteen-week tournament pits national teams against one another to contend for the world championship. Other Frisbee games include Guts Frisbee, Dog-Bee, and Frisbee Golf, which at the height of its popularity drew 10,000 players a week in Los Angeles alone. Wham-O sponsors the yearly U.S. Open Flying Disc Championship in which 260 Frisbee hurlers vie for tens of thousands of dollars in prize money.

The aerodynamic design of the Frisbee caught the attention of the U.S. Navy in 1969. It spent $400,000 for secret studies molding the discs into flares to be launched from airplanes. Unfortunately, the Frisbees flew up instead of down and were quickly retired from the armed forces.

The International Frisbee Association numbered 70,000 members by 1973 and even boasted a canine corps, made up of dogs who prefer catching a Frisbee to a stick or a bone.

Frisbees have been hurled everywhere from the White House lawn to the Great Wall of China, where it was first tossed between presidential daughter Susan Ford Bales and cartoonist Garry Trudeau. Since the heady days of the 1970s, the Frisbee has sagged some in popularity, although total sales by Wham-O alone have topped $100 million.

For the record, the farthest a Frisbee has been thrown is 190 meters (208 yards). The maximum time aloft is 16.72 seconds, and the highest speed thrown is 90 miles per hour.

—S.A.O.

VIDEO GAMES AND TETRIS

Video games may have started in the United States, but they owe their most recent world success to a tough Japanese businessman and a mild-mannered Russian computer scientist.

The Nintendo company of Japan was founded in 1889 as a manufacturer of playing cards. Nintendo means "work hard, but in the end, it is in heaven's hands." Since 1949 Nintendo has been in the hands of Hiroshi Yamauchi, the great-grandson of the company's founder. With a combination of ingenuity and ruthlessness, Yamauchi parlayed a small family company into the most successful business in Japan, surpassing Toyota in 1991.

Yamauchi expanded the company holdings to include everything from instant rice to a hotel that catered to hour-long trysts. Intrigued by the success of Atari and other American companies with arcade and home video games in the 1970s, Yamauchi came out with his first arcade video game, Donkey Kong. His employees were horrified at the silly name he chose and were convinced it would sink without a trace amid the more macho-oriented arcade competition. But the less threatening, humorous Donkey Kong appealed to kids and adults alike and became an international hit. In 1983 Nintendo put out Japan's first family computer, called Famicon. By pitting his game designers against one another, Yamauchi developed such popular games as Super Mario Brothers and the Legend of Zelda.

By the time Nintendo arrived in America in 1985, the U.S. video market had nearly bottomed out. Nintendo revitalized it, selling 34 million systems in the United States by 1995 and a total of 50 million worldwide.

Oddly enough, Yamauchi himself had no interest in or aptitude for the video games he produced, claiming "I have better things to do." One of those things was developing a portable video game, GameBoy, which became another runaway best-seller in the late 1980s.

In more recent years, Nintendo's domination in the game field has been seriously challenged by another Japanese company, Sega, which came out with Sega Genesis, a more powerful and sophisticated video system, in 1989. As the company slogan proudly proclaimed, "Sega Genesis does what Nintendon't." Two years later Yamauchi came back with a system that matched Genesis's power, Super NES (Nintendo Entertainment System), but the damage had been done. Sega had become a major player and continues to cut into Nintendo's market share. Besieged with lawsuits from other companies it allegedly stole ideas and technology from, Nintendo suffered another major blow in August 1994 when a federal court ordered it to pay $208.3 million to a bankrupt computer company for patent violation.

No one could be more different in character from ruthless executive Yamauchi than Aleksei Pazhitnov, a Russian computer scientist and the creator of the most popular computer game in the world today. He invented the game in 1985 on his antiquated microcomputer to stave off boredom at work in a computer laboratory in Moscow's Academy of Science. Pazhitnov based his simple game on the ancient Roman puzzle called Pentamino, in which players had to arrange twelve pieces in five squares into a perfect rectangle. He reduced the five squares to four and called the game Tetris, from the Greek *tetra*, meaning four. The game caught on like wildfire in the computer labs, reaching the point where one lab director banned it in order to get employees back to work.

But there was no stopping Tetris. Pazhitnov copied the game onto disks and gave them to friends. The game was eventually smuggled out of Russia to Budapest, Hungary, where it was grabbed up by such video game giants as Atari and Nintendo. Because the Soviets at the time had no means of copyrighting software, these companies easily bought up the rights to Tetris and quickly turned it into the most popular computer game in the world.

Both Pazhitnov and the Soviet government were flabbergasted by the news of the game's success. The Soviets slapped lawsuits on the manufacturers and now receive millions of dollars in royalties. Not so for the game's creator. As a private citizen under pre-perestroika laws, Pazhitnov had no claim on his invention and received not a penny for it. However, he quickly became a media star when, on a one-month tour of the United States, he was swamped by fans wanting his autograph on their Tetris boxes. Pazhitnov has since developed a three-dimensional expansion of Tetris, called Welltris, for which he is being well paid by Spectrum HoloByte—a happy ending to a modern-day computer fairy tale.

—S.A.O.

> We are closer to the ants than to the butterflies.
> Very few people can endure much leisure.
> Gerald Brenan, *Thoughts in a Dry Season*, 1979

FASHION FIRSTS

The same costume will be	
Indecent	10 years before its time
Shameless	5 years before its time
Outré (daring)	1 year before its time
Smart	
Dowdy	1 year after its time
Hideous	10 years after its time
Ridiculous	20 years after its time
Amusing	30 years after its time
Quaint	50 years after its time
Charming	70 years after its time
Romantic	100 years after its time
Beautiful	150 years after its time

James Laver, *Taste and Fashion*, 1937

1900—Button-Down Collars: John Brooks, of the celebrated men's outfitters Brooks Brothers, found a day out at the polo grounds in New Bedford a profitable experience. He noticed that some of the visiting British players had the collars of their shirts buttoned down and learned that it was to prevent their riding up into their faces on the field of play. Brooks had a special line of shirts made up with button-down collars, which he launched as the Polo. Originally the buttoned-down look was adopted only for sportswear, but it was adopted on Ivy League campuses for general wear in the early 1950s.

1906—Permanent Waving: German-born Karl Ludwig Nessler was working as a hair stylist in a London salon when he first tried out his new technique of permanent waving on a customer.

The boss spotted him and he was instantly dismissed. This was fortuitous, as it was exactly the spur he needed to go into business on his own account. On October 8, 1906, he introduced his Nessler Permanent Waving at his salon in London's Oxford Street. At first customers were few. They had to wear a dozen heavy brass curlers weighing 1¾ pounds each, the process took six hours to complete, and the cost was beyond all but the very rich at fifty-five dollars. Success came only when Nessler emigrated to the United States on the outbreak of World War I to avoid being interned as an enemy alien. Soon after his arrival the fashionable exhibition dancer Irene Castle introduced "bobbed" hair, and permanent waving became a craze that swept America.

1909—One-Piece Bathing Suit: Australian-born swimmer Annette Kellerman caused public outrage by appearing in public on a California beach wearing the first one-piece bathing dress. No stranger to controversy, in 1915 she gave the moral guardians of America something more to chew on when she dispensed with a bathing suit altogether to frolic in and out of the water naked in the Fox movie *Daughter of the Gods*.

1909—Sportswoman to Wear Trousers: Scion of a Boston Brahmin family, Eleanor Sears was a superb all-around athlete who believed that women would never be able to play team games effectively until they abandoned their skirts. In 1909 she strode onto the polo ground at the

Burlingame Country Club wearing jacket and trousers and asked to be allowed to join in a match against a team from England. Miss Sears's blow for dress reform was premature. The captain of the English team was rendered speechless with indignation and the coach of the American team ordered her off the field. Attitudes toward rational dress for women relaxed during World War I, when there was little time for sport but many women donned pants for workwear. Just ten years after Eleanor Sears's frustrated effort, a Leeds, England, schoolgirl named Elaine (later Baroness) Burton appeared in shorts for the first time at a track and field event in the Northern Counties (England) Ladies' Athletics Championships—and nobody ordered her off.

1913—Zipper: The zip fastener as we know it today was patented on April 29, 1913, by Gideon Sundback, a young Swedish engineer from Hoboken, New Jersey. There had been earlier attempts to produce a slide fastener, but they all suffered from the fatal flaw of coming apart under pressure. Sundback's improved version worked on the principle of identical units mounted on parallel tapes and was completely reliable. Initially, though, it met with no greater commercial success than its inferior predecessors. The navy put them on pilot's overalls, the army on the pockets of uniforms, and the air corps found a use for them never contemplated by the inventor—zipping the fabric onto the wings of airplanes. After the war the fasteners began to be incorporated into footwear, the B. F. Goodrich Company coining the name "Zipper" when they used them on their rubber galoshes. But although zippers were sometimes used on sports clothing, the high priests and priestesses of haute couture disdained anything so practical until Elsa Schiaparelli started to put them on the back of women's dresses at her Paris fashion house in 1931. Menswear finally succumbed in 1935, when fly buttons on men's pants were first replaced with the far more efficient, though occasionally painful, zip fastener.

1914—Backless Brassiere: The first patent for a brassiere was taken out by New York debutante Mary Phelps Jacob on November 13, 1914. But was it the very first brassiere? What the French called soutien-gorge was already known in Paris, but as a large, cumbersome garment full of frills and furbelows. Jacob's was the first elasticized, backless brassiere, designed to release women from the tyranny of the corset and enable them to participate in sports and other outdoor activities without physical restraint. Her prototype, though, had consisted of no more than two pocket handkerchiefs and a piece of pink ribbon. She conceived the idea while changing for a ball, the thought of

dancing the night away in a tight, whaleboned corset inspiring her to find a looser and less constricting substitute. Within half an hour her French maid had stitched together this ultralightweight bust supporter and Jacob was able to enjoy the ball with a new sense of freedom. Friends to whom she confided her secret asked her to produce bras for them, and then one day a letter arrived from a total stranger asking for one and enclosing a dollar bill. Realizing that there was a market for her invention, Jacob hired a designer to produce a detailed specification for her patent application, then sold the patent to the Warner Corset Company for $1,500 outright. Had she opted for royalties instead, she would have earned at least a hundredfold.

1914—Fashion Show: The first fashion parade with live models in the United States was organized by Edna Woolman Chase, editor of American Vogue, and held in the ballroom of the Ritz-Carlton Hotel in New York on November 4, 1914. (The first in the world had been held in London in 1899.) The object was to showcase American fashion, imports of Parisian couture having been suspended because of the war, though Mrs. Chase admitted in her memoirs to an ulterior motive—with no new designs from Paris, she had nothing with which to fill the pages of Vogue. Among the fashion houses represented were Bendel, Mollie, O'Hara, Bergdorf-Goodman, Gunther, Tappi, Maison Jacqueline, and Kurzman. The models appeared on a stage, turned left, turned right, descended a short flight of steps, and paraded down the center aisle. The only essential difference between the first fashion show and those of today was that the catwalk had yet to be invented.

1915—Lipstick: Coloring for the lips had been sold in pots for centuries, even though it was seldom used by respectable women. It was not until 1915 that it became available in stick form, retailed in a metal cartridge container by American cosmetician Maurice Levy.

1916—Liquid Nail Polish: No sooner had women started applying lipstick than they were shocking their menfolk by varnishing their nails. The first nail polish was Cutex, introduced by Northma Warren.

1921—Chanel No. 5: Ernst Beaux created the first "designer perfume" for legendary Paris couturier Coco Chanel while they were staying in Biarritz. And what about Chanel Nos. 1–4? They never existed. The 5 was coined because the perfume was launched in 1921 on the fifth day of the fifth month.

1923—Varnished Toenails: Pola Negri, eccentric Polish-born superstar of the Hollywood silents, pioneered the practice of polishing toenails. She later recalled that the first time she went out in public wearing sandals and scarlet toenails, a woman glanced at her feet and then shrieked, "She's bleeding!"

1926—Bare Legs: Although Pola Negri had started to go bare-legged at the same time that she began painting her toenails (see above), it was some years before the practice caught on among the other denizens of Hollywood. Joan Crawford claimed to have pioneered the fashion for bare legs with evening wear, abandoning her stockings when hemlines reached the knee in 1926 and only putting them on again when long frocks came back into fashion in 1930. What was acceptable in private, however, took some daring in public. In 1927 blond starlet Rita Carewe began going stockingless for comfort in the hot Los Angeles summer, but in order to preserve the proprieties she polished her tanned legs to look as if they were clad in silk. At the Wimbledon championships that same year, teenage South African tennis star "Billie" Tapscott was booed by the crowd for appearing on court with her legs bare.

1928—Women's Pants for Evening Wear: Women had started wearing colorful "beach pajamas" on the French Riviera in 1926, but they were definitely only for the *plage*. Two years later British actress Hermione Baddeley defied convention when she wore pants for an evening reception to celebrate her wedding to the aristocrat the Honorable David Tennant.

1930—Women's Pants For Day Wear: The movies have always exerted a strong influence on fashion and never more so than when Marlene Dietrich appeared in slacks in Josef von Sternberg's classic picture *Morocco*. The women of America took to pants with an eagerness that might have been more restrained had they understood von Sternberg's intention to signal the lesbian tendency of the character portrayed by the alluring Dietrich.

1935—Men's Briefs: Introduced by the Cooper Underwear Company of Kenosha, Wisconsin, the first briefs with an open seam went on sale at Marshall Field's in Chicago in January. When they were launched in Britain in 1938, the manufacturers advised left-handers to wear them inside out.

1935—Women's Jeans: No one knows for sure when women started to wear jeans, though one thing is sure—they *never* wore them to ride the range as depicted in movies of the old West. In the new West, it seems to have had more to do with dude ranching. The May 15, 1935, issue of *Vogue* depicts two chic and sophisticated Manhattanites improbably dressed as cowgirls. Part

Marlene Dietrich, pioneer of women's trousers, accompanied by Maurice Chevalier and Gary Cooper, 1930.

of the costume, *Vogue* explained, was "simple-but-severe blue jeans or Levis, turned up at the bottom once, laundered before wearing (to eliminate stiffness), cut straight and tight fitting, worn low on the hips, in the manner of your favorite dude wrangler." By the following year jeans for women had headed east. It was reported that the free spirits of Mrs. Hallie Flanagan's drama course at top women's school Vassar had abandoned their skirts in favor of blue jeans.

1936—Loafers: The penny loafer was designed by the G. H. Bass Company of Wilton, Maine, as an adaptation of the Norwegian slipper moccasins that had become fashionable on the French Riviera the previous year. Bass called them Weejuns, as a contraction of "Norwegian." They went on sale in men's fittings only at Rogers Peet of New York at twelve dollars a pair, with women's fittings following the next year. The origin of the practice among preppies of inserting a penny into the saddle of their loafers is, according to Bass, completely unknown.

1939—Nylon Stockings: The first women to wear nylon stockings were employees of the DuPont nylon yarn plant at Wilmington, Delaware, in February 1939. They were available to other Wilmington ladies the following month, when they went on sale at a few selected stores in the town. There was the odd problem with these experimental batches. They had a tendency to turn yellow after a while. And they generated so much static electricity that in dry weather ladies might find that preparations for bed were accompanied by the crackle of sparks.

1942—T-Shirts: The U.S. Navy called it a T-Type when they issued specifications for a knitted cotton shirt with round neck and short sleeves set at right angles to the front and back panels. While the navy saw its chief virtue as "greater sweat absorption under the arms," sailors were more impressed with the striking effect it had on girls. After the war it formed part of another kind of uniform as teenagers of both sexes sported T-shirts with blue jeans and sneakers—the first unisex leisure-wear costume.

1946—Bikini: Micheline Bernardini entered fashion history—and subsequently received 50,000 fan letters—when she modeled the first bikini at a Paris fashion show in July 1946. The creation of automotive engineer and swimsuit designer Louis Réard, the skimpy two-piece was made up of a fabric printed with newspaper text. And the name? On July 1, the Americans had detonated an atomic bomb at Bikini Atoll in the South Pacific. The suit was dubbed the bikini because of its explosive impact on the fashion world.

1949—Trainer: The German sportswear manufacturer Addas (later Adidas) introduced their "three-strip" running shoe, designed by Adolf Dassler. All the trainers in the world trace their descent from this prototype.

1957—Pants with Permanent Creases: The Siro-set process was developed at the Textile Industry Division of the Australian government's scientific research laboratory CSIRO in Melbourne. Not many governments show that much concern about the drudgery of ironing pants.

1959—Pantyhose: Launched as Panti-Legs by Glen Raven Mills of Glen Raven, North Carolina, pantyhose were a fine-denier version of the tights worn by ballet dancers and beatnik girls. Glen Raven's chief executive, Allen Gant, had been asked to develop them by his pregnant wife because she found having to wear stockings with a constrictive garter belt too uncomfortable. The original Panti-Legs had a seam running up the calf to make them indistinguishable from stockings. This was changed at the behest of veteran fan dancer Sally Rand, vaudeville star of the 1920s and 1930s, who was still performing as the 1960s dawned. She reckoned Panti-Legs would be ideal for wearing on drafty stages, but as she was supposed to be naked behind her fans, the seams were a giveaway. When the new seamless Panti-Legs were launched in 1961, Ms. Rand was able to perform

before goggle-eyed audiences who remained wholly unaware of her innocent deception.

1960—Lycra: The synthetic polyurethane fiber with the elastic properties of rubber was developed by DuPont and named Lycra. In December 1960 the Warner Lingerie Company introduced the Little Godiva step-in girdle, the first garment made of Lycra.

1961—Afro Hairstyle: Bronx teenager Barbara Terry had a date but found that she had no time to hot-press and curl her hair. Fortunately her father was proprietor of a hairdressing salon, Nelson's Tonsorial Parlor. With his help Barbara was on time to meet her beau, with her hair frizzed out in a style that other young black women—and eventually men—emulated.

1964—Miniskirt: In March *British Vogue* announced the sensation of the 1960s. The hemline had reached the knee in 1926, during the era of the flappers, but did not rise above it in the fashion world until Paris couturier André Courrèges took it four inches above the knee in 1964. British designer Mary Quant took it even higher than that three years later.

1964—Topless Swimsuit: When California fashion designer Rudi Gernreich was asked to predict trends in swimwear, he offhandedly remarked that topless swimsuits would soon be popular. Orders for such a suit poured in, and Gernreich had to fulfill his own prediction.

Winners of the first Miss Miniskirt contest on the Côte d'Azur, August 23, 1966.

Peggy Moffitt, who modeled the prototype, admitted that she wore the suit only once—for the photo shoot.

> Weird clothing is de rigueur for teenagers, but today's generation of teens is finding it difficult to be sufficiently weird. This is because the previous generation of teens, who went through adolescence in the sixties and seventies, used up practically all the available weirdness. After what went on in that twenty-year period, almost nothing looks strange to anyone.
>
> P. J. O'Rourke, Modern Manners, 1983

1979—Air-Cushioned Trainers: Aerospace engineer Frank Rudy developed the concept of the Nike Tailwind after studying the pressurized gasbags that enabled lunar modules to make safe landings.

1989—Inflatable Trainers: The Reebok Pump is a basketball boot designed to give the wearer a customized fit when it is inflated by pressing a small compressor, shaped like a basketball, in the tongue.

1993—Long-Lasting Perfume: Shiseido Eau de Cologne was launched in Japan in May. It contains hydroxy-propyl-cyclodexrin to inhibit evaporation, and the scent remains clear and strong for eight or nine hours. A conventional eau de cologne loses its fragrance after only one or two hours.

—P.H.R.

FOOTNOTE PERSON

ANNA JARVIS (1864–1948)

The creator of the modern Mother's Day was never a mother herself. Mothers have been honored for thousands of years. The ancient Greeks and Romans held festivals dedicated to mother goddesses.

In medieval England there was a Mothering Sunday, the fourth Sunday in Lent, when children who had been away from home as apprentices returned to see their mothers, usually bringing the gift of a simnel, or mothering, cake, a fruitcake with almond paste, meant to be eaten on mid-Lent Sunday.

The evolution of Mother's Day, as it exists today, began in the United States in 1890 when Miss Mary T. Sasseen, of Kentucky, suggested to a gathering of teachers that annual homage be paid to mothers every April 20, her own mother's birthday. Nothing came of the suggestion. In 1892 Robert K. Cummins, head of the Sunday school of the Universalist Church of Our Father in Baltimore, Maryland, proposed an annual memorial service on the Sunday closest to May 22, the date on which Mrs. Emily C. Pullman, mother of the church's pastor as well as mother of the inventor of the Pullman sleeping car, had died. This service was undertaken, although later the annual service was dedicated not merely to Mrs. Pullman but to all mothers worldwide. While this service was repeated for many years, it did not catch on nationally. In 1904 Fred E. Hering, of Indiana, appealed to the Fraternal Order of Eagles to support a national observance dedicated to mothers. This proposal, too, failed to excite interest.

Finally, the crusade for such a holiday achieved fulfillment through the tireless efforts of one individual. The actual creator of the modern Mother's Day observance was a Philadelphia woman, Anna M. Jarvis, who remained a spinster throughout her eighty-four years.

Jarvis's own mother, Anna Reeves Jarvis, was a Sunday school teacher who devoted herself to good works. Following the Civil War in the United States, she organized a "Mother's Friendship Day" to bring together families that had been split by the Union-Confederate rivalry. She lectured on "great mothers of the world" and suggested a "Memorial Mother's Day" to honor all mothers. Mrs. Jarvis's own family life was a difficult one. She gave birth to eleven children, but only four survived to adulthood. She was so fond of her elder daughter, Anna Jarvis, that her other daughter, Lillie, who was blind, once wrote to Anna to complain: "It has been your aim to render me virtually Motherless. . . . Nothing would help and encourage me like your death." Anna had a hard time moving away from home. When she was twenty-seven her uncle tried to lure her to Chattanooga to get a job and fulfill her potential. Mrs. Jarvis's tears won the day and Anna stayed home.

The following year, however, she was allowed to join her brother Claude in Philadelphia, leaving her mother behind to care for her bedridden, alcoholic father and her blind sister. Anna took a position as an advertising writer for an insurance company. Her father died in 1902 and the saintly Mrs. Jarvis followed on May 9, 1905.

Anna Jarvis brooded about her mother's death and blamed herself for choosing the wrong doctor to care for her. After two years, her obsessive grief began to worry her friends and relatives. Finally a cousin suggested that Anna "take up some of your Mother's life work, and

Anna Jarvis, left, who founded Mother's Day in honor of her mother, Anna Reeves Jarvis. It was first observed in 1908.

carry it on for her." This was the breakthrough she needed. Recalling her mother's dream of a "Memorial Mother's Day," she devoted her spare time to the cause.

On May 10, 1908, Miss Jarvis instigated simultaneous Mother's Day services in churches in Grafton, West Virginia, and Philadelphia, Pennsylvania. These services were held mainly to honor her own mother. Miss Jarvis suggested the wearing of white carnations, her mother's favorite flower. Following these memorials, Miss Jarvis began a strenuous letter-writing campaign, bombarding congressmen, state governors, influential businessmen, clergymen, and members of the press with proposals that a day be set aside dedicated to mothers, both living and dead. Gradually her hurricane of correspondence began to overcome resistance. In 1910 the governors of West Virginia, Oklahoma, and Washington proclaimed official Mother's Day holidays. Within a year every other state in the nation had followed suit.

Encouraged, Miss Jarvis gave up her job and incorporated herself as the Mother's Day International Association in December 1912. In less than two years Miss Jarvis saw her idea become a reality. Both houses of the U.S. Congress passed resolutions requesting the chief executive to proclaim such a holiday. On May 9, 1914,

President Woodrow Wilson issued a proclamation directing "government officials to display the United States flag on all government buildings" and inviting "the people of the United States to display the flag at their homes or other suitable places on the second Sunday in May as a public expression of our love and reverence for the mothers of our country."

The holiday quickly caught on elsewhere and was soon being observed in more than forty nations.

Despite her triumph, Miss Jarvis's life turned sour. It wasn't long before she lost control of Mother's Day. Politicians were quick to appropriate the day for their own benefit. Opponents of woman suffrage used it to remind people that a woman's place was in the home, not out working and voting. Anna Jarvis, however, supported women's right to vote and contended that Mother's Day was necessary to counteract the male bias of the American holiday calendar. "Washington's Birthday," she liked to point out, "is for the 'Father of our Country'; Memorial Day for our 'Heroic Fathers'; Fourth of July for 'Patriot Fathers'; Labor Day is for 'Laboring Fathers'; Thanksgiving Day for 'Pilgrim Fathers'; and even New Year's Day is for 'Old Father Time.' "

Church leaders, too, exploited Mother's Day

in hopes of bringing in larger audiences. But what really galled Anna Jarvis was the commercialization of Mother's Day, which she had conceived as a "holy day," not a "holiday." She regularly attacked the greeting card industry and the confectionery trade. "A printed card," she complained, "means nothing except that you are too lazy to write to the woman who has done more for you than anyone in the world. And candy! You take a box to mother—and then eat most of it yourself." Worst of all, by far, were the florists who tried to convert Mother's Day from a celebration of pious tributes to one of obligatory gift giving. Just as Montgomery Ward had invented Rudolph the Red Nosed Reindeer and Westinghouse had created Mrs. Santa Claus, the florists used a jingle to increase sales of red carnations as well as the white ones Jarvis had promoted:

White flowers for Mother's memory.
Bright flowers for Mothers living.

In 1920 Jarvis publicly denounced the floral industry and urged people to stop buying flowers on Mother's Day and to wear celluloid buttons instead. In 1923 she disrupted a conven-

tion of the Associated Retail Confectioners, and in 1925 she was arrested for disturbing the peace when she tried to stop the American War Mothers from selling white carnations. When the U.S. Postal Service decided to issue a Mother's Day stamp in 1934 featuring James Whistler's famous portrait of his mother, Anna Jarvis convinced them to remove the words *Mother's Day* and instead add a vase of carnations to Whistler's painting.

She wrote so many letters and collected so many clippings related to Mother's Day that she had to buy an extra house just to store them. Living alone with her sister Lillie, she continued to rant against the "charlatans, bandits, pirates, racketeers, kidnappers and other termites" whose greed had ruined her movement. After decades of increasing bitterness and paranoia, she was finally placed in a sanitarium by friends in 1943. She died on November 24, 1948, and was buried next to her mother. She never knew that during her final years some of her expenses were paid anonymously by the very florists she had so despised. Fifty years after her death Mother's Day was generating $7.5 billion in sales every year.

—I.W. and D.W.

10 MEMORABLE KISSES

1. THE MOVIE WITH 191 KISSES (1926)

In 1926 Warner Brothers studios starred John Barrymore in *Don Juan*. During the course of the film (two hours, forty-seven minutes), the amorous adventurer bestows a total of 191 kisses on a number of beautiful señoritas—an average of one every fifty-three seconds.

2. THE KISS AT L'HOTEL DE VILLE (1950)

A famous 1950 photograph of a young couple kissing on the streets of Paris—"Le Baiser de l'Hotel de Ville"—found itself under an international media spotlight when, four decades after the picture was taken, the photo became a commercial success, drawing out of the woodwork dozens of people who claimed to have been the photo's unidentified kissers. The black-and-white snapshot—originally taken for *Life* magazine by Robert Doisneau as part of his series on the Parisian working class—made Doisneau wealthy when, between 1986 and 1992, it became a best-seller through poster and postcard reprints. Among those who subsequently identified themselves as the kissers were Denise and Jean-Louis Lavergne, who sued Doisneau for $100,000 after he rejected their claim. They lost their case when it was determined, in 1993, that the kissers were

actually two professional models (and real-life lovers), Françoise Bornet and Jacques Cartaud.

3. THE MAJORCA, SPAIN, KISS-IN (1969)

In 1969 an effort was made to crack down on young lovers who were smooching in public in the town of Inca on the island of Majorca. When the police chief began handing out citations that cost offenders 500 pesetas (around seven dollars) per kiss, a group of thirty couples protested by staging a kiss-in at the harbor at Cala Figuera. Following a massive roundup by police, the amorous rebels were fined 45,000 pesetas for their defiant smooching and then released.

4. THE HOMOSEXUAL KISS IN *SUNDAY BLOODY SUNDAY* (1971)

One cinema kiss that turned heads among the moviegoing public was between two male actors, Peter Finch and Murray Head, in the 1971 film *Sunday Bloody Sunday*. The British tale of a bisexual love triangle included a medium close-up shot of this kiss in a scene originally planned to have featured only an embrace from afar. Director John Schlesinger commented that Finch and Head "were certainly less shocked by the kiss than the technicians on the set were.

When Finch was asked about that scene by somebody on TV, he said, 'I did it for England.' "

5. THE KISS OF HUMILITY (1975)

In an unprecedented gesture of humility, Pope Paul VI kissed the feet of Metropolitan Meliton of Chalcedon, envoy of Patriarch Demetrios I, who was head of the Eastern Orthodox Church, during a mass at the Sistine Chapel in Rome in 1975. The two men were commemorating the tenth anniversary of the lifting of excommunications that the churches of Constantinople and Rome had conferred on each other during the eleventh century. Taken aback by the pontiff's dramatic action, Meliton attempted to kiss the pope's feet in return but was kept from doing so by Paul. Meliton instead kissed the pope's hand.

6. THE KISS THAT DIDN'T HAPPEN (1975)

King Faisal of Saudi Arabia was engaged in discussions with the Kuwaiti oil minister when the king's nephew, Prince Faisal ibn Mussad Abdel Aziz, burst into the office unannounced. The king stood and, assuming that the prince wished to offer him holy greetings for Muhammad's birthday, lowered his head and waited for the traditional kiss. It never arrived. Instead the prince fired a bullet into the king's head, and then another into his neck, killing him.

7. THE KISS THAT COST $1,260 (1977)

Ruth van Herpen visited an art museum in Oxford, England, in 1977 and kissed a painting by American artist Jo Baer, leaving red lipstick stains on the $18,000 work. Restoration costs were reported to be as much as $1,260. Appearing in court, van Herpen explained, "I only kissed it to cheer it up. It looked so cold."

8. THE KISS THAT CAUSED A CENSORSHIP DEBATE (1978)

The first kiss to reach the movie screen in India was between actor Shashi Kapoor and actress Zeenat Aman in the 1978 Indian film Love Sublime. This landmark kiss, a product of new film guidelines, triggered a nationwide debate over censorship. Kapoor felt that the increased creative freedom would only add logic to Indian love stories and result in less cinema violence. Chief minister and film actor M. G. Ramachandran called for a mass protest, labeling the kissing scenes "an insult."

9. THE LONGEST KISS ON RECORD (1984)

The longest kiss was held between Eddie Levin and Delphine Crha in Chicago, Illinois, for a period of seventeen days, ten and a half hours. The record was set with the parting of their lips on September 24, 1984.

10. THE FIRST LESBIAN KISS ON AMERICAN COMMERCIAL TELEVISION (1994)

The first visible kiss between two women on an American network television series took place on the March 1, 1994, ABC-TV broadcast of the situation comedy Roseanne. In a controversial scene well publicized in the press, guest star Mariel Hemingway kisses series star Roseanne Arnold on the mouth. The kiss occurs in a "gay bar" setting, and Hemingway portrays a lesbian stripper whose kiss causes Roseanne to question her own sensibilities. The episode (whose script originally included a second kiss between two additional women) became the subject of much high-profile bickering between ABC executives and series producers Tom and Roseanne Arnold during the weeks prior to its airing. Up to the eleventh hour, the very inclusion of the kiss appeared to remain in question, prompting protests by gay rights organizations. ABC finally let the kiss happen, but added a viewer warning at the start of the episode.

—D.B.

> I kissed my first woman and smoked my first cigarette on the same day. I have never had time for tobacco since.
>
> Arturo Toscanini
>
> When women kiss it always reminds one of prizefighters shaking hands.
>
> H. L. Mencken, Chrestomathy, 1949

MORAL GUARDIANS

JIM BAKKER (b. 1940)

Jim Bakker, one of the foremost televangelists of the 1980s, inherited from his paternal forebears a tradition of spiritual devotion, dysfunctional personality, and hypocrisy on a grand scale. His grandfather, Joe Bakker, was a disliked and dismissed proselytizer who was active in the Pentecostal movement in America during the early twentieth century. Grandfather Joe began a prayer group that evolved into the Central Assembly of God. His bigotry, misplaced zealotry, and boorish eccentricity antagonized his congregation so much that he was banished from the church and forced to turn to a black church in order to attend services. The irony of his being a white bigot in a black church was compounded by the fact that this preacher/blue collar laborer was anti-Semitic even though his wife was Jewish.

Raleigh Bakker, Jim's father, also exhibited the kind of duality that later became the hallmark of his son. Raleigh was piously dedicated to Pentecostal orthodoxy but still managed to gain a reputation for flirtatiousness.

Jim Bakker was born on January 2, 1940, in Muskegon, Michigan. The fourth and final son, he was delivered five weeks premature. His youth was marked by poor grades and an inferiority complex. It was speculated, even by his parents, that he might prove to be a midget.

His academic life continued to founder in high school, but he shone in theatrics. He loved being on the stage as well as taking charge of production. Bakker initiated annual variety shows as benefits for the school paper. Not only did these extravaganzas allow him to exhibit his showmanship, but they also gave him the opportunity to demonstrate great ability as a producer.

He brought in amateur talent as well as local professionals whom he solicited to volunteer . . . wooing them with the likes of limousine services. The limousine would inevitably turn out to be a hearse donated for the day. Bakker's choice to headline his first big benefit show (1957) was an Elvis Presley imitator named Marlene Way. She was a twenty-one-year-old graduate of Muskegon High who had been on the Tonight Show (hosted by Steve Allen) earlier in the year. She had, in fact, been a guest on it twice in one week. Her appearance in Jim's school show led to the quadrupling of expected show profits. Bakker had become a star in the making.

He certainly seemed destined for show business; friends thought he'd soon be off to Broadway, but he didn't graduate with his class. His forced repeat of senior year, however, saw him become editor of the school newspaper and a successful student political campaign manager.

His final benefit production was truly a grand, last hurrah for the whole town. Its cast of 300, with thirty acts on the lineup, included Miss Michigan—the state beauty queen—a black rock group, and a Marilyn Monroe impersonator. It was pure Jim Bakker as a teenager and a foreshadowing of who he would become.

Another event, though, put a different spin on his future. High school student Jim Bakker was behind the wheel of a 1957 Cadillac when the car struck a three-year-old boy. The boy was badly hurt but survived and Bakker claims the experience changed his life . . . setting him firmly on a path toward spiritual redemption.

He began his formal theological training at North Central Bible College in Minneapolis, Minnesota, in 1959, where he met a fellow student named Tammy Faye LaValley. The two became college sweethearts who, because of a rule forbidding student marriages, were forced to quit school when they wed on April Fool's Day, 1961.

The young couple went to North Carolina, where they teamed up as preachers serving a circuit of small textile-manufacturing towns. In 1965 they were hired by Pat Robertson and went to work for his Christian Broadcasting Network, which headquartered in Portsmouth, Virginia. Jim's star truly began to rise in November of 1966 when Robertson had him launch what is considered to be the first Christian TV talk show. Robertson's mentorship lasted for six years, coming to an end when Bakker claimed that God had told him to "resign your job at CBN today."

Bakker's next career move was to partner with Pastor Paul Crouch, with whom he co-founded Trinity Broadcasting Systems, based in Santa Ana, California. A dispute between the two led to Bakker's exit, in 1973, and relocation to Charlotte, North Carolina, where he took over the hosting job on a WRET-TV talk show. Jim rechristened the show The PTL Club—initials that stand for "Praise the Lord" as well as "People that love."

The PTL Club was so successful that it enabled Bakker to start construction of Heritage USA—a religiously themed resort and business park. Worth an estimated $150 million, the complex grew to include a TV studio, a 504-room hotel, an executive office building in the shape of a pyramid, campsites, a shopping mall, condominiums, a $10 million water park, and neighboring tracts of private homes.

Jim and Tammy Faye had been married for nineteen years and had built an evangelical empire when, in December of 1980, their foundations began to crumble. It was the month that the forty-year-old preacher met a church secretary named Jessica Hahn in Clearwater, Florida. Bakker and Hahn had an hour-long tryst in a hotel room there, and no public mention of it was made for years. Hahn, however, began to complain privately about having suffered psychological damage from the sexual encounter.

Richard Dortch, a top aide to Bakker, brokered a deal with Hahn to make sure the matter remained private. She received an up-front payment of $115,000 and monthly interest from a $150,000 trust fund. The deal specified that if Hahn kept her silence and filed no complaint for a term of twenty years, the fund's principal would be transferred to her in its entirety.

The matter might have ended there if not for a leak of the scandalous secret, which came to the attention of Bakker's chief televangelical rival, the Reverend Jimmy Swaggart. Bakker had been furiously and hypocritically condemning Swaggart for the latter's sexual misconduct. Swaggart got even by instigating the leadership of the Assemblies of God—an overseer body of gospel churches—to begin an investigation into Bakker's ministry.

In March 1987, after a whirlwind of press coverage, Bakker publicly admitted his adultery as well as his involvement in the cover-up and pay-off schemes. Six years of silence and secrecy that shielded his sins ended with a blast and backlash that tarnished the reputations and severely crippled the fund-raising efforts of gospel ministries across the nation. The church leaders were not pleased by what they found in their investigation, and they defrocked Bakker on May 6, 1987. Reverend Jerry Falwell temporarily assumed the stewardship of the PTL organization.

The Hahn allegations led the IRS to scrutinize Bakker's financial dealings. He was eventually charged with mail and wire fraud in the sale of $158 million of mostly nonexistent timeshares to PTL fans who wanted to vacation at Heritage USA. He was convicted in October 1989 and sentenced to forty-five years in federal prison. The sentence was subsequently reduced to eight years.

Tammy Faye filed for divorce in March 1992 and married multimillionaire Roe Messner, Jim's close friend and a business partner, later that same year.

Jim Bakker was released from prison in July of 1994 after four and a half years behind bars and was remanded to a Salvation Army halfway house in Asheville, North Carolina. He was finally freed in December 1994.

—R.N.K.

Censorship is more depraving and corrupting than anything pornography can produce.

Tony Smythe

What progress we are making. In the Middle Ages they would have burned me. Now they are content with burning my books.

Sigmund Freud, referring to the public burning of his books in Berlin, letter to Ernest Jones, 1933

ANTHONY COMSTOCK (1844–1915)

A veteran of the Civil War and a stalwart of the YMCA, Anthony Comstock embarked on a lifetime crusade to remove all that was "lewd and lascivious" from art and literature. Born on a 163-acre farm in Connecticut, he was of Puritan ancestry. His mother died when he was ten, and he determined to dedicate his life to pursuits that would honor her memory. At eighteen, remorseful at having gotten drunk for the first and the last time in his life, he broke into the local liquor store, opened the spigots on the kegs, and let the liquor pour out on the floor.

The liquor store escapade, however, may have been a bit more than merely the result of guilt over a drinking bout. Prior to spilling out the liquor, Comstock had become a local hero for shooting and killing a mad dog that was roaming the streets. The dog was owned by the proprietor of the local liquor store. Just as he had protected the citizens from the mad dog, Comstock and his break-in saved the citizens from the evil work of the dog's owner. The two incidents became symbolic of his later crusades, and he often used the term *mad dogs* to refer to those he prosecuted.

With demon rum out of the way, pornography was his next target. At twenty-four, learning that a friend had been "led astray and corrupted and diseased" by an erotic book, Comstock determined to avenge this wrong. In so doing he found his lifelong vocation. Until then he had worked at a variety of clerking jobs. Now he became a full-time censor.

Comstock established the New York Society for the Suppression of Vice in 1873. Later he became an official agent of the U.S. Post Office. He alone was responsible for obtaining the stronger laws that barred obscenity from the mails. As a result, publishers were forced to convert explicit language in their books into euphemisms—*pregnant* fell from their pages to be replaced by *enceinte*. According to Comstock, sensual passages in books could overpower readers and plunge them helplessly into a state of lust. And lust, he said, "defiles the body, debauches the imagination, corrupts the mind, deadens the will, destroys the memory, sears the conscience, hardens the heart, and damns the soul."

Among the books Comstock successfully had banned or destroyed were *Fanny Hill, The Lustful Turk, Peep Behind the Curtains of a Female Seminary, A Night in a Moorish Harem,* and *Love on the Sly.* Despite rising opposition— "Jesus was never moved from the path of duty, however hard, by public opinion," said Comstock—he was responsible for the censorship of 500,000 reproductions of drawings and paintings, among them the innocent candy-box nude, *September Morn,* by Paul Chabas, a French artist. Comstock's idea of what was wrong in art was simple. As he told a reporter: "Anything which tends to destroy the dignity of womanhood or to display the female form in an irreverent manner is immoral. No one reveres the female form more than I do. In my opinion there is nothing else in the world so beautiful as the form of a beautiful maiden woman— nothing. But the place for a woman's body to be denuded is in the privacy of her own apartments with the blinds down."

Ironically, Comstock's fight to suppress *September Morn* turned the French painting into a huge financial success. The painting, considered mediocre and inoffensive by most critics, was not selling well when reproductions hit the U.S. market in 1913. Then New York publicist Harry Reichenbach struck a deal with a New York art dealer to generate sales: put the painting in the window; call Comstock and complain about it; let the ensuing publicity pull in the customers. The plan worked. As soon as Comstock raised a ruckus, the painting became famous, and the art dealer sold out his substantial quantity of reproductions. Comstock denied that he had been the victim of a hoax.

His censorship was indiscriminate. His five-foot-ten-inch, 210-pound blunderbuss presence, his muttonchop whiskers and black frock coat (Bible in its pocket), could be seen everywhere as he flayed out, smashing the good along with the bad. He was instrumental in getting Margaret Sanger's books on birth control banned in New York. He had the Department of the Interior fire Walt Whitman for *Leaves of Grass*. He had three thousand people arrested for obscenity. They ranged from Victoria Woodhull, female candidate for president, to Margaret Sanger's husband, who was charged with selling his wife's books. Only 10 percent of these victims were eventually convicted. Proudly, he took credit for hounding sixteen persons to their deaths, most from suicide and all sacrificed to his fanatical Puritanism.

In 1913 he told the *New York Evening World*: "In the forty-one years I have been here I have convicted persons enough to fill a passenger train of sixty-one coaches, sixty coaches containing sixty passengers and the sixty-first almost full. I have destroyed one hundred and sixty tons of obscene literature."

One of the few times that he met his match was when he tried to remove from the stage the play *Mrs. Warren's Profession* by George Bernard Shaw, whom Comstock referred to as an "Irish smut-dealer." Enraged, Shaw thundered back: "Comstockery is the world's standing joke at the expense of the United States. It confirms the deep-seated conviction of the Old World that America is a provincial place, a second-rate country town."

Comstock's only relaxations were his wife and his hobbies. He had married Margaret Hamilton, daughter of a Presbyterian elder, when he was twenty-seven. His senior by ten years, she weighed eighty-two pounds, always wore black, and rarely spoke a word. He had one child by Margaret, a daughter, Lillie, who died at six months. He and his wife then adopted a newborn girl, Adele, who turned out to be retarded, although he never acknowledged this fact. (After his death, forty-year-old Adele was confined to an institution.) His other loves were his collections of postage stamps and Japanese vases.

In 1915 President Woodrow Wilson appointed Comstock U.S. delegate to the International Purity Congress meeting at the San Francisco Exposition. At the convention he weakened himself by "overdoing," contracted pneumonia, returned home, and died. He was buried in Brooklyn's Evergreen Cemetery. His tombstone bore the epitaph: "In memory of a fearless witness."

But columnist Heywood Broun wrote a less sentimental obituary: "Anthony Comstock may have been entirely correct in his assumption that the division of living creatures into male and female was a vulgar mistake, but a conspiracy of silence about the matter will hardly alter the facts."

—I.W.

CHARLES COUGHLIN (1891–1974)

America's first radio talk star appeared in 1926. He was Father Charles E. Coughlin, a tall, charismatic priest with a mellifluous voice deepened by chain-smoking. Coughlin's career is best summarized by H. L. Mencken's definition of a demagogue: "One who preaches doctrines he knows to be untrue, to men he knows to be idiots."

Coughlin hoped his radio sermons would attract attention to his tiny church, the Shrine of the Little Flower, in Royal Oak, Michigan. He was right. In less than a decade, he was receiving as many as 10,000 fan letters a day. By 1935 the local post office reported that Coughlin's organization had cashed $4 million worth of money orders in a twenty-month period.

Like many radio (and TV) preachers who would follow him, Coughlin injected his religion with a high-octane blend of politics and economics. Abysmally ignorant in both subjects, he gained instant authority because his voice was heard by more than 30 million depression-weary Americans every Sunday at 3:00 P.M. Coughlin preached that the world's problems were caused by Communists and bankers, two words Coughlin believed to be synonymous with "Jewish."

A 1934 popularity poll reported that Coughlin was second only to President Franklin D. Roosevelt. Initially an FDR backer, by 1934 Coughlin was blasting Roosevelt as "the great liar" and "the scab President."

With fellow demagogues Francis Townsend and Gerald L. K. Smith, Coughlin formed the Union Party for the 1936 presidential election. His anti-Roosevelt rants grew more strident and his sermons more bigoted and hateful. NBC and CBS dropped him. The Vatican hinted that the Detroit archdiocese should restrain Coughlin. He moved to a network of independent radio stations, ignored the Vatican, and kept talking.

After the Union Party failed, Coughlin moved closer to America's more outré political leaders: William Dudley Pelley, founder of the storm-trooping Silver Shirts, and Fritz Kuhn, bargain-basement führer of the openly pro-Nazi German-American Bund. Coughlin also came under the spell of another anti-Semitic priest, Denis Fahey (1883–1954).

Like Senator Joseph McCarthy, Fahey "proved" his paranoid theories with hard numbers: of fifty-nine leaders in the Soviet Communist Party's Central Committee, fifty-six were Jews (the remaining three, Fahey said, were married to Jews). After World War II, Fahey was one of the first people to claim that the Holocaust was a hoax.

Coughlin enthusiastically quoted Fahey and distributed his books. The Fahey byline appeared in Coughlin's slick magazine, *Social Justice*. On November 7, 1938, synagogues all over Germany burned and Jews died during the Kristallnacht (Night of Broken Glass). In his November 20 sermon, Coughlin hinted that the Jews were getting just what they deserved.

A storm of controversy followed, and some radio stations canceled Coughlin. However, he remained powerful. As World War II loomed, Coughlin became a staunch isolationist and opposed an alliance with the "effete" British. The Catholic Church finally ordered Coughlin to give up his radio career in 1940. The federal government shut down *Social Justice* in 1942. With its frank admiration of Hitler and Mussolini, Coughlin's brand of social justice in wartime America was very close to treason.

In 1966 Coughlin retired. His sunset years were vexed by legal abortion and radical left-wing priests such as the Berrigan brothers, though Coughlin allowed that he himself was a "pioneer" of activist priests. He died in 1974.

—**M.S.S. and B.F.**

FATHER DIVINE (1879?–1965)

His followers often chanted, "He is God, he is God, he is God, God, God!" The women among them wore sweaters with a V for "virgin," and, slightly modified, a popular tune of the period serenaded him with the words "I can't give you anything but love, Father." The bald, paunchy little man—he was five feet two inches—wore $500 silk suits and was chauffeured about in a Duesenberg or flew with his army of secretaries in a private plane. The "Heavens" established by his disciples (some 10 million of them, he claimed) made him rich, but he owned next to nothing in his own name. He didn't even have a bank account. He fed, clothed, and housed the poor of all races at his missions, helped Fiorello La Guardia get elected mayor of New York City, and consoled thousands searching for some faith to hold on to during the Great Depression. Yet husbands sued him, claiming that their wives frolicked in his heavenly boudoir, "the Sun Dial," and one domestic-relations judge denounced him from the bench as a methodical home wrecker. To some, Father Divine was a

Father Divine's "Angels" march through Harlem in 1938.

saint or folk hero, to others a black Elmer Gantry or P. T. Barnum.

Father Divine claimed that he'd arrived on earth intact in a puff of smoke at "about the time of Abraham" to spread a creed of peace, communal living, celibacy, honesty, and racial equality. More likely he was born George Baker in Rockville, Maryland, in about 1879. There were few opportunities open to him, and from childhood he worked at odd jobs. He moved to Baltimore at the age of twenty, working as a gardener and on the waterfront, and encountering the many storefront churches that were springing up to offer African Americans an alternative to the mainstream black churches of the day. Here Baker found nourishment and training, teaching Sunday school and refining his evangelistic and oratorical skills. He also began to formulate his own theology, which borrowed from Methodism, Catholicism, the black religious tradition, and New Thought, a nineteenth-century precursor of twentieth-century New Age ideology that emphasized self-help and the healing power of positive thinking. In 1907 he went on a missionary visit to California—even then a headquarters for mind-power enthusiasts—where he encountered William Seymour, a black minister whose followers spoke in tongues and had the habit of being visited by God and collapsing in frenzied trances on the streets of downtown Los Angeles. Back in Baltimore, Baker became a follower of Sam Morris, a black man calling himself "Father Jehovah," and then joined a group called Live

Ever, Die Never. His experiences with these sects allowed him to further refine his message, and he was soon promoting himself along similar lines.

By 1915 Father Divine, as he was now known, had gone forth to Harlem, where he began persuading thousands of followers that he was God. His logic and language often were not of this world. "God is not only personified and materialized," he once said. "He is repersonified and rematerialized. He rematerialized and He rematerializes. He rematerialates and He is rematerializatable. He repersonificates and He repersonificatizes." Such indescribable tortuosities, and others such as "repersonifiably metaphysicalizationally," were probably uttered to both impress and confuse his followers and thus convince them of his divine origins. Though not so intended, they can be viewed as the ultimate satire on the semantics of the hucksterism that has pervaded American life before and since him.

Father Divine began building the financial base for his empire by putting his followers "out to work in the service," which meant placing them in jobs from which his movement received a kickback. Soon he was able to open his first "Heaven," a communal dwelling that he established in 1919 at Sayville, Long Island. But it was the philosophy and organization of the Kingdom of Peace movement that made it so popular—and so well endowed. For example, Father Divine preached that those who joined his kingdom entered a new life, and that they could never die while they believed in him. In fact, no one associated with him ever did die, for as soon as someone came down with an illness likely to be fatal, the person would be turned out of Heaven and dropped in a nearby flat, thus enabling the preacher to say truthfully, "No one dies in My House."

Father Divine's Peace Mission movement was widely controversial. In some ways it can be described as one of the first mass civil-rights movements, one that taught many African Americans that they could, even in a thoroughly racist society, assume command over their own lives. During the movement's heyday in the 1930s, however, Father Divine was extensively criticized within the black community. The head of the Universal Negro Improvement Association, Marcus Garvey—no mean trickster himself—called the Peace Mission movement "a colossal racket," and mainstream black religious leaders disparaged both Divine's methods and his message, which discounted racism as a factor in American society and often blamed blacks for their own inferior status.

The Heavens provided rooms for as little as five dollars a week and meals at about thirty-five cents (five cents during the depression), and indigent followers ate and slept free. The spiritual observances accompanying this mass cooperative or primitive communism were based on the Last Supper, and while there were songs and impromptu sermons, there were no formal services. Disciples rich and poor, black and white, male and female, ate from a banquet table often laden with as many as fifty different dishes. In accord with Father Divine's teachings, they adopted names such as Positive Love, Miss Charity, and Holy Quietness, discarding their family names.

Father Divine preached purity of the body and mind, which included sexual abstinence, and he forbade his followers to drink, smoke, swear, use cosmetics, go to the movies, or accept gifts or tips. "Peace" became the standard greeting and farewell of all members because hello began with a swear word. Despite its shortcomings, the Kingdom attracted millions who wanted peace, who wanted to believe that life was wonderful and that they could be virtuous, honest, reliable, and clean. The movement gained a worldwide membership, attracting even millionaires (one man left Father Divine an estate worth $10 million), and the Heavens eventually numbered seventy-five or more. All were united behind the motto "Father will provide."

Father did indeed provide. Money poured into the Heavens for the preacher and his disciples. In fact, they once toted more than $500,000 in rumpled bills, stuffed into old Gladstones and purses, to a Philadelphia bank. As for his divinity, he never really denied it and banners on the walls of all the movement's missions and houses read "Father Divine is God." The legend of his extraterrestrial connections grew when a judge who sentenced him to jail for a disorderly conduct charge dropped dead a few days later. "I hated to do it," said Father Divine from his cell. Later he would claim that he had had a hand in dropping the atomic bomb on Hiroshima. "I am the author and finisher of atomic energy," he said. "I have harnessed it." There was much truth in his only lengthy public statement on his divinity: "I don't have to say I'm God, and I don't have to say I'm not God. I said there are thousands of people who call me God. Millions of them. And there are millions of them call me the Devil, and I don't say I am God, and I don't say I am the Devil. But I produce God and shake the earth with it."

The preacher nonpareil, the minister of the malapropism could be just as evasive about sex—which he thoroughly enjoyed, even though he denied its pleasures to his disciples. It's said that when he seemed to be violating his own tenets, he'd explain to his partner of the night: "I am bringing your desire to the surface so that I can eliminate it." His policy of separating even married couples at his Heavens led to much speculation, and one of his confidential lady "secretaries" revealed the line he whispered invariably at the moment of seduction—"Mary wasn't a virgin."

In 1946 Father Divine married his "Sweet Angel," a twenty-two-year-old white Canadian previously named Edna Rose Kitchings, who became Mother Divine. He explained at the time that he had transferred the spirit of his first wife, a black woman, into the person of his second—stressing that they were one and the same. Then he added that after his "bodily disappearance" from Earth, his spirit would be possessed by the new Mother Divine.

Father Divine lived with his "Spotless Virgin Bride" until his death in 1965. His movement's worth at the time was estimated at more than $10 million. Eighteen secretaries were at his side to record his last words. When the doelike eyes in his round cherubic face were finally closed, Mother Divine announced that there would be no period of mourning but instead an extensive period of sumptuous feasting. Father, she explained, wouldn't have wanted it any other way.

—R.H. and E.H.B.

AIMEE SEMPLE MCPHERSON (1890–1944)

From John and Charles Wesley in the eighteenth century down to Billy Graham in the late twentieth century, Americans have always loved their evangelists. Yet no revivalist in U.S. history has been more enthusiastically loved— or more thoroughly disgraced—than Aimee Semple McPherson, who became a national institution in the 1920s.

Though she was ultimately to make millions through her preaching, Aimee's career got off to a shaky start. In 1907, while a farm girl of seventeen, she married an itinerant preacher named Robert Semple, who took her to China and died shortly thereafter, leaving his young wife pregnant and destitute. After the birth of her daughter, Aimee found her way back to the United States, where she married Harold Mc-Pherson, who fathered her second child, a son. But restlessness soon overcame her. Packing up her mother, two children, and a large tent, she set out in a battered car for a career as a traveling revivalist.

Her first great success came in southern California, which provided fertile ground for her ecstatic, optimistic rendering of the gospel. In 1921, while Sister Aimee was speaking at an outdoor rally in San Diego, an inspired old woman rose from her wheelchair and tottered toward the podium. She was followed by hundreds of other cripples as hysteria swept the arena. Overnight, Aimee Semple McPherson developed a national reputation as a faith healer. Nevertheless, Sister Aimee remained modest about her miracles. "I am not a healer," she said. "Jesus is the healer. I am only the little office girl who opens the door and says 'Come.' "

Soon Sister Aimee had raised enough money to open the Angelus Temple near downtown Los Angeles, which was to serve as a permanent base for her activities. This building, which cost $1.5 million to build (a handsome sum in 1923), was topped by a huge rotating lighted cross that could be seen for a distance of fifty miles. There was also a powerful in-house broadcasting station that sent the message of Sister Aimee's "Foursquare Gospel" around the world. A special "Miracle Room" displayed stacks of crutches, wheelchairs, and braces left over from faith cures. The main temple provided seats for 5,000 of the faithful, and Sister Aimee was able to attract a full house nearly every time she preached.

Instead of the familiar fire and brimstone of traditional evangelists, Sister Aimee stressed a gentler brand of salvation that emphasized the pleasures of heaven rather than the torments of hell. Her dramatic stage presence and her fashionably bobbed hair added powerfully to her appeal. There was always a good deal of show-business pageantry in Aimee's services. In her "Throw Out the Lifeline" number, a dozen maidens clad in white clung desperately to a storm-lashed Rock of Ages, while special-effects men labored mightily to create thunder, lightning, and wind. Just when all seemed lost, out jumped Sister Aimee in an admiral's uniform to order a squad of lady sailors to the rescue. They tossed out the blessed lifeline, while the male chorus, dressed as coast-guardsmen, swept the mechanical waves with searchlights. The virgins were saved, trumpets blared, and the congregation cheered while the American flag waved triumphantly over all.

Unfortunately, no one was available to rescue Sister Aimee when she herself needed it most. After reaching her peak in 1925, she was soon to suffer a spectacular fall from grace. In mid-May of 1926, Aimee drove to a hotel facing the Pacific Ocean, changed to a swimsuit, and then sat on the crowded beach, working on a sermon. Her secretary, Emma Schaffer, left for a short while, and when she returned Sister Aimee had disappeared. The supposition was that the great revivalist had gone out for a swim, suffered a cramp or some other difficulty, and drowned.

Thousands of the faithful camped along the sands while airplanes and boats patrolled off-shore, searching for a clue. One grief-stricken girl actually committed suicide. A young man jumped into the water, shouting, "I'm going after her," and drowned. A professional diver died of exhaustion.

Meanwhile, police and newsmen scoured the West for some clue to Sister Aimee's fate. For a month every lead brought authorities to a dead end. Then, on the thirty-first day, a ransom note was delivered to the Angelus Temple: it stated that Sister Aimee had been kidnapped and would be released in exchange for $500,000.

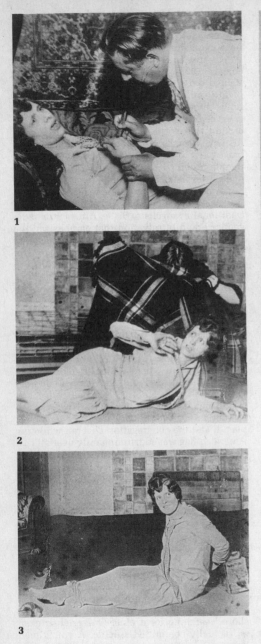

1

2

3

4

Aimee Semple McPherson reenacts her terrible "kidnapping." She shows how (1) her fingers were burned by a cigar, (2) the kidnappers wrapped her in blankets, (3) she was tied up, and (4) she escaped through a window.

The following day, around one o'clock in the morning, Sister Aimee suddenly turned up in the Mexican border town of Agua Prieta. She confirmed that she had been abducted from the beach and had been held prisoner in a remote desert shack. Her three captors—one woman and two men—called themselves the Avengers. Sister Aimee had finally escaped from them through a window and stumbled for miles across burning desert sands to safety.

The police were suspicious. Authorities scoured the desert and could find no shack. She showed no evidences of captivity or flight. Her dress was neat, her pale skin untouched by the desert sun. Reporters, equally suspicious, began chasing clues. The possibility had been raised that Sister Aimee, who had been divorced by her husband a few years before, had been having an affair with one Kenneth Ormiston, the former operator of her radio station. Coincidentally, Ormiston had disappeared from sight earlier in 1926 and his wife had filed a missing person report on him.

When Los Angeles district attorney Asa Keyes launched a formal investigation, witnesses came forward stating that during the time of her alleged captivity, Sister Aimee and her married lover, Ormiston, had indeed been seen together in several hotels and at a seaside cottage in Carmel, California. Keyes was about to start criminal proceedings against Aimee and four others believed to be involved in the deception, when her friend William Randolph Hearst, the publishing tycoon, supposedly intervened on her behalf. The charges were dropped. One of the main witnesses against Aimee, meantime, had been discredited—she had once been committed to an insane asylum because of the wild stories she made up.

Aimee's story could neither be proved nor disproved. Had she been kidnapped? The police had foiled at least three other real plots to kidnap or harm her. Had this one been real? Whatever the truth, the great evangelist now appeared to be a "woman with a past." Ormiston, who turned himself in to the police in December 1927, was ruined by the scandal and his wife divorced him.

Aimee struggled to continue her career and regain her former image. Love came again to Aimee in 1931 at the age of forty, but two days after her marriage to roly-poly Dale Hutton, he was sued by another female for breach of promise. Aimee fainted, fell, and hit her head on some flagstones, and after her recovery the couple divorced.

Through all these troubles, a sizable number of the Foursquare faithful stood by Sister Aimee; her services at the Angelus Temple continued to provide one of the best shows in town. Her popularity, though greatly diminished, continued into the 1940s.

On a September evening in 1944, Sister Aimee spoke to an enthusiastic crowd in Oakland, California. The next morning she was found unconscious in her hotel room and died soon afterward. Then came sad news. The coroner's verdict was that Sister Aimee had died from an overdose of sleeping pills.

—M.S.M.

CARRY NATION (1846–1911)

Carry Nation, the saloon-smashing Amazon who terrorized drunkards at the turn of the century, was born Carry Moore in Garrard County, Kentucky, on November 25, 1846. She was well equipped by Providence for the career of destruction to which the Lord summoned her: She stood nearly six feet tall and weighed more than 175 pounds.

A touch of strangeness ran through Carry's family. In the words of Robert Lewis Taylor in his biography, *Vessel of Wrath*, "An aunt, during certain lunar phases, made repeated attempts to clamber up on the roof and convert herself into a weather vane. A cousin, at the age of forty, unexpectedly returned to all fours." Carry's mother spent her adult life convinced that she was Queen Victoria. Carry herself spent most of four years, between the ages of eleven and fifteen, in bed with a mystery ailment that disappeared when her family moved from Texas to Missouri.

When she was nineteen years old she fell in love with a physician named Charles Gloyd. It wasn't until they married two years later that Carry discovered he was a drunkard. She left him and he quickly drank himself to death. In 1877 she remarried. This time her unfortunate choice of mates was David Nation, an incompetent preacher-lawyer-farmer. When the Nations eventually settled in Medicine Lodge, Kansas, Carry established herself as an advocate of the disadvantaged. She started a sewing circle to make clothes for the poor and invited them into her home on Thanksgiving and Christmas. She was also elected county chairman of the Women's Christian Temperance Union and it was in the field of prohibition that she would gain her fame.

At that point in history, Kansas was technically a "dry" state, but a U.S. Supreme Court ruling in 1890 legalized the importation of alcohol in "original packages" and this permitted saloons to flourish in every city and town. Carry Nation was naturally disgusted at such hypocrisy and she wrote passionate letters of protest to the governor, the attorney general, the sheriff of Barber County, and various local newspapers. When she received not a single response, she decided to take matters into her own hands. After a period of prayer and divination, she heard a voice from above, which she later described in her autobiography. "Take something in your hands," she was told, "and throw at these places and smash them!"

Carry knew how to follow orders. The next day—June 7, 1899—singing hymns and full of holy fire, she picked up a collection of bricks and stones from her backyard and wrapped them in old newspapers. Then she hitched up the buggy and drove to the town of Kiowa, nearly twenty miles away.

As she walked into one of the town's saloons, the men at the bar turned in amazement to see this fifty-two-year-old woman, dressed in black, invading their all-male inner sanctum.

"Men," Carry announced, "I have come to save you from a drunkard's fate!" Without further ado, she began heaving her stones with stunning accuracy. Within minutes every bottle in the place had been smashed, not to mention the mirror behind the bar and both of the front windows.

Carry resolved to move on to bigger and better things and turned her sights to "the murder mills of the metropolis of Wichita." Her first target was the most elegant bar in all of Kansas, located in the basement of the Hotel Carey. This establishment featured a huge $1,500 plate-glass mirror, surrounded by hundreds of sparkling electric lights. There was also a popular painting (for men only) entitled *Cleopatra at the Bath*. When Carry Nation beheld this lewd work of art she stopped dead in her tracks. She reflected—so she wrote later—that woman is stripped of everything by the saloons. Her husband is torn from her. She is robbed of her sons. Then they take away her clothes and her dignity. Trembling with rage, Carry approached the bartender.

"Young man," she demanded, "what are you doing in this hellhole!"

"I'm sorry, madam," he answered, "but we do not serve ladies."

"Serve me!" screamed Carry. "Do you think I'd drink your hellish poison!" She waved a furious finger at Cleopatra. "Take that filthy thing down and close this murder mill!"

When her request was ignored, Carry set to work. A barrage of rocks shattered the immense mirror and tore the offending canvas. "Glory to God!" she shouted. "Peace on earth, good will to men!"

Terrified, the drinkers and bartender managed to escape through the rear doorway as Carry began overturning tables and slashing chairs. She sent row upon row of bottles crashing to the floor. When Detective Park Massey of the Wichita police arrived on the scene, she had lifted one of the finest and biggest brass cuspidors (spittoons) in Kansas to the top of the cherry-wood bar and was beating it furiously.

"Madam," said the officer, "I must arrest you for defacing property."

"Defacing?" she screamed. "I am defacing nothing! I am destroying!"

In the trial that followed, many Kansas citizens rallied to Carry Nation's defense. After all, the establishments she had dismantled were supposed to be illegal under Kansas law. When the charges against her were finally dropped, Carry had won a moral victory as well as a good deal of national publicity.

In the next year alone, Carry launched more than twenty successful raids and became the most notorious female in the United States. The mere mention of her name was enough to strike terror into a saloonkeeper's heart, and when she arrived in a town, the taverns would either close down for the day or hire a special detachment of armed guards. As her rampage continued, Carry perfected her technique. She began to use metal hatchets in her work of destruction and these hatchets soon became her trademark. She was arrested more than thirty times for her escapades, and she paid her fines with proceeds from the sale of souvenir hatchets, inscribed with her name. During some of her raids, this matronly woman accomplished prodigious feats of strength: she tore icebox doors clean off their hinges and once ripped a huge cash register off its moorings on a bar, hoisted it over her head, and sent it sailing into the street.

Carry had little respect for authority figures. In court she referred to judges as "Your Dishonor," while policemen were "whiskey-swilled, saturn-faced tosspots." In fact, men in general were "nicotine-soaked, beer-besmeared, whiskey-greased, red-eyed devils" and "two-legged animated whiskey flasks."

Although it was her crusade against alcohol that made her famous, she also directed her wrath against other targets such as tobacco smoking, necking couples, harlotry, and skirts of improper length. She also favored woman suffrage, opposed corsets, and, most surprisingly, advocated sex education for children.

Carry Nation with her trusty hatchet.

"Ignorance is not innocence," she said, "but is the promoter of crime." She supported her views on sex education with a quote from the Bible: " 'My people are destroyed for lack of knowledge.' Hosea 4:6."

As her notoriety grew, Carry took to the lecture circuit, speaking not only in the United States but also in England and Scotland. She even began publication of a weekly newspaper, the *Smasher's Mail*, which included opposing viewpoints printed in a section entitled "Letters from Hell." Another column, "Private Talks to Boys and Girls," was so explicit that one reader called it a "blueprint for masturbation." Women throughout the country were inspired by Carry's example, and saloon smashers sprang up in many cities. Few, however, could rival the effectiveness of Carry's "hachetations," as she called them.

When she was sixty-two years old, she undertook one of her most ambitious raids, in Washington, D.C., wreaking havoc in the famous barroom of the Union Depot with the aid of three hatchets named Faith, Hope, and Charity.

Carry's last raid took place in Butte, Montana, in 1910. A few months later she collapsed while speaking against saloons and saloonkeepers in Eureka Springs, Arkansas, and died in Evergreen Hospital, Leavenworth, Kansas, on June 9, 1911.

—M.S.M.

QUOTEBOOK: FAMILY

MARRIAGE

Love, the strongest and deepest element in all lives, the harbinger of hope, of joy, of ecstasy; love, the defier of all laws, of all conventions; love, the freest, the most powerful molder of human destiny; how can such an all-compelling force be synonymous with that poor little State and Church-begotten weed, marriage?
Emma Goldman

Marriage is a very alienating institution, for men as well as for women. . . . It's a very dangerous institution—dangerous for men who find themselves trapped, saddled with a wife and children to support; dangerous for women, who aren't financially independent and end up depending on men who can throw them out when they are age forty; and dangerous for children because their parents vent all their frustration on them.
Simone de Beauvoir, interview, New York Times Magazine, June 2, 1974

Any intelligent woman who reads the marriage contract, and then goes into it, deserves all the consequences.
Isadora Duncan, My Life, 1927

Marriage is for women the commonest mode of livelihood, and the total amount of undesired sex endured by women is probably greater in marriage than in prostitution.
Bertrand Russell, Marriage and Morals, 1929

I am happy now that Charles calls on my bedchamber less frequently than of old. As it is, I now endure but two calls a week and when I hear his steps outside my door I lie down on my bed, close my eyes, open my legs and think of England.
Lady Hillingdon, Journal, 1912

When you see what some girls marry, you realize how much they must hate to work for a living.
Helen Rowland, Reflections of a Bachelor Girl, 1903

In recent years it has become common to hear people all over the country speak of long-term marriage in a tone of voice that assumes it to be inextricably intertwined with the music of Lawrence Welk.
Calvin Trillin, "Old Marrieds," The Nation, August 3, 1985

The concept of two people living together for 25 years without having a cross word suggests a lack of spirit only to be admired in sheep.
A. P. Herbert, News Chronicle, 1940

American women expect to find in their husbands a perfection that English women only hope to find in their butlers.
W. Somerset Maugham, A Writer's Notebook, 1949

The reason husbands and wives do not understand each other is because they belong to different sexes.
Dorothy Dix

I have certainly known more men destroyed by the desire to have a wife and child and to keep them in comfort than I have seen destroyed by drink and harlots.
William Yeats, attributed

Marriage is the only thing that affords a woman the pleasure of company and the perfect sensation of solitude at the same time.
Helen Rowland

I have never married because there was no need. I have three pets at home which answer the same purpose as a husband. I have a dog which growls every morning, a parrot which swears all the afternoon and a cat that comes home late at night.
Marie Corelli, quoted in What the Doctor Thought, by James Crichton-Browne

I married beneath me—all women do.
Nancy Astor

Of course, I do have a slight advantage over the rest of you. It helps in a pinch to be able to remind your bride that you gave up a throne for her.
Edward, Duke of Windsor, king of the United Kingdom, abdicated 1936, attributed

You never really know a man until you have divorced him.
Zsa Zsa Gabor

You never realize how short a month is until you pay alimony.
John Barrymore

PARENTS AND CHILDREN

One of the most obvious facts about grown-ups to a child is that they have forgotten what it is like to be a child.
Randall Jarrell, The Third Book of Criticism, 1965

Children have never been very good at listening to their elders, but they have never failed to imitate them.
James Baldwin, Esquire, 1960

It is not just Mowgli who was raised by a couple of wolves; any child is raised by a couple of grown-ups. Father and Mother may be nearer and dearer than anyone will ever be again—still, they are members of a different species.
Randall Jarrell, The Third Book of Criticism, 1965

They fuck you up, your Mum and Dad.
They may not mean to, but they do.
And give you all the faults they had
And add some extra, just for you.
                    Philip Larkin, This Be the Verse, 1974

If there is anything that we wish to change in the child,
we should first examine it and see whether it is not
something that could better be changed in ourselves.
            Carl Gustav Jung, Von Werden der Persönlichkeit
            (On the Development of Personality), 1932

No culture on earth outside of mid-century suburban
America has ever deployed one woman per child
without simultaneously assigning her such major
productive activities as weaving, farming, gathering,
temple maintenance, and tent building. The reason is
that full-time, one-on-one child-raising is not good for
women or children.
            Barbara Ehrenreich, "Stop Ironing the Diapers,"
                    The Worst Years of Our Lives, 1989

No matter how old a mother is she watches her
middle-age children for signs of improvement.
            Florida Scott-Maxwell, The Measure of My Days,
                                            1968

One reason you are stricken when your parents die is
that the audience you've been aiming at all your life—
shocking it, pleasing it—has suddenly left the theatre.
Katharine Whitehorn, the Observer, December 4, 1983

There are no illegitimate children—only illegitimate
parents.
            Leon R. Yankwich, opinion, Zipkin v. Mozon,
                                            June 1928

THE STAGES OF LIFE

THE YOUNG AND THE OLD

The young have aspirations that never come to pass,
the old have reminiscences of what never happened.
                    Saki, Reginald at the Carlton, 1904

The dead might as well try to speak to the living as the
old to the young.
                    Willa Cather, One of Ours, 1922

From the earliest times the old have rubbed it into the
young that they are wiser than they, and before the
young had discovered what nonsense this was they
were old too, and it profited them to carry on the
imposture.
            W. Somerset Maugham, Cakes and Ale, 1930

YOUTH

Youth is like spring, an over-praised season—
delightful if it happen to be a favoured one, but in
practice very rarely favoured and more remarkable, as

a general rule, for biting east winds than genial
breezes.
            Samuel Butler, The Way of All Flesh, 1903

Youth would be an ideal state if it came a little later in
life.
                    Lord Herbert Henry Asquith, 1923

The young always have the same problem—how to
rebel and conform at the same time. They have now
solved this by defying their parents and copying one
another.
            Quentin Crisp, The Naked Civil Servant, 1968

I hope I die before I get old.
                    Peter Townshend, "My Generation," 1965

The most prolific period of pessimism comes at
twenty-one, or thereabouts, when the first attempt is
made to translate dreams into reality.
            Heywood Broun, Pieces of Hate and Other
                                    Enthusiasms, 1922

A child becomes an adult when he realizes that he has
a right not only to be right but also to be wrong.
                    Thomas Szasz, The Second Sin, 1973

MIDDLE AGE

The only time you really live fully is from thirty to
sixty. . . . No, the young are slaves to dreams; the old
servants to regrets.
                    Hervey Allen, Anthony Adverse, 1933

It is sobering to consider that when Mozart was my age
he had already been dead for a year.
                                    Tom Lehrer, 1965

Years ago we discovered the exact point, the dead
center of middle age. It occurs when you are too young
to take up golf and too old to rush up to the net.
                    Franklin P. Adams, Nods and Becks, 1944

Middle age is when you've met so many people that
every new person you meet reminds you of someone
else.
                            Ogden Nash, Versus, 1949

At fifty, everyone has the face he deserves.
                    George Orwell, final entry in
                    his working notebook, April 17, 1949

After the age of fifty we begin to die little by little in the
deaths of others.
                    Julio Cortazar, A Certain Lucas, 1979

The years between fifty and seventy are the hardest.
You are always being asked to do things and yet you
are not decrepit enough to turn them down.
                    T. S. Eliot, Time, October 23, 1950

OLD AGE

The older I grow the more I distrust the familiar doctrine that age brings wisdom.

H. L. Mencken, Prejudices, 1922

The denunciation of the young is a necessary part of the hygiene of older people, and greatly assists the circulation of the blood.

Logan Pearsall Smith, Afterthoughts, 1931

Old age is better for women than for men. First of all, they have less far to fall, since their lives are more mediocre than those of most men.

Simone de Beauvoir

Being over seventy is like being engaged in a war. All our friends are going or gone and we survive amongst the dead and the dying as on a battlefield.

Muriel Spark, Memento Mori, 1959

Growing old is like being increasingly penalized for a crime you haven't committed.

Anthony Powell, Temporary Kings, 1973

When you're old, everything you do is sort of a miracle.

Millicent Fenwick

When one has reached eighty-one . . . one likes to sit back and let the world turn by itself, without trying to push it.

Sean O'Casey, New York Times, September 25, 1960

I will never be an old man. To me, old age is always fifteen years older than I am.

Bernard Baruch, 1955

If I'd known how old I was going to be I'd have taken better care of myself.

Adolph Zukor,
on the approach of his hundredth birthday;
quoted in Benny Green, Radio Times,
February 17, 1979

Said the little boy, "Sometimes I drop my spoon."
Said the little old man, "I do that too."
The little boy whispered, "I wet my pants."
"I do that too," laughed the little old man.
Said the little boy, "I often cry."
The old man nodded, "So do I."
"But worst of all," said the boy, "it seems
Grown-ups don't pay attention to me."
And he felt the warmth of a wrinkled old hand.
"I know what you mean," said the little old man.
Shel Silverstein, "The Little Boy and the Old Man,"
A Light in the Attic, 1974

Chapter 17

SPORTS

HISTORY OF THE OLYMPICS

SUMMER GAMES

1896 ATHENS
Competitors: 245
Nations: 14
Dates: April 6–15

Heroes: *James Connolly*, from a poor family, was self-educated but was accepted to Harvard. He dropped out of school to travel to Athens for the first modern Olympic Games. He became the first Olympic champion in 1,527 years when he won the triple jump. The Greek hosts were rewarded when the showcase event, the marathon, was won by *Spiridon Louis*, a local shepherd turned post office messenger.

Controversies: The swimming contests were held in the open sea around the Bay of Zea in 55-degree-Fahrenheit (12-degree-Celsius) water. During the 1,200-meter race, the contestants had to fight twelve-foot waves. The winner, *Alfréd Hajos* of Hungary, proclaimed, "My will to live completely overcame my desire to win."

MEDAL TOTALS OF LEADING NATIONS

	G*	S	B
United States	11	7	1
Greece	10	17	22
Germany	7	5	4
France	5	4	2
Great Britain	3	3	3
Hungary	2	1	4
Austria	2	1	2
Australia	2	0	1
Denmark	1	2	3
Switzerland	1	2	0

1900 PARIS
Competitors: 1,335
Nations: 23
Dates: May 20–October 28

*G = gold, S = silver, B = bronze

Heroes: In tennis, Wimbledon champion *Charlotte Cooper* became the first female champion of the modern games. *Alvin Kraenzlein* of the United States won four gold medals in three days in two hurdle events, the long jump, and the 60-meter dash. On July 16 former polio victim *Ray Ewry* of Lafayette, Indiana, won three gold medals in the standing high jump, standing long jump, and standing triple jump. He repeated his sweep in 1904. He settled for a double in 1908 because the standing triple jump was eliminated from the program.

Controversies: The Games were poorly organized, a mere appendage to the Paris World Exhibition. Some of the athletes were unaware that the meet they were taking part in was the Olympics. Kraenzlein's victory in the long jump came in disputed circumstances. The world record holder, Meyer Prinstein of Syracuse University, led after the qualifying round, which, at the time, counted toward the final placings. The final was held on a Sunday. The Syracuse team leader refused to let Prinstein compete on a Sunday even though he was Jewish. In the final Kraenzlein beat Prinstein's mark by one centimeter. Incompetence on the part of the regatta officials made it necessary to hold two separate finals in the coxed fours rowing event.

MEDAL TOTALS OF LEADING NATIONS

	G	S	B
France	26	39	30
United States	20	17	16
Great Britain	18	8	12
Switzerland	6	1	1
Belgium	5	5	5
Germany	3	2	2
Denmark	2	3	2
Italy	2	2	0
Australia	2	0	4
Hungary	1	2	2

1904 ST. LOUIS
Competitors: 687
Nations: 12
Dates: July 1–November 23

Hero: *George Eyser* won five medals in gymnastics, including two gold, despite the fact that he had a wooden leg.

Controversies: Again the games were poorly organized and many events attracted no foreign athletes. The only non-American team entered in the water polo event, a German squad, refused to take part when they learned that the Americans used a deflated ball and followed different rules. Swimmer Zoltán Halmay of Hungary won the 50-yard freestyle, but the U.S. judge declared that the winner was American J. Scott Leary. A brawl broke out and the race was rerun. This time Halmay won clearly. The marathon was held in 90-degree-Fahrenheit (32-degree-Celsius) weather, run on a dusty course with officials in automobiles preceding the runners. The first runner into the stadium, Fred Lorz of New York, was disqualified when it was discovered that he had ridden eleven miles in a car.

MEDAL TOTALS OF LEADING NATIONS

	G	S	B
United States	80	86	72
Germany	5	4	6

Cuba	5	3	3
Canada	4	1	1
Hungary	2	1	1
Austria	1	1	1
Greece	1	0	1
Switzerland	1	0	1
Ireland	1	0	0
Great Britain	0	1	1

1908 LONDON
Competitors: 2,035
Nations: 23
Dates: April 27–October 31

Heroes: New York City policeman *John Flanagan* won the hammer throw for the third straight time. One of the most dramatic moments in Olympic history occurred in the marathon when *Dorando Pietri* of Italy entered the stadium in first place but then collapsed. Officials helped him across the finish line, but he was disqualified for receiving assistance.

Controversies: In the 400-meter run, American John Carpenter was disqualified by British officials for interfering with the only non-American in the race, Wyndham Halswelle, a London-born Scot. The race was ordered rerun, but the other American finalists refused to take part and Halswelle ran alone. Another British-American altercation took place in, of all things, the tug-of-war. After the Liverpool police team

One of the most dramatic moments in the history of the modern Olympics: Dorando Pietri entered the stadium in first place in the 1908 marathon, but he collapsed and had to be helped across the finish line. The outside aid, although well-intentioned, caused him to be disqualified.

defeated the U.S. team, the Americans accused the Liverpudlians of wearing illegal boots with steel cleats and heels. The British maintained that the boots met the rules because they were standard police issue. When their protest was denied, the Americans withdrew from the remainder of the competition.

MEDAL TOTALS OF LEADING NATIONS

	G	S	B
Great Britain	56	50	39
United States	23	12	12
Sweden	8	6	11
France	5	5	9
Germany	3	5	5
Hungary	3	4	2
Canada	3	3	10
Norway	2	3	3
Italy	2	2	0
Belgium	1	5	2

1912 STOCKHOLM
Competitors: 2,545
Nations: 28
Dates: May 5–July 22

Heroes: *Jim Thorpe*, a Native American from Oklahoma Territory, won the decathlon and the pentathlon. Thorpe was probably the greatest all-around athlete of the century. His performance in the decathlon was so impressive that it would still have earned him the silver medal in the 1948 Olympics. Finland's *Hannes Kolehmainen* won three gold medals in long-distance races, setting a world record in the 5,000 meters. Cyclist *Okey Lewis* of South Africa won the longest race in Olympic history, completing the 199-mile (320-kilometer) race around Lake Mälar in ten hours, forty-two minutes, and thirty-nine seconds. The longest wrestling bout in Olympic history, a semifinal matchup in the 75-kilogram (165.5-pound) division was won by Estonian *Martin Klein* when he pinned his Finnish opponent, *Alfred Asikainen*, after eleven hours. In the 90-kilogram (198.5-pound) division, the final between *Anders Ahlgren* of Sweden and *Ivar Böhling* of Finland was declared a draw after nine hours.

Controversies: The Stockholm Games were relatively free of controversy. However, in the modern pentathlon, one of the American entrants missed out on the gold medal when he missed the target entirely on one shot during the shooting competition. The American, an army lieutenant by the name of George S. Patton Jr., claimed that his bullet hadn't missed the target, it had gone straight through a previously made hole. His argument was not accepted by the judges.

Jim Thorpe, star of the 1912 Olympics and perhaps the greatest athlete of the century.

MEDAL TOTALS OF LEADING NATIONS

	G	S	B
United States	25	18	20
Sweden	23	24	17
Great Britain	10	15	16
Finland	9	8	9
France	7	4	3
Germany	5	13	7
South Africa	4	2	0
Norway	3	2	5
Hungary	3	2	3
Canada	3	2	2

1916 BERLIN—Canceled because of war

1920 ANTWERP
Competitors: 2,668
Nations: 29
Dates: April 20–September 12

Heroes: Eight years after his triple-gold performance, *Hannes Kolehmainen* came back to win the closest men's marathon in Olympic history. The 100-meter dash was won by the popular American sprinter *Charley Paddock* with his famous flying finish. In the fencing competitions, Italian *Nedo Nadi* earned gold medals in five of the six events.

Controversies: The only incident of the Antwerp Games occurred in the equestrian dressage competition when third-place finisher Colonel Gutlaf-Adolf Boltenstern Sr. of Sweden was disqualified for practicing in the ring before the competition began.

The great Finnish distance runner, Paavo Nurmi (second from left), poses with the 1936 1,500-meter medalists, Glenn Cunningham, Jack Lovelock, and Luigi Beccali.

MEDAL TOTALS OF LEADING NATIONS

	G	S	B
United States	41	27	27
Sweden	19	21	24
Finland	15	10	9
Great Britain	14	15	13
Belgium	13	11	11
Norway	13	9	9
Italy	13	5	5
France	9	19	13
Holland	4	2	5
Denmark	3	9	1

1924 PARIS
Competitors: 3,092
Nations: 44
Dates: May 4–July 27

Heroes: American *Bud Houser* won both the shot put and the discus, the last male athlete to do so. The 100-meter dash and the 400-meter run were won by England's *Harold Abrahams* and Scotland's *Eric Liddell*. The award-winning film *Chariots of Fire* was based on their quests. In the swimming pool the most popular winner was *Johnny Weissmuller*, who won three gold medals as well as taking a bronze in water polo. Weissmuller also entertained the Parisian crowd by performing a comedy diving act between races. He later became even more famous as Hollywood's Tarzan. The biggest star of the Paris Games was grim-faced *Paavo Nurmi* of Finland, who won the 1,500-meter run, rested for fifty-five minutes, and then won the 5,000 meters. He also won three gold medals in cross-country and team races. Between 1920 and 1928 he earned nine gold medals and three silver medals.

Controversies: What the previous two Olympics lacked in controversy was more than made up for in Paris. More than 30,000 French fans watched in horror as their rugby team was thrashed by the upstart squad from the United States. Incensed by the Americans' rough play, the French taunted American spectators. Fights broke out and an art student from De Kalb, Illinois, was knocked unconscious. At the awards ceremony, the "Star-Spangled Banner" was drowned out by the whistling and booing of the crowd. At the wrestling venue the famous Greco-Roman champion Claes Johansson of Sweden defeated local favorite Henri Deglane. The French protested and the Jury of Appeal ordered the two men to wrestle for another six minutes, after which Deglane was declared the winner. Over at the tennis courts, Kitty McKane of Great Britain was breezing through her semifinal encounter with Didi Vlasto of France when another match at center court ended and a large crowd moved over to watch McKane and Vlasto. Soon the audience was in an uproar because the South African umpire refused to call the score in French rather than English. McKane, who had been leading 6–0, 3–0, lost her composure, allowing Vlasto to win thirteen of the next sixteen games and take the victory. The biggest disruptions took place at the boxing tournament. When an English referee, T. H. Walker, disqualified an Italian welterweight named Giuseppi Oldani, his supporters pelted Walker with a variety of objects until he was escorted from the arena by a bodyguard of Anglo-Saxon boxers and wrestlers. Two nights later, Roger Brousse, a French middleweight, was disqualified for biting his British opponent, Harry Mallin. Hundreds of demonstrators tried to enter the ring. Police quelled the riot after a half hour, but attacks against the judges and referees continued for the rest of the evening. The following night fighting broke out between Argentinian and Belgian fans. The arena was still in an uproar when Harry Mallin entered the ring for the middleweight final and the French spectators joined the chaos. Disputes engendered by the 1924 Olympics did not end with the Games themselves. Two separate conflicts between Italian and Hungarian fencing teams led to real duels that were held after the Games were over.

MEDAL TOTALS OF LEADING NATIONS

	G	S	B
United States	45	27	27
Finland	14	13	10
France	13	15	10
Great Britain	9	13	12
Italy	8	3	5
Switzerland	7	8	10
Norway	5	2	3
Sweden	4	13	12
Holland	4	1	5
Belgium	3	7	3

1928 AMSTERDAM
Competitors: 3,014
Nations: 46
Dates: May 17–August 12

Heroes: No new stars emerged. *Johnny Weissmuller* and *Paavo Nurmi* won more gold medals, but the only athlete to earn three golds was Swiss gymnast *Georges Miez*.

Controversies: Czech and American boxing fans staged vociferous protests, but the most important incident took place at the track. For the first time women were allowed to run a race longer than 200 meters. Lina Radke of Germany broke her own world record in winning the 800 meters. After the race several of the finalists collapsed in exhaustion and some were given aid. Antifeminists in the press and in the International Amateur Athletic Federation (IAAF) were so appalled by the spectacle that the IAAF banned races of more than half a lap and women didn't get to run 800 meters again until 1960.

MEDAL TOTALS OF LEADING NATIONS

	G	S	B
United States	22	18	16
Germany	10	7	14
Finland	8	8	9
Sweden	7	6	12
Italy	7	5	7
Switzerland	7	4	4
France	6	10	5

Holland	6	9	4
Hungary	4	5	0
Canada	4	4	7

1932 LOS ANGELES
Competitors: 1,408
Nations: 37
Dates: July 30–August 14

Hero: The heroine of the Los Angeles Games was Texan *Babe Didrikson*, who qualified for five track and field events but was allowed to enter only three. She won the javelin throw and the 80-meter hurdles and took a silver in the high jump despite setting a world record.

Controversies: Official incompetence marred the track and field competition. Discus thrower Jules Noël of France lofted a great throw that appeared to be good enough for the lead. Unfortunately, every one of the discus officials was distracted by the tense proceedings at the pole vault event nearby and none of them saw where the discus landed. They awarded Noël an extra throw, but it was a mediocre attempt and he finished fourth. The steeplechase runners were forced to complete an extra lap because the lap checker forgot to change the lap count the first time the runners passed by. The extra lap allowed Thomas Everson of Great Britain to pass Joseph McCluskey of the United States. Embarrassed officials offered to have the race rerun, but McCluskey, a good sport, declined. The most dramatic race was the 5,000 meters. In the last fifty yards American Ralph Hill tried twice to pass Finnish world-record-holder Lauri Lehtinen, but Lehtinen cut him off both times and reached the finish line first. The American crowd started to boo, but announcer Bill Henry cut them off, reminding them that "these people are our guests." Hill, like McCluskey, refused to file a protest. The water polo tournament was disrupted when the Brazilian team attacked a Hungarian referee and the police had to be called in. But the most scandalous incident of the Los Angeles Olympics took place in the dressage event. Bertil Sandström of Sweden placed second but was relegated to last place for encouraging his horse by making clicking noises. Sandström claimed that the noises were really made by a creaking saddle, but the Jury of Appeal was not convinced.

MEDAL TOTALS OF LEADING NATIONS

	G	S	B
United States	41	32	30
Italy	12	12	12
France	10	5	4
Sweden	9	5	9
Japan	7	7	4
Hungary	6	4	5
Finland	5	8	12

Great Britain	4	7	5
Germany	3	12	5
Australia	3	1	1

1936 BERLIN
Competitors: 4,066
Nations: 49
Dates: August 1–16

Heroes: The hero of heroes was American *Jesse Owens*, who won the 100 meters, the 200 meters, and the long jump and earned a fourth gold medal in the 4x100-meter relay. German fans ignored the Nazis' racial propaganda and hailed Owens as the star of the Berlin Games. Among their own heroes was equestrian lieutenant *Konrad Freiherr von Wangenheim*. During the steeplechase portion of the three-day event he was thrown by his horse and broke his collarbone. Knowing that his team would be disqualified if he failed to finish, von Wangenheim remounted and completed the course. The next day, in the jumping competition, his horse fell and landed on him. Again he remounted and finished, allowing Germany to take the gold medal. In one of the greatest races in Olympic history, *John Lovelock* of New Zealand set a world record in the 1,500-meter run, defeating Glenn Cunningham of Elkhart, Kansas, and defending champion Luigi Beccali of Italy.

Controversies: In 1931, when Berlin was chosen as the site for the 1936 Olympics, few people could foresee that a mere five years would see the rise to power of Adolf Hitler and the Nazi Party. The Nazis tried to make the Olympics a showcase for their "Aryan superrace," but when German long jumper Luz Long befriended black American Jesse Owens on the field in full view of 100,000 spectators, the audience sided with Long and Owens and not with Hitler. The ugliness of bigotry spread to the American team as well when U.S. coaches pulled Marty Glickman and Sam Stoller, the only Jews on the

Jesse Owens, the hero of the 1936 Olympics, was publicly befriended by his German rival, Luz Long.

U.S. track squad, from the relay team at the last minute. Another American athlete who never got to compete was defending backstroke champion Eleanor Holm, who was kicked off the team for getting drunk and shouting out obscenities during the boat trip to Germany. During a quarter-final soccer match, Peruvian fans rushed onto the field and attacked one of the Austrian players. Peru won the match, but a Jury of Appeal ordered it to be replayed. The Peruvians refused and, along with the Colombians, pulled out of the Games. A stranger controversy developed in the women's 100-meter dash. Missouri farm girl Helen Stephens defeated Polish favorite Stella Walsh (who really lived in Cleveland). Some Poles accused Helen Stephens of being a man and German officials were forced to give her a sex check, which she passed. Helen Stephens may not have had male sexual organs, but in 1980, when Stella Walsh died, an autopsy revealed that *she* did.

MEDAL TOTALS OF LEADING NATIONS
	G	S	B
Germany	33	26	30
United States	24	20	12
Hungary	10	1	5
Italy	8	9	5
Finland	7	6	6
France	7	6	6
Sweden	6	5	9
Holland	6	4	7
Japan	5	4	7
Great Britain	4	7	3

1940 TOKYO; HELSINKI—Canceled because of war

1944 LONDON—Canceled because of war

1948 LONDON
Competitors: 4,099
Nations: 59
Dates: July 29–August 14

Heroes: Of the nine women's track and field events included in the 1948 program, Dutch housewife *Fanny Blankers-Koen* won four of them. She probably could have won the long jump as well, considering that the winning leap was twenty inches shorter than Blankers-Koen's world record. On the men's side, Californian *Bob Mathias* caused a sensation by winning the decathlon at age seventeen. He remains the youngest male to win a track and field gold medal. In 1938 *Károly Takács* was a member of the Hungarian world-champion pistol-shooting team when a grenade exploded in his right hand—his pistol hand—and shattered it completely. Takács taught himself to shoot with his left hand and, ten years later, won an Olympic gold medal.

Controversies: In the men's 4x100-meter relay, the U.S. team crossed the finish line first but was disqualified when a British track official accused them of passing beyond the legal zone. The British team was awarded the gold instead. But three days later a Jury of Appeal reviewed films of the race and the disqualification was rescinded. Hungarian and Argentinian boxing fans took turns protesting decisions by storming the jurors' table. Once again the dressage competition was marred by a shocking breach of the rules: the first-place Swedish team was disqualified when it was learned that one of its members, Gehnäll Persson, who had been entered as an officer, was really only a noncommissioned officer. The 1948 games also saw the first political defection when Marie Provaznikova, the leader of the Czech women's team, refused to return to Czechoslovakia.

MEDAL TOTALS OF LEADING NATIONS

	G	S	B
United States	38	27	19
Sweden	16	11	17
France	10	6	13
Hungary	10	5	12
Italy	8	12	9
Finland	8	7	5
Turkey	6	4	2
Czechoslovakia	6	2	3
Switzerland	5	10	5
Denmark	5	7	8

1952 HELSINKI
Competitors: 4,925
Nations: 69
Dates: July 19–August 3

Heroes: Czech distance runner *Emil Zátopek* became the only athlete in Olympic history to win the 5,000 meters, the 10,000 meters, and the marathon in the same year, even though he had never competed in a marathon race before. His wife, Dana, won the javelin throw. In 1948 the Jamaican 4x400-meter relay team of *George Rhoden, Leslie Laing, Arthur Wint,* and *Herb McKenley* had been convinced they could upset the favorites from the United States, but Wint, running the third leg, pulled a muscle and they were unable to finish. The foursome stuck together and four years later in Helsinki they beat the Americans by one yard. The silver medal in the dressage competition was won by *Lis Hartel* of Denmark, who had been paralyzed below the knees following an attack of polio and had to be helped on and off her horse.

Controversies: The Helsinki games were the first at which the Soviet Union took part and many people feared unpleasant confrontations between the Soviets and the Americans. Instead, all was friendly and the Finnish organizers set the standard for hospitality and competence.

MEDAL TOTALS OF LEADING NATIONS

	G	S	B
United States	40	19	17
Soviet Union	22	30	19
Hungary	16	10	16
Sweden	12	13	10
Italy	8	9	4
Czechoslovakia	7	3	3
France	6	6	6
Finland	6	3	13
Australia	6	2	3
Norway	3	2	0

1956 MELBOURNE
Competitors: 3,342
Nations: 67
Dates: November 22–December 8

Heroes: There were many records set in 1956. "The Vaulting Vicar," the Reverend *Bob Richards* of California, became the first and only repeat winner of the pole vault. *Lars Hall* of Sweden became the first and only repeat winner of the modern pentathlon. Californian *Pat McCormick* became the only woman to win both the springboard and platform diving events twice. *László Papp* of Hungary became the first boxer to win three gold medals. Kayaker *Gert Fredriksson* of Sweden won both the 1,000-meter and the 10,000-meter races, the third time he had won the former and the second time he had won the latter. And the *U.S. basketball team,* led by future Boston Celtics stars Bill Russell and K. C. Jones, won their eight games by an average margin of more than fifty-three points—a record that has still not been surpassed.

Controversies: Because of Australian quarantine laws, the equestrian competitions were held in Stockholm—the only time the Olympics were split between two countries. Less than three weeks before the Olympics began, Soviet troops invaded Hungary. When water polo teams from the two nations played against each other in Melbourne, a brawl broke out and police had to be called in to prevent spectators from joining in the attack on the Soviets. This year also saw the first two boycotts of the modern Olympics. Holland, Spain, and Switzerland protested the Soviet invasion of Hungary, and Egypt, Iraq, and Lebanon protested the Israeli-led takeover of the Suez Canal.

MEDAL TOTALS OF LEADING NATIONS

	G	S	B
Soviet Union	37	29	32
United States	32	25	17
Australia	13	8	14
Hungary	9	10	7
Italy	8	8	9
Sweden	8	5	6
Great Britain	6	7	11

West Germany	5	9	6
Romania	5	3	5
Japan	4	10	5

1960 ROME
Competitors: 5,348
Nations: 83
Dates: August 25–September 10

Heroes: The marathon was won in dramatic fashion by an unknown Ethiopian, *Abebe Bikila*, who ran barefoot. Tennessee sprinter *Wilma Rudolph* earned three gold medals and *Cassius Clay*, a gregarious eighteen-year-old boxer from Louisville, Kentucky, handily won the light-heavyweight division. Later, as Muhammad Ali, he would become the most famous athlete in the world. Danish Finn class yachtsman *Paul Elvström* became the first athlete in any sport to win the same event four times. In the grand tradition of Konrad von Wangenheim, forty-five-year-old *Bill Roycroft* of Australia broke his collarbone in a fall during the three-day equestrian competition but left his hospital bed to take part in the jumping test so that Australia would qualify for the gold medal.

Controversies: Lance Larson of the United States appeared to edge out John Devitt of Australia to win the 100-meter freestyle. Devitt congratulated Larson. The unofficial electronic timers showed Larson winning by one-tenth of a second, with Larson touching four inches ahead of Devitt. But the judges awarded the

victory to Devitt and four years of protests failed to change their decision. Danish cyclist Knut Jensen collapsed from sunstroke, fractured his skull, and died. It was later determined that he had taken a blood circulation stimulant. The only other athlete to die during an Olympic competition was 1912 Portuguese marathon runner Francisco Lazaro.

MEDAL TOTALS OF LEADING NATIONS

	G	S	B
Soviet Union	43	29	31
United States	34	21	16
Italy	13	10	13
West Germany	10	10	6
Australia	8	8	6
Turkey	7	2	0
Hungary	6	8	7
Japan	4	7	7
Poland	4	6	11
East Germany	3	9	7

1964 TOKYO
Competitors: 5,140
Nations: 93
Dates: October 10–24

Heroes: *Abebe Bikila* became the first repeat winner of the marathon. *Peter Snell* of New Zealand won the 800-meter run for a second time and added a 1,500-meter gold as well. The 10,000 meters was won by Native American *Billy Mills*, who was such an outsider that not a single journalist had interviewed him before the race. *Mary Rand* became the first British woman to win an Olympic gold in track and field when she set a world record in the long jump. Australian swimmer *Dawn Fraser* won the 100-meter freestyle for the third straight time, while American *Don Schollander* became the first swimmer to earn four gold medals at one Olympics. Russian rower *Vyacheslav Ivanov* won the single sculls for the third time, and Ukrainian gymnast *Larysa Latynina* won six medals to bring her career total to an all-time record of eighteen—nine gold, five silver, and four bronze. The local heroes were the members of the *Japanese women's volleyball team*, whose final victory over the Soviet Union gained an 80 percent audience rating on Japanese television.

Controversies: The most shocking incident occurred during a pre-Olympic soccer qualifying match between Peru and Argentina in Lima, Peru. When the Uruguayan referee nullified a Peruvian goal, two spectators attacked him. The referee suspended the game and the incensed crowd surged onto the field. Police fired tear-gas grenades, fighting spilled out into the streets, and before the night was out 328 people had been killed.

Wilma Rudolph streaks to victory in the 1960 4 x 100-meter relay.

MEDAL TOTALS OF LEADING NATIONS

	G	S	B
United States	36	26	28
Soviet Union	30	31	35
Japan	16	5	8
Italy	10	10	7
Hungary	10	7	5
West Germany	7	14	14
Poland	7	6	10
Australia	6	2	10
Czechoslovakia	5	6	3
Great Britain	4	12	2

1968 MEXICO CITY

Competitors: 5,531

Nations: 112

Dates: October 12–27

Heroes: *Wyomia Tyus* of Griffin, Georgia, became the first sprinter to win the same event twice when she won the 100-meter dash. American discus thrower *Al Oerter* won his event for the fourth straight time. Long jumper *Bob Beamon* broke the world record by 21¾ inches, breaking the 29-foot barrier before anyone had even jumped 28 feet. United States high jumper *Dick Fosbury* caused a sensation by going over with his back to the bar. He won the gold medal, and the "Fosbury flop" became the standard technique. The most popular athlete at the Mexico City Olympics was Czech gymnast *Vera Cáslavská*, who defended her all-around title, added three more golds on individual apparatuses, and then capped off her week by getting married while a crowd of 10,000 Mexican fans surrounded the church. The four-man Swedish entry in the cycling team time trial was made up of four brothers, *Erik, Gösta, Sture,* and *Tomas Pettersson*. They finished in second place.

Controversies: Ten days before the Opening Ceremony, government troops fired on unarmed student protesters in Mexico City, killing hundreds of young people. Remarkably, this outrage attracted far less attention from the press than did a nonviolent protest by two African-American athletes two weeks later. Tommie Smith and John Carlos won the gold and bronze medals in the 200-meter dash. During the playing of the "Star-Spangled Banner" at the victory ceremony, Smith and Carlos protested racism in the United States by bowing their heads and raising clenched fists in Black Power salutes. Smith and Carlos were kicked out of the Olympic Village by the U.S. Olympic Committee under pressure from the International Olympic Committee, which had just dismissed the killing of student demonstrators as "an internal affair." Swedish modern pentathlete Hans-Gunnar Liljenvall gained the dubious distinction of being the first Olympic athlete to be disqualified for using prohibited drugs. His

crime?—drinking alcohol to steady his nerves before the shooting contest. The soccer tournament was marred by brawling. Fighting between the teams from Ghana and Israel continued back at the athletes' village, and the match between Czechoslovakia and Guatemala was also disrupted by fighting. Many people felt the Olympics should not have been held in Mexico City at all because of its altitude of 7,347 feet. The rarefied air proved disastrous to many athletes engaged in endurance events.

MEDAL TOTALS OF LEADING NATIONS

	G	S	B
United States	45	28	34
Soviet Union	29	32	30
Japan	11	7	7
Hungary	10	10	12
East Germany	9	9	7
France	7	3	5
Czechoslovakia	7	2	4
West Germany	5	11	10
Australia	5	7	5
Great Britain	5	5	3

1972 MUNICH

Competitors: 7,147

Nations: 122

Dates: August 26–September 10

Heroes: American swimmer *Mark Spitz* won an unprecedented seven gold medals to add to the two he had won in 1968. *Lasse Viren* of Finland won the 10,000-meter run even though he fell midway through the race. Later he won the 5,000 meters as well. Russian wrestler *Ivan Yarygin* won the 100-kilogram (220-pound) division by pinning all seven of his opponents. He was on the mat for a total of seventeen minutes and eight seconds. The media star of the Munich Games was Belorussian gymnast *Olga Korbut*, whose dramatic cycle of success, failure, and success captured hearts even in the United States, where Cold War antipathy to the Soviet Union was widespread.

Controversies: On September 5, 1972, the Olympic movement was permanently scarred when eight Palestinian terrorists broke into the Olympic Village, killed two members of the Israeli team, and took nine more hostage. An ensuing battle with West German police left all the hostages dead, as well as five of the terrorists and one policeman. The Olympics were suspended for thirty-four hours and a memorial service was held in the main stadium. (See page 167.) All other controversies paled in comparison with this tragedy, but this is not to say that they didn't occur anyway. Chief among them was the men's basketball final, in which the United States' sixty-two-game Olympic win streak was broken by the Soviet Union. Actually the game ended with the United States ahead, but twice the clock was set back until the Soviets finally scored the winning basket. That same day the Pakistani men's field hockey team lost a bitter 1–0 final to West Germany. Pakistani fans poured water on the president of the International Hockey Federation and at the medal ceremony several Pakistani players refused to face the German flag during the playing of the German national anthem. The International Olympic Committee banned the Pakistani players for life, but then reinstated them in time for the next Olympics. Another incident concerned Rick DeMont, a sixteen-year-old swimmer from San Rafael, California, who won the 400-meter freestyle but was disqualified for taking the banned drug ephedrine, which was contained in his asthma medicine. U.S. team officials had failed to check whether his medicine contained components on the prohibited list.

MEDAL TOTALS OF LEADING NATIONS

	G	S	B
Soviet Union	50	27	22
United States	33	31	30
East Germany	20	23	23
West Germany	13	11	16
Japan	13	8	8
Australia	8	7	2
Poland	7	5	9
Hungary	6	13	16
Bulgaria	6	10	5
Italy	5	3	10

1976 MONTREAL
Competitors: 6,085
Nations: 92
Dates: July 17–August 1

Heroes: *Lasse Viren* repeated his 5,000- and 10,000-meters double. *Victor Saneyev* of Soviet Georgia won his third triple jump gold medal. Four years later he came within 4½ inches of winning a fourth. Poland's *Irena Szewińska* set a world record in the 400-meter run. It was her fourth Olympics, during which she won seven medals in five different events. American swimmer *John Naber* won four gold medals and one silver. Fourteen-year-old Romanian gymnast *Nadia Comaneci* made Olympic history when she was awarded the first perfect scores of ten for her performance on the uneven bars and the balance beam. Japanese gymnast *Shun Fujimoto* broke his knee while finishing his floor exercises routine during the team event. Not wanting to cause concern among his coaches or fellow team members, he kept his injury to himself and continued performing. But when he dismounted from the rings he landed on his feet and compounded his injury by dislocating his knee. The pain was so intense that he finally had to withdraw.

Controversies: Twenty-two African nations boycotted the Montreal Games to protest the fact that New Zealand was allowed to compete even though a rugby team from that nation had toured South Africa. The situation was a bit awkward, since rugby was not an Olympic sport and South Africa had been ousted from the Olympics in 1964 because of its racial policies. Still, the Africans persisted and the Games went on without them. The women's swimming events were dominated by the East Germans, who won eleven of thirteen events even though they had failed to win a single gold medal four years earlier in Munich. The reason for their improvement was obvious to opposing swimmers and coaches: they were taking banned performance-enhancing drugs. But the International Swimming Federation did nothing to expose the East German violations. Scandal rocked the modern pentathlon competition when Soviet army major Boris Onischenko was caught cheating during the fencing contest. He had rigged his sword with a well-hidden push-button circuit breaker that allowed him to register a hit whenever he wanted. He was forever after known as Boris Dis-Onischenko.

MEDAL TOTALS OF LEADING NATIONS

	G	S	B
Soviet Union	49	41	35
East Germany	40	25	25
United States	34	35	25
West Germany	10	12	17
Japan	9	6	10
Poland	7	6	13
Bulgaria	6	9	7
Cuba	6	4	3
Romania	4	9	14
Hungary	4	5	13

1980 MOSCOW
Competitors: 5,353
Nations: 80
Dates: July 19–August 3

Heroes: East German *Waldemar Cierpinski* matched Abebe Bikila's feat of winning the marathon twice. Cuban boxer *Teófilo Stevenson* won the heavyweight title for the third straight time. *Yuri Sedykh* of Russia set a world record in the hammer throw to win his second gold medal in the event. Eight years later he added a silver. British runners *Sebastien Coe* and *Steve Ovett* were favored to win the 800 meters and 1,500 meters respectively, but each won the other's race.

Controversies: U.S. president Jimmy Carter initiated a boycott of the Moscow Games as part of a package of sanctions to protest the Soviet invasion of Afghanistan. Sixty-four countries joined the U.S. boycott and ten more declined to participate in the Opening Ceremony.

MEDAL TOTALS OF LEADING NATIONS

	G	S	B
Soviet Union	80	69	46
East Germany	47	37	42
Bulgaria	8	16	17
Cuba	8	7	5
Italy	8	3	4
Hungary	7	10	15
Romania	6	6	13
France	6	5	3
Great Britain	5	7	9
Poland	3	14	15

1984 LOS ANGELES
Competitors: 7,078
Nations: 140
Dates: July 28–August 12

Heroes: *Carl Lewis* matched Jesse Owens's feat of winning the 100 meters, 200 meters, long jump, and 4x100-meter relay. *Sebastian Coe* became the first repeat winner of the 1,500 meters. Great Britain's *Daley Thompson* won the decathlon for a second time, and *Edwin Moses* of the United States won the 400-meter hurdles, just as he had eight years earlier in Montreal. *Joan Benoit* of Freeport, Maine, triumphed in the inaugural women's marathon. In 1972 sixteen-year-old West German high jumper *Ulrike Meyfarth* had become the youngest-ever winner of an individual event in track and field. Twelve years later, in Los Angeles, Meyfarth became the *oldest* person to win an Olympic high jump competition. Finnish rower *Pertti Karpinnen* earned his third gold medal in the single sculls.

Controversies: With the Olympics in the United States, the Soviet government launched a revenge boycott that was joined by twelve other nations. Of the thirty-eight boxing matches involving U.S. boxers that were decided by decision, thirty-seven were won by the American contender. This led the president of the Nigerian Boxing Association to attack a boxing official with his walking stick and caused South Korean boxing leaders to threaten revenge when the Olympics came to their country four years hence. Oddly enough, the most controversial call was made *against* an American boxer, Evander Holyfield, who was disqualified for a late hit even though his opponent, Kevin Barry of New Zealand, argued that Holyfield had beaten him fairly. The most publicized incident took place in the women's 3,000-meter run when local favorite Mary Decker tripped on the heels of Zola Budd, a South African competing for Great Britain. Decker was unable to continue and the crowd booed Budd for the rest of the race even though she hadn't fouled Decker intentionally. A bizarre incident enlivened the rowing regatta when it was discovered that someone had sabotaged one of the oarlock gates on the French men's eights boat. The culprit was never found.

After the Olympics were over, it was revealed that eight members of the U.S. cycling squad, including gold medalist Steve Hegg, had injected other people's blood into their veins to increase their hemoglobin level and endurance.

MEDAL TOTALS OF LEADING NATIONS

	G	S	B
United States	83	61	30
Romania	20	16	17
West Germany	17	19	23
China	15	8	9
Italy	14	6	12
Canada	10	18	16
Japan	10	8	14
New Zealand	8	1	2
Yugoslavia	7	4	7
South Korea	6	6	7

1988 SEOUL
Competitors: 9,421
Nations: 159
Dates: September 17–October 2

Heroes: *Carl Lewis* became the first male repeat winner in both the 100-meter dash and the long jump. *Jackie Joyner-Kersee* won both the long jump and the heptathlon, while her sister-in-law *Florence Griffith-Joyner* won both sprints. Joyner-Kersee was victorious in the heptathlon again in 1992. *Christa Luding-Rothenburger* earned a silver medal in the cycling match sprint to become the only athlete ever to win medals in the Winter and Summer Olympics in the same year. Seven months earlier she had won gold and silver medals in speed skating. American swimmer *Matt Biondi* won seven medals, including five gold, and East German swimmer *Kristin Otto* won six golds. Otto's achievements were tarnished by her subsequent admission of the use of prohibited performance-enhancing drugs. *Janet Evans* of the United States won all three of the longest women's swimming events, and *Vladimir Salnikov* of Ukraine, who was thought to be washed up, won the 1,500-meter freestyle, just as he had eight years earlier in Moscow. Californian *Greg Louganis* became the first male diver to win both the springboard and platform events twice, even though he hit his head on the board and required stitches. The weightlifting star was five-foot-tall *Naim Suleymanoğlü*, who had defected from Bulgaria and now was competing for Turkey.

Controversies: Prior to the Seoul Games, thirty-six Olympic athletes had been disqualified for using forbidden drugs, but the sports world was rocked when one of the heroes of the Games, Canadian sprinter Ben Johnson, tested positive for anabolic steroids after setting a world record in the 100 meters. Wild scenes, reminiscent of the 1924 Paris Olympics, plagued the boxing

Roy Jones, referee Aldo Leoni, and Park Si-hun react with shock at the announcement of Park's victory in the 1988 Olympics.

tournament. The worst incident took place when a South Korean bantamweight, Byun Jong-il, was penalized twice for head butting and lost the fight as a result. The New Zealand referee, Keith Walker, was attacked not by spectators but by Korean boxing officials and security guards. More than six years after the Seoul Games ended, Greg Louganis revealed that he had been HIV positive when he hit his head on the springboard and bled in the pool.

MEDAL TOTALS OF LEADING NATIONS

	G	S	B
Soviet Union	55	31	46
East Germany	37	35	30
United States	36	31	27
South Korea	12	10	11
West Germany	11	14	15
Hungary	11	6	6
Bulgaria	10	12	13
Romania	7	11	6
France	6	4	6
Italy	6	4	4

1992 BARCELONA
Competitors: 9,367
Nations: 169
Dates: July 25–August 9

Heroes: *Carl Lewis* won the long jump a third time and then gained his eighth gold medal when he anchored the U.S. 4x100-meter relay team. Gymnast *Vitaly Scherbo* of Belarus earned

six gold medals—in fact, he won four in one day. *Derartu Tulu* of Ethiopia outkicked South Africa's Elana Meyer to win the 10,000-meter run. She was the first black African woman to win a medal in the Olympics. Less than three months before the Games began, Canada's world champion sculler, *Silken Laumann,* was injured when she was hit by another boat while warming up. Her leg was shattered and it was feared she would never compete again. Incredibly, she fought back, made the Canadian team, and won a bronze medal. *Derek Redmond* of Great Britain injured his right hamstring during a semifinal heat of the 400 meters and fell to the ground. He got up and, in tears, dragged himself along the track. His father rushed out of the stands to help his son and together they crossed the finish line. The most popular athletes at the Barcelona Olympics were the members of the *U.S. men's basketball team,* "the Dream Team." They were led by Magic Johnson, Larry Bird, Michael Jordan, Charles Barkley, and Patrick Ewing.

Controversies: The bitter rivalry in long-distance running between Morocco and Kenya reached a peak—or a valley—in the 10,000-meter race when Hammou Boutayeb of Morocco, a lap behind the leaders, blocked the path of Kenya's Richard Chelimo in order to help his own countryman Khalid Skah. Race officials disqualified Skah but then reinstated his victory the following day. Weightlifter Ibragim Samadov of Russia, outraged that the audience had cheered when he failed his last lift, refused his bronze medal and stalked off the podium during the medal ceremony. He was disqualified and banned for life from further international competition. The normally placid world of synchronized swimming was disrupted during the solo competition. The Brazilian judge punched in the wrong score for Canada's Sylvie Frechette. When she tried to correct her mistake and give Frechette a higher score, the American referee refused to allow the change. As it turned out, the error cost Frechette the gold medal, which went to Kristen Babb-Sprague of the United States instead. The following year, Frechette was awarded a gold medal, although Babb-Sprague was allowed to keep hers as well.

MEDAL TOTALS OF LEADING NATIONS

	G	S	B
Soviet Union	45	38	28
United States	37	34	37
Germany	33	21	28
China	16	22	16
Cuba	14	6	11
Spain	13	7	2
South Korea	12	5	12
Hungary	11	12	7
France	8	5	16
Australia	7	9	11

1996 ATLANTA—July 19–August 1

2000 SYDNEY—September 15–October 1

WINTER GAMES

1924 CHAMONIX
Competitors: 294
Nations: 16
Dates: January 25–February 4

Heroes: The first winner of the Winter Olympics was *Charles Jewtraw*, a speed skater from a poor family in Lake Placid, New York. Jewtraw won the 500 meters event on January 26, 1924. Finnish speed skater *Clas Thunberg* earned five medals, including three gold, and added two more golds in 1928. The *Toronto Granites* ice hockey team, representing Canada, outscored their five opponents 110 to 3. They beat Switzerland 33–0 and Czechoslovakia 30–0, but squeaked by the United States by the tight score of 6–1.

Controversies: Fifty years after the Chamonix Games, a sports historian, Toralf Strömstad (himself a silver medalist), discovered an error in the computation of the scores in the 1924 ski jump. It turned out that Norwegian-born American Anders Haugen, who had placed fourth,

should have been third. Haugen, who by then was eighty-three years old, was awarded his bronze medal in a special ceremony in Oslo.

MEDAL TOTALS OF LEADING NATIONS

	G	S	B
Norway	4	7	6
Finland	4	3	3
Austria	2	1	0
United States	1	2	1
Switzerland	1	0	1
Canada	1	0	0
Sweden	1	0	0
Great Britain	0	1	2
Belgium	0	0	1
France	0	0	1

1928 SAINT MORITZ
Competitors: 495
Nations: 25
Dates: February 11–19

Heroes: Thirty-four-year-old *Gillis Grafström* of Sweden won his third straight gold medal in men's figure skating (figure skating having been included in the 1920 Summer Olympics). On the women's side, fifteen-year-old *Sonja Henie* of Norway won the first of her gold medals.

MEDAL TOTALS OF LEADING NATIONS

	G	S	B
Norway	6	4	5
United States	2	2	2
Sweden	2	2	1
Finland	2	1	1
Canada	1	0	0
France	1	0	0
Austria	0	3	1
Belgium	0	0	1
Czechoslovakia	0	0	1
Germany	0	0	1
Great Britain	0	0	1
Switzerland	0	0	1

1932 LAKE PLACID
Competitors: 306
Nations: 17
Dates: February 4–15

Heroes: In 1920 *Eddie Eagan* had won the light-heavyweight boxing title at the Antwerp Olympics. Twelve years later, in Lake Placid, he joined the U.S. four-man bobsled team led by *Billy Fiske* and became the only person in history to earn gold medals in both the Summer and Winter Olympics.

Controversies: European speed skaters were shocked to discover that the American organizers were imposing something known as the North American Rules, in which the competitions were held as actual races with mass starts instead of in pairs against the clock. Clas

Eddie Eagan (second from left) is the only person to win gold medals in both the Summer and Winter Olympics.

Thunberg was so outraged that he refused to participate. The Americans further exasperated their guests by disqualifying skaters for "loafing": not doing their share to set the pace.

gian speed skater *Ivan Ballangrud* earned three gold medals and one silver to add to the gold, silver, and bronze he had collected in the last two Olympics.

MEDAL TOTALS OF LEADING NATIONS

	G	S	B
United States	6	4	2
Norway	3	4	3
Sweden	1	2	0
Canada	1	1	5
Finland	1	1	1
Austria	1	1	0
France	1	0	0
Switzerland	0	1	0
Germany	0	0	2
Hungary	0	0	1

MEDAL TOTALS OF LEADING NATIONS

	G	S	B
Norway	7	5	3
Germany	3	3	0
Sweden	2	2	3
Finland	1	2	3
Switzerland	1	2	0
Austria	1	1	2
Great Britain	1	1	1
United States	1	0	3
Canada	0	1	0
France	0	0	1
Hungary	0	0	1

1936 GARMISCH-PARTENKIRCHEN
Competitors: 755
Nations: 28
Dates: February 6–16

Heroes: *Sonja Henie*, now a mature twenty-three, won her third straight gold medal. Norwe-

1940 SAPPORO; SAINT MORITZ; GARMISCH-PARTENKIRCHEN—Canceled
because of war

1944 CORTINA D'AMPEZZO—Canceled
because of war

1948 SAINT MORITZ
Competitors: 713
Nations: 28
Dates: January 30–February 8

Hero: Alpine skiing was added to the Olympic program for the first time. There were three men's events. France's *Henri Oreiller* won two of them and placed second in the other.

Controversies: Two ice hockey teams arrived in Saint Moritz to represent the United States. One was sanctioned by the American Olympic Committee, the other by the International Ice Hockey Federation (IIHF). The International Olympic Committee banned both teams, but the Swiss organizers allowed the IIHF-approved team to compete anyway. They placed fourth.

MEDAL TOTALS OF LEADING NATIONS

	G	S	B
Norway	4	3	3
Sweden	4	3	3
Switzerland	3	4	3
United States	3	4	2
France	2	1	2
Canada	2	0	1
Austria	1	3	4
Finland	1	3	2
Belgium	1	1	0
Italy	1	0	0

1952 OSLO
Competitors: 732
Nations: 30
Dates: February 14–25

Heroes: Harvard senior *Dick Button* dazzled the judges with his triple loop to defend the figure skating title he had won in 1948. Local hero *Hjalmar Andersen* won three of the four men's speed skating events. His 24.8-second margin of victory in the 10,000 meters was the largest in Olympic history.

MEDAL TOTALS OF LEADING NATIONS

	G	S	B
Norway	7	3	6
United States	4	6	1
Finland	3	4	2
Germany	3	2	2
Austria	2	4	2
Canada	1	0	1
Italy	1	0	1
Great Britain	1	0	0
Holland	0	3	0
Sweden	0	0	4

1956 CORTINA D'AMPEZZO
Competitors: 818
Nations: 32
Dates: January 26–February 5

Hero: Austria's *Toni Sailer* swept the three alpine skiing events.

MEDAL TOTALS OF LEADING NATIONS

	G	S	B
Soviet Union	7	3	6
Austria	4	3	4
Finland	3	3	1
Switzerland	3	2	1
Sweden	2	4	4
United States	2	3	2
Norway	2	1	1
Italy	1	2	0
West Germany	1	0	0
Canada	0	1	2

1960 SQUAW VALLEY
Competitors: 665
Nations: 30
Dates: February 18–28

Heroes: The underdog *U.S. ice hockey team* came from behind to upset the defending champions from the Soviet Union, then came from behind again in their final match against Czechoslovakia to win a surprise gold medal.

MEDAL TOTALS OF LEADING NATIONS

	G	S	B
Soviet Union	7	5	9
United States	3	4	3
Norway	3	3	0
Sweden	3	2	2
Finland	2	3	3
West Germany	2	2	1
Canada	2	1	1
East Germany	2	1	0
Switzerland	2	0	0
Austria	1	2	3

1964 INNSBRUCK
Competitors: 1,186
Nations: 36
Dates: January 29–February 9

Heroes: Sweden's *Sixten Jernberg* won the 50-kilometer cross-country ski race, just as he had eight years earlier. When he gained another gold medal in the 4x10-kilometer relay, he closed out his Olympic career with four gold medals, three silver, and two bronze. Russian speed skater *Lydia Skoblikova* swept all four women's races, adding to the two gold medals she had won in Squaw Valley. French sisters *Christine* and *Marielle Goitschel* finished first and second in the slalom, then reversed their placings two days later in the giant slalom.

MEDAL TOTALS OF LEADING NATIONS

	G	S	B
Soviet Union	11	8	6
Austria	4	5	3

Norway	3	6	6
Finland	3	4	3
France	3	4	0
Sweden	3	3	1
East Germany	2	2	0
United States	1	2	3
Holland	1	1	0
West Germany	1	0	3

1968 GRENOBLE
Competitors: 1,293
Nations: 37
Dates: February 6–18

Hero: Local favorite *Jean-Claude Killy* swept the alpine events, matching Toni Sailer's feat of twelve years earlier.

Controversies: Killy's final race was the slalom, in which he was challenged by Austrian star Karl Schranz. Schranz sped through the fog, then skidded to a halt in the middle of his run, claiming a mysterious figure in black had crossed the course. He was granted a rerun, beat Killy's time, and was hailed as the winner. Two hours later it was announced that Schranz had missed two gates before his encounter with the mysterious interloper. An ugly debate between the French and Austrians ended in a 3–2 vote by the Jury of Appeal in favor of Killy. The three East German women who finished first, second, and fourth in the luge event were disqualified for illegally heating their runners.

MEDAL TOTALS OF LEADING NATIONS
	G	S	B
Norway	6	6	2
Soviet Union	5	5	3
France	4	3	2
Italy	4	0	0
Austria	3	4	4
Holland	3	3	3
Sweden	3	2	3
West Germany	2	2	3
United States	1	5	1
Finland	1	2	2
East Germany	1	2	2

1972 SAPPORO
Competitors: 1,232
Nations: 35
Dates: February 3–13

Heroes: *Ard Schenk* of Holland won three speed skating gold medals while Russian *Galina Kulakova* won all three women's cross-country races. The host fans were thrilled when Japanese ski jumpers *Yukio Kasaya, Akitsugu Konno,* and *Seiji Aochi* swept the medals in the normal hill event. No Japanese ski jumper had ever finished higher than seventh before.

Controversies: Karl Schranz again met Olympic frustration when the eighty-four-year-old president of the International Olympic Committee, Avery Brundage, banned him from competition for earning money as a "tester and designer" for ski product manufacturers. Brundage's hypocrisy was shown by the fact that the eventual winner of the downhill, Bernhard Russi of Switzerland, allowed his name and photo to be used in a huge pre-Olympic advertising campaign by a Swiss insurance company.

MEDAL TOTALS OF LEADING NATIONS
	G	S	B
Soviet Union	8	5	3
East Germany	4	3	7
Switzerland	4	3	3
Holland	4	3	2
United States	3	2	3
West Germany	3	1	1
Norway	2	5	5
Italy	2	2	1
Austria	1	2	2
Sweden	1	1	2

1976 INNSBRUCK
Competitors: 1,128
Nations: 37
Dates: February 4–15

Heroes: *Rosi Mittermaier* of West Germany won the downhill and the slalom, but finished one-eighth of a second too slow in the giant slalom and missed becoming the first woman to sweep the alpine events. On the men's side, Austria's *Franz Klammer* caused a sensation with his wild go-for-broke victory run in the downhill.

MEDAL TOTALS OF LEADING NATIONS
	G	S	B
Soviet Union	13	6	8
East Germany	7	5	7
United States	3	3	4
Norway	3	3	1
West Germany	2	5	3
Finland	2	4	1
Austria	2	2	2
Switzerland	1	3	1
Holland	1	2	3
Italy	1	2	1

1980 LAKE PLACID
Competitors: 1,071
Nations: 37
Dates: February 14–23

Heroes: American *Eric Heiden* won all five speed skating events. Russian figure skater *Irina Rodnina* earned her third pairs victory. The legendary Swede *Ingemar Stenmark* won both slalom races. And the *U.S. ice hockey team*, in an eerie replica of 1960, came from behind to upset the Soviet favorites, then came from behind again in their final match to defeat Finland and secure the gold medal.

MEDAL TOTALS OF LEADING NATIONS

	G	S	B
Soviet Union	10	6	6
East Germany	9	7	7
United States	6	4	2
Austria	3	2	2
Sweden	3	0	1
Liechtenstein	2	2	0
Finland	1	5	3
Norway	1	3	6
Holland	1	2	1
Switzerland	1	1	3

1984 SARAJEVO
Competitors: 1,277
Nations: 49
Dates: February 7–19

Heroes: Ice dancers *Jayne Torvill* and *Christopher Dean* of Nottingham, England, earned the first perfect scores of 6.0 in the event's history. Beautiful East German *Katarina Witt* charmed the judges to defend her women's figure skating title. Finnish nordic skier *Marja-Liisa Hämäläinen* gained revenge over her nation's sportswriters who said she was over the hill by earning three gold medals. And, shades of the Goitschel sisters, brothers *Phil* and *Steve Mahre* of the United States took first and second in the slalom.

MEDAL TOTALS OF LEADING NATIONS

	G	S	B
East Germany	9	9	6
Soviet Union	6	10	9
United States	4	4	0
Finland	4	3	6
Sweden	4	2	2
Norway	3	2	4
Switzerland	2	2	1
Canada	2	1	1
West Germany	2	1	1
Italy	2	0	0

1988 CALGARY
Competitors: 1,428
Nations: 57
Dates: February 13–28

Heroes: *Matti Nykänen* of Finland earned gold medals in all three ski jump events. Dutch speed skater *Yvonne van Gennip* upset the East German favorites to win three gold medals of her own.

MEDAL TOTALS OF LEADING NATIONS

	G	S	B
Soviet Union	11	9	9
East Germany	9	10	6
Switzerland	5	5	5
Finland	4	1	2
Sweden	4	0	2
Austria	3	5	2
Holland	3	2	2
West Germany	2	4	2
United States	2	1	3
Italy	2	1	2

1992 ALBERTVILLE
Competitors: 1,801
Nations: 64
Dates: February 8–23

Heroes: Norway's *Bjorn Dahlie* and *Vegard Ulvang* between them won every men's nordic skiing race, while Russian *Lyubov Yegorova* gained medals in every women's race—three gold and two silver. Yegorova's teammate *Raisa Smetanina* became the first winter athlete to earn ten Olympic medals. She also became the only athlete to win medals in five Winter Olympics, and, twelve days shy of her fortieth birthday, she was the oldest female medalist in the history of the Winter Olympics. On the other hand, ski jumper *Toni Nieminen* of Finland became the youngest male winter gold medalist. He was sixteen years old. The most popular star of the Albertville Games was Italy's *Alberto Tomba*. In Calgary he had won both the slalom and the giant slalom. In 1992 he won the giant slalom again to become the first alpine skier to win the same event twice.

MEDAL TOTALS OF LEADING NATIONS

	G	S	B
Germany	10	10	6
Soviet Union	9	6	8
Norway	9	6	5
Austria	6	7	8
United States	5	4	2
Italy	4	6	4
France	3	5	1
Finland	3	1	3
Canada	2	3	2
South Korea	2	1	1

1994 LILLEHAMMER
Competitors: 1,737
Nations: 67
Dates: February 12–27

Heroes: Local hero *Johann Olav Koss* set world records in the 1,500-, 5,000-, and 10,000-meter speed skating events. American *Dan Jansen* ended ten years of Olympic frustration by winning the 1,000-meter event in world-record time. *Bonnie Blair* of the United States, who had earned gold and bronze in speed skating in 1988 and added two golds in 1992, won two more gold medals in Lillehammer, this time by her biggest margins ever. All of the women's nordic races were won by either *Lyubov*

Yegorova of Russia or *Manuela Di Centa* of Italy. The *Italian men's 4x10-kilometer relay team* gained an upset victory over the favored Norwegians, winning the 101-minute race by two-fifths of a second.

Controversies: The women's figure skating contest was thrown into turmoil when American Tonya Harding was implicated in a physical attack on her rival Nancy Kerrigan. Both competed in Lillehammer, Kerrigan placing second and Harding eighth. The ice dance competition ended in dispute when Jayne Torvill and Christopher Dean, attempting a comeback after ten years, were marked down for violating the strict rules of the event, while the blatant violations of gold medalists Oksana Grichuk and Yevgeny Platov were ignored. In short-track speed skating, China's Zhang Yanmei, infuriated by the rough tactics of 500-meter winner Cathy Turner

of the United States, stormed off the victory podium in the middle of the award ceremony.

MEDAL TOTALS OF LEADING NATIONS

	G	S	B
Russia	11	8	4
Norway	10	11	5
Germany	9	7	8
Italy	7	5	8
United States	6	5	2
South Korea	4	1	1
Canada	3	6	4
Switzerland	3	4	2
Austria	2	3	4
Sweden	2	1	0

1998 NAGANO—February 7–22

2002 SALT LAKE CITY—February 9–26

—**D.W.**

SOCCER: THE WORLD CUP

Football's not a matter of life and death. It's much more serious than that.

Bill Shankly

1930 HOST: URUGUAY
Uruguay 4, Argentina 2

Goals: Dorado (URU)   12
        Peucelle (ARG)   20
        Stàbile (ARG)   37
        Cea (URU)   57
        Iriarte (URU)   68
        Castro (URU)   89

Having outbid five other nations for the right to host the inaugural World Cup—thanks, in part, to its promise to pay the travel and hotel expenses of all the visiting teams—it was only fitting that Uruguay should emerge as the first champion. The two-time defending Olympic gold medalists breezed through the tournament, beating their first three opponents by a combined score of 11–1 before rallying to defeat Argentina in the final, 4–2.

Uruguay folded the World Cup into the nation's centennial celebrations. Construction crews worked around the clock to complete a 100,000-seat stadium in Montevideo in time for Uruguay's opening match (a 1–0 win over Peru on Independence Day), and players such as José Andrade, Pedro Cea, and Héctor Scarone quickly became household names. But it was center-forward Héctor Castro, who had lost part of his left arm in a childhood accident, who came to symbolize Uruguay's gutsy determination, scoring the only goal against Peru before playing a pivotal role in the final.

Still, European anger over the staging of the first World Cup in South America prompted many nations to either boycott the competition or send makeshift teams. Countries such as Italy, England, Spain, and Holland were no-shows, while Romania took part only because King Carol, a die-hard fan, personally intervened and handpicked the squad. The United States, meanwhile, entered a team of predominantly transplanted British professionals and advanced all the way to the semifinals.

But in 1930 the World Cup final was an all–South American affair, as neighbors Uruguay and Argentina squared off on July 30, 1930, before a crowd of 93,000 in Montevideo's Centenary Stadium. The match was a replay of the 1928 Olympic final, and thousands of Argentine fans (many chanting "victory or death") crossed the Río de la Plata by boat either to attend the match or to mill around outside. Soldiers with fixed bayonets were stationed throughout the grounds to keep the crowds moving, while anybody entering the stadium was searched for weapons.

Uruguay was buoyed by the return of Castro to the starting lineup after a mysterious two-game benching, and the hosts took a 1–0 lead in the twelfth minute when midfielder Pablo Dorado scored through the legs of goalkeeper Juan Botasso. But Argentina rallied to take a 2–1 lead into halftime thanks to strikes by Carlos Peucelle and Guillermo Stàbile, although the latter appeared to have been offside.

Nevertheless, Uruguay emerged from the locker room determined to settle the score, and they evened things at 2–2 when Cea followed a brilliant dribble by beating Botasso in the fifty-seventh minute. From there, goals by Santos Iriarte and Castro—who notched his country's first and last goals of the tournament—secured the World Cup title, and Uruguay took possession of the 50,000-franc Jules Rimet trophy.

It has been said that other nations have their history and Uruguay has its soccer, a fact borne out by the mad celebrations that followed Uruguay's victory. A national holiday was declared, and there was dancing in the streets of Montevideo. Meanwhile, Argentina served notice that it took soccer just as seriously. Following the loss, enraged fans stoned the Uruguayan Embassy in Buenos Aires.

1934 HOST: ITALY
Italy 2, Czechoslovakia 1

Goals: Puc (CZE)   70
        Orsi (ITA)   81
        Schiavio (ITA) 95

After struggling to find entrants for the first World Cup, organizers of the second tournament, in Italy, found themselves with too many. As a result, a worldwide playoff competition was staged to winnow the field of thirty-two teams to sixteen, including a ludicrous playoff between the United States and Mexico held 8,000 miles away in Rome (the U.S. team advanced). Uruguay, meanwhile, became the first and only champion not to defend its title, when it withdrew prior to the competition, the result of a players' strike back home and lingering bad feelings left over from Italy's boycott four years earlier.

Italy, after defeating Greece in a playoff to qualify for its own tournament, became the second straight host to win the World Cup when it beat Czechoslovakia in the final in extra time, 2–1. Bolstered by three members of the 1930 Argentine squad now playing in the Italian League—midfielder Luis Monti, winger Raimundo Orsi, and defender Enrique Guaita—the Italians defended their inclusion by noting they were all of Italian heritage and could be called up for the Italian army. "If they can die for Italy," declared head coach Vittorio Pozzo, "they can play football for Italy." But of greater concern was the role of Italian dictator Benito Mussolini, who appropriated both the host team and the tournament for his own propaganda purposes, demanding total victory at all costs.

After routing the United States in the opener, 7–1, Italy narrowly squeaked by Spain in the second round—a 1–1 tie was followed by a 1–0 replay victory the next day—and a 1–0 win against Austria in the semifinals came despite heavy rains that flooded the field. A string of injuries also forced Italy to rely increasingly on a rough, physical style of play that intimidated opponents and officials alike. Pitted against

Czechoslovakia in the finals on June 10, 1934, the Italians faced a team that was drawn entirely from two clubs (Sparta and Slavia) and played with incredible cohesiveness and imagination. Nevertheless, it was seventy minutes before a goal was scored, as Czech winger Antonin Puc rifled home a shot along a sharp angle that gave Czechoslovakia a 1–0 lead and silenced the crowd of 55,000 at Rome's PNF Stadium.

Following a couple of near misses by the Czechs, Italy rallied to tie the score on an incredible goal by Orsi with less than nine minutes left to play. Taking a pass from his fellow Argentine Guaita, Orsi faked a pass with his left foot, then looped a shot with his right that dipped over the hands of goalkeeper Frantisek Planicka to make it 1–1. Although Orsi insisted the shot was no fluke, he tried to repeat it for photographers the next day and failed.

Forced to play overtime, Italy, utterly exhausted and decimated by injuries incurred during the tournament, quickly went to work. Midfielder Giuseppe Meazza shook off an injury to cross the ball to Guaita, who fed Schiavio the game winner that touched off mad celebrations all across Italy. Showered with gifts by Mussolini and other Fascist officials, the Italian players showed little remorse for the intimidation and fanaticism they had loosed on world soccer.

1938 HOST: FRANCE
Italy 4, Hungary 2

Goals: Colaussi (ITA) 5
        Titkos (HUN)   7
        Piola (ITA)   16
        Colaussi (ITA) 35
        Sárosi (HUN)   70
        Piola (ITA)   82

With Hitler on the move and Europe teetering on the brink of war, it's no surprise that the 1938 World Cup was plagued by political problems long before it began. Still, thirty-four nations entered the qualifying competition, and Italy, led by forward Silvio Piola, survived a tough field en route to a 4–2 win over Hungary to capture its second straight World Cup title.

Although France was considered a "neutral" site for the tournament, the world was too politically charged by 1938 for that to be so. Spain sent no team because it was embroiled in a civil war; Austria was considered a pretournament favorite until the nation was annexed by Germany, which simply drafted the top four Austrian players into the German squad; Argentina withdrew when it was not allowed to host the tournament; Uruguay backed out rather than risk losing to Europeans; England kept up the boycott it had begun in 1930; and so on, leaving Hungary and Czechoslovakia as the only teams capable of challenging the Italians.

Italy coasted into the finals, beating the host French (3–1) and an overconfident Brazilian side (2–1) that made the mistake of resting two key players for the final. Such errors were fatal against the Italians, who relied on the savvy and skill of coach Vittorio Pozzo to exploit any advantage. For instance, when the streets of Paris proved too crowded for the team bus to reach the Colombes Stadium for the final, Pozzo ordered the driver to return to the hotel and wait for the masses to disperse rather than have his players sit aboard the bus and fret. Hungary, meanwhile, played a fluid, attacking style that had given its World Cup opponents fits. The Magyars rolled up thirteen goals in their first three matches, including seven by center-forward Gyula Zsengeller.

Italy struck first on a goal by Gino Colaussi in the fifth minute, but Hungary equalized two minutes later when Pal Titkos drove a shot into the net from a sharp angle. Piola then put the defending champions back in front in the sixteenth minute when he completed an intricate four-pass move by slotting the ball past goalkeeper Antal Szabo for a 2–1 lead. Colaussi's second goal of the match—and fourth of the tournament—in the thirty-fifth minute gave Italy a two-goal lead heading into halftime.

Yet Hungary refused to quit. A goal by team captain Gyorgy Sárosi in the seventieth minute cut Italy's lead to one, and the Magyars continued to press right up to the end. But Piola, who had already been named "Player of the Tournament," added his second goal of the game with eight minutes left to play, allowing Italy to clinch its second straight World Cup title.

Only Giuseppe Meazza and Giovanni Ferrari remained from the 1934 championship team, while the trio of Alfredo Foni, Pietro Rava, and Ugo Locatelli added World Cup medals to their 1936 Olympic gold medals. Pozzo, meanwhile, had crafted two straight World Cup winners and looked set to go for three. But any further winning streak would have to wait. Europe burst into flames a little more than a year after Italy's victory over Hungary, and any future scores would have to be settled on the battlefield.

1950 HOST: BRAZIL
Uruguay 2, Brazil 1

Goals: Friaça (BRA)   48
           Schiaffino (URU) 66
           Ghiggia (URU) 79

With most of Europe still in ruins as a result of World War II, South America was the logical place to stage the next World Cup. And with Brazil's passion for the game approaching epidemic proportions—so much so that no other nation entered a bid to host the 1950 tournament—it was the obvious choice. But even though the Brazilians unveiled the style and skill that would alter the face of world soccer forever, it was Uruguay that emerged as champion, beating the Brazilians, 2–1, in Maracana Stadium before a crowd of 200,000, still the largest ever to watch a World Cup final.

Not surprisingly, the World Cup field was dramatically affected by World War II. Czechoslovakia and Hungary, the last two runners-up, could not field teams, and Austria decided its makeshift squad was too young. Germany, meanwhile, was banned from even entering the qualifying competition. But Great Britain, one of the few superpowers still standing after the war, dropped its FIFA (Fédération Internationale de Football Association) boycott and sent both England and Scotland to the finals, although Scotland later withdrew and England suffered a humiliating 1–0 loss to the United States.

With South America largely untouched by the war, Brazil and Uruguay were the premier teams, and they advanced to the final match on July 16, 1950. Yet it was not the championship game as such. Owing to a complex pool playoff system devised by FIFA, the final round consisted of four teams playing a round-robin schedule, and it just so happened that the Brazil-Uruguay game—which was slated last—wound up featuring the two best teams.

Brazil entered the match having scored thirteen goals in its last two games, and forward Ademir already had nine to his credit. Although needing only a tie to clinch the World Cup title, the hosts, urged on by their boisterous fans, chose instead to attack. And Brazil's efforts were rewarded less than three minutes into the second half when Ademir set up Friaça for the game's first goal.

Satisfied that his team was now in command, Brazilian coach Flavio Costa ordered his players to drop back and defend the lead. But the Brazilians never got the instructions. Instead, they continued to go forward and attack, a tactical error that left them vulnerable on defense and led to Uruguay's first goal. Right-winger Alcides Ghiggia gathered in a pass from Obdulio Jacinto Varela in the sixty-sixth minute and crossed the ball to Juan Alberto Schiaffino, who headed home the equalizer to make it 1–1.

Brazil answered Uruguay's challenge by stepping up its offense even more, but Uruguay never faltered. Instead the Uruguayans notched what turned out to be the game winner with eleven minutes left to play, when Ghiggia again carried into the left corner and instead of crossing the ball into the penalty area as before, raced in on goal and beat goalkeeper Moacir

Barbosa with a shot to the near post that made it 2–1. As the final whistle blew, the stunned Brazilians and their fans wept openly, but there was no denying the truth: the World Cup trophy—which had reportedly been stored under the bed of FIFA president Jules Rimet during the war—was once again in Uruguay's possession.

1954 HOST: SWITZERLAND
West Germany 3, Hungary 2

Goals:		
	Puskás (HUN)	6
	Czibor (HUN)	8
	Morlock (GER)	10
	Rahn (GER)	18
	Rahn (GER)	84

Readmitted to FIFA in 1950, Germany (now competing as West Germany) quickly returned to its prewar form, even though it fielded a team of players who had not seen international action in almost a decade. Led by stars such as Maximilian Morlock and Fritz Walter, the unseeded West Germans defeated Hungary, 3–2, in one of the greatest World Cup finals ever, and served notice they would be a force to be reckoned with in the years to come.

West Germany and Hungary met in the first round of the tournament, with Hungary prevailing 8–3. But West German coach Sepp Herberger had benched most of his starters for the game, realizing that a loss would give West Germany an easier route to the next round. By the time the two teams reached the final on July 4, 1954, in Berne's Wankdorf Stadium, Hungary (which had not lost an international match since May 1950) was overconfident and West Germany was almost unstoppable.

Despite a driving rain that turned the field into a quagmire, Hungary, which featured some of the game's all-time greats in Ferenc Puskás, Sandor Kocsis, and Josef Bozik, jumped out to a 1–0 lead when Puskás scored on a rebound in the sixth minute. Two minutes later, midfielder Zoltan Czibor stole a back pass from the German defense and scored, to make it 2–0. But West Germany quickly rallied. Morlock cut the lead in half with a blistering shot that split the Hungarian defenders in the tenth minute, and Helmut Rahn made it 2–2 eight minutes later, capitalizing on a mistake by goalkeeper Gyula Grosics to score off a cross.

Hungary hammered away at the West Germans in the second half, as Nandor Hidegkuti hit the post with a shot, Puskás hit the crossbar, and West German goalkeeper Anton Turek made one incredible save after another. Finally, with six minutes left to play, Rahn put his team ahead for good, stealing a half-hearted clearing pass from Mihaly Lantos and slipping a shot past the diving Grosics. Yet Hungary refused to concede, and they appeared to knot the score at

3–3 when Puskás beat Turek with two minutes left. But the play was ruled offside, making West Germany the first—and only—unseeded team ever to win the World Cup.

1958 HOST: SWEDEN
Brazil 5, Sweden 2

Goals:		
	Liedholm (SWE)	4
	Vavá (BRA)	10
	Vavá (BRA)	32
	Pelé (BRA)	55
	Zagalo (BRA)	68
	Simonsson (SWE)	80
	Pelé (BRA)	89

In a word, Pelé. The youngest player ever to appear in the World Cup finals up to that time, the seventeen-year-old forward made his debut an unforgettable one as he led Brazil to its first World Cup title. Pelé scored six goals—including two in the 5–2 win over Sweden in the final—as the Brazilians became the first team to win the World Cup on a continent other than its own.

Yet Pelé was not the only star of a team many regard as one of the best in history. Players such as Vavá, Garrincha, Didi, and Mario Zagalo all became superstars in their own right, and coach Vincent Feola's revolutionary 4-2-4 lineup system changed soccer forever. But it was Pelé who did the most damage. Despite not playing in Brazil's first two games, Pelé scored the goal that beat Wales in the quarterfinals, then notched a hat trick against France in the semifinals. By the time Brazil squared off against Sweden in the finals in Solna on June 29, 1958, Pelé was the talk of world soccer.

Sweden, meanwhile, was no slouch, and the country's decision to allow professional players into the national team made for a lineup that included European stars such as Nils Liedholm, Gunnar Gren, and Kurt Hamrin. Sweden even took the early lead in the final—the first time Brazil had trailed in the entire tournament —as Liedholm scored in the fourth minute, touching off mad celebrations among the crowd of 49,737 at Rasunda Stadium. But Brazil, a team many thought might fold if ever forced to play catch-up, switched into high gear instead, as Garrincha twice fed Vavá for goals to take a 2–1 lead.

The second half was all Pelé, as he made it 3–1 in the fifty-fifth minute by trapping a pass with his chest, swerving around his defender, then volleying a drive into the net. Following goals by Zagalo and Sweden's Agne Simonsson, Pelé closed out the scoring when he back-heeled a pass to Zagalo, then headed home the return cross to make it 5–2. As the winners took a victory lap carrying both the World Cup trophy and the Swedish flag in their arms, there was little doubt Brazil and Pelé would be heard from again.

1962 HOST: CHILE
Brazil 3, Czechoslovakia 1

Goals: Masopust (CZE) 15
        Amarildo (BRA) 18
        Zito (BRA)   68
        Vavá (BRA)   77

When a massive earthquake struck Chile during the bidding process to organize the 1962 World Cup, the president of the Chilean Football Federation turned the disaster to his advantage. "We have nothing," he told FIFA officials. "That is why we must have the World Cup." But if Chile rose miraculously from the ashes—erecting two new stadiums and countless hotels in time for the opening match—the World Cup itself crashed to earth. Gone was the exhilarating style of the Brazilians four years earlier, replaced by some of the most crude, defensive, and downright ugly soccer ever played.

Brazil beat Czechoslovakia, 3–1, in the final, to join Italy as the only nations to successfully defend their titles, but this victory lacked joy. Pelé suffered an injury in the second game of the tournament and did not play again, and the 4-2-4 alignment had been temporarily shelved in favor of a more "defensive" 4-3-3 lineup. Meanwhile, Garrincha's place in the final was only secured by special FIFA decree, which ruled that his ejection in the semifinals against Chile did not merit the standard one-game suspension.

Czechoslovakia reached the finals for the first time since 1934, but few gave the East Europeans much of a chance. A first-round match against Brazil resulted in a 0–0 tie, and the Czechs scored a total of just six goals entering the finals on June 17, 1962. So when Josef Masopust raced on to a pass from Adolf Scherer and slipped the ball past Brazilian goalkeeper Gilmar in the fifteenth minute, most in the crowd of 68,679 at National Stadium were stunned. But not the Brazilians. Four of the six previous World Cup winners had fallen behind, and Brazil needed just two minutes to wipe out Masopust's goal, as Amarildo, playing in place of Pelé, scored to make it 1–1.

Brazil took the lead for good in the sixty-eighth minute when Zito passed the ball to Amarildo, then dashed toward the goal and headed home the return pass for a 2–1 edge. The final goal came with thirteen minutes left, as Vavá scored on a fumble by goalkeeper Viliam Schorojf, allowing Brazil to join Uruguay and Italy as the only two-time winners.

1966 HOST: ENGLAND
England 4, West Germany 2

Goals: Haller (GER)   12
        Hurst (ENG)   18
        Peters (ENG)   78
        Weber (GER)   89
        Hurst (ENG)   100
        Hurst (ENG)   119

As the nation that invented soccer and boasted one of the most glamorous professional leagues in the world, it was only a matter of time before England was granted the right to host the World Cup. It is fortunate, then, that the 1966 World Cup was given to England at a time when its national team was peaking, allowing the English to capture on their home ground their only title, with a 4–2 win over West Germany.

The 1966 World Cup was a colorful, memorable event from start to finish. The theft of the Jules Rimet Trophy prior to the start of the tournament (and its subsequent recovery one week later by a dog named Pickles) made headlines, as did North Korea's sensational 1–0 upset of Italy and Brazil's first-round exit. Then there was Argentine captain Antonio Rattin, who refused to leave the field after being ejected in a game against England, sitting down on the turf for eight minutes instead.

However, none of that mattered by the time England and West Germany met in the finals on July 28, 1966, in London's Wembley Stadium. The crowd of 96,924 on hand—not to mention millions around the world watching via a satellite television feed—was treated to one of the most exciting games in World Cup history. West Germany scored first, capitalizing on a weak clearing pass by Ray Wilson in the twelfth minute as Helmut Haller intercepted the ball and easily scored. England equalized six minutes later, however, when Bobby Moore threaded a free-kick pass to teammate Geoff Hurst, who headed home the cross to make it 1–1.

England went ahead in the seventy-eighth minute as Hurst's shot rebounded to Martin Peters, who banged the ball into the net, but the West Germans managed to tie the score once again with just seconds left to play. Awarded a free kick deep in English territory, Lothar Emmerich lobbed the ball into the penalty area, where teammate Wolfgang Weber stabbed it past goalkeeper Gordon Banks to force extra time.

Ten minutes into overtime, Hurst scored the goal that ranks as one of the most controversial in history. Taking a pass from teammate Alan Ball, Hurst drove a shot on goal that ricocheted off the crossbar straight down into the goal mouth and then back into play. But while the English were celebrating, the referee was still not sure it was a goal. Only after a long discussion with his linesman did he declare the shot a goal, giving England a 3–2 lead. Hurst then took advantage of West Germany's gambling defense to add another goal in the 120th minute, making him the first and only player ever to score a hat trick in the World Cup final.

1970 HOST: MEXICO
Brazil 4, Italy 1

Goals: Pelé (BRA)   18
        Boninsegna (ITA)   37
        Gérson (BRA)   66
        Jairzinho (BRA)   71
        Carlos Alberto (BRA) 86

With all five former champions having qualified for the 1970 World Cup, the tournament was one of the most entertaining ever. All-time greats such as Pelé, Franz Beckenbauer, and Bobby Charlton took part; attacking soccer returned in full force; and not a single player was ejected from the competition. In fact, the only drawback was the venue, Mexico, where sweltering summer temperatures in excess of 100 degrees and altitude adjustment problems at 7,000 feet left several teams gasping for breath.

In the end, it came down to a battle of two-time champions—Brazil and Italy—with the Brazilians posting a decisive 4–1 victory. The match was also Pelé's farewell to international soccer, a fitting send-off for a man who had become synonymous with the sport. Although he threatened retirement after being badly mauled by defenders in the 1966 World Cup, Pelé's final tournament saw Brazil return to the fluid, dynamic attack that had been so successful in the past, even though legends such as Vavá and Garrincha had been replaced by names such as Jairzinho, Tostão, and Roberto Rivelino.

Yet the Brazilians entered the final on June 21, 1970, in Mexico City's Azteca Stadium under a cloud of doubt. The team's defense had been shaky throughout the tournament and goalkeeper Felix had already allowed six goals. But the decidedly pro-Latin crowd of 107,000 had little reason to worry, as Pelé put Brazil ahead in the eighteenth minute, heading home a cross from Rivelino that marked his country's hundredth goal in World Cup competition.

Italy fought right back, however, as midfielder Alessandro Mazzola drove the offense forward and Roberto Boninsegna capitalized on a Brazilian defensive lapse to knot the score at 1–1. Intercepting a lazy back-heel pass from Brito in the thirty-seventh minute, Boninsegna raced around Felix and slotted the ball into the net.

But the Italians failed to press their attack any further and Brazil dictated the pace the rest of the way. A booming left-footed shot by Gérson whistled past goalkeeper Enrico Albertosi in the sixty-sixth minute to make it 2–1, and Jairzinho made World Cup history five minutes later when he converted a pass from Pelé that made him the first (and only) player to score in every round. Brazil closed out the scoring with four minutes to play, as Pelé set up team captain Carlos Alberto for the final goal.

The victory made Brazilian coach Mario Zagalo the first man to win World Cup titles as both a player and a coach, and earned his country permanent possession of the Jules Rimet Trophy. And even though the trophy was stolen years later and never recovered—officials believe it was melted down—the memory of Brazil's finest hour still burns bright.

1974 HOST: WEST GERMANY
West Germany 2, Holland 1

Goals: Neeskens (HOL)   1, penalty
        Breitner (GER)   25, penalty
        Müller (GER)   43

The World Cup underwent many changes prior to the 1974 finals in West Germany. FIFA was now run by João Havelange of Brazil, the first non-European ever to be elected president, and a new eighteen-carat-gold World Cup trophy was commissioned for the winners. A new tournament format was also devised whereby second-round group winners would advance directly to the finals, eliminating the need for the semifinals altogether. The fact that established nations such as England, France, Portugal, and Spain failed to qualify for the finals only underscored the dawn of a new era.

But not entirely. West Germany, the reigning European champion, fielded a team that included at least a half dozen starters from its 1970 squad and strode impressively to its second World Cup title. Led by the elegant Franz Beckenbauer and goal-getter Gerd Müller, West Germany defeated Holland, 2–1, to become the fourth host nation to win the cup.

Although memories of the terrorist attack on the Munich Olympics two years earlier prompted stifling security, a crowd of 77,833 packed Munich's Olympic Stadium for the final on July 7, 1974, and was quickly swept up in the action. Less than one minute into the game—and without West Germany even touching the ball—Holland was awarded a penalty kick after Johan Cryuff was tripped in the penalty area. Johan Neeskens converted the kick for a 1–0 lead, but West Germany charged back to tie in the twenty-fifth minute on a penalty kick of its own. This time it was Bernd Holzenbein who had been fouled, and Paul Breitner scored to even the match at 1–1.

Although Holland's revolutionary "Total Football" attack had dazzled both fans and opponents in the tournament and given Cryuff the freedom to play as he liked, the thin Dutchman was shackled by West Germany's close midfield marking and eventually got so frustrated that he received a yellow card for unsportsmanlike conduct. Injuries to starters Wim Rijsbergen and Rob Rensenbrink in the final match further hampered Holland's attack.

Fittingly enough, it was Müller who scored West Germany's game winner. Taking a cross from Rainer Bonhof in the forty-third minute, Müller turned and slammed a brilliant shot past goalkeeper Jan Jonbloed to make it 2–1.

1978 HOST: ARGENTINA
Argentina 3, Holland 1

Goals:	Kempes (ARG)	38
	Nanninga (HOL)	81
	Kempes (ARG)	104
	Bertoni (ARG)	114

Argentina spent forty years lobbying for the right to host the World Cup, then nearly let political turmoil ruin the 1978 tournament once it got it. The military overthrow of Argentine dictator Isabelle Peron in 1976—coupled with a state of siege and widespread arrests and torture—terrified FIFA officials, as did the assassination of the president of Argentina's World Cup Organizing Committee. Several nations threatened to boycott the tournament, and superstar midfielder Johan Cryuff quit the Dutch national team rather than take part. But the military government promised a "trouble-free" World Cup, and the competition eventually took place under heavy security.

Given all the turmoil, it's not surprising that Argentina wound up the champion. Hailed by both government and guerrilla leaders as a symbol of the country's rebirth, the Argentine players were showered with ticker-tape confetti prior to each game and cheered by fans everywhere they went. Led by forward Mario Kempes—the only Argentine playing abroad—Argentina turned in a thrilling, brutal performance en route to a 3–1 win over Holland in extra time in the final.

The Dutch still employed the "Total Football" system that had stunned the experts in 1974, but the absence of Cryuff proved impossible to overcome. Still, Holland reached its second straight final on June 25, 1978, in Buenos Aires' Monumental Stadium and actually roughed up the Argentines for the first fifteen minutes. But Argentina refused to be intimidated, and they opened the scoring in the thirty-eighth minute when Kempes redirected a cross from Osvaldo Ardiles for a 1–0 lead.

With nine minutes left to play, Holland fought back to tie the score on a goal by reserve forward Dick Nanninga, then nearly won the game in regulation when Rob Rensenbrink slammed a shot off the post with one minute to go.

Once the thirty-minute overtime period commenced, it was all Argentina. Kempes beat three defenders and drove the ball past goalkeeper Jan Jongbloed in the 104th minute for his sixth goal of the tournament, and then set up Daniel Bertoni for the insurance goal with five minutes left. Argentina, which had flirted with soccer excellence as South American neighbors Brazil

and Uruguay won a combined five World Cups, finally joined the elite.

1982 HOST: SPAIN
Italy 3, West Germany 1

Goals:	Rossi (ITA)	57
	Tardelli (ITA)	68
	Altobelli (ITA)	81
	Breitner (GER)	83

The World Cup was expanded to twenty-four teams in 1982, and Third World nations such as Cameroon, Kuwait, Algeria, and Honduras justified their presence by recording some of the biggest upsets in tournament history. Algeria's 2–1 win over West Germany stunned everyone, as did Honduras's ties against Spain and Northern Ireland. But by the time the final rolled around, two venerable World Cup warhorses—Italy and West Germany—were vying to see who would join Brazil as three-time winners of the World Cup.

Italy's 3–1 victory in the final was a triumph of tenacity more than talent. Tied by its first three opponents and pilloried by the rabid press back home, Italy finally burst to life behind forward Paolo Rossi, the team's leading scorer in 1978, who had since served a two-year suspension for match fixing. Rossi rang up five goals in the second round alone and gave Italy much-needed momentum heading into the final on July 11, 1982, in Madrid's Bernabeau Stadium.

But disaster struck when injuries knocked Italian starters Giancarlo Antognoni and Francesco Graziani from the lineup, and Antonio Cabrini compounded matters in the twenty-fifth minute when he became the first man in World Cup history to miss a penalty kick. But Rossi saved the day, heading home a cross from Claudio Gentile in the fifty-seventh minute for a 1–0 lead. Marco Tardelli added a booming left-foot shot to make it 2–0 in the sixty-eighth minute, and substitute Alessando Altobelli sealed the win by redirecting a cross from Bruno Conti in the eighty-first minute.

By the time West Germany's Paul Breitner scored in the eighty-third minute to cut the lead to 3–1, Italy was already assured of victory—and a place in history.

1986 HOST: MEXICO
Argentina 3, West Germany 2

Goals:	Brown (ARG)	22
	Valdano (ARG)	56
	Rummenigge (GER)	73
	Völler (GER)	82
	Burruchaga (ARG)	84

When economic collapse made it impossible for Colombia to host the 1986 World Cup as planned, Mexico stepped in with three years to go. But en route to becoming the first two-time host in World Cup history, Mexico had to overcome problems of its own: economic depression, political chaos, and, worst of all, the devastating earthquake that hit Mexico City eight months prior to kickoff and left 25,000 dead. Such problems vanished in the wake of the 1986 World Cup, a rich, entertaining spectacle that climaxed with Argentina's dramatic 3–2 win over West Germany in the final.

Led by its midfield maestro, Diego Maradona, Argentina quickly emerged as the class of the competition, even as it won in controversial style. In the quarterfinals, a pair of Maradona goals allowed Argentina to beat England 2–1, even though Maradona clearly used his fist to knock in the first goal. Asked about it later, Maradona shrugged and credited the goal to "the hand of God."

Argentina was the clear favorite as it took the field against West Germany on June 29, 1986, in Mexico City's Azteca Stadium, and the crowd of 114,590 littered the turf with confetti. Argentina did not disappoint, taking a 1–0 lead in the twenty-second minute when Jorge Burruchaga floated across to José Luis Brown for an easy header and a 1–0 lead. Eleven minutes into the second half, Jorge Valdano's fourth goal of the tournament made it 2–0.

Diego Maradona's "hand of God" goal against England in the 1986 World Cup.

West Germany stepped up its attack, however, and was rewarded in the seventy-third minute when Karl-Heinz Rummenigge fought through a crowd in front of the Argentine goal to head home a cross from Andreas Brehme and cut the lead in half. West Germany then tied the score on substitute Rudi Völler's goal with eight minutes left to play.

But with West Germany still celebrating and the game seemingly headed for overtime, Maradona worked one last miracle. He slipped a long pass through the West German defense to Burruchaga, who beat goalkeeper Harald Schumacher with six minutes to go for the 3–2 lead that would make Argentina world champions once again.

1990 HOST: ITALY
West Germany 1, Argentina 0

Goal: Brehme (GER) 85, penalty

It is estimated that a record worldwide television audience of 1.6 billion tuned in to the 1990 World Cup final between West Germany and Italy, almost three times the number that watched the final four years earlier. Pity. For what they saw was one of the worst matches in World Cup history, a game so crude and tactically deficient that FIFA immediately set to work overhauling the so-called simplest game.

West Germany's 1–0 win allowed it to join Italy and Brazil as the only three-time winners and marked a fitting end to the era of German disunity. Slated to rejoin East Germany as one nation later that fall, West Germany retired with a record six appearances in the final, including four of the last five. West Germany's thirty-six World Cup victories also placed it second on the all-time list behind Brazil (forty-four).

But the 1990 World Cup final on July 8, 1990, in Rome's Olympic Stadium was doomed from the start. Argentina, which won only two of its matches in regulation and had several key players suspended from the final, played brutal, boring soccer designed to allow the team to reach sudden-death penalties. Diego Maradona had evolved from the game's greatest player into a boorish crybaby, and when Gustavo Dezotti was ejected with three minutes left to play, Maradona and other Argentine players surrounded the referee, angrily pushing and shoving him.

West Germany, meanwhile, simply had a bad game. After several near misses in the first half, forward Rudi Völler was tripped by Argentina's Roberto Sensini in the eighty-fifth minute in the penalty area. Andreas Brehme calmly slotted the penalty into the lower left-hand corner of the net, a just—if decidedly unimpressive—outcome.

1994 HOST: UNITED STATES
Brazil 0, Italy 0 (3–2 on penalty kicks)
The penalty-kick shootout that FIFA adopted in 1982 to settle ties in World Cup competition finally came back to haunt the organizers in 1994. After a splendid tournament that smashed all records for attendance (3.4 million) and profits ($50 million)—not to mention producing some breathtaking soccer—the World Cup stumbled at the final hurdle when Brazil and Italy were forced to decide the final on penalty kicks, with Brazil winning 3–2.

The matchup was an organizer's dream, especially in the United States, where the World Cup had finally stirred the nation's interest in soccer. A crowd of 94,194 wedged itself into the Rose Bowl in Pasadena, California, on July 17, 1994, to watch Brazil and Italy vie to become the first to win four World Cups. But, under a scorching sun, neither team scored during regulation play, nor during the two fifteen-minute overtime periods held afterward. So the best-of-five penalty-kick shootout system that has increasingly come to determine the winner in major international matches took over.

Italy got off to an inauspicious start when team captain Franco Baresi missed the goal, but Brazil was no better as Marcio Santos had his shot blocked. Both teams made their next two kicks, to stay even at 2–2, but then Daniele Massaro of Italy had his attempt blocked by Brazilian goalkeeper Claudio Taffarel. Brazilian midfielder Dunga then drove his shot home for a 3–2 lead, leaving it up to Italian superstar Roberto Baggio to keep his team alive.

But Baggio, the European player of the year who had single-handedly carried Italy to the final, sailed his kick well over the goal, allowing Brazil to capture its fourth World Cup title.
—D.W.C.

BASKETBALL

NBA FINALS

									Wins
1947	PHILADELPHIA WARRIORS	84*	85*	75	73	83*			4
	Chicago Stags	71	75	72*	74*	80			1
1948	BALTIMORE BULLETS	60	66	72*	78*	82	88*		4
	Philadelphia Warriors	71*	63*	70	75	91*	73		2
1949	MINNEAPOLIS LAKERS	88*	76*	94	71	66	77*		4
	Washington Capitols	84	62	74*	83*	74*	56		2
1950	MINNEAPOLIS LAKERS	68	85	91*	77*	76	110*		4
	Syracuse Nationals	66*	91*	77	69	83*	95		2
1951	ROCHESTER ROYALS	92*	99*	78	73	89*	73	79*	4
	New York Knicker-bockers	65	84	71*	79*	92	80*	75	3
1952	MINNEAPOLIS LAKERS	83*	72*	82	89	102*	68	82*	4
	New York Knicker-bockers	79(OT)	80	77*	90*(OT)	89	76*	65	3
1953	MINNEAPOLIS LAKERS	88*	73*	90	71	91			4
	New York Knicker-bockers	96	71	75*	69*	84*			1
1954	MINNEAPOLIS LAKERS	79*	60*	81	69	84	63*	87*	4
	Syracuse Nationals	68	62	67*	80*	73*	65	80	3
1955	SYRACUSE NATIONALS	86*	87*	89	102	71	109*	92*	4
	Fort Wayne Pistons	82	84	96*	109*	74*	104	91	3

*Home team
OT = Overtime

Year	Team	1	2	3	4	5	6	7	W
1956	PHILADELPHIA WARRIORS	98*	83	100*	107	99*			4
	Fort Wayne Pistons	94	84*	96	105*	88			1
1957	BOSTON CELTICS	123*	119*	98	123	124*	94	125*	4
	St. Louis Hawks	125(2OT)	99	100*	118*	109	96*	123(2OT)	3
1958	ST. LOUIS HAWKS	104	112	111*	98*	102	110*		4
	Boston Celtics	102*	136*	108	109	100*	109		2
1959	BOSTON CELTICS	118*	128*	123	118				4
	Minneapolis Lakers	115	108	110*	113*				0
1960	BOSTON CELTICS	140*	103*	102	96	127*	102	122*	4
	St. Louis Hawks	122	113	86*	106*	102	105*	103	3
1961	BOSTON CELTICS	129*	116*	120	119	121*			4
	St. Louis Hawks	95	108	124*	104*	112			1
1962	BOSTON CELTICS	122*	122*	115	115	121*	119	110*	4
	Los Angeles Lakers	108	129	117*	103*	126	105*	107(OT)	3
1963	BOSTON CELTICS	117*	113*	99	108	119*	112		4
	Los Angeles Lakers	114	106	119*	105*	126	109*		2
1964	BOSTON CELTICS	108*	124*	91	98	105*			4
	San Francisco Warriors	96	101	115*	95*	99			1
1965	BOSTON CELTICS	142*	129*	105	112	129*			4
	Los Angeles Lakers	110	123	126*	99*	96			1
1966	BOSTON CELTICS	129*	129*	120	122	117*	115	95*	4
	Los Angeles Lakers	133(OT)	109	106*	117*	121	123*	93	3
1967	PHILADELPHIA 76ERS	141*	126*	124	122	109*	125		4
	San Francisco Warriors	135(OT)	95	130*	108*	117	122*		2
1968	BOSTON CELTICS	107*	113*	127	105	120*	124		4
	Los Angeles Lakers	101	123	119*	119*	117(OT)	109*		2
1969	BOSTON CELTICS	118	112	111*	89*	104	99*	108	4
	Los Angeles Lakers	120*	118*	105	88	117*	90	106*	3
1970	NEW YORK KNICKERBOCKERS	124*	103*	111	115	107*	113	113*	4
	Los Angeles Lakers	112	105	108*(OT)	121*(OT)	100	135*	99	3
1971	MILWAUKEE BUCKS	98*	102	107*	118				4
	Baltimore Bullets	88	83*	99	106*				0
1972	LOS ANGELES LAKERS	92*	106*	107	116	114*			4
	New York Knickerbockers	114	92	96*	111*(OT)	100			1
1973	NEW YORK KNICKERBOCKERS	112	99	87*	103*	102			4
	Los Angeles Lakers	115*	95*	83	98	93*			1
1974	BOSTON CELTICS	98	96	95*	89*	96	101*	102	4
	Milwaukee Bucks	83*	105*(OT)	83	97	87*	102(2OT)	87*	3
1975	GOLDEN STATE WARRIORS	101	92*	109*	96				4
	Washington Bullets	95*	91	101	95*				0
1976	BOSTON CELTICS	98*	105*	98	107	128*	87		4
	Phoenix Suns	87	90	105*	109*	126(3OT)	80*		2
1977	PORTLAND TRAIL BLAZERS	101	89	129*	130*	110	109*		4
	Philadelphia 76ers	107*	107*	107	98	104*	107		2
1978	WASHINGTON BULLETS	102	106*	92*	120	94	117*	105	4
	Seattle SuperSonics	106*	98	93	116*(OT)	98*	82	99*	3
1979	SEATTLE SUPERSONICS	97	92	105*	114*	97			4
	Washington Bullets	99*	82*	95	112(OT)	93*			1
1980	LOS ANGELES LAKERS	109*	104*	111	102	108*	123		4
	Philadelphia 76ers	102	107	101*	105*	103	107*		2

Year	Team	1	2	3	4	5	6	7	W
1981	BOSTON CELTICS	98*	90*	94	86	109*	102		4
	Houston Rockets	95	92	71*	91*	80	91*		2
1982	LOS ANGELES LAKERS	124	94	129*	111*	102	114*		4
	Philadelphia 76ers	117*	110*	108	101	135*	104		2
1983	PHILADELPHIA 76ERS	113*	103*	111	115				4
	Los Angeles Lakers	107	93	94*	108*				0
1984	BOSTON CELTICS	109*	124*	104	129	121*	108	111*	4
	Los Angeles Lakers	115	121(OT)	137*	125*(OT)	103	119*	102	3
1985	LOS ANGELES LAKERS	114	109	136*	105*	120*	111		4
	Boston Celtics	148*	102*	111	107	111	100*		2
1986	BOSTON CELTICS	112*	117*	104	106	96	114*		4
	Houston Rockets	100	95	106*	103*	111*	97		2
1987	LOS ANGELES LAKERS	126*	141*	103	107	108	106*		4
	Boston Celtics	113	122	109*	106*	123*	93		2
1988	LOS ANGELES LAKERS	93*	108*	99	86	94	103*	108*	4
	Detroit Pistons	105	96	86*	111*	104*	102	105	3
1989	DETROIT PISTONS	109*	108*	114	105				4
	Los Angeles Lakers	97	105	110*	97*				0
1990	DETROIT PISTONS	105*	105*	121	112	92			4
	Portland Trail Blazers	99	106(OT)	106*	109*	90*			1
1991	CHICAGO BULLS	91*	107*	104	97	108			4
	Los Angeles Lakers	93	86	96*(OT)	82*	101*			1
1992	CHICAGO BULLS	122*	104*	94	88	119	97*		4
	Portland Trail Blazers	89	115(OT)	84*	93*	106*	93		2
1993	CHICAGO BULLS	100	111	121*	111*	98*	99		4
	Phoenix Suns	92*	108*	129(3OT)	105	108	98*		2
1994	HOUSTON ROCKETS	85*	83*	93	82	84	86*	90*	4
	New York Knicks	78	91	89*	91*	91*	84	84	3
1995	HOUSTON ROCKETS	120	117	106*	113*				4
	Orlando Magic	118*	106*	103	101				0
1996	CHICAGO BULLS	107*	92*	108	86	78	87*		4
	Seattle SuperSonics	90	88	86*	107*	89*	75		2

NBA FINALS HIGHLIGHTS

1951: In 1951 the NBA was only four years old, a mere sports infant. There were no superstars, no endorsements, no high fiving and high flying. But even in its infancy, the league managed to contribute its share of sports drama. The 1951 championship series, between the New York Knickerbockers and the Rochester Royals, went to seven games in a classy display of heart and grit. The Knicks, coached by Joe Lapchick, survived a rugged battle with the Syracuse Nationals in the semifinals to make it to the finals against the Royals, who had defeated the Knicks three times in the regular season, twice in overtime. The Royals, having upset the favored Minneapolis Lakers in their semifinal series, humiliated the Knicks 92–65 in the opener, then beat them 99–84 in the second game. The remarkable Royals went on to a 3–0 series lead with a 78–71 win in game three. But the Knicks came roaring back with three straight wins to even the series. In game seven the Knicks overcame a fourteen-point second-period deficit to edge in front 74–72 with two minutes to play, and it looked as though they might score the comeback of the young decade. With fifty-nine seconds remaining and the score tied at 75–75, the Royals' Bob Davies was fouled by Dick McGuire and sank both free throws to put the Royals in front for good. A last-second basket by Jack Coleman capped a well-deserved 79–75 Royals victory.

1955: Ah, the fifties, when an Easter dinner of prime rib au jus cost $1.05 and basketball was played by . . . well, by men of pale complexion and limited leaping ability. The Fort Wayne Pistons and Syracuse Nationals met in the NBA finals to determine which of these NBA power-houses would be the new champion of round-ball. The Nationals were well stocked with talent, including Dick Farley and Dolphe Schayes. Farley sparked a fourth-quarter rally for the Nationals' opening-game victory of 86–82. The Nationals won the second game, 87–84, this time behind Dolph Schayes's last-quarter spurt, and seemed well on their way to a sweep of the

Pistons. Game three saw the Pistons, playing before a home crowd in Indianapolis, blow a fifteen-point lead but hang on for a 96–89 win. With seven men scoring in double digits, the Pistons evened the series 2–2 in game four, 109–102, and then won game five, 74–71. The series went back to Syracuse, where the Nationals took their twenty-seventh game at home from the Pistons. The game was tied at 103 with a minute and a half left on the clock. John Kerr's jump shot and Dick Farley's tap-in clinched the victory for the Nationals. In the decisive seventh game, George King was the hero for Syracuse, sinking a free throw with twelve seconds left, to lift the Nationals to a hard-fought 92–91 victory—and a place in the NBA record books for Syracuse.

1957: The sports fans of Boston had not had much to celebrate in their long and anguished history. No World Series flag flying at Fenway Park, no NBA championship banner hanging in the Boston Garden. But in 1957 Boston's sports fortunes would change, and the Celtics would become a dynasty the likes of which had never before been seen in American sports. This road to respectability was not an easy one—the St. Louis Hawks won three games by two points, including a double-overtime opener in which Jack Coleman hit a desperation fifteen-footer with thirty seconds left. Bob Pettit's jumper with forty-four seconds left capped a Hawks rally for a 100–98 victory in game three, and Cliff Hagen's last-second tip-in in game six lifted the Hawks to a 96–94 win, setting up a seventh-game showdown. Boston center Bill Russell, unable to sleep the night before the game, spent hours praying for his teammates. Perhaps it was an answer to prayer, perhaps the Almighty decided that Boston sports fans had suffered enough. In the second overtime, the Garden rocking with the deafening screams of 13,000 spectators, Boston led by two points with two seconds left on the clock. Hawks reserve Alex Hannum threw a length-of-the-court pass to Bob Pettit, who put the ball up. It rolled around the rim—and dropped out. The Celtics had their first NBA title, and a dynasty was born.

1962: The seventh game of the NBA finals. Celtics versus Lakers. The score is tied 100–100, seven seconds left on the clock, the Lakers have the ball. Will they pull off the upset of the century, denying Boston its fourth straight championship? The Lakers came into the finals a hungry young team spoiling for an upset. After being routed in the opening game, they won the next two, behind the sharp shooting of Jerry West and Elgin Baylor. Indeed, West lived up to his nickname of Mr. Clutch in game three—after scoring two pressure-packed free throws, he stole the ball from Bob Cousy, the great Celtics guard, and scored a buzzer-beating basket to hand Los Angeles a 117–115 win. Both West and

Cousy were crying at the end of this emotional contest. The seasoned Celtics tied the series in game four, only to see the Lakers regain the advantage in game five behind Elgin Baylor's brilliant sixty-one-point outburst. The self-effacing Baylor shunned credit for the victory, calling it a team effort. But the Celtics, who moaned about the officiating in game five, took their revenge in game six, 119–105. On to game seven. The score tied at 100 each, Baylor hits two free throws, then Russell slam-dunks to even the score. The Bearded One finishes off with three more points in overtime, backed up with two buckets by Sam Jones. Celtics win, 110–107. But it took the luck of the Irish—and a valiant performance by Russell—to get them their fourth straight title.

1966: The Boston Celtics had won seven NBA championships in a row and seemed invincible. True, they no longer had Cousy and Sharman. But they had Bill Russell, considered by many to be the greatest defensive center ever to play the game, and they had John Havlicek, their valuable sixth man, who became so valuable that coach Red Auerbach had to make him a starter. But the upstart Los Angeles Lakers had other ideas. In the opener, Jerry West scored forty-one points for the Lakers and Gail Goodrich came up big off the bench to spark the Lakers to a 133–129 overtime win. The Celtics demonstrated their world-championship demeanor, winning the next three games (despite a forty-five-point Jerry West performance in game four). But Elgin Baylor's forty-one-point performance in game five helped the Lakers spoil the Boston party with a 121–117 victory. The improbable Lakers did it again in game six, Goodrich pouring in twenty-eight points and West scoring thirty-two, to pace Los Angeles to a 123–115 win. In game seven a screaming mob of more than 13,000 rabid Celtics fans packed into the Boston Garden to watch the showdown between the Lakers and the Celtics. Bill Russell rallied his weary troops, pulling down thirty-two rebounds and scoring twenty-five points as Boston barely pulled out a 95–93 win. Auerbach, who was retiring as Celtics coach, lit his famous victory cigar, savoring an unprecedented eighth straight NBA championship.

1969: It was billed as the Battle of the Big Men—Bill Russell, the Boston Celtics' great defensive center, and Wilt "the Stilt" Chamberlain, the problematic Laker star who had paced his team to the Western Conference title. The Celtics, having defeated Philadelphia 4–1 in the first round of the playoffs, beat the New York Knicks for their twelfth Eastern playoff title in thirteen years. The Lakers, led by Jerry West and Chamberlain, beat San Francisco in the first round and rolled over Atlanta 4–1, to advance to the finals. While Russell versus Chamberlain promised to be a classic matchup, it was the smaller men—Jerry West, and the Celtics' John Havlicek and Sam Jones—who carried their teams to a decisive seventh-game showdown. In the fifth game, Los Angeles would have eliminated Boston and won the championship had not Jones in the fourth game, made an unbelievable off-balance shot with three seconds left. He released the shot off his left foot, falling away; it hit the front of the rim, then the back, and then split the cords. Jones, stunned, just stared. Jerry West commented succinctly, "The Lord's will." The Celtics won the sixth game; the seventh game, despite a brilliant performance by West, saw an indefatigable Havlicek lead the Celtics to their eleventh world championship in thirteen years, outlasting the Lakers 108–106.

1971: It seemed a foregone conclusion that the Milwaukee Bucks, led by Lew Alcindor (later Kareem Abdul-Jabbar), would face the New York Knicks in the NBA finals. Except that someone forgot to inform the Baltimore Bullets, who upset the vaunted Knicks 4–3, to win the Eastern Conference championship. The Bullets neutralized Knicks star Willis Reed, who was hobbled by an injury—and by the Bullets' great center, Wes Unseld. By the time the series ended, Unseld had grabbed twice as many rebounds as Reed and held his opponent to a shooting average below 40 percent. Walt Frazier, the only Knick to perform consistently,

Wilt Chamberlain (right) moves against Bill Russell during the 1969 NBA playoffs.

was not enough to carry his team over the Bullets, whose slow-down tempo kept the much quicker Knicks out of sync. The Bucks, meanwhile, decimated a badly banged Laker team, who were without stars Elgin Baylor, Jerry West, and Keith Erickson, to win the Western Conference championship. The Bucks made it clear that they considered the Knicks to be the more worthy opponent—the perfect prelude to an upset by an underrated opponent. But heavily favored Milwaukee, paced by Lew Alcindor and Oscar Robertson, played with their usual unemotional efficiency, sweeping the Bullets in four games for the championship in the most one-sided final in NBA history. Alcindor had now won national titles at the high-school, college, and pro levels—and further basketball greatness awaited him with the Los Angeles Lakers.

1974: Celtics pride was once again on the line as Boston faced the Milwaukee Bucks for the NBA championship. Not since 1969, when the great center Bill Russell retired, had the Celtics been in the finals, a long drought for a city that had become accustomed to seeing championship flags hanging from the rafters of the Boston Garden. The Bucks, who had blown through the Los Angeles Lakers and the Chicago Bulls to reach the finals, did not figure to be a pushover. They had the best center in the league, one Kareem Abdul-Jabbar (formerly Lew Alcindor), a dominant presence in the low post. Abdul-Jabbar had once scored fifty-three points against Boston center Dave Cowens. This rematch—of Celtics pride versus the Bucks' hunger to prove themselves—saw Boston enjoying a 3–2 advantage going into game six, which proved to be one of the most dramatic playoff games in NBA history. The score was tied 86–86 at the end of regulation, both teams playing outstanding defense. The first extra period ended with Boston guard Don Chaney making a steal and Havlicek putting back his own miss to send the game into a second overtime. John Havlicek scored nine points for the Celtics, but Abdul-Jabbar's perfect fifteen-foot hook shot gave Milwaukee a thrilling 102–101 win. In game seven, Cowens went again to his long game, hitting six of nine long jumpers in the second half, plus a Bucks-stopping hook shot with 4.5 seconds left, leading the team to a 102–87 victory and the championship.

1988: It seemed almost sacrilege that the Lakers, the dominant team of the 1980s, would not be playing Larry Bird and the Boston Celtics in the 1988 NBA championship series. This time they were facing a new and possibly more dangerous opponent, the Detroit Pistons. The Bad Boys of Detroit, who defeated the Celtics in the Eastern Conference finals, had two of the NBA's toughest characters in center Bill Laimbeer and rebound maven Dennis Rodman. A dirty team? No one would come right out and say, but they were definitely "blue collar," a rugged lunch-pail team in contrast to the Lakers' sleek showtime style. Game six found the Lakers down by a game to the Pistons, who had won games one, four, and five by an average of nearly sixteen points. Game six, in the Forum in Inglewood, was a classic contest in which the Pistons, paced by a hobbled Isiah Thomas, were up 102–99 with a minute left. After a Byron Scott jumper brought the Lakers to within one, the Lakers got the ball back and gave it to—who else?—Magic Johnson. Magic whipped the ball to Kareem Abdul-Jabbar, who was fouled by Laimbeer. Abdul-Jabbar calmly sank the two free throws. Joe Dumars's layup did not go in for Detroit, the rebound slid out of Rodman's hands, and the Lakers had tied the series 6–6. Game seven was almost anticlimactic as the Lakers beat the Bad Boys to win back-to-back NBA championships.

1993: Michael Jordan, perhaps the greatest basketball player ever to lace up a hightop, led the Chicago Bulls to a "three-peat" of the NBA championship in 1993. There was nothing foregone about this conclusion—the Bulls were up against the Phoenix Suns, who had the irrepressible Charles Barkley, the deadly shooting of Dan Majerle, and the backcourt quickness of Kevin Johnson. The Suns had survived a first-round scare by the Magic-less Los Angeles Lakers, who shocked them—at home—in the first two games. The Suns prevailed over the Lakers, then went on to defeat the Houston Rockets and outlast the gritty Seattle SuperSonics. The Bulls had defeated their Eastern Conference rivals, the New York Knicks, four games to two in a bruising physical series. Now the showdown was set between the Bulls and the Suns. Jordan versus Barkley. The Best Player Ever versus the NBA's Most Valuable Player for 1993. In the sixth and decisive game, the Bulls allowed themselves to be caught by the Suns in the fourth quarter, but Jordan's breakaway layup drew Chicago to within two points, 98–96. With 3.9 seconds remaining, John Paxson hit a three-point shot for a thrilling 99–98 victory and the Bulls' third straight championship. Jordan, who scored thirty-three points and a team-high seven assists, could retire (albeit temporarily) at the pinnacle of his sport. He abandoned his brief, undistinguished baseball career to return to the Chicago Bulls and the NBA just prior to the 1995 playoffs.

—L.C.

BASEBALL

THE WORLD SERIES

Year	Team									Wins
1903	BOSTON RED SOX (A)	3*	3*	2*	4	11	6	7	3*	5
	Pittsburgh Pirates (N)	7	0	4	5*	2*	3*	3*	0	3
1904	not held									
1905	NEW YORK GIANTS (N)	3	0*	9	1*	2*				4
	Philadelphia Athletics (A)	0*	3	0*	0	0				1
1906	CHICAGO WHITE SOX (A)	2	1*	3	0*	8	8*			4
	Chicago Cubs (N)	1*	7	0*	1	6*	3			2
1907	CHICAGO CUBS (N)	3*	3*	5*	6	2				4
	Detroit Tigers (A)	3(12)†	1	1	1*	0*				0
1908	CHICAGO CUBS (N)	10	6*	3*	3	2				4
	Detroit Tigers (A)	6*	1	8	0*	0*				1
1909	PITTSBURGH PIRATES (N)	4*	2*	8	0	8*	4	8		4
	Detroit Tigers (A)	1	7	6*	5*	4	5*	0*		3
1910	PHILADELPHIA ATHLETICS (A)	4*	9*	12	3	7				4
	Chicago Cubs (N)	1	3	5*	4*(10)	2*				1
1911	PHILADELPHIA ATHLETICS (A)	1	3*	3	4*	3	13*			4
	New York Giants (N)	2*	1	2*(11)	2	4*(10)	2			2
1912	BOSTON RED SOX (A)	4	6*	1*	3	2*	2	4*	3*	4
	New York Giants (N)	3*	6(11)	2	1*	1	5*	11	2(10)	3

*Home team   A = American League
†Extra innings   N = National League

Year	Team	1	2	3	4	5	6	7	8	W
1913	PHILADELPHIA ATHLETICS (A)	6	0*	8	6*	3				4
	New York Giants (N)	4*	3(10)	2*	5	1*				1
1914	BOSTON BRAVES (N)	7	1	5*	3*					4
	Philadelphia Athletics (A)	1*	0*	4(12)	1					0
1915	BOSTON RED SOX (A)	1	2	2*	2*	5				4
	Philadelphia Phillies (N)	3*	1*	1	1	4*				1
1916	BOSTON RED SOX (A)	6*	2*	3	6	4*				4
	Brooklyn Dodgers (N)	5	1(14)	4*	2*	1				1
1917	CHICAGO WHITE SOX (A)	2*	7*	0	0	8*	4			4
	New York Giants (N)	1	2	2*	5*	5	2*			2
1918	BOSTON RED SOX (A)	1	1	2	3*	0*	2*			4
	Chicago Cubs (N)	0*	3*	1*	2	3	1			2
1919	CINCINNATI REDS (N)	9*	4*	0	2	5	4*	1*	10	5
	Chicago White Sox (A)	1	2	3*	0*	0*	5(10)	4	5*	3
1920	CLEVELAND INDIANS (A)	3	0	1	5*	8*	1*	3*		5
	Brooklyn Dodgers (N)	1*	3*	2*	1	1	0	0		2
1921	NEW YORK GIANTS (N)	0*	0	13*	4	1*	8	2*	1	5
	New York Yankees (A)	3	3*	5	2*	3	5*	1	0*	3
1922	NEW YORK GIANTS (N)	3*	3	3*	4	5*				4
	New York Yankees (A)	2	3*(10)	0	3*	3				0
1923	NEW YORK YANKEES (A)	4*	4	0*	8	8*	6			4
	New York Giants (N)	5	2*	1	4*	1	4*			2
1924	WASHINGTON SENATORS (A)	3*	4*	4	7	2	2*	4*		4
	New York Giants (N)	4(12)	3	6*	4*	6*	1	3(12)		3
1925	PITTSBURGH PIRATES (N)	1*	3*	3	0	6	3*	9*		4
	Washington Senators (A)	4	2	4*	4*	3*	2	7		3
1926	ST. LOUIS CARDINALS (N)	1	6	4*	5*	2*	10	3		4
	New York Yankees (A)	2*	2*	0	10	3(10)	2*	2*		3
1927	NEW YORK YANKEES (A)	5	6	8*	4*					4
	Pittsburgh Pirates (N)	4*	2*	1	3					0
1928	NEW YORK YANKEES (A)	4*	9*	7	7					4
	St. Louis Cardinals (N)	1	3	3*	3*					0
1929	PHILADELPHIA ATHLETICS (A)	3	9	1*	10*	3*				4
	Chicago Cubs (N)	1*	3*	3	8	2				1
1930	PHILADELPHIA ATHLETICS (A)	5*	6*	0	1	2	7*			4
	St. Louis Cardinals (N)	2	1	5*	3*	0*	1			2
1931	ST. LOUIS CARDINALS (N)	2*	2*	5	0	5	1*	4*		4
	Philadelphia Athletics (A)	6	0	2*	3*	1*	8	2		3
1932	NEW YORK YANKEES (A)	12*	5*	7	13					4
	Chicago Cubs (N)	6	2	5*	6*					0
1933	NEW YORK GIANTS (N)	4*	6*	0	2	4				4
	Washington Senators (A)	2	1	4*	1*	3*				1
1934	ST. LOUIS CARDINALS (N)	8	2	4*	4*	1*	4	11		4
	Detroit Tigers (A)	3*	3*(12)	1	10	3	3*	0*		3
1935	DETROIT TIGERS (A)	0*	8*	6	2	1	4*			4
	Chicago Cubs (N)	3	3	5*(11)	1*	3*	3			2
1936	NEW YORK YANKEES (A)	1	18	2*	5*	4*	13			4
	New York Giants (N)	6*	4*	1	2	5(10)	5*			2
1937	NEW YORK YANKEES (A)	8*	8*	5	3	4				4
	New York Giants (N)	1	1	1*	7*	2*				1
1938	NEW YORK YANKEES (A)	3	6	5*	8*					4
	Chicago Cubs (N)	1*	3*	2	3					0
1939	NEW YORK YANKEES (A)	2*	4*	7	7					4
	Cincinnati Reds (N)	1	0	3*	4*(10)					0
1940	CINCINNATI REDS (N)	2*	5*	4	5	0	4*	2*		4
	Detroit Tigers (A)	7	3	7*	2*	8*	0	1		3

Year	Team	1	2	3	4	5	6	7	W
1941	NEW YORK YANKEES (A)	3*	2*	2	7	3			4
	Brooklyn Dodgers (N)	2	3	1*	4*	1*			1
1942	ST. LOUIS CARDINALS (N)	4*	4*	2	9	4			4
	New York Yankees (A)	7	3	0*	6*	2*			1
1943	NEW YORK YANKEES (A)	4*	3*	6*	2	2			4
	St. Louis Cardinals (N)	2	4	2	1*	0*			1
1944	ST. LOUIS CARDINALS (N)	1*	3*	2	5	2	3*		4
	St. Louis Browns (A)	2	2(11)	6*	1*	0*	1		2
1945	DETROIT TIGERS (A)	0*	4*	0*	4	8	7	9	4
	Chicago Cubs (N)	9	1	3	1*	4*	8*(12)	3*	3
1946	ST. LOUIS CARDINALS (N)	2*	3*	0	12	3	4*	4*	4
	Boston Red Sox (A)	3(10)	0	4*	3*	6*	1	3	3
1947	NEW YORK YANKEES (A)	5*	10*	8	2	2	6*	5*	4
	Brooklyn Dodgers (N)	3	3	9*	3*	1*	8	2	3
1948	CLEVELAND INDIANS (A)	0	4	2*	2*	5*	4		4
	Boston Braves (N)	1*	1*	0	1	11	3*		2
1949	NEW YORK YANKEES (A)	1*	0*	4	6	10			4
	Brooklyn Dodgers (N)	0	1	3*	4*	6*			1
1950	NEW YORK YANKEES (A)	1	2	3*	5*				4
	Philadelphia Phillies (N)	0*	1*(10)	2	2				0
1951	NEW YORK YANKEES (A)	1*	3*	2	6	13	4*		4
	New York Giants (N)	5	1	6*	2*	1*	3		2
1952	NEW YORK YANKEES (A)	2	7	3*	2*	5*	3	4	4
	Brooklyn Dodgers (N)	4*	1*	5	0	6(11)	2*	2*	3
1953	NEW YORK YANKEES (A)	9*	4*	2	3	11	4*		4
	Brooklyn Dodgers (N)	5	2	3*	7*	7*	3		2
1954	NEW YORK GIANTS (N)	5*	3*	6	7				4
	Cleveland Indians (A)	2(10)	1	2*	4*				0
1955	BROOKLYN DODGERS (N)	5	2	8*	8*	5*	1	2	4
	New York Yankees (A)	6*	4*	3	5	3	5*	0*	3
1956	NEW YORK YANKEES (A)	3	8	5*	6*	2*	0	9	4
	Brooklyn Dodgers (N)	6*	13*	3	2	0	1*(10)	0*	3
1957	MILWAUKEE BRAVES (N)	1	4	3*	7*	1*	2	5	4
	New York Yankees (A)	3*	2*	12	5(10)	0	3*	0*	3
1958	NEW YORK YANKEES (A)	3	5	4*	0*	7*	4	6	4
	Milwaukee Braves (N)	4*(10)	13*	0	3	0	3*(10)	2*	3
1959	LOS ANGELES DODGERS (N)	0	4	3*	5*	0*	9		4
	Chicago White Sox (A)	11*	3*	1	4	1	3*		2
1960	PITTSBURGH PIRATES (N)	6*	3*	0	3	5	0*	10*	4
	New York Yankees (A)	4	16	10*	2*	2*	12	9	3
1961	NEW YORK YANKEES (A)	2*	2*	3	7	13			4
	Cincinnati Reds (N)	0	6	2*	0*	5*			1
1962	NEW YORK YANKEES (A)	6	0	3*	3*	5*	2	1	4
	San Francisco Giants (N)	2*	2*	2	7	3	5*	0*	3
1963	LOS ANGELES DODGERS (N)	5	4	1*	2*				4
	New York Yankees (A)	2*	1*	0	1				0
1964	ST. LOUIS CARDINALS (N)	9*	3*	1	4	5	3*	7*	4
	New York Yankees (A)	5	8	2*	3*	2*(10)	8	5	3
1965	LOS ANGELES DODGERS (N)	2	1	4*	7*	7*	1	2	4
	Minnesota Twins (A)	8*	5*	0	2	0	5*	0*	3
1966	BALTIMORE ORIOLES (A)	5	6	1*	1*				4
	Los Angeles Dodgers (N)	2*	0*	0	0				0
1967	ST. LOUIS CARDINALS (N)	2	0	5*	6*	1*	4	7	4
	Boston Red Sox (A)	1*	5*	2	0	3	8*	2*	3

Year	Team	1	2	3	4	5	6	7	W
1968	DETROIT TIGERS (A)	0	8	3*	1*	5*	13	4	4
	St. Louis Cardinals (N)	4*	1*	7	10	3	1*	1*	3
1969	NEW YORK METS (N)	1	2	5*	2*	5*			4
	Baltimore Orioles (A)	4*	1*	0	1(10)	3			1
1970	BALTIMORE ORIOLES (A)	4	6	9*	5*	9*			4
	Cincinnati Reds (N)	3*	5*	3	6	3			1
1971	PITTSBURGH PIRATES (N)	3	3	5*	4*	4*	2	2	4
	Baltimore Orioles (A)	5*	11*	1	3	0	3*(10)	1*	3
1972	OAKLAND A's (A)	3	2	0^	3^	4^	1	3	4
	Cincinnati Reds (N)	2*	1*	1	2	5	8*	2*	3
1973	OAKLAND A's (A)	2*	7*	3	1	0	3*	5*	4
	New York Mets (N)	1	10(12)	2*(11)	6*	2*	1	2	3
1974	OAKLAND A's (A)	3	2	3*	5*	3*			4
	Los Angeles Dodgers (N)	2*	3*	2	2	2			1
1975	CINCINNATI REDS (N)	0	3	6*	4*	6*	6	4	4
	Boston Red Sox (A)	6*	2*	5(10)	5	2	7*(12)	3*	3
1976	CINCINNATI REDS (N)	5*	4*	6	7				4
	New York Yankees (A)	1	3	2*	2*				0
1977	NEW YORK YANKEES (A)	4*	1*	5	4	4	8*		4
	Los Angeles Dodgers (N)	3(12)	6	3*	2*	10*	4		2
1978	NEW YORK YANKEES (A)	5	3	5*	4*	12*	7		4
	Los Angeles Dodgers (N)	11*	4*	1	3(10)	2	2*		2
1979	PITTSBURGH PIRATES (N)	4	3	4*	6*	7*	4	4	4
	Baltimore Orioles (A)	5*	2*	8	9	1	0*	1*	3
1980	PHILADELPHIA PHILLIES (N)	7*	6*	3	3	4	4*		4
	Kansas City Royals (A)	6	4	4*(10)	5*	3*	1		2
1981	LOS ANGELES DODGERS (N)	3	0	5*	8*	2*	9		4
	New York Yankees (A)	5*	3*	4	7	1	2*		2
1982	ST. LOUIS CARDINALS (N)	0*	5*	6	5	4	13*	6*	4
	Milwaukee Brewers (A)	10	4	2*	7*	6*	1	3	3
1983	BALTIMORE ORIOLES (A)	1*	4*	3	5	5			4
	Philadelphia Phillies (N)	2	1	2*	4*	0*			1
1984	DETROIT TIGERS (A)	3	3	5*	4*	8*			4
	San Diego Padres (N)	2*	5*	2	2	4			1
1985	KANSAS CITY ROYALS (A)	1*	2*	6	0	6	2*	11*	4
	St. Louis Cardinals (N)	3	4	1*	3*	1*	1	0	3
1986	NEW YORK METS (N)	0*	3*	7	6	2	6*	8*	4
	Boston Red Sox (A)	1	9	1*	2*	4*	5(10)	5	3
1987	MINNESOTA TWINS (A)	10*	8*	1	2	2	11*	4*	4
	St. Louis Cardinals (N)	1	4	3*	7*	4*	5	2	3
1988	LOS ANGELES DODGERS (N)	5*	6*	1	4	5			4
	Oakland Athletics (A)	4	0	2*	3*	2*			1
1989	OAKLAND A's (A)	5*	5*	13	9				4
	San Francisco Giants (N)	0	1	7*	6*				0
1990	CINCINNATI REDS (N)	7*	5*	8	2				4
	Oakland Athletics (A)	0	4(10)	3*	1*				0
1991	MINNESOTA TWINS (A)	5*	3*	4	2	5	4*	1*	4
	Atlanta Braves (N)	2	2	5*(12)	3*	14*	3(11)	0(10)	3
1992	TORONTO BLUE JAYS (A)	1	5	3*	2*	2*	4		4
	Atlanta Braves (N)	3*	4*	2	1	7	3*(11)		2
1993	TORONTO BLUE JAYS (A)	8*	4*	10	15	0	8*		4
	Philadelphia Phillies (N)	5	6	3*	14*	2*	6		2
1994	not held								
1995	ATLANTA BRAVES	3*	4*	6	5	4	1*		4
	Cleveland Indians	2	3	7*(11)	2*	5*	0		2

WORLD SERIES HIGHLIGHTS

1912: As the 1912 World Series got under way, all anybody talked about were household names such as Christy Mathewson, Tris Speaker, Rube Marquard, and Smokey Joe Wood. By the time it was over, Fred Snodgrass and Fred Merkle were the only names anybody remembered.

The New York Giants breezed through the regular season virtually untouched, winning 103 games and giving manager John McGraw his second straight National League pennant. Led by the pitching duo of Marquard, who won a record nineteen straight decisions to open the season, and the ageless Mathewson (twenty-three wins at age thirty-three), the Giants squared off against the Boston Red Sox, who captured the American League title thanks in large part to the phenomenal performances of Wood (thirty-four wins, including ten shutouts) and Speaker (a .383 batting average).

Although Boston won the opening game behind Wood's eleven strikeouts, the two teams were tied at 6–6 in the eleventh inning of game two when darkness fell and the result was declared a tie. The Giants won three of the next five—including a complete-game gem by Marquard in game six—to force a deciding eighth game in Boston.

Mathewson, still winless and pitching for the third time in seven days, carried the Giants through nine tense innings tied at 1–1. But after taking a 2–1 lead on Merkle's single in the top of the tenth, New York perfected a collapse in the bottom of the inning that defied the odds.

It began when pinch hitter Clyde Engle led off with a routine fly ball to center that Snodgrass, normally a reliable fielder, camped under—then inexplicably dropped. Engle reached second on the error, then took third two out later. Following a walk, Speaker stepped up to the plate and hit a short pop foul down the first-base line. In what came to be known as Merkle's boner, the Giants' first baseman made little or no attempt to catch the ball, even though it fell just a few feet away.

Given a reprieve, Speaker singled home Engle with the tying run, and the Red Sox won it all behind Larry Gardner's sacrifice fly moments later, 3–2. For the stunned Giants, two fielding errors added a nightmare postscript to an otherwise dream season.

1919: So much myth and hyperbole now shroud the legend of the 1919 "Black Sox" scandal that it is important to remember two things: (1) the eight Chicago White Sox players charged with "fixing" the 1919 World Series were acquitted in court, and (2) Chicago nearly won the Series anyway.

Playing an extended best-of-nine format designed to capitalize on the nation's postwar passion for baseball, the Cincinnati Reds needed three hits and four RBIs from Edd Roush in game eight to finally clinch the championship. But not before Chicago pitcher Dickey Kerr posted two heroic victories and some of the so-called Black Sox chipped in with standout performances. For instance, "Shoeless" Joe Jackson batted a Series-high .375 and homered in the final game; third baseman Buck Weaver hit .324; and first baseman Chick Gandil had two game-winning hits. Even pitcher Eddie Cicotte, one of the supposed ringleaders of the fix, hurled a one-run victory in game seven.

Still, a sharp drop in the betting odds of the highly favored White Sox prior to the Series was the first sign that something was amiss, and rumors were rampant that gamblers had gotten to some of the Chicago players. Strange occurrences—such as Cicotte's two errors in the fifth inning of game four, or shortstop Swede Risberg's anemic .080 batting average—only added to the suspicion.

The eight Black Sox were cleared by the courts in 1921, but baseball commissioner Kenesaw Mountain Landis imposed lifetime bans anyway because of their undeniable link to gamblers. That effectively keeps Jackson out of the Hall of Fame to this day, and his plight has become part of American lore through books and films such as *Eight Men Out* and *Field of Dreams*. Still, there is no evidence that a little boy confronted him outside the courtroom during the trials with the famous words, "Say it ain't so, Joe."

1924: It is only fitting that one of the closest, most dramatic World Series ever—one that included four one-run games and two extra-inning affairs—should have been decided by a tiny pebble.

No longer the fabled cellar dwellers of the American League, the Washington Senators reached the World Series for the first time in team history thanks to yet another standout season from thirty-six-year-old pitcher Walter Johnson. Pitching in his eighteenth season, the "Big Train" won twenty-three games and led the league with a 2.72 ERA. John McGraw's New York Giants, meanwhile, had captured their eighth pennant in the past fourteen years behind the usual galaxy of stars such as Bill Terry, Fred Lindstrom, and Frankie Frisch.

But beating the Senators proved no easy task, and the two teams were deadlocked at three games apiece heading into the tense, winner-take-all game seven in Washington's Griffith Stadium. New York nursed a 3–1 lead going into the eighth, but a bizarre pair of bad-hop hits soon scuttled the Giants' chances.

First, the Senators had loaded the bases with one out when Buck Harris rapped a grounder down the third-base line. But the ball hit a small rock in the infield and skipped over the head of third baseman Lindstrom, allowing two runs to

score. Then, after failing to capitalize on a
golden scoring opportunity against Johnson
(pitching in relief) in the top of the ninth, the
Giants were again faced with the inexplicable in
the bottom of the twelfth. A two-on grounder by
Earl McNeely toward Lindstrom again hopped
crazily over the third baseman's head after
striking a pebble, allowing the winning run to
score.

In the tradition of so many other Giants
postseason oddities, the infamous "pebble hit"
quickly took its place in New York lore. In the
process it added a fitting coda to the career of
McGraw, whose ninth and final World Series
was as strange as many of the others.

1932: Nobody knows for sure *what* Babe Ruth
was doing when he raised his hand while
batting in the fifth inning of game three of the
1932 World Series. Some say he was gesturing
at Chicago Cubs pitcher Charlie Root. Others
believe he was motioning toward the Cubs'
dugout. Still others believe the New York
Yankees slugger was keeping track of the balls
and strikes.

But legend has it that Ruth pointed toward
the center field bleachers to indicate where the
next pitch would end up, and the massive star
seemed to back it up. With the game tied at 4–4
and a count of two balls and two strikes on him,
Ruth appeared to point to straightaway center,
then smashed the next pitch all the way to the
base of the flagpole in center field. His electrifying "called shot" gave the Yankees a three-
games-to-none lead en route to a Series sweep.

Lou Gehrig finished with three home runs
and eight RBIs as New York scored an incredible
thirty-seven runs in the four games, yet Ruth's
homer was all anybody talked about. "What do
you think of the nerve of that big monkey
calling his shot and getting away with it?"
Gehrig asked reporters the next day, inadvertently fanning the flames. But Root steadfastly
denies Ruth tried to show him up. "If he had, I
would have knocked him down with the next
pitch," Root said. Scratchy newsreel footage
and wildly varying newspaper accounts do
little to set the record straight.

Ruth, meanwhile, was content to let the myth
take care of itself, especially so late in his career.
Although still the world's best-known athlete,
Ruth's skills had begun to erode, and he would
retire two years later. Fittingly, the "called shot"
was Ruth's fifteenth—and last—home run in
World Series play.

1956: Up until the events of October 8, 1956,
Don Larsen was a little-known pitcher whose
credits included (a) losing twenty-one games for
Baltimore in 1954; (b) being part of a seventeen-
player trade that same year, the biggest in
baseball history at that time; and (c) posting an
11.25 ERA in the 1955 World Series.

But because Larsen pitched so brilliantly in
game five of the 1956 World Series, he is known
as the only player ever to throw a perfect game
in postseason history. Larsen's dazzling performance proved to be the jewel in the crown of
the Yankees' sixth Series title in the last eight
years.

Larsen's performance was all the more remarkable because the Brooklyn Dodgers had
scored a combined twenty-three runs off the
Yankees through the first four games of the
Series. Larsen himself had been victimized in
game two, failing to last two full innings before
surrendering four runs en route to a 13–8 loss.
Yet there he was three days later in game five,
setting the Dodgers down in order and striking
out seven in the process.

Larsen's opponent in game five was former
New York Giants ace Sal Maglie, who fiddled
with a perfect game himself for three-plus
innings and allowed only two runs and five hits
on the day. But a solo home run by Mickey
Mantle and an RBI single by Hank Bauer gave
Larsen all the offensive support he needed, and
Mantle chipped in with a great one-handed
catch of a Gil Hodges liner in the fifth.

It came down to the ninth inning for Larsen,
with a crowd of 64,519 at Yankee Stadium on its
feet and three tough Dodgers hitters left to face.
But Carl Furillo flied out, Roy Campanella
grounded out to second, and pinch hitter Dale
Mitchell, a career .312 hitter, took a called third
strike to end the game and secure Larsen's place
in history.

1960: Simply stated, the Pittsburgh Pirates had
no business still playing baseball. Tagged for
forty-eight runs and seventy-eight hits by the
New York Yankees over the past week, the
Pirates should have long since run up the white
flag and surrendered. But appearing in the
World Series for the first time since 1927—and
clearly not awed by the Yankee dynasty—
Pittsburgh found itself tied with New York at
three games apiece heading into game seven of
the 1960 World Series.

The story had been one of excess and finesse.
While the Yankees bludgeoned Pittsburgh with
scores such as 16–3 (game two), 10–0 (game
three), and 12–0 (game six), the Pirates doggedly fashioned enough hit-and-run victories to
stay close. But a three-run home run by Yogi
Berra in the sixth inning staked New York to a
5–4 lead in game seven, and the Yankees added
two more runs in the eighth.

The Pirates rallied in the bottom of the
inning, however, taking an improbable 9–7 lead
on RBI singles by Dick Groat and Roberto
Clemente and a three-run home run over the
left-field wall from Hal Smith. Pittsburgh manager Danny Murtaugh turned to Bob Friend, an
eighteen-game winner during the regular season, to seal the win, but neither Friend nor

veteran Harvey Haddix could prevent New York from once again tying the score at 9–9.

That set the stage for Bill Mazeroski, Pittsburgh's scrappy little second baseman, who stepped to the plate to lead off the bottom of the ninth. Although never a power hitter, Mazeroski had poked a homer in game one, and he looked at one ball from pitcher Ralph Terry. He swung viciously at the next pitch, lining the ball over the wall in left field and touching off pandemonium in Pittsburgh's Forbes Field. Mazeroski was forced to weave through delirious fans as he rounded the bases and headed for home, and his home run gave the Pirates their first World Series championship in thirty-five years and the Yankees a taste of their own medicine.

> Baseball is very big with my people. It figures. It's the only time we can get to shake a bat at a white man without starting a riot.
>
> Dick Gregory, From the Back of the Bus, 1962

1972: At first glance the Oakland A's and the Cincinnati Reds could not have seemed more different. Yet the 1972 World Series proved the two teams to be a lot closer than anyone ever imagined.

Oakland was a mod, freewheeling ball club styled after its owner, Charlie Finley, a baseball maverick whose innovations included garish uniforms, bizarre nicknames, and bonuses for any player or coach willing to grow a mustache. In fact, Finley had the word *Swingin'* and a pair of white cleats worked into the A's logo, just in case anybody missed how really *cool* the team was. Cincinnati, meanwhile, was a no-nonsense organization from the top down. The players were forbidden to wear long sideburns or facial hair, and clubhouse boys were employed to paint out the manufacturer's stripes on the team's shoes.

But the 1972 Series turned out to be a nailbiter from the start. Six of the seven games were decided by one run, including several heartstopping finishes that are still being talked about today. In game two Oakland entered the bottom of the ninth with a 2–0 lead thanks to a home run by Joe Rudi. The Reds put one runner aboard, however, and followed with a drive to deep left field by Dennis Menke that looked certain to tie the score. But Rudi chased the ball down and made a leaping, backhanded catch off the wall to kill the rally.

In game four, the A's rallied from a 2–1 deficit with one out in the bottom of the ninth. Four consecutive singles—the last by pinch hitter Angel Mangual—gave Oakland a 3–2 win and a three-game-to-one lead in the Series. But Cincinnati won game five, taking a 5–4 victory in the bottom of the ninth when Oakland pinch runner John "Blue Moon" Odom tried to score from third with one out on a pop foul. Reds second baseman Joe Morgan made the catch, momentarily slipped, then recovered to throw out Odom at the plate.

Game six was the only rout of the Series, an 8–1 slugfest by the Reds, but the deciding seventh game returned to form. Little-known catcher Gene Tenace drove in two runs with a single and a double to spark Oakland, while manager Dick Williams turned to three all-star pitchers in relief (Jim "Catfish" Hunter, Ken Holtzman, and Rollie Fingers) to nail down a 3–2 win and the A's first World Series title since 1930, when the club was still located in Philadelphia.

1975: Game six of the 1975 World Series is considered by many to be the greatest postseason game ever, and the image of Carlton Fisk waving his twelfth-inning home run toward fair territory is already part of baseball lore.

But Fisk's shot overshadows the fact that the entire 1975 Series between Cincinnati and Boston was one of the most thrilling, controversial, and downright enjoyable World Series ever. Five of the games were decided by one run, subplots abounded, a three-day rain delay added to the suspense, and some of the game's all-time greats—Pete Rose, Carl Yastrzemski, Johnny Bench, and Luis Tiant—played central roles. Midway through game six, Rose stepped out of the batter's box, turned to Fisk behind the plate, and asked, "Isn't this fun?"

This Series had several big plays. In game two, the Reds overcame a 2–1 deficit with two outs in the ninth to win on Ken Griffey Sr.'s RBI double. Game three, meanwhile, is famous for a collision between Fisk and Reds pinch hitter Ed Armbrister, who attempted to bunt his way on in the tenth inning, then appeared to block Fisk's path to the ball. Boston players screamed for an interference call—and never got it—and the Reds seized the momentum and won on Morgan's bases-loaded hit.

Tiant pitched his second complete-game victory of the Series to win game four, but Tony Perez clubbed a pair of home runs in game five to give Cincinnati a three-games-to-two edge. Driving rains forced game six to be postponed for three days, only adding to the tension of a game that came with plenty of its own. Fisk's home run ended game six more than four hours after it started, surely one of the most compelling moments in baseball history, especially after Boston rallied from three runs down in the bottom of the eighth and tied the game on Bernie Carbo's pinch-hit home run.

It remained for Reds second baseman Joe Morgan to decide the Series on a two-out single in the ninth inning of game seven. With runners on first and third, Morgan looped a soft hit to right for a 4–3 lead, and reliever Will McEnaney retired Boston in order in the bottom of the inning to clinch Cincinnati's first championship in thirty-five years.

1986: According to baseball legend, the Boston Red Sox franchise has been cursed ever since the day in 1919 when Babe Ruth was traded away. The 1986 World Series stands as testament to that curse.

One strike away from winning its first World Series since Ruth posted two victories as a pitcher in the 1918 classic, Boston instead suffered a collapse that made winners of the New York Mets. The fateful scenario occurred in game six, with the Red Sox nursing a 5–3 lead in the tenth inning thanks to Dave Henderson's home run and an RBI single by Marty Barrett. After retiring the first two batters, reliever Calvin Schiraldi surrendered base hits to Gary Carter and pinch hitter Kevin Mitchell, but slipped two quick strikes past Ray Knight.

One strike away from victory, the Red Sox were instead denied as Knight slapped a hit to center, scoring Carter and bringing on relief pitcher Bob Stanley. What happened next is still being talked about in bars all over New England, as Stanley and the batter, Mookie Wilson, waged a tense, ten-pitch battle in front of 55,078 anxious fans in New York's Shea Stadium. Stanley again brought Boston within a pitch of victory after working the count to 2–2, but then he threw a wild pitch that allowed Mitchell to score from third and tie the game.

Moments later Wilson rapped a sharp grounder toward first baseman Bill Buckner, a ball that Buckner allowed to scoot through his legs for an error, giving Knight the chance to race home with the winning run.

Having tied the Series at three games apiece in such an emotional fashion, the Mets rallied to win game seven on home runs by Knight and Darryl Strawberry and the relief pitching of Jesse Orosco. By that time the Red Sox were too cursed to respond.

1991: Most World Series feature an underdog to root for. The 1991 Series, however, had two.

Both the Minnesota Twins and the Atlanta Braves finished dead last in their respective divisions in 1990, moribund teams struggling to come to grips with the free-agent era. But the Twins and the Braves each completed "worst-to-first" turnabouts in 1991 and entered the Series with nothing to lose. Seven breathtaking baseball games were the result, yet the Twins' world championship—the club's second in five years—might just as easily have gone to the Braves.

The home team won every time in the 1991 World Series, often in nerve-racking fashion. Five of the games were decided by one run, including three in extra innings. In game two rookie Scott Leius snapped a 2–2 tie with an eighth-inning home run, and game three went to the Braves on a two-out single by Mark Lemke in the twelfth inning. Lemke also won game four when he raced home from third to score on a fly ball, narrowly avoiding the tag by catcher Brian Harper.

The Twins staved off elimination in game six thanks to the heroics of center fielder Kirby Puckett, who made a circus catch off Ron Gant in the third inning, then won the game with a solo home run in the bottom of the eleventh.

Game seven dragged on for nine and a half scoreless, torturous innings as Minnesota's Jack Morris and Atlanta's John Smoltz hooked up in one of the classic pitching duels of postseason play. Both teams loaded the bases in the eighth but failed to score, and Braves reliever Alejandro Pena struck out pinch hitter Paul Sorrento to kill a Twins rally in the ninth.

Finally, Minnesota pinch hitter Gene Larkin singled home Dan Gladden with the winning run in the bottom of the tenth, the last great act in nine days of high drama.

—D.W.C

Babe Ruth hits his record-breaking 60th home run of the year on September 30, 1927.

Henry Aaron watches his 715th career home run on April 8, 1974, topping Babe Ruth's record of 714.

FOOTBALL

SUPER BOWL

1967 (at Los Angeles)
GREEN BAY PACKERS 7 7 14 7 35
Kansas City Chiefs   0 10 0 0 10

1st Quarter
8:56 Green Bay   TD McGee 37-yard pass
                       from Starr (Chandler
                       kick)
2nd Quarter
4:20 Kansas City TD McClinton 17-yard
                       pass from Dawson
                       (Mercer kick)
10:23 Green Bay   TD Taylor 14-yard run
                       (Chandler kick)
14:06 Kansas City FG Mercer 31 yards
3rd Quarter
2:27 Green Bay   TD Pitts 5-yard run
                       (Chandler kick)
14:09 Green Bay   TD McGee 13-yard pass
                       from Starr (Chandler
                       kick)
4th Quarter
8:25 Green Bay   TD Pitts 1-yard run
                       (Chandler kick)

1968 (at Miami)
GREEN BAY PACKERS 3 13 10 7 33
Oakland Raiders   0 7 0 7 14

1st Quarter
5:07 Green Bay   FG Chandler 39 yards
2nd Quarter
2:08 Green Bay   FG Chandler 20 yards
4:10 Green Bay   TD Dowler 62-yard pass
                       from Starr (Chandler
                       kick)
8:45 Oakland   TD Miller 23-yard pass
                       from Lamonica
                       (Blanda kick)
14:59 Green Bay   FG Chandler 43 yards
3rd Quarter
9:06 Green Bay   TD Anderson 2-yard run
                       (Chandler kick)
14:58 Green Bay   FG Chandler 31 yards
4th Quarter
3:57 Green Bay   TD Adderley 60-yard in-
                       terception return
                       (Chandler kick)
5:47 Oakland   TD Miller 23-yard pass
                       from Lamonica
                       (Blanda kick)

1969 (at Miami)
NEW YORK JETS 0 7 6 3 16
Baltimore Colts 0 0 0 7 7

2nd Quarter
5:57 New York   TD Snell 4-yard run
                       (Turner kick)

3rd Quarter
4:52 New York   FG Turner 32 yards
11:02 New York   FG Turner 30 yards
4th Quarter
1:34 New York   FG Turner 9 yards
11:41 Baltimore   TD Hill 1-yard run (Mi-
                       chaels kick)

1970 (at New Orleans)
KANSAS CITY CHIEFS 3 13 7 0 23
Minnesota Vikings   0 0 7 0 7

1st Quarter
8:08 Kansas City FG Stenerud 48 yards
2nd Quarter
1:40 Kansas City FG Stenerud 32 yards
7:08 Kansas City FG Stenerud 25 yards
9:26 Kansas City TD Garrett 5-yard run
                       (Stenerud kick)
3rd Quarter
10:28 Minnesota   TD Osborn 4-yard run
                       (Cox kick)
13:38 Kansas City TD Taylor 46-yard pass
                       from Dawson
                       (Stenerud kick)

1971 (at Miami)
BALTIMORE COLTS 0 6 0 10 16
Dallas Cowboys   3 10 0 0 13

1st Quarter
9:28 Dallas   FG Clark 14 yards
2nd Quarter
0:08 Dallas   FG Clark 30 yards
0:50 Baltimore   TD Mackey 75-yard pass
                       from Unitas (kick
                       blocked)
7:07 Dallas   TD Thomas 7-yard pass
                       from Morton (Clark
                       kick)
4th Quarter
7:25 Baltimore   TD Nowatzke 2-yard run
                       (O'Brien kick)
14:55 Baltimore   FG O'Brien 32 yards

1972 (at New Orleans)
DALLAS COWBOYS 3 7 7 7 24
Miami Dolphins   0 3 0 0 3

1st Quarter
13:37 Dallas   FG Clark 9 yards
2nd Quarter
13:45 Dallas   TD Alworth 7-yard pass from
                       Staubach (Clark kick)
14:56 Miami   FG Yepremian 31 yards
3rd Quarter
5:17 Dallas   TD D. Thomas 3-yard run
                       (Clark kick)
4th Quarter
3:18 Dallas   TD Ditka 7-yard pass from
                       Staubach (Clark kick)

1973 (at Los Angeles)
MIAMI DOLPHINS 7 7 0 0 14
Washington Redskins 0 0 0 7 7

1st Quarter
14:59 Miami TD Twilley 28-yard pass from Griese (Yepremian kick)
2nd Quarter
14:42 Miami TD Kiick 1-yard run (Yepremian kick)
4th Quarter
12:53 Washington TD Bass 49-yard fumble return (Knight kick)

1974 (at Houston)
MIAMI DOLPHINS 14 3 7 0 24
Minnesota Vikings 0 0 0 7 7

1st Quarter
9:33 Miami TD Csonka 5-yard run (Yepremian kick)
13:28 Miami TD Kiick 1-yard run (Yepremian kick)
2nd Quarter
8:58 Miami FG Yepremian 28 yards
3rd Quarter
6:16 Miami TD Csonka 2-yard run (Yepremian kick)
4th Quarter
1:35 Minnesota TD Tarkenton 4-yard run (Cox kick)

1975 (at New Orleans)
PITTSBURGH STEELERS 0 2 7 7 16
Minnesota Vikings 0 0 0 6 6

2nd Quarter
7:49 Pittsburgh SA White tackled Tarkenton in end zone
3rd Quarter
1:35 Pittsburgh TD Harris 12-yard run (Gerela kick)
4th Quarter
4:27 Minnesota TD T. Brown recovered block punt in end zone (kick failed)
11:29 Pittsburgh TD L. Brown 4-yard pass from Bradshaw (Gerela kick)

1976 (at Miami)
PITTSBURGH STEELERS 7 0 0 14 21
Dallas Cowboys 7 3 0 7 17

1st Quarter
4:36 Dallas TD D. Pearson 29-yard pass from Staubach (Fritsch kick)
9:03 Pittsburgh TD Grossman 7-yard pass from Bradshaw (Gerela kick)

2nd Quarter
0:15 Dallas FG Fritsch 36 yards
4th Quarter
3:32 Pittsburgh SA Harrison blocked punt out of end zone
6:19 Pittsburgh FG Gerela 36 yards
8:23 Pittsburgh FG Gerela 18 yards
11:58 Pittsburgh TD Swann 64-yard pass from Bradshaw (kick failed)
13:12 Dallas TD P. Howard 34-yard pass from Staubach (Fritsch kick)

1977 (at Pasadena)
OAKLAND RAIDERS 0 16 3 13 32
Minnesota Vikings 0 0 7 7 14

2nd Quarter
0:48 Oakland FG Mann 24 yards
7:50 Oakland TD Casper 1-yard pass from Stabler (Mann kick)
11:27 Oakland TD Banaszak 1-yard run (kick failed)
3rd Quarter
9:44 Oakland FG Mann 40 yards
14:13 Minnesota TD S. White 8-yard pass from Tarkenton (Cox kick)
4th Quarter
7:21 Oakland TD Banaszak 2-yard run (Mann kick)
9:17 Oakland TD Brown 75-yard interception return (kick failed)
14:35 Minnesota TD Voigt 13-yard pass from Lee (Cox kick)

1978 (at New Orleans)
DALLAS COWBOYS 10 3 7 7 27
Denver Broncos 0 0 10 0 10

1st Quarter
10:31 Dallas TD Dorsett 3-yard run (Herrera kick)
13:29 Dallas FG Herrera 35 yards
2nd Quarter
3:44 Dallas FG Herrera 43 yards
3rd Quarter
2:28 Denver FG Turner 47 yards
8:01 Dallas TD Johnson 45-yard pass from Staubach (Herrera kick)
9:21 Denver TD Lytle 1-yard run (Turner kick)
4th Quarter
7:56 Dallas TD Richards 29-yard pass from Newhouse (Herrera kick)

1979 (at Miami)
PITTSBURGH STEELERS 7 14 0 14 35
Dallas Cowboys 7 7 3 14 31

1st Quarter
5:13 Pittsburgh TD Stallworth 28-yard pass from Bradshaw (Gerela kick)

15:00 Dallas TD Hill 39-yard pass from Staubach (Septien kick)

2nd Quarter
2:52 Dallas TD Hegman 37-yard fumble return (Septien kick)

4:35 Pittsburgh TD Stallworth 75-yard pass from Bradshaw (Gerela kick)

14:34 Pittsburgh TD Bleier 7-yard pass from Bradshaw (Gerela kick)

3rd Quarter
12:24 Dallas FG Septien 27 yards
4th Quarter
7:50 Pittsburgh TD Harris 22-yard run (Gerela kick)

8:09 Pittsburgh TD Swann 18-yard pass from Bradshaw (Gerela kick)

12:37 Dallas TD Dupree 7-yard pass from Staubach (Septien kick)

14:38 Dallas TD Johnson 4-yard pass from Staubach (Septien kick)

1980 (at Pasadena)
PITTSBURGH STEELERS 3 7 7 14 31
Los Angeles Rams   7 6 6   0 19

1st Quarter
7:29 Pittsburgh FG Bahr 41 yards
12:16 Los Angeles TD Bryant 1-yard run (Corral kick)
2nd Quarter
2:08 Pittsburgh TD Harris 1-yard run (Bahr kick)

7:39 Los Angeles FG Corral 31 yards
14:46 Los Angeles FG Corral 45 yards
3rd Quarter
2:48 Pittsburgh TD Swann 47-yard pass from Bradshaw (Bahr kick)

4:45 Los Angeles TD R. Smith 24-yard pass from McCutcheon (kick failed)

4th Quarter
2:56 Pittsburgh TD Stallworth 73-yard pass from Bradshaw (Bahr kick)

13:11 Pittsburgh TD Harris 1-yard run (Bahr kick)

1981 (at New Orleans)
OAKLAND RAIDERS 14 0 10 3 27
Philadelphia Eagles   0 3   0 7 10

1st Quarter
6:04 Oakland TD Branch 2-yard pass from Plunkett (Bahr kick)

14:51 Oakland TD King 80-yard pass from Plunkett (Bahr kick)

2nd Quarter
4:32 Philadelphia FG Franklin 30 yards
3rd Quarter
2.30 Oakland TD Branch 29-yard pass from Plunkett (Bahr kick)

10:25 Oakland FG Bahr 46 yards
4th Quarter
1:01 Philadelphia TD Krepfle 8-yard pass from Jaworski (Franklin kick)

6:31 Oakland FG Bahr 35 yards

1982 (at Pontiac)
SAN FRANCISCO 49ERS 7 13 0   6 26
Cincinnati Bengals   0   0 7 14 21

1st Quarter
9:08 San Francisco TD Montana 1-yard run (Wersching kick)

2nd Quarter
8:07 San Francisco TD Cooper 11-yard pass from Montana (Wersching kick)

14:45 San Francisco FG Wersching 22 yards
14:58 San Francisco FG Wersching 26 yards
3rd Quarter
3:35 Cincinnati TD Anderson 5-yard run (Breech kick)

4th Quarter
4:54 Cincinnati TD Ross 4-yard pass from Anderson (Breech kick)

9:35 San Francisco FG Wersching 40 yards
13:03 San Francisco FG Wersching 23 yards
14:44 Cincinnati TD Ross 3-yard pass from Anderson (Breech kick)

1983 (at Pasadena)
WASHINGTON REDSKINS 0 10 3 14 27
Miami Dolphins   7 10 0   0 17

1st Quarter
6:49 Miami TD Cefalo 76-yard pass from Woodley (Von Schamann kick)

2nd Quarter
0:21 Washington FG Moseley 31 yards
9:00 Miami FG Von Schamann 20 yards

13:09 Washington TD Garrett 4-yard pass
                        from Theismann
                        (Moseley kick)
13:22 Miami   TD Walker 98-yard kick-
                        off return (Von
                        Schamann kick)
3rd Quarter
 6:51 Washington FG Moseley 20 yards
4th Quarter
 4:59 Washington TD Riggins 43-yard run
                        (Moseley kick)
13:05 Washington TD Brown 6-yard pass
                        from Theismann
                        (Moseley kick)

1984 (at Tampa)
        LOS ANGELES RAIDERS 7 14 14 3 38
        Washington Redskins   0   3   6 0   9

1st Quarter
 4:52 Los Angeles TD Jensen recovered
                         blocked punt in end
                         zone (Bahr kick)
2nd Quarter
 5:46 Los Angeles TD Branch 12-yard pass
                         from Plunkett (Bahr
                         kick)
11:56 Washington   FG Moseley 24 yards
14:53 Los Angeles TD Squirek 5-yard inter-
                         ception return (Bahr
                         kick)
3rd Quarter
 4:08 Washington   TD Riggins 1-yard run
                         (kick blocked)
 7:54 Los Angeles TD Allen 5-yard run
                         (Bahr kick)
15:00 Los Angeles TD Allen 74-yard run
                         (Bahr kick)
4th Quarter
12:36 Los Angeles FG Bahr 21 yards

1985 (at Stanford)
        SAN FRANCISCO 49ERS   7 21 10 0 38
        Miami Dolphins   10   6   0 0 16

1st Quarter
 7:36 Miami   FG Von Schamann 37
                           yards
11:48 San Francisco TD Monroe 33-yard
                           pass from Mon-
                           tana (Wersching
                           kick)
14:15 Miami   TD D. Johnson 2-yard
                           pass from Marino
                           (Von Schamann
                           kick)
2nd Quarter
 1:25 San Francisco TD Craig 8-yard pass
                           from Montana
                           (Wersching kick)
 8:02 San Francisco TD Montana 6-yard
                           run (Wersching
                           kick)

12:55 San Francisco TD Craig 2-yard run
                           (Wersching kick)
14:38 Miami   FG Von Schamann 31
                           yards
15:00 Miami   FG Von Schamann 30
                           yards
3rd Quarter
 4:48 San Francisco FG Wersching 27
                           yards
 8:42 San Francisco TD Craig 16-yard pass
                           from Montana
                           (Wersching kick)

1986 (at New Orleans)
        CHICAGO BEARS   13 10 21 2 46
        New England Patriots   3   0   0 7 10

1st Quarter
 1:12 New England FG Franklin 36 yards
 5:40 Chicago   FG Butler 28 yards
13:34 Chicago   FG Butler 24 yards
14:37 Chicago   TD Suhey 11-yard run
                         (Butler kick)
2nd Quarter
 7:36 Chicago   TD McMahon 2-yard
                         run (Butler kick)
15:00 Chicago   FG Butler 24 yards
3rd Quarter
 7:38 Chicago   TD McMahon 1-yard
                         run (Butler kick)
 8:44 Chicago   TD Phillips 28-yard in-
                         terception return
                         (Butler kick)
11:38 Chicago   TD Perry 1-yard run
                         (Butler kick)
4th Quarter
 1:46 New England TD Fryar 8-yard pass
                         from Grogan
                         (Franklin kick)
 9:24 Chicago   SA Waechter tackled
                         Grogan in end
                         zone

1987 (at Pasadena)
        NEW YORK GIANTS   7   2 17 13 39
        Denver Broncos   10   0   0 10 20

1st Quarter
 4:09 Denver   FG Karlis 48 yards
 9:33 New York TD Mowatt 6-yard pass
                      from Simms (Allegre
                      kick)
12:54 Denver   TD Elway 4-yard run
                      (Karlis kick)
2nd Quarter
12:14 New York SA Martin tackled Elway
                      in end zone
3rd Quarter
 4:52 New York TD Bavaro 13-yard pass
                      from Simms (Allegre
                      kick)
11:06 New York FG Allegre 21 yards

14:36 New York TD Morris 1-yard run
                      (Allegre kick)
4th Quarter
 4:04 New York TD McConkey 6-yard
                      pass from Simms
                      (Allegre kick)
 8:59 Denver   FG Karlis 28 yards
10:42 New York TD Anderson 2-yard run
                      (kick failed)
12:54 Denver   TD V. Johnson 47-yard
                      pass from Elway
                      (Karlis kick)

1988 (at San Diego)
WASHINGTON
REDSKINS   0 35 0 7 42
Denver Broncos   10 0 0 0 10

1st Quarter
 1:57 Denver   TD Nattiel 56-yard pass
                      from Elway (Karlis
                      kick)
 5:55 Denver   FG Karlis 24 yards
2nd Quarter
 0:53 Washington TD Sanders 80-yard
                      pass from Williams
                      (Haji-Sheikh kick)
 4:45 Washington TD Clark 27-yard pass
                      from Williams
                      (Haji-Sheikh kick)
 8:33 Washington TD Smith 58-yard run
                      (Haji-Sheikh kick)
11:14 Washington TD Sanders 50-yard
                      pass from Williams
                      (Haji-Sheikh kick)
13:56 Washington TD Didier 8-yard pass
                      from Williams
                      (Haji-Sheikh kick)

4th Quarter
 1:51 Washington TD Smith 4-yard run
                      (Haji-Sheikh kick)

1989 (at Miami)
SAN FRANCISCO 49ERS 3 0 3 14 20
Cincinnati Bengals   0 3 10 3 16

1st Quarter
11:46 San Francisco FG Cofer 41 yards
2nd Quarter
13:45 Cincinnati   FG Breech 34 yards
3rd Quarter
 9:21 Cincinnati   FG Breech 43 yards
14:10 San Francisco FG Cofer 32 yards
14:26 Cincinnati   TD Jennings 93-yard
                        kickoff return
                        (Breech kick)

4th Quarter
 0:57 San Francisco TD Rice 14-yard pass
                        from Montana
                        (Cofer kick)
11:40 Cincinnati   FG Breech 40 yards
14:26 San Francisco TD Taylor 10-yard
                        pass from Mon-
                        tana (Cofer kick)

1990 (at New Orleans)
SAN FRANCISCO 49ERS 13 14 14 14 55
Denver Broncos   3 0 7 0 10

1st Quarter
 4:54 San Francisco TD Rice 20-yard pass
                        from Montana
                        (Cofer kick)
 8:13 Denver   FG Treadwell 42
                        yards
14:57 San Francisco TD Jones 7-yard pass
                        from Montana
                        (kick failed)
2nd Quarter
 7:45 San Francisco TD Rathman 1-yard
                        run (Cofer kick)
14:26 San Francisco TD Rice 38-yard pass
                        from Montana
                        (Cofer kick)
3rd Quarter
 2:12 San Francisco TD Rice 28-yard pass
                        from Montana
                        (Cofer kick)
 5:16 San Francisco TD Taylor 35-yard
                        pass from Mon-
                        tana (Cofer kick)
 8:07 Denver   TD Elway 3-yard run
                        (Treadwell kick)
4th Quarter
 0:03 San Francisco TD Rathman 4-yard
                        run (Cofer kick)
 1:13 San Francisco TD Craig 1-yard run
                        (Cofer kick)

1991 (at Tampa)
NEW YORK GIANTS 3 7 7 3 20
Buffalo Bills   3 9 0 7 19

1st Quarter
 7:46 New York FG Bahr 28 yards
 9:09 Buffalo   FG Norwood 23 yards
2nd Quarter
 2:30 Buffalo   TD D. Smith 1-yard run
                      (Norwood kick)
 6:33 Buffalo   SA Hostetler sacked by B.
                      Smith in end zone
14:35 New York TD Baker 14-yard pass
                      from Hostetler (Bahr
                      kick)
3rd Quarter
 9:29 New York TD Anderson 1-yard run
                      (Bahr kick)
4th Quarter
 0:08 Buffalo   TD Thomas 31-yard run
                      (Norwood kick)
 7:40 New York FG Bahr 21 yards

1992 (at Minneapolis)
WASHINGTON REDSKINS 0 17 14 6 37
Buffalo Bills   0 0 10 14 24

2nd Quarter
 1:58 Washington FG Lohmiller 34 yards

5:06   Washington   TD   Byner 10-yard pass
                         from Rypien
                         (Lohmiller kick)
7:43   Washington   TD   Riggs 1-yard run
                         (Lohmiller kick)

3rd Quarter
0:16   Washington   TD   Riggs 2-yard run
                         (Lohmiller kick)
3:01   Buffalo   FG   Norwood 21 yards
9:02   Buffalo   TD   Thomas 1-yard run
                         (Norwood kick)
13:36 Washington   TD   Clark 30-yard pass
                         from Rypien
                         (Lohmiller kick)

4th Quarter
0:06   Washington   FG   Lohmiller 25 yards
3:24   Washington   FG   Lohmiller 39 yards
9:01   Buffalo   TD   Metzelaars 2-yard
                         pass from Kelly
                         (Norwood kick)
11:05 Buffalo   TD   Beebe 4-yard pass
                         from Kelly (Nor-
                         wood kick)

1993   (at Pasadena)
DALLAS COWBOYS   14 14 3 21 52
Buffalo Bills   7   3 7   0 17

1st Quarter
5:00   Buffalo   TD   Thomas 2-yard run
                      (Christie kick)
13:24 Dallas   TD   Novacek 23-yard pass
                      from Aikman (Elliott
                      kick)
13:39 Dallas   TD   J. Jones 2-yard fumble re-
                      turn (Elliott kick)
2nd Quarter
11:36 Buffalo   FG   Christie 21 yards
13:06 Dallas   TD   Irvin 19-yard pass from
                      Aikman (Elliott kick)
13:24 Dallas   TD   Irvin 18-yard pass from
                      Aikman (Elliott kick)
3rd Quarter
6:39   Dallas   FG   Elliott 20 yards
15:00 Buffalo   TD   Beebe 40-yard pass from
                      Reich (Christie kick)
4th Quarter
4:56   Dallas   TD   Harper 45-yard pass
                      from Aikman (Elliott
                      kick)
6:48   Dallas   TD   E. Smith 10-yard run (El-
                      liott kick)
7:29   Dallas   TD   Norton 9-yard fumble re-
                      turn (Elliott kick)

1994   (at Atlanta)
DALLAS COWBOYS   6   0 14 10 30
Buffalo Bills   3 10   0   0 13

1st Quarter
2:19   Dallas   FG   Murray 41 yards
4:41   Buffalo   FG   Christie 54 yards
11:05 Dallas   FG   Murray 24 yards

2nd Quarter
2:34   Buffalo   TD   Thomas 4-yard run
                      (Christie kick)
15:00 Buffalo   FG   Christie 28 yards
3rd Quarter
0:55   Dallas   TD   J. Washington 46-yard
                      fumble return (Murray
                      kick)
6:18   Dallas   TD   E. Smith 15-yard run
                      (Murray kick)
4th Quarter
5:10   Dallas   TD   E. Smith 1-yard run
                      (Murray kick)
12:10 Dallas   FG   Murray 20 yards

1995   (at Miami)
SAN FRANCISCO 49ERS   14 14 14   7 49
San Diego Chargers   7   3   8   8 26

1st Quarter
1:24   San Francisco   TD   Rice 44-yard pass
                            from Young
                            (Brien kick)
4:55   San Francisco   TD   Watters 51-yard
                            pass from Young
                            (Brien kick)
12:16 San Diego   TD   Mean 1-yard run
                            (Carney kick)
2nd Quarter
1:58   San Francisco   TD   Floyd 5-yard pass
                            from Young
                            (Brien kick)
10:16 San Francisco   TD   Watters 8-yard
                            pass from Young
                            (Brien kick)
13:16 San Diego   FG   Carney 31 yards
3rd Quarter
5:25   San Francisco   TD   Watters 9-yard
                            run (Brien kick)
11:42 San Francisco   TD   Rice 15-yard pass
                            from Young
                            (Brien kick)
11:59 San Diego   TD   Coleman 98-yard
                            kickoff return
                            (Seay pass from
                            Humphries)
4th Quarter
1:11   San Francisco   TD   Rice 7-yard pass
                            from Young
                            (Brien kick)
12:35 San Diego   TD   Martin 30-yard
                            pass from Hum-
                            phries (Pupunu
                            pass from Hum-
                            phries)

1996   (at Tempe)
DALLAS COWBOYS   10 3 7   7 27
Pittsburgh Steelers   0 7 0 10 17

1st Quarter
2:55   Dallas   FG   Boniol 42 yards
9:37   Dallas   TD   Novacek 3-yard pass

from Aikman (Boniol kick)

2nd Quarter
8:57   Dallas   FG   Boniol 35 yards
9:47   Pittsburgh TD   Thigpen 6-yard pass from O'Donnell (N. Johnson kick)

3rd Quarter
8:18   Dallas   TD   E. Smith 1-yard run (Boniol kick)

4th Quarter
3:40   Pittsburgh FG   N. Johnson 46 yards
8:24   Pittsburgh TD   Morris 1-yard run (N. Johnson kick)
11:17   Dallas   TD   E. Smith 4-yard run (Boniol kick)

SUPER BOWL HIGHLIGHTS

Super Bowl I—January 15, 1967, at Los Angeles (Green Bay Packers 35, Kansas City Chiefs 10): After years of feuding, after a signing war to get the services of professional football's best players, the first Super Bowl was the culmination of a peace treaty between the National Football League and the American Football League.

> *Football always has been reflective of modern life: violence punctuated by committee meetings.*
>   George Will, *Washington Post*, August 26, 1982
>
> *Football isn't a contact sport, it's a collision sport. Dancing is a contact sport.*
>   Duffy Daugherty

Although the media covering the event referred to the game as the Super Bowl, conservative league bosses did not think the name was dignified and it was officially called AFL versus NFL World Championship Game. Later the NFL would own the rights to the name "Super Bowl" and guard it like a jealous lover.

In its first year the game was not the "event" it was later to become. It was held in the cavernous 90,000-seat Los Angeles Coliseum—but only 61,946 fans showed up.

Despite the fact that many expected it to be a Super Blowout, it was a surprisingly competitive game—especially in the first half. Vince Lombardi's more experienced NFL champion Green Bay Packers were clearly the better team. But the upstarts from the newer AFL, the Kansas City Chiefs, put up a respectable battle.

"The Pack," led by quarterback Bart Starr, who completed sixteen of twenty-three passes for 250 yards and two touchdowns, never trailed in the contest.

Green Bay jumped out to a 7–0 lead in the first quarter. For trivia buffs, the first touchdown in Super Bowl history came 8 minutes, 56 seconds into the game as Starr threw a thirty-seven-yard pass to Max McGee.

Kansas City, led by quarterback Len Dawson, tied the game at 7–7 early in the second half on a seventeen-yard Dawson pass to Curtis McClinton. It would be the Chiefs' only touchdown of the day.

Green Bay, which led 14–10 at halftime, broke the game open with three second-half touchdowns—two on short runs by Elijah Pitts and the other on another Starr-to-McGee pass.

One of the quirkiest moments in Super Bowl history came as the second half opened. Both CBS and NBC (the networks with contracts with the NFL and the AFL) televised the first Super Bowl. When the second-half kickoff took place, NBC was still in a commercial break. So the officials simply nullified the play and had the kickoff take place all over.

Super Bowl III—January 12, 1969, at Miami (New York Jets 16, Baltimore Colts 7): If a man could walk on the moon, then the AFL could beat the NFL to win a Super Bowl—in 1969 both events occurred. And to sports fans, New York Jets quarterback Joe Namath's accomplishments were at least a close second to Neil Armstrong's.

In many ways 1969 defined the Super Bowl and helped turn it into a national event. The first two Super Bowls had been one-sided wins by Vince Lombardi's Green Bay Packers, and Super Bowl III, if anything, was expected to be worse.

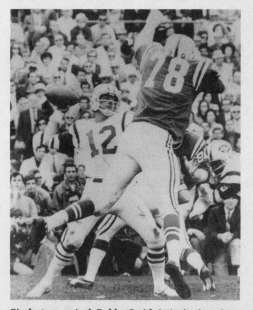

Six-foot seven-inch Bubba Smith (78) tries in vain to block a pass by Joe Namath during the 1969 Super Bowl.

The Baltimore Colts went through the regular season with an incredible 13–1 record, prompting some to call this Colt team one of the best ever. The Jets got through the season with an 11–3 mark, but the Jets were from the still lightly regarded AFL. The only person who seemed to believe the Jets had a chance was their young quarterback, appropriately nicknamed "Broadway" Joe Namath, who brashly guaranteed the underdogs would win. Namath made his prediction to reporters as he was lying near the pool at the Jets' Miami hotel.

In front of 75,389 fans, Namath lived up to his word. The Jets shocked the Colts and the football world, controlling the game and jumping out to a 7–0 halftime lead, then extending it to 16–0 early in the fourth quarter.

Broadway Joe led New York in the air, completing seventeen of twenty-eight passes for 206 yards, and Matt Snell led the way on the ground, rushing for 121 yards and the Jets' lone touchdown in the second quarter. All the other Jets points came from the sure-footed Jim Turner, who kicked three second-half field goals. The Colts never could get on track as their quarterback Earl Morrall threw three interceptions in the first half.

This was the first game where the NFL grudgingly used the term *Super Bowl*, and it turned into one of the most famous of them all.

Super Bowl V—January 17, 1971, at Miami (Baltimore Colts 16, Dallas Cowboys 13): The first four Super Bowls matched the champions of the NFL and the AFL. With the merger of the two leagues now complete, the AFL ceased to exist, and this was the first Super Bowl to match the champions of the newly designated and realigned National Football Conference and American Football Conference.

The Baltimore Colts were one of three old establishment NFL teams (along with the Pittsburgh Steelers and Cleveland Browns) that had moved over to the AFC, while the Dallas Cowboys were in the early stages of earning the title "America's Team."

Super Bowl V was not the most artistic game, with the two teams combining for eleven turnovers—the Colts lost the ball seven times and the Cowboys lost it four times. Still it turned out to be one of the most exciting Super Bowls ever—at least the ending was thrilling for the 79,204 at the Orange Bowl.

The Cowboys jumped out to a 6–0 lead early in the second quarter following two Mike Clark field goals from fourteen and thirty yards. The two teams then traded touchdowns and Dallas led at halftime 13–6.

That is the way it stood until the fourth quarter, when the Colts came back. First Baltimore tied the game—with 7:35 left in regulation, the Colts made it 13–13 on a two-yard run by Tom Nowatzke.

Appropriately, it was a turnover—number eleven—that led to the deciding score. With less than two minutes left, a pass by Dallas quarterback Craig Morton ended up in the arms of Colt linebacker Mike Curtis, who returned the ball to the Cowboy twenty-eight.

That set the stage for twenty-three-year-old field-goal kicker Jim O'Brien, known by his teammates as Lassie because of his long hair. With five seconds left, O'Brien kicked a thirty-two-yard field goal and the Colts became Super Bowl champions.

This Super Bowl marked the first time the NFL anointed the game with a Roman numeral—in this case V for five. It was also the first time that the Super Bowl trophy was given the name the Vince Lombardi Trophy, after the former Packer coach who had died earlier in the season.

Super Bowl X—January 18, 1976, at Miami (Pittsburgh Steelers 21, Dallas Cowboys 17): The Super Bowl celebrated its tenth year with one of the more exciting games and nearly a classic blunder as the Pittsburgh Steelers held on to beat the Dallas Cowboys 21–17.

Pittsburgh's triumph, in front of 80,187 spectators at the Orange Bowl, made the Steelers the third team ever to win back-to-back Super Bowls (after Green Bay and Miami).

The game highlighted the spectacular circus-like catches of Steeler wide receiver Lynn Swann, who grabbed four passes from quarterback Terry Bradshaw for 161 yards.

Dallas jumped out to a 7–0 lead less than five minutes into the game as Cowboy quarterback Roger Staubach threw a twenty-nine-yard pass to Drew Pearson.

But the Steelers came back later in the first quarter to tie the game 7–7, thanks in large part to Swann's first acrobatic feat of the day—a leaping thirty-two-yard fingertip grab of a Bradshaw pass. Swann's catch set up the eventual eight-yard touchdown pass from Bradshaw to Randy Grossman. Dallas moved back in front, 10–7, fifteen seconds into the second quarter on a thirty-six-yard field goal by Tony Fritsch.

That is the way it stood until the fourth quarter, when the Steelers took control. Pittsburgh scored four times in the final quarter—on a safety, two field goals, and a sixty-four-yard Bradshaw-to-Swann touchdown pass—to move in front 21–10.

The Bradshaw-Swann play was memorable. Bradshaw heaved the ball into the air as he was about to be knocked nearly unconscious and Swann made another leaping catch at the five-yard line before going into the end zone.

The Cowboys responded quickly as Staubach threw a thirty-four-yard pass to Percey Howard with less than two minutes left. But that only made it 21–17.

Next came a nearly grave error. With 1:22 left and the ball near midfield, the Steelers went for it on the fourth down rather than punt. Pittsburgh coaches later said they misunderstood a rule that stops the clock after the ball changes possession. The Cowboys got their chance but couldn't capitalize as Staubach threw an interception in the end zone on the game's final play.

Super Bowl XIII—January 15, 1979, at Miami (Pittsburgh Steelers 35, Dallas Cowboys 31): When the Pittsburgh Steelers met the Dallas Cowboys in Super Bowl XIII, it was truly a heavyweight matchup between professional football's top two teams.

The Cowboys were the defending champions, having beaten the Denver Broncos the year before in Super Bowl XII. The Steelers were winners in the ninth and tenth Super Bowls. That second triumph had come at the hands of the Cowboys in one of the most exciting Super Bowls ever.

Between them Dallas and Pittsburgh had won three of the last four Super Bowls. And to the victor would come the distinction of being the first three-time Super Bowl winner.

Each team had a powerful leader at quarterback—Terry Bradshaw for the Steelers and Roger Staubach for the Cowboys.

In the end it was Bradshaw and his Pittsburgh teammates who reigned supreme. Bradshaw had a game to remember, completing seventeen of thirty passes for 318 yards and throwing a Super Bowl record four touchdown passes. It overshadowed an otherwise excellent day for Staubach, who threw three touchdown passes of his own and should have had a fourth.

For the first three quarters the Steelers and Cowboys were like two great boxers throwing and taking hard punches and fighting back.

Pittsburgh struck first, five minutes into the game, with the first of Bradshaw's four scoring passes—a twenty-eight-yard toss to John Stallworth giving the Steelers a 7–0 lead. The Cowboys evened things at 7–7 on the final play of the first quarter as Staubach threw a thirty-nine-yard pass to Tony Hill. Dallas moved in front 14–7 early in the second quarter on a thirty-seven-yard fumble return by Mike Hegman, who literally ripped the ball away from Bradshaw.

This time it was Pittsburgh's turn to come back, and they did—two more touchdown passes by Bradshaw (one of them a seventy-five-yard toss to Stallworth) put the Steelers on top at halftime, 21–14.

Late in the third quarter came the play that might have turned the game around. Staubach had the Cowboys driving at the Steeler ten-yard line when he lobbed a pass to a wide-open Jackie Smith in the end zone. Smith dropped it and the Cowboys had to settle for a field goal, which cut the margin to 21–17.

Pittsburgh put the game away in the fourth quarter, scoring two touchdowns within nineteen seconds of each other, thanks to a fumble on the kickoff by Dallas.

Even with the score 35–17, the Cowboys didn't give up—Staubach connected on two late touchdown passes to make the score a close 35–31.

But it was the Steelers who became the first three-time Super Bowl champions.

Super Bowl XIV—January 20, 1980, at Pasadena (Pittsburgh Steelers 31, Los Angeles Rams 19): For the first time a Super Bowl had a hometown flavor as the Los Angeles Rams traveled twenty miles from the Los Angeles Coliseum to Pasadena's Rose Bowl.

But even with the hometown support and a record Super Bowl crowd of 103,985, the Rams became just another victim of the Steelers as Pittsburgh won its record fourth Super Bowl.

The Rams, who had the losingest regular season (9–7) of any previous Super Bowl team, made the Steelers fight hard, however. Los Angeles led after the first quarter, second quarter, and third quarter. When it counted, though, in the fourth quarter, Pittsburgh came back with two unanswered touchdowns. The game was thrilling, with the lead changing hands six times.

Again it was the Pittsburgh quarterback, Terry Bradshaw, who led the way as the Steelers captured their fourth title in just six years—the greatest Super Bowl run ever.

The Rams, who had been clear underdogs, played surprisingly tough, taking a 7–3 lead in the first quarter and holding a 13–10 advantage by halftime.

Pittsburgh came out of the locker room determined after the halftime break, and the Steelers quickly regained the lead, 17–13, on their opening drive as Bradshaw threw a forty-seven-yard pass to Lynn Swann. It was lead change number four.

Next it was the Rams' turn to respond, and they did, less than two minutes later taking a 19–13 lead as running back Lawrence McCutcheon threw an option pass to Ron Smith.

So it stood entering the fourth quarter. Then Bradshaw took over—he threw a seventy-three-yard touchdown bomb to John Stallworth to put Pittsburgh on top for good, 24–19. It was Bradshaw's ninth Super Bowl touchdown pass and the last in his remarkable career.

Los Angeles tried to come back yet again but Steeler Jack Lambert intercepted a pass at the Pittsburgh fourteen with just five minutes left to play. The Steelers added another touchdown to put the game out of reach.

Super Bowl XVII—January 30, 1983, at Pasadena (Washington Redskins 27, Miami Dolphins 17): The 1982 regular season was plagued by the NFL's first players strike. For seven weeks there was no professional football.

The dispute resulted in a shortened season (nine games instead of sixteen) but an additional round of playoff games—and the season ended with one of the more memorable Super Bowls.

The Redskins put together an unusual cast of characters—the offensive line was nicknamed the Hogs and the corps of wide receivers was nicknamed the Fun Bunch. But clearly the biggest, strangest, and most bizarre character was the Redskins' star running back, John Riggins. Riggins was known to do strange things—he once painted his toenails green, one year he got a Mohawk haircut, another year he shaved his hair off completely. Perhaps Riggins's most bizarre moment came years later when he was sitting, drunk, at a black-tie Washington dinner at a table with U.S. Supreme Court Justice Sandra Day O'Connor. Riggins looked at Justice O'Connor and declared, "Loosen up, Sandy baby!"

In Super Bowl XVII it was Riggins who loosened up the Miami defense as he became a workhorse, carrying the ball thirty-eight times for 166 yards and a memorable touchdown that won the game for the Redskins.

The game itself was close almost from start to finish. The Dolphins scored first on a seventy-six-yard pass from quarterback David Woodley to Jimmy Cefalo, to take a 7–0 lead. After the two traded field goals, the Skins tied the game, 10–10, with two minutes left in the first half on Joe Theismann's four-yard toss to Alvin Garrett.

The tie didn't last long—on the ensuing kickoff Miami's Fulton Walker took it all the way back to give the Dolphins a 17–10 halftime lead. Washington cut the lead to 17–13 with a third-quarter Mike Moseley field goal.

The play of the game took place nearly five minutes into the fourth quarter—again John Riggins played the central role. Washington had the ball, fourth down and one yard to go, at the Miami forty-three-yard line. The Redskins decided to go for the first down and handed the ball off to Riggins, who moved to his left and was never stopped. He scampered all the way into the end zone in what proved to be the winning score.

After the game Riggins declared, "Reagan may be President, but for today, I am King!"

Super Bowl XVIII—January 22, 1984, at Tampa (Los Angeles Raiders 38, Washington Redskins 9): The Washington Redskins entered Super Bowl XVIII as the defending champions determined to become only the fourth team to win back-to-back Super Bowl titles.

The Skins entered the game with eleven straight victories and thirty-one triumphs in their last thirty-four games. When the Redskins left the field, they had suffered one of the most one-sided Super Bowl defeats, as the maverick Los Angeles Raiders easily beat the defending champs 38–9.

The player of the game was Los Angeles running back Marcus Allen, who came through with a magical performance, gaining 191 yards and scoring two touchdowns, including one on a spectacular seventy-four-yard run.

Los Angeles dominated every aspect of the game in front of 72,920 fans at Tampa Stadium. Whether it was offense, defense, or special teams, the Silver and Black of the Raiders was in charge.

The domination began in the first quarter as the Raiders' Derrick Jensen blocked a Washington punt at the thirty-yard line, then chased the ball and fell onto it in the end zone. Los Angeles made it 14–0 in the second quarter on a twelve-yard pass from Jim Plunkett to Cliff Branch.

After the Redskins made it 14–3, Los Angeles struck again dramatically. The special-team unit and the offensive unit had already scored once—now it was time for the defense. With seven seconds left in the half and the ball on the Redskin five, Washington quarterback Joe Theismann decided to throw the ball. It turned out to be a mistake. Los Angeles defensive back Jack Squirek, remembering a similar call by Theismann during the regular season, intercepted the pass and ran it into the end zone to give the Raiders a 21–3 halftime advantage.

The third quarter belonged to Allen. After Washington cut the margin to 21–9, Allen responded with a five-yard touchdown to make it 28–9.

Then, as time expired in the quarter, came Allen's magical touchdown. With the ball on the Los Angeles twenty-six-yard line, Allen ran to the left and found no room. With nowhere to go, he turned completely around, making a U-turn, and, finding an opening, ran seventy-four yards. It was Los Angeles 35, Washington 9.

"You always dream of something like this happening. I never stopped to think about what to do. I just let the instincts take over," Allen said later.

Los Angeles added a field goal in the fourth quarter.

Super Bowl XXIII—January 22, 1989, at Miami (San Francisco 49ers 20, Cincinnati 16): Joe Montana had led the San Francisco 49ers to two previous Super Bowl victories—in 1982 against the Cincinnati Bengals in Super Bowl XVI and in 1985 against the Miami Dolphins in Super Bowl XIX. This triumph in Super Bowl XXIII, once more against the Bengals, would add another chapter to the legendary career of quarterback Montana as he put together a game-winning last-minute drive.

Despite the fact that San Francisco was a huge favorite, the Bengals matched them play for play and score for score in front of a crowd of 75,129 at Joe Robbie Stadium.

The first half was a battle of field goals. San Francisco's Mike Cofer kicked a forty-one-yard field goal in the first quarter to take a 3–0 lead, but Cincinnati's Jim Breech responded in the second quarter with a thirty-four-yarder to even the game 3–3 at halftime.

In the third quarter the two teams again exchanged field goals, first the Bengals, then the 49ers, to make it 6–6. Then, late in the third quarter and early in the fourth quarter, San Francisco and Cincinnati exchanged touchdowns to even the contest again at 13–13.

With three minutes and twenty seconds left in the game, the underdog and unheralded Bengals moved on top 16–13 on Breech's forty-yard field goal, his third of the game. That set the stage for Super Joe, and he lived up to his fans' expectations.

A penalty on the kickoff put the ball on the San Francisco eight-yard line with just 3:10 left. It was plenty of time for Montana and he choreographed a classic last-minute drive. Over the next two and a half minutes the 49ers drove ninety-two yards in eleven plays. Eight of the plays were Montana pass completions, and number eight was the game-winning touchdown—a 10-yard pass to John Taylor.

For the entire game Montana completed twenty-three of thirty-six passes for 357 yards, including eleven passes to his favorite receiver, Jerry Rice, who was named the game's Most Valuable Player.

After the game Cincinnati receiver Chris Collingsworth said, "Joe Montana is not human. I don't want to call him a God, but he's definitely somewhere in between."

Super Bowl XXV—January 27, 1991, at Tampa (New York Giants 20, Buffalo Bills 19): Under the shadow of the Persian Gulf War, under tight security fit for a president or a king, Super Bowl XXV may have been the greatest of them all as the New York Giants and the Buffalo Bills battled until the final seconds.

This game even had some international intrigue. U.S. military officials in Saudi Arabia felt Iraq's Saddam Hussein might launch a Scud missile attack during the game to disrupt the game's television coverage.

Because of fears of a terrorist attack, all the 73,813 fans at Tampa Stadium had to go through security checks. A six-foot chain-link fence was built around the stadium, and a concrete barrier was built around the fence. In the end there were no terrorist attacks and no missile launches—only a great game and an even greater ending.

The first quarter saw the Giants and the Bills trade field goals, making it 3–3 after the first fifteen minutes.

In the second quarter Buffalo moved on top 12–3, scoring twice in the first seven minutes—first on a one-yard touchdown run by Don Smith, then on a safety by Bruce Smith, who caught New York's Jeff Hostetler in the end zone. Just before the first half ended, with twenty-five seconds left, the Giants fought back with a critical touchdown on a fourteen-yard toss from Hostetler to Stephen Baker, to cut the Buffalo margin to 12–10.

In the third quarter New York moved on top, 17–12, on a one-yard run by Ottis Anderson, culminating a fourteen-play drive that consumed more than nine minutes.

On the first play of the fourth quarter the Bills moved on top again, 19–17, as Buffalo running back Thurman Thomas ran thirty-one yards for a touchdown. In this back-and-forth contest, it was next the Giants' turn to stage a comeback, and they did—taking a 20–19 lead on a field goal with seven minutes left in the game.

That is the way the score stood when the Bills took over at their own ten-yard line with 2:16 left in the game. Buffalo began to move the ball and soon the Bills were in Giants territory. The drive stalled and with time running out, the Bills turned the game over to field-goal kicker Scott Norwood. With eight seconds left, Norwood came into the game for a make-or-break forty-seven-yard field-goal try.

Norwood sent the ball sailing toward the goal posts. The kick had plenty of power but the ball sailed just slightly to the right, to give the Giants Super Bowl XXV.

—S.F.

HOCKEY

STANLEY CUP FINALS

					Wins
1914	TORONTO BLUESHIRTS	5*	6*	2*	3
	Victoria Aristocrats	2	5	1	0
1915	VANCOUVER MILLIONAIRES	6*	8*	12*	3
	Ottawa Senators	2	3	3	0

*Home team   OT = overtime

Year	Team	1	2	3	4	5	6	7	
1916	MONTREAL CANADIENS	0*	2*	6*	5*	2*			3
	Portland Rosebuds	2	1	3	6	1			2
1917	SEATTLE METROPOLITANS	4*	6*	4*	9*				3
	Montreal Canadiens	8	1	1	1				1
1918	TORONTO ARENAS	5*	4*	6*	1*	2*			3
	Vancouver Millionaires	3	6	3	8	1			2
1919	Finals halted because of influenza epidemic								
1920	OTTAWA SENATORS	3*	3*	1*	2†	6†			3
	Seattle Metropolitan	2	0	3	5	1			2
	† played in Toronto								
1921	OTTAWA SENATORS	1	4	3	2	2			3
	Vancouver Millionaires	2*	3*	2*	3*	1*			2
1922	TORONTO ST. PATS	3*	2*	0*	6*	5*			3
	Vancouver Millionaires	4	1(OT)	3	0	1			2
1923	OTTAWA SENATORS	2†	1†						2
	Edmonton Eskimos	1(OT)	0						0
	† played in Vancouver								
1924	MONTREAL CANADIENS	6*	3						2
	Calgary Tigers	1	0†						0
	† played in Ottawa								
1925	VICTORIA COUGARS	5*	3*	2*	6*				3
	Montreal Canadiens	2	1	4	1				1
1926	MONTREAL MAROONS	3*	3*	2*	2*				3
	Victoria Cougars	0	0	3	0				1
1927	OTTAWA SENATORS	0	3	1	3				2
	Boston Bruins	0*(OT)	1*	1*(OT)	1*				0
1928	NEW YORK RANGERS	0	2	1	1	2			3
	Montreal Maroons	2*	1*(OT)	2*	0*	1*			2
1929	BOSTON BRUINS	2*	2						2
	New York Rangers	0	1*						0
1930	MONTREAL CANADIENS	3	4						2
	Boston Bruins	0*	3*						0
1931	MONTREAL CANADIENS	2	1	2*	4*	2*			3
	Chicago Black Hawks	1*	2*(OT)	3(OT)	2	0			2
1932	TORONTO MAPLE LEAFS	6	6	6*					3
	New York Rangers	4*	2†	4					0
	† played in Boston								
1933	NEW YORK RANGERS	5*	3	2	1				3
	Toronto Maple Leafs	1	1*	3*	0*(OT)				1
1934	CHICAGO BLACK HAWKS	2	4	2*	1*				3
	Detroit Red Wings	1*(OT)	1*	5	0(2OT)				1
1935	MONTREAL MAROONS	3	3	4*					3
	Toronto Maple Leafs	2*	1*	1					0
1936	DETROIT RED WINGS	3*	9*	3	3				3
	Toronto Maple Leafs	1	4	4*(OT)	2*				1
1937	DETROIT RED WINGS	1	4*	0*	1*	3*			3
	New York Rangers	5*	2	1	0	0			2
1938	CHICAGO BLACK HAWKS	3	1	2*	4*				3
	Toronto Maple Leafs	1*	5*	1	1				1
1939	BOSTON BRUINS	2*	2*	3	2	3*			4
	Toronto Maple Leafs	1	3(OT)	1*	0*	1			1
1940	NEW YORK RANGERS	2*	6*	1	0	2	3		4
	Toronto Maple Leafs	1(OT)	2	2*	3*	1*(OT)	2*(OT)		2
1941	BOSTON BRUINS	3*	2*	4	3				4
	Detroit Red Wings	2	1	2*	1*				0
1942	TORONTO MAPLE LEAFS	2*	2*	2	4	9*	3	3*	4
	Detroit Red Wings	3	4	5*	3*	3	0*	1	3
1943	DETROIT RED WINGS	6*	4*	4	2				4
	Boston Bruins	2	3	0*	0*				0
1944	MONTREAL CANADIENS	5*	3	3	5*				4
	Chicago Black Hawks	1	1*	2*	4				0
1945	TORONTO MAPLE LEAFS	1	2	1*	3*	0	0*	2	4
	Detroit Red Wings	0*	0*	0	5	2*	1(OT)	1*	3

Year	Team								W
1946	MONTREAL CANADIENS	4*	3*	4	2	6*			4
	Boston Bruins	3(OT)	2(OT)	2*	3*(OT)	3			1
1947	TORONTO MAPLE LEAFS	0	4	4*	2*	1	2*		4
	Montreal Canadiens	6*	0*	2	1	3*	1		2
1948	TORONTO MAPLE LEAFS	5*	4*	2	7				4
	Detroit Red Wings	3	2	0*	2*				0
1949	TORONTO MAPLE LEAFS	3	3	3*	3*				4
	Detroit Red Wings	2*(OT)	1*	1	1				0
1950	DETROIT RED WINGS	4*	1	4	3*	1*	5*	4*	4
	New York Rangers	1	3†	0†	4(OT)	2(OT)	4	3(2OT)	3
	† played in Toronto								
1951	TORONTO MAPLE LEAFS	3*	2*	2	3	3*			4
	Montreal Canadiens	2(OT)	3(OT)	1*(OT)	2*(OT)	2(OT)			1
1952	DETROIT RED WINGS	3	2	3*	3*				4
	Montreal Canadiens	1*	1*	0	0				0
1953	MONTREAL CANADIENS	4*	1*	3	7	1*			4
	Boston Bruins	2	4	0*	3*	0(OT)			1
1954	DETROIT RED WINGS	3*	1*	5	2	0*	1	2*	4
	Montreal Canadiens	1	3	2*	0*	1	4*	1(OT)	3
1955	DETROIT RED WINGS	4*	7*	2	3	5*	3	3*	4
	Montreal Canadiens	2	1	4*	5*	1	6*	1	3
1956	MONTREAL CANADIENS	6*	5*	1	3	3*			4
	Detroit Red Wings	4	1	3*	0*	1			1
1957	MONTREAL CANADIENS	5*	1*	4	0	5*			4
	Boston Bruins	1	0	2*	2*	1			1
1958	MONTREAL CANADIENS	2*	2*	3	1	3*	5		4
	Boston Bruins	1	5	0*	3*	2(OT)	3*		2
1959	MONTREAL CANADIENS	5*	3*	2	3	5*			4
	Toronto Maple Leafs	3	1	3*	2*	3			1
1960	MONTREAL CANADIENS	4*	2*	5	4				4
	Toronto Maple Leafs	2	1	2*	0*				0
1961	CHICAGO BLACK HAWKS	3*	1	3*	1	6*	5		4
	Detroit Red Wings	2	3*	1	2*	3	1*		2
1962	TORONTO MAPLE LEAFS	4*	3*	0	1	8*	2		4
	Chicago Black Hawks	1	2	3*	4*	4	1*		2
1963	TORONTO MAPLE LEAFS	4*	4*	2	4	3*			4
	Detroit Red Wings	2	2	3*	2*	1			1
1964	TORONTO MAPLE LEAFS	3*	3*	3	4	1*	4	4*	4
	Detroit Red Wings	2	4(OT)	4*	2*	2	3*(OT)	0	3
1965	MONTREAL CANADIENS	3*	2*	1	1	6*	1	4*	4
	Chicago Black Hawks	2	0	3*	5*	0	2*	0	3
1966	MONTREAL CANADIENS	2*	2*	4	2	5*	3		4
	Detroit Red Wings	3	5	2*	1*	1	2*(OT)		2
1967	TORONTO MAPLE LEAFS	2	3	3*	2	4	3*		4
	Montreal Canadiens	6*	0*	2(2OT)	6	1*	1		2
1968	MONTREAL CANADIENS	3	1	4*	3*				4
	St. Louis Blues	2*(OT)	0*	3(OT)	2				0
1969	MONTREAL CANADIENS	3*	3*	4	2				4
	St. Louis Blues	1	1	0*	1*				0
1970	BOSTON BRUINS	6	6	4*	4*				4
	St. Louis Blues	1*	2*	1	3(OT)				0
1971	MONTREAL CANADIENS	1	3	4*	5*	0	4*	3	4
	Chicago Black Hawks	2*(2OT)	5*	2	2	2*	3	2*	3
1972	BOSTON BRUINS	6*	2*	2	3	2*	3		4
	New York Rangers	5	1	5*	2*	3	0*		2
1973	MONTREAL CANADIENS	8*	4*	4	4	7*	6		4
	Chicago Black Hawks	3	1	7*	0*	8	4*		2
1974	PHILADELPHIA FLYERS	2	3	4*	4*	1	1*		4
	Boston Bruins	3*	2*(OT)	1	2	5*	0		2
1975	PHILADELPHIA FLYERS	4*	2*	4	2	5*	2		4
	Buffalo Sabres	1	1	5*(OT)	4*	1	0*		2
1976	MONTREAL CANADIENS	4*	2*	3	5				4
	Philadelphia Flyers	3	1	2*	3*				0

Year	Team	G1	G2	G3	G4	G5	G6	G7	Series
1977	MONTREAL CANADIENS	7*	3*	4	2				4
	Boston Bruins	3	0	2*	1*(OT)				0
1978	MONTREAL CANADIENS	4*	3*	0	3	4*	4		4
	Boston Bruins	1	2(OT)	4*	4*(OT)	1	1*		2
1979	MONTREAL CANADIENS	1*	6*	4	4	4*			4
	New York Rangers	4	2	1*	3*(OT)	1			1
1980	NEW YORK ISLANDERS	4	3	6*	5*	3	5*		4
	Philadelphia Flyers	3*(OT)	8*	2	2	6*	4(OT)		2
1981	NEW YORK ISLANDERS	6*	6*	7	2	5*			4
	Minnesota North Stars	3	3	5*	4*	1			1
1982	NEW YORK ISLANDERS	6*	6*	3	3				4
	Vancouver Canucks	5(OT)	4	0*	1*				0
1983	NEW YORK ISLANDERS	2	6	5*	4*				4
	Edmonton Oilers	0*	3*	1	2				0
1984	EDMONTON OILERS	1	1	7*	7*	5*			4
	New York Islanders	0*	6*	2	2	2			1
1985	EDMONTON OILERS	1	3	4*	5*	8*			4
	Philadelphia Flyers	4*	1*	3	3	3			1
1986	MONTREAL CANADIENS	3	3	5*	1*	4			4
	Calgary Flames	5*	2*(OT)	3	0	3*			1
1987	EDMONTON OILERS	4*	3*	3	4	3*	2	3*	4
	Philadelphia Flyers	3	2(OT)	5*	1*	4	3*	1	3
1988	EDMONTON OILERS	2*	4*	6	3‡	6*			4
	Boston Bruins	1	2	3*	3*‡	3			0
	‡Suspended: power failure								
1989	CALGARY FLAMES	3*	2*	3	4	3*	4		4
	Montreal Canadiens	2	4	4*	2*	2	2*		2
1990	EDMONTON OILERS	3	7	1*	5*	4			4
	Boston Bruins	2*(3OT)	2*	2	1	1*			1
1991	PITTSBURGH PENGUINS	4*	4*	1	5	6*	8		4
	Minnesota North Stars	5	1	3*	3*	4	0*		2
1992	PITTSBURGH PENGUINS	5*	3*	1	6				4
	Chicago Black Hawks	4	1	0*	5*				0
1993	MONTREAL CANADIENS	1*	3*	4	3	4*			4
	Los Angeles Kings	4	2(OT)	3*(OT)	2*(OT)	1			1
1994	NEW YORK RANGERS	2*	3*	5	4	3*	1	3*	4
	Vancouver Canucks	3(OT)	1	1*	2*	6	4*	2	3
1995	NEW JERSEY DEVILS	2	4	5*	5*				4
	Detroit Red Wings	1*	2*	2	2				0
1996	COLORADO AVALANCHE	3*	8*	3	1				4
	Florida Panthers	1	1	2*	0*(3OT)				0

STANLEY CUP HIGHLIGHTS

1921: Hockey's transition from a brawling, regional minor league sport into a truly national game was marked by the 1921 finals, which pitted the National Hockey League champion Ottawa Senators against the Pacific Coast Hockey Association champs, the Vancouver Millionaires. A sellout crowd of 11,000—at the time the largest in the world to see a hockey game—attended game one at Vancouver's Denman Arena, with another 2,000 left standing outside, and the five-game series drew a combined attendance of 51,000.

Ottawa took the finals, three games to two, thereby becoming the first back-to-back Stanley Cup champion. But it wasn't easy. The Senators won all three games by one goal, including the deciding fifth game, which still ranks among the most tense and savage of all time.

Vancouver struck first, capturing game one 3–1, but Ottawa rallied to take the next two games. Wily veteran Jack Darragh led four different scorers in a 4–3 win in game two, then notched the game winner as the Senators took game three 3–2. The Millionaires collected themselves in time to secure a 3–2 win in game four, a rugged, penalty-filled affair that set up the winner-take-all game five.

Both Ottawa and Vancouver came out swinging in the final—literally. Senators defensemen Eddie Gerard and Sprague Cleghorn—a World War I veteran who was once arrested for beating his wife with a crutch—combined for ten penalties, meaning Ottawa played a man short for much of the game. Gerard and Cleghorn were eventually ejected for fighting with Vancouver's Bun Cook and given twenty-five-dollar fines. Lost amid the melee was Ottawa's 2–1 victory, giving coach Peter Green and the NHL their second straight Stanley Cup.

1942: To call the 1942 Stanley Cup finals a mismatch was to state the obvious. Toronto had reached five of the last seven championship rounds, then righted a so-so regular season by upsetting the first-place New York Rangers to reach the finals again. Detroit, meanwhile, came in fifth that year, then struggled to get by Montreal and Boston in the playoffs.

But World War II had done crazy things to the talent pool and the consistency of the NHL, and the Stanley Cup finals were no exception. The Red Wings reeled off three straight victories to come within one game of sweeping the finals, spurring Toronto to mount the greatest comeback in hockey history. In fact, the Maple Leafs are the only team in any professional sport ever to rally from a three-game deficit.

The comeback began in game four in Detroit, when coach Hap Day addressed his stunned Leafs with the immortal words, "We're taking the series one game at a time." That said, future Hall-of-Famer Syl Apps responded by scoring the tying goal and setting up teammate Nick Metz for the game winner in the 4–3 victory. Detroit coach "Jolly" Jack Adams was so incensed at his team's blowing a 2–0 lead that he charged onto the ice and punched referee Mel Harwood and was promptly suspended for the rest of the series.

Back home in Maple Leaf Gardens for game five, Toronto ripped off seven goals in the first two periods and cruised to a 9–3 win as Don Metz notched three goals, Apps a pair. Game six also went to Toronto (3–0), although the match is best remembered for featuring no penalties after an NHL front office edict to cut out the rough stuff.

A crowd of 16,218 squeezed into Maple Leaf Gardens for the deciding seventh game. Detroit took an early lead on a goal by Syd Howe, but Sweeney Schriner tied it up and Toronto goalkeeper Turk Broda held Detroit at bay the rest of the way. A goal by Peter Langelle and Schriner's second of the night were enough to give the Maple Leafs a 3–1 win.

1945: Although Toronto nearly squandered a three-games-to-none lead—giving Detroit a shot at either revenge or repeating the history of 1942—the Maple Leafs eventually held on. But this series said more about the remarkable players born of the World War II era than about the NHL finals.

Frank McCool was a minor league goaltender of modest talent when he was summoned to replace the legendary Turk Broda as the Toronto Maple Leafs' starter for the 1944–45 season. Despite ulcers that often left him doubled over in pain, McCool played all fifty games that season for Toronto, posting a 3.22 goals-against average and winning the Calder Award as the NHL's rookie of the year. But it was in the postseason play that McCool truly shone.

First, Toronto upset the Montreal Canadiens in six games as McCool outdueled Bill Durnan, the league's top goalie. Then came the Stanley Cup finals, where McCool posted three straight shutouts against Detroit—part of a finals-record 193 straight scoreless minutes that still stands—to give the Maple Leafs a seemingly insurmountable three-games-to-none lead.

But the Red Wings rallied, taking the next three games behind their hot rookie goaltender, Harry Lumley. Game seven was played at Detroit's Olympic Arena, where Babe Pratt broke a 1–1 tie with a power-play goal late in the third period and McCool made several key saves to give the Maple Leafs the Stanley Cup.

McCool's celebrity was short lived, however. He demanded a $500 pay raise for the 1945–46 season and threatened to sit out if he didn't get it. But with the war over and Broda back with the Maple Leafs—and the team off to a horrendous 3–10 start—McCool quickly fell from favor and he retired later that year.

1950: The New York Rangers ended years of mediocrity by reaching the Stanley Cup finals in 1950, but they were given little chance against Detroit, a team appearing in its third straight finals. The fact that the Rangers had been ousted from their home ice at Madison Square Garden by the Ringling Brothers' Circus during the series—meaning two crucial "home" games would have to be played in Toronto's Maple Leaf Gardens, with the rest at Detroit's Olympia Arena—only made matters worse. (Amazingly, all tickets to the two games in Toronto were gone forty-five minutes after they went on sale, which underscores that city's reputation as a serious hockey town.)

Still, New York's valiant performance in the 1950 finals was remarkable. With the Red Wings playing without superstar Gordie Howe, who suffered a concussion and nearly died as a result of a brutal check against Toronto in the semifinals, the Rangers won three of the first five games and threatened to capture their first Stanley Cup in a decade in game six.

But Detroit, led by winger Ted Lindsay, rallied for a 6–5 win, then twice overcame deficits in game seven to tie the game at 3–3 on an "impossible" shot by Jim McFadden that slipped past New York goalie Chuck Rayner from a sharp angle. Forced to play overtime to decide the Stanley Cup champion, the Rangers nearly won in the first sudden-death period as a shot by Nick Mickoski beat Harry Lumley but hit the post.

Detroit finally put New York away in the second overtime period when Pete Babando, a little-known benchwarmer from Braeburn, Pennsylvania, collected the puck from a face-off in the New York zone and whistled a backhander through a crowd for the winning goal, 4–3. Devastated, the Rangers retreated to their locker room, where Red Wing captain Sid Abel visited them. Looking around the room, he asked, "Don't you guys know when to quit?"

1951: Called the Sudden Death Series because all five games went into overtime, the 1951 Stanley Cup finals were aptly named for another, more grisly reason: Maple Leafs defenseman "Bashing Bill" Barilko—whose incredible, game-winning goal in game five gave Toronto the cup—died in an airplane crash shortly after the playoffs.

Toronto had won twelve of the fourteen games against Montreal during the regular season and stayed true to form when Sid Smith poked in the game winner in overtime in game one. But the Canadiens tied the series when Maurice Richard scored in sudden death to win game two.

The Maple Leafs won the next two games to take a three-games-to-one lead into game five. Yet Toronto needed the heart-stopping goal from Tod Sloan—his second of the game—with thirty-two seconds left in regulation to force another overtime. There, Barilko, a player Montreal manager Frank Selke said he hated so much that he wanted him on his team, drove a slapshot past goaltender Gerry McNeil at 2:53 of sudden death, giving the Maple Leafs their fourth Stanley Cup in five years.

But Toronto's joy was cut short. Barilko, who became a national hero in Canada, embarked on a camping trip several weeks later in northern Ontario with a friend who piloted a small plane. The plane crashed in dense forest and, despite a massive search, was given up for lost. Years later the wreckage of the plane was found with both bodies still inside.

1954: When Detroit and Montreal met in the 1954 Stanley Cup finals, it was the first of three straight championship bouts between the dynasties. But the 1954 series—and in particular game seven—is all anybody really remembers.

Both teams were in their golden eras. The Red Wings were led by future Hall of Famers such as Gordie Howe, Ted Lindsay, and Alex Delvecchio, and were midway through an incredible seven straight regular-season titles. Montreal, meanwhile, featured colorful superstars such as Maurice "Rocket" Richard, Jean Beliveau, and Bernie "Boom Boom" Geoffrion, and had just brought up goaltender Jacques Plante, who invented the goalie mask en route to making the Hall of Fame.

With the series tied at three games apiece, Detroit and Montreal skated to a 1–1 tie in regulation in game seven. With almost four and a half minutes gone in overtime, Detroit's Tony Leswick fired an innocent shot at Montreal goalie Gerry McNeil, who rose up to make the save. But Canadiens defenseman Doug Harvey reached up to deflect the shot, allowing the puck to skip off his glove and fly past McNeil and into the net, giving the Red Wings an improbable 2–1 win.

The result did more than decide the NHL champion—it also touched off more than a decade of bad blood between the clubs. The Canadiens did not congratulate Detroit after the win, in part because general manager Frank Selke and coach Dick Irvin supposedly frowned on athletes who "jumped over tennis nets." Yet Montreal—beaten by the Red Wings in seven games in the 1955 finals—had to wait until the 1956 Stanley Cup to get revenge.

1971: Montreal's victory in the 1971 Stanley Cup finals, the club's third in four years, was also its most bizarre. For starters, coach Al MacNeil was hated by his players, and team captain Henri Richard called him "one of the worst" coaches he'd ever played for. MacNeil quit less than a month after the Canadiens' triumph.

The team was also in the grips of a difficult transition. Legendary players such as Jean Beliveau and John Ferguson were fading fast, and Montreal failed even to make the playoffs in 1970. The Canadiens went through three coaches in four seasons. And then there was goalie Ken Dryden, a lanky Cornell University graduate who had exactly six NHL games under his belt when the 1971 playoffs began.

But Montreal rallied mightily around Dryden's spectacular play, bumping off the defending champion Bruins in the preliminaries before extending Chicago to seven games in the finals. Blessed with a red-hot goaltender of their own in Tony Esposito, the Black Hawks nursed a 2–0 lead midway through game seven at Chicago Stadium when Montreal stirred to life.

First, Jacques Lemaire beat Esposito with a long, sinking shot, then Richard tied the score with the forty-ninth postseason goal of his career. Finally, the man they called "Pocket Rocket"—in deference to his elder brother, Maurice "Rocket" Richard—smashed in the game winner, giving Montreal another classic win.

1994: According to hockey lore, the New York Rangers were cursed—not once, but twice—shortly after capturing the 1940 Stanley Cup. First, team president General John Reed Kilpatrick angered the hockey gods in 1941 when he celebrated paying off the mortgage on Madison Square Garden by burning the papers in the Stanley Cup. Second, the Garden's original hockey tenants, the New York Americans, folded in 1942, and embittered coach and general manager Red Dutton blamed the Rangers, vowing they'd never win the cup in his lifetime.

Dutton died in 1987, which meant the Rangers' incredible 1994 Stanley Cup triumph was actually overdue. But New Yorkers took it anyway, anxious to end a fifty-three-year drought that had become one of the most daunting in sports.

Wayne Gretzky in action during the 1985 NHL playoffs.

Led by team captain Mark Messier, one of six players recruited from the Edmonton Oilers' glory team of the mid-1980s, the Rangers staved off elimination in the semifinals to take a three-games-to-one lead over Vancouver in the finals. But the Rangers faltered (shades of the curse, perhaps?), dropping the next two games to force a winner-take-all seventh game in Madison Square Garden. To make matters worse, word leaked out prior to the game that Rangers coach Mike Keenan planned to join the Detroit Red Wings after the season, only adding to the confusion and pressure. (Keenan did leave, although his Detroit contract was ruled invalid, allowing him to sign with the St. Louis Blues instead.)

Messier, who rescued New York throughout the playoffs, stepped up one last time, scoring the winning goal in the heart-stopping 3–2 win that gave the Rangers their first Stanley Cup title since before World War II. "I've never experienced anything like the last two months," Messier said. "I wasn't saying much, but in my own mind, I was saying: 'This is absolutely incredible.' "

—D.W.C.

QUOTEBOOK: SPORTS

Sports develops not character, but characters.
　　　　Anonymous, in James A. Michener's *Sports in America*, 1976

Float like a butterfly,
Sting like a bee,
Your hands can't hit
What your eyes can't see!
　　　　Drew "Bundini" Brown

It's just a job. Grass grows, birds fly, waves pound the sand. I beat people up.
　　　　Muhammad Ali, *New York Times*, April 6, 1977

For when the One Great Scorer comes to mark
*　against your name,*
He writes—not that you won or lost—but how
*　you played the Game.*
　　　　Grantland Rice, "Alumnus Football," 1930

Playing a cheater is the real test of sportsmanship.
　　　　Jack Barnaby, 1979

No country which has cricket as one of its national games has yet gone Communist.
　　　　Lord Wyatt, 1979

Chapter 18

RELIGION

MAJOR WORLD RELIGIONS

ANIMISM

Background and Beliefs: Derived from the Latin word *animus*, meaning "spirit," animism is the belief that all beings, objects, and natural phenomena have souls or spirits. Animism is considered by many to be the original religion and is still widespread today, particularly in Africa, South America, and parts of Asia. Indeed, traces of Animism can be found in many of the "advanced" religions of the modern world. Beliefs and forms of worship vary widely from place to place and tribe to tribe.

Twentieth-Century History: E. B. Taylor, who coined the term *animism* in his book *Primitive Culture*, died in 1917. Although Taylor had no university education, he was a major contributor to the emerging field of anthropology and was the first anthropology professor at Oxford University in England. His writings on animism ignited the twentieth-century debates among philosophers and social scientists on the origin and evolution of religion.

JUDAISM

Background and Beliefs: The religion of the Jewish people, Judaism is the oldest of the monotheistic (one god) religions, and both Christianity and Islam are based on its principal beliefs. The words *Judaism* and *Jew* are derived from "Judah," the name of the ancient Jewish kingdom of southern Palestine.

Judaism was founded by Abraham, who made an agreement with God that he and his offspring would spread the doctrine that there was only one God. In return, God promised Abraham the land of Canaan (Israel) for his descendants.

The Jews first came into being as a nation in the thirteenth century B.C., when the prophet Moses led the Jews out of Egypt, where they had

been slaves, and into the land of Canaan. Since that time Judaism has had to struggle to survive. The Jews were kept captive by the Babylonians from 586 B.C. to 537 B.C., and in 70 A.D. Jerusalem was destroyed by the Roman army and the Jews were either massacred or dispersed. The Jews suffered much the same treatment at the hands of the Russians in the late 1800s.

The basic principles of Judaism are a love of learning (in ancient times, on the first day of school, children were fed honey cakes in the shapes of the letters of the alphabet so that they would associate learning with sweetness); the worship of God out of love, not out of fear; the performing of heartfelt good deeds without concern about rewards; and the importance of family.

Judaism is based upon two fundamental texts: the Hebrew Bible (the Old Testament) and the Talmud, a compendium of laws, traditions, poetry, anecdotes, biographies, and prophecies of the ancient Jews. The Talmud, a sixty-volume work, chronicles the debates among the most learned rabbis from 200 B.C. to 500 A.D.

Twentieth-Century History: In the early part of the twentieth century, the Jews of czarist Russia were victims of pogroms—organized persecutions and massacres. Jews in Germany suffered a similar fate in the 1930s and then the unspeakable horrors of the Nazi Holocaust during World War II. In 1995 commemorations were held in Europe on the fiftieth anniversary of the liberation of the extermination camps, and there is now a permanent memorial to the victims in the United States—the Holocaust Museum in Washington, D.C.

After the war the Zionist movement lobbied world leaders to reestablish a country of their own for the Jews. In 1948 the United Nations partitioned Palestine and proclaimed the state of Israel, leading to a massive immigration of Holocaust survivors and Jews from Muslim countries. There are now 4 million Jews living in Israel, but a still-larger population of Diaspora Jews lives outside the Jewish state; out of 17 million Jews worldwide, nearly a third live in the United States.

As Jews have come under secular influences and have assimilated the different cultures in which they live, Judaism has undergone changes. There are now four schools of the religion: Orthodox, Reformed, Conservative (which tries to strike a balance between Orthodox and Reformed), and Reconstructionist. The three main areas of customs that separate Orthodox Jews from the newer movements are the Sabbath observance, the dietary laws, and laws concerning family and sexual matters. Non-Orthodox Judaism still emphasizes tradition in liturgy and ritual, but the newer schools of Judaism accept women as cantors and rabbis, something unheard of in an Orthodox temple, where men and women must sit separately to worship.

Reconstructionist Jews also depart from tradition in their theological and social outlook. This movement, which was founded in the United States in 1934 by Rabbi Mordecai Kaplan, believes that economic justice, social action, and environmentalism are religious ideals. The forward-looking Rabbi Kaplan created America's first bas mitzvah for his own daughter in 1922. (The bar mitzvah is a Jewish ceremony welcoming an adolescent boy into the adult community; girls had never had a ceremony to celebrate their womanhood.) The Reconstructionists also believe that God is a force "who makes us more generous, sensitive, and caring people," rather than an omnipotent power who intervenes in our lives and in history. Conservative Jews who criticize this movement have said that the Reconstructionists pray "to whom it may concern."

Even within Orthodox Jewry there are moderates and extremists. One extreme group is the Lubavitch Hasidic sect headquartered in Crown Heights, Brooklyn. Hasidism is a two-hundred-year-old spiritual tradition that originated in western Russia. It proclaims the imminence of the apocalypse and the arrival of the Messiah, who will bring world peace and restore the Jewish temple. Under the charismatic leadership of Rabbi Menachem Schneerson from 1950 until his death in 1994, the Lubavitch Hasidim (named after the Rabbi's hometown in Russia) grew to 250,000 followers with 1,600 centers, called Chabad Houses, around the world. In New York City, they took to the streets in converted campers ("mitzvah-mobiles") to spread the word, attempting to draw Reformed and Conservative Jews back to a traditional religious life. Many believed that Rabbi Schneerson himself was the Messiah.

Another messianic influence on Judaism is Christianity. There are several evangelical groups, including Jews for Jesus (led by Richard Harvey, a Texas Jew), who believe in Jesus as the Messiah while claiming to retain their Jewish faith and practicing its traditions. Some 100,000 American Jews are said to be involved in such groups. There are far fewer converts in Israel. Being a Jew is a requirement for Israeli citizenship, and Jewish immigrants who proclaim Jesus as the Messiah do not qualify.

> A Jewish man with parents alive is a fifteen year old boy, and will remain a fifteen-year-old boy until they die.
>
> Philip Roth, *Portnoy's Complaint*, 1969

HINDUISM

Background and Beliefs: The word *Hinduism* is derived from "Hindu," the old Persian name for India, and it describes the religious as well as the social practices and beliefs that the Indian people have developed over more than fifty centuries.

One of the distinguishing elements of Hinduism is the caste system. Historically, India has four major castes, or divisions, of society, each created from a different part of Brahma, the Infinite Being who pervades all reality. Highest are the Brahmans, who originated from Brahma's face and are the caste of priests and intellectuals. The second caste, the Kshatriyas, were created out of Brahma's arms. They are the rulers and men of war and have the same privileges as the Brahmans. The third group, the Vaishyas, sprang from Brahma's thighs. They are farmers, artisans, and merchants. The Shudras were made from his feet and it is their duty to serve the three castes above them. Far beneath the four castes are the pariahs, or "untouchables." Mahatma Gandhi renamed the pariahs Harijans, or "Children of God."

Although a person is bound to his caste for life, he is not bound to it through eternity. Hindus believe that after the individual dies, the soul takes up a new life. Whether it will be better or worse than the previous one depends on karma, which in Sanskrit means "work" or "action." The doctrine of karma has its counterpart in the Judeo-Christian religions, expressed in the biblical saying "Whatsoever a man soweth, that shall he also reap."

Hinduism is rich in sacred scriptures such as the Vedas, which date back to around 2500 B.C. and include the Upanishads ("secret doctrine"), which provide the basis for modern philosophic Hinduism; and the Mahabharata, which includes the Bhagavad Gita, or "Song of the Lord," a dramatic poem that discusses the questions of killing, salvation, and attachment.

Three deities dominate popular Hinduism: Brahma, the Creator; Vishnu, the Preserver; and Siva (Shiva), the Destroyer. Other popular gods are Kali, goddess of death, wife of Siva; Krishna, god of love, an incarnation of Vishnu; and Lakshmi, who brings good fortune.

Twentieth-Century History: Hinduism, politics, and other social structures are inextricably linked in twentieth-century India. In 1947, when the British withdrew, India was founded as a secular nation and Pakistan was separated as an Islamic state (East Pakistan became Bangladesh). More than half a million Hindus and Muslims died in the struggle for statehood and Mahatma Gandhi was assassinated for the cause in 1948. Since the 1970s there has been a growing political movement to transform the secular nation of India into a Hindu state.

In December 1992, 200,000 armed Hindu fundamentalists destroyed a Muslim mosque in northern India, claiming the site rightfully belonged to them, since a temple to their warrior god Ram had once stood there. Their action set off four days of rioting across India and resulted in 1,000 deaths. The Indian government responded by arresting 700 extremists and outlawing several fundamentalist groups, both Hindu and Muslim.

The government has also tried through legislation to end traditional Hindu practices such as discrimination against the untouchables (outlawed in 1950) and the payment of a "bride price," or dowry (declared illegal in 1961). While these laws have brought changes in the urban areas where there is a growing middle class, they have not had great success in the rural areas—home to 70 percent of India's population. As recently as the 1990s, there have been instances of "bride burning" (murder of a woman when her dowry was not paid) and demonstrations by members of the Brahman class against affirmative action for the education of untouchables.

Debates about reproduction have a different context in India than they do in the West. Indian women considering abortion have used the medical procedure of amniocentesis to determine the sex of their fetus (a practice that is now illegal). If the fetus was male, they usually decided to bear the child, since male children are highly prized in society. Opponents of abortion in India have objected to it because "rebirth is powerfully interrupted by the abortion process."

While two-thirds of the world's 750 million Hindus live in India, there are growing numbers in the West as a result of immigration, interest in Eastern mysticism, and the New Age movement. Media attention on such fringe groups as the Hare Krishna and on the practices of yoga and Transcendental Meditation (which bills itself as a technique rather than a religious sect) have affected the public's perception of a major world religion. Some U.S.-born Hindus characterize Western stereotypes of Hinduism as "simplistic foolishness."

BUDDHISM

Background and Beliefs: Buddhism is both an ethical philosophy and a religion, deriving from the teaching of Gautama Buddha. *Buddha*, in Sanskrit, means "the enlightened one" and the title was first given to an Indian philosopher named Siddhartha (c. 563–483 B.C.), whose family name was Gautama. Born at the foot of the Himalayas in Lumbini in southern Nepal, Buddha was the son of a rajah of the Sakya clan and a member of the second Hindu caste, the Kshatriyas (warriors and rulers). It had been prophesied that he would be a universal teacher or a universal ruler. To keep him from becoming a teacher, his father tried to shield him from experiences that would reveal the misery of the world to him. Nonetheless, at twenty-nine, in the royal park, Buddha chanced to see a dead body, a sick man, an old man, and a yellow-robed monk with a begging bowl. The first three revealed the misery of the world to him, while the peace of the beggar suggested a suitable goal for his life. Leaving his wife, his child, and his princely inheritance behind, he became a wandering hermit in search of enlightenment.

For years Buddha sought but did not find it. Finally he seated himself under a wild fig tree and resolved not to get up before he understood the cause of human misery. For forty-nine days he stayed there, holding out against the temptations of the Wicked One, Mara. Finally he achieved nirvana, or enlightenment, after he realized that all suffering is the result of desire and the transcendence of desire would cause suffering to cease. For the rest of his life, until he died at the age of eighty, he preached this new gospel.

Buddha taught a way of life that he called the Middle Path because it avoids the extremes of self-denial and self-indulgence. The aim of Buddhism is to achieve nirvana, which in Sanskrit means "cessation." In nirvana, desire, passion, and the ego are extinguished and the individual achieves the end of suffering—the serenity of utter extinction.

Buddhism, in its original form, is a democratic do-it-yourself religion in which salvation can be achieved directly without using intermediaries such as gods and priests. But, like so many religions, as it spread Buddhism became more and more like those it replaced, and Buddha was worshipped as a god surrounded by other gods and served by an elaborate structure of monastic orders, priesthoods, temples, and ritual.

The two main schools of Buddhism are Hinayana ("the lesser vehicle") and Mahayana ("the greater vehicle"). Hinayana—or Theravada ("the doctrine of the elders"), as it is also known—emphasizes that each individual is responsible for his or her own salvation. It is dominant in Southeast Asia—Burma, Cambodia, Thailand, Vietnam, and Sri Lanka.

Mahayana lays stress on universal salvation, saying that all beings are tied together. It established itself firmly in China and spread to Korea and Japan, producing a diversity of sects including Nichiren, Lamaism, and Zen.

Nichiren Shoshu is a native Japanese phenomenon. Founded by Nichiren (1222–82) in an age when Japan was ruled by feudal lords, it adapted Buddhism to the Bushido warrior cult by teaching that the state and religion should be a unity. Lamaism, the religion of Tibet and neighboring regions, blended Mahayanist teachings with native spirit worship and the erotic practices of tantrism.

Zen Buddhism was brought to China from southern India in the sixth century by the philosopher Bodhidharma. Stressing self-reliance and meditation, Zen seeks to substitute intuitive awareness for intellect and logic. It is intended to train the mind to jump beyond the limits of thought, to leap from thinking to knowing.

Twentieth-Century History: Today there are almost 309 million Buddhists in the world, most of whom live in Asia, although there is a growing population in Europe and the United States.

During the second half of the twentieth century, Communist regimes in Asia (whose ideology encompassed Marx's statement that "religion is the opium of the people") suppressed Buddhist culture and destroyed thousands of monasteries after confiscating their art and other treasures. Atrocities were committed against Buddhists in Laos and Cambodia, especially under the Pol Pot government in the 1970s. Tibetan Buddhists suffered equally at the hands of the People's Republic of China, who occupied Tibet in 1950 and tried to extinguish the religion during Mao Zedong's Cultural Revolution from 1966 to 1973. In Burma and Sri Lanka, many monks set aside their contemplative life to campaign for independence from British colonial rule and to fight for political power against the minority Hindu population.

The disenfranchisement of the Tibetan Buddhists has been highly visible to the world community owing to the work of the Dalai Lama, the exiled spiritual leader or "god-king" of more than 6 million Tibetan Buddhists. When the Chinese clamped down on a 1959 uprising in Tibet, the Dalai Lama fled his home country in an arduous trip over the Himalayas to India, where he established a government in Dharmasala. More than 100,000 Tibetan Buddhists live in exile today.

The Chinese government reopened Tibet to the outside world in 1984; the monasteries are now a lucrative part of the tourist trade. Unconvinced that religious freedom has been achieved, the highest lama, who received the Nobel Prize for peace in 1989, has yet to accept the govern-

A child monk in Burma, 1988.

ment's invitation to return. In a 1991 interview, he said, "Once bitten by a snake, you feel suspicious even when you see a rope."

Tibetan Buddhism has been beset by internal, as well as external, conflict. In 1992 the line of succession was challenged in the Karma Kagyu order, the oldest of the four main subgroups of Tibetan Buddhism, sometimes referred to as Black Hat Buddhism because the master lama, or karmapa, wears a black hat. According to the religious tradition, the karmapa is reincarnated each generation. Before he dies he leaves cryptic clues for his followers so they can locate his successor. After the sixteenth Karmapa, Ranjung Rigpe Dorje, died in Chicago in 1981, it was eight years before his written clues were uncovered—one of his regents found the message in a prayer amulet given to him by the leader. A search party located a young boy, Ugen Thinley, in Tibet whose qualities, birthplace, and parentage matched the prediction. The Dalai Lama confirmed the choice through his own dreams, and the young boy was officially enthroned in September 1992.

In the meantime, the sixteenth Karmapa's nephew had challenged the amulet message as a forgery and located another young boy as the contender. There have been allegations of murder (a regent in the first search party was killed in a car accident) and political chicanery (backed by the Chinese). What's at stake is the leadership of 1 million Buddhists and the sect's assets, worth $1.2 billion. Those who side with the Dalai Lama and the first boy chosen cite a prophesy by a fourteenth-century karmapa: an evil being will appear at the time of the seventeenth Karmapa's reign; his name will be Na-tha, which translates as relative or nephew.

Dissension is also occurring among Buddhists in Japan. New religious movements, such as Rissho Kosei Kai and Soka Gakkai, grew rapidly in Japan after World War II and have spread to other parts of the world. Soka Gakkai, the largest of the new organizations, with 10 million members, is a lay group that was formed to support the 700-year-old teachings of Nichiren Shoshu Buddhism, especially the truths found in the Lotus Sutra, and to take the Mahayana principle of compassion into the world through social activism. Soka Gakkai members have had an aggressive recruitment policy and are active in education and politics; their support is behind the Komeito (Clean Government Party), which has had the swing vote in the upper house of the Japanese government. At the end of 1991, the priests of Nichiren Shoshu excommunicated the lay leaders of Soka Gakkai, charging that they had strayed from orthodox teachings under the temptation of money and power. In response, Soka Gakkai accused the priests of living in the Middle Ages and being subject to graft and greed themselves. The split, which one Soka Gakkai leader likened to the Reformation, has caused dissension in the international organization as well.

Buddhism became popular in the West among non-Asian followers largely thanks to the books of Daisetsu T. Suzuki, a Zen teacher who died in 1966. His work influenced the 1960s counterculture movement and writers such as Jack Kerouac, Gary Snyder, and Thomas Merton, a Christian monk. The poet Allen Ginsberg became associated with the Tibetan Buddhism of Chogyam Trungpa Rimpoche. Formerly an abbot of a large monastery in Tibet, Trungpa promoted Buddhism in the United States for nearly two decades before his death in 1987.

The spread of Hinayana Buddhism in the West is primarily attributable to the large numbers of Asian immigrants in recent years. Thai Buddhist communities are especially strong; the largest temple is in Los Angeles.

Buddhists the world over are increasingly coming to terms with the secular influences of the modern world. Monks in Japan can now marry and have children, and their income is taxable. There are Buddhist movements concerned with ecology, animal rights, and prison conditions. One notable international group is the Buddhist Peace Fellowship. Inspired by the contemporary Zen teachings of Thich Nhat Hanh, a Vietnamese writer and activist, the organization works to further world peace among all nationalities and religions.

CHRISTIANITY

Background and Beliefs: Jesus Christ (c. 6 B.C.–30 A.D.) is considered to be the inspiration for Christianity, although the word Christian was not used in his lifetime. The primary source of information about him is the New Testament—in particular the Gospels of Matthew, Mark, Luke, and John, and the Acts of the Apostles. Bible archaeology has revealed no indisputable evidence of his existence, but early non-Christian historians such as Suetonius, Tacitus, and Josephus refer to him in their discussions of the then new Christian movement. His name was actually Joshua, which means "Jehovah is salvation" in Hebrew; "Jesus" is the Greek for Joshua. "Christ" is from a Greek word meaning "anointed one"; it is a translation of the Hebrew word Messiah.

Born in Bethlehem, in Judea, Jesus was the son of a carpenter, Joseph, and his wife, Mary. According to the New Testament, his birth was foretold to his mother by the archangel Gabriel and was attended by miracles. Jesus was thirty when he was baptized by John the Baptist and took up his religious mission. For three years he preached a doctrine of charity, brotherly love, and repentance, with a promise of salvation to believers. During his ministry, he is said to have performed numerous miracles. His claim that he was the Son of God and the Savior of the Jews foretold by the Hebrew prophets brought him into conflict with the leaders of the Jewish people. Accused of sedition and other crimes against the state, he was tried by Pontius Pilate, the Roman procurator of Judea, and sentenced to death by crucifixion. His followers reported that he rose from the dead on the third day and appeared to them before ascending to heaven.

From a small sect at first limited to Palestinian Jews, Christianity spread throughout the Roman world. Because they refused to worship the Roman emperor as a god, Christians were persecuted for nearly 300 years. With the conversion of the emperor Constantine to Christianity in 312, the Christian sect was granted recognition and freedom to practice its beliefs openly. As its membership grew, the church was torn by theological controversies. When a variety of differences arose between the Church of Rome and the patriarchate of Constantinople, the pope excommunicated the patriarch (1054); the Eastern Orthodox churches date their origin from that event. Five hundred years later, the Protestant Reformation, an attempt to reform the Roman Church, led to a further division and the formation, eventually, of more than 250 Protestant sects, more than 200 of which are represented in the United States.

Twentieth-Century History: Christianity today has more than 1.8 billion adherents. Although the religion claims more followers than any other, the percentage of increase of Christians compared with the total world population has slowed slightly in the twentieth century. For the first time since the seventh century, the majority of Christians are not of European origin. The number of the faithful is growing in Asia, Africa, and especially Latin America, where there is a high birth rate and the number of lapsed Christians is nominal. In 1981, 15.6 percent of Christians spoke Spanish as their native tongue—more than the second-most-common language, English (14.8 percent).

Even with such cultural diversity, the three main traditions of the Christian church have kept continuity in the twentieth century. The Roman Catholic Church is unified by the see of Rome; the broader catholic traditions of Anglicanism and Eastern Orthodoxy trace their authority to an episcopal ministry, a succession of bishops; and Protestants emphasize the faith of the community of believers in their concept of the church.

Christianity has had to make provisions for the diversity of its followers. The ecumenical movement, which began in the nineteenth century, aims to unite Christian churches and clarify the identity of Christianity. Institutionalized in 1948 when the World Council of Churches was formed in Amsterdam, the movement brought together more than 260 Eastern Orthodox, Anglican, and Protestant denominations with more than 400 million members. The purpose of the council is to act together in matters of common interest and to engage in an ongoing dialogue concerning doctrine and the appropriate "life and work" of Christians. With the Second Vatican Council (1962–65), the Roman Catholic Church entered the process by affirming its connection with "separated brethren." In the late twentieth century, the strength of the ecumenical movement is being threatened not so much on theological grounds as on "life and work" issues, including the role of women, reproductive rights, and social activism.

The Christian church has long been a force in social and political change, both as an oppressor and as a champion for the oppressed. In this century, Christian movements and leaders have been part of the political upheavals in South Africa, the Philippines, Lebanon, Latin America, Poland, and many other areas. While Christianity was viewed as an enemy and suppressed in Communist Russia and China, Marxist revolutionary movements in Latin America in the 1970s found an ally in the church and its so-called liberation theology, the notion that Christ, who loved the poor and downtrodden, overcame suffering.

The church in eastern Europe and Russia was closely aligned with the monarchs and the czar against whom the Communists revolted, an alliance that can be explained in part by church organization. In the Eastern Orthodox tradition, each national church operates autonomously. The patriarch of Constantinople is not the Eastern "pope"; instead, he is the first honored among equal patriarchs in other countries and doesn't speak for the entire Orthodox Church. Because of this tradition, the Christian churches of eastern Europe and Russia have traditionally owed more loyalty to their national culture than to a central church, making them more likely to be used as pawns of the state. The unified church of Rome, on the other hand, has had a more oppositional role to political regimes in the twentieth century.

One of the most divisive issues facing Christianity today is the role of women, both in church and in the family. Women began to make inroads in the Protestant clergy in the 1950s, and today nearly one-third of the students in Protestant seminaries are women. While there is entrenched opposition to women in the ministry among the Catholic, Mormon, and black Baptist churches, the Anglican Church has grudgingly admitted women—most successfully in the United States. In England one-third of the Anglican priests refuse to acknowledge the women in their ranks, and the resistance to Anglican women clergy in Australia is even stronger. Although a majority of American Catholics favor women priests, there is not a glimmer of hope that the Vatican will retract its opposition as long as Pope John Paul II heads the Roman Church.

The issue of reproductive rights, especially abortion, is another women's issue that has mobilized the Catholic Church and other conservative denominations to social activism. The pope opposes abortion because it violates the commandment "Thou shalt not kill" (ironically, official church doctrine condones the death penalty in the case of extreme crimes). Conservative Protestants oppose the legal procedure for the same reason and also for the threat it poses to "family values."

The conservative movement is one of the most significant developments in twentieth-century Christianity, a movement that is increasing in numbers while the mainstream Christian denominations are decreasing. It is composed of three branches: Pentecostalism, Fundamentalism, and Evangelicalism.

Pentecostalism developed from the Methodist

Wesleyan Holiness movements in the United States at the end of the nineteenth century. It is characterized by the religious experience of "speaking in tongues," as the first Christians did when the Holy Spirit descended upon them in a "second baptism." Pentecostalists prophesy and engage in healings, believing that the miraculous healings that occurred in Christ's time are still possible today. The movement gained strength in the South and then spread in the 1960s to the Lutheran, Presbyterian, and other mainstream U.S. churches as the "charismatic" movement. It is now worldwide in influence, particularly in the Assemblies of God churches and in sub-Saharan Africa among the African Independent Churches.

The Fundamentalist movement also dates from the late nineteenth century, in the tradition of premillennialism, the belief that the second coming of Christ will occur before the millennium. Its central premise is that the Bible is the word of God and is literal truth. Arising as a reaction to Darwinism and the questioning of liberal theologians, Fundamentalism gained steam during the famous Scopes trial of 1925, when lawyer William Jennings Bryan argued against the teaching of evolution in schools and defended the Genesis story of creation as being scientific. Fundamentalists established a network of Bible colleges and have used radio, television, and publishing ventures to spread their beliefs, such as opposition to abortion and the right to prayer in public schools. Groups such as the Christian Coalition, with 1.5 million members, and the now-defunct Moral Majority, Inc., which was headed by Jerry Falwell, have been effective in the political arena. Moral Majority was instrumental in the election of Ronald Reagan to two terms in office. Fundamentalists are especially strong in the Southern Baptist Church.

The Evangelical movement has also used television to reach out to a large audience. Its most noted spokesman is Billy Graham, who began his first tour in 1949, the year the Communists gained power in China and suppressed Christian worship (a condition that lasted in China for thirty years). Evangelicals hold the same basic tenets as Fundamentalists but are more conciliatory in their style and more ecumenical in their approach; many millions of them remain affiliated with mainstream denominations.

All three of these modern Christian movements emphasize a personal conversion, a giving of oneself to Christ that is a profound emotional experience. After this personal salvation, one must witness for Christ by evangelizing to others and by leading a life of moral perfection. During the 1980s some of the "televangelists" were shown to fall short of perfection in scandals concerning sexual escapades and misuse of church funds. Despite these setbacks, the revival movements that make use of mass media reflect a growing trend in Christianity.

> In other religions, one must be purified before he can knock at the door. In Christianity, one knocks on the door as a sinner, and He Who answers to us heals.
> Fulton J. Sheen, *Peace of Soul*, 1949

> What makes Christ's teachings difficult is that they obligate us to do something about them.
> John J. Wade, *Conquering with Christ*, 1942

> Millions have died for Him, but only a few lived for Him.
> Dagobert D. Runes

> Once the apostle Paul had laid down universal love between all men as the foundation of his Christian community, the inevitable consequence in Christianity was the utmost intolerance towards all who remained outside of it.
> Sigmund Freud, *Civilization and Its Discontents*, 1930

> It was great for God to send his only son, but I'm waiting for him to send his only daughter. Then things will really be great.
> Candace Pert

ROMAN CATHOLICISM

Background and Beliefs: Roman Catholicism, which recognizes the bishop of Rome, the pope, as its head, is the largest of the branches of Christendom. Its early history is identical with the early history of Christianity. Over the centuries the church acquired vast amounts of land and wealth in the various countries of Europe, arousing the envy of divers rulers and governments. A 900-year struggle began when kings and emperors claimed the right to a voice in the appointment of bishops and the popes opposed them with the threat of excommunication.

During the Renaissance the church gained a widespread reputation for extravagance, corruption, and failure to practice what it preached. Throughout Europe a sweeping theological revolution got under way that resulted in the birth of the Protestant churches. Later centuries saw a continuous weakening of the power of the church from the pressures of philosophical movements and modern secularism.

Roman Catholics have traditionally believed that theirs is the only true religion. A faithful Catholic is one who accepts the teachings of Christ as revealed in the Bible, the sacraments and canon law of the church, and the encyclicals of the popes (according to the doctrine of papal infallibility of 1870, the pope is never in error in matters of faith and morals when he speaks as the head of the church). Roman

Catholics believe in the Trinity, holding that there is only one God in three persons, the Father, the Son, and the Holy Ghost, who are distinct from and equal to each other. According to the doctrine of original sin, when Adam disobeyed God in the Garden of Eden, all of his descendants shared in his sin. Christ was placed on earth to redeem mankind by sacrificing himself on the cross.

Catholics hold that the soul is immortal. At death each man and woman will be sent to heaven or hell, depending on which he or she has earned by deeds during life and his or her obedience to the laws of God; before entering heaven, many souls must spend some time in purgatory until they have been made pure. Christ is to come to earth a second time, whereupon all humans will be resurrected bodily and Christ will sit in judgment upon them.

Twentieth-Century History: The Roman Catholic Church has almost 1 billion members, including 98 million in North America and 412 million in Latin America.

The Roman Catholic Church in the twentieth century has been shaped by the external forces of two world wars and an internal democratization brought about by the Second Vatican Council (1962–65). With the end of the dynastic governments in World War I, the church was forced to deal with new regimes—democratic, Communist, and Fascist. In 1929 the Fascist Italian government under Benito Mussolini signed the Lateran Treaty, which normalized relations with the church, established Roman Catholicism as the state religion, and gave Vatican City (a tract of 108 acres within Rome) to the pope as his independent domain.

After World War II, when heavily Catholic countries such as Poland and Hungary fell to the Communists, the Vatican redefined its teachings on war and peace and made doctrinal changes in an effort to survive. An important papal bull (official declaration) was issued in 1950; Pope Pius XII proclaimed that Mary, mother of Christ (and a popular saint with the masses), was taken up bodily into heaven.

In 1962, two years after John F. Kennedy was elected the first Roman Catholic president of the United States, church leaders gathered to begin the Second Vatican Council, a watershed event in the modernization of the church. The council simplified church ritual to focus on the sacrament of the Eucharist, dropped Latin as the universal church language, encouraged greater participation of lay members, and de-emphasized the role of the priest as mediator between the faithful and God. The council also adopted an ecumenical outlook, moving away from the concept of "one true religion" toward a respect for the freedom of individuals to come to terms with their own conscience and religious convictions.

In the 1990s the church is becoming increasingly polarized into liberal and conservative factions; most of the ideological disputes focus on education, sex roles, and human sexuality. Under the conservative leadership of Pope John Paul II, the Vatican has reaffirmed the ban on the ordination of women (1994), forbidden dissension of theologians who teach at Catholic institutions (1990), and directed U.S. bishops to oppose actively any legislation that would promote public acceptance of homosexuality (1992). The pope also remains adamantly opposed to allowing the clergy to marry and to acknowledging a second marriage unless the first was formally annulled by the church. He believes the Catholic Church in the United States has been too lax in granting annulments (divorce is still not an option for strict Catholics). In the area of reproductive rights, the Vatican has condemned artificial insemination, test-tube babies, and surrogate motherhood, and it carries on an active campaign against abortion.

COPTIC CHURCH

Background and Beliefs: A theological controversy in the fifth century led to the formalization of the Coptic Church, the native Christian church of Egypt. The Catholic Church held that Christ had two natures, human and divine. The Copts maintained that Christ had only a single divine nature. Labeled as heretics by the Church of Rome in 451 A.D., they went their own way, only to be persecuted. Many Copts fled from Alexandria, where they had established advanced centers of learning, into the safety of the desert. Over the next few centuries, they expanded by missionary work into the Sudan and Ethiopia.

Twentieth-Century History: Today there are 7 to 8 million Copts, most of whom live in Upper Egypt and the cities of Cairo and Alexandria. The church in Ethiopia became an independent Orthodox Church in 1936 after the country was conquered by the Italians. In Egypt Copts now call themselves the Coptic Orthodox Church; they agree with Eastern Orthodox beliefs in all but the concept of the "monophysite" nature of Christ.

For centuries Egyptian Copts coexisted peacefully as a minority among their Muslim countrymen, until their religious freedom was threatened by the fundamentalist movement that sought to make Egypt more Islamic. In 1981, one month before his assassination, President Anwar Sadat arrested Pope Shenouda III, the Coptic patriarch, and thirty clergy members for "encouraging hostility toward the regime." Pope Shenouda was released after three years of house arrest at a monastery, and relations improved under the government of Hosni Mubarak.

In the 1990s Muslim extremists began a series of violent attacks on Coptic Christians in the slums of Cairo, as well as in the towns and countryside to the south. The Egyptian Parliament passed an antiterrorism act in 1992 and sent in troops to quell the disturbances. Many Copts, who felt the government's protection was too late and too little, took action to emigrate from their home country.

EASTERN ORTHODOXY

Background and Beliefs: The Eastern Orthodox churches, or Eastern communion, came into existence as the result of a lengthy series of theological, political, and cultural differences with the Church of Rome. The Byzantine Church, the branch of the Catholic Church presided over by the patriarch of Constantinople, had disagreed strongly with the popes on the use of icons; Rome favored the use of images in worship and Constantinople opposed them (in the form of statues, although formal religious paintings are venerated). Under Pope Nicholas I, in the ninth century, Rome asserted its claim to sovereignty over the entire church, but the patriarch insisted he and the heads of the other main divisions—the patriarchs of Syria, Antioch, and Jerusalem—had jurisdiction in their own territories. But perhaps the greatest source of irritation to the Byzantines was that the pope had crowned Charlemagne emperor of the West in 800 while the traditional Roman emperor still reigned in Constantinople. In the eleventh century the disagreements between East and West broke out with redoubled bitterness, and Pope Leo IX excommunicated the patriarch Michael Caerularius in 1054. The breach widened still further in 1204 when the Crusaders took Constantinople, sacked the Cathedral of Saint Sophia, confiscated church buildings, and tried to convert the Orthodox to the Roman faith.

Eastern Orthodox churches are bound together by a belief in the Trinity, the human and divine nature of Christ, and other dogmas established by the first seven councils of the church, held between 325 A.D. and 787 A.D. However, the Eastern communion does not accept more recent Catholic dogmas such as the infallibility of the pope and the Immaculate Conception, although it reveres Mary as the mother of Christ. In contrast to Roman Catholics, who hold that the Holy Ghost proceeds from God and Christ, the Orthodox believe it proceeds from God alone. Other Orthodox doctrines not subscribed to by Catholics are that Christ is the sole head of the church, and that the church's authority resides within its members, "the totality of the people of God." Salvation is regarded as possible only through the church, good works, and belief in Christ. Heaven and hell are considered real places.

Twentieth-Century History: The Eastern communion includes, besides the patriarchates of Constantinople, Jerusalem, Antioch, and Alexandria (all of which are quite small in membership), the national churches of Greece, Russia, Ukraine, Moldova, Georgia, Romania, Cyprus, the former Yugoslavia, Albania, Bulgaria, and the Czech and Slovak republics. American adherents number more than 4 million, the largest group being Greek Orthodox. World membership in Eastern Orthodox churches is estimated to be about 170 million.

After World War I, the Orthodox Church almost disappeared in Asia Minor, was completely regrouped in the Balkans, and was subjected to state control in the Soviet Union. With the collapse of Communism in the Soviet Union in 1991, there has been a flowering of interest in religion. The Russian Orthodox Church, however, is facing competition for membership from Protestant and Greek-Catholic denominations, as well as from its own ranks—the dioceses in Ukraine and Moldova have declared themselves independent Orthodox churches.

In 1988, when Mikhail Gorbachev formally declared an end to the state's war against religion, the first monastery (which had been used as a prison by the Communists) was returned to the Russian Orthodox Church. Some 6,000 monasteries and churches have been opened since that time. Russian Orthodox bishops gathered in 1990 to elect a new patriarch, Metropolitan Aleksei of Leningrad—the first church election to be free of atheistic influence since the Bolshevik revolution in 1917. Boris Yeltsin, the first freely elected president of Russia, affirmed the status of the church (and his own profession of faith) by inviting the patriarch to stand with him on the dais during his inauguration.

In the eyes of many, however, the Orthodox Church, which coexisted with the Soviet state for decades, is not yet free of the taint of Communism. Many bishops and priests have been accused of being agents of, or collaborating with, the KGB. In the 1990s the church is trying to steer clear of politics—both left and right, and especially the anti-Semitic movement—to focus on the task of rebuilding its spiritual tradition.

LUTHERANISM

Background and Beliefs: Lutheranism grew out of the teachings of Martin Luther (1483–1546), a German priest. First an ascetic Catholic monk and then a professor of theology, he became convinced, by the study of the Scriptures, that salvation was obtained through the grace of God and not through the mediation of the priesthood. This principle conflicted with the fundamental Roman Catholic practice of the sale of indulgences, which entitled the purchaser to forgiveness of sins. Luther attacked this custom in his Ninety-five Theses (1517), and when he failed to withdraw his charges, he was excommunicated (1521).

From the start, Luther and his followers were in conflict with Rome and its adherents. This helped to produce an armed conflict: from 1618 to 1648 Catholic and Protestant princes grappled in a religious and territorial struggle known as the Thirty Years' War, which devastated Germany.

The term *Lutheran* was first used as an expression of reproach in a papal bull; Luther himself favored "Evangelical" as a name for his church.

The basic Lutheran principle is "justification by faith"—that man's faith in God, rather than man's good works, will bring about his salvation. If people have faith in Christ, repent their sins, study the Scriptures, and receive the sacraments, Lutherans assert, their hearts will be altered and they will live the true Christian life. Lutherans regard the Bible as their sole guide; although they employ ordained ministers, they believe that every person is a priest and can approach God directly. They accept the Trinity and the virgin birth of Christ.

Twentieth-Century History: More than 55 million people are Lutherans today. Lutheranism is the religion of half the people of Germany. In Iceland, Finland, Norway, and Sweden it is the established church and receives support from the state. In the United States, membership is more than 8 million.

The trend in Lutheranism in the twentieth century has been toward consolidation. In 1947 the Lutheran World Federation was formed to aid refugees and others who suffered during World War II, as well as to serve as a cooperative agency for Lutheran churches worldwide. Twenty years later the U.S. Lutherans formed a similar umbrella agency at the national level—the Lutheran Council, whose membership includes 95 percent of all American Lutherans.

The Missouri Synod, a small federation of Lutheran churches, joined the council for only ten years. The synod holds more conservative views than mainstream Lutherans, including the view that women should not be in the ministry. The synod itself later split internally over this issue and others, leading to the formation of the Evangelical Lutheran Church in America.

Similar to other Christian denominations, the Lutherans have debated the place of homosexuals in the church. With the gay-rights movement begun in the 1970s and the effect of the AIDS epidemic on the gay community, many homosexuals have looked for solace and a voice in the church. In 1986 the Lutheran Church in America published a sympathetic report concerning same-sex unions. While it stopped short of proposing that such unions could meet "the standard of a covenant of fidelity" in marriage, it did acknowledge that "it is impossible not to be moved by the authenticity" of faithful same-sex relationships. A more complete policy statement of the Lutherans' stand on human sexuality caused an uproar in 1993 at their national assembly. The Lutherans decided to recommend "further study" and put off any official vote until a later time.

ANGLICANISM

Background and Beliefs: Anglicanism is a Protestant branch of Christianity with churches throughout the world that have the same form of worship as the Church of England. American adherents call their church the Episcopal or Protestant Episcopal Church. The term *Anglicanism* comes from the Latin word for "English"; *Episcopal* comes from *episkopos*, a Greek word meaning "bishops."

Anglicanism began in England after Henry VIII (1497–1547) declared that the king, not the pope, was the supreme head of the English church. Although Henry took this step because he wanted to annul his marriage to Catherine of Aragon and the pope had refused the annulment, the break with Rome came as the climax to more than a hundred years of protest by Englishmen against the authority of the Pope and the heavy financial burden of supporting the church. King Henry suppressed the monastic communities in England to prevent a threat to his newly claimed authority. The archbishop of Canterbury was made the religious head of the Church of England, which prepared its own prayer book (the Book of Common Prayer) and statement of doctrine (the Thirty-nine Articles).

Anglicanism was introduced into America in Jamestown, Virginia, in 1607. Many of the founding fathers of the United States were Episcopalians and more U.S. presidents have been Episcopalian than any other religion. Sometimes called the "bridge church," Anglicanism agrees with Roman Catholicism on most issues, but like other Protestant groups, Anglicans reject the authority of the pope. They believe that the Bible represents the final statement of life and religion, but it is not always to be interpreted literally. In general, Episcopalians do not believe in a physical heaven or hell and hold that God, after the Last Judgment, will re-create man with a "spiritual body"; however, members differ in their beliefs to some degree.

The clergy of the Anglican Church, like the Roman Catholics, are referred to as priests, but unlike Catholics, they are not required to be celibate and are allowed to marry. The Anglican Church has kept many Roman Catholic traditions in liturgy, the church calendar, and the structure of church government; Anglican bishops are sacramentally appointed in a line of succession that goes back to Jesus' original twelve apostles.

Twentieth-Century History: The worldwide Anglican Church today has 60 million members. Membership has declined overall about 10 percent in the last thirty years, and nearly 28 percent in the U.S. Episcopal Church. Episcopal conservatives credit the diminished membership to the liberal leanings of the church, which—compared with other Protestant denominations—allows members a wide berth of belief without censure. For example, some liberal dioceses have blessed same-sex marriages and ordained homosexual clergy, contrary to official Episcopal doctrine.

The biggest twentieth-century controversy in the church has concerned the ordination of women into the clergy. There have been women priests in the U.S. and Canadian branches of the church since the mid-1970s. However, when a Bostonian woman priest, Barbara Harris, was elected suffragan (assistant) bishop in 1988, conservatives felt the (male) apostolic tradition dating back to Christ was being threatened. They questioned whether the sacraments, including marriage and the ordination of priests, would be valid when administered by a female bishop. A group of 2,000 Episcopalians met in Fort Worth, Texas, and formed the Episcopalian Synod of America—effectively a church within a church. They proposed that their clergy would minister to conservative members of parishes who did not wish to follow women clergy or more liberal male priests. The synod also adopted for their worship the 1928 Book of Common Prayer. In the midst of the controversy she ignited, Bishop Harris has tried to remain uncontroversial. But as a divorced woman, an African American, and a former civil-rights activist, she was bound to attract media attention. She criticized her own congregation for being racist and sexist and said of herself, "I could be a combination of the Virgin Mary, Lena Horne, and Madame Curie," and still be unaccepted by some of the members.

England postponed the controversy of accepting women priests until 1992. In that year Dr. George Carey, the archbishop of Canterbury, announced that church leaders had approved the ordination of women by a mere two votes over the two-thirds majority needed to pass the measure. Traditionalists were outraged, in part because it meant the Church of England would have to abandon its thirty-year-long attempt to reconcile with the Vatican, which is firmly against women clergy. In protest, 600 Anglican priests in England resigned from their church and converted to Roman Catholicism.

PRESBYTERIANISM
Background and Beliefs: Presbyterianism was inspired by the teachings of the Swiss Protestant reformer John Calvin (1509–64), who started a movement that spread to France, Germany, and other parts of Europe. On the Continent, the Reformed Church came into being in response to his message. The fiery John Knox (1505?–72), a friend of Calvin's, brought his doctrines to Scotland. When Puritanism took power in seventeenth-century England, the Presbyterians were the largest faction within it.

Presbyterianism was first introduced to America by the Dutch Reformed in New Amsterdam and by the Scots-Irish Puritans in New England. Large numbers of Scottish immigrants spread the faith throughout the Colonies; by the time of the Revolution, Presbyterians were an important element in America.

The Westminster Confession (1645–47), the most famous statement of English Calvinism, is the basis of the Presbyterian creed. Presbyterians believe that the Scriptures are "the only infallible rule of faith and practice." They also believe in the Trinity and the existence of heaven and hell. A once important Calvinist tenet, predestination (holding that God, not the individual, determines the individual's fate) is no longer emphasized. Church rule is democratic. The individual church is governed by the "session," consisting of a teaching elder (an ordained minister) and ruling elders (members elected from the congregation).

Twentieth-Century History: The world membership of the Presbyterian Church has been estimated at nearly 40 million, including more than 2.9 million members in the United States. In Scotland, Presbyterianism is the established religion. In the United States, the Presbyterian Church U.S.A. was formed in 1983 when the North and South branches of the church finally bridged a schism dating from before the Civil War, a split caused by the slavery issue and theological differences. The 1983 creed of the reconciled church's beliefs was carefully worded so as not to offend the more conservative southerners. The more liberal members in the North were satisfied with the creed's emphasis on social concerns, including ecology, and the acceptance of women as ministers.

The church's stand on sexual morality was tested in 1991 when a committee prepared a report titled "Keeping Body and Soul Together" for discussion at the national convention. The report recommended a new ethic that allowed singles to be sexually active before marriage, accepted masturbation as normal and healthy, and did not view homosexuality as fundamentally immoral. The report caused a furor and sold 27,000 copies before it was voted down at the General Assembly by the large majority who remembered their Calvinist roots.

Presbyterians were riled again in 1993 by an interdenominational women's conference in Minneapolis, called "Reimagining God," where women explored the feminine aspects of God, invoked in prayer "Sophia" (Greek for "wisdom"), and ended the conference with a ritual of drinking milk and honey. Twenty-five percent of the attendees were Presbyterian and their church had donated $70,000 to the conference organizers. Conservative members of the church were outraged, accusing the women of goddess worship and threatening to withhold millions of dollars in donations from the national church. To stay the tide and protect the coffer, the General Assembly at its 1994 meeting reaffirmed Presbyterians' belief in "the one triune God," the Father, Son, and Holy Ghost.

BAPTISTS

Background and Beliefs: A Protestant denomination, the Baptists hold that only believers (not infants) may be baptized and that baptism must be administered by immersion (rather than by sprinkling).

The Baptist Church has no recognized founder. Some Baptists trace its development directly from John the Baptist, others from the Anabaptists of sixteenth-century Europe. Early Baptists were split into two groups: the General Baptists, who believed that Christ died for all people, and the Particular Baptists, who held the Calvinist doctrine that Christ died only for the elect. In 1608 a group of English Puritans, seeking to escape persecution, settled in Amsterdam and founded the first Baptist Church. In 1611 members of this congregation returned to England and established the first Baptist Church there. In the United States the first Baptist Church was established by Roger Williams at Providence, Rhode Island, in 1639, after he was banished from the Massachusetts Bay Colony.

Baptists hold that the Bible is the supreme authority in every matter of faith. Many Baptists are Fundamentalists: they accept the Bible as literal truth. Many believe that heaven and hell are real places and that there will be a physical resurrection of the dead on the Day of Judgment. In general, they believe in the Trinity and the virgin birth of Christ and hold that one is saved by faith in Christ and by the grace of God. Baptist worship focuses on the sermon and includes hymn singing and sometimes extemporaneous prayer.

Twentieth-Century History: About four-fifths of the 31 million Baptists in the world live in the United States. Baptist missionaries have been highly successful in recruiting converts in the former Soviet Union and in leading underground churches in the People's Republic of China.

The Baptist Church in the United States today is divided by North and South distinctions that date to pre–Civil War times. Fundamentalists have controlled the 14-million-member Southern Baptist Convention (SBC) since 1979 and have used their leadership position to reshape the denomination's views. They believe in the inerrancy of the Bible (that the Bible is the historical, scientific, and religious truth), advocate prayer in school, strongly oppose abortion, and tend to favor a strong national military and support conservative political candidates.

In 1991, 6,000 disaffected moderate Baptists broke from the SBC to set up their own organization. Naming themselves the Cooperative Baptist Fellowship, they expressed a desire to connect with the American Baptist churches in the North and the large black Baptist denominations in the South.

The black Baptist churches, which were organized after the Civil War by freed slaves, have played an important role in the black community in this century—not only as a spiritual and social center but as a political force as well. Led by the Reverend Martin Luther King Jr., the churches were instrumental in the civil-rights movement of the 1960s and in political action through the 1980s, when they backed the Reverend Jesse Jackson for president.

Baptist churches in the South continue to remain largely segregated, but the Southern Baptist Convention hopes to draw more blacks. As part of its expansion plans to more than triple in size by the year 2,000, the SBC has targeted 1,800 black communities for potential new members.

METHODISM

Background and Beliefs: Methodism was born in England out of the teachings of an Anglican clergyman, John Wesley (1703–91). The word *Methodism* was originally applied in derision because of the methodical way Wesley and his associates studied and performed their religious duties.

Wesley underwent a profound religious experience in London in 1738: "I felt I did trust in Christ, Christ alone, for salvation," he wrote in his *Journal.* Setting out as an evangelical preacher, stressing conversion and holiness in place of the formalism of the Church of England, he sought to breathe new life into the Episcopal faith. Although he always considered himself a loyal Anglican, he was often forbidden to preach in Anglican churches, and by the end of the eighteenth century his movement had its own flourishing societies in Great Britain and the young United States. By 1850 the Methodists were the largest Protestant group in the United States.

Although Methodists accept the Trinity and practice baptism and communion, they hold that individual love of God and individual religious experience mean more than formal doctrine. Salvation is achieved by a life of holiness, repentance, and faith and is available to everyone. Most believe in judgment after death, in which the morally good will be rewarded and the wicked punished.

Twentieth-Century History: The United Methodist Church is the second-largest Protestant denomination in the United States today. It has a strong missionary tradition. In 1991 a Methodist pastor, Dwight Ramsey, from Shreveport, Louisiana, helped a group of Russians in founding a Methodist congregation—the first new church with legal status in Russia since the Bolshevik revolution.

In general Methodist factions in the United States have moved toward unification in the twentieth century. The nineteenth-century "holiness" movement of Methodism, however, remains independent in the Assemblies of God and other Pentecostal denominations. While the Methodists of the North and South branches (which had split over slavery) officially reunited in 1939, they assigned black Methodist churches a "separate but equal" status within the United Methodist Church. It was not until 1974 that district divisions based on race were abolished.

During the Vietnam War era, the Methodist Church was called to accountability for its investment policy of church funds. In 1972 a study made by the Corporate Information Center of the National Council of Churches on the stockholdings of churches in corporations working on military contracts revealed that the United Methodist Church owned more than $59 million worth. The United Presbyterian Church was a close second, but all major Protestant denominations were on the list. "Ethical and moral concerns have not been expressed through the investment policies and responsibilities of the Church," the report declared, pointing out that Protestant groups were assisting in the manufacture and use of weapons of mass human and environmental destruction.

In the late twentieth century, one of the most controversial issues facing the Methodists is homosexuality. In 1987 an openly gay woman minister was officially tried by Methodist leaders—the first such trial since the early 1900s, when Methodist seminary professors were accused of heresy. The thirteen clergy members of the jury found her guilty of violating Methodist law and suspended her from ministerial duties. At its General Conference in 1992, the church reaffirmed its position that homosexuality conflicts with Christian teaching, although it did recommend further study of the issue at the local level.

LATTER-DAY SAINTS (Mormons)
Background and Beliefs: The Church of Jesus Christ of Latter-day Saints, whose members are generally known as Mormons, was founded in the United States in 1830 at Fayetteville, New York. Its headquarters today are in Salt Lake City, Utah.

Two men played outstanding roles in the founding and development of Mormonism: Joseph Smith (1805–44) and Brigham Young (1801–77). Smith, son of a poor New England farmer, declared in 1827 that an angel named Moroni had led him to dig up golden plates covered with sacred writings. The writings, which Smith translated into *The Book of Mormon*, told the sacred history of an Israelite people who had lived in North America. As a result of other revelations, Smith affirmed that he had been chosen as a priest and was to found a new religion. Believers flocked to him, but the hostility of neighbors repeatedly forced him and his followers in the new movement to travel onward—first to Ohio, then to Missouri and Illinois. In 1844, after introducing polygamy as a practice in the sect, he and his brother were murdered by a mob.

Brigham Young, a New York painter and glazier, was selected to head the Mormons after Smith's death. Under his leadership the Mormons trekked west in 1846–47, settling in Salt Lake City. With Young in command, the church flourished, and when Utah was made a federal territory he was appointed its first governor. Young, who continued to promote polygamy among the Mormons, had twenty-seven wives.

Mormons believe in a purposeful universe in which humans have been placed to make themselves more like God by faith and works. While they believe in Jesus as savior, their doctrines and sacraments go beyond the traditional tenets of Christianity. Their holy scriptures, considered equal to the Bible, include *The Book of Mormon* and other revelations; the head of their church is considered a living prophet to whom God speaks directly. They view the holy Trinity as separate gods and teach that God the Father, who once lived in human form, has a wife and gives birth to spiritual children, Jesus being one of them; faithful Mormons, too, may become gods.

Mormons also believe that marriages blessed in the temple are binding for eternity, not just on Earth, and that families are reunited in heaven (relatives who die as nonbelievers may be baptized in a special rite to ensure their afterlife). Mormons stress missionary work, especially among young adults, who typically volunteer two years of their lives as missionaries. Church members follow a dietary code known as the Word of Wisdom, which forbids coffee, tea, and alcohol.

Twentieth-Century History: The Mormons' missionary work has been highly effective in recent years. From 1982 to 1994, the church grew from 5 million to 8.7 million worldwide; half its members live outside the United States. The church, which refused to admit blacks to the priesthood until 1978, now has converts of all races in 149 countries. Its annual income is estimated to be $4.7 billion, second in U.S.

churches only to the Southern Baptists, who have double the membership.

One of the appeals of the Mormon Church is that it encourages secular activities, such as sports and music, within the context of a strong family. Families are required to gather one night a week for a "home evening" of prayer, study, and entertainment. Modern economic pressures, however, have reduced the size of the typical Mormon family.

The tenets of the Mormon Church, which owns Brigham Young University, are being challenged today by its own scholars and feminist members of the church. Some intellectuals have questioned the official version of the church's nineteenth-century origins, noting that there is no archaeological evidence to support the claim of an historic Israelite community in North America. Other critics believe that church founders usurped Masonic rituals for Mormon worship, rather than the rites' being received through divine revelation.

Some Mormon women are trying to show that the little-known doctrine of God's wife, "God the Mother," validates their quest for a larger leadership role. While women are allowed to lead prayers and give sermons, they are not allowed into the male hierarchy of priesthood, in which boys begin to participate at the age of twelve. In 1993 the church censored feminist members and excommunicated five women for their outspoken views. It has, however, made some concessions to women; in the marriage ceremony, they now vow obedience to God and not their husbands. Although polygamy has officially been banned since 1890, fringe groups of Mormons continue the practice in the 1990s.

JEHOVAH'S WITNESSES
Background and Beliefs: Although Jehovah's Witnesses has fewer members than many other Christian sects, energetic proselytizing has made it extremely well known.

The movement was founded by Charles Taze Russell (1852–1916), a Congregationalist haberdasher from Allegheny, Pennsylvania. His followers were first known as Russellites. In the tradition of millennialist prophets, Russell predicted the end of the world and Christ's Second Coming. When it did not occur in 1914, the year he had named, he revised his teachings.

The Witnesses believe that Christ became the king of heaven in 1914 and cast out Satan, thus beginning great troubles on earth that will climax in the Battle of Armageddon, Christ's victory on earth, and the destruction of Satan. They believe that exactly 144,000 followers will go to heaven and the rest of the Witnesses will live in a paradise on earth. Jehovah's Witnesses believe that theirs is the only true faith and the only way to salvation. Their only allegiance is to God, and they refuse to salute flags or participate in military service.

Twentieth-Century History: Today the sect, which was named Jehovah's Witness (for Jehovah, God) in 1931, has 2.6 million members worldwide. All members are considered ministers, and they take their ministry door to door seeking converts. The church keeps detailed records of the number of visits made, Bible classes attended, and printed materials distributed. Its two magazines—*Awake!* and *Watchtower*—translated into eighty languages, reached 10 million people a year during the 1980s.

In the years between 1973 and 1983, membership had declined by nearly 1 million, in part owing to the voice of a small group of dissenters who accused the church of being an Orwellian society that ruled every aspect of its followers' lives. Former Witnesses complain that the church discourages higher education and has unreasonable grounds for "disfellowship," its term for excommunication. The practice of shunning former members was strengthened in 1981 when church leaders forbade parents and siblings to speak to family members who had fallen away.

Faithful Jehovah's Witnesses continue to wait for the Battle of Armageddon and paradise on earth. The apocalyptic event has been predicted by the church for certain dates five times in this century. The last forecasted date that passed without the prophesy's coming true was in 1975.

CHRISTIAN SCIENCE
Background and Beliefs: Christian Science is a system of spiritual healing and a religion based on the principles taught by Mary Baker Eddy (1821–1910), who, while suffering from an injury in 1866, experienced a remarkable recovery that she declared came about after she read, in the Gospel of Saint Matthew, how Jesus healed. In 1875 she published *Science and Health with Key to the Scriptures*, and four years later she founded the Church of Christ, Scientist.

According to Eddy, belief in the truths of the Bible makes it possible to heal the sicknesses of the body. God is spirit, and humans created in his image are also spirit; matter does not exist, nor illness, except as an illusion; a person can overcome sickness if faith is strong enough. What others call death, Christian Science refers to as "only an incident in the dream of mortality."

The worship of Christian Scientists centers on reading the writings of Mary Baker Eddy and accounts of people who have been cured of illness.

Twentieth-Century History: Christian Science in the late twentieth century has 3,000 congregations in fifty-six countries with an estimated 150,000 members (church policy, as outlined by

Mary Baker Eddy, founder of the Christian Science movement.

Mary Baker Eddy, forbids publishing membership statistics). The size of the movement in the United States is about half what it was in the 1930s and 1940s; most recent growth has occurred in Third World countries.

Only since the 1960s have scholars begun to treat Eddy as a respectable Christian theologian. She believed in the spiritual equality of men and women and thought that social and political structures should reflect that equality. Women in the Christian Science Church have traditionally had a strong leadership role.

In the 1990s the church has been beset by legal challenges to the practice of its beliefs. The lack of medical care for children of Christian Scientists has become an issue as the incidence of divorce has risen and parents have taken opposing views. In 1993 the church lost its first civil suit for the wrongful death of a child, a suit brought by the child's father against his ex-wife, her new husband, and the church. The court ruled that the church had "deliberately ignored the rights and safety of the child," whose life would likely have been saved with medical intervention. From the Christian Science point of view, medical treatment is anti-Christian, and such legal rulings threaten their religious rights.

The church has also suffered setbacks in the 1990s as a result of expansion and mismanagement in its media empire. In an effort to make up for the financial losses of the *Christian Science Monitor* newspaper, the five-member board of

The Mother Church spent $400 million on radio and cable-TV news programs. The failed business enterprise resulted in bankruptcy for the church and divisiveness among its members. In 1994, hoping to recoup some losses, a member group sued the directors and trustees.

UNITED CHURCH OF CHRIST

Background and Beliefs: The United Church of Christ, one of America's newest Protestant groups, came into being in 1957. It is a union of several organizations that have their roots in two traditions: European Protestantism (brought to the American Colonies by immigrants from Switzerland and the German states) and Congregationalism. Congregationalism began in sixteenth-century England, where it was known as a Separatist movement because its members wanted to break away from the Church of England, for they were strongly opposed to bishops and presbyteries. After exile in Holland, a small group, called the Pilgrims, migrated to America, establishing their first church in the New World at Plymouth, Massachusetts, in 1620. Congregationalism became the established religion in some of the Colonies. Always active in education, it founded Harvard, Yale, and many other colleges.

The members of the United Church of Christ are free to interpret God's word in their own way, so worship varies with the individual church.

Twentieth-Century History: The first alliance that preceded the formation of the United Church of Christ occurred in 1934 when the Reformed Church in the United States and the Evangelical Synod of North America joined forces. Both of these groups were in the European Protestant tradition. In 1957 they united with the General Council of the Congregational Churches of the United States to form the United Church of Christ, which, in the 1990s, has approximately 1.6 million members.

Although the church is predominantly white, it was the first major U.S. denomination to issue a pastoral letter urging "reform of racist attitudes and institutions across the country." The statement was signed by fifty-four ministers and issued in 1991 on Martin Luther King Jr.'s birthday.

In its missionary work outside the United States during the 1980s, the church, along with other Protestant denominations, was labeled by some governments and media reports as "pro-Communist." In the Philippines in the late 1980s, when antigovernment insurgents and those simply suspected of being pro-Communist were being threatened and tortured, the United Church of Christ appeared on a Philippine military list of alleged "Communist front" groups. The military and military-backed vigilantes harassed and tortured church members and even murdered one of its executive committee members. Top officials from the United

Council of Churches in the United States visited lawmakers in Washington, D.C., to voice their objection to U.S. backing of the Philippine military. While members of the U.S. House of Representatives expressed concern over human rights abuses in the Philippines, they increased military aid to the newly democratic government of Corazon Aquino.

SHINTO

Background and Beliefs: The native religion of Japan, Shinto developed out of primitive worship of ancestors and natural forces, but it has been influenced by Confucianism and Buddhism. The word *Shinto*, which is Chinese (*shin tao*), means "the way of the gods." Shinto places great emphasis on physical and mental purity and on the belief in many deities and spirits, called *kami*, who are honored at shrines and festivals.

After Buddhism became established in Japan, it overshadowed Shinto for centuries. In 1868, however, the emperor Meiji seized power from the shogun and revived Shinto. It was made the state religion and was taught in the schools. Since Shinto emphasized the divine origin of the emperor's family, the military lords of Japan strongly promoted it, using it to justify their expansionist policies.

Twentieth-Century History: After the surrender of Japan in 1945, General Douglas MacArthur disestablished Shinto as a state religion. Emperor Hirohito, renouncing his claims to divinity, declared that the throne depended on the people's confidence and affection, not divine right. The separation of church and state was written into the Japanese constitution of 1947. Although Shinto is no longer the official national religion, it has retained some military associations. Members of the government make semiofficial yearly visits to the Yasukuni shrine, where spirits of the war dead are venerated.

Shinto is very much part of Japanese culture today. Marriages are conducted before Shinto shrines, and Shinto priests provide blessings on everything from automobiles to construction sites. Shinto followers continue to honor local deities at rural shrines and believe in the sacredness of three mountains—Kirishima, Miwa, and Fuji.

Several new Shinto-based sects have gained popularity in the postwar years. Three of the new movements—Seicho No Ie, Sekai Kyuseikyo, and Sekai Mahikari—are concerned primarily with spiritual healing powers that can overcome physical illness.

Today there are about 3.5 million followers of Shinto, many of whom are also practicing Buddhists.

ISLAM

Background and Beliefs: The word *Islam* means "submission" (to the will of God) in Arabic, and the followers of Islam are known as Muslims (from the Arabic for "those who submit").

Muhammad (c. 570–632), prophet and founder of Islam, was born in Mecca (located in Saudi Arabia), where he passed his youth as a shepherd and trader. At twenty-four he married his employer, Khadija, a rich widow fifteen years older than he was. He was a well-to-do merchant of forty when he had a vision in which the archangel Gabriel revealed to him that he had been selected to be the prophet and teacher of the worship of one God, Allah; at the time, his people worshipped idols and animistic spirits. Other revelations followed, which were later set down in the Qur'an (Koran), the sacred book of Islam. Preaching the new faith, Muhammad began to gather followers; but at the same time, he aroused hostility in Mecca, where an ancient black stone, fixed in a corner of a shrine called the Kaaba, was worshipped. In 622, to escape a plot to murder him, Muhammad fled to Yathrib (now called Medina). The Islamic era is dated from the year of his flight, called the Hegira.

In 630 Muhammad led his followers against Mecca, which surrendered to him; battles and treaties with other cities and tribes made him supreme in Arabia.

Muhammad preached a holy war against nonbelievers, and his followers made it a reality. Within a hundred years after the prophet's death, Egypt and Syria were Muslim countries and the faith had penetrated as far as Algeria and Tunis. Over the centuries the teachings of Islam have spread far and wide.

Muslims express their belief in one god in the official confession of faith, the Shahada: La ilaha illa Allah, wa Muhammadun rasulu Allu. ("There is no god but Allah, and Muhammad is his messenger.") All-powerful and gracious, Allah rewards the good and punishes the sinful.

Islam has twenty-eight prophets, most of whom are familiar from the Old and New Testaments: they include Adam, Abraham (the first Muslim), Noah, Jacob, Moses, David, Solomon, Elijah, Jesus (who did not die on the cross but was lifted up to heaven by Allah), and John the Baptist. Another is Alexander the Great. All of these prophets prepared the way for the final prophet, Muhammad. Muslims believe that each of the prophets brought revelations from Allah but man turned away from them, so God sent other prophets to repeat his message. Differences between the beliefs expressed in the Bible and the Koran are said to be due to errors in the Bible text.

To be a Muslim in good standing, one must obey the Five Pillars of Islam: (1) Repeat the confession of faith every day. (2) Pray five times a day—at dawn, at noon, in the middle of the afternoon, at dusk, and after dark. The faithful must pray facing the Kaaba, which is in the center of the Great Mosque at Mecca. Bowing the head to the ground acknowledges the greatness of Allah. (3) Give alms. The believer is obliged to contribute a prescribed amount, traditionally a fortieth part of his income. (4) Fast. This is compulsory all through the daylight hours of the month of Ramadan, the ninth month of the Muslim calendar, which commemorates the first revelation of the Koran. (Abstinence from sex is part of the fast.) (5) Make a pilgrimage to Mecca at least once, if health and finances permit. While there, the believer must walk around the Great Mosque seven times and kiss and touch the Kaaba Stone.

Twentieth-Century History: Islam is the second-largest world religion in the twentieth century, with some 950 million followers. There are at least seventy-three identified sects of the religion, most of which have national and cultural ties that identify them as much as their religious beliefs. The variety of expressions of the faith is summed up by the popular saying, "In any country where there are two Islamists, there are three movements."

The largest sects of Islam are the Sunnis (80 percent) and the Shiites (12 percent). The schism dividing the two groups concerns the line of succession of caliphs, or leaders of the faith. The Shiites believe the rightful heirs to Islam are descendants of Muhammad through Ali—the fourth caliph, who married Muhammad's daughter Fatima—and his two grandsons. The Sunnis believe in the succession as it occurred in history. Ali was assassinated and the leadership passed to a caliph who was not part of Muhammad's bloodline.

In the twentieth century, the world's attention has focused primarily on Islamic movements and conflicts in the Middle East: the Arab-Israeli wars of 1967 and 1973, the Intifada of 1987, Lebanon, and the Iranian revolution of 1979. Muslims in this region, however, account for only 20 percent of Islam. There are 60 to 70 million Muslims in the former Soviet Union, and 25 percent of the world's Muslims live in southern Asia (India, Pakistan, and Bangladesh). Indonesia has the largest Islamic population of any country, but it is also a very secular nation with a past of strong Buddhist and Hindu traditions.

Despite this diversity, media attention has centered on the Muslim fundamentalists and terrorists in the Middle East, whose goal is to undermine Israel and secular governments and establish Islamic states. An "Islamic state," however, means different things to different Muslim groups. There is a wide spectrum of tactics and beliefs even on the religious right regarding what social customs should be enforced in an Islamic state and what the policies should be regarding other religions and the secular world. One of the more mainstream conservative groups is the Muslim Brotherhood, the first mass movement of Muslims in the twentieth century. The brotherhood has significant political power in Egypt and Jordan, although it was outlawed in Syria in 1982.

In the former Soviet Union, there is a resurgence of interest in Islam. New mosques are being built (many were destroyed in the Stalin era) and the faithful are learning Arabic in order to study the Koran. Most of these Muslims are Sunnis, although the Azerbaijanis are Shiites.

A completely American offshoot of Islam is the black-nationalist movement known as the Black Muslims (or the Nation of Islam), which was founded in Detroit in 1930 by Wali Farad, who was known to his followers as "the Savior" or "the Great Mahdi." An anti-integrationist movement, the Black Muslims identify themselves with an ancient lost tribe of Muslims, the Shabazz. Members take Muhammadan names in place of Western ones and are required to give up vices such as alcohol and drugs.

After Farad disappeared in 1934, he was succeeded by his disciple Elijah Muhammad. With the help of an outstanding preacher named Malcolm X, who was assassinated in 1965 (see page 152), membership grew to 100,000. The Nation of Islam, now headed by Louis Farrakhan, is much smaller today.

African Americans make up 42 percent of the 6 million Muslims in the United States. Most American Muslims are second- to fifth-generation children of immigrants and are well assimilated into the middle class. In the 1990s, American Muslims rallied around the plight of Bosnian Muslims; they spoke out against the rapes and other war atrocities and lobbied U.S. politicians to intervene in the former Yugoslavia.

SCIENTISM

Background and Beliefs: The word *science* comes from the Latin word *sciens*, which means "knowing." Followers of scientism are called scientists, a term that was first used by William Whewell in 1840. The study of science began as a hobby among Greek intellectuals. For centuries those who acquired scientific knowledge kept it secret and although this practice is less common today, there are still many scientists who believe that their knowledge would be misused if it were spread to noninitiates. From a small sect, scientism has risen to the heights of respectability and its basic principles are taught to schoolchildren throughout the world.

Scientists believe that the order of the universe can be determined by systematic study and analysis. They believe that theirs is the only true path and that other paths are "mere superstitions." Over the years scientism has split into more than 1,200 different sects or "fields," each with its own sacred texts.

Twentieth-Century History: It is estimated that the worldwide scientific community has more than 3 million members, although the number of believers is much greater.

During the twentieth century, especially the latter half, scientism has been heavily influenced by a group known as physicists. They have developed new doctrines about the nature and origin of the universe in what amounts to a new scientific cosmology. A few notable members of the movement, including its founder, Albert Einstein, have voiced the heretical opinion that the concept of God is allowable within the framework of scientism. This point of view, however, has not swayed the majority of scientists.

COMMUNISM

Background and Beliefs: Communism is an atheistic ideology of social and economic equality founded by the nineteenth-century philosophers Karl Marx and Friedrich Engels. Marx called religion the "opium of the people"—a drug that intoxicates the working man, or proletariat, with visions of spiritual gifts and an afterlife while numbing him to his life on this earth, a life of oppression under capitalistic and imperialistic institutions. Communism calls for revolutionary changes in society: a redistribution of land and wealth and self-government by peasants and workers.

Twentieth-Century History: The Russian V. I. Lenin took on himself the mission that Karl Marx summarized in his epitaph: "Workers of all lands unite. The philosophers have only interpreted the world in various ways; the point is to change it." Lenin led the Bolshevik movement in its overthrow of the czar in 1917. A year later he established the Decree on the Separation of Church and State—and disestablished the Russian Orthodox Church. Five years earlier, Lenin had written in a letter to Maksim Gorky, "Every religious idea, every idea of God,

even every flirtation with this idea of God, is unutterable vileness."

The Communist Party came to dominate nearly all aspects of Russian life. While Lenin purported that "the dictatorship of the proletariat" was just a phase in the revolution to pure communism, Soviet society never made the transition. His successor, Joseph Stalin, was ultimately charged with the most heinous abuses of dictatorial power, even by Soviet leaders who came after him.

Marxism-Leninism spread to China in the 1920s, where Mao Zedong led the revolution that established the People's Republic of China in 1949. Maoism espoused faith in the Communist Party, faith in the masses, and transcendence of personal desires in order to serve the people as a whole. Pictures of Mao were displayed like icons and all literate Chinese read *Quotations from the Works of Chairman Mao Zedong* and referred to it for help with problems in daily living.

The tide of Communism that moved through regimes and wars in countries around the world during the twentieth century was turned on November 9, 1989, when the Berlin Wall fell. The new government established in East Germany included four clergymen and several Christian laymen among its twenty-three ministers. When the Soviet Union disbanded two years later, the Russians were left wondering what to do with a monument in Moscow's Red Square—the mausoleum that held Lenin's embalmed body.

ATHEISM

When the atheist is confronted with one of the natural outrages against the dignity and decency of life he is tempted to act for the moment as if God existed simply in order to have something on which to unloose his outraged feelings.
> Philip Toynbee, *Observer,* "Death of Mother,"
> April 17, 1969

Thanks to God, I am still, an atheist.
> Luis Buñuel, *Le Monde,* December 16, 1959

—F.D., D.W., and L.A.C.

SECTS AND CULTS

What's a cult? It just means not enough people to make a minority.
> Robert Altman

THE AMISH

The Amish are more a denomination of the Christian Mennonite Church than a cult or

secret society. They live spiritually rich and peaceful but materially austere lives, most of them refusing to make use of technological advances and modern farming techniques. They are basically a rural, agricultural people. Their horses and buggies are unique, quaint, and familiar sights along the country roads of Lancaster County, Pennsylvania, one of the areas of greatest Amish concentration.

Birth: Led by Elder (Bishop) Jacob Ammann, the Alsatian Anabaptist sect that came to be known as the Amish broke from the Swiss Mennonite Anabaptists during the period of 1693 to 1697. Ammann strove to induce the Mennonite elders of Emmental, Switzerland, to practice a strict *Meidung*, or shunning of excommunicated persons. Ammann insisted that those who lied, for example, should be excommunicated, and he questioned the belief that all truehearted persons could gain salvation. He forbade attendance at state churches and instituted communion twice yearly (as opposed to the Mennonite yearly practice). He declared those ministers who disagreed to be excommunicated.

Growth: Persecuted as pacifists, the Germanic Amish migrated to the lands of enlightened European rulers, who recognized their reliability and farming skills. Amish numbers once in Europe cannot be estimated, but none have been there for decades. The first Amish came to Pennsylvania in the 1720s. They are now in twenty American states and also in Canada and Central and South America. In 1900 the Amish numbered 8,000; in 1950, 33,000; in 1970, 70,000; and by the 1990s, 135,000. The U.S. population of Amish is concentrated in Pennsylvania, Ohio, and Indiana.

Practices and Beliefs: The Old Order, as they became known in 1845, has clung to the spirit of Ammann. The practice of shunning serves to protect the integrity of the community and its faith. The Amish believe in Christian values such as charity, humility, and brotherly love. They have a strong pacifist tradition of turning the other cheek and believe that leading a simple, communal life (without electricity, mechanized tools, or frivolous entertainment) leads one closer to God. They are opposed to capital punishment, military service, and interference from the government or any other agency that threatens their self-sufficiency and the obligation of their church to take care of its own. Living in districts, the Amish take turns holding services in their homes. Each district has a bishop, two or more assisting preachers, and a deacon, chosen by lot. The Old Order baptizes qualified applicants approaching adulthood by affusion (pouring). As the newly baptized person stands, the bishop gives his hand to a male applicant and greets him with a "holy kiss." He also shakes hands with a female applicant, who is then kissed by the bishop's wife. The holy kiss is also exchanged among ordained men on Sunday mornings. Footwashing, the handshake, and the holy kiss are observed separately among men and women at the communion of bread and wine, still practiced twice yearly. Amish services, conducted in German, take several hours, and their hymns, sung in unison without accompaniment, may

last twenty minutes or more. Backless benches are taken by wagon from home to home as the church meeting site changes. Infants and children attend, and a modest meal follows the service.

Amish men wear black hats and plain shirts and trousers. Suspenders and hook-and-eye coat fasteners are still used in some regions. Men grow beards and wear their hair long and unparted. The upper lip is shaved. Boys' clothing resembles that of men. Women and girls also wear long hair, always braided, and dress simply. They wear plain white prayer caps from infancy on. Full bonnets guard against weather when needed. An Amish bride dresses in blue.

Early marriage and large families are encouraged. Most Amish marry in their early twenties. Following an extensive courtship, the ceremony is reverently undertaken. A honeymoon consists of an extended horse-and-buggy trip to relatives' homes.

The Amish generally use horses and mules for farm power and the horse and buggy for transportation, although some churches have permitted tractors, without pneumatic tires, as economic necessities. Young men of courting age drive a single-seated buggy, pulled by a spirited horse. A family travels in a larger, enclosed buggy. Regionally, buggy colors vary from black to light gray to yellow.

Elderly Amish are cherished and cared for within a family home or in a separate house in the farm compound. Social Security and government agricultural subsidies are not accepted. Photographs are forbidden, as are radios, movies, and television. Ownership and use of an automobile would bring excommunication and shunning by the Old Order. But life is not without enjoyment. The Amish love their own singing and traditional folk games. Pride is avoided. Humility is natural. Visiting friends and relatives is the greatest Amish joy.

The community does not allow schooling beyond the eighth grade. High school is considered worldly. Amish parents have initiated legal suits to fight compulsory education laws; some have gone to jail rather than back down from their convictions. In 1972 the United States Supreme Court, in the case of *Wisconsin v. Yoder*, decided that Amish parents may have control over their children's elementary and middle school education by establishing their own schools, and that laws forcing children to attend high school violate the First Amendment.

The Amish have also tangled with the Internal Revenue Service and the armed forces to preserve their religious freedom. In 1955 Congress extended the twenty-year-old Social Security program to include self-employed farmers. Amish farmers refused to pay taxes into the system since they had no use for the benefits; their church and not the government would take care of its own poor, sick, and elderly. The IRS responded by attaching Amish bank accounts and confiscating land and livestock. When an Amish man, Valentine Y. Byler, was arrested in 1961 for delinquent taxes and his horses sold by the IRS during spring plowing season, public outcry caused the IRS to call a moratorium on their tax collecting. In 1965 Congress passed the Medicare bill with a clause exempting self-employed Amish from the health insurance system and from Social Security as well. In 1988 the legislature granted another exemption, on payroll taxes for Amish employees who work for Amish employers.

Military service has long been another area of contention between the government and the Old Order. Based on their belief in Christian nonresistance, Amish men typically have claimed conscientious objector status in wartime, a choice for which some men were subjected to physical abuse during World War I. In 1952, during the Korean War, the government established a mandatory alternative work program (Selective Service code 1-W) for conscientious objectors. This program put young Amish men to work in the cities. Some of them refused to work in the alienating urban areas away from their families and were fined and jailed. During the last years of the Vietnam War, the government compromised by granting farm deferments, whereby Amish men served their two years working land leased to the government by their church.

The agricultural basis of the Amish community has changed since 1970 as surburban development has encroached. In Lancaster County, Pennsylvania, for example, 3,000 to 5,000 acres of farmland are being lost annually to new housing tracts, industrial parks, and retirement facilities. The attendant increase in land prices has frequently left the Amish, who divide their large farms for the next generation, with smaller farms and no place to expand. Today, 40 percent of the Amish work in other industries—construction, tourism, or home-based craft businesses.

Their spirit and sense of community, however, have not diminished. In 1992 six Amish barns in central Pennyslvania were burned by vandals. Public sympathy and donations amounting to $700,000 poured in from around the country. Since the properties were restored in the traditional barn-raising manner, most of the money stayed in the bank. The Amish decided to send the balance to Los Angeles, to help rebuild the riot-torn city.

During the first half of the twentieth century, a variety of experiences, stresses, and accommodations befell the Old Order. Many became regular Mennonites. In 1927 the Beachy Amish (named for their leader, Moses Beachy) split from the Old Order, rejecting the practice of strict shunning, and eventually began to use automobiles and modern appliances. To the outsider the Old Order may seem austere, but they continue their attempts to preserve their customs, language, and religion as they were 300 years ago. The order has grown steadily over the last fifty years, as more and more young people have decided to remain in the faith and community of their parents. Not seeking converts, the Amish remain a closed society whose sincerity and simplicity are admired but rarely emulated.

—F.W.S. and L.A.C.

THE BRANCH DAVIDIANS

An obscure splinter group of the Adventist Church, the Branch Davidians gained worldwide notoriety in the spring of 1993 when leader David Koresh and eighty-one other members died following a bloody, fifty-one day standoff with the federal government at the group's headquarters near Waco, Texas. More than a hundred agents of the Bureau of Alcohol, Tobacco, and Firearms (ATF) stormed the compound on April 19 with armored vehicles, guns, and tear gas, but a fire many believe was set intentionally by the cult members quickly consumed the buildings, killing almost all of the men, women, and children inside. Only nine cultists escaped the flames. Meanwhile, four federal agents were killed and twenty injured at the start of the seven-week siege, prompting criticism of the ATF's tactics and forcing an overhaul of the bureau's top staff. President Bill Clinton and Attorney General Janet Reno shoulder much of the blame. As for the Branch Davidians, the apocalyptic theology that formed the backbone of the group eventually consumed it, and it is virtually nonexistent today.

Birth: The Branch Davidians were founded in 1935 by Victor Houteff, a Bulgarian immigrant who had been expelled six years earlier from the Los Angeles Adventist Church. Gripped by a passage in the Book of Ezekiel in which an angel of God separates the sinners from the faithful before Jerusalem's fall to the Babylonians, Houteff perceived that as a warning to Adventists. He established his own splinter church on the outskirts of Waco, deep in the heart of the Texas Bible Belt. Houteff led the congregation until his death twenty years later, whereupon his widow, Florence, assumed control. But she dissolved the church after her prediction that the last days of creation would begin April 22, 1959, proved incorrect.

Growth: The church members who stayed on in Waco clung to Benjamin Roden, a charismatic preacher who believed himself to be the actual successor to King David of Israel. A power struggle soon developed between Roden's son, George, who inherited the church and ran it with his mother, Lois, and Vernon Howell, a would-be rock guitarist/zealot who had been expelled from a congregation of the Seventh-day Adventist Church. Howell—who legally changed his name to David Koresh in 1990—joined the Davidians in 1984 and quickly rose among their ranks. Brash, clever, and a gifted speaker, Howell was born in Houston in 1959 and grew up in the Dallas area as an indifferent student but a passionate devotee of the Scriptures. He used rock music to spread his gospel, and the walls of the otherwise spartan compound in Waco came to be decorated with posters of heavy-metal acts such as Ted Nugent and Megadeath.

Roden's grip on the sect was too strong for Howell to break initially, and he was driven off at gunpoint, forming his own splinter group that resided in tents and packing crates near Palestine, Texas, in the mid-1980s. Shortly after Roden disinterred the corpse of a female Davidian church member with the intention of bringing her back to life, Howell and his followers returned to the Waco compound seeking to overthrow him. Charges of attempted murder against Howell and his group were never proven, but Roden was judged unable to stand trial for a murder he claimed Howell ordered him to commit. Roden was remanded over to a state mental hospital in 1990 and remains there today. One important fact became clear as a result of the conflict: the Davidians were heavily armed.

Howell moved quickly to consolidate his power as head of the Branch Davidians by 1988, and soon began recruiting members from overseas. At its largest, the Branch Davidian Church near Waco numbered around 130 members. Demanding absolute faith and loyalty of his followers, Howell completed his transformation as head of the cult when he changed his name to Koresh, Hebrew for "Cyrus," the Persian king who allowed the Jews to return to Israel after their captivity in Babylon.

Practices and Beliefs: The principles of the Branch Davidians were subject to the whims and paranoia of their leader. Koresh's belief that a final, all-consuming battle with nonbelievers lay ahead formed the basis for much of the apocalyptic theology that governed the Davidians. When this belief was cross-pollinated with his own brand of secular survivalism, the cult soon developed a bunker mentality that led to the stockpiling of weapons and food to wait out the battle. In fact, members considered renaming the compound "Ranch Apocalypse."

As if shipments of tons of automatic and semiautomatic weapons, hand grenades, and ammunition weren't enough, Koresh strengthened his followers with strict weight training, military-style drills, and dietary fasts. In addition, he fortified their psyches by constantly showing his favorite war films such as Platoon and Full Metal Jacket, or testing their resolve with random questions such as "Which of your two children are you prepared to sacrifice?"

Not surprisingly, the Branch Davidians abided by a harsh code of conduct. Men were essentially laborers, while women performed household chores and schooled the children. Cult members donated their paychecks and Social Security benefits to fund the church, and the daily diet was strictly rationed vegetarian fare. Television was forbidden. In its place were Koresh's monologues—fiery, twisted takes on the Scriptures that would last long into the night.

Children, meanwhile, were treated extremely harshly in the community. Separated from their parents—whom Koresh referred to as dogs—as infants and reared by group mothers, the children were abused in every sense of the word. Boys were schooled in the art of war; girls became part of Koresh's sexual harem as early as twelve years of age. Beatings with a wooden paddle (called "the helper") sometimes lasted thirty minutes. Child-abuse charges were filed against Koresh in Texas and California, but nothing was proven.

Koresh, meanwhile, had a different set of rules for himself. Beer, meat, MTV, and air-conditioning were available to him, as were the cult women, whom Koresh used to father as many as five children. Yet many believe Koresh was a gifted theologian, and he was working on a detailed interpretation of the Seven Seals of the Bible's Book of Revelation at the time of his death.

It was Koresh's passion for firearms that proved most dangerous, and he and his followers spent almost $200,000 on weapons in the seventeen months prior to the first ATF raid. When armed federal agents tried to serve Koresh with a search warrant on February 28, 1993—a badly botched battle plan that had been revealed to the Branch Davidian leader almost an hour earlier—they were pinned down by such heavy automatic weapons fire that some agents never got off a single shot.

When it was over, four federal agents were dead and twenty were wounded. Six cult members died in the exchange, with Koresh among the wounded. Over the next fifty-one days, thirty-seven members of the church—including twenty-one children—were allowed to leave the compound as the ATF sought to wait Koresh out. But Attorney General Reno finally approved the raid of April 19, saying she feared the child abuse inside the compound would worsen.

The aftermath of the Waco standoff was emotional. Two government reports criticized the ATF's handling of the affair, forcing an overhaul of the top brass and renewing calls that the bureau be folded into the FBI and the Internal Revenue Service. Meanwhile, eleven surviving Branch Davidians were tried for the murders of the federal agents but were acquitted, although eight were convicted of lesser charges, including voluntary manslaughter and weapons violations. Then there are the twenty-one Branch Davidian children, some of whom were orphaned by the siege and all of whom bore scars. According to a Baylor College of Medicine psychiatrist who studied the children for two months, their world was upside down, and "they learned to substitute the word love with fear."

—D.W.C.

CARGO CULTS

The cargo cults are based on a simple premise, yet they are often misunderstood by outsiders who cannot conceive of the state of mind, the naïveté, the hope and faith that could lead to the emergence of the cults. Essentially, the cargo cults sprang from the have/have-not relationship between the colonial powers and the islanders where the cults exist. The natives, upon seeing the unfamiliar and immense material wealth of the white men, made a cult out of the expectation of receiving such wealth for themselves.

Birth: In the South Pacific, off the northeast coast of Australia, lie the chain of islands that make up Melanesia: the Solomon, Santa Cruz, Fiji, Banks, Loyalty, New Hebrides, and New Caledonia Islands. They are sometimes called the Black Islands because of the skin color of the natives. It is here that cargo cults are found.

As the islands vary, so do the cults, but the basic concept is the same. The natives want the goods, or "cargo," that the white colonists have, goods they are denied—but will have one day in abundance. Melanesians explain the natural and social order of the world in terms of divine intervention. They believe the spirits of their ancestors live among them, looking after the health and reproduction of the tribe and its crops. The living must lead moral lives and practice rituals so the ancestor gods will continue to favor them. The islanders value material goods—such as land, gardens, and pigs—because they show that the spirit world is well pleased with them. They generously share their wealth as a means of expressing their status in society.

The notion of cargo arrived with the traders and explorers of the eighteenth and nineteenth centuries. For example, an island in the New Hebrides called Tanna, which today has the strongest and most messianic cargo cult, was discovered in 1774 by an English explorer, Captain James Cook. The British and, later, French and American trader ships that followed brought tools and trinkets that impressed the natives as treasures from heaven.

With no knowledge of production, the natives assumed the white men had received these treasures from the spirit world. White men who didn't give them any cargo, they reasoned, were trying to withhold the religious secrets by which such cargo could be obtained. The arrival of these pale men was made even more confusing by the fact that the Melanesians had traditionally associated the color white with corpses and spirits.

Under colonial subjugation, the islanders became indentured and contract laborers in gold and copper mines and in the harvesting of such crops as coffee, rubber, and cocoa. The cargo cults arose as a religious expression of rebellion and as a way to explain the wealth and strange customs of the Europeans. Prophets of the cults foretold of a day when the ancestor spirits would return in a ship laden with cargo. This momentous event would signal the beginning of a new spiritual age, a time of peace and prosperity, a time when the dignity and autonomy of the islanders would be restored. Some prophets predicted that black and white men would be brothers, while others said the whites had been keeping back cargo intended for the natives and would therefore be relegated to a lower status in the new world order.

Growth: When missionaries arrived in Melanesia, principally after 1914, many tribe members adopted Christianity, thinking this was the key to the strangers' sharp knives and bright cloth. Later some native mission workers, being closest to the source of goods, became full-fledged cargo cult prophets. But neither pagan nor Christian rituals brought the longed-for cargo.

There was an upsurge of cult activity during World War I when the first airplanes arrived in the region. Under "Vailala Madness," as it was called, the islanders looked for their ancestors and the cargo to arrive via the airways.

World War II also brought increased millennial zeal and several new prophets. The United States Army, including several thousand black soldiers, arrived on some of the islands in 1942 to fight the Japanese. The American GIs were equipped with a wealth of cargo (tins of food, refrigerators, lamps, guns, bulldozers, and jeeps), and they were more generous in sharing the goods than the colonial British and French or the Japanese invaders had been.

Perhaps it was the natives' affinity for the friendly Americans that gave rise to the popularity of two mythical beings in cargo cult folklore—John Frum, on the island of Tanna, and Alagh, in southeastern Papua New Guinea. In both stories it is said that the spirits of the dead, who have turned white, live in America. The spirit heroes, Frum and Alagh, go on a journey to America, promising to return with the ancestors and cargo for the people. Cultists try to lure back the heroes through practicing various rituals.

During the 1940s a prophet named Burigia pronounced that Alagh would not return until the islanders had killed all whites and people of mixed race. He and a band of followers murdered several government officials and a plantation owner, leading to the arrest and execution of Burigia and eight others.

The John Frum sect took a more pacifist approach. One follower summed up their fortitude (in the Pidgin English spoken on Tanna), "Back at the end of the century we heard that Jesus Christ was coming. . . . Jesus never come. Then Isaac appeared, sometime 1930s, thereabouts. Isaac promised John and disappeared. . . . John came and spoke to us. John he speak in many ways, many times, full of wisdom. We will have a cataclysm. . . . The earth will rise. . . . One land one people. John will return to bring us an era of peace and joy. The whites will leave. . . . We will regain our youth. . . . Custom will return."

Maybe the name Frum comes from "broom," to sweep out the whites, or from the name of an American pilot or a generous quartermaster; it's not clear. What is clear, to his followers, is that he heralds the millennium of unlimited cargo.

"Every day, after work, John appears to [some] men. . . . He tells them many wondrous things. The Americans are coming. The Americans come. They give us presents. . . . John has spoken Truth."

Natives in the Solomon Islands thought the black American soldiers in World War II were descendants of natives kidnapped by explorers centuries back. They assumed the black soldiers would join them in fighting to bring in the new age, when blacks could have all the white men's cargo to themselves. But when the war ended, all the soldiers—black and white—departed, and so did the cargo.

In 1964 the islanders of New Hanover had a novel idea for attaining cargo. Rather than voting for local candidates in the first elections held for the Papua New Guinea Parliament, they wrote in the name of Lyndon Johnson, hoping Johnson would represent them and reveal the secret of cargo. When the American president declined to be drafted, the citizens pooled the money they would have paid in taxes to "buy" LBJ. Although Johnson couldn't be bought, he did volunteer to send Barry Goldwater, his opponent in the 1964 elections.

Practices and Beliefs: In anticipation of the return of their ancestors on a plane or ship, the cargo cultists have engaged in a variety of rituals, both traditional and innovative, to please the spirit gods. Ceremonial washing and feasting are often part of the practices. On occasion, cult members have destroyed their own gardens, slaughtered all their livestock, and thrown their possessions into the sea, convinced that the arrival of the "spirit plane" with its abundant cargo is imminent. Sexual mores have been disrupted, with a ritual preparation time calling for either abstinence or group sex.

In an attempt to emulate the success of foreigners in securing cargo from the gods, islanders imitated European customs in their rituals. They prepared docks, constructed airstrips, built warehouses to store the cargo, and set up rudimentary "offices" where they passed pieces of paper back and forth. After their contact with cargo-rich GIs, they marched in mock drills carrying bamboo "rifles" and wore improvised uniforms or painted "U.S.A." on their bodies. They spoke into empty beer cans as the Americans had into microphones, telling the planes to land.

Even today cult members believe that John Frum lives in the United States. To please him, they emphasize traditional costume and ritual, such as dancing and drinking kava, the local narcotic drink made from the root of the *Piper methysticum* plant. Both these practices were often against colonial law. John Frum has been described by natives as a "mysterious little man with bleached hair, a high-pitched voice, and a coat with shining buttons." Many claim to have seen him "in the faint light of a fire" under the influence of kava.

On the island of Tanna, scarlet crosses and wooden gates are erected to Frum, especially around the volcano in which his men are believed to live. Carved bamboo chapels are built. In one chapel was found a life-size effigy of John Frum, face painted white, leg lifted as if flying or running. The headquarters of the John Frum Custom Movement is in Sulphur Bay on Tanna. Each day, cult members start their morning with prayers, then a flag-raising ceremony and a military-style parade. Traditional dancing and songs wind up the service. Questioned about their unswerving faith in John Frum's return, one member answered that "the [Christian] people [have] been waiting a long time for Jesus, too," and yet they still believe in Him.

—P.F. and L.A.C.

THE NATIVE AMERICAN CHURCH

The Native American Church is made up of individuals from a number of American Indian tribes. While the roots of the church lie in both Christianity and traditional Indian belief, the church's religious rituals center on the use of the sacred plant peyote to bring the church members closer to themselves and to God.

Peyote is a species of small, spineless cactus that grows in Mexico and Texas. The top of the plant is harvested and cut into buttons, then made into tea or chewed. The alkaloid cactus has hallucinogenic properties and, though it has a bitter taste that can induce vomiting, it is not harmful or addictive.

Birth: The origins of the Native American Church date back to pre-Columbian times, when Aztec priests made use of peyote for healing and as a means of contact with the supernatural. After the Spanish defeated the Aztecs in 1521, the Catholic Church passed a decree against the use of drugs. Offenders were tried in Inquisition courts and faced the same punishment as heretics. However, in northern Mexico, where the peyote cactus is indigenous, the church was not successful in preventing annual peyote pageants, which combined elements of Christianity with ancient rituals. These peyote practices were first introduced into the United States by Quanah Parker, whose mother was white and whose father was a Comanche chief. Parker fostered its use as a sacrament and medicine among his people.

Growth: As peyote rituals evolved in the 1880s among the Kiowa in the south, the Ghost Dance religion—which promised the disappearance of the white man and the return of the buffalo— was gaining popularity among the Plains Indians. When the Ghost Dance failed to prevent the massacre of 300 Indians at the Battle of Wounded Knee in 1890, the tribes at last lost faith in its power. Threatened with the possibility of cultural annihilation, many Plains Indians turned to the rituals of peyote.

By the early 1900s peyote use had become common among the Cheyenne, Comanche, Osage, Arapaho, Sioux, and most other tribes of the southern and northern plains and the Great Basin. Legal authorities and missionaries eager to convert the tribes to Christianity tried to have peyote classified as an intoxicant, and by 1910 laws prohibiting the possession and transportation of peyote were passed in many states.

As pressure mounted on Congress to legislate against the use of peyote, James Mooney of the Smithsonian Institution called for the formation of the Native American Church to give the peyote rituals a more respectable veneer. Beginning with its first chapter in Oklahoma, chartered in 1918, the Native American Church is now incorporated in seventeen states and Canada, with a membership estimated to be between 100,000 and 225,000. Some branches of the church—including the original Oklahoma church and the one in Navajoland, Arizona— operate independently of the international organization. The church remains a minority religion even among Native Americans, and it continues to battle for its First Amendment rights.

In 1978 Congress passed the American Indian Religious Freedom Act, which protects the rights of Native Americans to celebrate the customs and ceremonies of their traditional religions. Because the act was viewed more as a policy statement than a charter of legally enforceable rights, Indian tribal leaders have tried to strengthen it through amendments and legal suits. There have been numerous recent court cases in which drug laws have been challenged for their application to the Native American Church's sacramental use of peyote.

The landmark cases in the fight are the *People v. Woody* and the *State of Arizona v. Janice and Fred Whittingham*. In the former, the California Supreme Court ruled that the arrest of Jack Woody and three other men during a peyote ceremony had violated their right to exercise their religion. In the Arizona case, the police arrested a couple who were having their marriage blessed in a Native American Church ceremony and charged them with possession of peyote. In 1973 the Arizona Court of Appeals sided with the defendants, again affirming the right to practice one's religion without government interference.

Practices and Beliefs: When it was founded in 1918, the Native American Church stated in its articles of incorporation that its purpose was

> to foster and promote the religious belief of the several tribes of Indians in the State of Oklahoma, in the Christian religion with the practice of the Peyote Sacrament commonly understood and used among the adherents of this religion ... and to teach the Christian religion with morality, sobriety, industry, kindly charity and right living and to cultivate a spirit of self-respect and brotherly union among the members of the Native Race of Indians.

The ethics of the church emphasize care of the family, self-reliance, and abstinence from alcohol.

The peyote services are all-night meetings that begin after sundown on Saturday night. The participants gather in a tepee and sit in a circle around a fire and an altar to sing, tell stories, and pray. There are two primary variations of the peyote ceremony. In the Half-Moon ceremony, the altar is molded sand shaped as a crescent moon, tobacco is used, and concepts such as the Great Spirit and Mother Earth play a key role. The Big Moon peyote ceremony, which was introduced after 1800, has more Christian elements, such as Bible readings, and features a large horseshoe-shaped altar.

In both ceremonies a line that represents the road of life (the Peyote Road) is drawn through the altar from end to end of the tepee. It is from this line that the leader—the road man—

derives his title. At the center of the altar, a large button of peyote, called the Chief Peyote, is placed and other buttons are present for consumption throughout the night. Everyone takes part in the ceremony, with special tasks assigned to the officers such as the fire man, the cedar man, the drum chief, and the road man. As cedar incense is burned and fanned, a staff and drum are passed around the circle. The person holding the staff chants a prayer or sings a sacred song while the person next to him drums. The songs, usually sung in an unstressed style, are often traditional but can be in either English or the tribal language and sometimes express Christian beliefs. Each person takes as many peyote buttons as he wants. Drumming and singing continue until midnight, at which time a woman enters with water for cleansing, and special midnight songs are sung. After midnight the mood changes from an emphasis on dispelling evil to a focus on testimonials and an acceptance of good.

Believing that attention to detail keeps thoughts in the right path, peyoteists give special concern to the sweeping of the fire's ashes and the length of the wood. The road man is trained to make sure no one becomes too withdrawn. If this does occur, he fans the person affected, splashes water on his face, and may pray with him. No one is permitted to leave the meeting after it has started. When the first trace of light is seen through the tepee hole, dawn songs are sung, and a woman brings in traditional food of beef, corn, and berries, which everyone eats from a communal dish. Then the tepee flap is opened, and members go out into the sunlight.

Throughout the service individuals seek solutions to their problems, and psychiatrists have noted that the meetings are ego strengthening. The participants value peyote for its divine power to teach and to heal. Members travel great distances to visit other tribes for services, and special meetings can be called at any time in case of emergency or for healing purposes. Women have always played a traditional part in the service as the water and food bearers, and some older women are full-fledged participants. It is a woman, too, who is said to have originated the peyote religion—at least in the Kiowa version of the myth. The story tells of a pregnant woman who became separated from her people while they were gathering food far from home. Alone and frightened, she gave birth to her child. The spirits took pity on her and advised her to eat from the peyote plant to revive her strength. She was then able to travel home, where she taught her tribe songs and rituals to celebrate the power of the sacred cactus. The woman of this myth is called Peyote Woman and her story is often told in peyote ceremonies.

Although the Native American Church makes use of Christian paraphernalia and is—as was the Ghost Dance—Christian oriented, hostility from many Protestants and Catholics still exists over the use of drugs for visionary experiences. Members of the church feel that they were chosen over the white man to use peyote, and that while the white man may pray to God, the Indian speaks to him face to face.

—V.H. and L.A.C.

THE PEOPLES TEMPLE

The Peoples Temple originated as a nondenominational Christian church founded by the Reverend Jim Jones in the 1950s. It was to become known as one of the most infamous cults of all time. The Temple's ranks included a contingent of white liberals, but African Americans eventually constituted about two-thirds of the total congregation. Initially considered to be a legitimate theologian, Jones drew much public support and generated controversy while striving to make community service one of the Temple's primary hallmarks. However, it is because of its singular act of self-destruction rather than its good deeds that the Temple made notorious history on November 18, 1977, when its members committed the largest mass suicide in recent times.

Birth: James Warren Jones was born in 1931 in Lynn, Indiana. He married Marceline Baldwin in 1949 and became a Christian pastor. Having founded, in 1953, the Christian Assembly of God Church—a Fundamentalist church preaching racial equality—Jones went on to establish the Indianapolis Peoples Temple Full Gospel Church in 1956. It became affiliated with the Disciples of Christ denomination, in which he was ordained as a minister in 1964. Jones and his wife, Marceline, were the first Caucasians in Indianapolis to adopt an African-American child. They also adopted three Korean children and an emotionally handicapped daughter of Native American heritage. He gave his clan the nickname "the Rainbow Family."

Growth: Jones was named to head the Indianapolis Human Rights Commission in 1961 and was accorded the Martin Luther King Junior Humanitarian Award in 1977. In marked contrast to his honors, he achieved notoriety for claiming to have raised forty people from the dead and by conducting fraudulent "miracle" healings. His cancer cure, for example, involved making it appear as if he were able to pull diseased tissue from victims. The cancerous organs he purported to have extracted from their bodies were, however, chicken innards.

One hundred members of his Indiana congregation followed Jones to the vicinity of Ukiah in the Redwood Valley of northern California in 1965. Chosen in the belief that this region of ancient, protected trees would somehow survive the nuclear Armageddon that Jones was predicting would occur, the community served the transplanted congregation very well. The Peoples Temple flourished there and was able, in 1971, to buy a Masonic temple in San Francisco. A second church was subsequently purchased in Los Angeles. To fulfill Jones's Utopian vision, a third Peoples Temple outpost, called Jonestown, was established in 1973 as an agricultural commune in Guyana.

Headquartered in San Francisco, Jones steadily built the Peoples Temple into an organization that served sectarian as well as theological ends. The organization operated successful day-care centers, rehabilitation programs, soup kitchens, nursing homes, a ranch for handicapped boys, and drug counseling services, and offered financial grants to the needy. Jones became a significant player in Democratic Party and San Francisco politics and served as that city's Housing Authority chairman from 1976 to 1977.

Practices and Beliefs: The tenets of the Peoples Temple were based on a mixture of Christian Fundamentalism and Jones's own political ideology. He preached racial equality and championed socialistic doctrines. Prophecy of apocalypse was one of his principal messages. He warned of a fascist takeover of the United States and of eventual nuclear annihilation. The concept of "revolutionary suicide," which calls for collective self-destruction, became a dominating element of Temple dogma and led to the disaster at Jonestown.

Intimidation, humiliation, and severe physical punishments were Jones's chosen methods of enforcing authoritarian discipline. Punishments included forced consumption of hot peppers, sexual abuse, electric shocks, and other means of torture. Forced false confessions, surveillance, physical isolation, and drugs such as Thorazine and Valium were used to reinforce mind-control techniques by which Jones maintained control over his flock. Jones, known to take amphetamines, Percodan, and Elavil, was suspected of being a heroin user as well.

The Peoples Temple reached the zenith of its popularity in the mid-1970s, when its membership swelled to approximately 4,000 and it had a band of communes in operation from Los Angeles to Vancouver. Reports of financial misappropriations, sexual improprieties, beatings, and other serious crimes and indiscretions led to journalistic exposés of the Temple and

Victims of the Jonestown mass suicide and massacre, 1978.

dramatically heightened Jones's own sense of paranoia. He left the United States in 1977 and took personal charge of operations in Jonestown. In October of that year he cut off its communications link with the outside world and initiated an exercise, called White Nights, that prepared the cult for the mass suicide.

In response to charges made by the press as well as those of former followers and several relatives of Temple members, Congressman Leo J. Ryan of San Francisco led a team of investigators and journalists in checking out conditions at Jonestown. The visitors spent a night in the jungle commune and then, shepherding a group of more than a dozen Temple defectors, headed for a nearby àirstrip for a flight out of Guyana. Jones, fearful that the world was about to learn the truth of his operations, sent a hit squad to the runway in order to prevent the party from taking off. Congressman Ryan, NBC reporter Don Harris, NBC cameraman Bob Brown, and San Francisco *Chronicle* photographer Greg Robinson were killed and others were wounded.

When Jones learned that the mission had been less than successful, he initiated the mass suicide. The commune's paramedics were ordered to dispense fruit-flavored, cyanide-spiked Flavoraid to everyone in Jonestown. Adults, children, and seniors were told to drink the poison punch, and syringes were used to spray it down the throats of infants. According to an eyewitness, eighty-five bursts of semiautomatic gunfire rang out as Jones's henchmen fired at those Temple members attempting to escape. Nine hundred and fourteen people died at Jonestown, including 276 children. Jones himself was felled by a bullet that pierced his temple. Most of the eighty-four people who survived the carnage, a group that included three of Jones's sons, did so because they fortuitously happened to be elsewhere at the time.

—R.N.K.

THE RASTAFARIANS

The Rastafarian religion traces its roots back to Marcus Garvey, a Jamaican nationalist who founded the Universal Negro Improvement Association and led a "back to Africa" movement in the 1920s. But it wasn't until Ras (Prince) Tafari was crowned Emperor Haile Selassie of Ethiopia in 1930—fulfilling Garvey's prophecy that a black man would become king in Africa— that blacks began to take notice. Jamaicans, in particular, began to scour the Bible, seizing upon a passage in the Book of Revelation that appeared to validate the centuries of black sufferance and confirm Selassie as the Messiah. Rastafarians, as they called themselves, based their principles on a mixture of racism—whites

were evil and inferior to blacks—and Black Judaism, which identified Hebrews of the Old Testament as black people. The Rastafarian movement is symbolized by reggae music, long hair curls called dreadlocks, and the smoking of marijuana, and still draws its strength from Jamaica, where its numbers continue to grow. Recent immigration trends indicate that as many as 5,000 Rastafarians reside in the United States.

Birth: Mosiah Marcus Garvey's fierce belief in black pride served as the springboard for the Rastafarian movement. Born in the rural parish of Saint Anne's, Jamaica, in 1887, he was schooled as a printer and became an active trade union member. It was there that Garvey got a firsthand look at racial segregation—white colonialists held the most power, followed by citizens of mixed race, and then blacks. Garvey began to agitate for an independent black nation in the African homeland, promoting dark pigmentation as a symbol of pride, and promised deliverance for his people.

Garvey took his movement to the United States in 1916, where he formed the Universal Negro Improvement Association in Harlem and began to preach his vision of black statehood to the poorest and most underprivileged segment of the African-American population. Garvey reached countless more through his newspaper *Negro World*, and even promoted a steamship company, the Black Star Shipping Line, to return blacks to the motherland. But Garvey found no allies among either established African-American leaders or edgy white lawmakers, and he was convicted of mail fraud in 1923 and sentenced to five years in jail. In 1927 he was deported back to Jamaica, and eventually he emigrated to England, were he died, lonely and bitter, in 1940.

But Garvey's prediction of black deliverance appeared to come true in 1930, when Haile Selassie was crowned emperor of Ethiopia. Among his many titles were "Conquering Lion of Judah," "King of Kings," and "Lord of Lords," leading many blacks to believe he was the Living God promised in Revelations 19:16, which said, "On his robe and on his thigh he has a name inscribed, King of Kings and Lord of Lords." Although Selassie never claimed to be a god, he was purportedly a direct descendent of the queen of Shebah and King Solomon, which was good enough for Garvey's disaffected followers.

Growth: That the Rastafarian movement took hold so quickly in Jamaica was largely due to the efforts of four ministers—Joseph Hibbert, Archibald Dunkley, Robert Hinds, and Leonard Howell. It was Howell who most aggressively promoted the new religion, selling postcards of Selassie that he told buyers were passports to Africa (a leap of faith that earned him two years

in jail for fraud), and later establishing a
commune, the Pinnacle, in the parish of Saint
Catherine's in 1940 that served as the headquarters of Rastafarianism for the next two decades.

Residents of the Pinnacle grew ganja (marijuana), among other crops, and closely allied
themselves with Ethiopia. Harassed endlessly
by the Jamaican authorities, they soon grew
militant and violent, referring to themselves as
"Ethiopian warriors" and growing their hair
into long dreadlocks, a style believed borrowed
from Masai and Somali tribesmen of East
Africa. By the time Howell was committed to a
Jamaican mental hospital in 1960, the Pinnacle
was practically a nation unto itself.

Rastafarian groups had spread throughout
Jamaica by then, with mixed results. Most
notable was an ill-fated attempt by Claudius
Henry, an ordained minister, to lead an exodus
back to Africa in the fall of 1959. The resulting
chaos did prompt the Jamaican government to
send missions to Africa and investigate the
possibility of repatriation. However, nothing
concrete could be worked out and most Rastafarians found themselves stuck in the Caribbean.

In 1961 a delegation of Rastafarians traveled to
Ethiopia and met Abuna, the archbishop of the
Ethiopian Orthodox Church, who told them
Haile Selassie would be very upset if he learned
that the Rastas worshipped him as God. Far from
being discouraged, the Rastafarians were convinced that this sign of humility was proof of
Selassie's divinity. When Haile Selassie himself
made an official state visit to Jamaica on April
21, 1966, thousands of Rastafarians rushed
forward to touch the airplane. It took one-half
hour for Selassie to deplane and the official
welcoming ceremony had to be canceled.

Bob Marley.

Practices and Beliefs: The customs of the
Rastafarian movement vary widely between
sects, but there are some basic principles. For
instance, Haile Selassie is the Living God—
despite his death in 1975—and Ethiopia is the
Promised Land. Jamaica and other countries
outside Ethiopia are part of Babylon, a living
hell. Reportedly, when Haile Selassie visited
Jamaica, he gave a communique to the Rastafarians urging them not to emigrate to Ethiopia
until they had liberated the people of Jamaica.

Black is holy and beautiful, while white is evil
and ugly. Rastafarians believe they are direct
descendants of the ancient Israelites, who were
persecuted by the whites, and the day is coming
when whites will become the black man's
servant. In fact, whites are regarded as so inferior
that a Rastafarian will not work under one.

Marijuana is referred to by Rastafarians as the
wisdom weed, and they believe it was found
growing on the grave of King Solomon. Many
believe it is holy, and smoking "ganja" makes
one closer to God. But most Rastafarians refuse
to touch alcohol, believing white men originally

used it to get Africans drunk and more easily
enslave them.

Rastafarian beliefs are spread casually,
through street conferences called grounations, a
conflation of the words ground and foundation.
Followers deliberately speak in a jivey patois
language designed to confuse outsiders. Ganja is
often smoked with a pipe—echoing the Pipe of
Peace used by Native Americans—and simple
foods such as a mixture of flour, macaroni, and
water are eaten. (Canned or chemical foods or
those from scavengers such as pigs and shellfish
are never eaten.)

Reggae music has proven to be the most
popular vehicle for transmitting the Rastafarian
message worldwide. Popular musicians such as
Bob Marley and Peter Tosh used Jamaican "ska"
and "rock-steady" beats to produce albums that
spoke directly to homeless, unemployed, and
sometimes violent masses everywhere. In fact,
Marley became such a musical force that his
power took on political overtones, and his
apparent support for the Socialists led to an
assassination attempt in 1976. Gunmen broke
into his Kingston home and shot Marley, his
wife, and two others (none died), but Marley
still managed to perform—albeit in bandages—
at a concert promoting national peace and unity
three days later.

In 1978 Marley was awarded the International Peace Medal by the African delegation to
the United Nations, and he was an official guest
at Zimbabwe's independence celebration two
years later, an honor Marley regarded as the
highest he ever received. Marley died of brain
cancer on May 11, 1981.

—D.W.C.

Chapter 19

DEATH

GREAT ESCAPES

HOUDINI ESCAPES THE WATER TORTURE CELL— 1912

Houdini is still the undisputed king of escapes, even though almost seventy years have passed since his death. He successfully challenged audiences around the world to construct traps from which he could not extricate himself. During his career he escaped from countless jails and prisons, usually after being stripped and searched by police physicians to show that he had nothing "up his sleeves." He escaped from a Siberian transport cell, from the chain-laced belly of a freak sea monster that had washed up on the shores of New England, from crates, bags, barrels, boxes, and coffins. But Houdini's most spectacular feat was his famous Water Torture Cell.

He first introduced the Water Torture Cell at Berlin's Circus Busch in 1912. The audience went into a frenzy of appreciation, and the escape continued to astound tremendous crowds until Houdini died fourteen years later.

One of the posters he used to publicize the escape showed a fanged giant holding the tank shut, with Houdini trapped inside. Never known for modesty, Houdini called it his own "original invention, the greatest sensational mystery ever attempted in this or any other age." At the bottom of the poster, Houdini offered a "$1,000 reward to anyone proving that it is possible to obtain air in the 'up-side down' position in which Houdini releases himself from his water-filled torture cell."

Houdini would begin the act by spending about five minutes explaining the construction and design of the cell. The metal-lined mahogany tank was less than six feet high and less than one yard square. There was an inch-thick sheet of glass in the front to give the audience an unobstructed view of the cell's interior. The

top of the cell was composed of a set of stocks that would entrap Houdini's ankles. The stocks would be enclosed in a steel frame that would be padlocked to the tank. A steel grille would completely surround Houdini in the tank to reduce his range of movement. Then the entire tank would be locked in steel bands. After going over all this in detail, Houdini would repeat his cash offer to anyone who could prove he could breathe in the tank.

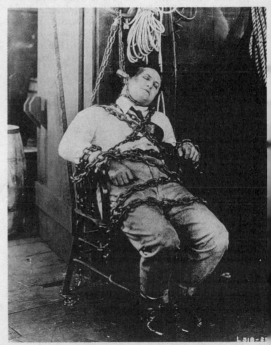

Harry Houdini relaxes before a performance.

Houdini would leave the stage to change clothes as his assistants filled the tank to the brim, using brass pails dipped in a giant tub of water. Houdini would return in a swimsuit and lie on a mat as the thick stocks were shut on his ankles. Then the steel frame was passed over his body and secured around the stocks so that they could not open. Each of these steps was inspected and supervised by a group of volunteers from the audience.

The grille was lowered into the tank; then Houdini was raised above it, head downward. He was lowered into the water, and the steel frame of the stocks was padlocked to the cell. The glass front was then covered to hide Houdini's method of escape.

The escape was extremely efficient and took twenty minutes to perform. Houdini eventually tired of it and repeatedly tried to come up with more spectacular feats—making an elephant vanish onstage, walking through a solid brick wall built before the audience by local masons, dismembering and reassembling a male assistant—but nothing drew crowds like the Water Torture Cell. He was forced to present it continually, no matter where he performed.

But despite all the hoopla, the Water Torture Cell was not Houdini's most difficult escape. While he had to depend on his superb physical conditioning and training to effect the escape, the cell was rigged, unlike all the prisons, manacles, straitjackets, and handcuffs he routinely slipped out of. This doesn't mean the feat was simple, however. In fact, there were two plugs in the bottom of the tank that Houdini could pull to drain the water in an emergency—a precaution he never would have considered if the rigged mechanism guaranteed escape.

The secret of the Water Torture Cell was in false rivets. By using the steel grille as a ladder, Houdini could pull himself into a fetal position. Though the tank had been filled to the brim, the immersion of his body had caused much of the water to flow out of the tank before the stocks were locked in place. Thus, when he curled up with his head at the top, the water level would drop by the amount of water displaced by his head and shoulders, an amount sufficient to allow him to breathe. Then he would work out the false rivets with his fingers. Removing these rivets would allow the frame around the stocks to come open, and Houdini could then free his feet, remove the stocks, and climb out without picking so much as one lock. Then he would replace the false rivets in the reassembled frame and wait until enough time had passed to make his escape dramatic.

Harry Houdini did not die in the Water Torture Cell—as shown in one popular movie about him. He died on Halloween, October 31, 1926, from an advanced case of appendicitis.

—C.B.

ESCAPE FROM SIBERIA— 1941

In the fall of 1939, the highly mechanized German blitzkrieg knifed into Poland from the west while the massive Red Army attacked from the east. In the doomed Polish army was twenty-four-year-old lieutenant Slavomir Rawicz. After suffering shrapnel wounds on the western front, Rawicz retreated east into the Russian-dominated area. Well-educated, fluent in Russian, and bred in a border town, he was soon arrested as a spy and found himself in the infamous Kharkov prison.

The torture master at Kharkov, known as "the Bull," subjected Rawicz to vicious beatings, knife slashings, cigarette burnings, icy water torture, and more, all in an effort to extort a confession. Yet after six months, the resolute Pole still had not confessed. To confess meant death, he feared, and he had a will to live. But the Bull, his reputation at stake, drugged his prisoner. In a stupor Rawicz signed a document he had not even been permitted to read. It was used as evidence against him in a mock trial, and he was sentenced to twenty-five years in a Siberian labor camp.

There were others with stories like Rawicz's, and thousands were assembled for the journey by rail into Siberia. Jammed against one another in unheated cattle cars, they had to stand for long periods, and many of the ill-nourished men died. The survivors left the train after a month, during which they had traveled more than 3,000 miles, for an even worse ordeal. Two columns of fifty men were handcuffed by one arm to a long chain. One end of the chain was then attached to a truck and the truck drove off north into the Siberian wilderness, pulling the convicts behind. Despite the fierce Siberian winter, with its blizzards, cutting winds, and drifting snow, the trucks enforced a constant pace of four miles an hour. As men passed the brink of exhaustion and died, they were uncuffed, stripped, and buried in the snow, while the survivors were moved forward on the chain. Soon a length of empty chain trailing in the snow told a tale of death.

After sixty days and more than a thousand miles, the decimated convoy finally reached camp number 303, deep in the Siberian forest about 350 miles south of the Arctic Circle. Slavomir Rawicz, assigned to a logging detail, immediately began plotting an escape. He volunteered for a job making wooden skis in return for increased rations—a chance to strengthen himself and to hoard supplies. After several months he volunteered to repair the commandant's radio, and he was befriended by the commandant's wife. With her help he obtained better clothing and more food for himself and his friends, and on a snowy night in April 1941 seven men crawled under the barbed wire, eluded guard dogs, and climbed the stockade.

There was no hesitation on the part of the desperate group as to which way to go. It had been decided in advance, reasoned through the long, frosty nights of whispered plotting in the barracks. They could not go east to the Kamchatka Peninsula 600 miles away. That route, though the shortest and easiest, was also the most obvious, and the risk of being apprehended would grow as they approached the heavily guarded and fortified Pacific coast. It was also certain capture or death to head back into the Siberian heartland and try to live out the war in hiding without the necessary working papers. So the treacherous southern route was the only alternative; south to Afghanistan or India and freedom.

Traveling by night and hiding by day, they avoided populated areas wherever possible. Near the great Lake Baikal they chanced on a young Polish girl, named Kristina, who had escaped from another labor camp, and she joined their party. In approximately sixty days, the group was some 1,200 miles from camp number 303, across the border in Outer Mongolia.

In Outer Mongolia the party traveled by day and mingled freely with the local populace, exchanging work for food. The Mongolians were hospitable even though the group was infested with lice. Still, they yearned for Allied territory and pressed forward toward India. After several weeks they entered the fearsome Gobi Desert and endured burning sun, long days without water, and three weeks with only snakes for food. In the Gobi, Kristina and one of the men died.

By October 1941 the six remaining fugitives reached the Himalayas. Fed and provisioned by friendly Tibetans, they began the climb. One morning one of the men simply did not awaken. The five continued, battling bitter cold, ripping winds, altitude sickness, and scurvy. Finally the crest of the last mountain range was behind them, and all that remained was the descent into India and safety.

Only one easy path of descent was available, and in the distance the men could see two creatures in that path. Approaching closer, the men saw a pair of rusty brown, eight-foot-tall beings looking like a cross between a bear and an ape. In his book The Long Walk, Rawicz described the encounter between the beasts and the group: "Two points struck me immediately. They were enormous and they walked on their hind legs. The picture is clear in my mind, fixed there indelibly by a solid two hours of observation. We just could not believe what we saw at first, so we stayed to watch. . . . I got the uncomfortable feeling they were challenging us to continue our descent across their ground. 'I think, they are laughing at us,' said Zaro. Mister Smith stood up—'It occurs to me they might take it into their heads to come up and investi-

gate us. It is obvious they are not afraid of us. I think we had better go while we are safe.' We pushed off around the rock and directly away from them. I looked back and the pair were standing still, arms swinging slightly, as though listening intently. What were they? For years they remained a mystery to me, but since recently I have read of scientific expeditions to discover the Abominable Snowman of the Himalayas and studied descriptions of the creature given by native hillmen, I believe that on that day we may have encountered two of the animals." Forced to make a treacherous detour, tragedy struck the group a final time. One of the men slipped off a rope and fell into a seemingly bottomless crevasse—an indirect victim of the "Abominable Snowman."

The group did not buckle but pressed on. They had not eaten for eight days when, on a sunny morning, they saw, in the distance, some men and dogs tending a flock of sheep. Their hopes raised, they kept going, looking like walking skeletons. Suddenly they spotted a band of soldiers marching toward them. They wanted to call out to them but were too weak and exhausted to do anything but stand and stare, their eyes filling with tears, as the military marchers approached. The group began to laugh and dance crazily before the astonished eyes of their uniformed rescuers, and one by one they collapsed on the ground. After nearly a year and 4,000 miles, the four survivors were at last safe and free.

After a lengthy recuperation in a Calcutta hospital, Slavomir Rawicz rejoined his Polish regiment fighting alongside the Allies in the Middle East.

—J.Z.

HENRI CHARRIERE (PAPILLON)—1941

Born in the south of France in 1906, the man who called himself Papillon ("butterfly" in French) has become known to the world as the quintessential escape artist. Blessed with an iron constitution, an endlessly inventive intelligence, a personality that could win over practically anyone he met, and an absolute determination to be free, Papillon staged one of the most bizarre escapes—after nine attempts—from the infamous prison on Devil's Island.

He later became famous through his autobiography, Papillon, and the film of the same title, which starred Steve McQueen and Dustin Hoffman.

Papillon grew up in Paris, a small player in the Montmartre underworld. In 1930 he was convicted of stabbing a pimp, a crime he steadfastly denied having committed, and sentenced to life in prison. As he descended into the hell of the French penal system, he quickly began to learn how to survive.

First, he discovered, every prisoner needed a *plan*, a smooth aluminum tube the size of a man's thumb that unscrewed in the middle so that tightly folded paper money could be secreted inside. The *plan* was then inserted in the anus, lodging far enough up in the colon so that guards could not discover it in the most probing of body searches.

Sentenced to a penal colony in French Guiana, he learned when he arrived that the life expectancy of prisoners was dismal. Every year 80 percent of the men were lost to leprosy, yellow fever, dysentery, tuberculosis, or malaria. And, of course, to murder and suicide. Suicide, indeed, stared him in the face for two years in solitary, his introduction to the world of prison.

No books, no paper, no pencil, the barest of human contact and that with brutal guards; a cement block for a chair, planks for a bed, a wooden pillow, and a cell with very little light but plenty of centipedes, rats, and mosquitoes—that was Papillon's world for two years.

"Here we don't try rehabilitation," said the prison director in his "welcoming" speech. "We know it's useless. We try to break you."

Papillon survived this stretch by exhausting himself physically each day by incessant pacing and then escaping inward to a rich fantasy life in which he could "roam among the stars." He wrote in his book, "I would not give in to the mental aberrations that complete isolation induced. . . . I had a good remedy: from the very start I would think of myself as free, healthy in mind and body."

His first escape was short-lived and brought him into the world of an isolated leper colony, among outcasts from society who befriended him and did what they could for him. He shared his meals with horribly ravaged men who had no noses and few fingers, and whose faces often lacked lips and eyelids.

As his obsession with escape grew he learned that most of the men in the penal colonies had adapted to life in a prison colony. He knew he could never adapt; he would escape or die.

In one escape attempt he and a friend constructed a raft, piece by piece, hiding the pieces in a grave in the island's cemetery. This attempt was also unsuccessful. He ended up in solitary confinement again, but his sentence was shortened when, on the one day prisoners were allowed to bathe in a makeshift pool at the edge of the sea, he made a dangerous attempt to save the life of a little girl who had been swept out into shark-infested waters.

Finally, Papillon was sent to Île du Diable, Devil's Island, which is actually one of three islands, the Îsles du Salut, that make up a triangle, with Royale and Saint-Joseph at the base and Diable at the top. It was on Diable that Dreyfus had been imprisoned, and Papillon took to sitting on the bench, high on the northernmost tip of the island, where Dreyfus himself had sat and dreamed of freedom.

It was 1941; Papillon had been in prison eleven years. He was thirty-five years old and had eight unsuccessful escapes behind him. He was about to start planning the most bizarre of them all, the one that would succeed—barely—in winning him his freedom.

On Diable there was no way to buy, steal, or make a boat or raft, and yet he knew he had to float away to freedom. The plan he came up with, like the work of so many creative geniuses, involved simple materials ready to hand.

He noticed that a giant wave came regularly after every six smaller waves, one that maybe, just maybe, if he timed it just right and leaped off the cliff into the water, would carry him away from the island—to shark-infested waters and a trip of several days, something no swimmer could hope to survive.

He needed a boat or—and here the second simple element of his escape scheme came to him—how about a big bag of coconuts? They floated, one by one, he knew that very well. With stones to simulate his own body weight, he began to experiment, tossing bags of coconuts off the cliff.

Finally he had the formula just right—if he tied himself to the perfect double bag of coconuts and leaped at just the right moment into the raging sea far below the cliff, he would be swept to sea. The currents, the tides, and the wind would take him to British Guiana, or Surinam, or Venezuela. Or it would kill him, and he well knew that death was a kind of escape too—but not the kind he craved.

With a fellow prisoner, Sylvain, he made the leap, each man with his own coconut raft and a small bag of supplies. The coconuts themselves, rich in liquid and vitamins, would provide sustenance for the trip.

Sylvain later perished in quicksand, but Papillon survived, eventually making his way to Venezuela, the land that was to be his home, the home of a free man finally. There he earned money as a tattoo artist, a restaurant keeper, the manager of a striptease joint in a bauxite mining town, and even at one point as impresario to a dancing cow.

With the publication of his book in 1970, he was able to spend his last years as a successful author. Papillon died in Madrid on July 29, 1973.

—R.W.S.

ESCAPE FROM GERMAN PRISONER-OF-WAR CAMP STALAG LUFT III—1943

It was not Lieutenant Oliver Philpot, hero of this story, who thought up the wooden-horse escape plan but his two comrades in the World

War II prisoner-of-war camp Stalag Luft III—Lieutenant R. Michael Codner, of the Royal Artillery, and Flight Lieutenant Eric "Bill" Williams, both of whom, like Philpot, were British. Instead of tunneling to safety from the prisoners' huts, it was logical to dig from the prison yard, which was closer to the edge of the compound. But they needed some kind of cover. The answer was a wooden horse, not so grand as the Trojans' but just as effective—a vaulting box, like the ones in high-school gyms, ostensibly to be used by the men to keep physically fit. While some men were vaulting over it, others would be under it, digging a path to freedom.

Accordingly, the horse was built: constructed of timber, paneled with wood from Red Cross tea chests, and with a top of solid boards padded with bedding. Looking like a sawhorse clothed in wood, it had a base measuring five feet by three feet, and it stood four and one-half feet high.

At first the men went through their two-hour vaulting sessions with the horse empty. One prisoner, deliberately awkward, knocked it over a couple of times to show the guards that nothing was going on underneath. The guards were justifiably suspicious, as they were at any peculiar activity engaged in by the men: at night they checked the horse over, breaking the fine black thread the men had rigged it with.

On July 8, 1943, tunneling began. Williams concealed himself in the box; then four men inserted two poles in each end of it and carried it out. While the men, dressed in shorts, vaulted one by one over the box, Williams removed a top layer of gray sand and put it into a cardboard box. Then he dug out yellow sand beneath, put it in bags made of pantlegs, and hung the bags (twelve in all) on the roof of the horse. Then he sank a bottomless and topless tea chest six inches below the surface to shore up the sides of the shaft, used the chest's lid as a cover, put the gray sand back, and knocked on the horse to be let out. After the horse was returned to the canteen, the men transferred the sand to long, sausagelike bags that hung inside their pants and let it trickle out around the compound yard.

In the next weeks, Codner and Williams took turns digging the shaft deeper and shoring it up below the tea chest with bricks. Then they began the horizontal tunnel, which they carefully lined with bed boards for the first twenty feet, so jolting caused by the vaulting wouldn't cave it in. It took two months to complete the first 40 of the 110 feet from the entrance point to 30 feet beyond the barbed wire. By then they were exhausted and started working together; one used a basin to collect the sand and the other pulled the basin back and bagged it. Since the men were getting bored with vaulting, Philpot was assigned as top-of-the-ground organizer to spur them on and lift their flagging spirits.

Meanwhile, using whatever makeshift tools they could devise, other prisoners were fashioning costumes and false passports for the potential escapees. The end results were works of art.

Once the tunnel caved in when a vaulter came down on a weak spot, but he had the presence of mind to fake a broken leg and lie across the telltale hole while Codner, who was in the tunnel, patched it up.

In the autumn, with time growing short (their railroad timetables would shortly expire, and their escape plans called for railroad travel), Williams pushed a poker up through the dirt at the end of the tunnel to see how far they had come. The end was nine feet short of a ditch where the searchlight would cast a shadow to provide them with some cover, so they dug on.

On October 29 the tunnel was complete. At 6:00 P.M. the three waited at the far end while another prisoner sealed up the entrance. Philpot later wrote about his final descent into the tunnel: "It was extraordinarily similar to plunging into a really cold sea."

Knowing the guard was coming through at 6:30 and their train would arrive at 7:00, the three men wasted no time. First Codner and Williams left the tunnel. Then it was Philpot's turn. In his pose as a Scandinavian businessman, he was wearing a suit, shirt, tie, and shoes; the name on his fake passport was Jon Jorgensen. Over his clothes he wore dyed Red Cross underwear to keep tunnel dirt off and to make him less conspicuous as he ran to safety. One of the men had given him a watch with a luminous dial, and he carried a homemade compass.

Poking his head up like a groundhog, he saw a tree and the lights of the compound. He knew the other two had gotten away safely, because there was no noise of pursuit. It was so bright that he felt "like an ant on a brilliantly lit billiards table." The guard was in his box eighty feet away, and a searchlight swept past. The tunnel seemed like home. In Philpot's words: "I could only think of boundary lights, search-lights, goons in boxes, harsh excited German shouts, and, above all, that cracking, splitting noise of shots disturbing a peaceful country night. I now almost wanted to pat the tunnel—as an old dog for which I had an affection. This earthwork was now no longer enemy but friend. It gave me cover. I had air now—and it was safe, and homely; I wanted to lie prone in it forever."

But it was time to go. He put his bundles of paraphernalia on the ground, climbed up, picked the bundles up, and ran across the road into the woods, which seemed more frighteningly open than he had imagined. From the camp he could hear prisoners singing loud hymns to cover the escape.

Without real incident, Philpot made it to the

train station and caught a train to Küstrin, then another to Danzig, where he arrived at 5:00 P.M. on October 30. He stowed away on a ship to Sweden and was subsequently flown home to England. Before he left, Philpot sent a friend at the camp a watch engraved with a smiling horse with three upraised tails.

Williams and Codner also made good their escape, though it took them two weeks, via a French labor camp and the Danish underground, to reach Sweden.

—A.E.

ESCAPE FROM ALCATRAZ—1962

Three bank robbers—Frank Morris and brothers Clarence and John Anglin—made the most elaborate and successful escape from Alcatraz in the twenty-nine-year history of the federal penitentiary known as "the Rock." The former prison is situated on a twelve-acre rocky island one and three-quarter miles off the shore of San Francisco. It once held military prisoners and later notorious criminals such as Al Capone and "Machine Gun" Kelly. Of the forty-one inmates who attempted escape from the maximum-security prison, twenty-six were recaptured, seven were shot to death, three drowned, and only two others besides Morris and the Anglins have never been found.

Morris and the Anglin brothers engineered their escape route from their cell. Working at night with a drill made from the motor of a vacuum cleaner, they enlarged the air-vent holes that ran from the cell to the larger ventilation-duct system. They worked only in the evening, when the prison's "music hour" masked the sounds of their labor, and they covered the growing hole with a piece of cardboard painted to resemble a metal grill. They dispensed of the concrete and plaster powder the next day during their exercise hour in the yard.

On June 11, the night of their escape, they put "sleeping dummies" in their beds to fool the guards, who kept them under almost constant watch (Alcatraz had 155 guards to 269 inmates, the highest per-prisoner ratio in any federal prison). The dummies' heads were constructed of soap and plaster, with facial features painted on. They were also adorned with human hair collected from the prison barber shop.

After crawling through the air vents to the ventilation corridor, the three escapees climbed up pipes to another air vent in the ceiling. Removing the screen, they reached the roof and raced atop the prison to the south wall, over the kitchen. There they slid down a fifty-foot pipe to reach the ground. Heading for the ocean, they had to scale at least one twelve-foot fence topped with barbed wire. Then, according to one account, they boarded a raft made of raincoats pilfered from the prison sewing shop and set out into the icy bay.

The next morning, about nine hours after their departure, the guards discovered the men were missing. A dragnet of the bay turned up a makeshift oar and a life vest on nearby Angel Island—indicating to officials that the three convicts had drowned. Nevertheless, the search was expanded to the city of San Francisco and the entire nation. No other evidence of Morris, Anglin,

Convicted bank robbers Frank Morris, John Anglin, and Clarence Anglin escaped from Alcatraz Island prison in 1962. It is not known whether they survived.

and Anglin—alive or dead—has ever been discovered. On the night of the escape, the ebb and flow of tides around Alcatraz was exceptionally mild, making it highly possible that Morris and the Anglin brothers, with their homemade life preservers and raft, did reach safety.

If the fugitives are living today, they would be in their early sixties. The hunt for them is still on. The U.S. marshal's office continues to investigate leads. As recently as 1993, marshals followed up on information provided by Thomas Kent, an ex-convict who had been incarcerated with Morris and the Anglin brothers. Kent appeared on the television program *America's Most Wanted*, receiving $2,000 in expenses for his interview. According to Kent, he was one of forty inmates who participated in the getaway preparations. While prison officials first thought that the excavation into the air vent was done with spoons, Kent supplied the detail that it had actually been done with a drill made from a vacuum cleaner motor.

Kent also related that the trio who escaped had learned Spanish in prison and that Clarence Anglin's girlfriend was set to meet them on shore and drive them to Mexico. Kent said he didn't join the escape because he had never learned to swim. Public interest in the fate of the escapees has always been strong—from the popularity of the movie *Escape from Alcatraz*, starring Clint Eastwood, to the recounting of the story by tour guides who conduct 1 million tourists a year through the former penitentiary. The ferryboat company that takes the tourists back and forth from Fisherman's Wharf to the island is offering a $1-million reward for information leading to the arrest of Frank Morris and Clarence and John Anglin.

For several years after the escape, the Anglin family received unsigned postcards, and at the 1987 funeral of the Anglins' mother, relatives noted two odd-looking women in heavy makeup.

—L.A.C.

SURVIVORS

MOUNT PELÉE SURVIVORS

On May 8, 1902, the volcano at the peak of Mount Pelée, which had been asleep for fifty-one years, erupted with sudden intensity, destroying the entire town of Saint Pierre, on the island of Martinique, and killing about 36,000 people. The island's largest volcano, standing 4,583 feet above sea level and dominating the northern end of Martinique, Mount Pelée had erupted only twice before, in 1767 and 1851. In 1902 there was increasing fear among the residents of the town after weeks of warnings, including earth tremors and mild eruptions. One corner of Saint Pierre was invaded by six-foot-long fer-de-lance snakes, which killed 50 people and 200 domestic animals (see page 100). Many people from areas closer to the volcano fled to Saint Pierre, while some residents of Saint Pierre tried to flee elsewhere. When the volcano finally erupted, most of the deaths were caused by steam, heated to 1,500 degrees Fahrenheit, mixed with lethal gases and volcanic dust.

Miraculously, there were three known survivors: Léon Comprère-Léandre, a shoemaker, who survived above ground; Harviva De Ilfrile, a young girl who hid in a coastal cave; and Auguste Ciparis, a convicted murderer, who was locked in an underground dungeon.

Léon Comprère-Léandre, a twenty-eight-year-old shoemaker, was sitting on the doorstep of his house in the southeastern part of Saint Pierre on the morning of May 8, when he felt a terrible wind blowing. The earth trembled and

the sky grew dark. He attempted to go into the house but felt his arms and legs burning. He watched people around him burn and fall dead while their clothing showed no signs of having been touched by fire. Many victims were coated with sulfuric lava, which burned hard and baked them alive.

With his legs bleeding and covered with burns, Léon Comprère-Léandre ran from his burning house to Fonds-Saint Denis, six kilometers east of Saint Pierre. The entire city was burning. Sixteen of eighteen ships in the harbor had capsized. Léandre somehow managed to escape breathing the lethal sulfur fumes that burned out people's tongues, larynges, and lungs.

Léandre was picked up by a rescue party at Le Trace and taken to a hospital in Fort-de-France. He later returned to Saint Pierre as a special constable employed as part of the force guarding the ruins against looters. He lived until 1936 and died a bachelor.

The second survivor was a young girl named Harviva De Ilfrile, who ran to a wharf, jumped into a small boat, and paddled to a cave, where she hid.

The final and most famous survivor was Auguste Ciparis, a young stevedore, who was confined in an underground prison cell for condemned prisoners when Mount Pelée erupted. The hut-shaped cell was completely solid except for a tiny window. The massive stone walls of the dungeon resisted the excessive heat and shock. As Ciparis was waiting for his breakfast on May 8, it suddenly got dark. Then hot air filled with ash came into his room through the narrow door grating on the side away from the volcano. His flesh was burned instantly. He called for help but to no avail. The intense heat that scorched him lasted only a minute. There was no smoke, no noise, no odor of burning gas. He was wearing his hat, shirt, and pants. None of his clothing caught fire, but his back and legs were severely burned by the hot air and ash.

He had no food for three days, only the water in his cell, which was not affected by the heat.

He took off his shirt, urinated on it, then wrapped the damp shirt around his head to keep himself from breathing in too much dust. His cell was half filled with rubble from the prison block, which had collapsed on top of it. He curled up in a corner and tried to avoid as much of the dust as possible. The dust piled up against the door of his cell until it blocked out the little light that had been able to seep in.

Three days after the disaster, Ciparis heard voices and cried for help. Search parties were nearby, and two salvage workers rescued him. He was badly burned, but his face, hands, and feet were not injured. He was taken to Morne Rouge, where he recovered.

Ciparis was pardoned and became widely known in carnival sideshows and the Barnum and Bailey Circus as "the Prisoner of Saint Pierre." Until his death in 1929, he earned his living by locking himself in an exact replica of his Saint Pierre cell.

—K.F.

POON LIM: MAN ON THE RAFT

Poon Lim, a Chinese seaman, holds the world's record as a survivor at sea alone on a life raft in the South Atlantic for 133 days. When told of his record, he said, "I hope no one will ever have to break it."

A twenty-four-year-old seaman from Hainan Island, off the south coast of China, Poon Lim shipped out as a second steward on the British merchant ship Ben Lomond. The ill-fated vessel left Cape Town, South Africa, bound for Dutch Guiana (Surinam) in South America, carrying a crew of fifty-five. It was torpedoed by a Nazi U-boat on November 23, 1942, off the northern coast of Brazil. The ship was sinking rapidly, so Poon Lim leaped over the side. Having tied a life jacket around himself, he surfaced and swam as quickly as he could away from the freighter and the futile calls for help of his shipmates.

When the ship's boilers exploded, the Ben Lomond sank below the surface of the Atlantic. Poon Lim paddled in the water, holding his head as high as he could above each wave in hopes of spotting a life raft. He saw one with several sailors clinging to it, but it drifted away.

Those five sailors were the only other survivors he noticed. Later, German reports listed ten survivors.

Poon Lim's first concern was simply to stay alive. He gulped air when he could and kept his head above the waves. After struggling for two hours, he saw a life raft several hundred feet away. He swam to it and climbed aboard.

His raft was built of timbers and was eight feet square. Tied to it were some tins of British biscuits, a ten-gallon water tank, some flares, and an electric torch. He estimated that, by allowing himself a few swallows of water and two biscuits in the morning and in the evening, he should be able to stay alive for at least a month.

On two occasions rescue seemed imminent: once when a freighter passed within close range, but inexplicably turned away, and once when a U.S. Navy patrol plane buzzed his raft and dropped a dye marker, but a sudden storm wiped out the marker and the pilot lost sight of him. These were the loneliest times for Poon Lim, with help so near and yet so far away. He was also spotted by a German U-boat, which chose to leave him to his fate rather than kill him. He soon realized that he couldn't expect help from others and must keep himself alive until he drifted to land.

To keep his body in shape, he swam routinely twice a day when the sea was quiet. He used the ocean swimmer's looping stroke as he circled the raft, always keeping his head above water, his eyes open for sharks. His skin got darker from the sun and broke out in saltwater boils. He lost weight but maintained his strength. When his food and water supply ran low, he formulated a new plan for survival.

He used the canvas covering of the life jacket as a receptacle to catch rainwater. He also utilized other materials that he had on board. He took apart the electric torch to get a wire, which he made into a fishhook. He spent days shaping the metal, using the water jug as a hammer. The tough hemp rope that held down his almost exhausted supplies of food and water served as a fishing line.

He used a piece of biscuit for bait. After finally catching a fish, he cut it in half with the edge of a biscuit tin and ate the raw flesh, using the remains as bait to catch his next meal.

About the end of the second month on the raft, he spotted sea gulls. Hoping to catch one, he gathered seaweed from the bottom of the raft, matted it in bunches, and molded it into a form that resembled a bird's nest. By this time he had caught several fish, which he baked in the sun to improve their taste. Some he ate and some he left next to the nest so that they would rot and the stench would attract the gulls.

When he finally saw a gull flying toward him, he lay still so it would land. As the gull attacked the fish, Poon Lim grabbed it by its neck. A fight ensued, which he won, but only after he was the victim of deep cuts from the bird's beak and claws.

He pried a loose nail from the raft's planking and used it to tear up an empty ration tin to make a knife. He used his shoe as a hammer to pound the metal. He quartered the bird, chewed its flesh, and sucked out the blood and the organs. He cut the rest of the bird into strips, which be chewed on until he caught the next bird or fish.

When he saw sharks, he did not swim. Instead he set out to catch one. He used the remnants of the next bird he caught as bait. The first shark to pick up the taste was only a few feet long. It gulped the bait and hit the line with full force, but in preparation Poon Lim had braided the line so it would have double thickness. He also had wrapped his hands in canvas to enable him to make the catch. But the shark attacked him after he brought it aboard the raft. He used the water container half-filled with seawater as a weapon. After his victory, Poon Lim cut open the shark and sucked the blood from its liver. Since it hadn't rained, he was out of water and this quenched his thirst. He sliced the fins and let them dry in the sun, a Hainan delicacy.

Poon Lim counted the days with notches on the side of the raft, and he counted the nights with X's. On the 131st day, he noticed that the water was pale green rather than black. Birds flew overhead and seaweed floated by. All of these were encouraging signs.

On the morning of the 133rd day, April 5, 1943, he saw a small sail on the horizon. He had no flares left, so he waved his shirt and jumped up and down in an effort to attract the crew's attention. The craft changed direction and headed for him.

The three men in the boat, Portuguese-speaking fishermen, took him aboard. They gave him water and beans before continuing their fishing. Eventually they headed west to Belém, a British colonial town at the mouth of the Amazon River in Brazil.

When they arrived three days later, Poon Lim was able to walk ashore unaided. The British consul took him to the hospital in Belém, where he stayed forty-five days. Poon had lost thirty pounds during his ordeal at sea, but other than having little appetite (he would only drink milk) and digestive problems, he suffered no severe medical consequences.

Poon's merchant marine company and the British Consul arranged for his transport to England via Miami and New York. As was standard with other wartime survivors, he was interviewed by the U.S. Navy in Miami. The Navy was so impressed by his survival skills that they arranged for a Chinese interpreter to conduct further interviews in New York. The Navy's Emergency Rescue Equipment section made a film of Poon with a replica raft built to his specifications. In the film, Poon reenacted how he fashioned his knife and fishing tackle and demonstrated his fishing skill. The film was used by navy recruiters, but when Poon later tried to enlist himself, he was refused for having flat feet.

In New York, Poon received numerous honors. King George VI awarded him the British Empire Medal, the highest civilian award. The British navy had booklets printed and placed in all life rafts, describing his survival techniques. His employers presented him with a gold watch and a pair of cufflinks, and the Chinese republican government granted him a Certificate of Honor.

The Chinese consul helped Poon obtain a temporary visa so he could remain in the United States. He worked as a parts inspector for an aeronautics company until the end of the war and was then employed as a messman by United States Lines.

Since the annual quota for Chinese immigrants was 105, Poon was denied his application for U.S. citizenship. Senator Warren G. Magnussen took up his cause, introducing a bill that was passed by the Senate and the House of Representatives. On July 27, 1949, President Harry Truman signed Private Law 178 to "provide for admission to, and the permanent residence in, the United States of Poon Lim."

When citizenship papers were completed in 1952, Poon married and settled with his wife in Brooklyn, New York, where they raised their four children. In 1983, after thirty-seven years with the shipping company, Poon retired as chief steward.

—K.F.

HIROO ONODA: THE LAST OF THE SAMURAI

No surrender! These words were drilled into young Hiroo Onoda's head by parents, peers, and superior officers. Onoda learned his lesson well. As a Japanese army lieutenant, he continued to fight World War II until 1974. Like a samurai of old, Onoda suffered through thirty grueling years carrying out his final order—to gather intelligence and direct guerrilla warfare on the small Philippine island of Lubang, only seventy-five miles southwest of Manila.

Onoda had been sent to Lubang to lead attacks against enemy airfields. According to Onoda's firsthand account in No Surrender— My Thirty-Year War, his exact orders, which he obeyed to the letter for the next thirty years, were: "You are absolutely forbidden to die by your own hand. It may take three years, it may take five, but whatever happens, we'll come back for you. Until then, so long as you have one soldier, you are to continue to lead. You may have to live on coconuts. If that's the case, live on coconuts! Under no circumstances are you to give up your life voluntarily."

When he arrived he found the men disheartened. His lack of any real authority earned him the nickname Noda Shoyu, after a brand of soy sauce, meaning he was seasoning and nothing more. On February 28, 1945, American troops attacked; after a four-day battle, the Japanese troops were decimated. The dazed survivors split up into small cells for safety. Onoda found himself with Private Kinshichi Kozuka and Corporal Shoichi Shimada.

Unknown to the men on the island, the Japanese forces surrendered on August 14, 1945.

All over the island, small pockets of resistance remained. In February 1946, Onoda's group was joined by Private Yuichi Akatsu, who clung to the group against Onoda's wishes in hopes of obtaining more food. In March forty-one Japanese soldiers surrendered. Onoda and his three comrades were the only Japanese resistance left on the island. They vowed to keep on fighting. Shimada, thirty-one, the only married man, was the best shot of the four and kept the others' spirits up with his cheerful conversation. Akatsu, whom Onoda didn't trust, was twenty-three. Kozuka, a quiet, introspective soldier, was twenty-five. Onoda, the leader, was twenty-four.

In September 1949 Akatsu deserted. The following July Onoda found a note from him saying, "When I surrendered [six months later] the Philippine troops greeted me as a friend." At this moment Onoda told the two remaining men his orders. They agreed that they must continue fighting.

In February 1952 aircraft leafleted the island explaining that the war had ended. They also dropped photographs and letters from Japanese relatives and friends. One photo showed Shimada's wife with two children, the girl presumably the child his wife was carrying when he left for war, but he doubted its authenticity.

In March 1952 a reporter who failed to contact them left behind a newspaper—the first they had seen in seven years—with a story circled for their attention. It described "the punitive mission against Japanese soldiers on Lubang." Onoda interpreted this as a clear meaning that the war continued.

In June 1953 Shimada was shot in the leg by an islander. Every day for four months Onoda bathed the wound and wrapped it in a loincloth dipped in cow fat. The wound healed, but Shimada grew steadily more despondent, frequently looking at the photograph of his wife and children. Once Onoda heard him saying softly to himself, "Ten years. Ten whole years."

On May 7, 1954, the three men were spotted by an island search party. Shooting began, and while Onoda and Kozuka dived for cover, Shimada stood upright and aimed his gun, but made no attempt to fire it. Suddenly he fell headfirst with a bullet between his eyebrows. Onoda could not understand why Shimada had not dived for cover.

By now the two remaining men had learned the laws of survival. For mending their clothes, they fashioned needles from wire netting and made cotton from a hemplike jungle plant. They brushed their teeth with the fiber from palm trees. They oiled their guns with palm oil. The palm leaves were their toilet paper. They always dug holes for their waste and examined their urine and feces to verify that their diet was correct. Their main food was bananas, coconut milk, and meat when they could kill a local cow once every two months. After eating fresh cow's meat, Onoda's temperature rose so dramatically that the soles of his feet burned. He learned to counter this fever by drinking green coconut milk. By stringently observing these rules, Onoda remained remarkably free from disease and had only two serious fevers during his entire ordeal. Kozuka also remained healthy; his only ailments were cuts on his feet caused by sharp thorns.

Sleep was always a threat to their safety. They never once slept without their trousers on, and in the dry season they slept on sloping ground so that, in the event of a surprise attack, they could instantly see all around without getting up. During the rainy season they lived in makeshift huts.

All their other needs they would "requisition" from the local natives on daring night raids, which they called "stepping out for the evening." The villagers called the two soldiers "the mountain devils."

There were many search parties over the years. One expedition cost $375,000 and used 13,000 men, but they didn't find the slightest trace of Onoda.

In May 1959 a search party arrived, led by Onoda's brother and Kozuka's brother. They stayed for six months and as a final effort to convince Onoda, Toshio Onoda, using a microphone, began to sing in the hope his brother would recognize his voice. But he was so emotionally overcome that his voice broke, and Onoda became convinced it was an impersonator. In 1972 another search party arrived, with Onoda's sister, Chie, and another brother, Tadao. This time Onoda decided that the voices were indeed those of his sister and brother, but this suggested to him only that Japan was about to recapture the island. In the meantime he would continue his vigil. When American military planes flew overhead, Onoda took it as a sign that World War II was still on. In fact, the planes were on their way to the Vietnam War.

On October 19, 1972, Onoda and Kozuka went on a dangerous "beacon raid." They set fire to the islanders' newly cut rice as a guerrilla tactic in order to prove to Japanese intelligence that they were still alive and awaiting fresh instructions. That night they were pinned down in a rice field by gunfire. Onoda dived for cover and heard his comrade say, "It's my chest. It's no use!" Kozuka's eyes went white, blood and foam gushed from his mouth, and he dropped forward, dead. Picking up Kozuka's rifle, Onoda ran through the forest screaming, "I'll get them for this! I'll kill them all! Kill them! Kill them! Kill them!" He was now utterly alone.

Forty-five days later he returned to the scene and found a large tombstone with incense and flowers, along with a note in his brother Tadao's handwriting. Onoda silently prayed for revenge as a Japanese flag, implanted there by the search party, flapped in the breeze.

In 1973 yet another search party tried unsuccessfully to bring Onoda back. After they had left, Onoda found a poem:

> Not even an echo
> Responds to my call in the
> Summery mountains.

It had been written by Onoda's aged father, who was among the search party.

On February 20, 1974, Onoda discovered a mosquito net beside a river. He crept up and caught a young man, who turned and saluted him. The man's name was Norio Suzuki, a young university dropout who had dedicated himself to travel and three pursuits: to find Lieutenant Hiroo Onoda, a panda, and the Abominable Snowman. His first ambition was achieved after only four days of searching. At first Onoda thought Suzuki was Filipino and was about to kill him when Suzuki suddenly spoke to him in Japanese.

Suzuki explained that the war was over and asked Onoda to return with him to Japan. Onoda refused, saying he would not give in until he received official orders from his immediate superior, Major Yoshima Taniguchi, rescinding all previous commands. Suzuki offered to return with those orders. Onoda allowed several photographs to be taken for the proof Suzuki said he would need before anyone would believe him. In one photo, Onoda allowed Suzuki to hold his gun. They prepared a meal, and Onoda was dumbfounded when he saw Suzuki pluck leaves off the trees for flavoring. In thirty years he had never seen natives cooking and wondered how this visitor could have picked up that knowledge in four days. His suspicions aroused, he waited to eat until his companion had taken several bites.

On March 7, 1974, Onoda went to a prearranged hiding place and discovered a message from Suzuki saying Major Taniguchi, Onoda's superior officer, was on his way to personally deliver new orders. Even at this moment Onoda believed that his orders would be a renewal of the original ones or an assignment against the Americans. He also saw, for the first time since he left Japan, his own face. Suzuki had left copies of two of the photographs; Onoda was struck by his resemblance to his uncles.

On the evening of March 9, 1974, as cau-

Hiroo Onoda (left) surrenders his sword to Major General Jose Rancudo of the Philippine Air Force, twenty-eight years after the end of World War II.

tiously as ever, Onoda crept toward the tent by the river—half expecting an ambush. Suzuki saw him and shouted for Major Taniguchi, who appeared from the tent. Onoda recognized the major and snapped to attention. He saluted and said, "Lieutenant Onoda, Sir, reporting for orders."

Taniguchi said, "Good for you," then patted him on the back and handed him a pack of cigarettes "from the Ministry of Health and Welfare."

Taniguchi, who was now employed in a bookshop, then proceeded to read his orders. In part they said: "The Fourteenth Area Army has ceased all combat activity.... Units and individuals under command of Special Squadron are to cease military activities and operations immediately...." The stunned Onoda tried to understand the full implications—the wasted years, the unnecessary deaths. Then he slowly pulled back the rifle bolt and unloaded the bullets. His thirty years of guerrilla fighting were over.

That night Onoda couldn't sleep and talked until dawn. He had an astounding memory for detail. Perhaps the most staggering fact of all was that he had kept a calendar, using nothing but the moon—and he was only six days behind the real calendar.

The following evening, March 10, 1974, he formally surrendered at the Lubang Radar Base to Major General Jose Rancudo of the Philippine Air Force. He ceremoniously presented his sword to the major general. As a mark of respect, it was immediately returned to the surprised Onoda. The following day the ceremony was repeated for the world's press when President Ferdinand Marcos again returned

Onoda's sword to him. He also pardoned Onoda for his crimes on Lubang, much to the disgust of the islanders Onoda had raided and shot at for the past thirty years.

Onoda was mobbed when he returned to Japan; 4,000 people swarmed into the airport to welcome him home. Onoda struck a responsive chord in his countrymen. They had watched the proceedings in the Philippines on TV and were impressed by the dignified old warrior. He had done his duty with true samurai spirit, fighting against hopeless odds until relieved by a superior. To modern, materialistic Japan, Onoda embodied the old, prewar ideals of duty and tradition.

But what had Onoda fought for? Back on Lubang, he left two close comrades and at least thirty Filipinos in their graves. They were casualties of a long-forgotten war because of one man's stubborn adherence to the samurai ways.

Onoda had a hard time adjusting to urban life, and with the earnings from his memoirs, he purchased a 2,780-acre ranch with 1,700 cattle in the Brazilian state of Mato Grosso do Sul. He was wed in 1976 to a woman who married him because "I didn't think he would find anyone else." He also began lecturing schoolchildren about nature and health, and in 1989 he opened a nonprofit camp, the Onoda Nature School. Unlike the aggressive survival schools popular in the United States, Onoda stresses harmony with nature rather than "conquering" nature through physical exercise. He does believe that "too much concrete and cleanliness makes for weak children" and that parents raise their children to be mentally weak by focusing more on school studies than life. "One reason why children have so many problems," he says, "is because their parents push them too hard and don't let them adjust to their own rhythm."

—J.B. and W.L.S.

ANDES PLANE CRASH

At approximately 3:30 P.M. on October 12, 1972, a Fairchild F-227 turboprop carrying forty-five passengers and crew to Santiago, Chile, crashed in a remote area of the Andes. The chartered aircraft belonged to the Uruguayan Air Force and was carrying a group of fifteen Uruguayan college boys, along with their friends and relatives and a crew of five. The boys belonged to prominent families from the prosperous Montevideo suburb of Carrasco and were members of an amateur rugby team, called the "Old Christians," scheduled for a series of matches in Santiago.

Owing to turbulent weather, the plane had made an overnight stop in Mendoza, Argentina. The next morning, while the plane was airborne over the Andes, the weather turned bad again. Since the mountain range is among the highest on earth, the F-227's ceiling limit of only 22,000 feet forced the pilots to fly through a pass, where a blanket of clouds obscured their vision of the ground beneath.

Because they'd prematurely begun their descent into Santiago, when visibility was restored they discovered they hadn't cleared the mountains and were shocked when they spotted giant peaks suddenly looming before them. With no time for the plane to climb again, the right wing crashed into the side of a mountain, snapped off, and somersaulted into the tail, severing it.

Instantly, two members of the crew and three of the boys were hurtled out the back of the plane into oblivion. A moment later the left wing and propeller were crushed, but a remarkable stroke of luck landed the fuselage smoothly onto the snow, where it slid on its belly like a toboggan at a speed of 230 miles per hour. A number of persons were either sucked out the back or crushed to death when the plane came to a sudden stop, forcing seats loose and hurling the strapped-in occupants forward.

The fuselage had settled approximately 12,000 feet above sea level. A number of those who had been on board were dead, missing, or critically impaired. Two of the boys, medical students with minimal training, attended to the injured as best they could.

The first night there was panic and hysteria from one corner of the fuselage to the other and no one got much sleep.

The next morning some of the sturdier survivors appraised their predicament. The good news was that rescue shouldn't take long and melted snow would provide unlimited water. The bad news was lack of medical facilities, thin mountain air, unbearable cold, psychological stress, and worst of all, scarcity of food.

After eight days of searching, the Chileans, Argentineans, and Uruguayans gave up. Apparently, from above the white fuselage was next to invisible against the snow.

When the survivors hooked up a transistor radio to the plane's battery, they were devastated to hear that the air search had been called off. They realized they were on their own, so inventiveness and improvisation were the orders of the day. They removed the plane's seat covers and used them as blankets. Pieces of tinted window glass doubled as sunglasses against the piercing glare of the snow.

Chocolate bars, crackers, some wine, and other tidbits were carefully rationed. Large chunks of aluminum from the wreckage were used as snowshoes and also shaped into small "solar-heat" tubs with spouts, which sufficed to melt enough snow for drinking. Sleeping bags were fashioned out of foam torn from the plane's insulation.

On the sixteenth night, survivors were surprised in their sleep by an avalanche that tore through the fuselage, fatally suffocating a number of them. By this time burying the dead, side by side in the snow, had become routine.

With virtually no food left after twenty days, an inevitable subject was broached. Without protein, bodies could not survive. The prospect of eating the flesh of their dead comrades became a reality for the living.

Although some were pragmatic, others had certain religious convictions. In the beginning, most were simply appalled and refused to indulge. As the prospect of survival grew dimmer, eventually a line was crossed. Sections of the dead bodies were hacked off with pieces of broken glass, cut into strips, and consumed for their precious protein content.

With precious little fuel to make fire, the flesh was usually eaten raw or sun-dried. The eligible cadavers were picked with discretion—no relatives and no one with external injuries that may have become infected.

As the practice became more acceptable, the participants became less selective in regard to body parts. The "food" would last longer if they ate what they'd previously avoided. Hands, feet, small intestines, even tongue and testicles became a feature on the menu.

One of the medical students pointed out the energy value of the glucose contained in the brains. This prompted skulls to be cracked open with an ax. Crude stews were concocted, and since there was a shortage of bowls, a few were created from the top halves of skulls.

Some justified their cannibalism by likening it to a heart transplant, taking the heart of one to keep another alive. Others contended that intentional starvation would have been suicide—a cardinal sin in the Catholic Church.

When it became very clear their party would never be found, two of the boys embarked on a very risky hike over the mountains. Ten days later they emerged from the white wilderness and were thrilled to encounter a shepherd.

They told him their incredible story, and within hours four climbers of Chile's Andean Rescue Corps helicoptered to the crash site and hauled out the remaining fourteen survivors, all male. It had been seventy-two days and some had lost as much as sixty pounds.

All told, thirteen had died in the initial crash. Two more died the first night, followed by two more over the next few days. Nine had perished as a result of the avalanche and three more from injuries over the remaining fifty-four days.

A pact among the survivors obliged them to claim their nutritional survival was due to chocolate, cheese, and fresh fish from a nearby lake, but it wasn't difficult for the rescuers to read the implications of the mutilated corpses. The families of the survivors refused to believe the gruesome evidence, but there was no argument once the survivors reluctantly admitted to what they'd resorted to.

The Chilean government decided to bury the dead bodies on the mountain rather than bring them down. The reasoning was that no parents should be subjected to identifying such remains as those on the mountain. The fuselage was burned where it lay, the dead copilot inside.

—J.L.

DUMPY THE DOG

Dumpy, as he would soon be known, was a three-year-old beagle-mix mongrel who lived on the streets of Salem, Ohio. One morning in January 1973 Dumpy was walking down the street when he was spotted by a local dogcatcher. The dogcatcher picked him up, threw him into the back of his van, gave him a dose of gas meant to kill him, and drove to the nearest dump.

When he got there, the dogcatcher, assuming Dumpy was dead, threw him in front of a moving bulldozer. But Dumpy suddenly awoke and tried to crawl away. The dogcatcher pulled out a gun and shot Dumpy four times, hitting him in the chest and foreleg. Dumpy kept moving forward. The bulldozer driver, James Gilbert, begged the dogcatcher to put Dumpy out of his misery, but the dogcatcher refused because he didn't want to dirty his boots. Instead he drove away. Gilbert called a relative, who called two friends, Joyce Guiler and Jean Fluharty. Guiler and Fluharty searched the dump in pouring rain until they found Dumpy, covered in mud and blood, hiding underneath a broken-down shack. They rushed the beagle to a veterinarian and saved his life. When word got out about what had happened, the dogcatcher received death threats and had to be given police protection. Eventually he was driven out of town.

As for Dumpy, 500 families offered to adopt him. When he later died of distemper, he was given a well-attended public funeral.

—D.W.

MEXICO CITY EARTHQUAKE BABIES

On the morning of September 19, 1985, a tremendous earthquake measuring 8.1 on the Richter scale struck Mexico City. Between 6,000 and 30,000 people were killed, and more than 400 buildings were completely destroyed and 5,700 damaged. Among the destroyed buildings were the multistory Benito Juarez Hospital and General Hospital, which collapsed, covering patients and staff with medical equipment, machinery, and concrete floors. For days afterward rescue workers searched through the rubble looking for survivors. Many were found, but more surprising was that several of them were newborn babies. In fact, the last two people to be saved—almost nine days after the quake—were babies. At least nineteen newborns survived, as did twenty-one-day-old Chuchito Figueroa, who was in an incubator being fed with intravenous liquids.

The question immediately arose as to how these babies, completely helpless and vulnerable, were able to survive without milk or water. Although there was speculation that adult survivors had taken care of some of the babies before they themselves died, the most popular theory is that the babies, deprived of sound, light, and any other stimuli, went into a sort of hibernation. They moved little, conserved energy, and used less oxygen and glucose than would normally be expected, allowing them to live longer. In addition, the newborn babies, having just emerged from the womb, did not know a disaster had struck, did not yet think logically, and were thus immune to the stress and panic that would have depleted the energy of adults or even of older children.

—D.W.

NONSURVIVORS

ROBERT FALCON SCOTT

Had we lived I should have had a tale to tell of the hardihood, endurance and courage of my companions which would have stirred the heart of every Englishman. These rough notes and our dead bodies must tell the tale.

Captain Robert Falcon Scott,
last message, March 29, 1912

In terms of sheer danger and daring, few feats of exploration rank alongside the conquering of the South Pole. Although Norwegian explorer Roald Amundsen led the first expedition there, nowhere has the enormity of the task been better illustrated than in the saga of Robert Falcon Scott, the forty-three-year-old British navy career officer who arrived at the pole thirty-five days after Amundsen.

Scott had led one previous Antarctic expedition in 1902 that brought him closer to the pole than anyone had ever been before. One of the members of that expedition, Lieutenant Ernest Shackleton, came closer yet in 1908 (within 120 miles).

Scott was born June 6, 1868, in the English naval port of Devonport, and he joined the Royal Navy in 1886. Though he had little experience in the Arctic, in 1901, at age thirty-two, he was recommended by Sir Clements Robert Markham to be given command of the National Antarctic Expedition, a scientific exploration of South Victoria Land and the ice barrier discovered by Sir James Clark Ross in 1841. This was to be followed by penetrating the interior of the Antarctic continent.

Scott's ship, the *Discovery*, took a course southward along the coast of South Victoria Land and eastward along the edge of Ross's ice barrier to the base of Mount Terror.

He ventured farther than any explorer before him and spotted uncharted land to the northeast, which he named King Edward VII Land after the reigning king of the United Kingdom and emperor of India. Scott finally entered Antarctic waters via McMurdo Sound, but he was unable to proceed because of the buildup of pack ice.

He had no choice but to back off and anchor in a small bay, where he would wait out the winter and try again. But even the summer couldn't break up the ice.

Frustrated and tired of waiting, Scott recruited two of his companions and attempted to cross the giant Ross Ice Shelf on dog sledges. After fifty-nine grueling days, the men, stricken with scurvy, turned back, and after another year, Scott eventually returned to England. Being hailed as a hero for having gotten closer to the Pole than anyone had before wasn't enough for him. He still longed to be the first man to actually set foot on the bottom of the world.

On June 1, 1910, he set out with a team of eleven men on the *Terra Nova*. Shortly after reaching Melbourne, Australia, on October 12, his resolve became stronger when he received word that the Norwegian, Roald Amundsen, was leading his own expedition toward the Pole. A race was on.

On January 4, 1911, the *Terra Nova* reached Ross Island. Scott and company spent the next months waiting out the weather and setting up supply depots across the Ross Ice Shelf for the return journey. Amundsen, at his base camp on the Bay of Whales, did the same. On November 1, Scott and his team set out for the Pole, using dogs, Siberian ponies, and motorized vehicles to haul their supplies. Amundsen had left his base camp two weeks earlier.

In a matter of days, Scott's motor vehicles gave out, and the last of the worn-out ponies had to be shot for food at the foot of Beardmore Glacier.

In addition to the men having to contend with vicious blizzards, Scott was driving them too hard. Seven of them returned to the base camp. He forged ahead with four loyal companions: Lawrence Oates, Edward A. Wilson, Henry Bowers, and Edgar Evans. Still optimistic, he wrote in his journal that "two long marches will land us at the Pole. . . . It ought to be a certain thing now. . . . The only appalling possibility is the sight of the Norwegian flag forestalling ours."

When Scott's team reached 10,560 feet, they began their descent and arrived at the Pole on January 18, 1912, only to discover the Norwegian flag that Amundsen had erected. Scott's heart sank. The Norwegians had gotten there on December 14. He wrote, "This is an awful place, and terrible enough for us to have laboured to it without the reward of priority."

The five men now faced an 800-mile return journey of frostbite, scurvy, and exhaustion. When they reached Beardmore Glacier, about halfway back to base, it was in the midst of a windstorm. Incredibly, Scott made the decision to continue with the scientific aspect of the expedition and spent weeks wandering about collecting geological specimens. Among them were rock samples with plant impressions indicating that Antarctica had once been forested.

This several-week delay was a tragic mistake. Food rations had to be cut in order to make Mid Glacier Depot, the last supply camp on the Beardmore Glacier. Seaman Edgar Evans crumbled under the strain. After falling twice and suffering a concussion, he died a short distance from the depot.

Hoping their strength wouldn't give out, the others crossed the Queen Maud Mountain Range and made the slow and painful march from one depot to another on the Ross Ice Shelf. Oates, suffering from extreme frostbite, knew he could go no farther. While the others huddled in the tent during a blizzard, he announced, "I am just going outside and may be some time." He was never seen again. His companions speculated that he had considered himself a burden and had committed an act of sacrifice so that they could push on to safety.

Scott, Wilson, and Bowers forged ahead toward One Ton Depot, less than 200 miles from base camp, where there were plenty of supplies, but a raging blizzard stopped them eleven miles short.

On March 29, 1912, Scott made his last journal entry, "Every day now, we have been ready to start for our depot eleven miles away, but outside the door of the tent, it remains a scene of swirling drift. I do not think we can hope for any better things now. We shall see it to the end, but we are getting weaker, of course. . . . It seems a pity, but I do not think I can write more. For God's sake look after our people."

Scott, Wilson, and Bowers were found dead in their sleeping bags by a search party on November 12, 1912, seven and a half months after Scott's last journal entry. His diaries, letters, photographs, and message to the public lay nearby along with the rock samples he'd refused to leave behind.

Months later, a monument of stones and a cross was built at the site of their death, in memory of all five of the men.

—J.L.

ANNE FRANK

As Anne Frank began her diary in 1943, she wrote that no one "will be interested in the unbosomings of a thirteen-year-old schoolgirl." For the next two years, until her capture, she used this small red-and-white plaid book to pour out her innermost thoughts and unmask well-concealed aspects of her personality. She had no idea that her secret diary would become the most human account of the most inhuman period in history.

Anne's real name was Annelies Marie. She was born in Frankfurt, the second daughter of a well-to-do middle-class Jewish family.

She was not a brilliant student, and she wrote with less feeling and imagination than many of her classmates. She was, by all accounts, a humorous, talkative, strong-willed girl who giggled and chattered with girlfriends, flirted with boys, played Ping-Pong, loved nice clothes, collected pictures of movie stars, and had a pen pal in Iowa. She had such a fondness for make-believe that she would often take a suitcase as she "traveled" on a one-hour visit next door.

Her family left Germany in 1933 to escape the reign of Nazi terror against the Jews and emigrated to Amsterdam. In 1940 the Netherlands fell to the Nazis, and strict anti-Jewish decrees were issued. The Franks did not change their daily routines at first, but Anne's father quietly made preparations to go into hiding should it become necessary.

In July 1942 Anne's sister, Margot, was called for deportation. One morning shortly thereafter, Otto and Edith Frank and their two daughters gathered their personal belongings and walked in the pouring rain across Amsterdam to their hiding place, a few attic rooms above Otto Frank's food products business. They were soon joined in this secret annex by four others: Hermann Van Daan, a business partner of Mr. Frank's; his wife, Petronella; their son, Peter; and a dentist named Albert Dussell.

During the next two years, Anne described in her diary their confinement in their cramped quarters. They could not venture outside, look through the curtain in the daylight, or speak above a whisper during working hours. Their links to the outside world were a radio and members of Mr. Frank's staff, who brought them supplies. Their tensions and quarrels developed into major personality conflicts because of their prisonlike existence.

Using life in the annex as a background, Anne wrote a moving account of her adolescence. She addressed her diary entries to an imaginary confidante named Kitty. With complete honesty she vividly described her bodily changes, the ecstasy of her first kiss, her budding sexuality, and her longings for companionship and fun. She revealed her resentment toward her mother,

Dit is een foto, zoals
ik me zou wensen,
altijd zo te zijn.
Dan had ik nog wel
een kans om naar
Holywood te komen.
Anne Frank.
10 Oct. 1942

(translation)
"This is a photo as I would wish
myself to look all the time. Then
I would maybe have a chance to
come to Hollywood."
Anne Frank, 10 Oct. 1942

Anne Frank's favorite photograph of herself.

her trust in her father, and her growing intimacy with Peter.

As the outside world shrank, her inner world grew. The more hatred, bitterness, and fear she saw, the greater her strength, courage, and compassion. From firsthand observations of the brutalities of war and people at their worst, she drew perceptive conclusions about the nature of people under duress and also about herself.

She became aware of her own duality, her cheerful and gloomy sides, and called herself a "little bundle of contradictions." Although she had the strength to endure her loneliness and longings, she had occasional moods of restlessness and depression. "The sun is shining, the sky is deep blue, there is a lovely breeze, and I'm longing—so longing—for everything. To talk, for freedom, for friends, to be alone. And I do so long to . . . cry." After ventilating such feelings, she would reproach herself, because she felt that self-pity and despair served no purpose.

Her overall attitude was positive, and the philosophy of life that emerged can only be described as miraculous in someone whose existence was constantly threatened. She was sure that her determination to survive and her joy in life would sustain her under any circumstances. In one of her last entries, she wrote that "in spite of everything I still believe that people are really good at heart. I simply can't build up my hopes on a foundation consisting of confusion, misery, and death. I see the world gradually being turned into a wilderness. I hear the ever-approaching thunder, which will destroy us too. I can feel the sufferings of millions, and yet, if I look up into the heavens, I think that it will all come right, that this cruelty too will end, and that peace and tranquillity will return again."

On August 4, 1944, four Nazi policemen stormed into the annex and arrested the inhabitants. In their haste to plunder the group's jewels and money, they emptied Mr. Frank's briefcase but barely glanced at the notebooks Anne had hidden in it. A week after the arrest, Miep Gies, an employee in Mr. Frank's business and one of the group's protectors, went upstairs to the annex, found the notebooks, and kept them in her desk drawer in the event that the girl would return.

The Franks, Van Daans, Dussell, and two of Mr. Frank's employees were taken to Gestapo headquarters. One of the employees was released, the other escaped. The Franks, Van Daans, and Dussell were sent to Westerbork, the prison for Jews in transit to Auschwitz. On September 3, 1944, they were herded onto the last train of Dutch Jews sent to Auschwitz. Two days later the Germans began their withdrawal from the Netherlands in face of the advancing Allied forces.

At Auschwitz the men and women were separated. Like the other women, Anne had her long hair clipped and her body hair shaved. The starving prisoners were subjected to "selections," where the weakest were marked for death. A fellow prisoner later recalled her memories of Anne: "I can still see [Anne] standing at the door and looking down the camp street as a herd of naked Gypsy girls were driven by to the crematory, and Anne watched them go and cried. And she cried also when we marched past Hungarian children who had already been waiting half a day in the rain in front of the gas chambers because it was not yet their turn. And Anne nudged me and said: 'Look, look. Their eyes . . .' "

After nearly two months in Auschwitz, Anne, Margot, and Petronella Van Daan were transferred to the Bergen-Belsen camp in Germany, where the conditions were nearly as horrifying. Separated from her daughters, Edith Frank died in Auschwitz on January 6, 1945.

A typhus epidemic at the crowded Bergen-Belsen camp claimed Margot's life in March. Anne, also sick with typhus, was not informed of her sister's death, but according to a surviving witness, she sensed what had happened. She died a few days later in a peaceful, quiet manner.

Otto Frank was the only one of the group who had been sequestered in the Amsterdam annex to survive the war. He was in the hospital at Auschwitz when the Russians liberated the camp. On his return to Amsterdam, Miep Gies gave Frank Anne's diary. He made a few copies for his mother and close friends as a memorial to his family. One friend gave it to a history professor, who prepared an article about it for a Dutch newspaper. He urged Frank to get it published. Two major Dutch publishers rejected it, but a third accepted it, and soon it was translated into more than twenty languages and adapted into a play. Frank retired from business to devote his life to Anne's legacy. He set up humanitarian projects with the book's royalties and personally answered the thousands of letters he received.

The most remarkable response came from Germany. In West Berlin a social work home bearing Anne's name was established, and elsewhere an organization to combat anti-Semitism was founded. On March 17, 1957, more than 2,000 young people marched, biked, or traveled by trains and buses to Bergen-Belsen to place flowers on the mass grave where Anne was buried.

The fiftieth anniversary of Anne Frank's death was marked by the publication of the definitive edition of her diary. It contains many entries that were not included in the earlier standard edition.

It has never been discovered who tipped off the Gestapo that Anne and the others were in hiding above Otto Frank's Amsterdam business. The Nazis rewarded such informants by paying them $1.40 for each Jew captured. As a result of this betrayal, Anne Frank died three months before her sixteenth birthday and less than two months before the war's end.

In a quiet, humble way, she succeeded in doing with her diary what postwar administrators had attempted, but failed, to do—make people feel the horrors of the Nazi regime.

—N.L.K. and L.A.C.

MOUNT OSUTAKA CRASH VICTIMS

At 6:12 P.M. on August 12, 1985, Japan Air Lines flight 123, a Boeing 747SR, took off from Tokyo's Haneda Airport for a one-hour trip to Osaka. Normally JAL 123 was a commuter flight for businessmen, but this time, because it was the beginning of the three-day Bon festival, there were also a lot of families on board. The plane was completely full—524 people, including the crew. But fifteen minutes after takeoff the pilot, Captain Masami Takahama, reported that he had lost control of the plane. For a half hour the plane lurched and twisted, while Takahama tried desperately to discover the problem and its solution.

While passengers around him were screaming in terror, Hirotsugu Kawaguchi, a fifty-two-year-old shipping line manager, pulled out his company diary and composed a farewell note to his wife and three children.

"Mariko, Tsuyoshi, Chiyoko—Please get along well with each other and help your mama," wrote Kawaguchi. "Papa feels very sorry I won't survive. I don't know the reason. Five minutes have passed."

He went on, "I never want to take an airplane again. Dear God, please help me. I didn't imagine that yesterday's dinner was going to be the last one with you all."

Then Kawaguchi described what had happened: "Something seems to have exploded in the airplane. Smoke is coming out. . . . Airplane is going down. I don't know where we are going and what is going to happen."

To his son he wrote, "Tsuyoshi—I do really count on you." And to his wife, "Honey—I feel very sorry about what is happening to me. Sayonara. Please take care of our children. It's six-thirty now. The airplane is spinning and going down quickly."

He closed with, "I'm very thankful to you that I was able to have a really happy life up to now."

At least two other passengers, Kayuo Yoshimura and Masakatsu Taniguchi, wrote short notes to their wives to take care of their children, Taniguchi on the back of a disposal bag that he then slipped into his pocket with his driver's license.

At 6:57 P.M. JAL 123 slammed into Mount Osutaka northwest of Tokyo. Of the 524 passengers and crew, only four survived. Hirotsugu Kawaguchi, Kayuo Yoshimura, and Masakatsu Taniguchi were not among them.

—D.W.

THE KILLING OF MICHAEL MALLOY

He was—at least up to a point—the most durable human being in American history, possibly in world history. More than thirty attempts were made to murder him. He survived all but one.

His name was Michael Malloy, and he was a bleary-eyed, unsteady, diminutive Irishman originally from County Donegal. While his insurance policy would later falsely give his age as forty-five, he was actually sixty years old. Once, in better times, he had been a fireman, but in 1933 his almost full-time occupation was alcoholic. He had been a habitué of all the lower-class bars of New York's Bronx, until they refused him any more credit and banned him. At the period of his finest hour, he was one of the derelicts and barflies who daily visited Tony Marino's speakeasy at 3804 Third Avenue, also in the Bronx.

For a while Michael Malloy had been hospitably received in Marino's speakeasy. At first he had seemed a sound credit risk. He worked, occasionally, as a janitor in the neighborhood, mostly sweeping floors, to pay for the rent on his cramped, dingy room and to obtain money for his drinks. But when his bar bill mounted and no payment was in sight, he was refused further drinks at Marino's and turned away from the free lunch tray. Still, he faithfully attended Marino's every day, usually managing to cadge a few drinks out of the more affluent customers, who were amused by his Irish charm and rambling anecdotes recounted with an assumed brogue.

Thus, Michael Malloy, living hand to mouth, in the dreary depression winter of January 1933, when he stood on the brink of immortality and came to the attention of the Murder Trust.

Actually, the members of the Murder Trust— later so named by New York City's tabloids— were less impressive than their grand organization title implied. They were a mixed, scruffy group of friends, some living barely within the law, some outside it. They had two things in common; they all hung out at Marino's, and they all desperately needed money.

The mainstays of the trust were five in number. There was twenty-seven-year-old Anthony Marino, proprietor of Marino's speakeasy and a natty dresser. There was twenty-eight-year-old Joseph Murphy, a onetime chemist who was now Marino's bartender. There was twenty-four-year-old Francis Pasqua, a newlywed and an undertaker who owned a funeral parlor on East 117th Street. There was Hershey, or Harry, Green, a taxicab driver. And there was twenty-nine-year-old Daniel Kreisberg, the father of three and a fruit vendor.

These five had enjoyed only one successful joint commercial venture together. In the early spring of 1932, desperate for cash, they had formed a partnership to take out an insurance policy on a young blonde named Betty Carlsen, the girlfriend of Anthony Marino, owner of the speakeasy and the beneficiary named in her policy. They had insured Miss Carlsen's life for $800. By a happy coincidence, this thoughtful investment had paid off. On a particularly cold night in the spring of 1932, Miss Carlsen, insensible from alcohol, had been helped back to her room. There she had been stripped naked, laid out on her bed, and doused with cold water. Then the windows of her room were thrown wide open to allow her the benefit of the bracing air. In the morning she was found dead. The coroner gave the cause of death as pneumonia compounded by alcoholism. The insurance company had routinely processed her life insurance policy and had paid $800 to Anthony Marino and company.

By early January of 1933, these riches had long since been dissipated, and Marino and his friends were in dire straits, once more desperately in need of cash. One evening, seated about a table behind the beaded curtain that separated the proprietor's back room from his bar, the five friends were discussing their immediate futures. The outlook was bleak. Not one of them had a creative idea. Then one of them remembered an old idea.

According to courtroom testimony months after, Marino had complained, "Business is bad."

Pasqua, the undertaker, staring out at the bar and the shabby figure of Michael Malloy trying to wheedle a drink, had said, "Why don't you take out insurance on Malloy? I'll do the rest."

With that brilliant inspiration, the Murder Trust was once more a going concern.

Malloy's whole life had brought him to this moment of truth. He was the perfect victim—a mindless, helpless, falling-down drunk when lubricated—with his own frantic need for an oasis and patrons.

First, for the Murder Trust, there was a formality. The members had to take out a life insurance policy or policies on Michael Malloy. On the face of it, this was not a simple matter. Normally, people were not insured without their knowledge. Exact details of how the policies were obtained never came to light. No doubt a cooperative insurance agent, one who did not ask questions and sought an easy commission, was found. Not one life insurance policy but three were taken out on Michael Malloy— actually on Nicholas Mallory—whose age was shaved from sixty to forty-five to keep the premiums low. He was identified as a relative, bartender Joseph Murphy's brother. One $800 policy was obtained from the Metropolitan Life Insurance Company. Two separate $494 policies were obtained from the Prudential Life Insurance Company. A double-indemnity clause was included. The $1,788 of insurance on Malloy would be worth $3,576 if the insured should die by accident.

The designated beneficiary of the policies was Anthony Marino. His four colleagues were to receive their portion of the take later.

The first day that the insurance policies were safely in pocket, the killing of Michael Malloy got under way. The only minor problem was the possibility that Malloy might become suspicious. Until now, at least in recent weeks, Malloy had been treated as a leper in Marino's. Suddenly he must be made welcome and plied with free drinks. Fortunately, there was a price war among the speakeasies in the Bronx, and Marino quickly made use of the fact. When Michael Malloy weaved into Marino's, the proprietor greeted him warmly, announcing that because of competition he was relaxing his credit restrictions and that Malloy, like all regulars, could take advantage of this. Malloy's watery eyes shone. Unbelievable good news. He clung to the bar like adhesive. He began to down shots of whiskey nonstop.

Initially Marino and company had theorized that Malloy was so weakened and debilitated by years of drinking, was in such bad shape, that an excessive amount of whiskey consumed in a short time would swiftly destroy him. Every day, for a week, Malloy drank like a fish from noon to night, then staggered out into the dark, while the trust waited for news of his death. Instead, each new day Malloy appeared in Marino's refreshed and ready for more.

As Marino's stock of alcohol neared depletion, without achieving the desired result, a sense of urgency infected the trust. They muttered, and they met to conspire on some new course of action. The bartender and former chemist, Murphy, still filled with chemistry lore, was asked for his advice. He suggested that they cease giving Malloy whisky and start serving him automobile-radiator antifreeze, which was wood alcohol and poisonous. The vote was unanimous in favor of using antifreeze to guarantee the quick demise of the insured.

Thus began what Bronx district attorney Samuel J. Foley would call "the most grotesque chain of events in New York criminal history." The next day Malloy appeared on schedule for his whiskey. Murphy passed him a few straight shots to soften him up for the lethal potion. Then came the antifreeze. Malloy gulped it down without blinking, smacked his lips, and asked for a refill. A half dozen shots of antifreeze were downed by Malloy before he passed out, collapsing to the barroom floor at three in the morning. The undertaker, Pasqua, examined him and announced that his heartbeat could hardly be heard and that he should be dead inside an hour. In an hour he was still alive, sound asleep on the floor. In three hours he sat up, got to his feet, apologized for his poor posture, and said he was thirsty.

The Murder Trust was astounded. Its leader, Marino, decided that Murphy had not given their victim enough antifreeze. For another week, day and night, Malloy was poured double and triple shots of antifreeze, enough to kill a battalion. At the end of each daily session he passed out, slept, woke up, and asked for more.

Bewildered, Marino changed the formula. No more antifreeze. From now on Malloy must be given turpentine. The Irishman accepted the turpentine, swallowed glass after glass of it, stumbled out into the night, and the following day bounced back for more of the same.

Soon turpentine was replaced by shots of undiluted horse liniment, sometimes lightened by rat poison. Malloy downed the fluid—and flourished.

Pasqua confided to his colleagues that he had once buried a man who had succumbed after combining raw oysters with whiskey. Marino ordered that the concoction be tried, except with one modification. It was to be tainted raw oysters and wood alcohol. Malloy steeped himself in the raw oysters and wood alcohol and wobbled out of Marino's toward his bed. Pasqua guaranteed that it would be his deathbed. The next afternoon Malloy was back, beaming and ready for seconds.

The mood of the Murder Trust was dark. Frustration led to more creative thinking. Finally Murphy came up with a positive sure thing. If Malloy could be fed some poisoned food from the free lunch tray, that would be certain to do him in. The suggestion was met with enthusiasm. The bartender was told to proceed. Immediately, Murphy opened an old can of sardines and put it outside to spoil. When it smelled foul and contamination was certain, Murphy spread the sardines on a slice of bread, mixed in some carpet tacks, worked in shavings of the sardine can a machine shop had obligingly prepared, laid on another piece of bread, and presented Malloy the sandwich. Delighted with the bartender's generosity, Malloy accepted the sandwich, chomped on it, chewing, swallowing, and finished it all, licking his fingers. Washing it down with a few more drinks of wood alcohol, he felt his way out of the bar and started for home.

The five members of the Murder Trust were gleeful as they waited for word of Malloy's death, either from ptomaine poisoning or from stomach hemorrhage. The following morning brought no word. The following afternoon brought Malloy in person, ready for a drink and another one of those appetizing sandwiches.

For the gang, this was too much. A small fortune was within their grasp, yet they could not claim it without a victim. And their victim defied them. They began to regard Michael Malloy as a phenomenon of nature. His stomach obviously was cast iron. Nothing taken into his digestive tract or bloodstream would harm him. If he were to be successfully obliterated, another and different means must be found. The trust members considered a variety of possibilities and settled on a surefire one they had employed before.

They acted on the coldest night of the winter. Outside there was a snowstorm and icy wind, and the temperature was fourteen degrees below zero. In Marino's, Malloy was encouraged to drink himself into a stupor. Marino and Pasqua carried the unconscious Malloy to Harry Green's taxi, waiting outside the door. After lifting Malloy into the backseat, the two men got in beside him. They drove to Claremont Park, where the coatless Malloy was carried from the road into the park and laid out on the wet snow behind some bushes. Opening his shirt, they poured a five-gallon tin of water over him and then left.

The next day the gang eagerly searched the afternoon papers for news of Malloy's death from exposure. The papers offered nothing. Perhaps it was too early. That evening Pasqua showed up with a bad head cold from the outing the night before. Then the speakeasy door opened, and there stood Michael Malloy, looking invigorated. He marched to the bar, calling out for his first drink.

That night the gang was frantic. They huddled and decided to consult an expert in mayhem. They called in a friend of Marino's: Anthony "Tough Tony" Bastone, a professional killer. After explaining their caper and what had been happening to date, they asked their consultant to advise them. He told them to stop the fancy stuff and just murder Malloy outright. Marino didn't want anything obvious that would alert the police. Bastone said it need not be obvious. It could be an accident.

The next night, at three in the morning, once more using Green's taxi, Marino and Bastone drove out to the deserted intersection of Baychester Avenue and Gun Hill Road. Malloy, who had passed out from drink hours before, sat slumped between them. They dragged him out into the intersection and held him up while Green backed up his taxi. Then Green catapulted his cab toward them at forty-five miles per hour. Marino and Bastone released Malloy and jumped aside as the speeding auto smashed full into Malloy, throwing him into the air, knocking him down, running him over. Leaving his corpse in the middle of the street, the victorious trio fled. The next day Malloy did not appear in Marino's. Nor did he appear the next or the next. Two weeks passed and no Malloy. The Murder Trust felt sure that he was dead at last, but they had to prove it to the insurance companies. They read the obituaries. No mention of Malloy. They visited the morgue. No Malloy. They phoned hospitals. No Malloy. He had vanished from the earth. Bastone suggested they waste no more time, find another bum, run him over, identify him as Malloy, and collect the insurance money. They tried it. The new victim clung to life in Fordham Hospital. The gang still did not have their dead man.

Then, in the third week of Malloy's disappearance, the habitués of Marino's were thrown into a turmoil. Michael Malloy himself walked in and settled at the bar. He apologized for his absence. He'd been in the hospital, which had neglected to list him as a patient. A car accident, Malloy explained. He'd suffered a concussion to the brain and a fractured shoulder. But now he was fine. "I'm sure ready for a drink," he said.

The Murder Trust was in despair and utterly routed. They had placed their chips on a human who was apparently indestructible. Once more Bastone suggested they stop using finesse, stop being clever, just get rid of Malloy the quickest way possible and cash in their insurance policies. All hands agreed. Murphy, the bartender, offered his room on Fulton Avenue. On Washington's Birthday the gang treated Malloy to his quota of drinks. He got drunk as usual and passed out. Kreisberg and Murphy took him to Murphy's room and dropped him down on the bed. One end of a rubber hose was attached to the gas jet, the other end was stuffed into Malloy's mouth. They let the gas fill him. "His face is all purple," Kreisberg reassured his collaborator.

In the morning Michael Malloy was found dead. Dr. Frank Manzella, an ex-alderman, was called in to write the death certificate. He certified that Michael Malloy had expired from lobar pneumonia, noting alcoholism as a contributing factor.

For a promise of a $400-share of the insurance payoff, undertaker Pasqua placed Malloy in a ten-dollar pine coffin and buried him in a twelve-dollar plot of ground in the Ferncliffe Cemetery in Westchester.

The durable Michael Malloy had lost in the end. Yet, though he would never know it, he would ultimately win.

The Murder Trust members were suspicious of one another and they talked too much. When Bastone tried to improve on his share of the insurance take, he was promptly liquidated. But the basic five continued to be indiscreet. The Bronx police began to hear rumors. When they checked and learned an actual Michael Malloy had died on Washington's Birthday, and there were policies on his life, they went to Ferncliffe Cemetery and exhumed Malloy's body. The coroner found Malloy had not died of pneumonia but had been eliminated by use of illuminating gas. Members of the trust were charged with murder.

The trial was held in the Bronx County Courthouse. The jury deliberated seven hours. Harry Green went to prison. Dr. Frank Manzella went to prison. On June 7, 1934, Anthony Marino, Frank Pasqua, and Daniel Kreisberg went to the electric chair in Sing Sing. On July 5, 1934, Joseph Murphy also died in the chair.

Because of his indestructibility, Michael Malloy had forced his killers to resort to obvious murder, and as a result, four of them died. They died, yet somehow Malloy lives.

—I.W.

FAMOUS LAST WORDS

Meher Baba: Indian guru, died 1969. The Baba's last words in 1925 preceded a lifetime of silence before his actual death: "Don't worry, be happy."

Max Baer: American boxer, died 1934. To the hotel operator who asked him if he wanted the house doctor: "No, get me a people doctor."

Saul Bowles: American journalist, died 1915. To his nurse: "You may be sure that in another world there is always one soul praying for you."

Feruccio Busoni: Italian pianist, died 1924. To his wife: "Dear Gerda, I thank you for every day we have been together."

Edith Cavell: British nurse, shot for spying, 1915. "I realize that patriotism is not enough. I must have no hatred or bitterness towards anyone. Don't think of me [as a heroine]. Think of me only as a nurse who tried to do her duty. . . . I am glad to die for my country."

"Cholly Knickerbocker" (Maury Paul): New York gossip columnist, died 1942. "Oh, Mother, how beautiful it is."

Grover Cleveland: American President, died 1908. "I have tried so hard to do right."

Jay Cooke: American banker, died 1905. Overhearing the reading of a prayer for the dead: "That was the right prayer."

Hart Crane: American poet, died 1932. As he jumped overboard to commit suicide: "Goodbye, everybody!"

Bruce Cummings: British biologist, died 1919. "My horizon has cleared. My thoughts are tinged with sweetness and I am content."

Gabriele D'Annunzio: Italian poet and novelist, died 1938. "I want to see again in springtime the city [Rome] that I love. I have been thinking about this trip with joy and with trembling."

Isadora Duncan: American interpretative dancer, died in auto accident, 1927. "Adieu my friends, I go on to glory!"

"Dutch Schultz" (Arthur Fleigenheimer): New York gangster, shot in 1935. Police stenogra-

Edith Cavell was executed as a spy by the Germans during World War I.

phers recorded the Dutchman's last ravings in an attempt to gain some information. They could make little sense of them: "Turn your back to me, please, Henry. I am so sick now. The police are getting many complaints. Look out. . . . I want that G-note. Look out for Jimmy Valentine, for he is an old pal of mine. Come on, Jim. . . . OK, OK, I am all through. I can't do another thing. . . . Look out! Mamma, Mamma! Look out for her. . . . Police, Mamma, Helen, Mother, please take me out. I will settle the indictment. Come on, Max, open the soap duckets. . . . The chimney sweeps. Talk to the sword. Shut up, you got a big mouth! Please help me up, Henry! Max! Come over here. French Canadian bean soup. I want to pay. Let them leave me alone."

Amelia Earhart: American aviator, died 1937(?). In a letter to her husband before her last flight: "Please know that I am quite aware of the hazards. I want to do it because I must do it. Women must try to do things as men have tried. When they fail, their failure must be but a challenge to others."

Thomas Edison: American inventor, died 1931. In a coma: "It is very beautiful over there."

Sir Charles Eliot: British diplomat and scholar, died 1931. "I see Mother."

Farouk: King of Egypt, deposed 1952, died in exile in Rome, 1965. "There will soon be only five Kings left: the Kings of England, Diamonds, Hearts, Spades and Clubs."

Hans Frank: Nazi war criminal, hung in 1946. "A thousand years will pass and the guilt of Germany will not be erased."

Charles Frohman: American theatrical manager, drowned in 1915 when the SS *Lusitania* was torpedoed by a German submarine. "Why fear death? It is the most beautiful adventure in life."

Sir William Schwenck Gilbert: British librettist, died 1911. Gilbert suffered a heart attack when he tried to rescue a girl from drowning on his estate: "Put your hands on my shoulders and don't struggle."

Radclyffe Hall: British author, died 1963. "What a life; but such as it is, I offer it to God."

Richard Halliburton: American explorer and writer, lost at sea, 1939. Last message: "Southerly gales, squalls, lee rail under water, wet bunks, hard tack, bully beef. Wish you were here, instead of me."

Oscar Hammerstein II: American lyricist, died 1960. Always a devoted baseball fan, he died reciting the names of his favorite players: "Ruth . . . Gehrig . . . Rizzuto . . ."

Joel Chandler Harris: American writer and creator of "Uncle Remus," died 1908. "I am about the extent of a tenth of a gnat's eyebrow better."

O. Henry (William S. Porter): American short-story writer, died 1910. "Turn up the lights. I don't want to go home in the dark."

Abram S. Hewitt: American industrialist and politician, died 1903. After removing the oxygen tube from his mouth: "And now I am officially dead."

Burton Holmes: American photographer and lecturer. Thinking of the ultimate show— heaven: "How I could pack them in with that one!"

Alfred Edward Housman: English poet, died 1936. After his doctor told him a "dirty" story: "Yes, that's a good one, and tomorrow I shall be telling it again on the Golden Floor."

Chris Hubbock: American TV news anchor, suicide by shooting, 1970. She made the news when she shot herself in the head on a prime-time news program: "And now, in keeping with Channel 40's policy of always bringing you the latest in blood and guts, in living color, you're about to see another first—an attempted suicide."

James Joyce: Irish novelist, died 1941. After being told he was being transfused with blood donated by two soldiers from Neuchâtel, Switzerland: "A good omen. I like Neuchâtel wine."

Kaliayev: Russian anarchist revolutionary, hung in 1905. He refused a crucifix on the scaffold: "I already told you that I am finished with life and am prepared for death. I consider my death as the supreme protest against a world of blood and tears."

Terry Kath: American rock musician, killed in 1978, playing Russian roulette with a loaded pistol: "Don't worry, it's not loaded."

Ronald Knox: British religious writer, died 1957. Asked if he would like to hear someone read a portion of his version of the Bible: "Awfully jolly of you to suggest it though."

Robert M. La Follette: American politician, died 1925. "I am at peace with all the world, but there is still a lot of work I could do. I don't know how the people will feel towards me, but I

756DEATH

shall take to the grave my love for them which has sustained me through life."

Gustav Mahler: Austrian composer, died 1911. "Mozart!"

Katherine Mansfield (Katherine Middleton Murry): New Zealand–born short-story writer, died 1923. "I believe . . . I'm going to die. I love the rain. I want the feeling of it on my face."

O. O. McIntyre: American newspaper columnist, died 1938. To his wife: "Snooks, will you please turn this way. I like to look at your face."

Elie Metchnikoff: Russian bacteriologist, died 1916. "You remember your promise? You will do my post-mortem? And look at the intestines carefully, for I think there is something there now."

Maria Montessori: Italian educator, died 1952. "Am I no longer of any use, then?"

Oscar: King of Sweden, died 1907: "Don't let them shut the theatres for me."

Carl Panzram: American mass murderer, hung in 1930. Asked if he had anything to say, Panzram, who admitted to his killings and resolutely refused any form of repentance, replied: "Yes. Hurry it up, you Hoosier bastard! I could hang a dozen men while you're fooling around."

Anna Pavlova: Russian prima ballerina, died 1931. "Get my 'Swan' costume ready."

Pablo Picasso: Spanish artist, died 1973. To his doctor: "You are wrong not to marry. It's useful."

Brian Piccolo: American football player, died of cancer, 1968. To his girlfriend: "Can you believe it, Joy? Can you believe this shit?"

Franklin Delano Roosevelt: American president, died 1945. "I have a terrific headache."

Theodore Roosevelt: American president, died 1919. "Please put out the lights."

Robbie Ross: British companion of Oscar Wilde, died 1918. Punning on Keats's famous farewell lines: "Here lies one whose name was written in hot water."

William Saroyan: American author, died 1981. "It's the most beautiful time of my life—and death."

Sir Ernest Shackleton: British explorer, died 1922. Complaining to his doctor: "You are always wanting me to give up something. What do you want me to give up now?"

George Bernard Shaw: English playwright, died 1950. To his nurse: "Sister, you're trying to keep me alive as an old curiosity, but I'm done, I'm finished, I'm going to die."

Carl "Alfalfa" Switzer: American star of the *Our Gang* film series, shot in 1959. His youthful stardom far behind him, Switzer was drunk in a bar; so was the man who shot him after he said: "I want the fifty bucks you owe me and I want it now!"

Ellen Terry: British actress, died 1928. Scribbled in the dust of her bedside table: "Happy."

Dylan Thomas: Welsh poet, died 1953. "I've had eighteen straight whiskies, I think that's the record. . . . After thirty-nine years, this is all I've done."

James Thurber: American cartoonist and humorist, died 1961. "God bless . . . God damn . . ."

Walter White: American black leader, died 1954. Asked by his daughter whether he liked her dress, White mocked the McCarthyite witch hunts of the time: "I plead the Fifth Amendment."

Edward Wilson: British doctor and explorer, died 1912. Wilson was lost with Scott's Antarctic expedition (see page 747); this letter was left for his wife: "God knows I am sorry to be the cause of sorrow to anyone in the world, but everyone must die and at every death there must be some sorrow. All the things I had hoped to do with you after this Expedition are as nothing now, but there are greater things for us to do in the world to come. My only regret is leaving you to struggle through your life alone, but I may be coming to you by a quicker way. I feel so happy now in having got time to write to you. One of my notes will surely reach you. Dad's little compass and Mother's little comb are in my pocket. Your little testament and prayer book will be in my hand or in my breast pocket when the end comes. All is well."

Thomas Wolfe: American novelist, died 1938. Greeting his sister: "All right, Mabel, I am coming."

Eugene Ysaye: Belgian violinist, died 1929. He had his Fourth Sonata played for his enjoyment: "Splendid, the finale is just a little too fast."

Florenz Ziegfeld: American theatrical producer, died 1932. In a delirium: "Curtain! Fast music! Lights! Ready for the last finale! Great! The show looks good. The show looks good."

For further reading: *Famous Last Words: The Ultimate Dictionary of Quotations,* by Jonathon Green. London: Chancellor Press, 1993.

20 STRANGE DEATHS

1. THE BURDEN OF MATRIMONY

William Shortis, a rent collector in Liverpool, England, and his wife, Emily Ann, had not been seen for several days. Worried friends and a policeman entered the house on August 13, 1903, and were horrified to discover William, dazed and dying, at the foot of the staircase pinned to the floor underneath the body of his 224-pound wife. A coroner's jury concluded that the elderly couple had been walking up the stairs when Emily Ann fell backward, carrying her husband with her. Mrs. Shortis died immediately from a concussion, but William remained in his unfortunate position for three days, too seriously injured to be able to extricate himself.

2. THE FATEFUL BATH

Pat Burke of Saint Louis, Missouri, took his first bath in twenty years on August 23, 1903. It killed him. Burke was the second victim of cleanliness in a week at the city hospital, and the third in its history. The first was Billy O'Rourke, who had been bathed on the previous Tuesday. Both men had been scrubbed with a broom.

3. THE WORST NIGHTMARE OF ALL

In 1924 British newspapers reported the bizarre case of a man who apparently committed suicide while asleep. Thornton Jones, a lawyer, woke up to discover that he had slit his throat. Motioning to his wife for a paper and pencil, Jones wrote, "I dreamt that I had done it. I awoke to find it true." He died eighty minutes later.

4. KILLED BY JAZZ

Seventy-nine-year-old cornetist and music professor Nicola Coviello had had an illustrious career, having performed before Queen Victoria, Edward VII, and other dignitaries. Realizing that his life was nearing its end, Coviello decided to travel from London to Saskatchewan to pay a final visit to his son. On the way he stopped in New York City to bid farewell to his nephews, Peter, Dominic, and Daniel Coviello. On June 13, 1926, the young men took their famous uncle to Coney Island to give him a taste of America. The elder Coviello enjoyed himself but seemed irritated by the blare of the jazz bands. Finally he could take it no longer. "That isn't music," he complained and he fell to the boardwalk. He was pronounced dead a few minutes later. Cause of death was "a strain on the heart."

5. TO DIE LAUGHING

Mr. and Mrs. Alex Mitchell of Brockley Green, Fairstead Estate, King's Lynn, England, were watching their favorite TV comedy, *The Goodies*, in 1975. During a scene about a new type of self-defense called "Ecky Thump," Alex Mitchell was seized by uncontrollable laughter. After a half hour of unrestrained mirth, he suffered a heart attack and died. His wife, Nessie, wrote to *The Goodies* thanking them for making her husband's last moments so happy.

6. TOO MUCH OF A GOOD THING

It is almost impossible to die of an overdose of water, but Tina Christopherson managed to do it. The twenty-nine-year-old Florida woman, who had an IQ of 189, became obsessed with the idea that she suffered from stomach cancer, a disease that had killed her mother. In an attempt to cleanse her body, Christopherson went on periodic water fasts, during which she ate no food but drank up to four gallons of water a day. By February 17, 1977, she had consumed so much water that her kidneys were overwhelmed and the excess fluid drained into her lungs. She died of internal drowning, otherwise known as water intoxication.

7. KILLED BY A ROBOT

Ford Motor Company's casting plant in Flat Rock, Michigan, employed a one-ton robot to fetch parts from a storage rack. When the robot malfunctioned on January 25, 1979, twenty-five-year-old Robert Williams was asked to climb up on the rack and get the parts. While he was performing the task, the robot suddenly reactivated and hit Williams in the head with its arm. Williams died instantly. Four years later a jury ordered Unit Handling Systems, the manufacturer of the robot, to pay Williams's family $10 million. Williams is believed to have been the first person killed by a robot.

8. THE PERILS OF POLITICS

Nitaro Ito, forty-one, a pancake shop operator in Higashiosaka, Japan, concluded that he needed an extra edge in his 1979 campaign for House of Representatives. He decided to stage an attack on himself and then draw sympathy by campaigning from a hospital bed. Ito's scheme was to have an employee, Kazuhiko Matsumo, punch him in the face on the night of September 17, after which Ito would stab himself in the leg. After Matsumo had carried out his part of the plan, Ito stabbed his right thigh. Unfortunately, he cut an artery and bled to death before he could reach his home fifty-five yards away.

9. WHAT A WASTE TO GO—PART ONE
The seventy-year-old mayor of Betterton, Maryland, Monica Myer, considered it part of her duties to check the sewage tanks at the municipal facility. On the night of March 19, 1980, she went to the Betterton treatment plant to test for chlorine and sediment. Unfortunately, she slipped on a catwalk, fell into a tank of human waste, and drowned.

10. THE DEADLY DANCE
In August 1981 eleven-year-old Simon Longhurst of Wigan, England, attended a Sunday afternoon junior disco session where, along with other youngsters, he performed the "head shake," a New Wave dance in which the head is shaken violently as the music gets faster and faster. The following day young Simon began suffering headaches and soon a blood clot developed. Three weeks later he died of acute swelling of the brain. The coroner ruled it "death by misadventure."

11. REVENGE OF THE PLANT KINGDOM
On February 4, 1982, twenty-seven-year-old David M. Grundman fired two shotgun blasts at a giant saguaro cactus in the desert outside Phoenix, Arizona. Unfortunately for Grundman, his shots caused a twenty-three-foot section of the cactus to fall on him, and he was crushed to death.

12. A FATAL TEMPER
On April 15, 1982, twenty-six-year-old Michael Scaglione was playing golf with friends at the City Park West Municipal Golf Course in New Orleans. After making a bad shot on the thirteenth hole, Scaglione became angry with himself and threw his club against a golf cart. When the club broke, the clubhead rebounded and stabbed Scaglione in the throat, severing his jugular vein. Scaglione staggered back and pulled the metal piece from his neck. Had he not done that, he might have lived, since the clubhead could have reduced the rapid flow of blood.

13. FATAL CURE FOR HEMORRHOIDS
Norik Hakpisan, a twenty-four-year-old music student of Sloane Terrace, Kensington, in London, was found dead on October 5, 1982, after being caught in a flash fire while trying to relieve a bad case of hemorrhoids with gasoline. The fumes from an open bottle of petrol had been ignited by a cooker hot plate. Hakpisan's brother Hiak said that relieving hemorrhoids with paraffin was an old family remedy, but that Norik had apparently used petrol instead.

14. STRANGLED BY A GARDEN HOSE
Thirty-five-year-old Richard Fresquez of Austin, Texas, became drunk on the night of May 7, 1983. He tripped on a garden hose, became tangled in it, and strangled to death while trying to break free.

15. AMONG THE MANY DANGERS OF THE SPIRITUAL WORLD
John Edward Blue, thirty-eight, of Dorchester, Massachusetts, was being baptized in Lake Cochituate, in Natick, Massachusetts, on August 13, 1984, when he and the minister performing the baptism slipped and fell backward into deep water. The minister survived, but Blue drowned.

16. DROWNED AT A LIFEGUARD'S PARTY
On August 1, 1985, lifeguards of the New Orleans Recreation Department threw a party to celebrate their first drowning-free season in memory. Although four lifeguards were on duty at the party and more than half the 200 party goers were lifeguards, when the party ended, one of the guests, Jerome Moody, thirty-one, was found dead on the bottom of the recreation department pool.

17. AMONG THE MANY DANGERS OF THE MATERIAL WORLD
Brink's armored car guard Hrand Arakelian, thirty-four, of Santee, California, was crushed to death by $50,000 worth of quarters. Arakelian was guarding a load of twenty-five-pound coin boxes in the back of a truck traveling down the San Diego Freeway on February 3, 1986, when the driver braked suddenly to avoid a car that had swerved in front of him. When he pulled over to check on his partner, he found Arakelian completely covered by boxes of coins.

18. AW CHUTE
Ivan McGuire was an experienced parachutist who spent the afternoon of April 2, 1988, in Louisburg, North Carolina, videotaping parachuting students as they jumped and jumping with them. On his third trip up, McGuire dropped from the airplane and began filming the instructor and student who followed him a second later. McGuire reached back and discovered that he had forgotten to put on his parachute. His videotape, which was shown on the news in nearby Raleigh, recorded McGuire's final words: "Uh-oh."

19. WHAT A WASTE TO GO—PART TWO
Carl Theuerkauf Sr. and his family ran the largest dairy farm in Michigan's Upper Peninsula.

Elmbrook Farm had been in the Theuerkauf family for 108 years. On the fateful day of July 27, 1989, Carl Sr.'s son Tom climbed through a narrow hole and down a ladder into a manure pit filled with twelve inches of liquefied manure. He was trying to clear a blocked drain. Unbeknownst to Tom, odorless but lethal methane gas had built up during a deadly heat wave. He lost consciousness and fell back into the manure. Tom's nephew Dan sent for help and then went down into the pit. Then Carl Sr.'s cousin Bill Hofer went down to help. When he was overcome, Carl Sr. tried to rescue his family. Finally Carl Jr. followed. By the time others on the farm could haul out everyone else, it was too late—five men had died.

20. BEAVER DAMN
When Nanette Meech, the first female trustee of the Minneapolis Institute of Arts, was seventy-six years old, she went kayaking on the Brule River in Wisconsin with her daughter and some friends. On July 15, 1993, Meech was hit on the head by a forty-foot poplar tree. The tree had been gnawed by a beaver the night before, but it didn't fall until the Meeches floated by. Nanette Meech died immediately.

—D.W.

PEOPLE MADE FAMOUS BY THEIR DEATH

CASEY JONES (April 30, 1900—Vaughan, Mississippi)
John Luther Jones (nicknamed Casey after his hometown of Cayce, Kentucky) was a career railroadman. According to legend, on the night of April 29, 1900, he pulled the Cannonball Express into Memphis and then volunteered to replace an ill engineer on the return home. Early the next morning he rode the express to its collision with a stalled train, after telling his fireman to jump. His body was found with one hand on the whistle cord and the other on the brake. His heroic death saved many lives, causing him ever afterward to be celebrated in song and legend.

HORST WESSEL (February 1930—Berlin, Germany)
A down-and-out ex-Brownshirt, Wessel was shot to death by a Communist during a period of Nazi-Communist street fighting. However, the killing was motivated not by politics but by rivalry over a prostitute. When Nazi propaganda chief Joseph Goebbels learned that Wessel had written a patriotic poem, "Up with the Flag," he made Wessel a party martyr and had him honored as an ideal Nazi youth. The poem was set to music and the "Horst Wessel Song" became the Nazi anthem.

—R.K.R.

KITTY GENOVESE (March 13, 1964—Kew Gardens, Queens, New York)
Her name would come to stand for a disquieting sense of late-twentieth-century urban isolation and an attitude of self-defensive noninvolvement in the lives of others. But in the early-morning hours of March 13, 1964, she was simply a young woman returning home from her job as a bar manager.

The home she tried to return to was an apartment in the very ordinary, middle-class suburb of Kew Gardens, Queens, in New York City. For a half hour, beginning at 3:20 A.M., thirty-eight respectable, ordinary neighbors heard her screams, and some saw her being attacked by a man with a knife.

Her killer returned twice after the initial attack, as she tried to make her way to safety, bleeding and dying. She screamed, "Oh, my God, he stabbed me! Please help me! Please help me!" And, "I'm dying! I'm dying!"

Railroad engineer Casey Jones sacrificed his life to save his passengers near Vaughan, Mississippi, on April 30, 1900.

Kitty Genovese did, in fact, die. Finally, at 3:50 someone did call the police, and they were there in two minutes, but too late to save the young woman's life.

Why did no one call earlier? "We thought it was a lover's quarrel," one couple said. "Frankly, we were afraid." "I didn't want my husband to get involved," another woman claimed. Asked why she hadn't called for help, another woman shrugged and said, "I don't know." Someone else put it this way: "I was tired. I went back to bed."

Unfortunately, by the 1990s urban criminals were so well armed and murderous attacks so common that cases of a victim's cries for help going unanswered are rarely considered newsworthy.

One positive change that grew out of Genovese's death was that New York City finally installed a 911 system so that calling for help became more convenient. Her killer, Winston Moseley, remained incarcerated as of September 1995.

MARY JO KOPECHNE (July 19, 1969— Chappaquiddick Island, Massachusetts)

Except for the circumstances of her death, there had been nothing unusually noteworthy in Mary Jo Kopechne's young life.

She had been drawn to politics since a year after her graduation from Caldwell College for Women in Caldwell, New Jersey. After a year of teaching in Montgomery, Alabama, Kopechne joined the staff of Florida senator George A. Smathers. In 1964 she started to work for Senator Robert F. Kennedy as a secretary to various speechwriters, and later as a secretary to Joseph Dolan, Kennedy's legal adviser.

Following Robert F. Kennedy's assassination in 1964 she went to work for Matt Reese Associates, a political consulting firm. She remained friendly with people she had met through her work with Kennedy.

The night of July 18, 1969, Kopechne attended a party at the Kennedy family compound on Martha's Vineyard. At about 11:15 she left the party in a car with Ted Kennedy on the way to the ferry to Edgartown. At about 12:50 A.M., July 19, the car went off a narrow bridge over a pond on Chappaquiddick Island

and overturned in the water. Kennedy was able to escape, but Kopechne drowned. Her name and the word Chappaquiddick entered the lexicon of the dark side of American politics.

Kennedy's behavior after the accident—he supposedly wandered dazed for hours, and he only reported the accident the following morning—and rumors of a cover-up of the true details of her death added to the string of lamentable events in the Kennedy family history.

CLAYTON HARTWIG (April 19, 1989— Battleship *Iowa*)

Clayton M. Hartwig, a U.S. Navy gunner's mate, was accused of suicide and mass murder in the April 19, 1989, explosion aboard the battleship *Iowa* that killed Hartwig and forty-six other sailors.

The navy's initial investigation was based on the supposed presence of foreign material in the breech of the huge gun; on interviews with Hartwig's shipmates that labeled him as "a loner" and a young man perhaps confused about his sexuality; on the fact that he had a life insurance policy made out to a shipmate; and on an FBI psychological profile that stated he "died as a result of his own actions, staging his death in such a fashion that he hoped it would appear to be an accident."

It was owing to the devotion and persistence of Hartwig's sister, Kathleen Kubicina, that his name was finally cleared. She led a public campaign to get independent scientific investigators to look at the case.

The navy had concluded that foreign material found in the breech after the explosion was from a homemade detonator placed there by Hartwig. The Sandia National Laboratories blew the navy's findings out of the water, however, ascribing the "foreign material" to seawater and gun-cleaning fluids. They staged experiments that showed that the explosion could have been accidentally caused by improper operation of the ramming device that compresses the gunpowder.

The navy conceded that it never had "clear and convincing evidence" that Hartwig had caused the explosion and formally apologized to Clayton Hartwig's family.

—R.W.S.

POSTHUMOUS FAME

PAUL GAUGUIN (1848–1903), French Painter
One of Gauguin's last letters sold in 1957 for 600,000 francs. The letter stated: "I am now down and out, defeated by poverty." For the gregarious ex-stockbroker from Paris who deserted home and family to live and paint in the South Pacific, the idealistic paradise he sought

never materialized. Nor did artistic success come during his lifetime, though he achieved recognition from a few European painters who were mostly as "down and out" as he was. Yet Gauguin's rebellion against "pretended rules," his efforts to convey emotional essence through painting technique, and his embrace of native

A self-portrait by Paul Gauguin.

culture as a fit subject of art revolutionized impressionist painting. "His end was his beginning," as one biographer stated. A small Gauguin memorial exhibition in the fall of 1903 laid the basis for his future reputation, even though the first postimpressionist exhibition, in 1910 in London—which included works by Gauguin, Van Gogh, and Matisse—evoked ridicule from the *Times*. Appreciation for Gauguin increased gradually by means of occasional exhibitions until 1942—a year that coincided with the appearance of the film *The Moon and Sixpence*, based on W. Somerset Maugham's 1919 novel about Gauguin. His journal, describing the last two years of his life, was published twenty years after his death. Since then, prices of his paintings have risen dramatically, until today his works number among the world's most expensive modern art.

SCOTT JOPLIN (1868–1917), U.S. Composer

The precocious son of a former slave, Scott Joplin taught himself to play the guitar, bugle, and piano before he was seven. Born near Texarkana, Texas, he received expert training in harmony, counterpoint, and classical music. Joplin left home at age fourteen, played honky-tonk piano in Texas and Louisiana and in bordellos in Mississippi, attended college in Sedalia, Missouri, and worked in Saint Louis and Chicago nightclubs. By the time he moved to New York, he had begun to publish numerous ragtime compositions in sheet-music form. The syncopated "ragged time" had evolved from an improvised mating of African-American folk music with the European march. Played in southern saloons and red-light districts, it was a grandparent of American jazz. Joplin treated the music as a serious art form, maintaining that "what is scurrilously called ragtime is an invention that is here to stay. . . . Syncopations are no indication of light or trashy music, and to shy bricks at 'hateful ragtime' no longer passes for musical culture." He structured and formalized the pattern in his own compositions, best known of which was the 1899 "Maple Leaf Rag." It was the first sheet music in the United States to sell a million copies, and Joplin earned a penny for each sheet. Joplin achieved recognition and a measure of prosperity within Harlem, but his name never traveled far beyond this cultural underground during his lifetime. In 1911 he completed his ragtime opera *Treemonisha*, which has as its theme the importance of education for blacks. He exhausted his financial, physical, and emotional resources in staging a single Harlem performance of *Treemonisha* in 1915. Interest in ragtime music faded with the new rhythms of Tin Pan Alley, and Joplin, sick with the ravages of syphilis and disillusioned at forty-nine, died in Manhattan State Hospital. The Joplin revival started in 1970, when Nonesuch Records issued a Joplin series played by classical pianists. Republication of his rags soon followed, and the 1973 film *The Sting* made Joplin's "The Entertainer" rag a national hit. Joplin's grave finally received a permanent marker; and *Treemonisha*, with elaborate orchestration, arrived on Broadway in 1975. Many of his works were lost, including an opera called *A Guest of Honor*, the score of which has never been found.

ROBERT HUTCHINGS GODDARD (1882–1945), U.S. Physicist, Rocketry Pioneer

Goddard taught physics for most of his career at Clark University in Worcester, Massachusetts. His now classic paper "A Method of Reaching Extreme Altitudes" (1919) predicted the development of spacecraft and the possibility of their reaching the moon and beyond. Over the next twenty-five years, he experimented, plotted trajectories, and tested several fuel and guidance systems, anticipating much of the later progress in rocketry. The *New York Times*, in a 1920 editorial, ridiculed his claim that rockets could fly to the moon, even though Goddard had clearly demonstrated that they could operate in a vacuum. In 1929 one of his rockets exploded and the state fire marshal banned him from further testing of his devices. The next year he moved his operation to Roswell, New Mexico. He was called moon mad, and his insights were ignored by both the general public and the government—although the German V-2 production of World War II adopted many of his ideas. Almost fifteen years after his death from throat cancer, the Soviet *Sputnik I* orbiter vindicated Goddard's theories. Since U.S. research could not proceed without infringing on many of his 214 patents, the government paid $1 million to his estate for the rights to them. In belated recognition of Goddard's skill and foresight, the NASA research facility at Greenbelt, Maryland, was named the Goddard Space Flight Center. And just a few days before the *Apollo 11* astronauts were to walk on the moon, the *New York Times*, on July 17, 1969, printed a formal retraction of its 1920 editorial.

FRANZ KAFKA (1883–1924), Austrian Author

Kafka, said poet W. H. Auden, bears the same relation to our age that Dante, Shakespeare, and Goethe bore to theirs. His novels *Amerika*, *The Trial*, and *The Castle* pose the spiritual and artistic problems that have occupied most serious twentieth-century writers and thinkers. The author was a typical victim of the urban rat race. As a harassed functionary of the Workers' Accident Insurance Institute in Prague, he struggled for free time from his job and his domineering family to write. He was the most sedentary of men, lonely, untraveled, and inexperienced except in business. Five slim volumes appeared and sank out of sight during his lifetime, and only a few friends realized that he was writing the novels that would help form the core of twentieth-century literature. These works remained incomplete and unpublished when tuberculosis killed him at age forty. After years of tortuous efforts to "begin my real life" and to describe a precise statement of his soul, Kafka considered his efforts a failure. In a last request, he asked his friend Max Brod to burn all of his papers and manuscripts. Brod indignantly refused, saying that if Kafka had really wanted them destroyed, he would not have given the task to the one person he knew would never consent to it. Thus Kafka's best-known novels, prophetic of the nightmare state of fascism, were first published in Germany in 1925 through 1927. Although the Nazis soon banned the books, translated editions surfaced in other countries. Kafka's reputation has steadily increased since the 1940s, and today the works of his critics and interpreters far outnumber his own.

LEON "BIX" BEIDERBECKE (1903–31), U.S. Jazz Musician

No jazz lover who has heard Bix Beiderbecke's pure cornet has ever forgotten it. Though he came from a musical family and studied classical music on his own, he never took a cornet lesson in his life but taught himself at age fourteen by playing along with Dixieland records. The shy, inarticulate boy from Davenport, Iowa, dropped out of school, and a succession of jobs with vagrant musical groups finally landed him his first steady work with Frank Trumbauer's band in 1925. He soon moved into Jean Goldkette's orchestra, where he often alternated between cornet and piano. In 1927 he joined Paul Whiteman's band, where he made $200 per week—the financial high point of his career. "Proud of his recordings with Whiteman," wrote Dan Morgenstern, "Bix religiously sent each record to his family; he was deeply hurt when by chance he looked into a closet at home and found it filled with his unopened packages." Whiteman often featured Beiderbecke's cornet solos, which attracted a devoted circle of fans, but the stress of the big band's commercial pace increased Beiderbecke's already severe alcohol problem. By 1929 he was no longer dependable on the stand, and Whiteman had to let him go. He played a few odd jobs for a while before he died of pneumonia at age twenty-eight. Beiderbecke remained forgotten until 1938, when Dorothy Baker published her *Young Man with a Horn*, a sentimental novel based on his life. The 1950 film of the same title, starring Kirk Douglas, was an even more romanticized version. Yet the novel marked the beginning of the Beiderbecke cult, and in time the true story of his life proved far more intriguing than the fictional one. In Beiderbecke's integration of impressionist composers, especially Debussy, his style and tone had lasting influence on jazz, and such recordings as "Singin' the Blues" and "In a Mist" have become classics. Today he is recognized as the first important jazz innovator among white musicians.

—J.E.

JOHN KENNEDY TOOLE (1937–68), U.S. Novelist

Every American novelist dreams of becoming published and winning a Pulitzer Prize. But John Kennedy Toole did not live to see his novel, *A Confederacy of Dunces*, published, nor was he on hand to accept his Pulitzer Prize for fiction, awarded in 1980.

Born in New Orleans in 1937 to a car salesman and a teacher, Toole demonstrated early on that he was precocious—by age sixteen he had graduated from high school and entered Tulane University, where he received a B.A. in 1958. During a two-year army stint in Puerto Rico, he wrote *A Confederacy of Dunces*, a seriocomic Dickensian tale set in New Orleans.

Robert Gottlieb, then an editor at Simon and Schuster, was interested enough to have Toole do several rewrites but finally passed on the novel, claiming that it would never sell. Toole made no further attempts to find a publisher. Instead, having become increasingly despondent, he was found in his car in 1968 in Biloxi, Mississippi, asphyxiated by carbon monoxide fumes.

Toole's mother, Thelma, sent off copies of

her son's manuscript to at least eight New York publishers, all of whom rejected it. In 1976 she talked novelist Walker Percy into reading it. At first skeptical, Percy ended up so impressed with the work that he approached Louisiana State University Press, who agreed to publish it. The novel was a huge critical success, winning the Pulitzer, hitting the *New York Times* best-seller list, and selling more than half a million copies in the Grove Press paperback edition.

—L.C.

QUOTEBOOK: DEATH

Death is psychologically as important as birth.... Shrinking away from it is something unhealthy and abnormal which robs the second half of life of its purpose.

Carl Gustav Jung

Why worry one's head over a thing that is inevitable? Why die before one's death?

Mohandas K. Gandhi

I'm not afraid to die, honey. In fact I'm kind of looking forward to it. I know that the Lord has his arms wrapped around this big, fat sparrow.

Ethel Waters, interviewed shortly before her death, 1977

I have never killed a man, but I have read many obituaries with a lot of pleasure.

Clarence Darrow

They shall grow not old, as we that are left grow old: Age shall not weary them, or the years condemn. At the going down of the sun and in the morning We will remember them.

Lawrence Binyon, poem in the *Times*, September 21, 1914

Do not go gentle into that good night, Old age should burn and rave at close of day; Rage, rage against the dying of the light.

Dylan Thomas "Do Not Go Gentle into That Good Night," 1952

The parrot is no more! It has ceased to be! It's expired and gone to meet its maker! This is a late parrot! It's a stiff! Bereft of life it rests in peace—if you hadn't nailed it to the perch it would be pushing up the daisies! It's rung down the curtain and joined the choir invisible! THIS IS AN EX-PARROT!

Graham Chapman, John Cleese, Terry Gilliam, Eric Idle, Terry Jones, and Michael Palin, *Monty Python's Flying Circus*, 1969

I recently visited an Eastern sage and asked him "Is it possible to live for ever?" "Certainly," he replied, "You must undertake to do two things." "What are they?" "Firstly, you must never again make any false statements." "That's simple enough. What is the second thing I must do?" "Every day you must utter the statement 'I will repeat this statement tomorrow.' If you follow these instructions faithfully you are certain to live forever."

Jacqueline Harman, letter to *Daily Telegraph*, October 8, 1985

Chapter 20

STRANGE STORIES

The world is so overflowing with absurdity that it is difficult for the humorist to compete.
Malcolm Muggeridge, on becoming editor of Punch

ODDITY HUNTERS

CHARLES FORT
(1874–1932)

For the last twenty-six years of his life, Charles Fort collected stories of happenings science could not explain: frogs, crabs, manna, and blood falling from the sky; light-wheels with 300-yard-long spokes; people bursting spontaneously into flame and burning to ashes; phantom bullets; poltergeists; strange disappearances; graveyards of animal bones. He professed to believe that there is a universe parallel to the one we perceive, that the earth rotates only once a year, and that God "drools comets and gibbers earthquakes." He also held that the sky is really a shell with holes that appear to be stars and through which things fall; that this shell is partly gelatinous, so that aviators might find themselves "stuck like currants" in it; that above the earth is an aerial Sargasso Sea in which things taken up from earth float and then are shaken loose by storms and other phenomena. Essentially, Fort taught that the world is full of surprises, that the principle of uncertainty reigns.

Fort's Victorian childhood in Albany, New York, was like something out of Charles Dickens. His mother died four years after his birth in 1874, and his father ran a tight ship. Children, who were supposed to be "seen and not heard," were beaten regularly. Charles never took it lying down. Once, his nose bloodied by a smash in the face from his father, Charles ran upstairs and wiped the gore all over the bedding, carpet, and curtains in the spare bedroom. His resentment generated in him a streak of cruelty. One of his hobbies was to collect birds; he killed them, cut off their wings and other parts, and mounted them on boards. Never a good student

(at least in school), he had a reputation as a clown. His inventive mind never stopped hatching schemes. If a friend had not backed out of a proposed plan for the two of them to run away to Burma to be elephant drivers, it is very likely, one suspects, that Charles would have gone through with it.

By the time he was seventeen, he was selling feature stories to a New York syndicate and the *Brooklyn World*, where a year later, through with formal schooling, he took a job as a writer. He went from the *World* to the *Woodhaven* (Queens) *Independent*, which folded after a short life and left him jobless. So he took off on a trip around the world, living on the cheap, sometimes a near hobo (he narrowly missed serving time on a chain gang in the American South), consorting with sailors and cowboys. In Africa he contracted a fever (probably malaria) and he came back to New York to recover. Anna Filing, a young Englishwoman he had known in Albany, took care of him, and in 1896 he married her. Four years older than he, she was nonliterary, a lover of movies and parakeets, a woman a contemporary described as "bustling" around the house.

In the first years of their marriage, the Forts lived in poverty. They broke up chairs to make firewood, pawned precious belongings, and suffered holes in their shoes. Charles worked at various odd jobs, then began to sell feature stories to newspapers and short stories to magazines. His short stories, which humorously chronicled the lives of his neighbors in the slums, appealed to Theodore Dreiser, who then worked for *Smith's Magazine*. Dreiser became a lifelong admirer and friend; he helped Fort get his books published.

Fort really wanted to be a novelist and

Charles Fort.

mass moves, a game could last as long as a week.

In the last year of his life, 1932, the fourth and last book of his collected notes and theories was published. The first, *The Book of the Damned*, had come out in 1919, with the help of Dreiser.

Here is a typical Charles Fort description of unexplained events:

> *Madras Mail*, May 13, 1907—a woman in the village of Manner, near Dinapore—flames that had consumed her body, but not her clothes—that two constables had found the corpse in a room, in which nothing else showed signs of fire, and had carried the smoldering body, in the unscorched clothes, to the District magistrate. *Toronto Globe*, Jan. 28, 1907—dispatch from Pittsburgh, Pa.—that Albert Houck had found the body of his wife, "burned to a crisp," lying upon a table—no sign of fire upon the table, nor anywhere else in the house. *New York Sun*, Jan. 24, 1930—coroner's inquiry, at Kingston, N.Y., into the death of Mrs. Stanley Lake. "Although her body was severely burned, her clothing was not even scorched."

Fort's other three books of notes and explanations—*New Lands* (1923), *Lo!* (1931), and *Wild Talents* (1932)—were written in a similar style. It was Fort who invented the now commonly used word *teleportation*.

In two unpublished books called *X* and *Y*, which he later burned, he advanced the theories that the earth was controlled by Martians ("I think we're property," he said) and that a civilization, unknown to most people, existed at the South Pole. He was also one of the first to speculate that unexplained lights in the sky might be vehicles from outer space.

A doubter, even of giants such as Galileo and Darwin, Fort did not reject science, but he was critical of the dogmatic "scientific priesthood" and their "damning" of facts and incidents that didn't fit into established theories. He also had the saving grace of finding even himself absurd. He was slightly misanthropic, had few friends except author Tiffany Thayer and Dreiser, refused to allow a telephone in his apartment, and said, "I have considerable liking for people, so long as I can stay away from them." With his fat face, mustache, and pince-nez, Fort greatly resembled Teddy Roosevelt. He was strong and tall, with a snub nose and calm eyes.

It's hard to say what Charles Fort thought of the Fortean Society, founded in 1931 by Tiffany Thayer to perpetuate Fort's name and works and to harass scientists. Many famous people of the day joined—Alexander Woollcott, John Cowper Powys, Ben Hecht—but Fort himself wouldn't, probably out of modesty and his antipathy toward all groups. In 1937 Thayer started the *Fortean Society Magazine* (later changed to *Doubt*), which published Fort's notes. As time went on, it became increasingly

estimated he put down more than 3 million words in novels, of which only one, *The Outcast Manufacturers*, published in 1909, made it into print.

In 1905 he began collecting notes about strange happenings. At one point he had 25,000 notes stuck into pigeonholes in a wall. (Also on the wall were framed specimens of spiders and butterflies.) More notes and clippings overflowed from shoe boxes. All were the result of years of research in the public libraries of New York; to collect them, he went at least twice through all the scientific periodicals written in English and French going back to 1880.

When Fort was forty years old, he inherited enough money to enable him to pursue full time what was now an obsession. Four years later he burned all the notes he had gathered and went with his wife to London, where he spent six months reading every day in the British Museum. At night he hung out with derelicts and loitered in Hyde Park or went to the movies with his wife. For many years he commuted between New York and London and accumulated 40,000 more notes.

Then he began to lose his sight (it returned briefly later), and since he was no longer able to read, he amused himself with a game he invented called super-checkers, which was played on a board with thousands of squares and with armies of men made of tacks and cardboard. Until he streamlined it by allowing

political, printing polemics against vaccination, fluoridation of water, and other technological advances and reporting embarrassments of scientists (for example, the time an astronomer fell off his telescope) with testy glee. In the ninth issue a new calendar (its year one being 1931) was introduced; its year contained a new month, Fort, sandwiched between August and September. The magazine folded in 1959. Now Fortean word is carried by the *Fortean Times* (Fenner, Reed & Jackson, P.O. Box 754, Manhasset, New York 11030) and by William Corliss's *Sourcebook Project* (P.O. Box 107, Glen Arm, Maryland 21057).

The last word belongs to Fort, who once said, "I believe nothing. I have shut myself away from the rocks and wisdoms of ages, and from the so-called great teachers of all time, and perhaps because of that isolation I am given to bizarre hospitalities. I shut the front door upon Christ and Einstein, and at the back door hold out a welcoming hand to little frogs and periwinkles."

—A.E.

ROBERT RIPLEY
(1890–1949)

Detractors and supporters have vehemently argued the veracity of Robert Leroy Ripley since his rise to fame in the 1920s as America's king of oddities. He was labeled the "world's greatest liar," yet his "Believe It or Not" cartoons had, at their height, a worldwide readership of 80 million people. His radio show announcer prattled off the following introduction, "That incomparable, inimitable, inestimable introducer of immeasurable, incalculable, and in-

Robert Ripley (seated, left), often accused of inaccuracy, submits to a test by William Marston's newly invented lie detector, December 1, 1931.

credible impossibilities." In his defense, Ripley could almost always produce documentation or an explanation for his cartoons and comments on the outlandish. However, that "proof" often took liberties with the truth. He once ran the headline "Buffalo Bill Never Shot a Buffalo." Of course the American buffalo is really a bison. Another cartoon claimed that a pound of feathers weighed more than a pound of gold. He backed this up with the logic that gold is usually weighed in the troy twelve-ounce pound. He was a storytelling lover of the bizarre who often considered the tale more important than the truth.

For him, embellishing reality was a way of life that he applied even to himself. He was born on December 26, 1890, but throughout his life he gave his birthday as Christmas Day. On three different passport applications, he gave his year of birth as 1891, 1892, and 1893. Books and articles on Ripley to this day usually list 1893 as the year he was born. Even his name changed. He was born LeRoy Ripley, with the Robert being unofficially added sometime in his early adulthood.

Whatever the accuracy of his material, Ripley was a grand entertainer in a tradition stretching from P. T. Barnum to the *National Enquirer*. In a more innocent and credulous age, he was a global explorer of the exotic and odd.

A large, active man with big buckteeth, a hawk nose, and dimples, he was full of two elements: energy and curiosity. It was often commented that he had a child's interest in the world and its magic and that, in fact, his whole life was an extended childhood. He traveled to primitive corners of the world, yet he was afraid of automobiles and telephones and had others do his driving and dialing. He was, himself, one of the curiosities that he loved to describe.

He was born in San Rafael, California, to a father who was a carpenter and a mother who had been born in a covered wagon on the Santa Fe Trail. In his youth he had two passions: drawing and baseball. He created the promotional posters for the semipro baseball team for which he was the pitcher. These posters caught the eye of a San Francisco newspaper editor who soon found Ripley work at the *Bulletin*. From there Ripley moved to the prestigious *San Francisco Chronicle*, where he worked for four years as an illustrator before being fired for asking for a $2.50-a-week raise.

Next, in 1913, Ripley was off to New York, where he found work with the *Globe* as a sports cartoonist. At the same time, he tried out for the New York Giants at their spring training. However, he broke his arm at practice, thus ending his chances at a professional baseball career.

On a slow sports-news day in December of 1918, he packaged nine sketches under the title "Champs and Chumps." These drawings depicted actual people who had accomplished such feats as running 100 yards backward in fourteen seconds, jumping rope 11,810 times in four hours, and holding their breath under water for six and one-half minutes. According to Ripley, his editor told him to come up with a better title and, in a flash of genius, he thought of "Believe It or Not!" However, the Ripley archives show that the "Believe It or Not" title did not actually appear for another year.

But the concept was an immediate success as Ripley spread out from sports into every subject imaginable. Cartoons featured a man who fell sixteen stories and suffered only bruises, and a will that was written on an eggshell. Another centered on Albert Smith, who was a one-armed paperhanger from Massachusetts with hives. Then there was Alexandre Patty, a "cranial hopper," who bounced down stairs on his head. Ripley discovered a gentleman named Ab C. Defghi, as well as two Ukrainians who slapped each other's face for thirty-six hours.

Ripley's truthful allegation that the "Star Spangled Banner" had never been officially adopted as the national anthem caused an uproar. The resulting 5-million-signature petition pushed Congress into passing the bill officially making it the national anthem in 1931. When Ripley asserted that Charles Lindbergh was the sixty-seventh man to fly nonstop across the Atlantic, 170,000 infuriated readers sent letters of protest. Ripley justified his statement by explaining that a two-man plane plus sixty-five people in two dirigibles had crossed the Atlantic prior to Lindbergh. The controversy only increased his popularity.

William Randolph Hearst picked up Ripley's contract in the early 1930s and syndicated his cartoons to 325 newspapers in thirty-three countries. Ripley published a series of books, starred in movie-short features, and had his own *Believe It or Not* weekly radio show. With a slight stutter and a nervous quaver to his voice, he was not very radiogenic, but listeners loved him anyway.

In the 1930s and 1940s, Ripley's "Believe It or Not" had become an industry receiving each year a million letters containing stories, photographs, and cartoons. In 1937 a twelve-year-old aspiring cartoonist from Minnesota named Charles Schulz submitted a cartoon featuring his dog who ate razor blades. The dog caricature eventually evolved into Snoopy of "Peanuts" fame.

Ripley made a fortune and spent a fortune. He bought mansions on Long Island, Palm Beach, and Manhattan. He threw lavish parties, owned and sailed a Chinese junk, and collected curios from around the world. And he traveled incessantly. His favorite country was China and his favorite sight was the Grand Canyon. Ripley claimed to have traveled the equivalent of eighteen times around the globe. Once he reported that he had traveled from New York to Cairo, 15,000 miles by airplane, 8,000 miles by ship, and 1,000 miles by camel, horse, and donkey.

He promoted his radio shows through special broadcasts while feeding sharks, visiting snake pits, or skydiving. During one broadcast from a canvas boat that was running the rapids of the Colorado River at night, he was accompanied by his local sponsor's son, Barry Goldwater.

Despite his appearance and shyness, Ripley was always surrounded by women. In 1919 he married Beatrice Roberts, a model and showgirl. The marriage foundered in only a few months and ended in divorce in 1925. Ripley never remarried but was never without women. At his estate on Long Island, he usually had four to five young women living with him, one currently in favor while the others waited their turn. His lovers were frequently Asian.

Ripley enjoyed life but never seemed satisfied with his success. As he grew older, alcohol, his other addiction besides women, took a heavier and heavier toll on him. He became bloated and went on more-frequent and longer drinking binges. When he started appearing on TV, he would often appear inebriated, slightly slurring his words. With high blood pressure, he suffered a series of strokes. Finally, in 1949 he checked into a New York hospital, where he died three days later of a heart attack.

Ripley considered himself a small-town boy who had made it big in the world. His radio producer, Doug Storer, characterized Ripley as "the greatest hayseed ever to succeed in show business." Today, Ripley Entertainment carries on his work. There are twenty-one Ripley Odditoriums around the world that purchase an average of 1,200 new oddities a year.

—R.J.F.

THE MCWHIRTER TWINS
(ROSS 1925–75; NORRIS b. 1925)

In 1955 Ross and Norris McWhirter were approached by an employee of Sir Hugh Beaver, managing director of the Guinness brewery, to coauthor a book of records to settle pub disputes. (The idea may have originated on a hunting expedition when Sir Hugh, having missed shooting a golden plover, wondered how fast the bird was flying.) The brothers, who were twins and shared a love of facts, drove to Park Royal, Sir Hugh's fifty-four-acre estate. During their conversation Sir Hugh talked about his experiences in Turkey, mentioning the problems of translating from English into Turkish. Norris pointed out that this shouldn't be a problem, as Turkish has only one irregular verb. Sir Hugh asked if he spoke Turkish, and Norris replied that he did not, but his interest in records and facts led him to this discovery about the Turkish language. Impressed, Sir Hugh decided that they were the right men for his project: the *Guinness Book of Records*.

From an early age, the McWhirter twins were fascinated by facts. Born August 12, 1925, of Scottish parents, they read scores of newspapers a week and their favorite book was *Whitaker's Almanac*. They even had a secret language, which they later abandoned. The twins remained inseparable until World War II, when Norris was assigned to a mine sweeper in the Pacific and Ross served in the Mediterranean. Though they were serving thousands of miles apart, they were to meet once during the war. To avoid hitting an Egyptian ship in the Malta harbor, Norris's ship rammed into the *Shillay*, the ship on which his brother Ross was serving.

After the war the McWhirter brothers pursued their interest in facts and records, forming McWhirter Twins, which did research for encyclopedias, periodicals, and other publications. Ross became a noted sportswriter, writing about tennis and rugby for the *Star*, while Norris covered track and field. Both men were superb athletes in their own right, becoming the only twins to win a national relay title—the 4×110-yard sprint relay in 1948.

Norris, who also covered the Olympic Games for the BBC from 1960 to 1972, was the public-address announcer at the historic 1954 track meet when Roger Bannister broke the four-

Norris and Ross McWhirter, founders of the Guinness Book of Records.

minute mile. Anticipating Bannister's success, he had carefully rehearsed his dramatic announcement of the event in his bathtub the night before.

Published in 1955, the first edition of the *Guinness Book of Records* contained not only British but world records as well (though, ironically, it omitted the record for the fastest bird). From an initial order for only six copies, the book reached England's best-seller list in four months. It arrived in the United States as *The Guinness Book of Superlatives* a year later, but did not sell well at first. It was re-titled as the *Guinness Book of World Records* and was given a new look. Demand grew in the 1960s, and the book began to come out in yearly editions in 1973. In 1974, 3.2 million paperback copies of it were printed in the United States. The McWhirters became the first authors to sell more than 25 million of a single title, and in 1994 the book reached worldwide sales of 74 million copies in 29 languages.

Amassing information for the book took a bit of finesse. When writing to experts, the brothers did not ask outright for information. Rather, they stated a fact that they figured must be close to the truth and asked the expert to correct it. As Norris explained, "People who have a total resistance to giving information often have an irresistible desire to correct other people's impressions."

Facts and publishing were not the McWhirters' only interests. Notorious for having a litigious nature, Ross was involved in nine court cases between 1954 and 1973. He brought action in 1954 against the National Union of Journalism because a union officer had defamed his brother's character. Ross won the judgment, plus damages and costs. In November 1968 he took on the Home Office single-handedly to challenge the miscounting of votes in local government elections in Enfield the previous May. He appealed to the High Court and won an injunction ordering the recount of the votes. In 1970 he took the Independent Broadcasting Authority (IBA) to court for transmitting subliminal advertising during a Labour Party broadcast—and lost. But his 1973 bid to have David Bailey's film about Andy Warhol banned from television was successful. Under the Television Act of 1964, anything that offended good taste and dignity was barred from being televised, and for McWhirter, the Bailey film came under that category. "I am not a fascist ogre of repression, or a self-appointed arbiter of good taste," he insisted. Rather, he saw himself as a libertarian who "liked to see the laws kept."

An ardent opponent of what he viewed as the stranglehold of unions, Ross went to court yet again to obtain an injunction against Eagle Ferry and the National Union of Seamen, which had impounded the cars of some forty passengers as a bargaining chip in a dispute. Ross obtained the injunction in nine minutes.

A vocal opponent of the Irish Republican Army's (IRA's) violent tactics, Ross founded an organization called Self Help, whose goals were to have the death penalty reinstated for terrorists and to require all Irish Republic nationals living in England to register and carry identity cards. In a pamphlet entitled *How to Stop the Bombers*, he offered a reward of £50,000 for information leading to the capture of the members of the IRA death squad believed to be responsible for the murder of eight civilians in car bombings. "I know the IRA have got me on their death list," Ross admitted, telling reporters that they might be writing his obituary soon.

His words proved prophetic. On November 27, 1975, as he opened his door to let in his wife, he was gunned down by two assassins. He was rushed to the hospital, where he died. On December 6 four members of the IRA gang believed to have been responsible for McWhirter's assassination were chased to a flat in Balcombe Street, where, after a six-day siege involving hostages, they were apprehended. All four terrorists received life sentences. Information they provided led the police to Brian Keenan, a.k.a. "Z," the notorious mastermind of the London bombing campaign. Keenan received a sentence of eighteen years.

After his brother's death, Norris McWhirter continued to enjoy a successful career as editor of *The Guinness Book*. In 1986 he relinquished his position as editor but remained as editorial advisor.

—L.C.

HOAXES

THE PROTOCOLS OF THE ELDERS OF ZION

The *Protocols of the Elders of Zion* was a 25,000-word manifesto calling for Jewish domination of the world. Drafted in secret by a conspiracy of high-placed Jewish leaders, it spoke of using bombs, biological warfare, and treachery to seize control of international banking and undermine the Christian way of life, and provided a blueprint for accomplishing it all. Not surprisingly, it furnished the Nazis with documentation of Jewish depravity—and with justification for moving ahead with the "final solution."

But the truth is that the *Protocols* was drafted by a group of Russian anti-Semites and reactionaries as a weapon against their political enemies. No Jew had anything to do with it.

The story of the *Protocols* broke in the *Banner*, a newspaper in Kishinev, Ukraine, in August 1903, under the headline "A Program for World Conquest by the Jews. Minutes of a Meeting of the Elders of Zion." Editor Paul Krushevan, an avowed Jew hater, gave no hint of his sources . . . only that the screed had been translated from French.

Two years later a more extensive rendering of the *Protocols* was published as part of *The Great in the Little*, a book by the Russian religious mystic Sergei Nilus. He traced the document's origins to a speech delivered in 1897 to the World Zionist Congress by Theodore Herzl, founder of the modern Zionist movement. It was this version on which all future speculation was based.

As presented by Nilus, the *Protocols* was a chilling document indeed. Among other things, it outlined a plan for Jews to conspire with freemasons, atheists, stock market manipulators, corrupt politicians, and other miscreants to conquer the world. The plot would begin insidiously, even invisibly, with the Jews leveraging their control of the press and financial markets to inflate prices, promote sexual deviance, undermine religious faith, and incite the masses to violence. Then, as the foundations of Christian civilization began to crack, the Jews would bomb the capitals of Europe and infect their populations with death dealing bacteria. Once in control, they would replace the gold standard with paper currency, banish dissent, and jail their opponents.

Nilus's version of the *Protocols* took Europe by storm. Few doubted its authenticity, although it was banned in Russia for a time as a fraud, despite the fact that anti-Semitism was a state policy. By the outset of World War I, the *Protocols* had been translated into most European languages and was growing in availability and influence. In Germany sales topped 120,000 copies in 1920, and the document may have incited the assassination of Foreign Minister Walter Rathenau, a Jew who was rumored to have been an Elder of Zion. In the early 1920s, as Germany suffered under the worst economic depression in history, Hitler commented that "according to the *Protocols of Zion*, the peoples are to be reduced to submission by hunger. The second revolution under the Star of David is the aim of the Jews in our time."

In the United States, industrialist Henry Ford—whose photograph Hitler kept on his desk—published excerpts of the *Protocols* in his virulently anti-Semitic newspaper, the *Dearborn Independent*.

In 1921 Philip Graves, Constantinople correspondent for the *Times* of London, came across an 1864 French political satire by Maurice Joly entitled *Dialogue in Hell Between Machiavelli and Montesque*. The publication of *Dialogue*, a pointed jibe at Emperor Napoleon III, got Joly thrown in jail. Though it was not in any way anti-Semitic, many of its passages were identical to those that later cropped up in the *Protocols*. Graves's conclusion: the *Protocols* was a hoax.

How the hoax originated is still open to question, but most likely it was masterminded by Pyotr Ivanovich Rachkovsky, one-time head of Okhrana, Russia's overseas secret police. Based in Paris from 1884 to 1902, Rachkovsky was an outspoken bigot who may well have created the *Protocols* as a way of savaging his political foes, destroying the Jews, and gaining points with Czar Nicholas II. Indeed, the anti-Semitic czar was only too happy to accept the *Protocols*' legitimacy. But eventually even he determined it was spurious and ordered it suppressed. It returned with a vengeance after the revolution. Indeed, White Russian factions battling the Bolsheviks in 1917 cited the *Protocols* as proof that the Jews were to blame for Russia's troubles, sparking pogroms that killed as many as 100,000 Jews.

At a 1934 trial in Russia, historian Vladimir Burtsev recalled being told by a number of czarist officials, including Rachkovsky and one of his aides, that the *Protocols* was bogus, and that Nilus had a hand in perpetrating it. Burtsev also pointed out suspicious similarities between the *Protocols* and yet another work—the 1866 novel *Biarritz*, by a German postal official, Hermann Gödsche. At one point Nilus himself had admitted that the *Protocols* was probably a hoax perpetrated by Rachkovsky; after the 1917 revolution, a Russian official visiting the former Paris headquarters of Okhrana was told by one of Rachkovsky's aides that the embittered old police chief had indeed concocted the *Protocols* himself.

Remarkably, even after the *Protocols* was discredited, it continued to grip the imagination of millions. In the United States, Father Charles Coughlin cited it often in his hate-filled weekly publication, *Social Justice*, in the late 1930s. Editions were widely circulated in the Middle East, Africa, and Latin America well into the 1970s, and the work was endorsed by such leaders as Egyptian president Abdel Nasser, Libyan strongman Muammar Gadhafi, King Faisal of Saudi Arabia, and Ugandan dictator Idi Amin. In 1984 Iran's supreme religious leader, the Ayatollah Khomeini, accused British troops of using the *Protocols* as an instruction manual in the commission of atrocities during the Falkland Islands War.

Postscript: In a case tried in Russia in 1993, editor Tancred Golenpolsky of the *Jewish Gazette* sued the radical nationalist group Pamyat for promoting anti-Semitism through its dissemination of the *Protocols*. The court found in favor of the plaintiff, fined the defendant $190, and pronounced the *Protocols* a forgery. Nearly a century after its first appearance, the *Protocols of the Elders of Zion* was again banned by the very nation that had originated it.

—B.F.

THE BOARDING OF HMS *DREADNOUGHT*

HMS *Dreadnought*, flagship of the British navy's Home Fleet, was anchored at Weymouth—an irresistible target for the practical joker and hoaxer Horace de Vere Cole. Cole was a wealthy young dilettante. He wrote poetry, studied art, and pulled pranks at every opportunity.

Prior to the *Dreadnought* affair, the highlight of Cole's career had been puncturing the vanity of a young member of Parliament named Oliver Locker-Lampson, who had boasted that an MP could never be arrested. Of the same social standing as the supercilious lawmaker, Cole arranged for the two of them to take a stroll together through Piccadilly. As they were walking, Cole slipped his gold watch into the young man's pocket and then suggested that they race a short distance. Cole quickly fell behind the sprinting MP and began shouting "Stop, thief!"

Captured by constables, the confused lawmaker was charged with stealing Cole's watch and was hauled off to police headquarters. Although Cole attempted to keep the entire incident out of the newspapers, the full story greeted the public the following morning. A two-hour speech of contrition was all that saved the once-proud politician from a forced resignation.

By comparison, the boarding of the *Dreadnought* was a far more complicated undertaking. For one thing, Cole was to be accompanied by five fellow conspirators, increasing the opportunity for human error—and consequent failure of the hoax—fivefold. For another, the victim would not be some obscure MP but the entire British navy.

In addition to Cole, the conspiratorial band consisted of author-naturalist Anthony Buxton; artist Duncan Grant; Guy Ridley, the son of a prominent judge; and a brother-sister combination, Adrian and Virginia Stephen. (Virginia Stephen would later become famous in another context entirely under her married name—Virginia Woolf.)

Of the six, four—Buxton, Grant, Ridley, and Virginia Stephen—were to don African robes and put on blackface in order to pose as Ethiopian royalty. Anthony Buxton would be the emperor, and the others princes. Virginia

Stephen cut her hair short for the occasion and donned a beard and mustache. Of the remaining two pranksters, Horace Cole assumed the role of Mr. Herbert Cholmondley of the Foreign Office, and Adrian Stephen became a German named Herr Kauffmann. Cholmondley was to be the British government's official escort for the Ethiopians, Kauffmann their interpreter.

Early on a February morning in 1910, the six transformed themselves into their temporary identities; four were in makeup and rented theatrical robes, turbans, and crosses, while Cole wore top hat and tails. When all preparations were completed, the bizarre group set off for Paddington Station, there to catch the train for Weymouth and a fate none of them could guess.

At Paddington Station, Cole informed the stationmaster of the royalty in attendance, and though mystified as to why he had not received prior notice, the stationmaster dutifully arranged for a spur-of-the-moment reception committee to observe the protocol procedures consistent with such an extraordinary situation. The royal party bowed politely, entered the train, and set off to Weymouth.

No sooner did the train pull out of Paddington Station than a seventh conspirator—whose identity was never revealed—fired off a telegram to the admiral of the Home Fleet, informing the officer of the prominent personages heading his way. The telegram concluded, "Kindly make all arrangements to receive them," and was signed with the name of the bona fide permanent head of the British Foreign Office, who would not be informed of the forgery until many days after the fact.

On the train bound for Weymouth, Cholmondley (Cole) and Kauffmann (Adrian Stephen) dined in a style befitting a career diplomat and a translator for royalty. But the emperor and his princes—at Cole's insistence—were forbidden to eat anything for fear of ruining their makeup. As the hunger situation grew desperate, however, Cole relented and allowed his errant Ethiopians to munch on some buns.

When the train at last reached Weymouth and the conspirators descended from their coach, they were amazed to find a red carpet spread across the station floor in their honor and beside the carpet a saluting naval officer in full ceremonial garb. Gawking spectators pressed against a hastily erected barrier as the hoaxers followed their official escort to a special car for the ride to the harbor.

Taken by launch from the harbor to the *Dreadnought*, Cole and his cohorts were received by Home Fleet admiral Sir William May.

The Dreadnought *hoaxers. (Horace Cole is misidentified as "William.")*

After inspecting a marine guard, the party was taken on a tour of the ship, during which Herr Kauffmann explained the various sights to the wide-eyed Ethiopians. Unsure of what sort of dialect to use, Adrian Stephen suddenly began spouting passages of Virgil's *Aeneid*, mispronouncing it sufficiently to make it unrecognizable as Latin. Later, when he could remember no more Virgil, he switched to Homer, mispronouncing the Greek in the same manner he had altered the Latin.

For their parts, the four in blackface could not have responded more enthusiastically to all that they were shown. Although Virginia Stephen—fearful of being discovered a woman—limited her commentary to an occasional "chuck-a-choi, chuck-a-choi," the others let go with loud exclamations of "bunga, bunga" at everything from an electric light bulb to the ship's heaviest armaments.

All was going perfectly until a light rain started to fall. Adrian Stephen was the first to detect the possible disaster that lay in store for all of them when he noticed Duncan Grant's false mustache beginning to lose its grip. Realizing that the precipitation would soon start everyone's makeup running, he hurriedly suggested to the captain that the Ethiopians would be more comfortable below the deck. Fortunately, Stephen's suggestion was acted on quickly, and Grant was able to repair his mustache surreptitiously as they proceeded inside. When the hoaxers left the ship, a band broke into the national anthem of Zanzibar, since they couldn't find the music for the national anthem of Ethiopia.

Forty minutes after boarding the *Dreadnought*, the conspirators were back ashore, and soon after reaching land, they were on a train back to London. But Horace Cole was still not satisfied. Maintaining his identity as Herbert Cholmondley of the Foreign Office, he politely but firmly informed the railroad personnel that the royal travelers could be served food only by individuals wearing white kid gloves. As a consequence, when the train stopped at Reading, one of the staff raced to a store in pursuit of the required gloves. Soon he returned triumphant, and only then did the ersatz Ethiopians eat.

Cole and his friends finally called a halt to the hoax when they arrived safely back in London. After posing for a group photograph, they cleaned off the blackface and returned the rented costumes. Then all but Horace Cole settled back to enjoy in private the delicious memories of how they had pulled the leg of the British navy.

Unable to keep the story of the successful prank a secret, Cole went to the newspapers. Within a week the group photograph and a complete account of the hoax were on the front pages of several London dailies. Although none of the conspirators' names appeared in the articles, some of the stuffier members of Parliament, investigators at Scotland Yard, officers of the Admiralty, and editors of the newspapers demanded that the rogues be captured and brought to justice. But the most serious criminal act committed, as even these humorless types were forced to admit, was the sending of a telegram under a false name.

For the most part, however, Britons recognized the comic dimension of the prank, and they quickly adopted the phrase "bunga, bunga" as a favorite exclamation to express delight or surprise. Naturally, the names of the participants finally leaked out, and after the public learned of Horace Cole's role in the *Dreadnought* hoax, he was granted the unofficial title of "prince of the practical jokers."

Two of the hoaxers apologized to the navy officials, but that was not enough to mollify them. Two naval officers went to Cole's house armed with canes. A very bizarre agreement was reached. Cole agreed to be caned if he could cane them too. A gentle mutual flogging was exchanged, and navy honor was almost restored.

A few days later another group of officers arrived at Duncan Grant's house and kidnapped him by taxi, with intent to cane. When Grant, in his bedroom slippers, refused to fight, the officers were distressed. Said one, "You can't cane a chap like that." After two token taps, the matter was ended.

Never again did Cole attempt so daring an escapade. In fact, his last years were a definite anticlimax to his stunt-filled youth. As the depression of the 1930s depleted his once substantial fortune, he drifted off into comparative obscurity, eventually moving to France, where he died of a heart attack in 1936 at the age of fifty-three.

—J.L.K. and A.W.

PILTDOWN MAN

For more than forty years, the discovery of Piltdown man was widely regarded as a landmark in the study of human evolution and one of the most important scientific breakthroughs of all time.

And it would have been, but for one catch. It was as phony as a three-eyed toad.

In 1908 Charles Dawson was strolling along a country road outside Piltdown Common, in Sussex, England, when some workmen showed him two bone fragments they'd dug up in a nearby gravel pit. Dawson, a country lawyer with a passion for paleontology, conducted his own search of the pit and found a humanoid skull, along with some primitive tools. He returned to the pit repeatedly over the next few years and excavated several more items. In 1912, believing his findings might be significant, he sent them to Arthur Smith Woodward, keeper of paleontology at the British Museum.

Woodward came out to Piltdown, where the two unearthed several more fragments, including a jawbone. It was an extraordinary find: the skull was strikingly human in appearance, but the jaw was that of an ape. Assuming the two pieces had come from the same toolmaking creature, Dawson and Woodward had located nothing less than the common ancestor of apes and humans—the evolutionary "missing link" whose existence had been postulated by Charles Darwin in 1871.

In 1913 Dawson presented his findings in the *Quarterly Journal of the Geological Society of London*. Eminent scientists, hungry for hard proof of Darwin's theory, offered quick and unquestioning acceptance. The respected British scientific journal *Nature* hailed the Dawson-Woodward find as "the most important discovery of its kind hitherto made in England." The name "Piltdown man" became part of the English language and Woodward prevailed on the British Museum to officially label the species *Eoanthropus dawsoni*—Dawson's dawn man—who was estimated to have lived a half-million years ago.

Additional bone fragments and implements were found at the pit over the next few years. Also discovered were the teeth and cranial bone fragments of a second creature—Piltdown II—two miles away. By now a number of prominent world figures had gotten into the act, including Arthur Conan Doyle, who personally offered to chauffeur Dawson around, and Jesuit priest Pierre Teilhard de Chardin, who assisted in the digging. Meanwhile, the minor village of Piltdown became a major tourist destination. Guided tours were offered of the area around the gravel pit, and the local pub changed its name from the Lamb Inn to the Piltdown Man.

As early as 1913, David Waterston, an anatomy instructor at King's College, said that, from where he sat, the "ancient" jawbone of the Piltdown man looked suspiciously like that of a modern-day chimpanzee. A few others raised doubts about Piltdown man's pedigree. But the skeptics had a tough time finding cracks in the Piltdown hypothesis because all the remains were kept under lock and key at the British Museum. Then in 1949 a geologist at the museum, Kenneth Oakley, gained access to a few fragments, with an eye to subjecting them to more rigorous scrutiny than had previously been applied.

It had long been known that buried bones absorb fluorine from groundwater and that by measuring the amount of fluorine they hold, one can estimate their relative age. Using this method, Oakley determined that the Piltdown man's cranial bones couldn't have been more than 50,000 years old.

Piltdown loyalists attacked Oakley and his methods. But others added their voices to his. Among them was Oxford University anthropologist J. S. Weiner, who showed that Piltdown man's teeth seemed to have come from an orangutan, and were mechanically filed and stained.

In 1953 Oakley retested the bones. This time he noticed a strong burning smell when he drilled into the jaw to remove a sample. Only new bone would emit a burning smell; the cranial bone, however, gave off no such odor, indicating that the two could not have come from the same person. There was also evidence that some of the bones had been dyed with potassium dichromate *before* they were taken out of the ground. Piltdown man, said Oakley, had never existed. He was no more than an "elaborate and carefully prepared hoax."

Oakley's revelation caught the scientific establishment with its pants down. Newspaper headlines waggishly proclaimed the century's most celebrated case of "skullduggery," and several members of Parliament angrily called on the British Museum to explain why that revered institution of research and learning had been so easily hornswoggled.

That Piltdown man was a fraud is no longer in question. Modern dating methods determined the jaw and the skull to be about 500 years old. But the identity of its perpetrator remains uncertain. Some point their finger at Dawson, for whom the Piltdown was a ticket into the Royal Society. Moreover, a neighbor of his, Harry Morris, claimed that Dawson often trafficked in bogus artifacts and once fobbed off a phony fossil on him in exchange for one of the most valuable items in Morris's collection. But Dawson was known to be a somewhat stuffy small-town lawyer, not given to practical jokes. Many of those who knew him doubted he could have planned and pulled off such a masterful ruse.

Over the years many others have been implicated and then exonerated. They include Teilhard de Chardin, who often joined Dawson on his bone hunts and would have had ample opportunity to plant the forged fossils, and Grafton Eliot Smith, an Australian anatomist whose theories about evolution would have been advanced by the Piltdown find.

In his 1990 book, *Piltdown: A Scientific Forgery*, anthropologist Frank Spencer suggests it was Dawson after all who planted the bones and artifacts, but that the mastermind of the hoax was Arthur Keith. An ambitious young anatomist in 1912, Keith would have had much to gain from popular acceptance of the Piltdown hoax, since it supported his own suppositions about the role of the brain in human development. In May 1996, British paleontologist Brian Gardiner, writing in *Nature*, put the blame on Martin Hinton, a young student who was angry with Arthur Smith Woodward because of a pay dispute over work Hinton had done for Woodward.

Postscript: In 1993 and 1994, four decades after the Piltdown fakery was exposed, paleontologists came upon the remains of seventeen apelike creatures in the Ethiopian desert. Dubbed *Ardipithecus ramidus*, they are thought to have lived 4.4 million years ago. That would make them the earliest human ancestors ever identified, and the closest thing yet discovered to a true "missing link." Though they had many humanoid characteristics, their jaws resembled those of a modern-day chimpanzee. Piltdown man may have been a scam, but its perpetrators knew their evolution.

—B.F.

ARTHUR MACHEN: THE RELUCTANT HOAXER

The popular theory that God is on the side of the big battalions received a damaging blow during World War I—if the account of the "angels of Mons" has any truth to it.

In late August of 1914, the British Expeditionary Force (BEF) of 70,000 men was under attack at Mons in Belgium, retreating before the advance of more than 160,000 German troops. The British commander, Field Marshal John Prince, had abandoned the other Allied forces in a misguided attempt to save his own troops. The British soldiers fought with courage and valor as they retreated, but it seemed inevitable that either capture or slaughter would be their fate.

Then—according to legend—there came heavenly intervention. Accounts speak of the appearance of Saint Michael and a legion of bowmen in the sky over Mons, terrifying the German troops and allowing the BEF to make its escape without great loss of life. Some soldiers spoke of seeing a figure swathed in white moving over the battlefield, untouched by the bullets; others saw a mounted knight in armor galloping toward the German lines; and still others spoke of a strange cloud in which a luminous cross could be seen.

Whatever happened on August 26, one fact remains: the British did escape from Mons with remarkably little loss of life, considering their dire situation. The nonsupernatural explanation, advanced by many military theorists, is that by this time the German forces were just too tired to pursue the retreating British and simply let them leave.

If the story of the angels of Mons was a hoax, it was a hoax perpetrated by its subjects rather than its author. That author was Arthur Machen (1863–1947), well known in England at the time as a superb writer of supernatural tales and stories; his books include *The Great God Pan, The House of Soul, Strange Roads*, and many others. Machen, upset at the way the war was going, was inspired to write a story of divine intervention at the battle of Mons; it was called *The Bowmen* and first appeared in the *London Evening Standard* on September 29, 1914. (It may well be that the appearance of the story in a newspaper rather than a magazine, so soon after the historical event, may have contributed to what followed.)

Machen was totally unprepared for what happened next: he was contacted by two British journals devoted to the supernatural, spiritual, and occult—*Light* and the *Occult Review*—both inquiring as to the "real story" of what happened at Mons. Machen assured both publications that it was entirely a fiction and had no basis in any real event, other than the retreat from Mons itself.

It might have been thought that Machen's definitive statement would end the matter. This did not happen; in subsequent letters to the magazines and interviews of visitors to their offices, others came forward to "verify" the appearance of the angels. These accounts varied widely: in some cases the leader of the heavenly host was clearly Saint Michael, in others an anonymous angel-soldier; sometimes the spectral host consisted of archers, sometimes knights in armor; and while one tale teller might speak of angel-like figures, another saw only the mysterious cloud; and so on.

What had happened, it seemed, was that Machen had tapped into a deep need in his readers. After the retreat from Mons, British soldiers and civilians alike had a need to know that God was indeed on their side, and they responded to Machen's story with an intensity that astonished him.

So great was this will to believe that it was seriously suggested that Machen had not created the story out of nothing but had been telepathically influenced by soldiers in the field at Mons. Further speculation was caused by a Red Cross nurse, Phyllis Campbell, who claimed that many of her charges had told her of the heavenly intervention. When Machen impatiently asked her to produce any evidence of these reports, or any such persons, Campbell refused.

It is worth noting that no military report of the conflict mentioned any supernatural incident until 1931, long after the story had been transformed into legend and had taken on its own reality. Writer Kevin McClure tracked down many stories and accounts, which he describes in *Visions of Bowmen and Angels*, a pamphlet of some thirty-two pages that is, thus far, the definitive study of the incident. McClure discovered many bizarre stories—including one in which the Germans had projected the images from planes, hoping to demoralize the British, and their scheme had turned against them—but could find little to suggest that anything of a supernatural nature occurred. While he believes that something strange may have happened at Mons, McClure can only conclude that "we all have our own thresholds of belief."

Arthur Machen's tale of the angels of Mons has now passed into real history; as late as the end of 1993, a *Time* magazine feature on angels recounted the story as a possibly true historical incident, and no mention is made of Machen or his fiction.

If, as is probable, the story of the angels of Mons was a hoax, it stands alone in the history of hoaxing as the one in which the readers tried to hoax its creator—instead of the other way around.

—T.A.W.

> Every time a child says "I don't believe in fairies" there is a fairy somewhere that falls down dead.
>   James M. Barrie, *Peter Pan*, 1904

A fairy offering a posy to Elsie Wright.

THE COTTINGLEY FAIRIES

Toward the end of the Great War, a pair of British schoolgirls astounded the world with several photographs they had taken of fairies, gnomes, and pixies at play. The pictures, which were widely circulated on both sides of the Atlantic, made the girls overnight media stars and were received with varying degrees of credulity by professional photographers and journalists.

They were a hoax, of course—although the "girls" didn't admit as much until 1976, when they were considerably advanced in years.

It all began in the quiet Yorkshire village of Cottingley in the summer of 1917, when Elsie Wright, age thirteen, and her ten-year-old cousin, Frances Griffiths, asked to borrow Elsie's father's new Midge camera. While playing in a glen behind the Wrights' house, the girls explained, they had made friends with a group of fairies and wanted to photograph them.

The girls took two photos, which Arthur Wright developed from glass negatives. In one, four fairies were dancing, with Frances looking on in the background, her hand resting on her chin; they were beguiling creatures with gossamer wings and ballerina's legs. The other showed Elsie, seated, with a winged gnome poised to leap into her lap. Charmed by their beauty, Mr. Wright assumed the photos were no more than a clever cut-and-paste job. When he searched the glen and Elsie's bedroom, however, he found no paper scraps or other evidence of trickery. The snapshots were stowed on a shelf and forgotten.

Three years later Edward Gardner, a prominent Theosophist, heard about the photos and got in touch with Frances's parents to ask if his friend Henry Snelling might have a look at them. A professional photographer, Snelling prided himself on his ability to tell authentic photos from fakes. He deemed the fairy snapshots the real thing.

"There is no trace whatever of studio work involving card or paper models, dark backgrounds, painted figures, etc.," he said. "In my opinion, they are both straight untouched pictures."

Around this time, Sir Arthur Conan Doyle was working on an article on fairies for the *Strand* magazine. Doyle's days as a mystery writer were long over; his main interest now—many called it an obsession—was spiritualism. He believed wholeheartedly in the existence of fairies, and when he got wind of the Cottingley photographs, he contacted Gardner. Doyle hoped to publish the photos with his article.

To ascertain their validity, Doyle brought the photos to Kodak. There was no "evidence of superimposition, or other tricks," the company's experts said. But they also insisted that Kodak had the technology and know-how to produce pictures every bit as realistic. Doyle was annoyed by their hedging but vowed to use the photos anyway. He never visited Cottingley or spoke directly with Frances or Elsie.

Meanwhile, Gardner did go to Cottingley and arranged for Frances and Elsie to take more snapshots of their fairy friends. Gardner saw nothing suspicious in the girls' request that he not accompany them on the photo shoot. He accepted their explanation that the sudden appearance of "strangers" might frighten the fairies and prevent them from emerging. Lest skeptics claim that the Wrights were promoting the pictures to score a quick profit, Gardner pointed out that the family had actually refused to accept payment for them, and even insisted that their names be omitted from Doyle's article.

On that 1920 outing, Frances and Elsie made three more photos, for a total of five. Doyle published them in an article entitled "An Epoch-Making Event—Fairies Photographed," in the November 1920 edition of the Strand; the issue sold out in three days. The rest of the pictures appeared in a second article, which came out the following spring, and in a 1922 book The Coming of the Fairies.

Though the writer himself wouldn't swear to the pictures' authenticity, many accepted them at face value, and Doyle found himself ridiculed in the press for his gullibility. The New York Herald Tribune claimed the fairies were actually dolls. The London Star ran an especially derisive article, illustrated by a picture of Doyle with fairies cavorting about his head. And in a letter to the New York World, one cynic wrote, "When Peter Pan called out to the audience in London at a recent performance the question about fairies, Conan Doyle was the first to give an affirmative."

Some skeptics noted that the Cottingley fairies sported modern hairstyles and the latest Paris fashions; others observed an uncanny resemblance between the fairies and figures in a popular ad campaign for candles. Could the Cottingley fairies have been the product of adolescent puckishness, a stack of magazines, and a gluepot? "One must freely admit that the children who could produce such fakes would be very remarkable children," observed a critic in the Spectator. "But then, the world, in point of act, is full not only of very, but of very, very remarkable children."

By today's standards the photos are hardly convincing. The fairies have a flat, pasted-on look. Moreover, Kodak experts have since pointed out that, given the light conditions under which the pictures were taken, the camera lens would have had to have been kept open for at least a full second—much longer than the girls had claimed. And that was too much time to have captured the fairies, with their beating wings, in such sharp detail.

Nonetheless, the two girls clung to their story well into old age. Finally, on a 1976 TV show called Calendar, Elsie came clean. "As for the photographs," she confessed, "let's say they were figments of our imagination—and leave it at that." In 1981 she and Frances, eighty and seventy-seven respectively, admitted to writer Joe Cooper that they had cut many of the pictures of fairies from a children's book called Princess Mary's Gift Book, and propped them up on leaves and twigs, holding them secure with hatpins (which Doyle mistook in one case for a fairy's navel). Said Elsie, "How on earth anyone could be so gullible as to believe that they were real was always a mystery to me."

—B.F.

THE LOCH NESS MONSTER PHOTO

The long neck, reptilian head, and single hump above the waterline has been the common image of the Loch Ness Monster in the public mind. A single photo of Nessie, taken in 1934 and called the Surgeon's Photograph, has been the "type" picture for all subsequent monster hunts. Dark, grainy, but still eerily distinct, the photo was one of the first and still the most popular photo of the creature ever taken.

And it's a fake.

In 1993 the last surviving hoaxer, ninety-year-old Christian Spurling, confessed the fraud to David Martin and Alastair Boyd—researchers on a Loch Ness biology and geography project—nearly sixty years after the fact and four months before his own death. The most famous image of the Loch Ness Monster was really a toy submarine from Woolworths, fitted with a sea serpent's head made of plastic wood.

The story of the Loch Ness Monster in modern times begins in 1933, when a new highway through Scotland opened the twenty-four-mile-long loch to passing traffic. With the opening of the highway came a sudden flap of sightings of a "queer beastie." The first report came on April 13, 1933, when Mr. and Mrs. John MacKay sighted an "enormous animal rolling and plunging" in the loch. The Inverness Courier carried the story, which quickly spread throughout the local press. By October there had been twenty additional sightings and the news had spread throughout Great Britain. London newspapers sent swarms of correspondents and desperately attempted to scoop each other. Automobiles lined the lochsides for miles. Radio stations interrupted their regular programs for the latest news from Loch Ness. A special passenger train service from Glasgow to Inverness was added to handle the crowds, and steamship tours of the loch became big business. It was 1933 and Britain was in the darkest part of the Great Depression. Media consumers were desperate for any stories that would mitigate the bleak news in the papers. Autumn of 1933 was perhaps simply a media circus waiting to happen, and the sudden appearance of the monster was all that was needed.

To cash in on firsthand knowledge of the monster, London's Daily Mail sent self-styled "big-game hunter" Duke Wetherell to track

The most famous photograph of the Loch Ness Monster, taken in 1934, was revealed as a hoax sixty years after the fact.

down the beast and scoop their rival newspaper, the *Daily Express*. Within forty-eight hours Wetherell had found two fresh footprints of "a very powerful soft-footed animal about twenty feet long." The *Mail* proudly published the first hard evidence of the Loch Ness Monster and sent plaster casts of the footprints to the Museum of Natural History for verification. The *Mail* was less than proud two weeks later when the museum reported that the two footprints were identical and came from a hippo-leg umbrella stand pressed into mud. Wetherell quietly sank out of sight.

Duke Wetherell was never again associated with the monster, and the incredible photo of Nessie a year later—from an unimpeachable source, a top London surgeon—helped the public forget the shabby hoax. Here at last was proof that Nessie did exist. It wasn't until 1993 that Wetherell's stepson explained the connection between the hoaxer and the famous photo.

Wetherell was apparently angry and humiliated by the blow to his reputation. "All right," he vowed to his twenty-one-year-old son, Ian, "we'll give them their monster." Also corralling his stepson Christian Spurling into the plan, Wetherell bought a toy submarine for two shillings and sixpence and gave it to the young

men to turn into a monster. Spurling built a head and neck of plastic wood over the sub's conning tower and sea trials were conducted in a local pond. With camera in hand Wetherell and Ian photographed the "monster" in the shallows of Loch Ness. When they heard a water bailiff approaching, Wetherell stuck out his foot and sank the Loch Ness Monster.

Wetherell showed the photo to his friend Maurice Chambers, who suggested the perfect "front" for the hoax: a London gynecologist he knew, Colonel Robert Wilson. Dr. Wilson was given the photo and a cover story and he sent them to the *Daily Mail*, which instantly trumpeted the news of *real* evidence for the Loch Ness Monster from an unimpeachable London surgeon. History was made, and the astonishing photo went on to launch the careers of a thousand cryptozoologists.

In fact, it was Boyd and Martin who discovered an obscure news story from 1975 in which Ian Wetherell, by now a pub owner, claimed that he and his father had faked a photo of the monster. The article didn't mention which photo, but it did name Maurice Chambers as coconspirator—and Boyd and Martin were already familiar with the name: articles from 1933 listed Maurice Chambers as a passenger in the car with Dr. Wilson when he took the photo. When the researchers tracked down the last surviving member of the hoax team in 1993, Wetherell's ninety-year-old stepson, Christian Spurling, he cheerfully admitted everything. Boyd and Martin looked forward to unveiling the hoax on the sixtieth anniversary of the photo in April 1994, but Spurling died before he could receive the fame—or infamy—he deserved.

The famous photo, the "type" artifact of the entire Loch Ness Monster hunt, was blown out of the water like so much tin and plastic wood. Does this make Nessie a clear fraud, joining the Piltdown man and cold fusion in the pantheon of exploded scientific hoaxes?

Well, not really, considering that the first mention of Nessie is recorded in 565 A.D. when Saint Columba had a run-in with a large water beast in Scotland. And considering that the original sighting by Mr. and Mrs. MacKay—the one that started off the whole furor—took place a year before the hoax photo ever appeared. Since the publication of the fraudulent Surgeon's Photo, literally hundreds of photos and thousands of feet of film and video have been taken of large unidentified and unexplained creatures in Loch Ness. Amid these millions of frames there is not one in which an undeniable, clearly identifiable creature can be seen. Yet the stories, the sightings, and the photos continue.

The Surgeon's Photo may be a hoax, but Nessie is clearly still a mystery.

—T. E.

THE AMITYVILLE HORROR

House hunting in the Long Island community of Amityville, New York, in November 1975, George and Kathy Lutz fell in love with a six-bedroom colonial with its own boathouse and swimming pool. They moved in on December 12.

They moved out on January 13.

In November 1974, a year before the Lutzes had ever heard of Amityville, the house had been the site of one of the area's grisliest crimes in recent memory. High on heroin, twenty-three-year-old Ronald DeFeo, eldest of five children who lived there with their parents, had come home late one night, grabbed a rifle from the gun rack, and moved from bedroom to bedroom, fatally shooting his parents and siblings. DeFeo was convicted of murder and drew six consecutive life terms in prison.

The Lutzes bought the house knowing full well what had taken place there. But what was past was past, they felt, and they were not superstitious people. They saw no rational reason to forego the purchase.

About a year later, New York writer Jay Anson heard from a book editor about the bizarre events that had befallen the Lutzes. He contacted the couple, who offered him exclusive rights to their story in return for an even split on any book royalties that might result. Anson agreed.

Throughout their month-long residency in Amityville, he learned, the Lutzes were traumatized by a terrifying array of supernatural events. It began the day they moved in, when Father Frank Mancuso, a family friend, dropped over to bless their new house. During benediction, a booming male voice ordered the priest, "Get out!"

Then things got really bad.

The Lutzes began hearing eerie "rappings" in the house; their dog became spooked and bolted around the house maniacally. The youngest of their three children, five-year-old Missy, described playful encounters in her room with a pig with glowing red eyes. Repulsive smells materialized from nowhere, green slime leaked from the hallway ceiling, houseflies swarmed around a window in the dead of winter. A heavy door was inexplicably ripped from its hinges; a large statue migrated from room to room. Doors and drawers opened and slammed shut without reason, windows shattered, and the telephone went haywire. Once, George saw Kathy levitating from their bed. She was also fondled by hands she couldn't see and unexplainable sores later broke out on her skin. Another time, George heard band music and left the living room to investigate. He failed to find the source, but when he returned to the living room, the rugs had been rolled up and the furniture had been moved.

"We thought we were going crazy," George later said. Finally, on January 13, in the midst of a torrential rainstorm, they bolted from the house, leaving all their furniture behind and forfeiting $28,000 in equity.

It was a chilling story, to be sure, and Anson made the most of it. His book, The Amityville Horror, was a hardcover best-seller, sold more than 6.5 million copies in paperback, and was made into a movie.

However, Anson never actually interviewed the Lutzes, nor did he ever set foot in the house at 112 Ocean Avenue. His main sources were forty-five hours of previously taped interviews handed to him by the couple, and a few live interviews with others associated with the case.

Did events happen as he described them? It's not likely. Reviewing Anson's book in the Washington Post, Curt Supplee said, "The demonic powers have been conducting themselves a little too carefully by William Friedkin/Universal City rules of diabolical etiquette—coming out at dramatic moments, but retiring modestly when the plot demands a quiet period of exposition, then building to a pleasing crescendo in the final pages. . . . The more deeply one looks, the more like fiction—even fantasy—this 'true story' seems."

What would have motivated the Lutzes to concoct such a tale? Money, certainly. Though the house was reasonably priced at $80,000, George and Kathy had budgeted for only half that amount, and they quickly realized they'd never be able to keep up with the payments. Abandoning it and cutting their losses may well have been a savvier move than it outwardly appeared—especially since the furniture they left behind was cheap and shoddy.

Claiming the place was haunted also turned out to be a financially astute move, given their 50 percent share of Anson's book royalties. Indeed, only two weeks after they vacated the house, they were in discussions with Ronald DeFeo's attorney, William Weber. Having failed to get his client acquitted on grounds of insanity, Weber now intended to build an appeal on the premise that the same demons that tormented the Lutzes had driven DeFeo to murder. The Lutzes, Weber later said, "were interested in developing the demonism aspect of the case." On a 1988 broadcast of the TV show *A Current Affair*, he said, "We took real-life incidents and transposed them. In other words, it was a hoax."

As it turned out, writer Paul Hoffman, not Anson, was the first writer to be hired to tell the Lutzes' story. That project was aborted, and in 1979 the Lutzes took Hoffman to court. Under oath, Lutz admitted that the incident involving the marching band and the displacement of carpeting and furniture had never happened. No door had ever been ripped from its hinges, he told the court, and he may have only dreamed that he saw his wife levitate. No, said Lutz, he never actually saw the pig, red-eyed or otherwise, that his daughter said she saw, and no priest blessed the house on moving day.

Other holes in the Lutz-Anson account were uncovered. In the book, Lutz claimed to have learned from the Amityville Historical Society that his home was built on an old Shinnecock Indian burial site. Nonsense, said society officials—there was never a burial site there, and, anyway, Lutz had never contacted them. Moreover, the "hurricane strength" rainstorm that knocked out electricity on January 13 and finally sent them fleeing seems to have been a total fabrication. Weather reports for that day indicate only traces of precipitation in the entire New York metropolitan region.

A year after the Lutzes moved out, another family—Barbara and James Cromarty and three of their five children—moved in. They never witnessed a single supernatural event. But they were plagued constantly by camera-toting tourists who flocked to the house for a close look. They later sued the Lutzes, Anson, and Prentice-Hall, publishers of *The Amityville Horror*, for $1.1 million. The suit was settled out of court for an undisclosed amount.

"Lutz has to be the greatest liar to come down the pike," James Cromarty told *People* magazine. Added Barbara, "The book is completely untrue. This is a lovely home."

Even Anson, who died in 1980, may have had doubts about the events at 112 Ocean Avenue as the Lutzes described them. "I never commit myself in the book," he said. "I leave it up to the reader to decide. But I believe these people believe that they went through all those things that they saw and heard."

—B.F.

THE TASADAY TRIBE

It was hailed as the greatest anthropological discovery of the twentieth century. A wealthy playboy politician named Manuel Elizalde Jr., the cultural minister for Ferdinand Marcos's Philippine government, convinced the world that a primitive tribe of cave dwellers called the Tasaday were leftovers from the Stone Age—the last human vestige on earth of that era, dating back some 40,000 years.

They were truly a unique anthropological find: a gentle, nonviolent tribe of twenty-six people who lived deep in the heart of the rain forest on the island of Mindanao, the second-largest and southernmost island in the Philippines. They lived on grubs, roots, wild fruit, yams, berries, bananas, and scooped-up crabs, tadpoles, and frogs from nearby streams. They wore loincloths made of orchid leaves, slept in caves, made fire from friction, used primitive tools made of stone and bamboo, and spoke in a primitive language with a limited vocabulary of only 800 words, which didn't include terms for war, weapon, or enemy.

Astonishingly, they remained isolated from nearby neighbors for centuries and undetected and uncontaminated from modern civilization until their discovery in 1971, when a native hunter named Defal penetrated their domain and befriended them. He taught them how to hunt and introduced them to metal knives.

Then word of their existence reached the Philippine government, specifically an agency created for the protection of indigenous minorities, headed by Manuel Elizalde Jr., who, in 1972, formally presented the tribe to journalists, anthropologists, TV news teams, linguists, environmentalists, ethnobotanists, and social scientists around the world.

National Geographic magazine was so convinced of their authenticity that they ran a cover story on the Tasaday. NBC-TV paid Elizalde a reported $50,000 to produce a documentary on their daily living habits. An Associated Press correspondent and nature journalist named

John Nance called them "the most significant anthropological discovery of the century." Even famed aviator Charles Lindbergh, by that time a well-known conservationist, proclaimed their virtues to the world, as did the BBC and other prominent news agencies.

Then, just as quickly as the Tasaday were introduced to the world, they were removed from sight. The Marcos government declared their domain a 46,300-acre preserve and installed an army of soldiers to protect the Tasaday from ruthless exploitation by loggers and mining companies intent on stripping the land of valuable mahogany and mining it for its rich mineral deposits.

Not until 1986, when the Marcos regime was finally toppled, did the world discover that the Tasaday tribe was a gigantic anthropological hoax personally engineered by Elizalde with the blessing of Ferdinand Marcos.

Without authorization, a Swiss journalist named Oswald Iten revisited the caves, only to discover that they were empty and that the small band of Stone Agers had relocated to nearby farming tribes.

He found them living in frame huts, wearing T-shirts and blue jeans, and sleeping on wooden beds, having easily adapted to their so-called new-found lifestyle. When confronted, they readily admitted their true identity. They confessed that they were ordinary peasants recruited by Elizalde, who promised them food, aid, money, and guns if they posed as Stone Age cave dwellers.

Other visiting journalists reported inconsistencies in their story as well. One reporter caught them smuggling cooked rice into the caves and noticed that the men were wearing colored undergarments beneath their loincloths and the women were wearing bras. ABC's *20/20* revealed that several members of the bogus Tasaday tribe laughed when they saw their naked pictures in *National Geographic* and confirmed that it had been one giant put-on fabricated by Elizalde himself, whom they called "Great man, God of the Tasaday."

But by that time Manuel Elizalde had fled to Costa Rica, taking $35 million of his National Minority Protection Bureau money, along with twenty-five tribal maidens. As the Philippines' Central Independent Television agency put it: "It was time to take the money and run."

But Elizalde's time had run out. Charged with racketeering, corruption of minorities, and prostitution, he fled from Costa Rica to the United States but was denied a visa.

Forced to return to the Philippines, he currently awaits trial on innumerable civil and criminal lawsuits while still adamantly maintaining that the Tasaday are the real thing.

Gintui with his two wives and two children, photographed during a preannounced visit in March 1986.

Gintui and family photographed by Oswald Iten a week earlier during an unannounced visit.

But the $64,000 question still persists. Why would one man go to such extremes to dupe the world into believing the Tasaday farce?

While investigators say that Elizalde had political ambitions and believed the national and international media attention focused on the Tasaday tribe and his affiliation with them would make him a household name, there was deeper motivation. In a word, greed.

The Marcos government created the Tasaday to endear themselves to the outside world as environmental protectionists while secretly gaining control over their tribal lands and obtaining the lucrative mining and logging rights exclusively for themselves. During the 1970s and 1980s, while they were in power, they successfully exploited the treasured preserve of untold millions in valuable mahogany and precious metals, including gold, copper, and silver. A French journalist discovered a huge open-pit copper mine built on the rain forest preserve, which he learned was owned by the North Davao Mining Company. The president of that company? Manuel Elizalde Jr.

—R.P.S.

PRACTICAL JOKERS

HUGH TROY (1906–64)

Nothing seemed unusual. In fact, it was a rather common occurrence in New York City. Five men dressed in overalls roped off a section of busy Fifth Avenue in front of the old Rockefeller residence, hung out MEN WORKING signs, and began ripping up the pavement. By the time they stopped for lunch, they had dug quite a hole in the street. This crew was different, however, from all the others that had descended on the streets of the city. It was led by Hugh Troy—the world's greatest practical joker.

For lunch, Troy led his tired and dirty crew into the dining room of a fashionable Fifth Avenue hotel that was nearby. When the head-waiter protested, Troy took him into his confidence. "It's a little gag the manager wants to put over," he told the waiter. The men ate heartily and seemed not to notice that indignant diners were leaving the premises. After lunch Troy and his men returned to their digging, and by late afternoon they had greatly enlarged the hole in the avenue. When quitting time arrived, they dutifully hung out their red lanterns, left the scene, and never returned. City officials discovered the hoax the next day but didn't learn who the pranksters were.

Hugh Troy was born in Ithaca, New York, where his father was a professor at Cornell University. After graduating from Cornell, Troy left for New York City, where he became a successful illustrator of children's books. When World War II broke out, he went into the army and eventually became a captain in the Twenty-first Bomber Command, Twentieth Air Force, under General Curtis LeMay. After the war he made his home for a short while in Garrison, New York, before finally settling in Washington, D.C., where he lived until his death. It was there that Tom Wolfe—then a young *Washington Post* reporter—dubbed Hugh Troy "America's all-time free-style practical joke champion."

As a youngster Troy became a friend of the painter Louis Agassiz Fuertes, who encouraged Troy to become an artist and may have encouraged the boy to become a practical joker as well. While Fuertes and Troy were out driving one day, Fuertes saw a JESUS SAVES sign and swiped it. Many a good laugh was had when several days later people saw the sign firmly planted in front of the Ithaca Savings Bank. The boy put up a few signs of his own. Fascinated by the word pinking, he posted a sign in front of his house: PINKING DONE. No one needed pinking done, but curiosity got the best of some, who stopped to ask what pinking was. "It's a trade secret," Troy quipped. The boy was also a member of a skating club, and when he needed some pocket money, he tacked an old cigar box near the entrance of the clubhouse, along with a PLEASE HELP sign. People naturally began dropping change into the box, change which Troy routinely pocketed.

The fun for Troy really began when he entered Cornell. Some of his celebrated antics involved a phony plane crash, reports on the campus radio station of an enemy invasion, an apparent ceiling collapse, and a cherry tree that one year miraculously bore apples. Troy's most successful stunt at Cornell concerned a rhinoceros. Using a wastebasket made from the foot of a rhinoceros, which he borrowed from his friend Fuertes, Troy made tracks across the campus and onto Cornell's frozen water reservoir, Beebe Lake, stopping at the brink of a large hole in the ice. Nobody knew what to make of the whole thing until campus zoologists confirmed the authenticity of the tracks. Townspeople then began to complain that their tap water tasted of rhinoceros. Not until the truth surfaced did the complaints subside.

Troy's antics did not stop when he graduated from Cornell. Shortly after moving to New York, he purchased a park bench, an exact duplicate of those used by the city. With the help of a friend, he hauled it into Central Park. As soon as Troy and his cohort spied a policeman coming down the path, they picked up the bench and started off with it. In no time the mischievous pair were in the local hoosegow. At that point the clever Troy produced his bill of sale, forcing the embarrassed police to release him and his pal. The two men repeated the caper several times before the entire force finally caught on.

As every New Yorker knows all too well, finding a parking place close to home can be nearly impossible. Not for Hugh Troy. He simply crafted a fake fire hydrant out of balsa wood and left it curbside in front of his residence. The space remained vacant until he parked his car there, after which he simply picked up his handiwork and stowed it in the trunk.

When the Museum of Modern Art sponsored the first American showing of van Gogh's work in 1935, Troy was on the scene again. The exhibit attracted large crowds of people who Troy suspected were more interested in the sensational aspects of the artist's life than in his paintings. To test his theory, Troy fashioned a replica of an ear out of a piece of dried beef and had it neatly mounted in a blue velvet display case. A small card telling the grisly story was attached: "This is the ear which Vincent van Gogh cut off and sent to his mistress, a French prostitute, December 24, 1888." The beef "ear" was then placed on a table in the gallery where van Gogh's paintings were displayed. Troy got immediate results. New York's "art lovers" flocked to the ear, which, as Troy suspected, was what they really wanted to see after all.

Hugh Troy's pranks were never vindictive, but once, when irked by the operator of a Greenwich Village movie theater, he got the last laugh. One evening he took a box full of moths into the theater and released them during the show. The moths flew directly for the light from the projector and made it impossible for anyone to see the picture. The manager was forced to call off the show and give the angry moviegoers passes for a future performance.

To protest the tremendous amount of paperwork in the army during World War II, Troy invented the special "flypaper report." Each day he sent this report to Washington to account for the number of flies trapped on the variously coded flypaper ribbons hanging in the company's mess hall. Soon the Pentagon, as might be expected, was asking other units for their flypaper reports.

Troy was also responsible for "Operation Folklore." While stationed on Saipan in the South Pacific, he and two other intelligence officers coached an island youngster in fantastic Troy-devised folktales, which the child then told to a gullible visiting anthropologist.

While some of his practical jokes were pure fun, many were designed to expose the smugness and gullibility of the American public. Annoyed by a recently announced course in ghostwriting at American University, Troy placed the following ad in the *Washington Post*: "Too Busy to Paint? Call on The Ghost Artists. We Paint It—You Sign It!! Why Not Give an Exhibition?" The response was more than he had bargained for. The hundreds of letters and phone calls only highlighted the fact that Americans' pretentiousness about art and their attempts to buy their way into "arty circles" had not waned since the van Gogh escapade.

Whether questioning the values of American society or simply relieving the monotony of daily life, Hugh Troy always managed to put a little bit of himself into each of his stunts. One day he stuffed a papier-mâché hand up his coat sleeve and took a trip through the Holland Tunnel. He had become annoyed with a toll collector who always grasped Troy's fingers when taking the toll ticket. As Troy reached the tollbooth, with his toll ticket taped between the fingers of the artificial hand, the toll taker seized both ticket and hand. Troy then sped away, leaving both ticket and hand in the grasp of the stunned tollbooth attendant.

—A.R. and P.E.

DICK TUCK (b. 1923)

As H. R. (Bob) Haldeman, President Richard Nixon's chief of staff, walked the corridor near the offices of the U.S. Senate Select Committee on Presidential Campaign Activities (Watergate Committee) several weeks before unwillingly giving testimony, he encountered a plump, jovial man. Haldeman's reaction was hostile. "You started all this, Tuck," he grumbled.

Not only Haldeman but other key Watergate witnesses told the Senate panel that planners of the 1972 Nixon campaign only sought to emulate the successes of Democratic political prankster Dick Tuck. And basically, the Watergate scandals did involve traditional political trickery gone berserk. Early on, the Nixon campaign hired Donald H. Segretti (later jailed for his activities) to be Tuck's GOP counterpart.

Unlike Segretti and his companions, however, Tuck has been rated by political commentators as a genius who elevated campaign trickery to "a minor black art." Here is a summary of Tuck's major pranks. Almost all involve Nixon.

Tuck first met Nixon in 1950 when the young congressman was seeking a U.S. Senate seat. Tuck, a GI Bill student, managed to get a job as advance man for a Nixon speech at the University of California in Santa Barbara even though he supported Nixon's opponent. Tuck scheduled the speech for the largest auditorium on campus in the late afternoon on a day when the campus was almost vacant. Tuck proceeded to send fleeing many of the diehards sitting in the cavernous hall with a marathon introduction that concluded, "Here is Mr. Nixon, who will speak to us about a subject of importance to all Californians—International Monetary Fund." After sputtering out some remarks, Nixon beckoned to Tuck and ominously informed him, "Dick Tuck, this is your last advance!"

In 1956 Vice President Nixon was in San Francisco for the Republican National Convention, hoping for renomination as President Dwight Eisenhower's running mate. Nixon's position was precarious. As buses brimming with Republicans rumbled down Bayshore Boulevard toward the Cow Palace, it became evident that Tuck had been busy during cover of darkness along this route, which also led to the city's landfill. Under each highway sign reading "Dump" was a pasteboard campaign sign reading "Nixon."

Tuck worked for John F. Kennedy in the 1960 race. After the first debate with Kennedy, Nixon, nervously awaiting indications of who would be considered the victor, flew from Chicago to Memphis. At the airport, a motherly type—cajoled by Tuck—rushed past television cameras to hug Nixon and cheer him by saying, "Don't worry, son. He beat you last night, but you'll get him next time."

In 1962 Nixon ran for governor of California against the Democratic incumbent, Pat Brown. Nixon was in San Francisco at a luncheon. It was a difficult time for Nixon, since his campaign had been seriously undermined by a report that his brother Donald had accepted a virtually unsecured loan of $205,000—for his Nixonburger business—from Howard Hughes. As Nixon spoke he noticed an inordinate amount of laughter from the press section. With dessert had come fortune cookies, and each contained Tuck's helpful message, "Ask him about the Hughes loan."

In Los Angeles' Chinatown, Nixon was met by a colorful group carrying pretty campaign signs: some in English, some in Chinese. Nixon spotted a particularly attractive Chinese placard and happily posed for photographs—until an elderly Chinese man whispered that the symbols translated to "How about the Hughes loan?" Nixon grabbed the placard and ripped it up.

Nixon lost, and entered temporary retirement. Tuck turned his attention to Barry Goldwater in the 1964 presidential contest. Goldwater decided on an old-fashioned railroad whistlestop tour through West Virginia, Ohio, and Indiana. Tuck had a friend board the train and by darkest night distribute a bogus newsletter—which incidentally bore Tuck's name. Among other things, the newsletter cautioned conservative Republicans against walking off the edge of the Earth and advised that to avoid confusion as the train rumbled through different time zones watches would be kept "on Washington time—George Washington, that is." The confederate—a known friend of Tuck's—was dramatically ordered off the train. "Young lady, you have made your last delivery!" Because CBS newsman Roger Mudd missed the shot, she reboarded and was thrown off again.

In 1968 Nixon was back as a presidential candidate. Tuck worked for Robert F. Kennedy. With Kennedy's assassination on June 5, little humor remained in Tuck that year. However, his mere presence was enough to trigger Republican panic. One day, just prior to a big Nixon rally in New York City, Tuck was standing near boxes of campaign buttons with slogans printed in several different languages. Spotting him, Nixon aide Herb Klein sprinted over to the boxes, peered at them for a minute, then ordered, "Destroy them." Klein sighed, "We just can't take the chance."

At that 1973 encounter with Haldeman outside the Watergate Committee offices when the former aide growled, "You started all this, Tuck," the prankster replied, "Yeah, Bob, but you guys ran it into the ground." Indeed, the transformation of practical jokes into "dirty tricks" put a damper on Tuck's exploits, as did the development of sophisticated "sound bite" campaigning. Tuck continued to be involved in politics, but not as a trickster.

—T.M.

ALAN ABEL (b. 1930)

"Alan Abel, a writer, musician, and film producer who specialized in satire and lampoons, died of a heart attack yesterday at Sundance, a ski resort near Orem, Utah, while investigating a location for a new film," began an obituary in the January 2, 1980, edition of the New York Times. What the paper's obit staff didn't know was that they had become victims of Abel's latest lampoon.

Abel was alive and well.

In tricking the Times into believing he was dead and publishing an admiring obituary, Abel was only demonstrating his impressive gifts for "challenging the obvious and uttering the outrageous," as his unwitting necrologists put it. Indeed, it was hardly the first time he'd pulled a fast one on a gullible public.

Four years out of Ohio State University, Abel perpetrated his first major hoax in 1959 as the mastermind of the Society for Indecency to Naked Animals (SINA). Working behind the scenes, Abel booked an appearance on the Today show for SINA president G. Clifford Prout Jr. In flawless deadpan, Prout inveighed against rampant animal nudity and urged

Americans to join SINA's campaign to provide proper attire for all pets, livestock, zoo animals, strays, and sundry fauna more than four inches tall. "A nude horse is a rude horse," he asserted.

Over the next few years, Prout, do-gooder heir to the Prout family fortune, showed up on several other network talk shows and was the subject of a front-page series in the San Francisco Chronicle. He chided First Lady Jacqueline Kennedy for allowing her horse to canter about in the altogether, advocated public rest rooms for animals, and promoted a line of free clothing patterns, including bikinis and half-slips for cows.

A lot of people took Prout seriously. Local SINA chapters were formed and members took to dressing their pets. One woman offered a $40,000 contribution, which was politely declined.

There was no SINA, of course. Abel had hatched the ruse, he later said, to protest "hypocrisy and extremism." There was no G. Clifford Prout Jr. either. The man who depicted him was actor Buck Henry, who was still sufficiently unknown to get away with the deception.

In 1964 Abel launched the election campaign of independent presidential candidate Yetta Bronstein. A Bronx grandmother with no political experience, Bronstein drew a respectable amount of media attention. If elected, she vowed, she would nail a suggestion box to the White House fence, institute federally subsidized bingo tournaments, and print a postage stamp bearing the nude likeness of Jane Fonda "to give a little pleasure for six cents to those who can't afford Playboy magazine." Her campaign slogan: "Vote for Yetta and watch things get better." Like SINA, Yetta Bronstein did not exist; in radio and TV interviews, she was portrayed by Abel's wife, Jeanne. And while the public got wise to her long before Election Day, she ran again in 1968.

Abel earns his living as a musician, humorist, and film producer. But clearly it is his pranks that get him out of bed in the morning—such as promoting a fictitious Sex Olympics or a scheme for selling advertising space on bald heads. He once lured several wary State Department and FBI officials and more than 150 reporters to a lavish wedding reception for Ugandan strongman Idi Amin at New York's Plaza Hotel. The "groom" was a 260-pound look-alike in a rented military uniform; his "bride" was blond and eighteen. "I thought it would be nice to give him a haven in the United States—make him a citizen by having him marry a WASP," Abel explained.

Following publication of the Bob Woodward and Carl Bernstein Watergate exposé, All the President's Men, Abel arranged a Washington press conference for the man touted as Deep Throat, the authors' confidential source. More than a hundred reporters showed up; so did Scott Meredith and Irving Lazar, two of New York's most high-powered literary agents. Both offered book contracts to "Deep Throat."

Abel also gulled legions of journalists into covering the arrival of the sham Topless String Quartet, whose unusual garb yielded a purer, more "unhampered" sound than that of conventionally attired ensembles; hundreds of fans wrote in for autographs, and Frank Sinatra offered the group a recording contract. Omar's School for Beggars, another Abel brainchild, purported to teach the finer points of panhandling. The very idea of it drew scathing comments from the *Wall Street Journal* and NBC's Tom Snyder, among others. And in 1990 Abel

hired actress Lee Chirillo to pose as Charlene Taylor, a cosmetician and sole winner of the $35 million New York State Lottery.

Ms. Chirillo-Taylor hosted reporters in a posh hotel suite, toasting herself with champagne, sailing dollar bills out the window, and autographing larger bills for the hotel staff. The *New York Post* went for the story in a big way: "$35M AND SHE'S SINGLE," was the front-page headline.

But the competing *Daily News* wasn't fooled for a moment. Its headline screamed, "IT'S A HOAX." How did the *News* know? The reporter it assigned to cover the press party spotted Abel and recognized him from a course of his she'd once taken. The subject: practical joking.

—B.F.

IMPOSTORS

BILLY TIPTON

For more than two decades, Billy Tipton was a popular jazz pianist and saxophonist. He married three times, adopted three sons, and was active in the Boy Scouts.

However, what no one knew—not his fellow musicians, nor his audiences, nor even his family—was that Billy Tipton was a woman. It was only after the musician's death in 1989 that his bizarre secret was revealed.

Little is known of Tipton's early years, other than that he was born in Oklahoma City in 1914 and raised in Kansas City. Eventually he made his way to Spokane, Washington, to pursue a career as a jazz musician. He assumed the sexual masquerade, most likely, because there was no other way of breaking into the predominantly male world of jazz.

"He gave up everything," said his third wife, Kitty Oakes. "There were certain rules and regulations in those days if you were going to be a musician."

Tipton performed in nightclubs from the 1940s until the 1960s, often with the Billy Tipton Trio. Some fans and colleagues claim he occasionally appeared with big band headliners Scott Cameron, Russ Carlyle, and Jack Teagarden. But Norma Teagarden denied that Tipton ever played a single gig with her brother, and drummer John Luppert, a contemporary of Tipton's, said Tipton's fame never extended beyond a small section of the Pacific Northwest.

"They speak of him playing with some of the great bands in the world," he said, "but he was a rather pedestrian piano player."

While Tipton struck some as "effeminate" in appearance, evidently no one ever suspected the deeper truth. In an interview with the *Los Angeles Times* a few weeks after the musician

died, his one-time hairstylist, Gene Chesurin, remembered Tipton as exceptionally image conscious and "fussy" about haircuts. "He was short and he liked to be tall," added Bob Woehrlin, the man who used to repair Tipton's shoes. "I'd build up his heels and that would throw his shoes out of balance."

Never once betraying his secret, Tipton flirted openly with female fans and married three times. His first two marriages were relatively short-lived; his third, to Kitty Oakes, lasted from 1960 until their divorce in 1979. "I never did do too good picking wives," Tipton later

When jazz leader Billy Tipton (center) died in 1989, an autopsy revealed that he was really a woman.

said. Perhaps his inability to keep a wife had something to do with an "injury" he claimed he had sustained that precluded "normal" sexual activity.

In old age Tipton's health declined, but he resolutely avoided doctors—most likely out of fear that his hidden self would be exposed. Living alone in a trailer for the last ten years of his life, he died of a bleeding ulcer in 1989. The paramedics summoned to aid him were the first, other than Oakes, to learn his true identity. Oakes had only found out after she and Tipton divorced.

It was a Spokane funeral director who broke the news to Tipton's adopted sons. They were shocked. "He'll always be dad," said one of them, Jon Clark. "But I think that he should have left something behind for us, something that would have explained the truth." Another adopted son, Scott Miller, said, "Now I know why I couldn't get him to a doctor. He had so much to protect."

—B.F.

FERDINAND DEMARA

Ferdinand Waldo Demara Jr. may or may not have been history's most cunning impostor. But he was certainly the most versatile. During his lifetime he assumed and shed so many convincing personas that it is difficult to say with certainty who—or what—Demara was.

Born in Lawrence, Massachusetts, on December 12, 1921, Demara fled home at sixteen to join a Trappist monastery, where he remained for two years. Tiring of the routine, he quit to join the army. But he quickly decided he had no taste for the enlisted man's life, so he outfitted himself with clipboard and bogus armband and masqueraded successfully as an orderly. It was the first of his many impostures.

Over the next three decades, Demara taught college classes in psychology as Dr. Robert Linton French, fobbed himself off as a zoologist named Cecil Haman, served as dean of the School of Philosophy at Pennsylvania's Gannon College, taught science at a Catholic boys' school, did cancer research in Seattle, worked as a civil engineer in the Yucatan, and directed a student counseling center. Remarkably, he had never finished high school, yet he was always able to learn enough about his profession du jour to perform competently and credibly.

Not that his excesses didn't trip him up on occasion. Once, Demara, posing as "Martin Godgart," was hired to teach Latin, English, and French at a high school on an isolated island off the Maine coast. He did well until his lack of formal credentials surfaced. He was fired and briefly jailed. In another incarnation, Demara served as a deputy sheriff in Washington State.

Looking into his past, authorities discovered he had deserted the navy. He was sentenced to eighteen months in prison—after conducting his own defense, naturally. Later Demara drew on his prison experience to give a believable performance as a law student and as the assistant warden of a Texas prison.

Demara's boldest deception occurred during the Korean War aboard the Canadian destroyer Cayuga. Posing as Dr. Joseph Cyr, a lieutenant-surgeon in the Royal Canadian Navy, he absorbed as much as he could from medical texts and journals, steeled himself with heavy drink, and successfully operated on dozens of wounded South Korean servicemen and civilians. Under less than ideal conditions, Demara removed a bullet lodged less than an inch from the patient's heart—an operation that would have challenged even a trained surgeon.

Hailed as the "miracle doctor," Demara was credited with saving many lives. But his new-won fame proved his undoing. The real Dr. Cyr, whose credentials Demara had stolen, got wind of the fraud and Demara was kicked out of the navy.

In his later years, Demara turned from deception to good works, living under his own name and counseling terminal patients at Good Samaritan Hospital in Anaheim, California. Most likely it wasn't an entirely voluntary career move: a Life magazine story and, later, a movie about him called The Great Imposter (starring Tony Curtis) blew his cover. Stripped of his power to deceive, Demara became "about the most miserably unhappy man I have ever known," according to his physician, Dr. John Zane. Demara died June 7, 1982.

—B.F.

DAVID HAMPTON

Six Degrees of Separation was the title of a 1993 film featuring Will Smith (star of television's Fresh Prince of Bel-Air); it told the story of a young man who made his entrée into New York society by posing as the son of Sidney Poitier. Many filmgoers probably assumed this was a fantasy from the mind of writer John Guare, from whose stage play the film was adapted—but it was based on a true story.

Born in 1964, David Hampton, the handsome son of a Buffalo attorney, seemed destined for trouble; he jumped from school to school as a teenager, finally giving up on formal education and settling for an equivalency diploma. In 1982, while on a visit to California, he was arrested in connection with a car theft, but the case was later dismissed.

The pivotal event in his life occurred in the summer of 1983, when, with a friend, he was turned away from Manhattan's fashionable Studio 54. Hampton decided that the son of a celebrity would get better treatment, and after considering Harry Belafonte (who did have a son named David, possibly known to Studio 54) and Sammy Davis Jr. (too glitzy and gaudy, Hampton thought), he decided to become the son of Sidney Poitier—who had six daughters but no male children.

The ruse worked; with his friend (who had now become Gregory Peck's son), Hampton was swept into the club with all due deference and respect, and he had a fine evening. Had he left it at that, all would have been well—but the imposture had been so successful and so easy that Hampton decided to see how far he could take it.

At first the scams were minor; Hampton would enter a restaurant as David Poitier, claiming he was to meet his famous father. The meal would be eaten, "dad" would never show up, and the restaurant would pick up the bill.

Then Hampton crossed over into new territory; he showed up at Melanie Griffith's apartment, claiming to be a friend of her husband's. Actor-director Gary Sinise, then apartment-sitting for Griffith, let him stay the night and lent him some money. Using the names from an address book he had acquired from a college student (stolen, said the student; given, insists Hampton), he repeated the scam several times, with such people as Jay Iselin (president of New York's Cooper Union), Osborn Elliott (an editor whose résumé included Newsweek magazine), and as many as a dozen others.

Becoming suspicious, several of the victims contacted the New York Police Department's Fraud Squad and shortly thereafter Hampton was arrested. Ordered by a judge to make restitution of the various "loans" and other charges he had accumulated, and to return to school, Hampton went back to Buffalo. He didn't stay long; when, after returning to Manhattan, he had an altercation with a taxi driver and refused to pay—and then forged a document he tried to use in his defense in court—Hampton was sent to Dannemora State Prison for twenty-one months.

Released, he went again to Buffalo, and then wandered for a while—by his own account living in California, Florida, England, and Europe at various times. When Guare's play opened at Lincoln Center in 1990, Hampton returned to New York and tried unsuccessfully to sue Guare, saying, "You don't take someone's life without contacting them," an observation containing a certain amount of irony.

—T.A.W.

PEOPLE WITH STRANGE POWERS

THE RAINMAKER

Nothing much distinguished the thirty-nine-year-old man who stood before the San Diego City Council on December 13, 1915—except his occupation. Although he modestly preferred to call himself a "moisture accelerator," Charles Mallory Hatfield would always be known as "the rainmaker." The Minnesota-born pluviculturist had been "persuading moisture to come down" in thirsty southern California since 1902, when he perfected his technique on his father's ranch near Bonsall. His credentials were impressive. In 1904 he raised the level of the Lake Hemet Land and Water Company's reservoir by twenty-two feet, and he collected $1,000 from the Los Angeles Chamber of Commerce for producing eighteen inches of rain during the first four months of 1905. He traveled to the Klondike the following year to fill the streams around Dawson City so the miners could pan for gold. And the farmers in California's San Joaquin Valley were so impressed with his work that he was invited to return for eight successive years. However, only the urging of the Wide Awake Improvement Club had induced the skeptical San Diego councilmen to request Hatfield's professional services. The city's population had doubled in four years, and an adequate water supply was necessary for continued growth. While the year's total rainfall had been average, it had been too intermittent to replenish the depleted reservoirs. The new 13-billion-gallon Morena Reservoir had never been more than half full, and on December 10 it held a scant 5 billion gallons of water. For $10,000 Hatfield promised he would fill this reservoir to overflowing before the end of 1916, and he agreed that if he failed the city would owe him nothing.

Hatfield immediately set out for the Morena Reservoir, located sixty miles east of San Diego in the lower elevations of the Laguna Mountains, where, with the assistance of his brother Paul, he built a "rain attraction and precipitation plant"—a twenty-four-foot wooden tower topped with a fenced twelve-foot-square platform to hold the vats from which his secret chemicals were dissipated into the atmosphere. Three dry days passed, but then 1.02 inches of rain fell on December 30. Using a formula that was "300 percent . . . stronger than ever before," the Hatfields worked around the clock. There were only a few showers during the next two weeks, but then a six-day storm that began on January 14 delivered 4.23 inches of rain to San Diego. DOWNPOUR LAYS MANTLE OF WEALTH ON

Rainmaker Charles Hatfield in 1929.

SAN DIEGO AND COUNTY RAIN RECORDS SMASHED read the headlines. By the time the rainmaker telephoned city hall on the seventeenth, 12.73 inches of rain had fallen at Morena. With a "loud, clear, and confident" voice, he explained, "Within the next few days I expect to make it rain right. . . . Just hold your horses until I show you a real rain."

The sky cleared on January 20, but another six-day storm rolled in four days later and brought 2.85 inches of rain to add to "Hatfield's Hatful." Since the ground was still saturated from the previous rains, disaster was inevitable. The San Diego River jumped its banks, and several houses floated out into San Diego Bay. Police in rowboats rescued stranded home owners and motorists, and one man, wiping the water from his eyes as he was hauled onboard, suggested, "Let's pay Hatfield $100,000 to stop." Ironically, the rain cut off the city's water supply, forcing people to seek out water holes. A variety of animals, including hundreds of snakes, appeared in the city's streets. The coastal highway to Los Angeles was impassable, boats were swept from their moorings in the bay, telegraph and telephone lines were felled, rail service to the area was discontinued because stretches of track had vanished, and 110 of the county's 112 bridges were washed away. Except for the arrival of an occasional relief steamer loaded with food, the city was completely isolated for a week.

Winds blowing up to sixty-two miles per hour were clocked on the morning of the twenty-sixth, and the north abutment of the Sweetwater Dam collapsed twenty-four hours later. On the evening of the twenty-seventh, the Lower Otay Dam burst "like the crack of doom," releasing 13 billion gallons of water. A fifty-foot wall of water drowned approximately twenty people and scoured the Otay Valley on its seven-mile journey to the San Diego Bay.

At Morena the Hatfields were oblivious to the destruction the rain had wreaked upon the rest of the county. When a band of farmers gathered at the base of their tower and yelled up at them to stop the rain, the brothers thought they were joking and continued their efforts to fill the reservoir. Charles explained, "I had a year to do the job, but I thought I might as well wind it up right away." By the end of January, forty-four inches of rain had fallen at Morena, and the water flowing over the top of the dam was four feet deep. Only when the brothers started into San Diego to claim their fee did they realize the magnitude of the storm damages. Since the road was gone, they had to walk, and they posed as the "Benson boys" to avoid being lynched by angry ranchers.

When Hatfield arrived in the city after four days of hiking, the city council refused to pay him. The rainmaker had been so eager to start to work that he had left San Diego before the contract was signed. When he threatened to sue the city for his fee, the council agreed to pay him only if he would assume responsibility for the $3.5 million in damage suits that had been filed against the city for hiring a rainmaker. (The rains were later judged to be "an act of God, not of Hatfield," and the city settled for five cents on the dollar.) Hatfield was philosophical about the loss and said, "It was worth the publicity, anyhow."

The rainmaker's reputation spread around the world after his feat in San Diego. In 1922 he was called to Naples by the Italian government to end a drought, and his last contract took him in 1930 to Honduras, where he doused a raging forest fire in ten days and produced a total of fifteen inches of rain in two months.

David Hatfield, Paul's son, claimed the brothers' greatest achievement occurred in 1922, on the California desert in unpopulated Sand Canyon, when they decided to "shoot the works." They hauled in barrels of chemicals, set up a tower, and waited two days for the rain. "It rained for about a day, but in one hour the weather bureau recorded 250 inches of rain," David reported. (The current Guinness record is 73.62 inches in twenty-four hours.) The canyon was destroyed, the Southern Pacific tracks were washed out for thirty miles, and a man living twenty miles away was "running for his very life."

Improved irrigation techniques reduced the need for Hatfield's services, and after 503 successful rainmaking attempts, Charles retired from the business and settled in Eagle Rock, a suburb of Los Angeles, where he sold sewing machines. Although rain aggravated his varicose veins in his later years, he was ready to return to San Diego to fill the reservoirs once again. In 1956 the eighty-one-year-old Hatfield attended the Hollywood premiere of *The Rainmaker*, a film that had been inspired by his career.

The Hatfields were offered large sums for their rainmaking process on several occasions. After Sand Canyon, Charles and Paul decided their formula was "too devastating a force to unleash to any one individual, or to a group of bureaucrats who might misuse it," David reported. "They looked around and they saw very few people of integrity, men who stood by their words at all costs, and they said, 'Well, the secret will die with us.' And that's what happened." Modern "weather modification" firms have been known to seed clouds with silver iodide crystals.

—L.S. and J.W.B.

THE ASTROLOGER

On November 2, 1939, Karl Ernst Krafft wired the Nazi State Security Office that between November 7 and 10 Hitler's life would be in danger. "There is a possibility of an attempt at assassination through the use of explosive material," predicted Krafft.

Krafft's telegram was pigeonholed in Berlin. Six days later, however, amid a Brownshirt beer-hall crowd, a bomb exploded. When the smoke cleared, the rostrum from which Hitler had earlier been addressing his cronies was a pile of rubble. Seven people were dead, sixty injured. Had Hitler not unexpectedly departed ahead of schedule, most certainly he too would have been a casualty.

Who was this man who apparently had foreseen the explosion? Small, dark-haired, and with eyes that "burned with an inner fire," Karl Ernst Krafft was a Swiss astrologer of German ancestry. Born May 10, 1900, he was brought up in an "oppressively bourgeois" household in Basel, Switzerland, where his father managed a local brewery. Krafft did well in school and showed a natural flair for mathematics. Over the protests of his parents, who hoped he would enter a practical profession such as banking, he enrolled as a science student at the University of Basel in 1919. That same year his younger sister died, and Krafft received his first exposure to occultism when seances were held in an attempt to contact her spirit. After that his interest in the occult sciences, astrology in particular, grew rapidly. In 1921, while a student at the University of Geneva, he began trying to discover an underlying statistical basis for astrological predictions—a study that was to consume the rest of his life. Considering himself a genius of Isaac Newton's caliber, his obsession with astrology bordered on the psychotic.

In 1938 Krafft laid the groundwork for his reputation when he analyzed the horoscopes of two anonymous individuals for Virgil Tilea, the Romanian minister in London. The first chart, Krafft said, indicated a person with Jewish blood who would probably not live beyond November 1938. The second chart showed a man of great prominence who would fall from his lofty position in September 1940. Krafft's astrological interpretations proved amazingly accurate. The first chart belonged to Corneliu Zelea-Codreanu, the half-Jewish leader of the Romanian Fascists, who was killed on November 30, 1938. The second chart was that of King Carol of Romania, who abdicated on September 6, 1940.

Confident that his own horoscope aligned him with the Nazi rulers, the highly ambitious Krafft was anxious to gain further attention. The day after the bomb exploded, he bypassed the bureaucracy and wired Deputy Führer Rudolf Hess of his successful prediction. Both Hitler and Minister for Propaganda Joseph Goebbels saw the telegram this time, and the following day the Gestapo arrested Krafft. After satisfying his interrogators that he was not involved in the assassination attempt, Krafft was released. Soon after that the Nazis decided that his talents could be put to good use.

Four centuries earlier the famous sixteenth-century seer Nostradamus had predicted that a man named "Hister" (Hitler?) would lead Germany in a great war. Supposedly, Nostradamus had also foreseen a major crisis in both Great Britain and Poland in 1939. Learning that the Swiss was an expert on this early seer, Goebbels enlisted Krafft to deduce from Nostradamus's writings the inevitability of a Nazi victory.

The first of Krafft's full-time studies for the Nazis foretold the imminent invasion of Holland and Belgium by German forces. Reputedly it contained additional astonishing predictions, but the material was so severely censored at the time that little of the original manuscript is extant today. After further study of Nostradamus, Krafft declared that southeast France—the seer's birthplace—would not be affected by hostilities. This prediction was quoted in leaflets that were scattered over France by plane. The result: thousands of French civilians made their way to southeast France, leaving the approaches to Paris and the ports of the English Channel relatively open when the German armies advanced.

Although Krafft was imbued with patriotic zeal for the "unjustly abused and slandered Third Reich," his predictions were not always optimistic. At a private gathering in the spring of 1940, he revealed to Nazi leaders Robert Ley and Hans Frank the results of his latest graph of Germany's future. Krafft warned that Germany would have a major military reversal in the winter of 1942–43. When Ley and Frank responded that the Fatherland would surely be victorious before then, they were badly mistaken. The war dragged on, and in January 1943, the predicted debacle occurred when German forces suffered a crushing defeat at Stalingrad.

As events soon proved, Krafft's fate was inextricably bound up with that of the Third Reich. On May 10, 1941, Rudolf Hess flew to Scotland, hoping to negotiate a peace with Winston Churchill. The Nazis alleged that Hess was acting on the advice of his astrologers. On June 9 the Nazis reacted to Hess's astrologically induced defection by cracking down on all "astrologers, fortune-tellers, and other swindlers" and hauling prominent occultists off to jails and concentration camps. Krafft was among them.

In prison Krafft was forced to misinterpret horoscopes of statesmen and other public figures. For example, he produced a false astrological analysis of President Franklin Roosevelt that was used for propaganda purposes. His observation that British field marshal Montgomery's lucky-in-war Scorpio sign was "certainly stronger" than his rival Rommel's was rudely dismissed. Only interpretations favorable to the Nazi cause were acceptable. Depressed and humiliated by the fact that a man of his reputation should be asked to provide astrological falsehoods for propaganda hacks, Krafft suffered a nervous breakdown. Early in March 1943, he contracted typhus.

On January 8, 1945, the forty-four-year-old astrologer died while being transferred to the infamous Buchenwald concentration camp. Although ill and in mental collapse, Krafft nonetheless had a parting prediction. He prophesied that British bombs would rain down on the German propaganda ministry as a punishment for its despicable conduct.

—P.G. and F.Br.

FAMOUS DISAPPEARANCES

AMBROSE BIERCE

Had Ambrose Bierce known that his death would be as controversial as his life, it no doubt would have afforded him grim amusement. Best known to modern readers for his *Devil's Dictionary* (almost continuously in print since its first publication in 1906)—and for the fictionalized portrayal by Gregory Peck in the 1989 film *Old Gringo*—"Bitter Bierce" had a cynical and sardonic view of the foibles of humanity and might have been amused at the speculation surrounding his disappearance in 1913.

Bierce came by his cynicism in a fashion both honest and horrific; as a boy of nineteen, in 1861, he enlisted in the Union Army and fought in several battles, among them Shiloh and Chickamauga. The latter conflict subsequently served as title and setting for what is still perhaps the most chilling short story ever written about the aftermath of battle.

Wounded three times, Bierce eventually attained the rank of major. Leaving the army, Bierce settled in San Francisco in 1868 and began the writing career that was to make him famous and, some said, furnish some clues as to the cause of his eventual disappearance.

In his newspaper column Bierce attacked fraud, hypocrisy, and venality wherever he found it—and then as now there was much to be found. No one was safe from his acid-dipped pen, from the lowliest of incompetent poets and clergymen to the most powerful of industrial magnates. Among the latter, a favored Bierce target was the railroad robber baron, for whom he coined the word *railrogue*. In a well-reported incident, one such railrogue—trying to avoid repaying the government $75 million—actually attempted to bribe Bierce on the steps of the Capitol. Asked to "Name your price!" Bierce coolly replied that his price was $75 million, made payable to the U.S. Treasury. Not long after, the railroads had to pay.

A man who cannot be bought is always bothersome; one who also has an audience can be dangerous. To many, the surprise was not that Bierce finally disappeared but that it took so long. Bierce's writing career stretched over four decades, much of it with the Hearst *San Francisco Examiner*—but he did not confine himself to newspaper work; he also wrote dozens of short stories. These ranged from the aforementioned *Chickamauga* and the classic *An Occurrence at Owl Creek Bridge* (arguably the most famous of Civil War stories) through many weird and fantastic stories to the grotesqueries of *Oil of Dog*.

If Bierce's professional life was successful, his personal affairs were in chaos. His marriage gave him two sons and a daughter but was unsuccessful, and eventually he separated from his wife; the two sons died young, one from pneumonia, the other a suicide after an unhappy romance. By 1908 Bierce seemed to have lost interest in the world and its foolishness; he broke with the Hearst papers and appeared to live an aimless life, wandering back and forth from San Francisco to the nation's capital several times.

Then—almost as a gift from the kind of vicious God Bierce might believe in—war broke out in Mexico, and the old soldier was inspired to cover, as he said to friends, "one last story." In a way, a war had created Ambrose Bierce; possibly he thought it fitting that it would take another war to destroy him.

Here begin the mysteries.

In a letter to his daughter, Helen, Bierce described his intention of covering the revolution, "to go down and see if these Mexicans can shoot straight!" Many see in this letter a good-bye and an intention of suicide. A good-bye it may well have been; Bierce knew what could happen on a battlefield, and that at seventy-one he was as vulnerable to a bullet as he had been at nineteen. Suicide—unless one considers the going to a war of a man of Bierce's age as suicidal in itself—is less likely. Though Bierce argued that suicide could be an act of bravery, throughout his own life he had bowed to no man and no power; if the Reaper wanted him, it is reasonable to think that Bierce would make it as difficult for that Shade as he had for everyone else.

In any case, in November of 1913 he saddled up and rode out of El Paso, Texas, south across the border. Given press credentials identifying him as an observer with Pancho Villa's Army of the Revolution, he headed to Chihuahua City. In a letter dated the day after Christmas, Bierce said that he was heading toward Ojinaga, where Villa's troops were laying siege to the town. That letter was the last anyone heard of Ambrose Bierce.

Many theories surfaced to account for his disappearance. Of these the most popular was that Bierce had been shot by Villa himself after an argument. Another was that he had "switched sides" and then been shot by Villa's soldiers as a traitor. Among the more fantastical theories was that Bierce had somehow got to England in time to meet with Lord Kitchener, then fighting his own Great War, and had died with Kitchener when his ship sank in 1916.

Some give credence to the first of these theories—that Villa shot Bierce—based on a biography written by a Bierce drinking partner, San Francisco dentist Adolph DeCastro. The dentist spun a tale of going to Mexico some years later, of meeting Villa and winning his confidence by criticizing Bierce. DeCastro said Villa told him that Bierce would not bother him any more: "He has passed." Both Villa and his brother told of Bierce's becoming drunk and insulting, and it is reasonable to assume that they could have lost patience with the "old gringo"—if anything of the sort ever happened. Aside from DeCastro's account, there is no evidence that it did.

None of the above theories, however, have the charm of that advanced by Charles Fort, the chronicler of the unusual and bizarre (see page 764). In his book *Wild Talents*, Fort noted that not long after Bierce's disappearance in Mexico, a man named Ambrose Small van-

ished in Canada and, like Bierce, was never found.

Fort asks us: Was somebody collecting Ambroses?

—T.A.W.

THE NORFOLK REGIMENT

The disappearance of a single person can often be the cause of clamor and speculation; the case of the Norfolk regiment is fascinating in that not one, or ten, or even twenty disappeared—more than 250 men were said to have marched into a mysterious cloud and forever vanished.

This event, which took place during the Gallipoli campaign of World War I, has been explained in various ways, ranging from the mundane (the soldiers were killed in battle and quickly buried by the enemy in mass graves) to the fantastic (an alien spacecraft, hidden within a cloud, took away the regiment for its own purposes). None of the explanations thus far advanced seem to cover all the facts.

The battle, fought between the Turks and the Allied forces, ranged across the Suvla Plain for nearly a year, beginning in January of 1915. It was costly, stupid, and notably pointless even within the greater pointlessness of war. On the evening of August 12, Britain's 163rd Brigade—consisting of regiments of the First-Eighth Hampshires, First-Fifth Suffolks, and First-Fifth Norfolks—was ordered to advance on Turkish positions. Most of the Allied force was pinned down and unable to move forward; the Fifth Norfolks, however, were able to advance into a wooded area. According to Sir Ian Hamilton's later report to Lord Kitchener: "Nothing more was seen or heard of any of them. They charged into the forest and were lost to sight and sound. None of them ever came back."

In the heat of battle, particularly one as bloody as this one, the loss of 267 men might have been thought tragic but not unusual. For them to simply disappear was something else again. Investigations after the war seemed to go nowhere, the Turks denying any knowledge of what had happened to the Norfolks.

The mystery deepened fully fifty years later, when three New Zealand soldiers, survivors of the battle, produced a signed statement of what they and their fellows had seen that afternoon: they described odd, dense clouds, shaped like loaves of bread, that had hovered close to the ground on an otherwise clear day. The Norfolk soldiers had marched directly into one of these clouds, said the witnesses, and as soon as the last had disappeared the cloud rose up and moved away—against the wind.

The statement has been attacked by skeptics on the grounds that (a) there was indeed low-lying mist on the ground that day, but no clouds reported, and (b) in the statement the regiment is misidentified as the First-Fourth rather than the Fifth. It was also averred that, from their position, the New Zealanders could not possibly have seen what they claimed.

There was, however, another report, possibly commissioned in secret by the royal family. Many of the Norfolks were drawn from the estate of King George V at Sandringham, so there was a personal concern. The report was made by Reverend Charles Pierrepoint Edwards, a chaplain to the Allied troops at Gallipoli who received the Military Cross for his bravery in rescuing the wounded. Edwards had for many years enjoyed a close relationship with the royal family.

His report was not published for more than half a century; when it finally came out, it revealed that 180 bodies had been found in a mass grave, and that some of these had been identified as members of the vanished Norfolk regiment.

To many it seems that the Edwards report raises more questions than it answers. If indeed 180 bodies were found, even if all of them belonged to the Norfolk regiment, what happened to the 87 others? Why would they not be found with their comrades? In a suppressed version of the report, Edwards is said to have stated that all the bodies found had died as the result of execution-style shooting in the head; this suggests that a full Norfolk regiment surrendered without a fight to the Turks, who were well known to shoot captured soldiers rather than take them prisoner. Such an event is theoretically possible—but then, so is kidnapping by alien spacecraft.

In his "Notes on the Graves in Gallipoli" at the end of the report, Edwards tells us that (a) the graves had been desecrated and all identifying marks removed; (b) the bodies were only bones, and in many cases badges and crests were absent; and (c) the bodies had been stripped of anything of value, including identification disks. For all that, Edwards was convinced he had solved the mystery.

The Vietnam war showed us that even with the best of military tracking technology and the most sophisticated record-keeping procedures, we could not account for all of those who vanish in battle. Theories—and "solutions"—about the disappearance of the Norfolk regiment will no doubt continue to be propounded. It is, however, unlikely that the mystery of these vanished soldiers will ever be truly solved.

—T.A.W.

JUDGE CRATER

On August 6, 1930, Judge Joseph Crater hailed a cab on West Forty-fifth Street in New York City, waved good-bye to the friends with whom he had dined at Billy Haa's Chophouse, and was not seen or heard from again.

To disappear completely is always difficult, and Crater was a well-known justice of the New York Supreme Court: age forty-one, height six feet, weight 185 pounds, well dressed (his suits were made by New York's most exclusive tailor), a popular clubman, and a respected lawyer, with, gossip related, a taste for showgirls.

He had recently returned from a vacation with his wife in Maine and was due back there on the ninth for her birthday. In New York he had collected a bulky file of legal papers from his office and had cashed two checks totaling $5,100, asking for large bills. These papers were never found. Mrs. Crater was unable to throw any light on her husband's disappearance, but some weeks later she found two envelopes in a desk, one containing $6,900 in cash and the other his life insurance policies for $30,000.

Judge Crater's name remained on the Missing Persons File (No. 1359S) from 1930 to 1979, when it was finally removed. Questioned in August 1974, the chief of the bureau said, "The chances are 100 percent that he will never be found." Twice the police had dug at places indicated by a clairvoyant, but without success.

There are no clues to Crater's fate, only suspicions. He disappeared at the time of the famous Seabury investigations into New York City graft and connections between Tammany Hall and politicians, officials, and judges. Had Crater been corrupted? Early in his career he had wanted only to teach law; later he realized that teaching could not provide the good things of life. "The best way to get ahead is to go into politics," he once said.

To obtain a nomination for a judgeship in New York in those days, a man expected to pay a full year's salary. In April, when Crater was appointed, he had withdrawn $23,000 from his bank. He may also have been mixed up in a shady deal involving a hotel receivership; the hotel was sold to the city for $75,000 and later resold for $2.8 million. Furthermore, he had received a telephone call in Maine that had upset him. He had to get back to New York right away, he had said, to "straighten those fellows out."

Was this a case of thieves falling out? Did associates kill Crater to increase their own shares, or to silence him? According to one theory, he suffered a heart attack, either while discussing a payoff with his partners or after being lured to the flat of a woman who was blackmailing him. Both such parties would have feared a murder charge arising from a death in the course of a felony, and so with the aid of underworld friends would have disposed of the body in classic gangland style—in a barrel filled with concrete and dropped into the river.

Or did Crater intentionally walk into oblivion? Deeply, perhaps dangerously, involved in city politics, did he seek a new life? While on vacation in Quebec in the previous year, he had called unexpectedly at a bank. Had he done that, as he announced, to change currency, or to deposit money for future eventualities?

The search for Crater was delayed until September, by which time the trail was lost. Why had his friends and associates not reported him missing? Perhaps they feared he had gone off on a toot with a showgirl, perhaps the same one he had taken to Atlantic City on August 1, five days before he disappeared.

—R.F.

AMELIA EARHART

Amelia Earhart, or "A.E." to her friends, was at one time or another a premed student, nurse's aide, telephone operator, truck driver, social worker, lecturer, writer, and editor. But her only constant love was aviation. She caught the flying bug while working in a Toronto military hospital during World War I. Wounded pilots talked fondly of their airborne derring-do and the sheer adventure of flying. Earhart was fascinated by their accounts and became hooked for life.

Born in Atchison, Kansas, in 1898, she graduated from high school in Chicago. After her Toronto stint, she moved to Los Angeles, where she learned to fly. In 1922 she bought her first airplane, and three months later she set a women's altitude record of 14,000 feet. But her big break came in 1928. On June 17 a strange trio—an alcoholic pilot, an ex-army mechanic, and Amelia Earhart—took off from Newfoundland in a trimotor Fokker flying boat and landed in Wales about twenty-one hours later.

Earhart, the first woman to cross the Atlantic by air, became an instant international celebrity, even though she was only a passenger. The tall, slender aviatrix with blond, close-cropped hair and an engaging smile captured everyone's heart. "Lady Lindy," they called her, an appellation she actually detested. In May 1932 she duplicated Lindbergh's feat by flying solo across the Atlantic, another first for a woman. Other records quickly followed: women's non-stop cross-country speed record of nineteen hours and five minutes (1932); first person to solo from Hawaii to California (January 1935); first to solo from Los Angeles to Mexico City (April 1935); first to solo from Mexico City to Newark, New Jersey (May 1935).

In 1937 Amelia Earhart was ready to realize her dream—to pilot a flight around the world. She received enthusiastic support from George Palmer Putnam, the wealthy publisher she had married six years earlier. Male pilots who had flown around the world across the northern hemisphere were rarely out of sight of land. Earhart would take the longest and most difficult route. It lay along the equator, a distance of about 27,000 miles, with extensive stretches over open ocean. "I want to do it because I must do it," she said. "Women must try to do things as men have tried. When they fail, their failure must be but a challenge to others."

Earhart's original intention was to fly from east to west. But after an aborted takeoff from Honolulu in March 1937, she reversed the direction. In May she flew from Oakland, California, to Miami, Florida. Then, on June 1, she took off again and headed south. With her was Frederick Noonan, forty-four, an experienced navigator but an alcoholic who had been sacked as a Pan Am pilot. Their plane was a twin-engine Lockheed Electra 10-E. Their route: Puerto Rico, Brazil, Africa, Pakistan, Burma, Singapore, Australia, New Guinea, Howland Island, Hawaii, and back to Oakland.

There were some delays and some malfunctioning of equipment, but Earhart and Noonan arrived safely at Lae, New Guinea, on June 30. The longest and most hazardous leg of their flight lay ahead. Their next stop, Howland Island, was a tiny speck in the Pacific, 2,556 miles to the east. At 10:30 A.M. on July 2, the Electra roared down the Lae runway for its last takeoff.

Amelia Earhart during a stopover in Calcutta shortly before her disappearance.

Waiting for them at Howland Island was the Coast Guard cutter *Itasca*, which was to maintain close radio contact and operate a direction finder set up on the island, where an airstrip had been built especially for Earhart and Noonan. At 2:45 A.M. on July 3, the first message arrived. "Cloudy and overcast," radioed Earhart, but static drowned out the rest. In subsequent messages, in a strained voice, she reported that gas was running low and asked the *Itasca* to take a bearing on her. But Earhart's transmissions were too short for the Coast Guard cutter to get a fix on her position. At 7:58 A.M. she reported, "We are circling but cannot see you." Then at 8:45 A.M., "We are on a line of position 157 dash 337. . . . We are running north and south." That was the last message received by the *Itasca*, which stayed around Howland for another hour, broadcasting continuously and making black smoke that would be visible for miles. The Coast Guard cutter then headed northwest into a severe squall, where the ship's captain believed Earhart's Electra had gone down. A large U.S. naval task force was dispatched to the area, including the aircraft carrier *Lexington*, with its ninety planes, the battleship *Colorado*, and a flotilla of smaller ships. Together they searched by land and by air the ocean and atolls both north and south of Howland. To the west along Earhart's intended line of flight, the British searched their Gilbert Island possessions for the missing aviators. The American government asked the Japanese for permission to search to the north and northwest through the Marshall Islands. However, the Japanese government refused and instead said their navy would scan the area for the lost plane. After covering 250,000 square miles over three weeks, at a cost of $4 million, in what was at the time the most massive sea search in history, the American searchers found no sign of Earhart, Noonan, or their plane. The official U.S. government version to this day is that Earhart and Noonan failed to locate tiny Howland Island in the fog and clouds, ran out of gas, and ditched into the sea, where their Electra went down, drowning them.

The late 1930s were a time when many Americans suspected the Japanese of planning war with the United States. These suspicions helped foster rumors that the Japanese were not telling all they knew about Earhart's disappearance. When war did break out, these suspicions grew. In 1943 RKO pictures distributed *Flight for Freedom*, in which a fictional famous aviatrix sacrifices her life on a spy mission over the Japanese-occupied Marshall Islands.

After American troops assaulted the Japanese stronghold of Saipan in July 1944, soldiers began reporting information relating to Earhart. An army sergeant claimed he saw an Electra in a hangar that carried the registry number NR 16020, the same as Earhart's. Reportedly, U.S. Marines found among the possessions of Japa-

nese POWs a picture album documenting Earhart's aviation career, a suitcase with Western women's clothing, and a locked book that had "10-year Diary of Amelia Earhart" inscribed on its cover. During interrogations, Saipanese natives reported having seen a white man and woman, captives of the Japanese, on the island in 1937. One report alleged that the woman died of disease and that the man was beheaded. Several marines claimed that they exhumed the bodies of two Westerners, possibly Earhart and Noonan, which were secretly carted off by their officers. But the allegations and rumors led to no reopening of the Earhart case.

Then in 1960 the *San Mateo Times* published the story of Josephine Akiyama, a Saipanese then living in California. She claimed that in 1937 she had witnessed the crash landing of an airplane in Saipan's Tanapag Harbor. She saw a white woman and man taken ashore who were arrested and possibly executed. This article caught the interest of Fred Goerner, a radio broadcaster who, with CBS backing, launched an investigation that lasted six years. During four journeys to Saipan, Goerner interviewed dozens of Saipanese who repeatedly told of a white man and woman who had arrived on their island in Japanese custody in 1937. Also, the publicity surrounding the new investigation brought the former U.S. servicemen who had been on Saipan in 1944 into contact with Goerner.

The story that Goerner put together held that Earhart had been on a spy mission for U.S. Naval Intelligence. She was to overfly the Mariana, Marshall, and Caroline Islands to gather information on the Japanese military buildup there. Unfortunately she became lost in a storm and made an emergency landing on a small atoll that she thought was in the British Gilbert Islands but was actually in the Japanese-held Marshall Islands. There she and Noonan set up their radio and powered it using one of the plane's engines. They sent out repeated SOS messages but could not accurately give their position. After the last message that the Coast Guard received on July 3, a Pan Am radio operator on Wake Island, a navy operator in Hawaii, and numerous ham operators reported receiving SOS messages for three more days from the marooned Earhart. At the time, these reports were ignored and not forwarded to the searchers, or possibly the U.S. Navy was aware of them but realized that they came from within Japanese waters. Finally, Earhart and Noonan were rescued—by the Japanese, who arrested them as spies. The Japanese held the two Americans in captivity because Earhart and Noonan had seen that the Japanese had indeed heavily fortified their island possessions. They died in captivity or were executed.

The Roosevelt administration knew of their probable fate but denied any knowledge, just as the Eisenhower administration would decades later when it lost a U-2 pilot over the Soviet Union. After the Saipan invasion, FDR most likely learned from military reports of Earhart's captivity and death but suppressed the information because of the negative impact that his administration's lack of action might have on the 1944 elections.

A member of Goerner's investigative team, Thomas Devine, was the soldier who claimed to have seen Earhart's Electra on Saipan in 1944. In fact, he claimed that he witnessed the burning of the aircraft at the personal orders of the secretary of the navy. In his book *Eyewitness: The Amelia Earhart Incident*, published in 1987, he added new information to the above theory and claimed to have found Earhart and Noonan's grave site.

After extensive investigation among the small islands of the Marshalls and in Tokyo, Vincent Loomis wrote *Amelia Earhart: The Final Story* in 1985. He asserts that Earhart and Noonan flew off course and crashed at Barre Island in Mili Atoll in the Japanese-occupied Marshall Islands. He tracked down a Japanese-born store owner in the Marshall Islands, who claimed he treated Noonan's crash-landing injuries as a medic in 1937. Loomis also states that Earhart and Noonan were transported by seaplane north to the headquarters island of Saipan. The seaplane carrying them landed in the Saipan harbor and this was the "crash" that Josephine Akiyama had witnessed. Loomis postulates that Earhart may have been deported to Tokyo, where she remained for most of the war.

With the Freedom of Information Act, author Randall Brink attacked the Earhart quest yet again in his *Lost Star* published in 1994. Brink's research shows that most likely Earhart was financed by the U.S. government and was flying a spy mission. Her plane was in fact not a civilian Electra 10 but a military version, which could fly faster, at higher altitudes, and for longer periods of time. Most previous studies thus based their theories on false assumptions of when Earhart would have run out of fuel and crashed. She could have flown thousands of miles farther than was previously suspected. Also, her plane was probably armed with secret aerial cameras that were used to photograph Japanese fortifications. In fact, Brink asserts that Earhart may have made a number of flights into Japanese airspace prior to her last takeoff. The Japanese, aware of her presence, had moved their super aircraft carrier *Akagi* into the area to capture her. On her last flight, as she flew through the Marshall Islands, Japanese fighter planes located her and fired on her plane, forcing her to land on a deserted sandbar. Brink shows from Japanese records that they never launched a search of their territories for Earhart, most likely because they knew exactly where to find her. Her last

message recorded by the civilian radio operators was, "He must be at least an admiral." Brink speculates that Earhart was transmitting the message that a Japanese landing party headed by a high-ranking officer was coming to capture her.

According to this theory, Earhart and Noonan were then taken to Saipan. He includes a picture obtained from a Saipanese police officer who worked with the Japanese during the war that shows a sickly and dispirited Earhart. Her wrecked plane was taken to the fortress island of Taroa, which was never taken by U.S. forces during World War II. Brink further reports that Earhart was later taken to Tokyo as a prisoner of war. Later she ended up in a POW camp in Weishien, China. At the end of the war, in 1945, someone sent the following priority telegram through the Canadian embassy to the U.S. War Department addressed to George Palmer Putnam (Earhart's husband), North Hollywood, California: CAMP LIBERATED ALL WELL VOLUMES TO TELL LOVE TO MOTHER

This document was found in a State Department file labeled "Amelia Earhart," with the reference number PW/8–2145. PW was the file designator for prisoners of war. What happened to Earhart from this point, Brink does not say. His final argument is that "a body of circumstantial evidence has been gathered that is both comprehensive and convincing, particularly since there is absolutely no evidence extant to prove that Earhart perished in the Pacific Ocean."

Another recent theory was advanced by a team of researchers called The International Group for Historic Aircraft Recovery (TIGHAR), led by Richard Gillespie. According to this group, Earhart, because of poor preparation and lack of technical knowledge of her radio equipment, and Noonan, because of a severe hangover, fouled up their navigation and got totally lost. They ran out of fuel and crash-landed on the small island of Nikumaroro in the Phoenix Islands. They salvaged their radio and continued to send out messages for three days. However, the island was without water, and after three days in the 120-degree heat, the two flyers died. The research group has supposedly recovered an aluminum fragment and a woman's shoe heel, both of which were tracked back through their manufacturers and proved to have belonged respectively to Earhart's plane and shoe. However, the authenticity of this research has recently been challenged.

Wild theories abound that Amelia Earhart was the infamous Tokyo Rose or that she was used by the Japanese to ensure the safety of their emperor at the end of the war and that she then returned to the United States anonymously and lived in New Jersey until 1970. The researchers who have spent years of their lives tracking down clues still hope to find definitive evidence: the submerged wreckage of her plane on a coral reef, a diary in an obscure file room in Tokyo, a lost file in the U.S. National Archives, or her grave on some Pacific island from which her body could be exhumed and the teeth tested against dental records. However, all of the above theories lack hard evidence. Therefore, the disappearance of Amelia Earhart remains an open case.

—R.J.R. and R.J.F.

D. B. COOPER

It was, truly, a dark and stormy night that Thanksgiving eve—November 24—of 1971. Visibility was zero and the freezing rain came down in sheets as the Boeing 727 bucked winds gusting up to seventy miles per hour, transporting its sole passenger at 10,000 feet. It was the passenger who had demanded that the Northwest Airlines jet fly so low and at just 200 miles per hour, a speed only slightly greater than the minimum needed to keep the plane from stalling and plunging into the densely wooded Cascade Mountains below. As the jet plowed through the storm, this tall dark man of about forty—wearing a business suit and overcoat—made his way to the aft door, opened it, and leaped into the raging tempest.

He was D. B. Cooper. No, make that Dan Cooper. A reporter made the error, but it really didn't make much difference. D. B. or Dan or Cooper—they were all phony. Dan Cooper was the name on his ticket for Northwest flight 305 from Portland, Oregon, to Seattle, Washington. In appearance a middle-aged businessman, he carried a briefcase that he placed on the unoccupied seat beside him. He ordered a drink, then handed the flight attendant a note. When she pocketed the paper, Cooper motioned that he wanted her to read it; in so doing he spilled his drink. She read the note and looked up to see the now open briefcase filled with wires and red cylinders. Flight 305 was being skyjacked.

It had happened before and it would happen again. But this time the motive was different. Whereas previous skyjackers had sought passage to Havana, Cooper demanded $200,000 (in $20 bills) and four parachutes—two backpack style and two chestpack style. He got everything he asked for when flight 305 landed in Seattle. In return, he allowed all thirty-six passengers to deplane. Then he ordered the jet aloft once again, this time headed southwest toward Mexico at the hazardously low speed and altitude. At Cooper's insistence, the aft door was unlocked and the flight crew confined to the forward cabin.

No one knows what became of D. B. Cooper or

D. B. Cooper, the mystery man who parachuted out of a skyjacked plane on November 24, 1971, and was never seen again.

all but about $6,000 of the money he presumably strapped around him before parachuting into the stormy night. None of the flight crew saw him make his now legendary exit from the rear of Flight 305, and none of the 300 army troops and uncounted fortune hunters who scoured the woods of southwestern Washington where he presumably landed ever turned up a parachute, body part, or the bulk of those 10,000 marked twenty-dollar bills that had once belonged to D. B. Cooper.

The only tangible evidence related to Cooper's skyjacking of flight 305 turned up in 1980. Eight-year-old Brian Ingram, picnicking with his family near Vancouver, Washington, came upon a soggy lump in the sand along the Columbia River. The lump turned out to be a packet of 299 twenty-dollar bills, many of which bore readable serial numbers traceable to the money paid to Cooper back in 1971. Ingram's accidental stumbling on the tattered bills was made all the more remarkable by the fact that none of the other cash turned over to Cooper that Thanksgiving eve has ever made it into circulation. Ingram eventually got to keep about half the loot; the FBI retained fourteen of the bills as evidence, and the rest went to reimburse Northwest Airlines' insurance company.

By the time Brian Ingram made his accidental discovery in 1980, D. B. Cooper was already the stuff of which legends are made. Whether he perished or prospered as a result of his daring act of November 24, 1971, made little difference. Whoever it was who skyjacked Flight 305 was quickly immortalized in song ("The Ballad of D. B. Cooper"), books (*Skyjacker's Guide— Or Please Hold This Bomb While I Go to the Bathroom*), T-shirts, bumper stickers, and an annual celebration in Ariel, Washington, near the site where the leaping looter presumably landed. The Saturday after Thanksgiving is D. B. Cooper Day in Ariel. Hundreds of cars from all over the Northwest jam Ariel's sole street, bands play all day and well into the next, beer and chili are consumed in great quantities, and everyone votes in the D. B. Cooper Look-Alike Contest—all in tribute to a man whose real name is still not known but whose daring turned him into a folk hero. "Cooper beat the system," said one celebrant in Ariel. Referring to the deed that D. B. Cooper Day commemorates, he went on: "It was a heroic act that didn't hurt anybody."

Could it be that the man who bought the ticket for flight 305 under the name Dan Cooper lived to enjoy his sizable earnings that night? Portland FBI agent Ralph Himmelsbach, assigned to the case the day it began and who never stopped searching for Cooper until he retired in 1980, was convinced that whoever leaped from that 727 back in 1971, in essence, committed suicide. "It's almost certain that when he hit that air at 200 miles an hour he tumbled ass over teakettle. . . . If he got [the parachute] open at all, I'm sure he was hurting pretty bad when he got down." Even a sprained ankle would have been a death sentence in that rugged terrain, and Himmelsbach surmised that if Cooper didn't die on impact, he never made it out of the wilderness. "Within a few months small animals would have taken care of his flesh and pretty much scattered the bones."

Richard Tosaw, another former FBI agent who spent years searching for the mysterious skyjacker, concurred that Cooper perished on or soon after that Thanksgiving eve. "He's on the bottom of the [Columbia] river near where the money was found between Portland and Vancouver. He's . . . probably tangled up in a sunken log or some other junk," with the missing $194,000 "still tied around his waist in a bag."

No matter how well informed they are, however, theories are only theories, and the fact is that the Cooper case remains the only unsolved airplane hijacking in American history. It is likely to remain so, particularly if the speculations of yet another former FBI agent and a U.S. probation and parole officer are valid. In 1991 Bernie Rhodes and Russell Calame wrote *D. B. Cooper, the Real McCoy*, in which they claim that Cooper was actually a Mormon Sunday school teacher named Richard McCoy. McCoy, who had served as a Green Beret in Vietnam, was convicted of the 1972 skyjacking of United Airlines flight 855 in what appeared to be nearly a carbon copy of Cooper's caper. McCoy extorted $500,000 from United before parachuting out the rear door. Rhodes and Calame helped crack the case and in so doing became convinced that Cooper and McCoy were the same person. In physical appearance, McCoy did look amazingly similar to the artist's sketch of the flight 305 skyjacker. In addition, both skyjackings followed almost identical patterns, varying only in a few refinements that showed that whoever commandeered the United flight had learned a few things from the earlier event. After capturing McCoy, authorities found newspaper articles about Cooper in McCoy's Volkswagen and a file of Cooper clippings at McCoy's house. McCoy, of course, never confessed to being D. B. Cooper, but he never denied it either.

But we'll never know for sure. Sentenced to forty-five years for skyjacking the United plane, Richard McCoy escaped from Pennsylvania's Lewisburg Penitentiary in August 1974. Betrayed by his wife, who wanted the reward money, McCoy was killed three months later in a shootout with pursuing authorities. If he was D. B. Cooper, Richard McCoy went to his grave with the secret. If not, D. B. Cooper may be anywhere—a corpse at the bottom of the Columbia River or, perhaps, very much alive and still in possession of several thousand twenty-dollar bills.

—J.L.K.

LORD LUCAN

Richard John Bingham, the seventh earl of Lucan, was born into a family that traces its wealth and its titles of nobility to the thirteenth century. His great-great-grandfather had been the officer who ordered the infamous charge of the Light Brigade during the Crimean War. Though blue-blood members of the aristocracy, Bingham's parents had socialist leanings and had been active in Labor Party politics. Their son, contrary to his upbringing, was an extreme right-winger.

After graduating from Eton, and following a two-year tour of duty spent as an officer in the army's elite Coldstream Guards regiment, he began his professional labors in the employ of a London bank. Bingham, however, decided to forego this work after six years, and in 1960 he became a professional, high-stakes gambler. Considered to be a dashing and rakish sort, he was, nonetheless, said to consider women to be inferior to men. He was known to spend most of his time in the company of males. What he did best was squander his considerable inherited fortune by gambling it away.

On the evening of Thursday, November 7, 1974, Lord Lucan went to the Clermont Club, a multimillionaire's hangout on Berkeley Square. On arrival he made some commotion with the club's doorman; however, when he left some time later, he did so as unobtrusively as possible. He returned to his apartment, where he changed from formal attire to casual clothes.

The thirty-nine-year-old Lord Lucan carried a U.S. Mail sack with him and a nine-inch length of lead pipe wrapped in adhesive medical tape as he left his place and headed for the elegant, five-story Georgian townhouse at 46 Lower Belgrave Street in which his estranged wife, Veronica, their ten- and four-year-old daughters, their seven-year-old son, and Sandra Rivett, the children's twenty-nine-year-old nanny, all lived.

Lucan knew that ordinarily it was the nanny's night off. On reaching the house, he surreptitiously let himself in with his own key and went into the kitchen. He then removed the light bulb from its socket and waited, in the dark, for his wife to appear. He knew she was upstairs with the kids. Soon, he figured, because the nanny was gone, she'd be coming down to make tea for herself.

It was just past 9:00 P.M. when footsteps could be heard descending the staircase. A female entered the kitchen and Lucan lashed out at the figure with the lead pipe. Blow after blow struck the woman, bloodying the room and causing her death. Lucan was just starting to stuff the body of his victim into the canvas mail sack he had brought along when he heard his wife, Veronica, call out for the nanny from the top of the stairs.

The lack of a response prompted Veronica to come down. Her husband attacked, whacking the lead pipe on her skull. Blood flowed from the wound as Veronica resisted the assault. She somehow managed to still Lucan's rage and convinced him to lead her to a sink and wash her wound. Then she fled the house. A mad run up the street took her into a neighborhood pub, where she was given first aid and a call was placed to the police. When they arrived at the scene, they found the bloodied mail bag holding the body of Sandra Rivett.

Lord Lucan took off right after his wife had fled from him. He drove to an undisclosed location and placed a telephone call to his mother, requesting that she get his children. He said there had been a "terrible accident." It was after midnight when he appeared at the home of close friends in Sussex. He told them that he had been walking in front of the Belgrave Street townhouse and, through a window, saw his wife being attacked by an intruder. He immediately made his way into the house and was sent sprawling by the slippery pools of blood that had gathered on the floor as the attacker escaped. In the darkness, in the turmoil—his wife confused him with the assailant. He felt condemned; no one would believe the truth.

Though he was drinking heavily as he told his story, Lucan managed to stay sober enough to pen letters to his brother-in-law that requested him to care for the children. He also informed his wife's brother that he would "lie doggo for a bit." Once finished with his letters, Lucan asked for and received sleeping pills and then, sometime after one in the morning, drove off into the night. The car he was driving, one borrowed from another friend, was found two days later, close by the terminal from which ferries cross the English Channel to France. The car was filled with bloodstains. Lord Lucan had disappeared. He has never been seen again.

His fate remains contested. Some who knew him well argue that he took his own life, that he realized that it would be impossible for someone as identifiable as he was to find sanctuary. Many believe he did, in fact, become a fugitive. It's surmised that he made his way to Portugal, aided by friends who owned private planes, and from Portugal to the safety of a remote farm in the south of Africa. Book-writing detectives claim he is alive and in hiding.

In the years following the disappearance, Lord Lucan's wife attempted suicide and spent some time in a mental institution to which she was committed. The children were raised by her sister and brother-in-law. Frances, the eldest, is a lawyer who practices in London. Daughter Camilla became a noted scholar in the classics at Oxford University. Their son, George, is a merchant banker. He has refused to assume his father's noble title as long as the mystery surrounding the disappearance remains unsolved.

—R.N.K.

THE *POET*

On October 24, 1980, the U.S. freighter *Poet*, bound for Egypt with a cargo of yellow corn and a crew of thirty-four, suddenly disappeared without even sending a distress signal. It was never found, nor was the crew.

A U.S. House of Representatives committee held hearings in 1981 to investigate the disappearance of the 12,000-ton freighter. It was established that seven and one-half hours after leaving Philadelphia on October 24, the *Poet* sent a message reporting a speed of fifteen knots on a course directly toward Gibraltar, with November 9 as its estimated date of arrival at Port Said. Later that day, Third Mate Robert Gove called his wife by ship-to-shore telephone. He reported no problems on board. That was the last communication from the ill-fated ship.

Two days later, on October 26, the *Poet* should have radioed again, according to routine practice. It did not. Its owner privately attempted to communicate with the freighter but waited until November 3 to alert the Coast Guard, which conducted a fruitless ten-day air search covering 300,000 square miles.

Two possible explanations to come out of the House hearings were that the *Poet* was hijacked in an underworld scheme to trade its cargo for heroin in Iran, or that it was carrying secret explosives to Egypt for the U.S. military. The official story, however, was that the ship was probably lost in a sudden storm at night, before the crew could send a message. But no debris was ever found, and the mystery remains unsolved.

—The Eds.

10 GOOD THINGS THAT HAPPENED ON FRIDAY THE THIRTEENTH

1. Alfred Dreyfus reinstated (July 13, 1906): The French government restored Dreyfus, a Jewish officer, to the army twelve years after he had been wrongly convicted of treason and banished to Devil's Island.

2. ASCAP organized (February 13, 1914): The American Society of Composers, Authors, and Publishers was formed in New York City to collect royalties when copyrighted music is performed in public for profit.

3. First woman flight instructor licensed (October 13, 1939): After completing 200 hours of flight, Evelyn Pinckert Kilgore received the first instructor's license ever issued to an aviatrix. During World War II she trained pilots in Pomona, California.

4. Greek patriots retake Athens (October 13, 1944): On this day the three-and-a-half-year Nazi occupation of Athens ended.

5. Announced return of the *Kitty Hawk* (February 13, 1948): Orville and Wilbur Wright gave their famous flying machine to the Science Museum in London in 1928. Twenty years later the museum sent it to the United States for permanent display at the Smithsonian Institution.

6. President Lyndon Johnson cracks down on sex discrimination (October 13, 1967): President Lyndon Johnson signed an executive order designed to rid the government of sex bias.

7. NASA selects first women astronauts (January 13, 1978): The National Aeronautics and Space Administration chose six women to join the astronaut corps, fifteen years after the first female Soviet cosmonaut orbited the earth forty-eight times.

8. Spycatcher vindicated (March 13, 1987): In a victory for press freedom, an Australian judge ruled that the memoirs of a British spy could be published in Australia. The British government had for months tried to prevent its publication for "security" reasons; they lost further attempts to thwart its release. It soon became a best-seller.

9. Poland privatizes companies (July 13, 1990): Poland's lower house of Parliament passed legislation to privatize 80 percent of the national economy, allowing workers to purchase shares in the companies for which they worked. Poland's senate approved the bill two weeks later.

10. Palestinians take control of security in Jericho (May 13, 1994): Israel handed over security and administrative control of the area of Jericho to Palestinian police and officials, and the first joint Israeli-Palestinian patrols of the main road began.

—The Eds.

FOOTNOTE PERSON

FRANCESCO LENTINI (1889–1966), "The Three-Legged Wonder"

He was billed as "the Three-Legged Wonder" because he had an almost full-size third leg extending from the right side of his body. Lentini toured for many years with both Ringling Brothers and the Barnum and Bailey Circus.

Frank Lentini was born in Rosolini, in the vicinity of Syracuse, Sicily, in 1889, the son of well-to-do parents. In a family of seven sisters and five brothers, he was the only one to have any physical abnormality. The midwife who delivered him was said to have hidden him under the bed and run screaming from the room.

Lentini's third leg was actually part of an undeveloped body, or incomplete twin, which was attached to his body at the base of the spine. The small body had a pelvic bone, a rudimentary set of male organs, and a tiny second foot growing out from the knee of the leg. It is believed that such abnormalities occasionally occur when a mother would have identical twins but, instead of dividing into two parts, the egg only partially divides. If both halves of the partially divided egg develop equally, Siamese twins result. If one of the twins fails to develop completely, a small body or appendage like Lentini's may appear on the fully formed twin.

Until age six, Lentini could reach the floor with his third leg. Then his other legs outpaced the third in growth, so that eventually one was thirty-nine inches, the other thirty-eight inches—but the third leg was only thirty-six inches, and the foot on it was clubbed.

Doctors had early determined that Lentini's extra appendage could not be removed surgically without grave danger of death or paralysis. Doomed to live as a human oddity, young Francesco suffered acutely from embarrassment and sank into a deep depression. Anxious to help their son adjust to his disability, Frank's parents took him to an institution for handicapped children, where he saw blind, crippled, and terribly deformed children who were far worse off than he was. "From that time to this," Lentini said later, recalling that visit, "I've never complained. I think life is beautiful and I enjoy living it."

When he was eight, Lentini's family went to the United States. For years his father held off circus impresarios who wanted to sign the boy for a tour. Instead, the youngster was allowed to complete his education. When he finished school, he could speak four languages. Only then did he begin touring. He traveled nineteen seasons with the Ringling Brothers and the Barnum and Bailey Circuses. He also toured with the Walter L. Main Circus, Buffalo Bill's Wild West Show, and others, as well as with his own carnival sideshow.

Lentini learned to cope well with his extra limb. He could walk, run, jump, ride a bicycle, ride a horse, ice-skate, roller-skate, and drive his own car. Although he had full control over the limb, he didn't walk on it, since it was so much shorter than the other two. But he did learn to kick a ball with it, which was a good stunt for his act. He also liked to use the extra leg as a stool, claiming that he was the only man who carried around his own chair. Lentini even insisted that the third limb was an asset when he swam, for he could use it as a rudder. When someone asked him how he bought three shoes, he replied, "I buy two pairs and give the extra left shoe to a one-legged friend. So, you see, every time I buy a pair of shoes I really do a good deed along with it!"

As an adult, Lentini weighed 175 pounds, and it was estimated that his extra appendage accounted for about twenty-five to thirty pounds. He liked to say that he ate about 15 percent more than the average man in order to feed his extra leg.

Francesco Lentini, the three-legged man, with one of his four children.

Frank Lentini married and with his wife, Helen, and their four children—all healthy and normal—made his home for many years in Wethersfield, Connecticut. In his old age he moved to Florida, but he never stopped touring. He was traveling with the Walter Wanous Side Show when he fell ill and was hospitalized in Jackson, Tennessee. There he died on September 22, 1966, at the age of seventy-seven. Although other people with three or even four legs have been recorded, Lentini is the only one who is known to have lived to such an advanced age.

—K.F.

BAD PREDICTIONS

As the twentieth century draws to a close and the twenty-first century looms larger, all manner of experts will appear in the media telling us what to expect of the new century. Don't believe them. Here's why:

THE SUBMARINE

I must confess that my imagination, in spite even of spurring, refuses to see any sort of submarine doing anything but suffocating its crew and floundering at sea.
H. G. Wells, British novelist, in *Anticipations*, 1901

The development of the submarine proceeded rapidly in the early twentieth century, and by World War I submarines were a major factor in naval warfare. They played an even more important role in World War II. By the 1960s and 1970s submarines were considered among the most important of all strategic weapons.

AIRCRAFT

May not our mechanisms . . . be ultimately forced to admit that aerial flight is one of that great class of problems with which man can never cope, and give up all attempts to grapple with it? . . . The construction of an aerial vehicle which could carry even a single man from place to place at pleasure requires the discovery of some new metal or some new force. Even with such a discovery we could not expect one to do more than carry its owner.
Simon Newcomb, U.S. astronomer, 1903

We hope that Professor [Samuel] Langley will not put his substantial greatness as a scientist in further peril by continuing to waste his time, and the money involved, in further airship experiments. Life is short, and he is capable of services to humanity incomparably greater than can be expected to result from trying to fly. . . . For students and investigators of the Langley type there are more useful employments.
The *New York Times*, December 10, 1903

Exactly one week later, the Wright brothers made the first successful flight at Kitty Hawk, North Carolina.

I confess that in 1901, I said to my brother Orville that man would not fly for fifty years. . . . Ever since, I have distrusted myself and avoided all predictions.
Wilbur Wright, U.S. aviation pioneer, 1908

The popular mind often pictures gigantic flying machines speeding across the Atlantic and carrying innumerable passengers in a way analogous to our modern steamships. . . . It seems safe to say that such ideas must be wholly visionary, and even if a machine could get across with one or two passengers the expense would be prohibitive to any but the capitalist who could own his own yacht.

Another popular fallacy is to expect enormous speed to be obtained. It must be remembered that the resistance of the air increases as the square of the speed and the work as the cube. . . . If with 30 horsepower we can now attain a speed of 40 miles per hour, then in order to reach a speed of 100 miles per hour we must use a motor capable of 470 horse-power. . . . It is clear that with our present devices there is no hope of competing for racing speed with either our locomotives or our automobiles.
William H. Pickering, U.S. astronomer, circa 1910, after the invention of the airplane

The first transatlantic commercial scheduled passenger air service was June 17 to 19, 1939, New York to England. The fare one way was $375, round trip $675—no more than a first-class fare on an ocean liner at the time. On October 14, 1922, at Mount Clemens, Michigan, a plane was flown 216.1 miles per hour.

HIGHWAYS

The actual building of roads devoted to motor cars is not for the near future, in spite of many rumors to that effect.
Harper's Weekly, August 2, 1902

Conceived in 1906, the Bronx River Parkway, New York, when completed in 1925, was the first auto express highway system in the United States.

RADIO

[Lee] De Forest has said in many newspapers and over his signature that it would be possible to transmit the

human voice across the Atlantic before many years. Based on these absurd and deliberately misleading statements, the misguided public ... has been persuaded to purchase stock in his company.

A U.S. district attorney prosecuting inventor Lee De Forest for selling stock fraudulently through the U.S. mails for his Radio Telephone Company, 1913

The first transatlantic broadcast of a human voice occurred on December 31, 1923, from Pittsburgh, Pennsylvania, to Manchester, England.

BOLSHEVISM

What are the Bolsheviki? They are representatives of the most democratic government in Europe.... Let us recognize the truest democracy in Europe, the truest democracy in the world today.
William Randolph Hearst, U.S. newspaper publisher, 1918

ROCKET RESEARCH

That Professor Goddard and his 'chair' in Clark College and the countenancing of the Smithsonian Institution does not know the relation of action to reaction, and of the need to have something better than a vacuum against which to react—to say that would be absurd. Of course he only seems to lack the knowledge ladled out daily in high schools.
The New York Times, January 12, 1920

The New York Times printed a formal retraction of this comment some forty-nine years later, on July 17, 1969, just prior to the Apollo landing on the moon.

No rocket will reach the moon save by a miraculous discovery of an explosive far more energetic than any known. And even if the requisite fuel were produced, it would still have to be shown that the rocket machine would operate at 459 degrees below zero—the temperature of interplanetary space.
Nikola Tesla, U.S. inventor, November 1928

The proposals as outlined in your letter ... have been carefully reviewed.... While the Air Corps is deeply interested in the research work being carried out by your organization ... it does not, at this time, feel justified in obligating further funds for basic jet propulsion research and experimentation.
Brigadier General George H. Brett, U.S. Army Air Corps, in a letter to rocket researcher Robert Goddard, 1941

AIR STRIKES ON NAVAL VESSELS

The day of the battleship has not passed, and it is highly unlikely that an airplane, or fleet of them,

could ever successfully sink a fleet of navy vessels under battle conditions.
Franklin D. Roosevelt, U.S. assistant secretary of the navy, 1922

As far as sinking a ship with a bomb is concerned, you just can't do it.
Rear Admiral Clark Woodward, U.S. Navy, 1939

JAPAN AND THE UNITED STATES

Nobody now fears that a Japanese fleet could deal an unexpected blow on our Pacific possessions.... Radio makes surprise impossible.
Josephus Daniels, former U.S. secretary of the navy, October 16, 1922

A Japanese attack on Pearl Harbor is a strategic impossibility.
George Fielding Eliot, "The Impossible War with Japan," American Mercury, September 1938

See newspaper headlines for December 7, 1941.

COMMERCIAL TELEVISION

While theoretically and technically television may be feasible, commercially and financially I consider it an impossibility, a development of which we need waste little time dreaming.
Lee De Forest, U.S. inventor and "father of the radio," 1926

[Television] won't be able to hold onto any market it captures after the first six months. People will soon get tired of staring at a plywood box every night.
Darryl F. Zanuck

REPEAL OF PROHIBITION

I will never see the day when the Eighteenth Amendment is out of the Constitution of the United States.
William Borah, U.S. senator, 1929

The Eighteenth Amendment was repealed in 1933. Borah was alive to see the day. He did not die until 1940.

HITLER

In this column for years, I have constantly laboured these points: Hitler's horoscope is not a war-horoscope.... If and when war comes, not he but others will strike the first blow.
R. H. Naylor, British astrologer for the London Sunday Express, 1939

THE ATOMIC BOMB

*That is the biggest fool thing we have ever done. . . .
The bomb will never go off, and I speak as an expert in
explosives.*

Admiral William Leahy, U.S. Navy officer speaking to
President Truman, 1945

INTERCONTINENTAL MISSILES

*There has been a great deal said about a 3,000-mile
high-angle rocket. In my opinion such a thing is
impossible for many years. The people who have been
writing these things that annoy me, have been talking
about a 3,000-mile high-angle rocket shot from one
continent to another, carrying an atomic bomb and so
directed as to be a precise weapon which would land
exactly on a certain target, such as a city.*

*I say, technically, I don't think anyone in the world
knows how to do such a thing, and I feel confident that
it will not be done for a very long period of time to
come. . . . I think we can leave that out of our thinking.
I wish the American public would leave that out of
their thinking.*

Dr. Vannevar Bush, U.S. engineer, in a report to a
Senate committee, 1945

LANDING ON THE MOON

*Landing and moving around the moon offers so many
serious problems for human beings that it may take
science another 200 years to lick them.*

Science Digest, August 1948

It took twenty-one years.

ATOMIC FUEL

*It can be taken for granted that before 1980 ships,
aircraft, locomotives, and even automobiles will be
atomically fueled.*

David Sarnoff, U.S. radio executive and former head
of RCA, 1955

THE VIETNAM WAR

The war in Vietnam is going well and will succeed.

Robert McNamara, U.S. secretary of defense,
January 31, 1963

*We are not about to send American boys 9,000 or
10,000 miles away from home to do what Asian boys
ought to be doing for themselves.*

Lyndon B. Johnson, U.S. president, October 21, 1964

*Whatever happens in Vietnam, I can conceive of
nothing except military victory.*

Lyndon B. Johnson, in a speech at West Point, 1967

FASHION IN THE 1970s

*So women will wear pants and men will wear skirts
interchangeably. And since there won't be any squea-
mishness about nudity, see-through clothes will only
be see-through for reasons of comfort. Weather permitting, both sexes will go about bare-chested, though
women will wear simple protective pasties.*

Rudi Gernreich, U.S. fashion designer, 1970
—K.H.J.

PHOTO CREDITS

INDEX

famous last words, 754–757
Fantasound, 416
Fantasticks, 514–515
Farad, Wali, 722
Faraday, David, 135
Farian, Frank, 443–444
Faris, Mohammad Al, 363
Farmer's Almanac, quote from, 8
Farnol, John Jeffery, 505
Farouk, King (Egypt), last words, 755
Faroux, Charles, 321
Farr, Jamie, 457, 458
Farrakhan, Louis, 154, 722
Farrar, Margaret Petherbridge, 624
Farrell, Charles, 433
Farrell, Mike, 457
Farrow, Mia, versus Woody Allen, 444–446
fashion firsts, 630–634
fashion in the 1970s, quote about, 803
fashion show, first, 631
Fantasia, 416
Fastest Forward, 425
Father Divine, 641–643
Fauntleroy, T. S., 330
fax machine, 582–583
fax (term), 384
Fay, Paul "Red," 54
  quoted, 58
FBI, Martin Luther King Jr. and, 157
feature film
  first, 409
  first directed by a woman, 412
feature-length talkie, first, 414
Federal Aid Road Act, 320
Federal Emergency Management
    Agency, quoted, 240
federal funding of roads, first, 320
federal gas tax, first, 321
Federal Reserve System, 37
Federal Trade Commission, 37
Feiffer, Jules, 250, 516
  quoted, 12, 379
Fellini, Federico, 388
Fellowship of Reconciliation, 279
fender skirts, first, 321
Feng Yula, quoted, 13
Fenwick, Millicent, quoted, 649
Feoktistov, Konstantin, 359
Feola, Vincent, 670
Ferber, Edna, 506
Ferlinghetti, Lawrence, 380
Fermi, Enrico, 230, 240, 388, 560
Ferrie, David, 149, 151
Fessenden, Reginald Aubrey, 576–577
Fhimah, Lamen Khalifa, 174
fiberglass-bodied car, first, 322
fiberglass (term), 384
fiber optics, 570–571
Fiddler on the Roof, 515–516
field emission microscope, 567
Field, Sally, 433
Fielding, Lewis, 471
field ion microscope, 567–568
Fields, W. C., 399–400, 405, 512
  quoted, 399–400
Fifth Extermination Campaign, 207
Figes, Eva, quoted, 11
Figone, Richard P., 202, 203
Figueiredo, João Baptista, doublespeak
    award, 394
Figueroa, Chuchito, 745
Fillmore, Millard, 543
film festival, first annual, 416
film score, first, 409
Finch, Peter, 636–637
Finck, Henry T., quoted, 15
Finley, Bernell, 156
Finley, Charlie, 686
Finn, Herb, 453
Finnegans Wake (Joyce), 389
Finney, Albert, 418
fire "demonstration," Gillingham, 101
fires
  Imperial Food Products, 83
  San Francisco, 80–81
  Triangle Shirtwaist factory, 81–83
first animalnaut, 287–288
First Draft of a Report on the EDVAC
    (von Neumann), 586
first surface crossing of the Arctic, 308
Fisch, Isidor, 121, 122
Fischbach, Fred, 434, 435
fish, falling from sky, 351

Fisher, Carl Graham, 320
Fisher, E. G., 585
Fisher, Harry "Bud," 427
Fiske, Billy, 662
Fitzgerald, F. Scott, 624
  quoted, 6, 8, 11, 13, 335, 408
Fitzgerald, John J. "Honey Fitz," 51–52,
    494
Fitzwater, Marlin, doublespeak award,
    396
Five Pillars of Islam, 721–722
"Five-Ton Mary," 294–295
Flaherty, Robert, 383
Flanagan, Hallie, 632
Flanagan, John, 651
flashback, first movie, 410
flashing turn signals, first, 322
Fleigenheimer, Arthur (Dutch Schultz),
    last words, 754–755
Fleischer, Richard, 430
Fleming, Ian, 586
  quoted, 15
Fleming, Sir Alexander, 558–559
Flintstones, 420
Flood, Charles Bracelen, quoted, 102
floods
  molasses, 100–101
  Yellow River, 89–90
floozy (term), 384
Florey, Howard, 559
Flow-matic, 586
Floyd, Charles "Pretty Boy," 189
flu. See influenza
Fluharty, Jean, 747
fluorescent lamp, 579
Flyer, 333
FM (frequency modulation) radio, 564
Foch, Ferdinand, quoted, 211
"Foggy Day, A," 497
Foley, Kevin, 204
Foley, Samuel J., quoted, 752
Folger, Abigail, 122–123
following orders (behavior experiment),
    614–615
Folsey, George, 443
Fonck, René, 334
Fonda, Jane, 433, 507
Fontanne, Lynn, 513
food firsts, 593–597
food product in aerosol can, first, 597
foodstuffs, falling from sky, 350, 351
football, 531–532
  Super Bowl, 689–694
  Super Bowl highlights, 694–699
footnote people
  Charles Atlas, 609–611
  Ota Benga, 310–311
  Alexandra David-Neel, 308–310
  John Howard Griffin, 316–318
  Anna M. Jarvis, 634–636
  James Kilroy, 406–407
  Timothy Leary, 611–612
  Francesco Lentini, 800–801
  "Typhoid Mary" Mallon, 107–108
  Hermann Rorschach, 612–613
footnote performers and artists, 520–528
Ford, Edsel, 326
Ford, Gerald, 72, 124, 150, 474, 538,
    620, 621
Ford, Glenn, 433
Ford, Henry, 325–326, 769
  affinity for soybeans, 326
  quoted, 327
Ford, John, 416, 426–427, 431–432
Ford Model T, 319, 325–326
foreign-owned auto factory, first, 323
Foreman, Percy, 158
Fore River Shipyard, 407
Forestier, G., 608
forgers, 197–199
forgiveness, quote about, 4
Forgy, Howell Maurice, quoted, 220
Forrester, Jay W., 587
Fort, Anna Filing (Mrs. Charles), 764
Fort, Charles, 764–766, 791
Fortas, Abe, 200
Fortean Society, 765–766
Fortean Society Magazine, 765–766
Fortean Times, 766
Fortier, Michael, 176
fortune cookies, 594
Fosbury, Dick, 384, 658
Fosbury flop, 658
Fosbury flop (term), 384

Foster, Fred, quoted, 5
Foster, Jodie, 433
Foster, Michael, 196
1492: Conquest of Paradise, 420
Fourteen Points, 37–38
Fox, William, 413
Fox *Movietone*, 415
Fracastoro, Girolamo, 609
France, Anatole (Jacques Anatole
    Thibault), quoted, 11
France, quote about, 4
Franchet d'Esperey, Louis-Félix-Marie-
    François, 212
Franchetti, Alberto, 493
Francis, Reuben X, 153
Franck, James, 231
Frank, Anne, 224, 748–750
Frank, Edith, 748, 749–750
Frank, Hans, 179–181, 232, 790
  last words, 755
Frank, Lawrence L., 596
Frank, Leo, 183–185
Frank, Margot, 748, 749–750
Frank, Otto, 748, 749–750
Frankenstein, 416
Frankenstein's monster, 421
Frankfurter, Felix, 115
Franklin, Myra, 427
Franklin, Rosalind, 561
Franks, Bobby, 116–117
Franz Ferdinand, Archduke (Austria), as-
    sassination of, 140–142
Franz Joseph, Emperor (Austria), 140
Fraser, Dawn, 657
Fraser, Simon Christopher (Baron
    Lovat), 226–227
Frasier (lion), 288–289
Frawley, William, 451
Fraze, Ermal Clayton, 597
Frazier, Buell, 150
Frazier, Robert A., 151
Frechette, Sylvie, 662
Freddie Bell and the Bellboys, 502
Frederick, Karl, 591
Fredriksson, Gert, 656
Freed, Arthur, 498
Freedman, Al, 441, 442
Freedman, Max, 501–502
freedom, quotes about, 4–5
Freedom of the Seas, The (Kenworthy),
    85
Free Speech League, 78
freeway (term), 384
freeze-frame device, first movie use of,
    413
French, Robert Linton, 786
French kiss, first movie, 418
Fresquez, Richard, 758
Freud, Clement, quoted, 598
Freud, Sigmund, 39, 77
  quoted, 15, 41, 639, 712
Freyer, Margret, 228
Frick, Henry Clay, 77
Frick, Wilhelm, 232
Friday the thirteenth, ten good things
    that happened on, 799–800
Friedman, Milton, quoted, 205
Friedman, Rose, quoted, 205
Friedman, William, 220
"friendly" fire, 244
Friend of the Humble, 528
friendship, quotes about, 5
Frisbee, 628–629
Frisch, Otto, 560
Fritts, Charles, 567
Fritzsche, Hans, 179
Frohman, Charles, last words, 755
Fromm, Erich, 103
  quoted, 106
Fromme, Lynette "Squeaky," 124
Frost, David, quoted, 3, 480
Frost, Robert
  1960 inaugural poem, 55
  quoted, 2
frozen food, 595–596
frozen orange juice concentrate, first,
    597
Frum, John, 727–728
Fry, Arthur, 584
Frykowski, Bartek, 124
Frykowski, Voytek, 122–123, 124
Fuchida, Mitsuo, quoted, 221–222
Fuchs, Klaus, 231, 248–249
Fuertes, Louis Agassiz, 782

PERPETUAL CALENDAR OF THE TWENTIETH CENTURY

Directions for use: Look for the year you want in the index below. The number opposite each year is the number of the calendar to use for that year (for example, the year 1900 is on calendar 2). Calendars for 1995 through 2000 are labeled as such for easy reference.

1 (1995)

JANUARY
```
S  M  T  W  T  F  S
1  2  3  4  5  6  7
8  9 10 11 12 13 14
15 16 17 18 19 20 21
22 23 24 25 26 27 28
29 30 31
```

MAY
```
S  M  T  W  T  F  S
      1  2  3  4  5  6
7  8  9 10 11 12 13
14 15 16 17 18 19 20
21 22 23 24 25 26 27
28 29 30 31
```

SEPTEMBER
```
S  M  T  W  T  F  S
                  1  2
3  4  5  6  7  8  9
10 11 12 13 14 15 16
17 18 19 20 21 22 23
24 25 26 27 28 29 30
```

FEBRUARY
```
S  M  T  W  T  F  S
         1  2  3  4
5  6  7  8  9 10 11
12 13 14 15 16 17 18
19 20 21 22 23 24 25
26 27 28
```

JUNE
```
S  M  T  W  T  F  S
            1  2  3
4  5  6  7  8  9 10
11 12 13 14 15 16 17
18 19 20 21 22 23 24
25 26 27 28 29 30
```

OCTOBER
```
S  M  T  W  T  F  S
1  2  3  4  5  6  7
8  9 10 11 12 13 14
15 16 17 18 19 20 21
22 23 24 25 26 27 28
29 30 31
```

MARCH
```
S  M  T  W  T  F  S
         1  2  3  4
5  6  7  8  9 10 11
12 13 14 15 16 17 18
19 20 21 22 23 24 25
26 27 28 29 30 31
```

JULY
```
S  M  T  W  T  F  S
                  1
2  3  4  5  6  7  8
9 10 11 12 13 14 15
16 17 18 19 20 21 22
23 24 25 26 27 28 29
30 31
```

NOVEMBER
```
S  M  T  W  T  F  S
         1  2  3  4
5  6  7  8  9 10 11
12 13 14 15 16 17 18
19 20 21 22 23 24 25
26 27 28 29 30
```

APRIL
```
S  M  T  W  T  F  S
                  1
2  3  4  5  6  7  8
9 10 11 12 13 14 15
16 17 18 19 20 21 22
23 24 25 26 27 28 29
30
```

AUGUST
```
S  M  T  W  T  F  S
      1  2  3  4  5
6  7  8  9 10 11 12
13 14 15 16 17 18 19
20 21 22 23 24 25 26
27 28 29 30 31
```

DECEMBER
```
S  M  T  W  T  F  S
                  1  2
3  4  5  6  7  8  9
10 11 12 13 14 15 16
17 18 19 20 21 22 23
24 25 26 27 28 29 30
31
```

2 (1900)

JANUARY
```
S  M  T  W  T  F  S
   1  2  3  4  5  6
7  8  9 10 11 12 13
14 15 16 17 18 19 20
21 22 23 24 25 26 27
28 29 30 31
```

MAY
```
S  M  T  W  T  F  S
      1  2  3  4  5
6  7  8  9 10 11 12
13 14 15 16 17 18 19
20 21 22 23 24 25 26
27 28 29 30 31
```

SEPTEMBER
```
S  M  T  W  T  F  S
                  1
2  3  4  5  6  7  8
9 10 11 12 13 14 15
16 17 18 19 20 21 22
23 24 25 26 27 28 29
30
```

FEBRUARY
```
S  M  T  W  T  F  S
            1  2  3
4  5  6  7  8  9 10
11 12 13 14 15 16 17
18 19 20 21 22 23 24
25 26 27 28
```

JUNE
```
S  M  T  W  T  F  S
               1  2
3  4  5  6  7  8  9
10 11 12 13 14 15 16
17 18 19 20 21 22 23
24 25 26 27 28 29 30
```

OCTOBER
```
S  M  T  W  T  F  S
1  2  3  4  5  6
7  8  9 10 11 12 13
14 15 16 17 18 19 20
21 22 23 24 25 26 27
28 29 30 31
```

MARCH
```
S  M  T  W  T  F  S
            1  2  3
4  5  6  7  8  9 10
11 12 13 14 15 16 17
18 19 20 21 22 23 24
25 26 27 28 29 30 31
```

JULY
```
S  M  T  W  T  F  S
1  2  3  4  5  6  7
8  9 10 11 12 13 14
15 16 17 18 19 20 21
22 23 24 25 26 27 28
29 30 31
```

NOVEMBER
```
S  M  T  W  T  F  S
               1  2  3
4  5  6  7  8  9 10
11 12 13 14 15 16 17
18 19 20 21 22 23 24
25 26 27 28 29 30
```

APRIL
```
S  M  T  W  T  F  S
1  2  3  4  5  6  7
8  9 10 11 12 13 14
15 16 17 18 19 20 21
22 23 24 25 26 27 28
29 30
```

AUGUST
```
S  M  T  W  T  F  S
         1  2  3  4
5  6  7  8  9 10 11
12 13 14 15 16 17 18
19 20 21 22 23 24 25
26 27 28 29 30 31
```

DECEMBER
```
S  M  T  W  T  F  S
                  1
2  3  4  5  6  7  8
9 10 11 12 13 14 15
16 17 18 19 20 21 22
23 24 25 26 27 28 29
30 31
```

3

JANUARY

S	M	T	W	T	F	S
		1	2	3	4	5
6	7	8	9	10	11	12
13	14	15	16	17	18	19
20	21	22	23	24	25	26
27	28	29	30	31		

FEBRUARY

S	M	T	W	T	F	S
					1	2
3	4	5	6	7	8	9
10	11	12	13	14	15	16
17	18	19	20	21	22	23
24	25	26	27	28		

MARCH

S	M	T	W	T	F	S
					1	2
3	4	5	6	7	8	9
10	11	12	13	14	15	16
17	18	19	20	21	22	23
24	25	26	27	28	29	30
31						

APRIL

S	M	T	W	T	F	S
	1	2	3	4	5	6
7	8	9	10	11	12	13
14	15	16	17	18	19	20
21	22	23	24	25	26	27
28	29	30				

MAY

S	M	T	W	T	F	S
			1	2	3	4
5	6	7	8	9	10	11
12	13	14	15	16	17	18
19	20	21	22	23	24	25
26	27	28	29	30	31	

JUNE

S	M	T	W	T	F	S
						1
2	3	4	5	6	7	8
9	10	11	12	13	14	15
16	17	18	19	20	21	22
23	24	25	26	27	28	29
30						

JULY

S	M	T	W	T	F	S
	1	2	3	4	5	6
7	8	9	10	11	12	13
14	15	16	17	18	19	20
21	22	23	24	25	26	27
28	29	30	31			

AUGUST

S	M	T	W	T	F	S
				1	2	3
4	5	6	7	8	9	10
11	12	13	14	15	16	17
18	19	20	21	22	23	24
25	26	27	28	29	30	31

SEPTEMBER

S	M	T	W	T	F	S
1	2	3	4	5	6	7
8	9	10	11	12	13	14
15	16	17	18	19	20	21
22	23	24	25	26	27	28
29	30					

OCTOBER

S	M	T	W	T	F	S
		1	2	3	4	5
6	7	8	9	10	11	12
13	14	15	16	17	18	19
20	21	22	23	24	25	26
27	28	29	30	31		

NOVEMBER

S	M	T	W	T	F	S
					1	2
3	4	5	6	7	8	9
10	11	12	13	14	15	16
17	18	19	20	21	22	23
24	25	26	27	28	29	30

DECEMBER

S	M	T	W	T	F	S
1	2	3	4	5	6	7
8	9	10	11	12	13	14
15	16	17	18	19	20	21
22	23	24	25	26	27	28
29	30	31				

4 (1997)

JANUARY

S	M	T	W	T	F	S
			1	2	3	4
5	6	7	8	9	10	11
12	13	14	15	16	17	18
19	20	21	22	23	24	25
26	27	28	29	30	31	

FEBRUARY

S	M	T	W	T	F	S
						1
2	3	4	5	6	7	8
9	10	11	12	13	14	15
16	17	18	19	20	21	22
23	24	25	26	27	28	

MARCH

S	M	T	W	T	F	S
						1
2	3	4	5	6	7	8
9	10	11	12	13	14	15
16	17	18	19	20	21	22
23	24	25	26	27	28	29
30	31					

APRIL

S	M	T	W	T	F	S
		1	2	3	4	5
6	7	8	9	10	11	12
13	14	15	16	17	18	19
20	21	22	23	24	25	26
27	28	29	30			

MAY

S	M	T	W	T	F	S
				1	2	3
4	5	6	7	8	9	10
11	12	13	14	15	16	17
18	19	20	21	22	23	24
25	26	27	28	29	30	31

JUNE

S	M	T	W	T	F	S
1	2	3	4	5	6	7
8	9	10	11	12	13	14
15	16	17	18	19	20	21
22	23	24	25	26	27	28
29	30					

JULY

S	M	T	W	T	F	S
		1	2	3	4	5
6	7	8	9	10	11	12
13	14	15	16	17	18	19
20	21	22	23	24	25	26
27	28	29	30	31		

AUGUST

S	M	T	W	T	F	S
					1	2
3	4	5	6	7	8	9
10	11	12	13	14	15	16
17	18	19	20	21	22	23
24	25	26	27	28	29	30
31						

SEPTEMBER

S	M	T	W	T	F	S
	1	2	3	4	5	6
7	8	9	10	11	12	13
14	15	16	17	18	19	20
21	22	23	24	25	26	27
28	29	30				

OCTOBER

S	M	T	W	T	F	S
			1	2	3	4
5	6	7	8	9	10	11
12	13	14	15	16	17	18
19	20	21	22	23	24	25
26	27	28	29	30	31	

NOVEMBER

S	M	T	W	T	F	S
						1
2	3	4	5	6	7	8
9	10	11	12	13	14	15
16	17	18	19	20	21	22
23	24	25	26	27	28	29
30						

DECEMBER

S	M	T	W	T	F	S
	1	2	3	4	5	6
7	8	9	10	11	12	13
14	15	16	17	18	19	20
21	22	23	24	25	26	27
28	29	30	31			

5 (1998)

JANUARY

S	M	T	W	T	F	S
				1	2	3
4	5	6	7	8	9	10
11	12	13	14	15	16	17
18	19	20	21	22	23	24
25	26	27	28	29	30	31

FEBRUARY

S	M	T	W	T	F	S
1	2	3	4	5	6	7
8	9	10	11	12	13	14
15	16	17	18	19	20	21
22	23	24	25	26	27	28

MARCH

S	M	T	W	T	F	S
1	2	3	4	5	6	7
8	9	10	11	12	13	14
15	16	17	18	19	20	21
22	23	24	25	26	27	28
29	30	31				

APRIL

S	M	T	W	T	F	S
			1	2	3	4
5	6	7	8	9	10	11
12	13	14	15	16	17	18
19	20	21	22	23	24	25
26	27	28	29	30		

MAY

S	M	T	W	T	F	S
					1	2
3	4	5	6	7	8	9
10	11	12	13	14	15	16
17	18	19	20	21	22	23
24	25	26	27	28	29	30
31						

JUNE

S	M	T	W	T	F	S
	1	2	3	4	5	6
7	8	9	10	11	12	13
14	15	16	17	18	19	20
21	22	23	24	25	26	27
28	29	30				

JULY

S	M	T	W	T	F	S
			1	2	3	4
5	6	7	8	9	10	11
12	13	14	15	16	17	18
19	20	21	22	23	24	25
26	27	28	29	30	31	

AUGUST

S	M	T	W	T	F	S
						1
2	3	4	5	6	7	8
9	10	11	12	13	14	15
16	17	18	19	20	21	22
23	24	25	26	27	28	29
30	31					

SEPTEMBER

S	M	T	W	T	F	S
		1	2	3	4	5
6	7	8	9	10	11	12
13	14	15	16	17	18	19
20	21	22	23	24	25	26
27	28	29	30			

OCTOBER

S	M	T	W	T	F	S
				1	2	3
4	5	6	7	8	9	10
11	12	13	14	15	16	17
18	19	20	21	22	23	24
25	26	27	28	29	30	31

NOVEMBER

S	M	T	W	T	F	S
1	2	3	4	5	6	7
8	9	10	11	12	13	14
15	16	17	18	19	20	21
22	23	24	25	26	27	28
29	30					

DECEMBER

S	M	T	W	T	F	S
		1	2	3	4	5
6	7	8	9	10	11	12
13	14	15	16	17	18	19
20	21	22	23	24	25	26
27	28	29	30	31		

6 (1999)

JANUARY

S	M	T	W	T	F	S
					1	2
3	4	5	6	7	8	9
10	11	12	13	14	15	16
17	18	19	20	21	22	23
24	25	26	27	28	29	30
31						

FEBRUARY

S	M	T	W	T	F	S
	1	2	3	4	5	6
7	8	9	10	11	12	13
14	15	16	17	18	19	20
21	22	23	24	25	26	27
28						

MARCH

S	M	T	W	T	F	S
	1	2	3	4	5	6
7	8	9	10	11	12	13
14	15	16	17	18	19	20
21	22	23	24	25	26	27
28	29	30	31			

APRIL

S	M	T	W	T	F	S
				1	2	3
4	5	6	7	8	9	10
11	12	13	14	15	16	17
18	19	20	21	22	23	24
25	26	27	28	29	30	

MAY

S	M	T	W	T	F	S
						1
2	3	4	5	6	7	8
9	10	11	12	13	14	15
16	17	18	19	20	21	22
23	24	25	26	27	28	29
30	31					

JUNE

S	M	T	W	T	F	S
		1	2	3	4	5
6	7	8	9	10	11	12
13	14	15	16	17	18	19
20	21	22	23	24	25	26
27	28	29	30			

JULY

S	M	T	W	T	F	S
				1	2	3
4	5	6	7	8	9	10
11	12	13	14	15	16	17
18	19	20	21	22	23	24
25	26	27	28	29	30	31

AUGUST

S	M	T	W	T	F	S
1	2	3	4	5	6	7
8	9	10	11	12	13	14
15	16	17	18	19	20	21
22	23	24	25	26	27	28
29	30	31				

SEPTEMBER

S	M	T	W	T	F	S
			1	2	3	4
5	6	7	8	9	10	11
12	13	14	15	16	17	18
19	20	21	22	23	24	25
26	27	28	29	30		

OCTOBER

S	M	T	W	T	F	S
					1	2
3	4	5	6	7	8	9
10	11	12	13	14	15	16
17	18	19	20	21	22	23
24	25	26	27	28	29	30
31						

NOVEMBER

S	M	T	W	T	F	S
	1	2	3	4	5	6
7	8	9	10	11	12	13
14	15	16	17	18	19	20
21	22	23	24	25	26	27
28	29	30				

DECEMBER

S	M	T	W	T	F	S
			1	2	3	4
5	6	7	8	9	10	11
12	13	14	15	16	17	18
19	20	21	22	23	24	25
26	27	28	29	30	31	

7

JANUARY
```
S  M  T  W  T  F  S
                  1
 2  3  4  5  6  7  8
 9 10 11 12 13 14 15
16 17 18 19 20 21 22
23 24 25 26 27 28 29
30 31
```

FEBRUARY
```
S  M  T  W  T  F  S
       1  2  3  4  5
 6  7  8  9 10 11 12
13 14 15 16 17 18 19
20 21 22 23 24 25 26
27 28
```

MARCH
```
S  M  T  W  T  F  S
       1  2  3  4  5
 6  7  8  9 10 11 12
13 14 15 16 17 18 19
20 21 22 23 24 25 26
27 28 29 30 31
```

APRIL
```
S  M  T  W  T  F  S
                1  2
 3  4  5  6  7  8  9
10 11 12 13 14 15 16
17 18 19 20 21 22 23
24 25 26 27 28 29 30
```

MAY
```
S  M  T  W  T  F  S
 1  2  3  4  5  6  7
 8  9 10 11 12 13 14
15 16 17 18 19 20 21
22 23 24 25 26 27 28
29 30 31
```

JUNE
```
S  M  T  W  T  F  S
          1  2  3  4
 5  6  7  8  9 10 11
12 13 14 15 16 17 18
19 20 21 22 23 24 25
26 27 28 29 30
```

JULY
```
S  M  T  W  T  F  S
                1  2
 3  4  5  6  7  8  9
10 11 12 13 14 15 16
17 18 19 20 21 22 23
24 25 26 27 28 29 30
31
```

AUGUST
```
S  M  T  W  T  F  S
    1  2  3  4  5  6
 7  8  9 10 11 12 13
14 15 16 17 18 19 20
21 22 23 24 25 26 27
28 29 30 31
```

SEPTEMBER
```
S  M  T  W  T  F  S
             1  2  3
 4  5  6  7  8  9 10
11 12 13 14 15 16 17
18 19 20 21 22 23 24
25 26 27 28 29 30
```

OCTOBER
```
S  M  T  W  T  F  S
                   1
 2  3  4  5  6  7  8
 9 10 11 12 13 14 15
16 17 18 19 20 21 22
23 24 25 26 27 28 29
30 31
```

NOVEMBER
```
S  M  T  W  T  F  S
       1  2  3  4  5
 6  7  8  9 10 11 12
13 14 15 16 17 18 19
20 21 22 23 24 25 26
27 28 29 30
```

DECEMBER
```
S  M  T  W  T  F  S
             1  2  3
 4  5  6  7  8  9 10
11 12 13 14 15 16 17
18 19 20 21 22 23 24
25 26 27 28 29 30 31
```

8

JANUARY
```
S  M  T  W  T  F  S
 1  2  3  4  5  6  7
 8  9 10 11 12 13 14
15 16 17 18 19 20 21
22 23 24 25 26 27 28
29 30 31
```

FEBRUARY
```
S  M  T  W  T  F  S
          1  2  3  4
 5  6  7  8  9 10 11
12 13 14 15 16 17 18
19 20 21 22 23 24 25
26 27 28 29
```

MARCH
```
S  M  T  W  T  F  S
             1  2  3
 4  5  6  7  8  9 10
11 12 13 14 15 16 17
18 19 20 21 22 23 24
25 26 27 28 29 30 31
```

APRIL
```
S  M  T  W  T  F  S
 1  2  3  4  5  6  7
 8  9 10 11 12 13 14
15 16 17 18 19 20 21
22 23 24 25 26 27 28
29 30
```

MAY
```
S  M  T  W  T  F  S
       1  2  3  4  5
 6  7  8  9 10 11 12
13 14 15 16 17 18 19
20 21 22 23 24 25 26
27 28 29 30 31
```

JUNE
```
S  M  T  W  T  F  S
                1  2
 3  4  5  6  7  8  9
10 11 12 13 14 15 16
17 18 19 20 21 22 23
24 25 26 27 28 29 30
```

JULY
```
S  M  T  W  T  F  S
 1  2  3  4  5  6  7
 8  9 10 11 12 13 14
15 16 17 18 19 20 21
22 23 24 25 26 27 28
29 30 31
```

AUGUST
```
S  M  T  W  T  F  S
          1  2  3  4
 5  6  7  8  9 10 11
12 13 14 15 16 17 18
19 20 21 22 23 24 25
26 27 28 29 30 31
```

SEPTEMBER
```
S  M  T  W  T  F  S
                   1
 2  3  4  5  6  7  8
 9 10 11 12 13 14 15
16 17 18 19 20 21 22
23 24 25 26 27 28 29
30
```

OCTOBER
```
S  M  T  W  T  F  S
    1  2  3  4  5  6
 7  8  9 10 11 12 13
14 15 16 17 18 19 20
21 22 23 24 25 26 27
28 29 30 31
```

NOVEMBER
```
S  M  T  W  T  F  S
             1  2  3
 4  5  6  7  8  9 10
11 12 13 14 15 16 17
18 19 20 21 22 23 24
25 26 27 28 29 30
```

DECEMBER
```
S  M  T  W  T  F  S
                   1
 2  3  4  5  6  7  8
 9 10 11 12 13 14 15
16 17 18 19 20 21 22
23 24 25 26 27 28 29
30 31
```

9 (1996)

JANUARY
```
S  M  T  W  T  F  S
    1  2  3  4  5  6
 7  8  9 10 11 12 13
14 15 16 17 18 19 20
21 22 23 24 25 26 27
28 29 30 31
```

FEBRUARY
```
S  M  T  W  T  F  S
             1  2  3
 4  5  6  7  8  9 10
11 12 13 14 15 16 17
18 19 20 21 22 23 24
25 26 27 28 29
```

MARCH
```
S  M  T  W  T  F  S
                1  2
 3  4  5  6  7  8  9
10 11 12 13 14 15 16
17 18 19 20 21 22 23
24 25 26 27 28 29 30
31
```

APRIL
```
S  M  T  W  T  F  S
    1  2  3  4  5  6
 7  8  9 10 11 12 13
14 15 16 17 18 19 20
21 22 23 24 25 26 27
28 29 30
```

MAY
```
S  M  T  W  T  F  S
          1  2  3  4
 5  6  7  8  9 10 11
12 13 14 15 16 17 18
19 20 21 22 23 24 25
26 27 28 29 30 31
```

JUNE
```
S  M  T  W  T  F  S
                   1
 2  3  4  5  6  7  8
 9 10 11 12 13 14 15
16 17 18 19 20 21 22
23 24 25 26 27 28 29
30
```

JULY
```
S  M  T  W  T  F  S
    1  2  3  4  5  6
 7  8  9 10 11 12 13
14 15 16 17 18 19 20
21 22 23 24 25 26 27
28 29 30 31
```

AUGUST
```
S  M  T  W  T  F  S
             1  2  3
 4  5  6  7  8  9 10
11 12 13 14 15 16 17
18 19 20 21 22 23 24
25 26 27 28 29 30 31
```

SEPTEMBER
```
S  M  T  W  T  F  S
 1  2  3  4  5  6  7
 8  9 10 11 12 13 14
15 16 17 18 19 20 21
22 23 24 25 26 27 28
29 30
```

OCTOBER
```
S  M  T  W  T  F  S
       1  2  3  4  5
 6  7  8  9 10 11 12
13 14 15 16 17 18 19
20 21 22 23 24 25 26
27 28 29 30 31
```

NOVEMBER
```
S  M  T  W  T  F  S
                1  2
 3  4  5  6  7  8  9
10 11 12 13 14 15 16
17 18 19 20 21 22 23
24 25 26 27 28 29 30
```

DECEMBER
```
S  M  T  W  T  F  S
 1  2  3  4  5  6  7
 8  9 10 11 12 13 14
15 16 17 18 19 20 21
22 23 24 25 26 27 28
29 30 31
```

10

JANUARY
```
S  M  T  W  T  F  S
       1  2  3  4  5
 6  7  8  9 10 11 12
13 14 15 16 17 18 19
20 21 22 23 24 25 26
27 28 29 30 31
```

FEBRUARY
```
S  M  T  W  T  F  S
                1  2
 3  4  5  6  7  8  9
10 11 12 13 14 15 16
17 18 19 20 21 22 23
24 25 26 27 28 29
```

MARCH
```
S  M  T  W  T  F  S
                   1
 2  3  4  5  6  7  8
 9 10 11 12 13 14 15
16 17 18 19 20 21 22
23 24 25 26 27 28 29
30 31
```

APRIL
```
S  M  T  W  T  F  S
       1  2  3  4  5
 6  7  8  9 10 11 12
13 14 15 16 17 18 19
20 21 22 23 24 25 26
27 28 29 30
```

MAY
```
S  M  T  W  T  F  S
             1  2  3
 4  5  6  7  8  9 10
11 12 13 14 15 16 17
18 19 20 21 22 23 24
25 26 27 28 29 30 31
```

JUNE
```
S  M  T  W  T  F  S
 1  2  3  4  5  6  7
 8  9 10 11 12 13 14
15 16 17 18 19 20 21
22 23 24 25 26 27 28
29 30
```

JULY
```
S  M  T  W  T  F  S
       1  2  3  4  5
 6  7  8  9 10 11 12
13 14 15 16 17 18 19
20 21 22 23 24 25 26
27 28 29 30 31
```

AUGUST
```
S  M  T  W  T  F  S
                1  2
 3  4  5  6  7  8  9
10 11 12 13 14 15 16
17 18 19 20 21 22 23
24 25 26 27 28 29 30
31
```

SEPTEMBER
```
S  M  T  W  T  F  S
    1  2  3  4  5  6
 7  8  9 10 11 12 13
14 15 16 17 18 19 20
21 22 23 24 25 26 27
28 29 30
```

OCTOBER
```
S  M  T  W  T  F  S
          1  2  3  4
 5  6  7  8  9 10 11
12 13 14 15 16 17 18
19 20 21 22 23 24 25
26 27 28 29 30 31
```

NOVEMBER
```
S  M  T  W  T  F  S
                   1
 2  3  4  5  6  7  8
 9 10 11 12 13 14 15
16 17 18 19 20 21 22
23 24 25 26 27 28 29
30
```

DECEMBER
```
S  M  T  W  T  F  S
    1  2  3  4  5  6
 7  8  9 10 11 12 13
14 15 16 17 18 19 20
21 22 23 24 25 26 27
28 29 30 31
```

11

JANUARY
```
 S  M  T  W  T  F  S
          1  2  3  4
 5  6  7  8  9 10 11
12 13 14 15 16 17 18
19 20 21 22 23 24 25
26 27 28 29 30 31
```

MAY
```
 S  M  T  W  T  F  S
                1  2
 3  4  5  6  7  8  9
10 11 12 13 14 15 16
17 18 19 20 21 22 23
24 25 26 27 28 29 30
31
```

SEPTEMBER
```
 S  M  T  W  T  F  S
       1  2  3  4  5
 6  7  8  9 10 11 12
13 14 15 16 17 18 19
20 21 22 23 24 25 26
27 28 29 30
```

FEBRUARY
```
 S  M  T  W  T  F  S
                   1
 2  3  4  5  6  7  8
 9 10 11 12 13 14 15
16 17 18 19 20 21 22
23 24 25 26 27 28 29
```

JUNE
```
 S  M  T  W  T  F  S
    1  2  3  4  5  6
 7  8  9 10 11 12 13
14 15 16 17 18 19 20
21 22 23 24 25 26 27
28 29 30
```

OCTOBER
```
 S  M  T  W  T  F  S
             1  2  3
 4  5  6  7  8  9 10
11 12 13 14 15 16 17
18 19 20 21 22 23 24
25 26 27 28 29 30 31
```

MARCH
```
 S  M  T  W  T  F  S
 1  2  3  4  5  6  7
 8  9 10 11 12 13 14
15 16 17 18 19 20 21
22 23 24 25 26 27 28
29 30 31
```

JULY
```
 S  M  T  W  T  F  S
          1  2  3  4
 5  6  7  8  9 10 11
12 13 14 15 16 17 18
19 20 21 22 23 24 25
26 27 28 29 30 31
```

NOVEMBER
```
 S  M  T  W  T  F  S
 1  2  3  4  5  6  7
 8  9 10 11 12 13 14
15 16 17 18 19 20 21
22 23 24 25 26 27 28
29 30
```

APRIL
```
 S  M  T  W  T  F  S
          1  2  3  4
 5  6  7  8  9 10 11
12 13 14 15 16 17 18
19 20 21 22 23 24 25
26 27 28 29 30
```

AUGUST
```
 S  M  T  W  T  F  S
                   1
 2  3  4  5  6  7  8
 9 10 11 12 13 14 15
16 17 18 19 20 21 22
23 24 25 26 27 28 29
30 31
```

DECEMBER
```
 S  M  T  W  T  F  S
       1  2  3  4  5
 6  7  8  9 10 11 12
13 14 15 16 17 18 19
20 21 22 23 24 25 26
27 28 29 30 31
```

12

JANUARY
```
 S  M  T  W  T  F  S
             1  2  3
 4  5  6  7  8  9 10
11 12 13 14 15 16 17
18 19 20 21 22 23 24
25 26 27 28 29 30 31
```

MAY
```
 S  M  T  W  T  F  S
                   1
 2  3  4  5  6  7  8
 9 10 11 12 13 14 15
16 17 18 19 20 21 22
23 24 25 26 27 28 29
30 31
```

SEPTEMBER
```
 S  M  T  W  T  F  S
          1  2  3  4
 5  6  7  8  9 10 11
12 13 14 15 16 17 18
19 20 21 22 23 24 25
26 27 28 29 30
```

FEBRUARY
```
 S  M  T  W  T  F  S
 1  2  3  4  5  6  7
 8  9 10 11 12 13 14
15 16 17 18 19 20 21
22 23 24 25 26 27 28
29
```

JUNE
```
 S  M  T  W  T  F  S
       1  2  3  4  5
 6  7  8  9 10 11 12
13 14 15 16 17 18 19
20 21 22 23 24 25 26
27 28 29 30
```

OCTOBER
```
 S  M  T  W  T  F  S
                1  2
 3  4  5  6  7  8  9
10 11 12 13 14 15 16
17 18 19 20 21 22 23
24 25 26 27 28 29 30
31
```

MARCH
```
 S  M  T  W  T  F  S
    1  2  3  4  5  6
 7  8  9 10 11 12 13
14 15 16 17 18 19 20
21 22 23 24 25 26 27
28 29 30 31
```

JULY
```
 S  M  T  W  T  F  S
             1  2  3
 4  5  6  7  8  9 10
11 12 13 14 15 16 17
18 19 20 21 22 23 24
25 26 27 28 29 30 31
```

NOVEMBER
```
 S  M  T  W  T  F  S
    1  2  3  4  5  6
 7  8  9 10 11 12 13
14 15 16 17 18 19 20
21 22 23 24 25 26 27
28 29 30
```

APRIL
```
 S  M  T  W  T  F  S
             1  2  3
 4  5  6  7  8  9 10
11 12 13 14 15 16 17
18 19 20 21 22 23 24
25 26 27 28 29 30
```

AUGUST
```
 S  M  T  W  T  F  S
 1  2  3  4  5  6  7
 8  9 10 11 12 13 14
15 16 17 18 19 20 21
22 23 24 25 26 27 28
29 30 31
```

DECEMBER
```
 S  M  T  W  T  F  S
          1  2  3  4
 5  6  7  8  9 10 11
12 13 14 15 16 17 18
19 20 21 22 23 24 25
26 27 28 29 30 31
```

13

JANUARY
```
 S  M  T  W  T  F  S
                1  2
 3  4  5  6  7  8  9
10 11 12 13 14 15 16
17 18 19 20 21 22 23
24 25 26 27 28 29 30
31
```

MAY
```
 S  M  T  W  T  F  S
 1  2  3  4  5  6  7
 8  9 10 11 12 13 14
15 16 17 18 19 20 21
22 23 24 25 26 27 28
29 30 31
```

SEPTEMBER
```
 S  M  T  W  T  F  S
             1  2  3
 4  5  6  7  8  9 10
11 12 13 14 15 16 17
18 19 20 21 22 23 24
25 26 27 28 29 30
```

FEBRUARY
```
 S  M  T  W  T  F  S
    1  2  3  4  5  6
 7  8  9 10 11 12 13
14 15 16 17 18 19 20
21 22 23 24 25 26 27
28 29
```

JUNE
```
 S  M  T  W  T  F  S
          1  2  3  4
 5  6  7  8  9 10 11
12 13 14 15 16 17 18
19 20 21 22 23 24 25
26 27 28 29 30
```

OCTOBER
```
 S  M  T  W  T  F  S
                   1
 2  3  4  5  6  7  8
 9 10 11 12 13 14 15
16 17 18 19 20 21 22
23 24 25 26 27 28 29
30 31
```

MARCH
```
 S  M  T  W  T  F  S
       1  2  3  4  5
 6  7  8  9 10 11 12
13 14 15 16 17 18 19
20 21 22 23 24 25 26
27 28 29 30 31
```

JULY
```
 S  M  T  W  T  F  S
                1  2
 3  4  5  6  7  8  9
10 11 12 13 14 15 16
17 18 19 20 21 22 23
24 25 26 27 28 29 30
31
```

NOVEMBER
```
 S  M  T  W  T  F  S
       1  2  3  4  5
 6  7  8  9 10 11 12
13 14 15 16 17 18 19
20 21 22 23 24 25 26
27 28 29 30
```

APRIL
```
 S  M  T  W  T  F  S
                1  2
 3  4  5  6  7  8  9
10 11 12 13 14 15 16
17 18 19 20 21 22 23
24 25 26 27 28 29 30
```

AUGUST
```
 S  M  T  W  T  F  S
    1  2  3  4  5  6
 7  8  9 10 11 12 13
14 15 16 17 18 19 20
21 22 23 24 25 26 27
28 29 30 31
```

DECEMBER
```
 S  M  T  W  T  F  S
             1  2  3
 4  5  6  7  8  9 10
11 12 13 14 15 16 17
18 19 20 21 22 23 24
25 26 27 28 29 30 31
```

14 (2000)

JANUARY
```
 S  M  T  W  T  F  S
                   1
 2  3  4  5  6  7  8
 9 10 11 12 13 14 15
16 17 18 19 20 21 22
23 24 25 26 27 28 29
30 31
```

MAY
```
 S  M  T  W  T  F  S
    1  2  3  4  5  6
 7  8  9 10 11 12 13
14 15 16 17 18 19 20
21 22 23 24 25 26 27
28 29 30 31
```

SEPTEMBER
```
 S  M  T  W  T  F  S
                1  2
 3  4  5  6  7  8  9
10 11 12 13 14 15 16
17 18 19 20 21 22 23
24 25 26 27 28 29 30
```

FEBRUARY
```
 S  M  T  W  T  F  S
       1  2  3  4  5
 6  7  8  9 10 11 12
13 14 15 16 17 18 19
20 21 22 23 24 25 26
27 28 29
```

JUNE
```
 S  M  T  W  T  F  S
             1  2  3
 4  5  6  7  8  9 10
11 12 13 14 15 16 17
18 19 20 21 22 23 24
25 26 27 28 29 30
```

OCTOBER
```
 S  M  T  W  T  F  S
 1  2  3  4  5  6  7
 8  9 10 11 12 13 14
15 16 17 18 19 20 21
22 23 24 25 26 27 28
29 30 31
```

MARCH
```
 S  M  T  W  T  F  S
          1  2  3  4
 5  6  7  8  9 10 11
12 13 14 15 16 17 18
19 20 21 22 23 24 25
26 27 28 29 30 31
```

JULY
```
 S  M  T  W  T  F  S
                   1
 2  3  4  5  6  7  8
 9 10 11 12 13 14 15
16 17 18 19 20 21 22
23 24 25 26 27 28 29
30 31
```

NOVEMBER
```
 S  M  T  W  T  F  S
          1  2  3  4
 5  6  7  8  9 10 11
12 13 14 15 16 17 18
19 20 21 22 23 24 25
26 27 28 29 30
```

APRIL
```
 S  M  T  W  T  F  S
                   1
 2  3  4  5  6  7  8
 9 10 11 12 13 14 15
16 17 18 19 20 21 22
23 24 25 26 27 28 29
30
```

AUGUST
```
 S  M  T  W  T  F  S
       1  2  3  4  5
 6  7  8  9 10 11 12
13 14 15 16 17 18 19
20 21 22 23 24 25 26
27 28 29 30 31
```

DECEMBER
```
 S  M  T  W  T  F  S
                1  2
 3  4  5  6  7  8  9
10 11 12 13 14 15 16
17 18 19 20 21 22 23
24 25 26 27 28 29 30
31
```